THE NEW BIBLE HYMN-BOOK

THE NEW BIBLE HYMN-BOOK

Compiled by Henry J. Waters

Henry Waters was brought up under the ministry of Stanley Delves who was Pastor at Forest Fold Baptist Chapel, Crowborough, Sussex from 1923 to 1977.

He became aware of the reality of spiritual life and the love of God after reading *Tortured for Christ* by Pastor Richard Wurmbrand, and hearing him preach following release from prison in Romania. He was baptised in 1969.

Since 1975 he has been a member of Providence Baptist Church, Hemlington, Middlesbrough, where he is a deacon. He worked as a General Medical Practitioner as well as in rheumatology, prison medicine and commissioning. He is now retired.

http://www.fast-print.net/bookshop

THE NEW BIBLE HYMN-BOOK

A catalogue record for this book is available from the British Library

ISBN 978-178456-290-8
(Also available as a paperback: ISBN 978-178456-289-2)

First Published 2016 by
Fast-Print Publishing of Peterborough, England.

For the New Bible Hymn-Book Charity (www.newbiblehymn-book.com)
Any profits from the sale of books will be used to promote the distribution of
Christian literature or aid in this country and abroad.

CONTENTS

HYMNS ON THE OLD TESTAMENT

HYMNS ON THE NEW TESTAMENT

Author	Hymn	Author	Hymn
Alexander, Cecil	679	Ken, Thomas	554
Ambrose	641	Kent, John	1480
Baker, Henry	254	Luther, Martin	353
Beddome, Benjamin	1158	Lyte, Henry	518
Berridge, John	1967	Matheson, George	928
Bonar, Horatius	1849	M'Cheyne, Robert	1224
Burnham, Richard	2012	Medley, Samuel	63
Byrom, John	1168	Midlane, Albert	966
Carmichael, Amy	1987	Milton, John	609
Cennick, John	1338	Monsell, John	1866
Clifford, Alan	1122	Montgomery, James	165
Conder, Josiah	1774	Newton, John	1714
Cowper, William	793	Ryland, John	319
Crosby, Fanny	592	Sleeper, William	1804
Deck, James	1828	Spafford, Horatio	145
Doddridge, Philip	25	Spurgeon, Charles	1289
Dudley-Smith, Timothy	1130	Stennett, Samuel	1764
Ellerton, John	546	Stone, Arthur	549
Elliott, Charlotte	1415	Swain, Joseph	1059
Fawcett, John	1734	Toplady, Augustus	1577
Gadsby, William	898	Watts, Isaac	2102
Gerhardt, Paulus	1386	Wesley, Charles	1789
Havergal, Frances	116	Wesley, John	1635
Haweis, Thomas	1404	Whitfield, Frederick	685
Herbert, George	409	Whittle, Daniel	1875
Higham, Vernon	1784	Williams, William	447
Hill, Rowland	1440	Winkworth, Catherine (translator)	650
Houghton, Frank	1184	Wordsworth, Christopher	1869
Irons, Joseph	1998	Zinzendorf, Nicholas von	846
Kelly, Thomas	1772		

Acknowledgements for pictures:

Bonar, H	Free Church of Scotland
Clifford, A	The Author
Dudley-Smith, T	The Author
Higham, W V	The Author

A few years ago I was asked to compile a selection of favourite hymns for a book that eventually became *Glorious Things*. In the course of choosing the 35 that had meant most to me in my life, I discovered that far from being merely functional aids to worship, many more hymns than I realised were of lasting worth in themselves. Among them are hymns of doubt and frailty as well as joy and optimism; hymns of quiet conviction and defiant hopefulness; hymns which belong to their culture but also reach out to the universal; hymns which convey a whiff of the eternal.

The New Bible Hymn-Book rather outdoes my 35. There are more than 2,000 hymns here from over 400 authors, imaginatively arranged and impeccably indexed. It is a marvellous collection – the fruit of a long labour of love. It's a collection to dive into, in confidence that wherever you plunge you will always draw out some pearl or another.

It is inevitable that in such a wide collection some hymns are better than others. After all, not everyone can be an Isaac Watts or a Charles Wesley. But taken together they capture the heart of the Bible narrative and the core of the Christian faith. And among them are some, such as Watts' "When I Survey the Wondrous Cross", which in their expression of profound emotion and complex theology also rank as sublime poetry.

Whether rediscovering hymns we have known since childhood or happening upon new ones for the first time, we will find much here to treasure.

Sally Magnusson

During the 1990s I came across a copy of *Gadsby's Hymns*; it was one of the hymn-books which I had used as a boy. I noted the verses on which each hymn was based and decided to index the hymns to the relevant verses in my Bible. I then did the same for *Denham's Selection, Grace Hymns and Hymns for Worship*. I have enjoyed reading hymns by Rev. W.Vernon Higham since student days and indexed his hymns as well.

In 2000 the Bible was stolen while we were on holiday in France and I decided to repeat the exercise. This time I also went through *Gospel Hymns, Spurgeon's Hymns, Olney Hymns* and *Christian Hymns*. I must say that I found it both helpful and enjoyable to look up the relevant hymns when reading a particular Bible chapter.

By 2005, it became clear that many of these traditional hymns had a great deal of intrinsic merit but many were not easily accessible. My mother-in-law, the late Mrs Marion Stone, suggested the possibility of producing a hymn-book. I decided to determine whether it was feasible to produce a book including most of the hymns from each of the source books. I discovered that of 7,062 hymns[1] only about 4,000 hymns were different. Of these around 1,000 hymns were relatively unsuitable for modern use and I arranged the remainder in Biblical reference order before making a final selection by comparing those on particular verses.

In addition to the hymns from the older source hymn-books, hymns by Rev. W. Vernon Higham and some by Bishop Timothy Dudley-Smith and Rev. Alan Clifford have been included, together with two hymns by the late Pastor Arthur Stone. A number of friends supplied a few other hymns from various sources.

This book of 2,146 hymns is the result. The hymns have been written by over 400 authors, not only by great poets and preachers but also by many lesser-known men and women. The hymns are firmly based on the Bible and taken together they capture the essence of the Christian faith.

---

[1] See table of Hymns Selected

More than ten hymns by the following authors have been included:
Harriet Auber, Benjamin Beddome, John Berridge, Horatius Bonar, Nicholas Brady, Richard Burnham, John Cennick, Josiah Conder, William Cowper, Fanny Crosby, David Denham, Philip Doddridge, Timothy Dudley-Smith, Charlotte Elliott, John Fawcett, William Gadsby, Joseph Hart, Frances Havergal, W.Vernon Higham, Joseph Irons, Thomas Kelly, John Kent, Henry Lyte, Samuel Medley, Albert Midlane, James Montgomery, John Newton, John Ryland, Charles Spurgeon, Anne Steele, Samuel Stennett, Joseph Swain, Augustus Toplady, Isaac Watts, Charles Wesley and William Williams.

The arrangement of the hymns led to the name: *The Bible Hymn-Book.* It is hoped that this will prove helpful for hymn selection and also for private Bible study. It should be noted that whereas some hymns are clearly based on a particular verse, other hymns have been attributed to one of a number of suitable verses.

This arrangement is not unique; indeed some of the earliest hymn-books were arranged in scriptural verse order: e.g. hymn-books by Isaac Watts in 1707, Philip Doddridge in 1755 and John Newton in 1779. The name is not original either, Horatius Bonar having compiled a hymn-book entitled, *The Bible hymn-book* in 1845.[2] For this reason I altered the title to *The New Bible Hymn-Book.*

The year 2011 marked the 400th Anniversary of the publication of the Authorised King James Version of the Bible. The vast majority of hymns in this selection have been inspired by the language of the King James Version and above almost every hymn there is a verse or part of a verse from the KJV; a few have a reference to a larger portion of scripture e.g. a psalm.

Many Christian believers derive much benefit and pleasure from the singing and reading of hymns: a single expression, verse, or a complete hymn can so often enhance worship or illuminate a Biblical truth. For those curious about Christianity, these hymns often explain the meaning of a verse in a memorable way. Some of the hymns are poems which are less suitable for singing but the vast majority could be used in public worship. It is hoped that that the hymns will be of interest and value to the General as well as the Christian Public.

---

[2] Faith Cook, *Our Hymn Writers and their Hymns* (Darlington:Evangelical Press 2005):81,201,296

None of us should underestimate our debt to the hymn-writers and to the compilers of the source hymn-books. Great effort was made to ensure that the best hymns known at the time were published. David Denham, for example, perused some 30,000 hymns for his selection of 1,192 hymns.

I would like to thank all those many friends who have made helpful suggestions over the years. I would especially like to record my thanks to Mr David Oldham, Mr B.A. Ramsbottom, Mr John Roberts, the late Pastor Fred Stone and the late Pastor Arthur Stone for their interest and encouragement.

I warmly thank Mrs Sally Hutter and Mr Jim Ransome for their proof-reading and much valuable advice but I of course take full responsibility for the final accuracy of the text. Mr John Perfect has helped me greatly with advice about hymn metres and indentations as well as by many other useful comments.

I thank my niece Caroline Waters for her work on the cover design and Pauline Tebbutt and her team at Printondemand-worldwide for their help and guidance. I would also record my gratitude to Neil Saunders of Ayton Computers who rescued the project on several occasions. I thank all the copyright holders for their permissions and advice.

I owe a great debt of gratitude to my mother, the late Mrs Olive Waters and her sister, the late Mrs Joyce Lovelock. My mother suggested 'The Bible Hymn-Book' as an appropriate title for the book and my aunt proved to be a great support despite her initial reservation that a wheelbarrow would be necessary to carry the book to church!

I also thank Sally Magnusson for her generous foreword.

Finally I thank my wife, Ruth, for her many suggestions and her support and encouragement, without which the book would not have been finished.

Henry Waters

The table shows the number of hymns and percentage selected from each of the main source hymn-books:

	TOTAL	SELECTED	PER CENT
Olney Hymns [3]	347	138	40%
Gadsby's Hymns[4]	1156	700	61%
Denham's Selection [5]	1192	633	53%
Spurgeon's Hymn Book [6]	1060	563	53%
Gospel Hymns [7]	1212	768	63%
Grace Hymn Book [8]	848	722	85%
Christian Hymns [9]	901	645	72%
Hymns for Worship [10]	184	163	89%
Hymns of W. Vernon Higham[11]	162	59	36%
Totals	7062	4387	62%

TUNES:
The New Bible Hymn-Book does not have its own tune book but currently the Christian Worship[12] tune book contains an excellent selection of suitable tunes and this is recommended.

ALTERATIONS:
I have altered a few hymns slightly and have indicated this by inserting (alt) at the head of the hymn. I have not usually indicated where a hymn has already been altered in one of the source hymn-books.

COPYRIGHT:
Although every effort has been made to trace the holders of copyright it has not been possible to make contact with everyone who may possibly own the copyright to some of the hymns and pictures. I apologise for any errors of this nature and if brought to my attention will be pleased to correct them in future reprints. H.J.W.

---

[3] Olney Hymns, First edition 1779, Facsimile edition 1979. (Banbury: The Trustees of The Cowper and Newton Museum, 2002)
[4] Gadsby's Hymns, Compiled by William Gadsby (1780-1844) and John Philpott (1802-1869); (London: Gospel Standard Publications,1987)
[5] The Saint's Melody, Compiled by David Denham (1791-1848); (London: Robert Banks and Son, 1837)
[6] "Our Own Hymn-Book", Compiled by C.H.Spurgeon (1834-1892); (2nd Reprint edn; Texas: Pilgrim Publications, 2002)
[7] Gospel Hymns, Compiled by the Strict and Particular Baptist Society (4th edn; London: Robert Stockwell,Ltd, 1950)
[8] Grace Hymns, (Guildford: Grace Publications Trust, 1975)
[9] Christian Hymns, eds Paul E Cook and Graham Harrison; (2nd edn; Bryntyrion, Bridgend: Evangelical Movement of Wales, 1988)
[10] Hymns for Worship, (Ossett, W Yorks: The Christian Bookshop, 1996)
[11] Hymns of W. Vernon Higham, (Stoke-on-Trent: Tentmaker Publications,1998)
[12] Christian Worship Tunes, (Cardiff: Christian Worship Publishing Trust, 2009)

AUTHORS	HYMNS	PERMISSIONS
Baughen, M. (1930-)	199	Words: © M. Baughen /The Jubilate Group.www.jubilate.co.uk Used by permission.
Briggs, G. W. (1875-1959)	1416	Words: George W. Briggs, Words © 1953 Ren. 1981 The Hymn Society (Admin. Hope Publishing Company,Carol Stream, IL 60188).
Carmichael, Amy (1867-1951)	1987	*The Collected Poems of Amy Carmichael: Mountain Breezes* by Amy Carmichael, © 1999 by The Dohnavur Fellowship. Used by permission of CLC Publications. May not be further reproduced. All rights reserved.
Chisholm, T. O. (1866-1960)	896	Words: Thomas O. Chisholm © 1923, Ren. 1951 Hope Publishing Company. Carol Stream, IL 60188. All rights reserved. Used by permission.
Clarke E.L.		see under A. B. Smith
Clarkson, E. M. (1915-2008)	1806	Words: Margaret Clarkson © 1957, Ren. 1985 Hope Publishing Company,Carol Stream, IL 60188. All rights reserved. Used by permission
Clifford, A. C. (1941-)	683 1122 1343 1412 1484 1760	The Author
Cook, P. E. G. (1932-)	1258 1824	The Author
Dudley- Smith, T. (1926-)	161 196 223 411 548 883 918 945 954 1130 1309 1957 2075 2104	Oxford University Press
Harris,T. (1874-1955)	713	© 1959 Nazarene Publishing House/Lillenas Publishing Company (Adm Music Services/Song Solutions www.songsolutions.org) All rights reserved. Used by permission.
Harrison, Eluned (1934-)	259	The Author
Harrison, G. S. (1935-2013)	271 555 598	Mrs Eluned Harrison
Higham, W. V. (1926-)	5 64 125 138 158 245 298 300 330 370 375 449 594 698 733 734 750 783 870 1086 1177 1185 1314 1327 1336 1378 1379 1389 1395 1477 1527 1535 1609 1628 1637 1656 1705 1708 1728 1744 1746 1765 1783 1784 1827 1864 1870 1874 1907 1925 1970 1993 1995 2007 2082 2131 2133 2137	The Author
Hine, S. K. (1899-1989)	524	Copyright © 1949 and 1953 by the Stuart Hine Trust. All rights in the USA its territories and possessions, except print rights, administered by Capitol Publishing.USA, North, Central and South America print rights administered by Hope Publishing Company. . All other non US Americas rights administered by the Stuart Hine Trust. Rest of the world rights administered by Integrity Music Europe, part of the David C Cook family, songs@integritymusic.com

ACKNOWLEDGMENTS and PERMISSIONS

AUTHORS	HYMNS	PERMISSIONS
Houghton, F. (1894-1972)	1184 1613 1651 1853 1909	The Overseas Missionary Fellowship
Hussey, J. E. (1874-1958)	1103	Words: Jennie E. Hussey,© 1921, Ren. 1949 Hope Publishing Company,Carol Stream, IL 60188. All rights reserved. Used by permission.
Idle, C. M. (1938-)	1913	Words: © C. Idle / The Jubilate Group. www.jubilate.co.uk. Used by permission.
Moore, J. M. (1925-)	1968	© 1952 New Spring Publishing/Brentwod Benson Publishing (Adm Capitolcmgpublishing.com UK&Eire Song Solutions www.songsolutions.org) All rights reserved. Used by permission.
Obbard, D. (1922-2011)	272	Mr Keith Obbard
Perry, N. R. (1909-2004)	324 362 1650	Mrs Rachel Westmacott
Rawley, F.H. (1854-1952)	1669	© 1937 HarperCollins Religious (Admn Song Solutions www.songsolutions.org) All rights reserved. Used by permission.
Rees, B.A. (1911-1983)	1947	Mr Alexander Scott
Saward, M. (1932-2015)	1665	Words: M. Saward © Mrs E. R. Hudson / The Jubilate Group. www.jubilate.co.uk Used by permission.
Seddon, J. E. (1915-1983)	604 1743	Words: J. E. Seddon © Mrs M. Seddon / The Jubilate Group. www.jubilate.co.uk Used by permission.
Sibomana, E.T. (1915-1975)	1698	Church Mission Society
Smith, A. B. (1916-2001) and Clark, E. L. (1925-1982)	154	© 1958 New Spring Publishing/Imagem (Adm Small Stone Media BV / Song Solutions www.songsolutions.org) All rights reserved. Used by permission.
Stone, A. (1924-2008)	549 1055	Mrs Carol Stone

TRANSLATOR	HYMNS	PERMISSIONS
Guillebaud, R.	1698	Church Mission Society
Harrison, G. S.(1935-2013)	391	Mrs Eluned Harrison
Higham, W. V. (1926)	1417 1700 1994	The Translator
Houghton, F. (1894-1972)	2010	The Overseas Missionary Fellowship
Jones, R. M. (1929-)	717	The Translator
Payne, E. (1902-1980)	1036	James Prain

HYMNS ON THE OLD TESTAMENT

Genesis and Exodus

1   Isaac Watts   CM

In the beginning God created the heaven and the earth. *Genesis 1:1*

I sing the almighty power of God,
   That made the mountains rise,
That spread the flowing seas abroad,
   And built the lofty skies.

I sing the wisdom that ordained
   The sun to rule the day;
The moon shines full at His command,
   And all the stars obey.

I sing the goodness of the Lord,
   That filled the earth with food;
He formed the creatures with His word,
   And then pronounced them good.

There's not a plant or flower below
   But makes His glories known;
And clouds arise and tempests blow,
   By order from His throne.

Creatures as numerous as they be,
   Are subject to His care;
There's not a place where we can flee
   But God is present there.

2   John Marriott   664 6664

And God said, Let there be light: and there was light. *Genesis 1:3*

Thou whose almighty word
Chaos and darkness heard,
   And took their flight;
Hear us we humbly pray,
And where the gospel day
Sheds not its glorious ray,
   Let there be light!

Thou who didst come to bring,
On Thy redeeming wing,
   Healing and sight,
Health to the sick in mind,
Sight to the inly blind;
O now to all mankind
   Let there be light!

Spirit of truth and love,
Life-giving, holy Dove,
   Speed forth Thy flight;
Move on the waters' face,
Bearing the lamp of grace,
And in earth's darkest place
   Let there be light!

Holy and blessèd Three,
Glorious Trinity,
   Wisdom, love, might;
Boundless as ocean's tide
Rolling in fullest pride,
Through the earth, far and wide,
   Let there be light!

3   George Bubier   76 76 D

And God saw everything that He had made, and, behold, it was very good. *Genesis 1:31*

'Twas God that made the ocean,
   And laid its sandy bed;
He gave the stars their motion,
   And built the mountain's head;
He made the rolling thunder,
   The lightning's flashing flame;
His works are full of wonder,
   All-glorious is His name.

And must it not surprise us
   That One so high and great,
Should see and not despise us,
   Poor sinners, at His feet?
Yet day by day He gives us
   Our raiment and our food;
In sickness He relieves us,
   And is in all things good.

But things that are far greater
   His mighty hand hath done,
And sent us blessings sweeter
   Through Christ His only Son,
Who, when He saw us dying
   In sin and sorrow's night,
On wings of mercy flying
   Came down with life and light.

He gives His word to teach us
   Our danger and our wants,
And kindly doth beseech us
   To take the life He grants.
His Holy Spirit frees us
   From Satan's deadly powers,
Leads us by faith to Jesus,
   And makes His glory ours.

4   Josiah Conder   88 88 88
I will make him an help meet for him.
Genesis 2:18

O God who didst from Adam's side
Fashion an help meet for his bride,
Flesh of his flesh, bone of his bone,
That both might feel and love as one!
    Make these Thy servants one in heart;
    Whom Thou hast joined let no man part.

Lord of the church, whose bleeding side
Gave life to Thy redeemèd bride;
Whose grace through every member spread
Joins the whole body to its Head:
    O let Thy love their model be,
    As they together live to Thee.

O Thou who once, a Guest divine,
Didst turn the water into wine!
Thy presence, not unsought, afford;
Fill Thou their cup, and bless them, Lord;
    And while each heart Thy word obeys,
    May all their joy be turned to praise.

Spirit of grace and holiness,
Who dost these bodies now possess,
As living temples, which to stain
Were God's own dwelling to profane,
    May these Thy servants, honouring Thee,
    Be kept in love and purity.

5   Vernon Higham   76 76 D
Where art thou? *Genesis 3:9*

The voice of God eternal
    Was heard in Eden far,
'Mid silence that was fearful,
    For sin had come to mar.
'Where art thou, child created,
    Where hidest thou from Me?'
For sin has man defeated,
    God's face he could not see.

A separation woeful
    From God and hope and life,
Despair and death so painful,
    A way of grief and strife.
The serpent so beguiling
    Enticed mankind to fall,
The whole creation writhing,
    From Satan's tempting call.

The Saviour to the victory
    From heaven to earth came down;
He came to show God's mercy
    And move the Father's frown.
Upon His blessèd shoulders
    Our Saviour took our shame,
And paid the price for sinners;
    Who can forget His name?

Where art thou, O poor sinner,
    In death and sin's dark night?
O listen to the wonder
    Of words of truth and light.
O turn thy gaze to Calvary
    Where Jesus calls thee back;
From hiding come for mercy,
    In Christ thou wilt not lack.

O wondrous restoration,
    An act of grace sublime!
The news of man's salvation
    Was planned by love divine.
What peace and joy is given
    To those who hear His voice
To come and be forgiven,
    And in His grace rejoice.

                © Author

6   John Newton   CM
Where art thou? *Genesis 3:9*

On man, in His own image made,
    How much did God bestow?
The whole creation homage paid,
    And owned him, Lord, below!

He dwelt in Eden's garden, stored
    With sweets for every sense;
And there with his descending Lord
    He walked in confidence.

But O by sin how quickly changed!
    His honour forfeited,
His heart from God and truth estranged,
    His conscience filled with dread!

Now from his Maker's voice he flees,
    Which was before his joy:
And thinks to hide amidst the trees,
    From an all-seeing eye.

Compelled to answer to his name;
    With stubbornness and pride
He cast, on God Himself, the blame,
    Nor once for mercy cried.

But grace, unasked, his heart subdued
    And all his guilt forgave;
By faith, the promised Seed he viewed,
    And felt His power to save.

Thus we ourselves would justify,
    Though we the law transgress;
Like him, unable to deny,
    Unwilling to confess.

But when by faith the sinner sees
    A pardon bought with blood;
Then he forsakes his foolish pleas,
    And gladly turns to God.

7   Alice Flowerdew   CM

While the earth remaineth, seedtime and harvest, and cold and heat, and summer and winter, and day and night shall not cease.
Genesis 8:22

Fountain of mercy, God of love,
  How rich Thy bounties are;
The rolling seasons, as they move,
  Proclaim Thy constant care.

When in the bosom of the earth
  The sower hid the grain;
Thy goodness marked its secret birth,
  And sent the early rain.

The spring's sweet influence, Lord, was Thine;
  The plants in beauty grew;
Thou gav'st the summer sun to shine,
  The mild refreshing dew.

These various mercies from above
  Matured the swelling grain;
A kindly harvest crowns Thy love,
  And plenty fills the plain.

We own and bless Thy gracious sway;
  Thy hand all nature hails;
Seed-time, nor harvest, night nor day,
  Summer nor winter fails.

8   Joseph Swain   LM

And they went forth to go into the land of Canaan. *Genesis 12:5*

Pilgrims we are, to Canaan bound;
  Our journey lies along this road;
This wilderness we travel round,
  To reach the city of our God.

And here, as travellers we meet,
  Before we reach the fields above,
To sit around our Master's feet,
  And tell the wonders of His love.

Oft have we seen the tempests rise;
  The world and Satan, hell and sin,
Like mountains, seemed to reach the skies,
  With scarce a gleam of hope between.

But still, as oft as troubles come,
  Our Jesus sends some cheering ray:
And that strong arm shall guide us home,
  Which thus protects us by the way.

9   John Newton   CM

Thou God seest me. *Genesis 16:13*

One glance of Thine, eternal Lord,
  Pierces all nature through;
Nor heaven, nor earth, nor hell afford
  A shelter from Thy view.

The mighty whole, each smaller part,
  At once before Thee lies;
And every thought of every heart
  Is open to Thine eyes.

Great God! from Thee there's nought concealed,
  Thou seest my inward frame;
To Thee I always stand revealed
  Exactly as I am!

Since I can hardly, therefore bear
  What in myself I see;
How vile and black must I appear,
  Most Holy God to Thee!

But since my Saviour stands between,
  In garments dyed in blood,
'Tis He, instead of me, is seen,
  When I approach to God.

Thus, though a sinner, I am safe;
  He pleads, before the throne,
His life and death in my behalf,
  And calls my sins His own.

What wondrous love, what mysteries,
  In this appointment shine!
My breaches of the law are His,
  And His obedience mine.

10   Richard Burnham   CM

Shall not the Judge of all the earth do right?
Genesis 18:25

Judge of the earth, Thou vital source
  Of wisdom, truth, and might,
Thine ancient counsels all divine,
  Are gracious, wise, and right.

Right is the gospel, right the laws,
  Right are the ways of God;
Right is the whole display of grace,
  And right the healing blood.

Right are the dealings of the Lord;
  And all His saints shall prove,
Whether He smiles, or frowns, or hides,
  All is in perfect love.

All the keen sorrows now we feel,
Through all this dreary night,
All are to lead from sin to God;
Then all are surely right.

Shines the whole providence of God,
With love divinely bright;
Whether He gives, withholds, or takes,
All is supremely right.

Soon may we well with raptures mount
The highest hill of light,
And sing with millions round the throne,
'The Lord doth all things right.'

Nothing but Jesus I esteem;
My soul is then sincere;
And everything that's dear to Him,
To me is also dear.

But ah! when these short visits end,
Though not quite left alone,
I miss the presence of my Friend,
Like one whose comfort's gone.

More frequent let Thy visits be,
Or let them longer last;
I can do nothing without Thee;
Make haste, O God, make haste.

---

11   Elizabeth Scott   CM
O let not the Lord be angry.
Genesis 18:32

When Abram full of sacred awe,
Before Jehovah stood,
And with a humble, fervent prayer,
For guilty Sodom sued;

With what success, what wondrous grace,
Was his petition crowned!
The Lord would spare, if in the place
Ten righteous men be found.

And could a single holy soul
So rich a boon obtain?
Great God, and shall Thy remnant cry
And plead with Thee in vain?

Britain, all guilty as she is,
Her several saints can boast;
And now their fervent prayers ascend;
And can those prayers be lost?

Are not Thy righteous dear to Thee
Now, as in ancient times?
Or does this guilty land exceed
Gomorrah in its crimes?

Still there are those who bear Thy name,
Here yet is Thine abode;
Long has Thy presence blessed our land;
Forsake us not, O God!

12   Joseph Hart   CM
And the LORD went His way, as soon as He had left communing with Abraham.
Genesis 18:33

When Jesus, with His mighty love,
Visits my troubled breast,
My doubts subside, my fears remove,
And I'm completely blest.

13   Horatius Bonar   SM
The everlasting God. *Genesis 21:33*

O everlasting Light,
Giver of dawn and day,
Dispeller of the ancient night
In which creation lay:

O everlasting Health
From which all healing springs;
Our bliss, our treasure, and our wealth,
To Thee our spirit clings.

O everlasting Truth,
Truest of all that's true;
Sure guide of erring age and youth,
Lead us, and teach us too.

O everlasting Strength,
Uphold us in the way;
Bring us, in spite of foes, at length
To joy, and light, and day.

O everlasting Love,
Well-spring of grace and peace,
Pour down Thy fulness from above,
Bid doubt and trouble cease.

14   John Newton   10 10 11 11
Jehovah-Jireh, 'The LORD will provide.'
Genesis 22:14

Though troubles assail and dangers affright,
Though friends should all fail and foes all unite,
Yet one thing secures us, whatever betide,
The Scripture assures us the Lord will provide.

When Satan appears to stop up our path,
And fills us with fears, we triumph by faith;
He cannot take from us, though oft he has tried,
This heart cheering promise, the Lord will provide.

His call we obey like Abram of old,
Not knowing our way, but faith makes us bold;
For though we are strangers we have a good
    Guide,
And trust, in all dangers, the Lord will provide.

No strength of our own or goodness we claim;
Yet, since we have known the Saviour's great
    name,
In this our strong tower for safety we hide,
The Lord is our power, the Lord will provide.

15   Thomas Kelly   87 87 77
In blessing I will bless thee.
Genesis 22:17

Saviour! follow with Thy blessing
    Truths delivered in Thy name;
Thus the word, Thy power possessing,
    Shall declare from whence it came.
Mighty let Thy gospel be,
Set the burdened sinner free.

Let the word be food to nourish
    Those whom Thou hast called Thy own;
Let Thy people's graces flourish;
    May they live to Thee alone.
May we all in Jesus live,
And to God the glory give.

16   Joseph Irons   SM
Come in, thou blessed of the LORD.
Genesis 24:31

Ye blessèd of the Lord,
    Whose souls hate every sin,
Why should you longer stand abroad?
    Since Jesus says, 'Come in.'

Your souls have often shared
    In blessings from above:
Your Father has His house prepared;
    Come in and taste His love.

Can you His kindness doubt?
    No, you can trust His grace;
Then wherefore stand you still without?
    Come in, and see His face.

Do many scruples rise?
    Does Satan bid you stay?
'Come in, thou blessèd,' Jesus cries;
    Then why should you delay?

Christ and His church invite,
    And you should glory win;
In heavenly things your souls delight;
    'Ye blessed of God, come in.'

17   Thomas Kelly   87 87 77
Come in, thou blessed of the LORD
Genesis 24:31

Welcome hither, friends belovèd,
    Ye to whom our Lord is dear:
They who are by Him approvèd,
    Ever shall be welcome here;
'Tis our privilege to know
Those who serve our Lord below.

Welcome, brethren, welcome hither,
    In our Saviour's name we meet.
While we now remain together,
    May our fellowship be sweet;
We will speak of things above,
All our theme, a Saviour's love.

'Tis to Him we owe our treasure,
    All we have and hope to have;
Come, ye saints, unite with pleasure,
    Sing of Jesus, strong to save;
Join the happy hosts above,
Celebrate the God of love.

18   Richard Burnham   CM
Hinder me not. *Genesis 24:56*

Now shall my soul on Jesus call,
    To feel redeeming love;
'Hinder me not,' I'll say to all,
    While seeking joys above.

Though num'rous evils make me sigh,
    There's none shall e'er confound;
'Hinder me not,' shall be my cry,
    For I'm to Canaan bound.

If men combine my soul to chase,
    Ne'er may I cease to say,
'Hinder me not,' for mighty grace
    Shall strength divine convey.

If gilded toys allure my sight,
    And court a short delay,
'Hinder me not,' I'll still repeat,
    And still pursue my way.

If snares abound and foes defy,
    And all their strength unite,
'Hinder me not' shall be my cry,
    Till crowned in realms of light.

19   John Ryland   CM
Hinder me not. *Genesis 24:56*

In all my Lord's appointed ways,
  My journey I'll pursue;
Hinder me not, ye much-loved saints,
  For I must go with you.

Through floods and flames, if Jesus lead,
  I'll follow where He goes;
'Hinder me not,' shall be my cry,
  Though earth and hell oppose.

Through duty, and through trials too,
  I'll go at His command;
Hinder me not, for I am bound
  To my Immanuel's land.

And when my Saviour calls me home,
  Still this my cry shall be,
Hinder me not, come, welcome death,
  I'll gladly go with Thee.

20   John Newton   77 77
And she went to enquire of the LORD.
Genesis 25:22

'Tis a point I long to know,
  Oft it causes anxious thought;
Do I love the Lord or no?
  Am I His, or am I not?

If I love, why am I thus?
  Why this dull and lifeless frame?
Hardly, sure, can they be worse
  Who have never heard His name.

When I turn my eyes within,
  All is dark, and vain, and wild;
Filled with unbelief and sin,
  Can I deem myself a child?

If I pray, or hear, or read,
  Sin is mixed with all I do;
You that love the Lord indeed,
  Tell me, is it thus with you?

Could I joy His saints to meet,
  Choose the ways I once abhorred,
Find at times the promise sweet,
  If I did not love the Lord?

Lord, decide the doubtful case;
Thou who art Thy people's Sun,
Shine upon Thy work of grace,
  If it be indeed begun.

Let me love Thee more and more,
  If I love at all, I pray;
If I have not loved before,
  Help me to begin today.

21   John Neale   LM
And he dreamed, and behold a ladder.
Genesis 28:12

When Jacob from his brother fled,
As he reposed his weary head,
He saw in vision, with surprise,
A ladder reaching to the skies.

Ascending and descending, here,
The angels of the Lord appear;
And from the top Jehovah spoke,
And thus in sweetest accents broke:

'I am thy God and thee I'll bless,
And keep thee safe in every place;
By night and day I will defend,
And be to thee a constant Friend.'

We in this mystic ladder trace
A view of Jesus and His grace;
In Him all blessings are bestowed,
In Him we find access to God.

22   John Newton   77 77
The LORD stood above it. *Genesis 28:13*

If the Lord our leader be,
  We may follow without fear;
East or West, by land or sea,
  Home with Him is everywhere.

When from Esau Jacob fled,
  Though his pillow was a stone,
And the ground his humble bed,
  Yet he was not left alone.

Lo! he saw a ladder reared,
  Reaching to the heavenly throne;
At the top the Lord appeared,
  Spake and claimed him for His own.

Well does Jacob's ladder suit
  To the gospel throne of grace;
We are at the ladder's foot,
  Every hour, in every place.

By assuming flesh and blood,
  Jesus heaven and earth unites;
We by faith ascend to God,
  God to dwell with us delights.

Should we traverse earth around,
  To the ladder still we come:
Every spot is holy ground,
  God is there – and He's our home.

23   Gerhard Tersteegen, tr. J Wesley
                                        88 88 88
**Surely the LORD is in this place; and I knew it
not.** *Genesis 28:16*

Lo, God is here! let us adore,
  And own how holy is this place!
Let all within us feel His power,
  And silent bow before His face;
Who know His power, His grace who prove,
Serve Him with awe, with reverence love.

Lo, God is here! Him day and night
  The united choirs of angels sing;
To Him, enthroned above all height,
  Heaven's host their noblest praises bring:
Disdain not, Lord, our meaner song,
Who praise Thee with a stammering tongue.

Being of beings! may our praise
  Thy courts with grateful fragrance fill;
Still may we stand before Thy face,
  Still hear and do Thy sovereign will;
To Thee may all our thoughts arise,
Ceaseless, accepted sacrifice.

24   John Kent   CM
He called the name of that place Bethel.
Genesis 28:19

Bethel, nor is the name forgot,
  That place was holy ground:
Jacob so named the sacred spot,
  For there his God he found.

'Twas here in holy vision blessed,
  While slumber sealed his eyes,
He saw on earth a ladder placed,
  Whose top surmounts the skies.

By this the Mediator's blood
  In lively type was shown,
The only way which peace from God,
  And grace and truth came down.

On errands of stupendous grace,
  Th'angelic host came down;
For Jesus is the meeting place
  Where heaven and earth are one.

Thy Bethel visits, Lord, repeat;
  O Jacob's God, draw near;
While we approach Thy mercy seat,
  In mercy bow Thine ear.

Through His atoning sacrifice,
  Of richest, sweetest smell,
Our offerings now ascend the skies,
  And please the Father well.

PHILIP DODDRIDGE 1702-1751

25   Philip Doddridge   CM
I am the God of Bethel. *Genesis 31:13*

O God of Bethel! by whose hand
  Thy people still are fed;
Who through this weary pilgrimage
  Hast all our fathers led:

Our vows, our prayers, we now present
  Before Thy throne of grace;
God of our fathers, be the God
  Of their succeeding race.

Through each perplexing path of life
  Our wandering footsteps guide;
Give us each day our daily bread,
  And raiment fit provide.

O spread Thy covering wings around,
  Till all our wanderings cease!
And at our Father's loved abode
  Our souls arrive in peace.

Such blessings from Thy gracious hand
  Our humble prayers implore;
And Thou shalt be our chosen God
  And portion evermore.

26   Charles Wesley   88 88 88
**There wrestled a man with him until the
breaking of the day.** *Genesis 32:24*

Come, O Thou Traveller unknown,
   Whom still I hold, but cannot see!
My company before is gone,
   And I am left alone with Thee;
With Thee all night I mean to stay,
And wrestle till the break of day.

I need not tell Thee who I am,
   My misery and sin declare;
Thyself hast called me by my name;
   Look on Thy hands, and read it there:
'But who,' I ask Thee, 'who art Thou?
Tell me Thy name, and tell me now.'

In vain Thou strugglest to get free;
   I never will unloose my hold!
Art Thou the Man that died for me?
   The secret of Thy love unfold:
Wrestling, I will not let Thee go,
Till I Thy name, Thy nature know.

Yield to me now; for I am weak,
   But confident in self-despair;
Speak to my heart, in blessings speak,
   Be conquered by my instant prayer;
Speak, or Thou never hence shalt move,
And tell me if Thy name is Love.

'Tis Love! 'tis Love! Thou diedst for me!
   I hear Thy whisper in my heart;
The morning breaks, the shadows flee,
   Pure, universal Love Thou art;
To me, to all, Thy mercies move:
Thy nature and Thy name is Love.

I know Thee, Saviour, who Thou art,
   Jesus, the feeble sinner's Friend;
Nor wilt Thou with the night depart,
   But stay and love me to the end;
Thy mercies never shall remove:
Thy nature and Thy name is Love.

27   John Newton   77 77
I will not let Thee go, except Thou bless me.
Genesis 32:26

Lord, I cannot let Thee go,
Till a blessing Thou bestow;
Do not turn away Thy face;
Mine's an urgent pressing case.

Thou didst once a wretch behold,
In rebellion blindly bold;
Scorn Thy grace; Thy power defy;
That poor rebel, Lord, was I.

Once a sinner near despair
Sought Thy mercy-seat by prayer;
Mercy heard and set Him free;
Lord, that mercy came to me.

Many days have passed since then;
Many changes I have seen;
Yet have been upheld till now;
Who could hold me up but Thou?

Thou hast helped in every need;
This emboldens me to plead;
After so much mercy past,
Canst Thou let me sink at last?

No; I must maintain my hold;
'Tis Thy goodness makes me bold;
I can no denial take,
When I plead for Jesus' sake.

28   Charles Wesley   CM
I will not let Thee go. *Genesis 32:26*

Shepherd divine, our wants relieve
   In this our evil day;
To all Thy tempted followers give
   The power to watch and pray.

Long as our fiery trial last,
   Long as the cross we bear,
O let our souls on Thee be cast
   In never-ceasing prayer.

The spirit of interceding grace
   Give us in faith to claim;
To wrestle till we see Thy face
   And know Thy hidden name.

Till Thou Thy perfect love impart,
   Till Thou Thyself bestow,
Be this the cry of every heart:
   'I will not let Thee go.'

I will not let Thee go unless
   Thou tell Thy name to me,
With all Thy great salvation bless,
   And make me all like Thee.

Then let me on the mountain-top
   Behold Thine open face,
Where faith in sight is swallowed up,
   And prayer in endless praise.

29 Samuel Crowhurst 66 66 88
And He blessed him there. *Genesis 32:29*

When Jacob feared to meet
  His brother in the way;
The sins of former years
  Upon his conscience lay;
Distressed, he cried to God in prayer,
Nor cried in vain, 'He blessed him there.'

The promise God had made
  Sustained him in the strife;
While struggling hard by faith,
  He wrestled for his life:
With Him prevailed whose gracious care
Had led him forth, 'He blessed him there.'

Dear Lord! when sins oppress,
  Or conscience us accuse,
When fears of wrath arise,
  Wilt Thou our prayer refuse?
O, leave us not in dark despair,
But meet us then, and bless us there!

Give us a word in power,
  A promise from Thy throne,
That we may wrestling plead,
  And hold Thee to Thine own:
Give faith to strive till Thou dost hear,
And we can say, 'He blessed me there.'

30 'Oligos', *Christian Magazine* 1790   LM
God hath dealt graciously with me.
Genesis 33:11

The gracious dealings of the Lord
Fill up the volumes of His word;
And every new-born soul can tell
Jehovah has done all things well.

Thy love is free, immensely great;
Thy blessings full, divinely sweet;
Thy kind protection, and Thy care,
Encourage hope and ardent prayer.

Thy visits do my soul inflame,
Thy sovereign love abides the same;
Thy purposes are fixed and sure,
And in Thy strength I shall endure.

Gracious Thy dealings, free Thy love;
I pant to soar and praise above;
There join the numerous blood-bought throng,
And grace shall be my endless song.

31 *Young People's Hymnal*   LM
I am Joseph your brother, whom ye sold into Egypt. *Genesis 45:4*

The Lord, how wondrous are His ways!
With humble awe repeat His praise;
His judgements are a deep profound,
Where all our scanty thoughts are drowned.

See how to Jacob's favourite son
He makes His power and wisdom known;
In him the secrets of His will
He doth mysteriously fulfil.

His brethren hate him, and contrive
His death, by whom they all must live;
He's sold at last, and made a slave,
That he their guilty lives might save.

Thus Jesus doth His brethren save,
For them His precious life He gave;
He's hated, sold, condemned, and slain,
But rises, o'er His church to reign.

His brethren bow before His throne,
And all their vile transgressions own:
Jesus, their Brother Jesus, lives,
And, with a smile, their guilt forgives.

32 *Young People's Hymnal*   SM
So now it was not you that sent me hither but God. *Genesis 45:8*

Yes, Joseph must be sold,
  A type of Christ, his Lord;
But God was with him, we are told,
  And kept him by His word.

How wondrous are the ways
  Of providence on earth!
The darkest and the saddest days
  Are often turned to mirth.

One day in prison seen,
  Another on the throne;
Yet every day the Lord has been
  The same toward His own.

33   Isaac Watts   LM
I have waited for Thy salvation, O LORD.
Genesis 49:18

Far from my thoughts, vain world, begone;
Let my religious hours alone;
Fain would my eyes my Saviour see;
I wait a visit, Lord from Thee.

My heart grows warm with holy fire,
And kindles with a pure desire;
Come, my dear Jesus, from above,
And feed my soul with heavenly love.

Blessed Jesus! What delicious fare!
How sweet Thy entertainments are!
Never did angels taste above,
Redeeming grace and dying love.

Hail, great Immanuel, all divine!
In Thee Thy Father's glories shine;
Thou brightest, sweetest, fairest One,
That eyes have seen or angels known.

34   Charles Wesley   88 88 D
From thence is the shepherd, the stone of Israel. *Genesis 49:24*

Thou Shepherd of Israel divine,
     The joy of the contrite in heart,
For closer communion we pine,
     Still, still we reside where Thou art.
The pasture Thy chosen shall find,
     Where all who their Shepherd obey
Are fed, on Thy bosom reclined,
     Are screened from the heat of the day.

Ah! show us that happiest place,
     The place of Thy people's abode,
Where saints in an ecstasy gaze
     And hang on their crucified Lord.
Thy love for lost sinners declare,
     Thy passion and death on the tree;
Our spirits to Calvary bear,
     To suffer and triumph with Thee.

'Tis there with the lambs of Thy flock,
     There only we'd covet to rest,
To lie at the foot of the Rock,
     Or rise to be hid in Thy breast:
'Tis there we would always abide,
     And never a moment depart,
Concealed in the cleft of Thy side,
     Eternally held in Thy heart.

35   Thomas Olivers   66 84 D
I am the God of thy father, the God of Abraham, the God of Isaac, and the God of Jacob. *Exodus 3:6*

The God of Abraham praise,
     Who reigns enthroned above,
Ancient of everlasting days,
     And God of love.
Jehovah! Great I AM!
     By earth and heaven confessed;
I bow and bless the sacred name
     For ever blessed.

The God of Abraham praise,
     At whose supreme command
From earth I rise, and seek the joys
     At His right hand.
I all on earth forsake—
     Its wisdom, fame, and power—
And Him my only portion make,
     My shield and tower.

The God of Abraham praise,
     Whose all-sufficient grace
Shall guide me all my happy days
     In all my ways.
He is my faithful Friend,
     He is my gracious God;
And He shall save me to the end
     Through Jesus' blood.

He by Himself hath sworn,
     I on His oath depend:
I shall, on eagles' wings upborne,
     To heaven ascend;
I shall behold His face,
     I shall His power adore,
And sing the wonders of His grace
     For evermore.

There dwells the Lord our King,
     The Lord our Righteousness,
Triumphant o'er the world and sin,
     The Prince of Peace;
On Zion's sacred height
     His kingdom He maintains,
And glorious with His saints in light
     For ever reigns.

The whole triumphant host
     Give thanks to God on high;
Hail, Father, Son, and Holy Ghost!
     They ever cry.
Hail, Abraham's God, and mine!
     I join the heavenly lays;
All might and majesty are Thine,
     And endless praise.

36   John Latchford   CM
**And the LORD went before them by day in a
pillar of a cloud.** *Exodus 13:21*

The cloudy pillar, Lord, I see,
  Unto Thy church of old,
A blessèd figure was of Thee,
  Whose love can ne'er be told.

It was to them defence and light,
  And such they did it prove;
A cloud by day, a fire by night,
  Which showed Thy care and love.

When that did rest, they rested too,
  And in their tents abode:
It was to them their journey through,
  A guide upon the road.

So, dearest Jesus, be to me
  My soul's defence and light,
My covering till Thy face I see,
  My guide by day and night.

37   Joseph Hart   CM
**Fear ye not, stand still, and see the salvation
of the LORD.** *Exodus 14:13*

Lord, let Thy Spirit prompt us when
  To go and when to stay;
Attract us with the cords of men,
  And we shall not delay.

Give power and will, and then command,
  And we will follow Thee;
And when we're frightened, bid us stand,
  And Thy salvation see.

38   Thomas Gill   87 87 887
**The LORD is my strength and song, and He is
become my salvation.** *Exodus 15:2*

We come unto our fathers' God:
  Their Rock is our salvation:
The eternal arms, their dear abode,
  We make our habitation;
We bring Thee, Lord, the praise they brought;
We seek Thee as Thy saints have sought
  In every generation.

The fire divine their steps that led,
  Still goeth bright before us;
The heavenly shield around them spread,
  Is still held high above us;
The grace those sinners that subdued,
The strength those weaklings that renewed,
  Doth vanquish, doth restore us.

The cleaving sins that brought them low
  Are still our souls oppressing;
The tears that from their eyes did flow
  Fall fast, our shame confessing;
As with Thee, Lord, prevailed their cry,
So our strong prayer ascends on high,
  And bringeth down Thy blessing.

Their joy unto their Lord we bring;
  Their song to us descendeth;
The Spirit who in them did sing
  To us His music lendeth.
His song in them, in us, is one;
We raise it high, we send it on,
  The song that never endeth!

Ye saints to come, take up the strain,
  The same sweet theme endeavour!
Unbroken be the golden chain!
  Keep on the song for ever!
Safe in the same dear dwelling-place,
Rich with the same eternal grace,
  Bless the same boundless Giver!

39   Richard Burnham   LM
**Thy right hand, O LORD, is become glorious in
power.** *Exodus 15:6*

God is my everlasting King;
God is my Strength, and I will sing;
His power upholds my feeble frame,
And I'm victorious through His name.

Through the Redeemer's precious blood,
I feel the mighty power of God;
Through the rich aid divinely given,
I rise from earth, and soar to heaven.

Dear Lord, thy weaker saints inspire,
And fill them with celestial fire;
On Thy kind arm may they rely,
And all their foes shall surely fly.

Now, Lord, Thy wondrous power exert,
And every ransomed soul support;
Give us fresh strength to wing our way
To regions of eternal day.

There may we praise the great I AM,
And shout the victories of the Lamb;
Raise every chorus to His blood,
And triumph in the power of God.

40   John Newton   CM
The waters were made sweet.
Exodus 15:25

Bitter indeed the waters are,
   Which in this desert flow;
Though to the eye they promise fair,
   They taste of sin and woe.

But there's a wonder-working wood,
   As all believers say,
Can make these bitter waters good,
   And take the curse away.

The cross on which the Saviour died,
   And conquered for His saints,
This is the tree, by faith applied,
   Which sweetens all complaints.

All who have found this blessed effect,
   No longer mourn their lot;
While on His sorrows they reflect,
   Their own are all forgot.

When they, by faith, behold the cross,
   Though many griefs they meet;
They draw again from every loss,
   And find the bitter sweet.

41   John Latchford   LM
The waters were made sweet.
Exodus 15:25

O Lord, to Thee I'll tell my mind,
   And on Thy precious name I'll call;
Because there is, I daily find,
   A secret something sweetens all!

The Lord to me indeed is kind;
   He knows my strength is very small;
But this He gives me still to find
   There's something secret sweetens all!

And when by sickness I'm confined,
   Then low before the Lord I'd fall,
And to my comfort always find
   There's something secret sweetens all!

To me there is no peace of mind
   From all that's on this earthly ball;
But yet there is in Christ, I find,
   A secret something sweetens all!

Soon death will come with message kind,
   And I shall hear my Jesus call;
I then indeed shall truly find
   There's something secret sweetens all!

42   John Kent (alt)   87 87
I am the LORD that healeth thee.
Exodus 15:26

Jesus heals the broken-hearted;
   O how sweet that sound to me!
Once beneath my sin He smarted,
   Groaned, and bled to set me free.

By His sufferings, death, and merits;
   By His Godhead, blood, and pain;
Broken hearts, or wounded spirits,
   Are at once made whole again.

Broken by the law's loud thunder,
   To the cross for refuge flee!
O'er His pungent sorrows ponder,
   'Tis His stripes that healeth thee.

Oil and wine to heal and cherish,
   Jesus still to Israel gives;
Nor shall e'er a sinner perish,
   Who in His dear name believes.

Seek, my soul, no other healing,
   But in Jesus' precious blood;
He, beneath the Spirit's sealing,
   Stands thy great High Priest with God.

43   William Cowper   CM
I am the LORD that healeth thee.
Exodus 15:26

Heal us, Immanuel; hear our prayer;
   We wait to feel Thy touch;
Deep-wounded souls to Thee repair
   And, Saviour, we are such.

Our faith is feeble, we confess;
   We faintly trust Thy word;
But wilt Thou pity us the less?
   Be that far from Thee, Lord!

Remember him who once applied
   With trembling for relief;
'Lord, I believe!' with tears he cried,
   'O help my unbelief!'

She, too, who touched Thee in the press,
   And healing virtue stole,
Was answered: 'Daughter, go in peace,
   Thy faith hath made thee whole.'

Like her, with hopes and fears we come
   To touch Thee, if we may:
'O send us not despairing home,
   Send none unhealed away.'

44   John Newton   CM
They gathered every man according to his eating. *Exodus 16:18*

Manna to Israel well supplied
  The want of other bread;
While God is able to provide,
  His people shall be fed.

Thus, though the corn and wine should fail
  And creature-streams be dry,
The prayer of faith will still prevail,
  For blessings from on high.

Of His kind care how sweet a proof!
  It suited every taste;
Who gathered most had just enough,
  Enough who gathered least.

'Twas daily bread, and would not keep,
  But must be still renewed;
Faith should not want a hoard or heap,
  But trust the Lord for food.

Nor can the best experience past,
  The life of faith maintain;
The brightest hope will faint at last,
  Unless supplied again.

Dear Lord, while we in prayer are found,
  Do Thou the manna give;
O! let it fall on all around,
  That we may eat and live.

45   Joseph Hart   SM
And the children of Israel did eat manna forty years. *Exodus 16:35*

When through the desert vast
  The chosen tribes were led,
They could not plough, nor till, nor sow,
  Yet never wanted bread.

Around their wandering camp,
  The copious manna fell;
Strewed on the ground, a food they found,
  But *what* they could not tell.

But better bread by far
  Is now to Christians given;
Poor sinners eat immortal meat,
  The Living Bread from heaven.

We eat the flesh of Christ,
  Who is the Bread of God;
Their food was coarse compared with ours,
  Though theirs was angels' food.

46   William Cowper   66 66 88
Jehovah-nissi, *'The Lord is my banner'*
Exodus 17:15

By whom was David taught
  To aim the dreadful blow,
When he Goliath fought,
  And laid the Gittite low?
No sword nor spear the stripling took,
But chose a pebble from the brook.

'Twas Israel's God and King,
  Who sent him to the fight,
Who gave him strength to sling
  And skill to aim aright;
Ye feeble saints, your strength endures,
Because young David's God is yours.

Who ordered Gideon forth,
  To storm the invader's camp,
With arms of little worth:
  A pitcher and a lamp?
The trumpets made his coming known,
And all the host was overthrown.

O! I have seen the day,
  When, with a single word,
God helping me to say,
  'My trust is in the Lord,'
My soul has quelled a thousand foes,
Fearless of all that could oppose.

But unbelief, self-will,
  Self-righteousness, and pride,
How often do they steal
  My weapon from my side!
Yet David's Lord and Gideon's Friend,
Will help His servant to the end.

47   John Kent   886 D
I will come unto thee, and I will bless thee.
Exodus 20:24

'Where two or three together meet,
My love and mercy to repeat,
  And tell what I have done;
There will I be,' says God, 'to bless,
And every burdened soul redress,
  Who worships at My throne.'

Make one in this assembly, Lord,
Speak to each heart some healing word,
  To set from bondage free;
Impart a kind celestial shower,
And grant that we may spend an hour
  In fellowship with Thee.

Guilt from the troubled heart remove,
Constrain the soul, by love, to love,
　Release from slavish fear;
Then, though in tents of sin we groan,
We'll sing like those around Thy throne,
　Till Thou shalt bring us there.

48　　　Fanny Crosby　　　10 7 10 7 +refrain
I love my master...I will not go out free.
Exodus 21:5

I am Thine, O Lord; I have heard Thy voice
　And it told Thy love to me;
But I long to rise in the arms of faith
　And be closer drawn to Thee.

　Draw me nearer, nearer, blessèd Lord,
　　To the cross where Thou hast died;
　Draw me nearer, nearer, nearer, blessèd Lord
　　To Thy precious, bleeding side.

Consecrate me now to Thy service, Lord,
　By the power of grace divine;
Let my soul look up with a steadfast hope
　And my will be lost in Thine.

O the pure delight of a single hour
　That before Thy throne I spend,
When I kneel in prayer and with Thee, my God,
　I commune as friend with friend.

There are depths of love that I cannot know
　Till I cross the narrow sea;
There are heights of joy that I may not reach
　Till I rest in peace with Thee.

49　　　John Newton　　　87 87 D
Behold the blood of the covenant.
Exodus 24:8

Dearest Saviour! we adore Thee,
　For Thy precious life and death;
Melt each stubborn heart before Thee;
　Give us all the eye of faith.
From the law's condemning sentence,
　To Thy mercy we appeal;
Thou alone canst give repentance;
　Thou alone our souls canst heal.

50　　　John Newton　　　CM
**I will commune with thee from above
the mercy seat.** *Exodus 25:22*

Approach, my soul, the mercy-seat,
　Where Jesus answers prayer;
There humbly fall before His feet,
　For none can perish there.

Thy promise is my only plea,
　With this I venture nigh;
Thou callest burdened souls to Thee
　And such, O Lord, am I!

Bowed down beneath the load of sin,
　By Satan sorely pressed,
By wars without and fears within,
　I come to Thee for rest.

Be Thou my Shield and Hiding-place,
　That, sheltered near Thy side,
I may my fierce accuser face
　And tell him Thou hast died.

O wondrous love! to bleed and die,
　To bear the cross and shame,
That guilty sinners, such as I,
　Might plead Thy gracious name.

51　　　William Cowper　　　LM
**I will commune with thee from above
the mercy seat.** *Exodus 25:22*

Jesus, where'er Thy people meet,
There they behold Thy mercy-seat;
Where'er they seek Thee Thou art found,
And every place is hallowed ground.

For Thou, within no walls confined,
Inhabitest the humble mind;
Such ever bring Thee where they come,
And going, take Thee to their home.

Dear Shepherd of Thy chosen few,
Thy former mercies here renew;
Here to our waiting hearts proclaim
The sweetness of Thy saving name.

Here may we prove the power of prayer,
To strengthen faith and sweeten care,
To teach our faint desires to rise,
And bring all heaven before our eyes.

Lord, we are few, but Thou art near,
Nor short Thine arm, nor deaf Thine ear;
O rend the heavens, come quickly down,
And make a thousand hearts Thine own!

52　　　John Newton　　　SM
**I will commune with thee from above
the mercy seat.** *Exodus 25:22*

　Behold the throne of grace,
　　The promise calls us near;
　There Jesus shows a smiling face,
　　And waits to answer prayer.

That rich atoning blood,
Which sprinkled round we see,
Provides for those who come to God
An all-prevailing plea.

Beyond our utmost wants
His love and power can bless;
To praying souls He always grants
More than they can express.

Thine image, Lord, bestow,
Thy presence and Thy love;
We ask to serve Thee here below,
And reign with Thee above.

Abiding in Thy faith,
Our will conformed to Thine,
Let us victorious be in death,
And then in glory shine.

53   John Newton   CM
And Aaron shall bear their names.
Exodus 28:12

Christ bears the name of all His saints,
Deep on His heart engraved;
Attentive to the state and wants
Of all His love has saved.

In Him a holiness complete,
Light, and perfection shine;
And wisdom, grace, and glory meet;
A Saviour all divine.

The blood, which, as a priest, He bears
For sinners, is His own;
The incense of His prayers and tears
Perfumes the holy throne.

In Him my weary soul has rest,
Though I am weak and vile;
I read my name upon His breast,
And see the Father smile.

54   Isaac Watts   CM
Once in the year shall he make atonement.
Exodus 30:10

Jesus, in Thee our eyes behold
A thousand glories more
Than the rich gems and polished gold
The sons of Aaron wore.

They first their own burnt-offerings brought,
To purge themselves from sin:
Thy life was pure, without a spot,
And all Thy nature clean.

Fresh blood, as constant as the day,
Was on their altar spilt:
But Thy one offering takes away
For ever all our guilt.

Their priesthood ran through several hands,
For mortal was their race:
Thy never-changing office stands
Eternal as Thy days.

Once, in the circuit of a year,
With blood, but not their own,
Did they within the veil appear,
Before the golden throne.

But Christ, by His own powerful blood,
Ascends above the skies;
And in the presence of our God
Shows His own sacrifice.

Jesus, the King of glory, reigns
On Zion's heavenly hill,
Looks like a Lamb that has been slain,
And wears His priesthood still.

He ever lives to intercede
Before His Father's face:
Give Him, my soul, thy cause to plead,
Nor doubt the Father's grace.

55   John Newton   LM
**Six days may work be done; but in the seventh
is the sabbath of rest, holy to the LORD.**
Exodus 31:15

How welcome to the saints, when pressed
With six days' noise, and care, and toil,
Is the returning day of rest,
Which hides them from the world awhile!

Now, from the throng withdrawn away,
They seem to breathe a different air;
Composed and softened by the day,
All things another aspect wear.

How happy if their lot is cast
Where statedly the gospel sounds!
The word is honey to their taste,
Renews their strength and heals their wounds.

With joy they hasten to the place
Where they their Saviour oft have met;
And while they feast upon His grace,
Their burdens and their griefs forget.

This favoured lot, my friends, is ours;
May we the privilege highly prize,
And find these consecrated hours
Sweet earnests of immortal joys.

56   Frances Havergal   65 65 65 D
Who is on the LORD'S side?
Exodus 32:26

Who is on the Lord's side?
   Who will serve the King?
Who will be His helpers
   Other lives to bring?
Who will leave the world's side?
   Who will face the foe?
Who is on the Lord's side?
   Who for Him will go?
By Thy call of mercy,
   By Thy grace divine,
We are on the Lord's side;
   Saviour, we are Thine.

Not for weight of glory,
   Not for crown and palm,
Enter we the army,
   Raise the warrior-psalm;
But for love that claimeth
   Lives for whom He died:-
He whom Jesus nameth
   Must be on His side.
By Thy love constraining,
   By Thy grace divine,
We are on the Lord's side;
   Saviour, we are Thine.

Jesus, Thou hast bought us,
   Not with gold or gem,
But with Thine own life-blood,
   For Thy diadem.
With Thy blessing filling
   Each who comes to Thee,
Thou hast made us willing,
   Thou hast made us free.
By Thy great redemption,
   By Thy grace divine,
We are on the Lord's side;
   Saviour, we are Thine.

Fierce may be the conflict,
   Strong may be the foe,
But the King's own army
   None can overthrow;
Round His standard ranging
   Victory is secure,
For His truth unchanging
   Makes the triumph sure.
Joyfully enlisting
   By Thy grace divine,
We are on the Lord's side;
   Saviour, we are Thine.

Chosen to be soldiers
   In an alien land,
Chosen, called and faithful
   For our Captain's band,
In the service royal
   Let us not grow cold;
Let us be right loyal,
   Noble, true and bold.
Master, Thou wilt keep us
   By Thy grace divine,
Always on the Lord's side,
   Saviour, always Thine.

57   James Edmeston   87 87 87
My presence shall go with thee, and I will give thee rest. *Exodus 33:14*

Lead us, heavenly Father, lead us
   O'er the world's tempestuous sea;
Guard us, guide us, keep us, feed us,
   For we have no help but Thee;
Yet possessing every blessing
   If our God our Father be.

Saviour, breathe forgiveness o'er us;
   All our weakness Thou dost know;
Thou didst tread this earth before us,
   Thou didst feel its keenest woe;
Lone and dreary, faint and weary,
   Through the desert Thou didst go.

Spirit of our God, descending,
   Fill our hearts with heavenly joy,
Love with every passion blending,
   Pleasure that can never cloy;
Thus provided, pardoned, guided,
   Nothing can our peace destroy.

58   John Fawcett   CM
My presence shall go with thee, and I will give thee rest. *Exodus 33:14*

Lord, in a wilderness I rove,
   With foes and fears oppressed;
Grant me the presence of Thy love,
   For that will give me rest.

Protect my soul from Satan's wiles,
   And ease my troubled breast;
Refresh me with Thy cheering smiles,
   For Thou canst give me rest.

Cheerful I'll walk the desert through,
   If with Thy presence blest;
Nor fear what earth or hell can do,
   For Thou wilt give me rest.

When snares and dangers fill the way,
    And I am sore distressed,
I'll fly to Thee, my strength and stay,
    For Thou wilt give me rest.

The happy day is drawing nigh
    When I shall be released,
And rise to dwell with Thee on high,
    In everlasting rest.

59   William Gadsby   CM
My presence shall go with thee, and I will give thee rest. *Exodus 33:14*

Jesus, Thou art our only rest
    From sin, and guilt, and fears;
We love to lean upon Thy breast,
    And on Thee cast our cares.

With anxious care and painful thought,
    We toiled and toiled again;
True holiness was what we sought,
    But this we sought in vain.

The works of nature, bad or good,
    Availèd nothing here;
Faith viewed the Saviour's precious blood,
    And banished guilt and fear.

Here's life, and light, and holiness,
    And righteousness divine;
A boundless treasure, all of grace,
    And faith says, 'All is mine.'

O what a rest is Christ to me!
    How precious and how true!
From guilt and sin He sets me free,
    And gives me glory too.

I have, I want no rest beside;
    Here's all a God can give;
Here would I constantly abide,
    And every moment live.

60   Joseph Irons   CM
I beseech Thee, show me Thy glory.
Exodus 33:18

'Show me Thy glory' dearest Lord,
    Which shines in Jesus' face;
A view of covenant love afford
    To subjects of Thy grace.

'Show me Thy glory' in the plan
    Which makes salvation free:
'Show me Thy glory' in the Man,
    Who lived and died for me.

Within that rock where Thou art seen,
    Thy glory, Lord, unfold,
Until, without a cloud between,
    Thy glory I behold.

61   William Gadsby   SM
I will make all my goodness pass before thee.
Exodus 33:19

Though we walk through this wilderness
    God's promise is our stay;
His goodness He will make to pass
    Before us in the way.

Goodness, immortal and divine,
    The bliss of endless day,
The Lord our God will make to pass
    Before us in the way.

The boundless treasures of His grace,
    He surely will display,
And all His goodness make to pass
    Before us in the way.

To make His saints His glory view,
    And sing their cares away,
The Lord will make His goodness pass
    Before them in the way.

62   William Gadsby   SM
I will proclaim the name of the LORD before thee. *Exodus 33:19*

The Lord proclaims His name;
    And sinners hear His voice;
His mercy ever stands the same,
    And we'll in Him rejoice.

His name is gracious still,
    And freely He bestows
The bounty of His sovereign will,
    On all who feel their woes.

His patience long endures,
    And savèd sinners know,
A God, long-suffering, still restores
    Their joy and peace below.

The thousands whom He loves
    He pardons and forgives,
Their persons He in Christ approves,
    And will while Jesus lives.

Lord, help us to believe,
    And make Thy name our choice;
Thy mercy freely to us give,
    And we'll in Thee rejoice.

SAMUEL MEDLEY 1738-99

63   Samuel Medley   CM
**The LORD, The LORD God, merciful and
gracious, longsuffering, and abundant in
goodness and truth.** *Exodus 34:6*

God shall alone the refuge be
   And comfort of my mind;
Too wise to be mistaken, He,
   Too good to be unkind.

In all His holy, sovereign will,
   He is, I daily find,
Too wise to be mistaken still,
   Too good to be unkind.

When I the tempter's rage endure,
   'Tis God supports my mind;
Too wise to be mistaken, sure!
   Too good to be unkind.

Though I cannot His goings see,
   Nor all His footsteps find;
Too wise to be mistaken, He,
   Too good to be unkind.

Hereafter He will make me know
   And I shall surely find,
He was too wise to err, and O
   Too good to be unkind!

64   Vernon Higham   DCM
**Then a cloud covered the tent of the
congregation, and the glory of the LORD filled
the tabernacle.** *Exodus 40:34*

O hear the cry of saints below,
   Although we are but few,
We long to see Thy mercy flow,
   And know Thy grace is true.
Almighty God, Redeemer King,
   Reveal Thy saving arm;
Display Thy majesty, and bring
   A myriad souls from harm.

O grant our hungry souls a sight
   Of glorious sovereign grace;
Yet clouds of mercy veil the light
   Of Jesus' smiling face.
O let Thy glory dress this tent,
   Our hearts with rapture fill
With certain hope, when Thou art bent
   Our longing hearts to thrill.

O leave us not in deep despair
   With dreaded word of loss;
Thy glory gone, and none to bear
   The tidings of Thy cross.
Revive Thy work, grant Thine embrace
   To us by day and night,
A shaft of fire, a cloud of grace:
   Display Thy word in might.

© Author

65   Horatius Bonar   76 76 D
**And he shall lay his hand upon the head of the
sin offering.** *Leviticus 4:29*

I lay my sins on Jesus,
   The spotless Lamb of God,
He bears them all and frees us
   From the accursèd load;
I bring my guilt to Jesus,
   To wash my crimson stains
White in His blood most precious,
   Till not a spot remains!

I lay my wants on Jesus,
   All fulness dwells in Him;
He heals all my diseases,
   He doth my soul redeem;
I lay my griefs on Jesus,
   My burdens and my cares,
He from them all releases,
   He all my sorrow shares.

I rest my soul on Jesus,
   This weary soul of mine,
His right hand me embraces,
   I on His breast recline;
I love the name of Jesus,
   Immanuel, Christ, the Lord;
Like fragrance on the breezes,
   His name abroad is poured.

I long to be like Jesus,
   Meek, loving, lowly, mild;
I long to be like Jesus,
   The Father's Holy Child!
I long to be with Jesus
   Amid the heavenly throng,
To sing with saints His praises,
   To learn the angels' song.

66   Samuel Medley   10 10 11 11
For today the LORD will appear unto you.
Leviticus 9:4

My soul, Lord, inflame with zeal from above.
Thy praise to proclaim, and sing of Thy love;
To lift up my voice in thanksgiving sincere,
This truth to rejoice in, 'the Lord will appear.'

How joyful this sound, while daily I find
Afflictions abound in body and mind!
It oft has afforded relief from my fear,
To find it recorded, 'the Lord will appear.'

I have, as I seem, when left in the dark,
Of light not a beam, of love not a spark:
And though thus in pain for an evidence clear,
I can't wait in vain, for 'the Lord will appear.'

A warfare I find without and within,
With legions combined, world, Satan, and sin;
Though sore they annoy me, I'll be of good cheer,
They shall not destroy me, 'the Lord will appear.'

My fears sometimes say, I never shall find
In death's awful day true peace in my mind;
But, though thus surrounded, yet, when I come
    there,
I can't be confounded, 'the Lord will appear.'

My dust He will raise, and glory He'll give,
And I to His praise in heaven shall live;
There He will deliver my soul from all fear,
And to me for ever 'the Lord will appear.'

67   William Horne   77 77
And the leper...shall cry, Unclean, unclean.
Leviticus 13:45

Jesus, Thou alone canst save,
    Thou canst raise the dead to life;
Thy reviving power I crave,
    To decide this inward strife.

Sin my every power defiles,
    Thought, and word, and action too;
Jesus, in Thy mercy smile;
    Cleanse, and make me white as snow.

Fierce, impetuous, o'er my head
    Billows of temptation roll;
Sorrows rise, and joys are fled;
    Darkness veils my shipwrecked soul.

'Midst the waves O bear me up;
    In Thy strength alone I stand;
In Thy promise is my hope;
    Guide me safe to Zion's land.

68   Hugh Stowell   LM
For I will appear in the cloud upon the mercy seat. *Leviticus 16:2*

From every stormy wind that blows,
From every swelling tide of woes,
There is a calm, a safe retreat;
'Tis found beneath the mercy-seat.

There is a place where Jesus sheds
The oil of gladness on our heads,
A place than all beside more sweet;
It is the blood-stained mercy-seat.

There is a spot where spirits blend,
Where friend holds fellowship with friend;
Though sundered far, by faith they meet
Around one common mercy-seat.

There, there, on eagles' wings we soar,
And time and sense seem all no more;
And heaven comes down our souls to greet,
And glory crowns the mercy-seat.

O let my hands forget their skill,
This tongue be silent, cold and still.
This bounding heart forget to beat
If I forget the mercy-seat.

69   Richard Burnham   CM
Ye shall be holy: for I the LORD your God am holy. *Leviticus 19:2*

The Father is a holy God;
    His holy Son He gave;
Who freely shed atoning blood,
    A guilty world to save.

The Spirit brings the chosen race,
    A holy Christ to view;
And while by faith they see His face,
    Their souls grow holy too.

In holiness the saints delight,
    While here on earth they dwell;
By faith they wrestle day and night,
    More holiness to feel.

The Holy Spirit leads them on,
    His holy truth to know;
Inscribes His laws in every son,
    And works obedience too.

He makes them feel the cleansing grace,
    That flows through Jesus' blood;
Unites in love the holy race,
    The new-born sons of God.

70   John Berridge, from John Cennick   CM
Ye shall inherit their land...a land that floweth with milk and honey.
Leviticus 20:24

Too long, alas, I vainly sought
    For happiness below,
But earthly comforts, dearly bought,
    No solid good bestow.

At length, through Jesus' grace, I found
    The good and promised land
Where milk and honey much abound
    And grapes In clusters stand.

My soul has tasted of the grapes,
    And now it longs to go
Where my dear Lord His vineyard keeps
    And all the clusters grow.

Upon the true and living Vine
    My famished soul would feast,
And banquet on the fruit divine,
    An everlasting guest.

71   Charles Wesley   66 66 88
Then shalt thou cause the trumpet of the jubilee to sound. *Leviticus 25:9*

Blow ye the trumpet, blow
    The gladly solemn sound;
Let all the nations know,
    To earth's remotest bound,
The year of jubilee is come,
Return, ye ransomed sinners, home!

Exalt the Lamb of God,
    The sin-atoning Lamb;
Redemption by His blood
    Through all the world proclaim:
The year of jubilee is come,
Return, ye ransomed sinners, home!

Ye who have sold for nought
    Your heritage above,
Shall have it back unbought,
    The gift of Jesus' love;
The year of jubilee is come,
Return, ye ransomed sinners, home!

Ye slaves of sin and hell,
    Your liberty receive
And safe in Jesus dwell
    And blest in Jesus live;
The year of jubilee is come,
Return, ye ransomed sinners, home!

Jesus, our great High Priest,
    Has full atonement made;
Ye weary spirits rest,
    Ye mournful souls be glad!
The year of jubilee has come,
Return, ye ransomed sinners, home!

72   John Fawcett   87 87 47
The LORD bless thee, and keep thee.
Numbers 6:24

Lord, dismiss us with Thy blessing;
    Fill our hearts with joy and peace;
Let us each, Thy love possessing,
    Triumph in redeeming grace.
        O refresh us!
    Travelling through this wilderness.

Thanks we give and adoration,
    For Thy gospel's joyful sound;
May the fruits of Thy salvation
    In our hearts and lives abound;
        May Thy presence
    With us evermore be found.

So, whene'er the signal's given,
    Us from earth to call away,
Borne on angels' wings to heaven,
    Glad the summons to obey,
        May we ever,
    Reign with Christ in endless day.

73   John Newton   SM
We are journeying unto the place of which the LORD said, I will give it you.
Numbers 10:29

From Egypt lately freed,
    By the Redeemer's grace,
A rough and thorny path we tread,
    In hopes to see His face.

The flesh dislikes the way,
    But faith approves it well;
This only leads to endless day
    All others lead to hell.

The promised land of peace,
    Faith keeps in constant view;
How different from the wilderness
    We now are passing through!

Here often from our eyes
    Clouds hide the light divine;
There we shall have unclouded skies,
    Our Sun will always shine.

Here griefs, and cares, and pains,
    And fears distress us sore;
But there eternal pleasure reigns,
    And we shall weep no more.

Lord, pardon our complaints;
We follow at Thy call;
The joy prepared for suffering saints,
Will make amends for all.

74   James Montgomery   CM
Come thou with us, and we will do thee good.
Numbers 10:29

Come in, thou blessèd of the Lord,
Stranger nor foe art thou;
We welcome thee with warm accord,
Our friend, our brother now.

The hand of fellowship, the heart
Of love, we offer thee:
Leaving the world, thou dost but part
From lies and vanity.

The cup of blessing which we bless,
The heavenly bread we break,
(Our Saviour's blood and righteousness),
Freely with us partake.

Come with us, we will do thee good,
As God to us hath done;
Stand but in Him, as those have stood,
Whose faith the victory won.

And when, by turns, we pass away,
As star by star grows dim,
May each, translated into day,
Be lost, and found in Him!

75   Isaac Watts   CM
God is not a man, that He should lie.
Numbers 23:19

Begin, my tongue, some heavenly theme,
And speak some boundless thing;
The mighty works, or mightier name,
Of our eternal King.

Tell of His wondrous faithfulness,
And sound His power abroad;
Sing the sweet promise of His grace,
And the performing God.

Proclaim, 'Salvation from the Lord,
For wretched dying men';
His hand has writ the sacred word
With an immortal pen.

Engraved as in eternal brass,
The mighty promise shines;
Nor can the powers of darkness rase
Those everlasting lines.

His every word of grace is strong
As that which built the skies;
The voice that rolls the stars along
Speaks all the promises.

76   John Newton   87 87 77
Hath He said, and shall He not do it?
Numbers 23:19

Yes! since God Himself hath said it,
On the promise I rely;
His good Word demands my credit,
What can unbelief reply?
He is strong, and can fulfil,
He is truth, and therefore will.

Sure the Lord thus far has brought me,
By His watchful, tender care;
Sure 'tis He Himself has taught me
How to seek His face by prayer.
After so much mercy past,
Will He give me up at last?

True, I am a foolish creature,
And have sinned against His grace!
But forgiveness is His nature,
Though He justly hides His face.
Ere He called me, well He knew
What a heart like mine would do.

In my Saviour's intercession,
Therefore I will still confide;
Lord, accept my free confession,
I have sinned, but Thou hast died:
This is all I have to plead,
This is all the plea I need.

77   Thomas Gibbons   LM
What hath God wrought! *Numbers 23:23*

'What hath God wrought!' might Israel say,
When Jordan rolled its waves away,
And gave a passage to their bands
To march secure across the sands.

'What hath God wrought!' might well be said
When Jesus, rising from the dead,
Scattered the shades of pagan night,
And blessed the nations with His light.

'What hath God wrought!' O blissful theme!
Are we redeemed and called by Him?
Shall we be led the desert through?
And safe arrive in glory too?

The news shall every harp employ
Fill every tongue with rapturous joy:
When we shall join the heavenly throng,
We'll swell the triumph and the song.

78   James Maxwell   CM
He was zealous for his God.
Numbers 25:13

Did Christ, believer, suffer shame,
    And bear the cross for thee;
And dost thou fear to own His name,
    Or bold for Jesus be?

Lord, may Thy people never dread
    To suffer shame or loss;
But in Thy footsteps may we tread.
    And glory in Thy cross.

Inspire our souls with zeal divine,
    And holy courage bold;
May knowledge, faith, and meekness shine,
    Nor let our love grow cold.

79   David Denham   SM
Who hath God so nigh unto them?
Deuteronomy 4:7

Who hath the Lord so nigh
    As Israel, whom He chose?
Kept as the apple of His eye,
    Amidst their raging foes.

In bonds of ancient love,
    He's nigh by sovereign choice,
Which all the ransomed millions prove,
    When called to hear His voice.

He's nigh to pardon sin,
    And heal each broken heart:
When Satan like a flood comes in,
    Jesus will strength impart.

He's nigh to do us good,
    When all our foes assail;
He will be nigh in Jordan's flood,
    When heart and flesh shall fail.

In hope of joys unknown,
    Let all the ransomed cry,
'All glory to the Three-in-One!
    For who hath God so nigh?'

80   David Denham   88 88 88
Teach them (to) **thy sons.**
Deuteronomy 4:9

Thou glorious source of light and love,
    Shine forth upon our rising race,
The darkness from their minds remove,
    And make them subjects of Thy grace:

Lord, send Thy Holy Spirit down,
And with success our efforts crown.

While we instruct them in Thy ways,
    Breathe on their souls, and life impart;
In babes and weaklings perfect praise;
    And write Thy laws within their heart:

The spirit of their minds renew,
    That they by faith may walk with God;
The love and power of sin subdue,
    And seal them Thine with Jesus' blood:

May all who in this work unite,
    Go on and prosper, never tire;
Be Thou their souls' supreme delight,
    And far exceed their hearts' desire:

Thus may Thy glorious kingdom spread,
    And millions more to Christ be given,
Till all for whom He fought and bled,
    Their loud hosannas sing in heaven.

81   *Gospel Magazine* 1778   SM
He will not forsake thee, neither destroy thee, nor forget the covenant of thy fathers.
Deuteronomy 4:31

The covenant of free grace,
    As made with Christ our Head,
Is stored with precious promises,
    By which our souls are fed.

The solemn oath of God
    Confirms each promise true;
And Jesus, with His precious blood,
    Has sealed the covenant, too!

Hence all our comforts flow,
    And balm for every fear;
May we by sweet experience know
    How choice, how rich they are.

82   Frances Alstyne   87 87 D
And thou shalt remember all the way which the LORD thy God led thee.
Deuteronomy 8:2

All the way my Saviour leads me:
    What have I to ask beside?
Can I doubt His tender mercy,
    Who through life has been my guide?
Heavenly peace, divinest comfort,
    Here by faith in Him to dwell!
For I know whate'er befall me,
    Jesus doeth all things well.

All the way my Saviour leads me:
    Cheers each winding path I tread,
Gives me grace for every trial,
    Feeds me with the living bread.

Though my weary steps may falter,
And my soul athirst may be,
Gushing from the rock before me,
Lo! a spring of joy I see.

All the way my Saviour leads me;
O the fulness of His love!
Perfect rest to me is promised
In my Father's house above.
When my spirit, clothed, immortal,
Wings its flight to realms of day,
This my song through endless ages—
Jesus led me all the way.

83 John Fawcett CM
And thou shalt remember all the way which the LORD thy God led thee.
Deuteronomy 8:2

Thus far my God has led me on,
And made His truth and mercy known;
My hopes and fears alternate rise,
And comforts mingle with my sighs.

Through this wide wilderness I roam,
Far distant from my blissful home;
Lord, let Thy presence be my stay,
And guard me in this dangerous way.

Temptations everywhere annoy,
And sins and snares my peace destroy;
My earthly joys are from me torn,
And oft an absent God I mourn.

My soul, with various tempests tossed,
Her hopes o'erturned, her projects crossed,
Sees every day new straits attend,
And wonders where the scene will end.

Is this, dear Lord, that thorny road
Which leads us to the mount of God?
Are these the toils Thy people know,
While in this wilderness below?

'Tis even so; Thy faithful love
Does all Thy children's graces prove;
'Tis thus our pride and self must fall
That Jesus may be all in all.

84 John Cennick LM
When thou hast eaten and art full, then thou shalt bless the LORD.
Deuteronomy 8:10

We bless Thee, Lord, for this our food,
But most of all for Jesus' blood:
May manna to our souls be given,
The bread of life sent down from heaven.

85 John Newton (alt) LM
That He might humble thee, and that He might prove thee, to do thee good at thy latter end.
Deuteronomy 8:16

I asked the Lord that I might grow
In faith, and love, and every grace,
Might more of His salvation know,
And seek more earnestly His face.

'Twas He Who taught me thus to pray,
And He, I trust, has answered prayer;
But it has been in such a way
As almost drove me to despair.

I hoped that in some favoured hour
At once He'd answer my request;
And, by His love's constraining power,
Subdue my sins, and give me rest.

Instead of this, He made me feel
The hidden evils of my heart,
And let the angry powers of hell
Assault my soul in every part.

'Lord, why is this?' I trembling cried,
'Wilt Thou pursue my soul to death?'
''Tis in this way', the Lord replied,
'I answer prayer for grace and faith.

'These inward trials I employ,
From self and pride to set thee free,
And break thy schemes of earthly joy,
That thou mayest seek thy all in Me.'

86 John Needham CM
What doth the LORD thy God require of thee, but to fear the LORD thy God, to walk in all His ways, and to love Him, and to serve the LORD thy God with all thy heart and with all thy soul.
Deuteronomy 10:12

Fear is a grace which ever dwells
With its fair partner, love;
Blending their beauties, both proclaim
Their source is from above.

Let terrors fright the unwilling slave,
The child with joy appears;
Cheerful he does his Father's will,
And loves as much as fears.

Let fear and love, most holy God,
Possess this soul of mine;
Then shall I worship Thee aright,
And taste Thy joys divine.

87   Benjamin Beddome   LM
Just and right is He. *Deuteronomy 32:4*

Great God! my Maker and my King,
Of Thee I'll speak, of Thee I'll sing;
All Thou hast done, and all Thou dost,
Declare Thee good, proclaim Thee just.

Thy ancient thoughts and firm decrees;
Thy threatenings and Thy promises;
The joys of heaven, the pains of hell,
What angels taste, what devils feel;

Thy terrors and Thy acts of grace;
Thy threatening rod, and smiling face;
Thy wounding and Thy healing word;
A world undone, a world restored;

While these excite my fear and joy,
While these my tuneful lips employ,
Accept, O Lord, the humble song,
The tribute of a trembling tongue.

88   Timothy Dwight   SM
He kept them as the apple of his eye.
Deuteronomy 32:10

I love Thy kingdom, Lord,
The house of Thine abode,
The church our blest Redeemer saved
With His own precious blood.

I love Thy church, O God:
Her walls before Thee stand,
Dear as the apple of Thine eye,
And graven on Thy hand.

For her my tears shall fall,
For her my prayers ascend,
To her my cares and toils be given,
Till toils and cares shall end.

Beyond my highest joy
I prize her heavenly ways,
Her sweet communion, solemn vows,
Her hymns of love and praise.

Jesus, Thou Friend divine,
Our Saviour and our King,
Thy hand from every snare and foe
Shall great deliverance bring.

Sure as Thy truth shall last,
To Zion shall be given
The brightest glories earth can yield,
And brighter bliss of heaven.

89   Isaac Watts   CM
And die in the mount. *Deuteronomy 32:50*

Lord, 'tis an infinite delight
To see Thy lovely face,
To dwell whole ages in Thy sight,
And feel Thy vital rays.

Thy love, a sea without a shore,
Spreads life and joy abroad;
O, 'tis a heaven worth dying for,
To see a smiling God!

Sweet was the journey to the sky
The wondrous prophet tried;
'Climb up the mount', says God, 'and die';
The prophet climbed and died.

Softly his fainting head he lay
Upon his Maker's breast,
His Maker kissed his soul away,
And laid his flesh to rest.

Thus in God's arms I'd leave my breath,
That His own Spirit gave;
This is the noblest road to death,
And this the sweetest grave.

90   John Adams   77 77
**The beloved of the LORD shall dwell in safety
by Him.** *Deuteronomy 33:12*

Lord, how many are my foes!
Many they that me oppose;
Thou my strong Protector be;
All my safety is in Thee.

Satan and my wicked heart
Often use their treacherous art;
Fain would make my soul to flee;
But my safety is in Thee.

Thou hast said and Thou art true,
'As I live, ye shall live too';
Thou my Rock wilt ever be;
All my safety is in Thee.

I'm a pilgrim here below;
Guide me all the desert through;
Let me, as I journey, see
All my safety is in Thee.

Then, when landed on that shore,
Where my mind was fixed before,
In sweet raptures I shall see
All my safety was in Thee.

91   James Montgomery   77 77
They shall call the people unto the mountain.
Deuteronomy 33:19

When on Sinai's top, I see
God descend in majesty,
To proclaim His holy law,
All my spirit sinks with awe.

When in ecstasy sublime,
Tabor's glorious height I climb.
In the too-transporting light,
Darkness rushes o'er my sight.

When on Calvary I rest,
God in flesh made manifest,
Shines in my Redeemer's face,
Full of beauty, truth, and grace.

Here I would for ever stay,
Weep and gaze my soul away;
Thou art heaven on earth to me,
Lovely, mournful Calvary.

92   John Fawcett   LM
As thy days, so shall thy strength be.
Deuteronomy 33:25

Afflicted saint, to Christ draw near,
Thy Saviour's gracious promise hear;
His faithful Word declares to thee,
That, as thy days, thy strength shall be.

Let not thy heart despond and say,
'How shall I stand the trying day?'
He has engaged by firm decree,
That, as thy days, thy strength shall be.

Thy faith is weak, thy foes are strong,
And if the conflict should be long,
The Lord will make the tempter flee:
For, as thy days, thy strength shall be.

Should persecutions rage and flame,
Still trust in thy Redeemer's name;
In fiery trials thou shalt see,
That, as thy days, thy strength shall be.

When called to bear the weighty cross,
Of sore affliction, pain, or loss,
Or deep distress or poverty,
Still, as thy days, thy strength shall be.

When ghastly death appears in view,
Christ's presence shall thy fears subdue;
He comes to set thy spirit free,
And, as thy days, thy strength shall be.

93   Anne Steele   CM
**The eternal God is thy refuge, and underneath
are the everlasting arms.**
Deuteronomy 33:27

Dear Refuge of my weary soul,
On Thee, when sorrows rise,
On Thee, when waves of trouble roll,
My fainting hope relies.

To Thee I tell each rising grief,
For Thou alone canst heal;
Thy word can bring a sweet relief
For every pain I feel.

But O! when gloomy doubts prevail,
I fear to call Thee mine;
The springs of comfort seem to fail,
And all my hopes decline.

Yet, gracious God, where shall I flee?
Thou art my only trust;
And still my soul would cleave to Thee,
Though prostrate in the dust.

Thy mercy-seat is open still;
Here let my soul retreat;
With humble hope attend Thy will,
And wait beneath Thy feet.

94   John Kent   11 11 11 11
**The eternal God is thy refuge, and underneath
are the everlasting arms.**
Deuteronomy 33:27

A refuge for sinners the gospel makes known;
'Tis found in the merits of Jesus alone;
The weary, the tempted, and burdened by sin,
Were never exempted from entering therein.

This refuge for sinners His love did ordain,
In Jesus the Lamb, from eternity slain;
And if God the Spirit reveal this to you,
Take refuge in Jesus, though hell should pursue.

The soul that shall enter in safety shall dwell;
There's no peradventure of sinking to hell;
The oath of Jehovah secures him from fear,
Nor shall the avenger of blood enter there.

Here's refuge for sinners, whose guilt shall appear
As black as the confines of endless despair;
Who, stripped of all merit whereon to rely,
Are taught by the Spirit to Jesus to fly.

Should conscience accuse us, as oft-times it may,
Here's blood that can take its defilement away.
In Jesus the Saviour, the sinner shall view
A city of refuge and righteousness too.

95   John Newton   CM
Happy art thou, O Israel.
Deuteronomy 33:29

Happy are they to whom the Lord
    His gracious name makes known!
And by His Spirit and His Word
    Adopts them for His own.

He calls them to a mercy-seat,
    And hears their humble prayer,
And when within His house they meet,
    They find His presence near.

The force of their united cries
    No power can long withstand;
For Jesus helps them from the skies,
    By His almighty hand.

Then mountains sink at once to plains,
    And light from darkness springs;
Each seeming loss improves their gains;
    Each trouble comfort brings.

Dear Lord, assist our souls to pay
    The debt of praise we owe;
That we enjoy a gospel-day,
    And heaven begun below.

96   Samuel Stennett   CM
**And the LORD showed him all the land of
Gilead, unto Dan.** *Deuteronomy 34:1*

On Jordan's stormy banks I stand,
    And cast a wishful eye
To Canaan's fair and happy land,
    Where my possessions lie.

O the transporting rapturous scene
    That rises to my sight!
Sweet fields arrayed in living green,
    And rivers of delight.

All o'er those wide-extended plains
    Shines one eternal day;
There God the Sun for ever reigns,
    And scatters night away.

When shall I reach that happy place,
    And be for ever blest?
When shall I see my Father's face,
    And in His bosom rest?

Filled with delight, my raptured soul
    Can here no longer stay,
Though Jordan's waves around me roll,
    Fearless I'd launch away.

97   Frederick Faber   CM
**Be strong and of a good courage; be not
afraid, neither be thou dismayed: for the LORD
thy God is with thee whithersoever thou goest.**
Joshua 1:9

Workman of God! O lose not heart,
    But learn what God is like,
And, in the darkest battle-field
    Thou shalt know where to strike.

Ah! God is other than we think;
    His ways are far above,
Far beyond reason's height, and reached
    Only by childlike love.

He hides Himself so wondrously,
    As though there were no God;
He is least seen when all the powers
    Of ill are most abroad.

Thrice blest is he to whom is given
    The instinct that can tell
That God is on the field, when He
    Is most invisible.

For right is right, since God is God,
    And right the day must win;
To doubt would be disloyalty,
    To falter would be sin.

98   John Kent   LM
**Thou shalt bind this line of scarlet thread in
the window which thou didst let us down by.**
Joshua 2:18

When God's own arm, His power to show,
Threw down the walls of Jericho,
In Rahab's house was safety found,
For there the scarlet thread was bound.

By faith she saw th'approaching storm,
And trembled at Jehovah's arm,
Received the spies in peace, 'tis said,
And bound the well-known scarlet thread.

By faith she saw the towering wall
Before the blast of rams' horns fall,
And did in that tremendous day,
The peaceful scarlet sign display.

'Come, kindred, here, make haste,' she cried,
'Destruction waits on every side;
No harm shall enter where we dwell,
The scarlet thread secures us well.'

Seven times she saw the troops go round,
And heard the rugged rams' horns sound;
But did no death nor danger fear,
Because the scarlet thread was there.

At length they blew the fatal blast,
When to the ground the walls were cast;
Vast was the slaughter, old and young,
Save where the scarlet thread was hung.

Like Israel, safe, whose favoured door
Was sprinkled well with paschal gore;
The sacred sign was just the same,
The scarlet thread or slaughtered lamb.

But we can nobler wonders tell,
By Jesus' blood redeemed from hell;
Secured by this from wrath divine,
We bless the sacred peaceful sign.

99   Henry Fowler   LM
**Come hither, and hear the words of the LORD
your God.** *Joshua 3:9*

Come hither, ye by sin distressed,
    And hear the Saviour's faithful word;
Soon ye shall enter into rest,
    And know that He's your conquering Lord.

Come hither, ye whose rising fears
    Forbid you to exult and sing;
Whose moments pass in sighs and tears,
    Feeling your guilt a dreadful sting.

Does Satan tempt you to give up,
    And call no more on Jesus' name?
Cast not away your little hope;
    Come hither, and behold the Lamb.

Come hither, to the Saviour come,
    Vile as thou art in every view;
In Jesus' house there still is room
    For needy sinners, such as you.

Power and love in Christ combine,
    An able, willing Saviour too;
Is He a Sun? On thee He'll shine.
    Is He thy God? He'll bring thee through.

100   Samuel Medley   CM
**Give me a blessing; for thou hast given me a
south land; give me also springs of water.**
Joshua 15:19

Now, dearest Lord, to praise Thy name,
    Let all our powers agree;
Worthy art Thou of endless fame;
    Our springs are all in Thee.

Here in Thy love will we rejoice,
    All sovereign, rich, and free;
Singing, we hope with heart and voice,
    Our springs are all in Thee.

To whom, dear Jesus, O to whom
    Shall needy sinners flee
But to Thyself, who bidst us come?
    Our springs are all in Thee.

Some tempted, weak, and trembling saint
    Before Thee now may be;
Let not his hopes or wishes faint;
    His springs are all in Thee.

The poor supply, the wounded heal,
    Let sinners such as we,
Salvation's blessings taste and feel;
    Our springs are all in Thee.

When we arrive at Zion's hill,
    And all Thy glory see,
Our joyful songs shall echo still,
    Our springs are all in Thee.

101   John Kent   88 88 D
But the Canaanites would dwell in that land.
Joshua 17:12

The Canaanites still in the land,
    To harass, perplex, and dismay,
Brought Israel of old at a stand,
    For Anak was stronger than they.
What God had designed they possessed,
    Supported and kept by His hand;
Yet, lest on their lees they should rest,
    The Canaanites dwelt in the land.

'Tis thus with the Israel on earth,
    Who groan with a body of sin,
Partake of a spiritual birth,
    The work of God's Spirit within;
Today, with a taste of His love,
    Jehovah their souls will expand,
Tomorrow He'll give them to prove
    The Canaanites still in the land.

Like Gad, by a troop overcome,
    They fall, through the workings of sin;
Yet glory they not in their shame,
    But mourn their defilement within.
On Zion's bright summit above,
    Victorious at last they shall stand,
Though now for a season they prove
    The Canaanites still in the land.

102   Garnet Terry   87 87 47
Show me a sign that Thou talkest with me.
Judges 6:17

Lord, now give me some true token
  That Thou hast my pardon sealed;
Let me know my heart is broken,
  And by Jesus' blood is healed:
    O come quickly,
    Art Thou not the sinner's Shield?

I am sinful altogether,
  Thou art holy, just, and good:
Tell, O tell me, Jesus, whether
  I've an interest in Thy blood.
    Precious Saviour,
    Fill my soul with heavenly food.

Dost Thou condescend to hear me,
  Thou who dost all worlds control?
Yes, I feel Thy presence cheer me;
  Love now animates my soul.
    Jesus whispers,
    'On Me all thy burdens roll.'

103   John Berridge   SM
**Should I leave my wine, which cheereth God
and man?** Judges 9:13

A wondrous wine there is,
  None can with it compare,
Creating most exalted bliss,
  Which God and man will cheer.

It is the wine of Love,
  That precious love divine
Which knits and cheers all hearts above,
  And makes their faces shine.

Believers know its taste,
  And can its virtues tell;
Oft when their hearts are sinking fast,
  One sip has made them well.

It is the cordial true;
  Lord, cheer me with it still;
Till at Thy seat I drink it new,
  And take my hearty fill.

104   *Dobell's Selection*   LM
If the LORD were pleased to kill us.
Judges *13:23*

Why should I yield to slavish fears?
God is the same to endless years;
Though clouds and darkness hide His face,
He's boundless both in truth and grace.

Would e'er the God of truth make known
The worth and glory of His Son;
His love and righteousness display,
And cast my soul at last away?

Would He reveal my sin and woe,
Teach me my numerous wants to know,
And help me in my darkest frame
To build my hopes on Jesus' name;

Would God preserve my soul from hell,
And make His love at times prevail,
Would He bestow such mercies past,
And yet reject my soul at last?

105   John Newton   CM
**Behold, there was a swarm of bees and honey
in the carcase of the lion.**
Judges 14:8

The lion that on Samson roared,
  And thirsted for his blood;
With honey afterwards was stored,
  And furnished him with food.

Believers, as they pass along,
  With many lions meet;
But gather sweetness from the strong,
  And from the eater, meat.

The lions rage and roar in vain,
  For Jesus is their shield;
Their losses prove a certain gain,
  Their troubles comfort yield.

The world and Satan join their strength,
  To fill their souls with fears;
But crops of joy they reap at length,
  From what they sow in tears.

Afflictions make them love the Word,
  Stir up their hearts to prayer;
And many precious proofs afford,
  Of their Redeemer's care.

The lions roar but cannot kill,
  Then fear them not, my friends,
They bring us, though against their will,
  The honey Jesus sends.

Though unbelief may long molest,
And sin and Satan break my rest,
Grace shall at last the victory get,
And make my conquest quite complete.

106   William Gadsby   SM
And let fall also some of the handfuls of purpose for her, and leave them, that she may glean them, and rebuke her not.
Ruth 2:16

When Ruth a-gleaning went,
  Jehovah was her guide;
To Boaz' field He led her straight,
  And she became his bride.

Jesus my Boaz is;
  My strength and portion too;
His Word of grace the precious field,
  Where I a-gleaning go.

O what a heavenly field!
  What handfuls it contains!
What strength and comfort gleaners get,
  To recompense their pains!

Rejoice, ye mourning souls;
  Ye broken hearts, be strong;
The field is ripe for harvest now,
  And ye shall glean ere long.

Ye gleaners, one and all,
  Let Christ be all your song;
He is your strength and portion too,
  And you to Him belong.

All blessings He contains;
  He cannot let you starve;
The meanest gleaner in His field,
  At length shall walk at large.

107   John Kent   LM
For thou art a near kinsman. *Ruth 3:9*

Ye weeping saints, whose souls are lean,
Seek in your Kinsman's field to glean;
Abundant store therein you'll find,
The Man is graciously inclined.

His name is Jesus, and you may
Glean in His field from day to day;
Ye need not of His bounty doubt,
He's kind, and will not cast you out.

Come, then, ye hungry souls, and fill
Out of His store: for 'tis His will
That all His kindred should be fed
With wholesome grain, with living bread.

But go not to another field,
For none but this can plenty yield;
Close by His chosen reapers stand,
And they will you from harm defend.

With them you'll find a rich supply,
To quench your thirst when you are dry;
With them you all may freely feed,
And find supply for every need.

Then you may to your brethren say,
'I've gleaned with pleasure all this day;
Out of my heavenly Kinsman's store,
I've plenty got, but still there's more.'

108   John Newton   LM
For thou art a near kinsman. *Ruth 3:9*

Now let us join with hearts and tongues,
And emulate the angels' songs;
Yea, sinners may address their King
In songs that angels cannot sing.

They praise the Lamb who once was slain,
But we can add a higher strain;
Not only say, 'He suffered thus,'
But that, 'He suffered all for us!'

Jesus, who passed the angels by,
Assumed our flesh to bleed and die;
And still He makes it His abode;
As Man He fills the throne of God.

Our next of kin, our Brother now,
He before whom the angels bow;
They join with us to praise His name,
But we the nearest interest claim.

O, glorious hour, it comes with speed,
When we, from sin and darkness freed,
Shall see His face who died for man,
And praise Him more than angels can!

109   Jean Ingelow   10 10 10 6
I will do the part of a kinsman to thee.
Ruth 3:13

And didst Thou love the race that loved not Thee?
And didst Thou take to heaven a human brow?
Dost plead with man's voice by the marvellous
     sea?
    Art Thou his kinsman now?

O God, O kinsman, loved, but not enough!
O Man, with eyes majestic after death!
Whose feet have toiled along our pathways rough,
    Whose lips drawn human breath!

By that one likeness which is ours and Thine,
By that one nature which doth hold us kin,
By that high heaven where, sinless, Thou dost
     shine,
    To draw us sinners in;

By Thy last silence in the judgment hall,
By long foreknowledge of the deadly tree,
By darkness, by the wormwood and the gall,
    I pray Thee, visit me.

Come, lest this heart should, cold and cast away,
Die ere the Guest adored she entertain—
Lest eyes that never saw Thine earthly day
    Should miss Thy heavenly reign.

110   John Berridge   CM
**Out of the abundance of my complaint and
grief have I spoken hitherto.**
1 Samuel 1:16

And does thy heart for Jesus pine,
   And make its secret moan?
He understands a sigh divine,
   And marks a secret groan.

These pinings prove that Christ is near,
   To testify His grace;
Call on Him with unceasing prayer
   For He will show His face.

Though much dismayed, take courage still,
   And knock at mercy's door;
A loving Saviour surely will
   Relieve His praying poor.

He knows how weak and faint thou art,
   And must appear at length;
A look from Him will cheer thy heart,
   And bring renewèd strength.

111   John Newton   66 66 88
**Out of the abundance of my complaint and
grief have I spoken hitherto.**
1 Samuel 1:16

   When Hannah, pressed with grief,
     Poured forth her soul in prayer,
   She quickly found relief,
     And left her burden there.
Like her in every trying case,
May we approach the throne of grace.

   When she began to pray,
     Her heart was pained and sad;
   But ere she went away,
     Was comforted and glad.
In trouble, what a resting place
Have they who know the throne of grace!

   Though men and devils rage,
     And threaten to devour,
   The saints, from age to age,
     Are safe from all their power.
Fresh strength they gain to run their race,
By waiting at the throne of grace.

   Numbers before have tried,
     And found the promise true;
   Nor has one been denied.
     Then why should I or you?
Let us, by faith, their footsteps trace,
And hasten to the throne of grace.

112   Isaac Watts   LM
My heart rejoiceth in the LORD.
1 Samuel 2:1

Lord, what a heaven of saving grace
Shines through the beauties of Thy face,
And lights our passions to a flame!
Lord, how we love Thy charming name!

When I can say, 'My God is mine,'
When I can feel Thy glories shine,
I tread the world beneath my feet,
And all that earth calls good or great.

While such a scene of sacred joys
Our raptured eyes and soul employs,
Here we could sit and gaze away,
A long, an everlasting day.

Well, we shall quickly pass the night
To the fair coasts of perfect light;
Then shall our joyful senses rove
O'er the dear Object of our love.

113   Richard Burnham   CM
There is none holy as the LORD.
1 Samuel 2:2

Jehovah is a holy God,
   His glorious Son He gave,
To make atonement by His blood,
   A guilty world to save.

His Spirit draws the chosen race,
   A holy Christ to view:
And while they see His holy face,
   Their souls grow holy too.

In holiness the saints delight,
   While here on earth they dwell:
O how they wrestle day and night,
   More holiness to feel!

Lord, may we all on Thee rely,
   And love Thy Holy Word;
O may we every evil fly,
   And Thy commands regard.

More may we feel the cleansing grace
   That flows through Jesus' blood;
More may we love the holy race:
   The happy sons of God.

May we, the objects of Thy love,
   Soon rise to Thy abode;
Sing with the holy choir above,
   The holiness of God.

114   William Gadsby   886 D.
He raiseth up the poor out of the dust, and lifteth up the beggar from the dunghill.
1 Samuel 2:8

A beggar, vile and base, I come,
Without a friend, without a home,
   And knock at mercy's door;
A friendless, helpless wretch indeed,
Nor have I one good work to plead,
   Yet crave a living store.

My wants are great and many too;
O Lamb of God, some pity show,
   Or I must surely die;
No other hand can help but Thee;
I've tried the rest, and plainly see
   They cannot me supply.

But though my wants are very great,
In Jesus they most richly meet;
   With Him I've all the rest;
And wilt Thou give Thyself to me?
From sin and Satan set me free?
   Then I'm completely blest.

Source of delight! Fountain of bliss!
In Thee I all things do possess;
   My treasure is divine;
With holy wonder I adore
The God who thus does bless the poor,
   And make their faces shine.

115   James Burns   66 66 88
The LORD called Samuel: and he answered, Here am I. *1 Samuel 3:4*

Hushed was the evening hymn,
   The temple courts were dark,
The lamp was burning dim
   Before the sacred ark
When suddenly a voice divine
Rang through the silence of the shrine.

The old man, meek and mild,
   The priest of Israel, slept;
His watch the temple child,
   The little Levite, kept;
And what from Eli's sense was sealed
The Lord to Hannah's son revealed.

O give me Samuel's ear,
   The open ear, O Lord,
Alive and quick to hear
   Each whisper of Thy word,
Like Him to answer at Thy call,
And to obey Thee first of all.

O give me Samuel's heart,
   A lowly heart that waits
Where in Thy house Thou art
   Or watches at Thy gates,
By day and night, a heart that still
Moves at the breathing of Thy will.

O give me Samuel's mind,
   A sweet, unmurmuring faith,
Obedient and resigned
   To Thee in life and death,
That I may read with childlike eyes
Truths that are hidden from the wise.

FRANCES HAVERGAL 1836-1879

116   Frances Havergal   87 87 77
Speak, LORD; for Thy servant heareth.
1 Samuel 3:9

Master, speak! Thy servant heareth,
    Waiting for Thy gracious word,
Longing for Thy voice that cheereth;
    Master, let it now be heard.
I am listening, Lord, for Thee;
What hast Thou to say to me?

Speak to me by name, O Master,
    Let me know it is to me;
Speak, that I may follow faster,
    With a step more firm and free,
Where the Shepherd leads the flock
In the shadow of the Rock

Master, speak! though least and lowest,
    Let me not unheard depart;
Master, speak! for O Thou knowest
    All the yearning of my heart;
Knowest all its truest need;
Speak, and make me blest indeed.

Master, speak! and make me ready,
    When Thy voice is truly heard,
With obedience glad and steady
    Still to follow every word.
I am listening, Lord, for Thee;
Master, speak! O speak to me!

117   Frances Havergal   LM
Speak, LORD; for Thy servant heareth.
1 Samuel 3:9

Lord, speak to me, that I may speak
    In living echoes of Thy tone;
As Thou hast sought, so let me seek
    Thy erring children, lost and lone.

O lead me, Lord, that I may lead
    The wandering and the wavering feet!
O feed me, Lord, that I may feed
    Thy hungering ones with manna sweet!

O strengthen me, that while I stand
    Firm on the Rock and strong in Thee,
I may stretch out a loving hand
    To wrestlers with the troubled sea!

O teach me, Lord, that I may teach
    The precious things Thou dost impart!
And wing my words, that they may reach
    The hidden depths of many a heart.

O fill me with Thy fulness, Lord,
    Until my very heart o'erflow
In kindling thought and glowing word,
    Thy love to tell, Thy praise to show!

O use me, Lord, use even me,
    Just as Thou wilt and when and where,
Until Thy blessèd face I see,
    Thy rest, Thy joy, Thy glory share!

118   Thomas Greene   CM
It is the LORD: let Him do what seemeth Him good. *1 Samuel 3:18*

It is the Lord, my covenant God,
    Whose claims are all divine,
Who has an undisputed right
    To govern me and mine.

It is the Lord! Should I distrust
    Or contradict His will,
Who cannot do but what is just
    And must be righteous still?

It is the Lord who gives me all,
    My wealth, my friends, my ease,
And of His bounties may recall
    Whatever part He please.

It is the Lord who can sustain
    Beneath the heaviest load,
From whom assistance I obtain
    To tread the thorny road.

It is the Lord, whose matchless skill
    Can from afflictions raise
Matter eternity to fill
    With ever-growing praise.

It is the Lord, my covenant God,
    Thrice blessèd be His name!
Whose gracious promise, sealed with blood,
    Must ever be the same.

119   Robert Robinson   87 87 D
Ebenezer, 'Hitherto hath the LORD helped us.'
1 Samuel 7:12

Come, Thou Fount of every blessing,
   Tune my heart to sing Thy grace!
Streams of mercy, never ceasing,
   Call for songs of loudest praise.
Teach me some melodious sonnet,
   Sung by flaming tongues above;
Praise the mount! O fix me on it!
   Mount of God's unchanging love.

Here I raise my Ebenezer;
   Hither by Thy help I'm come;
And I hope, by Thy good pleasure
   Safely to arrive at home.
Jesus sought me when a stranger,
   Wandering from the fold of God;
He, to save my soul from danger,
   Interposed His precious blood.

O to grace how great a debtor
   Daily I'm constrained to be!
Let that grace, Lord, like a fetter,
   Bind my wandering heart to Thee.
Prone to wander, Lord, I feel it;
   Prone to leave the God I love;
Here's my heart, Lord, take and seal it;
   Seal it from Thy courts above!

120   James Bell   86 886
Ebenezer, 'Hitherto hath the LORD helped us.'
1 Samuel 7:12

Another year of labour gone
   And now, O Lord, we meet
To bless Thee for the light that shone
And led us with its radiance on
   And brought us to Thy feet.

To Thee we raise no mournful song,
   No note of sad despair,
But joyful praise from heart and tongue,
For all our hopes to Thee belong,
   All mercies rich and rare.

O Father, help Thy people here
   As oft in seasons gone,
To hear the voice that conquers fear
And fills the soul with heavenly cheer
   While months and years roll on.

For Thine is all the work we do,
   All light and grace are Thine;
From day to day our faith renew
And keep us to the truth more true,
   More full of love divine.

121   Anon 1745   664 6664
**And all the people shouted, and said, God
save the king.** *1 Samuel 10:24*

God save our gracious Queen,
Long live our noble Queen,
   God save our Queen!
Send her victorious,
Happy and glorious,
Long to reign over us,
   God save our Queen!

Through every changing scene,
O Lord, preserve the Queen,
   Long may she reign!
Her heart inspire and move
With wisdom from above
And in a nation's love
   Her throne maintain.

Thy choicest gifts in store
On her be pleased to pour,
   Long may she reign!
May she defend our laws
And ever give us cause
To sing with heart and voice,
   'God save the Queen!'

122   Samuel Medley   LM
**The Strength of Israel will not lie nor repent:
for He is not a man, that he should repent.**
1 Samuel 15:29

Jehovah is a God of might;
   He framed the earth, He built the sky;
And what He speaks is surely right,
   'The Strength of Israel will not lie.'

Ye weary souls, with sin oppressed,
   To Him in every trouble fly;
His promise is, 'I'll give you rest,'
   'The Strength of Israel will not lie.'

Then why sunk down beneath despair?
   To Jesus' throne of grace apply;
His promise plead, He'll hear your prayer,
   'The Strength of Israel will not lie.'

Ask what you will in Jesus' name,
   He never will your suit deny;
To save you from the curse He came:
   'The Strength of Israel will not lie.'

Behold! I come, most gracious Lord,
   And on Thy promise now rely;
In my distress, how sweet this word:
   'The Strength of Israel will not lie!'

123 William Gadsby 10 10 11 11
**David therefore departed thence, and escaped
to the cave Adullam.**
1 Samuel 22:1

When Jesse's young son was honoured of
God,
  The stripling began to publish abroad
The love of Jehovah; His strength and His might;
Which brought down Goliath in Israel's sight.

What joy in the land at once did appear!
  Hosanna was sung to David, we hear;
But soon he was forced into Adullam's cave,
And thousands pursued him his life to bereave.

To Adullam's cave the wretched all run;
  Which David must have, their captain become;
And thus he is furnished with men, to be sure,
But, O be astonished! they're helpless and poor.

In David I see a Greater by far;
  'Tis Jesus, 'tis He who saves from despair;
No sinner dejected that flees to the Lamb,
Shall e'er be neglected, for David's His name.

124 John Berridge 77 77
**Every one that was in distress, and every one
that was in debt, and every one that was
discontented, gathered themselves unto him;
and he became a captain over them.**
1 Samuel 22:2

All in debt or in distress,
Discontented more or less,
All who would protection have,
Haste away to David's cave.

All who find their sinful debt
Deep and deeper growing yet;
All who have been Satan's tool,
Much his madman or his fool;

All who discontented are,
Full of guilt and full of fear;
Every soul who would not die,
Unto Jesus' cave must fly.

Haste, and seek the Saviour's face;
Rise, and bless Him for His grace;
To His scornèd cave repair;
He will wash and feast you there.

125 Vernon Higham 11 10 11 10
**And let it be, when thou hearest the sound of a
going in the tops of the mulberry trees, that
then thou shalt bestir thyself.**
2 Samuel 5:24

What is this sound among the mulberry bushes?
  What is this movement of Thy tender grace?
What is this sign that wondrous blessing ushers?
  Who is this One with majesty of place?

Whence came this host with myriad voices
    praising?
  Whence came the sound of melody so sweet?
This is the triumph, hear the angels singing
  'Glory to God!' and fall before His feet.

Happy the throng, the breeze of heaven feeling;
  Happy the hearts enveloped in Thy love.
Blessèd the hour of God's times of refreshing!
  Windows of heaven that open from above.

These are the armies of the God of mercy,
  Mighty in favour and sweeping all away;
No foe can stand or ever hope for glory —
  His is the victory, so be it Lord alway.
                                        © *Author*

126 Ludwig von Zinzendorf, tr. C Clemens
And let Thy name be magnified for ever.
2 Samuel 7:26 76 76

O Jesus Christ, most holy,
  Head of the church, Thy bride,
Each day in us more fully
  Thy name be magnified!

O may in each believer
  Thy love its power display,
And none among us ever
  From Thee, our Shepherd, stray.

127 John Newton CM
**But the thing that David had done displeased
the LORD.** *2 Samuel 11:27*

How David, when by sin deceived,
  From bad to worse went on!
For when the Holy Spirit's grieved
  Our strength and guard are gone.

His eye on Bathsheba once fixed,
  With poison filled his soul;
He ventured on adult'ry next,
  And murder crowned the whole.

So from a spark of fire at first,
  That has not been described;
A dreadful flame has often burst,
  And ravaged far and wide.

When sin deceives it hardens too,
For though he vainly fought
To hide his crimes from public view,
Of God he little thought.

He neither would, or could repent,
No true compunction felt;
'Till God in mercy Nathan sent,
His stubborn heart to melt.

The parable held forth a fact,
Designed his case to show;
But though the picture was exact,
Himself he did not know.

'Thou art the man,' the prophet said,
That word his slumber broke;
And when he owned his sin, and prayed,
The Lord forgiveness spoke.

Let those who think they stand, beware,
For David stood before;
Nor let the fallen soul despair,
For mercy can restore.

128 Benjamin Beddome 66 66 88
Who can tell whether GOD will be gracious to me, that the child may live?
2 Samuel 12:22

Great God! to Thee I'll make
My griefs and sorrows known;
And with a humble hope
Approach Thy awful throne;
Though by my sins deserving hell,
I'll not despair, for who can tell?

To Thee, who by a word
My drooping soul canst cheer,
And by Thy Spirit form
Thy glorious image there;
My foes subdue, my fears dispel;
I'll daily seek, for who can tell?

Endangered or distressed,
To Thee alone I'll fly.
Implore Thy powerful help,
And at Thy footstool lie;
My case bemoan, my wants reveal,
And patient wait, for who can tell?

My heart misgives me oft,
And conscience storms within;
But one sweet smile from Thee
At once would make me clean.
If Thou be mine, all will be well;
And why not so? for who can tell?

129 Margaret Clarkson CM
As for God, His way is perfect.
2 Samuel 22:31

His way is perfect! Though He lead
Through paths of grief and pain,
Who follows steadfast to the end
Finds everlasting gain.

His way is perfect! Though the sky
Be overcast and dim,
It shines until the perfect day
For those who walk with Him.

His way is perfect! Though the storm
Rage through the deepening night
The soul that leans upon its God
Knows that He leads aright.

His way is perfect! O my soul,
Trust where you cannot see!
Lift up faith's radiant, sightless eyes
And heed God's mystery!

130 John Kent CM
He hath made with me an everlasting covenant, ordered in all things, and sure.
2 Samuel 23:5

Come, saints, and sing in sweet accord,
With solemn pleasure tell,
The covenant made with David's Lord;
In all things ordered well.

This covenant stood ere time began,
That God with man might dwell;
Eternal wisdom drew the plan;
In all things ordered well.

This covenant, O believer, stands,
Thy rising fears to quell;
Sealed by thy Surety's bleeding hands;
In all things ordered well.

'Twas made with Jesus, for His bride,
Before the sinner fell;
'Twas signed, and sealed, and ratified;
In all things ordered well.

In glory, soon, with Christ their King,
His saints shall surely dwell;
And this blest covenant ever sing;
In all things ordered well.

131   Philip Doddridge   CM
**He hath made with me an everlasting
covenant, ordered in all things, and sure.**
2 Samuel 23:5

My God, the covenant of Thy love
  Abides for ever sure:
And, in its matchless grace, I feel
  My happiness secure.

What though my house be not with Thee
  As nature could desire!
To nobler joys than nature gives
  Thy servants all aspire.

Since Thou, the everlasting God,
  My Father art become;
Jesus, my Guardian and my Friend!
  And heaven my final home.

I welcome all Thy sovereign will,
  For all that will is love;
And when I know not what Thou dost,
  I'll wait the light above.

Thy covenant the last accent claims
  Of this poor faltering tongue;
And that shall the first notes employ
  Of my celestial song.

132   John Kent   LM
**And David longed, and said, Oh that one
would give me drink of the water of the well of
Bethlehem, which is by the gate!**
2 Samuel 23:15

How welcome to the soul oppressed,
In sorrow's vale, by raging thirst,
Scorched by the sun's meridian beam,
Is the sweet well of Bethlehem!

Prophets of old, and saints the same,
In every age, of every name,
Drank of this soul-reviving stream,
The water sweet of Bethlehem.

Water so pure, or half so good,
From nature's fountains never flowed;
There's curse and death in every stream,
Save in the well of Bethlehem.

To cheer when faint, when sick to heal,
Its wondrous virtues must prevail;
My sins to crush, my fears to quell,
Spring up, O stream! from Bethlehem's well.

When nature sinks beneath her load,
Amidst the din of Jordan's flood;
With this my every fear dispel,
One sip of Bethlehem's sacred well.

133   John Newton   77 77
Ask what I shall give thee. *1 Kings 3:5*

Come, my soul, Thy suit prepare,
Jesus loves to answer prayer;
He Himself has bid Thee pray,
Therefore will not say thee nay.

Thou art coming to a King;
Large petitions with thee bring;
For His grace and power are such,
None can ever ask too much.

With my burden I begin;
Lord, remove this load of sin;
Let Thy blood, for sinners spilt,
Set my conscience free from guilt.

Lord, I come to Thee for rest;
Take possession of my breast;
There Thy blood-bought right maintain,
And without a rival reign.

As the image in the glass
Answers the beholder's face,
Thus unto my heart appear;
Print Thy own resemblance there.

While I am a pilgrim here,
Let Thy love my spirit cheer;
As my Guide, my Guard, my Friend,
Lead me to my journey's end.

Show me what I have to do;
Every hour my strength renew;
Let me live a life of faith;
Let me die Thy people's death.

134   John Newton   LM
Ask what I shall give thee. *1 Kings 3:5*

If Solomon for wisdom prayed,
  The Lord before had made him wise
Else he another choice had made,
  And asked for what the worldlings prize.

Thus He invites His people still,
  But first instructs them how to choose,
Then bids them ask whate'er they will,
  Assured that He will not refuse.

And dost Thou say, 'Ask what thou wilt'?
  Lord, I would seize the golden hour;
I pray to be released from guilt,
  And freed from sin and Satan's power.

More of Thy presence, Lord, impart,
  More of Thy image let me bear;
Erect Thy throne within my heart,
  And reign without a rival there.

Give me to read my pardon sealed,
And from Thy joy to draw my strength;
To have Thy matchless love revealed
In all its height, and breadth, and length.

Grant these requests, I ask no more,
But to Thy care the rest resign;
Sick or in health, or rich or poor,
All will be well if Thou art mine.

135   William Gadsby   66 66 88
Have Thou respect unto the prayer of Thy servant. *1 King 8:28*

Within these walls, dear Lord,
  Display Thy matchless grace;
Thy constant aid afford,
  And show Thy smiling face;
And may Thy blessèd family
Enjoy salvation full and free.

Here may the eternal Three
  His glorious power make known,
Set captive sinners free,
  Bring wandering sinners home;
Display the wonders of His love,
And fix His children's hearts above.

May watchmen, taught of God,
  Jehovah's love declare;
Proclaim a Saviour's blood,
  To vanquish guilty fear;
And may the heavenly Paraclete,
Their message seal in Zion's heart.

136   Charles Wesley   CM
Let your heart therefore be perfect with the LORD our God, to walk in His statutes, and to keep His commandments, as at this day.
1 King 8:61

O for a heart to praise my God,
  A heart from sin set free,
A heart that's sprinkled with the blood
  So freely shed for me.

A heart resigned, submissive, meek;
  The great Redeemer's throne;
Where only Christ is heard to speak,
  Where Jesus reigns alone.

A humble, lowly, contrite heart,
  Believing, true, and clean,
Which neither life nor death can part
  From Him that dwells within.

A heart in every thought renewed
  And full of love divine,
Perfect and right and pure and good:
  A copy, Lord, of Thine.

Thy nature, gracious Lord, impart;
  Come quickly from above;
Write Thy new name upon my heart,
  Thy new, best name of Love.

137   Philip Doddridge   LM
I have hallowed this house, which thou hast built, to put My name there for ever. *1 King 9:3*

And will the great, eternal God,
On earth establish His abode?
And will He, from His radiant throne,
Avow our temples for His own?

These walls we to Thy honour raise;
Long may they echo with Thy praise,
And Thou, descending, fill the place
With choicest tokens of Thy grace.

Here let the great Redeemer reign,
With all the graces of His train,
While power divine His word attends,
To conquer foes, and cheer His friends.

And in the great decisive day,
When God the nations shall survey,
May it before the world appear
That crowds were born to glory here.

138   Vernon Higham   DCM
Behold, the half was not told me.
1King 10:7

I heard about the Son of Man,
  His beauty failed to see;
And wandered far, and vainly ran,
  Believing I was free.
And then Thy kind restraining grace
  Upon my soul took hold.
I stood amazed, and saw Thy face —
  The half had not been told!

Thy mercy led me through the vale;
  My heart, with sorrow laid,
With trembling trust and visage pale,
  Beheld the price He paid.
Such majesty and dignity!
  Though piercing crown was worn;
This blood and sacrifice to me
  Brought peace and I was born.

O blessèd Jesus, lovely name,
  A rose amongst the thorns!
I cannot see why men defame,
  And this my heart now mourns.
O gracious Lord, hear now my praise,
  I on Thy bosom lean;
Immortal source, eternal grace,
  Thy beauty I have seen.

© Author

139   John Newton   88 88 D
And the ravens brought him bread and flesh in the morning, and bread and flesh in the evening; and he drank of the brook. *1King 17:6*

Elijah's example declares,
　　Whatever distress may betide,
The saints may commit all their cares
　　To Him who will surely provide;
When rain long withheld from the earth
　　Occasioned a famine of bread,
The prophet, secured from the dearth,
　　By ravens was constantly fed.

More likely to rob than to feed,
　　Were ravens, which live upon prey;
But when the Lord's people have need,
　　His goodness will find out a way.
This instance to those may be strange
　　Who know not how faith can prevail;
But sooner all nature shall change,
　　Than one of God's promises fail.

How safe and how happy are they
　　Who on the Good Shepherd rely;
He gives them out strength for their day,
　　Their wants He will surely supply.
He ravens and lions can tame!
　　All creatures obey His commands!
Then let us rejoice in His name,
　　And leave all our cares in His hands.

140   John Newton   CM
And the barrel of meal wasted not, neither did the cruse of oil fail, according to the word of the LORD. *1 King 17:16*

By the poor widow's oil and meal,
　　Elijah was sustained,
Though small the stock, it lasted well
　　For God the store maintained.

Thus to His poor He still will give
　　Just for the present hour;
But for to-morrow they must live
　　Upon His word and power.

And thus, though faint it often seems,
　　He keeps our grace alive;
Supplied by His refreshing streams,
　　Our drooping hopes revive.

Though in ourselves we have no stock,
　　The Lord is nigh to save;
His door flies open when we knock,
　　And 'tis but 'ask and have.'

141   W.T.   CM
And the God that answereth by fire, let Him be God. *1King 18:24*

Elijah prayed in holy zeal,
　　Obtained the full desire;
His glory then did God reveal,
　　And answered him by fire.

False teachers, idols, perish all,
　　Vain helps that would deceive;
The God that answers when we call,
　　Still helps us to believe,

In Israel's Triune God we seek
　　Our help in time of need;
To know and grant before we speak
　　He must be God indeed.

142   Josiah Conder   LM
Then the fire of the LORD fell.
1 Kings 18:38

Lord! with Thy grace our hearts inspire,
Answer our sacrifice by fire,
And by Thy mighty acts declare,
Thou art the God who heareth prayer.

Faith asks no signal from the skies,
To show that prayers accepted rise;
Our Priest is in the holy place,
And answers from the throne of grace.

143   Charles Wesley   77 77 D
Behold, there ariseth a little cloud out of the sea, like a man's hand. *1 King 18:44*

See how great a flame aspires,
　　Kindled by a spark of grace!
Jesus' love the nations fires,
　　Sets the kingdoms on a blaze;
Fire to bring on earth He came;
　　Kindled in some hearts it is:
O that all might catch the flame,
　　All partake the glorious bliss!

When He first the work begun,
　　Small and feeble was His day:
Now the word doth swiftly run,
　　Now it wins its widening way;
More and more it spreads and grows,
　　Ever mighty to prevail;
Sin's strongholds it now o'erthrows,
　　Shakes the trembling gates of hell.

Sons of God, your Saviour praise;
  He the door hath opened wide,
He hath given the word of grace,
  Jesus' word is glorified;
Jesus, mighty to redeem,
  He alone the work hath wrought;
Worthy is the work of Him,
  Him who spake a world from nought.

Saw ye not the cloud arise,
  Little as a human hand?
Now it spreads along the skies,
  Hangs o'er all the thirsty land;
Lo! the promise of a shower
  Drops already from above;
But the Lord will shortly pour
  All the Spirit of His love.

144 Charles Wesley 76 76 77 76
**And after the earthquake a fire; but the LORD
was not in the fire: and after the fire a still
small voice.** *1 Kings 19:12*

Open, Lord, my inward ear,
  And bid my heart rejoice;
Bid my quiet spirit hear
  Thy comfortable voice;
Never in the whirlwind found,
  Or where earthquakes rock the place,
Still and silent is the sound,
  The whisper of Thy grace.

From the world of sin, and noise,
  And hurry I withdraw;
For the small and inward voice
  I wait with humble awe;
Silent am I now and still,
  Dare not in Thy presence move;
To my waiting soul reveal
  The secret of Thy love.

Thou didst undertake for me,
  For me to death wast sold;
Wisdom in a mystery
  Of bleeding love unfold;
Teach the lesson of Thy cross,
  Let me die with Thee to reign;
All things let me count but loss,
  So I may Thee regain.

Show me, as my soul can bear,
  The depth of inbred sin;
All the unbelief declare,
  The pride that lurks within;
Take me, whom Thyself hast bought,
  Bring into captivity
Every high aspiring thought
  That would not stoop to Thee.

Lord, my time is in Thy hand,
  My soul to Thee convert;
Thou canst make me understand,
  Though I am slow of heart;
Thine in whom I live and move,
  Thine the work, the praise is Thine;
Thou art wisdom, power, and love,
  And all Thou art is mine.

HORATIO SPAFFORD 1828-88

145 Horatio Spafford 11 8 11 9 + refrain
**Is it well with thee? is it well with thy
husband? is it well with the child? And she
answered, It is well.** *2 Kings 4:26*

When peace, like a river, attendeth my way,
  When sorrows like sea billows roll;
Whatever my lot, Thou hast taught me to say,
  'It is well, it is well with my soul.'

    *It is well with my soul;
    It is well, it is well with my soul.*

Though Satan should buffet, though trials should
      come,
  Let this blest assurance control,
That Christ has regarded my helpless estate
  And has shed His own blood for my soul.

My sin, O the bliss of this glorious thought!
  My sin, not in part but the whole,
Is nailed to the cross and I bear it no more;
  Praise the Lord, praise the Lord, O my soul!

O Lord, haste the day when my faith shall be
      sight,
  The clouds be rolled back as a scroll,
The trump shall resound and the Lord shall
      descend;
  Even so, it is well with my soul.

146   John Newton   LM
**And Gehazi passed on before them, and laid
the staff upon the face of the child.**
2 Kings 4:31

The Shunamite, oppressed with grief,
   When she had lost the son she loved,
Went to Elisha for relief,
   Nor vain her application proved.

He sent his servant on before
   To lay a staff upon his head;
This he could do, but do no more,
   He left him, as he found him, dead.

But when the Lord's almighty power
   Wrought with the prophet's prayer, and faith,
The mother saw a joyful hour,
   She saw her child restored from death.

Thus, like the weeping Shunamite,
   For many, dead in sin we grieve;
Now, Lord, display Thine arm of might,
   Cause them to hear Thy voice and live.

Thy preachers bear the staff in vain,
   Though at Thine own command we go;
Lord, we have tried, and tried again,
   We find them dead, and leave them so.

Come then Thyself; to every heart
   The glory of Thy name make known
The means are our appointed part,
   The power and grace are Thine alone.

147   John Newton   66 66 88
**Then went he down, and dipped himself seven
times in Jordan.** *2 Kings 5:14*

Before Elisha's gate
   The Syrian leper stood
But could not brook to wait,
   He deemed himself too good:
He thought the prophet would attend,
And not to him a message send.

'Have I this journey come,
   And will he not be seen?
I were as well at home,
   Would washing make me clean:
Why must I wash in Jordan's flood?
Damascus' rivers are as good.'

Thus by his foolish pride
   He almost missed a cure;
Howe'er at length he tried,
   And found the method sure:
Soon as his pride was brought to yield,
The leprosy was quickly healed.

Leprous and proud as he,
   To Jesus thus I came;
From sin to set me free,
   When first I heard His fame:
'Surely,' thought I, 'my pompous train
Of vows and tears will notice gain.'

My heart devised the way
   Which I supposed He'd take;
And when I found delay,
   Was ready to go back:
Had He some painful task enjoined,
I to performance seemed inclined.

When by His word He spake,
   That fountain opened see;
'Twas opened for thy sake,
   'Go wash, and thou art free:'
O! how did my proud heart gainsay,
I feared to trust this simple way.

At length I trial made,
   When I had much endured;
The message I obeyed,
   I washed, and I was cured:
Sinners this healing fountain try,
Which cleansed a wretch so vile as I.

148   John Newton   LM
**And he answered, Fear not: for they that be
with us are more than they that be with them.**
2 Kings 6:16

'Alas!' Elisha's servant cried,
When he the Syrian army spied;
But he was soon released from care,
In answer to the prophet's prayer.

Straitway he saw, with other eyes,
A greater army from the skies;
A fiery guard around the hill,
Thus are the saints preservèd still.

When Satan and his host appear,
Like him of old, I faint and fear;
Like him, by faith, with joy I see
A greater host engaged for me.

The saints espouse my cause by prayer,
The angels make my soul their care;
Mine is the promise sealed with blood,
And Jesus lives to make it good.

149   Joseph Hart   66 66 88

And Elisha died, and they buried him. And the bands of the Moabites invaded the land at the coming in of the year.
2 Kings 13:20

Once more the constant sun,
  Revolving round his sphere,
His steady course has run,
  And brings another year.
He rises, sets, but goes not back,
Nor ever quits his destined track.

Hence let believers learn
  To keep a forward pace
Be this our main concern,
  To finish well our race:
Backsliding shun, with patience press
Towards the Sun of Righteousness.

What now should be our task?
  Or rather, what our prayer?
What good thing shall we ask,
  To prosper this New Year?
With one accord our hearts we'd lift,
And ask our Lord some New Year's gift.

No trifling gift or small,
  Should friends of Christ desire.
Rich Lord, bestow on all
  Pure gold, well tried by fire.
Faith that stands fast when devils roar,
And love that lasts for evermore.

150   Joseph Hart   88 88 88

And Jabez called on the God of Israel, saying, O that Thou wouldest bless me indeed, and enlarge my coast.
I Chronicles 4:10

A saint there was in days of old
  Though we but little of him hear
In honour high, of whom is told
  A short, but an effectual prayer.
This prayer, my brethren, let us view,
And try if we can pray so too.

He called on Israel's God, 'tis said;
  Let us take notice first of that;
Had he to any other prayed,
  To us it had not mattered what;
For all true Israelites adore
One God, Jehovah, and no more.

'O that Thou wouldst me bless indeed,
  And that Thou wouldst enlarge my bound;
And let Thy hand in every need
  A guide and help be with me found;
That Thou wouldst, cause that evil be
No cause of pain and grief to me.'

What is it to be blest indeed,
  But to have all our sins forgiven;
To be from guilt and terror freed,
  Redeemed from hell, and sealed for heaven;
To worship an incarnate God,
And know He saved us by His blood?

And next, to have our coast enlarged
  Is, that our hearts extend their plan
From bondage and from fear discharged,
  And filled with love to God and man;
To cast off every narrow thought,
And use the freedom Christ has brought.

To use this liberty aright,
  And not the grace of God abuse,
We always need His hand, His might,
  Lest what He gives us we should lose;
Spiritual pride would soon creep in,
And turn His very grace to sin.

This prayer, so long ago preferred,
  Is left on sacred record thus;
And this good prayer by God was heard,
  And kindly handed down to us.
Thus Jabez prayed, for that's his name.
May all believers pray the same.

151   John Newton   CM

And Jabez called on the God of Israel, saying, Oh that Thou wouldest bless me indeed, and enlarge my coast.
I Chronicles 4:10

Jesus who bought us with His blood,
  And makes our souls His care,
Was known of old as Israel's God,
  And answered Jabez' prayer.

Jabez! a child of grief! the name
  Befits poor sinners well!
For Jesus bore the cross and shame,
  To save our souls from hell.

Teach us, O Lord, like him to plead
  For mercies from above:
O come, and bless our souls indeed
  With light, and joy, and love.

The gospel's promised land is wide,
  We fain would enter in,
But we are pressed on every side
  With unbelief and sin.

Arise, O Lord, enlarge our coast,
  Let us possess the whole!
That Satan may no longer boast
  He can Thy work control.

O! may Thy hand be with us still
Our Guide and Guardian be,
To keep us safe from every ill,
Till death shall set us free!

Help us on Thee to cast our care,
And on Thy word to rest.
That Israel's God, who heareth prayer,
Will grant us our request.

152   Joseph Hart   886 D
**Give unto the LORD, ye kindreds of the
people, give unto the LORD glory and
strength.** *1 Chronicles 16:28*

Ye saints on earth, your voices raise,
And sing the eternal Father's praise,
And glorify the Son;
Give glory to the Holy Ghost,
And join with all the angelic host
To bless the great Three-One.

153   Horatius Bonar   87 87 47
**Give unto the LORD the glory due unto His
name: bring an offering, and come before Him:
worship the LORD in the beauty of holiness.**
1 Chronicles 16:29

Glory be to God the Father,
Glory be to God the Son,
Glory be to God the Spirit,
Great Jehovah, Three in One:
Glory, glory,
While eternal ages run!

Glory be to Him who loved us,
Washed us from each spot and stain;
Glory be to Him who bought us,
Made us kings with Him to reign:
Glory, glory,
To the Lamb that once was slain!

Glory to the King of angels,
Glory to the church's King,
Glory to the King of nations,
Heaven and earth, your praises bring:
Glory, glory,
To the King of glory bring!

'Glory, blessing, praise eternal!'
Thus the choir of angels sings;
'Honour, riches, power, dominion!'
Thus its praise creation brings.
Glory, glory,
Glory to the King of kings!

154   Sylvanus Phelps   64 64 66 64
**And who then is willing to consecrate his
service this day unto the LORD?**
1 Chronicles 29:5

Saviour! Thy dying love
Thou gavest me;
Nor should I aught withhold,
My Lord, from Thee;
In love my soul would bow,
My heart fulfil its vow,
Some offering bring Thee now,
Something for Thee.

At the blest mercy seat,
Pleading for me,
My feeble faith looks up,
Jesus, to Thee;
Help me the cross to bear,
Thy wondrous love declare,
Some song to raise, or prayer,
Something for Thee.

Give me a faithful heart,
Likeness to Thee,
That each departing day
Henceforth may see
Some work of love begun,
Some deed of kindness done,
Some wanderer sought and won,
Something for Thee.

All that I am and have,
Thy gifts so free,
In joy, in grief, through life,
O Lord, for Thee!
And when Thy face I see,
My ransomed soul shall be,
Through all eternity,
Something for Thee.

155   William Bathurst   CM
**All things come of Thee, and of Thine own
have we given Thee.**
1 Chronicles 29:14

Lord, when our offerings we present
Before Thy gracious throne,
We but return what Thou hast lent,
And give Thee of Thine own.

The earth with all its wealth is Thine,
The heavens with all their host;
Why should we then in want repine,
Or in abundance boast?

The power and willingness to give
Alike proceed from Thee;
We still are debtors, since we live
Only by Thy decree.

Ourselves, our all, to Thee we owe;
　　And, if we come behind
What others of their wealth bestow,
　　Accept our willing mind.

156　Anon　　　66 66 D (iambic)
Now bless the LORD your God.
1 Chronicles 29:20

Come, brethren, ere we part,
　　Bless the Redeemer's name;
Join every tongue and heart,
　　To adore and praise the Lamb.
Jesus, the sinner's Friend,
　　Him, whom our souls adore,
His praises have no end;
　　Praise Him for evermore.

Lord, in Thy grace we came,
　　That blessing still impart:
We met in Jesus' name,
　　In Jesus' name we part.
Jesus, the sinner's Friend,
　　Him, whom our souls adore,
His praises have no end;
　　Praise Him for evermore.

If here we meet no more,
　　May we in realms above,
With all the saints adore
　　Redeeming grace and love.
Jesus, the sinner's Friend,
　　Him, whom our souls adore,
His praises have no end;
　　Praise Him for evermore.

157　Benjamin Francis and C H Spurgeon
　　　　　　　　　　66 66 88
**And when they lifted up their voice with the
…instruments of music, and praised the LORD
saying, For He is good: for His mercy endureth
for ever: that then the house was filled with a
cloud, even the house of the LORD.**
2 Chronicles 5:13

Great King of Zion, now
　　Display Thy matchless grace;
In love the heavens bow,
　　With glory fill this place:
Beneath this roof, O deign to show
How God can dwell with men below!

Here may Thine ears attend
　　Our interceding cries,
And grateful praise ascend
　　All fragrant to the skies:
Here may Thy word melodious sound,
And spread celestial joys around.

Here may th' attentive throng
　　Imbibe Thy truth and love.
And converts join the song
　　Of seraphim above;
And willing crowds surround Thy board
With sacred joy and sweet accord.

Here may our unborn sons
　　And daughters sound Thy praise,
And shine, like polished stones,
　　Through long succeeding days;
Here, Lord, display Thy saving power,
Until the last triumphant hour.

158　Vernon Higham　　　　CM
**If My people, which are called by My name,
shall humble themselves, and pray, and seek
My face, and turn from their wicked ways; then
will I hear from heaven, and will forgive their
sin, and will heal their land.** *2 Chronicles 7:14*

Come let us praise that Holy name,
　　Loved and exalted high!
The name above all men and fame,
　　That brings salvation nigh.

We are the people of His choice,
　　Called by His holy name.
Help us to listen to His voice
　　That takes away our shame.

Humble us now to pray and seek,
　　The beauty of Thy face;
Grant that we ever shall be meek,
　　Never Thy truth deface.

Turn us away from wicked ways,
　　O Lord, we now implore;
Come to us quickly, with us stay,
　　That we may Thee adore.

The land is healed when Thou dost touch
　　Thy people with Thy hand;
Come quickly, Lord, our need is such,
　　The grip of sin disband.

Happy the people who enjoy
　　The precious presence sweet;
Happy the land that does employ
　　Its days Thy name to greet.
　　　　　　　　　　© Author

159   Edith Cherry   11 10 11 10
**Help us, O LORD our God; for we rest on Thee,
and in Thy name we go against this multitude.**
2 Chronicles 14:11

We rest on Thee our Shield and our Defender!
  We go not forth alone against the foe;
Strong in Thy strength, safe in Thy keeping
    tender,
  We rest on Thee, and in Thy name we go.

Yes, in Thy name, O Captain of salvation!
  In Thy dear name, all other names above:
Jesus our Righteousness, our sure Foundation,
  Our Prince of glory and our King of love.

We go in faith, our own great weakness feeling,
  And needing more each day Thy grace to know:
Yet from our hearts a song of triumph pealing;
  We rest on Thee, and in Thy name we go.

We rest on Thee our Shield and our Defender!
  Thine is the battle, Thine shall be the praise;
When passing through the gates of pearly
    splendour,
  Victors we rest with Thee, through endless days.

160   John Newton   77 77
**Help us, O LORD our God; for we rest on Thee,
and in Thy name we go against this multitude.**
2 Chronicles 14:11

In themselves as weak as worms,
  How can poor believers stand,
When temptations, foes, and storms,
  Press them close on every hand?

Weak, indeed, they feel they are,
  But they know the Throne of Grace;
And the God who answers prayer,
  Helps them when they seek His face.

Though the Lord awhile delay,
  Succour they at length obtain;
He who taught their hearts to pray,
  Will not let them cry in vain.

Wrestling prayer can wonders do;
  Bring relief in deepest straits!
Prayer can force a passage through
  Iron bars and brazen gates.

For the wonders He has wrought,
  Let us now our praises give;
And, by sweet experience taught,
  Call upon Him while we live.

161   Timothy Dudley-Smith   88 88 88
**He humbled himself greatly before the God of
his fathers.** *2 Chronicles 33:12*

Almighty Lord Most High draw near
  Whose awesome splendour none can bear;
Eternal God, in mercy hear,
  Receive once more the sinners' prayer;
Upon Your word of grace we call
Whose word of power has ordered all.

How measureless Your mercies stand,
  The hope and pledge of sins forgiven;
Those sins, unnumbered as the sand,
  That hide the very stars of heaven:
O God of grace, to us impart
A penitent and contrite heart.

From such a heart we bend the knee
  And all our sin and shame confess.
Lord, Your unworthy servants see,
  And clothe us round with righteousness;
That loved and pardoned, healed and blest,
We taste Your mercies manifest.

So lift on high the Saviour's praise
  With all the hosts of heaven above,
And sing through everlasting days
  The God of glory, grace and love.
The Lord of all let all adore,
For ever and for evermore!

162   Richard Burnham   SM
**But many,... when the foundation of this
house was laid before their eyes, wept with a
loud voice; and many shouted aloud for joy.**
Ezra 3:12

  Come, all ye saints of God,
    Your grateful tongues employ;
Sing of a Saviour's pardoning blood,
    And shout aloud for joy.

  Once were ye sunk in earth,
    But now ye dwell on high;
Partakers of a glorious birth,
    Then shout aloud for joy.

  Though evils still arise,
    And many fears annoy,
Up to the Saviour lift your eyes,
    And shout aloud for joy.

View the eternal crown,
The powers of hell defy:
Keep in full view the Saviour's throne,
And shout aloud for joy.

Lord, raise our hearts above
Every delusive toy;
The fulness of salvation prove,
And shout aloud for joy.

Soon may Thy tender hand
Wipe every weeping eye;
Soon may we enter Canaan's land,
And shout aloud for joy.

But where the Lord has planted grace,
And made His glories known,
There fruits of heavenly joy and peace
Are found, and there alone.

A bleeding Saviour seen by faith,
A sense of pardoning love,
A hope that triumphs over death,
Give joys like those above.

To take a glimpse within the veil,
To know that God is mine;
Are springs of joy that never fail,
Unspeakable! Divine!

163   Richard Burnham   SM
Grace hath been showed from the LORD our God. *Ezra 9:8*

Grace moved the Triune God
Lost sinners to redeem;
Grace is the source of every good,
And grace shall be my theme.

Grace, what a pleasing sound!
How it delights my ear!
How it revives my languid hope,
And drowns my every fear!

Through grace I conquer hell
And break infernal chains;
Through grace my soul aspires to heaven,
Where the Redeemer reigns.

Grace the good work begins,
And grace completes the same;
Grace shall constrain my soul to raise
Hosannas to the Lamb.

From His abounding grace,
Daily I draw supplies;
Grace is the never-ceasing spring
Of all my swelling joys.

And when I meet my Lord,
And join the gracious throng,
Grace shall inspire my soul to sing,
And grace be all the song.

164   John Newton   CM
The joy of the LORD is your strength.
Nehemiah 8:10

Joy is a fruit that will not grow
In nature's barren soil;
All we can boast, till Christ we know,
Is vanity and toil.

JAMES MONTGOMERY 1771-1854

165   James Montgomery   SM
Stand up and bless the LORD your God.
Nehemiah 9:5

Stand up, and bless the Lord,
Ye people of His choice:
Stand up, and bless the Lord your God
With heart and soul and voice.

Though high above all praise,
Above all blessing high,
Who would not fear His holy Name,
And praise and magnify?

O for the living flame
From His own altar brought,
To touch our lips, our minds inspire,
And wing to heaven our thought!

God is our strength and song,
And His salvation ours;
Then be His love in Christ proclaimed
With all our ransomed powers.

Stand up, and bless the Lord,
The Lord your God adore;
Stand up, and bless His glorious name
Henceforth for evermore.

166   John Newton   CM
Moreover Thou leddest them in the day by a cloudy pillar; and in the night by a pillar of fire.
Nehemiah 9:12

When Israel by divine command,
    The pathless desert trod,
They found, though 'twas a barren land,
    A sure resource in God.

A cloudy pillar marked their road,
    And screened them from the heat,
From the hard rocks the water flowed,
    And manna was their meat.

Like them we have a rest in view,
    Secure from adverse powers;
Like them, we pass a desert too,
    But Israel's God is ours.

His word a light before us spreads,
    By which our path we see;
His love, a banner o'er our heads,
    From harm preserves us free.

Jesus, the Bread of life, is given
    To be our daily food;
We drink a wondrous stream from heaven,
    'Tis water, wine, and blood.

Lord, 'tis enough, I ask no more,
    These blessings are divine;
I envy not the worldling's store,
    If Christ and heaven are mine.

167   James Montgomery   77 77
Songs of praise and thanksgiving unto God.
Nehemiah 12:46

Songs of praise the angels sang,
Heaven with hallelujahs rang,
When Jehovah's work begun,
When He spake, and it was done.

Songs of praise awoke the morn,
When the Prince of Peace was born:
Songs of praise arose when He
Captive led captivity.

Heaven and earth must pass away,
Songs of praise shall crown that day;
God will make new heavens and earth,
Songs of praise shall hail their birth.

And shall man alone be dumb
Till that glorious kingdom come?
No; the church delights to raise
Psalms, and hymns, and songs of praise.

Saints below, with heart and voice,
Still in songs of praise rejoice;
Learning here, by faith and love,
Songs of praise to sing above.

Borne upon their latest breath,
Songs of praise shall conquer death;
Then, amidst eternal joy,
Songs of praise their powers employ.

168   Thomas Haweis   CM
Remember me, O my God, for good.
Nehemiah 13:31

O Thou from whom all goodness flows,
    I lift my heart to Thee;
In all my sorrows, conflicts, woes,
    Jesus, remember me.

When on my mourning, burdened heart,
    My sins lie heavily;
My pardon speak, Thy peace impart;
    In love remember me.

Temptations sore obstruct my way,
    And ills I cannot flee;
O give me strength, Lord, as my day;
    For good remember me.

If on my face for Thy dear name,
    Shame and reproaches be,
All hail reproach, and welcome shame!
    If Thou remember me.

The hour is near, consigned to death,
    I own the just decree;
Saviour, with my last parting breath,
    I'll cry, 'Remember me.'

169   Edmund Jones   CM
So will I go in unto the king, which is not according to the law: and if I perish, I perish.
Esther 4:16

Come, humble sinner in whose breast
    A thousand thoughts revolve;
Come, with your guilt and fear oppressed,
    And make this last resolve.

'I'll go to Jesus, though my sin
    Hath like a mountain rose;
I know His courts, I'll enter in
Whatever may oppose.

'Prostrate I'll lie before His throne,
    And there my guilt confess;
I'll tell Him I'm a wretch undone
    Without His sovereign grace.

'I'll to the gracious King approach,
    Whose sceptre pardon gives;
Perhaps He may command my touch,
    And then the suppliant lives.

'Perhaps He will admit my plea,
    Perhaps will hear my prayer,
But if I perish, I will pray,
    And perish only there.

'I can but perish if I go;
    I am resolved to try;
For, if I stay away, I know
    I must for ever die.

'But if I die, with mercy sought,
    When I the King have tried,
This were to die (delightful thought!)
    As sinner never died.'

170   Joseph Hoskins   LM
So will I go in unto the king, which is not
according to the law: and if I perish, I perish.
Esther 4:16

Sinners, exposed to endless woe,
Arise, and to King Jesus go,
Your guilt confess, His favour seek,
And wait to hear what God will speak.

Fear not the law, 'tis grace that reigns,
Jesus the sinner's cause maintains.
He ransomed rebels with His blood,
And now He intercedes with God.

To Him approach with fervent prayer,
And if you perish, perish there,
Resolved at Jesus' feet to lie,
Suing for mercy till you die.

Like Esther, venture near His throne,
And make your supplications known;
Tell Him the cause of all your grief,
And He will grant you quick relief.

Thrice happy souls, who thus address
The God of love, and boundless grace;
Jesus will such completely save,
And life eternal they shall have.

171   John Kent   CM
Hast not Thou made an hedge about him?
Job 1:10

Around a saint who feared His name,
    With whom the devil strove,
Jehovah fixed a wall of flame,
    And hedged him up with love.

From everlasting love's embrace,
    Nor hell nor sin could tear;
For God had hedged him round with grace,
    Deep as His counsels are.

In vain the tempter summoned all
    His black infernal crew;
They ne'er could cause this fence to fall,
    Or force a passage through.

Fruitless and vain his efforts prove,
    He here no mine could spring;
His darts by God were dipped in love,
    And blunted on the wing.

Like him, our refuge is the same,
    In safety we abide;
With walls of everlasting flame,
    Hedged round on every side.

Hedged in by God's tremendous name,
    Believer, cease thy fears;
Ten thousand chariots, all of flame,
    Thy God for thee prepares.

At every time, in every place,
    In safeguard thou shalt be;
For God hath fixed a wall of grace
    Betwixt thy foes and thee.

172   Samuel Medley   CM
There the weary be at rest. *Job 3:17*

Weary of earth, myself, and sin,
    Dear Jesus, set me free,
And to Thy glory take me in,
    For there I long to be.

Burdened, dejected, and oppressed,
    Ah! whither shall I flee
But to Thy arms, for peace and rest?
    For there I long to be.

Empty, polluted, dark, and vain,
    Is all this world to me;
May I the better world obtain;
    For there I long to be.

Lord, let a tempest-tossèd soul
    That peaceful harbour see,
Where waves and billows never roll;
    For there I long to be.

Let a poor labourer here below,
    When from his toil set free,
To rest and peace eternal go;
    For there I long to be.

173   William Cowper   CM
He shall deliver thee in six troubles: yea, in seven there shall no evil touch thee. *Job 5:19*

O Lord, my best desire fulfil,
　And help me to resign
Life, health, and comfort to Thy will,
　And make Thy pleasure mine.

Why should I shrink at Thy command,
　Whose love forbids my fears?
Or tremble at the gracious hand
　That wipes away my tears?

No; let me rather freely yield
　What most I prize to Thee,
Who never hast a good withheld,
　Or wilt withhold from me.

Thy favour all my journey through,
　Thou art engaged to grant;
What else I want, or think I do,
　'Tis better still to want.

Wisdom and mercy guide my way;
　Shall I resist them both:
A poor blind creature of a day,
　And crushed before the moth?

But ah! my inmost spirit cries,
　Still bind me to Thy sway,
Else the next cloud that veils my skies
　Drives all these thoughts away.

174   Isaac Watts   CM
My days are swifter than a weaver's shuttle, and are spent without hope. *Job 7:6*

Time! what an empty vapour 'tis!
　And days how swift they are!
Swift as an Indian arrow flies,
　Or like a shooting star.

Yet, mighty God! our fleeting days
　Thy lasting favours share;
Yet with the bounties of Thy grace,
　Thou load'st the rolling year.

'Tis sovereign mercy finds us food,
　And we are clothed with love;
While grace stands pointing out the road
　That leads our souls above.

His goodness runs an endless round;
　All glory to the Lord!
His mercy never knows a bound;
　And be His name adored.

Thus we begin the lasting song,
　And, when we close our eyes,
Let the next age Thy praise prolong
　Till time and nature dies.

175   C.W.C.   SM
How should man be just with God?
Job 9:2

　Answer for me, my Lord;
　On Thee my cause I lay;
I dare not stand and plead myself;
　Answer for me, I pray!

　Condemned beneath the law,
　I hear its awful word:
'The soul that sinneth it shall die';
　Answer for me, my Lord!

　Without the spotless Lamb,
　Without the blood outpoured,
There is no pardon for my soul;
　Answer for me, my Lord!

　Answer for me till life
　Hath loosed her silver cord;
And as I sink in death's embrace,
　Answer for me, my Lord!

　No righteousness of mine
　A shelter can afford;
But when I stand before the throne,
　Answer for me, my Lord!

176   James Relly   LM
Though I were perfect, yet would I not know my soul: I would despise my life. *Job 9:21*

Could I of all perfection boast,
As pure as that which Adam lost,
I'd say that Christ alone was good,
And glory only in His blood.

Were I, as Abraham, strong in faith,
And boldly faithful unto death,
I'd bid my faithfulness adieu,
And Jesus only faithful view.

If I more meek than Moses were,
Free from all anger, strife, or fear,
Yet this I gladly would despise,
And Jesus' meekness only prize.

Were I, as Job, submissive, still,
Patient, resigned to every ill,
Yet, when I look at Jesus' cross,
I count all this no more than dross.

If I were wise as Solomon,
Like Him with zeal and ardour shone,
Like Him I'd vain and foolish see
My wisdom, zeal, yea, all but Thee!

Had I an angel's purity,
Yet even this I would deny;
Nor good confess, in name or thing,
Except in Christ, my Lord and King.

177   John Newton   77 77 77
Job 10

Saviour shine and cheer my soul,
  Bid my dying hopes revive;
Make my wounded spirit whole,
  Far away the tempter drive:
Speak the word and set me free,
Let me live alone to Thee.

Shall I sigh and pray in vain,
  Wilt Thou still refuse to hear;
Wilt Thou not return again,
  Must I yield to black despair?
Thou hast taught my heart to pray,
Canst Thou turn Thy face away?

Once I thought my mountain strong,
  Firmly fixed no more to move;
Then Thy grace was all my song,
  Then my soul was filled with love:
Those were happy golden days,
Sweetly spent in prayer and praise.

When my friends have said, 'Beware,
  Soon or late you'll find a change;'
I could see no cause for fear,
  Vain their caution seemed and strange:
Not a cloud obscured my sky,
Could I think a tempest nigh?

Little, then, myself I knew,
  Little thought of Satan's power;
Now I find their words were true,
  Now I feel the stormy hour!
Sin has put my joys to flight,
Sin has changed my day to night.

Satan asks, and mocks my woe,
  'Boaster, where is now your God?'
Silence, Lord, this cruel foe,
  Let Him know I'm bought with blood:
Tell him, since I know Thy name,
Though I change Thou art the same.

178   John Newton   CM
**Behold, He breaketh down, and it cannot be
built again: He shutteth up a man, and there
can be no opening.** *Job 12:14*

All outward means, till God appears,
  Will ineffectual prove;
Though much the sinner sees and hears,
  He cannot learn to love.

But let the stoutest sinner feel
  The softening warmth of grace,
Though hard as ice, or rocks, or steel,
  His heart dissolves apace.

Feeling the blood which Jesus spilt,
  To save his soul from woe,
His hatred, unbelief, and guilt,
  All melt away like snow.

Jesus, we in Thy name entreat;
  Reveal Thy gracious arm;
And grant Thy Spirit's kindly heat,
  Our frozen hearts to warm.

179   Thomas Pollock   86 84
**How many are mine iniquities and sins? make
me to know my transgression and my sin.**
Job 13:23

Show me myself, O holy Lord;
  Help me to look within;
I will not turn me from the sight
  Of all my sin.

Just as it is in Thy pure eyes
  Would I behold my heart;
Bring every hidden spot to light,
  Nor shrink the smart.

Not mine, the purity of heart
  That shall at last see God;
Not mine, the following in the steps
  The Saviour trod;

Not mine, the life I thought to live
  When first I took His name;
Mine but the right to weep and grieve
  Over my shame.

Yet, Lord, I thank Thee for the sight
  Thou hast vouchsafed to me;
And humbled to the dust, I shrink
  Closer to Thee;

And if Thy love will not disown
  So frail a heart as mine,
Chasten and cleanse it as Thou wilt,
  But keep It Thine!

180   David Denham   CM
Are the consolations of God small with thee?
Job 15:11

The consolations of our God
  Are ancient, full, and free,
Flowing through the Redeemer's blood,
  To me, the sinner, me.

It's everlasting in its source,
  And in duration too;
No change in us can turn its course,
  In God, 'tis always new.

Its blessings, countless as the sands,
  Shine in our sins forgiven;
Through our great Surety's piercèd hands,
  Who seals our peace with heaven.

Its strength was proved by saints of old,
  Its strength our souls sustain;
But all its virtues can't be told
  Till we its fulness gain.

Should faith be weak, and comforts few,
  Our spring in Christ is sure;
Our strength as eagles' He'll renew,
  And our diseases cure.

Our streams of consolation here
  Lead to a sea above,
Where, like our Lord, we shall appear,
  Perfect in light and love.

181   Samuel Medley   CM
Behold, my witness is in heaven, and my record is on high. *Job 16:19*

My soul, arise! shake off thy fears,
  And wipe thy sorrows dry;
Jesus in heaven thy witness bears,
  Thy record is on high.

Above this world of sins and pains,
  Beyond the glittering sky,
My Witness still in heaven remains,
  My record is on high.

Cheerful I'll bow to all His will,
  And at His footstool lie;
My Witness lives in heaven, and still
  My record is on high.

Behold, my soul, whate'er betides,
  Thou shalt not, canst not die;
My Witness still in heaven abides,
  My record is on high.

Thus, while I sing of Christ, my Lord,
  And angels' harps outvie,
My Witness lives in heaven adored,
  My record is on high.

182   Henry Fowler   11 8 11 8
The righteous also shall hold on his way.
Job 17:9

Ye pilgrims of Zion, and chosen of God,
  Whose spirits are filled with dismay,
Since ye have eternal redemption thro' blood,
  Ye cannot but hold on your way.

As Jesus, in covenant love, did engage
  A fulness of grace to display,
The powers of darkness in malice may rage,
  The righteous shall hold on his way.

This truth, like its Author, eternal shall stand,
  Though all things in nature decay,
Upheld by Jehovah's omnipotent hand,
  The righteous shall hold on his way.

They may on the main of temptation be tossed;
  Their sorrows may swell as the sea;
But none of the ransomed shall ever be lost;
  The righteous shall hold on his way.

Surrounded with sorrows, temptations, and cares,
  This truth with delight we survey,
And sing, as we pass through this valley of tears,
  'The righteous shall hold on his way.'

183   Samuel Medley   LM
For I know that my Redeemer liveth, and that He shall stand at the latter day upon the earth.
Job 19:25

I know that my Redeemer lives—
What comfort this sweet sentence gives!
He lives, He lives, who once was dead,
And reigns, my ever-living Head!

He lives, triumphant from the grave;
He lives, eternally to save;
He lives all glorious in the sky;
He lives, exalted there on high.

He lives to silence all my fears,
To wipe away my falling tears,
To soothe and calm my troubled heart,
All needed blessings to impart.

He lives, and grants me daily breath;
Through Him my soul shall conquer death:
He's gone my mansion to prepare;
He lives to bring me safely there.

All glory to His sacred name!
  He lives, my Jesus, still the same;
O the sweet joy this sentence gives—
  I know that my Redeemer lives!

184   Fanny Crosby   Irregular
For I know that my Redeemer liveth, and that
He shall stand at the latter day upon the earth.
Job 19:25

Praise Him! praise Him!
Jesus, our blessèd Redeemer;
  Sing, O earth!
His wonderful love proclaim!
  Hail Him! hail Him!
highest arch-angels in glory;
  Strength and honour
give to His holy name.
  Like a shepherd,
Jesus will guard His children,
  In His arms
He carries them all day long.
  O ye saints
that dwell in the mountains of Zion!
  Praise Him! praise Him!
ever in joyful song.

Praise Him! praise Him!
Jesus our blessèd Redeemer,
  For our sins
He suffered and bled and died!
  He, our Rock,
our hope of eternal salvation,
  Hail Him! hail Him!
Jesus the Crucified—
  Loving Saviour,
meekly enduring sorrow,
  Crowned with thorns
that cruelly pierced His brow;
  Once for us
rejected, despised, and forsaken,
  Prince of glory,
ever triumphant now.

Praise Him! praise Him!
Jesus, our blessèd Redeemer,
  Heavenly portals,
loud with hosannas ring!
  Jesus, Saviour,
reigneth for ever and ever;
  Crown Him! crown Him!
Prophet and Priest and King!
  Death is vanquished!
Tell it with joy, ye faithful;
  Where is now
Thy victory, boasting grave?
  Jesus lives!
no longer Thy portals are cheerless;
  Jesus lives,
the mighty and strong to save.

185   Joseph Swain   886 D
Whom I shall see for myself, and mine eyes
shall behold. *Job 19:27*

Sweet is the thought that I shall know
The Man who suffered here below,
  To manifest His love
For me and those whom I love best,
Or here, or with Himself at rest,
  In the bright realms above!

Not all things else are half so dear
As His delightful presence here;
  What must it be on high!
His word, as in the churches known,
Falls like a shower of blessings down,
  And makes them shout for joy.

But how must His celestial voice
Make our enraptured hearts rejoice,
  When from His glorious throne
He calls us to come near His seat,
And we, at His once-piercèd feet,
  Our diadems cast down!

'Come in, thou blessèd, sit by Me,
With My own life I ransomed thee,'
  The Lord to each will say:
'Thou now shalt dwell with Me at home;
Ye blissful mansions, make him room,
  For ever here to stay.'

When Jesus thus invites us in,
How will the heavenly host begin
  To shout us welcome home!
'Come in! come in!' the blissful sound
Will make the crystal walls resound
  For joy that we are come.

186 David Denham LM
Why persecute we him, seeing the root of the matter is found in me? *Job 19:28*

The root of death is in me found,
By nature vile, in heart unsound;
Yet through Jehovah's kind decree.
The root of life is found in me!

The root of evil makes me groan
Before my God, my Father's throne:
But from the reign of sin made free,
The root of grace is found in me!

The root of folly, shame, and pride,
In my poor heart doth still abide;
Yet taught of God (to Christ I flee),
The root of wisdom's found in me.

The root of unbelief and fear
Shows how I need my Saviour near:
But since His death is all my plea,
The root of faith is found in me!

The root of hatred is subdued,
And peace with Zion's sons pursued;
In union to the Lord I see
The root of love is found in me!

The root of discontent and war,
My peace and choicest comforts mar;
But through Christ's sufferings on the tree,
The root of peace is found in me!

The root of all that's vile on earth,
Doth oft debase my heavenly birth;
Yet one with God, the Holy Three,
The root of glory's found in me!

187 Isaac Watts CM
Oh that I knew where I might find Him.
Job 23:3

O that I knew the secret place
  Where I might find my God!
I'd spread my wants before His face,
  And pour my woes abroad.

I'd tell Him how my sins arise,
  What sorrows I sustain;
How grace recedes and comfort dies,
  And leaves my heart in pain.

He knows what arguments I'd take
  To wrestle with my God;
I'd plead for His own mercy's sake,
  And for my Saviour's blood.

But stay, my soul, to hope give place
  He'll banish every fear;
He calls thee to His throne of grace,
  To spread thy sorrows there.

188 Charles Wesley LM
Oh that I knew where I might find Him.
Job 23:3

O that my load of sin were gone!
  O that I could at last submit
At Jesus' feet to lay it down,
  To lay my soul at Jesus' feet!

When shall my eyes behold the Lamb,
  The God of my salvation see?
Weary, O Lord, Thou know'st I am;
  Yet still I cannot come to Thee.

Rest for my soul I long to find;
  Saviour, if mine indeed Thou art,
Give me Thy meek and lowly mind,
  And stamp Thy image on my heart.

I would, but Thou must give me power,
  My heart from every sin release;
Bring near, bring near, the joyful hour,
  And fill me with Thy heavenly peace.

189 William Parker 84 884
But He knoweth the way that I take.
Job 23:10

God holds the key of all unknown
  And I am glad;
If other hands should hold the key
Or if He trusted it to me,
  I might be sad.

What if tomorrow's cares were here
  Without its rest!
I'd rather He unlocked the day,
And, as the hours swing open, say,
  'My will is best.'

I cannot read His future plans;
  But this I know:
I have the smiling of His face
And all the refuge of His grace
  While here below.

Enough; this covers all my wants
  And so I rest!
For what I cannot, He can see
And in His care I saved shall be--
  For ever blest.

190   Mary Brainerd   Irregular
But He knoweth the way that I take.
Job 23:10

I know not what awaits me;
   God kindly veils mine eyes,
And o'er each step of my onward way
   He makes new scenes to rise:
And every joy He sends me comes
   A sweet and glad surprise.

Where He may lead I'll follow,
   My trust in Him repose;
And every hour in perfect peace
   I'll sing. 'He knows! He knows!'

One step I see before me;
   'Tis all I need to see;
The light of heaven more brightly shines
   When earth's illusions flee;
And sweetly through the silence comes
   His loving—'Follow Me!'

O, blissful lack of wisdom!
   'Tis blessèd not to know;
He holds me with His own right hand
   And will not let me go;
And lulls my troubled soul to rest
   In Him who loves me so.

So on I go—not knowing,
   I would not if I might;
I'd rather walk in the dark with God,
   Than go alone in the light;
I'd rather walk by faith with Him,
   Than go alone by sight.

191   Isaac Watts   CM
But He is in one mind, and who can turn Him?
and what His soul desireth, even that He
doeth. *Job 23:13*

Keep silence, all created things,
   And wait your Maker's nod;
My soul stands trembling, while she sings
   The honours of our God.

Life, death, and hell, and worlds unknown,
   Hang on His firm decree;
He sits on no precarious throne,
   Nor borrows leave to be.

Chained to His throne a volume lies,
   With all the fates of men,
With every angel's form and size,
   Drawn by the eternal pen.

His providence unfolds the book,
   And makes His counsels shine;
Each opening leaf, and every stroke,
   Fulfils some deep design.

My God, I would not long to see
   My fate with curious eyes—
What gloomy lines are writ for me,
   Or what bright scenes may rise.

In Thy fair book of life and grace,
   O may I find my name
Recorded in some humble place,
   Beneath my Lord the Lamb.

192   Thomas Rowe   66 66 88
The Spirit of God hath made me, and the
breath of the Almighty hath given me life.
Job 33:4

Almighty Spirit, we
   Thy Godhead now adore;
We bring our praise to Thee,
   And thanks for evermore;
For once we slept in darkness deep,
But Thou hast raised us from the sleep.

Through all Thy work within,
   Thy greatness we admire;
It breaks the reign of sin,
   And lights the sacred fire,
To make us burn with love to God,
Through the atoning Saviour's blood.

Thy power and grace divine
   Has raised us from the dead:
And taught our souls to twine
   Around our living Head;
And none but God could bless us so,
Or raise us from such depths of woe.

To Jesus Thou dost lead
   Our souls for life and rest;
And on Himself to feed
   Till we are truly blest:
We now to Thee our praises bring,
And thus Thy glorious Godhead sing.

193   John Cennick   886 D
I have found a ransom. *Job 33:24*

Great God! if Thou shouldst bring me near,
To answer at Thy awful bar,
   And my own self defend;
If Jesus did Himself withdraw,
I know Thy holy, fiery law
   My soul to hell would send.

A sinner self-condemned I come,
Worthy that Thou shouldst me consume,
   But, O! one thing I plead:
The every mite to Thee I owed,
Christ Jesus, with His own heart's blood,
   In pity for me paid.

Now shouldst Thou me to judgment call,
Though Moses faced me there, and all
   My dreadful sins appeared,
I should not fear, but boldly stand;
Through Jesus' piercèd heart and hand,
   I know I should be spared.

My full receipt should there be showed,
Written with iron pens in blood,
   On Jesus' hands and side.
'I'm safe!' I'll shout, 'O law and sin,
Ye cannot bring me guilty in,
   For Christ was crucified!'

194   John Monsell   CM
**Teach us what we shall say unto Him; for we
cannot order our speech by reason of
darkness.** *Job 37:19*

When cold our hearts, and far from Thee
   Our wandering spirits stray,
And thoughts and lips move heavily,
   Lord, teach us how to pray.

Too vile to venture near Thy throne,
   Too poor to turn away,
Depending on Thy help alone,
   Lord, teach us how to pray.

We know not how to seek Thy face
   Unless Thou lead the way;
We have no words unless Thy grace,
   Lord, teach us how to pray.

Here every thought and fond desire
   We on Thine altar lay;
And when our souls have caught Thy fire,
   Lord, teach us how to pray.

195   Isaac Watts   66 66 88
With God is terrible majesty. *Job 37:22*

The Lord Jehovah reigns;
   His throne is built on high,
The garments He assumes
   Are light and majesty:
His glories shine with beams so bright,
No mortal eye can bear the sight.

The thunders of His hand
   Keep the wide world in awe;
His wrath and justice stand
   To guard His holy law;
And where His love resolves to bless,
His truth confirms and seals the grace.

Through all His mighty works
   Amazing wisdom shines,
Confounds the powers of hell,
   And breaks their dark designs;
Strong is His arm, and shall fulfil
His great decrees and sovereign will.

And will this mighty King
   Of glory condescend?
And will He write His name
   My Father and my Friend?
I love His name, I love His Word,
Join all my powers to praise the Lord.

196   Timothy Dudley-Smith   DCM
Job 38

Whose mighty word the heavens made?
   Who gave the planets birth,
And on its sure foundations laid
   The cornerstone of earth?
Creation's everlasting King,
   Whom morning stars proclaim,
And we with them rejoice to sing
   The splendours of His name.

The darkness fled at His decree,
   He gave the winds their breath.
He set the bounds of shore and sea,
   He formed the gates of death.
The Pleiades obey His will,
   By Him Orion shines;
The stars His purposes fulfil,
   The heavens His designs.

The thunder tells His name aloud,
  For Him the rivers flow;
He numbers every passing cloud,
  The treasures of the snow.
Our world of sea and sky and land,
  With living creatures stored,
Bears witness to its Maker's hand,
  Creation's King and Lord.

Who by His word the heavens made,
  The starry hosts on high,
But He whose Son our ransom paid,
  Who came in Christ to die?
To such a God, with all our powers,
  Let songs of praise ascend,
For we are His and He is ours,
  Our Father and our Friend.

*'Whose mighty word the heavens made?' by
Timothy Dudley-Smith (b.1926). © Timothy
Dudley-Smith in Europe and Africa. © Hope
Publishing Company in the United States of
America and the rest of the world. Reproduced by
permission of Oxford University Press . All rights
reserved.*

197   John Newton   SM
Behold, I am vile; what shall I answer Thee?
Job 40:4

O Lord, how vile am I,
  Unholy and unclean!
How can I dare to venture nigh
  With such a load of sin?

Is this polluted heart
  A dwelling fit for Thee?
Swarming, alas! in every part,
  What evils do I see!

If I attempt to pray,
  And lisp Thy holy name;
My thoughts are hurried soon away,
  I know not where I am.

If in Thy word I look,
  Such darkness fills my mind;
I only read a sealèd book,
  And no relief can find.

Thy gospel oft I hear,
  But hear it still in vain;
Without desire, or love, or fear,
  I like a stone remain.

Myself can hardly bear
  This wretched heart of mine!
How hateful, then, must it appear
  To those pure eyes of Thine!

And must I, then, indeed,
  Sink in despair and die?
Fain would I hope that Thou didst bleed
  For such a wretch as I.

That blood which Thou hast spilt,
  That grace which is Thy own,
Can cleanse the vilest sinner's guilt,
  And soften hearts of stone.

Low at Thy feet I bow;
  O pity and forgive!
Here will I lie, and wait till Thou
  Shalt bid me rise and live.

198   Isaac Watts   CM
Psalm 1

Blessed is the man who shuns the place
  Where sinners love to meet;
Who fears to tread their wicked ways,
  And hates the scoffer's seat:

But In the statutes of the Lord
  Has placed his chief delight;
By day he reads or hears the word,
  And meditates by night.

He, like a plant of generous kind,
  By living waters set,
Safe from the storms and blasting wind,
  Enjoys a peaceful state.

Green as the leaf, and ever fair,
  Shall his profession shine;
While fruits of holiness appear
  Like clusters on the vine.

Not so the impious and unjust;
  What vain designs they form!
Their hopes are blown away like dust,
  Or chaff before the storm.

Sinners in judgment shall not stand
  Amongst the sons of grace,
When Christ, the Judge, at His right hand
  Appoints His saints a place.

His eye beholds the path they tread;
  His heart approves it well:
But crooked ways of sinners lead
  Down to the gates of hell.

199   Michael Baughen   Irregular
Psalm 1

Blessèd is the man,
the man who does not walk
In the counsel of the ungodly
—blessèd is that man.
He who rejects the way,
rejects the way of sin
And who turns away from scoffing
—blessèd is that man.
But his delight
—by day and night—
Is the law of God Almighty.

He is like a tree
—a tree that flourishes
Being planted by the water
—blessèd is that man.
He will bring forth fruit
—his leaf will wither not—
For in all he does he prospers
—blessèd is that man.
For his delight
—by day and night—
Is the law of God Almighty.

The ungodly are not so
—for they are like the chaff
Which the wind blows clean away
—the ungodly are not so.
The ungodly will not stand
—upon the judgment day
Nor belong to God's own people
—the ungodly will not stand:
But God knows the
way of righteous men
And ungodly ways will perish.

Blessèd is the man,
the man who does not walk
In the counsel of the ungodly
—blèssed is that man.

Words: © M. Baughen / The Jubilate Group.
www.jubilate.co.uk USED BY PERMISSION

200   William Goode   66 66 44 44
Psalm 2

Though sinners boldly join,
   Against the Lord to rise,
Against His Christ combine,
   Th' Anointed to despise;
Though earth disdain,
   And hell engage,
   Vain is their rage,
Their counsel vain.

Jesus the Saviour reigns,
   On Zion is His throne;
The Lord's decree sustains
   His own begotten Son:
Up from the grave
   He bids Him rise
   And mount the skies,
With power to save.

O serve the Lord with fear,
   And reverence His command;
With sacred joy draw near,
   With solemn trembling stand;
Kneel at His throne,
   Your homage bear,
   His power declare,
And kiss the Son.

201   Thomas Kelly   87 87 47
Serve the LORD with fear, and rejoice with
trembling. *Psalm 2:11*

In Thy name O Lord, assembling,
   We Thy people now draw near,
Teach us to rejoice with trembling,
   Speak, and let Thy servants hear;
   Hear with meekness;
   Hear Thy word with godly fear.

Grant us, Lord, some gracious token
   Of Thy love before we part;
Crown Thy word which will be spoken,
   Life and peace to each impart,
   And all blessings
   Which will sanctify the heart.

While our days on earth are lengthened,
   May we give them Lord, to Thee;
Cheered by hope, and daily strengthened,
   May we run, nor weary be;
   Till Thy glory,
   Without clouds, in heaven we see.

There, in worship purer, sweeter,
   All Thy people shall adore;
Tasting of enjoyment greater
   Than they could conceive before;
   Full enjoyment,
   Full, unmixed, and evermore.

202   Henry Lyte   LM
Psalm 3

Thy promise, Lord, is perfect peace,
And yet my trials still increase;
Till fears at times my soul assail,
That Satan's rage must yet prevail.

Then, Saviour, then I fly to Thee,
And in Thy grace my refuge see:
Thou heard'st me from Thy holy hill.
And Thou wilt hear and help me still.

Beneath Thy wings secure I sleep;
What foe can harm while Thou dost keep?
I wake, and find Thee at my side,
My omnipresent Guard and Guide!

O why should earth or hell distress,
With God so strong, so nigh to bless?
From Him alone salvation flows;
On Him alone, my soul, repose.

203   Augustus Toplady   88 88 D *anapaestic*
But Thou, O LORD, art a shield for me; my
glory, and the lifter up of mine head.
Psalm 3:3

A sovereign Protector I have,
    Unseen, yet for ever at hand,
Unchangeably faithful to save,
    Almighty to rule and command.
He smiles and my comforts abound;
    His grace as the dew shall descend
And walls of salvation surround
    The soul He delights to defend.

Kind Author and ground of my hope,
    Thee, Thee for my God I avow;
My glad Ebenezer set up
    And own Thou hast helped me till now.
I muse on the years that are past
    Wherein my defence Thou hast proved;
Nor wilt Thou relinquish at last
    A sinner so signally loved.

Inspirer and Hearer of prayer,
    Thou Shepherd and Guardian of Thine,
My all to Thy covenant care
    I sleeping and waking resign.
If Thou art my Shield and my Sun,
    The night is no darkness to me;
And, fast as my moments roll on,
    They bring me but nearer to Thee.

204   Isaac Watts   CM
Salvation belongeth unto the LORD: thy
blessing is upon thy people. *Psalm 3:8*

Blessed are the souls that hear and know
    The gospel's joyful sound;
Peace shall attend the path they go,
    And light their steps surround.

Their joy shall bear their spirits up,
    Through their Redeemer's name;
His righteousness exalts their hope,
    Nor Satan dares condemn.

The Lord, our glory and defence,
    Strength and salvation gives:
Israel, Thy King for ever reigns.
    Thy God for ever lives.

205   Nahum Tate, Nicholas Brady   CM
Psalm 4

Lord of my life, my hopes, my joys,
    My never-failing Friend,
Thou hast been all my help till now,
    O help me to the end!

While worldly minds impatient grow,
    More prosperous times to see.
O let the glories of Thy face
    Shine brighter, Lord, on me!

So shall my heart o'erflow with joy
    More lasting and more true
Than theirs, possessed of all that they
    So eagerly pursue.

Then down in peace I'll lay my head,
    And take my needful rest:
No other guard I ask or need,
    Of Thee, O Lord, possessed.

206   Anne Steele   LM
Stand in awe, and sin not: commune with your
own heart upon your bed, and be still.
Psalm 4:4

Hence vain, intruding world, depart
No more allure nor vex my heart;
Let every vanity be gone;
I would be peaceful and alone.

Here let me search my inmost mind,
And try its real state to find,
The secret springs of thought explore,
And call my words and actions o'er.

Eternity, tremendous sound!
To guilty souls a dreadful wound;
But O, if Christ and heaven be mine,
How sweet the accents, how divine!

Be this my great, my only care,
My chief pursuit, my ardent prayer,
An interest in the Saviour's blood,
My pardon sealed, and peace with God.

Search, Lord, O search my inmost heart,
And light, and hope, and joy impart;
From guilt and error set me free,
And guide me safe to heaven and Thee.

207   Thomas Kelly   77 77
Who will shew us any good? LORD, lift Thou up the light of Thy countenance upon us.
Psalm 4:6

'Who will show us any good?'
   Thus the hopeless worldling cries;
Pleasure, though with zeal pursued,
   Still from his embraces flies.

Is there nothing here below
   Can supply the soul with food?
Hear the general answer, 'No!
   Who will show us any good?'

Must we then all hope resign?
   Is there nought can yield repose?
Saviour, make Thy face to shine,
   This is what will heal our woes.

208   Thomas Kelly   87 87 77
I will both lay me down in peace, and sleep: for Thou, LORD, only makest me dwell in safety.
Psalm 4:8

Through the day Thy love hath spared us;
   Now we lay us down to rest;
Through the silent watches guard us,
   Let no foe our peace molest:
Jesus, Thou our Guardian be;
Sweet it is to trust in Thee.

Pilgrims here on earth and strangers,
   Dwelling in the midst of foes,
Us and ours preserve from dangers;
   In Thine arms may we repose!
And, when life's sad day is past,
Rest with Thee in heaven at last.

209   Isaac Watts   CM
Psalm 5

Lord, in the morning Thou shalt hear
   My voice ascending high;
To Thee will I direct my prayer,
   To Thee lift up mine eye.

Up to the hills where Christ is gone
   To plead for all His saints;
Presenting at His Father's throne
   Our songs and our complaints.

Thou art a God before whose sight
   The wicked shall not stand;
Sinners shall ne'er be Thy delight,
   Nor dwell at Thy right hand.

But to Thy house will I resort,
   To taste Thy mercies there;
I will frequent Thy holy court,
   And worship in Thy fear.

O may Thy Spirit guide my feet
   In ways of righteousness!
Make every path of duty straight,
   And plain before my face.

210   Michael Bruce   CM
Give ear to my words, O LORD, consider my meditation. *Psalm 5:1*

Almighty Father of mankind,
   On Thee my hopes remain;
And when the day of trouble comes,
   I shall not trust in vain.

In early days Thou wast my guide,
   And of my youth the Friend:
And as my days began with Thee,
   With Thee my days shall end.

I know the power in whom I trust,
   The arm on which I lean;
He will my Saviour ever be,
   Who has my Saviour been.

My God, who causedst me to hope,
   When life began to beat,
And when a stranger in the world,
   Didst guide my wandering feet;

Thou wilt not cast me off when age
   And evil days descend!
Thou wilt not leave me in despair,
   To mourn my latter end.

Therefore in life I'll trust to Thee,
   In death I will adore,
And after death I'll sing Thy praise,
   When time shall be no more.

211   Thomas Ken   LM

My voice shalt Thou hear in the morning, O LORD; in the morning will I direct my prayer unto Thee, and will look up.
Psalm 5:3

Awake, my soul, and with the sun
Thy daily stage of duty run,
Shake off dull sloth, and joyful rise
To pay Thy morning sacrifice.

Thy precious time mis-spent redeem,
Each present day thy last esteem;
Improve Thy talent with due care;
For the great day thyself prepare.

Let all thy converse be sincere;
Thy conscience as the noonday clear;
Think how all-seeing God thy ways
And all thy secret thoughts surveys.

By influence of the light divine
Let thy own light in good works shine;
Reflect all heaven's propitious ways
In ardent love and cheerful praise.

Wake, and lift up thyself, my heart,
And with the angels bear thy part,
Who all night long unwearied sing
High praise to the eternal King.

Praise God, from whom all blessings flow;
Praise Him, all creatures here below;
Praise Him above, ye heavenly host;
Praise Father, Son, and Holy Ghost.

212   William Burleigh   10 10 10 10

Lead me, O LORD. *Psalm 5:8*

Lead us, O Father, in the paths of peace;
  Without Thy guiding hand we go astray,
And doubts appal and sorrows still increase;
  Lead us through Christ, the true and living Way.

Lead us, O Father, in the paths of truth;
  Unhelped by Thee, in error's maze we grope,
While passion stains and folly dims our youth,
  And age comes on uncheered by faith and hope.

Lead us, O Father, in the paths of right;
  Blindly we stumble when we walk alone,
Involved in shadows of a darkening night;
  Only with Thee we journey safely on.

Lead us, O Father, to Thy heavenly rest,
  However rough and steep the path may be,
Through joy or sorrow, as Thou deemest best,
  Until our lives are perfected in Thee.

213   Isaac Watts   SM

Let them also that love Thy name be joyful in Thee. *Psalm 5:11*

Come, we that love the Lord,
  And let our joys be known;
Join in a song with sweet accord,
  And thus surround the throne.

The sorrows of the mind
  Be banished from the place;
Religion never was designed
  To make our pleasures less.

Let those refuse to sing
  That never knew our God;
But children of the heavenly King
  May speak their joys abroad.

The hill of Zion yields
  A thousand sacred sweets
Before we reach the heavenly fields,
  Or walk the golden streets.

There shall we see His face,
  And never, never sin;
There from the rivers of His grace
  Drink endless pleasures in.

Then let our songs abound,
  And every tear be dry;
We're marching through Immanuel's ground
  To fairer worlds on high.

214   Henry Lyte   77 77
Psalm 6

Gently, gently lay Thy rod
On my sinful head, O God;
Stay Thy wrath, in mercy stay,
Lest I sink before its sway.

Heal me, for my flesh Is weak;
Heal me, for Thy grace I seek;
This my only plea I make.
Heal me for Thy mercy's sake.

Who within the silent grave
Shall proclaim Thy power to save?
Lord, my trembling soul reprieve,
Speak, and I shall rise and live.

Lo! He comes! He heeds my plea!
Lo! He comes! the shadows flee!
Glory round me dawns once more;
Rise, my spirit, and adore!

215 Samuel Medley   LM
Have mercy upon me, O LORD; for I am weak:
O LORD, heal me; for my bones are vexed.
Psalm 6:2

Regard, great God! my mournful prayer;
Make my poor trembling soul Thy care;
For me in pity undertake,
And save me for Thy mercies' sake.

My soul's cast down within me, Lord,
And only Thou canst help afford;
Let not my heart with sorrow break,
But save me for Thy mercies' sake.

Such dismal storms are raised within,
By Satan and indwelling sin,
Which all my soul with horror shake;
O save me for Thy mercies' sake.

I've foes and fears of every shape,
Nor from them can my soul escape;
Upon me, Lord, some pity take,
And save me for Thy mercies' sake.

I've scarce a glimmering ray of light;
With me 'tis little else but night;
O for my help do Thou awake,
And save me for Thy mercies' sake.

To me, dear Saviour, turn once more;
To my poor soul Thy joys restore;
Let me again Thy smiles partake.
Lord, save me for Thy mercies' sake.

216 Henry Lyte   77 77 D
Psalm 7

Lord, my God, in Thee I trust;
Save, O save Thy trembling dust,
 From the roaring lion's power.
 Seeking whom he may devour;
From a thousand waves that roll
Shipwreck o'er my sinking soul;
 God Omnipotent, I flee
 From them all to Thee, to Thee.

Thou my inmost wish canst read,
Thou canst help my utmost need;
 Let the world Thy goodness see,
 Let them mark Thy grace in me.
Lay the wicked in the dust,
Raise the feeble, guide the just:
 Searcher of the heart, I flee
 From myself to Thee, to Thee.

217 Isaac Watts   CM
Psalm 8

O Lord our Lord, how wondrous great
 Is Thine exalted name!
The glories of Thine heavenly state
 Let men and babes proclaim.

When I behold Thy works on high,
 The moon that rules the night,
And stars that well adorn the sky,
 Those moving worlds of light:

Lord, what is man, or all his race,
 Who dwells so far below,
That Thou shouldst visit him with grace
 And love his nature so?

218 Nahum Tate, Nicholas Brady CM
Psalm 9

To celebrate Thy praise, O Lord,
 I will my heart prepare;
To all the listening world Thy works
 Thy wondrous works declare.

The thought of them shall to my soul
 Exalted pleasure bring;
Whilst to Thy name, O Thou most High
 Triumphant praise I sing.

All those who have His goodness proved
 Will in His truth confide;
Whose mercy ne'er forsook the man
 That on His help relied.

His suffering saints, when most distressed,
 He ne'er forgets to aid;
Their expectations shall be crowned,
 Though for a time delayed.

Sing praises, therefore, to the Lord
 From Zion, His abode;
Proclaim His deeds, till all the world
 Confess no other God.

219 Philip Doddridge   CM
They that know Thy name will put their trust in
Thee. *Psalm 9:10*

Saviour divine! we know Thy name,
 And in that name we trust;
Thou art the Lord our righteousness,
 Thou art Thine Israel's boast.

Guilty we plead before Thy throne,
  And low in dust we lie,
Till Jesus stretch His gracious arm
  To bring the guilty nigh.

The sins of one most righteous day
  Might plunge us in despair;
Yet all the crimes of numerous years
  Shall our great Surety clear.

That spotless robe, which He hath wrought,
  Shall deck us all around;
Nor by the piercing eye of God
  One blemish shall be found.

Pardon, and peace, and lively hope,
  To sinners now are given;
Israel and Judah soon shall change
  The wilderness for heaven.

With joy we taste that manna now
  Thy mercy scatters down;
We seal our humble vows to Thee,
  And wait the promised crown.

220 Charles Wesley 664 6664
Sing praises to the LORD. *Psalm 9:11*

Come, Thou Almighty King,
Help us Thy name to sing,
  Help us to praise:
Father all-glorious,
O'er all victorious,
Come and reign over us,
  Ancient of days!

Jesus, our Lord, arise;
Scatter our enemies,
  And make them fall:
Let Thine almighty aid
Our sure defence be made,
Our souls on Thee be stayed;
  Lord, hear our call!

Come, Thou Incarnate Word,
Gird on Thy mighty sword,
  Our prayer attend:
Come, and Thy people bless,
And give Thy word success;
Spirit of holiness,
  On us descend!

Come, Holy Comforter,
Thy sacred witness bear
  In this glad hour:
Thou who almighty art,
Now rule in every heart,
And ne'er from us depart,
  Spirit of power!

To the great One-in-Three,
Eternal praises be,
  Hence, evermore!
His sovereign majesty
May we in glory see,
And to eternity
  Love and adore!

221 Joseph Swain 668 D
Sing praises to the LORD. *Psalm 9:11*

How pleasant is the gate
  Where willing converts wait
For fellowship with Zion here;
  Where they with wonder tell
  How they escaped from hell,
And hope in glory to appear.

With wonder we attend,
  While they the sinners' Friend,
With tears of holy joy, extol;
  Each heart, once hard as steel,
  Now made for sin to feel,
Bears tokens of a ransomed soul.

No more of self they boast,
  But humbly own the cost
Of their salvation freely paid;
  The sins which make them groan,
  And must have sunk them down,
They now behold on Jesus laid.

222 Anna Hudson 66 66 + refrain
I will rejoice in Thy salvation. *Psalm 9:14*

Dear Saviour, Thou art mine,
  How sweet the thought to me!
Let me repeat Thy name
  And lift my heart to Thee.

  Mine! mine! mine! I know Thou art mine;
  Saviour, dear Saviour, I know Thou art mine.

Thou art the sinner's Friend,
  So I Thy friendship claim,
A sinner saved by grace
  When Thy sweet message came.

My hardened heart was touched;
  Thy pardoning voice I heard;
And joy and peace came in
  While listening to Thy word.

So let me sing Thy praise,
  So let me call Thee mine;
I cannot doubt Thy word,
  I know that I am Thine.

223   Timothy Dudley-Smith   77 77
Psalm 10

In my hour of grief or need
When a friend is friend indeed,
Now, when Satan walks abroad,
Be not far from me, O Lord.

When the powers of evil ride
Through the world in open pride,
Flaunted sins and boasted shame
Bring contempt upon Your name.

When the godless host are strong,
When their mouth is filled with wrong,
Bitterness, deceit and fraud,
Be not far from me, O Lord.

When the poor becomes their prey,
When the weak are led astray,
Right is wrong and truth is lies,
Then, O Lord our God, arise!

Powers of darkness bring to grief,
Break the hold of unbelief,
Sound anew the quickening word,
Rise and come among us, Lord!

Then shall vice and falsehood fail,
Truth and righteousness prevail,
All His ransomed people sing
God, their everlasting King!

224   Ralph Wardlaw   SM
Arise, O LORD. *Psalm 10:12*

O Lord our God, arise,
The cause of Truth maintain,
And wide o'er all the peopled world
Extend her blessèd reign.

Thou Prince of Life, arise,
Nor let Thy glory cease;
Far spread the conquests of Thy grace,
And bless the earth with peace!

Thou, Holy Ghost, arise,
Expand Thy quickening wing,
And o'er a dark and ruined world
Let light and order spring.

All on the earth arise,
To God the Saviour sing!
From shore to shore, from earth to heaven,
Let echoing anthems ring!

225   Harriet Auber   LM
Psalm 11

When all bespeaks a Father's love,
O wherefore, fearful as the dove,
Should we in times of peril flee
To any refuge, Lord, but Thee?

In vain the wicked bend their bow,
And seek to lay the righteous low,
Thou from Thine everlasting throne
With watchful care regard'st Thine own.

Thy voice shall seal the sinner's fate,
Just vengeance shall his crimes await;
While the bright beams of grace divine,
Shall on Thy faithful servants shine.

226   William Matson   668 668 33 66
The LORD is in His holy temple.
Psalm 11:4

God is in His temple,
The Almighty Father,
Round His footstool let us gather:
Him with adoration
Serve, the Lord most holy,
Who hath mercy on the lowly;
Let us raise
Hymns of praise,
For His great salvation:
God is in His temple!

Christ comes to His temple:
We, His word receiving,
Are made happy in believing.
Lo! from sin delivered,
He hath turned our sadness,
Our deep gloom, to light and gladness!
Let us raise
Hymns of praise,
For our bonds are severed:
Christ comes to His temple!

Come and claim Thy temple,
Gracious Holy Spirit!
In our hearts Thy home inherit:
Make in us Thy dwelling,
Thy high work fulfilling,
Into ours Thy will instilling,
Till we raise
Hymns of praise,
Beyond mortal telling,
In the eternal temple.

227 William Gadsby   SM
The LORD trieth the righteous.
Psalm 11:5

The Lord the righteous tries;
    Yet we'll adore His name;
He never will their cause despise,
    Nor put their hope to shame.

He brings them to the test,
    And tries them by His law;
Then leads them to the promised rest,
    From whence they comfort draw.

Then He His face conceals,
    And lets them grope within;
And by His Spirit's power reveals
    The dreadful plague of sin.

We straightway cry, 'Unclean!
    A monstrous mass of woe!
What can such hosts of evil mean?
    And whither can we go?'

'Look here,' the Lord replies;
    'Thy beauty's all in Me;
'Tis Thine to flee from self, and prize
    Salvation full and free.

'Whate'er My wisdom does,
    Or lets the tempter do,
Thy guilt and ruin to disclose,
    One thing I keep in view:

'To teach thee how to live
    By faith in Jesus' name;
For guilt and sin to mourn and grieve,
    And sing the Lamb once slain.'

228 John Berridge   66 66 88
Help, LORD; for the godly man ceaseth.
Psalm 12:1

Send help, O Lord, we pray,
    And Thy own gospel bless;
For godly men decay,
    And faithful pastors cease;
The righteous are removèd home,
And scorners rise up in their room.

While Satan's troops are bold,
    And thrive in number too,
The flocks in Jesus' fold,
    Are growing lank and few;
Old sheep are moving off each year,
And few lambs in the fold appear.

Old shepherds, too, retire,
    Who gathered flocks below,
And young ones catch no fire,
    Or worldly-prudent grow;
Few run with trumpets in their hand,
To sound alarms by sea and land.

O Lord, stir up Thy power,
    To make the gospel spread;
And thrust out preachers more,
    With voice to raise the dead;
With feet to run where Thou dost call;
With faith to fight and conquer all.

The flocks that long have dwelt
    Around fair Zion's hill,
And Thy sweet grace have felt,
    Uphold and feed them still;
But fresh folds build up everywhere,
And plenteously Thy truth declare.

As one Elijah dies,
    True prophet of the Lord,
Let some Elisha rise
    To blaze the gospel-word;
And fast as sheep to Jesus go,
May lambs recruit His fold below.

229 Nahum Tate, Nicholas Brady   CM
Psalm 13

How long wilt Thou forget me, Lord?
    Must I for ever mourn?
How long wilt Thou withdraw from me,
    O! never to return?

O, hear, and to my longing eyes
    Restore Thy wonted light:
Revive my soul, nor let me sleep
    In everlasting night.

Since I have always placed my trust
    Beneath Thy mercy's wing,
Thy saving health will come, and then
    My heart with joy shall spring.

Then shall my song, with praise inspired,
    To Thee, my God, ascend,
Who to Thy servant in distress
    Such bounty didst extend.

230   Henry Lyte   76 76
O that the salvation of Israel were come out of Zion! *Psalm 14:7*

O that the Lord's salvation
  Were out of Zion come,
To heal His ancient nation,
  To lead His outcasts home.

How long the holy city
  Shall heathen feet profane?
Return, O Lord, in pity,
  Rebuild her walls again.

Let fall Thy rod of terror,
  Thy saving grace impart;
Roll back the veil of error,
  Release the fettered heart.

Let Israel home returning,
  Her lost Messiah see;
Give oil of joy for mourning,
  And bind Thy church to Thee.

231   Charles Spurgeon   SM
Psalm 15

Lord, I would dwell with Thee,
  On Thy most holy hill:
O shed Thy grace abroad in me,
  To mould me to Thy will.

Thy gates of pearl stand wide
  For those who walk upright;
But those who basely turn aside
  Thou chasest from Thy sight.

O tame my tongue to peace,
  And tune my heart to love;
From all reproaches may I cease,
  Made harmless as a dove.

The vile, though proudly great,
  No flatterer find in me;
I count Thy saints of poor estate
  Far nobler company.

Faithful, but meekly kind;
  Gentle, yet boldly true;
I would possess the perfect mind
  Which in my Lord I view.

But, Lord, these graces all
  Thy Spirit's work must be:
To Thee, through Jesus' blood I call.
  Create them all in me.

232   Isaac Watts   LM
Psalm 16

Preserve me, Lord, in time of need;
  For succour to Thy throne I flee,
But have no merits there to plead;
  My goodness cannot reach to Thee.

Oft have my heart and tongue confessed
  How empty and how poor I am;
My praise can never make Thee blessed,
  Nor add new glories to Thy name.

Yet, Lord, Thy saints on earth may reap
  Some profit by the good we do;
These are the company I keep,
  These are the choicest friends I know.

Let others choose the sons of mirth
  To give a relish to their wine;
I love the men of heavenly birth,
  Whose thoughts and language are divine.

233   Charles Wesley   LM
I have set the LORD always before me: because He is at my right hand, I shall not be moved. *Psalm 16:8*

Forth in Thy name, O Lord, I go,
  My daily labour to pursue,
Thee, only Thee, resolved to know
  In all I think, or speak, or do.

The task Thy wisdom hath assigned
  O let me cheerfully fulfil,
In all my works Thy presence find,
  And prove Thy good and perfect will.

Thee may I set at my right hand,
  Whose eyes my inmost substance see,
And labour on at Thy command,
  And offer all my works to Thee.

Give me to bear Thy easy yoke
  And every moment watch and pray,
And still to things eternal look,
  And hasten to Thy glorious day:

For Thee delightfully employ
  Whate'er Thy bounteous grace hath given,
And run my course, with even joy,
  And closely walk with Thee to heaven.

234   Isaac Watts   SM

Thou wilt shew me the path of life: in Thy presence is fulness of joy; at Thy right hand there are pleasures for evermore.
Psalm 16:11

My God, my Life, my Love,
  To Thee, to Thee I call,
I cannot live if Thou remove,
  For Thou art all in all.

Thy shining grace can cheer
  This dungeon where I dwell;
'Tis paradise when Thou art here;
  If Thou depart, 'tis hell.

The smilings of Thy face,
  How amiable they are!
'Tis heaven to rest in Thy embrace,
  And nowhere else but there.

To Thee, and Thee alone,
  The angels owe their bliss;
They sit around Thy gracious throne,
  And dwell where Jesus is.

Not all the harps above
  Can make a heavenly place,
If God His residence remove,
  Or but conceal His face.

Nor earth, nor all the sky,
  Can one delight afford;
No, not a drop of real joy,
  Without Thy presence, Lord.

Thou art the sea of love,
  Where all my pleasures roll;
The circle where my passions move,
  And centre of my soul.

To Thee my spirits fly,
  With infinite desire;
And yet how far from Thee I lie;
  Dear Jesus, raise me higher.

235   Charles Wesley   LM

Thou wilt shew me the path of life: in Thy presence is fulness of joy; at Thy right hand there are pleasures for evermore.
Psalm 16:11

How glorious is the life above,
  Which in this wilderness we taste!
The fulness of eternal love,
  That joy which shall for ever last!

That heavenly life in Christ concealed,
  These earthen vessels could not bear;
The past which now we find revealed,
  No saint or angel can declare.

The light of life eternal darts
  Into our souls a dazzling ray;
A drop of heaven o'erflows our hearts,
  And sweeps all earthly cares away!

Sure pledge of ecstacies unknown,
  Shall this divine communion be;
The ray shall rise into a sun!
  The drop shall swell into a sea!

236   George Herbert   CM

O LORD, attend unto my cry, give ear unto my prayer. *Psalm 17:1*

Behold dear Lord, we come again,
  To supplicate Thy grace;
We feel our leanness and our wants;
  We want to see Thy face.

Thou know'st, dear Lord, for what we're come;
  Each heart is known to Thee.
Lord, give our burdened spirits rest,
  And bid us all go free.

We've nothing of our own to plead,
  We come just as we are;
And who can tell but God may bless,
  And drive away our fear?

While one is pleading with our God,
  May each one wrestle too;
And may we feel the blessing come,
  And cheer us ere we go.

Then shall we sing of sovereign grace
  And feel its power within;
And glory in our Surety, Christ,
  Who bore our curse and sin.

For this we come, for this we plead,
  In spite of every foe;
Until Thou give this blessing, Lord,
  We would not let Thee go.

237   Joseph Irons   CM
Hold up my goings in Thy paths, that my footsteps slip not. *Psalm 17:5*

Ye heaven-born souls, who stand complete
  In Christ your righteousness,
Your Father's hand shall guide your feet
  To everlasting bliss.

Weakness itself is found in you,
  And darkness when you pray;
But fear not, Christian, God is true,
  You shall hold on your way.

Let earth molest, and Satan rage,
  And troubles crowd each day,
Fear not, your Father does engage
  You shall hold on your way.

The oath of God and covenant love,
  And Jesus' blood, all say,
You shall His Spirit's influence prove,
  And still hold on your way.

Till sin is slain, and death o'ercome;
  Till everlasting day;
Till you arrive in heaven your home,
  You shall hold on your way.

238   Isaac Watts   LM
As for me, I will behold Thy face in righteousness: I shall be satisfied, when I awake, with Thy likeness. *Psalm 17:15*

Lord, I am Thine, but Thou wilt prove
My faith, my patience, and my love;
When men of spite against me join,
They are the sword, the hand is Thine.

Their hope and portion lie below;
'Tis all the happiness they know;
'Tis all they seek; they take their shares
And leave the rest among their heirs.

What sinners value I resign;
Lord, 'tis enough that Thou art mine.
I shall behold Thy blissful face,
And stand complete in righteousness.

This life's a dream, an empty show,
But the bright world to which I go,
Has joys substantial and sincere;
When shall I wake and find me there?

O glorious hour! O blest abode!
I shall be near, and like my God!
And flesh and sin no more control
The sacred pleasures of my soul.

My flesh shall slumber in the ground,
  Till the last trumpet's joyful sound;
Then burst the chains with sweet surprise,
  And in my Saviour's image rise.

239   W G Lewis   LM
I shall be satisfied, when I awake, with Thy likeness. *Psalm 17:15*

My dear Redeemer, faithful Friend,
On Thee alone would I depend;
Hast Thou not sworn Thou'lt not forsake,
Till in Thy likeness I awake?

No solid pleasure can be found,
Tho' I should search this world around;
Nor lasting bliss can I partake,
Till in Thy likeness I awake.

Here I complain of grief and sin,
Of foes without, and worse within,
And this complaint I still shall make,
Till in Thy likeness I awake.

O happy hour! O glorious day!
When Thou shalt summon me away,
Thy face to see, my crown to take,
And in Thy likeness to awake.

240   Nahum Tate, Nicholas Brady   LM
Psalm 18

No change of times shall ever shock
  My firm affection. Lord, to Thee;
For Thou hast always been my Rock,
  A Fortress and Defence to me.

Thou my Deliverer art, my God,
  My trust is in Thy mighty power;
Thou art my Shield from foes abroad,
  At home my Safeguard and my Tower.

Let the eternal Lord be praised,
  The Rock on whose defence I rest;
O'er highest heavens His name be raised,
  Who me with His salvation blest.

Therefore to celebrate His fame
  My grateful voice to heaven I'll raise;
And nations, strangers to His name,
  Shall thus be taught to sing His praise.

241 Johann Scheffler, tr. J Wesley 88 88 88
I will love Thee, O LORD, my strength.
Psalm 18:1

Thee will I love, my Strength, my Tower;
  Thee will I love, my Joy, my Crown;
Thee will I love, with all my power,
  In all Thy works, and Thee alone;
Thee will I love, till the pure fire
Fills my whole soul with strong desire.

I thank Thee, uncreated Sun,
  That Thy bright beams have on me shined;
I thank Thee, who hast overthrown
  My foes, and healed my wounded mind;
I thank Thee, Lord, whose quickening voice
Bids my freed heart in Thee rejoice.

Uphold me in the doubtful race,
  Nor suffer me again to stray;
Strengthen my feet with steady pace
  Still to press forward in Thy way;
My soul and flesh, O Lord of might,
Transfigure with Thy heavenly light.

Thee will I love, my Joy, my Crown,
  Thee will I love, my Lord, my God;
Thee will I love, beneath Thy frown
  Or smile, Thy sceptre or Thy rod;
What though my flesh and heart decay?
Thee shall I love in endless day!

242 David Denham SM
The LORD is my Rock. *Psalm 18:2*

Christ Jesus is our Rock,
  Where we find strength and shade;
The firm foundation of His church,
  On which her hope is laid.

The objects of His love
  In Him securely dwell;
He is our bulwark and defence
  From all the powers of hell.

For us this Rock was smote,
  That we might life receive;
Whence flows a rich eternal stream,
  Whereof we drink and live!

Let all the ransomed sing
  Amidst earth's greatest shock;
In joy or sorrow, life or death,
  We're always in the Rock.

Though thrones and empires fall,
  Our Rock can never move;
Yea, when the world is wrapped in flames,
  Christ will our refuge prove.

243 Isaac Watts LM
As for God, His way is perfect.
Psalm 18:30

Just are Thy ways and true Thy word,
  Great Rock of my secure abode;
Who is a God beside the Lord?
  Or where's a refuge like our God?

'Tis He that girds me with His might;
  Gives me His holy sword to wield;
And while with sin and hell I fight,
  Spreads His salvation for my shield.

He lives (and blessèd be my Rock),
  The God of my salvation lives;
The dark designs of hell are broke;
  Sweet is the peace my Father gives.

To David and his royal seed
  Thy grace for ever shall extend;
Thy love to saints, in Christ their Head,
  Knows not a limit nor an end.

244 Nicolaus Zinzendorf, tr. Jane Borthwick
As for God, His way is perfect. 55 88 55
Psalm 18:30

Jesus, still lead on,
  Till our rest be won;
And although the way be cheerless,
We will follow, calm and fearless:
  Guide us by Thy hand
  To our fatherland.

If the way be drear,
  If the foe be near,
Let not faithless fears o'ertake us,
Let not faith and hope forsake us;
  For, through many a foe,
  To our home we go.

When we seek relief
  From a long-felt grief,
When oppressed by new temptations,
Lord, increase and perfect patience;
  Show us that bright shore
  Where we weep no more.

Jesus, still lead on
  Till our rest be won;
Heavenly Leader, still direct us,
Still support, console, protect us,
  Till we safely stand
  In our fatherland.

245   Vernon Higham   DCM
As for God, His way is perfect.
Psalm 18:30

Thy perfect law is my delight,
  O Lord of truth and grace;
In all Thy ways a beauteous sight
  To aid us in our race.
To love the Lord my God above,
  My neighbour as my own,
Is Thy command, O Lord of love,
  Thy Spirit now has shown.

Thy perfect law now dwells within
  And whispers peace to me;
The breath of pardon for my sin
  Thy pain at Calvary.
O may this love now richly flow,
  And grant me sweet increase;
Thus let my heart forever know
  The touch of heaven's peace.

Thy perfect name a melody
  Of grace I will endear;
Yet Satan fears and devils flee
  The name they dread to hear.
Now in my heart He is my King,
  My Sovereign Lord of all;
I humbly bow and gladly sing —
  'Tis fragrance to my soul.

© Author

246   Isaac Watts   LM
The heavens declare the glory of God.
Psalm 19:1

The heavens declare Thy glory, Lord,
  In every star Thy wisdom shines;
But when our eyes behold Thy word,
  We read Thy name in fairer lines.

The rolling sun, the changing light,
  And nights and days Thy power confess:
And the blest volume Thou hast writ
  Reveals Thy justice and Thy grace.

Sun, moon, and stars convey Thy praise
  Round the whole earth, and never stand;
So, when Thy truth begun its race,
  Destined to spread to every land:

Nor shall Thy living gospel rest,
  Till through the world Thy truth has run;
Till Christ has all the nations blessed
  That see the light, or feel the sun.

Great Sun of righteousness, arise,
  Bless the dark world with heavenly light;
Thy gospel makes the simple wise,
  Thy laws are pure, Thy judgments right.

Thy noblest wonders here we view,
  In souls renewed, and sins forgiven;
Lord, cleanse my sins, my soul renew,
  And make Thy word my guide to heaven.

247   Philip Bliss   87 87 D
**Let the words of my mouth, and the meditation
of my heart, be acceptable in Thy sight, O
LORD, my Strength, and my Redeemer.**
Psalm 19:14

I will sing of my Redeemer,
  And His wondrous love to me;
On the cruel cross He suffered,
  From the curse to set me free.

  Sing, O sing, of my Redeemer!
    With His blood He purchased me,
  On the cross He sealed my pardon,
    Paid the debt and made me free.

I will tell the wondrous story,
  How my lost estate to save,
In His boundless love and mercy,
  He the ransom freely gave.

I will praise my dear Redeemer,
  His triumphant power I'll tell,
How the victory He giveth
  Over sin and death and hell.

I will sing of my Redeemer,
  And His heavenly love to me;
He from death to life hath brought me,
  Son of God, with Him to be.

248   John Berridge   CM
Save, LORD: let the king hear us when we call.
Psalm 20:9

Eternal Father, Lord of all,
  By heaven and earth adored,
Regard Thy guilty creatures' call,
  Who would revere Thy word.

Lord Jesus, Son of God most high,
  Of all the rightful Heir,
Adored by hosts above the sky,
  And by Thy people here;

Thee, Saviour of the lost, we own,
  Incarnate God and Lord,
Refresh us now, and send us down
  The blessings of Thy word.

Thou, Holy Ghost, who dost reveal
  The secret things of grace;
And knowest well the Father's will,
  And His deep mind can trace;

Disclose the heavenly mysteries,
  And bring the gospel feast;
Give gracious hearts and opened eyes,
  That we may see and taste.

249   Charles Spurgeon   LM
Psalm 21

Thy strength, O Lord, makes glad our King,
  Who once in weakness bowed the head,
Salvation makes His heart to sing,
  For Thou hast raised Him from the dead.

Thou hast bestowed His heart's desires,
  Showered on His path Thy blessings down;
His royal pomp all heaven admires;
  Thou on His head hast set the crown.

A life eternal as Thy years,
  A glory infinite like Thine,
Repays Him for His groans and tears,
  And fills His soul with joy divine.

O King, belovèd of our souls,
  Thine own right hand shall find Thy foes;
Swift o'er their necks Thy chariot rolls,
  And earth Thy dreadful vengeance knows.

As glowing oven is Thy wrath,
  As flame by furious blast upblown;
With equal heat Thy love breaks forth,
  Like wall of fire around Thine own.

Be Thou exalted, King of kings,
  In Thine own strength sit Thou on high,
Thy church Thy triumph loudly sings,
  And lauds Thy glorious majesty.

250   Isaac Watts   LM
Psalm 22

Now let our mournful songs record
The dying sorrows of our Lord,
When He complained in tears and blood,
As One forsaken of His God.

They wound His head, His hands, His feet,
Till streams of blood each other meet;
By lot His garments they divide,
And mock the pangs in which He died.

But God, His Father, heard His cry;
Raised from the dead, He reigns on high;
The nations learn His righteousness,
And humble sinners taste His grace.

251   *Old and New Versions*   CM
Psalm 22

All ye that fear Him, praise the Lord;
  His sacred name adore;
And ye His chosen Israel,
  Praise Him for evermore.

Let all the glad converted world
  To Him their homage pay,
And scattered nations of the earth
  One sovereign Lord obey.

With humble worship to His throne
  Let all for aid resort;
That power which first their being gave,
  Alone can give support.

Let them, O Lord, Thy truth declare,
  And show Thy righteousness;
That children, yet unborn may learn
  Thy glory to confess.

252   Joseph Hart   76 76 78 76
But Thou art holy. *Psalm 22:3*

Jesus, Lord of life and peace,
  To Thee we lift our voice;
Teach us at Thy holiness
  To tremble and rejoice.
Sweet and terrible's Thy word;
  Thou and Thy word are both the same.
Holy, holy, holy Lord,
  We love Thy holy name.

Burning seraphs round Thy throne,
  Beyond all brightness bright,
Bow their bashful heads, and own
  Their own diminished light.
Worthy Thou to be adored,
  Lord God Almighty, great I AM!
Holy, holy, holy Lord,
  We love Thy holy name.

Saints, in whom Thy Spirit dwells,
  Pour out their souls to Thee;
Each his tale in secret tells,
  And sighs to be set free.
Christ admired, themselves abhorred,
  They cry with awe, delight, and shame,
Holy, holy, holy Lord,
  We love Thy holy name.

253   William Cowper   CM
Our fathers trusted in Thee. *Psalm 22:4*

The saints should never be dismayed,
   Nor sink in hopeless fear;
For when they least expect His aid,
   The Saviour will appear.

Blest proofs of power and grace divine
   That meet us in His word;
May every deep-felt care of mine
   Be trusted with the Lord.

Wait for His seasonable aid,
   And though it tarry, wait;
The promise may be long delayed,
   But cannot come too late.

HENRY WILLIAMS BAKER 1821-1877

254   Henry Baker   87 87 (iambic)
Psalm 23

The King of love my Shepherd is,
   Whose goodness faileth never;
I nothing lack if I am His
   And He is mine for ever.

Where streams of living water flow
   My ransomed soul He leadeth,
And, where the verdant pastures grow,
   With food celestial feedeth.

Perverse and foolish oft I strayed,
   But yet in love He sought me,
And on His shoulder gently laid
   And home rejoicing brought me.

In death's dark vale I fear no ill
   With Thee, dear Lord, beside me;
Thy rod and staff my comfort still,
   Thy cross before to guide me.

Thou spread'st a table in my sight;
   Thy unction grace bestoweth:
And O what transport of delight
   From Thy pure chalice floweth!

And so through all the length of days
   Thy goodness faileth never;
Good Shepherd, may I sing Thy praise
   Within Thy house for ever.

255   *Scottish Psalter 1650*   CM
Psalm 23

The Lord's my Shepherd, I'll not want:
   He makes me down to lie
In pastures green; He leadeth me
   The quiet waters by.

My soul He doth restore again
   And me to walk doth make
Within the paths of righteousness,
   E'en for His own name's sake.

Yea, though I walk in death's dark vale,
   Yet will I fear none ill:
For Thou art with me; and Thy rod
   And staff me comfort still.

My table Thou hast furnishèd
   In presence of my foes;
My head Thou dost with oil anoint
   And my cup overflows.

Goodness and mercy all my life
   Shall surely follow me;
And in God's house for evermore
   My dwelling-place shall be.

256   Mary Duncan   87 87
The LORD is my shepherd; I shall not want.
Psalm 23:1

Jesus, tender Shepherd, hear me;
   Bless Thy little lamb tonight;
Through the darkness be Thou near me;
   Keep me safe till morning light.

All this day Thy hand has led me,
   And I thank Thee for Thy care;
Thou hast clothed me, warmed and fed me;
   Listen to my evening prayer.

Let my sins be all forgiven;
   Bless the friends I love so well;
Take me, when I die, to heaven,
   Happy there with Thee to dwell.

257   Charles Wesley (alt)   LM
Psalm 24

Our Lord is risen from the dead!
    Our Jesus is gone up on high!
The powers of hell are captive led,
    Dragged to the portals of the sky.

There His triumphal chariot waits,
    And angels chant the solemn lay:
Lift up your heads, ye heavenly gates;
    Ye everlasting doors, give way.

Loose all your bars of solid light,
    And wide unfold the ethereal scene:
He claims these mansions as His right;
    Receive the King of glory in!

Who is this King of glory? who?
    The Lord that all our foes o'ercame,
The world, sin, death, and hell o'erthrew;
    And Jesus is the Conqueror's name.

Lo! His triumphal chariot waits,
    And angels chant the solemn lay:
Lift up your heads, ye heavenly gates;
    Ye everlasting doors, give way!

Who is this King of glory? who?
    The Lord, of glorious power possessed;
The King of saints, and angels too,
    God over all, for ever blessed!

258   *Psalter 1912*   11 11 11 11
Psalm 24

The earth and the fulness, with which it is stored,
The world and its dwellers, belong to the Lord.
For He on the seas its foundation hath laid,
And firm on the waters its pillars hath stayed.

What man shall the hill of Jehovah ascend?
And who in the place of His holiness stand?
The man of pure heart, and of hands without
    stain,
Who swears not to falsehood, nor loves what is
    vain.

He shall from Jehovah the blessing receive;
The God of salvation shall righteousness give;
For this is the people, yea, this is the race,
The Israèl true that are seeking His face.

Ye gates everlasting, be lifted on high;
The great King of glory to enter draws nigh.
O who is the King that in glory draws near?
Jehovah, the mighty in battle, is here.

Ye doors everlasting, be lifted on high;
The great King of glory to enter draws nigh.
This great King of glory, O who can He be?
Jehovah of hosts, King of glory is He.

259   Eluned Harrison   68 88
Who shall ascend into the hill of the LORD?
Psalm 24:3

    O Lord, who shall ascend
    That holy hill to seek Thy face?
Where is the man who dares to stand
    And worship in Thy holy place?

    The man whose hands are clean,
    With lowly heart, and lips kept pure,
Who knows the cleansing of Christ's blood,
    Has access there that will endure.

    To such the Lord shall give
    The blessing of His righteousness:
He calls His saints to seek His face
    And throng His courts that He may bless.

© Author

260   Francis Rous, W. Barton   DCM + *coda*
**Lift up your heads, O ye gates; and be ye lift
up, ye everlasting doors; and the King of glory
shall come in.** *Psalm 24:7*

Ye gates, lift up your heads on high;
    Ye doors that last for aye,
Be lifted up, that so the King
    Of glory enter may!
But who of glory is the King?
    The mighty Lord is this,
E'en that same Lord that great in might
    And strong in battle is.

Ye gates, lift up your heads; ye doors,
    Doors that do last for aye,
Be lifted up, that so the King
    Of glory enter may!
But who is He that is the King
    Of glory? who is this?
The Lord of hosts, and none but He,
    The King of glory is.

    Coda:
    Hallelujah! Hallelujah!
    Hallelujah! Hallelujah! Hallelujah!
    Amen, Amen, Amen.

261   Charles Wesley   77 77 + Hallelujahs
**Lift up your heads, O ye gates; and be ye lift
up, ye everlasting doors; and the King of glory
shall come in.** *Psalm 24:7*

Hail the day that sees Him rise, *Hallelujah!*
To His throne above the skies;
Christ, awhile to mortals given,
Reascends His native heaven.

There the glorious triumph waits;
Lift your heads, eternal gates!
Christ hath vanquished death and sin;
Take the King of glory in!

Him though highest heaven receives,
Still He loves the earth He leaves;
Though returning to His throne,
Still He calls mankind His own.

See! He lifts His hands above;
See! He shows the prints of love;
Hark! His gracious lips bestow
Blessings on His church below.

Still for us He intercedes;
His prevailing death He pleads;
Near Himself prepares our place,
First-fruits of the human race.

Grant, though parted from our sight,
Far above yon azure-height,
Grant our hearts may thither rise,
Seeking Thee beyond the skies.

There we shall with Thee remain,
Partners of Thine endless reign;
There Thy face unclouded see,
Find our heaven of heavens in Thee.

262   Gerhard Tersteegen, tr. C Winkworth
                       87 87 77 77
**Lift up your heads, O ye gates; and be ye lift
up, ye everlasting doors; and the King of glory
shall come in.** *Psalm 24:7*

Conquering Prince and Lord of glory,
   Majesty enthroned in light;
All the heavens are bowed before Thee,
   Far beyond them spreads Thy might;
Shall not I fall at Thy feet,
And my heart with rapture beat,
Now Thy glory is displayed,
Thine ere yet the worlds were made?

As I watch Thee far ascending
   To the right hand of the throne,
See the host before Thee bending,
   Praising Thee in sweetest tone;
Shall not I too at Thy feet
Here the angels' strain repeat,
And rejoice that heaven doth ring
With the triumph of my King?

Power and Spirit are o'erflowing,
   On me also be they poured;
Every hindrance overthrowing,
   Make Thy foes Thy footstool, Lord!
Yea, let earth's remotest end
To Thy righteous sceptre bend,
Make Thy way before Thee plain,
O'er all hearts and spirits reign.

Lo! Thy presence now is filling
   All Thy church in every place;
Fill my heart too; make me willing
   In this season of Thy grace;
Come, Thou King of glory, come,
Deign to make my heart Thy home,
There abide and rule alone,
As upon Thy heavenly throne!

263   Thomas Kelly   77 77 77
**Who is this King of glory? The LORD of hosts,
He is the King of glory. Selah.**
Psalm 24:10

Glory, glory, to our King!
   Crowns unfading wreathe His head;
Jesus is the name we sing;
   Jesus, risen from the dead;
Jesus, spoiler of the grave;
Jesus, mighty now to save.

Jesus is gone up on high:
   Angels come to meet their King;
Shouts triumphant rend the sky,
   While the Victor's praise they sing;
'Open now, ye heavenly gates!
'Tis the King of glory waits.'

Now behold Him high enthroned!
   Glory beaming from His face;
By adoring angels owned,
   Lord of holiness and grace:
O for hearts and tongues to sing,
'Glory, glory to our King.'

Jesus, on Thy people shine;
   Warm our hearts and tune our tongues
That with angels we may join,
   Share their bliss and swell their songs:
Glory, honour, praise, and power,
Lord, be Thine for evermore.

264   Isaac Watts   SM
Psalm 25

Mine eyes and my desire
Are ever to the Lord;
I love to plead His promises,
And rest upon His word.

When shall the sovereign grace
Of my forgiving God,
Restore me from those dang'rous ways
My wandering feet have trod?

The tumult of my thoughts
Doth but enlarge my woe;
My spirit languishes, my heart
Is desolate and low.

With every morning-light
My sorrow new begins;
Look on my anguish and my pain,
And pardon all my sins.

O keep my soul from death,
Nor put my hope to shame;
For I have placed my only trust
In my Redeemer's name.

With humble faith I wait
To see Thy face again;
Of Israel it shall ne'er be said,
'He sought the Lord in vain.'

265   William Gadsby   87 87 47
Lead me in Thy truth, and teach me: for Thou art the God of my salvation.
Psalm 25:5

Jesus, mighty God and Saviour,
  Lead me forth by Thy right hand;
And be it my fixed endeavour,
  To obey Thy sweet command;
    Let me never
  At a trifling distance stand.

Guide, O guide me by Thy Spirit;
  Leave me not to walk alone;
And by faith may I inherit
  The eternal Three-in-One;
    And with boldness,
Make Thy matchless wonders known.

May my soul be sweetly fillèd,
  With the treasures of my God;
And my tongue be rightly skillèd,
  To proclaim Thy truth abroad;
    And with pleasure,
God's eternal love record.

266   Simon Browne   LM
Lead me in Thy truth, and teach me: for Thou art the God of my salvation.
Psalm 25:5

Come gracious Spirit, heavenly Dove,
With light and comfort from above,
Be Thou our Guardian, Thou our Guide,
O'er every thought and step preside.

Conduct us safe, conduct us far
From every sin and hurtful snare;
Apply Thy word that rules must give,
And teach us lessons how to live.

The light of truth to us display,
And make us know and choose Thy way.
Plant holy fear in every heart,
That we from God may ne'er depart.

Lead us to Christ, the living Way,
Nor let us from His pasture stray;
Lead us to holiness, the road
That we must take to dwell with God.

Lead us to God, our only rest,
And in His love may we be blest,
Lead us to heaven, the seat of bliss,
Where pleasure in perfection is.

267   Josiah Conder   77 77
Lead me in Thy truth, and teach me: for Thou art the God of my salvation.
Psalm 25:5

Heavenly Father! to whose eye
Future things unfolded lie,
Through the desert, where I stray,
Let Thy counsels guide my way.

Lord, uphold me day by day,
Shed a light upon my way;
Guide me through perplexing snares;
Care for me in all my cares!

Help Thy servant to maintain
A profession free from stain;
That my sole reproach may be
Following Christ and fearing Thee.

Should Thy wisdom, Lord, decree
Trials long and sharp for me,
Pain or sorrow, care or shame,
Father, glorify Thy name!

Let me neither faint nor fear,
Feeling still that Thou art near;
In the course my Saviour trod,
Tending still to Thee, my God.

268   John Fawcett   LM
For Thy name's sake, O LORD, pardon mine iniquity; for it is great. *Psalm 25:11*

With melting heart and weeping eyes,
My guilty soul for mercy cries;
What shall I do, or whither flee,
To escape the vengeance due to me?

Till late, I saw no danger nigh;
I lived at ease, nor feared to die;
Wrapped up in self-conceit and pride,
'I shall have peace at last,' I cried.

But when, great God, Thy light divine
Had shone on this dark soul of mine,
Then I beheld, with trembling awe,
The terrors of Thy holy law.

How dreadful now my guilt appears,
In childhood, youth, and growing years;
Before Thy pure discerning eye,
Lord, what a filthy wretch am I!

Should vengeance still my soul pursue,
Death and destruction are my due;
Yet mercy can my guilt forgive,
And bid a dying sinner live.

Does not Thy sacred word proclaim
Salvation free in Jesus' name?
To Him I look, and humbly cry,
'O save a wretch condemned to die!'

269   William Bullock   66 66
LORD, I have loved the habitation of Thy house, and the place where Thine honour dwelleth. *Psalm 26:8*

We love the place, O God,
    Wherein Thine honour dwells;
The joy of Thine abode
    All earthly joy excels.

It is the house of prayer,
    Wherein Thy servants meet;
And Thou, O Lord, art there,
    Thy chosen flock to greet.

We love the word of life,
    The word that tells of peace,
Of comfort in the strife
    And joys that never cease.

We love to sing below
    Of mercies freely given;
But O we long to know
    The triumph song of heaven!

Lord Jesus, give us grace,
    On earth to love Thee more,
In heaven to see Thy face,
    And with Thy saints adore.

270   Isaac Watts   CM
LORD, I have loved the habitation of Thy house, and the place where Thine honour dwelleth. *Psalm 26:8*

My soul, how lovely is the place
    To which Thy God resorts!
'Tis heaven to see His smiling face,
    Though in His earthly courts.

There the great Monarch of the skies
    His saving power displays,
And light breaks in upon our eyes
    With kind and quickening rays.

With His rich gifts the heavenly Dove
    Descends and fills the place,
While Christ reveals His wondrous love,
    And sheds abroad His grace.

There, mighty God, Thy words declare
    The secrets of Thy will;
And still we seek Thy mercy there,
    And sing Thy praises still.

Lord, at Thy threshold I would wait,
    While Jesus is within,
Rather than fill a throne of state,
    Or live in tents of sin.

Could I command the spacious land
    And the more boundless sea,
For one blest hour at Thy right hand
    I'd give them both away.

271   Graham Harrison   DCM
Psalm 27

Whom shall I fear on earth below
    With such a God on high?
My light to guide, my strength to save—
    Thou, Lord, art ever nigh.
Let wicked men, my enemies,
    Rise in malicious pride,
In this will I be confident:
    Safe in my Lord I hide.

One thing desired I of the Lord,
One thing alone I've sought:
That long as life shall last on earth
I may to Thee be brought.
Within Thy house my days I'd spend,
Thy beauty to behold,
Enquire of Thee, and sing that praise
Whose end can ne'er be told.

He'll hide me in His secret place
When trouble rages sore;
Upon the rock of steadfast love
My feet are set secure.
He lifts my head in triumph high
Mine enemies above;
And so with joy my praise shall rise
To God, the King of love.

Hear, gracious Lord, this voice that cries;
Have mercy, is my plea:
Let not Thine anger hide Thy face
Far, far away from me.
Thou only hast my Helper been;
Forsake me not, I sigh;
Lift up Thy lovely face, and shine
Its beauty from on high.

Unless I had believed to see
His goodness while below,
What else in this sad land of sin
But faintness would I know?
Wait on the Lord, with courage wait,
And Thy weak heart shall find
The mighty strength of God within
Thy heart and soul and mind.

© Mrs.Eluned Harrison

272   David Obbard   88 88 D
Psalm 27

The Lord is my Saviour and Light,
In Him is my confidence stayed;
The Lord is the strength of my life,
Of whom shall I then be afraid?
When wicked, implacable foes,
Determined to slay me, they fell,
Though hosts should unite to oppose,
In God shall my confidence dwell.

One thing this I seek and desire,
To dwell in the house of the Lord,
His beauty to see, and enquire
Of His own infallible word.
In trouble my soul He will hide
Within His pavilion of peace,
The rock that surmounts every tide,
Though foes like a flood shall increase.

I therefore will offer Him praise,
The sweet sacrifices of joy,
My tongue, all the length of my days,
I shall in His worship employ.
Lord, hear when I cry with my voice,
Have mercy upon me, and speak,
Thou saidst, 'Seek My face and rejoice,'
I answered, 'Thy face, Lord, I seek.'

O hide not Thy face, is my plea,
Nor put me in anger away,
Thou hast been my help, ever be,
God of my salvation, I pray.
When father and mother forsake,
My God shall protection afford,
Then teach me Thy way, so to make
The path plain before me, O Lord.

Because of my enemies' cries,
Deliver me not to their will,
False witness against me arise,
And such as breathe cruelty still.
Unless I believed that the Lord
Would bless me, my hope would depart;
Take courage, and wait on the Lord,
Wait, and He will strengthen thy heart.

© K Obbard

273   Benjamin Beddome, John Rippon   CM
Hide not Thy face far from me; put not Thy servant away in anger: Thou hast been my help. *Psalm 27:9*

Dear Lord! why should I doubt Thy love
Or disbelieve Thy grace?
Sure Thy compassions ne'er remove,
Although Thou hide Thy face.

Thy smiles have freed my heart from pain,
My drooping spirits cheered:
And wilt Thou not appear again
Where Thou hast once appeared?

Hast Thou not formed my soul anew,
And told me I am Thine?
And wilt Thou now Thy work undo,
Or break Thy word divine?

Dost Thou repent? wilt Thou deny
The gifts Thou hast bestowed?
Or are those streams of mercy dry,
Which once so freely flowed?

Lord! let no groundless fears destroy
The mercies now possessed;
I'll praise for blessings I enjoy,
And trust for all the rest.

274   Isaac Watts   CM
Teach me Thy way, O LORD, and lead me in a plain path, because of mine enemies.
Psalm 27:11

O that the Lord would guide my ways
　To keep His statutes still;
O that my God would grant me grace
　To know and do His will!

O send Thy Spirit down to write
　Thy law upon my heart;
Nor let my tongue indulge deceit,
　Nor act the liar's part!

From vanity turn off my eyes;
　Let no corrupt design,
Nor covetous desires arise
　Within this soul of mine.

Order my footsteps by Thy word,
　And make my heart sincere;
Let sin have no dominion, Lord,
　But keep my conscience clear.

Make me to walk in Thy commands;
　'Tis a delightful road;
Nor let my head, or heart, or hands,
　Offend against my God.

275   Mansell Ramsey   64 64 66 64
Teach me Thy way, O LORD, and lead me in a plain path, because of mine enemies.
Psalm 27:11

Teach me Thy way, O Lord,
　Teach me Thy way!
Thy gracious aid afford,
　Teach me Thy way!
Help me to walk aright,
More by faith, less by sight;
Lead me with heavenly light;
　Teach me Thy way!

When doubts and fears arise,
　Teach me Thy way!
When storms o'erspread the skies,
　Teach me Thy way!
Shine through the cloud and rain,
Through sorrow, toil and pain;
Make Thou my pathway plain;
　Teach me Thy way!

Long as my life shall last,
　Teach me Thy way!
Where'er my lot be cast,
　Teach me Thy way!
Until the race is run,
Until the journey's done,
Until the crown is won,
　Teach me Thy way!

276   Music by Samuel Wesley   Irregular
Teach me Thy way, O LORD, and lead me in a plain path, because of mine enemies.
Psalm 27:11 (also Psalm 5:8 and 4:8)

Lead me, Lord, lead me in Thy righteousness;
　Make Thy way plain before my face.
Lead me, Lord, lead me in Thy righteousness;
　Make Thy way plain before my face.

For it is Thou, Lord, Thou, Lord, only,
　That makest me dwell in safety.
For it is Thou, Lord, Thou, Lord, only,
　That makest me dwell in safety.

277   James Merrick   77 77
Psalm 28

Lord, my strength, to Thee I pray;
Turn not Thou Thine ear away;
Gracious to my vows attend,
While the humble knee I bend.

On Thy long-experienced aid
See my hope for ever stayed:
Thou my Shield, my Fortress art;
Thou the Refuge of my heart.

Grant me, Lord, Thy love to share,
Feed me with a Shepherd's care;
Save Thy people from distress.
And Thy fold for ever bless.

278   John Kent   77 77
The LORD is my strength and my shield; my heart trusted in Him, and I am helped.
Psalm 28:7

Now to grace as debtors we,
Spared another year to see,
Mercies past would still review;
God hath helped us hitherto.

When the slaves of sin we lay,
Thou in love didst us survey;
This we now recall to view;
God hath helped us hitherto.

In temptation's hottest day,
On the mount, or through the sea,
We have found Thy promise true:
God hath helped us hitherto.

Oft by Zion's foes annoyed,
Oft cast down, but not destroyed;
Still to grace the praise is due;
God hath helped us hitherto.

When our sins deserved Thy rod,
Thee we found a peaceful God;
Lord, Thy visits now renew;
Thou hast helped us hitherto.

Tossed with tempests we have been,
In the deep Thy footsteps seen;
Sorrows, sins, temptations through,
God hath helped us hitherto.

God of love, forgive the sin;
We have long ungrateful been:
Now Thy name and love to praise,
Stones of help and songs we raise.

279   William Gadsby   886 D
**Save Thy people, and bless Thine inheritance:
feed them also, and lift them up for ever.**
Psalm 28:9

Again, dear Lord, we would be fed;
We come to seek for living bread,
   And feast on love divine;
Dear Father, let Thy presence be
Enjoyed by all Thy family,
   And make each face to shine.

In Thee all blessings richly meet;
Come, then, and give our souls a treat,
   And let us feast indeed;
O let us banquet with the King,
And love, and pray, and praise, and sing,
   As sons from bondage freed.

May faith be strong, and pierce the skies,
And we with pleasure realise
   The glory now prepared;
Commune with Jesus as our Friend;
Upon Him live; His love commend;
   And carnal things discard.

If this be granted, we'll adore
The hand that gives, yet keeps in store
   A boundless stock of grace;
In every time of need we'll cry,
And Thou shalt all our needs supply,
   And that with smiling face.

280   Thomas Kelly   87 87 47
Save Thy people, and bless Thine inheritance.
Psalm 28:9

God of our salvation, hear us;
   Bless, O bless us, ere we go;
When we join the world, be near us,
   Lest Thy people careless grow;
      Saviour, keep us,
   Keep us safe from every foe.

In the day of Thy appearing,
   When the trump of God shall sound,
May we hear it, nothing fearing,
   Though all nature sinks around,
      By our Saviour
   Raised, and then with glory crowned.

281   Thomas Sternhold   CM
Psalm 29

Ascribe to God, ye sons of men,
   Ascribe with one accord,
All praise and honour, might and strength,
   To Him the living Lord!

Give glory to His holy name,
   And honour Him alone;
Give worship to His majesty,
   And bow before His throne.

The Lord doth sit upon the floods,
   Their fury to restrain;
He reigns above, both Lord and King,
   And evermore shall reign.

The Lord shall give His people strength,
   And bid their sorrows cease;
The Lord shall bless His chosen race
   With everlasting peace.

282   John Monsell   13 10 13 10
Worship the LORD in the beauty of holiness.
Psalm 29:2

O worship the Lord in the beauty of holiness,
   Bow down before Him, His glory proclaim;
With gold of obedience, and incense of lowliness,
   Kneel and adore him, the Lord is His name.

Low at His feet lay thy burden of carefulness,
   High on His heart He will bear it for thee,
Comfort thy sorrows and answer thy
      prayerfulness,
   Guiding thy steps as may best for thee be.

Fear not to enter His courts in the slenderness
   Of the poor wealth thou would'st reckon as thine;
Truth in its beauty, and love in its tenderness,
   These are the offerings to lay on His shrine.

These, though we bring them in trembling and
      fearfulness,
   He will accept for the name that is dear;
Mornings of joy give for evenings of tearfulness,
   Trust for our trembling, and hope for our fear.

O worship the Lord in the beauty of holiness,
   Bow down before Him, His glory proclaim;
With gold of obedience, and incense of lowliness,
   Kneel and adore Him, the Lord is His name.

283   John Ryland   87 87
Sing unto the LORD, O ye saints of His, and give thanks at the remembrance of His holiness. *Psalm 30:4*

Sing, ye saints, admire and wonder,
   Jesus' matchless love adore:
Sing, for Sinai's awful thunder
   Shall upon you burst no more.

Sing, in spite of Satan's lying;
   Sing, though sins are black and large;
Sing, for Jesus, by His dying,
   Set you free from every charge.

Sing, though sense and carnal reason
   Fain would stop the joyful song:
Sing, and count it highest treason
   For a saint to hold his tongue.

Sing ye loud, whose holy calling
   Your election plainly shows;
Sing, nor fear a final falling,
   Jesus' love no changes knows.

Sing, for you shall heaven inherit,
   Sing, and ne'er the song have done:
Sing to Father, Son, and Spirit,
   One in Three, and Three in One.

284   John Newton   LM
And in my prosperity I said, I shall never be moved. *Psalm 30:6*

The peace of which I had a taste
   When Jesus first His love revealed,
I fondly hoped would always last,
   Because my foes were then concealed.

But when I felt the tempter's power
   Rouse my corruptions from their sleep,
I trembled at the stormy hour,
   And saw the horrors of the deep.

Now on presumption's billows borne,
   My spirit seemed the Lord to dare,
Now, quick as thought, a sudden turn
   Plunged me in gulfs of black despair.

'Lord, save me, or I sink,' I prayed;
   He heard, and bade the tempest cease;
The angry waves His word obeyed,
   And all my fears were hushed to peace.

The peace is His, and not my own,
   My heart (no better than before)
Is still to dreadful changes prone;
   Then let me never trust it more.

285   John Berridge   CM
LORD, by Thy favour Thou hast made my mountain to stand strong: Thou didst hide Thy face, and I was troubled.
Psalm 30:7

If but a single moment's space,
   My Lord Himself withdraws,
Dark clouds and storms come on apace,
   And debts, and broken laws.

My heart reveals its dross and dung,
   And loathsome is my breath;
My harp is on the willows hung,
   And Esau vows my death.

My eyes refuse to lend a tear;
   My throat is hoarse and dry;
I lisp and falter in my prayer,
   And sick and faint am I.

If Jesus loves the gospel-poor,
   That broken-hearted be,
A mourner waiteth at Thy door,
   Who wants a sight of Thee.

Look from the windows of Thy grace,
   And cheer a drooping heart;
A single smile from Thy sweet face
   Will bid my griefs depart.

Thou art the life of all my joys;
   Thy presence makes my heaven;
Whatever else my Lord denies,
   Thy presence, Lord, be given.

286   William Gadsby   10 10 10 10
Thou didst hide Thy face, and I was troubled.
Psalm 30:7

When my dear Jesus hides His smiling face,
Nor lets me feel the unction of His grace;
I feel my loss, nor can my spirit rest,
Till with His lovely presence I am blest.

I mourn like one bereft of home and friend,
And often wonder where the scene will end;
Tortured with anxious care, without repose,
I feel as one immersed in gloomy woes.

The means of grace afford no sweet relief,
But often tend to aggravate my grief;
I cannot rest without my resting-place;
Sweet Jesus, come, and let me Thee embrace.

287   Harriet Auber   DCM
Psalm 31

The Lord who hath redeemed our souls
    From death and endless woe,
Whose wisdom each event controls,
    From whom all mercies flow
He hath decreed that even here
    His faithful sons shall prove,
In weal and woe, 'midst toil and fear,
    The riches of His love.

But, O! when life's brief term is o'er.
    And heaven unfolds her gates,
For them what blessings are in store,
    For them what glory waits!
Praise, then, the Lord, all ye His saints,
    To Him devote your hearts;
He hears, He pities your complaints,
    Health, strength, and joy imparts.

288   Jonathan Franklin (alt)   CM
I will be glad and rejoice in Thy mercy: for Thou hast considered my trouble.
Psalm 31:7

In all my troubles and distress,
    The Lord my soul does own;
Jehovah does my griefs redress,
    And makes His mercy known.

He helps me on Him to rely;
    He is my Strength and Tower;
'Tis He that hears me when I cry,
    And manifests His power.

In every storm, in every sea,
    My Jesus makes a way;
His light shall make the darkness flee,
    And turn the shade to day.

'Tis He in trouble bears me up,
    And leads me safely through;
My Jesus does maintain my cup,
    And daily strength renew.

289   Charles Wesley   55 11 D
But I trusted in Thee, O LORD: I said, Thou art my God. *Psalm 31:14*

My God, I am Thine;
    What a comfort divine,
What a blessing to know that my Jesus is mine!
    In the heavenly Lamb
    Thrice happy I am,
And my heart it doth dance at the sound of His
    name.

True pleasures abound
    In the rapturous sound;
And whoever hath found it hath paradise found.
    My Jesus to know,
    And feel His blood flow,
'Tis life everlasting, 'tis heaven below.

Yet onward I haste
    To the heavenly feast:
That, that is the fulness; but this is the taste!
    And this I shall prove,
    Till with joy I remove,
To the heaven of heavens in Jesus' great love.

290   Benjamin Beddome   CM
My times are in Thy hand. *Psalm 31:15*

My times of sorrow and of joy,
    Great God, are in Thy hand;
My choicest comforts come from Thee,
    And go at Thy command.

If Thou shouldst take them all away,
    Yet let me not repine;
Before they were possessed by me,
    They were entirely Thine.

Nor let me drop a murmuring word,
    Though the whole world were gone;
But seek enduring happiness
    In Thee, and Thee alone.

291   John Newton   LM
My times are in Thy hand. *Psalm 31:15*

Upheld by Thy supporting hand,
    We pass, O Lord, from year to year;
And still we meet, at Thy command,
    To seek Thy gracious presence here.

Oft feed us Lord, beneath this vine,
    Through the new year, with heavenly bread;
Oft clothe Thy word with power divine,
    To break the rocks and raise the dead.

Oft by a Saviour's dying love,
    To many a wounded heart revealed,
Temptations, fears, and guilt remove,
    And be our Sun, and Strength, and Shield.

292   Henry Lyte   SM
My times are in Thy hand. *Psalm 31:15*

My times are in Thy hand:
My God, I wish them there;
My life, my friends, my soul I leave
    Entirely to Thy care.

My times are in Thy hand,
Whatever they may be;
Pleasing or painful, dark or bright,
    As best may seem to Thee.

My times are in Thy hand,
Why should I doubt or fear?
A Father's hand will never cause
    His child a needless tear.

My times are in Thy hand,
Jesus the Crucified;
The hand my cruel sins have pierced
    Is now my guard and guide.

My times are in Thine hand:
I'll always trust in Thee;
And, after death at Thy right hand
    I shall for ever be.

293   William Havergal   SM
My times are in Thy hand. *Psalm 31:15*

My times are in Thy hand,
Their best and fittest place:
I would not have them at command
    Without Thy guiding grace.

My times, and yet not mine;
I cannot them ordain;
Not one e'er waits from me a sign,
    Nor can I one detain.

My times, O Lord, are Thine,
And Thine their oversight:
Thy wisdom, love, and power combine
    To make them dark or bright.

I know not what shall be,
When passing times are fled;
But all events I leave with Thee,
    And calmly bow my head.

And when my times shall cease,
And life shall fade away,
Then bid me, Lord, depart in peace,
    To realms of endless day!

294   Christopher Wordsworth   LM
My times are in Thy hand. *Psalm 31:15*

Another year has now begun
With silent pace its course to run;
Our hearts and voices let us raise
To God in prayer and songs of praise.

Father, Thy bounteous love we bless,
For gifts and mercies numberless;
For life and health, for grace and peace,
For hope of joys that never cease.

O Son of God, in faith and fear
Teach us to walk as strangers here,
With hearts in heaven, that we may come
To where Thou art, our Father's home.

Grant us, O Comforter, Thy grace,
And speed us on our earthly race,
In body, spirit, and in soul,
Right onward to the heavenly goal.

Thou, Lord, who makest all things new,
O give us hearts both pure and true;
That we, as jewels, ever Thine,
In new Jerusalem may shine.

Blest Three in One, to Thee we pray;
Defend and guide us on our way;
That we at last with joy may see
The new year of eternity!

295   Henry Collins   88 88 88
O love the LORD, all ye His saints.
Psalm 31:23

Jesus, my Lord, my God, my All,
Hear me, blest Saviour, when I call;
Hear me, and from Thy dwelling-place
Pour down the riches of Thy grace:

    Jesus my Lord I Thee adore;
    O make me love Thee more and more.

Jesus, too late I Thee have sought;
How can I love Thee as I ought?
And how extol Thy matchless fame,
The glorious beauty of Thy name?

Jesus, what didst Thou find in me,
That Thou hast dealt so lovingly?
How great the joy that Thou hast brought,
So far exceeding hope or thought!

Jesus, of Thee shall be my song;
To Thee my heart and soul belong;
All that I have or am is Thine,
And Thou, blest Saviour, Thou art mine.

296 Isaac Watts CM
Psalm 32

Happy the man to whom his God
 No more imputes his sin;
But, washed in the Redeemer's blood,
 Hath made his garments clean!

Happy beyond expression he,
 Whose debts are thus discharged;
And from the guilty bondage free,
 He feels his soul enlarged.

While I my inward guilt suppressed
 No quiet could I find;
Thy wrath lay burning in my breast,
 And racked my tortured mind.

Then I confessed my troubled thoughts,
 My secret sins revealed;
Thy pardoning grace forgave my faults,
 Thy grace my pardon sealed.

This shall invite Thy saints to pray;
 When, like a raging flood,
Temptations rise, our strength and stay
 Is a forgiving God.

297 Joseph Hart LM
**Blessed is he whose transgression is forgiven,
whose sin is covered.**
Psalm 32:1

Blessèd are they whose guilt is gone,
 Whose sins are washed away with blood,
Whose hope is fixed on Christ alone,
 Whom Christ has reconciled to God.

Though travelling through this vale of tears,
 He many a sore temptation meet,
The Holy Ghost this witness bears,
 He stands in Jesus still complete.

This pearl of price no works can claim;
 He that finds this is rich indeed;
This pure white stone contains a name,
 Which none but who receives can read.

This precious gift, this bond of love,
 The Lord oft gives His people here;
But what we all shall be above
 Does not, my brethren, yet appear.

Yet this we safely may believe,
 'Tis what no words will e'er express;
What saints themselves cannot conceive,
 And brightest angels can but guess.

298 Vernon Higham 87 87 887
**For day and night Thy hand was heavy upon
me.** *Psalm 32:4*

Thy living word my heart did break
 When I beheld the Saviour;
From paths of sorrow I did wake
 To seek Thy mighty favour.
Mercy of God, atoning love,
Spirit of joy, flow from above,
 Thy gentle grace revealing.

Thy searching eye exposed my sin
 And motives so unworthy;
Shame and remorse now welled within;
 Thy gaze was full of pity.
Mercy of God disturbing me,
Spirit of truth and purity,
 Thy gentle grace revealing

Thy loving hand restrained my way,
 In righteousness to follow;
Thy will prevailed lest I should stray,
 And cause my soul to sorrow.
Mercy of God, constraining care,
Spirit of light beyond compare,
 Thy gentle grace revealing.

Thy tender dealing with my heart,
 Most painful, yet with healing;
This grace that bids me not depart,
 Pours balm with love constraining.
Mercy of God, eternal, strong,
Spirit of grace with victor's song,
 Thy gentle grace revealing.

© *Author*

299 John Brewer LM
Thou art my hiding place. *Psalm 32:7*

Hail sovereign love, that first began
The scheme to rescue fallen man!
Hail, matchless, free, eternal grace,
That gave my soul a hiding-place!

Against the God who rules the sky
I fought with hand uplifted high;
Despised the mention of His grace,
Too proud to seek a hiding-place.

But thus the eternal counsel ran:
'Almighty love, arrest that man!'
I felt the arrows of distress,
And found I had no hiding-place.

Indignant Justice stood in view;
To Sinai's fiery mount I flew;
But Justice cried, with frowning face,
'This mountain is no hiding-place!'

Ere long a heavenly voice I heard,
And Mercy's angel-form appeared;
She led me on, with placid pace,
To Jesus, as my Hiding-place.

On Him almighty vengeance fell,
That must have sunk a world to hell;
He bore it for a chosen race,
And thus became their Hiding-place.

A few more rolling suns, at most,
Will land me on fair Canaan's coast,
Where I shall sing the song of grace,
And see my glorious Hiding-place.

300   Vernon Higham   886 D
Thou art my hiding place. *Psalm 32:7*

O Lord what work of grace is this,
That brought my soul from grief to bliss.
  O blessèd, wondrous name!
It is the Lord, whose mighty hands
Outstretched to meet the law's demands,
  And brought me from my shame.

My silent tongue but hid my pain,
My stricken conscience roared in vain;
  My moisture turned to drought.
Then mercy came and caused my soul
To come to Thee to make it whole,
  Dispelling all my doubt.

In gentle ways, Thy tender grace
Now led my soul to seek Thy face;
  Thy glory to behold.
My hiding place is found in Thee,
Thy merit is my only plea;
  And this shall make me bold.

For there are times when Thou art found,
When floods of sorrows surge around
  To drive me to despair.
The name of Christ, I will confess,
And in this hiding place will rest;
  Secure in Jesus' care.

                    © *Author*

301   John Berridge   10 10 11 11
**I will instruct thee and teach thee in the way
which thou shalt go: I will guide thee with Mine
eye.** *Psalm 32:8*

  O where shall I find a guide to direct,
    Right skilful and kind, and brave to protect?
  To lovely Mount Zion my heart is now bound,
  But many a lion is in the way found.

'Tis Jesus can teach the way ye should go,
  And out His arm reach to help you on too;
The doubts that perplex you, the fears that
    distress,
The tempers that vex you, His grace can redress

Then may the Lord give me faith in His name.
  A faith that will live in water and flame,
A faith that endureth, and feasts on His blood;
A faith that assureth my sonship with God.

O teach me to love Thy Person most sweet,
  Nor let my heart rove, but keep at Thy feet;
Be with Thee delighted, and clasp Thee and
    twine,
Most firmly united to Thy living Vine.

And further, I seek the charms of Thy mind,
  The grace to be meek, and lowly, and kind;
Forbearing, forgiving, and loving always,
And only be living to publish Thy praise.

302   John Fawcett   87 87
**I will instruct thee and teach thee in the way
which thou shalt go: I will guide thee with Mine
eye.** *Psalm 32:8*

Jesus, Thou Almighty Saviour,
  Prostrate at Thy feet I lie;
Humbly I entreat Thy favour,
  Condescend to hear my cry.

When I was to Thee a stranger,
  Wandering in forbidden ways,
From the paths of sin and danger
  Thou didst call me by Thy grace.

Let not, then, my foes confound me,
  Thou art all my help and hope;
Let Thy arms of love surround me,
  Let Thy mercy hold me up.

Grant me Thy divine direction
  In the way that I should go;
Let Thy hand be my protection
  From the power of every foe.

Gracious Saviour, never leave me,
  While my toils and conflicts last;
To Thy kind embrace receive me,
  When the storms of life are past.

303 Nahum Tate, Nicholas Brady CM
Psalm 33

Let all the just to God with joy
    Their cheerful voices raise;
For well the righteous it becomes
    To sing glad songs of praise.

For faithful is the word of God,
    His works with truth abound;
He justice loves, and all the earth
    Is with His goodness crowned.

By His almighty word at first
    The heavenly arch was reared;
And all the beauteous hosts of light
    At His command appeared.

Whate'er the Mighty Lord decrees,
    Shall stand for ever sure;
The settled purpose of His heart
    To ages shall endure.

How happy, then, are they to whom
    The Lord for God is known;
Whom He, from all the world besides,
    Has chosen for His own!

Our soul on God with patience waits,
    Our help and shield is He;
Then, Lord, let still our hearts rejoice.
    Because we trust in Thee.

The riches of Thy mercy, Lord,
    Do Thou to us extend,
Since we, for all we want or wish,
    On Thee alone depend.

304 Philip Doddridge LM
The earth is full of the goodness of the LORD.
Psalm 33:5

Eternal Source of every joy!
Well may Thy praise our lips employ,
While in Thy temple we appear
To hail Thee Sovereign of the year.

Wide as the wheels of nature roll,
Thy hand supports and guides the whole!
The sun is taught by Thee to rise,
And darkness when to veil the skies.

The flowery spring, at Thy command,
Perfumes the air and paints the land;
The summer rays with vigour shine
To raise the corn and cheer the vine.

Thy hand in autumn richly pours
Through all our coast redundant stores,
And winters, softened by Thy care,
No more, the face of horror wear.

Seasons and months, and weeks and days
Demand successive songs of praise:
And be the grateful homage paid
With morning light and evening shade.

Here in Thy house let incense rise,
And circling Sabbaths bless our eyes,
Till to those lofty heights we soar,
Where days and years revolve no more.

305 Nahum Tate, Nicholas Brady CM
Psalm 34

Through all the changing scenes of life,
    In trouble and in joy,
The praises of my God shall still
    My heart and tongue employ.

Of His deliverance I will boast,
    Till all that are distressed
From mine example comfort take
    And charm their griefs to rest.

The hosts of God encamp around
    The dwellings of the just;
Protection He affords to all
    Who make His name their trust.

O magnify the Lord with me,
    With me exalt His name;
When in distress to Him I called,
    He to my rescue came.

O make but trial of His love,
    Experience will decide
How blest are they, and only they,
    Who in His truth confide.

Fear Him, ye saints, and you will then
    Have nothing else to fear;
Make but His service your delight;
    Your wants shall be His care.

306 *Gospel Magazine* 87 87 D
The young lions do lack, and suffer hunger:
but they that seek the LORD shall not want
any good thing. *Psalm 34:10*

Tell us O our best Belovèd,
　Where Thou feed'st Thy tender flock;
Where they rest at noon, discover;
　Shelter us beneath that rock!
Let no idol e'er divide us
　From Thee, Lord, in whom we live;
By Thy loving counsel guide us,
　And our souls at last receive.

Show us, Lord, Thy great salvation;
　Keep us till the storm shall cease;
In the world we've tribulation,
　But in Thee a solid peace.
No good thing shall be denied us;
　Thou wilt grace and glory give;
By Thy counsel Thou wilt guide us,
　And at last our souls receive.

307　Thomas Kelly　LM
Depart from evil, and do good; seek peace,
and pursue it. *Psalm 34:14*

While contests rend the Christian church,
　O may I live the friend of peace;
The sacred mine of Scripture search,
　And learn from man, vain man, to cease.

O teach me, Lord, Thy truth to know,
　And separate from all beside;
This I would guard from every foe,
　Nor fear the issue to abide.

But keep me, Lord, from party zeal,
　That seeks its own and not Thy praise:
This temper I would never feel,
　Or when I do, would own it base.

Be mine to recommend Thy grace,
　That sinners may believe and live;
That they who live may run the race,
　And then a crown of life receive.

Lord, search my heart; O search me through!
　Detect, destroy what's not Thy own;
Whene'er I speak, whate'er I do,
　O may I seek Thy praise alone.

308　Henry Lyte　CM
Psalm 35

O plead my cause, my Saviour, plead,
　I trust it all to Thee!
O Thou Who didst for sinners bleed,
　A sinner save in me!

Assure my weak, desponding heart,
　My threatening foes restrain;
O tell me Thou my helper art,
　And all their rage is vain!

When round Thy cross they rushed to kill,
　How was their fury foiled:
Their madness only wrought Thy will,
　And on themselves recoiled.

The great salvation there achieved
　My hope shall ever be;
My soul has in her Lord believed,
　And He will rescue me.

309　Anne Steele　CM
Say unto my soul, I am thy salvation.
Psalm 35:3

Eternal Source of joys divine,
　To Thee my soul aspires;
O could I say, 'The Lord is mine,'
　'Tis all my soul desires.

Thy smile can give me real joy,
　Unmingled and refined;
Substantial bliss, without alloy,
　And lasting as the mind.

Thy smile can gild the shades of woe,
　Bid stormy trouble cease,
Spread the fair dawn of heaven below,
　And sweeten pain to peace.

My hope, my trust, my life, my Lord,
　Assure me of Thy love;
O speak the kind transporting word,
　And bid my fears remove.

Then shall my thankful powers rejoice,
　And triumph in my God,
Till heavenly rapture tune my voice
　To spread Thy praise abroad.

310　Isaac Watts　CM
And my soul shall be joyful in the LORD.
Psalm 35:9

Salvation! O the joyful sound!
　'Tis pleasure to our ears,
A sovereign balm for every wound,
　A cordial for our fears.

Buried in sorrow and in sin,
　At hell's dark door we lay;
But we arise by grace divine,
　To see a heavenly day.

Salvation! let the echo fly
    The spacious earth around;
While all the armies of the sky
    Conspire to raise the sound.

From those that know Thee may Thy love
    And mercy ne'er depart,
And may Thy justice still protect
    And bless the upright heart.

311   Isaac Watts   LM
Psalm 36

High in the heavens, eternal God,
    Thy goodness in full glory shines;
Thy truth shall break through every cloud
    That veils and darkens Thy designs.

For ever firm Thy justice stands,
    As mountains their foundations keep;
Wise are the wonders of Thy hands;
    Thy judgments are a mighty deep.

Thy providence is kind and large,
    Both man and beast Thy bounty share;
The whole creation is Thy charge,
    But saints are Thy peculiar care.

My God, how excellent Thy grace,
    Whence all our hope and comfort springs!
The sons of Adam in distress
    Fly to the shadow of Thy wings.

Life, like a fountain rich and free,
    Springs from the presence of the Lord;
And in Thy light our souls shall see
    The glories promised in Thy word.

312   *Psalter* 1912   CM
Psalm 36

Thy mercy and Thy truth, O Lord,
    Transcend the lofty sky;
Thy judgments are a mighty deep,
    And as the mountains high.

Lord, Thou preservest man and beast;
    Since Thou art ever kind,
Beneath the shadow of Thy wings
    We may a refuge find.

With the abundance of Thy house
    We shall be satisfied;
From rivers of unfailing joy
    Our thirst shall be supplied.

The fountain of eternal life
    Is found alone with Thee,
And in the brightness of Thy light
    We clearly light shall see.

313   Philip Doddridge   LM
They shall be abundantly satisfied.
Psalm 36:8

O Lord, descend and fill this place
With choicest tokens of Thy grace!
These walls we do Thy honour raise;
Long may they echo with Thy praise

Here let the great Redeemer reign,
With all the graces of His train;
While power divine His word attends,
To conquer foes and cheer His friends.

314   David Denham   11 8 11 8
They shall be abundantly satisfied.
Psalm 36:8

How pleasant to wait on the God of all grace,
    And taste the sweet streams of His love:
The wonders of sovereign mercy to trace,
    As onward to Canaan I move!

I'm bound for the city of Zion above,
    Where Satan shall never molest,
But where the redeemed at the fountain of love
    Shall be through eternity blest.

Though Satan, the world, and my sins all unite,
    To keep me from Jesus my God;
Upheld and led forth by the Spirit to fight,
    My conquest is sure through His blood.

While errors are spreading and Satan doth roar
    Against the dear lambs of Thy flock.
May I the sure Scriptures more fully explore,
    Abiding in Jesus the Rock.

Thou art my full portion which cannot decrease
    My Strength, my Salvation, and Rest,
My great All in all in a cov'nant of peace,
    In whom I'm eternally blest.

Thus may I rejoice, and at all times confide
    In Thee, my Redeemer, alone;
Made strong in Thy grace the last storm to
        outride,
    And rise to Thy glorious throne.

315   John Berridge   LM
In Thy light shall we see light. *Psalm 36:9*

In darkness born, I went astray,
And wandered from the gospel way;
And since the Saviour gave me sight,
I cannot see without His light.

So poor, and blind, and lame I am,
My all is bound up in the Lamb;
And blessèd am I when I see
My spirit's inmost poverty.

I cannot walk without His might,
I cannot see without His light;
I can have no access to God,
But through the merits of His blood.

It makes me feel my ruined state,
It lays my soul at mercy's gate;
And Jesus smiles at such a guest;
And cheers Him with a heavenly feast.

316   Henry Lyte   CM
Psalm 37

O God of love, how blest are they
   Who in Thy ways delight!
Thy presence guides them all the day,
   And cheers them all the night.

Whene'er they faint, a mighty arm
   Is nigh them to uphold;
And sin or Satan cannot harm
   The feeblest of Thy fold.

The Lord is wise, the Lord is just,
   The Lord is good and true.
And they who on His promise trust
   Will find it bear them through.

His word will stay their sinking hearts;
   Their feet shall never slide:
The heavens dissolve, the earth departs,
   They safe in God abide.

317   *Scottish Version*   CM
Psalm 37

Set thou thy trust upon the Lord,
   Do good and know no care,
For so thou in the land shalt dwell,
   And God thy food prepare.

Delight thyself in God, He'll give
   Thine heart's desire to Thee:
Commit thy way to God alone,
   It brought to pass shall be.

And like unto the light He shall
   Thy righteousness display;
And He thy judgment shall bring forth,
   Like noontide of the day.

318   Georg Neumark, tr. Catherine Winkworth
                                          88 88 88
Trust in the LORD, and do good.
Psalm 37:3

Leave God to order all thy ways
   And hope in Him whate'er betide;
Thou'lt find Him in the evil days
   Thy all sufficient strength and guide:
Who trusts in God's unchanging love
Builds on the Rock that nought can move.

Only, thy restless heart keep still,
   And wait in cheerful hope, content
To take whate'er His gracious will,
   His all-discerning love, hath sent;
Nor doubt our inmost wants are known
To Him who chose us for His own.

Sing, pray and swerve not from His ways,
   But do thine own part faithfully;
Trust His rich promises of grace,
   So shalt they be fulfilled in thee:
God never yet forsook at need
The soul that trusted Him indeed.

JOHN RYLAND 1753-1825

319   John Ryland   CM
Delight thyself also in the LORD.
Psalm 37:4

O Lord, I would delight in Thee
   And on Thy care depend;
To Thee in every trouble flee,
   My best, my only Friend.

When all created streams are dried,
   Thy fulness is the same;
May I with this be satisfied,
   And glory in Thy name.

No good in creatures can be found,
   But may be found in Thee;
I must have all things and abound,
   While God is God to me.

O that I had a stronger faith,
   To look within the veil!
To credit what my Saviour saith,
   Whose word can never fail!

He that has made my heaven secure,
   Will here all good provide;
While Christ is rich, can I be poor?
   What can I want beside?

O Lord, I cast my care on Thee;
   I triumph and adore:
Henceforth my great concern shall be
   To love and please Thee more.

320   Paulus Gerhardt, tr. J Wesley   SM
Commit Thy way unto the LORD.
Psalm 37:5

Commit thou all thy griefs
   And ways into His hands,
To His sure truth and tender care,
   Who heaven and earth commands.

Who points the clouds their course,
   Whom winds and seas obey,
He shall direct thy wandering feet,
   He shall prepare thy way.

Thou on the Lord rely,
   So safe shalt thou go on;
Fix on His work thy steadfast eye,
   So shall thy work be done.

No profit canst thou gain
   By self-consuming care:
To Him commend thy cause; His ear
   Attends the softest prayer.

Thy everlasting truth,
   Father, Thy ceaseless love,
Sees all Thy children's wants, and knows
   What best for each will prove.

Thou everywhere hast sway
   And all things serve Thy might;
Thy every act pure blessing is,
   Thy path unsullied light.

When Thou arisest, Lord,
   What shall Thy work withstand?
Whate'er Thy children need Thou givest;
   And who shall stay Thy hand?

321   Horatius Bonar   DCM
Rest in the LORD, and wait patiently for him.
Psalm 37:7

I heard the voice of Jesus say,
   'Come unto Me and rest;
Lay down, thou weary one, lay down
   Thy head upon My breast.'
I came to Jesus as I was,
   Weary and worn and sad,
I found in Him a resting-place,
   And He has made me glad.

I heard the voice of Jesus say,
   'Behold I freely give
The living water, thirsty one.
   Stoop down and drink and live.'
I came to Jesus and I drank
   Of that life-giving stream,
My thirst was quenched, my soul revived
   And now I live in Him.

I heard the voice of Jesus say,
   'I am this dark world's light,
Look unto Me, thy morn shall rise
   And all thy day be bright.'
I looked to Jesus and I found
   In Him my Star, my Sun;
And in that light of life I'll walk,
   Till travelling days are done.

322   Jean Pigott   87 85 D
Rest in the LORD, and wait patiently for Him.
Psalm 37:7

Jesus! I am resting, resting
  In the joy of what Thou art;
I am finding out the greatness
    Of Thy loving heart.
Thou hast bid me gaze upon Thee,
  And Thy beauty fills my soul,
For, by Thy transforming power,
    Thou hast made me whole.

O how great Thy loving-kindness,
  Vaster, broader than the sea!
O how marvellous Thy goodness,
    Lavished all on me!
Yes, I rest in Thee, Belovèd,
  Know what wealth of grace is Thine,
Know Thy certainty of promise,
    And have made it mine.

Simply trusting Thee, Lord Jesus,
  I behold Thee as Thou art,
And Thy love so pure, so changeless,
    Satisfies my heart;
Satisfies its deepest longings,
  Meets, supplies its every need,
Compasseth me round with blessings;
    Thine is love indeed!

Ever lift Thy face upon me
  As I work and wait for Thee;
Resting 'neath Thy smile, Lord Jesus,
    Earth's dark shadows flee.
Brightness of my Father's glory,
  Sunshine of my Father's face,
Keep me ever trusting, resting,
    Fill me with Thy grace.

323   Augustus Toplady   SM
Rest in the LORD, and wait patiently for Him.
Psalm 37:7

O may I never rest
  Till I find rest in Thee,
Till of my pardon here possessed
  I feel Thy love to me!

Turn not Thy face away,
  Thy look can make me clean;
Me in Thy wedding robes array,
  And cover all my sin.

Tell me, my God, for whom
  Thy precious blood was shed;
For sinners? Lord, as such I come,
  For such the Saviour bled.

Then raise a fallen wretch,
  Display Thy grace in me;
I am not out of mercy's reach.
  Nor too far gone for Thee.

324   Norman Perry   86 84
**The steps of a good man are ordered by the
LORD.** *Psalm 37:23*

Give me, O Lord, a faith serene
  That rests in Thee alone,
Assured that grace divine has made
  Me all Thine own.

Teach me, O Lord, to understand
  Even in the darkest night,
When storms are high and seas are wild,
  Thy way is right.

Upon me, Lord, Thy peace bestow
  When foes assail my heart;
Appoint me some sweet meeting place
  With Thee apart.

Grant me, O Lord, to feel Thy hand
  Of tenderness and power
Is holding mine and leading me
  Each day, each hour.

So may I, Lord, upheld by Thee
  Live only to Thy praise
Depending on Thy mercy now
  And all my days.
             © *Mrs R Westmacott*

325   Philip Doddridge   LM
The righteous shall inherit the land.
Psalm 37:29

O Thou the Hope of Israel's host,
Their Strength, their Helper, and their Boast;
How oft their Saviour hast Thou been,
In times of trouble and of sin!

And have not we beheld Thy face?
Thy visits crowned the means of grace;
Oh come again, indulgent Lord,
With all the joy Thy smiles afford.

Enter our hearts, Redeemer blest,
Enter, Thou ever-honoured Guest;
Enter, and make our hearts Thine own,
Thy house, Thy temple, and Thy throne.

And stay, not only for a night,
To bless us with a transient sight;
But with us dwell, through time; and then
In heaven for evermore; Amen.

326   Isaac Watts   CM
Psalm 38

Amidst Thy wrath remember love;
   Restore Thy servant, Lord:
Nor let a Father's chastening prove
   Like an avenger's sword.

All my desire to Thee is known,
   Thine eye counts every tear;
And every sigh and every groan
   Is noticed by Thine ear.

Thou art my God, my only hope:
   My God will hear my cry;
My God will bear my spirit up
   When Satan bids me die.

My God, forgive my follies past,
   And be for ever nigh;
O Lord of my salvation haste,
   Before Thy servant die!

327   Thomas Kelly (alt)   LM
O LORD, rebuke me not in Thy wrath.
Psalm 38:1

Deal gently with Thy servant, Lord,
   And if the rod should needful be,
Thy seasonable aid afford;
   My soul in trouble flies to Thee.

Thy frown is terrible to bear,
   But grace a spring of hope supplies;
Thy anger more than death I fear,
   Thy favour more than life I prize.

But much I fear, lest in some hour
   Of sore temptation I may fall;
And, yielding to the tempter's power,
   Faithless may prove, and give up all.

Lord, save Thou me, for Thou alone
   Canst keep me in the trying hour;
Thy help I trust to, not my own,
   Thy love, Thy wisdom, and Thy power.

When chastisement shall needful be,
   Correct Thou me, but not in wrath;
A Father's hand I fain would see;
   A Father's rod no terror hath.

328   Charles Spurgeon   CM
Psalm 39

Behold, O Lord, my days are made
   A handbreadth at the most;
Ere yet 'tis noon my flower must fade,
   And I give up the ghost.

Then teach me, Lord, to know mine end,
   And know that I am frail;
To heaven let all my thoughts ascend,
   And let not earth prevail.

What is there here that I should wait,
   My hope's in Thee alone;
When wilt Thou open glory's gate
   And call me to Thy throne?

A stranger in this land am I,
   A sojourner with Thee;
O be not silent at my cry,
   But show Thyself to me,

Though I'm exiled from glory's land.
   Yet not from glory's King;
My God is ever near at hand,
   And therefore I will sing.

329   *Scottish Psalter 1650*   CM
Psalm 40:1-5

I waited for the Lord my God
   And patiently did bear;
At length to me He did incline
   My voice and cry to hear.

He took me from a fearful pit
   And from the miry clay,
And on a rock He set my feet,
   Establishing my way.

He put a new song in my mouth,
   Our God to magnify;
Many shall see it and shall fear,
   And on the Lord rely.

O blessèd is the man whose trust
   Upon the Lord relies,
Respecting not the proud, nor such
   As turn aside to lies.

O Lord my God, full many are
   The wonders Thou hast done;
Thy gracious thoughts to us-ward far
   Above all thoughts are gone.

Thy tender mercies, Lord, from me
   O do Thou not restrain;
Thy loving-kindness and Thy truth,
   Let them still maintain.

330   Vernon Higham   DCM
I waited patiently for the LORD.
Psalm 40:1

I waited sadly for the Lord,
   But darkness veiled His face;
I clung to sin and shunned His Word;
   Yet longed to prove His grace.
A heavy burden on me lay
   And conflict tore my heart;
No satisfaction from each way;
   Despair was all my part.

The Lord inclined and heard my cry
   And saw my dreadful plight:
A path of sin and pit of clay,
   A place of dismal night.
He brought me out of unbelief,
   And showed me truth divine;
With quickening touch with life so brief,
   Immortal breath was mine.

My feet upon a Rock I found,
   His blessing on life's race,
A song of joy with sweetest sound,
   A melody of grace.
I'll praise the God of Abraham,
   Who saw how I had roamed,
For worthy, worthy is the Lamb,
   Who on the cross atoned.

© *Author*

331   Charlotte Homer   888 6 + refrain
He brought me up also out of an horrible pit.
Psalm 40:2

In loving kindness Jesus came,
My soul in mercy to reclaim
And from the depths of sin and shame
   Through grace He lifted me.

   From sinking sand He lifted me;
   With tender hand He lifted me;
   From shades of night to plains of light,
   O praise His Name, He lifted me!

He called me long before I heard,
Before my sinful heart was stirred;
But when I took Him at His word,
   Forgiven, He lifted me.

His brow was pierced with many a thorn,
His hands by cruel nails were torn,
When from my guilt and grief, forlorn,
   In love He lifted me.

Now on a higher plane I dwell,
And with my soul I know it's well;
Yet how or why, I cannot tell,
   He should have lifted me.

332   William Rozzell   CM
And He hath put a new song in my mouth.
Psalm 40:3

O let my voice proclaim the joys
   My heart has known and felt;
And let my tongue declare the woes
   My soul has known by guilt.

Long in the paths of sin I trod,
   And, in her foulest way,
Provoked a kind and gracious God,
   And grieved Him day by day.

I tried His patience with my crimes,
   By days and years of sin;
Resolved to mend in aftertimes,
   And wash the leper clean.

But when the Lord His arm made bare,
   And took my heart in hand,
Effectual cleansing work was there,
   Which I could not withstand.

He doomed me in the dust to lie,
   In sorrows sharp and long;
Then changed my sadness into joy,
   My mourning to a song.

333   Fanny Crosby   76 76 D
And He hath put a new song in my mouth.
Psalm 40:3

My song shall be of Jesus:
   His mercy crowns my days;
He fills my cup with blessings,
   And tunes my heart to praise.
My song shall be of Jesus,
   The precious Lamb of God,
Who gave Himself my ransom,
   And bought me with His blood.

My song shall be of Jesus,
   When, sitting at His feet,
I call to mind His goodness,
   In meditation sweet,
My song shall be of Jesus,
   Whatever ill betide;
I'll sing the grace that saves me,
   And keeps me at His side.

My song shall be of Jesus,
   While pressing on my way
To reach the blissful region
   Of pure and perfect day.
And when my soul shall enter
   The gate of Eden fair,
A song of praise to Jesus
   I'll sing for ever there.

334 Charles Spurgeon 77 77
Psalm 41

Jesus, poorest of the poor!
  Man of sorrows! Child of grief!
Happy they whose bounteous store
  Ministered to Thy relief.

Jesus, though Thy head is crowned,
  Crowned with loftiest majesty.
In Thy members Thou art found,
  Plunged in deepest poverty.

Happy they who wash Thy feet,
  Visit Thee in Thy distress!
Honour great, and labour sweet,
  For Thy sake the saints to bless!

Thou wilt keep their soul alive;
  From their foes protect their head;
Languishing their strength revive,
  And in sickness make their bed.

Thou wilt deeds of love repay;
  Grace shall gen'rous hearts reward
Here on earth, and in the day
  When they meet their reigning Lord.

335 Magnus Landstat, tr. C Döving 88 88 88
I said, LORD, be merciful unto me: heal my soul. *Psalm 41:4*

Before Thee, God, who knowest all,
With grief and shame I prostrate fall.
I see my sins against Thee, Lord,
The sins of thought, of deed and word.
  They press me sure; I cry to Thee:
  'O God, be merciful to me!'

O Lord, my God, to Thee I pray:
O cast me not in wrath away!
Let Thy good Spirit ne'er depart,
But let Him draw to Thee my heart
  That truly penitent I be:
  O God, be merciful to me!

O Jesus, let Thy precious blood
Be to my soul a cleansing flood.
Turn not, O Lord, Thy guest away,
But grant that justified I may
  Go to my house at peace with Thee:
  O God, be merciful to me!

336 John Monsell 77 77
I said, LORD, be merciful unto me: heal my soul. *Psalm 41:4*

Sinful, sighing to be blest;
  Bound and longing to be free;
Weary, waiting for my rest;
  God be merciful to me.

Goodness I have none to plead,
  Sinfulness in all I see,
I can only bring my need;
  God be merciful to me.

Broken heart and downcast eyes
  Dare not lift themselves to Thee;
Yet Thou canst interpret sighs:
  God be merciful to me.

From this sinful heart of mine
  To Thy bosom I would flee:
I am not my own, but Thine:
  God be merciful to me.

There is One beside the throne,
  And my only hope and plea
Are in Him and Him alone:
  God be merciful to me.

He my cause will undertake,
  My Interpreter will be;
He's my all; and for His sake
  God be merciful to me.

337 David Denham SM
By this I know that Thou favourest me.
Psalm 41:11

  Thou favourest me, I know,
    By everlasting choice;
This makes me triumph o'er the foe,
    And in Thy name rejoice.

  Thou favourest me, I see,
    With Christ accounted one;
From guilt and condemnation free,
    Glory is now begun.

  Thou favourest me, I feel,
    When all my foes assail;
And blest with God the Spirit's seal,
    I shall at last prevail.

  Thou favourest me, I prove,
    In answer to my cries;
And strong in Thy eternal love,
    My soul each foe defies.

338   Nahum Tate, Nicholas Brady   CM
Psalm 42

As pants the hart for cooling streams
  When heated in the chase,
So longs my soul, O God, for Thee
  And Thy refreshing grace!

For Thee, my God, the living God,
  My thirsty soul doth pine;
O when shall I behold Thy face,
  Thou Majesty divine!

God of my strength, how long shall I
  Like one forgotten mourn?
Forlorn, forsaken and exposed
  To my oppressor's scorn?

Why restless, why cast down, my soul?
  Hope still and thou shalt sing
The praise of Him who is thy God,
  Thy health's eternal spring.

339   William Gadsby   87 87 47
**As the hart panteth after the water brooks, so
panteth my soul after Thee, O God.** *Psalm 42:1*

Precious Jesus! Friend of sinners;
  We, as such, to Thee draw near;
Let Thy Spirit now dwell in us,
  And with love our souls inspire;
    Fill, O fill us
With that love which casts out fear.

Matchless Saviour! let us view Thee
  As the Lord our Righteousness;
Cause each soul to cleave unto Thee,
  Come, and with Thy presence bless
    Dear Immanuel,
Feast us with Thy sovereign grace.

Open now Thy precious treasure:
  Let the blessings freely flow;
Give to each a gracious measure
  Of Thy glory here below;
    Loving Bridegroom,
'Tis Thyself we want to know.

Come, and claim us as Thy portion,
  And let us lay claim to Thee;
Leave us not to empty notion,
  But from bondage set us free;
    King of glory!
We would live and reign with Thee.

340   William Cowper   LM
My soul thirsteth for God, for the living God.
Psalm 42:2

I thirst, but not as once I did,
  The vain delights of earth to share;
Thy wounds, Immanuel, all forbid
  That I should seek my pleasures there.

It was the sight of Thy dear cross
  First weaned my soul from earthly things;
And taught me to esteem as dross
  The mirth of fools and pomp of kings.

I want that grace that springs from Thee,
  That quickens all things where it flows,
And makes a wretched thorn like me
  Bloom as the myrtle or the rose.

Dear Fountain of delight unknown,
  No longer sink below the brim;
But overflow and pour me down
  A living and life-giving stream!

For sure, of all the plants that share
  The notice of Thy Father's eye,
None prove less grateful to His care,
  Or yields Him meaner fruit, than I.

341   David Denham   CM
My soul thirsteth for God, for the living God.
Psalm 42:2

I thirst for God, the living God,
  The Fountain of free-grace;
I thirst for Jesus' cleansing blood,
  Which always suits my case.

I thirst the Spirit's power to prove,
  Who wounds, and then makes whole;
I thirst for everlasting love
  To satisfy my soul.

I thirst for nearness to the Lord,
  For visits from His throne;
I thirst for unction with His word,
  To serve Him as a son.

I thirst to see His count'nance shine,
  To hear His pard'ning voice;
I thirst for faith to call Him mine,
  And in Himself rejoice.

I thirst in prayer that I may feel
  My heart to heaven aspire;
I thirst for God's new covenant seal
  To fill my soul's desire.

I thirst upon His oath to feed,
    And humbly bear each rod;
I thirst to know Him in all need,
    My fulness and my God.

I thirst for keeping in His fear,
    Lest I His name disown;
I thirst in Him much fruit to bear,
    And on Him put the crown.

I thirst the conquest to obtain
    O'er all His foes and mine;
I thirst with Him to live and reign,
    And in His likeness shine.

342 John Berridge CM
**O my God, my soul is cast down within me:
therefore will I remember Thee.** *Psalm 42:6*

Why so cast down, dejected soul?
    A loving Christ is near;
Thy broken bones He can make whole,
    And drooping spirit cheer.

If guilty stings thy conscience feel,
    And pierce thee through and through,
Yet past backslidings Christ can heal,
    And love thee freely too.

If justice draw its flaming sword,
    And seems intent to kill,
On Jesus call, and trust His word,
    And thou shalt praise Him still.

Thy soul with tempests may be tossed,
    And Satan sorely thrust;
Yet sure no soul shall e'er be lost
    Who makes the Lord his trust.

Dear Jesus, show Thy smiling face,
    And Calvary's peace impart,
Display the power of saving grace,
    And cheer a troubled heart.

Refresh his eye with sweeter light,
    And whisper in his ear,
'Thy soul is precious in My sight,
    No need thou hast to fear.'

343 Edward Caswall CM
**Why art thou cast down, O my soul? and why
art thou disquieted within me? hope thou in
God.** *Psalm 42:11*

'O why so heavy, O my soul?'
    Thus to myself I said:
'O why so heavy, O my soul,
    And so disquieted?

'Hope thou in God; He still shall be
    Thy glory and thy praise;
His saving grace shall comfort thee
    Through everlasting days.

'His goodness made thee what thou art
    And yet will thee redeem:
O be thou of a steadfast heart,
    And put thy trust in Him.'

344 *Scottish Psalter 1650* DCM
O send out Thy light and Thy truth.
Psalm 43:3

O send Thy light forth and Thy truth;
    Let them be guides to me,
And bring me to Thine holy hill,
    E'en where Thy dwellings be.
Then will I to God's altar go,
    To God, my chiefest joy;
Yea, God, my God, Thy name to praise
    My harp I will employ.

Why art thou then cast down, my soul?
    What should discourage thee?
And why with vexing thoughts art thou
    Disquieted in me?
Still trust in God; for Him to praise
    Good cause I yet shall have;
He of my countenance is the health,
    My God that doth me save.

345   Charles Spurgeon   CM
Psalm 44

Our ears have heard, O glorious God,
   What work Thou didst of old:
And how the heathen felt Thy rod
   Our fathers oft have told.

'Twas not Thy people's arm or sword,
   But only Thy right hand,
Which scattered all the race abhorred,
   And gave Thy tribes their land.

Thou hadst a favour to the seed
   Which sprang of Jacob's line,
And still on men afore decreed
   Doth love electing shine.

These shall the heritage obtain,
   And drive out every sin
E'en death and hell shall rage in vain,
   They must the conquest win.

From grace alone their strength shall spring,
   Nor bow nor sword can save;
To God alone, their Lord and King,
   Shall all their banners wave.

In Thee alone we make our boasts,
   And glory all day long;
Arise at once, Thou Lord of hosts,
   And fill our mouth with song.

346   Joseph Irons   87 87 47
Psalm 45

Warm with love, my heart's inditing
   Cherished thoughts on sacred things;
With my tongue like ready writing,
   I'll extol the King of kings;
      Of whose glory
   Ev'ry saint and angel sings.

Thou of all the sons art fairest,
   Yea, Thy lips are fllled with grace;
All Thy fulness, Lord, Thou sharest
   'Mongst Thy chosen, ransomed race;
      And in glory
   They shall see Thee face to face.

O most mighty, O most blessèd,
   Gird Thy sword upon Thy thigh;
Be Thy Majesty confessèd,
   Bring Thy blood-bought trophies nigh;
      Let Thy glory
   All Thy stubborn foes defy.

Truth and righteousness, and meekness,
   Are the weapons of Thy hand;
All Thy foes shall know their weakness;
   None can Jesus' power withstand;
      'Tis Thy glory,
   Rebels bow at Thy command.

347   Isaac Watts   CM
Psalm 45

I'll speak the honours of my King.
   His form divinely fair;
None of the sons of mortal race
   May with the Lord compare.

Sweet is Thy speech, and heavenly grace
   Upon Thy lips is shed;
Thy God with blessings infinite
   Has crowned Thy sacred head.

Gird on Thy sword, victorious Prince,
   Ride with majestic sway;
Thy terror shall strike through Thy foes
   And make the world obey.

Thy throne, O God, for ever stands;
   Thy word of grace shall prove
A peaceful sceptre in Thy hands,
   To rule Thy saints by love.

Justice and truth attend Thee still,
   But mercy is Thy choice;
And God, Thy God, Thy soul shall fill
   With most peculiar joys.

348   Benjamin Wallin, A Toplady   CM
In thy majesty ride prosperously because of truth and meekness and righteousness.
Psalm 45:4

Hail, mighty Jesus! How divine
   Is Thy victorious sword!
The stoutest rebel must resign
   At Thy commanding word.

Deep are the wounds Thy arrows give;
   They pierce the hardest heart;
Thy smiles of grace the slain revive
   And joy succeeds to smart.

Still gird Thy sword upon Thy thigh,
   Ride with majestic sway
Go forth, sweet Prince, triumphantly
   And make Thy foes obey

And when Thy victories are complete,
   When all the chosen race
Shall round the throne of glory meet,
   To sing Thy conquering grace.

O may my blood-washed soul be found
   Among that favoured band!
And I, with them, Thy praise will sound
   Throughout Immanuel's land.

349   John Ryland   87 87 47
Thou lovest righteousness. *Psalm 45:7*

Let us sing the King Messiah,
   King of righteousness and peace;
Hail Him, all His happy subjects,
   Never let His praises cease:
     Ever hail Him;
   Never let His praises cease.

How transcendent are Thy glories,
   Fairer than the sons of men,
While Thy blessèd mediation
   Brings us back to God again:
     Blest Redeemer,
   How we triumph in Thy reign!

Gird Thy sword on, mighty Hero!
   Make the word of truth Thy car;
Prosper in Thy course majestic;
   All success attend Thy war!
     Gracious Victor,
   Let mankind before Thee bow!

Majesty combined with meekness,
   Righteousness and peace unite
To ensure Thy blessèd conquests;
   On, great Prince, assert Thy right:
     Ride triumphant
   All around the conquered globe.

Blest are all that touch Thy sceptre;
   Blest are all that own Thy reign,
Freed from sin, that worst of tyrants,
   Rescued from its galling chain:
     Saints and angels,
   All who know Thee bless Thy reign.

350   Joseph Irons   66 66 88
I will make Thy name to be remembered in all generations: therefore shall the people praise Thee for ever and ever.
Psalm 45:17

To speak my Saviour's name,
   And set His glory forth,
To sound abroad His fame,
   And estimate His worth,
Would well employ th' angelic throng,
And shall engage our thankful tongue.

His Person, grace, and might,
   His offices and love,
Are sources of delight
   To ransomed souls above.
In their loud songs I'll bear a part,
For Christ is precious in my heart.

My Brother, Surety, Friend;
   My Prophet, Priest, and King;
Faith's Author, Object, End;
   Around His cross I'll cling:
His precious blood redeemed my soul;
He found me maimed, and made me whole.

In comfort and distress,
   In freedom and in thrall,
'Tis He alone can bless,
   For He is All in all:
In life, and death, O may I find
My Jesus precious to my mind!

351   Isaac Watts   LM
Psalm 46

God is the refuge of His saints,
   When storms of sharp distress invade;
Ere we can offer our complaints,
   Behold Him present with His aid.

Let mountains from their seats be hurled
   Down to the deep, and buried there,
Convulsions shake the solid world,
   Our faith shall never yield to fear.

Loud may the troubled ocean roar;
   In sacred peace our souls abide,
While every nation, every shore,
   Trembles, and dreads the swelling tide.

There is a stream whose gentle flow
   Supplies the city of our God;
Life, love and joy, still gliding through,
   And watering our divine abode.

That sacred stream, Thy holy word,
   Our grief allays, our fear controls;
Sweet peace Thy promises afford,
   And give new strength to fainting souls.

Zion enjoys her Monarch's love,
   Secure against a threatening hour;
Nor can her firm foundations move,
   Built on His truth, and armed with power.

352 *Psalter* 1912   DCM
Psalm 46

God is our Refuge and our Strength,
   Our ever present aid,
And, therefore, though the earth remove,
   We will not be afraid;
Though hills amidst the seas be cast,
   Though foaming waters roar,
Yea, though the mighty billows shake
   The mountains on the shore.

A river flows whose streams make glad
   The city of our God,
The holy place wherein the Lord
   Most High has His abode;
Since God is in the midst of her,
   Unmoved her walls shall stand,
For God will be her early help,
   When trouble is at hand.

The nations raged, the kingdoms moved,
   But when His voice was heard
The troubled earth was stilled to peace
   Before His mighty word.
The Lord of Hosts is on our side,
   Our safety to secure;
The God of Jacob is for us
   A Refuge strong and sure.

O come, behold what wondrous works
   Jehovah's hand has wrought;
Come, see what desolation great
   He on the earth has brought.
To utmost ends of all the earth
   He causes war to cease;
The weapons of the strong destroyed,
   He makes abiding peace.

Be still and know that I am God,
   O'er all exalted high;
The subject nations of the earth
   My name shall magnify.
The Lord of Hosts is on our side.
   Our safety to secure;
The God of Jacob is for us
   A refuge strong and sure.

MARTIN LUTHER 1483-1546

353   Martin Luther, tr. T Carlyle   87 87 66 667
God is our refuge and strength, a very present help in trouble.
Psalm 46:1

A safe stronghold our God is still,
   A trusty shield and weapon;
He'll help us clear from all the ill
   That hath us now o'ertaken.
      The ancient prince of hell
      Hath risen with purpose fell;
      Strong mail of craft and power
      He weareth in this hour;
On earth is not his fellow.

With force of arms we nothing can,
   Full soon were we down-ridden;
But for us fights the proper Man,
   Whom God Himself hath bidden.
      Ask ye, who is this same?
      Christ Jesus is His name,
      The Lord Sabaoth's Son;
      He, and no other one,
Shall conquer in the battle.

And were this world all devils o'er,
   And watching to devour us,
We lay it not to heart so sore;
   Not they can overpower us.
      And let the prince of ill
      Look grim as e'er he will,
      He harms us not a whit:
      For why? His doom is writ;
A word shall quickly slay him.

God's word, for all their craft and force,
   One moment will not linger,
But, spite of hell, shall have its course;
   'Tis written by His finger.
      And though they take our life,
      Goods, honour, children, wife,
      Yet is their profit small:
      These things shall vanish all;
The city of God remaineth

354 Thomas Kelly   87 87 47
There is a river, the streams whereof shall make glad the city of God.
Psalm 46:4

See from Zion's sacred mountain,
  Streams of living water flow;
God has opened there a fountain,
  That supplies the plains below;
    They are blessèd
  Who its sovereign virtues know.

Through ten thousand channels flowing,
  Streams of mercy find their way;
Life, and health, and joy bestowing,
  Making all around look gay;
    O believer!
  All Thy sins are washed away.

Gladdened by the flowing treasure,
  All enriching as it goes;
Lo, the desert smiles with pleasure,
  Buds and blossoms as the rose;
    Every sinner
  Sings for joy where'er it flows.

Trees of life the banks adorning,
  Yield their fruit to all around,
Those who eat are saved from mourning;
  Pleasure comes and hopes abound;
    Fair their portion!
  Endless life with glory crowned.

355 Samuel Medley   LM
There is a river, the streams whereof shall make glad the city of God. *Psalm 46:4*

While the dear saints of God below
Travel this vale of sin and woe,
There is a river through the road,
Makes glad the city of our God.

This river is His heavenly love,
Proceeding from the throne above;
And all its streams which here are found,
With comfort, joy, and peace abound.

Blest river! great its virtues are;
Pure river, O how sweet and clear!
Deep river, through the desert way;
Full river, never to decay!

Ye thirsty, poor, and needy souls,
For you this wondrous river rolls.
Though sin and sorrow make you sad,
Yet drink, and let your hearts be glad.

Drink, and for ever bless His name,
From whom these streams of mercy came:
Drink, for the fountain's open still;
Drink, for He says, 'Whoever will.'

356 Samuel Medley   LM
Be still, and know that I am God.
Psalm 46:10

Let me, Thou sovereign Lord of all,
Low at Thy footstool humbly fall;
And while I feel affliction's rod,
Be still and know that Thou art God.

Let me not murmur nor repine,
Under these trying strokes of Thine;
But while I walk the mournful road
Be still and know that Thou art God.

When and wherever Thou shalt smite,
Teach me to own Thy sovereign right;
And underneath the heaviest load,
Be still and know that Thou art God.

Still let this truth support my mind,
Thou canst not err nor be unkind;
And thus approve Thy chastening rod,
And know Thou art my Father, God!

When this afflicted soul shall rise
To ceaseless joys above the skies,
I shall, as ransomed by Thy blood,
For ever sing, 'Thou art my God!'

357 Kathrina von Schlegel, tr. J Borthwick
10 10 10 10 10 10
Be still, and know that I am God. *Psalm 46:10*

Be still, my soul, the Lord is on thy side;
  Bear patiently the cross of grief or pain;
Leave to thy God to order and provide;
  In every change He faithful will remain.
Be still, my soul, thy best, thy heavenly Friend
Through thorny ways leads to a joyful end.

Be still, my soul, thy God doth undertake
  To guide the future as He has the past.
Thy hope, thy confidence, let nothing shake;
  All now mysterious shall be bright at last.
Be still, my soul, the waves and winds still know
His voice who ruled them while He dwelt below.

Be still, my soul, the hour is hastening on
  When we shall be for ever with the Lord,
When disappointment, grief and fear are gone,
  Sorrow forgot, love's purest joys restored.
Be still, my soul, when change and tears are past,
All safe and blessèd we shall meet at last.

358 Isaac Watts CM
Psalm 47

O for a shout of sacred joy,
  To God, the sovereign King:
Let every land their tongues employ,
  And hymns of triumph sing.

Jesus our God ascends on high;
  His heavenly guards around
Attend Him rising through the sky,
  With trumpet's joyful sound.

While angels shout and praise their King,
  Let mortals learn their strains;
Let all the earth His honours sing;
  O'er all the earth He reigns.

Rehearse His praise with awe profound,
  Let knowledge lead the song;
Nor mock Him with a solemn sound
  Upon a thoughtless tongue.

In Israel stood His ancient throne;
  He loved that chosen race;
But now He calls the world His own,
  And heathens taste His grace.

359 Charles Wesley 77 77
Psalm 47

Clap your hands, ye people all,
Praise the God on whom ye call;
Lift your voice and shout His praise,
Triumph in His sovereign grace!

Glorious is the Lord most high,
Terrible in majesty;
He His sovereign sway maintains,
King o'er all the earth He reigns.

Jesus is gone up on high,
Takes His seat above the sky:
Shout the angel-choirs aloud,
Echoing to the trump of God.

Sons of earth, the triumph join:
Praise Him with the host divine;
Emulate the heavenly powers;
Their victorious Lord is ours.

Shout the God enthroned above,
Trumpet forth His conquering love;
Praises to our Jesus sing,
Praises to our glorious King!

Power is all to Jesus given,
Power o'er hell, and earth, and heaven;
Power He now to us imparts:
Praise Him with believing hearts.

Wonderful in saving power,
  Him let all our hearts adore;
Earth and heaven repeat the cry:
  'Glory be to God most high!'

360 Horatius Bonar 66 66 (iambic)
He shall choose our inheritance for us, the
excellency of Jacob whom He loved. Selah.
Psalm 47:4

Thy way, not mine, O Lord,
  However dark it be;
Lead me by Thine own hand,
  Choose Thou the path for me.

Smooth let it be or rough,
  It will be still the best;
Winding or straight, it leads
  Right onward to Thy rest.

I dare not choose my lot;
  I would not if I might;
Choose Thou for me, my God,
  So shall I walk aright.

The kingdom that I seek
  Is Thine, so let the way
That leads to it be Thine,
  Else I must surely stray.

Take Thou my cup and it
  With joy or sorrow fill
As best to Thee may seem;
  Choose Thou my good or ill.

Choose Thou for me my friends,
  My sickness or my health;
Choose Thou my cares for me,
  My poverty or wealth.

Not mine, not mine the choice,
  In things or great or small;
Be Thou my Guide, my Strength,
  My Wisdom and my All.

361 Isaac Watts, alt. J Wesley DLM
God is gone up with a shout, the LORD with
the sound of a trumpet. *Psalm 47:5*

He dies! the Friend of sinners dies;
  Lo! Salem's daughters weep around
A solemn darkness veils the skies;
  A sudden trembling shakes the ground;
Come, saints, and drop a tear or two
  For Him who groaned beneath your load
He shed a thousand drops for you,
  A thousand drops of richer blood.

Here's love and grief beyond degree,
    The Lord of glory dies for men:
But lo! what sudden joys we see—
    Jesus the dead revives again.
The rising God forsakes the tomb:
    Up to His Father's courts He flies;
Cherubic legions guard Him home.
    And shout Him welcome to the skies.

Break off your tears, ye saints, and tell
    How high our great Deliverer reigns,
Sing how He spoiled the hosts of hell,
    And led the monster, death, in chains.
Say, 'Live for ever, wondrous King,
    Born to redeem, and strong to save;'
Then ask the monster, 'Where's thy sting?'
    And 'Where's thy victory, boasting grave?'

362   Norman Perry   10 4 10 4 10 10
For this God is our God for ever and ever: He will be our guide even unto death.
Psalm 48:14

Guide me safe home, I tremble in the way,
    Guide me safe home:
Without Thine aid O Lord I go astray,
    Guide me safe home:
Hold thou my hand through life's dark wilderness.
Without Thine aid, I falter in distress.

Guide me safe home, the way is known to Thee,
    Guide me safe home:
Life often rages like a trackless sea,
    Guide me safe home:
Thy word can hush the wildest winds to peace,
And cause the fierce and angry storms to cease.

Guide me safe home, the way is sure if Thou
    Guide me safe home:
For I am trusting, resting in Thee now,
    Guide me safe home:
Enduring to the end I shall be saved,
My name is ever on Thy heart engraved.

Guide me safe home, I trust in Thee alone,
    Guide me safe home:
The way and harbour both to Thee are known,
    Guide me safe home:
Home to the place where Christ my Saviour
    dwells,
And heaven's sweet music everlasting swells.

© Mrs R Westmacott

363   Philip Doddridge   LM
For this God is our God for ever and ever: He will be our guide even unto death.
Psalm 48:14

Great God, we sing that guiding hand,
By which supported still we stand;
The opening year Thy mercy shows,
Let mercy crown it till it close.

By day, by night, at home, abroad,
Still are we guarded by our God,
By His incessant bounty fed,
By His unerring counsel led.

With grateful hearts the past we own;
The future, all to us unknown,
We to Thy guardian care commit,
And peaceful leave before Thy feet.

In scenes exalted or depressed,
Be Thou our joy and Thou our rest;
Thy goodness all our hopes shall raise,
Adored through all our changing days.

When death shall interrupt these songs,
And seal in silence mortal tongues,
Our Helper, God, in whom we trust,
In better worlds our souls shall boast.

364   Francis Pott   85 85 843
Whoso offereth praise glorifieth Me.
Psalm 50:23

Angel voices ever singing
    Round Thy throne of light,
Angel harps for ever ringing,
    Rest not day nor night;
Thousands only live to bless Thee,
      And confess Thee
        Lord of might.

Thou who art beyond the farthest
    Mortal eye can scan,
Can it be that Thou regardest
    Songs of sinful man?
Can we know that Thou art near us
      And wilt hear us?
        Yes, we can.

Yes, we know that Thou rejoicest
    O'er each work of Thine;
Thou didst ears and hands and voices
    For Thy praise design;
Craftsman's art and music's measure
      For Thy pleasure
        All combine.

In Thy house, great God, we offer
Of Thine own to Thee,
And for Thine acceptance proffer,
All unworthily,
Hearts and minds and hands and voices
In our choicest
Psalmody.

Honour, glory, might, and merit
Thine shall ever be,
Father, Son, and Holy Spirit,
Blessed Trinity.
Of the best that Thou hast given
Earth and heaven
Render Thee.

365   Henry Lyte   CM
Psalm 49

Jehovah speaks, let man be awed,
And deep attention give;
Ye sinners, hear the way to God!
Ye dead, arise and live!

Trust not in earthly wealth and show,
Vain, vain are they to save;
Gold cannot buy release from woe,
Or ransom from the grave.

Worlds cannot reach the mighty price
Of one immortal soul;
No, Lord, Thy blood and sacrifice
Alone can make us whole.

In Thee be our salvation sure.
No other wealth we seek;
We're rich in Thee, however poor,
And strong, however weak.

366   Isaac Watts   CM
Psalm 50

The Lord, the Judge, before His throne,
Bids the whole earth draw nigh,
The nations near the rising sun,
And near the Western sky.

No more shall bold blasphemers say,
'Judgment will ne'er begin;'
No more abuse His long delay
To impudence and sin.

Throned on a cloud our God shall come,
Bright flames prepare His way:
Thunder and darkness, fire and storm,
Lead on the dreadful day.

Heaven from above His call shall hear,
Attending angels come,
And earth and hell shall know and fear
His justice and their doom.

367   John Bradford   LM
**Offer unto God thanksgiving; and pay Thy
vows unto the most High.**
Psalms 50:14

This day, O Lord, Thy servants meet,
And fall before Thy mercy-seat;
Our grateful thanks and praise we bring,
And of Thy mercies great we sing.

We bless Thy overruling hand
Which still protects this favoured land:
And, as a nation, we must own
Great things for us the Lord hath done.

The gospel word, from place to place,
Proclaims the sound of sovereign grace;
And thousands in this gospel day
The call of Zion's King obey.

Whatever course things here may take,
'Tis all, we know, for Zion's sake;
Thou hast declared Thy sovereign will
To set Thy King on Zion's hill.

In common bounties all may share,
Yet Israel is Thy special care;
Preserved in Christ, the chosen seed
In Him shall find a Friend indeed.

In heaven Thou hast prepared Thy throne,
And earth does Thy dominion own:
Angels Thy potent word obey,
And earthly kings confess Thy sway.

368   Isaac Watts (alt)   LM
Psalm 51

Show pity, Lord; O Lord, forgive;
Let a repenting rebel live;
Are not Thy mercies large and free?
May not a sinner trust in Thee?

My sins are great, but don't surpass
The power and glory of Thy grace;
Great God! Thy nature has no bound,
So let Thy pardoning love be found.

O wash my soul from every sin,
And make my guilty conscience clean;
Here on my heart the burden lies,
And past offences pain my eyes.

My lips with shame my sins confess,
Against Thy law, against Thy grace;
Lord, should Thy judgments grow severe,
I am condemned, but Thou art clear.

Yet save a trembling sinner, Lord,
Whose hope, still hovering round Thy word,
Would light on some sweet promise there,
Some sure support against despair.

369   Isaac Watts   CM
Psalm 51

O God of mercy, hear my call;
    My load of guilt remove;
Break down this separating wall,
    That bars me from Thy love.

Give me the presence of Thy grace,
    Then my rejoicing tongue
Shall speak aloud Thy righteousness,
    And make Thy praise my song.

No blood of goats, nor heifers slain
    For sin could e'er atone:
The death of Christ shall still remain
    Sufficient and alone.

A soul oppressed with sin's desert
    The Lord will ne'er despise;
A humble groan, a broken heart,
    Is our best sacrifice.

370   Vernon Higham   DSM
Against Thee, Thee only, have I sinned.
Psalm 51:4

    Against Thee have I sinned,
    Before the King divine
And all my evil is exposed
    Before my eyes and Thine.
    O hear me as I cry,
    Have mercy on my soul;
I come to Thee, O hear my sigh,
    Forgive and make me whole.

    There is no worthiness
    Within my broken heart,
My fallen nature, sore distress
    Shall surely be my part;
    Unless Thy grace lays hold
    With glorious truth to share
And grants me mercy to be bold
    When Thou hast shown Thy care.

    Create, O God, within
    A heart both pure and clean;
Restore my spirit, blot my sin
    And let me on Thee lean.
    Thy Holy Spirit give,
    O never take away!
And grant that He may in me live
    To give me joy this day.

    Thy presence is my light,
    Lord, never leave Thine own!
But fill my breast with pure delight
    That I am Thine alone.
    O take my lips this day,
    Thy wonders to proclaim,
To tell of Thy redeeming way,
    And magnify Thy fame.

    What dost Thou ask of me,
    What sacrifice to please?
For nothing in my hands can be
    Sufficient to appease.
    O look upon my heart,
    Now broken, Lord, by grace;
My contrite spirit will not part,
    I'll ever seek Thy face.

                              © *Author*

371   Philip Doddridge   SM
Against Thee, Thee only, have I sinned.
Psalm 51:4

    Once more we meet to pray,
    Once more our guilt confess;
Turn not, O Lord, Thine ear away
    From creatures in distress.

    Our sins to heaven ascend,
    And there for vengeance cry;
O God, behold the sinner's Friend,
    Who intercedes on high.

    Though we are vile indeed,
    And well deserve Thy curse,
The merits of Thy Son we plead,
    Who lived and died for us.

    Now let Thy bosom yearn,
    As it hath done before;
Return to us, O God, return,
    And ne'er forsake us more.

372   Isaac Watts   CM
Purge me with hyssop, and I shall be clean.
Psalm 51:7

How sad our state by nature is!
  Our sin how deep it stains!
And Satan binds our captive minds
  Fast in His slavish chains.

But there's a voice of sovereign grace
  Sounds from the sacred word—
Ho! ye despairing sinners, come,
  And trust upon the Lord.

My soul obeys the almighty call,
  And runs to this relief;
I would believe Thy promise, Lord;
  O help my unbelief!

To the dear fountain of Thy blood,
  Incarnate God, I fly;
Here let me wash my guilty soul
  From crimes of deepest dye.

A guilty, weak and helpless wretch,
  On Thy kind arms I fall;
Be Thou my strength and righteousness,
  My Jesus and my all.

373   John Stocker   77 77
Restore unto me the joy of Thy salvation.
Psalm 51:12

Gracious Spirit, Dove divine,
Let Thy light within me shine;
All my guilty fears remove,
With atoning blood and love.

Speak Thy pardoning grace to me;
Set the burdened sinner free;
Lead me to the Lamb of God;
Wash me in His precious blood.

Life and peace to me impart;
Seal salvation on my heart;
Breathe Thyself into my breast,
Earnest of immortal rest.

Let me never from Thee stray,
Keep me in the narrow way,
Fill my soul with joy divine,
Keep, me, Lord, for ever Thine.

374   Joseph Carlyle   CM
The sacrifices of God are a broken spirit.
Psalm 51:17

Lord, when we bend before Thy throne
  And our confessions pour,
Teach us to feel the sins we own
  And hate what we deplore.

Our broken spirits pitying see,
  True penitence impart;
Then let a kindling glance from Thee
  Beam hope upon the heart.

When we disclose our wants in prayer,
  May we our wills resign;
That not a thought may enter there
  Which is not wholly Thine.

May faith each weak petition fill
  And waft it to the skies,
And teach our hearts 'tis goodness still
  That grants it or denies.

375   Vernon Higham   CM
The sacrifices of God are a broken spirit.
Psalm 51:17

O tell me, Lord, what pleaseth Thee:
  Is there an offering meet?
For in my heart I long to see
  Thy smile of grace so sweet.

Search as I may in all my way
  And all my work and toil,
I cannot find a worthy day
  That sin has failed to soil.

This heart of mine with depths profound
  Yields disappointment keen,
And every effort I have found
  Has leaned to self and sin.

Then I beheld the purest One,
  With heart of love and peace,
Who shed His blood, a victory won,
  And floods of joy release.

My heart is broken at the sight
  Of such humility;
I stand amazed and bathe in light
  Of this new dignity.

Now I can see my life is vain,
   Contrition breaks my heart;
For now I know and feel the pain
   That sin and shame impart.

Yet in some strange and wondrous way
   This breaking pleaseth Thee;
For Thou wilt not despise or slay
   A holy sorrow's plea.

I feel Thy smile upon my face,
   And I rejoice to know
The blessèd bliss of Thine embrace
   In lifting one so low.

© Author

376   Henry Lyte   CM
Psalm 52

In vain the powers of darkness try
   To work the church's ill,
The Friend of sinners reigns on high,
   And checks them at His will.

Though mischief in their hearts may dwell,
   And on their tongues deceit,
A word of His their pride can quell.
   And all their aims defeat.

My trust is in His grace alone;
   His house shall be my home,
How sweet His mercies past to own,
   And hope for more to come.

377   Charles Spurgeon   CM
Psalm 53

The foes of Zion quake for fright,
   Where no fear was they quail;
For well they know that sword of might
   Which cuts through coats of mail.

The Lord of old defiled their shields,
   And laughed their spears to scorn;
Their bones lay scattered o'er the field,
   By dogs and vultures torn.

Let Zion's foes be filled with shame;
   Her sons are blessed of God;
Though scoffers now despise their name
   The Lord shall break the rod.

O would our God to Zion turn,
   God with salvation clad;
Then Judah's harps should music learn,
   And Israel be glad.

378   Henry Lyte   75 75 77
Psalm 54

Save me by Thy glorious name;
   Lord, that name is Love,
Help from Thee I humbly claim,
   Send it from above;
Hear, O hear my suppliant voice!
Hear, and bid my heart rejoice.

Foes to Christ and every good
   Fiercely throng on me;
Soon my soul must be subdued,
   Without aid from Thee:
But with Thee to make me strong,
Lord, they shall not triumph long.

Lo, He comes, He takes my part,
   All my struggles cease.
Rise in praise, my grateful heart.
   Bless the Prince of Peace.
God Himself has set me free,
God my worship ever be!

379   Robert Seagrave   76 76 77 76
**And I said, Oh that I had wings like a dove! for
then would I fly away, and be at rest.**
Psalm 55:6

Rise, my soul, and stretch thy wings,
   Thy better portion trace:
Rise from transitory things
   Toward heaven, thy native place.
Sun and moon and stars decay,
   Time shall soon this earth remove;
Rise, my soul, and haste away
   To seats prepared above.

Rivers to the ocean run,
   Nor stay in all their course;
Fire, ascending, seeks the sun;
   Both speed them to their source:
So a soul that's born of God
   Pants to view His glorious face,
Upward tends to His abode,
   To rest in His embrace.

Cease, ye pilgrims, cease to mourn;
   Press onward to the prize;
Soon our Saviour will return
   Triumphant in the skies:
Yet a season, and ye know
   Happy entrance will be given,
All our sorrows left below,
   And earth exchanged for heaven.

380 David Denham SM
**Cast thy burden upon the LORD, and He shall
sustain thee.** *Psalm 55:22*

Though sorrows cast thee down,
And sins thy soul oppress,
A precious Christ is on His throne,
To give His church redress.

On Him your burdens roll,
Who resteth in His love;
He'll cleanse, restore, and make you whole
And ever faithful prove.

He will His church maintain,
And all His words perform;
Her strength in weakness, ease in pain,
And refuge in the storm.

He will not suffer thee
From Him to be removed;
He cannot alter His decree,
Nor cast out one beloved.

Thy name is on His heart,
Of everlasting love;
In all thy griefs He bears a part,
And pleads for thee above.

Then roll thy cares on Him,
Plead His sufficient grace;
Since all who live in His esteem,
Shall dwell before His face.

381 Rowland Hill 77 77
**Cast thy burden upon the LORD, and He shall
sustain thee.** *Psalm 55:22*

Cast thy burden on the Lord;
Only lean upon His word;
Thou wilt soon have cause to bless
His eternal faithfulness.

He sustains thee by His hand;
He enables thee to stand;
Those whom Jesus once hath loved
From His grace are ne'er removed.

Human counsels come to nought;
That will stand which God hath wrought;
His compassion, love and power
Are the same for evermore.

Heaven and earth may pass away,
God's free grace shall not decay;
He hath promised to fulfil
All the pleasure of His will.

Jesus, Guardian of Thy flock,
Be Thyself our constant rock;
Make us, by Thy powerful hand,
Strong as Zion's mountain stand.

382 Isaac Watts CM
Psalm 56

God counts the sorrows of His saints,
Their groans affect His ears;
Thou hast a book for my complaints,
A bottle for my tears.

When to Thy throne I raise my cry.
The wicked fear and flee:
So swift is prayer to reach the sky;
So near is God to me.

In Thee, most holy, just and true,
I have reposed my trust;
Nor will I fear what man can do,
The offspring of the dust.

Thy solemn vows are on me, Lord;
Thou shalt receive my praise:
I'll sing, 'How faithful is Thy word;
How righteous all Thy ways!'

Thou hast secured my soul from death;
O set Thy prisoner free!
That heart and hand, and life and breath,
May be employed for Thee.

383 Charles Wesley 77 77 D
**In the shadow of Thy wings will I make my
refuge.** *Psalm 57:1*

Jesus Lover of my soul,
Let me to Thy bosom fly,
While the raging billows roll,
While the tempest still is high.
Hide me, O my Saviour, hide,
Till the storm of life is past;
Safe into the haven guide;
O receive my soul at last!

Other refuge have I none,
Hangs my helpless soul on Thee;
Leave, ah! leave me not alone;
Still support and comfort me.
All my trust on Thee is stayed;
All my help from Thee I bring;
Cover my defenceless head
With the shadow of Thy wing.

Thou, O Christ, art all I want;
  All in all in Thee I find;
Raise the fallen, cheer the faint,
  Heal the sick, and lead the blind.
Just and holy is Thy name;
  I am all unrighteousness;
Vile and full of sin I am;
  Thou art full of truth and grace.

Plenteous grace with Thee is found;
  Grace to pardon all my sin;
Let the healing streams abound;
  Make and keep me pure within.
Thou of life the Fountain art;
  Freely let me take of Thee;
Spring Thou up within my heart,
  Rise to all eternity.

384 Philip Doddridge   LM
My heart is fixed, O God, my heart is fixed: I will sing and give praise.
Psalm 57:7

O happy day that fixed my choice
  On Thee, my Saviour and my God!
Well may this glowing heart rejoice
  And tell its raptures all abroad.

O happy bond, that seals my vows
  To Him who merits all my love!
Let cheerful anthems fill His house,
  While to that sacred place I move.

'Tis done! the great transaction's done!
  I am my Lord's and He is mine;
He drew me and I followed on,
  Charmed to confess the voice divine.

Now rest, my long-divided heart,
  Fixed on this blissful centre, rest,
With ashes who would care to part,
  When called on angels' bread to feast?

High heaven that heard the solemn vow,
  That vow renewed shall daily hear;
Till in life's latest hour I bow
  And bless in death a bond so dear.

385 Thomas Kelly   87 87 47
My heart is fixed, O God, my heart is fixed: I will sing and give praise.
Psalm 57:7

Gracious Lord, my heart is fixèd,
  Sing I will, and sing of Thee,
Since the cup that justice mixèd,
  Thou hast drank, and drank for me:
    Great Deliverer!
  Thou hast set the prisoner free.

Many were the chains that bound me,
  But the Lord has loosed them all;
Arms of mercy now surround me.
  Favours these, nor few nor small:
    Saviour, keep me!
  Keep Thy servant lest he fall.

Fair the scene that lies before me,
  Life eternal Jesus gives;
While He waves His banner o'er me.
  Peace and joy my soul receives:
    Sure His promise!
  I shall live because He lives.

When the world would bid me leave Thee,
  Telling me of shame and loss,
Saviour, guard me, lest I grieve Thee,
  Lest I cease to love Thy cross:
    This is treasure!
  All the rest I count but dross.

386 Charles Spurgeon   LM
Psalm 58

Lord, make my conversation chaste,
  And all my understanding purge,
Lest with the wicked throng I haste
  And down to hell my pathway urge.

They from the womb are all estranged,
  The serpent's poison fills each vein,
They're not by wise persuasion changed,
  But like the adder deaf remain.

As lions' teeth the hunters break;
  As angry torrents soon are dry;
So shall Thy bow swift vengeance take
  Upon the proud who truth defy.

As melts the snail with slimy trail;
  As thorns consume in rapid blaze;
Before Thy wrath Thy foes shall fail,
  Thy whirlwinds shall their souls amaze.

387 William Allen 77 77
Psalm 59

I am hated, Lord, by those
  Who Thy holy truth despise;
Save me from my wicked foes,
  Lord of hosts, arise, arise!

Thou'rt my rock and my defence;
  Thou a tower unto Thy saints;
Thee I make my confidence,
  Thee I'll trust, though nature faints.

Glad Thy mercies will I sing,
  All Thy power and love confess;
Thou hast been, O heavenly King,
  My safe refuge in distress!

Songs with every morning's light,
  Lord, shall rise up to Thy throne;
All Thy saints shall praise Thy might,
  And Thy mercy shall make known.

388 Augustus Toplady CM
**But I will sing of Thy power; yea, I will sing
aloud of Thy mercy in the morning.**
Psalm 59:16

Kind Guardian of my sleeping hours!
  Accept the thanks I bring;
Beneath Thy smiles, my feeble powers
  Thy morning mercies sing.

Give me Thyself, the only good,
  And ever with me stay;
Whose faithful mercies are renewed
  With each returning day.

Ah! guide me with a Father's eye,
  Nor from my soul depart;
But let the Day-star from on high
  Illuminate my heart.

This day preserve me without sin,
  Unspotted in Thy ways;
And hear me, while I usher in
  The welcome morn with praise.

Far as the East from West remove
  Each earthly vain desire,
And raise me on the wings of love,
  O raise me daily higher.

Let all my words and all my ways
  Declare that I am Thine,
That so the light of truth and grace
  Before the world may shine.

389 Charles Spurgeon LM
Psalm 60

O God, Thou hast cast off Thy saints;
  Thy face Thou dost in anger hide.
And lo, Thy church for terror faints,
  While breaches all her walls divide!

Hard things Thou hast upon us laid,
  And made us drink most bitter wine;
But still Thy banner we've displayed,
  And borne aloft Thy truth divine.

Our courage fails not, though the night
  No earthly lamp avails to break.
For Thou wilt soon arise in might,
  And of our captors captives make.

Through Thee we shall most valiant prove,
  And tread the foe beneath our feet;
Through Thee our faith shall hills remove,
  And small as chaff the mountains beat.

390 William Horne LM
Lead me to the rock that is higher than I.
Psalm 61:2

O for a heart to seek my God,
Encouraged by His gracious word,
To view my Saviour all complete,
And lie submissive at His feet!

To Thee, almighty God, to Thee,
My Rock and Refuge, would I flee;
Now tides of sorrow, rolling high,
Appear to mingle earth and sky.

To see Thy saints in mourning clad,
And foes by their distress made glad,
O'erwhelms my soul with poignant grief;
Lord, send Thy servants sweet relief.

Though safe in Christ Thy saints abide,
Nor can their life be e'er destroyed;
While Thy dear cause is thus suppressed,
My burdened soul can take no rest.

Arise, O God, Thy cause defend;
Deliverance unto Zion send.
Arise, arise, O God of might,
And put Thy threatening foes to flight.

Pity Thy poor, dejected few;
Our souls revive, our strength renew;
Collect Thy scattered flock once more,
And open wide the gospel-door.

391   S J Griffith, tr. G Harrison   87 87 D
Lead me to the rock that is higher than I.
Psalm 61:2

Lead, Lord Jesus, my frail spirit
   To that Rock so strong and high,
Standing sure midst surging tempest,
   Safe when pounding waves are nigh:
In the Rock of Ages hiding,
   Come there flood or fiery blaze,
When the whole creation crumbles,
   Rock of Ages, Thee I'll praise.

When earth's rocks are cleft asunder
   By the terror of that day,
When, as cruel storms beat on them,
   Strong men cringe in fear away,
That sure Rock will still be standing,
   Midst the waters, midst the blaze;
There on heaven's eternal ocean,
   Rock of Ages, Thee I'll praise.

© *Mrs.Eluned Harrison*

392   Benjamin Beddome   CM
For Thou, O God, hast heard my vows.
Psalm 61:5

Witness ye men and angels now,
   Before the Lord we speak;
To Him we make our solemn vow,
   A vow we dare not break.

That long as life itself shall last
   Ourselves to Christ we yield;
Nor from His cause will we depart,
   Or ever quit the field.

We trust not in our native strength
   But on His grace rely,
That, with returning wants, the Lord
   Will all our need supply.

O guide our doubtful feet aright
   And keep us in Thy ways;
And while we turn our vows to prayers,
   Turn Thou our prayers to praise.

393   William Bennett   11 11 11 11
He only is my rock and my salvation.
Psalm 62:2

Convinced as a sinner, to Jesus I come,
Informed by the gospel for such there is room;
O'erwhelmèd with sorrow for sin, will I cry;
'Lead me to the Rock that is higher than I.'

O blessèd be Jesus, for answering prayer,
And raising my soul from the pit of despair;
In every new trial, to Him will I cry,
'Lead me to the Rock that is higher than I.'

The world, flesh, and Satan oft try to deceive,
And fain would persuade me my Saviour to leave;
But through His fresh succour, their power I defy;
Held fast to the Rock that is higher than I.

When sorely afflicted, and ready to faint,
Before my Redeemer I'll spread my complaint;
'Midst storms and distresses, my soul shall rely
On Jesus, the Rock that is higher than I.

The time will soon come when my journey will
      end;
And then, face to face, I shall see my best Friend:
For ever enjoy His blest presence on high,
And dwell in the Rock that is higher than I.

394   William Cushing
   11 11 11 11 + refrain
He only is my rock and my salvation.
Psalm 62:2

O safe to the Rock that is higher than I,
My soul in its conflicts and sorrows would fly,
So sinful, so weary, Thine, Thine would I be,
Thou blest Rock of Ages, I'm hiding in Thee!

   Hiding in Thee! hiding in Thee!
   Thou blest Rock of Ages, I'm hiding in Thee!

In the calm of the noontide, in sorrow's lone hour,
In times when the tempter casts o'er me His
      power;
In the tempests of life, on its wide heaving sea,
Thou blest Rock of Ages, I'm hiding in Thee!

How oft in the conflict, when pressed by the foe,
I have fled to my refuge, and breathed out my
      woe:
How often, when trials, like sea-billows roll,
Have I hidden in Thee, O Thou Rock of my soul!

395 Thomas Kelly   LM
He only is my rock and my salvation.
Psalm 62:2

Salvation is of God alone,
The glorious plan is all His own;
In love He formed the great design,
And here His grace and wisdom shine.

Salvation is of God alone;
One only victim could atone
For human guilt; that Victim He
Who claims with God equality.

Salvation is of God alone;
'Tis He who breaks the heart of stone,
Who makes self-righteousness to cease,
And gives the troubled conscience peace.

Salvation is of God alone;
'Tis He who leads His people on;
'Tis He who makes their burdens light,
And shields them in the day of fight.

Salvation is of God alone;
This truth let all His people own,
And to His name the praise be given
By saints on earth and saints in heaven!

396 William Gadsby (alt)   66 66 88
My soul, wait thou only upon God.
Psalm 62:5

What foolish folk are we!
    How prone to start aside,
And in our troubles flee
    From Jesus' wounded side;
To wait on self, or something base,
Instead of trusting sovereign grace!

O that our souls could wait
    At all times on the Lord;
And watch at wisdom's gate,
    Whose mercy will afford
A constant flow of every good,
To souls that trust alone in God.

The Lord is rich indeed,
    And richly will supply
The waiting sinner's need,
    With blessings from on high;
My expectation is from God;
Then wait, my soul, upon the Lord.

If darkness Him surround,
    His mercy's still the same;
He never will confound
    The soul that waits on Him;
He is my All; of Him I'll boast;
On Him I'll wait, and in Him trust.

397 John Berridge   66 66 88
Power belongeth unto God. *Psalm 62:11*

How sinners vaunt of power
    A ruined soul to save,
And count the fulsome store
    Of worth they seem to have,
And by such visionary props
Build up and bolster sandy hopes!

But God must work the will,
    And power to run the race;
And both through mercy still,
    A work of freest grace;
His own good pleasure, not our worth,
Brings all the will and power forth.

Disciples who are taught
    Their helplessness to feel,
Have no presumptuous thought,
    But work with care and skill;
Work with the means, and for this end,
That God the will and power may send.

They feel a daily need
    Of Jesus' gracious store,
And on His bounty feed,
    And yet are always poor;
No manna can they make or keep;
The Lord finds pasture for His sheep.

Renew, O Lord, my strength
    And vigour every day,
Or I shall tire at length,
    And faint upon the way;
No stock will keep upon my ground;
My all is in Thy storehouse found.

398 Henry Lyte   CM
Psalm 63

O God of love, my God Thou art;
    To Thee I early cry;
Refresh with grace my thirsty heart,
    For earthly springs are dry.

Thy power, Thy glory let me see,
    As seen by saints above;
'Tis sweeter, Lord, than life to me,
    To share and sing Thy love.

I freely yield Thee all my powers,
    Yet ne'er my debt can pay;
The thought of Thee at midnight hours
    Turns darkness into day.

Lord, Thou hast been my help, and Thou
    My refuge still shalt be;
Follow hard Thy footsteps now—
    O! when Thy face to see?

399   James Montgomery   LM
Psalm 63

O God, Thou art my God alone:
    Early to Thee my soul shall cry:
A pilgrim in a land unknown,
    A thirsty land, whose springs are dry.

O that it were as it hath been,
    When praying in the holy place,
Thy power and glory I have seen,
    And marked the footsteps of Thy grace.

Yet through this rough and thorny maze,
    I follow hard on Thee, my God:
Thy hand unseen upholds my ways;
    I safely tread where Thou hast trod.

Thee, in the watches of the night,
    When I remember on my bed,
Thy presence makes the darkness light,
    Thy guardian wings are round my head.

Better than life itself Thy love,
    Dearer than all beside to me;
For whom have I in heaven above.
    Or what on earth compared with Thee?

Praise with my heart, my mind, my voice,
    For all Thy mercy I will give;
My soul shall still In God rejoice;
    My tongue shall bless Thee while I live.

400   John Monsell   66 66
My soul thirsteth for Thee. *Psalm 63:1*

I hunger and I thirst;
    Jesus, my manna be;
Ye living waters, burst
    Out of the rock for me.

Thou bruised and broken Bread,
    My life-long wants supply;
As living souls are fed,
    O feed me, or I die.

Thou true life-giving Vine,
    Let me Thy sweetness prove;
Renew my life with Thine,
    Refresh my soul with love.

Rough paths my feet have trod,
    Since first their course began;
Feed me, Thou Bread of God;
    Help me, Thou Son of man.

For still the desert lies
    My fainting soul before
O living waters, rise
    Within me evermore.

401   Philip Doddridge   LM
Thou hast been my help. *Psalm 63:7*

My Helper, God! I bless His name,
Whose love for ever is the same;
The tokens of whose gracious care
Open, and crown, and close the year.

I midst ten thousand dangers stand,
Supported by His guardian hand,
And see, when I review my ways,
Ten thousand monuments of praise.

Thus far His arm hath led me on,
Thus far I make His mercy known;
And while I tread this desert land,
New mercies shall new songs demand.

My grateful soul, on Jordan's shore,
Shall raise one sacred pillar more;
Then bear in His bright courts above
Inscriptions of immortal love.

402   Henry Lyte   87 87
Psalm 64

Hear, O Lord, our supplication;
    Let our souls on Thee repose!
Be our refuge, our salvation,
    'Mid ten thousand threatening foes.

Lord, Thy saints have many troubles,
    In their path lies many a snare:
But before Thy breath, like bubbles,
    Melt they soon in idle air.

Cunning are the foe's devices,
    Bitter are his words of gall;
Sin on every side entices;
    Lord, conduct us safe through all.

Be our foes by Thee confounded,
    Let the world Thy goodness see,
While, by might and love surrounded,
    We rejoice, and trust in Thee.

403   Isaac Watts   CM
Psalm 65

Good is the Lord, the heavenly King,
  Who makes the earth His care;
Visits the pastures every spring.
  And bids the grass appear.

The clouds, like rivers, raised on high,
  Pour out at Thy command
Their watery blessings from the sky,
  To cheer the thirsty land.

The softened ridges of the field
  Permit the corn to spring;
The valleys rich provision yield,
  And the poor labourers sing.

The little hills on every side
  Rejoice at falling showers;
The meadows, dressed in all their pride.
  Perfume the air with flowers.

The various months Thy goodness crowns;
  How bounteous are Thy ways!
The bleating flocks spread o'er the downs,
  And shepherds shout Thy praise.

404   Samuel Medley   SM
Praise waiteth for Thee, O God, in Zion.
Psalm 65:1

Great God! before Thy throne
  We joyfully appear,
In songs to make Thy glories known,
  And thus begin the year.

What favours all divine;
  What mercies shall we share;
What blessings all around us shine
  To open this new year!

Indulgent goodness spares
  And still preserves us here,
And bounty all divine prepares
  Supplies for this new year.

Our follies past forgive;
  Our souls divinely cheer:
And help us more to Thee to live,
  Dear Lord, in this new year.

Prepare us for Thy will,
  Whatever may appear;
And let Thy loving-kindness still
  Preserve us through the year.

Confirm our souls in Thee,
  In faith and holy fear;
And let a precious Jesus be
  Our song through all the year.

405   John Newton   SM
We shall be satisfied with the goodness of thy house. *Psalm 65:4*

Hungry and faint, and poor,
  Behold us, Lord, again,
Assembled at Thy mercy's door,
  Thy bounty to obtain!

Thy word invites us nigh,
  Or we must starve indeed;
For we no money have to buy,
  Nor righteousness to plead.

The food our spirits want,
  Thy hand alone can give;
O hear the prayer of faith, and grant
  That we may eat and live!

406   Ellen Felkin   87 87 D + refrain
Thou crownest the year with Thy goodness.
Psalm 65:11

Now the year is crowned with blessing
  As we gather in the grain;
And, our grateful thanks expressing,
  Loud we raise a joyous strain.
Bygone days of toil and sadness
  Cannot now our peace destroy;
For the hills are clothed with gladness,
  And the valleys shout for joy.

    To the Lord their first-fruits bringing,
      All His thankful people come,
    To the Father praises singing
      For the joy of harvest home.

In the spring the smiling meadows
  Donned their robes of living green,
As the sunshine chased the shadows
  Swiftly o'er the changing scene;
In the summer-time the story
  Of a riper hope was told;
Then the rich autumnal glory
  Decked the fields in cloth of gold.

Shall not we, whose hearts are swelling
  With the thought of former days,
Sing a joyous song foretelling
  Future gladness, fuller praise?
For the cloud the bow retaineth
  With its covenant of peace,
That, as long as earth remaineth,
  Harvest-time shall never cease.

407 David Denham CM
Thou crownest the year with Thy goodness.
Psalm 65:11

'Tis by Jehovah's sovereign grace,
  His counsel and His care,
We've been preserved in every place,
  Throughout another year.

Though oft cast down, but not destroyed,
  God has been always near;
His glorious arm has been employed
  For us all through the year.

His wondrous love and faithful word
  In all things are made dear;
And the great goodness of the Lord
  Closes and crowns the year.

408 Isaac Watts CM
Psalm 66

Sing, all ye nations to the Lord,
  Sing with a joyful noise;
With melody of sound record
  His honours and your joys.

Say to the power that shakes the sky,
  How terrible art Thou!
Sinners before Thy presence fly,
  Or at Thy feet they bow.

O bless our God and never cease,
  Ye saints, fulfil His praise;
He keeps our life, maintains our peace,
  And guides our doubtful ways.

Lord, Thou hast proved our suffering souls
  To make our graces shine;
So silver bears the burning coals,
  The metal to refine.

Through watery deeps and fiery ways
  We march at Thy command;
Led to possess the promised place
  By Thine unerring hand.

GEORGE HERBERT 1593-1633

409 George Herbert Irregular
**All the earth shall worship Thee, and shall sing
unto Thee.** *Psalm 66:4*

Let all the world in every corner sing,
  'My God and King!'
  The heavens are not too high,
  His praise may thither fly:
  The earth is not too low;
  His praises there may grow.
Let all the world in every corner sing,
  'My God and King!'

Let all the world in every corner sing,
  'My God and King!'
  The church with psalms must shout,
  No door can keep them out:
  But, above all, the heart
  Must bear the longest part.
Let all the world in every corner sing,
  'My God and King!'

410 Henry Lyte 77 77 77
Psalm 67

God of mercy! God of grace!
Show the brightness of Thy face;
Shine upon us, Saviour shine,
Fill Thy church with light divine;
And Thy saving health extend
Unto earth's remotest end.

Let the people praise Thee, Lord;
Be by all that live adored;
Let the nations shout and sing
Glory to their Saviour King;
At Thy feet their tribute pay,
And Thy holy will obey.

Let the people praise Thee, Lord;
Earth shall then her fruits afford;
God to man His blessing give;
Man to God devoted live;
All below, and all above,
One in joy and light and love.

411   Timothy Dudley-Smith   77 77
Psalm 67

Mercy, blessing, favour, grace,
   Saving power to us be shown;
Brightness of the Father's face
   To the nations now be known.

Shout in triumph, sing in praise!
   Peoples all, proclaim His worth:
Just and righteous are His ways,
   Sovereign Lord of all the earth.

Harvests year by year proclaim
   Blessings new in plenty poured;
All the earth shall fear His name,
   All His people praise the Lord.

412   Charlotte Elliott   LM
God be merciful unto us, and bless us; and cause His face to shine upon us; Selah.
Psalm 67:1

Thou glorious Sun of Righteousness,
   Risen on high to set no more,
Shine on us now, to heal and bless,
   With brighter beams than e'er before.

Shine on Thy work of grace within,
   On each celestial blossom there;
O, crush each bitter root of sin,
   And make Thy garden fresh and fair!

Shine on Thy pure, eternal word,
   Its mysteries to our souls reveal;
And whether read, remembered, heard,
   O let it quicken, strengthen, heal!

Shine on the temples of Thy grace,
   In holy robes Thy priests be clad;
Unveil the brightness of Thy face,
   And make Thy chosen people glad.

Shine, till Thy glorious beams shall chase
   The brooding cloud from every eye!
Till every heart Thy dwelling-place
   Shall hail the Dayspring from on high!

Shine on, shine on, eternal Sun!
   Pour richer floods of life and light,
Till that bright Sabbath be begun,
   That glorious day which knows no night.

413   Edward Welch   76 76 (iambic)
Then shall the earth yield her increase; and God, even our own God, shall bless us.
Psalm 67:6

We lift our hearts, O Father,
   To Thee our voices raise
For these Thy suppliant servants
   In mingled prayer and praise:

Praise for the joy of loving,
   All other joys above,
Praise for the priceless blessing
   Of love's response to love;

Prayer that the glad surrender
   Of self may perfect be,
That each be one with other
   And both be one in Thee;

Prayer that Thou wilt accomplish
   The promise of today
And crown the years with blessing
   That shall not pass away.

414   *Scottish Psalter 1650*   CM
Psalm 68 part 1

Let God arise, and scatterèd
   Let all His enemies be;
And let all those that do Him hate
   Before His presence flee.

As smoke is driven so drive Thou them;
   As fire melts wax away,
Before God's face let wicked men
   So perish and decay.

But let the righteous all be glad:
   Let them before God's sight
Be very joyful; yea, let them
   Rejoice with all their might.

To God sing praise, to God sing praise:
   Extol Him with your voice,
He rides on heaven, by His name JAH,
   Before His face rejoice.

415   Harriet Auber   77 77 D
Psalm 68 part 2

As Thy chosen people, Lord,
   Once oppressed, in numbers few,
Trusted to Thy steadfast word,
   And a mighty nation grew;
So Thy church on earth begun.
   By Thy blessing shall increase,
While the course of time shall run,
   Till Messiah's reign of peace.

Soon shall every scattered tribe
To her bosom be restored;
Every heart and tongue ascribe
Praise and glory to the Lord;
Militant awhile below
Rest and joy shall soon be given;
Then in rapturous strains shall flow
Her triumphant song in heaven.

416   Isaac Watts   LM
Psalm 68 part 3

Kingdoms and thrones to God belong,
Crown Him, ye nations, in your song:
His wondrous names and powers rehearse;
His honours shall enrich your verse.

Proclaim Him King, pronounce Him blessed;
He's your defence, your joy, your rest;
When terrors rise and nations faint,
God is the strength of every saint.

417   Philip Doddridge   CM
Thou wentest forth before Thy people.
Psalm 68:7

My soul, triumphant in the Lord,
Shall tell its joys abroad;
And march with holy vigour on,
Supported by its God.

Through all the winding maze of life,
His hand hath been my guide;
And in that long-experienced care,
My heart shall still confide.

His grace through all the desert flows,
An unexhausted stream:
That grace on Zion's sacred mount
Shall be my endless theme.

Beyond the choicest joys of earth
These distant courts I love;
But O I burn with strong desire
To view Thy house above!

Mingled with all the shining band,
My soul would there adore;
A pillar in Thy temple fixed,
To be removed no more.

418   Joseph Hart   87 87 D
O God, hast prepared of Thy goodness for the poor. *Psalm 68:10*

O how good our gracious God is!
What rich feasts does He provide!
Bread and wine to feed our bodies;
But much more is signified:
All His sheep (amazing wonder!)
Feeds He with His flesh and blood;
Where's the power can ever sunder
Souls united thus to God?

When we take the sacred symbols
Of His body, bread and wine;
While the heart relents and trembles,
We rejoice with joy divine;
Jesus makes the weakest able,
Feeds us with His flesh and blood;
Needy beggars at His table
Are the welcome guests of God.

Cease thy fears, then, weak believer;
Jesus Christ is still the same,
Yesterday, today, for ever,
Saviour is His unctuous name;
Lowliness of heart, and meekness
To the bleeding Lamb belong;
Trust to Him, and by thy weakness
Thou shalt prove that Christ is strong.

419   Emma Toke   SM
Thou hast ascended on high, Thou hast led captivity captive. *Psalm 68:18*

Thou art gone up on high!
Triumphant o'er the grave,
And captive led captivity,
Thy ransomed ones to save.

Thou art gone up on high,
To mansions in the skies;
And round Thy throne unceasingly
The songs of praise arise.

Thou art gone up on high:
But Thou didst first come down,
Through earth's most bitter agony
To pass unto Thy crown;

Thou art gone up on high;
But Thou shalt come again.
With all the bright ones of the sky
Attendant in Thy train.

O! by Thy saving power,
So make us live and die,
That we may stand, in that dread hour,
At Thy right hand on high!

420   Henry Lyte   CM
Psalm 69

Lord, I would stand with thoughtful eye
  Beneath Thy fatal tree,
And see Thee bleed, and see Thee die,
  And think, 'What love to me!'

Dwell on the sight, my stony heart,
  Till every pulse within
Shall into contrite sorrow start,
  And hate the thought of sin.

Didst Thou for me, my Saviour, brave
  The scoff, the scourge, the gall,
The nails, the thorns, the spear, the grave,
  While I deserved them all?

O help me some return to make,
  To yield my heart to Thee,
And do and suffer for Thy sake
  As Thou didst then for me.

421   Henry Fowler   LM
Your heart shall live that seek God.
Psalm 69:32

'Seek ye My face,' the Saviour cries;
My soul, where canst thou find supplies
But in the Lamb, for sinners slain,
Who has not shed His blood in vain?

Does bitter anguish fill thy heart,
And make thee from the promise start?
Does Satan tempt thee to give up,
No more in Jesus' name to hope?

Art thou afflicted, sore distressed,
Embarrassed and by guilt oppressed?
Anxious to know thy sins forgiven,
And find an open way to heaven?

Thou shalt obtain the blessing yet;
Jesus will not thy cries forget;
Wait on the Lord, take courage still;
His promise surely He'll fulfil.

422   Charles Spurgeon   LM
Psalm 70

Make haste, O God, my soul to bless!
  My help and my deliverer Thou;
Make haste, for I'm in deep distress,
  My case is urgent; help me now.

Make haste, O God, make haste to save!
  For time is short, and death is nigh;
Make haste ere yet I'm in my grave,
  And with the lost for ever lie.

Make haste, O God, and hear my cries
  Then with the souls who seek Thy face
And those who Thy salvation prize,
  I'll magnify Thy matchless grace.

423   Isaac Watts   CM
Psalm 71

My Saviour, my almighty Friend,
  When I begin Thy praise,
Where will the growing numbers end,
  The numbers of Thy grace?

Thou art my everlasting trust;
  Thy goodness I adore;
And since I knew Thy graces first,
  I speak Thy glories more.

My feet shall travel all the length
  Of the celestial road;
And march with courage in Thy strength,
  To see my Father God.

When I am filled with sore distress
  For some surprising sin,
I'll plead Thy perfect righteousness,
  And mention none but Thine.

How will my lips rejoice to tell
  The victories of my King!
My soul redeemed from sin and hell,
  Shall Thy salvation sing.

Awake, awake, my tuneful powers;
  With this delightful song
I'll entertain the darkest hours,
  Nor think the season long.

424   Frances Havergal   85 83
In Thee, O LORD, do I put my trust.
Psalm 71:1

I am trusting Thee, Lord Jesus,
  Trusting only Thee!
Trusting Thee for full salvation,
  Great and free.

I am trusting Thee for pardon,
  At Thy feet I bow;
For Thy grace and tender mercy,
  Trusting now.

I am trusting Thee for cleansing,
  In the crimson flood;
Trusting Thee to make me holy,
  By Thy blood.

I am trusting Thee to guide me,
　Thou alone shalt lead;
Every day and hour supplying
　　All my need.

I am trusting Thee for power;
　Thine can never fail;
Words which Thou Thyself shalt give me
　　Must prevail.

I am trusting Thee, Lord Jesus;
　Never let me fall;
I am trusting Thee for ever
　　And for all.

425　Henry Lyte　　　　　　　SM
In Thee, O LORD, do I put my trust.
Psalm 71:1

My spirit on Thy care,
　Blest Saviour, I recline;
Thou wilt not leave me to despair,
　For Thou art Love divine.

In Thee I place my trust,
　On Thee I calmly rest;
I know Thee good, I know Thee just,
　And count Thy choice the best.

Whate'er events betide,
　Thy will they all perform;
Safe in Thy breast my head I hide,
　Nor fear the coming storm.

Let good or ill befall,
　It must be good for me;
Secure of having Thee in all,
　Of having all in Thee.

426　John Bailey　　　　　76 76 D
I am as a wonder unto many. *Psalm 71:7*

By night I sometimes wonder,
　And wonder oft by day;
I wonder now, and wonder
　Shall, while on earth I stay
'Twill be a pleasing wonder,
　When I shall safely come
Through every storm to Zion,
　My peaceful, happy home.

Yes, earth and heaven will wonder
　That I the conquest gain,
After so often groaning,
　Half dead among the slain;
'Twill be an endless wonder
　That I should safe arrive,
Through seas of tribulation,
　To Canaan's land alive.

The saints will greatly wonder.
　And shout the victor's song;
And I, the greatest wonder,
　There singing in the throng:
A wonder above wonders,
　To see one black as I,
White, without spot or blemish,
　Among the host on high.

427　Richard Burnham　　　　LM
Cast me not off in the time of old age.
Psalm 71:9

Ne'er was a sinner cast away
Whom the Redeemer taught to pray;
He loves such souls by far too well,
Than e'er to cast them down to hell.

Come, praying soul, thy God draws near,
And listens to each broken prayer;
Pleased, He attends thy every groan,
And soon in mercy will come down.

He ne'er was known to disappoint
A praying, waiting, humble saint;
But such a soul He'll ever bless
With all the glories of His grace.

428　William Hurn　　　　　CM
But I will hope continually. *Psalm 71:14*

Hope is the anchor of the soul,
　A grace of heavenly birth;
When tempests rage and billows roll,
　We learn its use and worth.

Our strength and fortitude may droop,
　And refuge seem to fail;
But we are still upheld by hope,
　Which looks within the veil.

When heavier storms assail us here,
　And darken all our way,
Hope sees the distant skies are clear,
　And waits a glorious day.

In all our troubles may we wait,
　And meekly kiss the rod;
Deliverance never comes too late
　To those who hope in God.

429   John Cennick   10 10 11 11
I will also praise Thee with the psaltery.
Psalm 71:22

Our Saviour alone, the Lord, let us bless,
Who reigns on His throne, the Prince of our
    peace;
Who evermore saves us by shedding His blood;
All hail, holy Jesus! our Lord and our God.

We thankfully sing Thy glory and praise,
Thou merciful Spring of pity and grace;
Thy kindness for ever to men we will tell,
And say, our dear Saviour redeemed us from hell.

Preserve us in love, while here we abide;
O never remove Thy presence, nor hide
Thy glorious salvation, till each of us see,
With joy, the blessed vision completed in Thee.

430   Isaac Watts   LM
Psalm 72

Jesus shall reign where'er the sun
Doth His successive journeys run;
His kingdom stretch from shore to shore,
Till moons shall wax and wane no more.

For Him shall endless prayer be made,
And princes throng to crown His head;
His name like sweet perfume shall rise
With every morning sacrifice.

People and realms of every tongue
Dwell on His love with sweetest song;
And infant voices shall proclaim
Their early blessings on His name.

Blessings abound where'er He reigns,
The prisoner leaps to loose His chains;
The weary find eternal rest,
And all the sons of want are blessed.

Where He displays His healing power,
Death and the curse are known no more;
In Him the tribes of Adam boast
More blessings than their father lost.

Let every creature rise and bring
Peculiar honours to our King;
Angels descend with songs again,
And earth repeat the loud Amen.

431   James Montgomery   76 76 D
He shall judge Thy people with righteousness.
Psalm 72:2

Hail to the Lord's Anointed,
    Great David's greater Son!
Hail, in the time appointed,
    His reign on earth begun!
He comes to break oppression,
    To set the captive free,
To take away trangression,
    And rule in equity.

He shall come down like showers
    Upon the fruitful earth,
And love, joy, hope, like flowers,
    Spring in His path to birth:
Before Him on the mountains
    Shall peace, the herald, go;
And righteousness, in fountains,
    From hill to valley flow.

Kings shall fall down before Him,
    And gold and incense bring;
All nations shall adore Him,
    His praise all people sing;
To Him shall prayer unceasing
    And daily vows ascend;
His kingdom still increasing,
    A kingdom without end.

He comes with succour speedy
    To those who suffer wrong;
To help the poor and needy,
    And bid the weak be strong;
To give them songs for sighing,
    Their darkness turn to light,
Whose souls, condemned and dying,
    Were precious in His sight.

O'er every foe victorious,
    He on His throne shall rest;
From age to age more glorious,
    All-blessing and all-blest:
The tide of time shall never
    His covenant remove;
His name shall stand for ever,
    His changeless name of Love.

432   German 18th Cent, tr. E Caswall   66 6 D
Daily shall He be praised. *Psalm 72:15*

When morning gilds the skies,
My heart awaking cries,
    'May Jesus Christ be praised!'
Alike at work and prayer
To Jesus I repair:
    May Jesus Christ be praised.

When sleep her balm denies,
My silent spirit sighs,
    'May Jesus Christ be praised!'
When evil thoughts molest,
With this I shield my breast,
    May Jesus Christ be praised.

In heaven's eternal bliss
The loveliest strain is this,
    May Jesus Christ be praised!
The powers of darkness fear
When this sweet chant they hear,
    May Jesus Christ be praised!

Let earth's wide circle round
In joyful notes resound,
    May Jesus Christ be praised!
Let air and sea and sky,
From depth to height, reply,
    May Jesus Christ be praised!

Be this, while life is mine,
My canticle divine,
    May Jesus Christ be praised!
Be this the eternal song,
Through all the ages long,
    May Jesus Christ be praised!

433   Joseph Swain   LM
Daily shall He be praised. *Psalm 72:15*

Praise your Redeemer, praise His name,
    Ye saints who live upon His grace;
Praise Him whose love remains the same
    Through every change of time and place.

Praise Him who opens mercy's door,
    To welcome every seeking soul;
Who gives salvation to the poor.
    And makes the wounded conscience whole.

Praise Him who came from heaven to bring
    Glad tidings of salvation down;
Praise Him, for you have cause to sing
    Who hope for an immortal crown.

Praise Him who loved you on the cross,
    Praise Him who loved you on His throne.
Praise Him who turns to gain your loss,
    And makes your crosses prove your crown.

Praise Him who loved you long before
    The wheels of time began to move;
Whose love, when time shall be no more,
    Will still be everlasting love.

434   David Denham   87 87
**Blessed be the LORD God, the God of Israel,
who only doeth wondrous things.** *Psalm 72:18*

O Thou wondrous Lord of glory!
    Self-existent, great I AM!
Let each ransomed soul adore Thee,
    Through our gracious Lord the Lamb.

Wondrous in Thy vast perfections,
    Which in all Thy works appear;
Wondrous in Thy grace relations,
    To Thy church for ever dear.

Wondrous love in God's Anointed,
    Brought Him from His heavenly throne!
At the time His grace appointed
    For His children to atone.

Wondrous blood to heal the wounded,
    Lepers cleanse, and captives free;
Wondrous righteousness imputed
    To the guilty, e'en to me!

Wondrous fulness ever flowing
    In ten thousand streams of love,
To refresh the saints while going
    To their Father's house above.

Wondrous theme of revelation;
    Wondrous Christ, Thy people's All!
We possess, in Thy salvation,
    Grace from which we cannot fall.

Wondrous love was fixed upon us!
    Wondrous wisdom made it known!
Wondrous mercy still supports us!
    Wondrous glory waits to crown!

435 Isaac Watts   LM
Psalm 73 part 1

Lord, what a thoughtless wretch was I,
  To mourn, and murmur, and repine,
To see the wicked placed on high,
  In pride and robes of honour shine.

But, O their end! their dreadful end!
  Thy sanctuary taught me so:
On slippery rocks I see them stand,
  And fiery billows roll below.

Now let them boast how tall they rise,
  I'll never envy them again:
There they may stand with haughty eyes,
  Till they plunge deep In endless pain.

Their fancied joys, how fast they flee!
  Just like a dream when man awakes:
Their songs of softest harmony
  Are but a preface to their plagues.

Now I esteem their mirth and wine
  Too dear to purchase with my blood;
Lord, 'tis enough that Thou art mine;
  My life, my portion, and my God.

436 Isaac Watts   CM
Psalm 73 part 2

God my supporter and my hope,
  My help for ever near,
Thine arm of mercy held me up,
  When sinking in despair.

Thy counsels, Lord, shall guide my feet
  Through this dark wilderness;
Thy hand conduct me near Thy seat,
  To dwell before Thy face.

Were I In heaven without my God
  'Twould be no joy to me:
And whilst this earth is mine abode,
  I long for none but Thee.

What if the springs of life were broke,
  And flesh and heart should faint?
God is my soul's eternal Rock,
  The strength of every saint.

Still to draw near to Thee, my God,
  Shall be my sweet employ;
My tongue shall sound Thy works abroad.
  And tell the world my joy.

437 Harriet Auber   CM
Psalm 73 part 3

Whom have we, Lord, in heaven but Thee
  And whom on earth beside;
Where else for succour shall we flee,
  Or in whose strength confide?

Thou art our portion here below,
  Our promised bliss above;
Ne'er can our souls an object know
  So precious as Thy love.

When heart and flesh, O Lord, shall fail,
  Thou wilt our spirits cheer;
Support us through life's thorny vale,
  And calm each anxious fear.

Yes, Thou, our only Guide through life,
  Shalt help and strength supply;
Support us in death's fearful strife,
  Then welcome us on high.

438 David Denham   11 11 11 11
And afterward receive me to glory.
Psalm 73:24

Mid scenes of confusion and creature complaints,
How sweet to my soul is communion with saints;
To find at the banquet of mercy there's room,
And feel in the presence of Jesus at home!

Sweet bonds that unite all the children of peace,
And thrice precious Jesus, whose love cannot
  cease;
Though oft from Thy presence in sadness I roam,
I long to behold Thee, in glory, at home!

I sigh from this body of sin to be free,
Which hinders my joy and communion with Thee;
Though now my temptations like billows may
  foam,
All, all will be peace when I'm with Thee at home!

While here in the valley of conflict I stay,
O, give me submission and strength as my day!
In all my afflictions to Thee would I come,
Rejoicing in hope of my glorious home.

Whate'er Thou deniest, O give me Thy grace!
The Spirit's true witness, and smiles of Thy face;
Indulge me with patience to wait at Thy throne,
And find, even now, a sweet foretaste of home.

I long, dearest Lord, in Thy beauties to shine,
No more as an exile in sorrow to pine:
But in Thy fair image arise from the tomb,
With glorified millions to praise Thee, at home!

439   Isaac Watts   CM
Whom have I in heaven but Thee?
Psalm 73:25

My God, my Portion, and my Love,
  My everlasting All,
I've none but Thee in heaven above,
  Or on this earthly ball.

To Thee we owe our wealth, and friends,
  And health, and safe abode;
Thanks to Thy name for meaner things,
  But they are not my God.

How vain a toy is glittering wealth,
  If once compared to Thee!
Or what's my safety or my health,
  Or all my friends to me?

Let others stretch their arms like seas,
  And grasp in all the shore;
Grant me the visits of Thy face,
  And I desire no more.

440   Charles Wesley   77 77
Whom have I in heaven but Thee?
Psalm 73:25

Jesus, all-atoning Lamb,
Thine, and only Thine, I am:
Take my body, spirit, soul;
Only Thou possess the whole.

Thou my one thing needful be;
Let me ever cleave to Thee;
Let me choose the better part;
Let me give Thee all my heart.

Fairer than the sons of men,
Do not let me turn again,
Leave the fountain-head of bliss,
Stoop to creature-happiness.

Whom have I on earth below?
Thee, and only Thee, I know;
Whom have I in heaven but Thee?
Thou art all in all to me.

All my treasure is above,
All my riches is Thy love:
Who the worth of love can tell?
Infinite, unsearchable.

441   Samuel Medley   LM
Whom have I in heaven but Thee?
Psalm 73:25

Jesus my Lord, my Life, my All,
Prostrate before Thy throne I fall;
Fain would my soul look up and see
My hope, my heaven, my all in Thee.

In vain from creatures help I seek;
Thou, only Thou, the word canst speak
To heal my wounds, and calm my grief,
Or give my mourning heart relief.

Without Thy peace and presence, Lord,
Not all the world can help afford.
O do not frown my soul away,
But smile my darkness into day.

I long to hear Thy pardoning voice;
O speak, and bid my soul rejoice;
Say, 'Peace, be still; look up and live;
Life, peace, and heaven are Mine to give.'

Then, filled with grateful, holy love,
My soul in praise would soar above;
And with delightful joy record
The wondrous goodness of the Lord.

442   H L Nicholson   LM
My flesh and my heart faileth: but God is the strength of my heart, and my portion for ever.
Psalm 73:26

In Christ, I've all my soul's desire;
His Spirit doth my heart inspire
With boundless wishes large and high,
And Christ will all my wants supply.

Christ is my Hope, my Strength, and Guide,
For me He bled, and groaned and died;
He is my Sun, to give me light.
He is my soul's supreme delight.

Christ is the source of all my bliss,
My Wisdom and my Righteousness;
My Saviour, Brother, and my Friend,
On Him alone I now depend.

Christ is my King, to rule and bless,
And all my troubles to redress;
He's my salvation, and my all,
Whate'er on earth shall me befall.

Christ is my strength and portion too,
My soul in Him can all things do;
Through Him I'll triumph o'er the grave,
And death and hell my soul outbrave.

443   Harriet Auber   886 D
Psalm 75

That Thou, O Lord, art ever nigh,
Though veiled in awesome majesty,
  Thy mighty works declare;
Thy hand this earthly frame upholds,
Thine eye the universe beholds
  With providential care.

Thou settest up, and pullest down;
To Thee the monarch owes His crown,
  The conqueror His wreath;
In Thee all creatures live and move;
Thou reign'st supreme In heaven above,
  And in the earth beneath.

Great King of kings, and Lord of lords,
Whose hand chastises and rewards,
  Thee only we adore;
To Thee the voice of praise shall rise,
In hallelujahs to the skies,
  When time shall be no more.

444   Henry Lyte   SM
Psalm 76

  God in His church is known,
  His name is glorious there;
He there sets up His earthly throne,
  And hears His people's prayer.

  The powers of death and hell
  In vain her peace oppose;
A word of His the storm can quell,
  And scatter all her foes.

  The Lord to judgment came;
  Earth trembled and was still;
'Tis His, 'tis His, the proud to tame,
  And shield the meek from ill.

  The fury of His foes
  Fulfils but His decree:
Ye saints, on Him your hopes repose,
  And He your strength will be.

445   Nahum Tate, Nicholas Brady   CM
Psalm 77

Will God for ever cast us off;
  His love return no more?
His promise, will it never give
  Its comfort as before?

Can His abundant love forget
  Its wonted aids to bring?
Has He in wrath shut up and sealed
  His mercy's healing spring?

I'll call to mind His works of old,
  The wonders of His might:
On them my heart shall meditate,
  Them shall my tongue recite.

Thy people, Lord, long since have Thee
  A God of wonders found:
Long since hast Thou Thy chosen seed
  With strong deliverance crowned.

446   Augustus Toplady   88 88 D
Will the Lord cast off for ever?
Psalm 77:7

Encompassed with clouds of distress,
  And tempted all hope to resign,
I pant for the light of Thy face,
  That I in Thy beauty may shine.
Disheartened with waiting so long,
  I sink at Thy feet with my load;
All plaintive I pour out my song,
  And stretch forth my hands unto God.

Shine, Lord, and my terror shall cease;
  The blood of atonement apply;
And lead me to Jesus for peace,
  The Rock that is higher than I
Speak, Saviour, for sweet is Thy voice;
  Thy presence is fair to behold;
I thirst for Thy Spirit, with cries
  And groanings that cannot be told.

If sometimes I strive, as I mourn,
  My hold of Thy promise to keep,
The billows more fiercely return,
  And plunge me again in the deep.
While harassed and cast from Thy sight,
  The tempter suggests with a roar,
'The Lord has forsaken Thee quite;
  Thy God will be gracious no more.'

Yet, Lord, if Thy love has designed
  No covenant blessing for me,
Ah! tell me, how is it I find
  Some sweetness in waiting for Thee?
Almighty to rescue Thou art,
  Thy grace is immortal and free;
Lord, succour and comfort my heart,
  And make me live wholly to Thee.

WILLIAM WILLIAMS 1717-91

447 William Williams, tr. P Williams 87 87 47
And He led them on safely, so that they feared not. *Psalm 78:53*

Guide me, O Thou great Jehovah!
  Pilgrim through this barren land;
I am weak, but Thou art mighty;
  Hold me with Thy powerful hand;
    Bread of heaven,
Feed me now and evermore.

Open Thou the crystal fountain,
  Whence the healing streams do flow;
Let the fiery, cloudy pillar
  Lead me all my journey through;
    Strong Deliverer,
Be Thou still my strength and shield.

When I tread the verge of Jordan,
  Bid my anxious fears subside;
Death of deaths, and hell's destruction,
  Land me safe on Canaan's side;
    Songs of praises,
I will ever give to Thee.

448 William Goode   SM
Psalm 79

  Thou gracious God, and kind,
  O cast our sins away;
Nor call our former guilt to mind,
  Thy justice to display.

  Thy tenderest mercies show,
  Thy richest grace prepare,
Ere yet, with guilty fears laid low,
  We perish in despair.

  Save us from guilt and shame,
  Thy glory to display;
And for the great Redeemer's name,
  Wash all our sins away.

So we Thy flock, Thy choice,
  The people of Thy love,
Through life shall in Thy care rejoice;
  But praise Thee best above.

449 Vernon Higham   8 10 10 4
Turn us again, O God, and cause Thy face to shine; and we shall be saved. *Psalm 80:3*

Turn us again, Shepherd Divine;
Cherubim praise and heaven declares Thy name:
Name of our Lord and name to us most dear;
  Kindle a flame.

Kindle a flame, within the hearts,
Stir us to seek and turn to God again:
O let Thy grace draw forth our souls to Thee,
  Thy name to claim.

Teach us to weep for godly gifts;
Tears in great measure grant to us today:
Tasting the bread, the sorrows of the Head,
  Whom men did slay.

O bless the fruit for it is Thine,
Pour forth Thy presence, see our cruel foes;
Stir up Thy strength and come, O come O Lord!
  Remove our woes.

Jerusalem is desolate,
Yet once was full with glory and with grace;
The shadow of Thy cross spread through the land:
  We seek Thy face.

Look down upon Thy heritage;
Let fruits of grace flow down as holy wine;
Revive Thy work, and cause Thine own to praise:
  Visit this vine!

© Author

450 Thomas Kelly   87 87 77
The vineyard which Thy right hand hath planted. *Psalm 80:15*

See the vineyard lately planted
  By Thy hand, O Lord of hosts!
Let Thy people's prayer be granted,
  Keep it safe from hostile boasts:
Many think Thy work to mar,
O remove the danger far!

'Tis Thine own, Thy hand has made it,
  Hide it from the wintry blast,
Let no foot of beast invade it,
  No rude hand its beauty waste:
Hear Thy people when they pray,
Keep Thy vineyard night and day.

Drooping plants revive and nourish,
   Let them thrive beneath Thy hand;
Let the weak grow strong and flourish,
   Blooming fair at Thy command:
Let the fruitful yield the more,
Laden with a richer store.

451   Harriet Auber   CM
Psalm 81

O God our strength, to Thee our song
   With grateful hearts we raise;
To Thee, and Thee alone belong
   All worship, love, and praise.

In trouble's dark and stormy hour
   Thine ear hath heard our prayer,
And graciously Thine arm of power
   Hath saved us from despair.

And Thou, O ever gracious Lord,
   Wilt keep Thy promise still,
If, meekly hearkening to Thy word,
   We seek to do Thy will.

Led by the light Thy grace imparts,
   Ne'er may we bow the knee
To idols which our wayward hearts
   Set up instead of Thee.

So shall Thy choicest gifts, O Lord,
   Thy faithful people bless,
For them shall earth its stores afford,
   And heaven its happiness.

452   Charles Spurgeon   CM
Psalm 82

The kings of earth are in the hands
   Of God who reigns on high;
He in their council-chamber stands,
   And sees with watchful eye.

Though foolish princes tyrants prove,
   And tread the godly down;
Though earth's foundations all remove;
   He weareth still the crown.

They proudly boast a godlike birth,
   In death like men they fall;
Arise, O God, and judge the earth,
   And rule the nations all.

When shall Thy Son, the Prince of Peace,
   Descend with glorious power?
Then only shall oppression cease:
   O haste the welcome hour.

453   David Denham   SM
Thy hidden ones. *Psalm 83:3*

Hidden by ancient choice,
   In Christ to life enrolled,
The saints are called to hear His voice
   And rest within His fold.

Hidden by heavenly birth,
   By hidden manna fed,
Pilgrims and strangers on the earth,
   In hidden paths we tread.

Hidden in Christ the Root,
   His branches grow and thrive,
From Him we all derive our fruit,
   And on His fulness live.

Hidden in His strong hand,
   From all that would destroy,
As monuments of grace we stand,
   Ordained to peace and joy.

Though hidden foes assail,
   To hinder faith and prayer,
Till they can over Christ prevail,
   We have no cause to fear.

We've hidden springs of grace,
   That shall o'er sin abound,
And hidden meetness for the place
   Where all the saints are crowned.

454   Isaac Watts   LM
Psalm 84

How pleasant, how divinely fair,
O Lord of Hosts, Thy dwellings are!
With long desire my spirit faints,
To meet the assemblies of Thy saints.

Blest are the saints who sit on high,
Around the throne of majesty;
Thy brightest glories shine above,
And all their work is praise and love.

Blest are the souls that find a place
Within the temple of Thy grace;
There they behold Thy gentler rays,
And seek Thy face, and learn Thy praise.

Blest are the men whose hearts are set
To find the way to Zion's gate;
God is their strength, and through the road
They lean upon their Helper, God.

Cheerful they walk with growing strength,
Till all shall meet in heaven at length,
Till all before Thy face appear,
And join in nobler worship there.

455   Isaac Watts   LM
Psalm 84

Great God! attend, while Zion sings
The joy that from Thy presence springs;
To spend one day with Thee on earth,
Exceeds a thousand days of mirth.

God is our Sun, He makes our day;
God is our Shield, He guards our way
From all the assaults of hell and sin,
From foes without, and foes within.

All needful grace will God bestow,
And crown that grace with glory too;
He gives us all things, and withholds
No real good from upright souls.

O God, our King, whose sovereign sway
The glorious hosts in heaven obey;
And devils at Thy presence flee;
Blest is the man who trusts in Thee.

456   John Milton   CM
Psalm 84

How lovely are Thy dwellings fair!
  O Lord of hosts, how dear
The pleasant tabernacles are,
  Where Thou dost dwell so near!

My soul doth long and almost die
  Thy courts, O Lord, to see;
My heart and flesh aloud do cry,
  O living God, for Thee.

Happy who in Thy house reside,
  Where Thee they ever praise!
Happy whose strength in Thee doth bide,
  And in their hearts Thy ways!

They journey on from strength to strength
  With joy and gladsome cheer,
Till all before our God at length
  In Zion do appear.

For God, the Lord, both Sun and Shield,
  Gives grace and glory bright;
No good from them shall be withheld
  Whose ways are just and right.

Lord God of hosts, that reign'st on high,
  That man is truly blest
Who only on Thee doth rely,
  And in Thee only rest.

457   Isaac Watts   SM
How amiable are Thy tabernacles, O LORD of hosts! *Psalm 84:1*

Welcome sweet day of rest,
  That saw the Lord arise;
Welcome to this reviving breast,
  And these rejoicing eyes.

The King Himself comes near,
  And feasts His saints today;
Here we may sit and see Him here,
  And love, and praise, and pray.

One day amidst the place
  Where my dear God has been,
Is sweeter than ten thousand days
  Of pleasurable sin.

My willing soul would stay
  In such a frame as this,
And sit and sing herself away
  To everlasting bliss.

458   Samuel Stennett   SM
How amiable are Thy tabernacles, O LORD of hosts! *Psalm 84:1*

How charming is the place,
  Where my Redeemer, God,
Unveils the beauties of His face,
  And sheds His love abroad!

Not the fair palaces
  To which the great resort,
Are once to be compared to this,
  Where Jesus holds His court.

Here, on the mercy-seat,
  With radiant glory crowned,
Our joyful eyes behold Him sit,
  And smile on all around.

To Him their prayers and cries
  Each humble soul presents;
He listens to their broken sighs,
  And grants them all their wants.

To them His sovereign will
  He graciously imparts;
And in return accepts with smiles,
  The tribute of their hearts.

Give me, O Lord, a place
  Within Thy blest abode,
Among the children of Thy grace,
  The servants of my God.

459   John Byrom   66 66
My soul longeth, yea, even fainteth for the courts of the LORD: *Psalm 84:2*

My spirit longs for Thee
  Within my troubled breast.
Unworthy though I be
  Of so divine a Guest.

Of so divine a Guest
  Unworthy though I be,
Yet has my heart no rest
  Unless it come from Thee.

Unless It come from Thee,
  In vain I look around;
In all that I can see
  No rest is to be found.

No rest is to be found
  But in Thy blessèd love!
Oh let my wish be crowned;
  And send it from above!

460   John Newton   LM
They go from strength to strength.
Psalm 84:7

As when the weary traveller gains
  The height of some o'erlooking hill,
His heart revives if 'cross the plains
  He eyes his home, though distant still.

While he surveys the much-loved spot,
  He slights the space that lies between;
His past fatigues are now forgot,
  Because his journey's end is seen.

Thus, when the Christian pilgrim views,
  By faith, his mansion in the skies,
The sight his fainting strength renews,
  And wings his speed to reach the prize.

The thought of home his spirit cheers,
  No more he grieves for troubles past,
Nor any future trial fears,
  So he may safe arrive at last.

'Tis there,' he says, 'I am to dwell,
  With Jesus, in the realms of day:
Then shall I bid my cares farewell,
  And He shall wipe my tears away.'

Jesus! on Thee our hope depends,
  To lead us on to Thine abode;
Assured our home will make amends
  For all our toil while on the road.

461   Joseph Swain   88 88 88
The Lord will give grace and glory.
Psalm 84:11

Lord, 'tis a heaven of joy and love
  To feel Thy gracious presence here!
And 'twill be heaven complete above,
  When we Thy perfect likeness bear,
And see Thy truth all-glorious shine,
Replete with rays of love divine.

All honour to Thy name alone,
  And thanks, eternal thanks, be given,
For Thou hast brought sweet mercy down,
  And raised our hearts and hopes to heaven,
And Thou alone canst keep our feet,
Till safe around Thy throne we meet.

Still let Thy grace sufficient prove
  To guide us on in wisdom's ways;
O, mould us by redeeming love,
  And make us fruitful to Thy praise!
That while our hearts rejoice in God,
Our lives may preach His name abroad.

But O, should sin disturb our peace,
  And awful fear our hearts alarm,
Saviour, appear for our release,
  And guilt of its dread sting disarm!
No balm but Thy rich blood can heal
The wounds which broken spirits feel.

462   Charles Cole   LM
Wilt Thou not revive us again?
Psalm 85:6

Revive Thy work in Zion, Lord,
There let Thy name be still adored;
There let Thy constant dwelling be,
Then will Thy saints rejoice in Thee.

Revive Thy work in every heart,
And heavenly blessings still impart;
Let grace increase abundantly,
Then will Thy saints rejoice in Thee.

Let faith, and hope, and love revive,
And humble zeal be kept alive;
Thy wondrous goodness let us see,
Then will Thy saints rejoice in Thee.

To Zion's hill let converts fly,
And let their number multiply,
To do Thy will let all agree,
Then will Thy saints rejoice in Thee.

Thus, Lord, attend to our request,
And let Thy churches thus be blest;
Let them enjoy prosperity,
Then will Thy saints rejoice in Thee.

Thus will the tree of life afford
　Both healing balm and heavenly food;
And we shall live and own the Lord
　Supremely wise, supremely good:
On earth proclaim redeeming love,
And sound it louder still above.

463　Joseph Hart　　　　　　　　LM
**Shew us Thy mercy, O LORD, and grant us
Thy salvation.** *Psalm 85:7*

Dimiss us with Thy blessing, Lord,
Help us to feed upon Thy word;
All that has been amiss forgive,
And let Thy truth within us live.

Though we are guilty, Thou art good;
Wash all our works in Jesus' blood;
Give every fettered soul release,
And bid us all depart in peace.

464　John Newton　　　　　　77 77 77
I will hear what God the LORD will speak.
Psalm 85:8

Safely through another week
　God has brought us on our way;
Let us now a blessing seek.
　On the approaching Sabbath-day;
Day of all the week the best,
Emblem of eternal rest.

Mercies multiplied each hour
　Through the week our praise demand;
Guarded by almighty power,
　Fed and guided by His hand:
Though ungrateful we have been,
Only made returns of sin.

While we pray for pardoning grace,
　Through the dear Redeemer's name,
Show Thy reconcilèd face,
　Shine away our sin and shame:
From our worldly care set free,
May we rest this night with Thee!

When the morn shall bid us rise,
　May we feel Thy presence near;
May Thy glory meet our eyes
　When we in Thy house appear!
There afford us, Lord, a taste
Of our everlasting feast.

May the gospel's joyful sound
　Conquer sinners, comfort saints,
Make the fruits of grace abound,
　Bring relief for all complaints:
Thus may all our Sabbaths prove,
Till we join the church above.

465　William Gadsby　　　　　87 87 47
**Mercy and truth are met together;
righteousness and peace have kissed each
other.** *Psalm 85:10*

Truth and mercy meet together,
　Righteousness and peace embrace;
Each perfection of Jehovah
　Meets and shines in Jesus' face;
　　Here the Father
　Can be just and save by grace.

What a field of consolation!
　Here no jarring notes are found;
Zion has a full salvation,
　And shall all her foes confound;
　　Each believer
　Has for hope a solid ground.

Justice has no loss sustainèd;
　Truth remains in perfect light;
Not an attribute is stainèd;
　All in one grand cause unite
　　Savèd sinners
　Must and shall in God delight.

Here's a cord which can't be broken;
　O my soul, with wonder tell;
God Himself the word has spoken,
　Zion in her Lord shall dwell;
　　And with Jesus
　Live in spite of earth and hell.

O ye much-esteemèd sinners,
　Who in Jesus Christ are found,
Rest assured you shall be winners,
　Soon with glory shall be crowned;
　　And for ever
　Shall the praise to Christ redound.

466　Isaac Watts　　　　　　　　LM
Mercy and truth are met together.
Psalm 85:10

Nature with open volume stands,
　To spread her Maker's praise abroad,
And every labour of His hands,
　Shows something worthy of a God.

But in the grace that rescued man,
　His brightest form of glory shines;
Here on the cross 'tis fairest drawn,
　In precious blood, and crimson lines.

O the sweet wonders of that cross,
　Where God the Saviour loved and died!
Her noblest life my spirit draws
　From His dear wounds and bleeding side.

I would for ever speak His name,
  In sounds to mortal ears unknown;
With angels join to praise the Lamb,
  And worship at His Father's throne.

467   William Tucker   LM
**Mercy and truth are met together;
righteousness and peace have kissed each
other.** *Psalm 85:10*

Infinite grace! and can it be
  That heaven's Supreme should stoop so low?
To visit one so vile as me—
  One who has been His bitt'rest foe?

Can holiness and wisdom join
  With truth, with justice, and with grace,
To make eternal blessings mine,
  And sin with all its guilt erase?

O love! beyond conception great,
  That formed the vast stupendous plan!
Where all divine perfections meet
  To reconcile rebellious man!

There wisdom shines in fullest blaze,
  And justice all her rights maintains,
Astonished angels stoop to gaze,
  While mercy o'er the guilty reigns.

Yes, mercy reigns, and justice too,
  In Christ they both harmonious meet;
He paid to justice all her due,
  And now He fills the mercy-seat.

Such are the wonders of our God,
  And such the amazing depths of grace,
To save from wrath's vindictive rod
  The chosen sons of Adam's race.

468   Annie Hawks   64 64 + refrain
I am poor and needy. *Psalm 86:1*

I need Thee every hour,
  Most gracious Lord;
No tender voice like Thine
  Can peace afford.

  *I need Thee, O I need Thee;
  Every hour I need Thee;
  O bless me now, my Saviour!
  I come to Thee.*

I need Thee every hour;
  Stay Thou near by;
Temptations lose their power
  When Thou art nigh.

I need Thee every hour,
  In joy or pain;
Come quickly and abide,
  Or life is vain.

I need Thee every hour;
  Teach me Thy will;
And Thy rich promises
  In me fulfil.

I need Thee every hour,
  Most Holy One;
O make me Thine indeed,
  Thou blessèd Son.

469   Richard Burnham   77 77
**Be merciful unto me, O Lord: for I cry unto
Thee daily.** *Psalm 86:3*

Jesus now Thyself reveal;
  Manifest Thy love to me;
Make me, Saviour, make me feel
  All my soul's delight in Thee.

All Thy ways I'd well approve,
  Under Thy dear wings abide;
Never from Thy cross I'd move,
  Never leave Thy wounded side.

Daily I'd repent of sin,
  Daily wash in Calvary's blood,
Daily feel Thy peace within,
  Daily I'd commune with God.

Daily I'd Thy name adore,
  Prize Thy word, and love to pray;
All Thy kindness well explore,
  Still press on to perfect day.

When with evils I'm beset,
  Foes advancing all around,
Down I'd fall at Thy dear feet,
  Wait to see Thy grace abound.

470   David Denham   77 77
Great is Thy mercy toward me.
Psalm 86:13

Mercy is a stream most sweet,
  Flowing from the sacred Three!
Mercy, love, and justice meet
  In the work of Christ for me.

Mercy my redemption planned,
  In the covenant ordered well;
Mercy plucked me, as a brand,
  From the fire of sin and hell!

Mercy in the Saviour's blood,
Heals my soul in deep distress;
Mercy leads me up to God,
In His perfect righteousness.

Mercy soothes my troubled breast
With a balm for all my woes;
Mercy sets my heart at rest,
Safe amidst my raging foes.

Mercy reconciles to grief,
When oppressed with gloomy care;
Mercy brings my soul relief
In the way of faith and prayer.

Mercy sheds a cheering light
On the purposes of heaven;
Mercy is the Lord's delight,
Shining in my sins forgiven.

Mercy gives me heavenly food,
Bread to strengthen, wine to cheer;
Mercy always does me good,
Seals my peace, subdues my fear.

Mercy, when my heart shall fail,
Will all needful help afford;
Mercy shall o'er death prevail:
Hallelujah to the Lord.

471   Charles Cole   LM
Shew me a token for good. *Psalm 86:17*

Show me some token, Lord, for good,
Some token of Thy special love;
Show me that I am born of God,
And that my treasure is above.

My supplication, Lord, is this,
That all my sins may be subdued;
That all Thy precious promises
May be to me and for my good.

O seal my pardon to my soul,
And then proclaim my peace with Thee;
Thus make my wounded conscience whole,
And that will be for good to me.

Let Thy good Spirit rule my heart,
And govern all my words and ways;
Let grace abound in every part,
And teach my tongue to sing Thy praise.

Thus may I see that I am Thine,
And feel my heart to Thee ascend;
Then shall I know that Thou art mine,
My God, my Father, and my Friend.

472   Thomas Kelly, John Rippon   87 87 47
Shew me a token for good. *Psalm 86:17*

Grant us, Lord, some gracious token
Of Thy love before we part;
Crown Thy word which has been spoken,
Life and peace to each impart!
And all blessings
Which shall sanctify the heart.

473   John Newton   87 87 D
Glorious things are spoken of thee, O city of God. *Psalm 87:3*

Glorious things of thee are spoken,
Zion, city of our God!
He whose word cannot be broken,
Formed thee for His own abode;
On the Rock of Ages founded,
What can shake thy sure repose?
With salvation's walls surrounded,
Thou may'st smile at all thy foes.

See! the streams of living waters,
Springing from eternal love,
Well supply thy sons and daughters,
And all fear of want remove.
Who can faint while such a river
Ever flows their thirst to assuage?
Grace, which, like the Lord, the Giver,
Never fails from age to age.

Round each habitation hovering,
See the cloud and fire appear!
For a glory and a covering,
Showing that the Lord is near.
Thus deriving from their banner,
Light by night and shade by day,
Safe they feed upon the manna
Which He gives them when they pray.

Blest inhabitants of Zion,
Washed in the Redeemer's blood!
Jesus, whom their souls rely on,
Makes them kings and priests to God:
'Tis His love His people raises
Over self to reign as kings;
And as priests, His solemn praises
Each for a thank-offering brings.

Saviour, if of Zion's city
I through grace a member am,
Let the world deride or pity,
I will glory in Thy name:
Fading is the worldling's pleasure,
All his boasted pomp and show;
Solid joys and lasting treasure,
None but Zion's children know.

474   Samuel Parrot   LM
All my springs are in Thee. *Psalm 87:7*

Jesus, Thy praise my soul would sing,
From whom my every blessing springs;
Taught by Thy grace, I feel and see,
Dear Lord, my springs are all in Thee.

Convinced of sin against my God,
I feel I need Thy pard'ning blood,
Which on the cross was shed for me:
Dear Lord, my pardon springs from Thee.

Clothed in Thy righteousness divine,
By precious faith I call it mine;
From condemnation I am free,
My hope of glory springs from Thee,

When to Thy fulness I apply,
My soul receives a sweet supply;
Abundant grace, both rich and free,
Dear Lord, my springs are all in Thee.

Since Thou hast led me to believe
On Thee, my cov'nant Head, I live,
Experience and Thy word agree
To prove my springs are all in Thee.

Yes, Lord, Thou art my All in all!
Upheld by Thee, I cannot fall;
In heaven I shall for ever sing,
Both grace and glory from Thee spring.

475   Henry Lyte   76 76 D
Psalm 88

Lord God of my salvation,
   To Thee, to Thee, I cry;
Oh let my supplication
   Arrest Thine ear on high.
Distresses round me thicken,
   My life draws nigh the grave;
Descend, O Lord, to quicken,
   Descend my soul to save.

Thy wrath lies hard upon me,
   Thy billows o'er me roll,
My friends all seem to shun me,
   And foes beset my soul.
Where'er on earth I turn me,
   No comforter is near;
Wilt Thou too Father, spurn me?
   Wilt Thou refuse to hear?

No! banished and heart-broken
   My soul still clings to Thee;
The promise Thou hast spoken
   Shall still my refuge be.
So present ills and terrors
   My future joy increase,
And scourge me from my errors
   To duty, hope, and peace.

476   John Stocker   11 11 11 11
I will sing of the mercies of the LORD for ever.
Psalm 89:1

Thy mercy, my God, is the theme of my song,
The joy of my heart, and the boast of my tongue;
Thy free grace alone, from the first to the last,
Hath won my affections, and bound my soul fast.

Thy mercy in Jesus exempts me from hell;
Its glories I'll sing and its wonders I'll tell;
'Twas Jesus, my Friend, when He hung on the
   tree,
Who opened the channel of mercy for me.

Thy mercy is more than a match for my heart,
Which wonders to feel its own hardness depart;
Dissolved by Thy goodness I fall to the ground,
And weep to the praise of the mercy I found.

The door of thy mercy stands open all day
To the poor and the needy who knock by the way;
No sinner shall ever be empty sent back,
Who comes seeking mercy for Jesus's sake.

Great Father of mercies, Thy goodness I own,
And the covenant love of Thy crucified Son;
All praise to the Spirit, whose whisper divine
Seals mercy, and pardon, and righteousness
   mine.

477   Joseph Addison   CM
I will sing of the mercies of the LORD for ever.
Psalm 89:1

When all Thy mercies, O my God,
   My rising soul surveys,
Transported with the view, I'm lost
   In wonder, love and praise.

Unnumbered comforts on my soul
   Thy tender care bestowed,
Before my infant heart conceived
   From whom these comforts flowed.

When worn with sickness oft hast Thou
   With health renewed my face;
And when in sins and sorrows sunk,
   Revived my soul with grace.

Ten thousand thousand precious gifts
My daily thanks employ;
Nor is the least a cheerful heart
That tastes those gifts with joy.

Through all eternity to Thee
A joyful song I'll raise;
But O, eternity's too short
To utter all Thy praise.

478   Charles Wesley   10 10 11 11
Blessed is the people that know the joyful sound. *Psalm 89:15*

O what shall I do my Saviour to praise,
So faithful and true, so plenteous in grace;
So strong to deliver, so good to redeem,
The weakest believer that hangs upon Him.

How happy the man whose heart is set free,
The people that can be joyful in Thee!
Their joy is to walk in the light of Thy face,
And still they are talking of Jesus's grace.

Their daily delight shall be in Thy name;
They shall, as their right, Thy righteousness
claim.
Thy righteousness wearing, and cleansed by
blood
Bold shall they appear in the presence of God.

For Thou art their boast, their glory, and power;
And I also trust to see the glad hour:
My soul's new creation, alive from the dead;
The day of salvation that lifts up my head.

Yes, Lord, I shall see the bliss of Thy own;
Thy secret to me shall soon be made known;
For sorrow and sadness I joy shall receive,
And share in the gladness of all that believe.

479   William Gadsby   66 66 88
Blessed is the people that know the joyful sound. *Psalm 89:15*

Thrice happy are the men,
Who know the joyful sound;
They glory in the Lamb;
Their hopes upon Him found;
They see how justice, truth, and grace,
Agree and shine in Jesus' face.

A joyful sound indeed,
To sinners in distress,
Who have no works to plead
But what are vile and base;
Who feel their hearts a dreadful den
Of every murderous, hateful sin.

For such to hear and know
Salvation is of God,
That Jesus will bestow
The riches of His love
On sinners who have nought to bring,
Will make their very souls to sing.

He pardons all their sins,
And makes them white as wool,
And the sweet Spirit sends,
To fill their vessels full
Of faith, and love, and joy, and peace,
And seal them sons and heirs of grace.

480   Henry Lyte   87 87 47
Blessed is the people that know the joyful sound. *Psalm 89:15*
.
O how blest the congregation
Who the gospel know and prize;
Joyful tidings of salvation
Brought by Jesus from the skies!
He is near them,
Knows their wants and hears their cries.

In His name rejoicing ever,
Walking in His light and love,
And foretasting, in His favour,
Something here of bliss above;
Happy people!
Who shall harm them? what shall move?

In His righteousness exalted,
On from strength to strength they go,
By ten thousand ills assaulted,
Yet preserved from every foe!
On to glory,
Safe they speed through all below.

God will keep His own anointed,
Nought shall harm them, none condemn;
All their trials are appointed,
All must work for good to them;
All shall help them
To their heavenly diadem.

481   Isaac Watts   CM
Then Thou spakest in vision to Thy holy one.
Psalm 89:19

Hear what the Lord in vision said,
And made His mercy known:
'Zion, behold, your help is laid
On My almighty Son.

'High shall He reign on David's throne
My people's better King;
My arm shall beat His rivals down,
And still new subjects bring.

'Me for His Father and His God
    He shall for ever own,
Call me His Rock, His high abode;
    And I'll support My Son.

'My first-born Son, arrayed in grace,
    At My right hand shall sit;
Beneath Him angels know their place,
    And monarchs at His feet.

'My covenant stands for ever fast;
    My promises are strong;
Firm as the heavens His throne shall last
    His seed endure as long.'

482   Benjamin Wallin   LM
My mercy will I keep for Him for evermore, and my covenant shall stand fast with him.
Psalm 89:28

Rejoice ye saints, in every state,
    Divine decrees remain unmoved;
No turns of providence abate
    God's care for those He once has loved.

Firmer than heaven His covenant stands,
    Though earth should shake and skies depart.
You're safe in your Redeemer's hands,
    Who bears your names upon His heart.

Our Surety knows for whom He stood
    And gave Himself a sacrifice:
The souls once sprinkled with His blood,
    Possess a life that never dies.

Though darkness spread around our tent,
    Though fear prevail and joy decline,
God will not of His oath repent:
    Dear Lord, Thy people still are Thine!

483   William Hammond   CM
My mercy will I keep for Him for evermore.
Psalm 89:28

For us the dear Redeemer died;
    Why are we then ashamed?
We stand for ever justified,
    And cannot be condemned.

Though we believe not, He is true;
    The work is in His hand;
His gracious purpose He will do,
    And all His word shall stand.

If once the love of Christ we feel
    Upon our hearts impressed,
The mark of that celestial seal
    Can never be erased.

The Lord will scourge us if we stray,
    And wound us with distress;
But He will never take away
    His covenant of peace.

The peace which Jesus' blood secures,
    And fixes in our hearts,
To all eternity endures,
    Nor finally departs.

484   Isaac Watts   CM
My covenant will I not break. *Psalm 89:34*

Our God, how firm His promise stands,
    E'en when He hides His face!
He trusts in our Redeemer's hands
    His glory and His grace.

Then why, my soul, these sad complaints,
    Since Christ and thou are one?
Thy God is faithful to His saints,
    Is faithful to His Son.

Beneath His smiles my heart has lived,
    And part of heaven possessed.
I'll praise His name for grace received,
    And trust Him for the rest.

485   Frances Havergal   LM
My covenant will I not break. *Psalm 89:34*

Jehovah's covenant shall endure,
All ordered, everlasting, sure!
O child of God, rejoice to trace
Thy portion in its glorious grace.

'Tis Thine, for Christ is given to be
The covenant of God to thee,
In Him, God's golden scroll of light,
The darkest truths are clear and bright.

O sorrowing sinner, well He knew,
Ere time began, what He would do!
Then rest thy hope within the veil;
His covenant mercies shall not fail.

O doubting one, eternal Three
Are pledged in faithfulness for thee;
Claim every promise sweet and sure,
By covenant oath of God secure.

O waiting one, each moment's fall
Is marked by love, that planned them all;
Thy times, all ordered by His hand,
In God's eternal covenant stand.

O feeble one, look up and see
Strong consolation sworn for thee;
Jehovah's glorious arm is shown,
His covenant strength is all thine own.

O mourning one, each stroke of love
A covenant blessing yet shall prove;
His covenant love shall be thy stay;
His covenant grace be as thy day.

O Love that chose, O Love that died,
O Love that sealed and sanctified,
All glory, glory, glory be,
O covenant, triune God, to Thee!

486   Isaac Watts   CM
Psalm 90

Our God, our help in ages past,
  Our hope for years to come,
Our shelter from the stormy blast
  And our eternal home;

Under the shadow of Thy throne
  Thy saints have dwelt secure;
Sufficient is Thine arm alone,
  And our defence is sure.

Before the hills in order stood,
  Or earth received her frame,
From everlasting Thou art God,
  To endless years the same.

A thousand ages in Thy sight
  Are like an evening gone;
Short as the watch that ends the night
  Before the rising sun.

Time, like an ever-rolling stream,
  Bears all its sons away;
They fly forgotten, as a dream
  Dies at the opening day.

Our God, our help in ages past,
  Our hope for years to come,
Be Thou our Guide while troubles last,
  And our eternal home.

487   Thomas Gill   87 87 887
Lord, Thou hast been our dwelling place in all generations. *Psalm 90:1*

Lord, Thou hast been our dwelling-place
  In every generation;
Thy people still have known Thy grace,
  And blessed Thy consolation;
Through every age Thou heard'st our cry;
Through every age we found Thee nigh,
  Our strength and our salvation.

Our cleaving sins we oft have wept,
  And oft Thy patience proved;
But still Thy faith we fast have kept,
  Thy name we still have lovèd:
And Thou hast kept and loved us well,
Hast granted us in Thee to dwell,
  Unshaken, unremovèd.

Lord, nothing from Thine arms of love
  Shall Thine own people sever:
Our helper never will remove,
  Our God will fail us never.
Thy people, Lord, have dwelt in Thee;
Our dwelling-place Thou still wilt be
  For ever and for ever.

488   Isaac Watts   CM
From everlasting to everlasting, Thou art God.
Psalm 90:2

Lord, raise my soul above the ground,
  And draw my thoughts to Thee;
Teach me, with sweet and solemn sound,
  To praise the eternal Three.

Long ere the lofty skies were spread,
  Jehovah filled His throne;
Or Adam formed, or angels made,
  The Maker lived alone.

His boundless years can ne'er decrease,
  But still maintain their prime;
Eternity's His dwelling-place,
  And ever is His time.

While like a tide our minutes flow,
  The present and the past,
He fills His own immortal now,
  And sees our ages waste.

The sea and sky must perish too,
  And vast destruction come!
The creatures! look how old they grow,
  And wait their fiery doom.

Well; let the sea shrink all away,
  And flame melt down the skies,
My God shall live an endless day
  When the old creation dies.

489   Frances Havergal   76 76D
We spend our years as a tale that is told.
Psalm 90:9

Another year is dawning;
   Dear Master, let it be,
In working or in waiting,
   Another year with Thee.
Another year of leaning
   Upon Thy loving breast,
Of ever-deep'ning trusting,
   Of quiet, happy rest.

Another year of mercies,
   Of faithfulness and grace,
Another year of gladness
   In shinings of Thy face.
Another year of progress,
   Another year of praise,
Another year of proving
   Thy presence 'all the days.'

Another year of service,
   Of witness for Thy love,
Another year of training
   For holier work above.
Another year is dawning;
   Dear Master, let it be,
On earth, or else in heaven,
   Another year for Thee!

490   David Denham   CM
**He that dwelleth in the secret place of the
most High shall abide under the shadow of the
Almighty.** *Psalm 91:1*

In Christ, the secret place of God,
   His chosen shall abide;
Blessed with redemption in His blood,
   And all their needs supplied.

He'll succour in each trying day,
   Nor let the weakest fail;
Mercy and truth He will display,
   Though earth and hell assail.

From every foe His arm shall save,
   Then why indulge a fear?
We soon shall every storm outbrave,
   And palms of victory bear.

Cheer up, ye saints, the crown's in view,
   We are for ever blest;
God has engaged to hear us through,
   And heaven must be possessed.

491   Cleland McAfee   CM + refrain
**He that dwelleth in the secret place of the
most High shall abide under the shadow of the
Almighty.** *Psalm 91:1*

There is a place of quiet rest,
   Near to the heart of God;
A place where sin cannot molest,
   Near to the heart of God.

   *O Jesus, blest Redeemer,
   Sent from the heart of God;
   Hold us, who wait before Thee,
   Near to the heart of God.*

There is a place of comforts sweet,
   Near to the heart of God;
A place where we our Saviour meet,
   Near to the heart of God.

There is a place of full release,
   Near to the heart of God;
A place where all is joy and peace,
   Near to the heart of God.

492   Thomas Ken   LM
He shall cover thee with His feathers.
Psalm 91:4

Glory to Thee, my God, this night,
For all the blessings of the light;
Keep me, O keep me, King of kings,
Under Thine own almighty wings!

Forgive me, Lord, for Thy dear Son,
The ills that I this day have done;
That, with the world, myself, and Thee,
I, ere I sleep, at peace may be.

Teach me to live, that I may dread
The grave as little as my bed:
Teach me to die, that so I may
Triumphing rise at the last day.

O, may my soul on Thee repose,
And with sweet sleep mine eyelids close—
Sleep, that shall me more vigorous make,
To serve my God when I awake!

If in the night I sleepless lie,
My soul with heavenly thoughts supply;
Let no ill dreams disturb my rest,
No powers of darkness me molest.

Praise God, from whom all blessings flow,
Praise Him, all creatures here below,
Praise Him above, ye heavenly host,
Praise Father, Son, and Holy Ghost.

493   John Newton   87 87 D
**He shall call upon me, and I will answer him: I
will be with him in trouble; I will deliver him
and honour him.** *Psalm 91:15*

Could the creatures help or ease us,
    Seldom should we think of prayer;
Few, if any, come to Jesus,
    Till reduced to self-despair.
Long we either slight or doubt Him,
    But, when all the means we try
Prove we cannot do without Him,
    Then at last to Him we cry.

Fear thou not, distressed believer;
    Venture on His mighty name;
He is able to deliver,
    And His love is still the same.
Can His pity or His power
    Suffer thee to pray in vain?
Wait but His appointed hour,
    And thy plea thou shalt obtain.

494   Isaac Watts   LM
Psalm 92 part 1

Sweet is the work, my God, my King,
To praise Thy name, give thanks and sing;
To show Thy love by morning light,
And talk of all Thy truth at night.

Sweet is the day of sacred rest,
No mortal care shall seize my breast;
O may my heart in tune be found,
Like David's harp of solemn sound.

My heart shall triumph in the Lord,
And bless His works and bless His word;
Thy works of grace, how bright they shine!
How deep Thy counsels, how divine!

Then shall I share a glorious part
When grace hath well refined my heart;
And fresh supplies of joy are shed,
Like holy oil, to cheer my head.

Sin, my worst enemy before,
Shall vex my eyes and ears no more;
My inward foes shall all be slain,
Nor Satan break my peace again.

Then shall I see, and hear, and know
All I desired or wished below;
And every power find sweet employ
In that eternal world of joy.

495   Isaac Watts   LM
Psalm 92 part 2

Lord, 'tis a pleasant thing to stand
In gardens planted by Thine hand:
Let me within Thy courts be seen,
Like a young cedar, fresh and green.

There grow Thy saints in faith and love,
Blessed with Thine influence from above;
Not Lebanon with all its trees
Yields such a comely sight as these.

The plants of grace shall ever live;
Nature decays, but grace must thrive;
Time, that doth all things else impair,
Still makes them flourish strong and fair.

Laden with fruits of age, they show
The Lord is holy, just, and true;
None that attend His gates shall find
A God unfaithful or unkind.

496   Isaac Watts   LM
Psalm 93

Jehovah reigns; He dwells in light,
Girded with majesty and might;
The world created by His hands,
Still on its first foundation stands.

But ere this spacious world was made,
Or had its first foundations laid,
Thy throne eternal ages stood,
Thyself the ever-living God.

Like floods the angry nations rise,
And aim their rage against the skies;
Vain floods, that aim their rage so high!
At Thy rebuke the billows die.

For ever shall Thy throne endure;
Thy promise stands for ever sure;
And everlasting holiness
Becomes the dwellings of Thy grace.

497   Harriet Auber   LM
Psalm 94

Can guilty man, indeed, believe
  That He, who made and knows the heart,
Shall not the oppressor's crimes perceive,
  Nor take His injured servants' part?

Shall He who, with transcendent skill,
  Fashioned the eye and formed the ear;
Who modelled nature to His will,
  Shall He not see? Shall He not hear?

Shall He, who framed the human mind,
  And bade its kindling spark to glow,
Who all its varied powers combined,
  O mortal, say—shall He not know?

Vain hope! His eye at once surveys
  Whatever fills creation's space;
He sees our thoughts, and marks our ways,
  He knows no bounds of time and place.

Surrounded by His saints, the Lord
  Shall armed with holy vengeance come;
To each His final lot award.
  And seal the sinner's fearful doom.

498   Charles Wesley   LM
Ye fools, when will ye be wise?
Psalm 94:8

God of my life, Thy gracious power
  Through varied deaths my soul has led;
Oft turned aside the fatal hour,
  Or lifted up my sinking head.

Whither, O whither should I fly,
  But to the loving Saviour's breast?
Secure within Thy arms to lie,
  And safe beneath Thy wings to rest.

I have no skill the snare to shun,
  But Thou, O Christ, my wisdom art:
I ever into ruin run,
  But Thou art greater than my heart.

Foolish, and impotent, and blind,
  Lead me the way Thy saints have known;
Bring me where I my heaven may find,
  The heaven of loving Thee alone.

499   Augustus Toplady   76 76
Thy comforts delight my soul.
Psalm 94:19

If my Lord Himself reveal,
  No other good I want;
Only Christ my wounds can heal,
  Or silence my complaint.

He that suffered in my stead,
  Shall my Physician be:
I will not be comforted
  Till Jesus comforts me.

500   Isaac Watts   SM
Psalm 95

  Come, sound His praise abroad,
    And hymns of glory sing:
Jehovah is the sovereign God,
    The universal King.

  He formed the deeps unknown,
    He gave the seas their bound;
The watery worlds are all His own,
    And all the solid ground.

  Come, worship at His throne;
    Come, bow before the Lord:
We are His works, and not our own;
    He formed us by His word.

  Today attend His voice,
    Nor dare provoke His rod;
Come, like the people of His choice,
    And own your gracious God.

501   *The Sower* 1878   LM
Let us come before His presence with thanksgiving, and make a joyful noise unto him with psalms. *Psalm 95:2*

O God in Christ, a covenant God,
In Jesus' name, through Jesus' blood,
Before Thy throne we now appear,
In worship to begin the year.

Fit us for all Thou hast designed;
Give us a calm, believing mind;
Free us from guilt and slavish fear;
Make this to us a blessèd year.

A year, if spared, of love and peace;
A year of fruit, through faith's increase;
A year of tender, godly fear,
A humbling and exalting year.

A year when Jesus Christ shall be
To us a deep reality;
Jesus to faith's blest sight be near,
By day, by night, throughout the year.

If this our closing year should be,
O, give us so to lean on Thee,
That we may meet without a fear
Our last on earth, our dying year!

502 Richard Baxter   66 66 44 44

O sing unto the LORD a new song: sing unto the LORD, all the earth. *Psalm 96:1*

Ye holy angels bright,
  Who wait at God's right hand,
Or through the realms of light
  Fly at your Lord's command,
    Assist our song,
      Or else the theme
      Too high doth seem
    For mortal tongue.

Ye blessèd souls at rest,
  Who see your Saviour's face,
Whose glory, even the least
  Is far above our grace.
    God's praises sound,
      As in His sight
      With sweet delight
    Ye do abound.

Ye saints, who toil below,
  Adore your heavenly King,
And, onward as ye go,
  Some joyful anthem sing;
    Take what He gives,
      And praise Him still
      Through good and ill,
    Who ever lives.

My soul, bear thou thy part,
  Triumph in God above,
And with a well tuned heart
  Sing thou the songs of love.
    Let all thy days
      Till life shall end,
      Whate'er He send,
    Be filled with praise.

503 Anne Steele   CM

Sing unto the LORD, bless His name; show forth his salvation from day to day. *Psalm 96:2*

Come, ye that love the Saviour's name,
  And joy to make it known;
The Sovereign of your heart proclaim,
  And bow before His throne.

Behold your King, your Saviour crowned
  With glories all divine;
And tell the wondering nations round
  How bright those glories shine.

Infinite power and boundless grace
  In Him unite their rays:
You that have e'er beheld His face,
  Can you forbear His praise?

When in His earthly courts we view
  The glories of our King,
We long to love as angels do,
  And wish like them to sing.

And shall we long and wish in vain?
  Lord, teach our songs to rise!
Thy love can animate the strain,
  And bid it reach the skies.

O, happy period! glorious day!
  When heaven and earth shall raise
With all their power, the raptured lay
  To celebrate Thy praise.

504 Harriet Auber (alt)   LM
Psalm 97

Jehovah reigns! O earth, rejoice;
Ye ransomed isles, exalt your voice:
Make every hill and vale around
Responsive to the welcome sound.

Though far removed from mortal eye,
He reigns in glorious majesty;
Himself in awesome clouds concealed,
His truth, His justice stands revealed.

Yes, Jesus reigns! the gospel's light
Beams with mild radiance on our sight;
And fallen man, redeemed, forgiven,
May lift his heart, his hopes to heaven.

O, then, obey His sacred word,
All ye who love and fear the Lord;
Go, publish through His wide domains
The glorious truth, Jehovah reigns!

505 Paulus Gerhardt, tr. J Wesley   SM

The LORD reigneth; let the earth rejoice.
Psalm 97:1

  Give to the winds thy fears;
    Hope and be undismayed;
God hears thy sighs and counts thy tears,
    God shall lift up thy head.

  Through waves and clouds and storms
    He gently clears thy way;
Wait thou His time; so shall this night
    Soon end in joyous day.

  Still heavy is thy heart?
    Still sink thy spirits down?
Cast off the weight, let fear depart,
    Bid every care be gone.

What though thou rulest not?
Yet heaven and earth and hell
Proclaim, God sitteth on the throne
And ruleth all things well!

Leave to His sovereign sway
To choose and to command;
So shalt thou wondering own His way,
How wise, how strong, His hand.

Far, far above thy thought
His counsel shall appear,
When fully He the work hath wrought
That caused thy needless fear.

Thou seest our weakness, Lord;
Our hearts are known to Thee;
O lift Thou up the sinking hand,
Confirm the feeble knee.

506　　Isaac Watts　　　　　　CM
Psalm 98

Joy to the world! the Lord is come!
Let earth receive her King,
Let every heart prepare Him room,
And heaven and nature sing.

Joy to the earth! the Saviour reigns!
Let men their songs employ;
While fields and floods, rocks, hills, and plains
Repeat the sounding joy.

No more let sins and sorrows grow,
Nor thorns infest the ground;
He comes to make His blessings flow
Far as the curse is found.

He rules the world with truth and grace,
And makes the nations prove
The glories of His righteousness,
And wonders of His love.

507　　William Gadsby　　　　CM
The LORD reigneth; let the people tremble.
Psalm 99:1

Great God! whose universal power
Through all the earth is known;
Who governs heaven and earth, nor sits
On a precarious throne;

Our wars and tumults all arise
As the effect of sin;
Sin is the cause of all the woes
The world has felt or seen.

Dear Lord, we fall before Thy face:
Our guilt and folly own;
And pray Thee, for Thy mercy's sake,
To make Thy goodness known.

In mercy put a stop to war;
In mercy send us peace;
Nor let Thy vengeance on us fall,
Almighty King of grace.

Yet, Lord, whate'er Thy will may be,
We pray to be resigned;
We know Thou art too wise to err,
Too good to be unkind.

508　　Isaac Watts (alt)　　　　LM
Psalm 100

Before Jehovah's awesome throne,
Ye nations bow with sacred joy;
Know that the Lord is God alone,
He can create, and He destroy.

His sovereign power, without our aid,
Made us of clay, and formed us men;
And when like wandering sheep we strayed,
He brought us to His fold again.

We are His people, we His care,
Our souls and all our mortal frame;
What lasting honours shall we rear,
Almighty Maker, to Thy name?

We'll crowd Thy gates with thankful songs,
High as the heavens our voices raise;
And earth, with her ten thousand tongues,
Shall fill Thy courts with sounding praise.

Wide as the world is Thy command,
Vast as eternity Thy love;
Firm as a rock Thy truth must stand,
When rolling years shall cease to move.

509　　William Kethe　　　　LM
Psalm 100

All people that on earth do dwell,
Sing to the Lord with cheerful voice;
Him serve with fear, His praise forth tell;
Come ye before Him and rejoice.

The Lord, ye know, is God indeed;
Without our aid He did us make:
We are His folk, He doth us feed,
And for His sheep He doth us take.

O, enter, then, His gates with praise,
Approach with joy His courts unto;
Praise Him, and bless His name always,
For it is seemly so to do!

For why? the Lord our God is good,
His mercy is for ever sure;
His truth at all times firmly stood,
And shall from age to age endure.

510   Henry Downton   76 76 D
I will sing of mercy and judgment: unto Thee O Lord will I sing. *Psalm 101:1*

My song shall be of mercy;
Come, ye who love the Lord,
Who know that He is gracious,
Who trust His faithful word;
Tell out His works with gladness,
With me exalt His name,
Whose love endures for ever,
To endless years the same.

My song shall be of judgment;
Ye who His chastenings feel,
O faint not, nor be weary;
He wounds that He may heal;
Yea, bless the hand that smiteth,
And in your grief confess
That all His ways are wisdom,
And truth, and righteousness.

Of mercy and of judgment
To Thee, O Lord, we sing,
O Father, Son, and Spirit,
O great eternal King;
For only Thou art holy,
For Thou art Lord alone,
And mercy still and judgment
Are pillars of Thy throne.

511   Joseph Hart   SM
I will sing of mercy and judgment.
Psalm 101:1

Thy mercy, Lord, we praise;
Of judgment too we sing;
For all the riches of Thy grace
Our grateful tribute bring.

Mercy may justly claim
A sinner's thankful voice;
And judgment joining in the theme,
We tremble and rejoice.

Thy mercies bid us trust;
Thy judgments strike with awe;
We fear the last, we bless the first,
And love Thy righteous law.

Who can Thy acts express,
Or trace Thy wondrous ways?
How glorious is Thy holiness;
How terrible Thy praise!

Thy goodness how immense
To those that fear Thy name!
Thy love surpasses thought or sense,
And always is the same.

Thy judgments are too deep
For reason's line to sound.
Thy tender mercies to Thy sheep
No bottom know, nor bound.

512   Isaac Watts   LM
O when wilt Thou come unto me?
Psalm 101:2

Come, dearest Lord, descend and dwell,
By faith and love, in every breast;
Then shall we know and taste and feel
The joys that cannot be expressed.

Come, fill our hearts with inward strength,
Make our enlargèd souls possess,
And learn the height and breadth and length
Of Thine immeasurable grace.

Now to the God, whose power can do
More than our thoughts or wishes know,
Be everlasting honours done
By all the church through Christ His Son.

513   Isaac Watts   CM
Psalm 102 part 1

Hear me, O God, nor hide Thy face,
But answer, lest I die;
Hast Thou not built a throne of grace,
To hear when sinners cry?

My days are wasted like the smoke,
Dissolving in the air;
My strength is dried, my heart is broke,
And sinking in despair.

Sense can afford no real joy
To souls that feel Thy frown;
Lord, 'twas Thy hand advanced me high,
Thy hand hath cast me down.

But Thou for ever art the same,
O my eternal God!
Ages to come shall know Thy name,
And spread Thy works abroad.

Thou wilt arise and show Thy face;
Nor will my Lord delay
Beyond the appointed hour of grace,
That long expected day.

514 *Scottish Version* 1641   CM
Psalm 102 part 2

Thou shalt arise, and mercy have
    Upon Thy Zion yet;
The time to favour her is come,
    The time that Thou hast set.

For in her rubbish and her stones
    Thy servants pleasure take;
Yea, they the very dust thereof
    Do favour for her sake.

So shall the heathen people fear
    The Lord's most holy name;
And all the kings on earth shall dread
    Thy glory and Thy fame.

When Zion by the mighty Lord
    Built up again shall be,
Then shall her gracious God appear
    In glorious majesty.

515   John Kent   LM
**Thou shalt arise, and have mercy upon Zion:
for the time to favour her, yea, the set time, is
come.** *Psalm 102:13*

There is a period known to God
When all His sheep, redeemed by blood,
Shall leave the hateful ways of sin,
Turn to the fold, and enter in.

At peace with hell, with God at war,
In sin's dark maze they wander far,
Indulge their lust, and still go on
As far from God as sheep can run.

But see how heaven's indulgent care
Attends their wanderings here and there;
Still hard at heel where'er they stray,
With pricking thorns to hedge their way.

When wisdom calls, they stop their ear,
And headlong urge the mad career;
Judgments nor mercies ne'er can sway
Their roving feet to wisdom's way.

Glory to God, they ne'er shall rove
Beyond the limits of His love;
Fenced with Jehovah's *shalls* and *wills,*
Firm as the everlasting hills.

The appointed time rolls on apace,
Not to propose but call by grace;
To change the heart, renew the will,
And turn the feet to Zion's hill.

516   Samuel Medley   SM
**He will regard the prayer of the destitute, and
not despise their prayer.**
Psalm 102:17

Come, praying souls, rejoice,
    And bless your Father's name;
Joyful to Him lift up your voice,
    And all His love proclaim.

Your mournful cry He hears,
    He marks your feeblest groan,
Supplies your wants, dispels your fears,
    And makes His mercy known.

To all His praying saints
    He ever will attend,
And to their sorrows and complaints
    Will timely succour send.

Then blessèd be the Lord,
    Who has not turned away
His mercy nor His precious word
    From those who love to pray.

No, still He bows His ear
    In gentle pity down;
For praying breath He loves to hear,
    And praying souls He'll crown.

Then let us still go on
    In His appointed ways,
Rejoicing in His name alone
    In prayer and humble praise.

517   Nahum Tate, Nicholas Brady   CM
**But Thou art the same, and Thy years shall
have no end.** *Psalm 102:27*

Through endless years Thou art the same,
    O Thou eternal God!
Ages to come shall know Thy name,
    And spread Thy praise abroad.

The strong foundations of the earth
    Of old by Thee were laid;
By Thee the beauteous arch of heaven
    With matchless skill was made.

Soon shall this goodly frame of things,
    Formed by Thy powerful hand,
Be like a vesture laid aside,
    And changed at Thy command.

But Thy eternal state, O Lord,
    No length of time shall waste:
Thy power and wisdom, truth and grace,
    From age to age shall last.

Then to the children of Thy saints
Shalt endless blessings give:
They in their fathers' God shall trust,
And in Thy presence live.

HENRY LYTE 1793-1847

518   Henry Lyte   87 87 47
Psalm 103

Praise, my soul, the King of heaven,
To His feet Thy tribute bring;
Ransomed, healed, restored, forgiven,
Who like Thee His praise should sing;
Praise Him! Praise Him!
Praise the everlasting King!

Praise Him for His grace and favour
To our fathers in distress;
Praise him, still the same for ever,
Slow to chide, and swift to bless;
Praise Him! Praise Him!
Glorious in His faithfulness.

Father-like, He tends and spares us;
Well our feeble frame He knows;
In His hands He gently bears us,
Rescues us from all our foes;
Praise Him! Praise Him!
Widely as His mercy flows.

Frail as summer's flower we flourish;
Blows the wind, and it is gone;
But while mortals rise and perish
God endures unchanging on.
Praise Him! Praise Him!
Praise the high eternal One.

Angels help us to adore him,
Ye behold Him face to face;
Sun and moon, bow down before him,
Dwellers all in time and space;
Praise Him! Praise Him!
Praise with us the God of grace.

519   Isaac Watts   SM
Psalm 103

O bless the Lord, my soul!
Let all within me join,
And aid my tongue to bless His name
Whose favours are divine.

O bless the Lord, my soul!
Nor let His mercies lie
Forgotten in unthankfulness,
And without praises die.

'Tis He forgives thy sins;
'Tis He relieves thy pain;
'Tis He that heals thy sicknesses,
And makes thee young again.

He crowns thy life with love,
When ransomed from the grave;
He that redeemed my soul from hell,
Hath sovereign power to save.

He fills the poor with good;
He gives the sufferers rest;
The Lord hath judgments for the proud,
And justice for the oppressed.

His wondrous works and ways
He made by Moses known;
But sent the world His truth and grace
By His belovèd Son.

520   Isaac Watts   SM
The LORD is merciful and gracious.
Psalm 103:8

My soul, repeat His praise,
Whose mercies are so great,
Whose anger is so slow to rise,
So ready to abate.

God will not always chide;
And, when His strokes are felt,
His strokes are fewer than our crimes,
And lighter than our guilt.

High as the heavens are raised
Above the ground we tread,
So far the riches of His grace
Our highest thoughts exceed.

His power subdues our sins,
And His forgiving love,
Far as the East is from the West,
Does all our guilt remove.

521   William Gadsby   SM

Like as a father pitieth his children, so the LORD pitieth them that fear Him.
Psalm 103:13

The Lord Jehovah is
  Our Father and our Friend;
Immortal majesty is His,
  Nor can His glory end.

He guards His children well,
  Nor shall they starve for want;
When they their needs unto Him tell,
  He'll answer their complaint.

He bids His saints draw nigh,
  Nor fear to call Him theirs;
And, though He reigns enthroned on high,
  He calls them sons and heirs.

His sympathising heart
  Feels for them in distress;
And love divine He will impart,
  With strength and righteousness.

Though they in darkness walk,
  He is their Father still;
And when insulting Ishmaels mock
  He will His grace reveal.

His children He supplies
  With food and raiment too;
He with His wisdom makes them wise,
  And will their strength renew.

Through all the scenes of time,
  He'll make His goodness known;
His sons, in every age and clime,
  His sovereign grace shall own.

522   Richard Burnham   CM

But the mercy of the LORD is from everlasting to everlasting upon them that fear Him.
Psalm 103:17

Mercy divine is sovereign, free,
  And infinitely great;
Ancient as vast eternity,
  And most divinely sweet.

The wondrous mercy of a God
  Saves an apostate race;
Applies the balm of Jesus' blood,
  And yields a sacred peace.

Pardon, and life, and heavenly joys,
  Flow from this living stream:
Streams of rich blessings ever rise,
  To make us louder sing.

'Tis sovereign mercy sweetly draws
  The heaven-born child of God,
To walk in all His Father's laws,
  And prize the Saviour's blood.

'Tis mercy buries all complaints,
  Gives pleasures ever new;
O how she triumphs o'er the saints,
  And makes them triumph too!

Great God of mercy, roll along
  Mercy to every soul;
May mercy be the blissful song
  Sounded from pole to pole.

523   Robert Grant   55 55 65 65
Psalm 104

O worship the King,
  All-glorious above;
O gratefully sing
  His power and His love:
Our Shield and Defender,
  The Ancient of Days,
Pavilioned in splendour
  And girded with praise.

O tell of His might,
  O sing of His grace,
Whose robe is the light,
  Whose canopy space;
His chariots of wrath
  The deep thunder-clouds form,
And dark is His path
  On the wings of the storm.

The earth, with its store
  Of wonders untold,
Almighty, Thy power
  Hath founded of old;
Hath stablished it fast,
  By a changeless decree,
And round it hath cast,
  Like a mantle, the sea.

Thy bountiful care
  What tongue can recite?
It breathes in the air,
  It shines in the light;
It streams from the hills,
  It descends to the plain,
And sweetly distils
  In the dew and the rain.

Frail children of dust,
  And feeble as frail,
In Thee do we trust,
  Nor find Thee to fail;
Thy mercies how tender,
  How firm to the end,
Our Maker, Defender,
  Redeemer, and Friend!

524 Stuart K Hine

11 10 11 10 + refrain

O LORD my God, Thou art very great.
Psalm 104:1

O Lord my God! When I in awesome wonder
  Consider all the works Thy hand hath made,
I see the stars, I hear the mighty thunder,
  Thy power throughout the universe displayed:

Then sings my soul, my Saviour God, to Thee,
  How great Thou art! How great Thou art!
Then sings my soul, my Saviour God, to Thee,
  How great Thou art! How great Thou art!

When through the woods and forest glades I
  wander
And hear the birds sing sweetly in the trees;
When I look down from lofty mountain grandeur,
  And hear the brook, and feel the gentle breeze:

And when I think that God His Son not sparing,
  Sent Him to die—I scarce can take it in.
That on the cross my burden gladly bearing,
  He bled and died to take away my sin:

When Christ shall come with shout of acclamation
  And take me home—what joy shall fill my heart!
Then shall I bow in humble adoration
  And there proclaim, my God, how great Thou
    art!

Copyright © 2015 Thankyou Music/Adm. by Capitol CMG
Publishing.excl.UK&Europe, adm.by Integrity Music, part
of the David C Cook family, songs@integritymusic.com

525 Philip Doddridge LM

I will sing unto the Lord as long as I live.
Psalm 104:33

God of my life, through all my days
My grateful powers shall sound Thy praise;
My song shall wait with opening light,
And cheer the dark and silent night.

When anxious cares would break my rest,
And griefs would tear my throbbing breast,
Thy tuneful praises, raised on high,
Shall check the murmur and the sigh.

When death o'er nature shall prevail,
And all the powers of language fail,
Joy through my swimming eyes shall break,
And mean the thanks I cannot speak.

But O when that last conflict's o'er,
And I am chained to earth no more,
With what glad accents shall I rise
To join the music of the skies!

Soon shall I learn the exalted strains
Which echo through the heavenly plains;
And emulate, with joy unknown,
The glowing seraphs round the throne.

The cheerful tribute will I give
Long as a deathless soul shall live;
A word so sweet, a theme so high,
Demands and crowns eternity.

526 Augustus Toplady CM

My meditation of Him shall be sweet: I will be
glad in the LORD. *Psalm 104:34*

When languor and disease invade
  This trembling house of clay,
'Tis sweet to look beyond our cage,
  And long to fly away.

Sweet to look inward, and attend
  The whispers of His love;
Sweet to look upward to the place
  Where Jesus pleads above.

Sweet to look back, and see my name
  In life's fair book set down;
Sweet to look forward, and behold
  Eternal joys my own.

Sweet to reflect how grace divine
  My sins on Jesus laid;
Sweet to remember that His blood
  My debt of suffering paid.

Sweet in His righteousness to stand,
  Which saves from second death;
Sweet to experience, day by day,
  His Spirit's quickening breath.

Sweet in His faithfulness to rest,
  Whose love can never end;
Sweet on His covenant of grace
  For all things to depend.

Sweet in the confidence of faith
  To trust His firm decrees;
Sweet to lie passive in His hands,
  And know no will but His.

If such the sweetness of the streams
  What must the fountain be
Where saints and angels draw their bliss
  Immediately from Thee!

527   Nahum Tate, Nicholas Brady   CM
Psalm 105

O render thanks and bless the Lord;
  Invoke His sacred name;
Acquaint the nations with His deeds,
  His matchless deeds proclaim.

Sing to His praise in lofty hymns,
  His wondrous works rehearse;
Make them the theme of your discourse,
  And subject of your verse.

Rejoice in His almighty name,
  Alone to be adored;
And let their hearts o'erflow with joy
  That humbly seek the Lord.

Seek ye the Lord, His saving strength
  Devoutly still implore;
And where He's ever present seek
  His face for evermore.

528   *The Scottish Psalter 1650*   CM
Praise ye the LORD. O give thanks unto the LORD. *Psalm 106:1*

Give praise and thanks unto the Lord,
  For bountiful is He;
His tender mercy doth endure
  Unto eternity.

God's mighty works who can express,
  Or show forth all His praise?
Blessèd are they that judgment keep,
  And justly do always.

Remember me, Lord, with that love
  Which Thou to Thine dost bear;
With Thy salvation, O my God,
  To visit me draw near,

That I Thy chosen's good may see,
  And in their joy rejoice,
And may with Thine inheritance
  Triumph with cheerful voice.

529   Fanny Crosby   98 98 + refrain
Let the redeemed of the LORD say so.
Psalm 107:2

Redeemed! how I love to proclaim it,
  Redeemed by the blood of the Lamb;
Redeemed through His infinite mercy,
  His child and forever I am.

Redeemed, redeemed,
Redeemed by the blood of the Lamb,
Redeemed, redeemed,
His child and for ever I am.

Redeemed and so happy in Jesus,
  No language my rapture can tell;
I know that the light of His presence
  With me doth continually dwell.

I know I shall see in His beauty,
  The King in whose law I delight;
Who lovingly guardeth my footsteps,
  And giveth me songs in the night.

530   John Newton   CM
And He led them forth by the right way.
Psalm 107:7

When Israel was from Egypt freed,
  The Lord, who brought them out,
Helped them in every time of need,
  But led them round about.

To enter Canaan soon they hoped,
  But quickly changed their mind;
When the Red Sea their passage stopped,
  And Pharaoh marched behind.

The desert filled them with alarms,
  For water and for food;
And Amalek, by force of arms,
  To check their progress stood.

They often murmured by the way,
  Because they judged by sight;
But were at length constrained to say,
  The Lord had led them right.

In the Red Sea that stopped them first,
  Their enemies were drowned.
The rocks gave water for their thirst,
  And manna spread the ground.

By fire and cloud their way was shown,
  Across the pathless sands;
And Amalek was overthrown,
  By Moses' lifted hands.

The way was right their hearts to prove,
  To make God's glory known;
And show His wisdom, power and love,
  Engaged to save His own.

Just so the true believer's path
  Through many dangers lies;
Though dark to sense, 'tis right to faith,
  And leads us to the skies.

531   Joseph Irons   LM
And He led them forth by the right way.
Psalm 107:7

Let saints proclaim Jehovah's praise,
And acquiesce in all His ways;
He keeps eternity in sight.
And what His hand performs is right.

'By the right way' His saints are led,
Which none but holy souls can tread:
The way that carnal reason hates,
Although it leads to heaven's bright gates.

''Tis the right way,' though dark and rough;
Mysterious, yet 'tis plain enough;
And we, when faith is changed to sight,
Shall know 'the ways of God were right.'

''Tis the right way' when pain and loss
Our flattering expectations cross;
And if our souls the end could view,
We should approve the pathway too.

''Tis the right way,' Lord lead me on
Through this vain world up to Thy throne;
Where reason fails, may faith approve,
And wait till all's explained above.

532   Joseph Gilmore   LM + refrain
And He led them forth by the right way.
Psalm 107:7

He leadeth me! O blessèd thought!
O words with heavenly comfort fraught!
Whate'er I do, where'er I be,
Still 'tis God's hand that leadeth me.

He leadeth me! He leadeth me!
By His own hand He leadeth me;
His faithful follower I would be,
For by His hand He leadeth me.

Sometimes 'mid scenes of deepest gloom,
Sometimes where Eden's bowers bloom,
By waters calm, o'er troubled sea,
Still 'tis God's hand that leadeth me.

Lord, I would clasp Thy hand in mine
Nor ever murmur nor repine;
Content, whatever lot I see,
Since 'tis my God that leadeth me.

And when my task on earth is done,
When, by Thy grace, the victory's won,
E'en death's cold waves I would not flee
Since Thou through Jordan leadeth me.

533   Latin 12th Cent., tr. Ray Palmer   LM
For He satisfieth the longing soul.
Psalm 107:9

Jesus, Thou Joy of loving hearts,
    Thou Fount of life, Thou Light of men,
From the best bliss that earth imparts,
    We turn unfilled to Thee again.

Thy truth unchanged hath ever stood;
    Thou savest those that on Thee call;
To them that seek Thee Thou art good,
    To them that find Thee, all in all.

We taste Thee, O Thou living Bread,
    And long to feast upon Thee still;
We drink of Thee, the Fountain-Head,
    And thirst our souls from Thee to fill.

Our restless spirits yearn for Thee
    Where'er our changeful lot is cast;
Glad, when Thy gracious smile we see;
    Blest, when our faith can hold Thee fast.

O Jesus, ever with us stay,
    Make all our moments calm and bright;
Chase the dark night of sin away;
    Shed o'er our souls Thy holy light.

534   William Whiting   88 88 88
He bringeth them out of their distresses.
Psalm 107:28

Eternal Father, strong to save,
Whose arm hath bound the restless wave,
Who bidst the mighty ocean deep
Its own appointed limits keep;
    O hear us, when we cry to Thee
    For those in peril on the sea!

O Christ, whose voice the waters heard
And hushed their raging at Thy word,
Who walkedst on the foaming deep
And calm amidst its rage didst sleep!
    O hear us, when we cry to Thee
    For those in peril on the sea!

Most Holy Spirit, who didst brood
Upon the chaos, dark and rude
And bid its angry tumult cease
And give, for wild confusion, peace;
    O hear us, when we cry to Thee
    For those in peril on the sea!

O Trinity of love and power,
Our brethren shield in danger's hour;
From rock and tempest, fire and foe,
Protect them wheresoe'er they go!
    Thus evermore shall rise to Thee
    Glad hymns of praise from land and sea.

535   Thomas Kelly   LM

He bringeth them unto their desired haven.
Psalm 107:30

The Christian navigates a sea
Where various forms of death appear;
Nor skill, alas! nor power has he,
Alright his dangerous course to steer.

Why does he venture, then, from shore,
And dare so many deaths to brave?
Because the land affrights him more
Than all the perils of the wave;

Because he hopes a port to find,
Where all his toil will be repaid;
And though unskilful, weak, and blind,
Yet Jesus bids him nothing dread.

His destined land he sometimes sees,
And thinks his toils will soon be o'er;
Expects some favourable breeze
Will waft him quickly to the shore.

But sudden clouds obstruct his view,
And he enjoys the sight no more;
Nor does he now believe it true
That he had ever seen the shore.

Though fear his heart should overwhelm,
He'll reach the port for which he's bound;
For Jesus holds and guides the helm,
And safety is where he is found.

536   Henry Lyte   LM
Psalm 109

Stranger and pilgrim here below,
   I turn for refuge, Lord, to Thee;
Thou know'st my every want and woe;
   O smite my foes, and rescue me!

Thy name is love; for that name's sake
   Sustain and cheer my sinking soul;
Low as I am, and poor, and weak,
   One word of Thine can make me whole.

Help, Lord! let all my foes perceive,
   'Tis Thine to comfort or condemn;
With Thee to bless me and relieve,
   I little heed reproach from men.

Arise then, on my soul arise;
   Thy sheltering wings around me cast:
And all that now afflicts or tries
   Shall work my peace, O Lord, at last.

537   Harriet Auber   77 77 D
Psalm 110

Jesus, Lord, to Thee we sing,
Thee our Saviour, Priest, and King,
   Who our guilt and woes sustained,
   And the cup of vengeance drained:
Now Thou sitt'st enthroned on high,
Crowned with power and victory;
   All Thy foes shall prostrate fall,
   Every nation hear Thy call.

As at morning's youthful hour,
Dewdrops gem each leaf and flower,
   So, O Lord, our sons unborn,
   Shall Thy crowded courts adorn;
Gladly own Thee for their King,
Gladly free-will offerings bring,
   Till Thy spreading empire prove
   Boundless as Thy wondrous love.

538   Augustus Toplady   10 10 11 11

Thy people shall be willing in the day of Thy power. *Psalm 110:3*

   How mighty Thou art, O Lord, to convert;
   Thou only couldst conquer so stubborn a heart,
For Thy love to lost man alone could constrain
So stiff-necked a rebel to love Thee again.

   Through Thee I embrace the ransoming grace,
   Of Him who has suffered and died in my place,
Though I strove to withstand the force of Thy
      hand,
Thy Spirit would conquer, and I was constrained.

   In vain I withstood, and fled from my God,
   For mercy would save me through Jesus's
      blood.
I felt it applied, and I joyfully cried,
   'Me, me Thou hast loved, and for me Thou hast
      died.'

For sinners like me Thy mercy is free,
Who hunger and thirst for redemption by Thee.
Lord, gather in more; make this the glad hour;
Compel them to yield in the day of Thy power.

539   John Cennick   CM

Thou art a priest for ever after the order of Melchizedek. *Psalm 110:4*

Thou dear Redeemer, dying Lamb,
   We love to hear of Thee;
No music's like Thy charming name
   Nor half so sweet can be.

O let us ever hear Thy voice;
In mercy to us speak;
And in our Priest we will rejoice,
Thou great Melchizedek.

Our Jesus shall be still our theme,
While in this world we stay;
We'll sing our Jesus' lovely name,
When all things else decay.

When we appear in yonder cloud
With all Thy favoured throng,
Then will we sing more sweet, more loud,
And Christ shall be our song.

540   John Wingrove   77 77
Thou art a priest for ever after the order of Melchizedek. *Psalm 110:4*

King of Salem, bless my soul!
Make a wounded sinner whole!
King of righteousness and peace,
Let not Thy sweet visits cease!

Come, refresh this soul of mine
With Thy sacred bread and wine!
All Thy love to me unfold,
Half of which cannot be told.

Hail, Melchizedek divine;
Great High Priest, Thou shalt be mine;
All my powers before Thee fall;
Take not tithe, but take them all.

541   Charles Spurgeon   87 87
Psalm 111

Praise the Lord; with exultation
My whole heart my Lord shall praise
'Midst the upright congregation,
Loftiest hallelujahs raise.

All His works are great and glorious,
Saints review them with delight;
His redemption all victorious
We remember day and night.

Meat He gives to those who fear Him,
Of His covenant mindful still;
Wise are those who much revere Him,
And rejoice to do His will.

For His grace stands fast for ever,
His decrees the saints secure;
From His oath He turneth never,
Every promise standeth sure.

Therefore be His praise unceasing,
Be His name for ever blest;
And with confidence increasing,
Let us on His promise rest.

542   Joseph Hart   LM
He hath made His wonderful works to be remembered. *Psalm 111:4*

How wondrous are the works of God,
Displayed through all the world abroad!
Immensely great! Immensely small!
Yet one strange work exceeds them all!

He formed the sun, fair fount of light;
The moon and stars, to rule the night;
But night and stars, and moon and sun,
Are little works compared with one.

He rolled the seas and spread the skies,
Made valleys sink and mountains rise;
The meadows clothed with native green,
And bade the rivers glide between.

But what are seas, or skies, or hills,
Or verdant vales, or gliding rills,
To wonders man was born to prove:
The wonders of redeeming love?

'Tis far beyond what words express,
What saints can feel or angels guess;
Angels, that hymn the great I AM,
Fall down and veil before the Lamb.

The highest heavens are short of this;
'Tis deeper than the vast abyss;
'Tis more than thought can e'er conceive,
Or hope expect, or faith believe.

Almighty God sighed human breath!
The Lord of life experienced death!
How it was done we can't discuss,
But this we know, 'twas done for us.

Blest with this faith, then let us raise
Our hearts in love, our voice in praise;
All things to us must work for good,
For whom the Lamb has shed His blood.

Trials may press of every sort;
They may be sore, they must be short;
We now believe, but soon shall view,
The greatest glories God can show.

543   Isaac Watts, J Needham   CM
Holy and reverend is His name.
Psalm 111:9

How shall I praise the eternal God,
  That infinite Unknown?
Who can ascend His high abode,
  Or venture near His throne?

Heaven's brightest lamps, with Him compared,
  How mean they look, and dim!
The holy angels have no spots,
  Yet can't compare with Him.

Holy is He in all His works,
  And truth is His delight;
But sinners, and their wicked ways,
  Shall perish from His sight.

None but His favourites may draw near,
  Who stand in Christ complete;
Those holy ones shall all appear
  And worship at His feet.

In Jesus' image shining bright
  With rapture they adore
The holy, holy, holy Lord,
  In glory evermore.

544   Joseph Hart   10 10 11 11
The fear of the LORD is the beginning of wisdom. *Psalm 111:10*

The fear of the Lord our days will prolong,
  In trouble afford a confidence strong,
Will keep us from sinning, will prosper our ways,
And is the beginning of wisdom and grace.

The fear of the Lord preserves us from death,
  Enforces His word, enlivens our faith,
It regulates passion, and helps us to quell
The dread of damnation and terrors of hell.

The fear of the Lord is soundness and health;
  A treasure well stored with heavenly wealth;
A fence against evil, by which we resist
World, flesh, and the devil, and imitate Christ.

The fear of the Lord is clean and approved;
  Makes Satan abhorred and Jesus beloved;
It conquers in weakness; is proof against strife;
A cordial in sickness; a fountain of life.

The fear of the Lord is lowly and meek;
  The happy reward of all that Him seek;
They only that fear Him the truth can discern,
For, living so near Him, His secrets they learn.

The fear of the Lord His mercy makes dear,
  His judgments adored, His righteousness clear,
Without its fresh flavour, in knowledge there's
  fault;
In doctrines no savour; in duties no salt.

The fear of the Lord confirms a good hope;
  By this are restored the senses that droop;
The deeper it reaches, the more the soul thrives;
It gives what it teaches, and guards what it gives.

The fear of the Lord forbids us to yield;
  It sharpens our sword and strengthens our
  shield.
Then cry we to heaven, with one loud accord,
That to us be given the fear of the Lord.

545   Charles Spurgeon   87 87 47
Psalm 112

Blessèd is the man that feareth,
  And delighteth in the Lord;
Wealth, the wealth which truly cheereth,
  God shall give Him for reward;
    And His children,
  Shall be blest around His board.

He shall not be moved for ever,
  Though with evil tidings tried;
Nought from God His faith shall sever,
  Fixed His heart shall still abide;
    For believers
  Are secured on every side.

To the upright light arises,
  Darkness soon gives place to day;
While the man who truth despises,
  And refuses to obey,
    In a moment,
  Cursed of God, shall melt away.

Therefore let us praise Jehovah:
  Sound His glorious name on high,
Sing His praises, and moreover
  By our actions magnify
    Our Redeemer,
  Who by blood has brought us nigh.

JOHN ELLERTON 1826-93

The sea beheld, and struck with dread,
Rolled all its billows back;
And Jordan, through his deepest bed,
Revealed their destined track.

What ailed thee, O thou mighty sea!
Why rolled thy waves in dread?
What bade thy tide, O Jordan, flee
And bare its deepest bed?

O earth, before the Lord, the God
Of Jacob, tremble still:
Who makes the waste a watered sod,
The flint a gushing rill.

546 John Ellerton 98 D

From the rising of the sun unto the going down of the same the LORD'S name is to be praised. *Psalm 113:3*

The day Thou gavest, Lord, is ended,
The darkness falls at Thy behest,
To Thee our morning hymns ascended,
Thy praise shall sanctify our rest.

We thank Thee that Thy church, unsleeping,
While earth rolls onward into light,
Through all the world her watch is keeping,
And rests not now by day or night.

As o'er each continent and island
The dawn leads on another day,
The voice of prayer is never silent,
Nor dies the strain of praise away.

The sun that bids us rest is waking
Our brethren 'neath the Western sky,
And hour by hour fresh lips are making
Thy wondrous doings heard on high.

So be it, Lord,Thy throne shall never
Like earth's proud empires pass away,
Thy kingdom stands and grows for ever,
Till all Thy creatures own Thy sway.

547 George Burgess CM
Psalm 114

When forth from Egypt's trembling strand
The tribes of Israel sped,
And Jacob in the stranger's land
Departing banners spread;

Then One, amid their thick array
His kingly dwelling made,
And all along the desert way
Their guiding sceptre swayed.

548 Timothy Dudley-Smith 87 87 D
Psalm 115

Not to us be glory given
But to Him who reigns above:
Glory to the God of heaven
For His faithfulness and love!
What though unbelieving voices
Hear no word and see no sign,
Still in God my heart rejoices,
Working out His will divine.

Not what human fingers fashion,
Gold and silver, deaf and blind,
Dead to knowledge and compassion,
Having neither heart nor mind,
Lifeless gods, yet some adore them,
Nerveless hands and feet of clay;
All become, who bow before them,
Lost indeed, and dead as they.

Not in them is hope of blessing,
Hope is in the living Lord:
High and low, His name confessing,
Find in Him their shield and sword.
Hope of all whose hearts revere Him,
God of Israel, still the same!
God of Aaron! Those who fear Him,
He remembers them by name.

Not the dead, but we the living
Praise the Lord with all our powers;
Of His goodness freely giving,
His is heaven; earth is ours.
Not to us be glory given
But to Him who reigns above:
Glory to the God of heaven,
For His faithfulness and love!

ARTHUR STONE 1924-2008

549   Arthur Stone   LM
I love the LORD. *Psalm 116:1*

I love the Lord! Praise God for this,
Joy, source and centre of my bliss.
O would I know and love much more,
But find my sins a dreadful sore.

I love the Lord, and now can see,
The reason's this, He first loved me,
O! How eternal is that love,
That brought my Saviour from above.

'Lovest thou Me?' the Saviour says,
Then walk in My appointed ways.
He that believes and is baptized,
Will ne'er of heaven be despised.

I love the Lord! He's heard my prayer,
Does this not testimony bear?
That Jesus lives and intercedes,
And all my supplications pleads.

And when that river comes in sight,
When clouds appear as dark as night,
Lord, strength and grace and peace afford,
And may I cry, 'I love the Lord.'

© Mrs Carol Evans

550   Isaac Watts   CM
Psalm 116

What shall I render to my God,
    For all His kindness shown?
My feet shall visit Thine abode,
    My songs address Thy throne.

Among the saints that fill Thine house,
    My offerings shall be paid:
There shall my zeal perform the vows
    My soul in anguish made.

How much is mercy Thy delight,
    Thou ever-blessèd God!
How dear Thy servants in Thy sight!
    How precious is their blood!

How happy all Thy servants are!
    How great Thy grace to me!
My life, which Thou hast made Thy care,
    Lord, I devote to Thee.

Now I am Thine, for ever Thine,
    Nor shall my purpose move!
Thy hand hath loosed my bands of pain,
    And bound me with Thy love.

Here in Thy courts I leave my vow,
    And Thy rich grace record:
Witness, ye saints, who hear me now,
    If I forsake the Lord.

551   John Newton   CM
What shall I render unto the LORD for all His benefits toward me? *Psalm 116:12*

For mercies countless as the sands,
    Which daily I receive
From Jesus, my Redeemer's hands,
    My soul, what canst thou give?

Alas! from such a heart as mine
    What can I bring Him forth?
My best is stained and dyed with sin,
    My all is nothing worth.

Yet this acknowledgment I'll make,
    For all He has bestowed—
Salvation's sacred cup I'll take,
    And call upon thy God.

The best returns for one like me,
    So wretched and so poor,
Is from His gifts to draw a plea,
    And ask Him still for more.

I cannot serve Him as I ought,
    No works have I to boast,
Yet would I glory in the thought
    That I should owe Him most.

552   Frances Havergal   66 66 66
What shall I render unto the LORD for all His benefits toward me? *Psalm 116:12*

Thy life was given for me,
   Thy blood, O Lord, was shed
That I might ransomed be
   And quickened from the dead.
Thy life was given for me;
What have I given for Thee?

Long years were spent for me
   In weariness and woe
That through eternity
   Thy glory I might know.
Long years ware spent for me;
Have I spent one for Thee?

Thy Father's home of light,
   Thy rainbow-circled throne,
Were left for earthly night,
   For wanderings sad and lone.
Yes, all was left for me;
Have I left aught for Thee?

Thou, Lord, hast borne for me
   More than my tongue can tell
Of bitterest agony
   To rescue me from hell.
Thou sufferedst all for me;
What have I borne for Thee?

And Thou hast brought to me
   Down from Thy home above
Salvation full and free,
   Thy pardon and Thy love.
Great gifts Thou broughtest me;
What have I brought to Thee?

O let my life be given,
   My years for Thee be spent,
World-fetters all be riven
   And joy with suffering blent.
To Thee my all I bring,
My Saviour and my King!

553   James Montgomery   77 77
Psalm 117

All ye nations, praise the Lord,
   All ye lands, your voices raise;
Heaven and earth with loud accord,
   Praise the Lord, for ever praise:

For His truth and mercy stand,
   Past, and present, and to be;
Like the years of His right hand,
   Like His own eternity.

Praise Him, ye who know His love;
   Praise Him from the depths beneath;
Praise Him in the heights above;
   Praise your Maker, all that breathe.

THOMAS KEN 1637-1711

554   Thomas Ken   LM
O praise the LORD, all ye nations.
Psalm 117:1

Praise God, from whom all blessings flow;
Praise Him all creatures here below;
Praise Him above, ye heavenly host;
Praise Father, Son, and Holy Ghost.

555   Graham Harrison   98 98 D
Psalm 118

Unto the Lord come, raise together
   Glad songs of praise from earth below;
To Him whose mercy lasts for ever
   True thankfulness now let us show:
When, in distress, my cry ascended,
   He answered me and set me free;
I will not fear, by Him defended:
   What can man do now unto me?

Better it is on Him relying
   Than confidence in man to place;
My enemies around defying,
   Undaunted in His name I'll face:
My strength, my song and my salvation,
   All has the Lord become to me!
Praise, then, with joyful acclamation,
   His hand that brings the victory.

Thee will I praise—Thou hast protected
   When Thou didst hear my helpless cry;
The stone by builders once rejected
   Now in its place is set on high.
Save, Lord, we plead, Thou great Defender,
   Send to us now prosperity;
With grateful hearts we then will render
Our sacrifice of praise to Thee.
© Mrs. Eluned Harrison

556   Carl Spitta, tr. S Findlater   11 10 11 10
The voice of rejoicing and salvation is in the tabernacles of the righteous.
Psalm 118:15

O happy home where Thou art loved the dearest,
Thou loving Friend, and Saviour of our race,
And where among the guests there never cometh
One who can hold such high and honoured place!

O happy home where two in heart united
In holy faith and blessèd hope are one,
Whom death a little while alone divideth
And cannot end the union here begun!

O happy home whose little ones are given
Early to Thee, in humble faith and prayer,
To Thee, their Friend, who from the heights of heaven
Guides them and guards with more than mother's care!

O happy home where each one serves Thee lowly,
Whatever His appointed work may be,
Till every common task seems great and holy,
When it is done, O Lord, as unto Thee!

O happy home where Thou art not forgotten
When joy is overflowing, full and free;
O happy home, where every wounded spirit
Is brought, Physician, Comforter, to Thee.

Until at last, when earth's day's work is ended,
All meet Thee in the blessèd home above,
From whence Thou camest, where Thou hast ascended,
Thy everlasting home of peace and love!

557   Isaac Watts   CM
This is the day which the LORD hath made; we will rejoice and be glad in it. *Psalm 118:24*

This is the day the Lord hath made,
  He calls the hours His own;
Let heaven rejoice, let earth be glad,
  And praise surround the throne.

Today He rose and left the dead,
  And Satan's empire fell:
Today the saints His triumph spread,
  And all His wonders tell.

Hosanna to the anointed King,
  To David's holy Son!
Make haste to help us, Lord, and bring
  Salvation from Thy throne.

Blest be the Lord, who comes to men
  With messages of grace;
Who comes in God His Father's name,
  To save our sinful race.

Hosanna, in the highest strains
  The church on earth can raise;
The highest heavens in which He reigns
  Shall give Him nobler praise!

558   Charles Wesley   88 88 88
This is the day which the LORD hath made; we will rejoice and be glad in it. *Psalm 118:24*

Come let us with our Lord arise,
Our Lord, who made both earth and skies;
Who died to save the world He made,
And rose triumphant from the dead;
  He rose, the Prince of life and peace,
  And stamped the day for ever His.

This is the day the Lord hath made,
That all may see His love displayed,
May feel His resurrection's power,
And rise again to fall no more,
  In perfect righteousness renewed,
  And filled with all the life of God.

Then let us render Him His own,
With solemn prayer approach the throne,
With meekness hear the gospel word,
With thanks His dying love record;
  Our joyful hearts and voices raise,
  And fill His courts with songs of praise.

Honour and praise to Jesus pay
Throughout His consecrated day;
Be all in Jesus' praise employed,
Nor leave a single moment void;
  With utmost care the time improve,
  And only breathe His praise and love.

559 John Kent 77 77
O LORD, I beseech Thee, send now prosperity.
Psalm 118:25

Jesus, Sovereign Lord of all,
At Thy feet we humbly fall;
Lift our hearts and eyes to Thee,
Send, O Lord, prosperity.

On Thy church Thy Spirit breathe;
Say, 'the Holy Ghost receive;'
Void of this, we ne'er shall see
Days of sweet prosperity.

Signs and wonders in Thy name
Here display, Thou bleeding Lamb;
Raise the dead, the captive free,
Send, O Lord, prosperity.

Here let rebels at Thy throne,
Lay their hostile weapons down:
Kiss Thy feet with suppliant knee,
Send, O Lord, prosperity.

Pastors send Thy fold to bless,
Crown their labours with success;
Preaching not themselves, but Thee:
Source of all prosperity.

In Thy temple, living stones,
Place our daughters and our sons;
Trophies to Thy grace to be,
Send, O Lord, prosperity.

560 *Lady Huntingdon's coll.* 87 87 47
Blessed be he that cometh in the name of the LORD. *Psalm 118:26*

Lord, we welcome Thy dear servant,
  Messenger of gospel grace!
O how beauteous are the feet of
  Him that brings good news of peace!
    Lord, we welcome
  Every servant sent of Thee.

Bless, O bless his message to us!
  Give us hearts to hear the word
Of redemption, dearly purchased
  By the death of Christ our Lord.
    O reveal it
  To our poor and helpless souls!

Lord, vouchsafe Thy grace and glory
  To Thy faithful labourer dear!
Let the incense of our hearts be
  Offered up in faith and prayer,
    Bless, O bless him
  Now, henceforth, for evermore!

561 Isaac Watts CM
Psalm 119

O how I love Thy holy law!
  'Tis daily my delight;
And thence my meditations draw
  Divine advice by night.

How doth Thy word my heart engage!
  How well employ my tongue!
And in my tiresome pilgrimage
  Yields me a heavenly song.

Am I a stranger, or at home,
  'Tis my perpetual feast:
Not honey dropping from the comb,
  So much allures the taste.

No treasures so enrich the mind,
  Nor shall Thy word be sold
For loads of silver well-refined,
  Nor heaps of choicest gold.

When nature sinks, and spirits droop,
  Thy promises of grace
Are pillars to support my hope,
  And there I write Thy praise.

562 *Psalter* 1912 LM
Wherewithal shall a young man cleanse his way? by taking heed thereto according to Thy word. *Psalm 119:9*

How shall the young direct their way?
  What light shall be their perfect guide?
Thy word, O Lord, will safely lead,
  If in its wisdom they confide.
Sincerely I have sought Thee, Lord,
  O let me not from Thee depart;
To know Thy will and keep from sin
  Thy word I cherish in my heart.

O blessèd Lord, teach me Thy law,
  Thy righteous judgments I declare;
Thy testimonies make me glad,
  For they are wealth beyond compare.
Upon Thy precepts and Thy ways
  My heart will meditate with awe;
Thy word shall be my chief delight,
  And I will not forget Thy law.

563   Clara Scott   88 98 888 4
**Open Thou mine eyes, that I may behold
wondrous things out of Thy law.**
Psalm 119:18

Open my eyes that I may see
  Glimpses of truth Thou hast for me;
Place in my hands the wonderful key
  That shall unclasp and set me free.
Silently now I wait for Thee,
  Ready, my God, Thy will to see;
Open my eyes, illumine me,
    Spirit divine!

Open my ears that I may hear
  Voices of truth Thou sendest clear;
And while the wave-notes fall on my ear,
  Everything false will disappear.
Silently now I wait for Thee,
  Ready, my God, Thy will to see;
Open my ears, illumine me,
    Spirit divine!

Open my mouth and let me bear
  Tidings of mercy everywhere;
Open my heart and let me prepare
  Love with Thy children thus to share.
Silently now I wait for Thee,
  Ready, my God, Thy will to see;
Open my heart, illumine me,
    Spirit divine!

Open my mind, that I may read
  More of Thy love in word and deed:
What shall I fear while yet Thou dost lead?
  Only for light from Thee I plead.
Silently now I wait for Thee,
  Ready, my God, Thy will to see;
Open my mind, illumine me,
    Spirit divine!

564   Mrs M A Chaplin   76 76 D
I have stuck unto Thy testimonies.
Psalm 119:31

Cleave to the words of Jesus,
  O hearts which sigh and ache;
They breathe a spell of quiet
  Which life-storms cannot break!
It lifts the heaviest burden,
  And lulls the strongest pain,
The hope of one day hearing
  That same sweet voice again.

Cleave to the words of Jesus,
  He says, 'Be not afraid;
Your heavenly Father knoweth
  The needs of all He made;
Let not your heart be troubled,
  While ye believe in Me,
For where My Father dwelleth,
  There shall My people be.'

Cleave to the words of Jesus
  Until He comes again;
And sing them till the weary
  Grow rested with the strain.
And while the words of others
  Lead many a soul astray,
Be ours to take the scriptures
  And tread the narrow way.

565   *Scottish Psalter 1615*   CM
Teach me, O LORD, the way of Thy statutes.
Psalm 119:33

Teach me, O Lord, the perfect way
  Of Thy precepts divine,
And to observe it to the end
  I shall my heart incline.

Give understanding unto me,
  So keep Thy law shall I;
Yea, ev'n with my whole heart I shall
  Observe it carefully.

In Thy law's path make me to go,
  For I delight therein;
My heart unto Thy testimonies,
  And not to greed, incline.

Turn Thou away my sight and eyes
  From viewing vanity;
And in Thy good and holy way
  Be pleased to quicken me.

566   John Newton   87 87 77
**This is my comfort in my affliction: for Thy
word hath quickened me.**
Psalm 119:50

Precious Bible! what a treasure
  Does the word of God afford!
All I want for life or pleasure,
  FOOD and MEDICINE, SHIELD and SWORD
Let the world account me poor,
Having this I need no more.

FOOD, to which the world's a stranger,
Here my hungry soul enjoys;
Of excess there is no danger;
Though it fills, it never cloys,
On a dying CHRIST I feed,
He is meat and drink indeed!

When my faith is faint and sickly,
Or when Satan wounds my mind,
Cordials to revive me quickly,
Healing MEDICINES, here I find,
To the promises I flee,
Each affords a remedy.

In the hour of dark temptation,
Satan cannot make me yield;
For the word of consolation
Is to me a mighty SHIELD:
While the scripture truths are sure,
From his malice I'm secure.

Vain his threats to overcome me,
When I take the Spirit's SWORD;
Then with ease I drive him from me;
Satan trembles at the word:
'Tis a sword for conquest made,
Keen the edge and strong the blade.

Shall I envy, then, the miser,
Doting on his golden store?
Sure I am, or should be, wiser;
I am rich, 'tis he is poor:
JESUS gives me in his word,
FOOD and MEDICINE, SHIELD and SWORD.

567 John Berridge   66 66 88
Thou art my portion, O LORD.
Psalm 119:57

I seek and hope to find
A portion for my soul,
To heal a feverish mind,
And make a bankrupt whole;
A cup of blessing for the poor,
That's free, and full, and flowing o'er.

No satisfying rest
Earth's fluttering joys impart;
The portion of a beast
Will not content my heart;
The God of spirits only can
Fill up the vast desires of man.

Then, Jesus, wilt Thou be
My portion and my all?
For I would wait on Thee,
And listen to Thy call;
My daily wants Thou canst supply,
And find me food, and bring me joy.

Whate'er I wish or want
Can come from Thee alone,
Thou canst my heart content;
Then let Thy grace be shown;
I'd choose Thee for my portion, Lord;
Supply me well from mercy's board.

568   *Original* 1790   LM
It is good for me that I have been afflicted.
Psalm 119:71

Lift up your heads, afflicted saints,
Suppress your murmurs and complaints,
And let this thought your grief remove,
That your afflictions are in love.

The wicked feel the scourging rod,
Yet neither know nor love our God,
But this should well be understood,
The Christian's trials are for good.

'Tis good that some should mourning go,
That they themselves may better know:
It makes them better love the Lord,
And value more His precious word.

'Tis good in youth to bear the yoke,
And to submit to every stroke:
Afflictions wean from sense and sin,
And make the graces grow within.

'Tis good that saints should trust the Lord,
And seek for comfort in His word:
There all they read will tend to prove
That their afflictions 'are in love.'

569   *Psalter* 1912   LM
For ever, O LORD, Thy word is settled in heaven. *Psalm 119:89*

For ever settled in the heavens,
Thy word, O Lord, shall firmly stand;
Thy faithfulness shall never fail;
The earth abides at Thy command.

Thy word and works unmoved remain,
Thine every purpose to fulfil;
All things are Thine and Thee obey,
And all as servants wait Thy will.

I should have perished in my woe
Had not I loved Thy law divine;
That law I never can forget;
O save me, Lord, for I am Thine.

The wicked would destroy my soul,
But in Thy truth is refuge sure;
Exceeding broad is Thy command,
And in perfection shall endure.

570   Anne Steele   CM
O how love I Thy law! it is my meditation all the day. *Psalm 119:97*

Father of mercies, in Thy word
    What endless glory shines!
For ever be Thy name adored
    For these celestial lines.

Here springs of consolation rise
    To cheer the fainting mind,
And thirsty souls receive supplies,
    And sweet refreshment find.

Here the Redeemer's welcome voice
    Spreads heavenly peace around;
And life and everlasting joys
    Attend the blissful sound.

O, may these hallowed pages be
    My ever dear delight!
And still new beauties may I see,
    And still increasing light.

Divine Instructor, gracious Lord,
    Be Thou for ever near;
Teach me to love Thy sacred word,
    And view my Saviour here.

571   Bernard Barton   CM
Thy word is a lamp unto my feet, and a light unto my path. *Psalm 119:105*

Lamp of our feet, whereby we trace
    Our path when wont to stray;
Stream from the fount of heavenly grace;
    Brook, by the traveller's way.

Bread of our souls, whereon we feed;
    True manna from on high;
Our guide and chart, wherein we read
    Of realms beyond the sky.

Pillar of fire, through watches dark,
    And radiant cloud by day:
When waves would whelm our tossing bark,
    Our anchor and our stay.

Word of the everlasting God,
    Will of His glorious Son,
Without thee how could earth be trod,
    Or heaven itself be won?

Yet to unfold thy hidden worth,
    Thy mysteries to reveal,
That Spirit who first gave thee forth,
    Thy volume must unseal.

Lord, grant that we aright may learn
    The wisdom it imparts,
And to its heavenly teaching turn,
    With simple, childlike hearts.

572   William How   76 76 D
Thy word is a lamp unto my feet, and a light unto my path. *Psalm 119:105*

O Word of God incarnate,
    O Wisdom from on high,
O Truth unchanged, unchanging,
    O Light of our dark sky,
We praise Thee for the radiance
    That from the hallowed page,
A lantern to our footsteps,
    Shines on from age to age.

The church from her dear Master
    Received the gift divine,
And still that light she lifteth,
    O'er all the earth to shine;
It is the golden casket
    Where gems of truth are stored;
It is the heaven-drawn picture
    Of Christ, the living Word.

It floateth like a banner
    Before God's host unfurled;
It shineth like a beacon
    Above the darkling world;
It is the chart and compass
    That, o'er life's surging sea,
'Mid mists, and rocks, and quick-sands,
    Still guides, O Christ, to Thee.

O make Thy church, dear Saviour,
    A lamp of burnished gold,
To bear before the nations
    Thy true light, as of old;
O teach Thy wandering pilgrims
    By this their path to trace,
Till, clouds and darkness ended,
    They see Thee face to face.

573   John Fawcett   CM
Thy word is a lamp unto my feet, and a light unto my path. *Psalm 119:105*

How precious is the Book divine,
    By inspiration given!
Bright as a lamp its doctrines shine,
    To guide our souls to heaven.

Its light, descending from above,
    Our gloomy world to cheer,
Displays a Saviour's boundless love,
    And brings His glories near.

It shows to man his wandering ways,
    And where his feet have trod;
And brings to view the matchless grace
    Of a forgiving God.

When once it penetrates the mind
    It conquers every sin;
The enlightened soul begins to find
    The path of peace divine.

It sweetly cheers our drooping hearts,
    In this dark vale of tears;
Life, light, and joy it still imparts,
    And quells our rising fears.

O'er all the strait and narrow way
    Its radiant beams are cast;
A light whose ever-cheering ray
    Grows brightest at the last.

This lamp through all the tedious night
    Of life shall guide our way,
Till we behold the clearer light
    Of an eternal day.

---

574   Albert Midlane   10 4 10 4 10 10
Thy word is a lamp unto my feet, and a light unto my path. *Psalm 119:105*

Thy word, O Lord, Thy precious word alone,
        Can lead me on;
By this, until the darksome night be gone,
        Lead Thou me on;
Thy word is light, Thy word is life and power,
By it, O guide me in each trying hour!

This all I have; around no light appears,
        O lead me on!
With eyes on Thee,though gazing through my
        tears,
        Lead Thou me on!
The good and best might lead me far astray,
Omniscient Saviour, lead Thou me, I pray!

Whate'er my path, led by Thy word, 'tis good,
        O lead me on!
Be my poor heart Thy blessèd word's abode,
        Lead Thou me on!
The Holy Spirit gives the light to see,
And leads me, by Thy word, close following Thee!

Led by aught else, I tread a devious way;
        O lead me on!
Speak, Lord, and help me ever to obey,
        Lead Thou me on!
My every step shall then be well defined,
And all I do according to Thy mind!

575   Edwin Hodder   CM
Thy law do I love. *Psalm 119:113*

Thy word is like a garden, Lord,
    With flowers bright and fair;
And every one who seeks may pluck
    A lovely garland there.

Thy word is like a deep, deep mine;
    And jewels rich and rare
Are hidden in its mighty depths,
    For every searcher there.

Thy word is like an armoury,
    Where soldiers may repair,
And find for life's long battle-day
    All needful weapons there.

O, may I love Thy precious word,
    May I explore the mine,
May I its fragrant flowers glean,
    May light upon me shine!

O, may I find my armour there,
    Thy word my trusty sword;
I'll learn to fight with every foe
    The battle of the Lord.

---

576   Isaac Watts   CM
Thy testimonies are wonderful.
Psalm 119:129

Great God, with wonder and with praise,
    Upon Thy works we look;
But still Thy wisdom, power, and grace,
    Shine brightest in Thy Book.

The stars that in their courses roll
    Have much instruction given;
But Thy good word informs the soul
    The way to life and heaven.

The fields provide us food, and show
    The goodness of the Lord;
But fruits of life and glory grow
    In Thy most holy word.

Here we are taught how Christ has died,
    To save from death and hell;
Not all the books on earth beside
    Such heavenly wonders tell.

Then let us love our Bible more,
    And take a fresh delight
By day to read these wonders o'er
    And meditate by night.

577 William Cowper CM
The entrance of Thy words giveth light.
Psalm 119:130

The Spirit breathes upon the word
  And brings the truth to sight;
Precepts and promises afford
  A sanctifying light.

A glory gilds the sacred page,
  Majestic, like the sun;
It gives a light to every age;
  It gives, but borrows none.

The hand that gave it still supplies
  The gracious light and heat;
Its truths upon the nations rise;
  They rise, but never set.

Let everlasting thanks be Thine,
  For such a bright display,
As makes a world of darkness shine
  With beams of heavenly day.

My soul rejoices to pursue
  The steps of Him I love;
Till glory breaks upon my view,
  In brighter worlds above.

578 Synesius; tr. A Chatfield SM
Look Thou upon me, and be merciful unto me.
Psalm 119:132

  Lord Jesus, think on me
  And purge away my sin;
From earthborn passions set me free
  And make me pure within.

  Lord Jesus, think on me
  With care and woe oppressed;
Let me Thy loving servant be
  And gain Thy promised rest.

  Lord Jesus, think on me
  Amid the battle's strife;
In all my pain and misery
  Be Thou my health and life.

  Lord Jesus, think on me
  Nor let me go astray;
Through darkness and perplexity
  Point Thou the heavenly way.

  Lord Jesus, think on me
  When flows the tempest high;
When on doth rush the enemy,
  O Saviour, be Thou nigh.

  Lord Jesus, think on me
  That, when this life is past,
I may the eternal brightness see
  And share Thy joy at last.

579 *Scottish Psalter 1615* CM
Thy law do I love.
Psalm 119:163 (also Psalm 19)

God's law is perfect, and converts
  The soul in sin that lies;
God's testimony is most sure,
  And makes the simple wise.

The statutes of the Lord are right,
  And do rejoice the heart;
The Lord's command is pure, and doth
  Light to the eyes impart.

Unspotted is the fear of God,
  And doth endure for ever;
The judgments of the Lord are true
  And righteous altogether.

Moreover, they Thy servants warn
  How he his life should frame;
A great reward provided is
  For them that keep the same.

The words which from my mouth proceed,
  The thoughts sent from my heart,
Accept, O Lord, for Thou my Strength
  And my Redeemer art.

580 John Berridge 66 66 88
I have longed for Thy salvation, O LORD.
Psalm 119:174

  Jesus I long for Thee,
    And sigh for Canaan's shore,
  Thy lovely face to see,
    And all my warfare o'er;
Here billows break upon my breast
And brooding sorrows steal my rest.

  I pant, I groan, I grieve
    For my untoward heart;
  How full of doubts I live,
    Though full of grace Thou art!
What poor returns I make to Thee
For all the mercy shown to me!

581 *Scottish Version*   CM
Psalm 120

Woe's me that I in Mesech am
  A sojourner so long;
That I in tabernacles dwell
  To Kedar that belong.

My soul with him that hateth peace
  Hath long a dweller been;
I am for peace; but when I speak,
  For battle they are keen.

My soul distracted mourns and pines
  To reach that peaceful shore,
Where all the weary are at rest,
  And troubles vex no more.

Fierce burning coals of juniper,
  And arrows of the strong,
Await those false and cruel tongues
  Which do the righteous wrong.

But as for me my song shall rise
  Before Jehovah's throne,
For He has seen my deep distress,
  And hearkened to my groan.

582   John Campbell   10 4 10 4 10 10
I will lift up mine eyes unto the hills.
Psalm 121:1

Unto the hills around do I lift up
      My longing eyes,
O whence for me shall my salvation come!
      From whence arise?
From God the Lord doth come my certain aid,
From God the Lord who heaven and earth hath
      made.

He will not suffer that thy foot be moved,
      Safe shalt thou be;
No careless slumber shall His eyelids close,
      Who keepeth thee;
Behold our God, the Lord, He slumbereth ne'er,
Who keepeth Israel in His holy care.

Jehovah is Himself thy keeper true,
      Thy changeless shade;
Jehovah thy defence on thy right hand
      Himself hath made;
And thee no sun by day shall ever smite,
No moon shall harm thee in the silent night.

From every evil shall He keep thy soul,
      From every sin;
Jehovah shall preserve thy going out,
      Thy coming in.
Above thee watching, He whom we adore
Shall keep thee henceforth, yea, for evermore.

583   Augustus Toplady   88 88 D
**Behold, He that keepeth Israel shall neither
slumber nor sleep.** *Psalm 121:4*

Inspirer and Hearer of prayer,
  Thou Shepherd and Guardian of Thine;
My all, to Thy covenant care,
  I sleeping and waking resign:
If Thou art my Shield and my Sun,
  The night is no darkness to me,
And fast as my moments roll on,
  They bring me but nearer to Thee.

Thy ministering spirits descend,
  To watch while Thy saints are asleep;
By day and by night they attend,
  The heirs of salvation to keep.
Bright seraphs dispatched from the throne,
  Repair to the stations assigned,
And angels elect are sent down
  To guard the elect of mankind.

584   Richard Burnham   CM
The LORD is thy keeper. *Psalm 121:5*

Christ is the Keeper of His saints,
  He guards them by His power;
Subdues their numerous complaints,
  In every gloomy hour.

What though they fear each dread alarm,
  Tried, and severely tossed;
Held by the Saviour's mighty arm,
  None, none can e'er be lost.

He'll lead them on fair Zion's road,
  Though weary, weak, and faint;
For O! they ne'er shall lose their God,
  Or God e'er lose a saint.

How sure His great salvation shines;
  How full the vast reward;
How firm the promise e'er remains:
  How faithful is the Lord!

585   Isaac Watts   668 D

I was glad when they said unto me, Let us go into the house of the LORD.
Psalm 122:1

How pleased and blest was I,
To hear the people cry,
'Come, let us seek our God today!'
Yes, with a cheerful zeal,
We haste to Zion's hill,
And there our vows and honours pay.

Zion, thrice happy place!
Adorned with wondrous grace,
And walls of strength embrace thee round;
In thee our tribes appear,
To pray, and praise, and hear
The sacred gospel's joyful sound.

There David's greater Son
Has fixed His royal throne;
He sits for grace and judgment there.
He bids the saints be glad;
He makes the sinner sad,
And humble souls rejoice with fear.

May peace attend thy gate,
And joy within thee wait,
To bless the soul of every guest;
The man that seeks thy peace,
And wishes thy increase,
A thousand blessings on him rest.

My tongue repeats her vows,
'Peace to this sacred house,'
For there my friends and kindred dwell;
And since my glorious God
Makes thee His blest abode,
My soul shall ever love thee well.

586   James Montgomery   77 77

I was glad when they said unto me, Let us go into the house of the LORD.
Psalm 122:1

To Thy temple we repair,
Lord, we love to worship there,
Where within the veil we meet
Christ before the mercy-seat.

While Thy glorious praise is sung,
Touch our lips, unloose our tongue,
That our joyful souls may bless
Thee, the Lord our righteousness.

While the prayers of saints ascend,
God of love, to ours attend;
Hear us, for Thy Spirit pleads;
Hear, for Jesus intercedes.

While we hearken to Thy law,
Fill our souls with humble awe,
Till Thy gospel to us be
Life and immortality.

From Thy house when we return,
May our hearts within us burn;
And at evening may we say,
'We have walked with God today.'

587   Henry Lyte   77 77
Psalm 123

Unto Thee I lift my eyes,
Thou that dwellest in the skies;
At Thy throne I meekly bow,
Thou canst save, and only Thou.

As a servant marks his lord,
As a maid her mistress' word,
So I watch and wait on Thee,
Till Thy mercy visit me.

Let Thy face upon me shine,
Tell me, Lord, that Thou art mine
Poor and little though I be,
I have all in having Thee.

Here to be despised, forgot,
Is Thy children's common lot;
But with Thee to make it up,
Lord, I ask no better cup.

588   John Ryland   LM

If it had not been the Lord who was on our side..
Psalm 124:1

'Had not the Lord,' my soul may cry,
'Had not the Lord been on my side;
Had He not brought deliverance nigh,
Then must my helpless soul have died.'

Had not the Lord been on my side,
My soul had been by Satan slain;
And Tophet, opening large and wide,
Would not have gaped for me in vain.

Lo, floods of wrath, and floods of hell,
In fierce impetuous torrents roll;
Had not the Lord defended well,
The waters had o'erwhelmed my soul.

As when the fowler's snare is broke,
The bird escapes on cheerful wings;
My soul, set free from Satan's yoke,
With joy bursts forth, and mounts, and sings.

She sings the Lord her Saviour's praise;
  Sings forth His praise with joy and mirth;
To Him her song in heaven she'll raise,
  To Him that made both heaven and earth!

589   Charles Wesley   SM
Psalm 125

Who in the Lord confide,
And feel His sprinkled blood,
In storms and hurricanes abide
Firm as the mount of God.

Steadfast and fIxed and sure,
His Zion cannot move;
His faithful people stand secure,
In Jesus' guardian love.

As round Jerusalem
The hilly bulwarks rise,
So God protects and covers them
From all their enemies.

On every side He stands,
And for His Israel cares;
And safe in His almighty hands
Their souls for ever bears.

But let them still abide
In Thee, all gracious Lord,
Till every soul is sanctified,
And perfectly restored.

The men of heart sincere
Continue to defend;
And do them good, and save them here,
And love them to the end.

590   Martin Rinckart, tr. Catherine Winkworth
                      67 67 66 66
**The LORD hath done great things for us;
whereof we are glad.** *Psalm 126:3*

Now thank we all our God,
  With heart and hands and voices,
Who wondrous things hath done,
  In whom His world rejoices;
Who from our mother's arms,
  Hath blessed us on our way
With countless gifts of love,
  And still is ours today.

O may this bounteous God
  Through all our life be near us,
With ever joyful hearts
  And blessèd peace to cheer us;
And keep us in His grace,
  And guide us when perplexed,
And free us from all ills
  In this world and the next.

All praise and thanks to God
  The Father now be given,
The Son, and Him who reigns
  With them in highest heaven—
The one eternal God,
  Whom earth and heaven adore;
For thus it was, is now,
  And shall be evermore.

591   David Denham   CM
**The LORD hath done great things for us;
whereof we are glad.** *Psalm 126:3*

Great things for us the Lord hath done,
  Before the world was made:
Beloved and chosen in His Son,
  On whom our help was laid.

Great things for us the Lord hath done,
  Redeemed from death and sin,
When Jesus did for us atone,
  And righteousness brought in.

Great things for us the Lord hath done,
  In Gospel truths revealed:
With God in covenant ever one,
  To endless glory sealed.

Great things for us the Lord hath done,
  In all our troubles past.
And all who trust in Christ alone
  Shall overcome at last.

Great things for us the Lord hath done,
  In providence and grace:
He will complete the work begun,
  And we shall see His face.

FANNY J CROSBY 1820-1915

592   Fanny Crosby   11 11 11 11 + refrain
**The LORD hath done great things for us;
whereof we are glad.** *Psalm 126:3*

To God be the glory! Great things He hath done!
So loved He the world that He gave us His Son,
Who yielded His life an atonement for sin
And opened the life-gate that we may go in.

Praise the Lord! praise the Lord!
Let the earth hear His voice!
Praise the Lord! praise the Lord!
Let the people rejoice!
O come to the Father through Jesus the Son;
And give Him the glory, great things He hath
done!

O perfect redemption, the purchase of blood!
To every believer the promise of God;
The vilest offender who truly believes,
That moment from Jesus a pardon receives.

Great things He hath taught us, great things He
    hath done
And great our rejoicing through Jesus the Son;
But purer and higher and greater will be
Our wonder, our transport, when Jesus we see!

593   John Ellerton   76 76 D
**Except the LORD build the house, they labour
in vain that build it.** *Psalm 127:1*

O Father all creating,
    Whose wisdom, love and power,
First bound two lives together
    In Eden's primal hour,
Today to these Thy children
    Thine earliest gifts renew,
A home by Thee made happy,
    A love by Thee kept true.

O Saviour, Guest most bounteous
    Of old in Galilee,
Vouchsafe today Thy presence
    With these who call on Thee;
Their store of earthly gladness
    Transform to heavenly wine,
And teach them in the tasting
    To know the gift is Thine.

O Spirit of the Father,
    Breathe on them from above;
So mighty in Thy pureness
    So tender in Thy love,
That, guarded by Thy presence,
    From sin and strife kept free,
Their lives may own Thy guidance,
    Their hearts be ruled by Thee.

Except Thou build it, Father,
    The house is built in vain;
Except Thou, Saviour, bless it,
    The joy will turn to pain;
But nought can break the union
    Of hearts in Thee made one;
And love Thy Spirit hallows
    Is endless love begun.

594   Vernon Higham   CM
**Except the LORD build the house, they labour
in vain that build it.** *Psalm 127:1*

We worship Thee, the King of grace,
    With heart and soul and voice;
O grant that mercy's smiling face
    May cause us to rejoice!

Along life's path we have been led
    By Thee, our Lord and Friend;
And we have tasted of the Bread
    Of Life, which Thou dost send.

We come to Thee for blessing now
Upon this wedding-day;
We ask Thee, Lord, Thy grace bestow
And may Thy presence stay.

We come our promises to make,
Present our vows to Thee;
Our humble prayer, O gently take,
That we may faithful be.

Upon our hearts, O grant Thy peace,
Thy guidance in our lives;
That we may walk the way of grace,
And be in all things wise.

Upon our home Thy blessing give,
A haven from the storm,
A place of comfort, where we live
In harmony and calm.

We look to Thee, our sovereign God,
For unction and for grace;
And when our journey we have trod,
We'll see Thy blessèd face.

© Author

595   Henry Lyte   LM
Psalm 128

How blest the man who fears the Lord,
Who walks by His unerring word;
His labours find a full increase,
His days are crowned with health and peace.

Domestic comfort builds her nest,
Beneath his roof, within his breast;
And earth's best blessings hourly rise
To cheer his pathway to the skies.

But earth's best gifts are poor to those
The Spirit on his soul bestows;
The earnest here of joys above,
The foretaste of eternal love.

Onward he goes from strength to strength,
Till heaven's bright morning breaks at length,
And calls him to his full reward:
How blest the man who fears the Lord!

596   John Beaumont   76 76 77 76
Psalm 129

Many times since days of youth,
May Israel truly say,
Foes devoid of love and truth
Afflict me day by day;
Yet they never can prevail,
God defends His people still;
Jesus' power can never fail
To save from all that's ill.

God hath Zion set apart
For His abiding place;
Sons of wrath and guileful art
He'll banish from His face:
God for Israel doth fight;
Israel, on thy God depend;
Christ shall keep thee day and night,
Till all thy troubles end.

597   John Ryland   CM
Psalm 130

Out of the depths of doubt and fear,
Depths of despair and grief,
I cry; my voice, O Jesus, hear,
And come to my relief!

Thy gracious ears, O Saviour, bow
To my distressful cries,
For who shall stand, O Lord, if Thou
Shouldst mark iniquities?

But why do I my soul distress?
Forgiveness is with Thee:
With Thee there is abundant grace,
That Thou mayst fearèd be.

Then for the Lord my soul shall wait,
And in His word I'll hope;
Continue knocking at His gate,
Till He the door shall ope.

Not weary guards who watch for morn,
And stand with longing eyes,
Feel such desires to see the dawn,
The joyful dawn arise!

They never feel such warm desires
As those which in me move,
As those wherewith my soul aspires
To see the God of love!

O God of mercy! let me not
Then hope for Thee in vain;
Nor let me ever be forgot,
And in despair remain.

598   Graham Harrison   87 87 887
Psalm 130

Out of the depths I cry to Thee;
   Lord, hear me, I implore Thee;
If Thou shouldst mark iniquity,
   Who, Lord, shall stand before Thee?
O may Thine ear attend my cry!
Lord, bid me to Thyself draw nigh,
   While now I call upon Thee.

'Tis Thee, O Lord, my soul doth seek,
   Upon Thy word relying;
Thou art a God who aids the meek,
   Their every need supplying.
Lord, may I Thy forgiveness know,
That I to Thee due fear may show,
   And humbly walk before Thee.

More doth my soul, Lord, for Thee wait
   Than those that long for morning,
Who through the darkest hours of night
   Are watching for the dawning.
From every sin, Lord, set me free;
Make my whole life bring praise to Thee,
   For Thou alone art worthy.

Hope thou, my soul, then, in the Lord,
   Whose plentiful redemption
And mercy shall to Thee afford
   The promise of salvation.
They hope in vain who think they can
Escape from sin by strength of man:
   God only can deliver.

© Mrs.Eluned Harrison

599   Martin Luther, tr. C Winkworth 87 87 887
Psalm 130

From deep distress I cry to Thee,
   Lord, hear me, I implore Thee;
Bend down Thy gracious ear to me,
   Regard my prayer before Thee;
If Thou rememberest each misdeed,
If each should have its rightful meed,
   Who may abide Thy presence?

Our pardon is Thy gift; Thy love
   And grace alone avail us;
Our works could ne'er our guilt remove,
   The strictest life would fail us;
That none may boast himself of aught,
But own in fear Thy grace hath wrought
   What in Him seemeth righteous.

And thus my hope is in the Lord
   And not in mine own merit;
I rest upon His faithful word
   To them of contrite spirit;
That He is merciful and just:
Here is my comfort and my trust;
   His help I wait with patience.

Though great our sins and sore our woes,
   His grace much more aboundeth;
His helping love no limit knows,
   Our utmost need it soundeth;
Our kind and faithful Shepherd He,
Who shall at last set Israel free
   From all their sin and sorrow.

600   Henry Baker   SM
**Out of the depths have I cried unto Thee, O
LORD.** *Psalm 130:1*

   Out of the deep I call
   To Thee, O Lord, to Thee.
Before the throne of grace I fall;
   Be merciful to me.

   Out of the deep I cry,
   The woeful deep of sin,
Of evil done in days gone by,
   Of evil now within.

   Out of the deep of fear
   And dread of coming shame;
All night till morning watch is near
   I plead the precious name.

   Lord, there is mercy now,
   As ever was, with Thee.
Before Thy throne of grace I bow;
   Be merciful to me.

601   John Newton   77 77 77
Psalm 131

Quiet, Lord, my froward heart;
   Make me teachable and mild,
Upright, simple, free from art;
   Make me as a weanèd child,
From distrust and envy free,
Pleased with all that pleases Thee.

What Thou shalt today provide
   Let me as a child receive;
What tomorrow may betide
   Calmly to Thy wisdom leave:
'Tis enough that Thou wilt care;
Why should I the burden bear?

As a little child relies
  On a care beyond his own,
Knows he's neither strong nor wise,
  Fears to stir a step alone,
Let me thus with Thee abide,
As my Father, Guard and Guide.

Thus preserved from Satan's wiles,
  Safe from dangers, free from fears,
May I live upon Thy smiles,
  Till the promised hour appears,
When the sons of God shall prove
All their Father's boundless love.

602 Isaac Watts LM
Until I find out a place for the LORD, an habitation for the mighty God of Jacob.
Psalm 132:5

Where shall we go to seek and find
  A habitation for our God;
A dwelling for the Eternal Mind,
  Amongst the sons of flesh and blood?

The God of Jacob chose the hill
  Of Zion, for His ancient rest;
And Zion is His dwelling still;
  His church is with His presence blessed.

'Here will I fix my gracious throne,
  And reign for ever,' says the Lord;
'Here shall My power and love be known,
  And blessings shall attend My word.

'Here I will meet the hungry poor,
  And fill their souls with living bread;
Sinners that wait before My door,
  With sweet provisions shall be fed.

Girded with truth, and full of grace,
  My priests, My ministers shall shine;
Not Aaron, in his costly dress,
  Made an appearance so divine.

'The saints, unable to contain
  Their inward joys, shall shout and sing,
The Son of David here shall reign,
  And Zion triumph in her King.'

603 John Harris CM
Arise, O LORD, into Thy rest; Thou, and the ark of Thy strength. *Psalm 132:8*

Light up this house with glory, Lord;
  Enter, and claim Thine own;
Receive the homage of our souls,
  Erect Thy temple-throne.

We ask no bright shekinah-cloud,
  To glorify the place:
Give, Lord, the substance of that sign—
  A plenitude of grace.

We rear no altar—Thou hast died;
  We deck no priestly shrine;
What need have we of creature-aid?
  The power to save is Thine.

O Thou, who, risen, cam'st to bless,
  Gently as comes the dew,
Here, entering, breathe on all around,
  Peace, peace be unto you.

No rushing mighty wind we ask;
  No tongues of flame desire;
Grant us the Spirit's quickening light,
  His purifying fire.

Light up this house with glory, Lord—
  The glory of that love
Which forms and saves a church below,
  And makes a heaven above.

604 James Seddon SM
Psalm 133

  How good a thing it is,
  How pleasant to behold—
When brethren learn to live at one,
  The law of love uphold.

  As perfume, by its scent,
  Breathes fragrance all around
So life itself will sweeter be
  Where unity is found.

  And like refreshing dew
  That falls upon the hills—
True union sheds its gentle grace,
  And deeper love instils.

  God grants His choicest gifts
  To those who live in peace;
To them His blessings shall abound
  And evermore increase.

Words: J. E. Seddon © Mrs M. Seddon / The Jubilate Group. www.jubilate.co.uk USED BY PERMISSION

605   Charles Wesley   77 77
Behold, how good and how pleasant it is for brethren to dwell together in unity!
Psalm 133:1

Jesus Lord, we look to Thee;
Let us in Thy name agree;
Show thyself the Prince of Peace;
Bid all strife for ever cease.

By Thy reconciling love,
Every stumbling-block remove;
Each to each unite, endear;
Come and spread Thy banner here.

Make us of one heart and mind,
Courteous, pitiful, and kind;
Lowly, meek, in thought and word,
Altogether like our Lord.

Let us each for other care;
Each another's burdens bear;
To Thy church the pattern give;
Show how true believers live.

Let us then with joy remove
To Thy family above;
On the wings of angels fly;
Show how true believers die.

606   James Montgomery   LM
There the LORD commanded the blessing, even life for evermore.
Psalm 133:3

Command Thy blessing from above,
  O God! on all assembled here:
Behold us with a Father's love,
  While we look up with filial fear.

Command Thy blessing, Jesus, Lord!
  May we Thy true disciples be;
Speak to each heart the mighty word,
  Say to the weakest, 'Follow Me.'

Command Thy blessing in this hour,
  Spirit of truth! and fill the place
With humbling and exalting power,
  With quickening and confirming grace.

O Thou, our Maker, Saviour, Guide,
  One true, eternal God confessed,
May nought in life or death divide
  The saints in Thy communion blest!

With Thee and Thine for ever found,
  May all the souls who here unite,
With harps and songs Thy throne surround,
  Rest in Thy love, and reign in light.

607   Henry Lyte   77 77 77
Psalm 134

Praise to God on high be given,
Praise from all in earth and heaven,
Ye that in His presence stand,
Ye that walk by His command,
Saints below, and hosts above,
Praise, O praise, the God of love!

Praise Him at the dawn of light,
Praise Him at returning night;
Strings and voices, hands and hearts,
In His praises bear your parts;
Thou that madest earth and sky,
Bless us in return from high!

608   Nahum Tate, Nicholas Brady   CM
Psalm 135

O praise the Lord with one consent,
  And magnify His name;
Let all the servants of the Lord
  His worthy praise proclaim.

Praise Him all ye that in His house
  Attend with constant care,
With those that to His outmost courts
  With humble zeal repair!

For God His own peculiar choice
  The sons of Jacob makes;
And Israel's offspring for His own
  Most valued treasure takes.

Let all with thanks His wondrous works
  In Zion's courts proclaim!
Let them in Salem, where He dwells,
  Exalt His holy name!

JOHN MILTON 1608-1674

609   John Milton   77 77
Psalm 136

Let us with a gladsome mind,
Praise the Lord, for He is kind:

For His mercies shall endure,
Ever faithful, ever sure.

He, with all commanding might,
Filled the new-made world with light:

All things living He doth feed,
His full hand supplies their need:

He His chosen race did bless
In the wasteful wilderness:

He hath with a piteous eye
Looked upon our misery:

Let us, then, with gladsome mind,
Praise the Lord, for He is kind:

610   Joseph Hart   CM
O give thanks unto the LORD; for He is good:
for His mercy endureth for ever. *Psalm 136:1*

God's mercy is for ever sure;
    Eternal is His name;
As long as life and speech endure,
    My tongue this truth proclaim.

I basely sinned against His love,
    And yet my God was good;
His favour nothing could remove,
    For I was bought with blood.

That precious blood atones all sin,
    And fully clears from guilt;
It makes the foulest sinner clean,
    For 'twas for sinners spilt.

He raised me from the lowest state,
    When hell was my desert;
I broke His law, and, worse than that,
    Alas! I broke His heart!

My soul, thou hast, let what will ail,
    A never-changing Friend;
When brethren, friends, and helpers fail,
    On Him alone depend.

611   James Hamilton   85 83
Who giveth food to all flesh: for His mercy
endureth for ever. *Psalm 136:25*

Praise, O praise the Lord of harvest,
    Providence and love!
Praise Him in His earthly temples,
    And above!

Praise Him, every living creature,
    By His goodness fed,
Whose rich mercy daily giveth
    Daily bread.

Sing Him thanks for all the bounties
    Of His gracious hand;
Smiling peace and welcome plenty
    O'er our land.

Speed, O speed, that glorious harvest
    Of the souls of men,
When Christ's members, here long scattered
    Meet again.

Glory to the Lord of harvests,
    Holy Three in One!
To the Father, Son and Spirit,
    Praise be done!

612   Augustus Toplady   SM
Psalm 137

Your harps, ye trembling saints,
    Down from the willows take;
Loud to the praise of love divine
    Bid every string awake.

Though in a foreign land,
    We are not far from home;
And nearer to our house above
    We every moment come.

His grace will to the end
    Stronger and brighter shine;
Nor present things, nor things to come,
    Shall quench the grace divine.

When we in darkness walk,
    Nor feel the heavenly flame,
Then is the time to trust our God,
    And rest upon His name.

Soon shall our doubts and fears
    Subside at His control;
His lovingkindness shall break through
    The midnight of the soul.

Blest is the man, O God,
    That stays himself on Thee,
Who wait for Thy salvation, Lord,
    Shall Thy salvation see.

613   Thomas Kelly   LM
**By the rivers of Babylon, there we sat down,
yea, we wept, when we remembered Zion.**
Psalm 137:1

O Zion, when I think on thee,
    I wish for pinions[13] like the dove,
And mourn to think that I should be
    So distant from the place I love.

A captive here, and far from home,
    For Zion's sacred walls I sigh;
To Zion all the ransomed come,
    And see the Saviour eye to eye.

While here, I walk on hostile ground;
    The few that I can call my friends
Are, like myself, with fetters bound,
    And weariness our steps attends.

But yet we shall behold the day,
    When Zion's children shall return;
Our sorrows then shall flee away,
    And we shall never, never mourn.

The hope that such a day will come
    Makes e'en the captive's portion sweet;
Though now we wander far from home,
    In Zion soon we all shall meet.

614   Thomas Kelly   LM
**We hanged our harps upon the willows in the
midst thereof.** *Psalm 137:2*

My harp on yonder willow lies,
    Silent, neglected, and unstrung;
My cheerful songs are turned to sighs;
    Sad is my heart and mute my tongue.

Once I could sound the note of praise,
    As loud as others I could sing;
But retrospect of former days
    No help in present grief will bring.

But why should I give way to grief?
    I see my remedy at hand;
Does not the gospel bring relief
    To such as self-convicted stand?

Yes, 'tis a faithful, cheering word,
    That Jesus came to save the lost;
This truth with richest grace is stored,
    And to the vilest yields the most.

615   Isaac Watts   LM
Psalm 138

With all my powers of heart and tongue,
I'll praise my Maker in my song:
Angels shall hear the notes I raise,
Approve the song, and join the praise.

I'll sing Thy truth and mercy, Lord,
I'll sing the wonders of Thy word;
Not all Thy works and names below,
So much Thy power and glory show.

To God I cried when troubles rose;
He heard me, and subdued my foes;
He did my rising fears control,
And strength diffused through all my soul.

Grace will complete what grace begins,
To save from sorrows or from sins;
The work that wisdom undertakes
Eternal mercy ne'er forsakes.

616   William Cowper   CM
In the day when I cried Thou answeredst me.
Psalm 138:3

To tell the Saviour all my wants
    How pleasing is the task?
Nor less to praise Him when He grants
    Beyond what I can ask.

My labouring spirit vainly seeks
    To tell but half the joy,
With how much tenderness He speaks,
    And helps me to reply.

But this with boldness I proclaim,
    Nor care if thousands hear;
Sweet is the ointment of His name;
    Not life is half so dear.

Trust me, I draw the likeness true,
    And not as fancy paints;
Such honour may He give to you,
    For such have all His saints.

617   *Psalter Hymnal* 1927   LM
Psalm 139

Lord, Thou hast searched me, and dost know
Where'er I rest, where'er I go;
Thou knowest all that I have planned,
And all my ways are in Thy hand.

---

[13] wing-feathers

My words from Thee I cannot hide;
I feel Thy power on every side;
O wondrous knowledge, awful might,
Unfathomed depth, unmeasured height!

Where can I go apart from Thee,
O whither from Thy presence flee?
In heaven? It is Thy dwelling fair;
In death's abode? Lo,Thou art there.

If I the wings of morning take,
And far away my dwelling make,
The hand that leadeth me is Thine,
And my support Thy power divine.

If deepest darkness cover me,
The darkness hideth not from Thee;
To Thee both night and day are bright,
The darkness shineth as the light.

618   John Kent   66 66 88
How precious also are Thy thoughts unto me.
Psalm 139:17

Indulgent God, how kind
    Are all Thy ways to me,
Whose dark benighted mind
    Was enmity with Thee;
Yet now, subdued by sovereign grace,
My spirit longs for Thy embrace!

How precious are Thy thoughts
    Which o'er my bosom roll!
They swell beyond my faults
    And captivate my soul;
How great their sum, how high they rise,
Can ne'er be known beneath the skies.

Preserved in Jesus when
    My feet made haste to hell;
And there should I have gone
    But Thou dost all things well;
Thy love was great, Thy mercy free,
Which from the pit delivered me.

A monument of grace,
    A sinner saved by blood,
The streams of love I trace
    Up to the fountain, God;
And in His wondrous mercy see
Eternal thoughts of love to me.

619   James Burns   SM
When I awake, I am still with Thee.
Psalm 139:18

Still with Thee, O my God,
    I would desire to be;
By day, by night, at home, abroad,
    I would be still with Thee.

With Thee, when dawn comes in
    And calls me back to care;
Each day returning, to begin
    With Thee, my God, in prayer.

With Thee, amid the crowd
    That throngs the busy mart;
To hear Thy voice 'mid clamour loud,
    Speak softly to my heart.

With Thee, when day is done
    And evening calms the mind;
The setting, as the rising sun,
    With Thee my heart would find.

With Thee, when darkness brings
    The signal of repose:
Calm in the shadow of Thy wings,
    Mine eyelids I would close.

With Thee, in Thee, by faith
    Abiding I would be;
By day, by night, in life, in death,
    I would be still with Thee.

620   Francis Bottome   CM
**Search me, O God, and know my heart: try me,
and know my thoughts.**
Psalm 139:23

Search me, O God! my actions try
    And let my life appear
As seen by Thine all-searching eye,
    To mine my ways make clear.

Search all my sense and know my heart,
    Who only canst make known
And let the deep, the hidden part
    To me be fully shown.

Throw light into the darkened cells
    Where passion reigns within;
Quicken my conscience till it feels
    The loathsomeness of sin.

Search all my thoughts, the secret springs,
    The motives that control;
The rebel heart where evil things
    Hold empire o'er the soul.

Search, till Thy fiery glance has cast
    Its holy light through all,
And I by grace am brought at last
    Before Thy face to fall.

Thus prostrate I shall learn of Thee,
    What now I feebly prove,
That God alone in Christ can be
    Unutterable love!

621   Henry Lyte   LM
Psalm 140

The Christian, like his Lord of old,
    Must look for foes and trials here:
Yet may the weakest saint be bold,
    With such a friend as Jesus near.

The lion's roar need not alarm,
    O Lord, the feeblest of Thy sheep;
The serpent's venom cannot harm,
    While Thou art nigh to watch and keep.

Before, when dangers round me spread,
    I cried to Thee, almighty Friend;
Thou coveredst my defenceless head;
    And shall I not on Thee depend?

O refuge of the poor and weak,
    Regard Thy suffering people's cry;
Humble the proud, uphold the meek,
    And bring us safe to Thee on high.

622   John Beaumont   77 77
Psalm 141

Lord, I daily call on Thee,
Hear my voice and answer me;
Save me, for in faith I pray,
Take, O take my sins away.

Let my prayer as incense rise,
Pure accepted sacrifice;
Let my life with virtue shine,
Fill my soul with love divine.

Keep, O keep my lips and heart,
Let me ne'er from Thee depart;
Holy, happy, may I be
Perfect, O my God, like Thee.

623   Gerhard Tersteegen, tr. S Jackson   LM
**Thou art my refuge and my portion in the land
of the living.** *Psalm 142:5*

Though all the world my choice deride,
    Yet Jesus shall my portion be;
For I am pleased with none beside;
    The fairest of the fair is He.

Sweet is the vision of Thy face,
    And kindness o'er Thy lips is shed;
Lovely art Thou and full of grace,
    And glory beams around Thy head.

E'en whilst I hated, Thou didst love,
    And o'er Thy rebel creature yearn;
For me Thou pleadest still above—
    And shall I not such love return?

Thy sufferings I embrace with Thee,
    Thy poverty and shameful cross;
The pleasures of the world I flee,
    And deem its treasures worthless dross.

Be daily dearer to my heart,
    And ever let me feel Thee near;
Then willingly with all I'd part,
    Nor count it worthy of a tear.

O keep my heart and love with Thee
    Until my mortal work is done;
And then in heaven Thy face I'll see,
    To be with Thee for ever one!

624   Anne Steele   LM
Psalm 143

Hear, O my God, with pity hear,
    My humble supplicating moan;
In mercy answer all my prayer,
    And make Thy truth and goodness known.

And O! let mercy still be nigh;
    Should awful justice frown severe,
Before the terrors of Thine eye,
    What trembling mortal can appear?

I call to mind the former days;
    Thy ancient works declare Thy name,
Thy truth, Thy goodness, and Thy grace;
    And these, O Lord, are still the same.

Come Lord, on wings of mercy fly,
    My spirit fails at Thy delay;
Hide not Thy face; I faint, I die,
    Without Thy blissful healing ray.

Teach me to do Thy sacred will;
    Thou art my God, my hope, my stay;
Let Thy good Spirit lead me still,
    And point the safe, the upright way.

Thy name, Thy righteousness I plead,
    O Lord revive my drooping heart;
Let these distressing fears recede,
    And bid my troubles all depart.

625   John Bull   77 77
I flee unto Thee to hide me. *Psalm 143:9*

Let my life be hid with Thee,
    Gracious Saviour, Lord of might!
Saved from sin, from dangers free,
    Lightened by Thy perfect light.

Let my life be hid with Thee,
    When my raging foes abound;
Covered by Thy panoply,
    Safe within Thy holy ground.

Let my life be hid with Thee,
    When my soul is vexed below;
Let me still Thy mercy see,
    When bowed down by grief and woe.

Let my life be hid with Thee,
    When in death I sink and fail,
Lest my raging enemy
    In that dying hour prevail.

Let my life be hid with Thee,
    Bound within Thy life above;
Living through eternity,
    In the realms of peace and love.

626   John Beaumont   SM
Psalm 144

I'll bless my Saviour God,
    Who doeth all things right;
Armed with His Spirit's two-edged sword,
    Against my foes I'll fight.

My goodness, and high tower,
    My fortress, and my shield;
Depending on His love and power
    I'll boldly take the field.

My Saviour shall subdue
    The powers of earth and hell;
Behold, He maketh all things new,
    He doeth all things well.

627   Joseph Irons   87 87 47
Happy is that people, whose God is the LORD.
Psalm 144:15

O the happiness arising
    From the life of grace within,
When the soul is realising
    Conquests over hell and sin!
      Happy moments!
Heavenly joys on earth begin.

On the Saviour's fulness living,
    All His saints obtain delight;
With the strength which He is giving,
    They can wrestle, they can fight.
      Happy moments!
When King Jesus is in sight.

Nearer, nearer, to Him clinging,
    Let my helpless soul be found,
All my sorrows to Him bringing,
    May His grace in me abound;
      Happy moments!
With new covenant blessings crowned.

628   John Newton   CM
Happy is that people, whose God is the LORD.
Psalm 144:15

O happy they who know the Lord,
    With whom He deigns to dwell!
He feeds and cheers them by His word;
    His arm supports them well.

He helped His saints in ancient days,
    Who trusted in His name:
And we can witness, to His praise,
    His love is still the same.

His presence sweetens all our cares,
    And makes our burdens light;
A word from Him dispels our fears,
    And gilds the gloom of night.

Lord, let us then most highly prize
    These tokens of Thy love,
Till Thou shalt bid our spirits rise
    To worship Thee above.

629   Isaac Watts   CM
Psalm 145 part 1

Long as I live I'll bless Thy name,
    My King, my God of love;
My work and joy shall be the same,
    In the bright world above.

Great is the Lord, His power unknown,
    And let His praise be great:
I'll sing the honours of Thy throne,
    Thy works of grace repeat.

Thy grace shall dwell upon my tongue;
    And, while my lips rejoice,
The men that hear my sacred song
    Shall join their cheerful voice.

Fathers to sons shall teach Thy name,
    And children learn Thy ways;
Ages to come Thy truth proclaim,
    And nations sound Thy praise.

Thy glorious deeds of ancient date
    Shall through the world be known;
Thine arm of power, Thy heavenly state,
    With public splendour shown.

The world is managed by Thy hands,
    Thy saints are ruled by love;
And Thine eternal kingdom stands,
    Though rocks and hills remove.

630   Isaac Watts   CM
Psalm 145 part 2

Sweet is the memory of Thy grace,
  O my God, my heavenly King;
Let age to age Thy righteousness
  In sounds of glory sing.

God reigns on high, but not confines
  His goodness to the skies;
Through the whole earth His bounty shines
  And every want supplies.

With longing eyes Thy creatures wait
  On Thee for daily food;
Thy liberal hand provides their meat,
  And fills their mouths with good.

How kind are Thy compassions, Lord!
  How slow Thine anger moves!
But soon He sends His pardoning word
  To cheer the souls He loves.

Creatures, with all their endless race,
  Thy power and praise proclaim;
But saints that taste Thy richer grace
  Delight to bless Thy name.

631   Richard Burnham   CM
Every day will I bless Thee. *Psalm 145:2*

Come, come, ye happy, happy saints,
  The heavenly Lamb adore;
Dwell on His everlasting love,
  And praise Him evermore.

Spread His dear name through all the earth.
  Sing His eternal power:
Shout the rich fountain of His blood;
  And praise Him evermore.

Up to the courts, where now He reigns,
  May all our spirits soar,
Fully survey the mercy-seat.
  And praise Him evermore.

Saints who surround the dazzling throne,
  Their tuneful voices raise;
Higher than angels bear their songs,
  The glorious songs of praise.

Come, Him my spirit, higher still,
  Swell the celestial lays;
Higher than all the heights of heaven.
  Sound Jesus' endless praise.

632   Ernst Lange, tr. J Wesley   LM
Great is the LORD, and greatly to be praised;
and His greatness is unsearchable.
Psalm 145:3

O God, Thou bottomless abyss!
  Thee to perfection who can know?
O height immense! what words suffice
  Thy countless attributes to show?

Unfathomable depths Thou art;
  O plunge me in Thy mercy's sea!
Void of true wisdom is my heart;
  With love embrace and cover me.

Eternity Thy fountain was,
  Which, like Thee, no beginning knew;
Thou wast ere time began His race,
  Ere glowed with stars the ethereal blue.

Greatness unspeakable is Thine,
  Greatness, whose undiminished ray,
When short-lived worlds are lost, shall shine,
  When earth and heaven are fled away.

Unchangeable, all-perfect Lord,
  Essential life's unbounded sea,
What lives and moves, lives by Thy word;
  It lives, and moves, and is from Thee.

High is Thy power above all height,
  Whate'er Thy will decrees is done;
Thy wisdom, equal to Thy might
  Only to Thee, O God, is known.

633   John Gurney   LM
The LORD is good to all. *Psalm 145:9*

Yes, God is good; in earth and sky,
  From ocean depths and spreading wood,
Ten thousand voices seem to cry,
  'God made us all, and God is good.'

The sun that keeps His trackless way,
  And downward pours His golden flood,
Night's sparkling host, all seem to say,
  In accents clear, that God is good.

The merry birds prolong the strain,
  Their song with every spring renewed;
And balmy air, and falling rain,
  Each softly whisper, 'God is good.'

I hear it in the rushing breeze;
  The hills that have for ages stood,
The echoing sky and roaring seas,
  All swell the chorus, 'God is good.'

Yes, God is good, all nature says,
    By God's own hand with speech endued;
And man, in louder notes of praise,
    Should sing for joy that God is good.

For all Thy gifts we bless Thee, Lord;
    But most for Thy redeeming blood,
Thy pardoning grace, Thy quickening word,
    These prompt our songs that God is good.

634 Isaac Watts LM
All Thy works shall praise Thee, O LORD.
Psalm 145:10

Give to our God immortal praise;
Mercy and truth are all His ways;
Wonders of grace to God belong,
Repeat His mercies in your song.

Give to the Lord of lords renown,
The King of kings with glory crown:
His mercies ever shall endure,
When lords and kings are known no more.

He built the earth, He spread the skies
And fixed the starry lights on high:
Wonders of grace to God belong,
Repeat His mercies in your song.

He fills the sun with morning light,
He bids the moon direct the night:
His mercies ever shall endure,
When suns and moons shall shine no more.

He sent His Son with power to save
From guilt, and darkness, and the grave:
Wonders of grace to God belong,
Repeat His mercies in your song.

Through this vain world He guides our feet,
And leads us to His heavenly seat:
His mercies ever shall endure,
When this vain world shall be no more.

635 George Conder 77 77 77
All Thy works shall praise Thee, O LORD.
Psalm 145:10

All things praise Thee, Lord, most high,
Heaven and earth, and sea and sky,
All were for Thy glory made,
That Thy greatness thus displayed,
    Should all worship bring to Thee;
    All things praise Thee: Lord, may we.

All things praise Thee, night to night
Sing in silent hymns of light;
All things praise Thee, day to day,
Chants Thy power in burning ray;
    Time and space are praising Thee:
    All things praise Thee: Lord, may we.

All things praise Thee, high and low,
Rain, and dew, and seven-hued bow,
Crimson sunset, fleecy cloud,
Rippling stream, and tempest loud,
    Summer, winter, all to Thee
    Glory render: Lord, may we.

All things praise Thee: gracious Lord,
Great Creator, powerful Word,
Omnipresent Spirit, now
At Thy feet we humbly bow;
    Lift our hearts in praise to Thee:
    All things praise Thee: Lord, may we.

636 Mathias Claudius, tr. J Campbell
76 76 D + refrain
Thou givest them their meat in due season.
Psalm 145:15

We plough the fields and scatter
    The good seed on the land,
But it is fed and watered
    By God's almighty hand;
He sends the snow in winter,
    The warmth to swell the grain,
The breezes and the sunshine
    And soft refreshing rain.

All good gifts around us
Are sent from heaven above,
    Then thank the Lord,
    O thank the Lord,
For all His love.

He only is the Maker
    Of all things near and far;
He paints the wayside flower;
    He lights the evening star;
The winds and waves obey Him;
    By Him the birds are fed;
Much more to us, His children,
    He gives our daily bread.

We thank Thee then, O Father,
    For all things bright and good,
The seed-time and the harvest,
    Our life, our health, our food.
No gifts have we to offer
    For all Thy love imparts,
But that which Thou desirest,
    Our humble, thankful hearts.

637   Isaac Watts   888 D
Psalm 146

I'll praise my Maker while I've breath;
And when my voice is lost in death,
  Praise shall employ my nobler powers;
My days of praise shall ne'er be past,
While life, and thought, and being last,
  Or immortality endures.

Happy the man whose hopes rely
On Israel's God! He made the sky,
  And earth, and sea, with all their train;
His truth for ever stands secure;
He saves the oppressed, He feeds the poor,
  And none shall find His promise vain.

The Lord gives eyesight to the blind;
The Lord supports the fainting mind;
  He sends the labouring conscience peace;
He helps the stranger in distress,
The widow, and the fatherless,
  And grants the prisoner sweet release.

I'll praise Him while He lends me breath;
And when my voice is lost in death,
  Praise shall employ my nobler powers;
My days of praise shall ne'er be past,
While life, and thought, and being last,
  Or immortality endures.

638   Augustus Toplady   77 77 D
**Happy is he that hath the God of Jacob for his
help, whose hope is in the LORD his God.**
Psalm 146:5

Happiness thou lovely name,
  Where's thy seat, O tell me, where?
Learning, pleasure, wealth, and fame,
  All cry out, 'It is not here.'
Not the wisdom of the wise
Can inform me where it lies;
  Not the grandeur of the great
  Can the bliss I seek create.

Object of my first desire,
  Jesus, crucified for me;
All to happiness aspire,
  Only to be found in Thee.
Thee to praise and Thee to know,
Constitute our bliss below;
  Thee to see and Thee to love,
  Constitute our bliss above.

Lord, it is not life to live,
  If Thy presence Thou deny;
Lord, if Thou Thy presence give,
  'Tis no longer death to die.
Source and Giver of repose,
Singly from Thy smile it flows;
  Happiness complete is Thine;
  Mine it is, if Thou art mine.

Whilst I feel Thy love to me,
  Every object teams with joy;
May I ever walk with Thee,
  Then into Thy presence die!
Let me but Thyself possess,
Total sum of happiness!
  Real bliss I then shall prove;
  Heaven below and heaven above.

639   Isaac Watts   LM
Psalm 147

Praise ye the Lord: 'tis good to raise
Our hearts and voices in His praise:
His nature and His works invite
To make this duty our delight.

The Lord builds up Jerusalem,
And gathers nations to His name:
His mercy melts the stubborn soul,
And makes the broken spirit whole.

He formed the stars, those heavenly flames;
He counts their numbers, calls their names;
His wisdom's vast, and knows no bound,
A deep where all our thoughts are drowned.

Great is our Lord, and great His might;
And all His glories infinite:
He crowns the meek, rewards the just,
And treads the wicked to the dust.

640   Isaac Watts   CM
**Great is our Lord, and of great power: His
understanding is infinite.**   *Psalm 147:5*

Great God! how infinite art Thou!
  What worthless dust are we!
Let the whole race of creatures bow,
  And pay their praise to Thee!

Thy throne eternal ages stood,
  Ere seas or stars were made;
Thou art the ever-living God,
  Were all the nations dead.

Nature and time quite naked lie
  To Thy immense survey,
From the formation of the sky,
  To the great burning day.

Eternity, with all its years,
  Stands present in Thy view;
To Thee there's nothing old appears—
  Great God! there's nothing new!

Our lives through various scenes are drawn,
  And vexed with trifling cares,
While Thy eternal thought moves on
  Thy undisturbed affairs.

Great God! how infinite art Thou!
What worthless dust are we!
Let the whole race of creatures bow,
And pay their praise to Thee!

AMBROSE C339-397

641   Ambrose, tr. C Wesley   88 88 88
Great is our Lord, and of great power: His understanding is infinite. *Psalm 147:5*

Infinite God, to Thee we raise
Our hearts in solemn songs of praise;
By all Thy works on earth adored,
We worship Thee, the common Lord;
    The everlasting Father own,
    And bow our souls before Thy throne.

Thee all the choir of angels sings,
The Lord of hosts, the King of kings;
Cherubs proclaim Thy praise aloud,
And seraphs shout the Triune God;
    And, 'Holy, holy, holy!' cry,
    Thy glory fills both earth and sky!

God of the patriarchal race,
The ancient seers record Thy praise,
The goodly apostolic band
In highest joy and glory stand;
    And all the saints and prophets join
    To extol Thy majesty divine.

Head of the martyrs' noble host,
Of Thee they justly make their boast;
The church, to earth's remotest bounds,
Her heavenly Founder's praise resounds;
    And strives, with those around the throne,
    To hymn the mystic Three in One.

Father of endless majesty,
All might and love they render Thee;
Thy true and only Son adore,
The same in dignity and power;
    And God the Holy Ghost declare,
    The saints' eternal Comforter.

642   William Dix   87 87 D (iambic)
He maketh peace in thy borders, and filleth thee with the finest of the wheat.
Psalm 147:14

To Thee, O Lord, our hearts we raise
    In hymns of adoration,
To Thee bring sacrifice of praise
    With shouts of exultation;
Bright robes of gold the fields adorn,
    The hills with joy are ringing,
The valleys stand so thick with corn
    That even they are singing.

And now, on this our festal day,
    Thy bounteous hand confessing,
Before Thee thankfully we lay
    The first-fruits of Thy blessing.
By Thee the souls of men are fed
    With gifts of grace supernal;
Thou who dost give us earthly bread,
    Give us the Bread eternal.

We bear the burden of the day
    And often toil seems dreary;
But labour ends with sunset ray
    And rest comes for the weary:
May we, the angel-reaping o'er,
    Stand at the last accepted,
Christ's golden sheaves for evermore
    To garners bright elected.

643   Henry Lyte   77 77
Psalm 148

Praise the Lord, His glories show,
Saints within His courts below,
Angels round His throne above,
All that see and share His love.

Earth to heaven, and heaven to earth,
Tell His wonders, sing His worth:
Age to age, and shore to shore,
Praise Him, praise Him, evermore.

Praise the Lord, His mercies trace;
Praise His providence and grace,
All that He for man hath done,
All He sends us through His Son.

Strings and voices, hands and hearts,
In the concert bear your parts;
All that breathe, your Lord adore,
Praise Him, praise Him, evermore!

644   Richard Burnham   66 66 88
Praise ye the LORD. *Psalm 148:1*

Love will I ever sing:
  Sing of its ancient date;
Love is the flowing spring
  Of blessings truly great;
Love is the pure immortal food,
Love is the height and depth of God.

Love is my comely dress,
  My glory and my crown,
My life, my joy, my peace,
  My heaven, and my throne;
Love is the pure immortal food,
Love is the height and depth of God.

Lord, may I soon be caught
  Up to the realms above,
And there be better taught
  The glories of Thy love;
And feast on this immortal food,
And triumph in the love of God.

645   Richard Burnham   LM
The children of Israel, a people near unto Him.
Psalm 148:14

O what a blessing 'tis to prove
  Sweet nearness to Mount Zion's King!
Then the dear saints, inflamed with love,
  Delight to pray, delight to sing.

Then O what fellowship with God,
  What sweet enjoyment of His grace!
Love in the heart is shed abroad,
  And all the soul is filled with peace.

Through the Redeemer's precious blood
  We for a growing nearness pray,
Till face to face we see our God
  In regions of eternal day.

646   William Gadsby   SM
Let the children of Zion be joyful in their King.
Psalm 149:2

Jesus, the Lord, is King,
  And be His name adored;
Let Zion with sweet pleasure sing
  The honours of her God.

His laws are just and mild,
  All pregnant with delight;
The church at large, and every child,
  Shall prove His burden light.

Let Christians all attend
  To His commanding voice;
His mercies never have an end;
  Then be His ways our choice.

On Zion's hill He reigns,
  And still displays His love;
Bids saints remember all His pains,
  And lift their hearts above.

647   Philip Doddridge   SM
He will beautify the meek with salvation.
Psalm 149:4

Ye humble souls, rejoice,
  And cheerful praises sing!
Wake all your harmony of voice,
  For Jesus is your King!

That meek and lowly Lord,
  Whom here your souls have known,
Pledges the honour of His word
  To avow you for His own.

He brings salvation near,
  For which His blood was paid;
How beauteous shall your souls appear,
  Thus sumptuously arrayed!

Sing, for the day is nigh
  When, near your Saviour's seat,
The tallest sons of pride shall lie
  The footstool of your feet.

Salvation, Lord, is Thine,
  And all Thy saints confess
The royal robes in which they shine
  Were wrought by sovereign grace.

648   William Cowper   LM
**This honour have all His saints. Praise ye the
LORD.** *Psalm 149:9*

Honour and happiness unite
  To make the Christian's name a praise.
How fair the scene, how clear the light,
  That fills the remnant of his days!

A kingly character he bears,
  No change his priestly office knows;
Unfading is the crown he wears,
  His joys can never reach a close.

Adorned with glory from on high,
  Salvation shines upon his face;
His robe is of th' ethereal dye,
  His steps are dignity and grace.

Inferior honours he disdains,
 Nor stoops to take applause from earth;
The King of kings Himself maintains
 The expenses of his heavenly birth.

The noblest creature seen below,
 Ordained to fill a throne above;
God gives him all He can bestow,
 His kingdom of eternal love!

My soul is ravished at the thought!
 Methinks from earth I see him rise!
Angels congratulate his lot,
 And shout him welcome to the skies!

649   Nahum Tate, Nicholas Brady   LM
Psalm 150

O praise the Lord in that blest place,
 From whence His goodness largely flows!
Praise Him in heaven, where He His face
 Unveiled in perfect glory shows!

Praise Him for all the mighty acts
 Which He in our behalf has done!
His kindness this return exacts,
 With which our praise should equal run.

Let all that vital breath enjoy.
 The breath He does to them afford,
In just returns of praise employ:
 Let every creature praise the Lord!

CATHERINE WINKWORTH 1829-1878

650 Joachim Neander, tr. Catherine Winkworth
                                14 14 478
**Let every thing that hath breath praise the
LORD.** *Psalm 150:6*

Praise to the Lord, the Almighty, the
 King of creation!
O my soul, praise Him for He is thy
 health and salvation!
 All ye who hear,
 Now to His temple draw near,
Join me in glad adoration.

Praise to the Lord, who o'er all things so
 wondrously reigneth,
Shelters thee under His wings, yea, so
 gently sustaineth:
 Hast thou not seen?
 All that is needful hath been
Granted in what He ordaineth.

Praise to the Lord, who doth prosper thy
 work and defend thee!
Surely His goodness and mercy here
 daily attend thee;
 Ponder anew,
 What the Almighty will do,
If with His love He befriend thee!

Praise to the Lord! O let all that is
 in me adore Him!
All that hath life and breath, come now with
 praises before Him!
 Let the Amen
 Sound from His people again;
Gladly for aye we adore Him.

651   Charles Wesley   LM
**Happy is the man that findeth wisdom, and the
man that getteth wisdom.** *Proverbs 3:13*

Happy the man who finds the grace,
The blessing of God's chosen race,
The wisdom coming from above,
And faith that sweetly works by love.

Happy beyond description he
Who knows, 'the Saviour died for me!'—
The gift unspeakable obtains,
And heavenly understanding gains.

Her ways are ways of pleasantness,
And all her paths are paths of peace;
Wisdom to silver we prefer,
And gold is dross compared with her.

He finds, who wisdom apprehends,
A life begun that never ends;
The tree of life divine she is,
Set in the midst of Paradise.

Happy the man who wisdom gains,
In whose obedient heart she reigns;
He owns, and will for ever own,
Wisdom, and Christ, and heaven are one.

652   James Boden   66 66 88
Her ways are ways of pleasantness, and all her paths are peace. *Proverbs 3:17*

The wisdom of the Lord,
  Descending from above,
Calls to the sons of men
  In language full of love:
Her ways are ways of pleasantness,
And all her paths are paths of peace.

Her riches are divine,
  Her treasures always full,
Brighter than rubies shine,
  And satisfy the soul:
Her ways are ways of pleasantness,
And all her paths are paths of peace.

On wisdom's pleasant ways
  The sun will always shine,
To cheer the soul with peace,
  And prospect all divine:
O come and try her pleasant ways,
And you shall find her paths of peace.

653   Mary Masters   77 77
Her ways are ways of pleasantness, and all her paths are peace. *Proverbs 3:17*

'Tis religion that can give
Sweetest pleasures while we live;
'tis religion must supply
Solid comfort when we die.

After death its joys will be
Lasting as eternity:
Be the living God my Friend,
Then my bliss shall never end.

654   Sabine Baring-Gould   65 65
Thou shalt lie down, and thy sleep shall be sweet. *Proverbs 3:24*

Now the day is over,
  Night is drawing nigh,
Shadows of the evening
  Steal across the sky.

Now the darkness gathers,
  Stars their watches keep,
Birds and beasts and flowers
  Soon will be asleep.

Jesus, give the weary
  Calm and sweet repose;
With Thy tenderest blessing
  May mine eyelids close.

Grant to little children
  Visions bright of Thee;
Guard the sailors tossing
  On the deep blue sea.

Comfort every sufferer
  Watching late in pain;
Those who plan some evil
  From their sin restrain.

When the morning wakens,
  Then may I arise
Pure and fresh and sinless
  In Thy holy eyes.

655   John Berridge   SM
Let thine eyes look right on.
Proverbs 4:25

To Canaan art thou bound?
  Walk on in Jesus' might;
But mark, the way is holy ground,
  And needs a heart upright.

Make Jesus all thy peace,
  And make Him all thy arm;
Rely alone upon His grace,
  To guard from every harm.

To Jesus some will pray,
  Yet not with single eye;
They turn their eyes another way,
  Some creature-help to spy.

In darkness such are held;
  And bound in legal fear;
A double eye is in the child,
  The heart is not sincere.

Such find no gospel rest,
  But into bondage fall,
The Lord will not uphold thy breast,
  Till He is all in all.

Lord, give me single sight,
  And make it strong and clear,
So will my soul be full of light,
  And feel the Saviour near.

656   Samuel Medley (alt)   CM
Hear; for I will speak of excellent things.
Proverbs 8:6

Wake, all our cheerful powers to praise
  And touch the tuneful strings,
While we our thankful voices raise,
  And sing of heavenly things.

Th' eternal sovereign love of God,
　　That source of all our bliss,
When by His Spirit shed abroad,
　　How excellent is this!

The Spirit's work of sovereign grace,
　　In age or youthful years,
Where'er this blessèd change takes place,
　　Most excellent appears.

Jesus, the Saviour, Brother, Friend,
　　Of such poor folk as we,
Whose lovingkindness knows no end:
　　How excellent is He!

The Saviour's blood and righteousness
　　Are great beyond compare;
Nor can our loftiest songs express
　　How excellent they are.

Cheerful, my soul, attend His word,
　　Believe, obey, and sing;
The gospel is (O, bless the Lord!)
　　So excellent a thing!

When I, at death, leave all things here,
　　And up to Jesus flee,
Then will these glorious things appear
　　Most excellent to me.

657 William Cowper　　　　76 76 D
**The LORD possessed me in the beginning of
His way.** *Proverbs 8:22*

Ere God had built the mountains,
　　Or raised the fruitful hills;
Before He filled the fountains
　　That feed the running rills;
In Me, from everlasting,
　　The wonderful I AM,
Found pleasures never wasting,
　　And Wisdom is My name.

When, like a tent to dwell in,
　　He spread the skies abroad;
And swathed about the swelling
　　Of ocean's mighty flood;
He wrought by weight and measure,
　　And I was with Him then;
Myself the Father's pleasure,
　　And Mine, the sons of men.

Thus Wisdom's words discover
　　Thy glory and Thy grace,
Thou everlasting Lover
　　Of our unworthy race!
Thy gracious eye surveyed us
　　Ere stars were seen above;
In wisdom Thou hast made us,
　　And died for us in love.

And couldst Thou be delighted
　　With creatures such as we!
Who when we saw Thee, slighted
　　And nailed Thee to a tree?
Unfathomable wonder,
　　And mystery divine!
The voice that speaks in thunder,
　　Says, Sinner I am thine!'

658 Joseph Swain　　　　LM
My delights were with the sons of men.
Proverbs 8:31

How free, how glorious was the grace,
　　How wonderful God's sovereign love
That chose our souls, our time and place,
　　Before He bade the planets move!

He fixed His children's future lot
　　When first He drew creation's plan,
Rejoicing in each favoured spot
　　Where He would dwell with fallen man.

Jesus with high delight surveyed,
　　On the vast map before His eye,
The place where He has since displayed
　　The great incarnate mystery.

No claim had we who now enjoy
　　The smiles of our redeeming God:
He only knows that chose us, why
　　Our hearts are His divine abode.

When we appear before His throne,
　　And He shall call our spirits hence,
We must be saved by grace alone.
　　For who can help Omnipotence?

659 Rowland Hill CM
The fear of the LORD is the beginning of wisdom. *Proverbs 9:10*

Happy the children who betimes
  Have learned to know the Lord;
Who, through His grace, escape the crimes
  Forbidden in His word.

Should they be early hence removed,
  He will their souls receive;
For they whom Jesus here hath loved
  With Him shall ever live.

The Saviour, whom they trusted here,
  Shall wipe their tears away;
No night of darkness shall be there,
  But one eternal day.

May we with those in bliss, O Lord,
  For ever numbered be!
Taught by Thy Spirit and Thy Word,
  To live alone to Thee.

660 William Gadsby SM
The memory of the just is blessed.
Proverbs 10:7

  Grace taught our friends to know
  What rebels they had been;
'Twas grace redeemed them from their woe,
  And made their conscience clean.

  Grace taught them to commune
  With Christ the Lamb once slain;
To hate the sins that made Him mourn,
  And put His soul to pain.

  Grace taught their souls to sing
  Salvation through His blood;
Through grace they loved Him as their King,
  Their Saviour, and their God.

  Grace must and will relieve
  From such a waste as this,
All souls that in the Lord believe,
  And take them to His bliss.

661 William Gadsby 88 88 D
The law of the wise is a fountain of life.
Proverbs 13:14

Sweet Jesus! how great is Thy love;
  Thy mercy and truth know no end;
And all that are born from above,
  Shall find Thee a permanent Friend;
Dear Saviour, enlighten my eyes,
  That I may the wonders behold
Contained in the law of the wise,
  Too grand and too great to be told.

O what a rich field of delight!
  How sweet and how fragrant the smell!
Its beauties astonish me quite,
  Nor am I yet able to tell
The half of the glory I see
  In that divine treasure of grace;
Sweet wonders are shown unto me,
  When I behold Jesus's face.

Dear Jesus! Thy glories unfold,
  Nor let me be wanting of sight;
O may I with pleasure behold
  Thy statutes, and in them delight.
I want to know nothing beside;
  Here's room for my soul to expand;
Nor can I be better employed,
  In Meshech's discouraging land.

662 John Berridge 886 D
The tongue of the wise useth knowledge aright. *Proverbs 15:2*

The means of grace are in my hand,
The blessing is at God's command,
  Who must the work fulfil;
But though I read and watch and pray,
Yet here the Lord directs my way.
  And worketh all things still.

I cannot speak a proper word,
Nor think aright, but from the Lord
  Preparing heart and tongue;
In nature I can see no good,
But all my good proceeds from God,
  And does to grace belong.

I see it now, and do confess
My utter need of Jesus' grace,
  And of His Spirit's light;
I beg His kind and daily care;
O Lord, my heart and tongue prepare
  To think and speak aright.

Prepare my heart to love Thee well,
And love Thy truth which doth excel,
  And love Thy children dear;
Instruct me how to live by faith,
And feel the virtue of Thy death,
  And find Thy presence near.

Prepare my tongue to pray and praise,
To speak of providential ways,
  And heavenly truth unfold;
To strengthen well a feeble soul,
Correct the wanton, rouse the dull,
  And silence sinners bold.

663   Joseph Hart   CM
The preparations of the heart in man, and the answer of the tongue, is from the LORD.
Proverbs 16:1

Once more we come before our God;
   Once more His blessing ask;
O may not duty seem a load,
   Nor worship prove a task.

Father, Thy quickening Spirit send,
   From heaven, in Jesus' name,
To make our waiting minds attend,
   And put our souls in frame.

May we receive the word we hear,
   Each in an honest heart;
Hoard up the precious treasure there,
   And never with it part.

To seek Thee all our hearts dispose;
   To each Thy blessings suit;
And let the seed Thy servant sows
   Produce a copious fruit.

Bid the refreshing North wind wake;
   Say to the South wind, 'Blow;'
Let every plant the power partake,
   And all the garden grow.

Revive the parched with heavenly showers;
   The cold with warmth divine;
And as the benefit is ours,
   Be all the glory Thine.

664   Thomas Kelly   87 87 47
Whoso trusteth in the LORD, happy is he.
Proverbs 16:20

Lord we plead with Thee for pardon;
   Who can need it more than we?
Make us as a watered garden,
   Fruitful let Thy people be;
      'Tis Thy pleasure
That Thy people live to Thee.

Keep us in a world of sorrow;
   When we call, O hear our prayer!
Let us trust Thee for the morrow,
   Free from boasting, free from care;
      When we trust Thee,
Truly happy then we are.

665   John Sammis   66 9 D + refrain
Whoso trusteth in the LORD, happy is he.
Proverbs 16:20

When we walk with the Lord
In the light of His word,
What a glory He sheds on our way!
While we do His good will,
He abides with us still,
And with all who will trust and obey!

*Trust and obey! for there's no other way
To be happy in Jesus but to trust and obey.*

Not a shadow can rise,
Not a cloud in the skies,
But His smile quickly drives it away;
Not a doubt nor a fear,
Not a sigh nor a tear,
Can abide while we trust and obey!

Not a burden we bear,
Not a sorrow we share,
But our toil He doth richly repay;
Not a grief nor a loss,
Not a frown nor a cross,
But is blest if we trust and obey .

But we never can prove
The delights of His love
Until all on the altar we lay;
For the favour He shows,
And the joy He bestows,
Are for them who will trust and obey.

Then in fellowship sweet
We will sit at His feet,
Or we'll walk by His side in the way;
What He says we will do,
Where He sends we will go,
Never fear, only trust and obey!

666   John Latchford   LM
The lot is cast into the lap. *Proverbs 16:33*

'The lot is cast' where I'm to go,
And what I am to do below,
With all the steps I am to tread
Till I arrive with Christ, my Head.

'The lot is cast' by love divine,
Then why, my foolish heart, repine?
God's mind is fixed both firm and sure,
And, like Himself, it will endure.

'The lot is cast,' and in His light,
I see it is both just and right;
And sure He may the same dispose
Without me asking what He does.

'The lot is cast' is very plain,
And all my murmuring is in vain;
Then may I sit submissive down,
Rejoicing Jesus wears the crown.

Lord, may this be my motto still,
'The lot is cast,' and at Thy will,
Whether the same's adverse or not,
I with Thy own shall have my lot.

---

667   Joseph Swain   CM
A friend loveth at all times.
Proverbs 17:17

A Friend there is, your voices join,
　Ye saints, to praise His name,
Whose truth and kindness are divine,
　Whose love's a constant flame.

When most we need His helping hand,
　This Friend is always near;
With heaven and earth at His command,
　He waits to answer prayer.

His love no end or measure knows;
　No change can turn its course;
Immutably the same, it flows
　From one eternal source!

When frowns appear to veil His face,
　And clouds surround His throne,
He hides the purpose of His grace,
　To make it better known.

And if our dearest comforts fall
　Before His sovereign will,
He never takes away our all:
　Himself He gives us still.

Our sorrows in the scale He weighs,
　And measures out our pains;
The wildest storm His word obeys;
　His word its rage restrains.

---

668   Jonathan Evans   LM
A brother is born for adversity.
Proverbs 17:17

When every scene this side the grave
　Seems dark and cheerless to the eye.
How sweet at such a time to have
　A Brother in adversity!

When father, mother, all are gone,
　When bursts affection's closest tie,
How sweet to claim, as still our own,
　A Brother in adversity!

And who is this, whom still we find,
　When father, mother, husband, die,
Still faithful, loving, tender, kind?
　A Brother in adversity.

Jesus, 'tis Thou—ah, who can trace
　Thy love, unchanging, full, and free?
Or tell the riches of Thy grace,
　Thou Brother in adversity?

Thy wounded hands and feet proclaim
　That love and mercy meet in Thee;
That Jesus is the sweetest name,
　The Brother in adversity!

Ye travellers in this wilderness,
　Who somewhat of His beauty see,
For ever, O! for ever bless
　This Brother in adversity.

---

669   Albert Midlane   86 76 76 76
**A friend loveth at all times, and a brother is
born for adversity.** *Proverbs 17:17*

There's a Friend for little children
　Above the bright blue sky,
A Friend who never changes,
　Whose love will never die.
Unlike our friends by nature,
　Who change with changing years,
This Friend is always worthy
　The precious name He bears.

There's a rest for little children
　Above the bright blue sky,
Who love the blessèd Saviour,
　And 'Abba, Father' cry—
A rest from every trouble,
　From sin and danger free,
Where every little pilgrim
　Shall rest eternally.

There's a home for little children
　Above the bright blue sky,
Where Jesus reigns in glory,
　A home of peace and joy;
No home on earth is like it,
　Or can with it compare;
For every one is happy,
　Nor could be happier, there.

There's a crown for little children
　Above the bright blue sky,
And all who look to Jesus
　Shall wear it by-and-by—
A crown of brightest glory,
　Which He will then bestow
On all who love the Saviour,
　And walk with Him below.

There's a song for little children
    Above the bright blue sky,
A song that will not weary
    Though sung continually,
A song which even angels
    Can never, never sing;
They know not Christ as Saviour,
    But worship Him as King.

670   John Berridge   886 D
There is a Friend that sticketh closer than a brother. *Proverbs 18:24*

There is a Friend, who sticketh fast,
And keeps His love from first to last,
    And Jesus is His name;
An earthly brother drops his hold,
Is sometimes hot and sometimes cold,
    But Jesus is the same.

He loves His people, great and small,
And, grasping hard, embraces all,
    Nor with a soul will part;
No tribulations which they feel,
No foes on earth, or fiends of hell,
    Shall tear them from His heart.

His love before all time began,
And through all time it will remain,
    And evermore endure;
Tho' rods and frowns are sometimes
    brought,
And man may change, He changes not;
    His love abideth sure.

Let all the ransomed of the Lord
Exalt His love with one accord,
    And hallelujah sing;
Adore the dying Friend of man,
And bless Him highly as you can;
    He is your God and King.

671   John Newton   87 87 77
There is a Friend that sticketh closer than a brother. *Proverbs 18:24*

One there is above all others,
    Well deserves the name of Friend;
His is love beyond a brother's,
    Costly, free, and knows no end:
They who once His kindness prove,
Find it everlasting love.

Which of all our friends to save us,
    Would consent to shed His blood?
But our Jesus died to have us
    Reconciled in Him to God:
This was boundless love indeed!
Jesus is a Friend in need.

When He lived on earth abasèd,
    Friend of sinners was His name;
Now, above all glory raisèd,
    He rejoices in the same:
Still He calls them brethren, friends,
And to all their wants attends.

Could we bear from one another
    What He daily bears from us?
Yet this glorious Friend and Brother
    Loves us, though we treat Him thus;
Though for good we render ill,
He accounts us brethren still.

O for grace our hearts to soften!
    Teach us, Lord, at length to love;
We, alas, forget too often
    What a Friend we have above!
But when home our souls are brought,
We shall love Thee as we ought.

672   Jonathan Evans   LM
There is treasure to be desired and oil in the dwelling of the wise. *Proverbs 21:20*

Jesus is all I wish or want
For Him I pray, I thirst, I pant;
Let others after earth aspire:
Christ is the treasure I desire.

Possessed of Him, I wish no more;
He is an all-sufficient store;
To praise Him all my powers conspire:
Christ is the treasure I desire.

If He His smiling face but hide,
My soul no comfort has beside;
Distressed, I after Him inquire:
Christ is the treasure I desire.

And while my heart is racked with pain,
Jesus appears and smiles again;
Why should my Saviour thus retire?
    Christ is the treasure I desire.

Come, humble souls, and view His charms,
Take refuge in His saving arms;
And sing, while you His worth admire:
'Christ is the treasure I desire.'

673   Joseph Irons   LM

As cold waters to a thirsty soul, so is good news from a far country.
Proverbs 25:25

No news can suit a ruined race
But sovereign, free, eternal grace;
No other gospel can impart
Joy, peace, and comfort to the heart.

But those are tidings good indeed,
Which tell me Jesus deigned to bleed,
To vanquish Satan, cancel sin,
And bring eternal glory in.

The only gospel we can own,
Sets Jesus Christ upon His throne;
Proclaims salvation full and free,
Obtained on Calvary's rugged tree.

The gospel is the news from heaven,
Of grace bestowed and sins forgiven—
Redeeming blood—electing love—
Of quickening grace—and joys above.

Lord, write this gospel in my heart,
And in its blessings give me part;
Until I see my Saviour's face,
And sing, 'I'm saved by gospel grace.'

674   David Denham   LM

The full soul loatheth an honeycomb; but to the hungry soul every bitter thing is sweet.
Proverbs 27:7

We ran the downward road in haste,
  Unconscious of our dreadful doom;
The slaves of sin, without a taste
  For Christ, the gospel honeycomb.

Though thus deceived in Satan's snare,
  Till God's set time of grace was come,
He brought us nigh, by faith and prayer—
  To Christ, the gospel honeycomb.

Great were the pangs of conscious guilt
  Which overspread our minds with gloom
Till Jesus, in the blood He spilt,
  Became our gospel honeycomb!

O precious Christ! who came to bless,
  Obey, and suffer in our room;
Thy person, love, and righteousness,
  Excels the luscious honeycomb.

In all the conflicts we may meet,
  When waves of trouble rounds us foam;
Each bitter thing affords a sweet
  In Thee, our precious honeycomb.

When summoned to resign our breath,
  In prospect of our heavenly home,
Then, in the bitter pains of death,
  Be Thou our sweetest honeycomb.

675   John Berridge   77 77

He that trusteth in his own heart is a fool: but whoso walketh wisely, he shall be delivered.
Proverbs 28:26

He that trusts in his own heart,
Acts a raw and foolish part;
Base it is, and full of guile,
Brooding mischief in a smile.

Does it boast of love within?
So it may, and yet may sin;
Peter loved his Master well,
Yet a loving Peter fell.

Does it feel a melting frame?
David also felt the same;
Yet he made a woeful trip,
And perceived his mountain slip.

Does it talk of faith, and boast
Abra'm had as much as most;
Yet, beguiled by unbelief,
Twice he durst deny his wife.

Every prop will, first or last,
Sink or fail, but Jesus Christ;
On this sure foundation stone
Let me build and rest alone.

676   Isaac Watts   LM

What is His name, and what is His Son's name, if thou canst tell? *Proverbs 30:4*

What is our God, or what His name,
  Nor men can learn, or angels teach;
He dwells concealed in radiant flame,
  Where neither eye nor thoughts can reach.

The spacious worlds of heavenly light,
  Compared with Him, how short they fall!
They are too dark, and He too bright:
  Nothing are they, and God is all.

He spoke the wondrous word, and lo,
  Creation rose at His command!
Whirlwinds and seas their limits know,
  Bound in the hollow of His hand.

There rests the earth, there roll the spheres;
  There nature leans and feels her prop:
But His own self-sufficience bears
  The weight of His own glories up.

The tide of creatures ebbs and flows,
　　Measuring their changes by the moon;
No ebb His sea of glory knows,
　　His age is one eternal noon.

677 John Newton CM
All is vanity. *Ecclesiastes 1:2*

The evils that beset our path
　　Who can prevent or cure?
We stand upon the brink of death
　　When most we seem secure.

If we today sweet peace possess,
　　It soon may be withdrawn;
Some change may plunge us in distress,
　　Before tomorrow's dawn.

Disease and pain invade our health
　　And find an easy prey;
And oft, when least expected, wealth
　　Takes wings and flies away.

A fever or a blow can shake
　　Our wisdom's boasted rule;
And of the brightest genius make
　　A madman or a fool.

The gourds, from which we look for fruit,
　　Produce us only pain;
A worm unseen attacks the root,
　　And all our hopes are vain.

I pity those who seek no more
　　Than such a world can give;
Wretched they are, and blind, and poor,
　　And dying while they live.

Since sin has filled the earth with woe,
　　And creatures fade and die;
Lord, wean our hearts from things below,
　　And fix our hopes on high.

678 John Ryland 77 77
To every thing there is a season.
Ecclesiastes 3:1

Sovereign Ruler of the skies,
Ever gracious, ever wise;
All my times are in Thy hand,
All events at Thy command.

His decree who formed the earth
Fixed my first and second birth;
Parents, native place, and time,
All appointed were by Him.

He that formed me in the womb,
He shall guide me to the tomb:
All my times shall ever be
Ordered by His wise decree.

Times of sickness; times of health;
Times of penury and wealth;
Times of trial and of grief;
Times of triumph and relief;

Times the tempter's power to prove;
Times to taste the Saviour's love;
All must come, and last, and end,
As shall please my heavenly Friend.

Plagues and deaths around me fly;
Till He bids, I cannot die;
Not a single shaft can hit,
Till the God of love sees fit.

CECIL ALEXANDER 1818-95

679 Cecil Alexander 76 76 + refrain
He hath made every thing beautiful in His time.
Ecclesiastes 3:11

All things bright and beautiful,
　　All creatures great and small,
All things wise and wonderful,
　　The Lord God made them all.

Each little flower that opens,
　　Each little bird that sings,
He made their glowing colours,
　　He made their tiny wings.

The purple-headed mountain,
　　The river running by,
The sunset, and the morning
　　That brightens up the sky;

The cold wind in the winter,
　　The pleasant summer sun,
The ripe fruits in the garden,
　　He made them every one.

He gave us eyes to see them,
　　And lips that we might tell
How great is God Almighty,
　　Who has made all things well.

680   Joseph Hart   SM
Surely I know that it shall be well with them that fear God. *Ecclesiastes 8:12*

The men that fear the Lord,
  In every state are blest;
The Lord will grant whate'er they want;
  Their souls shall dwell at rest.

His secrets they shall share,
  His covenant shall learn;
Guided by grace, shall walk His ways,
  And heavenly truths discern.

He pities all their griefs;
  When sinking, makes them swim;
He dries their tears, relieves their fears,
  And bids them trust in Him.

In His remembrance-book
  The Saviour sets them down,
Accounting each a jewel rich,
  And calls them all His own.

This fear's the spirit of faith,
  A confidence that's strong;
An unctuous light to all that's right,
  A bar to all that's wrong.

It gives religion life
  To warm, as well as light;
Makes mercy sweet, salvation great,
  And all God's judgments right.

681   David Denham   66 66 88
Surely I know that it shall be well with them that fear God. *Ecclesiastes 8:12*

With all that fear our God,
  It shall be ever well;
Redeemed by precious blood,
  From Satan, death, and hell,
And called from darkness into light,
They now aspire to all that's right.

'Tis well this fear is given,
  And is by God maintained;
Well that it leads to heaven,
  And sin is now restrained;
Well that its subjects cannot fail,
But shall through life and death prevail.

Well in the love of God,
  With all the chosen race;
Well in the Saviour's blood,
  And rich abounding grace;
Well in the Spirit's work complete,
Who makes the saints for glory meet,

682   James Montgomery   SM
In the morning sow thy seed.
Ecclesiastes 11:6

Sow in the morn thy seed,
  At eve hold not thine hand;
To doubt and fear give thou no heed,
  Broadcast it o'er the land.

Thou knowest not which may thrive
  The late or early sown;
Grace keeps the chosen germ alive,
  When and wherever strown.

And duly shall appear
  In verdure, beauty, strength,
The tender blade, the stalk, the ear,
  And the full corn at length.

Thou canst not toil in vain,
  Cold, heat and moist and dry
Shall foster and mature the grain
  For garners in the sky.

Then when the glorious end,
  The day of God, is come,
The angel-reapers shall descend
  And heaven cry, 'Harvest-home!'

683   Alan Clifford   11 11 11 11
Remember now thy Creator in the days of thy youth. Ecclesiastes 12:1

Remember the Lord
  In the days of your youth,
Acknowledge His word
  And hold fast to His truth;
When troubles appear
  And perplexities come,
The Lord will be near
  To protect you from harm.

He'll lift up your head
  And reveal His rich grace,
He'll strengthen your heart
  To pursue the straight race;
Turn not to the left
  And turn not to the right,
Don't wander or drift
  But keep Jesus in sight.

Let Him be your Guide
  In your every concern,
With Jesus beside
  You will wisely discern;
As years come and go
  In the journey of grace,
His presence you'll know
  While beholding His face.

You'll bless Him for all
   That He taught you in youth,
For hearing the call
   Of His mercy and truth;
At last you will prove
   In the heavenly land,
How wise was His love
   And how kind was His hand.

© Author

684   Fanny Crosby   LM + refrain
Or ever the silver cord be loosed.
Ecclesiastes 12:6

Some day the silver cord will break,
   And I no more as now shall sing;
But O the joy when I shall wake
   Within the palace of the King!

    And I shall see Him face to face,
    And tell the story— 'Saved by grace!'
    And I shall see Him face to face,
    And tell the story— 'Saved by grace!'

Some day my earthly house will fall,
   I cannot tell how soon 'twill be;
But this I know— my All in all
   Has now a place in heaven for me.

Some day, when fades the golden sun
   Beneath the rosy-tinted West,
My blessèd Lord shall say, 'Well done!'
   And I shall enter into rest.

Some day; till then I'll watch and wait—
   My lamp all trimmed and burning bright—
That when my Saviour opes the gate,
   My soul to Him may take its flight.

FREDERICK WHITFIELD 1829-1904

685   Frederick Whitfield   CM
Thy name is as ointment poured forth.
Song 1:3

Jesus the name I love so well,
   The name I love to hear!
No saint on earth its worth can tell,
   Nor heart conceive how dear.

It bids my trembling soul rejoice,
   And dries each rising tear;
It tells me in a 'still small voice,'
   To trust and not to fear.

This name shall shed its fragrance still
   Along the thorny road,
Shall sweetly smooth the rugged hill
   That leads me up to God.

And there, with all the blood-bought throng,
   From sin and sorrow free,
I'll sing the new, eternal song,
   Of Jesus' love to me.

686   John Newton   CM
Thy name is as ointment poured forth.
Song 1:3

How sweet the name of Jesus sounds
   In a believer's ear!
It soothes his sorrows, heals his wounds,
   And drives away his fear.

It makes the wounded spirit whole.
   And calms the troubled breast;
'Tis manna to the hungry soul,
   And to the weary rest.

Dear Name! the Rock on which I build,
   My Shield and Hiding-place;
My never-failing Treasury, filled
   With boundless stores of grace.

Jesus, my Shepherd, Husband, Friend,
   My Prophet, Priest and King;
My Lord, my Life, my Way, my End,
   Accept the praise I bring.

Weak is the effort of my heart,
   And cold my warmest thought;
But when I see Thee as Thou art,
   I'll praise Thee as I ought.

Till then I would Thy love proclaim,
   With every fleeting breath;
And may the music of Thy name
   Refresh my soul in death!

687 John Adams 77 77
Draw me, we will run after Thee. *Song 1:4*

Draw my soul to Thee, my Lord;
Make me love Thy precious word!
Bid me seek Thy smiling face;
Willing to be saved by grace.

Dearest Jesus, bid me come;
Let me find Thyself my home;
Thou the Refuge of my soul,
Where I may my troubles roll.

Lord, Thy powerful work begun,
Thou wilt never leave undone;
Teach me to confide in Thee;
Thy salvation's wholly free.

688 Benjamin Beddome, J Rippon CM
Draw me, we will run after Thee. *Song 1:4*

If Thou hast drawn a thousand times,
    O draw me, Lord, again;
Around me cast Thy Spirit's bands,
    And all my powers constrain.

Draw me from all created good,
    From self, the world, and sin,
To the dear fountain of Thy blood,
    And make me pure within.

O lead me to Thy mercy-seat;
    Attract me nearer still;
Draw me, like Mary, to Thy feet,
    To sit and learn Thy will.

O draw me all the desert through
    With cords of heavenly love,
And when prepared for going hence,
    Draw me to dwell above.

689 Joseph Swain LM
We will be glad and rejoice in Thee.
Song 1:4

Jesus, Thy saints assemble here,
Thy power and goodness to declare;
O, may these happy seasons prove
That we have known redeeming love.

And while of mercies past we speak,
And sing of endless joys to come,
Let Thy full glories on us break,
And every thought give Jesus room!

Engrave Thy name on every heart,
And give us all, before we part,
The life-restoring joys to know
Which from Thy veins in rivers flow.

No other food may we desire,
No other theme our bosoms fire,
But sovereign, rich, redeeming love,
While here, and when we dwell above!

Thine everlasting love we sing,
The source whence all our pleasures spring;
How deep it sinks! how high it flows!
No saint can tell, no angel knows!

Its length and breadth no eye can trace,
No thought explore the bounds of grace;
Like its dear Author's name, it shines
In infinite unfolded lines!

690 Rowland Hill 77 77
**Tell me, O Thou whom my soul loveth, where
Thou feedest, where Thou makest Thy flock to
rest at noon.** *Song 1:7*

Tell me, Saviour, from above,
Dearest Object of my love,
Where Thy little flocks abide,
Sheltered near Thy bleeding side!

Say, Thou Shepherd all divine,
Where I may my soul recline.
Where for refuge shall I fly,
While the burning sun is high?

Never had I sought Thy name,
Never felt the inward flame,
Had not love first touched my heart,
Given the painful, pleasant smart.

Turn, and claim me as Thy own;
Be my portion, Lord, alone.
Deign to hear a sinner's call;
Be my everlasting all!

691 Isaac Watts LM
**Tell me, O Thou whom my soul loveth, where
Thou feedest, where Thou makest Thy flock to
rest at noon.** *Song 1:7*

Thou whom my soul admires above
All earthly joy and earthly love,
Tell me, dear Shepherd, let me know,
Where doth Thy choicest pasture grow?

Where is the shadow of that Rock
That from the sun defends Thy flock?
Fain would I feed among Thy sheep,
Among them rest, among them sleep.

The footsteps of Thy flock I see;
Thy sweetest pastures here they be:
A wondrous feast of love appears,
Bought with Thy wounds and groans and tears.

His dearest flesh He makes my bread,
For wine His richest blood is shed:
Here to these hills my soul will come,
Till my Belovèd leads me home.

692   Samuel Stennett   CM
**While the king sitteth at His table, my
spikenard sendeth forth the smell thereof.**
Song 1:12

Lord! at Thy table I behold
   The wonders of Thy grace:
But most of all admire that I
   Should find a resting-place:

What strange surprising grace is this
   That such a soul has room!
My Saviour takes me by the hand,
   My Jesus bids me come.

'Eat, O My friends,' the Saviour cries,
   'The feast was made for you;
For you I groaned, and bled, and died,
   And rose and triumphed too.'

Ye saints below, and hosts of heaven,
   Join all your praising powers;
No theme is like redeeming blood,
   No Saviour is like ours.

693   I Bridgman   CM
**I am the Rose of Sharon, and the Lily of the
valleys.** *Song 2:1*

The sweetest flower that ever grew
   Upon this bed of earth;
The flower I covet most to view,
   In Bethlehem sprang forth—

A Lily, white as purest snow,
   As fragrant as the spring:
A flower so rare as this below,
   Made angels look and sing.

The Lily had not long been there,
   Amidst a thorny group,
But powers of darkness sought to tear
   This beauteous flower up.

And when this lovely Lily died,
   It left, as flowers do,
A kindred seed, which must abide
   Some thorny scourges too.

This Lily lives, no more to die,
   The joy of Paradise;
And all the seed shall, bye-and-bye
   To those fair mansions rise.

694   Isaac Watts   LM
**I am the Rose of Sharon, and the Lily of the
valleys.** *Song 2:1*

Behold the Rose of Sharon here,
The Lily which the valleys bear.
Behold the Tree of Life, that gives
Refreshing fruit and healing leaves.

Among the thorns so lilies shine;
Amongst wild gourds the noble vine;
So in mine eyes my Saviour proves,
Amidst a thousand meaner loves.

Beneath His cooling shade I sit
To shield me from the burning heat;
Of heavenly fruit He spreads a feast,
To feed mine eyes and please my taste.

With living bread and generous wine
He cheers this sinking heart of mine:
And opening His own heart to me,
He shows His thoughts how kind they be.

695   Frances Havergal   76 76
**I sat down under His shadow with great
delight.** *Song 2:3*

Sit down beneath His shadow
   And rest with great delight;
The faith that now beholds Him
   Is pledge of future sight.

Our Master's love remember,
   Exceeding great and free;
Lift up thy heart in gladness,
   For He remembers thee.

Bring every weary burden,
   Thy sin, thy fear, thy grief;
He calls the heavy laden
   And gives them kind relief.

A little while, though parted,
   Remember, wait and love;
Until He comes in glory,
   Until we meet above.

Till in the Father's kingdom
   The heavenly feast is spread
And we behold His beauty,
   Whose blood for us was shed!

696   John Kent   LM
I sat down under His shadow with great delight. *Song 2:3*

Beneath the shadow of my Lord,
Jesus, by every saint adored,
My soul was once indulged to be,
And found His fruit was sweet to me.

His dying love my soul o'ercame,
I felt its sweet seraphic flame;
Could say in faith, from doubting free,
'How sweet Thy fruit and shade to me.'

Sheltered from every hostile ray
That issued from the fount of day,
My raptured soul could trace and see
How sweet Thy fruit and shade to me.

O! sweet repast of heavenly love,
How rich those royal dainties prove!
In Thine embrace 'tis life to be,
So sweet Thy fruit and shade to me.

Thus He appeared my soul's delight,
I chide the moments' hasty flight,
And still beneath life's healing tree,
In life and death desire to be.

697   John Kent   LM
He brought me to the banqueting house, and His banner over me was love.
Song 2:4

To banquet once the spouse was led,
By Him who for her pardon bled;
There was her soul indulged to prove
His looks divine, and banner love.

Like her, my soul, beneath the word,
Was led to banquet with my Lord;
His flesh I ate, His love I sung,
While o'er my head His banner hung.

'Twas then I found a heaven within,
And pardoning blood for every sin;
While love eternal, great and free,
Was still His banner over me.

Thus in His favour I have found.
Whose temples once with thorns were crowned;
While o'er my head, a wretch depraved
In folds of love His banner waved.

O! sweet repast of living bread!
'Here let me die, my Lord,' I said;
'I'm sick of love, and faint to see
Thy banner thus spread over me.'

''Twas for thy sin, My love,' He said,
'Those poignant thorns surround My head;
I groaned and bled on Calvary's tree,
To spread this banner over thee.'

Jesus when Thou shalt call, I'll fly,
To join the marriage feast on high;
And o'er Thy glorious fulness rove,
And pay my Saviour love for love.

698   Vernon Higham   DCM
He brought me to the banqueting house, and His banner over me was love.
Song 2:4

The Lord drew near my love to find,
  And called me to His side.
With sad reluctance I declined,
  And turned away to hide.
My lonely soul in sudden fear,
  Cried out His lovely name:
But He was gone, I knew not where,
  And left me in my shame.

What have I done, this soul of mine,
  To grieve the dearest One?
To drive Him from my breast, yet pine
  Not to be left alone.
Shunned by my friends, and all did spurn,
  In bitter tears I mourn;
Return, O Holy One, return,
  My soul shall no more roam.

O daughters of Jerusalem,
  Belovèd is His name:
Turn not away, do not condemn
  And leave me in my shame.
O let me of my longing share
  For Jesus Christ my Lord.
He is the One, my soul does care
  To stay in sweet accord.

He is the Rose of Sharon rare,
  The Lily of the Vale,
His countenance so fine, most fair,
  His strength can never fail.
He is the Lover of my heart,
  My yearning soul desires:
My ravished heart will not depart:
  My eager soul inspires.

I hear a sound, a gentle sound,
  Yet strong in powerful grace:
At last my soul by Him is found,
  I shall behold His face.
He is the Bright and Morning Star,
  This Christ of Calvary.
O'er hill and vale and mountains far
  He calls, He comes for me.

© Author

699   Isaac Watts   CM
He brought me to the banqueting house, and His banner over me was love.
Song 2:4

Lord, how divine Thy comforts are!
  How heavenly is the place
Where Jesus spreads the sacred feast
  Of His redeeming grace!

There the rich bounties of our God,
  And sweetest glories shine;
There Jesus says that I am His,
  And my Belovèd's mine.

What shall we pay our heavenly King,
  For grace so vast as this?
He brings our pardon to our eyes,
  And seals it with a kiss.

Let such amazing loves as these
  Be sounded all abroad,
Such favours are beyond degrees,
  And worthy of a God.

To Him that washed us in His blood
  Be everlasting praise,
Salvation, honour, glory, power,
  Eternal as His days.

700   William Williams   87 87 47
The voice of my beloved! behold, He cometh leaping upon the mountains, skipping upon the hills. *Song 2:8*

Hark! the voice of my Belovèd,
  Lo, He comes in greatest need,
Leaping on the lofty mountains,
  Skipping over hills with speed,
    To deliver,
  Me unworthy from all woe.

In a dungeon deep He found me,
  Without water, without light,
Bound in chains of horrid darkness,
  Gloomy, thick, Egyptian night;
    He recovered
  Thence my soul with price immense.

And for this let men and angels,
  All the heavenly hosts above,
Choirs of seraphim elected,
  With their golden harps of love,
    Praise and worship,
  My Redeemer without end.

Let believers raise their anthems;
  All the saints in one accord,
Mixed with angels and archangels,
  Sing their dear Redeeming Lord;
    Love eternal,
  Inconceivable, unknown.

701   John Berridge   SM
My beloved spake, and said unto me, Rise up, My love, My fair one, and come away.
Song 2:10

If Jesus kindly say,
  And with a whispering word,
'Arise, My love, and come away,'
  I run to meet my Lord.

My soul is in my ears;
  My heart is all on flame;
My eyes are sweetly drowned in tears,
  And melted is my frame.

My raptured soul will rise,
  And give a cheerful spring,
And dart through all the lofty skies,
  To visit Zion's King.

He meets me with a kiss,
  And with a smiling face;
I taste the dear, enchanting bliss,
  And wonder at His grace.

The world now drops its charms;
  My idols all depart;
Soon as I reach my Saviour's arms,
  I give Him all my heart.

A soft and tender sigh
  Now heaves my hallowed breast;
I long to lay me down and die,
  And find eternal rest.

702 John Newton 77 77 D
For, lo, the winter is past, the rain is over and gone. *Song 2:11*

Pleasing spring again is here
Trees and fields in bloom appear;
  Hark! the birds, with artless lays,
  Warble their Creator's praise!
Where, in winter all was snow,
Now the flowers in clusters grow!
  And the corn, in green array,
  Promises a harvest day.

What a change has taken place!
Emblem of the spring of grace;
  How the soul in winter mourns,
  Till the Lord, the Sun, returns;
Till the Spirit's gentle rain
Bids the heart revive again:
  Then the stone is turned to flesh,
  And each grace springs forth afresh.

Lord, afford a spring to me!
Let me feel like what I see;
  Ah! my winter has been long,
  Chilled my hopes, and stopped my song!
Winter threatened to destroy
Faith, and love, and every joy;
  If Thy life was in the root,
  Still I could not yield the fruit.

Speak, and by Thy gracious voice
Make my drooping soul rejoice;
  O belovèd Saviour, haste,
  Tell me all the storms are past;
On Thy garden deign to smile,
Raise the plants, enrich the soil:
  Soon Thy presence will restore
  Life to what seemed dead before.

Lord, I long to be at home,
Where these changes never come!
  Where the saints no winter fear,
  Where 'tis spring throughout the year!
How unlike this state below!
There the flowers unwithering blow!
  There no chilling blasts annoy!
  All is love, and bloom, and joy.

703 William Hammond 77 77
My Beloved is mine, and I am His.
Song 2:16

Christ is mine, and I am His;
Centre, source, and sum of bliss;
Earth and hell in vain combine
Me and Jesus to disjoin.

Thou my fortress art and tower;
Having Thee, I want no more.
Strong in Thy full strength I stand;
None can pluck me from Thy hand.

Nothing in myself I am;
All I have is in the Lamb.
While His face on me does shine,
All in heaven and earth is mine.

In my Jesus' arms secure,
To the end I shall endure;
Join with me, ye angels, join!
Praise His name in hymns divine.

704 Joseph Irons CM
My Beloved is mine, and I am His.
Song 2:16

Jesus, the glories of Thy face
  My songs of praise record:
I sing the overflowing grace
  Of my belovèd Lord.

Thou art the Father's chief delight:
  Thy beauty angels view:
Thou art all fair in Zion's sight,
  And my Belovèd too.

Of Thee the ancient prophets wrote:
  Of Thee let Israel sing;
And heaven's vast choir, in every note,
  Praise my belovèd King.

Thy precious name shall joy impart
  To all that are Thine own:
In life and death, O may my heart
  Be my Belovèd's throne.

705 Charles Mudie 64 64 10 10
My Beloved is mine, and I am His.
Song 2:16

I lift my heart to Thee,
  Saviour divine;
For Thou art all to me
  And I am Thine.
Is there on earth a closer bond than this;
That my Belovèd's mine and I am His?

Thine am I by all ties;
  But chiefly Thine,
That through Thy sacrifice
  Thou, Lord, art mine.
By Thine own cords of love, so sweetly wound
Around me, I to Thee am closely bound.

To Thee, Thou dying Lamb,
  I all things owe;
All that I have, and am,
  And all I know.
All that I have is now no longer mine
And I am not my own; Lord, I am Thine.

How can I, Lord, withhold
  Life's brightest hour
From Thee; or gathered gold,
  Or any power?
Why should I keep one precious thing from Thee,
When Thou hast given Thine own dear self for
  me?

I pray Thee, Saviour, keep
  Me in Thy love,
Until death's holy sleep
  Shall me remove
To that fair realm where, sin and sorrow o'er,
Thou and Thine own are one for evermore.

706   William Cowper   CM
Saw ye Him whom my soul loveth?
Song 3:3

To those who know the Lord I speak,
  Is my Belovèd near?
The Bridegroom of my soul I seek,
  O! when will He appear?

Though once a Man of grief and shame,
  Yet now He fills a throne,
And bears the greatest, sweetest name
  That earth or heaven have known.

Grace flies before, and love attends
  His steps where'er He goes;
Though none can see Him but His friends,
  And they were once His foes.

Such Jesus is, and such His grace,
  O may He shine on you!
And tell Him, when you see His face,
  I long to see Him too.

707   Isaac Watts   LM
Let my beloved come into his garden.
Song 4:16

We are a garden walled around,
Chosen and made peculiar ground;
A little spot enclosed by grace,
Out of the world's wide wilderness.

Like trees of myrrh and spice we stand,
Planted by God the Father's hand;
And all His springs in Zion flow
To make the young plantation grow.

Awake, O heavenly Wind, and come,
Blow on this garden of perfume;
Spirit divine, descend and breathe
A gracious gale on plants beneath.

Make our best spices flow abroad,
To entertain our Saviour, God;
And faith, and love, and joy appear,
And every grace be active here.

Let my Belovèd come and taste
His pleasant fruits at His own feast.
'I come, My spouse, I come,' He cries,
With love and pleasure in His eyes.

Our Lord into His garden comes,
Well pleased to smell our poor perfumes;
And calls us to a feast divine,
Sweeter than honey, milk, or wine:

'Eat of the tree of life, My friends;
The blessings that My Father sends;
Your taste shall all My dainties prove,
And drink abundance of My love.'

Jesus, we will frequent Thy board,
And sing the bounties of our Lord;
But the rich food on which we live
Demands more praise than tongue can give.

708   John Kent   LM
Awake, O north wind; and come, thou south.
Song 4:16

When Zion's sons, great God! appear
In Zion's courts for praise and prayer,
There, in Thy Spirit, deign to be
As one with those who worship Thee.

Without Thy sovereign power, O Lord,
No sweets the gospel can afford;
No drops of heavenly love will fall
To cheer the weary, thirsting soul.

Winds from the North and South, awake,
Take of the things of Jesus, take;
Diffuse Thy kind celestial dew,
Bring pardon, peace, and healing too.

Then shall we count the season dear
To those who speak or those who hear;
And all conspire with sweet accord,
In hymns of joy, to praise the Lord.

709   John Newton   CM
Awake, O north wind; and come, thou south.
Song 4:16

Breathe from the gentle South, O Lord,
  And cheer me from the North;
Blow on the treasures of Thy word,
  And call the spices forth.

Cold as I feel this heart of mine,
  Yet since I feel it so,
It yields some hope of life divine
  Within, however low.

I seem forsaken and alone;
  I hear the lion roar;
And every door is shut but one,
  And that is mercy's door.

Here would I wait, and hope, and pray,
  Till needed mercy come;
But lest I faint, or turn away,
  Lord, do not tarry long.

710   John Berridge   88 88 88
**What is thy Beloved more than another
beloved?** *Song 5:9*

If gazing strangers want to know
What makes me sing of Jesus so;
I love His name, 'tis very dear,
And would His loveliness declare:

    *A single smile from Jesus given
    Will lift a drooping soul to heaven.*

His eyes are full of melting love,
More soft and sparkling than the dove;
And sweet instruction He conveys,
To warm my heart and guide my ways:

No sinful taint His bosom knows,
But with amazing kindness glows;
He wrought a righteousness divine,
And gives me faith to call it mine:

His mercies, like Himself, endure,
And like His love are ever sure;
And when our eyes His worth can view,
Our hearts will love and trust Him too.

711   Joseph Swain   88 88 D
**My Beloved is white and ruddy, the chiefest
among ten thousand.** *Song 5:10*

When on my Belovèd I gaze,
  So dazzling His beauties appear,
His charms so transcendently blaze,
  The sight is too melting to bear.
When from my own vileness I turn
  To Jesus exposed on the tree,
With shame and with wonder I burn.
  To think what He suffered for me.

My sins, O how black they appear,
  When in that dear bosom they meet!
Those sins were the nails and the spear
  That wounded His hands and His feet.
'Twas justice that wreathed for His head
  The thorns that encircled it round;
Thy temples, Immanuel, bled,
  That mine might with glory be crowned.

The wonderful love of His heart,
  Where He has recorded my name,
On earth can be known but in part;
  Heaven only can bear the full flame.
In rivers of sorrow it flowed,
  And flowed in those rivers for me,
My sins are all drowned in His blood;
  My soul is both happy and free.

712   Augustus Toplady   CM
**My Beloved is white and ruddy, the chiefest
among ten thousand.** *Song 5:10*

Compared with Christ, in all beside
  No comeliness I see;
The one thing needful, dearest Lord,
  Is to be one with Thee.

The sense of Thy expiring love,
  Into my soul convey;
Thyself bestow, for Thee alone,
  My All in all, I pray.

Less than Thyself will not suffice
  My comfort to restore;
More than Thyself I cannot crave,
  And Thou canst give no more.

Loved of my God, for Him again
  With love intense I'd burn;
Chosen of Thee ere time began,
  I choose Thee in return.

Whate'er consists not with Thy love,
  O teach me to resign;
I'm rich to all the intents of bliss,
  If Thou, O God, art mine.

713   Thoro Harris   87 87 D
My Beloved is white and ruddy, the chiefest among ten thousand. *Song 5:10*

Who can cheer the heart like Jesus,
  By His presence all divine?
True and tender, pure and precious,
  O how blest to call Him mine!

All that thrills my soul is Jesus;
  He is more than life to me;
And the fairest of ten thousand,
  In my blessèd Lord I see.

Love of Christ so freely given,
  Grace of God beyond degree,
Mercy higher than the heaven,
  Deeper than the deepest sea.

What a wonderful redemption!
  Never can a mortal know
How my sin, though red like crimson,
  Can be whiter than the snow.

Every need His hand supplying,
  Every good in Him I see;
On His strength divine relying,
  He is all in all to me.

By the crystal-flowing river
  With the ransomed I will sing,
And for ever and for ever
  Praise and glorify the King.

714   Joseph Irons   LM
He is altogether lovely. *Song 5:16*

Let Zion hear while I proclaim
My precious Saviour's matchless name;
He's wise and holy, just and true,
And altogether lovely too.

He's lovely from His head to feet,
His heart is love—His mouth most sweet;
Angels and saints delight to sing
Their altogether lovely King.

Essential deity He claims,
Reveals Himself in lovely names;
He lives, and dies, and reigns for us—
He's altogether lovely thus.

His loveliness has won my heart;
Dear Jesus, let us never part:
I'll sound Thy lovely name abroad,
My altogether lovely Lord.

Up to His throne I soon shall go,
  More of His loveliness to know,
While ransomed millions shall declare
  He's altogether lovely there.

715   John Newton   LM
This is my Beloved, and this is my Friend. *Song 5:16*

Poor, weak, and worthless though I am,
  I have a rich, almighty Friend;
Jesus, the Saviour, is His name;
  He freely loves, and without end.

He ransomed me from hell with blood,
  And by His power my foes controlled;
He found me wandering far from God,
  And brought me to His chosen fold.

He cheers my heart, my needs supplies,
  And says that I shall shortly be
Enthroned with Him above the skies;
  O what a Friend is Christ to me!

716   Samuel Stennett (alt)   CM
He is altogether lovely. *Song 5:16*

To Christ the Lord let every tongue
  Its noblest tribute bring:
When He's the subject of the song,
  Who can refuse to sing?

Survey the beauties of His face,
  And on His glories dwell;
Think of the wonders of His grace,
  And all His triumphs tell.

Majestic sweetness sits enthroned
  Upon His awesome brow;
His head with radiant glories crowned,
  His lips with grace o'erflow.

No mortal can with Him compare,
  Among the sons of men;
Fairer He is than all the fair
  That fill the heavenly train.

He saw me plunged in deep distress,
  He flew to my relief:
For me He bore the shameful cross,
  And carried all my grief.

To heaven, the place of His abode,
  He brings my weary feet:
Shows me the glories of my God,
  And makes my joys complete.

717   William Williams, tr. R Jones   87 87 47
He is altogether lovely. *Song 5:16*

Jesus, Jesus, all-sufficient,
  Beyond telling is Thy worth;
In Thy name lie greater treasures
  Than the richest found on earth.
    Such abundance
  Is my portion with my God.

In Thy gracious face there's beauty
  Far surpassing every thing
Found in all the earth's great wonders
  Mortal eye hath ever seen.
    Rose of Sharon,
  Thou Thyself art heaven's delight.

                    © *Translator*

718   George Robinson   77 77 D
I am my Beloved's, and my Beloved is mine.
Song 6:3

Loved with everlasting love,
  Led by grace that love to know;
Spirit, breathing from above,
  Thou hast taught me it is so!
O this full and perfect peace!
  O this transport all divine!
In a love which cannot cease,
  I am His and He is mine.

Heaven above is softer blue,
  Earth around is sweeter green;
Something lives in every hue
  Christless eyes have never seen;
Birds with gladder songs o'erflow,
  Flowers with deeper beauties shine,
Since I know as now I know,
  I am His and He is mine.

Things that once were wild alarms
  Cannot now disturb my rest;
Closed in everlasting arms,
  Pillowed on the loving breast.
O to lie for ever here,
  Doubt and care and self resign,
While He whispers in my ear—
  I am His and He is mine.

His for ever, only His;
  Who the Lord and me shall part?
Ah, with what a rest of bliss
  Christ can fill the loving heart!
Heaven and earth may fade and flee,
  Firstborn light in gloom decline;
But, while God and I shall be,
  I am His and He is mine.

719   William Gadsby   11 11 11 11
**What will ye see in the Shulamite? As it were
the company of two armies.**
Song 6:13

In every believer two armies are seen,
The new man of grace, and the old man of sin;
In Christ he is perfect, and free from all guilt,
Yet in himself evils are both seen and felt.

As one in the Lord, he's a true son of peace;
In himself, he is nothing but sin and disgrace;
His body's the temple of the Holy Ghost,
And Christ in him dwelleth as King of one host.

When Christ takes possession, and proves
  Himself King,
Then sin, world, and Satan, their forces will bring!
Nor will they be wanting of gun-shot from hell;
The old prince of darkness will furnish them well.

Yet such is the power and love of our King,
In spite of all hell we of victory sing;
For though sin and devils against us unite,
'Tis Christ fights our battles, and puts them to
  flight.

The victory is thine! then let hell do its worst;
For Christ will still reign, and of Christ thou shalt
  boast;
And when the fight's ended, the crown thou shalt
  wear,
And glory immortal with Christ thou shalt share.

720   Charles Wesley   886 D
**How fair and how pleasant art Thou, O Love,
for delights!** *Song 7:6*

O Love divine, how sweet Thou art!
When shall I find my willing heart
  All taken up by Thee?
I thirst, I faint, I die to prove
The greatness of redeeming love,
  The love of Christ to me.

Stronger His love than death or hell;
Its riches are unsearchable;
  The first-born sons of light
Desire in vain its depths to see;
They cannot reach the mystery,
  The length and breadth and height.

God only knows the love of God;
O that it now were shed abroad
In this poor stony heart!
For love I sigh, for love I pine;
This only portion, Lord, be mine,
Be mine this better part!

O that I could for ever sit
With Mary at the Master's feet!
Be this my happy choice;
My only care, delight and bliss,
My joy, my heaven on earth, be this,
To hear the Bridegroom's voice.

721   Isaac Watts   LM
**Who is this that cometh up from the
wilderness, leaning upon her Beloved?**
Song 8:5

Who is this fair one in distress,
That travels from this wilderness;
And, pressed with sorrows and with sins,
On her belovèd Lord she leans?

This is the spouse of Christ our God,
Bought with the treasures of His blood;
And her request and her complaint
Is but the voice of every saint:

'O let my name engraven stand
Both on Thy heart and on Thy hand;
Seal me upon Thy arm, and wear
That pledge of love for ever there.

'Stronger than death Thy love is known,
Which floods of wrath can never drown;
And hell and earth in vain combine,
To quench a fire so much divine.

'But I am jealous of my heart,
Lest it should once from Thee depart;
Then let Thy name be well impressed,
As a fair signet, on my breast.

'Till Thou hast brought me to Thy home,
Where fears and doubts can never come,
Thy countenance let me often see,
And often Thou shalt hear from me.'

722   John Kent   SM
**Who is this that cometh up from the
wilderness, leaning upon her Beloved?**
Song 8:5

From sin's dark thorny maze,
To Canaan's fertile plains,
A travelling fair one in distress,
On her Belovèd leans.

Through fire and flood she goes,
A weakling, more than strong;
Vents in His bosom all her woes,
And leaning moves along.

When dangers round her press,
And darkness veils the skies,
She leans upon His righteousness;
From thence her hopes arise.

When guilt, a mighty flood,
Her trembling conscience pains,
Then on His peace-securing blood
This travelling fair one leans.

She views the covenant sure;
Her hopes all centre there;
And on His bosom leans secure,
Whose temples bled for her.

723   Joseph Irons   LM
**Who is this that cometh up from the
wilderness, leaning upon her Beloved?**
Song 8:5

On yonder barren, rugged ground,
Behold a traveller upward bound:
And as she leaves this wilderness,
The wondering world says, 'Who is this?'

Fatigued with hills, and foes, and thorns!
The desert's husks her spirit scorns;
She treads on worlds, leaves sin's abyss,
And angry fiends say, 'Who is this?'

She leans upon the Prince of grace,
And, as she moves with steady pace
Through worlds of light, to heavenly bliss,
Angelic hosts say, 'Who is this?'

With heaven-born hope she still aspires,
Leaning on Christ, whom she admires:
And while to heaven she claims access,
Her smiling God says, 'Who is this?'

Jehovah asked, and then replied.
'This is My jewel, temple, bride,
She bears My image, is My own,
And shall be partner of My throne.'

724   John Newton   CM
Why should ye be stricken any more?
Isaiah 1:5

Physician of my sin-sick soul,
    To Thee I bring my case;
My raging malady control,
    And heal me by Thy grace.

Pity the anguish I endure,
    See how I mourn and pine;
For never can I hope a cure
    From any hand but Thine.

I would disclose my whole complaint,
    But where shall I begin?
No words of mine can fully paint
    That worst distemper, sin.

It lies not in a single part,
    But through my frame is spread;
A burning fever in my heart,
    A palsy in my head.

Lord, I am sick, regard my cry,
    And set my spirit free:
Say, canst Thou let a sinner die,
    Who longs to live to Thee?

725   Isaac Watts   CM
**Come now, and let us reason together, saith
the LORD: though your sins be as scarlet, they
shall be as white as snow; though they be red
like crimson, they shall be as wool.** *Isaiah 1:18*

Why does your face, ye humble souls,
    Those mournful colours wear?
What doubts are these that try your faith,
    And nourish your despair?

What though your numerous sins exceed
    The stars that fill the skies,
And, aiming at the eternal throne,
    Like pointed mountains rise?

What though your mighty guilt beyond
    The wide creation swell,
And has its cursed foundations laid
    Low as the deeps of hell?

See, here an endless ocean flows
    Of never-failing grace;
Behold, a dying Saviour's veins
    The sacred flood increase!

It rises high, and drowns the hills;
    Has neither shore nor bound;
Now if we search to find our sins,
    Our sins can ne'er be found.

Awake, our hearts, adore the grace
That buries all our faults;
And pardoning blood that swells above
Our follies and our thoughts.

726   Augustus Toplady   SM
**Though your sins be as scarlet, they shall be
as white as snow.** *Isaiah 1:18*

Jesus, Thy light impart,
    And lead me in Thy path;
I have an unbelieving heart;
    But Thou canst give me faith.

Unrivalled reign within;
    My only Sovereign be;
O crucify the man of sin,
    And form Thyself in me.

Thy blood's renewing might
    Can make the foulest clean;
Can wash the Ethiopian white,
    And change the leopard's skin.

Fulfil Thy gracious word,
    And show my guilt forgiven;
Bid me embrace my dying Lord,
    And mount with Thee to heaven.

727   Michael Bruce   CM
**The mountain of the LORD'S house shall be
established in the top of the mountains.**
Isaiah 2:2

Behold! the mountain of the Lord
    In latter days shall rise
On mountain-tops, above the hills,
    And draw the wondering eyes.

To this the joyful nations round,
    All tribes and tongues, shall flow;
Up to the hill of God, they'll say,
    And to His house we'll go.

The beam that shines from Zion's hill
    Shall lighten every land;
The King that reigns in Salem's towers
    Shall all the world command.

Among the nations He shall judge;
    His judgments truth shall guide;
His sceptre shall protect the just,
    And quell the sinner's pride.

No strife shall vex Messiah's reign,
    Or mar those peaceful years;
To ploughshares men shall beat their swords,
    To pruning-hooks their spears.

Come, then! O come from every land,
  To worship at His shrine,
And walking in the light of God,
  With holy beauties shine.

728   John Milton   CM
The LORD alone shall be exalted in that day.
Isaiah 2:17

The Lord will come and not be slow,
  His footsteps cannot err;
Before Him righteousness shall go,
  His royal harbinger.

Mercy and truth that long were missed,
  Now joyfully are met;
Sweet peace and righteousness have kissed,
  And hand in hand are set.

Truth from the earth, like to a flower,
  Shall bud and blossom then;
And justice, from her heavenly bower,
  Look down on mortal men.

Rise, God, judge Thou the earth in might,
  This wicked earth redress;
For Thou art He who shalt by right
  The nations all possess.

The nations all, whom Thou hast made
  Shall come, and all shall frame
To bow them low before Thee, Lord,
  And glorify Thy name.

For great Thou art, and wonders great
  By Thy strong hand are done:
Thou in Thy everlasting seat
  Remainest God alone.

729   John Kent   SM
**Say ye to the righteous, that it shall be well
with him.** *Isaiah 3:10*

What cheering words are these;
  Their sweetness who can tell?
In time and to eternal days,
  ''Tis with the righteous well.'

In every state secure,
  Kept as Jehovah's eye,
'Tis well with them while life endure,
  And well when called to die.

Well when they see His face,
  Or sink amidst the flood;
Well in affliction's thorny maze
  Or on the mount of God.

Well when the gospel yields
  Pure honey, milk, and wine;
Well when thy soul her leanness feels
  And all her joys decline.

'Tis well when joys arise;
  'Tis well when sorrows flow;
'Tis well when darkness veils the skies,
  And strong temptations blow.

'Tis well when at His throne
  They wrestle, weep, and pray;
'Tis well when at His feet they groan,
  Yet bring their wants away.

'Tis well when they can sing
  As sinners bought with blood;
And when they touch the mournful string,
  And mourn an absent God.

'Tis well when on the mount
  They feast on dying love;
And 'tis as well, in God's account,
  When they the furnace prove.

'Tis well when Jesus calls,
  'From earth and sin arise,
Join with the host of virgin souls,
  Made to salvation wise.'

730   Samuel Medley   886 D
**Now will I sing to my wellbeloved a song of my
Beloved touching His vineyard.** *Isaiah 5:1*

O could I speak the matchless worth,
O could I sound the glories forth
  Which in my Saviour shine!
I'd soar and touch the heavenly strings,
And vie with Gabriel while he sings
  In notes almost divine.

I'd sing the precious blood He spilt,
My ransom from the dreadful guilt
  Of sin, and wrath divine;
I'd sing His glorious righteousness,
In which all perfect, heavenly dress
  My soul shall ever shine.

I'd sing the character He bears,
And all the forms of love He wears,
  Exalted on His throne;
In loftiest songs of sweetest praise,
I would to everlasting days
  Make all His glories known.

Well, the delightful day will come
When my dear Lord will bring me home,
  And I shall see His face;
Then with my Saviour, Brother, Friend,
A blest eternity to spend,
  Triumphant in His grace.

731   Richard Mant   87 87 D
Holy, holy, holy, is the LORD of hosts.
Isaiah 6:3

Round the Lord in glory seated,
　　Cherubim and seraphim
Filled His temple, and repeated
　　Each to each the alternate hymn:

　　'Lord, Thy glory fills the heaven:
　　　Earth is with its fulness stored;
　　Unto Thee be glory given,
　　　Holy, holy, holy Lord!'

Heaven is still with glory ringing;
　　Earth takes up the angels' cry,
Holy, holy, holy, singing,
　　Lord of hosts, Thou Lord most high!

With His seraph train before Him,
　　With His holy Church below,
Thus conspire we to adore Him,
　　Bid we thus our anthem flow:

732   James Montgomery   77 77 D
Holy, holy, holy, is the LORD of hosts.
Isaiah 6:3

Holy, holy, holy Lord!
　　God of Hosts, when heaven and earth
Out of darkness, at Thy word,
　　Issued into glorious birth,
All Thy works before Thee stood,
And Thine eye beheld them good;
　　While they sang with sweet accord,
　　Holy, holy, holy Lord!

Holy, holy, holy! Thee,
　　One Jehovah evermore,
Father, Son and Spirit, we,
　　Dust and ashes would adore:
Lightly by the world esteemed,
From that world by Thee redeemed,
　　Sing we here with glad accord,
　　Holy, holy, holy Lord!

Holy, holy, holy! all
　　Heaven's triumphant choirs shall sing,
When the ransomed nations fall
　　At the footstep of their King:
Then shall saints and seraphim,
Harps and voices, swell one hymn,
　　Blending in sublime accord,
　　Holy, holy, holy Lord!

733   Vernon Higham   64 64 66 64
**Then said I, Woe is me! for I am undone;
because I am a man of unclean lips, and I
dwell in the midst of a people of unclean lips:
for mine eyes have seen the King, the LORD of
hosts.** *Isaiah 6:5*

Create in us, O Lord,
　　A holy fire;
Thy word a flaming sword
　　Our hearts inspire.
Thy glories to declare,
Thy grace beyond compare,
Thy love with Thee to share,
　　We now aspire.

Descend, O Holy Dove,
　　With words of peace,
With blaze of truth and love
　　On earth increase.
O stir our souls today
To seek Thy wondrous way;
For Thou hast come to stay:
　　Then grace release.

Repeat Thy word of joy
　　To us on earth.
And make Thy church employ
　　Its saving worth.
O grant a refuge sweet,
A place for us to meet,
Thy holy presence greet:
　　To hope give birth.
　　　　　　　　　　　　　　© *Author*

734   Vernon Higham   87 87 D
**And I heard the voice of the Lord, saying,
Whom shall I send, and who will go for us?
Then said I, Here am I; send me.** *Isaiah 6:8*

Have you heard the voice of Jesus
　　Softly pleading with your heart?
Have you felt His presence glorious,
　　As He calls your soul apart,
With a love so true and loyal,
　　Love divine that ever flows
From a Saviour, righteous, royal,
　　And a cross that mercy shows?

Have you heard the voice of mercy
　　Granting peace and pardon pure?
Have you felt the balm of Calvary
　　Binding all your wounds secure?
Was there ever such salvation?
　　Was there ever care like this?
See the Saviour's grief and passion,
　　Grace and mercy's gentle kiss.

Have you heard the Saviour calling
  All to leave and follow Him?
Have you felt His Person drawing
  With compulsion lives to win?
Hearken to His invitation,
  To the music of God's grace;
Let the peace of God's salvation
  Fill your soul, and love embrace.

Will you hear the voice of Jesus
  Calling home to mansions fair?
Will you know the promise precious,
  And the Shepherd's tender care?
Yes, if you in life responded
  To God's grace and gospel sound:
For they never are confounded
  Who believed and Jesus found.

© Author

735   Charles Spurgeon   87 87
Whom shall I send, and who will go for Us?
Then said I, Here am I; send me. *Isaiah 6:8*

Lord, Thy church, without a pastor,
  Cries to Thee in her distress;
Hear us, gracious Lord and Master,
  And with heavenly guidance bless.

Walking midst Thy lamps all golden,
  Thou preservest still the light;
Stars in Thy right hand are holden,
  Stars to cheer Thy church's night.

Find us, Lord, the man appointed
  Pastor of this flock to be
One with holy oil anointed,
  Meet for us, and dear to Thee.

Send a man, O King in Zion.
  Made according to Thine heart,
Meek as lamb, and bold as lion,
  Wise to act a shepherd's part.

Grant us now Thy heavenly leading,
  Over every heart preside,
Now, in answer to our pleading,
  All our consultations guide.

736   John Newton   77 77
Behold, a virgin shall conceive, and bear a
Son, and shall call His name Immanuel.
Isaiah 7:14

Sweeter sounds than music knows
  Charm me in Immanuel's name:
All her hopes my spirit owes
  To His birth, and cross, and shame.

When He came, the angels sung
  'Glory be to God on high;'
Lord, unloose my stammering tongue;
  Who should louder sing than I?

Did the Lord a Man become
  That He might the law fulfil,
Bleed and suffer in my room,
  And canst thou, my tongue, be still?

No; I must my praises bring,
  Though they worthless are, and weak;
For should I refuse to sing,
  Sure the very stones would speak.

O my Saviour, Shield, and Sun,
  Shepherd, Brother, Husband, Friend—
Every precious name in One!
  I will love Thee without end.

737   Mary Macdonald, tr. L Macbean   555 3 D
Behold, a virgin shall conceive, and bear a
Son, and shall call His name Immanuel.
Isaiah 7:14

Child in the manger,
  Infant of Mary;
Outcast and stranger,
  Lord of all!
Child who inherits
  All our transgressions,
All our demerits
  On Him fall.

Once the most holy
  Child of salvation
Gently and lowly
  Lived below;
Now as our glorious
  Mighty Redeemer,
See Him victorious
  O'er each foe.

Prophets foretold Him,
  Infant of wonder;
Angels behold Him
  On His throne;
Worthy our Saviour
  Of all their praises;
Happy for ever
  Are His own.

738 Ann Cousin 76 76 76 75
Thy land, O Immanuel. *Isaiah 8:8*

The sands of time are sinking;
  The dawn of heaven breaks;
The summer morn I've sighed for,
  The fair, sweet morn, awakes:
Dark, dark hath been the midnight,
  But day-spring is at hand,
And glory, glory dwelleth
  In Immanuel's land.

The King there, in His beauty,
  Without a veil is seen;
It were a well-spent journey,
  Though seven deaths lay between;
The Lamb with His fair army
  Doth on Mount Zion stand,
And glory, glory dwelleth
  In Immanuel's land.

O Christ, He is the fountain,
  The deep, sweet well of love;
The streams on earth I've tasted,
  More deep I'll drink above;
There, to an ocean fulness,
  His mercy doth expand,
And glory, glory dwelleth
  In Immanuel's land.

With mercy and with judgment
  My web of time He wove,
And aye the dews of sorrow
  Were lustred with His love:
I'll bless the hand that guided,
  I'll bless the heart that planned,
When throned where glory dwelleth
  In Immanuel's land.

The bride eyes not her garment,
  But her dear Bridegroom's face;
I will not gaze at glory,
  But on my King of grace;
Not at the crown He giveth,
  But on His piercèd hand:
The Lamb is all the glory
  Of Immanuel's land.

I've wrestled on towards heaven,
  'Gainst storm and wind and tide;
Now, like a weary traveller
  That leans upon his guide,
Amid the shades of evening,
  While sinks life's lingering sand,
I hail the glory dawning
  From Immanuel's land.

739 David Denham LM
And He shall be for a sanctuary.
Isaiah 8:14

While passing through this vale of tears,
Exposed to sorrows, sins, and fears,
O what a source of joy to see
Christ will my Sanctuary be.

By Sinai's law condemned to die,
To Thy dear arms, O Christ! I fly;
In Thy atoning blood I see
Thou wilt my Sanctuary be.

Thou art my only resting-place,
The fountain head of sovereign grace;
In all my conflicts may I see
Thou wilt my Sanctuary be.

Though sin and Satan oft assail,
Thy promises can never fail;
My times in Thy good hands; I see
Thou wilt my Sanctuary be.

With such a mighty God to save,
I shall each storm of life outbrave;
And in the hour of death shall see
Thou wilt my Sanctuary be.

In Father, Son, and Holy Ghost,
I shall for ever make my boast;
While through eternity I see
God will my Sanctuary be.

740 Samuel Medley LM
And He shall be for a sanctuary.
Isaiah 8:14

Jesus before Thy face I fall,
My Lord, my Life, my Hope, my All;
For I have nowhere else to flee,
No sanctuary, Lord, but Thee.

In Thee I every glory view,
Of safety, strength, and beauty too;
Belovèd Saviour, ever be
A Sanctuary unto me.

Whatever woes and fears betide,
In Thy dear bosom let me hide;
And, while I pour my soul to Thee,
Do Thou my Sanctuary be.

Through life and all its changing scenes,
And all the grief that intervenes,
'Tis this supports my fainting heart,
That Thou my Sanctuary art.

Apace the solemn hour draws nigh,
When I must bow my head and die;
But O what joy this witness gives,
Jesus, my Sanctuary, lives!

He from the grave my dust will raise;
I in the heavens will sing His praise;
And when in glory I appear,
He'll be my Sanctuary there.

741   John Morison   CM
The people that walked in darkness have seen a great light. *Isaiah 9:2*

The race that long in darkness pined
  Have seen a glorious Light;
The people dwell in day, who dwelt
  In death's surrounding night.

To hail Thy rise, Thou better Sun,
  The gathering nations come,
Joyous, as when the reapers bear
  The harvest-treasures home.

To us a Child of hope is born,
  To us a Son is given;
Him shall the tribes of earth obey,
  Him all the hosts of heaven.

His name shall be the Prince of peace,
  For evermore adored;
The Wonderful, the Counsellor,
  The great and mighty Lord.

His power increasing still shall spread;
  His reign no end shall know:
Justice shall guard His throne above,
  And peace abound below.

742   Charles Wesley   87 87 D
The people that walked in darkness have seen a great light. *Isaiah 9:2*

Light of those whose dreary dwelling
  Borders on the shades of death,
Come, and,Thy bright beams revealing,
  Dissipate the clouds beneath.
The new heaven's and earth's Creator,
  In our deepest darkness rise,
Scattering all the night of nature,
  Pouring day upon our eyes.

Still we wait for Thy appearing;
  Life and joy Thy beams impart,
Chasing all our fears, and cheering
  Every poor benighted heart.
Come, and manifest the favour
  Thou hast for the ransomed race;
Come, Thou dear exalted Saviour!
  Come, and bring Thy gospel grace.

Save us in Thy great compassion,
  O Thou mild, pacific Prince!
Give the knowledge of salvation,
  Give the pardon of our sins.
By Thy all-sufficient merit
  Every burdened soul release;
By the shining of Thy Spirit,
  Guide us into perfect peace.

743   James Montgomery   664 6664
They joy before Thee according to the joy in harvest. *Isaiah 9:3*

The God of harvest praise;
In loud thanksgiving raise
  Hand, heart and voice!
The valleys laugh and sing,
Forests and mountains ring,
The plains their tribute bring,
  The streams rejoice!

Yes, bless His holy name
And joyous thanks proclaim
  Through all the earth!
To glory in your lot
Is comely, but be not
God's benefits forgot
  Amid your mirth.

The God of harvest praise;
Hands, hearts and voices raise
  With sweet accord.
From fields to garner throng
Bearing your sheaves along
And in your harvest song,
  Bless ye the Lord.

744   William Styles   77 77
They joy before Thee according to the joy in harvest. *Isaiah 9:3*

Let us all with one accord
Praise the ever-living Lord,
Through whose goodness we all come
Thus to hail the harvest home.

Mindful of His covenant, yet
He can ne'er His word forget;
So the seasons onward roll,
Urged by His divine control.

Nature owns her sovereign King,
Winter hours give place to spring,
And the summer follows fast,
Autumn crowns the whole at last.

He is Lord of frost and snow,
By His will the breezes blow;
And, through Him, the sunbeams bright
Flood the gladdened world with light.

See the stacks of corn appear,
Produce of the circling year,
Silent messengers, to tell
That He doeth all things well.

And can He prove faithful thus,
And unmindful be of us,
Who, though we are sinful dust,
Calmly in the Saviour trust?

Gracious God, our faith increase,
Whisper to us thoughts of peace:
Till the joyful time shall come
Of the final harvest home.

745   William Gadsby   CM
For every battle of the warrior is with confused noise, and garments rolled in blood. *Isaiah 9:5*

Jesus our heavenly Warrior is,
    He fights our battles well;
His wisdom, love, and power displays,
    And conquers death and hell.

When this almighty Warrior stood
    The church's woes to bear,
Sin, Satan, and the curse of God,
    In blazing wrath drew near.

He bore their every poisonous dart,
    Nor from God's vengeance fled;
Hell seized His agonisèd heart,
    And, lo! He bowed His head.

He stained His garments in their blood,
    And, O victorious King!
In triumph rose the conquering God,
    Sweet victory to sing.

He satisfied the claims of law,
    In that tremendous day;
Let saints from hence their comfort draw,
    And sing their cares away.

O for a living faith to view
    The victories of the Lamb;
And sweetly lean upon Him too,
    Nor fear to trust His name.

746   Christopher Wordsworth   77 77 77
His name shall be called Wonderful, Counsellor, The mighty God, The everlasting Father, The Prince of Peace.
Isaiah 9:6

Sing, O sing, this blessèd morn!
Unto us a Child is born,
Unto us a Son is given,
God Himself comes down from heaven.

Sing, O sing this blessèd morn,
Jesus Christ today is born!

God of God and Light of light
Comes with mercies infinite,
Joining in a wondrous plan
Heaven to earth, and God to man:

God with us, Immanuel,
Deigns for ever now to dwell;
He on Adam's fallen race
Sheds the fulness of His grace:

God comes down that man may rise,
Lifted by Him to the skies,
Christ is Son of Man that we
Sons of God in Him may be:

O renew us, Lord, we pray,
With Thy Spirit day by day,
That we ever one may be,
With the Father and with Thee:

747   Charles Wesley   87 87 D
The Prince of Peace. *Isaiah 9:6*

Peace be to this habitation;
    Peace to all that dwell therein;
Peace, the earnest of salvation,
    Peace, the fruit of pardoned sin;
Peace that speaks the heavenly Giver,
    Peace to worldly minds unknown;
Peace divine that lasts for ever;
    Peace that comes from God alone.

Jesus, Prince of Peace, be near us,
    Fix in all our hearts Thy home;
With Thy gracious presence cheer us,
    Let Thy sacred kingdom come.
Raise to heaven our expectation;
    Give our ransomed souls to prove
Glorious and complete salvation
    In the realms of bliss above.

748   John Berridge   66 66 88
His rest shall be glorious. *Isaiah 11:10*

When Jesus' gracious hand
    Has touched our eyes and ears,
O what a dreary land
    The wilderness appears!
No healing balm springs from its dust;
No cooling stream to quench the thirst.

Yet long I vainly sought
    A resting-place below;
And that sweet land forgot
    Where living waters flow;
I hunger now for heavenly food,
And my poor heart cries out for God.

Lord, enter in my breast,
　And with me sup and stay;
Nor prove a hasty Guest,
　Who tarries but a day;
Upon my bosom fix Thy throne,
And pull each fancy idol down.

My sorrow Thou canst see,
　For Thou dost read my heart;
It pineth after Thee,
　And yet from Thee will start;
Reclaim Thy roving child at last,
And fix my heart and bind it fast.

749　William Cowper　　　77 77
O LORD, I will praise Thee. *Isaiah 12:1*

I will praise Thee every day
Now thine anger's turned away!
Comfortable thoughts arise
From the bleeding sacrifice.

Here, in the fair gospel field,
Wells of free salvation yield
Streams of life, a plenteous store,
And my soul shall thirst no more.

Jesus, is become, at length.
My salvation and my strength;
And His praises shall prolong,
While I live, with grateful song.

Praise ye, then, His glorious name,
Publish His exalted fame!
Still His worth your praise exceeds,
Excellent are all His deeds.

Raise again the joyful sound,
Let the nations roll it round!
Zion, shout, for this is He!
God the Saviour dwells in thee.

750　Vernon Higham　　　77 77 D
O LORD, I will praise Thee. *Isaiah 12:1*

Lord Almighty, King Divine,
　Thou Who knowest all mankind,
Gazed upon this life of mine,
　Satisfaction could not find.
Yet Thine anger turned away,
　Undeserving mercy flowed;
And Thy comfort was my stay,
　When I saw Thy love unfold.

Love immense and love so sweet,
　Love beyond my dearest dream;
Love that gives, this love I greet,
　For it flows an endless stream.
Such a fount is God alone,
　Source of all His saving wealth;
Christ alone does now atone,
　Died and rose to give us health.

Here I'll trust, and will not fear,
　In Jehovah, God supreme;
Strong in heart with song endear;
　Hear my praises and redeem.
From this wealth salvation flows,
　He will always meet my needs;
Praise His name, my longing knows,
　As I drink, my soul He feeds.

© *Author*

751　John Newton　　　55 55 65 65
God is my salvation; I will trust, and not be afraid. *Isaiah 12:2*

Begone, unbelief!
　My Saviour is near,
And for my relief
　Will surely appear.
By prayer let me wrestle
　And He will perform;
With Christ in the vessel
　I smile at the storm.

If dark be my way,
　Since He is my guide,
'Tis mine to obey,
　'Tis His to provide;
Though cisterns be broken
　And creatures all fail,
The word He hath spoken
　Shall surely prevail.

His love in time past
　Forbids me to think
He'll leave me at last
　In trouble to sink;
Each sweet Ebenezer
　I have in review,
Confirms His good pleasure
　To help me quite through.

Determined to save,
　He watched o'er my path,
When, Satan's blind slave,
　I sported with death;
And can He have taught me
　To trust in His name,
And thus far have brought me
　To put me to shame?

Why should I complain
    Of want or distress,
Temptation or pain?
    He told me no less;
The heirs of salvation,
    I know from His word,
Through much tribulation
    Must follow their Lord.

Since all that I meet
    Shall work for my good,
The bitter is sweet,
    The medicine is food;
Though painful at present,
    'Twill cease before long;
And then, O how pleasant
    The conqueror's song!

752   John Kent   77 77

With joy shall ye draw water out of the wells of salvation. *Isaiah 12:3*

Water from salvation's wells,
    Thirsty sinner, come and draw;
Grace in Jesus' fulness dwells,
    More than men or angels know.

'Twas in God, the fount supreme,
    Till the day that Adam fell;
Then the first all-healing stream
    Watered Eden's garden well.

Far and wide the cleansing flood
    O'er the sin-cursed garden ran;
Preaching peace by Jesus' blood—
    Blissful sound to rebel man.

Thousands now around the throne
    Water from this fountain drew;
Felt their griefs and sorrows gone;
    Hymned His praise; and why not you?

Bring no money, price, or aught,
    No good deeds, nor pleasing frames,
Mercy never can be bought;
    Grace is free; and all's the Lamb's.

753   Richard Burnham   66 66 88

Praise the LORD, call upon His name, declare His doings among the people. *Isaiah 12:4*

Lord of the skies, look down,
    And hearken to our prayers;
Shine from Thy gracious throne,
    And chase away our fears:
Then to Thy name a song we'll raise,
And every note shall swell with praise,

Enlighten every mind,
    Fill every heart with grace:
May every spirit find
    That God is in the place;
Then to His name a song we'll raise,
And every note shall swell with praise.

Soon shall the Saviour give
    Our souls their full desire,
And we with Him shall live,
    And all His grace admire!
Then to His name a song we'll raise,
And every note shall swell with praise.

754   John Kent (alt)   CM

Praise the LORD, call upon His name, declare His doings among the people. *Isaiah 12:4*

Children of light, assist my song,
    Come swell the sacred tone:
A sweeter note the blood-bought throng
    Ne'er sung before the throne.

'Tis to the Lamb, for ever dear,
    By God, made sin to be.
Whose sacred side received the spear,
    Whose hands were pierced for me.

On love like this reflect, my soul,
    Here's heights and depths to view.
And lengths that stretch from pole to pole,
    The gospel mystery through.

He passed the rebel angels by,
    Creatures of nobler powers,
While rebel souls are raised on high;
    This sinful flesh of ours.

The sins of all the ransomed race
    That's found throughout the world,
By this one act of sovereign grace
    Were in oblivion hurled.

When thine elect on Zion meet,
    We'll lift Thy name on high,
And every act of grace repeat,
    And shout with holy joy.

755   Samuel Medley   LM

I will make a Man more precious than fine gold. *Isaiah 13:12. (see also 1 Peter 2:7)*

'Jesus is precious,' says the word;
What comfort does this truth afford!
And those who in His name believe,
With joy this precious truth receive.

To them He is more precious far
Than life and all its comforts are;
More precious than their daily food;
More precious than their vital blood.

Not health, nor wealth, nor sounding fame,
Nor earth's deceitful, empty name,
With all its pomp and all its glare,
Can with a precious Christ compare.

He's precious in His precious blood,
That pardoning and soul-cleansing flood;
He's precious in His righteousness,
That everlasting, heavenly dress.

In every office He sustains,
In every victory He gains,
In every counsel of His will,
He's precious to His people still.

As they draw near their journey's end,
How precious is their heavenly Friend!
And when in death they bow their head,
He's precious on a dying bed.

In glory, Lord, may I be found,
And, with Thy precious mercy crowned,
Join the glad song, and there adore
A precious Christ for evermore.

756 Thomas Kelly 87 87 47
The LORD hath founded Zion, and the poor of His people shall trust in it.
Isaiah 14:32

Zion stands by hills surrounded,
    Zion kept by power divine;
All her foes shall be confounded,
    Though the world in arms combine:
        Happy Zion,
    What a favoured lot is thine!

Every human tie may perish;
    Friend to friend unfaithful prove;
Mothers cease their own to cherish;
    Heaven and earth at last remove;
        But no changes
    Can attend Jehovah's love.

Zion's Friend in nothing alters,
    Though all others may and do;
His is love that never falters,
    Always to its object true.
        Happy Zion!
    Crowned with mercies ever new.

If thy God should show displeasure,
    'Tis to save, and not destroy;
If He punish, 'tis in measure;
    'Tis to rid thee of alloy.
        Be thou patient;
    Soon thy grief shall turn to joy.

757 Elizabeth Clephane 76 86 86 86
Thou hast been a strength to the poor, a strength to the needy in his distress, a refuge from the storm, a shadow from the heat.
Isaiah 25:4

Beneath the cross of Jesus
    I fain would take my stand,
The shadow of a mighty rock
    Within a weary land;
A home within the wilderness,
    A rest upon the way,
From the burning of the noontide heat
    And the burden of the day.

O safe and happy shelter!
    O refuge tried and sweet!
O trysting-place where heaven's love
    And heaven's justice meet!
As to the holy patriarch
    That wondrous dream was given,
So seems my Saviour's cross to me
    A ladder up to heaven.

There lies, beneath its shadow,
    But on the farther side,
The darkness of an awful grave
    That gapes both deep and wide:
And there between us stands the cross,
    Two arms outstretched to save;
Like a watchman set to guard the way
    From that eternal grave.

Upon that cross of Jesus
    Mine eyes at times can see
The very dying form of One
    Who suffered there for me;
And from my smitten heart, with tears,
    Two wonders I confess—
The wonders of His glorious love,
    And my own worthlessness.

I take, O cross, thy shadow,
    For my abiding place;
I ask no other sunshine than
    The sunshine of His face;
Content to let the world go by,
    To know no gain nor loss—
My sinful self my only shame,
    My glory all —the cross.

758   *Scottish Paraphrases*   CM
**We have a strong city; salvation will God
appoint for walls and bulwarks.**
Isaiah 26:1

How glorious Zion's courts appear,
    The city of our God!
His throne He hath established here,
    Here fixed His loved abode.

Its walls, defended by His grace,
    No power shall e'er o'erthrow,
Salvation is its bulwark sure
    Against the assaulting foe.

Lift up the everlasting gates,
    The doors wide open fling;
Enter, ye nations, who obey
    The statutes of our King.

Here shall ye taste unmingled joys,
    And dwell in perfect peace,
Ye, who have known Jehovah's name,
    And trusted in His grace.

Trust in the Lord, for ever trust,
    And banish all your fears;
Strength in the Lord Jehovah dwells,
    Eternal as His years.

759   Catesby Paget   CM
**Thou wilt keep him in perfect peace, whose
mind is stayed on Thee.**
Isaiah 26:3

A mind at perfect peace with God;
    O what a word is this!
A sinner reconciled through blood,
    This, this indeed is peace!

By nature and by practice far—
    How very far from God!
Ye now by grace brought near to Him,
    Through faith in Jesus' blood.

So near, so very near to God,
    I cannot nearer be;
For in the Person of His Son
    I am as near as He.

So dear, so very dear to God,
    More dear I cannot be;
The love wherewith He loves the Son—
    Such is His love to me!

Why should I ever anxious be,
    Since such a God is mine?
He watches o'er me night and day,
    And tells me, 'Mine is thine.'

760   Edward Bickersteth   10 10
**Thou wilt keep him in perfect peace, whose
mind is stayed on Thee.**
Isaiah 26:3

Peace, perfect peace, in this dark world of sin?
The blood of Jesus whispers peace within.

Peace, perfect peace, by thronging duties
        pressed?
To do the will of Jesus, this is rest.

Peace, perfect peace, with sorrows surging
        round?
In Jesus' presence nought but calm is found.

Peace, perfect peace, with loved ones far away?
In Jesus' keeping we are safe, and they.

Peace, perfect peace, our future all unknown?
Jesus we know, and He is on the throne.

Peace, perfect peace, death shadowing us and
        ours?
Jesus has vanquished death and all its powers.

It is enough; earth's struggles soon shall cease,
And Jesus call us to heaven's perfect peace.

761   Thomas Kelly   77 77
The way of the just is uprightness.
Isaiah 26:7

When we cannot see our way,
Let us trust and still obey;
He who bids us forward go
Cannot fail the way to show.

Though the sea be deep and wide,
Though a passage seem denied,
Fearless let us still proceed,
Since the Lord vouchsafes to lead.

Though it be the gloom of night,
Though we see no ray of light,
Since the Lord Himself is there,
'Tis not meet that we should fear.

Night with Him is never night;
Where He is, there all is light;
When He calls us, why delay?
They are happy who obey.

Be it ours, then, while we're here,
Him to follow without fear;
Where He calls us, there to go,
What He bids us, that to do.

762   Charles Wesley   CM
O LORD, have we waited for Thee; the desire of our soul is to Thy name, and to the remembrance of Thee. *Isaiah 26:8*

Up to the hills I lift mine eye,
    Thy promised aid I claim;
Father of mercies, glorify
    Thy favourite Jesus' name.

Salvation in that name is found,
    Balm of my grief and care;
A medicine for every wound:
    All, all I want is there.

Faith to be healed, Thou know'st I have,
    For Thou that faith hast given:
Thou canst, Thou wilt the sinner save,
    And make me meet for heaven.

Thou canst o'ercome this heart of mine,
    Thou wilt victorious prove:
For everlasting strength is Thine,
    And everlasting love.

Bound down with twice ten thousand ties,
    Yet let me hear Thy call:
My soul in confidence shall rise—
    Shall rise and break through all.

Deliverance to my soul proclaim,
    And life and liberty;
Show forth the virtue of Thy name,
    And Jesus prove to me!

763   John Kent   CM
With my soul have I desired Thee in the night; yea, with my spirit within me will I seek Thee early. *Isaiah 26:9*

'Twas in the night, when troubles came,
    I sought, my God, for Thee,
But found no refuge in that name
    That once supported me.

I sought Thee, but I found Thee not,
    For all was dark within;
Thy tender mercy I forgot
    To me when dead in sin.

With cords of His eternal love,
    'Twas thus my soul He drew,
And taught my wretched heart to prove
    His oath and promise true.

At length my Sun's refulgent beam
    Through the dark cloud appeared;
My night of woe was like a dream;
    My soul was blessed and cheered.

764   Charles Wesley   CM
LORD, thou wilt ordain peace for us: for thou also hast wrought all our works in us.
Isaiah 26:12

Father, to Thee my soul I lift,
    My soul on Thee depends,
Convinced that every perfect gift
    From Thee alone descends.

Mercy and grace are Thine alone,
    And power and wisdom, too;
Without the Spirit of the Son,
    We nothing good can do.

We cannot speak one useful word,
    One holy thought conceive.
Unless, in answer to our Lord,
    Thyself the blessing give.

Thou all our works in us hast wrought,
    Our good is all divine;
The praise of every virtuous thought
    And righteous work is Thine.

From Thee, through Jesus, we receive
    Power on Thee to call!
In Thee, we are, and move, and live,
    Our God is All in All!

765   Charles Cole   LM
The great trumpet shall be blown.
Isaiah 27:13

Hark! how the gospel trumpet sounds!
Christ and free grace therein abounds;
Free grace to such as sinners be;
And if free grace, why not for me?

The Saviour died, and by His blood
Brought rebel sinners near to God;
He died to set the captives free;
And why, my soul, why not for thee?

The blood of Christ, how sweet it sounds,
To cleanse and heal the sinner's wounds!
The streams thereof are rich and free;
And why, my soul, why not for thee?

Thus Jesus came the poor to bless,
To clothe them with His righteousness;
The robe is spotless, full, and free;
And why, my soul, why not for thee?

Eternal life by Christ is given,
And ruined rebels raised to heaven,
Then sing of grace so rich and free,
And say, my soul, why not for thee?

766   Samuel Barnard   LM

Behold, I lay in Zion for a foundation a stone, a tried stone, a precious corner stone, a sure foundation. *Isaiah 28:16*

Christ is the sure foundation Stone,
Proved by His saints who hence are gone;
Could we converse with them, they'd say,
This precious Stone did not give way.

It stood in every trying hour,
We proved its strength, we proved its power;
We proved it strong, our souls to bear,
Nor had we ever cause to fear.

Other foundations there are none,
But this one precious, living Stone;
Those laid by men, however wise,
Are only refuges of lies.

The Lord Himself this stone did lay,
And tried it, but it ne'er gave way;
A sure foundation it doth prove
To all the objects of His love.

When all foundations else shall fail,
Those built on this shall then prevail;
And lift their heads with joyful praise,
To Him who this foundation lays.

767   John Newton   CM

And therefore will the LORD wait, that He may be gracious unto you. *Isaiah 30:18*

Now, gracious Lord, Thy arm reveal,
   And make Thy glory known ;
Now let us all Thy presence feel,
   And soften hearts of stone.

Help us to venture near Thy throne,
   And plead a Saviour's name,
For all that we can call our own
   Is vanity and shame.

From all the guilt of former sin
   Let mercy set us free ;
And let the year we now begin,
   Begin and end with Thee.

Send down Thy Spirit from above,
   That saints may love Thee more,
And sinners now may learn to love,
   Who never loved before.

And when before Thee we appear,
   In our eternal home,
May growing numbers worship here,
   And praise Thee in our room.

768   Samuel Medley   CM

He will be very gracious unto thee at the voice of thy cry. *Isaiah 30:19*

When in my heart Jehovah's love
   Is freely shed abroad,
How joyfully He makes me prove
   He is my gracious God!

When, borne on faith's adventurous wing,
   I mount to His abode,
Then, while I soar, I sweetly sing,
   'He is my gracious God!'

When Jesus to my sinful soul
   Applies His precious blood,
To pardon, cleanse, and make me whole,
   I praise my gracious God!

In all my trials here below,
   O may I kiss His rod;
For this, through grace, I surely know—
   He's still my gracious God!

In all the storms through which I've passed,
   And all the paths I've trod,
It ever has appeared at last
   He's still my gracious God!

769   William Cowper   LM

He will be very gracious unto thee at the voice of thy cry; when He shall hear it, He will answer thee. *Isaiah 30:19*

What various hindrances we meet,
In coming to the mercy-seat!
Yet who that knows the worth of prayer,
But wishes to be often there?

Prayer makes the darkened cloud withdraw,
Prayer climbs the ladder Jacob saw;
Gives exercise to faith and love;
Brings every blessing from above.

Restraining prayer, we cease to fight;
Prayer makes the Christian's armour bright;
And Satan trembles when he sees
The weakest saint upon his knees.

While Moses stood with arms spread wide,
Success was found on Israel's side;
But when, through weariness, they failed,
That moment Amalek prevailed.

Have you no words? ah! think again;
Words flow apace when you complain,
And fill your fellow-creatures' ear
With the sad tale of all your care.

Were half the breath thus vainly spent,
  To heaven in supplication sent,
Your cheerful song would oftener be,
  'Hear what the Lord has done for me.'

770   William Cowper   LM
As birds flying, so will the LORD of hosts
defend Jerusalem; defending also He will
deliver it; and passing over He will preserve it.
Isaiah 31:5

As birds their infant brood protect,
  And spread their wings to shelter them,
Thus saith the Lord to His elect,
  'So will I guard Jerusalem.'

And what, then, is Jerusalem,
  This darling object of His care?
What is its worth in God's esteem?
  Who built it? Who inhabits there?

Jehovah founded it in blood,
  The blood of His incarnate Son;
There dwell the saints once foes to God,
  The sinners whom He calls His own.

There, though besieged on every side,
  Yet much beloved, and guarded well,
From age to age they have defied
  The utmost force of earth and hell.

Let earth repent, and hell despair,
  The city has a sure defence:
Her name is called, 'The Lord is there!'
  And who has power to drive Him thence?

771   George Herbert   LM
And a Man shall be as an hiding place from the
wind. *Isaiah 32:2*

Amidst the sorrows of the way,
Lord Jesus, teach my soul to pray;
And let me taste Thy special grace,
And run to Christ, my Hiding-place.

Thou know'st the vileness of my heart,
So prone to act the rebel's part;
And when Thou veil'st Thy lovely face,
Where can I find a hiding-place?

Lord, guide my silly, wandering feet,
And draw me to Thy mercy-seat.
I've nought to trust but sovereign grace;
Thou only art my Hiding-place.

O how unstable is my heart!
Sometimes I take the tempter's part,
And slight the tokens of Thy grace,
And seem to want no hiding-place.

But when thy Spirit shines within,
And makes me feel the plague of sin;
Then how I long to see Thy face!
'Tis then I want a hiding-place.

Lord Jesus, shine, and then I can
Feel sweetness in salvation's plan;
And as a sinner, plead for grace,
Through Christ, the sinner's Hiding-place.

772   William Gadsby   77 77
The shadow of a great rock in a weary land.
Isaiah 32:2

Jesus Christ, the sinner's Friend,
Loves His people to the end;
And that they may safe abide,
He's the Rock in which they hide.

As a rock, He guards them well
From the rage of sin and hell.
Such a rock is Christ to me,
I am safe, though thousands flee!

Sheltered in His wounded side,
Now no ill can me betide;
From the tempest covered o'er;
One with Him for evermore.

773   John Kent   LM
The shadow of a great rock in a weary land.
Isaiah 32:2

Great Rock, for weary sinners made,
  When storms of sin distress the soul,
Here let me rest my weary head,
  When lightnings blaze and thunders roll.

Within the clefts of His dear side,
  There all His saints in safety dwell.
And what from Jesus shall divide?
  Not all the rage of earth or hell.

Blessed with the pardon of her sin,
  My soul beneath Thy shade would lie,
And sing the love that took me in,
  While others sank in sin to die.

O sacred covert from the beams
  That on the weary traveller beat,
How welcome are Thy shade and streams;
  How blessed, how sacred, and how sweet!

774   Isaac Watts   CM
Thine eyes shall see the King in His beauty:
they shall behold the land that is very far off.
Isaiah 33:17

There is a land of pure delight,
  Where saints immortal reign;
Infinite day excludes the night,
  And pleasures banish pain.

There everlasting spring abides,
  And never-withering flowers;
Death, like a narrow sea, divides
  This heavenly land from ours.

O could we make our doubts remove,
  These gloomy doubts that rise,
And see the Canaan that we love
  With unbeclouded eyes;

Could we but climb where Moses stood,
  And view the landscape o'er,
Not Jordan's stream, nor death's cold flood,
  Should fright us from the shore.

775   Charles Wesley   88 88 D
Thine eyes shall see the King in His beauty:
they shall behold the land that is very far off.
Isaiah 33:17

I long to behold Him arrayed
  With glory and grandeur above;
The King in His beauty displayed—
  His beauty of holiest love;
I trust through His grace to be there,
  Where Jesus has fixed His abode;
O, when shall we meet in the air,
  And fly to the mountain of God?

With Him I on Zion shall stand
  (For Jesus hath spoken the word),
The breadth of Immanuel's land
  Survey by the light of the Lord;
And when on Thy bosom reclined,
  Thy face I am strengthened to see,
My fulness of bliss I shall find,
  My heaven of heavens, in Thee.

How happy the people that dwell
  At rest in the city above!
No pain the inhabitants feel,
  No sickness or sorrow they prove.
Physician of souls, unto me
  A part in Thy righteousness give;
So shalt Thou, when death sets me free
  My soul to the city receive.

776   Philip Doddridge   LM
In the wilderness shall waters break out, and
streams in the desert. *Isaiah 35:6*

Blest Jesus! source of grace divine,
What soul-refreshing streams are Thine;
O, bring these healing waters nigh,
Or we must droop, and fall, and die.

No traveller through desert lands,
Midst scorching suns and burning sands,
More needs the current to obtain,
Or to enjoy refreshing rain.

Our longing souls aloud would sing,
'Spring up, celestial fountain, spring;
To a redundant river flow,
And cheer this thirsty land below.'

May this blest torrent, near my side,
Through all the desert gently glide;
Then, in Immanuel's land above,
Spread to a sea of joy and love!

777   William Gadsby   66 66 88
And the ransomed of the LORD shall return,
and come to Zion with songs and everlasting
joy upon their heads: they shall obtain joy and
gladness, and sorrow and sighing shall flee
away. *Isaiah 35:10*

The ransomed of the Lord
  Shall unto Zion come;
A faithful, loving God
  Will surely bring them home;
He gave His life a ransom-price,
And Zion shall in Him rejoice.

The promise of the Lord
  Shall stand for ever good,
And Zion shall record
  The wonders of His love.
Redemption's glorious work is done;
The ransomed shall to Zion come.

The Holy, Wise, and Just,
  His Well-Belovèd gave;
And shall the man be cursed
  That Jesus came to save?
Shall sin and Satan Jesus cheat,
Or prove the ransom incomplete?

O vanity extreme!
  And base that heart must be
Whose tongue can dare proclaim
  The ransomed damned shall be.
The debt is paid; the victory won;
The ransomed shall to Zion come.

They shall rejoice in Him,
    And in Him they shall boast;
He saves from wrath and sin,
    From guilt, law, and the curse.
To Zion they shall all be led,
And joy shall rest upon their head.

'Tis no uncertain sound
    The gospel-trumpet gives;
The church in Christ is found,
    And by and in Him lives;
While Jesus lives to bring them home,
The ransomed shall to Zion come.

778   Garnet Terry   CM
O LORD, I am oppressed; undertake for me.
Isaiah 38:14

The Lord will undertake the cause
    Of all that are oppressed;
Then cast on Him your every care,
    And on His promise rest.

Are you bowed down with sin and shame?
    Fear not this plea to make—
'Lord Jesus, I am sore oppressed,
    But do Thou undertake.'

Or does thy soul in darkness dwell?
    By prayer still importune:
King Hezekiah used this plea,
    And was delivered soon.

Be this my everlasting song,
    Be this my only plea—
Jesus has died, and rose, and lives,
    To undertake for me.

779   William Gadsby   87 87 47
And the glory of the LORD shall be revealed.
Isaiah 40:5

O what matchless condescension
    The eternal God displays;
Claiming our supreme attention,
    To His boundless works and ways.
        His own glory
He reveals in gospel days.

In the person of the Saviour,
    All His majesty is seen!
Love and justice shine for ever;
    And, without a veil between,
        We approach Him,
And rejoice in His dear name.

Would we view His brightest glory,
    Here it shines in Jesus' face;
Sing and tell the pleasing story,
    O ye sinners saved by grace;
        And with pleasure,
Bid the guilty Him embrace.

In His highest work, redemption,
    See His glory in a blaze;
Nor can angels ever mention
    Aught that more of God displays;
        Grace and justice
Here unite to endless days.

True, 'tis sweet and solemn pleasure,
    God to view in Christ the Lord;
Here He smiles and smiles for ever;
    May my soul His name record;
        Praise and bless Him,
And His wonders spread abroad.

780   Charles Wesley   77 77
He shall feed His flock like a shepherd: He shall gather the lambs with His arm, and carry them in His bosom, and shall gently lead those that are with young. *Isaiah 40:11*

Happy soul, that, free from harms,
Rests within his Shepherd's arms!
Who his quiet shall molest
Who shall violate his rest?

Jesus does his spirit bear,
Far removes each anxious care;
He who found the wandering sheep
Loves and still delights to keep.

O! that I might so believe;
Steadfastly to Jesus cleave;
Only on His love rely,
Smile at the destroyer nigh;

Free from sin and servile fear,
Feel the Saviour always near;
All His care rejoice to prove,
All the blessings of His love!

Shepherd, seek Thy wandering sheep;
Bring me back, and lead, and keep;
Take on Thee my every care;
Bear me, in Thy bosom bear.

Let me know Thy gentle voice,
More and more in Thee rejoice;
From Thy fulness grace receive;
Ever in Thy Spirit live.

781   Isaac Watts   CM
**Hast thou not known? hast thou not heard,
that the everlasting God, the LORD, the
Creator of the ends of the earth, fainteth not,
neither is weary?** *Isaiah 40:28*

Hast thou not known, hast thou not heard,
  That firm remains on high
The everlasting throne of Him
  Who formed the earth and sky?

Art thou afraid His power shall fail
  When comes thy evil day?
And can an all-creating arm
  Grow weary or decay?

Supreme in wisdom as in power
  The Rock of ages stands;
Though Him thou canst not see, nor trace
  The working of His hands.

He gives the conquest to the weak,
  Supports the fainting heart;
And courage in the evil hour
  His heavenly aids impart.

Mere human power shall fast decay,
  And youthful vigour cease;
But they who wait upon the Lord
  In strength shall still increase.

They with unwearied feet shall tread
  The path of life divine,
With growing ardour onward move,
  With growing brightness shine.

782   Isaac Watts   CM
He giveth power to the faint. *Isaiah 40:29*

Whence do our mournful thoughts arise?
  And where's our courage fled?
Has restless sin and raging hell
  Struck all our comforts dead?

Have we forgot the almighty name
  That formed the earth and sea?
And can an all-creating arm
  Grow weary, or decay?

Treasures of everlasting might
  In our Jehovah dwell;
He gives the conquest to the weak,
  And treads their foes to hell.

Mere mortal power shall fade and die,
  And youthful vigour cease;
But we that wait upon the Lord
  Shall feel our strength increase.

The saints shall mount on eagles' wings,
  And taste the promised bliss,
Till their unwearied feet arrive
  Where perfect pleasure is.

783   Vernon Higham   77 77 D
**They that wait upon the LORD shall renew
their strength; they shall mount up with wings
as eagles; they shall run, and not be weary;
and they shall walk, and not faint.** *Isaiah 40:31*

Everlasting is the Word
  Strong in power and rich in grace;
Every promise of the Lord
  Shines with glory from His face.
Never weary in His way
  Is the King who made the earth;
Great Creator, who dost sway
  Sovereign rule and priceless worth.

To the faint He giveth aid;
  To the weak a way of joy;
Strong shall faint and young shall fade,
  Yet His grace shall love employ.
Blessèd is our happy place,
  He has moved the darkness dim;
See His mercy as we trace
  Love and justice dwell in Him.

They that on the Lord do wait,
  Now mount up with eagle's flight—
Wings of majesty so great,
  Glorious is the wondrous sight.
They shall run and never tire;
  They shall walk and never fall;
For the Lord is their desire,
  God of grace and all in all.
                                        © *Author*

784   Anne Steele   LM
Fear thou not; for I am with thee.
Isaiah 41:10

Why sinks my weak, desponding mind?
  Why heaves my heart the anxious sigh?
Can sovereign goodness be unkind?
  Am I not safe, since God is nigh?

He holds all nature in His hand;
  That gracious hand on which I live
Does life, and time, and death command,
  And has immortal joys to give.

'Tis He supports this fainting frame;
  On Him alone my hopes recline;
The wondrous glories of His name,
  How wide they spread, how bright they shine!

Infinite wisdom! boundless power!
Unchanging faithfulness and love!
Here let me trust, while I adore,
Nor from my Refuge e'er remove.

My God, if Thou art mine indeed,
Then I have all my heart can crave;
A present help in times of need;
Still kind to hear, and strong to save.

Forgive my doubts, O gracious Lord!
And ease the sorrows of my breast;
Speak to my heart the healing word,
That Thou art mine, and I am blest.

785   Benjamin Beddome   CM
Fear thou not; for I am with thee.
Isaiah 41:10

Ye trembling souls, dismiss your fears,
Be mercy all your theme;
Mercy, which like a river flows
In one continual stream.

Fear not the powers of earth and hell,
God will these powers restrain,
His mighty arm their rage repel,
And make their efforts vain.

Fear not the want of outward good
He will for His provide:
Grant them supplies of daily food,
And all they need beside.

Fear not that He will e'er forsake,
Or leave His work undone;
He's faithful to His promises,
And faithful to His Son.

You, in His wisdom, power and grace,
May confidently trust;
His wisdom guides, His power protects,
His grace rewards the just.

786   Frances Havergal   65 65 D
Fear thou not; for I am with thee.
Isaiah 41:10

Standing at the portal
Of the opening year,
Words of comfort meet us,
Hushing every fear;
Spoken through the silence
By our Father's voice,
Tender, strong and faithful,
Making us rejoice.

Onward then and fear not,
Children of the day!
For His word shall never,
Never pass away.

I, the Lord, am with thee,
Be thou not afraid!
I will keep and strengthen,
Be thou not dismayed!
Yea, I will uphold thee
With my own right hand;
Thou art called and chosen
In My sight to stand.

For the year before us,
O what rich supplies!
For the poor and needy
Living streams shall rise;
For the sad and sinful
Shall His grace abound;
For the faint and feeble
Perfect strength be found.

He will never fail us,
He will not forsake;
His eternal covenant
He will never break;
Resting on His promise,
What have we to fear?
God is all-sufficient
For the coming year.

787   John Newton   CM
Fear thou not; for I am with thee.
Isaiah 41:10

Incarnate God! the soul that knows
Thy name's mysterious power,
Shall dwell in undisturbed repose,
Nor fear the trying hour.

Angels, unseen, attend the saints,
And bear them in their arms,
To cheer their spirit when it faints,
And guard their life from harms.

The angels' Lord Himself is nigh
To them that love His name;
Ready to save them when they cry,
And put their foes to shame.

Crosses and changes are their lot,
Long as they sojourn here;
But since their Saviour changes not,
What have His saints to fear?

788   John Newton   77 77 D
Fear thou not; for I am with thee: be not dismayed; for I am thy God: I will strengthen thee; yea, I will help thee; yea, I will uphold thee with the right hand of My righteousness.
Isaiah 41:10

Pensive doubting, fearful heart,
    Hear what Christ the Saviour says;
Every word should joy impart,
    Change thy mourning into praise.
Yes, He speaks, and speaks to thee,
    May He help thee to believe!
Then thou presently wilt see
    Thou hast little cause to grieve:

'Fear thou not, nor be ashamed;
    All thy sorrows soon shall end,
I, who heaven and earth have framed,
    Am thy Husband and thy Friend;
I, the High and Holy One,
    Israel's God, by all adored,
As thy Saviour will be known,
    Thy Redeemer and thy Lord.

'For a moment I withdrew,
    And thy heart was filled with pain
But My mercies I'll renew;
    Thou shalt soon rejoice again;
Though I seem to hide My face,
    Very soon My wrath shall cease;
'Tis but for a moment's space,
    Ending in eternal peace.

'Though afflicted, tempest-tossed,
    Comfortless awhile thou art,
Do not think thou canst be lost,
    Thou art graven on My heart;
All thy wastes I will repair;
    Thou shalt be rebuilt anew;
And in thee it shall appear
    What the God of love can do.'

789   William Gadsby   66 66 88
Behold my Servant, whom I uphold; mine Elect, in whom my soul delighteth.
Isaiah 42:1

Behold with wondering eyes,
    The Servant of the Lord;
On wings of love He flies,
    His counsels to unfold!
He comes, He comes with truth and grace!
And Zion shall behold His face.

Behold Him as your Head;
    Your Husband, and your Friend;
Your Saviour, and your God,
    Your Way, your Life, your End.
Behold Him as your Shepherd dear,
And on Him rest when danger's near.

Behold Him as your King,
    Whose laws are peace and love;
Mercy and judgment sing,
    And set your minds above.
Behold Him as your great High Priest,
With Zion's name upon His breast.

Your Counsellor to plead,
    Your Prophet He to teach;
A Daysman He is made,
    To make up every breach.
On Him depend; before Him fall;
Behold Him as your All in All.

790   Samuel Stennett   LM
A bruised reed shall He not break.
Isaiah 42:3

How soft the words my Saviour speaks,
    How kind the promises He makes!
A bruisèd reed He never breaks,
    Nor will He quench the smoking flax.

The humble poor He'll not despise,
    Nor on the contrite sinner frown;
His ear is open to their cries,
    And quickly sends salvation down.

He sees the struggles that prevail
    Between the powers of grace and sin,
He kindly listens while they tell
    The bitter pangs they feel within.

Though pressed with fears on every side,
    They know not how the strife may end;
Yet He will soon the cause decide,
    And judgment unto victory send.

791   Fanny Crosby   11 10 11 10
I the LORD have called thee in righteousness, and will hold thine hand, and will keep thee.
Isaiah 42:6

Hold Thou my hand! so weak I am and helpless,
    I dare not take one step without Thy aid;
Hold Thou my hand! for then, O loving Saviour,
    No dread of ill shall make my soul afraid.

Hold Thou my hand! and closer, closer draw me
    To Thy dear self—my hope, my joy, my all;
Hold Thou my hand, lest haply I should wander,
    And missing Thee, my trembling feet should fall.

Hold Thou my hand! the way is dark before me
    Without the sunlight of Thy face divine;
But when by faith I catch its radiant glory,
    What heights of joy, what rapturous songs are mine!

Hold Thou my hand! that when I reach the margin,
   Of that lone river Thou didst cross for me,
A heavenly light may flash along its waters
   And every wave like crystal bright shall be.

792   Isaac Watts   CM
Let the inhabitants of the rock sing, let them shout from the top of the mountains.
Isaiah 42:11

Arise my soul, my joyful powers,
   And triumph in thy God;
Awake, my voice, and loud proclaim
   His glorious grace abroad.

He raised me from the depths of sin,
   The gates of gaping hell;
And fixed my standing more secure
   Than 'twas before I fell.

The arms of everlasting love
   Beneath my soul He placed,
And on the Rock of Ages set
   My slippery footsteps fast.

The city of my blessed abode
   Is walled around with grace;
Salvation for a bulwark stands,
   To shield the sacred place.

Satan may vent his sharpest spite,
   And all his legions roar;
Almighty mercy guards my life,
   And bounds his raging power.

Arise, my soul! awake my voice,
   And tunes of pleasure sing;
Loud hallelujahs shall address
   My Saviour and my King.

WILLIAM COWPER 1731-1800

793   William Cowper   CM
And I will bring the blind by a way that they knew not; I will lead them in paths that they have not known: I will make darkness light before them, and crooked things straight.
Isaiah 42:16

God moves in a mysterious way
   His wonders to perform;
He plants His footsteps in the sea,
   And rides upon the storm.

Deep in unfathomable mines
   Of never-failing skill,
He treasures up His bright designs,
   And works His sovereign will.

Ye fearful saints, fresh courage take;
   The clouds ye so much dread
Are big with mercy, and shall break
   In blessings on your head.

Judge not the Lord by feeble sense,
   But trust Him for His grace;
Behind a frowning providence
   He hides a smiling face.

His purposes will ripen fast,
   Unfolding every hour;
The bud may have a bitter taste,
   But sweet will be the flower.

Blind unbelief is sure to err,
   And scan His work in vain;
God is His own interpreter,
   And He will make it plain.

794   Joseph Addison   CM
I will make darkness light before them, and crooked things straight. *Isaiah 42:16*

How are Thy servants blest, O Lord!
   How sure is their defence!
Eternal Wisdom is their Guide,
   Their help Omnipotence.

From all my griefs and fears, O Lord,
   Thy mercy sets me free,
Whilst in the confidence of prayer
   My heart takes hold on Thee.

In midst of dangers, fears and death,
   Thy goodness I'll adore,
And praise Thee for Thy mercies past,
   And humbly hope for more.

My life, while Thou preserv'st my life,
   Thy sacrifice shall be;
And O may death, when death shall come,
   Unite my soul to Thee!

795   Augustus Toplady   886 D
Fear not: for I have redeemed thee, I have called thee by thy name; thou art Mine.
Isaiah 43:1

From whence this fear and unbelief?
Hast Thou, O Father, put to grief
  Thy spotless Son for me?
And will the righteous Judge of men
Condemn me for that debt of sin
  Which, Lord, was charged on Thee?

Complete atonement Thou hast made,
And to the utmost farthing paid
  Whate'er Thy people owed;
How then can wrath on me take place,
If sheltered in Thy righteousness,
  And sprinkled with Thy blood?

If Thou hast my discharge procured,
And freely in my room endured
  The whole of wrath divine,
Payment God cannot twice demand,
First at my bleeding Surety's hand,
  And then again at mine.

Turn, then, my soul, unto thy rest;
The merits of thy great High Priest
  Speak peace and liberty;
Trust in His efficacious blood,
Nor fear thy banishment from God,
  Since Jesus died for thee.

796   John Kent   77 77
When thou passest through the waters, I will be with thee. *Isaiah 43:2*

Christ exalted is our song,
Hymned by all the blood-bought throng;
To His throne our shouts shall rise,
God with us by sacred ties.

Shout, believer, to thy God!
He has once the wine-press trod;
Peace procured by blood divine;
Cancelled all thy sins and mine.

Here thy bleeding wounds are healed;
Sin condemned and pardon sealed;
Grace her empire still maintains;
Christ without a rival reigns.

Through corruption, felt within,
Darkness, deadness, guilt, and sin,
Still to Jesus turn thy eyes—
Israel's hope and sacrifice.

In thy Surety thou art free;
His dear hands were pierced for thee;
With His spotless vesture on,
Holy as the Holy One.

O the heights, the depths of grace,
Shining with meridian blaze!
Here the sacred records show
Sinners black but comely too.

Saints dejected, cease to mourn;
Faith shall soon to vision turn;
Ye the kingdom shall obtain,
And with Christ exalted reign.

797   Joseph Swain   87 87
Since thou wast precious in My sight, thou hast been honourable, and I have loved thee.
Isaiah 43:4

On the wings of faith uprising,
  Jesus crucified I see;
While His love, my soul surprising,
  Cries, 'I suffered all for thee.'

Then beneath the cross adoring,
  Sin does like itself appear;
When, the wounds of Christ exploring,
  I can read my pardon there.

Here I'd feast my soul for ever;
  While this balm of life I prove,
Every wound appears a river
  Flowing with eternal love.

Who can think without admiring?
  Who can hear and nothing feel
See the Lord of life expiring,
  Yet retain a heart of steel?

Angels here may gaze and wonder,
  What the God of love could mean,
When He tore the heart asunder,
  Never once defiled with sin.

798   William Gadsby   87 87 47
I, even I, am the LORD; and beside Me there is no Saviour. *Isaiah 43:11*

Jesus is a mighty Saviour;
  Helpless souls have here a Friend;
He has borne their misbehaviour,
  And His mercy knows no end;
    O ye helpless,
  Come, and on His grace depend.

He, to save your souls from ruin,
  Shed His blood upon the tree!
O ye needy, haste unto Him;
  His salvation's full and free;
    Vilest sinners
  Shall His great salvation see.

Whatsoe'er your age or case be,
None can save you but the Lamb;
If in prison, He can set free,
And a full release proclaim;
He is mighty,
And to save the lost He came.

Yes, the very worst of sinners,
Who upon His grace rely,
Shall of endless bliss be winners;
And shall sing, beyond the sky,
Songs of praises
To the Lamb that once did die.

799   Horatius Bonar   CM
They shall shew forth my praise.
Isaiah 43:21

Fill Thou my life, O Lord my God,
In every part with praise,
That my whole being may proclaim
Thy being and Thy ways.

Not for the lip of praise alone,
Nor e'en the praising heart,
I ask, but for a life made up
Of praise in every part:

Praise in the common things of life,
Its goings out and in;
Praise in each duty and each deed,
However small and mean.

Fill every part of me with praise;
Let all my being speak
Of Thee and of Thy love, O Lord,
Poor though I be and weak.

So shalt Thou, Lord, from me, e'en me,
Receive the glory due;
And so shall I begin on earth
The song for ever new.

So shall no part of day or night
From sacredness be free;
But all my life, in every step,
Be fellowship with Thee.

800   Joseph Irons   LM
**For I will pour water upon him that is thirsty,
and floods upon the dry ground: I will pour My
Spirit upon thy seed, and My blessing upon
thine offspring.** *Isaiah 44:3*

Blest be the God of sovereign grace,
Who owns His word within this place,
Pours out His Spirit like a shower,
And makes poor sinners feel His power.

Here hungry souls have oft been fed
With savoury meat and living bread;
Truth clothed with power unfolds free grace,
And sanctifies the chosen race.

Here gospel liberty is known,
While gospel fruits are daily shown;
Here pleasures like a river flow,
And Jesus sees His kingdom grow.

Here God the Father's love is named,
Here God the Saviour is proclaimed;
Here God the Spirit sets His seal,
And souls once dead begin to feel.

Here, then, we'll sound Jehovah's praise,
Glad to behold and feel His grace;
Joy in the wonders He has done,
Still praying, 'let Thy work go on.'

801   Charles Wesley   SM
Fear ye not, neither be afraid. *Isaiah 44:8*

Away my needless fears,
And doubts no longer mine;
A ray of heavenly light appears,
A messenger divine.

Thrice comfortable hope
That calms my troubled breast;
My Father's hand prepares the cup
And what He wills is best.

If what I wish is good
And suits the will divine;
By earth and hell in vain withstood
I know it shall be mine.

Still let them counsel take
To frustrate His decree,
They cannot keep a blessing back
By heaven designed for me.

Here then I doubt no more,
But in His pleasure rest,
Whose wisdom, love, and truth and power
Engage to make me blest.

To accomplish His design
The creatures all agree;
And all the attributes divine
Are now at work for me.

802   John Berridge   CM
He shall let go my captives. *Isaiah 45:13*

Art thou by sin a captive led?
  Is sin thy daily grief?
The Man who brake the serpent's head
  Can bring thee sweet relief.

His name is Jesus, for He saves,
  And setteth captives free;
His office is to purchase slaves,
  And give them liberty.

No money for thy ransom take,
  But mercy much entreat;
Go, with the chains about thy neck,
  And fall before His feet.

Tell how thy bosom tyrants lash,
  And rage without control;
Show where the fetters gall thy flesh,
  And bruise thy inmost soul.

The sight will melt His piteous heart,
  Soon touched with human woe;
And healing up thy guilty smart,
  His freed-man thou shalt go.

803   Samuel Medley   LM
Assemble yourselves and come; draw near together. *Isaiah 45:20*

My soul, take courage from the Lord;
Believe and plead His holy word;
To Him alone do thou complain,
Nor shalt thou seek His face in vain.

Upon Him call in humble prayer,
Thou still art His peculiar care;
He'll surely turn and smile again,
Nor shalt thou seek His face in vain.

However sinful, weak, and poor,
Still wait and pray at mercy's door;
Faithful Jehovah must remain,
Nor shalt thou seek His face in vain.

Though the vile tempter's hellish rage
Will, with his darts, thy soul engage,
God through the fight shall thee sustain,
Nor shalt thou seek His face in vain.

Though the corruptions of thy heart
Daily new cause of grief impart,
Pray that thy lusts may all be slain,
Nor shalt thou seek His face in vain.

Though sharp afflictions still abound,
  And clouds and darkness thee surround,
Still pray, for God will all explain,
  Nor shalt thou seek His face in vain.

In Him, and Him alone, confide;
  Still at the throne of grace abide;
Eternal victory thou shalt gain,
  Nor shalt thou seek His face in vain.

804   John Bradford   77 77
There is no God else beside Me; a just God and a Saviour; there is none beside Me. *Isaiah 45:21*

O the power of love divine!
  Who its heights and depths can tell—
Tell Jehovah's grand design,
  To redeem our souls from hell?

Mystery of redemption this:
  All my sins on Christ were laid;
My offence was reckoned His;
  He the great atonement made!

Fully I am justified;
  Free from sin, and more than free;
Guiltless, since for me He died;
  Righteous, since He lived for me.

Jesus, now to Thee I bow;
  Let Thy praise my tongue employ.
Saved unto the utmost now,
  Who can speak my heartfelt joy?

805   John Newton   76 76 D
Look unto Me, and be ye saved, all the ends of the earth: for I am God, and there is none else. *Isaiah 45:22*

How lost was my condition
  Till Jesus made me whole!
There is but one Physician
  Can cure a sin-sick soul.
Next door to death He found me,
  And snatched me from the grave;
To tell to all around me,
  His wondrous power to save.

The worst of all diseases
  Is light, compared with sin;
On every part it seizes,
  But rages most within:
'Tis palsy, plague, and fever,
  And madness—all combined;
And none but a believer
  The least relief can find.

From men great skill professing
  I thought a cure to gain;
But this proved more distressing,
  And added to my pain:
Some said that nothing ailed me,
  Some gave me up for lost;
Thus every refuge failed me,
  And all my hopes were crossed.

At length this great Physician,
  How matchless is His grace!
Accepted my petition,
  And undertook my case:
First gave me sight to view Him,
  For sin my eyes had sealed;
Then bid me look unto Him,
  I looked, and I was healed.

A dying, risen Jesus,
  Seen by the eye of faith;
At once from danger frees us,
  And saves the soul from death:
Come then to this Physician,
  His help He'll freely give;
He makes no hard condition,
  ''Tis only—look and live.'

806   Amelia Hull   Irregular
Look unto Me, and be ye saved.
Isaiah 45:22

There is life for a look at the Crucified One;
  There is life at this moment for thee;
Then look, sinner,look unto Him, and be saved,—
  Unto Him who was nailed to the tree.

  Look,look, look and live!
  There is life for a look at the Crucified One,
  There is life at this moment for thee.

It is not thy tears of repentance or prayers,
  But the blood that atones for the soul:
On Him, then, who shed it, believing at once
  Thy weight of iniquities roll.

His anguish of soul on the cross hast thou seen?
  His cry of distress hast thou heard!
Then why, if the terrors of wrath He endured,
  Should pardon to thee be deferred?

Then doubt not thy welcome, since God has
    declared,
  There remaineth no more to be done;
That once in the end of the world He appeared,
  And completed the work He begun.

But take, with rejoicing, from Jesus at once
  The life everlasting He gives:
And know, with assurance, thou never canst die
  Since Jesus, thy righteousness, lives.

807   John Kent   87 87 47
Behold, I have refined thee, but not with silver;
I have chosen thee in the furnace of affliction.
Isaiah 48:10

Sons of God, in tribulation,
  Let your eyes the Saviour view;
He's the Rock of our salvation,
  He was tried and tempted too;
    All to succour
  Every tempted, burdened son.

'Tis if need be, He reproves us,
  Lest we settle on our lees;
Yet He in the furnace loves us;
  'Tis expressed in words like these:
    'I am with thee,
  Israel, passing through the fire.'

To His church, His joy, and treasure,
  Every trial works for good;
They are dealt in weight and measure,
  Yet how little understood!
    Not in anger,
  But from His dear covenant love.

If today He deigns to bless us
  With a sense of pardoned sin,
Perhaps tomorrow He'll distress us,
  Make us feel the plague within;
    All to make us
  Sick of self and fond of Him.

808   John Monsell   77 77 4
Sing, O heavens; and be joyful, O earth.
Isaiah 49:13

Sing, O heavens! O earth, rejoice!
Angel harp, and human voice,
Round Him, as He rises, raise
Your ascending Saviour's praise.
    Hallelujah!

Bruisèd is the serpent's head,
Hell is vanquished, death is dead,
And to Christ gone up on high,
Captive is captivity.
    Hallelujah!

All His work and warfare done
He into His heaven is gone,
And beside His Father's throne,
Now is pleading for His own:
    Hallelujah!

Asking gifts for sinful men,
That He may come down again,
And, the fallen to restore,
In them dwell for evermore.
    Hallelujah!

Sing, O heavens! O earth, rejoice!
Angel harp, and human voice,
Round Him, in His glory, raise
Your ascended Saviour's praise.
    Hallelujah!

809   Augustus Toplady   CM
**Behold, I have graven thee upon the palms of
My hands.** *Isaiah 49:16*

Redeemed offender, hail the day
  That sees thy sins forgiven;
Jesus has borne thy guilt away,
  And pleads for thee in heaven.

Imprinted on His hands thou art,
  In characters of blood:
The streams that issued from His heart
  Shall waft thee safe to God.

For me, the great, the holy Lamb,
  His Father's wrath did bear;
I see His feet, and read my name
  Engraven deeply there.

My faith looks back and sees Him bleed,
  A thorny crown He wears;
To set upon the sinner's head
  A shining crown of stars.

Thy righteousness my robe shall be,
  Thy sacrifice my hope!
For my offence, upon the tree
  My Lord was lifted up.

For me the Saviour's blood avails,
  Almighty to atone;
The hands He gave to piercing nails,
  Shall lead me to His throne.

810   William Shrubsole   LM
**Awake, awake, put on strength, O arm of the
LORD.** *Isaiah 51:9*

Arm of the Lord, awake, awake!
Put on Thy strength, the nations shake;
And let the world adoring see
Triumphs of mercy wrought by Thee.

Say to the heathen from Thy throne,
'I am Jehovah, God alone;'
Thy voice their idols shall confound,
And cast their altars to the ground.

Let Zion's time of favour come;
O bring the tribes of Israel home!
And let our wandering eyes behold
Gentiles and Jews in Jesus' fold.

Almighty God, Thy grace proclaim
In every clime, of every name;
Let adverse powers before Thee fall
And crown the Saviour Lord of all.

811   John Cennick   77 77
**Therefore the redeemed of the LORD shall
return, and come with singing unto Zion; and
everlasting joy shall be upon their head: they
shall obtain gladness and joy; and sorrow and
mourning shall flee away.** *Isaiah 51:11*

Children of the heavenly King,
As ye journey, sweetly sing;
Sing your Saviour's worthy praise,
Glorious in His works and ways.

Ye are travelling home to God
In the way the fathers trod;
They are happy now, and ye
Soon their happiness shall see.

O ye banished seed, be glad;
Christ your Advocate is made;
You to save, your flesh assumes;
Brother to your souls becomes.

Shout, ye little flock, and blest;
You on Jesus' throne shall rest;
There your seat is now prepared,
There your kingdom and reward.

Fear not, brethren, joyful stand
On the borders of your land;
Jesus Christ, your Father's Son,
Bids you undismayed go on.

Lord, submissive make us go,
Gladly leaving all below;
Only Thou our Leader be,
And we still will follow Thee.

812   Mrs Vokes   SM
**How beautiful upon the mountains are the feet
of him that bringeth good tidings, that
publisheth peace.** *Isaiah 52:7*

Ye messengers of Christ,
  His sovereign voice obey;
Arise! and follow where He leads,
  And peace attend your way.

The Master whom you serve
  Will needful strength bestow;
Depending on His promised aid,
  With sacred courage go.

Mountains shall sink to plains,
And hell in vain oppose,
The cause is God's and must prevail,
In spite of all His foes.

Go, spread a Saviour's fame,
And tell His matchless grace
To the most guilty and depraved
Of Adam's numerous race.

We wish you, in His name,
The most divine success;
Assured that He who sends you forth
Will your endeavours bless.

813   Philip Doddridge   CM
Break forth into joy, sing together, ye waste places of Jerusalem: for the LORD hath comforted His people, He hath redeemed Jerusalem. *Isaiah 52:9*

Sing, ye redeemèd of the Lord,
   Your great Deliverer sing;
Pilgrims for Zion's city bound,
   Be joyful in your King.

A hand divine shall lead you on
   Through all the blissful road,
Till to the sacred mount you rise,
   And see your smiling God.

There garlands of immortal joy
   Shall bloom on every head,
While sorrow, sighing, and distress,
   Like shadows, all are fled.

March on in your Redeemer's strength,
   Pursue His footsteps still;
And let the prospect cheer your eye,
   While labouring up the hill.

814   Priscilla Owens   73 73 77 73
All the ends of the earth shall see the salvation of our God. *Isaiah 52:10*

We have heard the joyful sound
   Jesus saves!
Spread the gladness all around
   Jesus saves!
Bear the news to every land,
Climb the steeps and cross the waves,
Onward! 'tis our Lord's command,
   Jesus saves!

Waft it on the rolling tide
   Jesus saves!
Tell to sinners far and wide
   Jesus saves!
Sing, ye islands of the sea,
Echo back, ye ocean caves,
Earth shall keep her jubilee,
   Jesus saves!

Sing above the battle's strife
   Jesus saves!
By His death and endless life
   Jesus saves!
Sing it softly through the gloom,
When the heart for mercy craves,
Sing in triumph o'er the tomb
   Jesus saves!

Give the winds a mighty voice
   Jesus saves!
Let the nations now rejoice,
   Jesus saves!
Shout salvation full and free,
Highest hills and deepest caves,
This our song of victory
   Jesus saves!

815   Arthur Russell   SM
His visage was so marred more than any man, and His form more than the sons of men. *Isaiah 52:14*

   More marred than any man's,
   The Saviour's visage see;
Was ever sorrow like to His
   Endured on Calvary?

   O hear that piercing cry!
   What can its meaning be?
'My God! my God! O! why hast Thou
   In wrath forsaken Me?'

   O 'twas because our sins
   On Him by God were laid;
He Who Himself had never sinned,
   For sinners, sin was made.

   Thus sin He put away
   By His one sacrifice,
Then, Conqueror o'er death and hell,
   He mounted to the skies.

   Therefore let all men know
   That God is satisfied;
And sinners all who Jesus trust,
   Through Him are justified.

816   Thomas Kelly   LM

Who hath believed our report? and to whom is the arm of the LORD revealed?
Isaiah 53:1

Now may the gospel's conquering power
  Be felt by all assembled here;
So shall this prove a joyful hour,
  And God's own arm of strength appear.

Lord! let Thy mighty voice be heard;
  Speak in the word, and speak with power;
So shall Thy glorious name be feared
  By those who never feared before.

O pity those who sleep in sin,
  Preserve them from the sinner's doom;
Show them the ark, and take them in,
  And save them from the wrath to come.

So shall Thy people joyful be,
  And angels shall more loudly sing,
And both ascribe the praise to Thee,
  To Thee, the everlasting King!

817   Philip Bliss   777 8

He is despised and rejected of men; a Man of sorrows, and acquainted with grief.   *Isaiah 53:3*

Man of Sorrows! what a name
For the Son of God who came
Ruined sinners to reclaim!
  Hallelujah! what a Saviour!

Bearing shame and scoffing rude,
In my place condemned He stood;
Sealed my pardon with His blood:
  Hallelujah! what a Saviour!

Guilty, vile, and helpless, we;
Spotless Lamb of God was He!
Full atonement—can it be?
  Hallelujah! what a Saviour!

Lifted up was He to die,
'It is finished!' was His cry;
Now in heaven exalted high:
  Hallelujah! what a Saviour!

When He comes, our glorious King,
All His ransomed home to bring,
Then anew this song we'll sing:
  'Hallelujah! what a Saviour!'

818   Thomas Kelly   87 87 D

He is despised and rejected of men.
Isaiah 53:3

'Stricken, smitten, and afflicted,'
  See Him dying on the tree!
'Tis the Christ by man rejected!
  Yes, my soul, 'tis He! 'tis He!
'Tis the long expected Prophet,
  David's Son, yet David's Lord;
Proofs I see sufficient of it;
  'Tis the true and faithful Word.

Tell me, ye who hear Him groaning,
  Was there ever grief like His?
Friends, through fear, His cause disowning,
  Foes insulting His distress.
Many hands were raised to wound Him,
  None would interpose to save,
But the awful stroke that found Him,
  Was the stroke that justice gave.

Ye who think of sin but lightly,
  Nor suppose the evil great,
Here may view its nature rightly,
  Here its guilt may estimate.
Mark the sacrifice appointed!
  See who bears the awful load!
'Tis the Word, the Lord's Anointed,
  Son of Man, and Son of God.

Here we have a firm foundation;
  Here's the refuge of the lost;
Christ's the Rock of our salvation;
  His the name of which we boast.
Lamb of God for sinners wounded!
  Sacrificed to cancel guilt!
None shall ever be confounded
  Who on Thee their hopes have built.

819   Joseph Swain   886 D

He is despised and rejected of men.
Isaiah 53:3

How vast the sufferings, who can tell,
When Jesus fought sin, death, and hell,
  And was in battle slain?
How great the triumph, who can sing,
When from the grave the immortal King
  Triumphant rose again?

Yet we'll attempt His name to bless,
While we pass through the wilderness
  To Canaan's happy shore.
But when we reach the plains above,
And every breath we draw is love,
  We'll sing His glories more.

820   Johann Heerman, tr. R Bridges

11 11 11 5

All we like sheep have gone astray; we have turned every one to his own way; and the LORD hath laid on Him the iniquity of us all.
Isaiah 53:6

Ah, holy Jesus, how hast Thou offended,
That man to judge Thee hath in hate pretended?
By foes derided, by Thine own rejected,
    O most afflicted.

Who was the guilty? who brought this upon Thee?
Alas, my treason, Jesus, hath undone Thee.
'Twas I, Lord Jesus, I it was denied Thee:
    I crucified Thee.

Lo, the good Shepherd for the sheep is offered:
The slave hath sinnèd, and the Son hath suffered:
For man's atonement, while he nothing heedeth,
    God intercedeth.

For me, kind Jesus, was Thine incarnation,
Thy mortal sorrow, and Thy life's oblation:
Thy death of anguish and Thy bitter passion,
    For my salvation.

Therefore, kind Jesus, since I cannot pay Thee,
I do adore Thee, and will ever pray Thee;
Think on Thy pity and Thy love unswerving,
    Not my deserving.

821   Charles Wesley   11 11 11 11

The LORD hath laid on Him the iniquity of us all. *Isaiah 53:6*

The Lord in the day of His anger, did lay
Our sins on the Lamb, and He bore them away.
He died to atone for our sins, not His own;
The Father has punished for us His dear Son.

With joy we approve the design of His love;
'Tis a wonder below and a wonder above.
Our Ransom, our Peace, and our Surety He is;
Come, see if there ever were sorrow like His.

He came from above, the law's curse to remove;
He loved, He has loved us, because He would
    love;
And, when time is no more, we still shall adore
That ocean of love, without bottom or shore.

Love moved Him to die, and on this we rely,
Our Jesus has loved us, we cannot tell why;
But this we can tell, that He loved us so well,
As to lay down His life to redeem us from hell.

822   Horatius Bonar   DSM

All we like sheep have gone astray; we have turned every one to his own way; and the LORD hath laid on Him the iniquity of us all.
Isaiah 53:6

  I was a wandering sheep,
  I did not love the fold;
I did not love my Shepherd's voice,
  I would not be controlled,
  I was a wayward child,
  I did not love my home;
I did not love my Father's voice,
  I loved afar to roam.

  The Shepherd sought His sheep,
  The Father sought His child;
They followed me o'er vale and hill,
  O'er deserts waste and wild:
They found me nigh to death,
  Famished and faint and lone;
They bound me with the bands of love,
  They saved the wandering one.

  I was a wandering sheep,
  I would not be controlled;
But now I love my Shepherd's voice,
  I love, I love the fold.
  I was a wayward child,
  I once preferred to roam;
But now I love my Father's voice,
  I love, I love His home.

823   Edward Denny   CM

For the transgression of My people was He stricken. *Isaiah 53:8*

To Calvary, Lord, in spirit now
  Our weary souls repair,
To dwell upon Thy dying love,
  And taste its sweetness there.

Sweet resting-place of every heart
  That feels the plague of sin.
Yet knows that deep mysterious joy,
  The peace of God within.

There through Thine hour of deepest woe,
  Thy suffering spirit passed;
Grace here its wondrous victory gained,
  And love endured its last.

Dear suffering Lamb, Thy bleeding wounds
  With cords of love divine,
Have drawn our willing hearts to Thee,
  And linked our life with Thine.

Our longing eyes would fain behold
  That bright and blessèd brow,
Once wrung with bitterest anguish, wear
  Its crown of glory now.

824   Anne Steele   LM
Yet it pleased the LORD to bruise Him.
Isaiah 53:10

Was it for sin, for mortal guilt,
   The Saviour gave His vital blood;
For sin amazing anguish felt,
   The wrath of an offended God?

And shall I harbour in my breast
   (Tremble, my soul, at such a deed)
This dreadful foe, this fatal guest,
   The sin fhat made the Saviour bleed?

Come, glorious Conqueror, gracious Lord,
   Thy all-prevailing power employ;
O come, with Thy resistless word,
   These hateful enemies destroy.

My hope, my all is fixed on Thee,
   For Thou alone hast power divine;
O come, and conquer, Lord, for me,
   And all the glory shall be Thine.

825   Augustus Toplady   886 D
He bare the sin of many, and made
intercession for the transgressors.
Isaiah 53:12

O Thou who didst Thy life-blood give,
Apostate sinners to retrieve
   From nature's deadly fall,
If Thou has bought me with a price,
My sins against me ne'er shall rise,
   For Thou hast borne them all.

And wast Thou punished in my stead?
Didst Thou without the city bleed,
   To expiate my stain?
On earth my God vouchsafed to dwell,
And made of glorious avail
   The sufferings of the Man.

Behold Him for transgressors given,
Behold the incarnate King of heaven
   For us, His foes, expire!
Amazed, O earth, the tidings hear!
He bore, that we might never bear,
   His Father's righteous ire.

Ye saints, the Man of Sorrows bless,
The God, for our unrighteousness
   Deputed to atone:
Praise till, with all the ransomed throng
Ye sing the never-ending song,
   And see Him on His throne.

826   Ralph Erskine   CM
For thy Maker is thine husband; the LORD of
hosts is His name. *Isaiah 54:5*

O happy soul, Jehovah's bride,
   The Lamb's belovèd spouse,
Strong consolation's flowing tide
   Thy Husband thee allows.

His precious name is Jesus—why?
   Because He saves from sin;
Redemption's right He won't deny,
   Thy Husband's near of kin.

His wounds have saved thee once from woes,
   His blood from vengeance screened;
When heaven, and earth, and hell were foes,
   Thy Husband was a friend.

And that He never will forsake,
   His credit fair he's given;
In hottest broils then courage take,
   Thy Husband's now in heaven.

Renounce Thine own ability,
   Lean to His promised might;
The Strength of Israel cannot lie,
   Thy Husband's always right.

827   William Cowper (alt)   LM
For a small moment have I forsaken thee; but
with great mercies will I gather thee.
Isaiah 54:7

When darkness long has veiled my mind,
   And smiling day once more appears,
Then, my Redeemer, then I find
   The folly of my doubts and fears.

I chide my unbelieving heart,
   And blush that I should ever be
Thus prone to act so base a part,
   Or harbour one hard thought of Thee.

O let me then at length be taught
   (What I am still so slow to learn)
That God is love, and changes not,
   Nor knows the shadow of a turn.

Sweet truth, and easy to repeat!
   But when my faith is sharply tried,
I find myself a learner yet,
   Unskilful, weak, and apt to slide.

But, O my Lord, one look from Thee
   Subdues the disobedient will;
Drives doubt and discontent away,
   And Thy rebellious one is still.

Thou art as ready to forgive
  As I am ready to repine;
Thou, therefore, all the praise receive;
  Be shame and self-abhorrence mine.

828   Anon   11 11 11 11
**In a little wrath I hid My face from thee for a
moment; but with everlasting kindness will I
have mercy on thee.** *Isaiah 54:8*

Everlasting kindness! hark, my soul! 'tis He,
Thy Jehovah Jesus, speaks this word to thee:
Everlasting kindness! speak that word once
  more;
O, my soul, still listen, trust it and adore!

Everlasting kindness e'en to such as I,
On whom wrath eternal might in justice lie;
But Jehovah Jesus speaks this word so free:
Everlasting kindness I have shown to thee.

Everlasting kindness, since the world began,
God's eternal kindness through the ages ran;
Hidden oft in shadows, dim to human sight,
In Jehovah Jesus now it shineth bright.

Everlasting kindness brought the Son of God
From the Father's bosom here to shed His blood:
Everlasting kindness all God's way shall crown,
When before our Jesus gladly we fall down.

Everlasting kindness never shall depart;
Well Jehovah Jesus knew my wandering heart,
Knew that lovingkindness, tender, true and free,
Everlasting kindness, only suited me.

829   John Berridge   88 88 88
**O thou afflicted, tossed with tempest, and not
comforted, behold, I will lay thy stones with
fair colours, and lay thy foundations with
sapphires.** *Isaiah 54:11*

Thou poor, afflicted, tempted soul,
  With fears, and doubts, and tempests tossed,
What if the billows rise and roll,
  And dash thy ship, it is not lost;
The winds and waves, and fiends may roar,
But Christ will bring thee safe on shore.

What ails those eyes bedewed with tears?
  Those labouring sighs that heave thy breast?
Those oft-repeated, broken prayers?
  Dost thou not long for Jesus' rest?
And can the Lord pass heedless by,
And see a mourning sinner die?

830   Robert Grant   11 11 11 11
**O thou afflicted, tossed with tempest, and not
comforted, behold, I will lay thy stones with
fair colours, and lay thy foundations with
sapphires.** *Isaiah 54:11*

O Zion afflicted with wave upon wave;
Whom no man can comfort, whom no man can
  save
With darkness surrounded, by terrors dismayed,
In toiling and rowing thy strength is decayed.

Loud roaring, the billows now nigh overwhelm;
But skilful's the Pilot who sits at the helm;
His wisdom conducts thee, His power thee
  defends,
In safety and quiet thy warfare He ends.

'O fearful, O faithless!' in mercy He cries;
'My promise, My truth, are they light in thy eyes?
Still, still I am with thee; My promise shall stand;
Through tempest and tossing, I'll bring thee to
  land.

'Forget thee I will not, I cannot; thy name
Engraved on My heart does for ever remain;
The palms of My hands while I look on I see
The wounds I receivèd when suffering for thee.

'I feel at My heart all thy sighs and thy groans,
For thou art most near Me, My flesh and my
  bones;
In all thy distresses thy Head feels the pain;
Yet all are most needful; not one is in vain.

'Then trust Me, and fear not; thy life is secure;
My wisdom is perfect, supreme is My power;
In love I correct thee, thy soul to refine,
To make thee at length in My likeness to shine.'

831   Joseph Hart   87 87 47
**Ho, every one that thirsteth, come ye to the
waters, and he that hath no money; come ye,
buy, and eat; yea, come, buy wine and milk
without money and without price.** *Isaiah 55:1*

Come ye sinners, poor and wretched,
  Weak and wounded, sick, and sore;
Jesus ready stands to save you,
  Full of pity, joined with power;
    He is able,
  He is willing; doubt no more.

Come, ye needy,come and welcome;
  God's free bounty glorify!
True belief and true repentance,
  Every grace that brings us nigh,
    Without money,
  Come to Jesus Christ and buy!

Let not conscience make you linger,
Nor of fitness fondly dream;
All the fitness He requireth,
Is to feel your need of Him,
This He gives you,
'Tis the Spirit's rising beam.

Come, ye weary, heavy laden,
Lost and ruined by the fall;
If you tarry till you're better,
You will never come at all.
Not the righteous,
Sinners Jesus came to call!

View Him prostrate in the garden;
On the ground your Maker lies;
Then on Calvary's tree behold Him,
Hear Him cry before He dies,
'It is finished!'
Sinner, will not this suffice?

Lo! the incarnate God ascended,
Pleads the merit of His blood;
Venture on Him, venture wholly,
Let no other trust intrude;
None but Jesus
Can do helpless sinners good.

832   John Cennick   88 88 88
Ho, every one that thirsteth, come ye to the waters. *Isaiah 55:1*

Ho, ye despairing sinners, hear,
Ye thirsty, sin-sick souls, draw near;
Here's water, whose all-powerful stream
Shall quench your thirst and wash you clean,
Its healing power has always wrought
Beyond the reach of human thought.

Bethesda's pool is not like this,
Nor heals nor cures such leprosies;
Nor Siloam's streams, nor Jordan's flood
Could to my heart seem half so good;
'Tis Jesus' blood, that crimson sea,
That washes guilt and filth away.

To this dear Fountain I'd repair,
With all the wounds and pains I bear;
I'd keep my station near its side,
And wash, and drink, and there abide;
Nor from the sacred streams remove,
Till taken to their source above.

833   John Fawcett   88 88 88
So shall My word be that goeth forth out of My mouth: it shall not return unto Me void, but it shall accomplish that which I please, and it shall prosper in the thing whereto I sent it.
Isaiah 55:11

Thy presence, gracious God, afford;
Prepare us to receive Thy word;
Now let Thy voice engage our ear,
And faith be mixed with what we hear;

Thus, Lord, Thy waiting servants bless,
And crown Thy gospel with success.

Distracting thoughts and cares remove,
And fix our hearts and hopes above;
With food divine may we be fed,
And satisfied with living bread.

To us the sacred word apply,
With sovereign power and energy;
And may we, in Thy faith and fear,
Reduce to practice what we hear.

Father, in us Thy Son reveal;
Teach us to know and do Thy will;
Thy saving power and love display,
And guide us to the realms of day.

834   Joseph Swain   LM
Mine house shall be called an house of prayer for all people. *Isaiah 56:7*

Jesus how heavenly is the place,
Where Thy dear people wait for Thee!
Where the rich fountain of Thy grace
Stands ever open, full, and free.

Hungry, and poor, and lame, and blind,
Hither the blood-bought children fly;
In Thy deep wounds a balsam find,
And live while they behold Thee die.

Here they forget their doubts and fears,
While Thy sharp sorrows meet their eyes;
And bless the hand that dries their tears,
And each returning want supplies.

O the vast mysteries of Thy love!
How high, how deep, how wide it rolls!
Its fountain springs in heaven above,
Its streams revive our drooping souls.

835   Frederick Faber   CM
The high and lofty One that inhabiteth eternity, whose name is Holy.
Isaiah 57:15

My God, how wonderful Thou art!
    Thy majesty how bright!
How beautiful Thy mercy-seat,
    In depths of burning light!

How dread are Thine eternal years,
    O everlasting Lord,
By prostrate spirits day and night
    Incessantly adored!

O how I fear Thee, living God,
    With deepest, tenderest fears,
And worship Thee with trembling hope
    And penitential tears!

Yet I may love Thee, too, O Lord,
    Almighty as Thou art,
For Thou hast stooped to ask of me
    The love of my poor heart.

No earthly father loves like Thee;
    No mother, e'er so mild,
Bears and forebears as Thou hast done
    With me, Thy sinful child.
How wonderful, how beautiful,
    The sight of Thee must be,
Thine endless wisdom, boundless power,
    And awful purity!

836   William Cowper   CM
I dwell in the high and holy place, with him also that is of a contrite and humble spirit, to revive the spirit of the humble, and to revive the heart of the contrite ones. *Isaiah 57:15*

The Lord will happiness divine
    On contrite hearts bestow;
Then tell me, gracious God, is mine
    A contrite heart, or no?

I hear, but seem to hear in vain;
    Insensible as steel;
If aught is felt, 'tis only pain,
    To find I cannot feel.

I sometimes think myself inclined
    To love Thee, if I could;
But often find another mind,
    Averse to all that's good.

My best desires are faint and few;
    I fain would strive for more;
But when I cry, 'My strength renew,'
    Seem weaker than before.

Thy saints are comforted, I know,
    And love Thy house of prayer;
I sometimes go where others go,
    But find no comfort there.

O make this heart rejoice or ache,
    Decide this doubt for me;
And if it be not broken, break,
    And heal it if it be.

837   Isaac Watts   CM
Thou shalt be like a watered garden, and like a spring of water, whose waters fail not.
Isaiah 58:11

My thoughts surmount these lower skies,
    And look within the veil;
There springs of endless pleasure rise,
    The waters never fail.

There I behold, with sweet delight,
    The blessed Three in One;
And strong affections fix my sight
    On God's incarnate Son.

His promise stands for ever firm,
    His grace shall ne'er depart;
He binds my name upon His arm,
    And seals it on His heart.

Light are the pains that nature brings;
    How short our sorrows are,
When with eternal future things
    The present we compare!

I would not be a stranger still
    To that celestial place,
Where I for ever hope to dwell,
    Near my Redeemer's face.

838   John Kent   LM
Then shalt thou delight thyself in the LORD.
Isaiah 58:14

Jesus, in Thee, my soul's delight,
What matchless beauties tempt my sight!
Compared with Thee, the solar ray
In shades and darkness dies away.

Thou art my Rock and Refuge too,
My Hiding-Place when foes pursue;
My Sun, my Shield, my Tower strong,
My sweetest note in every song.

Thou art the Prize to which I press,
My Wisdom, and my Righteousness;
My Surety, bound my debts to pay;
My Light, my Life, my Love, my Way.

My Advocate before the throne,
My stable base, my Corner-stone;
My Anchor sure, when storms arise,
My Bread descending from the skies.

Thou art my Peace, amidst the din
Of horrid war 'twixt grace and sin;
My Pilot wise, to guide my way,
In safety, o'er life's troubled sea.

My ransom Thou, when Adam's fall
In guilt and ruin deluged all;
My Tree of Life, whose leaves have been
A balm to heal the wounds of sin.

My Fountain, open every day
To take the stains of sin away.
Of sovereign, rich, atoning blood;
In this my soul draws nigh to God.

While life endures, and breath remains,
In pungent sorrows, joys, or pains,
Still let my song Thy love proclaim,
And tell the wonders of Thy name.

839   William Horne   CM
Then shalt thou delight thyself in the LORD.
Isaiah 58:14

We sing the Sabbath of the Lord,
    The saints' eternal rest:
For Jesus, in the heavens adored,
    Our Sabbath is confessed.

The end of every Jewish rite,
    Our Sacrifice, our Peace,
Our Life, our Righteousness, our Might,
    Our Sabbath Jesus is.

The Sabbath's Lord descends to die,
    And puts our foes to flight;
Before Him all the shadows fly,
    Like darkness chased by light.

In Christ, our Sabbath, our delight,
    The holy of the Lord,
His people walk in spotless white:
    Then be His name adored.

Honour His name in every way,
    All honour is His due,
Whose presence makes our Sabbath day,
    Whose mercy's ever new.

For rest like this, ye ransomed, join
    With notes of sweetest chord.
And sing in sounds, and joys divine,
    'Our Sabbath is the Lord.'

840   Joseph Hoskins   LM
**Arise, shine; for thy light is come, and the
glory of the LORD is risen upon thee.**
Isaiah 60:1

Great Light of life, Thou nature's Lord,
Bring light from darkness by Thy word;
Shine in our hearts, in mercy shine,
To give the light of truth divine.

Light of our souls! Thyself reveal;
Thy power and presence let us feel;
And know and see the wondrous things
Concealed from prophets, priests, and kings.

In the dear face of Christ, our God,
His righteousness and pardoning blood,
May we behold our all in all,
And at His foot of mercy fall.

There Thy perfections shine most bright;
May we behold them with delight;
And see how justice, truth, and grace
Unite, and smile in Jesus' face.

Great Sun of Righteousness! arise,
Open our long-benighted eyes;
Shine, Jesus, shine from day to day,
Till all that's dark be done away.

841   Joseph Swain   LM
**The city of the LORD, the Zion of the Holy One
of Israel.** *Isaiah 60:14*

No earthly city can compare
With Zion, when her Lord is there!
Her gifts like golden turrets rise,
Her fervent graces reach the skies.

Her stately walls are girt with power,
Safety and strength compose her tower;
Firm on a Rock her palace stands,
The glory of the Builder's hands.

A river, full of peace and love,
Forever flowing from above,
Makes her inhabitants rejoice,
And tunes with praise each mourner's voice.

Faith, like an eagle from her nest,
Mounts up in search of heavenly rest;
And love, like incense from the fire,
Ascends in flames of strong desire.

Patience, that long enduring, still
Submissive waits Jehovah's will;
And lively hope, that lifts her head
Beyond the regions of the dead.

Here all the heaven-born sons of grace
Proclaim the King of Zion's praise,
Whose precious name, from every tongue,
Flows on in one delightful song.

842   Isaac Watts   LM
**But thou shalt call thy walls Salvation, and thy
gates Praise.** *Isaiah 60:18*

Happy the church, thou sacred place;
The seat of thy Creator's grace;
Thy holy courts are His abode,
Thou earthly palace of our God!

Thy walls are strength, and at thy gates
A guard of heavenly warriors waits;
Nor shall thy deep foundations move,
Fixed on His counsels and His love.

Thy foes in vain designs engage;
Against His throne in vain they rage:
Like rising waves with angry roar,
That dash and die upon the shore.

Then let our souls in Zion dwell,
Nor fear the wrath of men or hell;
His arms embrace this happy ground,
Like brazen bulwarks built around.

God is our Shield, and God our Sun;
Swift as the fleeting moments run;
On us He sheds new beams of grace,
And we reflect His brightest praise.

843   William Gadsby   11 11 11 11
**The Spirit of the Lord GOD is upon Me;
because the LORD hath anointed Me to preach
good tidings unto the meek; He hath sent Me
to bind up the brokenhearted, to proclaim
liberty to the captives, and the opening of the
prison to them that are bound.** *Isaiah 61:1*

The gospel brings tidings, glad tidings indeed,
To mourners in Zion, who want to be freed
From sin, and from Satan, and Mount Sinai's
    flame,
Good news of salvation, through Jesus the Lamb.

What sweet invitations the gospel contains,
To men heavy laden with bondage and chains;
It welcomes the weary to come and be blessed
With ease from their burdens, in Jesus to rest.

For every poor mourner, who thirsts for the Lord,
A fountain is opened in Jesus the Word;
Their poor parchèd conscience to cool and to
    wash
From guilt and pollution, from dead works and
    dross.

A robe is provided, their shame now to hide,
In which none are clothèd but Jesus's bride;
And though it be costly, yet is the robe free,
And all Zion's mourners shall decked with it be.

A ring that denotes His unchangeable love,
Is put on the finger, God's kindness to prove,
This love no beginning can know, nor an end,
And Zion shall wear it in praise of her Friend.

844   Philip Doddridge   CM
**The Spirit of the Lord GOD is upon Me;
because the LORD hath anointed Me to preach
good tidings unto the meek; He hath sent Me
to bind up the brokenhearted, to proclaim
liberty to the captives, and the opening of the
prison to them that are bound.** *Isaiah 61:1*

Hark, the glad sound, the Saviour comes,
    The Saviour promised long;
Let every heart prepare a throne,
    And every voice a song.

He comes the prisoners to release,
    In Satan's bondage held;
The gates of brass before Him burst,
    The iron fetters yield.

He comes from thickest films of vice
    To clear the mental ray,
And on the eyeballs of the blind
    To pour celestial day.

He comes the broken heart to bind,
    The bleeding soul to cure,
And with the treasures of His grace,
    To enrich the humble poor.

Our glad hosannas, Prince of peace,
    Thy welcome shall proclaim;
And heaven's eternal arches ring
    With Thy belovèd name.

845 William Kingsbury LM
**But ye shall be named the Priests of the
LORD: men shall call you the Ministers of our
God.** *Isaiah 61:6*

Great Lord of all Thy churches, hear
Thy ministers' and people's prayer;
Perfumed by Thee, O may it rise
Like fragrant incense to the skies.

Revive Thy churches with Thy grace,
Heal all our breaches, grant us peace;
Rouse us from sloth, our hearts inflame
With ardent zeal for Jesus' name.

May young and old Thy word receive,
Dead sinners hear Thy voice and live,
The wounded conscience healing find,
And joy refresh each drooping mind.

May agèd saints, matured with grace,
Abound in fruits of holiness;
And when transplanted to the skies,
May younger in their stead arise.

Thus we our suppliant voices raise,
And weeping, sow the seed of praise,
In humble hope that Thou wilt hear
Thy ministers' and people's prayer.

NICOLAUS VON ZINZENDORF 1700-1760

846 Nicolaus Zinzendorf, tr. J Wesley LM
**He hath covered me with the robe of
righteousness.** *Isaiah 61:10*

Jesus, Thy blood and righteousness
My beauty are, my glorious dress;
'Midst flaming worlds, in these arrayed,
With joy shall I lift up my head.

When from the dust of death I rise
To claim my mansion in the skies,
E'en then shall this be all my plea,
'Jesus has lived and died for me.'

Bold shall I stand in that great day,
For who aught to my charge shall lay?
Fully absolved through these I am,
From sin and fear, from guilt and shame.

This spotless robe the same appears,
When ruined nature sinks in years!
No age can change its glorious hue;
The robe of Christ is ever new.

O let the dead now hear Thy voice,
Bid Lord, Thy banished ones rejoice;
Their beauty this, their glorious dress,
Jesus, the Lord our righteousness.

847 Thomas Kelly 87 87 77
**Who is this that cometh from Edom, with dyed
garments from Bozrah?** *Isaiah 63:1*

Who is this that comes from Edom,
    All His raiment stained with blood,
To the slave proclaiming freedom,
    Bringing and bestowing good,
Glorious in the garb He wears,
Glorious in the spoil He bears?

'Tis the Saviour, now victorious,
    Travelling onward in His might;
'Tis the Saviour, O how glorious
    To His people is the sight!
Jesus now is strong to save,
Mighty to redeem the slave.

Why that blood His raiment staining?
    'Tis the blood of many slain:
Of His foes there's none remaining—
    None the contest to maintain;
Fallen they are, no more to rise;
All their glory prostrate lies.

This the Saviour has effected
    By His mighty arm alone;
See the throne for Him erected!
    'Tis an everlasting throne;
'Tis the great reward He gains,
Glorious fruit of all His pains.

Mighty Victor, reign for ever;
    Wear the crown so dearly won;
Never shall Thy people, never
    Cease to sing what Thou hast done.
Thou hast fought Thy people's foes;
Thou wilt heal Thy people's woes.

848   William Gadsby (alt)   886 D
I that speak in righteousness, mighty to save.
Isaiah 63:1

Mighty to save is Christ the Lamb;
Let all the saints adore His name,
    And make His goodness known;
With one accord proclaim abroad,
The wonders of their Saviour, God,
    Whose blood did once atone.

Mighty to save! nor all sin's power
Can hold the sinner in that hour
    When Jesus calls him home;
Nor Moses, with his iron rod,
Can keep the trembling soul from God,
    When the set time is come.

Mighty to save! He saves from hell;
A mighty Saviour suits me well;
    A helpless wretch am I;
With sin oppressed, by law condemned,
With neither feet nor legs to stand,
    Nor wings from wrath to fly.

Mighty to save! He saves from death:
O may I, with my latest breath,
    His mighty power proclaim.
Ye sinners lost, and wretched too,
He came to save such souls as you,
    And mighty is His name.

Mighty to save! let Zion sing
The honours of her God and King,
    Whose love no change can know.
With cheerful hearts, and cheerful voice,
We'll in the mighty God rejoice,
    And sing His praise below.

And when the icy hand of death
Shall steal away our mortal breath,
    Our joy shall still increase;
Yes, with a loud immortal tongue,
We'll sing, and Christ shall be our song,
    In realms of endless peace.

849   Samuel Medley   LM
I will mention the lovingkindnesses of the
LORD. *Isaiah 63:7*

Awake my soul, in joyful lays,
And sing thy great Redeemer's praise;
He justly claims a song from me;
His lovingkindness, O how free!

He saw me ruined in the fall,
Yet loved me notwithstanding all;
He saved me from my lost estate,
His lovingkindness, O how great!

Though numerous hosts of mighty foes,
Though earth and hell my way oppose,
He safely leads my soul along;
His lovingkindness, O how strong!

When trouble, like a gloomy cloud,
Has gathered thick and thundered loud,
He near my soul has always stood;
His lovingkindness, O how good!

Often I feel my sinful heart
Prone from my Saviour to depart;
But though I have Him oft forgot,
His lovingkindness changes not!

Soon shall I pass the gloomy vale;
Soon all my mortal powers must fail;
O may my last expiring breath
His lovingkindness sing in death!

Then let me mount and soar away
To the bright world of endless day,
And sing with rapture and surprise,
His lovingkindness in the skies.

850   Philip Doddridge   SM
For He said, Surely they are My people,
children that will not lie: so He was their
Saviour. *Isaiah 63:8*

Dear Saviour, I am Thine
    By everlasting bands;
My name, my heart, I would resign;
    My soul is in Thy hands.

To Thee I still would cleave
    With ever-growing zeal:
If millions tempt me Christ to leave,
    They never shall prevail.

His Spirit shall unite
    My soul to Him my head;
Shall form me to His image bright,
    And teach His path to tread.

Death may my soul divide
    From this abode of clay;
But love shall keep me near Thy side
    Through all the gloomy way.

Since Christ and we are one,
    Why should we doubt or fear?
If He in heaven hath fixed His throne,
    He'll fix His members there.

851   William Gadsby   77 77
In His love and in His pity He redeemed them.
Isaiah 63:9

Jesus lived, and loved, and died,
Rose, and lives to intercede;
And with Zion on His breast,
He has said He'll ever rest.

Long before this world was made,
Or that monster, Sin, appeared,
God was love, and loved the men
He designèd to redeem.

Love constrained the Lamb to die,
For a wretch so vile as I;
Love, immensely great and free,
Christ has shown to worthless me.

Once I rolled in guilt and sin,
Heeded not a heart unclean;
But I now with wonder tell,
Jesus saved my soul from hell.

852   John Langford   77 77
In His love and in His pity He redeemed them.
Isaiah 63:9

Now begin the heavenly theme;
Sing aloud in Jesus' name;
Ye who His salvation prove,
Triumph in redeeming love.

Ye who see the Father's grace
Beaming in the Saviour's face,
As to Canaan on you move,
Praise and bless redeeming love.

Mourning souls, dry up your tears;
Banish all your guilty fears;
See your guilt and curse remove,
Cancelled by redeeming love.

Welcome all by sin oppressed,
Welcome to His sacred rest;
Nothing brought Him from above,
Nothing but redeeming love.

When His Spirit leads us home,
When we to His glory come,
We shall all the fulness prove
Of our Lord's redeeming love.

He subdued the infernal powers,
Those tremendous foes of ours
From their cursèd empire drove,
Mighty in redeeming love.

Hither, then, your music bring;
Strike aloud each cheerful string;
Join, ye saints, the hosts above;
Join to praise redeeming love.

853   Anne Steele   CM
Thou, O LORD, art our Father, our Redeemer;
Thy name is from everlasting.
Isaiah 63:16

My God, my Father, blissful name!
   O may I call Thee mine?
May I with sweet assurance claim
   A portion so divine?

This only can my fears control,
   And bid my sorrows fly;
What harm can ever reach my soul
   Beneath my Father's eye?

Whate'er Thy providence denies
   I calmly would resign,
For Thou art just, and good, and wise;
   O bend my will to Thine.

Whate'er Thy sacred will ordains,
   O give me strength to bear;
And let me know my Father reigns,
   And trust His tender care.

If pain and sickness rend this frame,
   And life almost depart,
Is not Thy mercy still the same,
   To cheer my drooping heart?

If cares and sorrows me surround,
   Their power why should I fear?
My inward peace they cannot wound,
   If Thou, my God, art near.

854   May Maude   77 77
We are Thine. *Isaiah 63:19*

Thine for ever! God of love,
Hear us from Thy throne above;
Thine for ever may we be,
Here and in eternity.

Thine for ever! Lord of life,
Shield us through our earthly strife;
Thou the Life, the Truth, the Way,
Guide us to the realms of day.

Thine for ever! O how blest
They who find in Thee their rest,
Saviour, Guardian, heavenly Friend,
O defend us to the end.

Thine for ever! Shepherd, keep
These Thy frail and trembling sheep;
Safe alone beneath Thy care,
Let us all Thy goodness share.

Thine for ever! Thou our Guide,
All our wants by Thee supplied,
All our sins by Thee forgiven,
Lead us, Lord, from earth to heaven.

855   Joseph Hart   LM
**Oh that Thou wouldest rend the heavens, that
Thou wouldest come down, that the
mountains might flow down at Thy presence.**
Isaiah 64:1

O for a glance of heavenly day,
To take this stubborn stone away:
And thaw, with beams of love divine,
This heart, this frozen heart of mine!

The rocks can rend, the earth can quake,
The seas can roar, the mountains shake;
Of feeling all things show some sign,
But this unfeeling heart of mine.

To hear the sorrows Thou hast felt,
Dear Lord, an adamant would melt;
But I can read each moving line,
And nothing move this heart of mine.

Thy judgments, too, unmoved I hear,
(Amazing thought!) which devils fear;
Goodness and wrath in vain combine
To stir this stupid heart of mine.

But something yet can do the deed,
And that dear something much I need;
Thy Spirit can from dross refine,
And move and melt this heart of mine.

856   Joseph Hart   10 10 11 11
**As when the melting fire burneth, the fire
causeth the waters to boil, to make Thy name
known to Thine adversaries, that the nations
may tremble at Thy presence!** *Isaiah 64:2*

The good hand of God has brought us again
(A favour bestowed, we hope not in vain)
To hear from our Saviour the word of His grace;
Then be our behaviour becoming the place.

Remember the ends for which we are met;
Alas! my dear friends, we're apt to forget;
The motives that brought us, the Lord only sees;
But if He has taught us, our ends should be these:

To worship the Lord with praise and with prayer;
To practise His word, as well as to hear,
To own with contrition the deeds we have done,
And take the remission God gives in His Son.

Blest Spirit of Christ, descend on us thus;
Thy servant assist; teach him to teach us;
O send us Thy unction, to teach us all good;
And touch with compunction, and sprinkle with
    blood.

857   Anne Steele   CM
We are the clay, and Thou our Potter.
Isaiah 64:8

And can my heart aspire so high
  To say, 'My Father, God?'
Lord, at Thy feet I fain would lie
  And learn to kiss the rod.

I would submit to all Thy will,
  For Thou art good and wise;
Let every anxious thought be still,
  Nor one faint murmur rise.

Thy love can cheer the darksome gloom,
  And bid me wait serene;
Till hopes and joys immortal bloom,
  And brighten all the scene.

858   John Berridge   CM
**For My people have committed two evils; they
have forsaken Me the fountain of living waters,
and hewed them out cisterns, broken cisterns,
that can hold no water.** *Jeremiah 2:13*

Of cistern waters art thou sick,
  And loath'st the mire they bring?
Then hither stretch thy thirsty neck,
  And taste a living spring.

A spring that issues from a rock,
  Where purest waters flow;
And rocky hearts, by Moses struck,
  May to these waters go.

No spring will quench a thirst like this;
  It makes a conscience whole,
Inspires the heart with heavenly bliss,
  And purifies the soul.

Whoe'er can truly say, 'I thirst,'
  May come and take his fill;
'Tis free for sinners, vile and lost;
  'Tis God who works the will.

Its Owner is a heavenly King;
  And by His winning ways,
He draws the thirsty to His spring,
  Who drink and sing His praise.

Lord, draw me by Thy secret touch,
  Or backward I shall start;
For sure I want entreating much,
  So fearful is my heart.

859   David Denham   CM
Wilt thou not from this time cry unto Me, My Father, Thou art the guide of my youth?
Jeremiah 3:4

God is my Father, then I see
  All good He will bestow;
In everlasting love to me
  His mercies daily flow.

God is my Father to chastise,
  Yet in compassion's near;
When humbled, He regards my cries,
  And proves Himself more dear.

God is my Father to perform
  All that His love decreed;
My hiding-place in every storm,
  And help in present need.

God is my Father to restore,
  Though oft by sin beguiled;
O may I love and serve Him more,
  Who calls me still His child.

God is my Father, then I know
  I am for ever blest;
His counsel marks my steps below,
  And leads to endless rest.

God is my Father to reveal
  The mysteries of His grace;
And all who have the Spirit's seal,
  In heaven shall have a place.

860   Anne Steele   CM
Return, thou backsliding Israel, saith the LORD. *Jeremiah 3:12*

How oft, alas, this wretched heart
  Has wandered from the Lord,
How oft my roving thoughts depart,
  Forgetful of His word!

Yet sovereign mercy calls, 'Return!'
  Dear Lord, and may I come?
My vile ingratitude I mourn;
  O take the wanderer home.

And canst Thou, wilt Thou yet forgive,
  And bid my crimes remove,
And shall a pardoned rebel live,
  To speak Thy wondrous love?

Almighty grace, Thy healing power
  How glorious, how divine!
That can to life and bliss restore
  So vile a heart as mine!

Thy pardoning love, so free, so sweet,
  Dear Saviour, I adore;
O keep me at Thy sacred feet,
  And let me rove no more.

861   Joseph Hart   LM
Return, thou backsliding Israel, saith the LORD. *Jeremiah 3:12*

Backsliding souls, return to God;
  Your faithful God is gracious still;
Leave the false ways ye long have trod,
  For God will your backslidings heal.

Your first espousals call to mind;
  'Tis time ye should be now reclaimed.
What fruit could ever Christians find
  In things whereof they're now ashamed?

The indignation of the Lord
  Awhile endure, for 'tis your due;
But firm and steadfast stands His word;
  Though you are faithless, He is true.

The blood of Christ, a precious blood!
  Cleanses from all sin, doubt it not,
And reconciles the soul to God,
  From every folly, every fault.

862   David Denham   CM
Turn, O backsliding children, saith the LORD; for I am married unto you.
Jeremiah 3:14

The heavenly Bridegroom's call I hear,
  In mercy rich and free;
'Turn, ye backsliders, and draw near,
  I'm married unto thee.

'I have espoused thee for My own,
  And with Me thou shalt be,
My Hephzibah, my glorious crown!
  I'm married unto thee.

'I bought thee with My own heart's blood,
  When dying on the tree;
And in the righteousness of God,
  I'm married unto thee.

'All the vast stores of covenant grace
  Are thine, by firm decree;
And thou in heaven shalt see My face,
  I'm married unto thee.

'In all thy losses, griefs, and snares,
  Thy Refuge I will be;
A present help in all thy cares,
  I'm married unto thee.

'In saving thee from death and hell,
  My attributes agree;
And, for eternity, all's well;
  I'm married unto thee.'

Hear, mourning souls, the Bridegroom's voice,
  And to His bosom flee;
He says, by love, by right, and choice,
  'I'm married unto thee.'

Lord, speak, now speak the gracious word
  To me, the sinner me!
O say, as my sin-pardoning Lord,
  'I'm married unto thee.'

Lord, make in me this union shine,
  That heaven and earth may see,
In heart and life, I'm truly Thine,
  And married unto Thee!

863   William Collyer   LM
**Return, ye backsliding children, and I will heal
your backslidings.** *Jeremiah 3:22*

Return, O wanderer, return
  And seek thy gracious Father's face;
Those warm desires that in thee burn
  Were kindled by redeeming grace.

Return, O wanderer, return
  And seek thy heavenly Father's heart,
Whose pitying eyes thy grief discern,
  Whose hand can heal thine inward smart.

Return, O wanderer, return!
  He heard thy deep repentant sigh;
He saw thy softened spirit mourn
  When no intruding ear was nigh.

Return, O wanderer, return!
  Thy Saviour bids thy spirit live;
Go to His bleeding feet and learn
  How freely Jesus can forgive.

Return, O wanderer, return
  And wipe away the falling tear;
'Tis God who says, 'No longer mourn,'
  'Tis mercy's voice invites thee near.

864   Charles Wesley   88 88 88
**Return, ye backsliding children, and I will heal
your backslidings.** *Jeremiah 3:22*

O Jesus, full of truth and grace,
  More full of grace than I of sin,
Yet once again I seek Thy face;
  Open Thine arms, and take me in,
And freely my backslidings heal,
And love the faithless sinner still.

Thou knowest the way to bring me back,
  My fallen spirit to restore:
O for Thy truth and mercy's sake,
  Forgive, and bid me sin no more;
The ruins of my soul repair,
And make my heart a house of prayer.

The stone to flesh again convert,
  The veil of sin again remove;
Sprinkle Thy blood upon my heart,
  And melt it by Thy dying love;
This rebel heart by love subdue,
And make it soft, and make it new.

Ah! give me, Lord, the tender heart
  That trembles at the approach of sin;
A godly fear of sin impart,
  Implant, and root it deep within,
That I may dread Thy gracious power,
And never dare to offend Thee more.

865   John Needham   CM
**He reserveth unto us the appointed weeks of
the harvest.** *Jeremiah 5:24*

To praise the ever-bounteous Lord,
  My soul, wake all thy powers;
He calls, and at His voice come forth
  The smiling harvest hours.

His covenant with the earth He keeps;
  My tongue, His goodness sing;
Summer and winter know their time,
  His harvest crowns the spring.

Well pleased the toiling swains behold
  The waving yellow crop;
With joy they bear the sheaves away,
  And sow again in hope.

Thus teach me, gracious God, to sow
  The seeds of righteousness:
Smile on my soul, and with Thy beams,
  The ripening harvest bless.

Then, in the last great harvest, I
  Shall reap a glorious crop;
The harvest shall by far exceed
  What I have sown in hope.

O, may the promised blissful hour,
  Thy welcome season come,
When all Thy servants shall unite
  To shout the harvest home!

A joyful harvest they shall have
  Who now in sadness sow;
And those shall live to sing above
  Who wept for sin below.

866   John Newton   LM
Stand ye in the ways, and see, and ask for the old paths. *Jeremiah 6:16*

By faith in Christ I walk with God,
  With heaven my journey's end in view;
Supported by His staff and rod,
  My road is safe and pleasant too.

I travel through a desert wide,
  Where many round me blindly stray;
But He vouchsafes to be my Guide,
  And will not let me miss my way.

Though snares and dangers throng my path,
  And earth and hell my course withstand,
I triumph over all by faith,
  Guarded by His almighty hand.

The wilderness affords no food,
  But God for my support prepares;
Provides me every needful good,
  And frees my soul from wants and cares.

With Him sweet converse I maintain;
  Great as He is, I dare be free;
I tell Him all my grief and pain,
  And He reveals His love to me.

Some cordial from His word He brings,
  Whene'er my feeble spirit faints;
At once my soul revives and sings,
  And yields no more to sad complaints.

867   William Gadsby   SM
Is not the LORD in Zion? is not her King in her? *Jeremiah 8:19*

The Lord is Zion's King;
  Let Zion in Him trust;
'Midst friends and foes His goodness sing,
  And of His mercy boast.

He rules on Zion's hill,
  With laws of peace and grace,
Laws that bespeak His kindness still,
  And human pride abase.

Let saints His sceptre own;
  His righteous laws obey;
Acknowledge Him the Lord alone,
  And walk the heavenly way.

868   David Denham   CM
Astonishment hath taken hold on me. *Jeremiah 8:21*

Astonished at myself I stood,
  Unclean before the Lord;
Yet Jesus washed me in His blood,
  And health of soul restored.

Astonished at His sovereign grace,
  I cried, 'O Lord, why me?'
He said, 'Though you are vile and base,
  My love is rich and free.'

Astonished at His rich repast,
  I sang of sins forgiven,
And thought the joy would always last,
  Till earth was changed for heaven.

Alas! how soon, by Satan moved,
  In darkest paths I trod!
Yet with astonishment I proved
  I changed, and not my God.

And still, though black, deserving hell,
  On Christ for help I call;
And O astonishing to tell,
  His merit covers all.

If with astonishment I see
  So much of God below,
What must the full fruition be
  Where pleasures ever flow!

869   Richard Burnham   87 87
Is there no balm in Gilead; is there no physician there? *Jeremiah 8:22*

Jesus is a wise Physician,
  Skilful and exceeding kind;
Through Him sinners find remission,
  And enjoy sweet peace of mind.

Moved with tenderest compassion,
  He relieves the wounded heart;
And the richest consolation
  His blest Spirit does impart.

This Physician understandeth
  All disorders of the soul;
And no payment He demandeth,
  When He makes the wounded whole.

Come, ye souls, who now are sighing
  Under guilt's distressing chains,
To the Saviour now be flying;
  He will ease you of your pains.

What though bad is your condition,
And your wounds you can't endure?
He, the sinner's wise Physician,
Will effect a perfect cure.

870   Vernon Higham   LM
Is there no balm in Gilead; is there no physician there? *Jeremiah 8:22*

What wounds are these within my breast,
What holy sorrow and distress?
Father of pity, God of grace,
Grant me a vision of Thy face.

With my poor soul now gently share,
Silent Intruder, love and care;
Kindly and firmly draw me nigh,
Removing all that caused my sigh.

The grief I caused forgive me, Lord;
Kindly forbear and peace afford;
Pardon and mercy are my plea;
These are the gifts that come from Thee.

Slowly my gaze will seek Thine own
And see Thy smile disperse Thy frown:
Full restoration and return,
Repentance Thou wilt never spurn.

Thy healing balm removes the pain
That disobedience must attain;
And I shall love Thy blessèd name,
For Thou hast touched and moved my shame.
© Author

871   Thomas Kelly   77 77
The portion of Jacob is not like them: for He is the former of all things; and Israel is the rod of His inheritance: The LORD of hosts is His name. *Jeremiah 10:16*

'Jacob's portion is the Lord;'
What can Jacob more require?
What can heaven more afford?
Or a creature more desire?

'Jacob's portion is the Lord;'
His is sure a pleasant lot;
Jacob's portion cannot fail,
'Tis the Lord who changes not.

Worldlings may their gold display,
Tell what pleasures they afford;
Jacob smiles at all they say,
'Jacob's portion is the Lord.'

Heaven and earth shall flee away;
Sinners with their idols fall;
Jacob shall survive the day;
Jacob's God is Lord of all.

Happy Jacob! Fear not thou!
Triumph when the Lord appears!
He who is thy portion now
Will be thine through endless years.

872   Richard Burnham   CM
O LORD, Thou knowest: remember me, and visit me. *Jeremiah 15:15*

Jesus, my kind and gracious Friend,
Simply I look to Thee,
Now in the richness of Thy love,
Dear Lord, remember me.

Remember Thy pure word of grace;
Remember Calvary's tree;
Remember all Thy dying groans,
And then remember me.

Thou wondrous Advocate with God,
I yield my soul to Thee;
While Thou art pleading on the throne,
Dear Lord, remember me.

I own I'm guilty, own I'm vile,
Yet Thy salvation's free;
Then in Thy all-abounding grace,
Dear Lord, remember me.

And when I close my eyes in death,
And human help shall flee.
Then, then, my dear redeeming God,
O then remember me.

873   John Stevens   SM
Blessed is the man that trusteth in the LORD, and whose hope the LORD is. *Jeremiah 17:7*

The Father chose the seed
In Christ, their chosen Head,
The Spirit makes them feel their need
Of hope in Him who bled.

Hope is a taste begun
Of great Jehovah's grace,
Revealed in Jesus Christ the Son,
To all the chosen race.

Hope is a lively act
Of Jesus' life within,
And grounded on the gospel fact
That Jesus died for sin.

Hope purifies the heart,
Through Jesus' cleansing blood,
Performs, like faith, a saving part,
Beneath the throne of God.

Good hope expects to meet
In Christ a rich supply;
And humbly waits around His seat,
With holy peace and joy.

Through grace good hope abides,
And shields us from despair;
Yields cordials to the heart besides,
And helps the saint in prayer.

Hope comforts through the cross,
Speaks sweetly of the Lamb,
And gospel hope will suffer loss,
To serve the great I AM.

Her nature's serpentine indeed;
Her strength could make a Samson yield;
Nor David could against her stand,
When David's God withheld His hand.

Good God! what can a mortal do,
With such a cursèd, artful foe!
Let grace divine my soul defend,
Nor let me to this monster bend.

Work in me, Lord, to will and do,
My way to Zion to pursue;
And while I tread the thorny road,
Teach me to lean upon my God.

874   Augustus Toplady   SM
**Blessed is the man that trusteth in the LORD,
and whose hope the LORD is.**
Jeremiah 17:7

Blest is the man, O God,
That stays himself on Thee;
Who waits for Thy salvation, Lord,
Shall Thy salvation see.

When we in darkness walk,
Nor feel the heavenly flame,
Then is the time to trust our God,
And rest upon His name.

Soon shall our doubts and fears
Subside at His control;
His lovingkindness shall break through
The midnight of the soul.

His grace will to the end
Stronger and brighter shine;
Nor present things, nor things to come,
Shall quench the life divine.

875   William Gadsby   LM
**The heart is deceitful above all things, and
desperately wicked: who can know it?**
Jeremiah 17:9

Sin has a thousand pleasing charms,
Which flatter to preserve from harms;
She richly gilds her pleasing baits,
And calls her trash delicious sweets.

Young men and maidens, rich and poor,
Are pleased with her deceptive ore;
There's scarce an eye that views the light,
But she can charm by day or night.

Nor are the vessels of the Lord
Free from the chirpings of this bird,
Her craft and spleen she'll make them feel,
And make them like a drunkard reel.

876   Adelaide Pollard   54 54 D
**Behold, as the clay is in the potter's hand, so
are ye in Mine hand, O house of Israel.**
Jeremiah 18:6

Have Thine own way, Lord,
Have Thine own way;
Thou art the Potter,
I am the clay.
Mould me and make me
After Thy will,
While I am waiting
Yielded and still.

Have Thine own way, Lord,
Have Thine own way;
Search me and try me,
Master, today.
Whiter than snow, Lord,
Wash me just now,
As in Thy presence
Humbly I bow.

Have Thine own way, Lord,
Have Thine own way;
Wounded and weary,
Help me, I pray.
Power, all power,
Surely is Thine;
Touch me and heal me,
Saviour divine.

Have Thine own way, Lord,
Have Thine own way;
Hold o'er my being
Absolute sway.
Fill with Thy Spirit
Till all shall see
Christ only, always,
Living in me.

877   Joseph Irons   CM
He shall be called, THE LORD OUR
RIGHTEOUSNESS. *Jeremiah 23:6*

Ye souls condemned by Sinai's law,
    And sunk in deep distress,
To Calvary look, and comfort draw,
    From Christ our Righteousness.

This is the name by which He's known,
    The name His saints confess:
Gaze on Him, humble souls, and own
    The Lord our Righteousness.

A title just, a pardon sealed,
    A spotless wedding dress:
Yea, grace and glory are revealed
    In Christ our Righteousness.

O, that my faith could Jesus claim,
    No more should doubts depress!
Fain would I triumph in this name:
    The Lord our Righteousness.

878   Robert M'Cheyne   11 11 11 11
He shall be called, THE LORD OUR
RIGHTEOUSNESS. *Jeremiah 23:6*

I once was a stranger to grace and to God,
I knew not my danger, and felt not my load;
Though friends spoke in rapture of Christ on the
    tree,
'Jehovah Tsidkenu' was nothing to me.

When free grace awoke me, by light from on high,
Then legal fears shook me, I trembled to die;
No refuge or safety in self could I see,
'Jehovah Tsidkenu' my Saviour must be.

My terrors all vanished before the sweet name.
My guilty fears banished, with boldness I came,
When sealed by the Spirit, through mercy most
    free,
'Jehovah Tsidkenu' was all things to me.

'Jehovah Tsidkenu' my treasure and boast,
'Jehovah Tsidkenu' I cannot be lost;
In Thee I shall conquer, by flood and by field,
My cable, my anchor, my breastplate and shield.

And treading the valley, the shadow of death
This watchword should rally my faltering breath;
For when from life's fever my God sets me free,
'Jehovah Isidkenu' my death-song shall be.

879   William Hammond   77 77
And ye shall seek me, and find me, when ye
shall search for me with all your heart.
Jeremiah 29:13

Lord, we come before Thee now,
At Thy feet we humbly bow;
O do not our plea disdain,
Shall we seek Thee, Lord, in vain?

In Thine own appointed way,
Now we seek Thee, here we stay;
Lord, from hence we would not go
Till a blessing Thou bestow.

Send some message from Thy word,
That may joy and peace afford:
Let Thy Spirit now impart
Full salvation to each heart.

Comfort those who weep and mourn,
Let the time of joy return;
Those who are cast down lift up,
Make them strong in faith and hope.

Grant that all may seek and find
Thee a God supremely kind;
Heal the sick, the captive free,
Let us all rejoice in Thee.

880   John Kent   LM
Yea, I have loved thee with an everlasting love:
therefore with lovingkindness have I drawn
thee. *Jeremiah 31:3*

'Twas with an everlasting love
    That God His own elect embraced;
Before He made the worlds above,
    Or earth on her huge columns placed.

Long ere the sun's refulgent ray
    Primeval shades of darkness drove,
They on His sacred bosom lay,
    Loved with an everlasting love.

Then in the glass of His decrees,
    Christ and His bride appeared as one;
Her sin, by imputation, His,
    Whilst she in spotless splendour shone.

O love, how high thy glories swell!
    How great, immutable, and free!
Ten thousand sins, as black as hell,
    Are swallowed up, O love, in thee!

Believer, here thy comfort stands:
    From first to last salvation's free,
And everlasting love demands
    An everlasting song from thee.

881   William Gadsby   CM
Yea, I have loved thee with an everlasting love: therefore with lovingkindness have I drawn thee. *Jeremiah 31:3*

Salvation O my soul, rejoice;
   Salvation is of God;
He speaks, and that almighty voice
   Proclaims His grace abroad.

How wonderful, how grand the plan!
   All Deity's engaged
To rescue rebel, ruined man
   From Satan's power and rage.

The Father loved us ere we fell,
   And will for ever love;
Nor shall the powers of earth or hell
   His love from Zion move.

'Twas love that moved Him to ordain
   A Surety just and good;
And on His heart inscribe the name
   Of all for whom He stood.

Nor is the Surety short of love;
   He loves beyond degree;
No less than love divine could move
   The Lord to die for me.

And O what love the Spirit shows!
   When Jesus He reveals
To men oppressed with sin and woes,
   He all their sorrows heals.

The Three-in-One and One-in-Three,
   In love for ever rest;
And Zion shall in glory be,
   And with His love be blessed.

882   Johann Scheffler, tr. J Wesley   88 88 88
Yea, I have loved thee with an everlasting love: therefore with lovingkindness have I drawn thee. *Jeremiah 31:3*

O Love, who formedst me to wear
   The image of Thy Godhead here;
Who soughtest me with tender care
   Through all my wanderings wild and drear:

   O Love, I give myself to Thee,
   Thine ever, only Thine to be.

O Love, who ere life's earliest dawn
   On me Thy choice hast gently laid;
O Love, who here as Man wast born
   And wholly like to us wast made:

O Love, who once in time wast slain,
   Pierced through and through with bitter woe;
O Love, who wrestling thus didst gain
   That we eternal joy might know:

O Love, who lovest me for aye,
   Who for my soul dost ever plead:
O Love, who didst my ransom pay,
   Whose power sufficeth in my stead:

O Love, who once shalt bid me rise
   From out this dying life of ours;
O Love, who once above yon skies
   Shalt set me in the fadeless bowers:

883   Timothy Dudley-Smith   11 10 11 10
The Lord hath appeared of old unto me, saying, Yea, I have loved thee with an everlasting love. *Jeremiah 31:3*

Lord, for the years Your love has kept and guided,
   Urged and inspired us, cheered us on our way,
Sought us and saved us, pardoned and provided,
   Lord of the years, we bring our thanks today.

Lord, for that word, the word of life which fires us,
   Speaks to our hearts and sets our souls ablaze,
Teaches and trains, rebukes us and inspires us,
   Lord of the word, receive Your people's praise.

Lord, for our land, in this our generation,
   Spirits oppressed by pleasure, wealth and care;
For young and old, for commonwealth and nation,
   Lord of our land, be pleased to hear our prayer.

Lord, for our world; when we disown and doubt Him,
   Loveless in strength, and comfortless in pain;
Hungry and helpless, lost indeed without Him,
   Lord of the world, we pray that Christ may reign.

Lord, for ourselves; in living power remake us,
   Self on the cross and Christ upon the throne;
Past put behind us, for the future take us,
   Lord of our lives, to live for Christ alone.

884   William Gadsby   LM
**I am a Father to Israel, and Ephraim is My
firstborn.** *Jeremiah 31:9*

God is a Father, just and wise,
And reigns enthroned above the skies;
Yet all His saints on earth shall know,
He condescends to dwell below.

He'll make His sons and daughters wise,
And teach them all His ways to prize;
He'll lead them forth with love and power,
And save them in a trying hour.

To them He will His secrets tell,
And save them from the power of hell;
And when they leave this world of woe,
He'll take them all to glory too.

885   Thomas Gibbons   CM
**Therefore they shall come and sing in the
height of Zion, and shall flow together to the
goodness of the LORD.**
Jeremiah 31:12

Thy goodness, Lord, our souls confess,
    Thy goodness we adore;
A spring whose blessings never fail,
    A sea without a shore!

Sun, moon, and stars Thy love attest
    In every golden ray;
Love draws the curtains of the night,
    And love brings back the day.

Thy bounty every season crowns
    With all the bliss it yields;
With joyful clusters load the vines,
    With strengthening grain the fields.

But chiefly Thy compassion, Lord,
    Is in the gospel seen:
There, like a sun, Thy mercy shines
    Without a cloud between.

Pardon, acceptance, peace, and joy,
    Through Jesus' name are given;
He on the cross was lifted high,
    That we might reign in heaven.

886   Joseph Hart   CM
**My people shall be satisfied with My
goodness, saith the LORD.**
Jeremiah 31:14

Lord help us on Thy word to feed;
    In peace dismiss us hence;
Be Thou, in every time of need,
    Our refuge and defence.

We now desire to bless Thy name,
    And in our hearts record,
And with our thankful tongues proclaim,
    The goodness of the Lord.

887   Emma Bevan   DCM
**My people shall be satisfied with My
goodness, saith the LORD.**
Jeremiah 31:14

O Christ, in Thee my soul hath found,
    And found in Thee alone,
The peace, the joy, I sought so long,
    The bliss till now unknown.

*Now none but Christ can satisfy,
    None other name for me:
There's love and life and lasting joy,
    Lord Jesus, found in Thee!*

I sighed for rest and happiness,
    I yearned for them, not Thee;
But while I passed my Saviour by,
    His love laid hold on me.

I tried the broken cisterns, Lord,
    But ah! the waters failed!
Even as I stooped to drink they fled
    And mocked me as I wailed.

The pleasures lost I sadly mourned,
    But never wept for Thee,
Till grace the sightless eyes received
    Thy loveliness to see.

888   Richard Burnham   88 88 88
**Turn Thou me, and I shall be turned; for Thou
art the LORD my God.**
Jeremiah 31:18

Great God, convert our souls to Thee,
And every evil may we flee:
Bow every heart before Thy throne,
And let us cleave to Thee alone.

*O turn us, turn us, by Thy grace,
Turn us to seek Thy glorious face.*

Turn us from Satan, sin, and hell,
And to our souls Thyself reveal;
Turn us from darkness unto light,
From earthly joys to pure delight.

Dear Lord, how careless have we been!
O turn us more from self and sin;
'Tis only Thou canst turn the heart,
And bid our evils all depart

More may we know our nature's loss,
And find our all in Jesus' cross!
There see our every sin forgiven,
And prove the way to God and heaven.

889   Joseph Irons   LM
And they shall be My people, and I will be their God. *Jeremiah 32:38*

Amidst the wealth of Bible stores,
And gems the eye of faith explores,
None with such joy and comfort fill,
As Jesus' covenant SHALL and WILL.

Delightful words! the king's decrees!
Which rule all heaven, and earth and seas;
All things in time, till time shall end,
Upon His SHALLS and WILLS depend.

Why are not feeble saints destroyed?
Why are not promises made void,
And sin my utter ruin proved?
His SHALLS and WILLS remain unmoved.

The weak become both strong and bold,
While on these words faith keeps her hold;
Mountains must melt and waves be still,
Obeying Jesus' SHALL and WILL.

These potent words subdued my heart,
And made the love of sin depart:
Christ said, 'My purpose I'll fulfil,
You SHALL submit and reign I WILL.'

These words a sovereign power conveyed,
Confirmed each promise He had made;
My IFs and BUTS I laid aside,
And now in SHALLS and WILLS abide.

890   Richard Burnham   LM
Come, and let us join ourselves to the LORD in a perpetual covenant that shall not be forgotten. *Jeremiah 50:5*

These honoured saints, redeemed by blood,
Now join the happy church of God;
Drawn by the force of sovereign grace,
In Zion now they take their place.

With pleasure we the saints behold,
Joining the great Redeemer's fold:
May we with them for ever prove,
A Gospel Church, the house of love.

891   John Newton   CM
They shall ask the way to Zion. *Jeremiah 50:5*

Zion! the city of our God,
  How glorious is the place!
The Saviour there has His abode,
  And sinners see His face!

Firm, against every adverse shock,
  Its mighty bulwarks prove;
'Tis built upon the living Rock,
  And walled around with love.

There, all the fruits of glory grow,
  And joys that never die;
And streams of grace, and knowledge flow
  The soul to satisfy.

Come, set your faces Zion-ward,
  The sacred road enquire;
And let a union to the LORD
  Be henceforth your desire!

The gospel shines to give you light,
  No longer, then, delay;
The Spirit waits to guide you right,
  And Jesus is the way.

O LORD, regard Thy people's prayer,
  Thy promise now fulfill;
And young and old, by grace prepare,
  To dwell on Zion's hill.

892   Joseph Hart   77 77 D
Is it nothing to you, all ye that pass by?
Lamentations 1:12

Much we talk of Jesus' blood;
But how little's understood!
  Of His sufferings so intense,
  Angels have no perfect sense.
Who can rightly comprehend
Their beginning or their end
  'Tis to God, and God alone,
  That their weight is fully known.

O thou hideous monster, Sin,
What a curse hast thou brought in!
  All creation groans through thee,
  Pregnant cause of misery.
Thou hast ruined wretched man,
Ever since the world began;
  Thou hast God afflicted too;
  Nothing less than that would do.

Would we then rejoice indeed
Be it that from thee we're freed:
　　And our justest cause to grieve
　　Is that thou wilt to us cleave.
Faith relieves us from thy guilt,
But we think whose blood was spilt;
　　All we hear, or feel, or see,
　　Serves to raise our hate to thee.

Dearly we are bought, for God
Bought us with His own heart's blood;
　　Boundless depths of love divine!
　　Jesus, what a love was Thine!
Though the wonders Thou hast done
Are as yet so little known,
　　Here we fix and comfort take—
　　Jesus died for sinners' sake.

893　　Charles Wesley　　55 11 D
Is it nothing to you, all ye that pass by?
Lamentations 1:12

　　All ye that pass by,
　　To Jesus draw nigh;
To you is it nothing that Jesus should die?
　　Your ransom and peace,
　　Your surety He is;
Come, see if there ever was sorrow like His.

　　He dies to atone
　　For sins not His own;
Your debt He hath paid, and your work He hath
　　　done.
　　Ye all may receive
　　The peace He did leave,
Who made intercession, 'My Father, forgive!'

　　For you and for me
　　He prayed on the tree:
The prayer is accepted, the sinner is free.
　　That sinner am I
　　Who on Jesus rely,
And come for the pardon God cannot deny.

　　His death is my plea;
　　My Advocate see,
And hear the blood speak that hath answered for
　　　me;
　　He purchased the grace,
　　Which now I embrace;
O Father, Thou know'st He hath died in my place.

894　　John Berridge　　66 66 88
He shutteth out my prayer. *Lamentations 3:8*

　　I hear a righteous man,
　　　A prophet good and great,
　　In deep distress complain,
　　　And thus his grief relate:
'I call on God and cry and shout,
But all my prayer He shutteth out.'

　　Let every drooping saint
　　　Keep waiting evermore;
　　And though exceeding faint,
　　　Knock on at mercy's door;
Still cry and shout till night is past,
For daylight will spring up at last.

　　If Christ do not appear,
　　　When His disciples cry,
　　He marketh every tear,
　　　And counteth every sigh;
In all their sorrows bears a part,
Beholds their grief, and feels their smart.

　　He lends an unseen hand,
　　　And gives a secret prop,
　　Which keeps them waiting stand,
　　　Till He complete their hope!
So let me wait upon this Friend,
And trust Him till my troubles end.

895　　John Keble　　LM
**It is of the LORD'S mercies that we are not
consumed, because His compassions fail not.**
Lamentations 3:22

New every morning is the love
Our wakening and uprising prove;
Through sleep and darkness safely brought,
Restored to life, and power, and thought.

New mercies each returning day
Hover around us while we pray:
New perils past, new sins forgiven,
New thoughts of God, new hopes of heaven.

If, on our daily course, our mind
Be set to hallow all we find,
New treasures still, of countless price,
God will provide for sacrifice.

The trivial round, the common task,
Will furnish all we ought to ask;
Room to deny ourselves—a road
To bring us daily nearer God.

Only, O Lord, in Thy dear love,
Fit us for perfect rest above;
And help us this and every day
To live more nearly as we pray.

896   Thomas Chisholm
11 10 11 10 + refrain (dactylic)
Great is Thy faithfulness.
Lamentations 3:23

Great is Thy faithfulness, O God my Father,
There is no shadow of turning with Thee;
Thou changest not, Thy compassions, they fail
    not;
As Thou hast been Thou for ever wilt be.

*Great is Thy faithfulness! Great is Thy
    faithfulness!
Morning by morning new mercies I see;
All I have needed Thy hand hath provided—
Great is Thy faithfulness, Lord, unto me!*

Summer and winter, and spring-time and harvest,
Sun, moon and stars in their courses above,
Join with all nature in manifold witness
To Thy great faithfulness, mercy and love.

Pardon for sin and a peace that endureth,
Thy own dear presence to cheer and to guide;
Strength for today and bright hope for tomorrow,
Blessings all mine, with ten thousand beside!

Great Is Thy Faithfulness
Words: Thomas O. Chisholm

897   Richard Burnham   66 66 88
Great is Thy faithfulness.
Lamentations 3:23

Mount Zion's faithful King
    Proclaims in faithfulness,
That every needful thing
    His children shall possess;
And they will ever sound abroad,
'Great is the faithfulness of God.'

He's faithful to regard
    The promises of grace;
And all He hath declared
    Shall surely come to pass;
And His dear saints will sound abroad,
'Great is the faithfulness of God.'

None could e'er truly say,
    They sought the Lord in vain;
He'll evermore display
    His love to seeking men;
And they delight to sound abroad,
'Great is the faithfulness of God.'

O Lord, Thy word fulfil,
    Thy presence now make known;
Now, now, dear Lord, reveal
    The glories of Thy throne:
Then will Thy children sound abroad,
'Great is the faithfulness of God.'

WILLIAM GADSBY 1773-1844

898   William Gadsby   10 10 10 10
**The LORD is my portion, saith my soul;
therefore will I hope in Him.**
Lamentations 3:24

Immortal honours rest on Jesus' head;
My God, my Portion, and my Living Bread;
In Him I live, upon Him cast my care;
He saves from death, destruction, and despair.

He is my Refuge in each deep distress;
The Lord my strength and glorious righteousness;
Through floods and flames He leads me safely on,
And daily makes His sovereign goodness known.

My every need He richly will supply;
Nor will His mercy ever let me die;
In Him there dwells a treasure all divine,
And matchless grace has made that treasure
    mine.

O that my soul could love and praise Him more,
His beauties trace, His majesty adore;
Live near His heart, upon His bosom lean;
Obey His voice, and all His will esteem.

899   William Cowper   CM
**The LORD is my portion, saith my soul;
therefore will I hope in Him.**
Lamentations 3:24

From pole to pole let others roam,
    And search in vain for bliss;
My soul is satisfied at home,
    The Lord my portion is.

Jesus, who on His glorious throne
  Rules heaven, and earth, and sea,
Is pleased to claim me for His own,
  And give Himself to me.

His person fixes all my love,
  His blood removes my fear;
And while He pleads for me above,
  His arm preserves me here.

His word of promise is my food,
  His Spirit is my Guide;
Thus daily is my strength renewed,
  And all my wants supplied.

For Him I count as gain each loss:
  Disgrace, for Him, renown;
Well may I glory in His cross,
  While He prepares my crown!

Let worldlings then indulge their boast!
  How much they gain or spend;
Their joys must soon give up the ghost,
  But mine shall know no end.

900   Anna Waring   DCM
**The LORD is my portion, saith my soul;
therefore will I hope in Him.**
Lamentations 3:24

My heart is resting, O my God;
  I will give thanks and sing;
My heart is at the secret source
  Of every precious thing.
Now the frail vessel Thou hast made
  No hand but Thine shall fill;
The waters of the earth have failed
  And I am thirsting still.

I thirst for springs of heavenly life
  And here all day they rise;
I seek the treasure of Thy love
  And close at hand it lies:
And a new song is in my mouth
  To long-loved music set;
Glory to Thee for all the grace
  I have not tasted yet.

I have a heritage of joy
  That yet I must not see;
The hand that bled to make it mine
  Is keeping it for me;
My heart is resting on His truth,
  Who hath made all things mine;
Who draws my captive will to Him
  And makes it one with Thine.

My heart is resting, O my God;
  My heart is in Thy care;
I hear the voice of joy and health
  Resounding everywhere.
'Thou art my portion,' saith my soul,
  Ten thousand voices say,
The music of their glad Amen
  Will never die away.

901   John Ryland   CM
**But though He cause grief, yet will He have
compassion according to the multitude of His
mercies.**
Lamentations 3:32

What, though God try by various ways
  Our faith and every grace!
Though for a while our Father please
  To hide His heavenly face!

May we not yield to unbelief,
  Since grace the same abides;
He pities, though He causes grief,
  Loves, though His face He hides.

Though hid behind a passing cloud
  Our sun doth still remain;
If He awhile His glory shroud,
  He'll soon break out again.

902   Benjamin Beddome   CM
**Thou hast heard my voice: hide not Thine ear
at my breathing, at my cry.** *Lamentations 3:56*

Prayer is the breath of God in man,
  Returning whence it came:
Love is the sacred fire within,
  And prayer the rising flame.

It gives the burdened spirit ease,
  And soothes the troubled breast:
Yields comfort to the mourning soul,
  And to the weary, rest.

The prayers and praises of the saints,
  Like precious odours sweet,
Ascend and spread a rich perfume
  Around the mercy-seat.

When God inclines the heart to pray,
  He hath an ear to hear;
To Him there's music in a groan,
  And beauty in a tear.

The humble suppliant cannot fail
  To have his wants supplied,
Since He for sinners intercedes
  Who once for sinners died.

903   Albert Midlane   LM
Remember, O LORD, what is come upon us:
consider, and behold our reproach.
Lamentations 5:1

Apart from every worldly care,
We bow before Thee, Lord, in prayer,
And as our one, our only claim,
We lisp our blessèd Jesus' name.

May the blest Spirit, Father, now,
Each heart in holy reverence bow;
And may our feeble breathings rise
To Thee, like holy sacrifice.

Our need Thou knowest, Thou art nigh,
And Thou canst every need supply;
Boundless, dear Father, is Thy store,
Remember us, we ask no more.

904   Joseph Irons   CM
A wheel in the middle of a wheel.
Exekiel 1:16

A wondrous wheel of providence,
   Held in Jehovah's hand;
Mysterious to the sons of sense,
   Moved by divine command.

Each of time's changes, like a spoke,
   Proceeds from God, its source;
Each fills its station, none are broke,
   All aid its wondrous course.

Its circle reaches earth's wide bound,
   Its axis is God's will;
On His decrees it must go round
   Till He shall say, 'Be still.'

Let atheists vainly talk of chance,
   I would this wheel adore.
Which rules and guides each circumstance
   Which angels can't explore.

Through seas, o'er hills, it makes its way,
   Though earth and hell oppose;
'Tis hastening on the last great day,
   Its wonders to disclose.

905   John Berridge   SM
Son of man, seest thou what they do?
Ezekiel 8:6

That image-chamber foul
   Which met Ezekiel's eye,
Points out the breast of every soul,
   Where lurking idols lie.

Yet ask for further light,
   And turn to see thy woe,
And God will clear thy misty sight,
   And deeper visions show.

As we the light can bear
   To break upon our eyes,
Still deeper idols shall appear,
   And more will after rise.

Thus pride is broken down,
   And humbled in the dust,
We view our vileness, and must own
   The Lord is all our trust.

May Jesus Christ disclose
   The plagues within my heart;
And as my soul more humbled grows,
   A brighter faith impart.

906   David Denham   SM
Set a mark upon the foreheads of the men that
sigh and that cry for all the abominations that
be done. *Ezekiel 9:4*

Distinguished from the rest
   Of Adam's fallen race,
The saints of God were ever blest,
   And marked as heirs of grace.

When dead in sin they lay,
   Their names were marked above,
And in the Lord's appointed way
   They each His kindness prove.

Marked with a sense of sin,
   They sigh and cry to God:
Who pardons, heals, and makes them clean,
   Through Jesus' precious blood.

Marked with His righteousness,
   They stand in Him approved;
His great and glorious name confess
   And are at all times loved.

Marked in each trying hour,
   Through grace they persevere;
And marked with God's almighty power,
   They overcome by prayer.

Thus marked, may we press on,
   Since Christ is on our side:
And meet at last upon His throne,
   With millions glorified.

907   Isaac Watts   LM
And I will give them one heart, and I will put a new Spirit within you. *Ezekiel 11:19 and 37:9*

This is the word of truth and love,
Sent to the nations from above;
Jehovah here resolves to show
What His almighty grace can do.

Lo! at its sound the dead revive,
Quickened by grace are made alive;
Dry bones are raised and clothed afresh,
And hearts of stone are turned to flesh.

May but this grace my soul renew,
Let sinners gaze and hate me too;
The word that saves me does engage
A sure defence from all their rage.

908   Thomas Kelly   87 87 77
Yea, I said unto thee when thou wast in thy blood, Live. *Ezekiel 16:6*

When we lay in sin polluted,
    Wretched and undone we were;
All we saw and heard was suited
    Only to produce despair;
Ours appeared a hopeless case;
Such it had been, but for grace.

As we lay exposed and friendless,
    Needing what no hand could give,
Then the Lord, whose praise be endless
    Passèd by, and bid us live;
This was help in time of need;
This was grace, 'twas grace indeed.

Yes, 'twas grace beyond all measure,
    When He bid such sinners live,
Laid aside His just displeasure,
    And determined to forgive;
But He chose our hopeless case,
With a view to show His grace.

And shall we be found forgetful
    Of the Lord, who thus forgave?
Lord, our hearts are most deceitful,
    'Tis in Thee our strength we have;
Should'st Thou let Thy people go,
They'd forget how much they owe.

Keep us, then, O keep us ever!
    While we stand, 'tis in Thy strength;
Leave us not, forsake us never,
    Till we see Thy face at length;
Hold Thy helpless people fast;
Save us, Lord, from first to last.

909   Daniel Whittle   Irregular
There shall be showers of blessing. *Ezekiel 34:26*

There shall be showers of blessing:
    This is the promise of love!
There shall be seasons refreshing
    Sent from the Saviour above.

    Showers of blessing,
        Showers of blessing we need;
    Mercy-drops round us are falling
        But for the showers we plead.

There shall be showers of blessing
    Precious reviving again;
Over the hills and the valleys,
    Sound of abundance of rain.

There shall be showers of blessing:
    Send them upon us, O Lord!
Grant to us now a refreshing:
    Come and now honour Thy word.

There shall be showers of blessing:
    O that today they might fall,
Now as to God we're confessing,
    Now as on Jesus we call!

910   Elizabeth Codner   87 87 3
There shall be showers of blessing. *Ezekiel 34:26*

Lord, I hear of showers of blessing,
    Thou art scattering full and free;
Showers the thirsty land refreshing;
    Let some drops descend on me,
        Even me.

Pass me not, O gracious Father;
    Sinful though my heart may be;
Thou might'st leave me, but the rather
    Let Thy mercy light on me,
        Even me.

Pass me not, O tender Saviour;
    Let me love and cling to Thee;
I am longing for Thy favour;
    When Thou comest, call for me,
        Even me.

Pass me not, O mighty Spirit;
    Thou canst make the blind to see;
Witnesser of Jesus' merit,
    Speak the word of power to me,
        Even me.

911   Charles Wesley   77 77
**A new heart also will I give you, and a new
Spirit will I put within you.**
Ezekiel 36:26

Dearest Lord, what must I do?
Only Thou the way canst show;
Thou canst save me in this hour;
I have neither will nor power.

God if over all Thou art,
Greater than the sinful heart;
Let Thy power in me be shown;
Take away the heart of stone.

Take away my darling sin,
Make me willing to be clean;
Make me willing to receive
What Thy goodness waits to give.

Teach me, Lord, with all to part;
Tear all idols from my heart;
Let Thy power on me be shown;
Take away the heart of stone.

Jesus, mighty to renew,
Work in me to will and do;
Turn my nature's rapid tide;
Stem the torrent of my pride.

Stop the whirlwind of my will;
Bid corruptions, Lord, be still;
Now Thy love almighty shew,
Cleanse my heart, my mind renew.

912   Cecil Alexander   LM
**And I will put My Spirit within you, and cause
you to walk in My statutes.**
Ezekiel 36:27

Spirit of God, that moved of old
   Upon the waters' darkened face,
Come, when our faithless hearts are cold,
   And stir them with an inward grace.

Thou that art power and peace combined,
   All highest strength, all purest love,
The rushing of the mighty Wind,
   The brooding of the gentle Dove.

Come, give us still Thy powerful aid,
   And urge us on, and make us Thine;
Nor leave the hearts that once were made
   Fit temples for Thy grace divine.

Nor let us quench Thy sevenfold light;
   But still with softest breathings stir
Our wayward souls, and lead us right,
   O Holy Ghost, the Comforter.

913   Augustus Toplady   87 87
**And I will put My Spirit within you, and cause
you to walk in My statutes.**
Ezekiel 36:27

Holy Ghost, dispel our sadness,
   Pierce the clouds of nature's night;.
Come, Thou Source of joy and gladness,
   Breathe Thy life, and spread Thy light.

Come, Thou best of all donations
   God can give, or we implore!
Having Thy sweet consolations,
   We on earth can wish no more.

Author of the new creation,
   Bid us now Thy influence prove;
Make our souls Thy habitation;
   Shed abroad the Saviour's love.

914   John Newton   LM
Ezekiel 37

Preachers may, from Ezekiel's case,
   Draw hope in this declining day;
A proof, like this, of sovereign grace
   Should chase our unbelief away.

When sent to preach to lifeless bones,
   Who could have thought he would succeed?
But well he knew, the Lord from stones
   Could raise up Abra'm's chosen seed.

Can these be made a num'rous host,
   And such dry bones new life receive?
The prophet answered, 'Lord Thou knowst
   They shall, if Thou commandment give.'

Like him, around I cast my eye,
   And O! what heaps of bones appear!
Like him, by Jesus sent, I'll try,
   For He can cause the dead to hear.

Hear, ye dry bones, the Saviour's word?
   He, who when dying, gasped, 'Forgive,'
That gracious, sinner-loving Lord,
   Says, 'Look to Me, dry bones, and live.'

Thou heavenly Wind awake and blow,
   In answer to the prayer of faith;
Now Thine almighty influence show,
   And fill dry bones with living breath.

O make them hear, and feel, and shake,
   And, at Thy call, obedient move;
The bonds of death and Satan break,
   And bone to bone unite in love.

915 Joseph Hart 886 D
Behold, I will cause breath to enter into you, and ye shall live. *Ezekiel 37:5*

Descend from heaven, celestial Dove,
With flames of pure seraphic love
  Our ravished breasts inspire;
Fountain of joy, blest Paraclete,
Warm our cold hearts with heavenly heat,
  And set our souls on fire.

Breathe on these bones, so dry and dead;
Thy sweetest, softest influence shed
  In all our hearts abroad;
Point out the place where grace abounds;
Direct us to the bleeding wounds
  Of our incarnate God.

Conduct, blest Guide, Thy sinner-train
To Calvary, where the Lamb was slain,
  And with us there abide;
Let us our loved Redeemer meet,
Weep o'er His piercèd hands and feet,
  And view His wounded side.

From which pure fountain if Thou draw
Water to quench the fiery law,
  And blood to purge our sin;
We'll tell the Father in that day,
(And Thou shalt witness what we say),
  'We're clean, just God, we're clean.'

Teach us for what to pray, and how;
And since, kind God, 'tis only Thou
  The throne of grace canst move,
Pray Thou for us, that we, through faith,
May feel the effects of Jesus' death,
  Through faith, that works by love.

Thou, with the Father and the Son,
Art that mysterious Three-in-One,
  God blest for evermore!
Whom though we cannot comprehend,
Feeling Thou art the sinner's Friend,
  We love Thee and adore.

916 Jane Leeson 77 77
And David my servant shall be king over them; and they all shall have one shepherd.
Ezekiel 37:24

Loving Shepherd of Thy sheep,
Keep me, Lord, in safety keep;
Nothing can Thy power withstand,
None can pluck me from Thy hand.

Loving Shepherd, Thou didst give
Thine own life that I might live;
May I love Thee day by day,
Gladly Thy sweet will obey.

I would praise Thee every day,
Gladly all Thy will obey,
Like Thy blessèd ones above
Happy in Thy precious love.

Loving Shepherd, ever near,
Teach me still Thy voice to hear;
Suffer not my feet to stray
From the strait and narrow way.

Where Thou leadest I would go,
Walking in Thy steps below;
Then before Thy Father's throne,
Jesus, claim me for Thy own.

917 John Kent CM
Afterward he measured a thousand; and it was a river that I could not pass over. *Ezekiel 47:5*

Beneath the sacred throne of God
  I saw a river rise,
The streams were peace and pardoning blood,
  Descending from the skies.

Angelic minds cannot explore
  This deep, unfathomed sea;
'Tis void of bottom, brim, or shore,
  And lost in Deity.

I stood amazed, and wondered when,
  Or why, this ocean rose,
That wafts salvation down to men,
  His traitors and His foes.

918 Timothy Dudley-Smith 66 66 44 44
Daniel answered and said, Blessed be the name of God for ever and ever: for wisdom and might are His... *Daniel 2:20-23*

Beyond all mortal praise
  God's name be ever blest,
Unsearchable His ways,
  His glory manifest;
    From His high throne
      In power and might
      By wisdom's light
    He rules alone.

Our times are in His hand
  To whom all flesh is grass,
While as their Maker planned
  The changing seasons pass.
    He orders all:
      Before His eyes
      Earth's empires rise,
    Her kingdoms fall.

He gives to humankind,
    Dividing as He will,
All powers of heart and mind,
    Of spirit, strength and skill:
        Nor dark nor night
            But must lay bare
            Its secrets, where
        He dwells in light.

To God the only Lord
    Our fathers' God, be praise;
His holy name adored
    Through everlasting days.
        His mercies trace
            In answered prayer,
            In love and care,
        And gifts of grace.

'Beyond all mortal praise' by Timothy Dudley-Smith (b.1926). © Timothy Dudley-Smith in Europe and Africa. © Hope Publishing Company in the United States of America and the rest of the world. Reproduced by permission of Oxford University Press . All rights reserved.

919   John Newton   CM
In the same hour came forth fingers of a man's hand. *Daniel 5:5*

Poor sinners! little do they think
    With whom they have to do!
But stand securely on the brink
    Of everlasting woe.

Belshazzar thus, profanely bold,
    The Lord of hosts defied;
But vengeance soon his boasts controlled,
    And humbled all his pride.

He saw a hand upon the wall
    (And trembled on his throne)
Which wrote his sudden dreadful fall
    In characters unknown.

Why should he tremble at the view
    Of what he could not read?
Foreboding conscience quickly knew
    His ruin was decreed.

See him o'erwhelmed with deep distress!
    His eyes with anguish roll;
His looks, and loosened joints, express
    The terrors of his soul.

His pomp and music, guests and wine,
    No more delight afford;
O sinner, ere this case be thine,
    Begin to seek the Lord.

The law like this hand-writing stands,
    And speaks the wrath of God;
But Jesus answers its demands,
    And cancels it with blood.

920   Robert Robinson (alt)   87 87 D
The Ancient of days *Daniel 7:9,13,22.*

Mighty God, while angels bless Thee,
    May a mortal lisp Thy name?
Lord of men, as well as angels,
    Thou art every creature's theme.
Lord of every land and nation,
    Ancient of eternal days,
Sounded through the wide creation
    Be Thy just and lawful praise.

For the grandeur of Thy nature,
    Grand beyond a seraph's thought;
For created works of power,
    Works with skill and kindness wrought;
For Thy providence, that governs
    Through Thine empire's wide domain,
Wings an angel, guides a sparrow;
    Blessèd be Thy gentle reign.

But Thy rich, Thy free redemption,
    Dark through brightness all along;
Thought is poor, and poor expression;
    Who dare sing that awesome song?
Brightness of the Father's glory,
    Shall Thy praise unuttered lie?
Fly, my tongue, such a guilty silence!
    Sing the Lord who came to die.

From the highest throne in glory,
    To the cross of deepest woe,
All to ransom guilty captives:
    Flow, my praise, for ever flow!
Go, return, immortal Saviour!
    Leave Thy footstool, take Thy throne;
Thence return, and reign for ever,
    Be the kingdom all Thine own!

921   William Gadsby   66 66 88
To finish the transgression, and to make an end of sins, and to make reconciliation for iniquity, and to bring in everlasting righteousness. *Daniel 9:24*

Ye servants of the Lord,
    Ye messengers of grace,
Go forth with one accord,
    Proclaim a full release:
Jesus has made an end of sin,
And righteousness divine brought in.

With tidings great and grand;
  Tidings immensely good;
Proclaim, through all the land,
  Redemption through His blood:
Jesus has made an end of sin,
And righteousness divine brought in.

Ye sinners in distress,
  The tidings are for you;
Salvation is of grace,
  And full salvation too:
Jesus has made an end of sin,
And righteousness divine brought in.

922   John Kent   LM
And I will betroth thee unto Me for ever.
Hosea 2:19

Betrothed, in love, ere time began,
  His blood-bought bride with Jesus see
Made by eternal union One,
  Who was, and is, and is to be.

Thus He became our covenant Head;
  Charged with her sin the Saviour stands,
To do and suffer in her stead
  All that the righteous law demands.

Here justice and the highest grace
  Met in the sinner's only Friend;
He freely took our lowest place;
  O! love that does all thought transcend.

When sunk in sin He'll not disown
  Those sacred ties that made her His,
But claim this partner of His throne,
  Through floods of wrath and deep distress.

Nor flood, nor flame, nor hell combined,
  Shall from His heart the church divide
His blood th' eternal covenant signed
  When for her sins in love He died.

Thus in His eyes she ever stood
  From wrinkle and from blemish free;
Loved with the dateless love of God,
  And blessed by the great sacred Three.

923   Samuel Pearce   87 87 47
In their affliction they will seek Me early.
Hosea 5:15

In the floods of tribulation,
  While the billows o'er me roll,
Jesus whispers consolation,
  And supports my fainting soul;
    Sweet affliction,
  That brings Jesus to my soul.

Floods of tribulation heighten,
  Billows still around me roar,
Those who know not Christ, they frighten;
  But my soul defies their power;
    Sweet affliction,
  Thus to bring my Saviour near.

In the sacred page recorded,
  Thus His word securely stands:
'Fear not, I'm in trouble near thee,
  Nought shall pluck thee from My hands;'
    Sweet affliction,
  Every word my love demands.

When I gain the weight of glory,
  Still the path I'll ne'er forget,
But, exulting, cry, 'It led me
  To my blessèd Saviour's seat:'
    Sweet affliction,
  Which has brought to Jesus' feet.

924   John Morison   CM
Come, and let us return unto the LORD.
Hosea 6:1

Come, let us to the Lord our God
  With contrite hearts return;
Our God is gracious, nor will leave
  The desolate to mourn.

His voice commands the tempest forth
  And stills the stormy wave;
And though His arm be strong to smite,
  'Tis also strong to save.

Long hath the night of sorrow reigned;
  The dawn shall bring us light;
God shall appear, and we shall rise
  With gladness in His sight.

Our hearts, if God we seek to know,
  Shall know Him and rejoice;
His coming like the morn shall be,
  Like morning songs His voice.

As dew upon the tender herb,
  Diffusing fragrance round;
As showers that usher in the spring,
  And cheer the thirsty ground;

So shall His presence bless our souls
  And shed a joyful light;
That hallowed morn shall chase away
  The sorrows of the night.

Firstborn of many brethren Thou;
  To Thee, lo! all our souls we bow;
To Thee our hearts and hands we give:
  Thine may we die, Thine may we live!

925   Eliza Hewitt   LM + refrain
Then shall we know, if we follow on to know the LORD. *Hosea 6:3*

More about Jesus would I know,
More of His grace to others show;
More of His saving fulness see,
More of His love who died for me.

> *More, more about Jesus,*
> *More, more about Jesus,*
> *More of His saving fulness see,*
> *More of His love who died for me.*

More about Jesus let me learn,
More of His holy will discern;
Spirit of God, my Teacher be,
Showing the things of Christ to me.

More about Jesus in His word,
Holding communion with my Lord;
Hearing His voice in every line,
Making each faithful saying mine.

More about Jesus on His throne,
Riches in glory all His own;
More of His kingdom's sure increase;
More of His coming, Prince of Peace.

926   Joseph Hart   SM
Then shall we know, if we follow on to know the LORD. *Hosea 6:3*

Once more before we part,
We'll bless the Saviour's name:
Record His mercies, every heart;
Sing, every tongue, the same.

Hoard up His sacred word,
And feed thereon and grow;
Go on to seek to know the Lord,
And practise what you know.

927   Philip Doddridge   CM
I drew them with cords of a Man, with bands of love. *Hosea 11:4*

My God, what cords of love are Thine!
How gentle, yet how strong!
While power, and truth, and love combine
To draw our souls along.

The guilt of twice ten thousand sins
One moment takes away;
And grace, when first the work begins,
Secures the crowning day.

Comfort, through all this vale of tears,
In rich profusion flows;
And glory of unnumbered years
Eternity bestows.

Drawn by such cords, we'll onward move
In love and union sweet;
Till, filled with perfect joy above,
Around Thy throne we meet.

GEORGE MATHESON 1842-1906

928   George Matheson   88 886
How shall I give thee up, Ephraim?
Hosea 11:8

O Love that wilt not let me go,
I rest my weary soul in Thee!
I give Thee back the life I owe,
That in Thine ocean depths its flow
May richer, fuller be.

O Light that followest all my way,
I yield my flickering torch to Thee;
My heart restores its borrowed ray,
That in Thy sunshine's blaze its day
May brighter, fairer be.

O Joy that seekest me through pain,
I cannot close my heart to Thee;
I trace the rainbow through the rain
And feel the promise is not vain
That morn shall tearless be.

O Cross that liftest up my head,
I dare not ask to fly from Thee;
I lay in dust life's glory dead,
And from the ground there blossoms red
Life that shall endless be.

929   Charles Wesley   LM
O Israel, thou hast destroyed thyself; but in Me is thine help. *Hosea 13:9*

Jesus in whom the Godhead's rays
   Beam forth with mildest majesty,
I see Thee full of truth and grace,
   And come for all I want to Thee.

Wrathful, impure, and proud I am;
   Nor constancy, nor strength, I have;
But Thou, O Lord, art still the same,
   And hast not lost Thy power to save.

Save me from pride, the plague repel;
   Jesus, Thy humble mind impart,
O let Thy Spirit within me dwell,
   And give me lowliness of heart.

Enter Thyself, and cast out sin;
   More of Thy purity bestow;
Touch me, and make the leper clean;
   Wash me, and I am white as snow.

930   Isaac Watts   CM
I will redeem them from death.
Hosea 13:14

O for an overcoming faith,
   To cheer my dying hours,
To triumph o'er the monster, Death,
   And all his frightful powers.

Joyful with all the strength I have
   My quivering lips should sing,
'Where is thy boasted victory, Grave
   And where's the monster's sting?'

If sin be pardoned, I'm secure;
   Death has no sting beside;
The law gives sin its damning power,
   But Christ, my ransom, died.

Now to the God of victory
   Immortal thanks be paid,
Who makes us conquerors, though we die,
   Through Christ our living Head.

931   Charles Wesley   88 88 88
O Israel, return unto the LORD thy God.
Hosea 14:1

Weary of wandering from the Lord,
   And now made willing to return,
I hear, and bow me to the rod;
   For now, not without hope, I mourn;
There is an Advocate above,
A Friend before the throne of love.

O Jesus! full of truth and grace,
   More full of grace than I of sin;
Yet once again I seek Thy face;
   Open Thy arms, and take me in!
All my backslidings freely heal,
And love the faithless sinner still.

Thou know'st the way to bring me back.
   My fallen spirit to restore;
O, for Thy truth and mercy's sake,
   Forgive, and bid me sin no more!
The ruins of my soul repair,
And make my heart a house of prayer.

Ah, give me, Lord, the tender heart,
   That trembles at the approach of sin;
A godly fear of sin impart,
   Implant and root it deep within;
That I may love Thy gracious power,
And never dare to offend Thee more.

932   Charles Wesley   76 76 77 76
I will heal their backsliding, I will love them freely. *Hosea 14:4*

Jesus, Friend of sinners, hear
   A feeble creature pray;
From my debt of sin set clear,
   For I have nought to pay.
Speak, O speak my kind release,
   A poor backsliding soul restore;

Love me freely, seal my peace,
   And let me rove no more.

Though my sins as mountains rise,
   And swell, and reach to heaven,
Mercy is above the skies,
   And I shall stand forgiven.
Mighty is my guilt's increase,
   But greater is Thy mercy's store!

From the oppressive weight of sin,
   My struggling spirit free;
Blood and righteousness divine
   Can rescue even me.
Holy Spirit, shed Thy grace,
   And let me feel the softening shower;

933   Albert Midlane   87 87 87
I will heal their backsliding, I will love them freely. *Hosea 14:4*

Love us *freely*, blessèd Jesus,
    For we have not aught to pay;
Saviour Thou, and we poor sinners,
    Is alone what we can say;
Love us freely, blessèd Jesus,
    For we have not aught to pay.

Love us *ever,* blessèd Jesus,
    We are changing as the wind;
If Thy love on us depended,
    We should ne'er salvation find;
Love us ever, blessèd Jesus,
    We are changing as the wind.

Love and *help* us, blessèd Jesus,
    Help us to be wholly Thine;
Every idol and enchantment,
    For Thy glory to resign;
Love and help us, blessèd Jesus,
    Help us to be wholly Thine.

Love and *keep* us, blessèd Jesus,
    Keep us from denying Thee;
Keep our wayward feet from straying
    Into paths of vanity;
Love and keep us, blessèd Jesus,
    Keep us from denying Thee.

934   David Denham   SM
I will be as the dew unto Israel.
Hosea 14:5

    God does in spring renew,
    And fruitful make the ground;
So Jesus is to us as dew,
    From Him our fruit is found.

    He keeps His plants in view,
    And does most gracious prove;
Descending gentle as the dew,
    In countless drops of love.

    His doctrine, like the dew,
    Falls silent on the soul;
Quickens to life, and forms anew
    His image on the whole.

    In changes not a few,
    Our need of Christ is felt;
But when He sends the softening dew,
    Our hearts begin to melt.

    Thus come, Lord Jesus, come,
    In blessings ever new;
And, till we meet in heaven at home,
    Be to us as the dew.

935   Joseph Hart   CM
Sanctify ye a fast, call a solemn assembly.
Joel 1:14

Lord look on all assembled here,
    Who in Thy presence stand
To offer up united prayer
    For this our sinful land.

Oft have we each in private prayed
    Our country might find grace;
Now hear the same petitions made
    In this appointed place.

Or, if among us some be met,
    So careless of their sin,
They have not cried for mercy yet,
    Lord, make them now begin.

Thou, by whose death poor sinners live,
    By whom their prayers succeed,
Thy Spirit of supplication give,
    And we shall pray indeed.

We will not slack, nor give Thee rest,
    But importune Thee so
That, till we shall by Thee be blest,
    We will not let Thee go.

Great God of Hosts, deliverance bring;
    Guide those that hold the helm;
Support the state, preserve the king,
    And spare the guilty realm

Or, must the dread decree be past,
    And we must feel the rod,
May faith and patience hold us fast
    To our correcting God.

Whatever be our destined case,
    Accept us in Thy Son;
Give us His gospel and His grace,
    And then, Thy will be done.

936 William Gadsby 66 66 88
Be glad then, ye children of Zion, and rejoice in the LORD your God. *Joel 2:23*

Christians, rejoice, and sing
Your Maker's lovely praise;
He is your God and King,
Ancient of endless days;
He lives, He reigns, and sits above,
The King of kings, and God of love.

No place can Him contain;
Immensity He fills;
He measures, with a span,
The world with all its hills;
In heaven He reigns your God and King,
And will you to His glory bring.

He saves you by His grace;
O matchless grace indeed,
That such a rebel race
From sin and Satan's freed!
His mercy, truth, and justice join,
To make you in full glory shine.

The time will shortly come,
When you, with sweet surprise,
Will find yourself at home
With Christ, above the skies;
With Him to live, with Him to reign,
And never, never part again.

937 David Denham 87 87
And ye shall eat in plenty, and be satisfied, and praise the name of the LORD your God, that hath dealt wondrously with you. *Joel 2:26*

O how great is the provision
In the gospel of our God!
Suited to our worst condition,
And procured by Jesus' blood.

'Tis a feast of God's providing,
Who well knew what we should need;
And in Christ our Head abiding.
Now He bids us come and feed.

Here is living water given,
And the Lamb of God for food,
Christ, the Bread of Life from heaven,
With abundant stores of good.

Here's the milk of consolation,
Grapes from Eshcol for the sad,
Here's the honey of salvation,
And God's wine to make us glad.

Here's strong meat of ancient flavour,
Firm decrees which cannot move,
Salt of grace retaining savour,
While Jehovah rests in love.

Here are promises applying
Precious cordials all divine,
Fruits to cheer the sick and dying,
Gathered from the living Vine.

This great feast has been proclaimèd
By commission from the Lord:
And the poor, the blind, and maimèd,
Are invited in His word.

All who have in Christ believèd,
Here have found a resting-place;
But since God my soul receivèd,
O how much I owe to grace!

938 James Montgomery LM
I will pour out My Spirit upon all flesh.
Joel 2:28

O Spirit of the living God,
In all the fulness of Thy grace,
Where'er the foot of man hath trod,
Descend on our apostate race.

Give tongues of fire and hearts of love,
To preach the reconciling word;
Give power and unction from above,
Whene'er the joyful sound is heard.

Be darkness, at Thy coming, light;
Confusion, order, in Thy path;
Souls without strength inspire with might;
Bid mercy triumph over wrath.

O Spirit of the Lord, prepare
All the round earth her God to meet;
Breathe Thou abroad like morning air
Till hearts of stone begin to beat.

Baptize the nations: far and nigh
The triumphs of the cross record;
The name of Jesus glorify,
Till every kindred call Him Lord.

God from eterninty hath willed
All flesh shall His salvation see;
So be the Father's love fulfilled,
The Saviour's sufferings crowned through Thee.

939   Philip Doddridge   LM
Beat your plowshares into swords, and your pruninghooks into spears: let the weak say, I am strong. *Joel 3:10*

Now let the feeble all be strong,
And make Jehovah's arm their song;
His shield is spread o'er every saint,
And thus supported, who shall faint?

What though the hosts of hell engage
With mingled cruelty and rage?
A faithful God restrains their hands,
And chains them down in iron bands.

Bound by His word, He will display
A strength proportioned to our day;
And when united trials meet,
Will show a path of safe retreat.

Thus far we prove that promise good,
Which Jesus ratified with blood;
Still is He gracious, wise, and just,
And still in Him let Israel trust.

940   Bartholomaus Ringwaldt   8787 887
    tr. William Collyer, Thomas Cotterill
Prepare to meet thy God. *Amos 4:12*

Great God, what do I see and hear?
    The end of things created!
The Judge of mankind doth appear
    On clouds of glory seated;
The trumpet sounds, the graves restore
The dead which they contained before:
    Prepare, my soul, to meet Him!

The dead in Christ shall first arise
    At the last trumpet's sounding,
Caught up to meet Him in the skies,
    With joy their Lord surrounding.
No gloomy fears their souls dismay,
His presence sheds eternal day
    On those prepared to meet Him.

But sinners, filled with guilty fears,
    Behold His wrath prevailing;
For they shall rise and find their tears
    And sighs are unavailing;
The joys of sin are past and gone,
    Trembling they stand before the throne,
All unprepared to meet Him.

Great God, what do I see and hear?
    The end of things created!
The Judge of mankind doth appear
    On clouds of glory seated;
Beneath His cross I view the day
When heaven and earth shall pass away,
    And thus prepare to meet Him.

941   Richard Burnham   LM
Prepare to meet thy God. *Amos 4:12*

O Jesus, now my soul incline
Ever to muse on things divine;
Only Thy will I'd now regard,
And be prepared to meet my Lord,

Ah! never may mere worldly charms
Allure my soul from Thy dear arms:
Swayed by the pure eternal word,
I'd stand prepared to meet my Lord.

To earth's vain toys I'd bid adieu,
And fully after God pursue,
Wrestling before a mercy-seat,
I'd stand prepared my God to meet.

May time-delights no more enthrall;
Away, ye dreams, I' d leave you all;
Jesus alone I'd now regard,
And stand prepared to meet my Lord.

Death's marching forth, I clearly see:
Soon, do I know, He'll call for me;
May Calvary's cross sweet peace afford,
While I go forth to meet my Lord.

942   John Newton   LM
Prepare to meet thy God. *Amos 4:12*

Oft as the bell, with solemn toll,
Speaks the departure of a soul,
Let each one ask himself, 'Am I
Prepared, should I be called to die?'

Only this frail and fleeting breath
Preserves me from the jaws of death;
Soon as it fails, at once I'm gone,
And plunged into a world unknown.

Then, leaving all I loved below,
To God's tribunal I must go;
Must hear the Judge pronounce my fate,
And fix my everlasting state.

Lord Jesus, help me now to flee,
And seek my hope alone in Thee;
Apply Thy blood, Thy Spirit give,
Subdue my sin, and let me live.

Then when the solemn bell I hear,
If saved from guilt, I need not fear;
Nor would the thought distressing be,
'Perhaps it next may toll for me!'

Rather, my spirit would rejoice,
And long, and wish, to hear Thy voice;
Glad when it bids me earth resign,
Secure of heaven, if Thou art mine.

943   David Denham   SM
Seek ye Me, and ye shall live. *Amos 5:4*

We seek the Lord our God,
  By faith and humble prayer;
Seek cleansing in the Saviour's blood,
  And find salvation there.

We seek our Father's face,
  And prove Him near at hand;
We seek His soul-transforming grace,
  And run at His command.

We seek Him in His word,
  Our sure unerring guide;
His love and faithfulness record,
  Who does all good provide.

We seek Him on His throne,
  For help in every need,
Seek life and peace from Him alone,
  And with His children feed.

O may we seek Him more,
  And all His will pursue;
Love Him, and trust Him, and adore,
  With heaven at last in view.

944   Thomas Kelly   CM
O Lord GOD, forgive, I beseech Thee: by whom shall Jacob arise? for he is small.
Amos 7:2

'BY whom shall Jacob now arise?'
  For Jacob's friends are few
And (what should fill us with surprise)
  They seem divided too.

'By whom shall Jacob now arise?'
  For Jacob's foes are strong;
I read their triumph in their eyes;
  They think he'll fail ere long.

'By whom shall Jacob now arise?'
  Can any tell by whom?
Say, shall this branch that withered lies,
  Again revive and bloom?

Lord, Thou canst tell—the work is Thine;
  The help of man is vain;
On Jacob now arise and shine,
  And he shall live again.

945   Timothy Dudley-Smith   CM
Arise, Go to Nineveh, that great city, and cry against it. *Jonah 1:2*

Whom God has summoned by His word,
  Shall they, like Jonah, flee,
Far from the presence of the Lord
  Across a waste of sea?

The waves and billows work His will,
  The storms His word obey;
So God provides a refuge still,
  And spurs the heart to pray.

When from the depths His people cry
  Their pleas are not in vain;
His grace and mercy make reply
  To grant them life again.

From grief and loss to joy restored,
  From death to life above!
How slow to anger is the Lord,
  How strong His steadfast love!

946 Joseph Hoskins CM
Then I said, I am cast out of Thy sight; yet I will look again toward Thy holy temple.
Jonah 2:4

Alas! the Lord my life is gone,
 The Saviour hides His face;
And I am left to walk alone,
 In this dark wilderness.

In vain I read, in vain I pray,
 Or hear salvation's word,
Unless a soul-reviving ray
 Beam from the glorious Lord.

Yet would I trust in Him that died,
 For Jesus is His name;
Yet would I in His grace confide,
 For He is still the same.

If once His grace renew the heart,
 Jesus will there remain;
He cannot finally depart,
 But must return again.

Then, dearest Lord, teach me to wait
 Thy own appointed time;
O change my captive, mournful state,
 And witness Thou art mine.

947 Samuel Medley LM
Then I said, I am cast out of Thy sight; yet I will look again toward Thy holy temple.
Jonah 2:4

See a poor sinner, dearest Lord,
Whose soul, encouraged by Thy word,
At mercy's footstool would remain,
And there would look, and look again.

How oft deceived by self and pride,
Has my poor heart been turned aside;
And, Jonah-like, has fled from Thee,
Till Thou hast looked again on me!

Ah! bring a wretched wanderer home,
And to Thy footstool let me come,
And tell Thee all my grief and pain,
And wait and look, and look again.

Take courage, then, my trembling soul;
One look from Christ shall make thee whole;
Trust thou in Him; 'tis not in vain;
But wait and look, and look again.

948 Isaac Watts 66 66 88
But I will sacrifice unto Thee with the voice of thanksgiving. *Jonah 2:9*

We give immortal praise
 To God the Father's love,
For all our comforts here,
 And better hopes above.
He sent His own eternal Son,
To die for sins that man had done.

To God the Son belongs
 Immortal glory too,
Who bought us with His blood
 From everlasting woe;
And now He lives, and now He reigns,
And sees the fruit of all His pains.

To God the Spirit's name
 Immortal worship give,
Whose new-creating power
 Makes the dead sinner live.
His work completes the great design,
And fills the soul with joy divine.

Almighty God, to Thee
 Be endless honours done,
The undivided Three,
 And the mysterious One,
Where reason fails, with all her powers,
There faith prevails and love adores.

949 John Newton CM
Salvation is of the LORD. *Jonah 2:9*

Salvation, what a glorious plan,
 How suited to our need!
The grace that raises fallen man
 Is wonderful indeed!

'Twas Wisdom formed the vast design
 To ransom us when lost;
And Love's unfathomable mine
 Provided all the cost.

Strict Justice, with approving look,
 The holy covenant sealed;
And Truth and Power undertook
 The whole should be fulfilled.

Truth, Wisdom, Justice, Power, and Love,
 In all their glory shone,
When Jesus left the courts above,
 And died to save His own.

Truth, Wisdom, Justice, Power, and Love
 Are equally displayed;
Now Jesus reigns, enthroned above,
 Our Advocate and Head.

Now sin appears deserving death,
Most hateful and abhorred:
And yet the sinner lives by faith,
And dares approach the Lord.

Soon we pass this desert dreary,
Soon we bid farewell to pain:
Never more are sad or weary,
Never, never sin again!

950   Horatius Bonar   SM
Salvation is of the LORD. *Jonah 2:9*

Not what my hands have done
Can save my guilty soul;
Not what my toiling flesh hath borne
Can make my spirit whole.

Not what I feel or do
Can give me peace with God;
Not all my prayers and sighs and tears
Can bear my awful load.

Thy work alone, O Christ,
Can ease this weight of sin;
Thy blood alone, O Lamb of God,
Can give me peace within.

Thy love to me, O God,
Not mine, O Lord, to Thee,
Can rid me of this dark unrest,
And set my spirit free.

Thy grace alone, O God,
To me can pardon speak;
Thy power alone, O Son of God,
Can this sore bondage break.

I bless the Christ of God;
I rest on love divine;
And with unfaltering lip and heart,
I call this Saviour mine.

951   Horatius Bonar   87 87
Arise ye, and depart; for this is not your rest.
Micah 2:10

This is not my place of resting,
Mine's a city yet to come;
Onward to it I am hasting:
On to my eternal home.

In it all is light and glory;
O'er it shines a nightless day:
Every trace of sin's sad story,
All the curse, hath passed away.

There the Lamb, our Shepherd, leads us,
By the streams of life along,
On the freshest pastures feeds us,
Turns our sighing into song.

952   William Gadsby   CM
The Breaker is come up before them.
Micah 2:13

The Breaker is gone forth in love,
With power and skill divine;
Descending from the realms above,
To quell His foes and mine.

In love to Zion, He has broke
The powers of death and hell;
And her from Sinai's dreadful yoke
Has broken off as well.

Though death, and law, and sin agree
This Breaker to arrest,
He breaks their bonds, Himself sets free,
With Zion on His breast.

He breaks His children's hearts in twain,
And brings proud nature down;
The hearts He breaks He heals again,
And on them puts a crown.

He breaks through every darksome cloud
And shows His lovely face;
Which makes the sinner sing aloud,
'Salvation is of grace.'

He breaks the traps and gins that lie
To catch poor pilgrims' feet;
And, when they stumble, makes them fly
To Him, their safe retreat.

He'll break the strings of nature soon,
And bid the prisoner fly
Beyond the reach of sin and gloom,
His glory to enjoy.

953   Samuel Medley   LM
The Breaker is come up before them.
Micah 2:13

Sing the dear Saviour's glorious fame.
Who bears the Breaker's wondrous name;
Sweet name! and it becomes Him well.
Who breaks down sin, guilt, death, and hell.

Almighty Breaker sure is He,
He broke my chains and set me free;
A gracious Breaker to my soul,
He breaks, and O He makes me whole.

Great Breaker! O Thy love impart
Daily to break my stony heart;
O, break it, Lord, and enter in,
And break, O break, the power of sin.

Break out and shine upon my soul.
One look from Thee will make me whole;
Break through my foes to my relief,
And break, O break, my unbelief.

By Thee I'll break through every foe,
And joyful on my way I'll go;
By Thee I'll break death's cold embrace,
And mount to heaven, and see Thy face.

954   Timothy Dudley-Smith   CM
Micah 4

Behold a broken world, we pray,
    Where want and war increase,
And grant us, Lord, in this our day,
    The ancient dream of peace:

A dream of swords to sickles bent,
    Of spears to scythe and spade,
The weapons of our warfare spent,
    A world of peace remade;

Where every battle-flag is furled
    And every trumpet stilled,
Where wars shall cease in all the world,
    A waking dream fulfilled.

No force of arms shall there prevail
    Nor justice cease her sway;
Nor shall their loftiest visions fail
    The dreamers of the day.

O Prince of peace, who died to save,
    A lost world to redeem,
And rose in triumph from the grave,
    Behold our waking dream.

Bring, Lord, Your better world to birth,
    Your kingdom, love's domain;
Where peace with God, and peace on earth,
    And peace eternal reign.

955   John Kent   LM
And this Man shall be the peace.
Micah 5:5

Peace by His cross has Jesus made;
The church's everlasting Head
O'er hell and sin has victory won,
And, with a shout, to glory gone.

When o'er thy head the billows roll,
And shades of sin obscure thy soul;
When thou canst no deliverance see,
Yet still this Man thy Peace shall be.

In tribulation's thorny maze,
Or on the mount of sovereign grace,
Or in the fire, or through the sea,
This glorious Man thy Peace shall be.

Yea, when thy eye of faith is dim,
Rest thou on Jesus, sink or swim,
And at His footstool bow the knee,
For Israel's God thy Peace shall be.

956   William Cowper   CM
What doth the LORD require of thee, but to do justly, and to love mercy, and to walk humbly with thy God? *Micah 6:8*

O for a closer walk with God,
    A calm and heavenly frame;
A light to shine upon the road
    That leads me to the Lamb.

Where is the blessedness I knew
    When first I saw the Lord?
Where is the soul-refreshing view
    Of Jesus and His word?

What peaceful hours I then enjoyed,
    How sweet their memory still!
But now I find an aching void
    The world can never fill.

Return, O holy Dove! return,
  Sweet messenger of rest!
I hate the sins that made Thee mourn,
  And drove Thee from my breast.

The dearest idol I have known,
  Whate'er that idol be;
Help me to tear it from Thy throne,
  And worship only Thee.

So shall my walk be close with God,
  Calm and serene my frame;
So purer light shall mark the road
  That leads me to the Lamb.

957   John Dobell   SM
Hear ye the rod, and who hath appointed it.
Micah 6:9

How gracious, and how wise
  Is our chastising God!
And O! how rich the blessings are,
  Which blossom from the rod!

He lifts it up on high,
  With pity in His heart,
That every stroke His children feel,
  May grace and peace impart.

Sweet fruits afflictions bring,
  Like those on Aaron's rod,
They bud and bloom divinely fair,
  Which proves them sent of God.

Dear Father! we consent
  To discipline divine,
And bless the pain that makes our souls
  Still more completely Thine.

Supported by Thy love,
  We tend to realms of peace,
Where every pain shall far remove,
  And every frailty cease.

958   Susannah Harrison   CM
Therefore I will look unto the LORD; I will wait for the God of my salvation: my God will hear me. *Micah 7:7*

My God! for I can call Thee mine,
  My Father and my Friend;
Am I not Thine, for ever Thine?
  To Thee my groans ascend.

My God! how pleasing is the sound!
  What can I wish for more?
In Thee, my God, my soul hath found
  An everlasting store.

My God! I still repeat the cry,
  Bring Thy salvation near;
My God, do Thou my wants supply,
  And manifest Thy care.

My God will hear me when I call,
  My God will send relief;
While Thou, my God, art All in all,
  I cannot yield to grief.

Eternal thanks to Thy great name,
  Whose grace has made me Thine;
Nothing shall put my soul to shame
  While I can call Thee mine.

959   Lucy Whitmore   10 10 10 10
He delighteth in mercy. *Micah 7:18*

Father, again in Jesus' name we meet,
And bow in penitence beneath Thy feet:
Again to Thee our feeble voices raise,
To sue for mercy, and to sing Thy praise.

O we would bless Thee for Thy ceaseless care,
And all Thy works from day to day declare:
Is not our life with hourly mercies crowned?
Does not Thine arm encircle us around?

Alas, unworthy of Thy boundless love,
Too oft with careless feet from Thee we rove;
But now, encouraged by Thy voice, we come,
Returning sinners to a Father's home.

O by that name in whom all fulness dwells,
O by that love which every love excels,
O by that blood so freely shed for sin,
Open blest mercy's gate, and take us in.

960   Samuel Davies   88 88 88
Who is a God like unto Thee, that pardoneth iniquity? *Micah 7:18*

Great God of wonders! all Thy ways
  Are worthy of Thyself divine;
And the bright glories of Thy grace
  Among Thine other wonders shine:

> *Who is a pardoning God like Thee?*
> *Or who has grace so rich and free?*

Pardon from an offended God!
  Pardon for sins of deepest dye!
Pardon bestowed through Jesus' blood!
  Pardon that brings the rebel nigh!

O may this glorious, matchless love,
  This God-like miracle of grace,
Teach mortal tongues, like those above,
  To raise this song of lofty praise:

961   David Denham   11 8 11 8
The LORD hath His way in the whirlwind and in the storm, and the clouds are the dust of His feet. *Nahum 1:3*

The Lord hath His way in the whirlwind and storm,
  The clouds are the dust of His feet;
The whole of His pleasure His hand shall perform,
  And all His intentions complete.

No foe can annoy me, or friend give a smile
  Unless He permit or constrain;
Tho' Satan may tempt and false brethren revile,
  My God will His purpose explain.

False charges against me, though painful to bear,
  In truth may be boldly withstood;
But since they afford me fresh matter for prayer,
  I know they are working for good!

I own I am vile, and repent in the dust,
  More worthy of hell than of heaven;
Yet in the atonement of Jesus I trust,
  Through whom I am freely forgiven.

Since God is my refuge, I must persevere,
  My cause I commit to His care;
Nor will I the tongue of the slanderer fear,
  But give myself wholly to prayer.

Now prostrate before Thee, my glorious Lord,
  Thy precepts, O bind to my heart;
And help me to walk as becometh Thy word,
  Nor from its instructions depart.

962   Jane Crewdson   87 87
Though it tarry, wait for it; because it will surely come, it will not tarry.
Habakkuk 2:3

Lord, we know that Thou art near us,
  Though Thou seem'st to hide Thy face;
And are sure that Thou dost hear us,
  Though no answer we embrace.

Not one promise shall miscarry;
  Not one blessing come too late;
Though the vision long may tarry,
  Give us patience, Lord, to wait!

While withholding, Thou art giving
  In Thine own appointed way;
And while waiting we're receiving
  Blessings suited to our day.

O the wondrous loving-kindness,
  Planning, working out of sight!
Bearing with us in our blindness!
  Out of darkness bringing light.

Weaving blessings out of trials;
  Out of grief evolving bliss:
Answering prayer by wise denials
  When Thy children ask amiss!

And when faith shall end in vision,
  And when prayer is lost in praise;
Then shall love, in full fruition,
  Justify Thy secret ways.

963   Samuel Turner   CM
But the just shall live by His faith.
Habakkuk 2:4

Christ is the Lord our Righteousness,
  (For so the Scripture saith);
And justified, through Him, by grace
  I live by precious faith.

Christ is the only way to God,
  To glory He's the path;
And through rich grace, in that sure road,
  I walk by precious faith.

Christ is the Living Bread from heaven
  Which saves from second death.
And on that Bread to me 'tis given
  To feed by precious faith.

Christ is my Captain, full of might,
  And whilst I dwell on earth,
He will enable me to fight
  The fight of precious faith.

Christ is my Rock, and though my foes
　Display their utmost wrath,
Yet in the power which He bestows
　I stand by precious faith.

Christ is my Guide, and will be so
　Till I resign my breath;
Then shall I bid this world adieu,
　And die in precious faith.

964　Bessie Head　　　　　　98 98
**O LORD, revive Thy work in the midst of the
years.** *Habakkuk 3:2*

O Breath of life, come sweeping through us,
　Revive Thy church with life and power.
O Breath of life, come, cleanse, renew us,
　And fit Thy church to meet this hour.

O Wind of God, come, bend us, break us,
　Till humbly we confess our need;
Then in Thy tenderness remake us,
　Revive, restore; for this we plead.

O Breath of love, come, breathe within us,
　Renewing thought and will and heart:
Come, love of Christ afresh to win us,
　Revive Thy church in every part.

Revive us, Lord! Is zeal abating
　While harvest fields are vast and white?
Revive us, Lord, the world is waiting,
　Equip Thy church to spread the light.

965　William Gadsby (alt)　　66 66 88
**O LORD, revive Thy work in the midst of the
years.** *Habakkuk 3:2*

Great God, to Thee we come,
　And solemnly confess,
Our hearts are prone to roam
　From paths of righteousness;
We view the year already past,
And see great cause to be abashed.

Thy sovereign love and care
　Thus far have brought us on,
'Midst sins, and woes, and fear,
　Thy goodness is made known.
That grace must needs be rich and free,
Which saves such sinful souls as we.

We now begin the year,
　Dependent on Thy grace;
May we possess Thy fear,
　And often see Thy face;
Lord, make us daily live by faith,
Triumphant over sin and death.

Revive Thy work within,
　And make us watch and pray;
Subdue each hateful sin,
　And guide us in Thy way;
In Jesus may we live and rest,
And sweetly lean upon His breast.

ALBERT MIDLANE 1825-1909

966　Albert Midlane　　　　SM
**O LORD, revive Thy work in the midst of the
years.** *Habakkuk 3:2*

Revive Thy work, O Lord!
Thy mighty arm make bare;
Speak with the voice that wakes the dead,
And make Thy people hear!

Revive Thy work, O Lord,
While here to Thee we bow;
Descend, O gracious Lord, descend:
O come and bless us now!

Revive Thy work, O Lord!
Exalt Thy precious name!
And may Thy love in every heart
Be kindled to a flame!

Revive Thy work, O Lord!
And bless to all Thy word!
And may its pure and sacred truth
In living faith be heard!

Revive Thy work, O Lord!
Create soul-thirst for Thee;
And hungering for the bread of life
O may our spirits be!

Revive Thy work, O Lord!
Give Pentecostal showers!
Be Thine the glory, Thine alone!
The blessing, Lord, be ours!

967 John Newton 87 87 D
O LORD, revive Thy work in the midst of the years. *Habakkuk 3:2*

Saviour, visit Thy plantation,
  Grant us Lord, a gracious rain;
All will come to desolation,
  Unless Thou return again:
Keep no longer at a distance,
  Shine upon us from on high;
Left, for want of thine assistance,
  Every plant should droop and die.

Surely, once Thy garden flourished,
  Every part looked bright and green;
Then Thy word our spirits nourished,
  Happy seasons we have seen!
But a drought has since succeeded,
  And a sad decline we see;
Lord, thy help is greatly needed,
  Help can only come from Thee.

Where are those we counted leaders,
  Filled with zeal, and love, and truth?
Old professors, tall as cedars,
  Bright examples to our youth!
Some in whom we once delighted,
  We shall meet no more below;
Some alas! we fear are blighted,
  Scarce a single leaf they show.

Younger plants, the sight how pleasant,
  Covered thick with blossoms stood;
But they cause us grief at present,
  Frosts have nipped them in the bud!
Dearest Saviour, hasten hither,
  Thou canst make us bloom again;
O permit us not to wither,
  None can hope in Thee in vain.

Let our mutual love be fervent,
  Make us prevalent in prayers;
Let each one esteemed Thy servant,
  Shun the world's bewitching snares:
Break the tempter's fatal power,
  Turn each stony heart to flesh;
And begin, from this good hour,
  To revive Thy work afresh.

968 William Cowper 76 76 D
Yet I will rejoice in the LORD, I will joy in the God of my salvation. *Habakkuk 3:18*

Sometimes a light surprises
  The Christian while he sings;
It is the Lord who rises
  With healing in His wings:
When comforts are declining,
  He grants the soul again
A season of clear shining,
  To cheer it after rain.

In holy contemplation,
  We sweetly then pursue
The theme of God's salvation,
  And find it ever new:
Set free from present sorrow,
  We cheerfully can say,
E'en let the unknown morrow
  Bring with it what it may.

It can bring with it nothing
  But He will bear us through;
Who gives the lilies clothing
  Will clothe His people too;
Beneath the spreading heavens,
  No creature but is fed;
And He who feeds the ravens
  Will give His children bread.

Though vine nor fig-tree neither
  Their wonted fruit should bear,
Though all the field should wither,
  Nor flocks nor herds be there,
Yet, God the same abiding,
  His praise shall tune my voice;
For, while in Him confiding,
  I cannot but rejoice.

969 David Denham CM
Therefore wait ye upon Me, saith the LORD. *Zephaniah 3:8*

Wait on the Lord, ye saints, in prayer,
  Whate'er your state or frame;
Wait on the Lord with every care,
  But wait in Jesus' name.

Wait on the Lord in every storm,
  His presence makes a calm;
Wait till He does His will perform,
  Reclining on His arm.

Wait on the Lord in all His ways,
  Encouraged by His word;
Wait on the Lord with songs of praise,
  His mighty acts record.

Wait on the Lord for fresh supplies
  From His abundant store!
Wait, till, with Christ in Paradise,
  The soul can hold no more.

Wait on the Lord, and never fear,
  He'll grace and glory give;
Wait, since the Lord is always near,
  In whom we always live.

Wait on the Lord with heaven in sight,
  And sin and death o'erthrown;
Wait, till, with Jesus crowned with light,
  We sit upon His throne.

970   Benjamin Beddome (alt)   LM
Therefore wait ye upon Me, saith the LORD.
Zephaniah 3:8

God's ways are just, His counsels wise;
No darkness can prevent His eyes;
No thought can fly, nor thing can move,
Unknown to Him that sits above.

He in the thickest darkness dwells;
Performs His works, the cause conceals;
But though His methods are unknown,
Judgment and truth support His throne.

In heaven, and earth, and air, and seas,
He executes His firm decrees;
And by His saints it stands confessed,
That what He does is ever best.

Wait, then, my soul, submissive wait,
Prostrate before His awesome seat;
And, 'midst the terrors of His rod,
Trust in a wise and gracious God.

971   Thomas Kelly   LM
**I will also leave in the midst of thee an afflicted
and poor people, and they shall trust in the
name of the LORD.** *Zephaniah 3:12*

'Poor and afflicted,' Lord, are Thine,
Among the great unfit to shine;
But, though the world may think it strange,
They would not with the world exchange.

'Poor and afflicted,' yes, they are;
Their cup is filled with grief and care;
But He who saved them by His blood,
Makes every sorrow work for good.

'Poor and afflicted;' yet they sing,
For Jesus is their glorious King;
'Through sufferings perfect,' now He reigns,
And shares in all their griefs and pains.

'Poor and afflicted;' but ere long
They'll join the bright celestial throng
Their sufferings then will reach a close,
And heaven afford them sweet repose.

And while they walk the thorny way,
They're often heard to sigh and say,
'Dear Saviour, come; O quickly come,
And take Thy mourning pilgrims home.'

972   John Kent   10 10 11 11
**The Lord thy God in the midst of thee is
mighty; He will save, He will rejoice over thee
with joy; He will rest in His love, He will joy
over thee with singing.** *Zephaniah 3:17*

Salvation by grace, how charming the song!
  With seraphim join the theme to prolong;
'Twas planned by Jehovah in council above,
Who to everlasting shall rest in His love.

This covenant of grace all blessings secures;
  Believers, rejoice, for all things are yours;
And God from His purpose shall never remove,
But love thee, and bless thee, and rest in His love.

But when, like a sheep that strays from the fold,
  To Jesus Thy Lord thy love shall grow cold,
Think not He'll reject thee, howe'er He reprove;
For though He correct thee, He'll rest in His love.

In Jesus, the Lamb, the Father's delight,
  The saints without blame appear in His sight;
And while He in Jesus their souls shall approve,
So long shall Jehovah abide in His love.

973 David Denham CM
I am with you, saith the LORD of hosts.
Haggai 2:4

Jehovah dwells in Zion still,
　Our ever-present Lord!
His ancient covenant to fulfil,
　And magnify His word.

He's with us in His pardoning blood,
　And Holy Spirit given;
He's with us, as our gracious God,
　In Christ, the way to heaven.

He's with us in temptation's hour,
　Fresh succour to impart;
He's with us in His love and power,
　To heal each broken heart.

He's with us in His faithfulness,
　In every fire and flood;
He's with us to correct and bless,
　And working all for good.

He will be with us to sustain
　When heart and flesh shall fail,
And we with Him shall live and reign
　In heaven, within the veil.

974 James Montgomery LM
Consider now, from the day that the
foundation of the LORD'S temple was laid,
consider it. *Haggai 2:18*

This stone to Thee, in faith we lay;
　We build a temple, Lord, to Thee:
Thine eye be open, night and day,
　Here, to protect Thy sanctuary.

Here, when Thy people seek Thy face,
　And dying sinners pray to live;
Hear Thou in heaven, Thy dwelling-place,
　And, when Thou hearest, O forgive.

Here, when Thy messengers proclaim
　The blessed gospel of Thy Son,
Still, by the power of His great name,
　Be mighty signs and wonders done.

Hosanna! to their heavenly King—
　When children's voices raise that song;
Hosanna! let the angels sing,
　And heaven with earth the strain prolong.

But will, indeed, Jehovah deign
　Here to abide no transient Guest?
Here will the great Redeemer reign?
　And here the Holy Spirit rest?

O, may Thy glory ne'er depart!
　Yet choose not, Lord, this house alone;
Thy kingdom come to every heart,
　In every bosom fix Thy throne.

975 John Newton 77 77
Sing and rejoice, O daughter of Zion: for, lo, I
come, and I will dwell in the midst of thee,
saith the LORD. *Zechariah 2:10*

Son of God! Thy people's shield!
　Must we still Thine absence mourn?
Let Thy promise be fulfilled,
　Thou hast said, 'I will return!'

Gracious Leader now appear,
　Shine upon us with Thy light!
Like the spring, when Thou art near,
　Days and suns are doubly bright.

As a mother counts the days
　Till her absent son she see;
Longs and watches, weeps and prays,
　So our spirits long for Thee.

Come, and let us feel Thee nigh,
　Then Thy sheep shall feed in peace;
Plenty bless us from on high,
　Evil from amongst us cease.

With Thy love, and voice, and aid,
　Thou canst every care assuage;
Then we shall not be afraid,
　Tho' the world and Satan rage.

Thus each day for Thee we'll spend,
　While our callings we pursue;
And the thoughts of such a Friend
　Shall each night our joy renew.

Let Thy light be ne'er withdrawn,
　Golden days afford us long!
Thus we pray at early dawn,
　This shall be our evening song.

976 Samuel Medley 10 10 11 11
Is not this a brand plucked out of the fire?
Zechariah 3:2

Of Jesus I sing, now reiging above,
　And to Him I bring this tribute of love:
For O I desire His love to commend,
Who me 'from the fire plucked out as a brand.'

He saw the disgrace and shame I lay in;
　Yet mercy took place, and pardoned my sin:
Sure I must admire the wonderful hand,
Which me 'from the fire plucked out as a brand.'

O what hath He done my soul to set free!
Of sinners not one more favoured than me;
Well may He require my heart and my hand,
Who me 'from the fire plucked out as a brand.'

The time will soon come when I shall appear
In heaven, my home, and worship Thee there;
In glorious attire before Thee I'll stand,
Who me 'from the fire plucked out as a brand.'

977   John Newton   87 87 47
**For behold the stone that I have laid before
Joshua.** *Zechariah 3:9*

Jesus Christ, the Lord's Anointed,
  Who His blood for sinners spilt,
Is the Stone by God appointed,
  And the church is on Him built;
    He delivers
  All who trust Him from their guilt.

Many eyes at once are fixèd
  On a Person so divine;
Love, with awful justice mixèd,
  In His great redemption shine:
    Mighty Jesus!
  Give me leave to call Thee mine.

By the Father's eye approvèd,
  Lo, a voice is heard from heaven,
'Sinners, this is my Belovèd,
  For your ransom freely given:
    All offences
  For His sake shall be forgiven.'

Angels with their eyes pursued Him,
  When He left His glorious throne;
With astonishment they viewed Him,
  Put the form of servant on:
    Angels worshipped
  Him who was on earth unknown.

Satan and his host, amazèd,
  Saw this Stone in Zion laid;
Jesus, though to death abasèd,
  Bruised the subtle serpent's head,
    When, to save us,
  On the cross His blood He shed.

When a guilty sinner sees Him,
  While he looks his soul is healed;
Soon this sight from anguish frees him
  And imparts a pardon sealed:
    May this Saviour
  Be to all our hearts revealed.

978   Isaac Watts   LM
**Not by might, nor by power, but by my Spirit,
saith the LORD of hosts.**
Zechariah 4:6

Eternal Spirit, we confess
And sing the wonders of Thy grace;
Thy power conveys our blessings down
From God the Father and the Son.

Enlightened by Thy heavenly ray,
Our shades and darkness turn to day;
Thy inward teachings make us know
Our danger and our refuge too.

Thy power and glory work within,
And break the chains of reigning sin;
Do our imperious lusts subdue,
And guide our roving feet anew.

The troubled conscience knows Thy voice;
Thy cheering words awake our joys;
Thy words allay the stormy wind,
And calm the surges of the mind.

979   John Dracup   CM
Grace, grace unto it. *Zechariah 4:7*

Free grace to every heaven-born soul
  Will be their constant theme;
Long as eternal ages roll,
  They'll still adore the Lamb.

Free grace alone can wipe the tears
  From our lamenting eyes;
Can raise our souls from guilty fears
  To joy that never dies.

Free grace can death itself outbrave,
  And take its sting away;
Can souls unto the utmost save,
  And them to heaven convey.

Our Saviour, by free grace alone,
  His building shall complete;
With shouting bring forth the head stone,
  Crying, 'Grace, grace to it.'

May I be found a living stone,
  In Salem's streets above;
And help to sing before the throne,
  Free grace and dying love.

980 Joseph Hart   CM
For who hath despised the day of small things? *Zechariah 4:10*

The Lord that made both heaven and earth,
   And was Himself made man,
Lay in the womb, before His birth,
   Contracted to a span.

Behold, from what beginnings small
   Our great salvation rose;
The strength of God is owned by all;
   But who His weakness knows?

Let not the strong the weak despise;
   Their faith, though small, is true;
Though low they seem in others' eyes,
   Their Saviour seemed so too.

Nor meanly of the tempted think;
   For O what tongue can tell
How low the Lord of life must sink,
   Before He vanquished hell?

As in the days of flesh He grew
   In wisdom, stature, grace,
So in the soul that's born anew,
   He keeps a gradual pace.

No less almighty at His birth,
   Than on His throne supreme;
His shoulders held up heaven and earth,
   When Mary held up Him.

981 Samuel Medley   CM
Even He shall build the temple of the LORD; and He shall bear the glory, and shall sit and rule upon His throne.
Zechariah 6:13

Jesus, how bright His glory shines
   In all His works above!
On earth His kind and wise designs
   His church and people love.

He plans the temple of the Lord,
   And all the building rears;
And be His holy name adored,
   He all the glory bears.

The vast materials all He forms,
   Nor love nor power He spares;
He guards the building from all harms,
   And all the glory bears.

In this blest building may my soul
   A living stone appear;
And he, the Builder of the whole,
   Shall all the glory bear.

When He the topmost stone shall bring
   To heaven, to see Him there,
We shall the Builder's praises sing,
   And He the glory bear.

982 Charles Wesley   CM
They made their hearts as an adamant stone.
Zechariah 7:12

Come, O Thou all-victorious Lord,
   Thy power to us make known;
Strike with the hammer of Thy word,
   And break these hearts of stone.

O that we all might now begin
   Our foolishness to mourn,
And turn at once from every sin,
   And to our Saviour turn!

Give us ourselves and Thee to know,
   In this our gracious day;
Repentance unto life bestow,
   And take our sins away.

Conclude us first in unbelief,
   And freely then release;
Fill every soul with sacred grief,
   And then with sacred peace.

Impoverish, Lord, and then relieve,
   And then enrich the poor;
The knowledge of our sickness give,
   The knowledge of our cure.

That blessèd sense of guilt impart,
   And then remove the load;
Trouble, and wash the troubled heart
   In the atoning blood.

Our desperate state through sin declare,
   And speak our sins forgiven;
In perfect holiness prepare,
   And take us up to heaven.

983 Theodulph of Orlèans, tr. J Neale 76 76 D
Thy King cometh unto thee... *Zechariah 9:9*

All glory, laud, and honour
   To Thee, Redeemer, King,
To whom the lips of children
   Made sweet hosannas ring!
Thou art the King of Israel,
   Thou David's royal Son,
Who in the Lord's name comest,
   The King and blessed One!

The people of the Hebrews
  With palms before Thee went;
Our praise and prayer and anthems
  Before Thee we present:
To Thee, before Thy passion,
  They sing their hymns of praise;
To Thee, now high exalted,
  Our melody we raise.

Thou didst accept their praises;
  Accept the prayers we bring,
Who in all good delightest,
  Thou good and gracious King!
All glory, praise, and honour
  To Thee, Redeemer, King,
To whom the lips of children
  Made sweet hosannas ring!

984   John Kent   LM

Turn you to the strong hold, ye prisoners of hope. *Zechariah 9:12*

Prisoners of hope, to Jesus turn;
  He's a Stronghold, ordained for you;
Gird up your loins, and cease to mourn,
  And to the Lamb your way pursue.

Though fast in Sinai's fetters bound,
  Held in the deepest bondage there,
Yet 'tis the gospel's joyful sound:
  'Sinners, to this Stronghold repair.'

Turn hither, ye who once were blessed
  With life the ways of God to run;
But now whose hearts are sore distressed,
  Because those golden hours are gone.

Turn hither, ye who oft have tried,
  By works, salvation to obtain;
See royal robes your shame to hide,
  And blood that takes out every stain.

His name a tower for strength renowned,
  Shall save His people from their sin;
Free grace shall o'er their sins abound;
  Ye fearing, doubting souls, turn in.

985   William Hammond   10 10 11 11

Turn you to the strong hold, ye prisoners of hope. *Zechariah 9:12*

Ye prisoners of hope, o'erwhelmèd with grief,
  To Jesus look up for certain relief;
There's no condemnation in Jesus the Lord,
But strong consolation His grace doth afford

Should justice appear a merciless foe,
  Yet be of good cheer, and soon shall you know
That sinners confessing their wickedness past,
A plentiful blessing of pardon shall taste.

Then dry up your tears, ye children of grief,
  For Jesus appears to give you relief;
If you are returning to Jesus, your Friend,
Your sighing and mourning in singing shall end.

'None will I cast out who come,' saith the Lord;
  Why, then, do you doubt? Lay hold of His word;
Ye mourners of Zion, be bold to believe,
For ever rely on your Saviour and live.

986   Charles Wesley   88 88 88

And I will strengthen them in the LORD; and they shall walk up and down in His name, saith the LORD. *Zechariah 10:12*

Thou hidden source of calm repose,
  Thou all-sufficient love divine;
My help and refuge from my foes,
  Secure I am, if Thou art mine:
And lo! from sin and grief and shame,
I hide me, Jesus, in Thy name.

Thy mighty name salvation is
  And keeps my happy soul above;
Comfort it brings, and power and peace
  And joy and everlasting love:
To me, with Thy dear name, are given
Pardon and holiness and heaven.

Jesus, my all in all Thou art,
  My rest in toil, mine ease in pain;
The medicine of my broken heart;
  In war, my peace; in loss, my gain;
My smile beneath the tyrant's frown;
In shame, my glory and my crown.

In want, my plentiful supply;
  In weakness, mine almighty power;
In bonds, my perfect liberty;
  My light in Satan's darkest hour;
My help and stay whene'er I call;
My life in death; my heaven, my all.

987   Charles Wesley   CM
And I will strengthen them in the LORD; and they shall walk up and down in His name, saith the LORD. *Zechariah 10:12*

Through Christ, when we together came,
  In singleness of heart,
We met, O Jesus, in Thy name,
  And in Thy name we part.

We part in body, not in mind,
  Our minds continue one:
And each to each in Jesus joined,
  We happily go on.

988   Joseph Hart   SM
I fed the flock. *Zechariah 11:7*

Here hungry souls appear,
And eat celestial bread;
The poor and needy banquet here,
With royal dainties fed.

Here thirsty souls approach,
And drink immortal wine;
The entertainment is for such,
Prepared by grace divine.

God bids us bring no price,
The feast is furnished free:
His bounteous hand the poor supplies,
And who more poor than we?

His Spirit from above
Our Father sends us down,
And looks with everlasting love
On all that love His Son.

989   Joseph Hart   CM
And they shall look upon Me whom they have pierced, and they shall mourn for Him, as one mourneth. *Zechariah 12:10*

Lord, who can hear of all Thy woe,
  Thy groans and dying cries,
And not feel tears of sorrow flow,
  And sighs of pity rise?

Much harder than the hardest stone
  That man's hard heart must be;
Alas! dear Lord, with shame we own
  That just such hearts have we.

The symbols of Thy flesh and blood
  Will (as they have been oft)
With unrelenting hearts be viewed,
  Unless Thou make them soft.

Dissolve these rocks; call forth the stream,
  Make every eye a sluice;
Let none be slow to weep for Him,
  Who wept so much for us.

And while we mourn, and sing, and pray,
  And feed on bread and wine,
Lord, let Thy quickening Spirit convey
  The substance with the sign.

990   James Allen, W Shirley   87 87 D
And they shall look upon Me whom they have pierced, and they shall mourn for Him, as one mourneth. *Zechariah 12:10*

Sweet the moments, rich in blessing,
  Which before the cross I spend,
Life, and health, and peace possessing
  From the sinner's dying Friend;
May I sit for ever viewing
  Mercy's streams in streams of blood;
Precious drops my soul bedewing,
  Plead and claim my peace with God!

Truly blessèd is this station,
  Low before His cross to lie,
While I see divine compassion
  Beaming in His languid eye.
Here it is I find my heaven,
  While upon the Lamb I gaze;
Love I much? I'm much forgiven;
  I'm a miracle of grace.

Love and grief my heart dividing,
  With my tears His feet I'll bathe;
Constant still in faith abiding,
  Life deriving from His death.
May I still enjoy this feeling,
  In all need to Jesus go;
Prove His wounds each day more healing,
  And Himself more deeply know!

991   John Newton   CM
And they shall look upon Me whom they have pierced, and they shall mourn for Him, as one mourneth. *Zechariah 12:10*

In evil long I took delight,
  Unawed by shame or fear,
Till a new object struck my sight,
  And stopped my wild career.

I saw One hanging on a tree,
  In agonies and blood,
Who fixed His languid eyes on me,
  As near His cross I stood.

Sure never till my latest breath
   Can I forget that look;
It seemed to charge me with His death,
   Though not a word He spoke.

My conscience felt and owned the guilt,
   And plunged me in despair;
I saw my sins His blood had spilt,
   And helped to nail Him there.

A second look He gave, which said,
   'I freely all forgive;
This blood is for thy ransom paid;
   I die that thou may'st live.'

It heals the soul of feverish heat,
And helps a pulse with grace to beat;
The fretful look, the wanton eye,
And lordly self before it fly.

No spring like this makes lepers whole,
Not that renowned Bethesda's pool,
Nor Siloam's stream, nor Jordan's flood,
Were altogether half so good.

Fast by this fountain let me stay,
And drink, and wash my sores away;
If but a moment I depart,
Sick is my head, and faint my heart.

992   William Cowper   CM
In that day there shall be a fountain opened.
Zechariah 13:1

There is a fountain filled with blood,
   Drawn from Immanuel's veins,
And sinners plunged beneath that flood,
   Lose all their guilty stains.

The dying thief rejoiced to see
   That fountain in his day;
And there have I, as vile as he,
   Washed all my sins away.

Dear dying Lamb! Thy precious blood
   Shall never lose its power,
Till all the ransomed church of God
   Be saved, to sin no more.

E'er since, by faith, I saw the stream
   Thy flowing wounds supply,
Redeeming love has been my theme,
   And shall be till I die.

But when this lisping, stammering tongue
   Lies silent in the grave,
Then, in a nobler, sweeter song,
   I'll sing Thy power to save.

993   John Cennick   LM
In that day there shall be a fountain opened.
Zechariah 13:1

A fountain! cries the man of God,
A fountain with a purple flood;
A fountain opened for the poor,
Where sickly souls may find a cure.

It softens well the heart of stone,
And kindly knits a broken bone,
Restoring hearing, speech, and sight,
And puts all guilty fears to flight.

994   Josiah Conder   87 87 D
In that day there shall be a fountain opened.
Zechariah 13:1

Praise the God of all creation,
   Praise the Father's boundless love;
Praise the Lamb, our expiation,
   Priest and King enthroned above.
Praise the Fountain of salvation,
   Him by whom our spirits live;
Undivided adoration
   To the One Jehovah give.

995   William Gadsby   77 77
**But it shall come to pass, that at evening time
it shall be light.** *Zechariah 14:7*

What am I, and where am I?
   Strange myself and paths appear;
Scarce can lift a thought on high,
   Or drop one heart-feeling tear.

Yet I feel I'm not at home,
   But know not which way to move:
Lest I farther yet should roam
   From the Object of my love.

Some small glimmering light I have,
   Yet too dark to see my way;
Jesus' presence still I crave;
   When, O when will it be day?

Is the evening time at hand
   Will it then indeed be light?
Will the sun its beams extend:
   Chase away the shades of night?

Then His love is rich and free;
   Jesus, let me feel its power,
And my soul will cling to Thee,
   Love and praise Thee and adore.

996   John Kent   CM

For the LORD, the God of Israel, saith that He hateth putting away. *Malachi 2:16*

Let Zion songs of triumph sing;
  Let gladness crown the day;
Jehovah is her God and King,
  He hates to put away.

'Graved on His hands divinely fair,
  Who did their ransom pay,
The golden letters still appear;
  He hates to put away.

Think not that He'll Thy cry reject,
  Or spurn Thy humble plea;
He hears the groans of His elect,
  And hates to put away.

When loathsome in thy sins and blood,
  He did thy state survey,
And for a stranger Surety stood;
  He hates to put away.

Salvation's of the Lord alone;
  Grace is a shoreless sea;
In heaven there's ne'er a vacant throne;
  He hates to put away.

997   Thomas Kelly   CM

Behold, I will send my messenger, and He shall prepare the way before me.
Malachi 3:1

He comes; the Saviour full of grace,
  By ancient prophets sung;
The smile of mercy on His face,
  And truth upon His tongue.

In Him the world no beauty sees,
  No form nor comeliness;
Rejected and despised He is,
  And plunged in deep distress.

But there's a people taught by grace
  To know His matchless worth;
They own Him, though accounted base,
  And show His praises forth.

They own Him as the Lord of all,
  Their Saviour and their God;
Before His feet they prostrate fall—
  The purchase of His blood.

998   John Newton   LM

And they shall be Mine, saith the LORD of hosts, in that day when I make up My jewels.
Malachi 3:17

Kindred in Christ, for His dear sake,
  A hearty welcome here receive:
May we together now partake
  The joys which only He can give.

To you and us by grace it's given
  To know the Saviour's precious name;
And shortly we shall meet in heaven,
  Our hope, our way, our end the same.

May He by whose kind care we meet,
  Send His good Spirit from above,
Make our communications sweet
  And cause our hearts to burn with love.

Forgotten be each worldly theme
  When Christians see each other thus:
We only wish to speak of Him
  Who lived and died and reigns for us.

We'll talk of all He did and said
  And suffered for us here below;
The path He marked for us to tread
  And what He's doing for us now.

Thus, as the moments pass away,
  We'll love and wonder and adore;
And hasten on the glorious day
  When we shall meet to part no more.

999   William Cushing   Irregular

And they shall be Mine, saith the LORD of hosts, in that day when I make up My jewels.
Malachi 3:17

When He cometh, when He cometh
  To make up His jewels,
All His jewels, precious jewels,
  His loved and His own.

Like the stars of the morning,
  His bright crown adorning,
They shall shine in their beauty,
  Bright gems for His crown.

He will gather, He will gather
  The gems for His kingdom;
All the pure ones, all the bright ones,
  His loved and His own.

Little children, little children,
  Who love their Redeemer,
Are the jewels, precious jewels,
  His loved and His own.

1000 William Gadsby SM

But unto you that fear My name shall the Sun of righteousness arise with healing in His wings. *Malachi 4:2*

Jehovah is my Sun;
  He shines into my heart;
Though clouds do often interpose,
  My Sun shall not depart.

This Sun has warmed my soul,
  When chilled by sin and death;
Its beams have shone with strength and heat,
  And made me strong in faith.

Whatever be my frame,
  My Sun no change can know;
Though I am dark, He still remains
  My light and glory too.

Nor death, nor sin, nor hell,
  Shall make Him cease to shine;
And, though I cannot always feel
  His beams, He's ever mine.

'Tis no precarious light
  That shines on Zion's hill;
'Tis God, essential light itself,
  And therefore cannot fail.

1001 Augustus Toplady CM

But unto you that fear My name shall the Sun of righteousness arise with healing in His wings. *Malachi 4:2*

Thou Sun of Righteousness arise,
  Shine, glorious source of light.
And with the brightness of Thy rays
  Now chase away the night.

Confused and blind, though oft I am,
  And prone to go astray;
Bid me receive my sight and I
  Shall clearly see my way.

Impart a ray of heavenly light,
  Pure fervent love inspire;
And may the Holy Spirit aid,
  And fan the sacred fire.

The captive at Thy word shall be
  From every chain released;
The broken heart shall sing for joy,
  The troubled sea shall rest.

Let not my hopes be overcast
  With shadows of despair;
Dart through my soul Thy quickening beam,
  And shine for ever there.

1002 Charles Wesley CM

But unto you that fear My name shall the Sun of righteousness arise with healing in His wings. *Malachi 4:2*

Eternal Sun of Righteousness,
  Display Thy beams divine,
And cause the glories of Thy face
  Upon my heart to shine.

Light in Thy light O may I see,
  Thy grace and mercy prove,
Revived and cheered and blessed by Thee,
  The God of pardoning love.

Lift up Thy countenance serene,
  And let Thy happy child
Behold, without a cloud between,
  The Godhead reconciled.

That all-comprising peace bestow
  On me, through grace forgiven;
The joys of holiness below,
  And then the joys of heaven.

HYMNS ON THE NEW TESTAMENT

Matthew

1003   Charles Wesley   CM
**Thou shalt call His name JESUS: for He shall
save His people from their sins.** *Matthew 1:21*

Jesus! the name high over all,
  In hell, or earth, or sky;
Angels and men before it fall,
  And devils fear and fly.

Jesus! the name to sinners dear,
  The name to sinners given;
It scatters all their guilty fear,
  It turns their hell to heaven.

Jesus! the prisoner's fetters breaks,
  And bruises Satan's head;
Power into strengthless souls it speaks,
  And life into the dead.

His only righteousness I show,
  His saving grace proclaim;
'Tis all my business here below
  To cry: 'Behold the Lamb!'

Happy, if with my latest breath
  I might but gasp His name;
Preach Him to all, and cry in death:
  'Behold, behold the Lamb!'

1004   Philips Brooks   DCM
They shall call His name Immanuel.
Matthew 1:23

O little town of Bethlehem,
  How still we see thee lie!
Above thy deep and dreamless sleep
  The silent stars go by:
Yet in thy dark streets shineth
  The everlasting Light;
The hopes and fears of all the years
  Are met in thee tonight.

O morning stars, together
  Proclaim the holy birth,
And praises sing to God the King,
  And peace to men on earth;
For Christ is born of Mary;
  And, gathered all above,
While mortals sleep, the angels keep
  Their watch of wondering love.

How silently, how silently,
  The wondrous gift is given!
So God imparts to human hearts
  The blessings of His heaven.
No ear may hear His coming;
  But in this world of sin,
Where meek souls will receive Him still
  The dear Christ enters in.

O holy Child of Bethlehem,
  Descend to us, we pray;
Cast out our sin, and enter in;
  Be born in us today.
We hear the Christmas angels
  The great glad tidings tell;
O come to us, abide with us,
  Our Lord Immanuel.

1005   Samuel Medley   LM
They shall call His name Immanuel.
Matthew 1:23

Now let a song of sacred joy
Our voices and our hearts employ;
While we on earth attempt to tell
The glories of Immanuel.

Seraphs and angels round His throne
Unite to make His glories known;
Yet does He all their praise excel,
So great is our Immanuel.

For us He left the worlds above
On wings of everlasting love.
With sinful folk on earth to dwell,
And thus appeared Immanuel.

Hail, great Redeemer, all divine:
In whom eternal glories shine;
With joy to all the world we tell
Our Jesus is Immanuel.

Accept, dear Lord! the highest praise
Our hearts and voices here can raise.
With Thee ere long we hope to dwell,
And ever sing Immanuel.

1006   John Rippon   77 77
They shall call His name Immanuel.
Matthew 1:23

God with us! O glorious name!
Let it shine in endless fame;
God and man in Christ unite;
O, mysterious depth and height!

God with us! His mighty love
Brought Him from His courts above;
Now, ye saints, His grace admire,
Swell the song with holy fire.

God with us! but tainted not
With the first transgressor's blot;
Yet did He our sins sustain,
Bear the guilt, the curse, the pain!

God with us! O wondrous grace!
We shall see Him face to face;
Then shall we Immanuel sing,
As we ought, our God and King.

1007   Joseph Hart   CM
**There came wise men from the east to
Jerusalem.** *Matthew 2:1*

Come ye redeemèd of the Lord,
    Your grateful tribute bring;
And celebrate, with one accord,
    The birthday of our King.

Let us with humble hearts repair
    (Faith will point out the road)
To little Bethlehem, and there
    Adore our infant God.

In swaddling bands the Saviour view!
    Let none His weakness scorn;
The feeblest heart shall hell subdue,
    Where Jesus Christ is born.

No pomp adorns, no sweets perfume
    The place where Christ is laid;
A stable serves Him for His room,
    A manger is His bed.

The crowded inn, like sinners' hearts,
    (O ignorance extreme!)
For other guests, of various sorts,
    Had room; but none for Him.

But see what different thoughts arise
    In our and angels' breasts;
To hail His birth *they* left the skies,
    We lodged Him with the beasts!

Yet let believers cease their fears,
    Nor envy heavenly powers;
If sinless innocence be theirs,
    Redemption all is ours.

1008   James Montgomery   87 87 47
Where is He that is born King of the Jews?
Matthew 2:2

Angels from the realms of glory,
    Wing your flight o'er all the earth;
Ye who sang creation's story,
    Now proclaim Messiah's birth;

        Come and worship,
    Worship Christ, the new-born King.

Shepherds in the field abiding,
    Watching o'er their flocks by night;
God with man is now residing,
    Yonder shines the infant-light:

Sages, leave your contemplations;
    Brighter visions beam afar;
Seek the great Desire of nations;
    Ye have seen His natal star.

Saints before the altar bending,
    Watching long in hope and fear,
Suddenly the Lord, descending,
    In His temple shall appear;

1009   Reginald Heber   11 10 11 10 (dactylic)
Where is He that is born King of the Jews?
Matthew 2:2

Brightest and best of the sons of the morning,
    Dawn on our darkness, and lend us thine aid;
Star of the East, the horizon adorning,
    Guide where our infant Redeemer is laid.

Cold on His cradle the dew-drops are shining;
    Low lies His head with the beasts of the stall;
Angels adore Him in slumber reclining,
    Maker, and Monarch, and Saviour of all.

Say, shall we yield Him, in costly devotion,
    Odours of Edom, and offerings divine,
Gems of the mountain and pearls of the ocean,
    Myrrh from the forest or gold from the mine?

Vainly we offer each ample oblation,
    Vainly with gifts would His favour secure;
Richer by far is the heart's adoration,
    Dearer to God are the prayers of the poor.

Brightest and best of the sons of the morning,
Dawn on our darkness, and lend us thine aid;
Star of the East, the horizon adorning,
Guide where our infant Redeemer is laid.

1010 Traditional 17th Cent. Irregular
**Lo, the star, which they saw in the east, went
before them, till it came and stood over where
the young Child was.**
Matthew 2:9

The first Nowell the angel did say
Was to certain poor shepherds in fields as they
lay;
In fields where they lay keeping their sheep,
On a cold winter's night that was so deep.

*Nowell, Nowell, Nowell, Nowell,
Born is the King of Israel.*

They lookèd up and saw a star,
Shining in the East, beyond them far,
And to the earth it gave great light,
And so it continued both day and night.

And by the light of that same star,
Three wise men came from country far;
To seek for a King was their intent,
And to follow the star wherever it went.

This star drew nigh to the North-West,
O'er Bethlehem it took its rest,
And there it did both stop and stay,
Right over the place where Jesus lay.

Then entered in those wise men three
Full reverently on bended knee,
And offered there, in His presence,
Their gold, and myrrh, and frankincense.

Then let us all with one accord
Sing praises to our heavenly Lord,
That hath made heaven and earth of nought,
And with His blood mankind hath bought.

1011 William Dix 77 77 77
**When they saw the star, they rejoiced with
exceeding great joy.** *Matthew 2:10*

As with gladness men of old
Did the guiding star behold,
   As with joy they hailed its light,
   Leading onward, beaming bright—
So, most gracious Lord, may we
Evermore be led to Thee.

As with joyful steps they sped,
Saviour, to Thy lowly bed,
   There to bend the knee before
   Thee, whom heaven and earth adore—
So may we with willing feet
Ever seek the mercy-seat.

As they offered gifts most rare
At Thy cradle rude and bare—
   So may we with holy joy,
   Pure, and free from sin's alloy,
All our costliest treasures bring,
Christ, to Thee, our heavenly King.

Holy Jesus, every day,
Keep us in the narrow way;
   And, when earthly things are past,
   Bring our ransomed souls at last
Where they need no star to guide,
Where no clouds Thy glory hide.

In the heavenly country bright
Need they no created light;
   Thou its light, its joy, its crown,
   Thou its sun which goes not down;
There for ever may we sing
Hallelujahs to our King.

1012 German 15th Cent., tr. Percy Dearmer
76 77 Irregular
**They saw the young Child with Mary His
mother, and fell down, and worshipped Him.**
Matthew 2:11

Unto us a Boy is born!
   King of all creation,
Came He to a world forlorn,
   The Lord of every nation.

Cradled in a stall was He
   With sleepy cows and asses;
But the very beasts could see
   That He all men surpasses.

Herod then with fear was filled:
   'A prince,' he said, 'in Jewry!'
All the little boys he killed
   At Bethlehem in his fury.

Now may Mary's Son, who came
   So long ago to love us,
Lead us all with hearts aflame
   Unto the joys above us.

Alpha and Omega He!
   Let the organ thunder,
While the choir with peals of glee
   Doth rend the air asunder!

1013   Charles Wesley   888 D
**He shall baptize you with the Holy Ghost, and
with fire.** *Matthew 3:11*

Come, Holy Ghost, all-quickening fire,
Come, and my hallowed heart inspire,
   Sprinkled with the atoning blood;
Now to my soul Thyself reveal,
Thy mighty working let me feel,
   And know that I am born of God.

Humble, and teachable, and mild,
O may I, as a little child,
   My lowly Master's steps pursue!
Be anger to my soul unknown,
Hate, envy, jealousy, be gone;
   In love create Thou all things new.

Let earth no more my heart divide,
With Christ may I be crucified,
   To Thee with my whole soul aspire;
Dead to the world and all its toys,
Its idle pomp, and fading joys,
   Be Thou alone my one desire!

My will be swallowed up in Thee;
Light in Thy light still may I see,
   Beholding Thee with open face;
Called the full power of faith to prove,
Let all my hallowed heart be love,
   And all my ransomed life be praise.

1014   James Montgomery   LM
**He shall baptize you with the Holy Ghost, and
with fire.** *Matthew 3:11*

Jesus, our best-belovèd Friend,
   Draw out our souls in pure desire;
Jesus, in love to us descend,
   Baptize us with Thy Spirit's fire.

On Thy redeeming name we call,
   Poor and unworthy though we be;
Pardon and sanctify us all;
   Let each Thy full salvation see.

Our souls and bodies we resign
   To fear and follow Thy commands;
O take our hearts, our hearts are Thine,
   Accept the service of our hands.

Firm, faithful, watching unto prayer,
   May we Thy blessèd will obey,
Toil in Thy vineyard here, and bear
   The heat and burden of the day.

Yet, Lord, for us a resting-place
   In heaven at Thy right hand prepare;
And till we see Thee face to face
   Be all our conversation there.

1015   John Fellows   CM
**Then cometh Jesus from Galilee to Jordan
unto John, to be baptized of him.**
Matthew 3:13

Dear Lord! and will Thy pardoning love
   Embrace a wretch so vile?
Wilt Thou my load of guilt remove,
   And bless me with Thy smile?

Hast Thou the cross for me endured,
   And all its shame despised?
And shall I be ashamed, O Lord,
   With Thee to be baptized?

Didst Thou the great example lead
   In Jordan's swelling flood?
And shall my pride disdain the deed
   That's worthy of my God?

Dear Lord, the ardour of Thy love
   Reproves my cold delays;
And now my willing footsteps move
   In Thy delightful ways.

1016   William Gadsby   66 66 88
**Then cometh Jesus from Galilee to Jordan
unto John, to be baptized of him.**
Matthew 3:13

With wonder and with love,
   We at Thy courts appear;
Thy ways our hearts approve,
   And Thy great name revere;
We own the Lamb, our Leader wise,
Nor would we dare His ways despise.

What Jesus does command,
   His children should obey;
He's King in Zion's land,
   And does His sceptre sway;
Let Zion, then, with one accord,
Obey the precepts of her Lord.

Can anything be mean,
   That's worthy of our God?
The King Himself was seen
   In Jordan's swelling flood;
And shall the subject scorn to tread
The path the King Himself has made?

Come, fill our souls with love,
   With faith, and peace, and joy,
Nor let the price of blood
   Against her God reply;
Dear Father, draw, and we will run,
In sweet obedience to Thy Son.

1017   Samuel Deacon   CM
**Then cometh Jesus from Galilee to Jordan
unto John, to be baptized of him.**
Matthew 3:13

Behold the Prince of glory go
   To be baptized by John,
While Jordon's honoured waters flow,
   Around God's holy One.

Though many memorable things
   Distinguished Jordan's shore,
It never had the King of kings
   Beneath its waves before.

The Holy Spirit, like a dove,
   Comes with His feathers spread,
Down from the shining realms of love,
   And settles on His head.

Now speaks the Father from His throne
   (Be earth and heaven amazed),
'Jesus is My belovèd Son,
   In whom I am well pleased.'

And shall not we behold this fact
   With wonder and delight
If God approve, we boldly act,
   The ordinance must be right,

1018   William Williams   87 87 47
**The people which sat in darkness saw great
light.** *Matthew 4:16*

O'er the gloomy hills of darkness
   Look, my soul; be still, and gaze;
All the promises do travail
   With a glorious day of grace;
     Blessèd jubilee!
Let Thy glorious morning dawn.

Kingdoms wide that sit in darkness,
   Grant them, Lord, Thy glorious light;
And from Eastern coast to Western
   May the morning chase the night,
     And redemption,
Freely purchased, win the day.

May the glorious day approaching,
   End their night of sin and shame;
And the everlasting gospel
   Spread abroad Thy holy name
     O'er the borders
Of the great Immanuel's land.

Fly abroad, thou mighty gospel,
   Win and conquer, never cease:
May Thy lasting, wide dominions
   Multiply and still increase;
     Sway Thy sceptre
Saviour, all the world around.

1019   Cecil Alexander   87 87
**And He saith unto them, Follow Me, and I will
make you fishers of men.**
Matthew 4:19

Jesus calls us! O'er the tumult
   Of our life's wild, restless sea,
Day by day His sweet voice soundeth,
   Saying, 'Christian, follow Me.'

As of old apostles heard it
   By the Galilean lake,
Turned from home and toil and kindred,
   Leaving all for His dear sake.

Jesus calls us from the worship
   Of the vain world's golden store:
From each idol that would keep us,
   Saying, 'Christian, love Me more.'

In our joys and in our sorrows,
   Days of toil and hours of ease,
Still He calls, in cares and pleasures,
   'Christian, love Me more than these.'

Jesus calls us, by Thy mercies,
   Saviour, may we hear Thy call,
Give our hearts to Thy obedience,
   Serve and love Thee best of all.

1020   Edward Plumptre   DCM
**And they brought unto Him all sick
people...and He healed them.**
Matthew 4:24

Thine arm, O Lord, in days of old,
   Was strong to heal and save;
It triumphed o'er disease and death,
   O'er darkness and the grave,
To Thee they went—the blind, the dumb,
   The palsied, and the lame,
The leper with his tainted life,
   The sick with fevered frame.

And, lo, Thy touch brought life and health,
   Gave speech, and strength, and sight;
And youth renewed and frenzy calmed
   Owned Thee, the Lord of light:
And now, O Lord, be near to bless,
   As mighty as before,
In crowded street, by restless couch,
   As by Gennesaret's shore.

Be Thou our great Deliverer still,
   Thou Lord of life and death;
Restore and quicken, soothe and bless,
   With Thine almighty breath;
To hands that work and eyes that see
   Give wisdom's heavenly lore,
That whole and sick, and weak and strong,
   May praise Thee evermore.

1021   Godfrey Thring   87 87 77
**And they brought unto Him all sick people and
He healed them.**
Matthew 4:24

Thou to whom the sick and dying
   Ever came, nor came in vain,
Still with healing words replying
   To the wearied cry of pain,
Hear us, Jesus, as we meet,
Suppliants at Thy mercy-seat.

Still the weary, sick and dying
   Need a brother's, sister's care;
On Thy higher help relying,
   May we now their burden share,
Bringing all our offerings meet,
Suppliants at Thy mercy-seat.

May each child of Thine be willing,
   Willing both in hand and heart,
All the law of love fulfilling,
   Ever comfort to impart,
Ever bringing offerings meet,
Suppliant to Thy mercy-seat.

1022   Anne Steele   LM
**Blessed are the poor in spirit: for theirs is the
kingdom of heaven.** *Matthew 5:3*

Ye humble souls, complain no more;
Let faith survey your future store.
How happy, how divinely blest,
The sacred words of truth attest.

In vain the sons of wealth and pride
Despise your lot, your hope deride;
In vain they boast their little stores;
Trifles are theirs, a kingdom yours.

A kingdom of immense delight,
Where health, and peace, and joy unite;
Where undeclining pleasures rise,
And every wish has full supplies.

A kingdom which can ne'er decay,
While time sweeps earthly thrones away;
The state which power and truth sustain,
Unmoved for ever must remain.

There shall your eyes with rapture view
The glorious Friend that died for you,
That died to ransom, died to raise
To crowns of joy and songs of praise.

Jesus! to Thee I breathe my prayer;
Reveal, confirm my interest there;
Whate'er my humble lot below,
This, this my soul desires to know.

1023   Samuel Medley   LM
**Blessed are the poor in spirit: for theirs is the
kingdom of heaven.** *Matthew 5:3*

How blessed are they who truly see
Their emptiness and poverty;
Whose souls are humbled in the dust,
And who in Jesus only trust!

Glad they renounce their former pride,
And wholly in His name confide;
Only in Him they make their boast,
Who came to seek and save the lost.

They're vile and poor in their own eyes,
But Jesus' love they highly prize;
They never think they're laid too low
If Jesus on them pity show.

To be the meanest they're content,
If Jesus but their souls present
With pardoning grace and heavenly love,
To fit them for the joys above.

These are the souls whom Christ will bless
With all the riches of His grace;
And these are they who soon shall rise
To a bright kingdom in the skies.

1024 Isaac Watts LM
Blessed are the poor in spirit: for theirs is the kingdom of heaven. *Matthew 5:3*

Blest are the humble souls that see
Their emptiness and poverty;
Treasures of grace to them are given,
And crowns of joy laid up in heaven.

Blest are the men of broken heart,
Who mourn for sin with inward smart;
The blood of Christ divinely flows,
A healing balm for all their woes.

Blest are the meek, who stand afar
From rage and passion, noise and war;
God will secure their happy state,
And plead their cause against the great.

Blest are the souls that thirst for grace,
Hunger and long for righteousness;
They shall be well supplied and fed,
With living streams and living bread.

Blest are the men whose hearts do move
And melt with sympathy and love;
From Christ the Lord shall they obtain
Like sympathy and love again.

Blest are the pure, whose hearts are clean
From the defiling powers of sin;
With endless pleasure they shall see
A God of spotless purity.

Blest are the men of peaceful life,
Who quench the coals of growing strife;
They shall be called the heirs of bliss,
The sons of God, the God of peace.

Blest are the sufferers who partake
Of pain and shame for Jesus' sake;
Their souls shall triumph in the Lord.
Glory and joy are their reward.

1025 Samuel Medley LM
Blessed are they that mourn: for they shall be comforted. *Matthew 5:4*

Jesus the glorious Head of grace,
Knows every saint's peculiar case;
What sorrows by their souls are borne,
And how for sin they daily mourn.

He knows how deep their groanings are,
And what their secret sighs declare;
And, for their comfort, has expressed
That all such mourning souls are blessed.

They're blessed on earth, for 'tis by grace
They see and know their mournful case;
Blessed mourners! they shall shortly rise
To endless comfort in the skies.

There all their mourning days shall cease,
And they be filled with joy and peace;
Comforts eternal they shall prove,
And dwell for ever in His love.

Dear Lord, may I a mourner be,
Over my sins and after Thee;
And when my mourning days are o'er,
Enjoy Thy comforts evermore.

1026 Charles Wesley 77 77
Blessed are they that mourn: for they shall be comforted. *Matthew 5:4*

Calmer of my troubled heart,
Bid my unbelief depart;
Speak, and all my sorrows cease;
Speak, and all my soul is peace.

Comfort me, whene'er I mourn,
With the hope of Thy return;
And, till I Thy glory see,
Help me to believe in Thee.

1027 Samuel Medley LM
Blessed are the meek: for they shall inherit the earth. *Matthew 5:5*

Jesus, the holy Lamb of God,
Who all the paths of meekness trod,
To copy Him, O may we seek,
Who in His word has blessed the meek.

Meekness, that bright celestial grace,
Shone in the Saviour's lovely face;
Meekness through all His conduct ran,
The glorious God! the wondrous Man!

O that our souls like Him may be
From pride and wrathful passion free;
And every word and action speak,
That we, like Him, are truly meek.

Meek souls are of a heavenly birth,
And such are truly blest on earth;
In Christ alone they comfort seek,
Who blesses and who loves the meek.

Jesus, to my poor sinful heart
This grace of meekness, O impart!
Fain would I, Lord, though poor and weak,
Be like Thyself, in all things meek.

1028   Samuel Medley   LM
Blessed are they which do hunger and thirst after righteousness: for they shall be filled.
Matthew 5:6

Jesus those happy souls does bless,
Who hunger for His righteousness;
Who seek the smilings of His face,
And thirst for fresh supplies of grace.

They cannot here contented live
On all the dainties earth can give;
Their souls can feast on nothing less
Than Christ's eternal righteousness.

Some sweet foretastes they have below,
But the bright world, to which they go,
Will them a glorious banquet yield;
There shall their souls be ever filled.

May this my blest experience be;
To hunger, Lord, and thirst for Thee,
And on Thy righteousness to live,
Which can both food and comfort give!

Then when at death my soul shall rise
To the blest banquet in the skies,
I shall partake the heavenly store,
And feast and sing for evermore.

1029   Samuel Medley   LM
Blessed are the merciful: for they shall obtain mercy. *Matthew 5:7*

Jesus to Thee our praise we bring;
Thy mercy, all divine, we sing;
Thou ever merciful and kind.
In Thee poor sinners mercy find.

When they on Thy dear name believe,
What wondrous mercy they receive!
This makes them merciful and kind,
Because in Thee they mercy find.

O to us all, dear Lord, impart
A merciful and tender heart;
And by our practice here attest
That Thou the merciful hast blest.

1030   Samuel Medley   LM
Blessed are the pure in heart: for they shall see God. *Matthew 5:8*

Jesus, before Thee I appear;
My earnest supplications hear;
Fountain of every grace Thou art,
O give me purity of heart.

The pure in heart Thy lips have blest;
They shall see God, and in Him rest;
This blessing, Lord, to me impart,
A real purity of heart.

I hate, dear Lord, my inbred sin;
It dwells, and O, it works within,
I feel its deep envenomed dart,
Yet long for purity of heart.

Let all my conduct be sincere;
Thy grace in heart and life appear;
Then heart and life shall ever be
A unison of praise to Thee.

Bring me, at last, by sovereign love,
Safe to the blessèd world above;
There to possess the glorious part,
A perfect purity of heart.

1031   John Keble, W Hall   SM
Blessed are the pure in heart: for they shall see God. *Matthew 5:8*

Blest are the pure in heart,
For they shall see their God,
The secret of the Lord is theirs,
Their soul is Christ's abode.

The Lord, who left the heavens,
Our life and peace to bring,
To dwell in lowliness with men,
Their Pattern and their King;

Still to the lowly soul
He doth Himself impart,
And for His dwelling and His throne
Chooseth the pure in heart.

Lord, we Thy presence seek;
May ours this blessing be;
Give us a pure and lowly heart,
A temple meet for Thee.

1032   Samuel Medley   LM
Blessed are the peacemakers: for they shall be called the children of God. *Matthew 5:9*

The souls who love and long for peace,
Who strive to make contention cease,
And seek the path by Jesus trod,
Are blessèd as the sons of God.

Peace from the Lord their souls have felt:
Peace, and the pardon of their guilt;
Peace which this world, do what it may,
Can neither give; nor take away.

A peace that's holy, pure, and good;
A peace procured by Jesus' blood:
A peace which only He can give;
A peace which shall for ever live.

Sweet peace they labour to restore,
And grieve that they succeed no more;
'Tis an employ they can't forsake,
For peace on earth they love to make.

Then, Lord, to prove my heavenly birth,
May I seek peace and truth, on earth;
And when upon a dying bed,
In peace with Thee lay down my head.

1033 James Montgomery SM
Our Father which art in heaven….
Matthew 6:9-13

Our heavenly Father, hear
The prayer we offer now;
Thy name be hallowed far and near,
To Thee all nations bow.

Thy kingdom come! Thy will
On earth be done in love,
As saints and seraphim fulfil
Thy perfect law above.

Our daily bread supply,
While by Thy word we live;
The guilt of our iniquity
Forgive, as we forgive.

From dark temptation's power,
From Satan's wiles defend;
Deliver in the evil hour,
And guide us to the end.

Thine, then, for ever be
Glory and power divine;
The sceptre, throne and majesty
Of heaven and earth are Thine.

1034 William Gadsby SM
**Thy kingdom come. Thy will be done in earth,
as it is in heaven.** *Matthew 6:10*

Great God! Thy kingdom come,
With reverence would we pray,
May the eternal Three-in-One
His sovereign sceptre sway.

May grace triumphant reign,
And Christ exalted be;
Sinners, deserving endless pain,
Thy great salvation see.

May mercy, truth, and peace,
Fill each believer's soul,
And the sweet kingdom of Thy grace,
Their raging lusts control.

May love and harmony
Among Thy saints abide,
Thy presence set each bosom free
From enmity and pride.

Go on, Thou mighty God,
Thy wonders to make known,
Till every sinner bought with blood,
Shall trust in Thee alone.

Thus let Thy kingdom come,
And free salvation reign,
Till all Thy saints arrive at home,
And never part again.

1035 Josiah Conder 77 77
Give us this day our daily bread.
Matthew 6:11

Day by day the manna fell;
O! to learn this lesson well,
Still by constant mercy fed,
Give me, Lord, my daily bread.

'Day by day,' the promise reads;
Daily strength for daily needs:
Cast foreboding fears away;
Take the manna of today.

Lord, my times are in Thy hand;
All my ardent hopes have planned
To Thy wisdom I resign,
And would make Thy purpose mine.

Thou my daily task shalt give;
Day by day to Thee I live:
So shall added years fulfil,
Not mine own—my Father's will.

Fond ambition, whisper not;
Happy is my humble lot:
Anxious, busy cares away!
I'm provided for today.

O to live exempt from care,
By the energy of prayer;
Strong in faith, with mind subdued;
Yet elate with gratitude!

1036   Anabaptist Ausbund, tr. Ernest Payne
87 87 887
For Thine is the kingdom, and the power, and the glory, for ever. Amen.
Matthew 6:13

Our Father God, Thy name we praise,
  To Thee our hymns addressing,
And joyfully our voices raise
  Thy faithfulness confessing;
Assembled by Thy grace, O Lord,
We seek fresh guidance from Thy word;
  Now grant anew Thy blessing.

Touch, Lord, the lips that speak for Thee;
  Set words of truth before us,
That we may grow in constancy,
  The light of wisdom o'er us.
Give us this day our daily bread;
May hungry souls again be fed;
  May heavenly food restore us.

As with our brethren here we meet,
  Thy grace alone can feed us.
As here we gather at Thy feet
  We pray that Thou wilt heed us.
The power is Thine, O Lord divine,
The kingdom and the rule are Thine.
  May Jesus Christ still lead us!
                              © *James Prain*

1037   Georgiana Taylor   888 3
But seek ye first the kingdom of God, and His righteousness; and all these things shall be added unto you. *Matthew 6:33*

Seek ye first, not earthly pleasure,
Fading joy and failing treasure;
But the love that knows no measure
    Seek ye first.

Seek ye first, not earth's aspirings,
Ceaseless longings, vain desirings;
But your precious soul's requirings
    Seek ye first.

Seek ye first God's peace and blessing,
Ye have all if this possessing;
Come, your need and sin confessing,
    Seek Him first.

Seek Him first; then, when forgiven,
Pardoned, made an heir of heaven,
Let your life to Him be given;
    Seek this first.

Seek this first; be pure and holy;
Like the Master, meek and lowly;
Yielded to His service wholly;
    Seek this first.

Seek the coming of His kingdom;
Seek the souls around to win them;
Seek to Jesus Christ to bring them;
    Seek this first.

Seek this first, His promise trying;
It is sure, all need supplying;
Heavenly things, on Him relying,
    Seek ye first.

1038   Sister Mary Xavier   84 84
Sufficient unto the day is the evil thereof.
Matthew 6:34

Lord, for tomorrow and its needs
    I do not pray;
Keep me, my God, from stain of sin,
    Just for today.

Let me do faithfully Thy work
    And duly pray;
Let me be kind in word and deed,
    Just for today.

Let me no wrong or idle word,
    Unthinking, say;
Set Thou a seal upon my lips,
    Just for today.

So for tomorrow and its needs
    I do not pray;
But keep me, guide me, hold me, Lord,
    Just for today.

1039   Hewett   77 77
Ask, and it shall be given you; seek, and ye shall find; knock, and it shall be opened unto you. *Matthew 7:7*

Come, poor sinner, come and see,
All thy strength is found in Me;
I am waiting to be kind,
To relieve thy troubled mind.

Dost thou feel thy sins a pain?
Look to Me and ease obtain:
All My fulness thou mayst share,
And be always welcome there.

Boldly come; why dost thou fear?
I possess a gracious ear;
I will never tell thee nay,
While thou hast a heart to pray.

Try the freeness of My grace,
Sure, 'twill suit thy trying case.
Mourning souls will ne'er complain,
Having sought My face in vain.

Knock, and cast all doubt behind,
Seek, and thou shalt surely find;
Ask, and I will give thee peace.
And thy confidence increase.

Will not this encourage thee,
Vile and poor to come to Me?
Sure thou canst not doubt My will!
Come, and welcome, sinner, still!

1040 Anne Brontë SM

Because strait is the gate, and narrow is the way, which leadeth unto life, and few there be that find it. *Matthew 7:14*

Believe not those who say
The upward path is smooth,
Lest thou shouldst stumble in the way
And faint before the truth.

It is the only road
Unto the realms of joy;
But he that seeks that blest abode
Must all his powers employ.

Arm, arm thee for the fight!
Cast useless loads away;
Watch through the darkest hours of night;
Toil through the hottest day.

To labour and to love,
To pardon and endure,
To lift thy heart to God above
And keep thy conscience pure.

Be this thy constant aim,
Thy hope, thy chief delight;
What matter who should whisper blame,
Or who should scorn or slight,

If but thy God approve
And if, within thy breast,
Thou feel the comfort of His love,
The earnest of His rest.

1041 Jane Taylor CM

Because strait is the gate, and narrow is the way, which leadeth unto life, and few there be that find it. *Matthew 7:14*

There is a path that leads to God,
All others go astray;
Narrow, but pleasant, is the road,
And Christians love the way.

It leads straight through this world of sin,
And dangers must be passed;
But those who boldly walk therein,
Will get to heaven at last.

How shall a little pilgrim dare
This dangerous path to tread?
For on the way is many a snare
For youthful travellers spread.

While the broad road, where thousands go,
Lies near, and opens fair;
And many turn aside, I know,
Who walk with sinners there.

But lest my feeble steps should slide,
Or wander from Thy way,
Lord, condescend to be my Guide,
And I shall never stray.

Then I may go without alarm,
And trust His word of old;
'The lambs He'll gather with His arm,
And lead them to the fold.'

1042 Edward Mote 88 88 88

And the rain descended, and the floods came, and the winds blew, and beat upon that house; and it fell not: for it was founded upon a rock. *Matthew 7:25*

My hope is built on nothing less
Than Jesus' blood and righteousness;
I dare not trust the sweetest frame,
But wholly lean on Jesus' name.

On Christ, the solid Rock, I stand;
All other ground is sinking sand.

When darkness veils His lovely face,
I rest on His unchanging grace;
In every rough and stormy gale
My anchor holds within the veil.

His oath, His covenant and His blood,
Support me in the 'whelming flood;
When all around my soul gives way,
He then is all my hope and stay.

When He shall come with trumpet sound
O may I then in Him be found!
Dressed in His righteousness alone,
Faultless to stand before the throne.

1043 John Berridge   SM
**And, behold, there came a leper and
worshipped Him, saying, Lord, if Thou wilt,
Thou canst make me clean.** *Matthew 8:2*

Defiled I am indeed;
Defiled throughout by sin;
Thy purple fountain, Lord, I need,
To wash a leper clean.

The fountain open stands.
Yet on its brink I dwell;
O put me in with Thy own hands,
And that will make me well.

1044 Henry Baker   CM
**Lord, I am not worthy that Thou shouldest
come under my roof: but speak the word only,
and my servant shall be healed.** *Matthew 8:8*

I am not worthy, holy Lord,
  That Thou shouldst come to me;
Speak but the word; one gracious word
  Can set the sinner free.

I am not worthy: cold and bare
  The lodging of my soul;
How canst Thou deign to enter there?
  Lord, speak, and make me whole.

I am not worthy; yet, my God,
  How can I say Thee nay;
Thee, who didst give Thy flesh and blood
  My ransom-price to pay?

O come in this appointed hour,
  Feed me with food divine;
And fill with all Thy love and power
  This worthless heart of mine.

1045 Rowland Hill   CM
**And Jesus said unto the centurion, Go thy
way; and as thou hast believed, so be it done
unto thee. And his servant was healed in the
selfsame hour.** *Matthew 8:13*

Thou, who a tender Parent art,
  Regard a parent's plea:
Our offspring, with an anxious heart,
  We now commend to Thee.

Our children are our greatest care,
  A charge which Thou hast given:
In all Thy graces let them share,
  And all the joys of heaven.

If a centurion could succeed,
  Who for his servant cried;
Wilt Thou refuse to hear us plead,
  For those so near allied?

On us Thou hast bestowed Thy grace,
  Be to our children kind;
Among Thy saints give them a place,
  And leave not one behind.

Happy we then shall live below,
  The remnant of our days:
And when to brighter worlds we go,
  Shall long resound Thy praise.

1046 Henry Alford   888 6 (trochaic)
Lord, save us: we perish. *Matthew 8:25*

Lo! the storms of life are breaking,
Faithless fears our hearts are shaking;
For our succour undertaking,
  Lord and Saviour, help us.

Lo! the world, from Thee rebelling,
Round Thy church in pride is swelling;
With Thy word their madness quelling,
  Lord and Saviour, help us.

On Thine own command relying,
We our onward task are plying,
Unto Thee for safety sighing,
  Lord and Saviour, help us.

Steadfast we, in faith abiding,
In Thy secret presence hiding,
In Thy love and grace confiding,
  Lord and Saviour, help us.

By Thy birth, Thy cross, Thy passion,
By Thy tears of deep compassion,
By Thy mighty intercession,
  Lord and Saviour, help us.

1047 Joseph Hart   CM
**Son, be of good cheer; thy sins be forgiven
thee.** *Matthew 9:2*

How high a privilege 'tis to know
  Our sins are all forgiven;
To bear about this pledge below,
  This special grant of heaven!

To look on this when sunk in fears,
  While each repeated sight,
Like some reviving cordial, cheers,
  And makes temptations light!

O what is honour, wealth, or mirth,
    To this well-grounded peace?
How poor are all the goods of earth,
    To such a gift as this!

This is a treasure rich indeed,
    Which none but Christ can give;
Of this the best of men have need;
    This I, the worst, receive.

1048 John Kent   LM
**They that be whole need not a physician, but
they that are sick.** *Matthew 9:12*

Who but the soul that's led to know
How just and holy is the law,
Will to the cross of Christ repair,
And seek salvation only there?

Jesus, my soul's compelled to flee
From all its wrath and curse to Thee;
Though oft, thro' pride, my stubborn will
To Sinai feels a cleaving still.

Sinner, if thou art taught to see
How great thy guilt and misery,
In every thought and act impure,
The blood of Christ thy soul can cure.

Daily to feel thyself undone,
Will make thee haste to kiss the Son,
And on thy knees for pardon sue,
And praise, and bless, and love Him too.

To feel thy shame and nakedness,
Will make thee love that glorious dress
That sets from condemnation free,
And from the curse delivers thee.

Without a seam this garment's wove,
Bequeathed in everlasting love;
Ere time began, designed to be
A royal robe to cover thee.

We seek no other blood or name,
To cleanse our guilt and hide our shame,
But that wrought out by Christ the Son,
Which God imputes, and faith puts on.

1049 Anne Steele   LM
**They that be whole need not a physician, but
they that are sick.** *Matthew 9:12*

Deep are the wounds which sin has made;
    Where shall the sinner find a cure?
In vain, alas! is nature's aid;
    The work exceeds all nature's power.

Sin, like a raging fever, reigns
    With fatal strength in every part;
The dire contagion fills the veins,
    And spreads its poison to the heart.

And can no sovereign balm be found?
    And is no kind physician nigh,
To ease the pain and heal the wound,
    Ere life and hope for ever fly?

There is a great Physician near;
    Look up, O fainting soul, and live.
See, in His heavenly smiles appear
    Such ease as nature cannot give.

See, in the Saviour's precious blood,
    Life, health, and bliss abundant flow!
Tis only this dear sacred flood
    Can ease thy pain and heal thy woe.

1050 John Kent   CM
**For she said within herself, If I may but touch
His garment, I shall be whole.** *Matthew 9:21*

Ye sin-sick souls, dismiss your fears,
    The halt, the blind, the lame;
Come, touch the garment Jesus wears,
    There's healing in the same.

'Till sick of every other way,
    You'll ne'er to Jesus go,
Whose words eternal life convey,
    Whose wounds with pardon flow.

Surrounded with ten thousand cares,
    And sad beyond degree;
Yet in this garment Jesus wears,
    There's healing still for thee.

Come, stretch the withered hand today,
    For Christ is passing by;
Thy case admits of no delay,
    Unless ye touch, ye die.

Could Jordan's streams at once remove
    Naaman's sore disease;
Far greater virtue sinners prove
    In Christ, the Prince of Peace.

One touch of this celestial robe
    Speaks pardon to the soul;
When sins more ponderous than the globe
    Across the conscience roll.

1051   Samuel Barnard   66 66 88
But when He saw the multitudes, He was
moved with compassion. *Matthew 9:36*

Jesus we come to meet
  With Thee, our Lord and King,
To bow before Thy feet,
  And here Thy praises sing:
Compassion on us have, we pray,
And empty send us not away.

May every worldly care
  Be banished from our mind;
May we with profit hear;
  And peace and comfort find:
Refresh us from Thy word, we pray,
And empty send us not away.

Our strength will soon decrease,
  Unless our souls be fed;
We feel our health and peace
  Depend on living Bread.
Thy gracious hand now, Lord, display,
And empty send us not away.

May all true mourners feel
  Their grief exchanged for joy;
Thy love to them reveal,
  And all their fears destroy:
That when they leave Thy house this day,
They may not empty go away.

May all Thy children prove
  The riches of Thy grace;
Each taste redeeming love,
  And see Thy smiling face:
So shall we all with pleasure say,
'We are not empty sent away.'

1052   Philip Doddridge   LM
Pray ye therefore the Lord of the harvest, that
He will send forth labourers into His harvest.
Matthew 9:38

Shepherd of Israel, bend Thine ear,
Thy servants' groans indulgent hear;
Perplexed, distressed, to Thee we cry,
And seek the guidance of Thine eye.

Send forth, O Lord, Thy truth and light
To guide our doubtful footsteps right;
Our drooping hearts, O God, sustain,
Nor let us seek Thy face in vain.

Return, in ways of peace return,
Nor let Thy flock neglected mourn;
May our blest eyes a Shepherd see,
Dear to our souls, and dear to Thee!

Fed by his care, our tongues shall raise
A cheerful tribute to Thy praise;
Our children learn the grateful song,
And theirs the cheerful notes prolong.

1053   Isaac Watts   CM
Are not two sparrows sold for a farthing? and
one of them shall not fall on the ground
without your Father.
Matthew 10:29

There's not a sparrow nor a worm
  But's found in God's decrees;
He raises monarchs to their thrones,
  And sinks them if He please.

If light attend the course I run,
  'Tis He provides those rays;
And 'tis His hand that hides my sun,
  If darkness cloud my days.

When He reveals the Book of Life,
  O may I read my name
Among the chosen of His love,
  The followers of the Lamb!

1054   John Berridge   886 D
But the very hairs of your head are all
numbered. *Matthew 10:30*

How watchful is the loving Lord,
How sweet His providential word,
  To children that believe!
Your very hairs are numbered all;
Not one by force or chance can fall
  Without your Father's leave.

No cross nor bliss, no loss nor gain,
No health nor sickness, ease nor pain,
  Can give themselves a birth;
The Lord so rules by His command,
Nor good nor ill can stir a hand,
  Unless He send them forth.

Since Thou so kind and watchful art,
To guard my head, and guard my heart,
  And guard my very hair,
Teach me with childlike mind to sit
And sing at my dear Saviour's feet,
  Without distrust or fear.

So, like a pilgrim, let me wait,
Contented well in every state,
  Till all my warfare ends,
Live in a calm and cheerful mood,
And find that all things work for good
  Which Jesus kindly sends.

1055 Arthur Stone LM
A Friend of publicans and sinners.
Matthew 11:19

I have a rich almighty Friend,
On whom my hopes of heaven depend;
My every need He well supplies,
And still on Him my hope relies.

Each day I call on Him in prayer,
The throne of grace proves He is there
To hear and answer my requests,
And so I am for ever blessed.

At last I'll reach the promised land,
Guarded and guided by His hand,
To join with all who love the Lord
The place where Jesus is adored.

© *Mrs Carol Evans*

1056 Isaac Watts CM
I thank Thee, O Father, Lord of heaven and earth, because Thou hast hid these things from the wise and prudent, and hast revealed them unto babes.
Matthew 11:25

Jesus the Man of constant grief,
A mourner all His days;
His spirit once rejoiced aloud,
And turned His joy to praise:

'Father, I thank Thy wondrous love,
That has revealed Thy Son
To men unlearnèd; and to babes
Has made the gospel known.

'The mysteries of redeeming grace
Are hidden from the wise;
While pride and carnal reasonings join
To swell and blind their eyes.'

Thus does the Lord of heaven and earth
His great decrees fulfil,
And order all His works of grace
By His own sovereign will.

1057 Isaac Watts LM
Come unto Me, all ye that labour and are heavy laden, and I will give you rest.
Matthew 11:28

Come hither, all ye weary souls,
Ye heavy laden sinners, come;
I'll give you rest from all your toils,
And raise you to My heavenly home.

'They shall find rest that learn of Me,
I'm of a meek and lowly mind;
But passion rages like a sea,
And pride is restless as the wind.

'Blessed is the man whose shoulders take
My yoke, and bears it with delight;
My yoke is easy to His neck,
My grace shall make the burden light.'

Jesus, we come at Thy command;
With faith, and hope, and humble zeal
Resign our spirits to Thy hand,
To mould and guide us at Thy will.

1058 William Lloyd 87 87
Come unto Me, all ye that labour and are heavy laden, and I will give you rest.
Matthew 11:28

Come, poor sinners, come to Jesus,
Weary, heavy laden, weak;
None but Jesus Christ can ease us,
Come ye all, His mercy seek.

'Come,' it is His invitation;
'Come to Me,' the Saviour says,
Why, O why such hesitation,
Gloomy doubts, and base delays?

Do you fear your own unfitness,
Burdened as you are with sin?
'Tis the Holy Spirit's witness;
Christ invites you— 'enter in.'

Do your sins and your distresses
'Gainst this sacred record plead?
Know that Christ most kindly blesses
Those who feel the most their need.

Hear His words, so true and cheering,
Fitted just for the distressed;
Dwell upon the sound endearing;
'Mourners, I will give you rest.'

Stay not pondering on your sorrow,
Turn from your own self away:
Do not linger till tomorrow,
Come to Christ without delay.

JOSEPH SWAIN 1761-96

Why art thou afraid to come?
Why afraid to tell thy case?
He will not pronounce thy doom;
Smiles are seated on His face.

Though His majesty be great,
Yet His mercy is no less;
Though He thy transgressions hate,
Jesus feels for thy distress.

Raise thy downcast eyes and see,
Numbers do His throne surround;
These were sinners once, like thee,
But have full salvation found.

Yield not, then, to unbelief;
Courage, soul, 'there yet is room!'
Though of sinners thou art chief,
Come, thou burdened sinner, come.

1059   Joseph Swain   87 87 47
**Come unto Me, all ye that labour and are
heavy laden, and I will give you rest.**
Matthew 11:28

Come, ye souls, by sin afflicted,
Bowed with fruitless sorrow down;
By the broken law convicted,
Through the cross behold the crown!
Look to Jesus;
Mercy flows through Him alone.

Sweet as home to pilgrims weary,
Light to newly-opened eyes,
Flowing springs in deserts dreary,
Is the rest the cross supplies;
All who taste it
Shall to rest immortal rise.

Blessèd are the eyes that see Him;
Blest the ears that hear His voice;
Blessèd are the souls that trust Him,
And in Him alone rejoice;
His commandments
Then become their happy choice.

But to sing the 'Rest remaining,'
Mortal tongues far short must fall;
Heavenly tongues are ever aiming,
But they cannot tell it all;
Faith believes it,
But it overwhelms them all.

1061   Anne Steele   LM
**Come unto Me, all ye that labour and are
heavy laden, and I will give you rest.**
Matthew 11:28

Come, weary souls, with sin distressed,
Come and accept the promised rest;
The gospel's gracious call obey,
And cast your gloomy fears away.

Oppressed with guilt (a painful load),
O come and spread your woes abroad,
Divine compassion, mighty love,
Will all the painful load remove.

Here mercy's boundless ocean flows,
To cleanse your guilt, and heal your woes;
Pardon, and life, and endless peace;
How rich the gift, how free the grace!

Dear Saviour, let Thy powerful love
Confirm our faith, our fears remove;
Forgiveness shed through every breast,
And guide us to eternal rest.

1060   John Newton   77 77
**Come unto Me, all ye that labour and are
heavy laden, and I will give you rest.**
Matthew 11:28

Christ has blessings to impart,
Grace to save thee from thy fears;
O the love that fills His heart!
Sinner, wipe away thy tears.

1062   William Gadsby   886 D
And in His name shall the Gentiles trust.
Matthew 12:21

How sweet and precious is the name
Of Jesus Christ, the Lord, the Lamb,
To sinners in distress!
A name just suited to their case;
Pregnant with mercy, truth, and grace,
With strength and righteousness.

His name, as Jesus, suits them well;
He saves from sin, wrath, law, and hell,
From guilt and slavish fears.
His name is Wonderful indeed;
An able Counsellor, to plead,
Just suits a case like theirs.

Immanuel! thrice-blessèd name!
The God we trust is still the same!
An endless Father, He;
A most illustrious Prince of Peace;
A Tower, a precious Hiding-place,
Is Jesus Christ to me.

Yes, if His name be Lord of Hosts,
Of His almighty power I'll boast;
He all my foes shall quell;
He's all the helpless soul can need;
No ointment put on Aaron's head,
Could give so sweet a smell.

In Him the Gentile church shall trust;
Of Him shall sing; of Him shall boast;
On Him cast all their care;
He is their God, and they shall know
What His almighty power can do,
Nor death, nor danger fear.

1063   William Cowper   CM
**And He spake many things unto them in
parables, saying, Behold, a sower went forth
to sow.** Matthew 13:3

Ye sons of earth prepare the plough,
Break up your fallow ground!
The Sower is gone forth to sow,
And scatter blessings round.

The seed that finds a stony soil,
Shoots forth a hasty blade;
But ill repays the sower's toil,
Soon withered, scorched, and dead.

The thorny ground is sure to baulk
All hopes of harvest there;
We find a tall and sickly stalk,
But not the fruitful ear.

The beaten path and highway side
Receive the seed in vain;
The watchful birds the spoil divide,
And pick up all the grain.

But where the Lord of grace and power
Has blessed the happy field;
How plenteous is the golden store
The deep-wrought furrows yield!

Father of mercies we have need
Of Thy preparing grace;
Let the same hand that gives the seed,
Provide a fruitful place.

1064   Jonathan Evans   87 87 47
**But he that received seed into the good
ground is he that heareth the word, and
understandeth it; which also beareth fruit.**
Matthew 13:23

Come, Thou soul-transforming Spirit,
Bless the sower and the seed;
Let each heart Thy grace inherit,
Raise the weak the hungry feed:
From the gospel
Now supply Thy people's need.

O may all enjoy the blessing
Which Thy word's designed to give;
Let us all, Thy love possessing,
Joyfully the truth receive;
And for ever
To Thy praise and glory live!

1065   Henry Alford   77 77 D
**But when the blade was sprung up, and
brought forth fruit, then appeared the tares
also.** Matthew 13:26

Come, ye thankful people, come,
Raise the song of harvest home!
All is safely gathered in
Ere the winter storms begin;
God our Maker doth provide
For our wants to be supplied;
Come to God's own temple, come,
Raise the song of harvest home!

All the world is God's own field
Fruit unto His praise to yield;
Wheat and tares together sown;
Unto joy or sorrow grown;
First the blade and then the ear,
Then the full corn shall appear;
Lord of harvest, grant that we
Wholesome grain and pure may be.

For the Lord our God shall come
And shall take His harvest home;
From His field shall in that day
All offences purge away;
Give His angels charge at last
In the fire the tares to cast;
But the fruitful ears to store
In His garner evermore.

Even so, Lord, quickly come
To Thy final harvest home;
  Gather Thou Thy people in,
  Free from sorrow, free from sin;
There for ever purified
In Thy presence to abide;
  Come, with all Thine angels, come,
  Raise the glorious harvest home!

1066   John Kent   LM

The enemy that sowed them is the devil; the harvest is the end of the world; and the reapers are the angels. *Matthew 13:39*

There is a day, 'tis hastening on,
  When Zion's God shall purge His floor;
His own elect shall then be known,
  For He shall count those jewels o'er.

Nought but the grains of gospel gold
  Will ever stand this trying day;
When, like a scroll, together rolled,
  The starry heavens shall pass away.

How stands the case, my soul, with thee?
  For heaven are thy credentials clear?
Is Jesus' blood thy only plea?
  Is He thy great Forerunner there?

Is thy proud heart subdued by grace
  To seek salvation in His name?
There's wisdom, power, and righteousness,
  All centering in the worthy Lamb.

Then thou mayest rest assured of this,
  And lift thy favoured head with joy,
Thy hopes of heaven's eternal bliss,
  Earth, hell, and sin shall ne'er destroy.

1067   John Mason   CM

Who, when he had found one pearl of great price, went and sold all that he had, and bought it. *Matthew 13:46*

I've found the pearl of greatest price,
  My heart doth sing for joy;
And sing I must, for Christ is mine,
  Christ shall my song employ.

Christ is my Prophet, Priest, and King:
  My Prophet full of light,
My great High Priest before the throne,
  My King of heavenly might.

For He indeed is Lord of lords,
  And He the King of kings;
He is the Sun of Righteousness,
  With healing in His wings.

Christ is my peace; He died for me,
  For me He gave His blood;
And, as my wondrous sacrifice,
  Offered Himself to God.

Christ Jesus is my All-in-all,
  My comfort and my love;
My life below; and He shall be
  My glory-crown above.

1068   William Williams   886 D

Who, when he had found one pearl of great price, went and sold all that he had, and bought it. *Matthew 13:46*

Dear Jesus, come, my soul doth groan
For nought but for Thyself alone,
  Thou art the pearl of price;
For Thee, I'd part with all below,
And every hardship undergo,
  Beneath the vaulted skies.

Thy presence can, without delay,
Drive all my numerous cares away,
  As chaff before the wind;
Compose my thoughts to adore and love
Thee, as an object far above,
  To Thee alone inclined.

Release me from my heavy chain,
Guilt, sin and shame, which still remain
  To bind me hand and foot;
O, glorious Conqueror, enter in,
Cast out my foes, destroy my sin,
  Both branch and spreading root.

Give me that knowledge pure, divine,
To know and feel that Thou art mine,
  And Thee my portion call;
That doubts and fears may flee away,
And faith unfeignèd win the day,
  And triumph over all.

1069   William Hammond   77 77
O thou of little faith, wherefore didst thou doubt? *Matthew 14:31*

Will my doubting ne'er be o'er?
Will the Lord return no more?
When shall I the Saviour see,
And be sure He died for me?

How I waver to and fro,
Rising high and sinking low!
Now to heaven I aspire,
Now to shades of death retire.

When a glimpse of hope appears,
Soon 'tis lost in doubts and fears.
O! I fear 'tis all a cheat!
Keep me, Lord, from self-deceit.

Lord, Thy light, Thy love display;
All my darkness chase away;
Everlasting peace restore;
Bid me disbelieve no more.

Put Thy Spirit in my heart;
Bid my doubts and fears depart;
When Thy face shall on me shine,
I shall know and feel Thee mine.

1070   Samuel Medley   CM
O thou of little faith, wherefore didst thou doubt? *Matthew 14:31*

Thus the Redeemer kindly saith,
   When fears are round about,
'Thou trembling soul of little faith,
   O wherefore didst thou doubt?'

What, though the fiercely raging storm
   Attend thy path throughout?
Christ thy deliverance will perform;
   Then wherefore dost thou doubt?

Soon all the saints on Canaan's shore
   Triumphantly shall shout;
And reign with God for evermore,
   Then wherefore dost thou doubt?

1071   Benjamin Beddome   SM
For out of the heart proceed evil thoughts, murders, adulteries, fornications, thefts, false witness, blasphemies. *Matthew 15:19*

Astonished and distressed,
   I turn my eyes within;
My heart with loads of guilt oppressed,
   The seat of every sin.

What crowds of evil thoughts,
   What vile affections there!
Distrust, presumption, artful guile,
   Pride, envy, slavish fear.

Almighty King of saints,
   These tyrant-lusts subdue;
Expel the darkness of my mind,
   And all my powers renew.

This done, my cheerful voice
   Shall loud hosannas raise;
My soul shall glow with gratitude,
   My lips proclaim Thy praise.

1072   John Newton   77 77
Have mercy on me, O Lord, Thou Son of David; my daughter is grievously vexed with a devil. *Matthew 15:22*

Prayer an answer will obtain,
   Though the Lord awhile delay;
None shall seek His face in vain,
   None be empty sent away.

When the woman came from Tyre,
   And for help to Jesus sought;
Though' He granted her desire,
   Yet at first He answered not.

Could she guess at His intent,
   When He to His followers said,
'I to Israel's sheep am sent,
   Dogs must not have childrens' bread.'

She was not of Israel's seed,
   But of Canaan's wretched race;
Thought herself a dog indeed;
   Was not this a hopeless case?

Yet although from Canaan sprung,
   Though a dog herself she styled:
She had Israel's faith and tongue,
   And was owned for Abraham's child.

From His words she draws a plea:
   'Though unworthy children's bread,
'Tis enough for one like me,
   If with crumbs I may be fed.'

Jesus then His heart revealed,
   'Woman canst thou thus believe?
I to thy petition yield,
   All that thou canst wish, receive.'

'Tis a pattern set for us,
   How we ought to wait and pray;
None who plead and wrestle thus,
   Shall be empty sent away.

1073   Fanny Crosby   85 85 + refrain
Then came she and worshipped Him, saying,
Lord, help me. *Matthew 15:25*

Pass me not, O gracious Saviour,
     Hear my humble cry;
While on others Thou art calling,
     Do not pass me by.

     Saviour! Saviour!
       Hear my humble cry,
     While on others Thou art calling,
       Do not pass me by.

Let me at a throne of mercy
     Find a sweet relief;
Kneeling there in deep contrition,
     Help my unbelief.

Trusting only in Thy merit,
     I would seek Thy face:
Heal my wounded, broken spirit,
     Save me by Thy grace.

Thou the spring of all my comfort,
     More than life to me,
Whom have I on earth beside Thee,
     Whom in heaven but Thee?

1074   Augustus Toplady   CM
Lord, help me. *Matthew 15:25*

Jesus, Redeemer, Saviour, Lord,
     The weary sinner's Friend;
Come to my help, pronounce the word,
     Bid my corruptions end.

Thou canst o'ercome this heart of mine,
     Thou canst victorious prove;
For everlasting strength is Thine
     And everlasting love.

Bound down with twice ten thousand ties,
     Yet let me hear Thy call,
My soul in confidence shall rise,
     Shall rise and break through all.

Speak and the deaf shall hear Thy voice,
     The blind his sight receive;
The dumb in songs of praise rejoice,
     The heart of stone believe.

1075   John Fawcett   CM
And she said, Truth, Lord: yet the dogs eat of
the crumbs which fall from their masters'
table. *Matthew 15:27*

A crumb of mercy, Lord, I crave,
     Unworthy to be fed
With dainties such as angels have,
     Or with the children's bread.

Have pity on my needy soul;
     Thy peace and pardon give;
Thy love can make the wounded whole,
     And bid the dying live.

Behold me prostrate at Thy gate;
     Do not my plea deny;
With longing eyes for Thee I wait;
     O help me, or I die.

When Thou dost give a heart to pray,
     Thou wilt incline Thy ear;
From me turn not Thy face away,
     But my petition hear.

So shall my joyful soul adore
     The riches of Thy grace;
No sinner needed mercy more,
     That ever sought Thy face.

1076   Samuel Medley   LM
Thou art Peter, and upon this Rock I will build
My church. *Matthew 16:18*

On Christ alone His Church is built;
He, only He, absolves from guilt;
To Him alone our praise we bring,
And Him, the great foundation, sing.

In Him salvation stands secure;
This strong foundation must endure;
Stronger than death His love is known.
Nor can His church be overthrown.

In the eternal plan of grace,
He undertook our wretched case:
Love, how amazing, how divine,
Throughout the whole transaction shine!

He is the 'Rock' believers have;
Born to redeem, and strong to save;
He stooped to take our flesh and blood,
The wondrous Man, th' incarnate God!

In vain combinèd hosts assail,
Nor shall the gates of hell prevail:
Nor force, nor fraud, the building shock,
Founded on Him, th' eternal Rock.

1077   Sabine Baring-Gould

65 65 D + refrain

That thou art Peter, and upon this Rock I will build my church; and the gates of hell shall not prevail against it. *Matthew 16:18*

Onward, Christian soldiers,
　Marching as to war,
Looking unto Jesus,
　Who is gone before:
Christ, the royal Master,
　Leads against the foe;
Forward into battle,
　See, His banners go!

Onward, Christian soldiers,
*　Marching as to war,*
Looking unto Jesus,
*　Who is gone before.*

At the name of Jesus,
　Satan's host doth flee;
On then, Christian soldiers,
　On to victory!
Hell's foundations quiver
　At the shout of praise:
Brothers, lift your voices:
　Loud your anthems raise.

Like a mighty army
　Moves the church of God;
Brothers, we are treading
　Where the saints have trod:
We are not divided,
　All one body we,
One in hope and doctrine,
　One in charity.

Crowns and thrones may perish,
　Kingdoms rise and wane;
But the church of Jesus
　Constant will remain:
Gates of hell can never
　'Gainst that church prevail;
We have Christ's own promise
　And that cannot fail.

Onward, then, ye people,
　Join our happy throng;
Blend with ours your voices
　In the triumph-song;
Glory, praise and honour
　Unto Christ the King;
This through countless ages
　Men and angels sing.

1078   Charles Everest　　　　　　LM

If any man will come after Me, let him deny himself, and take up his cross, and follow Me.
Matthew 16:24

'Take up thy cross,' the Saviour said,
　'If thou wouldst My disciple be;
Deny thyself, the world forsake
　And humbly follow after Me.'

Take up thy cross; let not its weight
　Fill thy weak soul with vain alarm:
His strength shall bear thy spirit up
　And brace thy heart and nerve thine arm.

Take up thy cross, nor heed the shame,
　Nor let thy foolish pride rebel;
Thy Lord for thee the cross endured
　To save thy soul from death and hell.

Take up thy cross then in His strength
　And calmly every danger brave;
'Twill guide thee to a better home
　And lead to victory o'er the grave.

Take up thy cross and follow Him,
　Nor think till death to lay it down;
For only he who bears the cross
　May hope to wear the glorious crown.

1079   John Giles　　　　　　87 87 47

If any man will come after Me, let him deny himself, and take up his cross, and follow Me.
Matthew 16:24

Hast Thou said, exalted Jesus,
　'Take thy cross and follow Me'?
Shall the word with terror seize us?
　Shall we from the burden flee?
　　Lord, I'll take it,
　And, rejoicing, follow Thee.

Sweet the sign that thus reminds me,
　Saviour, of Thy love for me;
Sweeter still the love that binds me
　In its deathless bond to Thee:
　　O what pleasure,
　Buried with my Lord to be!

Then, baptized in love and glory,
　Lamb of God, Thy praise I'll sing;
Loudly with the immortal story
　All the harps of heaven shall ring:
　　Saints and angels
　Sound it loud from every string.

1080 Samuel Turner LM

Again I say unto you, That if two of you shall agree on earth as touching any thing that they shall ask, it shall be done for them of My Father which is in heaven. *Matthew 18:19*

We have Thy promise, gracious Lord,
  Thou wilt be where Thy people meet;
O, then, fulfil Thy gracious word,
  And make our happiness complete.

Thy promise is to two or three,
  Who meet together in Thy name;
That for whatever they agree
  To ask, they surely shall obtain.

We ask Thy gracious presence here,
  The sweet enjoyment of Thy love;
From worldly thoughts O keep us clear,
  And set our hearts on things above.

We ask Thy Holy Spirit's aid,
  Whilst we're engaged in prayer and praise;
We ask from our great living Head
  To be supplied with every grace.

We ask for faith a sweet increase,
  To find our doubts and fears removed,
To feel the powerful reign of peace,
  And every sinful thought subdued.

We ask to feel a union sweet,
  We ask a blessing on Thy word;
We ask—but all our askings meet
  In this—we ask Thy presence, Lord!

1081 Samuel Stennett LM

For where two or three are gathered together in My name, there am I in the midst of them. *Matthew 18:20*

'Where two or three, with sweet accord,
Obedient to their sovereign Lord,
Meet to recount His acts of grace,
And offer solemn prayer and praise;

'There,' says the Saviour, 'will I be
Amid this little company;
To them unveil My smiling face,
And shed My glories round the place.'

We meet at Thy command, dear Lord;
  Relying on Thy faithful word;
Now send Thy Spirit from above;
Now fill our hearts with heavenly love.

1082 Charles Wesley SM

For where two or three are gathered together in My name, there am I in the midst of them. *Matthew 18:20*

Jesus, we look to Thee,
  Thy promised presence claim;
Thou in the midst of us shalt be,
  Assembled in Thy name.

Thy name salvation is
  Which now we come to prove;
Thy name is life and joy and peace
  And everlasting love.

We meet the grace to take
  Which Thou hast freely given;
We meet on earth for Thy dear sake
  That we may meet in heaven.

Present we know Thou art,
  But O Thyself reveal;
Now Lord let every waiting heart
  Thy mighty comfort feel.

O may Thy quickening voice
  The death of sin remove
And bid our inmost souls rejoice
  In hope of perfect love.

1083 Thomas Kelly LM

For where two or three are gathered together in My name, there am I in the midst of them. *Matthew 18:20*

How sweet to leave the world awhile,
  And seek the presence of the Lord!
Dear Saviour, on Thy people smile,
  And come according to Thy word.

From busy scenes we now retreat,
  That we may here converse with Thee;
Ah, Lord, behold us at Thy feet!
  Let this the 'gate of heaven' be.

'Chief of ten thousand,' now appear,
  That we by faith may see Thy face!
O speak, that we Thy voice may hear,
  And let Thy presence fill this place.

Then let the worldling boast his joys,
  We've meat to eat he knows not of;
We count his treasures worthless toys,
  While we possess a Saviour's love.

1084   Richard Burnham   CM
**But Jesus said, Suffer little children, and
forbid them not, to come unto Me: for of such
is the kingdom of heaven.**
Matthew 19:14

Dear Lord, these children now we bring
   Moved by Thy great command;
Offer them up in sacred prayer,
   And leave them in Thy hand.

Now may rich mercy, all divine,
   Flow from the Prince of Peace;
Planting in each immortal soul
   The seed of heavenly grace.

Lord, bring them up in Thy good ways,
   And make them love Thy word;
O may they prove a holy seed,
   A seed to serve the Lord.

And may their parents, blessèd Lord,
   Through Thy rich counsel given,
Counsel their offspring in Thy fear,
   And train them up for heaven.

May every root and every branch
   Be watered from above:
May each increasingly enjoy
   The blessings of Thy love.

Let them all travel Zion's road,
   And ever live in peace;
Parents and children rise at length
   To heaven's eternal bliss.

1085   Henry Milman   LM
**Hosanna to the Son of David: Blessed is He
that cometh in the name of the Lord; Hosanna
in the highest.** *Matthew 21:9*

Ride on, ride on in majesty!
Hark, all the tribes 'Hosanna!' cry;
O Saviour meek, pursue Thy road,
With palms and scattered garments strowed.

Ride on, ride on in majesty!
In lowly pomp ride on to die:
O Christ, Thy triumphs now begin
O'er captive death and conquered sin.

Ride on, ride on in majesty!
The angel armies of the sky
Look down with sad and wondering eyes
To see the approaching sacrifice.

Ride on, ride on in majesty!
Thy last and fiercest strife is nigh:
The Father on His sapphire throne
Awaits His own anointed Son.

Ride on, ride on in majesty!
In lowly pomp ride on to die:
Bow Thy meek head to mortal pain,
Then take, O God, Thy power, and reign.

1086   Vernon Higham   87 87 47
**And when He was come into Jerusalem, all the
city was moved, saying, Who is this?**
Matthew 21:10

Who is this with joy approaching
   Happy men who see His face?
'Tis the Saviour, healing, speaking,
   Full of truth and full of grace.
      Son of David,
   Grant me sight, and Thine embrace.

Who is this, with men acclaiming,
   Born the Son of David's line,
Hallelujahs, palm leaves waving?
   'Tis the Christ, the Son Divine.
      Loud Hosannas!
   Come, O Lord, for Thee we pine.

Who is this, on cross so lonely,
   Hanging there for men to see?
Tis the Lord of all the glory,
   Bearing penalty for me.
      O forgive me!
   Plead my cause eternally.

Who is this in glory standing,
   Victor over death and shame,
Risen glorious, ever pleading?
   'Tis a sweet and wondrous name!
      Blessèd Jesus!
   Praise the Lord who took my blame!

                                    © *Author*

1087   John Henley   77 77 + refrain

**The children crying in the temple, and saying,
Hosanna to the Son of David.**
Matthew 21:15

Children of Jerusalem
Sang the praise of Jesus' name:
Children, too, of modern days,
Join to sing the Saviour's praise.

   *Hark! while infant voices sing
   Loud hosannas to our King.*

We are taught to love the Lord,
We are taught to read His word.
Wc are taught the way to heaven:
Praise for all to God be given.

Parents, teachers, old and young,
All unite to swell the song;
Higher and yet higher rise,
Till hosannas reach the skies.

1088   John Newton   88 88 D
What think ye of Christ? Whose Son is He?
They say unto Him, The Son of David.
Matthew 22:42

What think you of Christ? is the test,
   To try both your state and your scheme;
You cannot be right in the rest,
   Unless you think rightly of Him.
As Jesus appears in your view,
   As He is belovèd or not;
So God is disposèd to you,
   And mercy or wrath are your lot.

Some take Him a creature to be,
   A man, or an angel at most:
Sure these have not feelings like me,
   Nor know themselves wretched and lost.
So guilty, so helpless am I,
   I durst not confide in His blood,
Nor on His protection rely,
   Unless I were sure He is God.

Some call Him a Saviour in word,
   But mix their own works with His plan;
And hope He His help will afford,
   When they have done all that they can:
If doings prove rather too light,
   (A little, they own, they may fail),
They purpose to make up full weight
   By casting His name in the scale.

Some style Him the Pearl of great price,
   And say he's the Fountain of joys;
Yet feed upon folly and vice,
   And cleave to the world and its toys:
Like Judas, the Saviour they kiss,
   And while they salute Him, betray;
Ah! what will profession like this
   Avail in His terrible day?

If asked what of Jesus I think,
   Though still my best thoughts are but poor
I say, He's my meat and my drink,
   My life, and my strength, and my store;
My Shepherd, my Husband, my Friend,
   My Saviour from sin and from thrall;
My hope from beginning to end,
   My portion, my Lord, and my All.

1089   George Matheson   DSM
One is your Master, even Christ; and all ye are
brethren. *Matthew 23:8*

   Make me a captive, Lord,
   And then I shall be free;
Force me to render up my sword
   And I shall conqueror be.
   I sink in life's alarms
   When by myself I stand;
Imprison me within Thine arms
   And strong shall be my hand.

   My heart is weak and poor
   Until it master find;
It has no spring of action sure,
   It varies with the wind;
   It cannot freely move
   Till Thou hast wrought its chain,
Enslave it with Thy matchless love,
   And deathless it shall reign.

   My will is not my own
   Till Thou hast made it Thine;
If it would reach the monarch's throne
   It must its crown resign;
   It only stands unbent,
   Amid the clashing strife,
When on Thy bosom it has leant
   And found in Thee its life.

1090   Frances Havergal   77 77 77
One is your Master, even Christ; and all ye are
brethren. *Matthew 23:8*

Jesus, Master, whose I am,
   Purchased Thine alone to be
By Thy blood, O spotless Lamb,
   Shed so willingly for me,
Let my heart be all Thine own,
Let me live to Thee alone.

Jesus, Master, I am Thine:
   Keep me faithful, keep me near;
Let Thy presence in me shine
   All my homeward way to cheer.
Jesus, at Thy feet I fall,
O be Thou my All in all.

Jesus, Master, whom I serve,
   Though so feebly and so ill,
Strengthen hand and heart and nerve
   All Thy bidding to fulfil.
Open Thou mine eyes to see
All the work Thou hast for me.

Lord, Thou needest not, I know,
Service such as I can bring;
Yet I long to prove and show
Full allegiance to my King.
Thou an honour art to me:
Let me be a praise to Thee.

1091   Richard Burnham   66 66 88
**And this gospel of the kingdom shall be
preached in all the world for a witness unto all
nations; and then shall the end come.**
Matthew 24:14

Great God, to Thee we pray,
Show Thy refulgent face;
Sinners convert to Thee,
And save them by Thy grace;
The gospel to all nations send,
And let them know the sinner's Friend.

May thoughtless mortals feel
The great Jehovah's rod;
Then to their souls reveal
The mercy of a God;
The gospel to all nations send,
And let them know the sinner's Friend.

Turn the self-righteous train
From their delusive dreams;
Cause them to fly from sin,
And wash in Calvary's streams;
The gospel to all nations send.
And let them know the sinner's Friend.

Look on the formal race,
On them Thy Spirit pour;
O let them see Thy grace,
And let them feel its power;
The gospel to all nations send,
And let them know the sinner's Friend.

1092   Daniel Whittle   Irregular
**And they shall see the Son of man coming in
the clouds of heaven with power and great
glory.** *Matthew 24:30*

Our Lord is now rejected,
And by the world disowned;
By the many still neglected,
And by the few enthroned.
But soon He'll come in glory;
The hour is drawing nigh
For the crowning-day that's coming
by-and-by!

*O! the crowning-day is coming—
Is coming by-and-by,
When our Lord shall come in power
And glory from on high!
O the glorious sight will gladden
Each waiting, watchful eye,
In the crowning-day that's coming
by-and-by!*

The heavens shall glow with splendour;
But brighter far than they
The saints shall shine in glory,
As Christ shall them array:
The beauty of the Saviour
Shall dazzle every eye,
In the crowning-day that's coming
by-and-by!

Our pain shall then be over,
We'll sin and sigh no more;
Behind us all of sorrow,
And nought but joy before—
A joy in our Redeemer,
As we to Him are nigh,
In the crowning-day that's coming
by-and-by!

Let all who look for, hasten
The coming joyful day;
By earnest consecration.
To walk the narrow way;
By gathering in the lost ones
For whom our Lord did die,
For the crowning-day that's coming
by-and-by!

1093   Joseph Hart   LM
**Heaven and earth shall pass away, but My
words shall not pass away.**
Matthew 24:35

The moon and stars shall lose their light,
The sun shall sink in endless night;
Both heaven and earth shall pass away;
The works of nature all decay.

But they that in the Lord confide,
And shelter in His wounded side,
Shall see the danger overpast,
Stand every storm, and live at last.

What Christ has said must be fulfilled;
On this firm rock, believers build;
His word shall stand, His truth prevail,
And not one jot or tittle fail.

His word is this (poor sinners, hear);
'Believe on Me, and banish fear;
Cease from your own works, bad or good,
And wash your garments in My blood.'

1094   Charles Wesley   66 66 88
But the wise took oil in their vessels with their lamps. *Matthew 25:4*

Ye slumbering souls, arise!
    With all the dead awake;
Unto salvation wise,
    Oil in your vessels take;
Upstarting at the midnight cry,
'Behold the heavenly Bridegroom nigh.'

He comes, He comes, to call
    The nations to His bar,
And take to glory all
    Who meet for glory are:
Made ready for your free reward,
Go forth with joy to meet your Lord.

Go, meet Him in the sky,
    Your everlasting Friend;
Your Head to glorify,
    With all His saints ascend;
Ye pure in heart, obtain the grace
To see, without a veil, His face!

Ye that have here received
    The unction from above,
And in His Spirit lived,
    And thirsted for His love,
Jesus shall claim you for His bride:
Rejoice with all the sanctified.

Rejoice in glorious hope
    Of that great day unknown,
When you shall be caught up
    To stand before His throne;
Called to partake the marriage feast,
And lean on our Immanuel's breast.

The everlasting doors
    Shall soon the saints receive,
Above yon angel powers
    In glorious joy to live;
Far from a world of grief and sin,
With God eternally shut in.

1095   John Kent   LM
And at midnight there was a cry made, Behold, the bridegroom cometh; go ye out to meet Him. *Matthew 25:6*

Hark! 'tis the solemn midnight cry,
    Virgins, arise, your lamps prepare;
The heavenly Bridegroom, from the sky,
    Doth in the clouds of heaven appear.

Go ye who for His coming wait,
    Whose lamps are bright with heavenly flame;
He comes to make your bliss complete,
    And show the glories of His name.

Not as the bare professing race,
    Whose lamp in total darkness dies;
But furnished with the oil of grace,
    Arise, ye virgin souls, arise.

Your sacred unction ne'er decays,
    But kindled once, remains the same;
Burning to everlasting days,
    For God Himself maintains the flame.

Without the Spirit's work within
    Profession's but unhallowed fire;
A name to live while dead in sin,
    That shall in endless night expire.

The church of Jesus, great and small,
    Are slumbering, yet not dead in sin!
For they shall hear the Master's call,
    And with the Bridegroom enter in.

1096   Charles Wesley   555 11
Well done, good and faithful servant.
Matthew 25:21,23

Come, let us anew
Our journey pursue,
Roll round with the year,
And never stand till the Master appear.

His adorable will
Let us gladly fulfil,
And our talents improve,
By the patience of hope and the labour of love.

Our life is a dream;
Our time as a stream
Glides swiftly away,
And the fugitive moment refuses to stay.

O that each in the day
Of His coming may say:
I have fought my way through,
I have finished the work Thou didst give me to do!

O that each from his Lord
May receive the glad word:
Well and faithfully done;
Enter into My joy, and sit down on My throne!

1097 William Gadsby (alt) 66 66 88
**When the Son of man shall come in His glory,
and all the holy angels with Him, then shall He
sit upon the throne of His glory.** *Matthew 25:31*

With great and awesome power,
Jesus, the Judge, shall come,
To bid His foes depart,
And take His children home;
How will the wicked quake and fear,
When they before Him must appear.

He comes, the world to judge,
Nor will He take a bribe;
His wrath none can escape,
But His belovèd bride;
Millions will unto mountains call,
To hide them and upon them fall.

Poor soul, what is thy hope?
On what dost thou depend?
Art thou a stranger still
To Christ, the sinner's Friend?
Soon thou must leave thy all below,
And then, O then, what wilt thou do?

Christians, lift up your heads;
Say, what has Jesus done?
His matchless grace to you
The Saviour has made known;
Yes, you shall all His glory see,
And from the second death be free.

1098 William Cowper CM
**Jesus took bread, and blessed it, and brake it,
and gave it to the disciples, and said, Take,
eat; this is My body.**
Matthew 26:26

This is the feast of heavenly wine,
And God invites to sup;
The juices of the living Vine
Were pressed to fill the cup.

O bless the Saviour, ye that eat,
With royal dainties fed;
Not heaven affords a costlier treat,
For Jesus is the bread.

The vile, the lost, He calls to them.
Ye trembling souls appear;
The righteous, in their own esteem,
Have no acceptance here.

Approach, ye poor, nor dare refuse
The banquet spread for you;
Dear Saviour, this is welcome news
Then I may venture too.

If guilt and sin afford a plea,
And may obtain a place,
Surely the Lord will welcome me,
And I shall see His face.

1099 John Fellows LM
**Jesus took bread, and blessed it, and brake it,
and gave it to the disciples, and said, Take,
eat; this is My body.**
Matthew 26:26

Children of Zion, ye who sing
The lofty praises of your King;
Who in His solemn temple dwell,
And of His boundless glory tell:

Come in, ye blessèd of the Lord,
Ye that believe His holy word,
Come! and receive our heavenly bread,
The food with which His saints are fed.

Your Saviour's boundless goodness prove,
And feast on His redeeming love:
Come! all ye happy souls that thirst:
The last is welcome as the first.

Come to His table, and receive
Whate'er a pardoning God can give;
His love through every age endures,
His promise and Himself are yours.

1100   Edward Denny   SM
But I say unto you, I will not drink henceforth of this fruit of the vine, until that day when I drink it new with you in My Father's kingdom.
Matthew 26:29

Sweet feast of love divine!
'Tis grace that makes us free
To feed upon this bread and wine
  In memory, Lord, of Thee.

Here every welcome guest
Waits, Lord, from Thee to learn
The secrets of Thy Father's breast
  And all Thy grace discern.

Here conscience ends its strife
And faith delights to prove
The sweetness of the bread of life,
  The fulness of Thy love.

Thy blood that flowed for sin
In symbol here we see
And feel the blessèd pledge within,
  That we are loved of Thee.

But if this glimpse of love
Is so divinely sweet,
What will it be, O Lord, above,
  Thy gladdening smile to meet!

To see Thee face to face,
Thy perfect likeness wear
And all Thy ways of wondrous grace
  Through endless years declare!

1101   Aaron Wolfe   SM
And when they had sung an hymn, they went out into the mount of Olives. *Matthew 26:30*

A parting hymn we sing
Around Thy table, Lord;
Again our grateful tribute bring,
  Our solemn vows record.

Here have we seen Thy face,
And felt Thy presence near;
So may the savour of Thy grace
  In word and life appear.

In self-forgetting love
Be our communion shown,
Until we join the church above,
  And know as we are known.

1102   Henry White   LM
And when they had sung an hymn, they went out into the mount of Olives. *Matthew 26:30*

Come, Christian brethren, ere we part
Join every voice and every heart,
One solemn hymn to God we raise,
The closing song of grateful praise.

Christians, we here may meet no more,
But there is yet a happier shore;
And there, released from toil and pain,
Dear brethren, we shall meet again.

And now to God, the Three in One,
Be everlasting glory done;
Raise, raise, ye saints, the sound again;
Ye nations join the loud Amen.

1103   Jenny Hussey   CM + refrain
Then cometh Jesus with them unto a place called Gethsemane. *Matthew 26:36*

King of my life, I crown Thee now,
  Thine shall the glory be;
Lest I forget Thy thorn-crowned brow,
  Lead me to Calvary.

    Lest I forget Gethsemane,
    Lest I forget Thine agony,
    Lest I forget Thy love for me,
      Lead me to Calvary.

Show me the tomb where Thou wast laid,
  Tenderly mourned and wept:
Angels in robes of light arrayed,
  Guarded Thee whilst Thou slept.

Let me, like Mary, through the gloom,
  Come with a gift to Thee;
Show to me now the empty tomb,
  Lead me to Calvary.

May I be willing, Lord, to bear
  Daily my cross for Thee;
Even Thy cup of grief to share,
  Thou hast borne all for me.

Fill me, O Lord, with Thy desire
  For all who know not Thee;
Then touch my lips with holy fire,
  To speak of Calvary.

Lead Me to Calvary
Words: Jennie E. Hussey
© 1921, Ren. 1949 Hope Publishing Company, Carol Stream, IL 60188. All rights reserved. Used by permission.

1104 Joseph Hart LM
Then cometh Jesus with them unto a place called Gethsemane. *Matthew 26:36*

Come hither, ye that fain would know
  The exceeding sinfulness of sin;
Come see a scene of matchless woe,
  And tell me what it all can mean.

Behold the darling Son of God
  Bowed down with horror to the ground,
Wrung at the heart, and sweating blood,
  His eyes in tears of sorrow drowned!

See how the Victim panting lies,
  His soul with bitter anguish pressed;
He sighs, He faints, He groans, He cries,
  Dismayed, dejected, shocked, distressed.

What pangs are these that tear His heart?
  What burden's this that's on Him laid?
What means this agony of smart?
  What makes our Maker hang His head?

'Tis Justice, with its iron rod,
  Inflicting strokes of wrath divine;
'Tis the avenging hand of God,
  Incensed at all your sins and mine.

Deep in His breast our names were cut;
  He undertook our desperate debt;
Such loads of guilt were on Him put,
  He could but just sustain the weight.

Then let us not ourselves deceive;
  For, while of sin we lightly deem,
Whatever notions we may have,
  Indeed we are not much like Him.

1105 William Gadsby 77 77
Watch and pray, that ye enter not into temptation. *Matthew 26:41*

Dangerous is the path we go,
In this wilderness below,
Savage beasts, of every kind,
Aiming to distress the mind.

Scarce an hour but pilgrims see
They from danger are not free;
In some unexpected way,
Something fills them with dismay.

Thus beset, they daily feel
They have neither strength nor skill
Rightly to oppose the foe,
Or to guard against the woe.

How, then, can they persevere?
Must they of the prize despair?
No; 'tis theirs to watch and pray,
For the Lord will guard the way.

Christ the Master, Lord of all,
Bids His children watch and call;
May it be our blessèd case,
Both to watch and seek His face.

When we watch, then may we pray,
And in prayer watch every day;
And with pleasure ever prove
All our strength is from above.

Thus supported, we shall be
More than conquerors, Lord, through Thee;
And when every danger's past,
Live and reign with Thee at last.

1106 Anne Steele CM
Watch and pray, that ye enter not into temptation. *Matthew 26:41*

Alas, what hourly dangers rise!
  What snares beset my way!
To heaven O let me lift my eyes,
  And hourly watch and pray.

How oft my mournful thoughts complain,
  And melt in flowing tears!
My weak resistance, ah, how vain!
  How strong my foes and fears!

O gracious God, in whom I live,
  My feeble efforts aid;
Help me to watch, and pray, and strive,
  Though trembling and afraid.

Increase my faith, increase my hope,
  When foes and fears prevail!
And bear my fainting spirit up,
  Or soon my strength will fail.

Whene'er temptations fright my heart,
  Or lure my feet aside,
O God, Thy powerful aid impart—
  My Guardian and my Guide.

O keep me in the heavenly way,
  And bid the tempter flee;
And let me never, never stray,
  From happiness and Thee.

1107 Charlotte Elliott   777 3
**Watch and pray, that ye enter not into
temptation.** *Matthew 26:41*

Christian! seek not yet repose,
Cast thy dreams of ease away,
Thou art in the midst of foes:
    Watch and pray.

Principalities and powers,
Mustering their unseen array,
Wait for thy unguarded hours:
    Watch and pray.

Gird thy heavenly armour on,
Wear it ever night and day;
Ambushed lies the evil one:
    Watch and pray.

Hear the victors who o'ercame;
Still they mark each warrior's way;
All with one sweet voice exclaim,
    'Watch and pray.'

Hear, above all, hear thy Lord,
Him thou lovest to obey;
Hide within thy heart His word,
    Watch and pray.

Watch, as if on that alone
Hung the issue of the day;
Pray that help may be sent down;
    Watch and pray.

1108 Charlotte Elliott   888 4
**O my Father, if this cup may not pass away
from Me, except I drink it, Thy will be done.**
Matthew 26:42

My God my Father while I stray
Far from my home on life's rough way,
O, teach me from my heart to say,
    'Thy will be done!'

If Thou shouldst call me to resign
What most I prize; it ne'er was mine;
I only yield Thee what was Thine;
    'Thy will be done!'

Should pining sickness waste away
My life, in premature decay;
My Father, still I strive to say,
    'Thy will be done!'

If but my fainting heart be blest
With Thy sweet Spirit for its guest,
My God, to Thee I leave the rest;
    'Thy will be done!'

Renew my will from day to day;
Blend it with Thine, and take away
All that now makes it hard to say,
    'Thy will be done!'

Then, when on earth I breathe no more,
The prayer, oft mixed with tears before,
I'll sing upon a happier shore,
    'Thy will be done!'

1109 John Chandler   87 87 47
And sitting down they watched Him there.
Matthew 27:36

Now, my soul, thy voice upraising,
    Sing aloud in mournful strain,
Of the sorrows most amazing,
    And the agonizing pain,
        Which our Saviour
    Sinless bore, for sinners slain.

He the ruthless scourge enduring,
    Ransom for our sins to pay;
Sinners by His own stripes curing,
    Raising those who wounded lay;
        Bore our sorrows,
    And removed our pains away.

He to liberty restored us
    By the very bonds He bare:
And His nail-pierced limbs afford us
    Each a stream of mercy rare:
        Lo! He draws us
    To the cross, and keeps us there.

When His painful life was ended,
    When the spear transfixed His side,
Blood and water thence descended,
    Pouring forth a double tide:
        This to cleanse us,
    That to heal us, is applied.

Jesus! may Thy promised blessing
    Comfort to our souls afford;
May we, now Thy love possessing,
    And at length our full reward,
        Ever praise Thee,
    As our ever-glorious Lord!

1110 Thomas Kelly   SM
He saved others; Himself He cannot save.
Matthew 27:42

    'Himself He cannot save,'
    Insulting foe, 'tis true;
The words a gracious meaning have,
    Though meant in scorn by you.

'Himself He cannot save,'
This is His highest praise.
Himself for others' sake He gave,
And suffers in their place.

It were an easy part
For Him the cross to fly;
But love to sinners fills His heart,
And makes Him choose to die.

'Tis love the cause unfolds,
The deep mysterious cause,
Why He who all the world upholds,
Hangs upon yonder cross.

Let carnal Jews blaspheme,
And worldly wisdom mock;
The Saviour's cross shall be my theme,
And Christ Himself my Rock.

1111   James Deck   CM
And, behold, the veil of the temple was rent in
twain from the top to the bottom; and the earth
did quake, and the rocks rent. Matthew 27:51

The veil is rent: lo! Jesus stands
Before the throne of grace;
And clouds of incense from His hands
Fill all that glorious place.

His precious blood is sprinkled there,
Before and on the throne;
And His own wounds in heaven declare
His work on earth is done.

'Tis finished!' on the cross, He said,
In agonies and blood;
'Tis finished!' now He lives to plead
Before the face of God.

'Tis finished!' here our souls can rest,
His work can never fail;
By Him, our Sacrifice and Priest,
We enter through the veil.

Within the holiest of all,
Cleansed by His precious blood,
Before Thy throne Thy children fall,
And worship Thee, our God.

1112   Samuel Stennett   CM
Truly this was the Son of God.
Matthew 27:54

Yonder: amazing sight! I see
Th' incarnate Son of God
Expiring on th' accursèd tree,
'Twas there He shed His blood.

The trembling earth, the darkened sky,
Proclaim the truth aloud;
And with th' amazed centurion, cry,
'This is the Son of God!'

So great, so vast a sacrifice
May well my hope revive:
If God's own Son thus bleeds and dies,
The sinner sure may live.

O that these cords of love divine
Might draw me, Lord, to Thee!
Thou hast my heart, it shall be Thine!
Thine it shall ever be!

1113   Charles Wesley   77 77 + Hallelujahs
He is not here: for He is risen, as He said.
Matthew 28:6

Christ, the Lord, is risen today:
    Hallelujah!
Sons of men and angels say,
    Hallelujah!
Raise your joys and triumphs high;
    Hallelujah!
Sing, ye heavens; thou earth, reply,
    Hallelujah!

Love's redeeming work is done;
Fought the fight, the battle won:
Lo! our Sun's eclipse is o'er;
Lo! He sets in blood no more.

Vain the stone, the watch, the seal,
Christ hath burst the gates of hell:
Death in vain forbids Him rise!
Christ hath opened paradise.

Lives again our glorious King!
Where, O death, is now thy sting?
Once He died our souls to save;
Where thy victory, O grave?

Soar we now where Christ hath led,
Following our exalted Head:
Made like Him, like Him we rise,
Ours the cross, the grave, the skies.

Hail the Lord of earth and heaven,
Praise to Thee by both be given;
Thee we greet triumphant now,
Hail, the Resurrection Thou!

1114   Thomas Kelly   87 87 47
He is not here: for He is risen, as He said.
Matthew 28:6

Come, ye saints, look here and wonder,
  See the place where Jesus lay;
He has burst His bands asunder,
  He has borne our sins away.
    Joyful tidings!
  Yes, the Lord is risen today.

Jesus triumphs! O sing praises!
  By His death He overcame:
Thus the Lord His glory raises;
  Thus He fills His foes with shame.
    O sing praises!
  Praises to the Victor's name.

Jesus triumphs! countless legions
  Come from heaven to meet their King;
Soon in yonder blessèd regions
  They shall join His praise to sing.
    Songs eternal
  Shall through heaven's high arches ring.

1115   Christopher Wordsworth   87 87 D
He is not here: for He is risen, as He said.
Matthew 28:6

Hallelujah! Hallelujah!
  Hearts to heaven and voices raise;
Sing to God a hymn of gladness,
  Sing to God a hymn of praise;
He, who on the cross a victim
  For the world's salvation bled,
Jesus Christ, the King of glory,
  Now is risen from the dead.

Christ is risen, Christ the first-fruits
  Of the holy harvest field,
Which will all its full abundance
  At His second coming yield;
Then the golden ears of harvest
  Will their heads before Him wave,
Ripened by His glorious sunshine
  From the furrows of the grave.

Christ is risen, we are risen;
  Shed upon us heavenly grace,
Rain, and dew, and gleams of glory,
  From the brightness of Thy face;
So that we, with hearts in heaven,
  Here on earth may fruitful be,
And by angel-hands be gathered,
  And be ever Lord with Thee.

Hallelujah! Hallelujah!
  Glory be to God on high;
Hallelujah to the Saviour,
  Who has gained the victory;
Hallelujah to the Spirit,
  Fount of love and sanctity;
Hallelujah! Hallelujah!
  To the Triune Majesty!

1116   Philip Doddridge   CM
He is not here: for He is risen, as He said.
Matthew 28:6

Ye humble souls that seek the Lord,
  Chase all your fears away;
And bow with rapture down to see
  The place where Jesus lay.

Thus low the Lord of life was brought,
  Such wonders love can do;
Thus cold in death that bosom lay,
  Which throbbed and bled for you.

But raise your eyes, and tune your songs;
  The Saviour lives again:
Not all the bolts and bars of death
  The Conqueror could detain.

High o'er the angelic bands He rears
  His once dishonoured head;
And through unnumbered years He reigns,
  Who dwelt among the dead.

With joy like His shall every saint
  His vacant tomb survey;
Then rise with His ascending Lord
  To realms of endless day.

1117   Thomas Baldwin   LM
He is not here: for He is risen, as He said.
Matthew 28:6

Come, happy souls, adore the Lamb,
Who loved our race ere time began,
Who veiled His Godhead in our clay,
And in the humble manger lay.

To Jordan's stream the Spirit led,
To mark the path His saints should tread,
With joy they trace the sacred way,
To see the place where Jesus lay.

Baptized by John in Jordan's wave,
The Saviour left His watery grave;
Heaven owned the deed, approved the way,
And blessed the place where Jesus lay.

Come, all who love His precious name:
Come, tread His steps and learn of Him;
Happy beyond expression they
Who find the place where Jesus lay.

1118   John Monsell   87 87 D + refrain
And go quickly, and tell His disciples that He is risen from the dead. *Matthew 28:7*

Christ is risen! Hallelujah!
    Risen our victorious Head!
Sing His praises! Hallelujah!
    Christ is risen from the dead.
Gratefully our hearts adore Him,
    As His light once more appears,
Bowing down in joy before Him,
    Rising up from grief and tears.

Christ is risen! Hallelujah!
    Risen our victorious Head!
Sing His praises! Hallelujah!
    Christ is risen from the dead.

Christ is risen! all the sadness
    Of His earthly life is o'er,
Through the open gates of gladness
    He returns to life once more;
Death and hell before Him bending,
    He doth rise, the Victor now,
Angels on His steps attending,
    Glory round His wounded brow.

Christ is risen! henceforth never
    Death or hell shall us enthral,
We are Christ's, in Him for ever
    We have triumphed over all;
All the doubting and dejection
    Of our trembling hearts have ceased:
'Tis His day of resurrection,
    Let us rise and keep the feast.

1119   Thomas Kelly   664 6664
Go ye therefore, and teach all nations, baptizing them in the name of the Father, and of the Son, and of the Holy Ghost.
Matthew 28:19

Sound, sound the truth abroad!
Bear ye the word of God
    Through the wide world!
Tell what our Lord has done
Tell how the day is won
And from His lofty throne
    Satan is hurled.

It is our Lord's command
Far over sea and land
    To bear His name;
Bear it to every shore,
Regions unknown explore,
Enter at every door,
    Silence is shame.

Speed on the wings of love,
Jesus, who reigns above,
    Bids us to fly;
They who His message bear
Should neither doubt nor fear:
He will their Friend appear,
    He will be nigh.

When on the mighty deep,
He will their spirits keep,
    Stayed on His word;
When in a foreign land,
No other friend at hand,
Jesus will by them stand,
    Jesus their Lord.

Ye who, forsaking all,
At your loved Master's call
    Comforts resign;
Soon will your work be done,
Soon will the prize be won,
Brighter than yonder sun,
    Then shall ye shine.

1120   Joseph Tritton   LM
Lo, I am with you alway, even unto the end of the world. *Matthew 28:20*

Head of the church and Lord of all,
Hear from Thy throne our suppliant call,
We come the promised grace to seek
Of which aforetime Thou didst speak.

'Lo, I am with you': that sweet word,
Lord Jesus, meekly be it heard
And stamped with all-inspiring power
On our weak souls this favoured hour.

Without Thy presence, King of saints,
Our purpose fails, our spirit faints,
Thou must our wavering faith renew,
Ere we can yield Thee service true.

Thy consecrating might we ask
Or vain the toil, unblessed the task,
And impotent of fruit will be
Love's holiest effort wrought for Thee.

'Lo, I am with you:' even so,
Thy joy our strength we fearless go,
And praise shall crown the suppliant's call,
Head of the church and Lord of all!

1121 Philip Doddridge CM

Lo, I am with you alway, even unto the end of the world. *Matthew 28:20*

Now let our mourning hearts revive,
  And all our tears be dry;
Why should those eyes be drowned in grief,
  Which view a Saviour nigh?

What though the arm of conquering death
  Does God's own house invade;
What though the prophet and the priest
  Be numbered with the dead?

Though earthly shepherds dwell in dust,
  The agèd and the young,
The watchful eye in darkness closed,
  And mute the instructive tongue;

The eternal Shepherd still survives,
  New comfort to impart;
His eye still guides us, and His voice
  Still animates our heart.

'Lo, I am with you,' saith the Lord,
  'My church shall safe abide;
For I will ne'er forsake My own,
  Whose souls in Me confide.'

Through every scene of life and death,
  This promise is our trust;
And this shall be our children's song,
  When we are cold in dust.

REV ALAN C CLIFFORD 1941-

1122 Alan Clifford DCM

I am with you alway. *Matthew 28:20*

In all the winding paths of life,
  Their troubles and their cares,
Our hearts they long to end the strife
  That burdens all our days;
Where do we rest, 'till glory breaks,
  In friends, in memories?
In Him we rest, who ever speaks,
  'I am with you always!'

The peaceful place, the carefree day,
  The most endearing friend,
Such snares become; they make us say,
  'O may they never end!'
In vain we cling to passing joys
  That vanish from our eyes,
In moments sad, recall the words,
  'I am with you always!'

Lift up your head, O child of God,
  And cast away your fears;
Your path the Lord of glory trod,
  With anguish, blood and tears!
He is your treasure, ever new,
  Your comfort all your days;
Rest in His word, who speaks to you,
  'I am with you always!'

© *Author*

1123 Henry Twells LM

And at even, when the sun did set, they brought unto Him all that were diseased, and them that were possessed with devils.
Mark 1:32

At even, ere the sun was set,
  The sick, O Lord, around Thee lay;
O in what divers pains they met!
  O with what joy they went away!

Once more 'tis eventide, and we,
  Oppressed with various ills, draw near,
What if Thy form we cannot see?
  We know and feel that Thou art here.

O Saviour Christ, our woes dispel!
  For some are sick and some are sad;
And some have never loved Thee well,
  And some have lost the love they had.

And some are pressed with worldly care,
  And some are tried with sinful doubt;
And some such grievous passions tear
  That only Thou canst cast them out.

And none, O Lord, have perfect rest,
  For none are wholly free from sin;
And they who fain would serve Thee best,
  Are conscious most of wrong within.

O Saviour Christ, Thou too art Man!
  Thou hast been troubled, tempted, tried;
Thy kind but searching glance can scan
  The very wounds that shame would hide.

Thy touch has still its ancient power;
  No word from Thee can fruitless fall;
Hear in this solemn evening hour,
  And in Thy mercy heal us all.

1124   Augustus Toplady   11 11 11 11
I came not to call the righteous, but sinners to repentance. *Mark 2:17*

The gospel brings tidings to each wounded soul,
That Jesus the Saviour can make it quite whole;
And what makes this gospel most precious to me,
It holds forth salvation so perfectly free!

The gospel declares that God, sending His Son
To die for poor sinners, gave all things in one;
This, too, makes the gospel most precious to me;
Because 'tis a gospel as full as 'tis free!

Since Jesus has saved me, and that freely too,
I fain would in all things my gratitude show;
But as to man's merit, 'tis hateful to me!
The gospel—I love it; 'tis perfectly free!

1125   Samuel Wesley   CM
Therefore the Son of man is Lord also of the sabbath. Mark 2:28

The Lord of Sabbaths let us praise
  In concert with the blest:
And in most sweet harmonious lays
  Employ this day of rest.

O may we still remember Thee,
  And more in knowledge grow
More of Thyself, dear Jesus, see,
  While waiting here below.

On this blest day a brighter scene
  Of glory was displayed
By God th' eternal Word, than when
  The universe was made.

He rises, who our pardon bought
  With grief and pain extreme;
'Twas great to speak our souls from nought,
  But greater to redeem.

A blest eternity we hope
  With Him in heaven to spend
Where congregations ne'er break up,
  And Sabbaths never end.

1126   Washington Gladden   LM
And He ordained twelve, that they should be with Him, and that He might send them forth to preach. *Mark 3:14*

O Master, let me walk with Thee
In lowly paths of service free;
Tell me Thy secret; help me bear
The strain of toil, the fret of care.

Help me the slow of heart to move
By some clear winning word of love;
Teach me the wayward feet to stay
And guide them in the homeward way.

Teach me Thy patience; still with Thee
In closer, dearer company,
In work that keeps faith sweet and strong,
In trust that triumphs over wrong;

In hope that sends a shining ray
Far down the future's broadening way;
In peace that only Thou canst give,
With Thee, O Master, let me live.

1127   Richard Burnham   CM
And with many such parables spake He the word unto them, as they were able to hear it. *Mark 4:33*

How wise and various are the ways
  The Saviour doth pursue,
In dealing with a chosen race,
  And forming them anew!

Some feel the piercing law of God,
  And vengeance seems to reign;
Then cry for mercy, plead, and wait,
  But all appears in vain.

At length the Lord of glory comes
  To wipe their streaming eyes,
Sweetly applies the healing blood,
  And guilt and terror dies.

Others are drawn with cords of love,
  And run with eager pace:
Soon they behold the pardoning God,
  And feel the sealing grace.

Others are led more gently on,
  Yet prayerful and sincere,
Kindly upheld with cheering hopes,
  But seldom free from fear.

Lord, look on all our waiting souls,
  And all our doubts remove:
Enter each heart, and reign alone,
  The God of truth and love.

1128   Edward Hopper   77 77 77
Peace, be still. *Mark 4:39*

Jesus, Saviour, pilot me,
Over life's tempestuous sea;
Unknown waves before me roll,
Hiding rock and treacherous shoal;
    Chart and compass come from Thee;
    Jesus, Saviour, pilot me!

As a mother stills her child,
Thou canst hush the ocean wild;
Boisterous waves obey Thy will
When Thou sayest to them, 'Be still!'
    Wondrous Sovereign of the sea,
    Jesus, Saviour, pilot me!

When at last I near the shore,
And the fearful breakers roar
Twixt me and the peaceful rest,
Then, when leaning on Thy breast,
    May I hear Thee say to me,
    'Fear not! I will pilot thee!'

1129   Dorothy Thrupp   CM
**What manner of man is this, that even the
wind and the sea obey Him?** *Mark 4:41*

A little ship was on the sea,
    It was a pretty sight;
It sailed along so pleasantly,
    And all was calm and bright.

When, lo! a storm began to rise,
    The wind grew loud and strong;
It blew the clouds across the skies,
    It blew the waves along.

And all but One were sore afraid
    Of sinking in the deep;
His head was on a pillow laid,
    And He was fast asleep.

'Master, we perish; Master, save!'
    They cried. Their Master heard:
He rose, rebuked the wind and wave,
    And stilled them with a word.

He to the storm says, 'Peace be still!'
    The raging billows cease:
The mighty winds obey His will,
    And all are hushed to peace.

O! well we know it was the Lord,
    Our Saviour and our Friend,
Whose care of those who trust His word,
    Will never, never end.

BISHOP TIMOTHY DUDLEY-SMITH 1926-

1130   Timothy Dudley-Smith   10 10 10 10
**Go home to thy friends, and tell them how
great things the Lord hath done for thee, and
hath had compassion on thee.**
Mark 5:19

Tell out, my soul, the greatness of the Lord!
    Unnumbered blessings, give my spirit voice;
Tender to me the promise of His word;
    In God my Saviour shall my heart rejoice.

Tell out, my soul, the greatness of His name!
    Make known His might, the deeds His arm has
        done;
His mercy sure, from age to age the same;
    His holy name, the Lord, the mighty One.

Tell out, my soul, the greatness of His might!
    Powers and dominions lay their glory by.
Proud hearts and stubborn wills are put to
        flight,
    The hungry fed, the humble lifted high.

Tell out, my soul, the glories of His word!
    Firm is His promise, and His mercy sure.
Tell out, my soul, the greatness of the Lord
    To children's children and for evermore!

1131 Edward Bickersteth 10 10 10 10
**And He said unto them, Come ye yourselves
apart into a desert place, and rest a while.**
Mark 6:31

Come ye yourselves apart and rest awhile,
  Weary, I know it, of the press and throng;
Wipe from your brow the sweat and dust of toil,
  And in My quiet strength again be strong.

Come ye aside from all the world holds dear,
  For converse which the world has never known;
Alone with Me and with My Father here,
  With Me and with My Father not alone.

Come, tell me all that ye have said and done,
  Your victories and failures, hopes and fears;
I know how hardly souls are wooed and won;
  My choicest wreaths are always wet with tears.

Come ye and rest: the journey is too great
  And ye will faint beside the way and sink;
The bread of life is here for you to eat
  And here for you the wine of love to drink.

Then, fresh from converse with our Lord, return
  And work till daylight softens into even;
The brief hours are not lost in which ye learn
  More of your Master and His rest in heaven.

1132 Charles Wesley CM
Be of good cheer: it is I; be not afraid.
Mark 6:50

Talk with us, Lord, Thyself reveal,
  While here on earth we rove;
Speak to our hearts, and let us feel
  The kindling of Thy love.

With Thee conversing, we forget
  All time and toil and care;
Labour is rest, and pain is sweet,
  If Thou, my God, art there.

Here then, my God, vouchsafe to stay,
  And bid my heart rejoice;
My bounding heart shall own Thy sway,
  And echo to Thy voice.

Thou callest me to seek Thy face,
  'Tis all I wish to seek;
To attend the whispers of Thy grace,
  And hear Thee inly speak.

Let this my every hour employ
  Till I Thy glory see,
Enter into my Master's joy,
  And find my heaven in Thee.

1133 Samuel Medley LM
He hath done all things well. *Mark 7:37*

O for a heart prepared to sing,
To God, my Saviour and my King!
While with His saints I join to tell,
My Jesus has done all things well.

All worlds His glorious power confess
His wisdom all His works express;
But O His love what tongue can tell?
My Jesus has done all things well.

How sovereign, wonderful, and free,
Is all His love to sinful me!
He plucked me as a brand from hell;
My Jesus has done all things well.

And since my soul has known His love,
What mercies has He made me prove:
Mercies which all my praise excel;
My Jesus has done all things well.

Whene'er my Saviour and my God
Has on me laid His gentle rod,
I know, in all that has befell,
My Jesus has done all things well.

Sometimes He's pleased His face to hide,
To make me pray, or stain my pride;
Yet am I helped on this to dwell,
My Jesus has done all things well.

Soon shall I pass the vale of death,
And in His arms shall lose my breath;
Yet then my happy soul shall tell,
My Jesus has done all things well.

And when to that bright world I rise,
And join the anthems in the skies,
Among the rest this note shall swell,
My Jesus has done all things well.

1134   John Newton   CM
Now the disciples had forgotten to take bread,
neither had they in the ship with them more
than one loaf. *Mark 8:14*

When the disciples crossed the lake
  With but one loaf on board;
How strangely did their hearts mistake
  The caution of their LORD.

'The leaven of the Pharisees
  Beware,' the Saviour said;
They thought, 'it is because He sees
  We have forgotten bread.'

It seems they had forgotten too,
  What their own eyes had viewed;
How with what scarce sufficed for few,
  He fed a multitude.

If five small loaves, by His command,
  Could many thousands serve;
Might they not trust His gracious hand,
  That they should never starve?

They oft His power and love had known,
  And doubtless were to blame;
But we have reason good to own
  That we are just the same.

How often has He brought relief,
  And every want supplied!
Yet soon, again, our unbelief
  Says, 'Can the Lord provide?'

Be thankful for one loaf today,
  Though that be all your store;
Tomorrow, if you trust and pray,
  Shall timely bring you more.

1135   John Wreford   CM
Lord, I believe; help Thou mine unbelief.
Mark 9:24

Lord, I believe; Thy power I own,
  Thy word I would obey;
I wander comfortless and lone
  When from Thy truth I stray.

Lord, I believe; but gloomy fears
  Sometimes bedim my sight;
I look to Thee with prayers and tears
  And cry for strength and light.

Lord, I believe; but Thou dost know
  My faith is cold and weak;
Pity my frailty and bestow
  The confidence I seek.

Yes, I believe; and only Thou
  Canst give my soul relief:
Lord, to Thy truth my spirit bow;
  Help Thou mine unbelief.

1136   Thomas Hastings   CM
And they brought young children to Him.
Mark 10:13

O Lord, behold us at Thy feet,
  A needy, sinful band:
As suppliants round Thy mercy-seat,
  We come at Thy command.

'Tis for our children we would plead,
  The offspring Thou hast given;
Where shall we go, in time of need,
  But to the God of heaven?

We ask not for them wealth or fame,
  Amid the worldly strife;
But, in the all-prevailing name,
  We ask eternal life.

We crave the Spirit's quickening grace,
  To make them pure in heart,
That they may stand before Thy face,
  And see Thee as Thou art.

1137   James Gabb   77 77
And they brought young children to Him.
Mark 10:13

Jesus, Thou wast once a child,
Meek, obedient, pure, and mild;
Such may our dear children be!
Teach them, Lord, to follow Thee.

Thou didst grow in grace and truth,
Up from infancy to youth;
May we, Lord, our children see,
Striving thus to copy Thee.

Subject to Thy parents' word,
When their least command was heard,
May we, Lord, our children see
Thus obedient unto Thee!

At Thy heavenly Father's voice,
Thou in duty didst rejoice;
Changed by grace, O Lord, would we
See our children follow Thee!

1138 Thomas Hastings 77 77
And they brought young children to Him.
Mark 10:13

God of mercy, hear our prayer
 For the children Thou hast given;
Let them all Thy blessings share,
 Grace on earth, and bliss in heaven!

In the morning of their days
 May their hearts be drawn to Thee;
Let them learn to lisp Thy praise
 In their earliest infancy.

Cleanse their souls from every stain,
 Through the Saviour's precious blood;
Let them all be born again,
 And be reconciled to God.

For this mercy, Lord, we cry;
 Bend Thine ever-gracious ear;
While on Thee our souls rely,
 Hear our prayer, in mercy hear!

1139 Walter Mathams 85 83
**Suffer the little children to come unto Me, and
forbid them not: for of such is the kingdom of
God.** *Mark 10:14*

Jesus, Friend of little children,
 Be a Friend to me;
Take my hand and ever keep me
 Close to Thee.

Teach me how to grow in goodness,
 Daily as I grow;
Thou hast been a child and surely
 Thou dost know.

Step by step, O lead me onward,
 Upward into youth!
Wiser, stronger still becoming
 In Thy truth.

Never leave me, nor forsake me,
 Ever be My Friend;
For I need Thee from life's dawning
 To its end.

1140 Charles Wesley 77 77
**Whosoever shall not receive the kingdom of
God as a little child, he shall not enter therein.**
Mark 10:15

Lord, if Thou Thy grace impart,
Poor in spirit, meek in heart,
I shall, as my Master, be
Rooted in humility.

Simple, teachable, and mild,
Changed into a little child;
Pleased with all the Lord provides;
Weaned from all the world besides.

Father, fix my soul on Thee;
Every evil let me flee;
Nothing want, beneath, above,
Happy in Thy precious love.

1141 Harriet McKeever 65 65
**And He took them up in His arms, put His
hands upon them, and blessed them.**
Mark 10:16

Jesus, high in glory,
 Lend a listening ear;
When we bow before Thee,
 Children's praises hear.

Though Thou art so holy,
 Heaven's almighty King,
Thou wilt stoop to listen
 While Thy praise we sing.

We are little children,
 Weak and apt to stray;
Saviour, guide and keep us
 In the heavenly way.

Save us, Lord, from sinning,
 Watch us day by day;
Help us now to love Thee,
 Take our sins away.

Then when Thou shalt call us
 To our heavenly home,
We will gladly answer,
 'Saviour, Lord, we come.'

1142 Philip Doddridge CM
**And He took them up in His arms, put His
hands upon them, and blessed them.**
Mark 10:16

See Israel's gentle Shepherd stand
 With all-engaging charms;
Hark, how He calls the tender lambs
 And folds them in His arms.

'Permit them to approach,' He cries,
 'Nor scorn their humble name;'
For 'twas to bless such souls as these
 The Lord of angels came.

We bring them, Lord, in thankful hands
 And yield them up to Thee;
Joyful that we ourselves are Thine,
 Thine let our offspring be.

1143   Charles Wesley   77 77
**And He took them up in His arms, put His
hands upon them, and blessed them.**
Mark 10:16

Gentle Jesus, meek and mild,
Look upon a little child;
Pity my simplicity,
Suffer me to come to Thee.

Fain I would be as Thou art;
Give me Thy obedient heart;
Thou art pitiful and kind;
Let me have Thy loving mind.

Above all, let me fulfil
God my heavenly Father's will,
Never His good Spirit grieve,
Only to His glory live.

Thou didst live to God alone;
Thou didst never seek Thine own;
Thou Thyself didst never please;
God was all Thy happiness.

Loving Jesus, gentle Lamb,
In Thy gracious hands I am;
Make me, Saviour, what Thou art;
Live Thyself within my heart.

I shall then show forth Thy praise,
Serve Thee all my happy days;
Then the world shall always see
Christ, the holy Child, in me.

1144   Anna Warner   77 77 + refrain
**And He took them up in His arms, put His
hands upon them, and blessed them.**
Mark 10:16

Jesus loves me, this I know,
For the Bible tells me so;
Little ones to Him belong,
They are weak, but He is strong.

Yes, Jesus loves me,
Yes, Jesus loves me,
Yes, Jesus loves me,
The Bible tells me so.

Jesus loves me! He who died
Heaven's gate to open wide;
He will wash away my sin,
Let His little child come in.

Jesus loves me! loves me still,
When I'm very weak and ill;
From His shining throne on high
Watches with me where I lie.

Jesus loves me! He will stay
Close beside me all the way;
If I love Him, when I die
He will take me home on high.

1145   Augustus Toplady   CM
**Who then can be saved? And Jesus looking
upon them saith, With men it is impossible,
but not with God: for with God all things are
possible.** *Mark 10:26,27.*

What though I cannot break my chain
    Or e'er throw off my load,
The things impossible to men
    Are possible to God.

Who, who shall in Thy presence stand,
    Or match Omnipotence;
Unfold the grasp of Thy right hand
    And pluck the sinner thence?

Faith to be healed I fain would have,
    O might it now be given;
Thou canst, Thou canst the sinner save,
    And make me meet for heaven.

Bound down with twice ten thousand ties,
    Yet let me hear Thy call;
My soul in confidence shall rise,
    Shall rise and break through all.

Thou canst o'ercome this heart of mine,
    Thou wilt victorious prove;
For everlasting strength is Thine,
    And everlasting love.

1146   Henry Lyte   87 87 D
We have left all, and have followed Thee.
Mark 10:28

Jesus, I my cross have taken,
    All to leave, and follow Thee;
Destitute, despised, forsaken,
    Thou from hence my all shalt be:
Perish every fond ambition,
    All I've sought, and hoped, and known;
Yet how rich is my condition!
    God and heaven are still mine own.

Let the world despise and leave me,
    They have left my Saviour too;
Human hearts and looks deceive me;
    Thou art not, like man, untrue:
And, while Thou shalt smile upon me,
    God of wisdom, love, and might,
Foes may hate, and friends may shun me;
    Show Thy face, and all is bright.

Man may trouble and distress me,
'Twill but drive me to Thy breast;
Life with trials hard may press me,
Heaven will bring me sweeter rest.
O 'tis not in grief to harm me,
While Thy love is left to me!
O 'twere not in joy to charm me,
Were that joy unmixed with Thee!

Take, my soul, thy full salvation;
Rise o'er sin, and fear, and care:
Joy to find in every station
Something still to do or bear.
Think what Spirit dwells within thee,
What a Father's smile is thine,
What a Saviour died to win thee:
Child of heaven, shouldst thou repine?

Haste then on from grace to glory,
Armed by faith, and winged by prayer;
Heaven's eternal day's before thee;
God's own hand shall guide thee there.
Soon shall close thine earthly mission,
Swift shall pass thy pilgrim days,
Hope soon change to glad fruition,
Faith to sight, and prayer to praise.

1147 Charlotte Elliott 888 6
He, casting away his garment, rose, and came to Jesus. *Mark 10:50*

Just as I am, without one plea,
But that Thy blood was shed for me
And that Thou bidd'st me come to Thee,
O Lamb of God, I come!

Just as I am, and waiting not
To rid my soul of one dark blot,
To Thee, whose blood can cleanse each spot,
O Lamb of God, I come!

Just as I am, though tossed about,
With many a conflict, many a doubt,
Fightings and fears within, without,
O Lamb of God, I come!

Just as I am, poor, wretched, blind;
Sight, riches, healing of the mind,
Yea, all I need, in Thee to find,
O Lamb of God, I come!

Just as I am, Thou wilt receive,
Wilt welcome, pardon, cleanse, relieve;
Because Thy promise I believe,
O Lamb of God, I come!

Just as I am, Thy love unknown
Has broken every barrier down;
Now to be Thine, yea, Thine alone,
O Lamb of God, I come!

Just as I am, of that free love
The breadth, length,depth, and height to prove,
Here for a season, then above,
O Lamb of God, I come.

1148 William Cowper LM
Is it not written, My house shall be called of all nations the house of prayer? but ye have made it a den of thieves. *Mark 11:17*

Thy mansion is the Christian's heart,
O Lord, Thy dwelling-place secure!
Bid the unruly throng depart,
And leave the consecrated door.

Devoted as it is to Thee,
A thievish swarm frequents the place;
They steal away my joys from me,
And rob my Saviour of His praise.

There, too, a sharp designing trade,
Sin, Satan, and the world maintain;
Nor cease to press me, and persuade
To part with ease and purchase pain.

I know them, and I hate their din;
Am weary of the bustling crowd;
But while their voice is heard within,
I cannot serve Thee as I would.

O for the joy Thy presence gives;
What peace shall reign when Thou art here;
Thy presence makes this den of thieves
A calm, delightful house of prayer.

And if Thou make Thy temple shine,
Yet, self-abased, will I adore;
The gold and silver are not mine;
I give Thee what was Thine before.

1149   John Newton   LM
And in the morning, as they passed by, they saw the fig tree dried up from the roots.
Mark 11:20

One awful word which Jesus spoke,
   Against the tree which bore no fruit;
More piercing than the lightenings stroke,
   Blasted and dried it to the root.

But could a tree the LORD offend,
   To make Him show His anger thus?
He surely had a farther end,
   To be a warning word to us.

The fig-tree by its leaves was known,
   But having not a fig to show;
It brought a heavy sentence down,
   'Let none hereafter on thee grow.'

Too many, who the gospel hear,
   Whom Satan blinds and sin deceives;
We to this fig-tree may compare,
   They yield no fruit, but only leaves.

Knowledge, and zeal, and gifts, and talk,
   Unless combined with faith and love,
And witnessed by a gospel walk,
   Will not a true profession prove.

Without the fruit the LORD expects
   Knowledge will make our state the worse;
The barren trees He still rejects,
   And soon will blast them with His curse.

O Lord! unite our hearts in prayer!
   On each of us Thy Spirit send;
That we the fruits of grace may bear,
   And find acceptance in the end.

1150   Frederick Faber   LM
And it was the third hour, and they crucified Him. *Mark 15:25*

O come and mourn with me awhile;
   O come ye to the Saviour's side;
O come together, let us mourn:
   Jesus, our Lord, is crucified.

Have we no tears to shed for Him,
   While soldiers scoff and Jews deride?
Ah! look how patiently He hangs;
   Jesus, our Lord, is crucified.

How fast His hands and feet are nailed;
   His throat with parching thirst is dried;
His failing eyes are dimmed with blood;
   Jesus, our Lord, is crucified.

Come let us stand beneath the cross;
   So may the blood from out His side
Fall gently on us drop by drop;
   Jesus, our Lord, is crucified.

A broken heart, a fount of tears
   Ask, and they will not be denied;
Lord Jesus, may we love and weep,
   Since Thou for us art crucified.

1151   Thomas Kelly   87 87 47
And the superscription of His accusation was written over, THE KING OF THE JEWS.
Mark 15:26

'Tis to Thee we owe allegiance,
   God our Saviour and our King;
May we render true obedience,
   Every day our tribute bring;
      And with rapture
   Of Thy love and glory sing.

May we bow to Thy dominion,
   Yielding to Thy righteous sway;
Careless of the world's opinion,
   May we all Thy will obey;
      Saviour, lead us,
   Lead us in the perfect way.

Thine is greatness never wasting,
   High Thou art, with glory crowned;
Thine a kingdom everlasting,
   Grace and truth Thy throne surround;
      While all others
   Vanish, and no more are found.

Happy they whom Thou dost govern!
   Great their peace, their honour great;
Thee beholding, Thee their Sovereign,
   Thee enthroned in royal state.
      Happy people!
   Who before Thee ever wait!

1152   John Ellerton   77 77 77
My God, My God, why hast Thou forsaken Me?
Mark 15:34

Throned upon the awful tree,
King of grief, I watch with Thee.
   Darkness veils Thine anguished face;
   None its lines of woe can trace;
None can tell what pangs unknown
Hold Thee silent and alone.

Silent through those three dread hours,
Wrestling with the evil powers.
    Left alone with human sin,
    Gloom around Thee and within,
Till the appointed time is nigh,
Till the Lamb of God may die.

Hark, that cry that peals aloud
Upward through the whelming cloud!
    Thou, the Father's only Son,
    Thou, His own Anointed One,
Thou dost ask Him—can it be?—
'Why hast Thou forsaken Me?'

Lord, should fear and anguish roll
Darkly o'er my sinful soul,
    Thou, who once wast thus bereft
    That Thine own might ne'er be left,
Teach me by that bitter cry
In the gloom to know Thee nigh.

1153   William Clarke   CM
There were also women looking on afar off.
Mark 15:40

In Thee, my Lord, I am complete,
    My name is on Thy breast;
This truth unto my soul is sweet,
    And gives me peace and rest.

Like Salem's daughters may I sit,
    And view Thy wounds and blood;
Then will my soul begin to melt
    With love to Thee, my God.

1154   William Cowper   CM
There were also women looking on afar off.
Mark 15:40

'Tis joy enough, my All in all,
    At Thy dear feet to lie;
Thou wilt not let me lower fall,
    And none can higher fly.

1155   Thomas Haweis   66 66 88
He is risen; He is not here. *Mark 16:6*

The happy morn is come;
    Triumphant o'er the grave,
The Saviour leaves the tomb,
    Omnipotent to save:

    Captivity is captive led,
    For Jesus liveth, who was dead.

Who now accuseth them
    For whom their Surety died?
Or who shall those condemn
    Whom God hath justified?

Christ hath the ransom paid;
    The glorious work is done;
On Him our help is laid,
    By Him our victory won:

Hail, Thou triumphant Lord!
    The Resurrection Thou;
Hail, Thou Incarnate Word!
    Before Thy throne we bow;

1156   Edward Bickersteth   87 87 D (iambic)
And He said unto them, Go ye into all the
world, and preach the gospel to every
creature. *Mark 16:15*

For My sake and the gospel's, go
    And tell redemption's story;
His heralds answer, 'Be it so,
    And Thine, Lord, all the glory!'
They preach His birth, His life, His cross,
    The love of His atonement,
For whom they count the world but loss,
    His Easter, His enthronement.

Hark, hark, the trump of jubilee
    Proclaims to every nation,
From pole to pole, by land and sea,
    Glad tidings of salvation.
As nearer draws the day of doom
    While still the battle rages,
The heavenly Day-spring, through the gloom,
    Breaks on the night of ages.

Still on and on the anthems spread
    Of hallelujah voices,
In concert with the holy dead,
    The warrior-church rejoices;
Their snow-white robes are washed in blood,
    Their golden harps are ringing;
Earth and the Paradise of God
    One triumph-song are singing.

He comes, whose advent-trumpet drowns
    The last of time's evangels,
Immanuel crowned with many crowns,
    The Lord of saints and angels:
O Life, Light, Love, the great I AM,
    Triune, who changest never,
The throne of God and of the Lamb
    Is Thine, and Thine for ever!

1157 Thomas Kelly 87 87 47
And He said unto them, Go ye into all the world, and preach the gospel to every creature. *Mark 16:15*

Speed Thy servants, Saviour, speed them;
　Thou art Lord of winds and waves:
They were bound, but Thou hast freed them;
　Now they go to free the slaves.
　　Be Thou with them:
　'Tis Thine arm alone that saves.

Friends, and home, and all forsaking,
　Lord, they go at Thy command;
As their stay Thy promise taking,
　While they traverse sea and land:
　　O be with them!
　Lead them safely by the hand.

When they think of home, now dearer
　Than it ever seemed before,
Bring the promised glory nearer,
　Let them see that peaceful shore,
　　Where Thy people
　Rest from toil and weep no more.

Where no fruit appears to cheer them,
　And they seem to toil in vain,
Then in mercy, Lord, draw near them,
　Then their sinking hopes sustain;
　　Thus supported,
　Let their zeal revive again.

In the midst of opposition,
　Let them trust, O Lord, in Thee;
When success attends their mission,
　Let Thy servants humbler be;
　　Never leave them,
　Till Thy face in heaven they see:

There to reap in joy for ever
　Fruit that grows from seed here sown,
There to be with Him who never
　Ceases to preserve His own,
　　And with gladness
　Give the praise to Him alone.

BENJAMIN BEDDOME 1717-95

1158 Benjamin Beddome LM
And they went forth, and preached every where, the Lord working with them.
Mark 16:20

Father of mercies, bow Thine ear,
Attentive to our earnest prayer;
We plead for those who plead for Thee;
Successful pleaders may they be!

How great their work, how vast their charge!
Do Thou their anxious souls enlarge:
Their best acquirements are our gain;
We share the blessings they obtain.

Clothe, then, with energy divine,
Their words, and let those words be Thine;
To them Thy sacred truth reveal,
Suppress their fear, inflame their zeal.

Teach them to sow the precious seed,
Teach them Thy chosen flock to feed;
Teach them immortal souls to gain,
Souls that will well reward their pain.

Let thronging multitudes around
Hear from their lips the joyful sound,
In humble strains Thy grace implore
And feel Thy new-creating power.

1159 Charlotte Elliott SM
To make ready a people prepared for the Lord.
Luke 1:17

　Prepare me, gracious God,
　To stand before Thy face;
Thy Spirit must the work perform,
　For it is all of grace.

　In Christ's obedience clothe,
　And wash me in His blood;
So shall I lift my head with joy
　Among the sons of God.

　Do Thou my sins subdue;
　Thy sovereign love make known,
The spirit of my mind renew,
　And save me in Thy Son.

　Let me attest Thy power;
　Let me Thy goodness prove,
Till my full soul can hold no more
　Of everlasting love.

1160   Joseph Hart   87 87 D
And Mary said, My soul doth magnify the Lord.
Luke 1:46

Jesus is our God and Saviour,
    Guide, and Counsellor, and Friend;
Bearing all our misbehaviour,
    Kind and loving to the end.
Trust Him, He will not deceive us,
    Though we hardly of Him deem;
He will never, never leave us;
    Nor will let us quite leave Him.

Nothing but Thy blood, O Jesus!
    Can relieve us from our smart;
Nothing else from guilt release us:
    Nothing else can melt the heart.
Law and terrors do but harden,
    All the while they work alone;
But a sense of blood-bought pardon
    Soon dissolves a heart of stone.

Teach us, by Thy patient Spirit,
    How to mourn and not despair;
Let us, leaning on Thy merit,
    Wrestle hard with God in prayer.
Whatsoe'er afflictions seize us,
    They shall profit, if not please;
But defend, defend us, Jesus,
    From security and ease.

Softly to Thy garden lead us,
    To behold Thy bloody sweat;
Though Thou from the curse hast freed us,
    Let us not the cost forget.
Be Thy groans and cries rehearsèd
    By the Spirit in our ears,
Till we, viewing whom we've piercèd,
    Melt in sympathetic tears.

1161   Charles Wesley   77 77 77
**Through the tender mercy of our God;
whereby the Dayspring from on high hath
visited us.** *Luke 1:78*

Christ, whose glory fills the skies,
    Christ, the true, the only Light,
Sun of righteousness, arise,
    Triumph o'er the shades of night;
Dayspring from on high, be near;
Daystar, in my heart appear.

Dark and cheerless is the morn
    Unaccompanied by Thee;
Joyless is the day's return,
    Till Thy mercy's beams I see;
Till they inward light impart,
Glad my eyes, and warm my heart.

Visit then this soul of mine,
    Pierce the gloom of sin and grief;
Fill me, radiancy divine,
    Scatter all my unbelief;
More and more Thyself display,
Shining to the perfect day.

1162   J Ormiston   87 87
**Through the tender mercy of our God;
whereby the Dayspring from on high hath
visited us.** *Luke 1:78*

Lord, how tender is Thy mercy,
    Free as tender, rich as free;
Pitying, pardoning chief of sinners,
    Pitying, pardoning, even me.

Mercy tender, pity tearful,
    Find their fount divine in Thee;
Flowing thence, they seek the thirsty;
    Seeking, find that thirst in me.

Tender mercy, Lord, befits Thee,
    Need like mine befits Thy grace;
Pity gentle Lord, Thy pity
    Finds in me its resting-place.

'Twas Thy mercy, 'twas Thy pity,
    Ere creation, sin or man,
Moved Thee, true and faithful Kinsman,
    To secure redemption's plan.

Then, when time had coursed the ages
    Mercy, pity, sped to earth;
Cam'st Thou forth, the Man of sorrows,
    For our sorrows, lo! Thy birth.

Born to bear Thy brethren's burdens,
    Born to carry even mine!
O, what matchless mercy, pity,
    Saviour, Jesus, in Thee shine!

Sweet Thy mercy, deep Thy pity,
    Sweeter, deeper, day by day;
Deeper as life's shadows deepen,
    Sweeter as earth's joys decay.

Soon, O! soon, in Salem's city,
    Midst the ransomed sinner-host,
I shall sing the Mercy-Triune,
    Father, Son, and Holy Ghost!

1163 Isaac Watts CM

To give light to them that sit in darkness and in the shadow of death, to guide our feet into the way of peace. *Luke 1:79*

My God, the spring of all my joys,
    The life of my delights,
The glory of my brightest days,
    And comfort of my nights.

In darkest shades if He appear,
    My dawning is begun;
He is my soul's sweet morning star,
    And He my rising sun.

The opening heavens around me shine
    With beams of sacred bliss,
While Jesus shows His heart is mine,
    And whispers, 'I am His.'

My soul would leave this heavy clay,
    At that transporting word,
Run up with joy the shining way,
    To embrace my dearest Lord.

Fearless of hell and ghastly death,
    I'd break through every foe;
The wings of love and arms of faith
    Should bear me conqueror through.

1164 Johann Heerman, tr. C Winkworth
LM

To give light to them that sit in darkness and in the shadow of death, to guide our feet into the way of peace. *Luke 1:79*

O Christ, our true and only Light,
Illumine those who sit in night,
Let those afar now hear Thy voice
And in Thy fold with us rejoice.

And all who else have strayed from Thee,
O gently seek! Thy healing be
To every wounded conscience given
And let them also share Thy heaven.

O make the deaf to hear Thy word
And teach the dumb to speak, dear Lord,
Who dare not yet the faith avow,
Though secretly they hold it now.

Shine on the darkened and the cold,
Recall the wanderers from Thy fold,
Unite those now who walk apart,
Confirm the weak and doubting heart.

So they with us may evermore
Such grace with wondering thanks adore,
And endless praise to Thee be given
By all Thy church in earth and heaven.

1165 Edmund Sears DCM

And all went to be taxed, every one into his own city. *Luke 2:3*

It came upon the midnight clear,
    That glorious song of old,
From angels bending near the earth
    To touch their harps of gold:
'Peace on the earth, goodwill to men,
    From heaven's all-gracious King!'
The world in solemn stillness lay
    To hear the angels sing.

Still through the cloven skies they come,
    With peaceful wings unfurled,
And still their heavenly music floats
    O'er all the weary world;
Above its sad and lowly plains
    They bend on hovering wing,
And ever o'er its Babel sounds
    The blessèd angels sing.

Yet with the woes of sin and strife
    The world has suffered long;
Beneath the angels' strain have rolled
    Two thousand years of wrong;
And man, at war with man, hears not
    The love-song which they bring:
O hush the noise, ye men of strife,
    And hear the angels sing.

And ye, beneath life's crushing load
    Whose forms are bending low,
Who toil along the climbing way
    With painful steps and slow,
Look up! for glad and golden hours
    Come swiftly on the wing;
O rest beside the weary road,
    And hear the angels sing.

For lo! the days are hastening on,
    By prophet bards foretold,
When with the ever-circling years
    Comes round the age of gold;
When peace shall over all the earth
    Its ancient splendours fling,
And the whole world send back the song
    Which now the angels sing.

1166   Anon   11 11 11 11
And she brought forth her firstborn son, and wrapped Him in swaddling clothes, and laid Him in a manger. *Luke 2:7*

Away in a manger, no crib for a bed,
The little Lord Jesus laid down His sweet head.
The stars in the bright sky looked down where He
     lay,
The little Lord Jesus asleep on the hay.

The cattle are lowing, the Baby awakes,
But little Lord Jesus no crying He makes.
I love Thee, Lord Jesus! look down from the sky,
And stay by my side until morning is nigh.

Be near me, Lord Jesus; I ask Thee to stay
Close by me for ever, and love me I pray.
Bless all the dear children in Thy tender care,
And fit us for heaven, to live with Thee there.

1167   Charlotte Elliott   Irregular
There was no room for them in the inn.
Luke 2:7

   Thou didst leave Thy throne
   And Thy kingly crown,
When Thou camest to earth for me;
   But in Bethlehem's home
   Was there found no room
For Thy holy nativity:
O come to my heart, Lord Jesus!
There is room in my heart for Thee.

   Heaven's arches rang
   When the angels sang,
Proclaiming Thy royal degree;
   But of lowly birth
   Cam'st Thou, Lord, on earth,
And in great humility:
O come to my heart, Lord Jesus!
There is room in my heart for Thee.

   Thou camest, O Lord,
   With the living word,
That should set Thy people free;
   But, with mocking scorn,
   And with crown of thorn,
They bore Thee to Calvary:
O come to my heart, Lord Jesus!
Thy cross is my only plea.

   When heaven's arches ring,
   And her choirs shall sing,
At Thy coming to victory,
   Let Thy voice call me home,
   Saying, 'Yet there is room,
There is room at My side for thee!'
And my heart shall rejoice, Lord Jesus!
When Thou comest and callest for me.

JOHN BYROM 1692-1763

1168   John Byrom   10 10 10 10 10 10
I bring you good tidings of great joy, which shall be to all people. *Luke 2:10*

Christians, awake, salute the happy morn,
Whereon the Saviour of mankind was born;
   Rise to adore the mystery of love
   Which hosts of angels chanted from above!
With them the joyful tidings first begun
Of God incarnate, of the virgin's Son.

Then to the watchful shepherds it was told,
Who heard the angelic herald's voice, 'Behold,
   I bring good tidings of a Saviour's birth
   To you and all the nations upon earth;
This day hath God fulfilled His promised word,
This day is born a Saviour, Christ the Lord.'

He spake; and straightway the celestial choir
In hymns of joy, unknown before, conspire;
   The praises of redeeming love they sang,
   And heaven's whole orb with hallelujahs rang;
God's highest glory was their anthem still,
Peace upon earth, and unto men goodwill.

To Bethlehem straight th' enlightened shepherds
     ran
To see the wonder God had wrought for man
   And found, with Joseph and the blessèd maid,
   Her Son, the Saviour, in a manger laid;
Then to their flocks, still praising God, return,
And their glad hearts with holy rapture burn.

O may we keep and ponder in our mind
God's wondrous love in saving lost mankind;
   Trace we the Babe who hath retrieved our loss
   From His poor manger to His bitter cross;
Tread in His steps, assisted by His grace,
Till man's first heavenly state again takes place.

Then may we hope, the angelic hosts among,
To sing, redeemed, a glad triumphant song:
   He that was born upon this joyful day
   Around us all His glory shall display;
Saved by His love, incessant we shall sing
Eternal praise to heaven's Almighty King.

1169   Nahum Tate   CM
**I bring you good tidings of great joy, which
shall be to all people.** *Luke 2:10*

While shepherds watched their flocks by night,
    All seated on the ground,
The angel of the Lord came down,
    And glory shone around.

'Fear not,' said he, for mighty dread
    Had seized their troubled mind;
'Glad tidings of great joy I bring
    To you and all mankind.

'To you, in David's town, this day,
    Is born, of David's line,
A Saviour, who is Christ the Lord;
    And this shall be the sign:

'The heavenly Babe you there shall find
    To human view displayed,
All meanly wrapped in swathing bands,
    And in a manger laid.'

Thus spake the seraph; and forthwith
    Appeared a shining throng
Of angels, praising God, who thus
    Addressed their joyful song:

'All glory be to God on high,
    And on the earth be peace;
Good-will henceforth from heaven to men,
    Begin and never cease.'

1170   Latin 17th Cent., tr. F Oakley
                               Irregular
**For unto you is born this day in the city of
David a Saviour, which is Christ the Lord.**
Luke 2:11

O come, all ye faithful,
    Joyful and triumphant,
Come ye, O come ye to Bethlehem;
    Come and behold Him,
Born the King of angels:

    O come, let us adore Him,
    O come, let us adore Him,
    O come, let us adore Him,
      Christ the Lord!

True God of true God,
    Light of Light eternal,
Lo! He abhors not the virgin's womb,
    Son of the Father,
Begotten not created:

Sing, choirs of angels,
    Sing in exultation,
Sing, all ye citizens of heaven above;
    Glory to God
In the highest:

Yea, Lord, we greet Thee,
    Born this happy morning,
Jesus, to Thee be glory given;
    Word of the Father,
Now in flesh appearing:

1171   Edward Caswall   77 77 D
**For unto you is born this day in the city of
David a Saviour, which is Christ the Lord.**
Luke 2:11

See, amid the winter's snow,
Born for us on earth below,
See, the Lamb of God appears,
Promised from eternal years.

    Hail, Thou ever-blessèd morn!
    Hail, redemption's happy dawn!
    Sing through all Jerusalem:
    Christ is born in Bethlehem!

Lo, within a manger lies
He who built the starry skies,
He who, throned in height sublime,
Sits amid the cherubim.

Say, ye holy shepherds, say,
What your joyful news today;
Wherefore have ye left your sheep
On the lonely mountain steep?

'As we watched at dead of night,
Lo, we saw a wondrous light:
Angels, singing peace on earth,
Told us of the Saviour's birth.'

Sacred Infant, all divine,
What a tender love was Thine,
Thus to come from highest bliss
Down to such a world as this!

Teach, O teach us, holy Child,
By Thy face so meek and mild,
Teach us to resemble Thee
In Thy sweet humility.

1172 Charles Wesley   77 77 D + refrain
And suddenly there was with the angel a
multitude of the heavenly host praising God.
Luke 2:13

Hark! the herald angels sing
Glory to the new-born King,
  Peace on earth, and mercy mild,
  God and sinners reconciled.
Joyful, all ye nations, rise,
Join the triumph of the skies;
  With the angelic host proclaim,
  'Christ is born in Bethlehem.'

  Hark! the herald angels sing
  Glory to the new-born King.

Christ, by highest heaven adored,
Christ, the Everlasting Lord,
  Late in time behold Him come,
  Offspring of a virgin's womb.
Veiled in flesh the Godhead see!
Hail the incarnate Deity!
  Pleased as Man with men to dwell,
  Jesus, our Immanuel.

Hail, the heaven-born Prince of Peace!
Hail, the Sun of Righteousness!
  Light and life to all He brings,
  Risen with healing in His wings.
Mild He lays His glory by,
Born that man no more may die,
  Born to raise the sons of earth,
  Born to give them second birth.

Come, Desire of nations, come,
Fix in us Thy humble home;
  Rise, the woman's conquering Seed,
  Bruise in us the serpent's head.
Now display Thy saving power,
Ruined nature now restore;
  Now in mystic union join
  Thine to ours, and ours to Thine!

1173 Charles Wesley   76 76 77 76
Glory to God in the highest, and on earth
peace, good will toward men. *Luke 2:14*

Glory be to God on high,
  And peace on earth descend:
God comes down, He bows the sky,
  And shows Himself our Friend:
God the invisible appears:
  God, the blest, the great I AM,
Sojourns in this vale of tears,
  And Jesus is his name.

Him the angels all adored,
  Their Maker and their King;
Tidings of their humbled Lord
  They now to mortals bring.
Emptied of His majesty,
  Of His dazzling glories shorn,
Being's source begins to be,
  And God Himself is born!

See the eternal Son of God
  A mortal Son of man;
Dwelling in an earthly clod,
  Whom heaven cannot contain.
Stand amazed, ye heavens, at this!
  See the Lord of earth and skies;
Humbled to the dust He is,
  And in a manger lies.

We, the sons of men, rejoice,
  The Prince of Peace proclaim;
With heaven's host lift up our voice,
  And shout Immanuel's name:
Knees and hearts to Him we bow;
  Of our flesh and of our bone,
Jesus is our Brother now,
  And God is all our own.

1174 Paulus Gerhardt, tr. Catherine Winkworth
8336 D
And they came with haste, and found Mary,
and Joseph, and the Babe lying in a manger.
Luke 2:16

All my heart this night rejoices,
  As I hear, far and near,
  Sweetest angel voices;
Christ is born! their choirs are singing
  Till the air everywhere
  Now with joy is ringing.

Hark! a voice from yonder manger,
  Soft and sweet, doth entreat:
  'Flee from woe and danger;
Brethren, come: from all that grieves you
  You are freed: all you need
  I will surely give you.'

Come, then, let us hasten yonder:
  Here let all, great and small,
  Kneel in awe and wonder;
Love Him who with love is yearning:
  Hail the star that from far
  Bright with hope is burning.

Ye who pine in weary sadness,
  Weep no more, for the door
  Now is found of gladness;
Cling to Him, for He will guide you
  Where no cross, pain or loss
  Can again betide you.

Blessèd Saviour, let me find Thee;
    Keep Thou me close to Thee;
    Cast me not behind Thee;
Life of life, my heart Thou stillest,
    Calm I rest on Thy breast,
    All this void Thou fillest.

Thee, dear Lord, with heed I'll cherish,
    Live to Thee, and with Thee
    Dying, shall not perish,
But shall dwell with Thee for ever
    Far on high, in the joy
    That can alter never.

1175 Martin Luther, tr. C Winkworth LM
**And they came with haste, and found Mary,
and Joseph, and the Babe lying in a manger.**
Luke 2:16

Give heed, my heart, lift up thine eyes;
Who is it in yon manger lies?
Who is this Child so young and fair?
The blessèd Christ-child lieth there.

Ah, dearest Jesus, holy Child,
Make Thee a bed, soft, undefiled,
Within my heart, that it may be
A quiet chamber kept for Thee.

My heart for very joy doth leap,
My lips no more can silence keep;
I too must sing with joyful tongue,
That sweetest ancient cradle-song:

'Glory to God in highest heaven,
Who unto men His Son hath given;'
While angels sing with pious mirth,
A glad new year to all the earth.

1176 Joseph Mohr Irregular
**And they came with haste, and found Mary,
and Joseph, and the Babe lying in a manger.**
Luke 2:16

Silent night! holy night!
All is calm, all is bright
Round yon virgin mother and Child,
Holy Infant so tender and mild,
    Sleep in heavenly peace!

Silent night! holy night!
Shepherds quake at the sight!
Glories stream from heaven afar,
Heavenly hosts sing hallelujah;
    Christ the Saviour is born!

Silent night! holy night!
Son of God, love's pure light
Radiant beams from Thy holy face,
With the dawn of redeeming grace,
    Jesus, Lord, at Thy birth.

1177 Vernon Higham DCM
**Then took he Him up in his arms, and blessed
God.** *Luke 2:28*

All praise and honour to the Child,
    In gentle arms who lay,
When Simeon took this undefiled,
    The Lord whom men did slay.
He gazed upon the little One,
    And gladness filled His breast;
His eyes beheld God's only Son,
    In whom all men are blest.

We rest in arms eternal, strong,
    Secure for evermore;
For we are found, to Him belong;
    Our souls He will restore.
The arms of grace encompass firm
    With pardon and with love;
Assurance does our hearts confirm,
    The gift of God above.

We gaze into the eyes of Him
    Who grants us peace of mind;
For we have seen the Saviour win
    Salvation for mankind.
We look to Jesus Christ our Lord,
    And rest in Him alone;
For we have hearkened to His word,
    The Lord who did atone.

The hope and light of all mankind,
    Immanuel now displayed;
He fills our eyes and, men to find,
    Behold the price He paid!
We worship Thee with heart and voice,
    And praise Thy sweetest grace;
Recline our souls as we rejoice
    To feel Thy blest embrace.
                                    © Author

1178 Isaac Watts   CM
Then took he Him up in his arms, and blessed God. *Luke 2:28*

Lord, at Thy temple we appear,
  As happy Simeon came,
And hope to meet our Saviour here;
  O make our joys the same!

With what divine and vast delight
  The good old man was filled,
When fondly in his withered arms
  He clasped the Holy Child.

'Now I can leave this world,' he cried,
  'Behold thy servant dies:
I've seen Thy great salvation, Lord,
  And close my peaceful eyes.

'This is the light prepared to shine
  Upon the Gentile lands,
Thine Israel's glory, and their hope
  To break their slavish bands.'

Jesus, the vision of Thy face
  Hath overpowering charms;
Scarce shall I feel death's cold embrace
  If Christ be in my arms.

Then while ye hear my heart-strings break,
  How sweet my minutes roll!
A mortal paleness on my cheek,
  But glory in my soul.

1179 Charles Wesley   87 87
Then took he Him up in His arms, and blessed God. *Luke 2:28*

Come, Thou long-expected Jesus,
  Born to set Thy people free;
From our sins and fears release us,
  Let us find our rest in Thee:

Israel's strength and consolation,
  Hope of all Thy saints Thou art;
Dear Desire of every nation,
  Joy of every longing heart.

Born Thy people to deliver,
  Born a child and yet a King;
Born to reign in us for ever,
  Now Thy gracious kingdom bring.

By Thine own eternal Spirit
  Rule in all our hearts alone;
By Thine all-sufficient merit
  Raise us to Thy glorious throne.

1180 Edwin Hood   CM
And Jesus increased in wisdom and stature, and in favour with God and man.
Luke 2:52

I love to think, though I am young,
  My Saviour was a child;
That Jesus walked this earth along,
  With feet all undefiled.

He kept His Father's word of truth,
  As I am taught to do;
And while He walked the path of youth,
  He walked in wisdom too.

I love to think that He who spake
  And made the blind to see,
And called the sleeping dead to wake,
  Was once a child like me:

That He who wore the thorny crown,
  And tasted death's despair,
Had a kind mother like my own,
  And knew her love and care.

I know 'twas all for love of me
  That He became a child,
And left the heavens, so fair to see,
  And trod earth's pathway wild.

Then Saviour, who was once a child,
  A child may come to Thee;
And O in all Thy mercy mild,
  Dear Saviour, come to me!

1181 Charles Wesley   LM
He shall baptize you with the Holy Ghost and with fire. *Luke 3:16*

O Thou who camest from above
  The pure celestial fire to impart,
Kindle a flame of sacred love
  On the mean altar of my heart.

There let it for Thy glory burn
  With inextinguishable blaze,
And trembling to its source return
  In humble prayer and fervent praise.

Jesus, confirm my heart's desire
  To work and speak and think for Thee;
Still let me guard the holy fire
  And still stir up Thy gift in me.

Ready for all Thy perfect will,
  My acts of faith and love repeat,
Till death Thy endless mercies seal
  And make the sacrifice complete

1182 John Fellows LM

And Jesus being full of the Holy Ghost returned from Jordan, and was led by the Spirit into the wilderness. *Luke 4:1*

When the eternal Son of God
Had been baptized in Jordan's flood,
To the lone desert He repairs,
And sore temptation firmly bears.

Should you, that now have been baptized,
Be thus with Satan's darts surprised,
Lift up to heaven your wistful eyes,
Your hope, your help, in Jesus lies.

Never presume to think or say,
The stream has washed your sins away;
Never depend on what's your own,
Nor trust to works or duties done.

Each rite which truth and love ordain
Points to the Lamb that once was slain:
Our wandering thoughts to Him they call:
The centre and the soul of all.

Baptized with Christ, be it your aim
To dignify the Christian name:
With Him aspire to things above,
And put on Christ in faith and love.

1183 Ralph Erskine CM

The Spirit of the Lord *is* upon Me, because He hath anointed Me to preach the gospel to the poor; He hath sent Me to heal the brokenhearted, to preach deliverance to the captives, and recovering of sight to the blind, to set at liberty them that are bruised.
Luke 4:18

Christ came to heal the broken heart,
    The bleeding soul to cure,
Treasures to bankrupts to impart,
    And riches to the poor.

To make a proclamation free
    Of pardon, grace, and peace,
The Lord Jehovah's jubilee,
    His year of sweet release.

For ashes He'll with beauty dress;
    For grief with joy anoint;
And for the spirit of heaviness,
    The robe of praise appoint.

That trees of righteousness might be
    Their proper name when tried,
The planting of the Lord, that He
    May thus be glorified.

Welcome the Preacher great, that comes
    For all these happy ends;
This office justly He assumes,
    Whom God the Father sends.

FRANK HOUGHTON 1894-1972

1184 Frank Houghton 76 76 D

And He said unto them, I must preach the kingdom of God to other cities also; for therefore am I sent. *Luke 4:43*

Facing a task unfinished,
    That drives us to our knees,
A need that, undiminished,
    Rebukes our slothful ease,
We, who rejoice to know Thee,
    Renew before Thy throne
The solemn pledge we owe Thee
    To go and make Thee known.

We bear the torch that flaming
    Fell from the hands of those
Who gave their lives proclaiming
    That Jesus died and rose.
Ours is the same commission,
    The same glad message ours,
Fired by the same ambition,
    To Thee we yield our powers.

O Father who sustained them,
    O Spirit who inspired,
Saviour, whose love constrained them
    To toil with zeal untired,
From cowardice defend us,
    From lethargy awake!
Forth on Thine errands send us
    To labour for Thy sake.

© Overseas Missionary Fellowship

1185   Vernon Higham   DCM
**He is like a man which built an house, and
digged deep, and laid the foundation on a
rock.** *Luke 6:48*

There is a Rock on which I stand
  And now I am secure;
Its mighty base within the land
  Of God's eternal shore.
It never moves, it never falls,
  Or fails to keep each saint
Who trusts in Christ, and on Him calls
  When Satan bids Him faint.

Upon this Rock I now will build
  My life, and live for Thee;
O daily grant my vessel filled
  With Thy serenity.
A heart of prayer, a loving way
  That will not Jesus fail;
So grace may flow to those who stray,
  And see Thy love prevail.

What is this Rock, this place of peace,
  Above the fears of life,
That grants me joy and gives me grace
  To live above the strife?
This Rock is Christ of Calvary
  Who took away my stain,
Whose life and death avail for me;
  Eternal life I gain.

© Author

1186   Isaac Watts   CM
A great prophet is risen up among us.
Luke 7:16

We bless the Prophet of the Lord,
  That comes with truth and grace;
Jesus, Thy Spirit and Thy word
  Shall lead us in Thy ways.

We reverence our High Priest above,
  Who offered up His blood,
And lives to carry on His love,
  By pleading with our God.

We honour our exalted King;
  How sweet are His commands!
He guards our souls from hell and sin
  By His almighty hands.

Hosanna to His glorious name,
  Who saves by different ways!
His mercies lay a sovereign claim
  To our immortal praise.

1187   'James B—R, 1780'   LM
**Behold a gluttonous man, and a winebibber, a
friend of publicans and sinners!** *Luke 7:34*

Jesus, th' incarnate God of love,
Rules all the shining worlds above;
And though His name the heavens transcend.
Yet He is still the sinner's Friend.

Before the rolling skies were made,
Or nature's deep foundations laid,
He saw our fall, and did intend
To show Himself the sinner's Friend.

Behold the condescending God
Awhile forsake His bright abode;
To our mean world see Him descend,
And groan and die the sinner's Friend.

When the appointed hour was come,
He burst the barriers of the tomb;
Then to the skies He did ascend,
Where still He lives the sinner's Friend.

Ye mourning souls, to Jesus come,
Cast off despair, there yet is room:
To His dear hands your cause commend,
Who only is the sinner's Friend.

1188   James Smith   87 87 47
**Behold a gluttonous man, and a winebibber, a
friend of publicans and sinners!** *Luke 7:34*

Trembling sinner, cease thy doubting,
  Look to Christ, the sinner's Friend!
He is now thy soul inviting—
  To His gracious words attend:
    'Come, poor sinner,
  Come to Me, the sinner's Friend.

I am ready to receive you:
  I will peace and pardon send:
Come to Me, I will relieve you,
  On My faithful word depend:
    Come, poor sinner,
  Come to Me, the sinner's Friend.'

1189 Joseph Hart CM
There was a certain creditor which had two debtors: the one owed five hundred pence, and the other fifty. *Luke 7:41*

Mercy is welcome news indeed
  To those that guilty stand;
Wretches that feel what help they need
  Will bless the helping hand.

Who rightly would his alms dispose
  Must give them to the poor.
None but the wounded patient knows
  The comforts of his cure.

We all have sinned against our God;
  Exception none can boast;
But he that feels the heaviest load
  Will prize forgiveness most.

No reckoning can we rightly keep,
  For who the sum can know?
Some souls are fifty pieces deep,
  And some five hundred owe.

But let our debts be what they may,
  However great or small,
As soon as we have nought to pay,
  Our Lord forgives us all.

'Tis perfect poverty alone
  That sets the soul at large;
While we can call one mite our own,
  We have no full discharge.

1190 John Newton CM
And when they had nothing to pay, he frankly forgave them both. Tell me therefore, which of them will love him most? *Luke 7:42*

Ten thousand talents once I owed,
  And nothing had to pay,
But Jesus freed me from the load,
  And washed my sin away.

Yet since the Lord forgave my sin,
  And blotted out my score,
Much more indebted I have been
  Than e'er I was before.

My guilt is cancelled quite, I know,
  And satisfaction made;
But the vast debt of love I owe,
  Can never be repaid.

The love I owe for sin forgiven,
  For power to believe,
For present peace and promised heaven,
  No angel can conceive.

That love of Thine! Thou sinner's Friend!
  Witness Thy bleeding heart!
My little all can ne'er extend
  To pay a thousandth part.

1191 John Wingrove 87 87 D
Seest thou this woman? *Luke 7:44-50*

Hail! my ever-blessèd Jesus,
  Only Thee I wish to sing;
To my soul Thy name is precious:
  Thou my Prophet, Priest, and King.
O! what mercy flows from heaven,
  O! what joy and happiness!
Love I much? I've much forgiven,
  I'm a miracle of grace.

Once with Adam's race in ruin,
  Unconcerned in sin I lay,
Swift destruction still pursuing,
  Till my Saviour passèd by:
Witness, all ye host of heaven,
  My Redeemer's tenderness;
Love I much? I've much forgiven,
  I'm a miracle of grace

Shout, ye bright angelic choir,
  Praise the Lamb enthroned above,
Whilst astonished I admire
  God's free-grace and boundless love;
That blest moment I received Him,
  Filled my soul with joy and peace;
Love I much? I've much forgiven,
  I'm a miracle of grace

1192 John Cawood CM
Now the parable is this: The seed is the word of God. *Luke 8:11*

Almighty God, Thy word is cast
  Like seed into the ground:
Now let the dew of heaven descend,
  And righteous fruits abound.

Let not the foe of Christ and man
  This holy seed remove:
But give it root in every heart,
  To bring forth fruits of love.

Let not the world's deceitful cares
  The rising plant destroy;
But let it yield a hundredfold
  The fruits of peace and joy.

Oft as the precious seed is sown,
  Thy quickening grace bestow;
That all whose souls the truth receive
  Its saving power may know.

1193   Richard de Courcey   66 66 88
And He said unto them, Let us go over unto the other side of the lake. And they launched forth. *Luke 8:22*

Jesus at Thy command
    I launch into the deep;
And leave my native land,
    Where sin lulls all asleep;
For Thee I would the world resign,
And sail to heaven with Thee and Thine.

Thou art my Pilot wise;
    My compass is Thy word;
My soul each storm defies,
    While I have such a Lord;
I trust Thy faithfulness and power,
To save me in the trying hour.

Though rocks and quicksands deep
    Through all my passage lie;
Yet Christ will safely keep,
    And guide me with His eye;
My anchor, hope, shall firm abide,
And I each boisterous storm outride.

By faith I see the land,
    The port of endless rest;
My soul, Thy sails expand,
    And fly to Jesus' breast!
O may I reach the heavenly shore,
Where winds and waves distress no more.

Whene'er becalmed I lie,
    And storms forbear to toss;
Be Thou, dear Lord, still nigh,
    Lest I should suffer loss;
For more the treacherous calm I dread,
Than tempests bursting o'er my head.

Come, Holy Ghost, and blow
    A prosperous gale of grace;
Waft me from all below
    To heaven, my destined place!
Then, in full sail, my port I'll find,
And leave the world and sin behind.

1194   Godfrey Thring   888 3
Then He arose, and rebuked the wind and the raging of the water: and they ceased, and there was a calm. *Luke 8:24*

Fierce raged the tempest o'er the deep,
Watch did Thine anxious servants keep,
But Thou wast wrapped in guileless sleep,
        Calm and still.

'Save, Lord, we perish,' was their cry,
'O save us in our agony!'
Thy word above the storm rose high,
        'Peace, be still!'

The wild winds hushed; the angry deep
Sank, like a little child, to sleep;
The sullen billows ceased to leap,
        At Thy will.

So, when our life is clouded o'er,
And storm-winds drift us from the shore,
Say, lest we sink to rise no more,
        'Peace, be still!'

1195   John Ryland   77 77
He received them, and spake unto them of the kingdom of God, and healed them that had need of healing. *Luke 9:11*

When the Saviour dwelt below,
    Pity in His bosom reigned;
Sympathy He loved to show,
    Nor the meanest plea disdained.

Round Him thronged the blind, the lame,
    Deaf and dumb, diseased, possessed;
None in vain for healing came,
    All the Saviour freely blessed.

He could make the leper whole;
    Thousands at a meal He fed;
Winds and waves could He control;
    By a word He raised the dead.

Listening sinners round Him pressed
    Whilst He taught the way to bliss;
Even enemies confessed,
    'No man ever spake like this.'

Be Thy love to me revealed;
    Be Thy grace by me possessed;
Touch me, and I shall be healed;
    Bless me, and I shall be blessed.

1196   Joseph Irons   CM

But whom say ye that I am? Peter answering said, The Christ of God. *Luke 9:20*

The church triumphant round the throne,
    Redeemed with precious blood,
In scenes of glory here unknown,
    Adore the Christ of God.

The church on earth, renewed by grace,
    Confide in Jesus' name;
And as they run the heavenly race.
    The Christ of God proclaim.

My soul shall gaze upon His face,
    In whom all glories shine;
This precious truth just suits my case,
    The Christ of God is mine.

Soon I shall join the heavenly throng,
    And in their pleasure share;
Shouting in one eternal song,
    The Christ of God is there!

1197   Anne Brontë   SM

And He said to them all, If any man will come after Me, let him deny himself, and take up his cross daily, and follow Me. *Luke 9:23*

Oppressed with sin and woe,
    A burdened heart I bear;
Opposed by many a mighty foe,
    Yet will I not despair.

With this polluted heart,
    I dare to come to Thee—
Holy and mighty as Thou art—
    For Thou wilt pardon me.

I feel that I am weak,
    And prone to every sin;
But Thou who givest to those who seek,
    Wilt give me strength within.

I need not fear my foes;
    I need not yield to care;
I need not sink beneath my woes,
    For Thou wilt answer prayer.

In my Redeemer's name
    I give myself to Thee;
And, all unworthy as I am,
    My God will welcome me.

1198   Joseph Grigg   LM

For whosoever shall be ashamed of Me and of My words, of him shall the Son of man be ashamed. *Luke 9:26*

Jesus and shall it ever be,
A mortal man ashamed of Thee
Ashamed of Thee, whom angels praise;
Whose glories shine to endless days?

Ashamed of Jesus! sooner far
Let evening blush to own a star;
He sheds His beams of light divine
O'er this benighted soul of mine.

Ashamed of Jesus! just as soon
Let midnight be ashamed of noon;
Tis midnight with my soul till He,
Bright Morning Star, bids darkness flee.

Ashamed of Jesus! that dear Friend,
On whom my hopes of heaven depend!
No; when I blush, be this my shame,
That I no more revere His name.

Ashamed of Jesus! yes, I may,
When I've no guilt to wash away;
No tear to wipe; no good to crave:
No fears to quell; no soul to save.

Till then, nor is my boasting vain,
Till then I boast a Saviour slain;
And O may this my glory be,
That Christ is not ashamed of me.

His institutions would I prize;
Take up my cross, the shame despise
Dare to defend His noble cause,
And yield obedience to His laws.

1199   Joseph Robinson   SM

When they were awake, they saw His glory, and the two men that stood with Him.
Luke 9:32

'Tis good, Lord, to be here!
    Thy glory fills the night;
Thy face and garments, like the sun,
    Shine with unborrowed light.

'Tis good, Lord, to be here,
    Thy beauty to behold,
Where Moses and Elijah stand,
    Thy messengers of old.

Fulfiller of the past!
    Promise of things to be!
We hail Thy body glorified
    And our redemption see.

Before we taste of death,
We see Thy kingdom come;
We fain would hold the vision bright
And make this hill our home.

'Tis good, Lord, to be here!
Yet we may not remain;
But since Thou bidst us leave the mount,
Come with us to the plain.

1200   Mary Gates   888 6
After these things the Lord appointed other seventy also, and sent them two and two before His face into every city and place, whither He Himself would come. *Luke 10:1*

Send Thou, O Lord, to every place
Swift messengers before Thy face,
The heralds of Thy wondrous grace,
   Where Thou Thyself wilt come.

Send men whose eyes have seen the King,
Whose ears have heard His summons ring;
Send such Thy lost ones home to bring;
   Send them where Thou wilt come.

To bring good news to souls in sin;
The bruised and broken hearts to win;
In every place to bring them in,
   Where Thou Thyself wilt come.

Gird each one with the Spirit's sword,
The sword of Thine own deathless word;
And make them conquerors, conquering Lord,
   Where Thou Thyself wilt come.

Raise up, O Lord, the Holy Ghost,
From this broad land a mighty host,
Their war-cry, 'We will seek the lost,
   Where Thou, O Christ, wilt come!'

1201   Henry Downton   87 87 D
The harvest truly is great, but the labourers are few: pray ye therefore the Lord of the harvest, that He would send forth labourers into His harvest. *Luke 10:2*

Lord, her watch Thy church is keeping;
   When shall earth Thy rule obey?
When shall end the night of weeping?
   When shall break the promised day?
See the whitening harvest languish,
   Waiting still the labourer's toil;
Was it vain—Thy Son's deep anguish?
   Shall the strong retain the spoil?

Tidings sent to every creature,
   Millions yet have never heard;
Can they hear without a preacher?
   Lord Almighty, give the word.
Give the word; in every nation
   Let the gospel-trumpet sound,
Witnessing a world's salvation
   To the earth's remotest bound.

Then the end: Thy church completed,
   All Thy chosen gathered in,
With their King in glory seated,
   Satan bound, and banished sin:
Gone for ever parting, weeping,
   Hunger, sorrow, death, and pain;
Lo! her watch Thy church is keeping;
   Come, Lord Jesus, come to reign!

1202   John Newton   LM
But a certain Samaritan, as he journeyed, came where he was: and when he saw him, he had compassion on him. *Luke 10:33*

How kind the good Samaritan
   To him who fell among the thieves!
Thus Jesus pities fallen man,
   And heals the wounds the soul receives.

O! I remember well the day,
   When sorely wounded, nearly slain,
Like that poor man I bleeding lay,
   And groaned for help, but groaned in vain.

But He whose name had been my scorn,
   (As Jews Samaritans despise)
Came, when He saw me thus forlorn,
   With love and pity in His eyes.

Gently He raised me from the ground,
   Pressed me to lean upon His arm,
And into every gaping wound
   He poured His own all-healing balm.

Unto His church my steps He led,
   The house prepared for sinners lost,
Gave charge I should be clothed and fed,
   And took upon Him all the cost.

Thus saved from death, from want secured,
   I wait till He again shall come
(When I shall be completely cured),
   And take me to His heavenly home.

There through eternal boundless days,
   When nature's wheel no longer rolls;
How shall I love, adore, and praise,
   This good Samaritan to souls.

1203 Philip Doddridge   LM
**But one thing is needful: and Mary hath
chosen that good part, which shall not be
taken away from her.** *Luke 10:42*

Beset with snares on every hand,
In life's uncertain path I stand;
Saviour divine, diffuse Thy light,
To guide my doubtful footsteps right.

Engage this roving, treacherous heart
To fix on Christ, my better part;
To scorn the trifles of a day,
For joys that none can take away.

Then let the wildest storms arise;
Let tempests mingle earth and skies;
No fatal shipwreck shall I fear,
But all my treasures with me bear.

If Thou, my Jesus, still be nigh,
Cheerful I live, and joyful die;
Secure, when mortal comforts flee,
To find ten thousand worlds in Thee.

1204 Samuel Medley   LM
**But one thing is needful: and Mary hath
chosen that good part, which shall not be
taken away from her.** *Luke 10:42*

Jesus engrave it on my heart,
That Thou the one thing needful art;
I could from all things parted be,
But never, never, Lord, from Thee.

Needful art Thou to make me live;
Needful art Thou all grace to give;
Needful to guide me, lest I stray;
Needful to help me every day.

Needful is Thy most precious blood;
Needful is Thy correcting rod;
Needful is Thy indulgent care;
Needful Thy all-prevailing prayer.

Needful Thy presence, dearest Lord,
True peace and comfort to afford;
Needful Thy promise to impart
Fresh life and vigour to my heart.

Needful art Thou, my soul can say,
Through all life's dark and thorny way;
In death Thou wilt most needful be,
When I yield up my soul to Thee.

Needful art Thou, to raise my dust
In shining glory with the just;
Needful when I in heaven appear,
To crown and to present me there.

1205 John Newton   CM
Lord, teach us to pray. *Luke 11:1*

Great Shepherd of Thy people, hear
    Thy presence now display;
As Thou hast given a place for prayer,
    So give us hearts to pray.

Show us some token of Thy love,
    Our fainting hope to raise;
And pour Thy blessings from above,
    That we may render praise.

Within these walls let holy peace
    And love and concord dwell;
Here give the troubled conscience ease,
    The wounded spirit heal.

The hearing ear, the seeing eye,
    The contrite heart bestow;
And shine upon us from on high,
    That we in grace may grow.

May we in faith receive Thy word,
    In faith present our prayers,
And in the presence of our Lord
    Unbosom all our cares.

And may the gospel's joyful sound,
    Enforced by mighty grace,
Awaken many sinners round,
    To come and fill the place.

1206 William Gadsby   77 77
Lord, teach us to pray. *Luke 11:1*

Blessèd Jesus, Lord of all,
Teach us on Thy name to call;
Help us to be much in prayer.
And upon Thee cast our care.

Draw us, Lord, by Thy sweet power,
In temptation's darkest hour;
Make us cry to Thee our Friend,
And upon Thy grace depend.

At all times, in every case,
Lead us to Thy Throne of Grace;
Let our needs be what they may,
Teach us how and what to pray.

Jesus, deign to bless us thus,
And to glory in Thy cross;
Then, though men and devils roar,
We will ever Thee adore.

1207   James Montgomery   CM
Lord, teach us to pray. *Luke 11:1*

Lord, teach us how to pray aright,
  With reverence and with fear;
Though dust and ashes in Thy sight,
  We may, we must draw near.

We perish if we cease from prayer;
  O grant us power to pray!
And when to meet Thee we prepare,
  Lord, meet us by the way.

Burdened with guilt, convinced of sin,
  In weakness, want and woe,
Fightings without, and fear within;
  Lord, whither shall we go?

God of all grace, we come to Thee
  With broken, contrite hearts;
Give what Thine eye delights to see,
  Truth in the inward parts.

Give deep humility; the sense
  Of godly sorrow give;
A strong desiring confidence
  To hear Thy voice and live.

Faith in the only sacrifice
  That can for sin atone;
To build our hopes, to fix our eyes,
  On Christ, on Christ alone.

Patience to watch and wait and weep,
  Though mercy long delay;
Courage, our fainting souls to keep,
  And trust Thee though Thou slay.

Give these, and then Thy will be done;
  Thus strengthened with Thy might;
We by Thy Spirit and Thy Son
  Shall pray and pray aright.

1208   Thomas Gill   CM
**Ask, and it shall be given you; seek, and ye
shall find; knock, and it shall be opened unto
you.** *Luke 11:9*

O fount of grace that runneth o'er,
  So full, so vast, so free!
Are none too worthless, none too poor,
  To come and take of Thee?

We come, O Lord, with empty hand,
  Yet turn us not away,
For grace hath nothing to demand,
  And suppliants nought to pay.

'Tis ours to ask and to receive;
  To take and not to buy;
'Tis Thine, in sovereign grace to give,
  Yes, give abundantly!

And thus, in simple faith we dare
  Our empty urn to bring;
O nerve the feeble hand of prayer,
  To dip it in the spring!

1209   Joseph Hart   SM
**How much more shall your heavenly Father
give the Holy Spirit to them that ask Him?**
Luke 11:13

  Come Holy Spirit, come;
    Let Thy bright beams arise;
  Dispel the darkness from our minds,
    And open all our eyes.

  Cheer our desponding hearts,
    Thou heavenly Paraclete;
  Give us to lie, with humble hope,
    At our Redeemer's feet.

  Revive our drooping faith:
    Our doubts and fears remove;
  And kindle in our breasts the flames
    Of never-dying love.

  Convince us of our sin,
    Then lead to Jesus' blood;
  And to our wondering view reveal
    The secret love of God.

  Show us that loving Man
    That rules the courts of bliss,
  The Lord of Hosts, the Mighty God,
    The eternal Prince of Peace.

  'Tis Thine to cleanse the heart,
    To sanctify the soul,
  To pour fresh life on every part,
    And new-create the whole.

  If Thou, celestial Dove,
    Thy influence withdraw,
  What easy victims soon we fall
    To conscience, wrath, and law!

  No longer burns our love;
    Our faith and patience fail;
  Our sin revives, and death and hell
    Our feeble souls assail.

  Dwell, therefore, in our hearts;
    Our minds from bondage free;
  Then shall we know, and praise, and love
    The Father, Son, and Thee.

1210 John Newton   CM
But when a stronger than he shall come upon him, and overcome him, he taketh from him all his armour wherein he trusted, and divideth his spoils.
Luke 11:22

The castle of the human heart,
    Strong in its native sin,
Is guarded well in every part
    By him who dwells within.

For Satan there in arms resides,
    And calls the place his own;
With care against assaults provides,
    And rules as on a throne.

But Jesus, stronger far than he,
    In His appointed hour,
Appears to set His people free
    From the usurper's power.

'This heart I bought with blood,' He says,
    'And now it shall be Mine.'
His voice the strong one armed dismays;
    He knows he must resign.

In spite of unbelief, and pride,
    And self, and Satan's art,
The gates of brass fly open wide,
    And Jesus wins the heart.

The rebel soul that once withstood
    The Saviour's kindest call;
Rejoices now, by grace subdued,
    To serve Him with her all.

1211 Anna Waring   76 76 D
Fear not, little flock. *Luke 12:32*

In heavenly love abiding,
    No change my heart shall fear;
And safe is such confiding,
    For nothing changes here:
The storm may roar without me,
    My heart may low be laid;
But God is round about me,
    And can I be dismayed?

Wherever He may guide me,
    No want shall turn me back;
My Shepherd is beside me
    And nothing can I lack:
His wisdom ever waketh,
    His sight is never dim;
He knows the way He taketh
    And I will walk with Him.

Green pastures are before me
    Which yet I have not seen;
Bright skies will soon be o'er me,
    Where the dark clouds have been.
My hope I cannot measure,
    My path to life is free;
My Saviour has my treasure
    And He will walk with me.

1212 Horatius Bonar   CM
Fear not, little flock. *Luke 12:32*

A little flock! so calls He thee,
    Who bought thee with His blood;
A little flock—disowned of men,
    But owned and loved of God.

A little flock! yes even so,
    A handful among men;
Such is the purpose of thy God,
    So willeth He: Amen!

A little flock! 'tis well, 'tis well;
    Such be her lot and name;
Through ages past it has been so,
    And now 'tis still the same.

But the Chief Shepherd comes at length
    Her feeble days are o'er,
No more a handful in the earth,
    A little flock no more.

No more a lily among thorns;
    Weary, and faint, and few,
But countless as the stars of heaven,
    Or as the early dew.

1213 William Gadsby   77 77
But I have a baptism to be baptized with; and how am I straitened till it be accomplished!
Luke 12:50

Precious Jesus! here we are,
Come to witness and declare
We are Thine, redeemed with blood,
Called and proved the sons of God.

Jesus, ere He gave His blood,
Was immersed in Jordan's flood,
There, and in that way, to show
What He had to undergo.

In the watery grave we see,
Looking through it, Lord, to Thee,
Jesus, overwhelmed in blood,
Sunk in wrath's tremendous flood.

And shall we for whom He died,
Rose, and lives to intercede,
Be too proud to be despised,
And with Him to be baptized?

No, dear Saviour, we will go
In the watery grave, to show
We are buried with our King,
And we rise His praise to sing.

Precious Spirit, make us see
Love immense, beyond degree;
Now, and when beneath the flood,
Fill us with the love of God.

1214   John Berridge   886 D
But when thou makest a feast, call the poor,
the maimed, the lame, the blind.
Luke 14:13

When Jesus would His grace proclaim,
He calls the simple, blind, and lame
    To come and be His guest;
Such simple folk the world despise;
Yet simple folk have sharpest eyes,
    And learn to walk the best.

They view the want of Jesus' light,
Of Jesus' blood, and Jesus' might,
    Which others cannot view;
They walk in Christ, the living Way,
And fight, and win the well-fought day,
    Which others cannot do.

They all declare, 'I nothing am,
My life is bound up in the Lamb,
    My wit and might are His;
My worth is all in Jesus found,
He is my Rock, my anchor-ground,
    And all my hope of bliss.'

Such simple soul I fain would be,
The scorn of man, the joy of Thee,
    Thy parlour guest and friend;
Do make me, Lord, a little child,
Right simple-hearted, meek and mild,
    And loving to the end.

1215   Albert Midlane   SM
Come; for all things are now ready.
Luke 14:17

'All things are ready, Come!'
    Come to the supper spread;
Come, rich and poor, come, old and young,
    Come, and be richly fed.

'All things are ready,' Come,
    The invitation's given.
Through Him who now in glory sits
    At God's right hand in heaven.

'All things are ready,' Come,
    The door is open wide;
O feast upon the love of God,
    For Christ, His Son, has died.

'All things are ready,' Come,
    All hindrance is removed;
And God, in Christ, His precious love,
    To fallen man has proved.

'All things are ready,' Come,
    Tomorrow may not be;
O sinner, come, the Saviour waits,
    This hour to welcome Thee!

1216   Josiah Conder   77 77
Come; for all things are now ready.
Luke 14:17

Welcome, welcome! sinner, hear!
Hang not back through shame or fear:
Doubt not, nor distrust the call;
Mercy is proclaimed to all.

Welcome, weeping penitent!
Grace has made thy heart relent:
Welcome, long estrangèd child!
God in Christ is reconciled.

Welcome to the cleansing fount
Springing from the sacred mount:
Welcome to the feast divine,
Bread of life and living wine.

All ye weary and distressed,
Welcome to relief and rest!
All is ready, hear the call,
There is ample room for all!

None can come that shall not find
Mercy called whom grace inclined!
Nor shall any willing heart
Hear the bitter word, 'Depart!'

O! the virtue of that price,
That redeeming sacrifice!
Come, ye bought, but not with gold,
Welcome to the sacred fold.

1217 Phippard 66 66 88
Bring in hither the poor, and the maimed, and the halt, and the blind. *Luke 14:21*

Ye sin-sick souls, draw near,
  And banquet with your King;
His royal bounties share,
  And loud hosannas sing:
Here mercy reigns, here peace abounds,
Here's blood to heal your dreadful wounds.

Here's clothing for the poor,
  Here's comfort for the weak;
Here's strength for tempted souls,
  And cordials for the sick;
Here's all an empty soul can need,
Laid up in Christ the living Head.

But may a soul like mine,
  All stained with guilt and blood,
Approach the throne of grace,
  And converse hold with God?
Yes, Jesus calls, 'Come, sinners, come,
In mercy's arms there yet is room!'

He's on the throne of grace,
  And waits to answer prayer;
What though thy sin and guilt
  Like crimson doth appear;
The blood of Christ divinely flows,
A healing balm for all thy woes.

O wondrous love and grace!
  Did Jesus die for me
Were all my numerous debts
  Discharged on Calvary?
Yes, Jesus died—the work is done,
He did for all my sins atone.

1218 Joseph Hart LM
And the servant said, Lord, it is done as Thou hast commanded, and yet there is room. *Luke 14:22*

Pity a helpless sinner, Lord,
Who would believe Thy gracious word,
But own my heart, with shame and grief,
A sink of sin and unbelief.

Lord, in Thy house I read there's room,
And, venturing hard, behold I come;
But can there, tell me, can there be
Amongst Thy children room for me?

I eat the bread, and drink the wine;
But O! my soul wants more than sign!
I faint unless I feed on Thee,
And drink the blood as shed for me.

For sinners, Lord, Thou cam'st to bleed;
And I'm a sinner vile indeed;
Lord, I believe, Thy grace is free,
O magnify that grace in me.

1219 Anne Steele CM
And the servant said, Lord, it is done as thou hast commanded, and yet there is room. *Luke 14:22*

Ye wretched, hungry, starving poor,
  Behold a royal feast!
Where mercy spreads her bounteous store
  For every humble guest.

See, Jesus stands with open arms;
  He calls, He bids you come:
Guilt holds you back and fear alarms,
  But see, there yet is room.

Room in the Saviour's bleeding heart;
  There love and pity meet.
Nor will He bid the soul depart
  That trembles at His feet.

In Him, the Father reconciled,
  Invites your soul to come;
The rebel shall be called a child
  And kindly welcomed home.

O come, and with His children taste
  The blessings of His love;
While hope attends the sweet repast
  Of nobler joys above.

There, with united heart and voice,
  Before the eternal throne,
Ten thousand, thousand souls rejoice
  In ecstasies unknown.

And yet, ten thousand, thousand more
  Are welcome still to come;
Ye longing souls, the grace adore;
  Approach, there yet is room.

1220   Erdman Neumeister, tr. Emma Bevan

77 77 D

This man receiveth sinners, and eateth with them. *Luke 15:2*

Sinners Jesus will receive;
    Sound this word of grace to all
Who the heavenly pathway leave,
    All who linger, all who fall!

    Sing it o'er and o'er again;
      Christ receiveth sinful men.
    Make the message clear and plain,
      Christ receiveth sinful men.

Come; and He will give you rest;
    Trust Him; for His word is plain;
He will take the very worst:
    Christ receiveth sinful men.

Now my heart condemns me not,
    Pure before the law I stand;
He who cleansed me from all spot,
    Satisfied its last demand.

Christ receiveth sinful men,
    Even me with all my sin;
Purged from every spot and stain,
    Heaven with Him I enter in.

1221   Joseph Hart   CM

This man receiveth sinners, and eateth with them. *Luke 15:2*

A Man there is, a real Man,
    With wounds still gaping wide,
From which rich streams of blood once ran,
    In hands, and feet, and side.

'Tis no wild fancy of our brains,
    No metaphor we speak;
The same dear Man in heaven now reigns,
    That suffered for our sake.

This wondrous Man of whom we tell,
    Is true Almighty God;
He bought our souls from death and hell;
    The price, His own heart's blood.

That human heart He still retains,
    Though throned in highest bliss;
And feels each tempted member's pains;
    For our affliction's His.

Come, then, repenting sinner, come;
    Approach with humble faith;
Owe what Thou wilt, the total sum
    Is cancelled by His death!

His blood can cleanse the blackest soul,
    And wash our guilt away;
He will present us sound and whole
    In that tremendous day.

1222   Albert Midlane   87 87 47

Joy shall be in heaven over one sinner that repenteth, more than over ninety and nine just persons, which need no repentance. *Luke 15:7*

Now we'll render to the Saviour,
    Praise for all that He has wrought;
For the precious, full salvation,
    Which has now to souls been brought.
      Hallelujah!
    Jesus shall have all the praise!

Heaven has rung with joy and transport,
    While we here have been convened,
Over the returning sinner,
    Numbered now with the redeemed:
      Hallelujah!
    Jesus shall have all the praise!

1223   Albert Midlane   87 87 D

I will arise and go to my father, and will say unto him, Father, I have sinned against heaven, and before thee.
Luke 15:18

'Tis the voice of mercy calls thee,
    Wanderer from the Father's home,
'Tis not God, in voice of thunder,
    'Tis a Father calls thee, 'Come!'
Yea, His loving heart still waiteth,
    And canst thou refuse Him still?
Nay, with contrite heart relenting,
    Say, 'Arise and come, I will.'

Come, in all thy filthy garments,
    Tarry not to cleanse or mend;
Come, in all thy destitution.
    As thou art, and He'll befriend,
By the tempter's vain allurements,
    Be no longer thou beguiled:
God the Father waits to own thee
    As His dear adopted child.

ROBERT M'CHEYNE 1813-43

1224   Robert M'Cheyne   77 77 77
How much owest thou unto my lord?
Luke 16:5

When this passing world is done,
When has sunk the radiant sun,
    When I stand with Christ on high,
    Looking o'er life's history,
Then, Lord, shall I fully know,
Not till then, how much I owe.

Chosen, not for good in me,
Wakened up from wrath to flee,
    Hidden in the Saviour's side,
    By the Spirit sanctified,
Teach me, Lord, on earth to show
By my love how much I owe.

When I stand before the throne,
Dressed in beauty not my own,
    When I see Thee as Thou art,
    Love Thee with unsinning heart,
Then, Lord, shall I fully know,
Not till then, how much I owe.

When the praise of heaven I hear,
Loud as thunders to the ear,
    Loud as many waters' noise,
    Sweet as harps' melodious voice,
Then, Lord, shall I fully know,
Not till then, how much I owe.

1225   Ralph Erskine, J Berridge   CM
**And there was a certain beggar named
Lazarus, which was laid at his gate, full of
sores.** *Luke 16:20*

My business lies at Jesus' gate,
    Where many a Lazar comes;
And here I sue, and here I wait
    For mercy's falling crumbs.

My rags and wounds my wants proclaim,
    And help from Him implore;
The wounds do witness I am lame,
    The rags that I am poor.

The Lord, I hear, the hungry feeds,
    And cheereth souls distressed;
He loves to bind up broken reeds,
    And heal a bleeding breast.

His name is Jesus, full of grace,
    Which draws me to His door;
And will not Jesus show His face,
    And bring His gospel store?

Supplies of every grace I want,
    And each day want supply;
And if no grace the Lord will grant,
    I must lie down and die.

1226   William Bathurst   CM
**And the apostles said unto the Lord, Increase
our faith.** *Luke 17:5*

O for a faith that will not shrink,
    Though pressed by many a foe;
That will not tremble on the brink
    Of poverty or woe;

That will not murmur or complain
    Beneath the chastening rod;
But in the hour of grief or pain
    Can lean upon its God.

A faith that shines more bright and clear
    When tempests rage without;
That when in danger knows no fear,
    In darkness feels no doubt.

A faith that keeps the narrow way
    Till life's last spark is fled,
And with a pure and heavenly ray
    Lights up the dying bed.

Lord, give me such a faith as this
    And then, whate'er may come,
I taste even now the hallowed bliss
    Of an eternal home.

1227   John Newton   SM
Men ought always to pray, and not to faint.
Luke 18:1

    Our Lord, who knows full well
    The heart of every saint;
Invites us, by a parable,
    To pray and never faint.

He bows His gracious ear,
  We never plead in vain;
Yet we must wait, till He appear,
  And pray, and pray again.

Tho' unbelief suggest,
  Why should we longer wait?
He bids us never give Him rest,
  But be importunate.

'Twas thus a widow poor,
  Without support or friend,
Beset the unjust judge's door,
  And gained, at last, her end.

For her he little cared,
  As little for the laws;
Nor God, nor man, did he regard,
  Yet he espoused her cause.

She urged him day and night,
  Would no denial take;
At length he said, ' I'll do her right,
  For my own quiet sake.'

And shall not Jesus hear
  His chosen, when they cry?
Yes, though He may awhile forbear,
  He'll help them from on high.

His nature, truth and love,
  Engage Him on their side;
When they are grieved, His mercies move,
  And can they be denied?

Then let us earnest be,
  And never faint in prayer;
He loves our importunity,
  And makes our cause His care.

1228 Samuel Medley   LM
God be merciful to me a sinner.
Luke 18:13

Hear, gracious God, a sinner's cry,
For I have nowhere else to fly;
My hope, my only hope's in Thee;
O God, be merciful to me!

To Thee I come, a sinner poor,
And wait for mercy at Thy door;
Indeed, I've nowhere else to flee:
O God, be merciful to me!

To Thee I come, a sinner weak,
And scarce know how to pray or speak;
From fear and weakness set me free;
O God, be merciful to me!

To Thee I come, a sinner vile;
Upon me, Lord, vouchsafe to smile;
Mercy, through blood, I make my plea;
O God, be merciful to me!

To Thee I come, a sinner great,
And well Thou knowest all my state;
Yet full forgiveness is with Thee;
O God, be merciful to me!

To Thee I come, a sinner lost,
Nor have I aught wherein to trust;
But where Thou art, Lord, I would be;
O God, be merciful to me!

To glory bring me, Lord, at last,
And there, when all my fears are past,
With all Thy saints I'll then agree,
God has been merciful to me!

1229 Charles Wesley   77 77
God be merciful to me a sinner.
Luke 18:13

Depth of mercy! can there be
Mercy still reserved for me?
Can my God His wrath forbear?
Me, the chief of sinners, spare?

I have long withstood His grace,
Long provoked Him to His face,
Would not hearken to His calls,
Grieved Him by a thousand falls.

Whence to me this waste of love?
Ask my Advocate above!
See the cause in Jesus' face,
Now before the throne of grace.

There for me the Saviour stands;
Shows His wounds and spreads His hands,
God is love; I know, I feel;
Jesus lives, and loves me still.

Jesus, answer from above:
Is not all Thy nature love?
Wilt Thou not the wrong forget?
Suffer me to kiss Thy feet?

If I rightly read Thy heart,
If Thou all compassion art,
Bow Thine ear, in mercy bow;
Pardon and accept me now.

1230 John Berridge   SM
God be merciful to me a sinner.
Luke 18:13

To Christ for help I fly,
The Friend of sinners lost,
A refuge sweet and sure and nigh,
And there is all my trust.

No help in self I find,
And yet have sought it well;
The native treasure of my mind
Is sin and death and hell.

Lord, grant me free access
Unto Thy piercèd side,
For there I seek my dwelling-place,
And there my guilt would hide.

In every time of need
My helpless soul defend,
And save me from all evil deed,
And save me to the end.

And when the hour is near
That flesh and heart will fail,
Do Thou in all Thy grace appear,
And bid my faith prevail.

1231 William Hutchings   Irregular
Suffer little children to come unto Me.
Luke 18:16

When mothers of Salem
Their children brought to Jesus,
The stern disciples drove them back
And bade them depart:
But Jesus saw them ere they fled,
And sweetly smiled, and kindly said,
'Suffer little children to come unto Me.'

For I will receive them,
And fold them in My bosom;
I'll be a Shepherd to those lambs,
O drive them not away!
For if their hearts to Me they give,
They shall with Me in glory live:
'Suffer little children to come unto Me.'

How kind was our Saviour
To bid those children welcome!
But there are many thousands who
Have never heard His name;
The Bible they have never read;
They know not that the Saviour said:
'Suffer little children to come unto Me.'

O soon may the heathen
Of every tribe and nation
Fulfil Thy blessèd word, and cast
Their idols all away;
O shine upon them from above,
And show Thyself the God of love;
Teach the little children to come unto Thee.

1232 Charles Wesley   88 88 88
**Zacchaeus, make haste, and come down; for
to day I must abide at thy house.**
Luke 19:5

Leader of faithful souls, and Guide
Of all that travel to the sky,
Come and with us, even us, abide,
Who would on Thee alone rely,
On Thee alone our spirits stay,
While held in life's uneven way.

Strangers and pilgrims here below,
This earth, we know, is not our place;
But hasten through the vale of woe,
And, restless to behold Thy face,
Swift to our heavenly country move,
Our everlasting home above.

We've no abiding city here,
But seek a city out of sight;
Thither our steady course we steer,
Aspiring to the plains of light,
Jerusalem, the saints' abode,
Whose founder is the living God.

Through Thee, who all our sins hast borne,
Freely and graciously forgiven,
With songs to Zion we return,
Contending for our native heaven;
That palace of our glorious King,
We find it nearer while we sing.

Raised by the breath of love divine,
We urge our way with strength renewed;
The church of the first-born to join,
We travel to the mount of God,
With joy upon our heads arise,
And meet our Captain in the skies.

1233   Anon, *Sankey's Songs and Solos*

10 10 10 6

For the Son of man is come to seek and to save that which was lost. *Luke 19:10*

Jesus, my Saviour, to Bethlehem came,
Born in a manger to sorrow and shame;
O, it was wonderful—blest be His name!
      Seeking for me, for me!

Jesus, my Saviour, on Calvary's tree,
Paid the great debt, and my soul He set free;
O, it was wonderful—how could it be?
      Dying for me, for me!

Jesus, my Saviour, the same as of old,
While I was wandering afar from the fold,
Gently and long did He plead with my soul,
      Calling for me, for me!

Jesus, my Saviour, shall come from on high—
Sweet is the promise as weary years fly;
O, I shall see Him descending the sky,
      Coming for me, for me!

1234   Benjamin Beddome   SM

And when He was come near, He beheld the city, and wept over it. Luke 19:41

Did Christ o'er sinners weep?
   And shall our cheeks be dry?
Let floods of penitential grief
   Burst forth from every eye.

The Son of God in tears!
   Angels with wonder see!
Be thou astonished, O my soul!
   He shed those tears for thee.

He wept that we might weep;
   Each sin demands a tear;
In heaven alone no sin is found,
   And there's no weeping there.

1235   Joseph Hart   CM

This do in remembrance of Me.
Luke 22:19

The King of heaven a feast has made,
   And to His much-loved friends,
The faint, the famished, and the sad,
   This invitation sends:

'Beggars, approach My royal board,
   Furnished with all that's good;
Come, sit at table with your Lord,
   And eat celestial food.

'My body and My blood receive,
   It comes entirely free;
I ask no price for all I give,
   But O remember Me!'

Lo, at Thy gracious bidding, Lord,
   Though vile and base, we come
O speak the reconciling word,
   And welcome wanderers home.

Rich wine, and milk, and heavenly meat,
   We come to buy and live;
Since nothing is the price that's set,
   And we have nought to give.

Impart to all Thy flock below
   The blessings of Thy death.
On every begging soul bestow
   Thy love, Thy hope, Thy faith.

May each, with strength from heaven endued,
   Say, 'My Beloved's mine:
I eat His flesh, and drink His blood,
   In signs of bread and wine.'

1236   Joseph Hart   CM

This do in remembrance of Me.
Luke 22:19

That doleful night before His death,
   The Lamb, for sinners slain,
Did almost with His latest breath
   This solemn feast ordain.

To keep Thy feast, Lord, are we met,
   And to remember Thee;
Help each poor trembler to repeat,
   'For me He died, for me.'

Thy sufferings, Lord, each sacred sign
   To our remembrance brings:
We eat the bread and drink the wine,
   But think on nobler things.

O tune our tongues, and set in frame
   Each heart that pants to Thee,
To sing, 'Hosanna to the Lamb,
   The Lamb that died for me!'

1237   George Perfect   64 64 66 64
Lord, I am ready to go with Thee, both into prison, and to death. *Luke 22:33*

Jesus was slain for me,
    At Calvary;
Crownèd with thorns was He
    At Calvary.
There He in anguish died,
There from His opened side
Poured forth the crimson tide,
    At Calvary.

Pardoned is all my sin,
    At Calvary;
Cleansed is my heart within,
    At Calvary.
Now robes of praise I wear,
Gone are my grief and care,
Christ bore my burdens there,
    At Calvary.

Wondrous His love for me,
    At Calvary;
Glorious His victory,
    At Calvary.
Vanquished are death and hell,
O, let His praises swell,
Ever my tongue shall tell
    Of Calvary.

1238   John Newton   LM
Lacked ye any thing? And they said, Nothing.
Luke 22:35

Be still, my heart! these anxious cares
To thee are burdens, thorns, and snares;
They cast dishonour on thy Lord,
And contradict His gracious word.

Brought safely by His hand thus far,
Why dost thou now give place to fear?
How canst thou want if He provide,
Or lose thy way with such a Guide?

When first, before His mercy-seat,
Thou didst to Him thy all commit,
He gave thee warrant from that hour
To trust His wisdom, love and power.

Did ever trouble yet befall,
And He refuse to hear thy call?
And has He not His promise passed,
That thou shalt overcome at last?

Like David, thou may'st comfort draw,
Saved from the bear's and lion's paw
Goliath's rage I may defy,
For God, my Saviour, still is nigh.

He who has helped me hitherto,
Will help me all my journey through;
And give me daily cause to raise
New Ebenezers to His praise.

Though rough and thorny be the road,
It leads thee home, apace, to God;
Then count thy present trials small,
For heaven will make amends for all.

1239   Joseph Swain   88 88 D
And being in an agony He prayed more earnestly. *Luke 22:44*

How willing was Jesus to die,
    That we fellow-sinners might live!
The life they could not take away,
    How ready was Jesus to give!
They piercèd His hands and His feet;
    His hands and His feet He resigned;
The pangs of His body were great,
    But greater the pangs of His mind.

That wrath would have kindled a hell
    Of never-abating despair,
In millions of creatures, which fell
    On Jesus, and spent itself there.
'Twas justice that burst in a blaze
    Of vengeance on Jesus, our Head;
Divinity's indwelling rays
    Sustained Him till nature was dead.

Divinity back to His frame
    The life He had yielded restored,
And Jesus entombed was the same
    With Jesus in glory adored.
No nearer we venture than this,
    To gaze on a deep so profound,
But tread, whilst we taste of the bliss,
    With reverence the hallowèd ground.

1240   Charles Gabriel   Irregular
And being in an agony He prayed more earnestly. *Luke 22:44*

I stand amazed in the presence
    Of Jesus the Nazarene,
And wonder how He could love me,
    A sinner, condemned, unclean.

How marvellous! how wonderful!
    And my song shall ever be:
How marvellous! how wonderful
    Is my Saviour's love for me!

For me it was in the garden
    He prayed, 'Not My will but Thine;'
He had no tears for His own griefs,
    But sweat drops of blood for mine.

In pity angels beheld Him
And came from the world of light
To comfort Him in the sorrows
He bore for my soul that night.

He took my sins and my sorrows,
He made them His very own;
He bore the burden to Calvary
And suffered and died alone.

When with the ransomed in glory
His face I at last shall see,
It will be joy through the ages
To sing of His love for me.

1241   Charles Wesley   76 76 78 76
And the Lord turned, and looked upon Peter.
Luke 22:61

Jesus let Thy pitying eye
Call back a wandering sheep:
False to Thee, like Peter, I
Would fain like Peter, weep;
Let me be by grace restored;
On me be all its freeness shown;
Turn, and look upon me, Lord,
And break my heart of stone.

Saviour, Prince, enthroned above,
Repentance to impart,
Give me, through Thy dying love,
The humble, contrite heart.
Give, what I have long implored,
A portion of Thy love unknown,
Turn, and look upon me, Lord,
And break my heart of stone.

Look as when Thy pitying eye
Was closed, that we might live;
'Father,' (at the point to die,
My Saviour gasped), 'forgive!'
Surely, with that dying word,
He turns, and looks, and cries, ''Tis done.'
O my loving, bleeding Lord,
This breaks the heart of stone.

1242   John Berridge   77 77
And the Lord turned, and looked upon Peter.
Luke 22:61

Jesus cast a look on me;
Give me sweet simplicity;
Make me poor, and keep me low,
Seeking only Thee to know.

All that feeds my busy pride,
Cast it evermore aside;
Bid my will to Thine submit;
Lay me humbly at Thy feet.

Make me like a little child,
Of my strength and wisdom spoiled,
Seeing only in Thy light,
Walking only in Thy might.

Leaning on Thy loving breast,
Where a weary soul may rest;
Feeling well the peace of God
Flowing from Thy precious blood.

In this posture let me live,
And hosannas daily give;
In this temper let me die,
And hosannas ever cry.

1243   Charles Wesley   SM
And the Lord turned, and looked upon Peter.
Luke 22:61

O! that I could repent,
With all my idols part,
And to Thy gracious eyes present
A humble, contrite heart.

A heart with grief oppressed,
For having grieved my God,
A troubled heart that cannot rest,
Till sprinkled with Thy blood.

Jesus on me bestow
The penitent desire:
With true sincerity of woe
My aching breast inspire.

With softening pity look,
And melt my hardness down;
Strike with Thy love's resistless stroke.
And break this heart of stone!

1244   James Montgomery   77 77
**And when they were come to the place, which
is called Calvary, there they crucified Him.**
Luke 23:33

When on Calvary I rest,
God in flesh made manifest
Shines in my Redeemer's face,
Full of beauty, truth and grace.

Here I would for ever stay,
Weep and gaze my soul away;
Thou art heaven on earth to me,
Lovely, mournful Calvary.

1245 John Newton CM
Father, forgive them; for they know not what they do. *Luke 23:34*

'Father, forgive', the Saviour said
  'They know not what they do:'
His heart was moved when thus He prayed
  For me, my friends, and you.

He saw, that as the Jews abused
  And crucified His flesh;
So He, by us, would be refused,
  And crucified afresh.

Through love of sin, we long were prone
  To act as Satan bid;
But now, with grief and shame we own,
  We knew not what we did.

We know not the desert of sin,
  Nor whom we thus defied;
Nor where our guilty souls had been,
  If Jesus had not died.

We knew not what a law we broke,
  How holy, just and pure!
Nor what a God we durst provoke,
  But thought ourselves secure.

But Jesus all our guilt foresaw,
  And shed His precious blood
To satisfy the holy law,
  And make our peace with God.

My sin, dear Saviour, made Thee bleed,
  Yet didst Thou pray for me!
I know not what I did, indeed,
  When ignorant of Thee.

1246 John Newton 77 77
If Thou be Christ, save Thyself and us.
Luke 23:39

Sovereign grace has power alone
To subdue a heart of stone;
And the moment grace is felt,
Then the hardest heart will melt.

When the Lord was crucified,
Two transgressors with Him died;
One with vile blaspheming tongue,
Scoffed at Jesus as he hung.

Thus he spent his wicked breath,
In the very jaws of death,
Perished, as too many do,
With the Saviour in his view.

But the other, touched with grace,
Saw the danger of his case;
Faith received to own the Lord,
Whom the scribes and priests abhorred.

'Lord,'he prayed, 'remember me,
When in glory Thou shalt be:'
'Soon with Me,' the Lord replies,
'Thou shalt rest in paradise.'

This was wondrous grace indeed,
Grace vouchsafed in time of need!
Sinners trust in Jesus' name,
You shall find Him still the same.

But beware of unbelief,
Think upon the hardened thief;
If the gospel you disdain,
Christ to you will die in vain.

1247 Richard Burnham CM
Remember me when Thou comest into Thy kingdom. *Luke 23:42*

Jesus! Thou art the sinner's Friend,
  As such I look to Thee:
Now, in the fulness of Thy love,
  O Lord! remember me.

Remember Thy pure word of grace,
  Remember Calvary;
Remember all Thy dying groans,
  And, then, remember me.

Thou wondrous Advocate with God!
  I yield myself to Thee,
While Thou art sitting on Thy throne,
  Dear Lord! remember me.

Lord! I am guilty, I am vile,
  But Thy salvation's free;
Then, in Thine all-abounding grace,
  Dear Lord! remember me.

And when I close my eyes in death,
  When creature-helps all flee,
Then, O my dear Redeemer-God!
  I pray, remember me.

1248 Robert Lowry Irregular
Why seek ye the living among the dead?
Luke 24:5

Low in the grave He lay—
  Jesus, my Saviour!
Waiting the coming day—
  Jesus, my Lord!

Up from the grave He arose,
With a mighty triumph o'er His foes;
He arose a victor from the dark domain,
And He lives for ever with His saints to reign!
He arose! He arose!
Hallelujah! Christ arose!

Vainly they watch His bed—
  Jesus, my Saviour!
Vainly they seal the dead—
  Jesus, my Lord!

Death cannot keep his prey—
  Jesus, my Saviour!
He tore the bars away—
  Jesus, my Lord!

1249 Edwin Paxton Hood   LM
Jesus Himself drew near, and went with them.
Luke 24:15

O walk with Jesus, wouldst thou know
How deep, how wide His love can flow!
They only fail His love to prove
Who in the ways of sinners rove.

Walk Thou with Him; that way is light,
All other pathways end in night;
Walk Thou with Him; that way is rest,
All other pathways are unblest.

O walk with Jesus! to thy view
He will make all things sweet and new;
Will bring new fragrance from each flower,
And hallow every passing hour.

Jesus, a great desire have we
To walk life's troubled path with Thee;
Come to us now, in converse stay;
And O walk with us day by day.

1250 John Keble   LM
Abide with us. *Luke 24:29*

Sun of my soul, Thou Saviour dear,
It is not night if Thou be near;
O, may no earth-born cloud arise,
To hide Thee from Thy servant's eyes!

Abide with me from morn till eve,
For without Thee I cannot live;
Abide with me when night is nigh,
For without Thee I fear to die.

When the soft dews of kindly sleep
My weary eyelids gently steep,
Be my last thought, 'how sweet to rest
For ever on my Saviour's breast!'

Come near and bless us when we wake,
Ere through the world our way we take,
Till, in the ocean of Thy love,
We lose ourselves in heaven above.

1251 Henry Lyte   10 10 10 10
Abide with us. *Luke 24:29*

Abide with me, fast falls the eventide;
The darkness deepens, Lord, with me abide,
When other helpers fail and comforts flee,
Help of the helpless, O abide with me.

Swift to its close ebbs out life's little day,
Earth's joys grow dim, its glories pass away;
Change and decay in all around I see;
O Thou who changest not, abide with me.

I need Thy presence every passing hour:
What but Thy grace can foil the tempter's power?
Who like Thyself my guide and stay can be?
Through cloud and sunshine, O abide with me.

I fear no foe with Thee at hand to bless;
Ills have no weight and tears no bitterness;
Where is death's sting? where, grave, thy victory?
I triumph still, if Thou abide with me.

Reveal Thyself before my closing eyes,
Shine through the gloom and point me to the
  skies;
Heaven's morning breaks and earth's vain
  shadows flee;
In life, in death, O Lord, abide with me.

1252 Thomas Kelly   SM
**The Lord is risen indeed, and hath appeared to
Simon.** *Luke 24:34*

The Lord is risen indeed,
  And are the tidings true?
Yes, they beheld the Saviour bleed,
  And saw Him living too.

The Lord is risen indeed,
  Then justice asks no more;
Mercy and truth are now agreed,
  Who stood opposed before.

The Lord is risen indeed,
  Then is His work performed:
The captive Surety now is freed,
  And death, our foe, disarmed.

The Lord is risen indeed,
  Then hell has lost its prey;
With Him is risen the ransomed seed,
  To reign in endless day.

1253 James Montgomery CM
He was known of them in breaking of bread.
Luke 24:35

Be known to us in breaking bread,
But do not then depart;
Saviour, abide with us, and spread
Thy table in our heart.

There sup with us in love divine,
Thy body and Thy blood,
That living bread, that heavenly wine,
Be our immortal food.

1254 William Pennyfather 65 65
**Jesus Himself stood in the midst of them, and
saith unto them, Peace be unto you.**
Luke 24:36

Jesus, stand among us,
In Thy risen power,
Let this time of worship
Be a hallowed hour.

Breathe Thy Holy Spirit
Into every heart,
Bid the fears and sorrows
From each soul depart.

Thus with quickened footsteps
We'll pursue our way,
Watching for the dawning
Of eternal day.

1255 John Cennick CM
**Jesus Himself stood in the midst of them, and
saith unto them, Peace be unto you.**
Luke 24:36

Here is the Lord! let us adore!
How glorious is the place!
This is the gate of heaven, ye poor,
Attend and beg for grace.

Here is the Lamb amidst us now,
He spreads His gracious hands;
With blessings for His church below
Our dear Redeemer stands.

Dear brethren, think how nigh you sit
To Him who bled for you;
Fall down and worship at His feet,
Who loves and meets us so.

1256 Katharine Kelly Irregular
**Then opened He their understanding, that they
might understand the scriptures.**
Luke 24:45

Give me a sight, O Saviour,
Of Thy wondrous love to me,
Of the love that brought Thee down to earth,
To die on Calvary.

*O make me understand it,
Help me to take it in,
What it meant to Thee, the Holy One,
To bear away my sin.*

Was it the nails, O Saviour,
That bound Thee to the tree?
Nay, 'twas Thine everlasting love,
Thy love for me, for me.

O, wonder of all wonders,
That through Thy death for me,
My open sins, my secret sins,
Can all forgiven be!

Then melt my heart, O Saviour,
Bend me, yes, break me down,
Until I own Thee Conqueror,
And Lord and Sovereign crown.

1257 Joseph Hart CM
**And it came to pass, while He blessed them,
He was parted from them, and carried up into
heaven.** *Luke 24:51*

Now for a theme of thankful praise
To tune the stammerer's tongue;
Christians, your hearts and voices raise,
And join the joyful song.

The Lord's ascended up on high,
Decked with resplendent wounds;
While shouts of victory rend the sky,
And heaven with joy resounds.

See, from the regions of the dead,
Through all the ethereal plains,
The powers of darkness captive led,
The dragon dragged in chains.

Ye eternal gates, your leaves unfold!
Receive the conquering King;
Ye angels, strike your harps of gold;
And saints, triumphant sing.

Sinners, rejoice! He died for you;
For you prepares a place;
Sends down His Spirit to guide you through
With every gift of grace.

His blood, which did your sins atone,
　For your salvation pleads;
And, seated on His Father's throne,
　He reigns and intercedes.

1258　Paul Cook　　　　　　　　CM
In the beginning was the Word.
John 1:1-18

From heaven's eternal throne there came
　A word of strong decree:
'Light up the world with grace and truth
　And set the captives free!'

Forth from the courts of heavenly bliss
　Down to this world of shame,
The Son of God with light and life
　In glad obedience came.

The Word made flesh in human form
　Entered the world He made;
The darkness fled and glory shone
　Around where He was laid.

While circling years in time revealed
　The plan of God in grace,
The Son of man unfurled the truth
　Prophets had learned to trace.

Borne to a cross by cruel hands
　Of men in darkness held,
Judgment and death eclipsed the Son,
　Whilst lies deceived the world.

Out from a tomb of dark despair
　The Prince of light arose;
The truth prevails and grace abounds,
　In all the world it flows.

Now fix your gaze, O sons of light,
　On heaven's exalted King!
The Lamb of God will soon return
　And full salvation bring.

© Author

1259　Oliver Holmes　　　　　　LM
**In Him was life; and the life was the light of
men.** *John 1:4*

Lord of all being, throned afar,
Thy glory flames from sun and star:
Centre and soul of every sphere,
Yet to each loving heart how near!

Sun of our life, Thy quickening ray
Sheds on our path the glow of day;
Star of our hope, Thy softened light
Cheers the long watches of the night.

Our midnight is Thy smile withdrawn;
Our noontide is Thy gracious dawn;
Our rainbow arch, Thy mercy's sign:
All, save the clouds of sin, are Thine!

Lord of all life, below, above,
Whose light is truth, whose warmth is love,
Before Thy ever-blazing throne
We ask no lustre of our own.

Grant us Thy truth, to make us free,
And kindling hearts that burn for Thee,
Till all Thy living altars claim
One holy light, one heavenly flame!

1260　William How　　　　　　87 87 D
**He was in the world, and the world was made
by Him, and the world knew Him not.**
John 1:10

Who is this so weak and helpless,
　Child of lowly Hebrew maid,
Rudely in a stable sheltered,
　Coldly in a manger laid?
'Tis the Lord of all creation,
　Who this wondrous path hath trod;
He is God from everlasting,
　And to everlasting God.

Who is this, a Man of Sorrows,
　Walking sadly life's hard way,
Homeless, weary, sighing, weeping
　Over sin and Satan's sway?
'Tis our God, our glorious Saviour,
　Who above the starry sky
Now for us a place prepareth,
　Where no tear can dim the eye.

Who is this? behold Him shedding
　Drops of blood upon the ground!
Who is this, despised, rejected,
　Mocked, insulted, beaten, bound?
'Tis our God, who gifts and graces
　On His church now poureth down;
Who shall smite in holy vengeance
　All His foes beneath His throne.

Who is this that hangeth dying
　While the rude world scoffs and scorns,
Numbered with the malefactors,
　Torn with nails, and crowned with thorns?
'Tis the God who ever liveth
　'Mid the shining ones on high,
In the glorious golden city,
　Reigning everlastingly.

1261 Isaac Watts   CM
He came unto His own, and His own received
Him not. *John 1:11*

How condescending and how kind,
    Was God's eternal Son!
Our misery reached His heavenly mind,
    And pity brought Him down.

When justice, by our sins provoked,
    Drew forth its dreadful sword,
He gave His soul up to the stroke
    Without a murmuring word.

He sunk beneath our heavy woes,
    To raise us to His throne;
There's ne'er a gift His hand bestows,
    But cost His heart a groan.

This was compassion like a God,
    That when the Saviour knew
The price of pardon was His blood,
    His pity ne'er withdrew.

Now though He reigns exalted high
    His love is still as great;
Well He remembers Calvary,
    Nor lets His saints forget.

Here let our hearts begin to melt
    While we His death record,
And, with our joy for pardoned guilt
    Mourn that we pierced the Lord.

1262 Samuel Medley   LM
Which were born, not of blood, nor of the will
of the flesh, nor of the will of man, but of God.
John 1:13

Assist my soul, my heavenly King,
Thy everlasting love to sing;
And joyful spread Thy praise abroad,
As one, through grace, that's born of God.

No, it was not the will of man
My soul's new heavenly birth began;
Nor will nor power of flesh and blood
That turned my heart from sin to God.

Herein let self be all abased,
And sovereign love alone confessed;
This be my song through all the road,
That born I am, and born of God.

O may this love my soul constrain
To make returns of love again;
That I, while earth is my abode,
May live like one that's born of God.

May I Thy praises daily show,
Who hast created all things new,
And washed me in a Saviour's blood
To prove that I'm a son of God.

And when the appointed hour shall come,
That Thou wilt call me to my home,
Joyful I'll pass the chilling flood,
And die as one that's born of God.

Then shall my soul triumphant rise
To its blest mansion in the skies;
And in that glorious, bright abode,
Sing then as one that's born of God.

1263 John Fawcett   10 10 11 11
And of His fulness have all we received, and
grace for grace. *John 1:16*

A fulness resides in Jesus our Head,
    And ever abides to answer our need;
The Father's good pleasure has laid up in store
A plentiful treasure, to give to the poor.

Whate'er be our wants, we need not to fear;
    Our numerous complaints His mercy will hear;
His fulness shall yield us abundant supplies;
His power shall shield us when dangers arise.

The fountain o'erflows, our woes to redress,
    Still more He bestows, and grace upon grace.
His gifts in abundance we daily receive;
He has a redundance for all that believe.

Whatever distress awaits us below,
    Such plentiful grace will Jesus bestow
As still shall support us and silence our fear,
For nothing can hurt us while Jesus is near.

When troubles attend, or danger, or strife,
    His love will defend and guard us thro' life;
And when we are fainting and ready to die,
Whatever is wanting, His grace will supply.

1264 Joseph Hart   CM
For the law was given by Moses, but grace and
truth came by Jesus Christ.
John 1:17

Is, then, the law of God untrue,
    Which He by Moses gave?
No! but to take it in this view,
    That it has power to save.

Legal obedience were complete,
    Could we the law fulfil;
But no man ever did so yet,
    And no man ever will.

The law was never meant to give
New strength to man's lost race;
We cannot act before we live,
And life proceeds from grace.

But grace and truth by Christ are given;
To Him must Moses bow;
Grace fits the new-born soul for heaven,
And truth informs us how.

By Christ we enter into rest,
And triumph o'er the fall;
Whoe'er would be completely blest
Must trust to Christ for all.

1265 Ralph Erskine CM
For the law was given by Moses, but grace and truth came by Jesus Christ.
John 1:17

Lo! in the law Jehovah dwells,
But Jesus is concealed;
Whereas the gospel's nothing else
But Jesus Christ revealed.

Both law and gospel here unite
In righteousness and peace;
While truth and mercy kindly meet
In our Immanuel's face.

1266 John Rees CM
Behold the Lamb of God, which taketh away the sin of the world. *John 1:29*

Sinners, behold the Lamb of God,
Who takes away our guilt;
Look to His precious, precious blood,
That Jews and Gentiles spilt.

Sinners, to Jesus now draw near,
Invited by His word;
The chief of sinners need not fear,
'Behold the Lamb of God.'

In every state, and time, and place,
Plead only Jesus' blood;
However wretched be your case,
'Behold the Lamb of God.'

Spirit of grace, to us apply
Immanuel's precious blood,
That we may, till we dwell on high,
'Behold the Lamb of God.'

1267 John Fellows 66 66 88
I saw the Spirit descending from heaven like a dove, and it abode upon Him.
John 1:32

Descend celestial Dove!
And make Thy presence known;
Reveal our Saviour's love,
And seal us for Thine own;
Unblessed by Thee, our works are vain,
Nor can we e'er acceptance gain.

When our incarnate God,
The sovereign Prince of Light,
In Jordan's swelling flood
Received the holy rite,
In open view Thy form came down,
And dove-like flew, the King to crown.

The day was never known,
Since time began its race,
On which such glory shone,
On which was shown such grace
As that which shed, in Jordan's stream,
On Jesus' head the heavenly beam.

Continue still to shine,
And fill us with Thy fire:
This ordinance is Thine;
Do Thou our souls inspire!
Thou wilt attend on all Thy sons,
Till time shall end, Thy promise runs.

1268 Charles Wesley 66 66 88
Rabbi, Thou art the Son of God; Thou art the King of Israel. *John 1:49*

Rejoice the Lord is King;
Your God and King adore;
Mortals, give thanks and sing,
And triumph evermore.
Lift up the heart, lift up the voice;
Rejoice aloud, ye saints, rejoice.

Rejoice, the Saviour reigns,
The God of truth and love;
When He had purged our stains,
He took His seat above;
Lift up the heart, lift up the voice;
Rejoice aloud, ye saints, rejoice.

His kingdom cannot fail;
He rules o'er earth and heaven;
The keys of death and hell
Are to our Jesus given;
Lift up the heart, lift up the voice;
Rejoice aloud, ye saints, rejoice.

He all His foes shall quell;
　　Shall all our sins destroy;
And every bosom swell
　　With pure seraphic joy;
Lift up the heart, lift up the voice;
Rejoice aloud, ye saints, rejoice.

Rejoice in glorious hope,
　　Jesus, the Judge, shall come,
And take His servants up
　　To their eternal home;
We soon shall hear the archangel's voice;
The trump of God shall sound, Rejoice!

1269　John Berridge　　　　　CM
**And the third day there was a marriage in
Cana of Galilee; and the mother of Jesus was
there.** *John 2:1*

Thou who at Cana didst appear,
　　To bless a marriage feast,
Vouchsafe Thy gracious presence here;
　　Be Thou with us as Guest.

Upon the bridal pair look down,
　　Who now have plighted hands;
Their union with Thy favour crown,
　　And bless their nuptial bands.

With gifts of grace their hearts endow,
　　Of all rich dowries best;
Their substance bless, and peace bestow
　　To sweeten all the rest.

In purest love their souls unite,
　　That they, with Christian care,
May make domestic burdens light,
　　By taking mutual share.

Through life their every step attend
　　With tokens of Thy love;
And, having reached their journey's end,
　　Complete their bliss above.

1270　William Sleeper　　　　Irregular
**Marvel not that I said unto thee, Ye must be
born again.** *John 3 :7*

A ruler once came to Jesus by night,
To ask Him the way of salvation and light;
The Master made answer in words true and plain:
'Ye must be born again!'

　　*'Ye must be born again!
　　Ye must be born again!
　　I verily, verily say unto Thee,
　　Ye must be born again!'*

Ye children of men, attend to the word,
So solemnly uttered by Jesus the Lord;
And let not this message to you be in vain:
'Ye must be born again!'

O ye who would enter that glorious rest,
And sing with the ransomed the song of the blest;
The life everlasting if ye would obtain:
'Ye must be born again!'

1271　Richard Burnham　　　　CM
Born of the Spirit. *John 3:8*

Lost in the ruins of the fall,
　　I lay in awful night,
Till great Jehovah changed my heart,
　　And gave me heavenly light.

Born of the Lord, I feel a power
　　That draws to Jesus' blood,
Loosens my soul from chains of guilt,
　　And ties it fast to God,

Born of the Lord, I can't allow
　　That sin should rule my heart,
But long that every evil thought
　　Might evermore depart.

Born of the Lord, I soon shall fly:
　　Fly to His bright abode;
Rise to the honours of His throne,
　　To live and reign with God.

1272　Isaac Watts　　　　　CM
**And as Moses lifted up the serpent in the
wilderness, even so must the Son of man be
lifted up.** *John 3:14*

So did the Hebrew prophet raise
　　The brazen serpent high;
The wounded felt immediate ease,
　　The camp forbore to die.

'Look upward in the dying hour.
　　And live,' the prophet cries:
But Christ performs a nobler cure
　　When faith lifts up her eyes.

High on the cross the Saviour hung,
　　High in the heavens He reigns;
Here sinners, by th'old serpent stung,
　　Look, and forget their pains.

When God's own Son is lifted up,
　　A dying world revives:
The Jew beholds the glorious hope,
　　The expiring Gentile lives.

1273 William Rees (vs.1,2), William Williams (vs.3,4), tr. William Edwards   87 87 D
For God so loved the world, that He gave His only begotten Son, that whosoever believeth in Him should not perish, but have everlasting life. *John 3:16*

Here is love, vast as the ocean,
  Lovingkindness as the flood,
When the Prince of life, our ransom,
  Shed for us His precious blood.
Who His love will not remember?
  Who can cease to sing His praise?
He can never be forgotten
  Throughout heaven's eternal days.

On the Mount of Crucifixion
  Fountains opened deep and wide;
Through the floodgates of God's mercy
  Flowed a vast and gracious tide.
Grace and love, like mighty rivers,
  Poured incessant from above,
And heaven's peace and perfect justice
  Kissed a guilty world in love.

Let me all Thy love accepting,
  Love Thee, ever all my days;
Let me seek Thy kingdom only
  And my life be to Thy praise;
Thou alone shalt be my glory,
  Nothing in the world I see.
Thou hast cleansed and sanctified me,
  Thou Thyself hast set me free.

In Thy truth Thou dost direct me
  By Thy Spirit through Thy Word;
And Thy grace my need is meeting,
  As I trust in Thee, my Lord.
Of Thy fulness Thou art pouring
  Thy great love and power on me,
Without measure, full and boundless,
  Drawing out my heart to Thee.

1274 William Hammond   77 77
For God so loved the world, that He gave His only begotten Son, that whosoever believeth in Him should not perish, but have everlasting life. *John 3:16*

Gracious Lord, incline Thy ear;
My requests vouchsafe to hear;
Hear my never-ceasing cry;
'Give me Christ, or else I die.'

Wealth and honour I disdain,
Earthly comforts, Lord, are vain;
These can never satisfy;
Give me Christ, or else I die.

Lord, deny me what Thou wilt,
Only ease me of my guilt.
Suppliant at Thy feet I lie;
Give me Christ, or else I die.

All unholy and unclean,
I am nothing else but sin;
On Thy mercy I rely;
Give me Christ, or else I die.

Thou dost freely save the lost;
In Thy grace alone I trust.
With my earnest plea comply;
Give me Christ, or else I die.

Thou dost promise to forgive
All who in Thy Son believe;
Lord, I know Thou canst not lie;
Give me Christ, or else I die.

1275 Arthur Pierson   66 66 88
For God so loved the world, that He gave His only begotten Son, that whosoever believeth in Him should not perish, but have everlasting life. *John 3:16*

The gospel of Thy grace
  My stubborn heart has won,
For God so loved the world,
  He gave His only Son
That: whosoever will believe
Shall everlasting life receivel

The serpent lifted up
  Could life and healing give,
So Jesus on the cross
  Bids me to look and live;
For: whosoever will believe
Shall everlasting life receive!

The soul that sins shall die!
  My awful doom I heard;
I was for ever lost
  But for Thy gracious word,
That: whosoever will believe
Shall everlasting life receive!

Not to condemn the world
  The Man of Sorrows came,
But that the world might have
  Salvation through His name.
For: whosoever will believe
Shall everlasting life receive!

Lord, help my unbelief!
  Give me the peace of faith,
To rest with child-like trust
  On what Thy gospel saith
That: whosoever will believe
Shall everlasting life receive!

1276   Robert Walmsley   10 4 10 7 4 10
For God so loved the world, that He gave His only begotten Son, that whosoever believeth in Him should not perish, but have everlasting life. *John 3:16*

Come, let us sing of a wonderful love,
 Tender and true;
Out of the heart of the Father above,
 Streaming to me and to you:
  Wonderful love
Dwells in the heart of the Father above.

Jesus, the Saviour, this gospel to tell
 Joyfully came;
Came with the helpless and hopeless to dwell,
 Sharing their sorrow and shame;
  Seeking the lost,
Saving, redeeming at measureless cost.

Jesus is seeking the wanderers yet;
 Why do they roam?
Love only waits to forgive and forget;
 Home! weary wanderer, home!
  Wonderful love
Dwells in the heart of the Father above.

Come to my heart, O Thou wonderful love!
 Come and abide,
Lifting my life till it rises above
 Envy and falsehood and pride,
  Seeking to be
Lowly and humble, a learner of Thee.

1277   John Stevens   SM
And John also was baptizing in Aenon near to Salim, because there was much water there: and they came, and were baptized. *John 3:23*

Near Salim John was found,
 And Aenon's streams he prized,
Because its waters did abound,
 'They came and were baptized.'

Thus all who are redeemed,
 And of God's will apprised,
By them the truth is much esteemed
 They come to be baptized.

Can water be forbid?
 Or ways of God disguised?
The path of Christ must not be hid:
 He surely was baptized.

Thou heavenly Lamb, come down,
 That truth be not despised:
Thy saints with saving blessings crown,
 While here they are baptized.

1278   John Kent   LM
He must needs go through Samaria. *John 4:4*

Once as the Friend of sinners dear,
A Man of sorrows sojourned here;
Eternal love ordained it so,
That through Samaria He must go.

But what could His dear feet incline,
(Unless compelled by love divine,
From whence salvation's blessings flow)
That He must through Samaria go?

There, wandering from the fold of God,
He saw the purchase of His blood:
And o'er this wretch, to lust a slave,
Did sovereign grace her banner wave.

Herein discriminating grace
Shone with a bright refulgent blaze;
While dead in sin ten thousands lie,
Grace brought this rebel harlot nigh.

Roused from her fond delusive dream,
As Israel's God she worshipped Him;
Drank of that living water pure,
That shall to endless years endure.

This object of eternal love,
Ordained to fill a throne above,
Shall in the gospel annals shine,
And prove election all divine.

Jesus, our Shepherd, God, and King,
Thy guardian care and love we sing,
And hail that grace both rich and free,
That brings Thy wandering sheep to Thee.

Glory to God, till this takes place,
Bulwarks of fire and walls of grace
Keep all His blood-bought flock secure,
Till calling proves election sure.

1279   John Newton   LM
The woman then left her waterpot, and went her way into the city, and saith to the men. *John 4:28*

Jesus, to what didst Thou submit
 To save Thy dear-bought flock from hell!
Like a poor traveller see Him sit,
 Athirst, and weary, by the well.

The woman who for water came,
 (What great events on small depend)
Then learnt the glory of His name,
 The Well of life, the sinner's Friend!

Taught from her birth to hate the Jews,
　And filled with party-pride; at first
Her zeal induced her to refuse
　Water, to quench the Saviour's thirst.

But soon she knew the gift of God,
　And Jesus whom she scorned before,
Unasked that drink on her bestowed,
　Which whoso tastes shall thirst no more.

His words her prejudice removed,
　Her sin she felt, relief she found;
She saw and heard, believed and loved,
　And ran to tell her neighbours round.

'O come, this wondrous Man behold!
　The promised Saviour! this is He,
Whom ancient prophecies foretold,
　Born, from our guilt to set us free.'

Like her, in ignorance content,
　I worshipped long I knew not what;
Like her, on other things intent,
　I found Him, when I sought Him not.

He told me all that e'er I did,
　And told me all was pardoned too;
And now, like her, as He has bid,
　I live to point Him out to you.

1280　Richard Burnham　　　　　　CM
**Jesus saith unto them, My meat is to do the
will of Him that sent Me, and to finish His
work.** *John 4:34*

Jesus, an unexampled Friend,
　One of exalted fame,
A great salvation undertakes,
　And finishes the same.

Hell trembled at the grand design,
　Opposed the glorious Son,
But He pursued the mighty work,
　Till the great All was done.

Justice was fully satisfied,
　Atonement fully made;
The law was fully magnified,
　And wondrous love displayed.

Salvation through the finished work,
　Strikes my attentive ear;
While I believe the record true,
　I lose each guilty fear.

''Tis finished'—what a sweet report!
　What pleasure it affords!
O, what a cordial to my heart,
　Are Jesus' dying words!

''Tis finished'—He again repeats,
　And at the blissful sound,
Ten thousand evils die away,
　And heavenly joys abound.

1281　John Monsell　　　　　　76 76 D
**Lift up your eyes, and look on the fields; for
they are white already to harvest.**
John 4:35

Lord of the living harvest
　That whitens o'er the plain,
Where angels soon shall gather
　Their sheaves of golden grain,
Accept these hands to labour,
　These hearts to trust and love
And deign with them to hasten
　Thy kingdom from above.

As labourers in Thy vineyard,
　Send us out, Christ, to be
Content to bear the burden
　Of weary days for Thee;
We ask no other wages,
　When Thou shalt call us home,
But to have shared Thy travail
　And see Thy kingdom come.

Come down, Thou Holy Spirit,
　And fill our souls with light;
Clothe us in spotless raiment,
　In linen clean and white;
Within Thy sacred temple
　Be with us, where we stand
And sanctify Thy people
　Throughout this happy land.

Be with us, God the Father,
　Be with us, God the Son,
Be with us, God the Spirit,
　O blessèd Three in One!
Make us a royal priesthood,
　Thee rightly to adore
And fill us with Thy fulness,
　Now and for evermore.

1282　John Newton　　　　　　SM
**Now there is at Jerusalem by the sheep market
a pool, which is called in the Hebrew tongue
Bethesda, having five porches.** *John 5:2*

　Beside the gospel-pool
　　Appointed for the poor,
From time to time my helpless soul
　　Has waited for a cure.

How often have I seen
The healing waters move;
And others, round me, stepping in
Their efficacy prove.

But my complaints remain;
I feel, alas! the same;
As full of guilt, and fear, and pain,
As when at first I came.

O would the Lord appear
My malady to heal!
He knows how long I've languishèd
And what distress I feel.

How often have I thought,
'Why should I longer lie?
Surely the mercy I have sought
Is not for such as I.'

But whither can I go?
There is no other pool
Where streams of sovereign virtue flow
To make a sinner whole.

Here then, from day to day,
I'll wait, and hope, and try;
Can Jesus hear a sinner pray,
Yet suffer him to die?

No; He is full of grace;
He never will permit
A soul that fain would see His face,
To perish at His feet.

1283   John Kent   CM
**Now there is at Jerusalem by the sheep market
a pool, which is called in the Hebrew tongue
Bethesda, having five porches.** *John 5:2*

As round the pool, Bethesda named,
The sick and wounded lay,
And went from hence, though sorely maimed,
Restored to health away;

So, at the gospel pool we wait,
Disordered all by sin;
In a polluted, dreadful state,
And lepers all unclean.

Lo, here are souls by Satan bound,
And who shall set them free?
Speak, Lord, there's mercy in the sound;
All power belongs to Thee.

Descend, descend, Thou God of grace,
Thy saving health display;
Thy mercy suit to every case;
Send none unhealed away.

1284   John Newton   CM
**Now there is at Jerusalem by the sheep market
a pool, which is called in the Hebrew tongue
Bethesda, having five porches.** *John 5:2*

Here at Bethesda's pool, the poor,
The withered, halt, and blind;
With waiting hearts expect a cure,
And free admittance find.

Here streams of wondrous virtue flow
To heal a sin-sick soul;
To wash the filthy white as snow,
And make the wounded whole.

The dumb break forth in songs of praise,
The blind their sight receive;
The cripple runs in wisdom's ways,
The dead revive, and live!

Restrained to no one case, or time,
These waters always move;
Sinners, in every age and clime,
Their vital influence prove.

Yet numbers daily near them lie,
Who meet with no relief;
With life in view they pine and die
In hopeless unbelief.

'Tis strange they should refuse to bathe,
And yet frequent the pool;
But none can even wish for faith,
While love of sin bears rule.

Satan their consciences has sealed,
And stupified their thought;
For were they willing to be healed,
The cure would soon be wrought.

Do Thou, dear Saviour, interpose,
Their stubborn wills constrain;
Or else to them the water flows,
And grace is preached in vain.

1285   Isaac Watts   66 66 88
**He that honoureth not the Son honoureth not
the Father which hath sent Him.**
John 5:23

To God the Father's throne
Perpetual honours raise;
Glory to God the Son;
To God the Spirit praise;
And while our lips their tribute bring,
Our faith adores the name we sing.

1286   John Newton   LM
The hour is coming, and now is, when the dead shall hear the voice of the Son of God: and they that hear shall live.
John 5:25

May this be a much-favoured hour
  To souls in Satan's bondage led!
Lord, clothe Thy word with sovereign power
  To break the rocks, and raise the dead.

To mourners speak a cheering word;
  On seeking souls vouchsafe to shine;
Let poor backsliders be restored,
  And all Thy saints in praises join.

1287   Richard Burnham   LM
He was a burning and a shining light: and ye were willing for a season to rejoice in his light.
John 5:35

O bless Thy servant, dearest Lord,
While he shall preach Thy gospel word;
May he declare delightful things,
Touching the glorious King of kings.

O grant him bright celestial views,
While he proclaims the gospel news;
With fiery zeal his soul inflame,
While he exalts the bleeding Lamb.

Give him clear light, and burning love;
Shower down Thy blessings from above;
O may we hear the Saviour's voice,
And in His precious name rejoice.

1288   John Kent   CM
Search the scriptures. *John 5:39*

'Go search the Scriptures,' saith our Lord,
  'They testify of Me;
'Tis truth's eternal, great record,
  From every error free.

'There My eternal Godhead shines
  With bright, refulgent rays;
There beam Jehovah's great designs
  From everlasting days.'

There the great gospel scheme behold,
  Chief of the works of God:
Replete with grace and love untold,
  And pardon bought with blood.

There's armour for the trying day,
  Both shield and helmet too:
And grace, the fainting soul to stay,
  And always something new.

There's balm to heal the wounds of sin,
  On life's fair tree it grows;
And blood to wash your garments in,
  From Jesus' side it flows.

O may the Spirit's influence sweet
  Shine on the glorious whole;
Its precepts guide my roving feet,
  And promise feast my soul.

Let revelation's glories shine,
  And spread from sea to sea;
Till reason stoops to faith divine,
  And owns her sovereign sway.

CHARLES HADDON SPURGEON 1834-1892

1289   Charles Spurgeon   87 87 47
And Jesus took the loaves; and when He had given thanks, He distributed to the disciples.
John 6:11

Heavenly Father, grant Thy blessing
  On the food before us spread,
All our tongues are now confessing,
    By Thy hand alone we're fed,
      And Thou givest,
  Best of all, the living bread.

1290   Charles Spurgeon   87 87
And Jesus took the loaves; and when He had given thanks, He distributed to the disciples.
John 6:11

Join to bless the bounteous Giver,
  For the food He here bestows;
From His goodness like a river
  Every earthly blessing flows.

1291   John Newton   88 88 D
**And when even was now come, His disciples
went down unto the sea.**
John 6:16

Constrained by their Lord to embark,
  And venture, without Him, to sea;
The season tempestuous and dark,
  How grieved the disciples must be!
But though He remained on the shore,
  He spent the night for them in prayer;
They still were as safe as before,
  And equally under His care.

They strove, though in vain, for a while,
  The force of the waves to withstand;
But when they were wearied with toil,
  They saw their dear Saviour at hand:
They gladly received Him on board,
  His presence their spirits revived;
The sea became calm at His word,
  And soon at their port they arrived.

We, like the disciples, are tossed
  By storms, on a perilous deep;
But cannot be possibly lost,
  For Jesus has charge of the ship:
Though billows and winds are enraged,
  And threaten to make us their sport;
This Pilot His word has engaged
  To bring us, in safety, to port.

If sometimes we struggle alone,
  And He is withdrawn from our view;
It makes us more willing to own,
  We nothing, without Him, can do:
Then Satan our hopes would assail,
  But Jesus is still within call;
And when our poor efforts quite fail,
  He comes in good time and does all.

Yet, Lord, we are ready to shrink
  Unless we Thy presence perceive;
'O save us!' we cry, 'or we sink,'
  We would, but we cannot believe:
The night has been long and severe,
  The winds and the seas are still high;
Dear Saviour, this moment appear,
  And say to our souls, 'It is I!'

1292   Charlotte Elliott   CM
But He saith unto them, It is I; be not afraid.
John 6:20

When waves of trouble round me swell,
  My soul is not dismayed:
I hear a voice I know full well—
  ''Tis I—be not afraid.'

When black the threatening skies appear,
  And storms my path invade,
Those accents tranquillize each fear,
  ''Tis I—be not afraid.'

There is a gulf that must be crossed;
  Saviour, be near to aid!
Whisper when my frail bark is tossed,
  ''Tis I—be not afraid.'

There is a dark and fearful vale,
  Death hides within its shade;
O say, when flesh and heart shall fail,
  ''Tis I—be not afraid.'

1293   Joseph Hart   SM
**Then said they unto Him, Lord, evermore give
us this bread.** *John 6:34*

Lord, send Thy Spirit down
  On babes that long to learn;
Open our eyes, and make us wise,
  Thy body to discern.

'Tis by Thy word we live,
  And not by bread alone;
The word of truth from Thy blest mouth,
  O make it clearly known.

With what we have received
  Impart Thy quickening power,
We would be fed with living bread,
  And live for evermore.

1294   Mary Lathbury   64 64 D
I am the bread of life. *John 6:35*

Break Thou the Bread of life,
  Dear Lord, to me,
As Thou didst break the bread
  Beside the sea;
Beyond the sacred page
  I seek Thee, Lord,
My spirit longs for Thee,
  Thou living Word.

Thou art the Bread of life,
  O Lord, to me,
Thy holy word the truth
  That saveth me;
Give me to eat and live
  With Thee above,
Teach me to love Thy truth,
  For Thou art love.

O send Thy Spirit, Lord,
　Now unto me,
That He may touch my eyes
　And make me see;
Show me the truth concealed
　Within Thy word,
And in Thy book revealed,
　I see Thee, Lord.

Bless Thou the Bread of life
　To me, to me,
As Thou didst bless the loaves
　By Galilee;
Then shall all bondage cease,
　All fetters fall,
And I shall find my peace,
　My All in all.

1295　John Fawcett　　　　　LM
I am the bread of life. *John 6:35*

Jesus! Thou art the living Bread,
By which our needy souls are fed;
In Thee alone Thy children find
Enough to fill the empty mind.

Without this Bread I starve and die;
No other can my need supply:
But this will suit my wretched case,
Abroad, at home, in every place.

'Tis this relieves the hungry poor,
Who ask for bread at mercy's door;
This living food descends from heaven,
As manna to the Jews was given.

This precious food my heart revives;
What strength, what nourishment it gives!
O, let me evermore be fed
With this divine, celestial Bread!

1296　William Dix　　　　　76 76 D
**All that the Father giveth Me shall come to Me;
and him that cometh to Me I will in no wise
cast out.** *John 6:37*

'Come unto Me, ye weary
　And I will give you rest.'
O blessèd voice of Jesus,
　Which comes to hearts oppressed.
It tells of benediction:
　Of pardon, grace and peace;
Of joy that has no ending:
　Of love which cannot cease.

'Come unto Me, ye wanderers
　And I will give you light.'
O loving voice of Jesus,
　Which comes to cheer the night!
Our hearts were filled with sadness
　And we had lost our way;
But morning brings us gladness
　And songs at break of day.

'Come unto Me, ye fainting
　And I will give you life.'
O cheering voice of Jesus,
　Which comes to aid our strife!
The foe is stern and eager,
　The fight is fierce and long!
But He has made us mighty
　And stronger than the strong.

'And whosoever cometh
　I will not cast him out.'
O welcome voice of Jesus,
　Which drives away our doubt:
Which calls us, very sinners,
　Unworthy though we be,
Of love so free and boundless,
　To come, dear Lord, to Thee.

1297　Fanny Crosby　　　　　CM
**All that the Father giveth Me shall come to Me;
and him that cometh to Me I will in no wise
cast out.** *John 6:37*

O precious words that Jesus said!
　'The soul that comes to Me,
I will in no wise cast him out,
　Whoever he may be.'

O precious words that Jesus said!
　'Behold, I am the Door;
And all that enter in by Me
　Have life for evermore.'

O precious words that Jesus said!
　'Come, weary souls oppressed,
Come, take My yoke and learn of Me
　And I will give you rest.'

O precious words that Jesus said!
　'The world I overcame;
And they who follow where I lead
　Shall conquer in My name.'

1298 Isaac Watts CM
And this is the Father's will which hath sent Me, that of all which He hath given Me I should lose nothing, but should raise it up again at the last day. *John 6:39*

Firm as the earth Thy gospel stands,
  My Lord, my Hope, my Trust;
If I am found in Jesus' hands,
  My soul can ne'er be lost.

His honour is engaged to save
  The meanest of His sheep;
All that His heavenly Father gave
  His hands securely keep.

Nor death, nor hell, shall e'er remove
  His favourites from His breast;
In the dear bosom of His love
  They must for ever rest.

1299 Leila Morris 9 10 9 10
No man can come to Me, except the Father which hath sent Me draw him: and I will raise him up at the last day.
John 6:44

Nearer, still nearer, close to Thy heart,
Draw me, my Saviour, so precious Thou art;
Fold me, O fold me close to Thy breast,
Shelter me safe in that 'Haven of Rest'.

Nearer, still nearer, nothing I bring,
Nought as an offering to Jesus my King;
Only my sinful, now contrite heart;
Grant me the cleansing Thy blood doth impart.

Nearer, still nearer, Lord, to be Thine,
Sin, with its follies, I gladly resign,
All of its pleasures, pomp and its pride:
Give me but Jesus, my Lord crucified.

Nearer, still nearer, while life shall last,
Till all its struggles and trials are past;
Then through eternity, ever I'll be
Nearer, my Saviour, still nearer to Thee.

1300 John Kent LM
He that believeth on Me hath everlasting life.
John 6:47

Saved is the sinner that believes.
  The sacred gospel annals show;
To him repentance Jesus gives,
  And sin's complete remission too.

He hears the Spirit's voice within;
  A sacred ray breaks on his eyes;
He bursts at once the sleep of sin,
  And naked now to Jesus flies.

Sprinkled with blood his conscience is;
  He feels the sweets of sin forgiven;
While Jesus' spotless righteousness
  Becomes his meetness now for heaven.

Jesus, Thy Godhead, blood, and name,
  O! 'tis eternal life to know;
Here let my soul her hold maintain,
  When pressed by conscience, wrath, or law.

Sin-burdened soul, with tempest tossed,
  Thy bark shall every storm outride;
Grace once received can ne'er be lost,
  Nor hell from Christ thy soul divide.

1301 Richard Burnham 88 88 88
I am the living bread which came down from heaven: if any man eat of this bread, he shall live for ever. *John 6:51*

Jesus, the church's glorious Head,
Behold, we wait for living bread;
O feed our souls with grace divine,
While on Thy bosom we recline:

  Cleansed in the fountain of Thy blood,
  We pray to feel the life of God.

Lord, every barren soul revive,
And keep Thy children all alive;
Gazing on Calvary's wondrous tree,
There the atoning Saviour see;

Jesus, Thy quickening grace impart,
And sweetly soften every heart,
To feel the gospel's joyful sound,
And find forgiving love abound:

Saviour, for life, for life we pray,
More of Thy life, and more convey:
Abounding life, O Lord, bestow;
A heavenly life we pant to know;

1302 Josiah Conder 77 77 77
For My flesh is meat indeed, and My blood is drink indeed. *John 6:55*

Bread of heaven! on Thee we feed,
For Thy flesh is meat indeed;
  Ever may our souls be fed
  With this true and living bread;
Day by day, with strength supplied,
Through the life of Him who died.

Vine of heaven! Thy blood supplies
This blest cup of sacrifice;
'Tis Thy wounds our healing give;
To Thy cross we look and live:
Thou, our life; O let us be
Rooted, grafted, built in Thee.

1303   Joseph Hart   CM
He that eateth My flesh, and drinketh My blood, dwelleth in Me, and I in Him.
John 6:56

The blest memorials of Thy grief,
  Thy sufferings, and Thy death,
We come, dear Saviour, to receive;
  But would receive with faith.

The tokens sent us to relieve
  Our spirits when they droop,
We come, dear Saviour, to receive;
  But would receive with hope.

The pledges Thou wast pleased to leave,
  Our mournful minds to move,
We come, dear Saviour, to receive;
  But would receive with love.

Here, in obedience to Thy word,
  We take the bread and wine,
The utmost we can do, dear Lord,
  For all beyond is Thine.

Increase our faith, and hope, and love;
  Lord, give us all that's good;
We would Thy full salvation prove,
  And share Thy flesh and blood.

1304   May Grimes   65 65
The words that I speak unto you, they are spirit, and they are life. *John 6:63*

Speak, Lord, in the stillness,
  While I wait on Thee;
Hushed my heart to listen
  In expectancy.

Speak, O blessèd Master,
  In this quiet hour;
Let me see Thy face, Lord,
  Feel Thy touch of power.

For the words Thou speakest,
  They are life indeed;
Living Bread from heaven,
  Now my spirit feed!

All to Thee is yielded,
  I am not my own;
Blissful, glad surrender,
  I am Thine alone.

Speak, Thy servant heareth!
  Be not silent, Lord;
Waits my soul upon Thee
  For the quickening word!

Fill me with the knowledge
  Of Thy glorious will;
All Thine own good pleasure
  In Thy child fulfil.

1305   William Gadsby   77 77
It is the spirit that quickeneth. *John 6:63*

Holy Ghost, we look to Thee;
Raise the dead; the captive free;
From the mighty take the prey,
Teach the weak to watch and pray.

Now, dear Lord, the heavens rend;
Make some haughty rebel bend;
Life, and light, and truth impart,
To some careless sinner's heart.

If it be Thy holy will,
Now Thy gracious word fulfil;
Quicken souls, and make them cry,
'Jesus, save me, or I die.'

Nor Thy mourning saints forget;
Thy sweet unction still repeat;
Daily lead us unto Christ,
As our Prophet, King, and Priest.

Thine it is the church to bless,
And to comfort in distress;
Trembling, helpless souls to guide,
Safe to Jesus' wounded side.

Out of self to Jesus lead!
For and in us intercede;
Guide us down to death, and there
Banish all our guilt and fear.

There and then support the mind;
May we be to death resigned;
And with an immortal song,
Haste to join the heavenly throng.

1306   John Newton   CM
Will ye also go away? *John 6:67*

When any turn from Zion's way,
  (Alas, what numbers do!)
Methinks I hear my Saviour say,
  'Wilt thou forsake Me too?'

Ah! Lord, with such a heart as mine,
  Unless Thou hold me fast,
I feel I must, I shall, decline,
  And prove like them at last,

Yet Thou alone hast power, I know,
  To save a wretch like me;
To whom, or whither, could I go,
  If I should turn from Thee?

Beyond a doubt I rest assured
  Thou art the Christ of God;
Who hast eternal life secured
  By promise and by blood.

The help of men and angels joined,
  Could never reach my case;
Nor can I hope relief to find,
  But in Thy boundless grace.

No voice but Thine can give me rest,
  And bid my fears depart;
No love but Thine can make me blest,
  And satisfy my heart.

What anguish has that question stirred:
  If I will also go?
Yet, Lord, relying on Thy word,
  I humbly answer, 'No.'

1307   Charles Wesley   SM
Lord, to whom shall we go? *John 6:68*

  Ah! whither should I go,
  Burdened, and sick, and faint?
To whom should I my troubles show,
  And pour out my complaint?

  My Saviour bids me come:
  Ah! why do I delay?
He calls the weary sinner home!
  And yet from Him I stay.

  What is it keeps me back,
  From which I cannot part,
Which will not let my Saviour take
  Possession of my heart?

  Jesus, the hindrance show,
  Which I have feared to see:
Yet let me now consent to know
  What keeps me out from Thee.

Searcher of hearts, in mine
  Thy trying power display;
Into its darkest corners shine,
  And take the veil away.

1308   Anne Steele   CM
If any man thirst, let him come unto Me, and drink. *John 7:37*

The Saviour calls—let anxious ears
  Attend the heavenly sound:
Ye doubting souls, dismiss your fears,
  Hope smiles reviving round.

For every thirsty longing heart
  Here streams of bounty flow;
And life, and health, and bliss impart,
  To banish mortal woe.

Here springs of sacred pleasure rise
  To ease your every pain,
Immortal fountain! full supplies!
  Nor shall you thirst in vain.

Dear Saviour, draw reluctant hearts;
  To Thee let sinners fly,
And take the bliss that love imparts;
  And drink and never die.

1309   Timothy Dudley-Smith   10 10 10 10
I am the light of the world: he that followeth Me shall not walk in darkness, but shall have the light of life. *John 8:12*

Christ be my leader by night as by day;
Safe through the darkness for He is the way.
Gladly I follow, my future His care,
Darkness is daylight when Jesus is there.

Christ be my teacher in age as in youth,
Drifting or doubting, for He is the truth.
Grant me to trust Him; though shifting as sand,
Doubt cannot daunt me; in Jesus I stand.

Christ be my Saviour in calm as in strife;
Death cannot hold me, for He is the life.
Not darkness nor doubting nor sin and its stain
Can touch my salvation: with Jesus I reign.

1310   Jonathan Evans   CM
If the Son therefore shall make you free, ye shall be free indeed. *John 8:36*

Ye captive souls, in fetters bound,
   Who feel your misery;
The way to liberty is found:
   The Son shall make you free.

Hear the Redeemer's gracious call:
   'Poor captives, come to Me;
Into My arms for freedom fall;
   Come, and I'll make you free.'

Why should you doubt His love or power?
   To Him for refuge flee;
This is the Lord's appointed hour;
   He waits to make you free.

The souls who are by Jesus freed,
   No more shall bondage see;
From sin and death they're free indeed;
   Dear Saviour, make me free.

Divorce my soul from every sin,
   Let me Thy servant be;
O make and keep my conscience clean
   To show that I am free.

1311   Charles Wesley   886 D
As long as I am in the world, I am the light of the world. *John 9:5*

Light of the world, Thy beams I bless;
On Thee, bright Sun of Righteousness,
   My faith hath fixed its eye;
Guided by Thee, through all I go,
Nor fear the ruin spread below,
   For Thou art always nigh.

Not all the powers of hell can fright
A soul that walks with Christ in light;
   He walks and cannot fall:
Clearly he sees and wins his way,
Shining unto the perfect day
   And more than conquers all.

I rest in Thine almighty power;
The name of Jesus is a tower
   That hides my life above;
Thou canst, Thou wilt, my Helper be:
My confidence is all in Thee,
   The faithful God of love.

Wherefore, in never-ceasing prayer,
My soul to Thy continual care
   I faithfully commend;
Assured that Thou through life shalt save
And show Thyself beyond the grave
   My everlasting Friend.

1312   Samuel Medley   LM
I am the door of the sheep. *John 10:7*

My soul, a joyful song prepare,
The Saviour's wondrous love declare,
Praise His dear name for evermore,
The only open, heavenly door.

Is Christ the Door? Then here I'll wait;
Thanks to His name! 'tis not too late;
Though late I come, and vile and poor,
God will receive me at this door.

Is Christ the Door? Let saints rejoice,
And bless Him with a cheerful voice;
Loud let your grateful praises sound,
For at this door you mercy found.

May we, when death's dark vale is passed,
Enter, by Him, to heaven at last;
And there, in songs, for evermore.
Exult in God, and bless this door.

1313   John Kent   CM
I am the door: by Me if any man enter in, he shall be saved, and shall go in and out, and find pasture. *John 10:9*

To gospel grace, a boundless store,
   Salvation full and free,
'I am,' saith Christ, 'the only Door;
   Come, enter in by Me.'

'Come, ye who feel the guilt of sin,
   Here's healing balm for you;
A living way to enter in,
   By blood divine, I show.

'Why will ye toil at Sinai now,
   When I was cursed for thee?
Come, learn at sovereign grace to bow,
   And enter in by Me.

'Thousands have tried, by holy deeds,
   In vain to enter in;
And struggled hard, by forms and creeds,
   Eternal life to win.

'The pastures of eternal love
   Your dwelling-place shall be;
There shall ye feed, and ne'er remove,
   Who enter in by Me.

'Divine forgiveness on his heart
   I'll seal, without a fee;
And to him heaven itself impart,
   Who enters in by Me.'

1314   Vernon Higham   88 88 88
I am the door. *John 10:9*

Thy gentle hand has touched my heart
With quickening life Thou didst impart;
I never knew such grace could be,
Or joy and peace from Calvary.
   Amazing grace, eternal Lord,
   This life abundant spread abroad.

Thy gentle hand has touched my life,
Leading me onwards through the strife;
Comfort and strength for daily needs;
Thy wondrous presence now me leads.
   In life or death or sore distress
   I rest on Thy great faithfulness.

Thy gentle hand has touched my soul,
And brought me to Thy chosen fold,
Never to lose my way again,
Or wander in the paths of pain.
   Now I rejoice in ways of grace,
   Happy to see and know Thy face.
                              © *Author*

1315   John Adams   87 87 47
**I am the good shepherd: the good shepherd
giveth His life for the sheep.**
John 10:11

Jesus Shepherd of Thy people,
   Lead us through this desert land;
We are weak, and poor, and feeble,
   Yet we trust Thy mighty hand;
      Great Protector!
   By Thy power alone we stand.

All Thy sheep shall come to Zion;
   With them Thou wilt never part;
Beasts of prey, nor roaring lion,
   None shall pluck them from Thy heart;
      All Thy chosen
   Cost Thee wounds, and blood, and smart.

In Thy bosom safely lodgèd,
   Thine shall rest from danger free;
They shall never more be judgèd,
   Nor shall condemnation see;
      Blessèd Jesus,
   Let us thus rejoice in Thee.

1316   William Gadsby   87 87 47
**As the Father knoweth Me, even so know I the
Father: and I lay down My life for the sheep.**
John 10:15

O my soul, admire and wonder;
   Jesus lived and died for thee;
He has broke the bands asunder,
   And from bondage set thee free.
      Sweet deliverance
   Jesus Christ has wrought for me.

I a slave to sin and Satan
   Once did live, and liked it well;
But the God of my salvation
   Died to save my soul from hell.
      Precious Saviour
   Let me ever with Thee dwell.

All the debts I had contracted,
   He, in mercy, called His own;
And lest I should be neglected,
   Drew me near His gracious throne;
      Paid all charges,
   Then, and for the time to come.

Soon I hope to see His glory,
   And, with all the saints above,
Sing and tell the pleasing story,
   In the highest strains of love:
      And for ever
   Live and reign with Him above.

1317   Philip Doddridge   SM
**My sheep hear My voice, and I know them, and
they follow Me.** *John 10:27*

   My soul, with joy attend,
      While Jesus silence breaks;
   No angel's harp such music yields
      As what my Shepherd speaks.

   'I know My sheep,' He cries;
      'My soul approves them well;
   Vain is the treacherous world's disguise,
      And vain the rage of hell.

   'I freely feed them now
      With tokens of My love.
   But richer pastures I prepare,
      And sweeter streams above.

   'Unnumbered years of bliss
      I to My sheep will give;
   And while My throne unshaken stands,
      Shall all My chosen live.

This tried almighty hand
Is raised for their defence;
Where is the power can reach them there,
Or what can force them thence?'

Enough, my gracious Lord,
Let faith triumphant cry;
My heart can on this promise live;
Can on this promise die.

1318   attr. Dorothy Thrupp   87 87 47
My sheep hear My voice, and I know them, and they follow Me. *John 10:27*

Saviour, like a shepherd lead us;
Much we need Thy tenderest care;
From Thy pleasant pastures feed us;
For our use Thy folds prepare.
Blessèd Jesus!
Thou hast bought us, Thine we are.

We are Thine; do Thou befriend us;
Be the Guardian of our way;
Keep Thy flock; from ill defend us;
Seek us when we go astray,
Blessèd Jesus!
Hear Thy children when they pray.

Thou hast promised to receive us,
Poor and sinful though we be;
Thou hast mercy to relieve us,
Grace to cleanse and power to free.
Blessèd Jesus!
Early let us turn to Thee.

Early let us seek Thy favour,
Early let us do Thy will.
Blessèd Lord, our only Saviour,
With Thyself our bosoms fill;
Thou hast loved us,
Blessèd Jesus, love us still!

1319   Charles Wesley (v.1), Paulus Gerhardt
tr. J Wesley   88 88 88
And I give unto them eternal life; and they shall never perish, neither shall any man pluck them out of My hand. *John 10:28*

Still nigh me, O my Saviour, stand
And guard in fierce temptation's hour;
Hide in the hollow of Thy hand,
Show forth in me Thy saving power;
Still be Thine arm my sure defence:
Nor earth nor hell shall pluck me thence.

Still let Thy love point out my way:
How wondrous things Thy love hath wrought!
Still lead me lest I go astray;
Direct my work, inspire my thought;
And, if I fall, soon may I hear
Thy voice, and know that Love is near.

In suffering be Thy love my peace,
In weakness be Thy love my power;
And when the storms of life shall cease,
Jesus, in that tremendous hour,
In death as life be Thou my Guide
And save me, who for me hast died.

1320   John Newton   CM
Jesus said unto her, I am the resurrection, and the life: he that believeth in Me, though he were dead, yet shall he live. *John 11:25*

'I am,' says Christ, 'your glorious Head'
(May we attention give,)
'The Resurrection of the dead,
The Life of all that live.

'By faith in Me the soul receives
New life, though dead before;
And he that in My name believes,
Shall live to die no more.

'The sinner sleeping in his grave
Shall at My voice awake,
And when I once begin to save,
My work I'll ne'er forsake.'

Fulfil Thy promise, gracious Lord,
On us assembled here;
Put forth Thy Spirit with the word,
And cause the dead to hear.

Preserve the power of faith alive
In those who love Thy name;
For sin and Satan daily strive
To quench the sacred flame.

Thy power and mercy first prevailed
From death to set us free;
And often since our life had failed,
Had it not been in Thee.

To Thee we look, to Thee we bow,
To Thee for help we call;
Our Life and Resurrection Thou,
Our Hope, our Joy, our All.

1321   Benjamin Beddome   LM
Jesus wept. *John 11:35*

So fair a face bedewed with tears;
What beauty e'en in grief appears!
He wept, He bled, He died for you;
What more, ye saints, could Jesus do?

Enthroned above, with equal glow
His warm affections downward flow;
In our distress He bears a part,
And feels a sympathetic smart.

Still His compassions are the same;
He knows the frailty of our frame;
Our heaviest burdens He sustains;
Shares in our sorrows and our pains.

1322   Samuel Partridge   76 76 D
Then said the Jews, Behold how He loved him!
John 11:36

How dearly God must love us
   And this poor world of ours,
To spread blue skies above us,
   And deck the earth with flowers!
There's not a weed so lowly,
   Nor bird that cleaves the air,
But tells, in accents holy,
   His kindness and His care.

He bids the sun to warm us,
   And light the path we tread;
At night, lest aught should harm us,
   He guards our welcome bed;
He gives our needful clothing,
   And sends our daily food;
His love denies us nothing
   His wisdom deemeth good.

The Bible, too, He sends us,
   That tells how Jesus came,
Whose word can save and cleanse us
   From guilt and sin and shame:
O may God's mercies move us
   To serve Him with our powers,
For O how He must love us
   And this poor world of ours!

1323   Charles Wesley   CM
**And when He thus had spoken, He cried with a
loud voice, Lazarus, come forth.**
John 11:43

Thou Son of God, whose flaming eyes
   Our inmost thoughts perceive,
Accept the humble sacrifice,
   Which now to Thee we give.

We bow before Thy gracious throne,
   And think ourselves sincere;
But show us, Lord, is every one
   Thy real worshipper?

Is here a soul that knows Thee not,
   Nor feels His want of Thee,
A stranger to the blood which bought
   His pardon on the tree?

Convince him now of unbelief;
   His desperate state explain;
And fill his heart with sacred grief,
   And penitential pain.

Speak with that voice which wakes the dead,
   And bid the sleeper rise!
And bid his guilty conscience dread
   The death that never dies.

1324   John Kent (alt)   CM
**And he that was dead came forth, bound hand
and foot with graveclothes.**
John 11:44

'Till God the sinner's mind illume,
   'Tis dark as night within;
Like Lazarus in the dreary tomb,
   Bound hand and foot by sin.

Yet though in solid fetters bound,
   To God's free grace a foe,
The gospel has a joyful sound:
   'Loose him, and let him go.'

Sinners shall hear this joyful sound,
   When God designs it so;
Grace shall beyond their sins abound;
   'Loose him, and let him go.'

Justice, beholding his attire,
   No more appears his foe;
He says, ' I've all that I require;
   Loose him, and let him go.'

He stands accepted in His name
   Whose blood for him did flow;
The holy law proclaims the same:
   'Loose him, and let him go.'

1325 Josiah Conder LM
Sir, we would see Jesus. *John 12:21*

Lord, in this blest and hallowed hour
Reveal Thy presence and Thy power;
Show to my faith Thy hands and side,
My Lord and God, the Crucified.

Fain would I find a calm retreat
From vain distractions near Thy feet;
And, borne above all earthly care,
Be joyful in Thy house of prayer.

Or let me through the opening skies
Catch one bright glimpse of Paradise,
And realize, with raptured awe,
The vision dying Stephen saw.

But if unworthy of such joy,
Still shall Thy love my heart employ:
For of Thy favoured children's fare
'Twere bliss the very crumbs to share.

Yet never can my soul be fed
With less than Thee, the living Bread;
Thyself unto my soul impart,
And with Thy presence fill my heart.

1326 Benjamin Beddome, J Rippon CM
Sir, we would see Jesus. *John 12:21*

Lord, let me see Thy beauteous face!
   It yields a heaven below;
And angels round the throne will say,
   'Tis all the heaven they know.

A glimpse, a single glimpse of Thee,
   Would more delight my soul
Than this vain world, with all its joys,
   Could I possess the whole.

1327 Vernon Higham CM
**Except a corn of wheat fall into the ground and
die, it abideth alone: but if it die, it bringeth
forth much fruit.**
John 12:24

A corn of wheat abides alone,
   Except it fall and die;
Deep in the ground new life is born,
   Yet there it has to lie.

Deep in the mystery of grace
   Of Thine eternal realm,
Thy blessèd Son took our disgrace,
   And thus fulfilled Thy plan.

Death worketh life on Calvary,
   And sinner's burden borne;
A place for man from wrath to flee,
   The Saviour's crown adorn.

We gaze upon an empty cross,
   And on a gaping grave:
The Saviour died, yet in His loss,
   Eternal life He gave.

Until we die to self and sin,
   Then we abide alone;
Yet when we die we live in Him,
   And stand before that throne.

Death worketh life — O image strange!
   Life that shall endless be,
Exquisite truth and sweet exchange —
   Thy gift at Calvary.
                                        © Author

1328 Richard Burnham 77 77
**And I, if I be lifted up from the earth, will draw
all men unto Me.** *John 12:32*

Jesus draws the chosen race
By His sweet resistless grace;
Causing them to hear His call,
And before His power to fall.

From the blissful realms above,
Swift as lightning flies His love;
Draws them to His tender breast;
There they find the gospel rest.

Then how eagerly they move
In the happy paths of love!
How they glory in the Lord,
Pleased with Jesus' sacred word!

When the Lord appears in view,
Old things cease, and all is new;
Love divine o'erflows the soul;
Love does every sin control.

1329   Samuel Crossman   66 66 44 44
**Having loved His own which were in the world,
He loved them unto the end.**
John 13:1

My song is love unknown,
　My Saviour's love to me;
Love to the loveless shown,
　That they might lovely be.
　　O who am I,
　　　That for my sake
　　　My Lord should take
　　Frail flesh, and die?

He came from His blest throne
　Salvation to bestow;
But men made strange, and none
　The longed-for Christ would know:
　　But O! my Friend,
　　　My Friend indeed,
　　　Who at my need
　　His life did spend.

Sometimes they strew His way,
　And His sweet praises sing;
Resounding all the day
　Hosannas to their King:
　　Then 'Crucify!'
　　　Is all their breath,
　　　And for His death
　　They thirst and cry.

They rise and needs will have
　My dear Lord made away;
A murderer they save,
　The Prince of life they slay;
　　Yet cheerful He
　　　To suffering goes
　　　That He His foes
　　From thence might free.

In life, no house, no home
　My Lord on earth might have;
In death, no friendly tomb,
　But what a stranger gave.
　　What may I say?
　　　Heaven was His home;
　　　But mine the tomb
　　Wherein He lay.

Here might I stay and sing,
　No story so divine;
Never was love, dear King!
　Never was grief like Thine.
　　This is my Friend,
　　　In whose sweet praise
　　　I all my days
　　Could gladly spend.

1330   William Gadsby   LM
**Having loved His own which were in the world,
He loved them unto the end.**
John 13:1

The love of Christ is rich and free;
Fixed on His own eternally;
Nor earth, nor hell, can it remove;
Long as He lives, His own He'll love.

His loving heart engaged to be
Their everlasting Surety;
'Twas love that took their cause in hand,
And love maintains it to the end.

Love cannot from its post withdraw;
Nor death, nor hell, nor sin, nor law,
Can turn the Surety's heart away;
He'll love His own to endless day.

Love has redeemed His sheep with blood;
And love will bring them safe to God;
Love calls them all from death to life;
And love will finish all their strife.

He loves through every changing scene,
Nor aught can Him from Zion wean;
Not all the wanderings of her heart
Can make His love from her depart.

At death, beyond the grave, He'll love;
In endless bliss, His own shall prove
The blazing glory of that love
Which never could from them remove.

1331   James Small   87 87 D (iambic)
**Having loved His own which were in the world,
He loved them unto the end.**
John 13:1

I've found a Friend, O such a Friend!
　He loved me ere I knew Him;
He drew me with the cords of love
　And thus He bound me to Him:
And round my heart still closely twine
　Those ties which nought can sever,
For I am His and He is mine,
　For ever and for ever.

I've found a Friend, O such a Friend!
　He bled, He died to save me;
And not alone the gift of life
　But His own self He gave me:
Nought that I have my own I call,
　I hold it for the Giver:
My heart, my strength, my life, my all,
　Are His, and His for ever.

I've found a Friend, O such a Friend!
　All power to Him is given
To guard me on my onward course
　And bring me safe to heaven.
The eternal glories gleam afar
　To nerve my faint endeavour;
So now to watch! to work! to war!
　And then—to rest for ever!

I've found a Friend, O such a Friend!
　So kind and true and tender,
So wise a Counsellor and Guide,
　So mighty a Defender:
From Him, who loves me now so well,
　What power my soul can sever?
Shall life or death or earth or hell?
　No! I am His for ever!

1332　Joseph Hart　　　　LM
**Having loved His own which were in the world,
He loved them unto the end.**
John 13:1

And why, dear Saviour, tell me why,
Thou thus wouldst suffer, bleed, and die?
What mighty motive could Thee move?
The motive's plain—'twas all for love!

For love of whom? Of sinners base,
A hardened herd, a rebel race,
That mocked and trampled on Thy blood,
And wantoned with the wounds of God.

They nailed Him to th'accursèd tree:
They did, my brethren, so did we!
The soldiers pierced His side, 'tis true,
But we have pierced Him through and through.

1333　Albert Midlane　　　77 77
**Having loved His own which were in the world,
He loved them unto the end.**
John 13:1

Sweet the theme of Jesus' love!
Sweet the theme all themes above;
Love unmerited and free,
Our triumphant song shall be.

Love, so vast that nought can bound;
Love, too deep for thought to sound;
Love, which made the Lord of all
Drink the wormwood and the gall.

Love, which led Him to the cross,
Bearing there unuttered loss;
Love, which brought Him to the gloom
Of the cold and darksome tomb.

Love which made Him hence arise
Far above the starry skies,
There with tender, loving care,
All His people's griefs to share.

Love, which will not let Him rest
Till His chosen all are blest;
Till they all for whom He died
Live rejoicing by His side.

1334　John Fawcett (alt)　　　CM
**Jesus answered and said unto him, What I do
thou knowest not now; but thou shalt know
hereafter.** *John 13:7*

Thy way, O God! is in the sea,
　Thy paths I cannot trace;
Nor comprehend the mystery
　Of Thy unbounded grace.

Here the dark veils of flesh and sense,
　My captive soul surround;
Mysterious deeps of providence
　My wond'ring thoughts confound.

When I behold Thy awesome hand
　My earthly hopes destroy,
In deep astonishment I stand,
　And ask the reason why.

As through a glass, I dimly see
　The wonders of Thy love,
How little do I know of Thee,
　Or of the joys above.

'Tis but in part I know Thy will,
　I bless Thee for the sight;
When will Thy love the rest reveal
　In glory's clearer light?

With rapture shall I then survey
　Thy providence and grace,
And spend an everlasting day
　In wonder, love, and praise.

1335   Nicolaus Zinzendorf, Anna Nitschmann
tr. John Wesley   LM
**Peter saith unto Him, Thou shalt never wash
my feet. Jesus answered him, If I wash thee
not, thou hast no part with Me.**
John 13:8

O come, Thou wounded Lamb of God!
Come, wash us in Thy cleansing blood;
Give us to know Thy love, then pain
Is sweet, and life or death is gain.

Take our poor hearts, and let them be
For ever closed to all but Thee;
Seal Thou our breasts, and let us wear
That pledge of love for ever there.

How can it be, Thou heavenly King,
That Thou shouldst man to glory bring;
Make slaves the partners of Thy throne,
Decked with a never-fading crown?

O Lord, enlarge our scanty thought,
To know the wonders Thou hast wrought;
Unloose our stammering tongues to tell
Thy love immense, unsearchable!

First-born of many brethren, Thou,
To Thee both heaven and earth must bow;
Help us to Thee our all to give,
Thine may we die, Thine may we live.

1336   Vernon Higham   66 84 D
**Let not your heart be troubled: ye believe in
God, believe also in Me.** *John 14:1*

The mansions of the Lord
Are fair beyond compare;
The house of God will peace afford:
To all declare.
See Jesus Christ has died
For those who once did roam;
And He alone can be our Guide
To bring us home.

'Let not your troubled heart
Dismay in doubt and die;
Believe in God, do not depart;'
Now hear His cry.
The way to God above
Is only through His Son;
No other path, but by His love
So dearly won.

Look to the Saviour now,
Embrace His glorious form;
The way, truth, life, He will endow
In gospel warm.
Complete in all He is,
Conforming to God's will;
A destined death by traitor's kiss
He did fulfil.

To all who trust in Him
God's word will never fall;
For He will guide and gather in
His children all.
The gentle Christ behold,
Who shed His blood so free;
Comes for His own, leads to the fold
His family.

The peace of God is strong,
And far above this earth;
It is the gift and happy song
Of heaven's worth.
This peace of heart and mind
That stays in storm and care,
Which God bestows to those who find
This Saviour fair.
© Author

1337   Cecil Alexander   CM
I go to prepare a place for you. *John 14:2*

The golden gates are lifted up,
The doors are opened wide;
The King of glory is gone in
Unto His Father's side.

Thou art gone up before us, Lord,
To make for us a place,
That we may be where now Thou art,
And look upon God's face.

And ever on our earthly path
A gleam of glory lies;
A light still breaks behind the cloud
That veiled Thee from our eyes.

Lift up our hearts, lift up our minds:
Let Thy dear grace be given,
That, while we wander here below,
Our treasure be in heaven;

That where Thou art at God's right hand,
Our hope, our love, may be.
Dwell Thou in us, that we may dwell
For evermore in Thee.

JOHN CENNICK 1718-55

1338   John Cennick   LM
**I am the way, the truth, and the life: no man
cometh unto the Father, but by Me.**
John 14:6

Jesus, my All, to heaven is gone,
He whom I fix my hopes upon;
His track I see, and I'll pursue
The narrow way, till Him I view.

The way the holy prophets went,
The road that leads from banishment,
The King's highway of holiness
I'll go, for all His paths are peace.

This is the way I long have sought,
And mourned because I found it not;
My grief, my burden long has been,
Because I could not cease from sin.

The more I strove against its power,
I sinned and stumbled but the more:
Till late I heard my Saviour say,
'Come hither, soul, I am the way.'

Lo! glad I come; and Thou, blest Lamb,
Shalt take me to Thee as I am;
Nothing but sin I Thee can give;
Nothing but love shall I receive.

Then will I tell to sinners round,
What a dear Saviour I have found;
I'll point to Thy redeeming blood,
And say, 'Behold the way to God.'

1339   William Gadsby   77 77
**I am the way, the truth, and the life: no man
cometh unto the Father, but by Me.**
John 14:6

Jesus is the way to God;
   Jesus is the way to bliss;
In this way the church has trod,
   Down from Adam's day to this.

Jesus is the living way;
   All beside to ruin lead;
They are safe, and only they,
   Who are one in Christ their Head.

Jesus is a holy way;
   Leads to endless joys above;
Holy men, and only they,
   Walk in this blest way of love.

Jesus is a humble way;
   Pride and self must be brought down;
Nothing like a beast of prey
   Ever can in this way run.

Jesus is the way of strength;
   Yet the strong this way can't come;
And the Lord will prove at length,
   Weaklings have the victory won.

Jesus is the way of peace,
   Paved from end to end with love;
Yes, this way abounds with grace,
   And the needy it approve.

All a helpless soul can need,
   All a faithful God can give,
In this way is to be had;
   Here the hungry eat and live.

1340   George Doane   CM
**I am the way, the truth, and the life: no man
cometh unto the Father, but by Me.**
John 14:6

Thou art the Way; to Thee alone
   From sin and death we flee;
And he, who would the Father seek,
   Must seek Him, Lord, by Thee.

Thou art the Truth; Thy word alone
   True wisdom can impart;
Thou only canst inform the mind,
   And purify the heart.

Thou art the Life; the rending tomb
   Proclaims Thy conquering arm;
And those who put their trust in Thee,
   Nor death, nor hell shall harm.

Thou art the Way, the Truth, the Life;
   Grant us that Way to know,
That Truth to keep, that Life to win,
   Whose joys eternal flow.

1341 Joseph Hart LM
I am the way, the truth, and the life: no man cometh unto the Father, but by Me.
John 14:6

Do any ask the heavenly road,
The shining way that leads to God?
Then hear the blessèd Jesus say,
'Come unto Me, I am the Way.'

Do any wish the truth to learn,
The good from evil to discern;
To shun the tempter in their youth?
The Saviour says: 'I am the Truth.'

Do any feel the plague of sin,
Satan and death at work within?
Jesus can quell the mortal strife,
For Jesus says: 'I am the Life.'

Do any feel their need of God,
To go the way the saints have trod,
To stay no longer in the night?
Then hear His words: 'I am the Light.'

1342 Harriet Auber 86 84
And I will pray the Father, and He shall give you another Comforter, that He may abide with you for ever.
John 14:16

Our blest Redeemer, ere He breathed
　His tender, last farewell,
A Guide, a Comforter bequeathed,
　　With us to dwell.

He came in semblance of a dove,
　With sheltering wings outspread,
The holy balm of peace and love
　　On each to shed.

He came in tongues of living flame
　To teach, convince, subdue;
All powerful as the wind He came,
　　As viewless too.

And His that gentle voice we hear,
　Soft as the breath of even,
That checks each fault, that calms each fear,
　And speaks of heaven.

And every virtue we possess,
　And every victory won,
And every thought of holiness,
　　Are His alone.

Spirit of purity and grace,
　Our weakness pitying see;
O, make our hearts Thy dwelling-place,
　　And meet for Thee!

1343 Alan Clifford DLM
He shall give you another Comforter.
John 14:16

Come, Holy Ghost, my heart assure,
Dispel my fears, that I no more
　May doubt that mercy now is mine,
　Nor question promises divine;
Impress the seal, Thine image leave,
Confirm in power that grace I have,
　That I may run the heavenly race
　With joy, beholding Jesus' face.

Come, blessèd Comforter divine,
Relieve this doubting heart of mine;
　Banish the clouds of unbelief,
　O liberate my soul from grief,
Illumine me with heavenly light,
Scatter the thoughts of darkest night!
　With anxious sighs I look above,
　Longing to know my Saviour's love.

Come, promise of the Father's love,
Abide within me, gentle Dove;
　My soul assured, I then shall rest
　On my Redeemer's tender breast,
Until I come to heaven at last,
With all my sins and troubles past;
　Truly to know that grace was sure,
　Happy to know, and doubt no more!
© Author

1344 Alfred Vine LM
He shall give you another Comforter.
John 14:16

O Breath of God, breathe on us now,
　And move within us while we pray;
The spring of our new life art Thou,
　The very light of our new day.

O, strangely art Thou with us, Lord,
　Neither in height nor depth to seek;
In nearness shall Thy voice be heard;
　Spirit to spirit Thou dost speak.

Christ is our Advocate on high:
　Thou art our Advocate within;
O, plead the truth, and make reply
　To every argument of sin.

But ah, this faithless heart of mine!
　The way I know, I know my Guide:
Forgive me, O my Friend divine
　That I so often turn aside.

Be with me when no other friend
　The mystery of my heart can share;
And be Thou known, when fears transcend,
　By Thy best name of Comforter.

1345 Charles Wesley   888 D
He shall give you another Comforter.
John 14:16

Father of everlasting grace,
Thy goodness and Thy truth we praise,
  Thy goodness and Thy truth we prove;
Thou hast, in honour of Thy Son,
The gift unspeakable sent down,
  The Spirit of life, and power, and love.

Send us the Spirit of Thy Son,
To make the depths of Godhead known,
  To make us share the life divine;
Send Him the sprinkled blood to apply,
Send Him our souls to sanctify,
  And show and seal us ever Thine.

So shall we pray, and never cease,
So shall we thankfully confess
  Thy wisdom, truth, and power, and love;
With joy unspeakable adore,
And bless and praise Thee evermore,
  And serve Thee as Thy hosts above.

Till, added to that heavenly choir,
We raise our songs of triumph higher,
  And praise Thee in a bolder strain,
Out-soar the first-born seraph's flight,
And sing, with all our friends in light,
  Thy everlasting love to man.

1346 Charles Wesley   87 87 D
The Spirit of truth. *John 14:17*

Love divine, all loves excelling,
  Joy of heaven, to earth come down!
Fix in us Thy humble dwelling;
  All Thy faithful mercies crown.
Jesus, Thou art all compassion;
  Pure unbounded love Thou art;
Visit us with Thy salvation;
  Comfort every trembling heart.

Breathe, O breathe Thy blessèd Spirit
  Into every troubled breast!
Let us all in Thee inherit;
  Let us find Thy promised rest.
Take away the love of sinning;
  Alpha and Omega be;
End of faith, as its beginning,
  Set our hearts at liberty.

Come, almighty to deliver,
  Let us all Thy grace receive!
Suddenly return, and never,
  Never more Thy temples leave;
Thee we would be always blessing,
  Serve Thee as Thy hosts above,
Pray and praise Thee without ceasing;
  Glory in Thy perfect love.

Finish then Thy new creation;
  Pure and holy may we be;
Let us see Thy great salvation
  Perfectly secured by Thee;
Changed from glory into glory,
  Till in heaven we take our place;
Till we cast our crowns before Thee,
  Lost in wonder, love, and praise.

1347 Samuel Medley   LM
I will not leave you comfortless: I will come to you. *John 14:18*

Come, ye who know the Saviour's love,
And His indulgent mercies prove;
In cheerful songs His praise express,
For He'll not leave you comfortless.

He ever acts the Saviour's part,
With strong compassions in His heart;
The least and weakest saints He'll bless,
Nor will He leave us comfortless.

His wisdom, goodness, power, and care,
We largely, sweetly, daily share;
He will our every fear suppress.
Nor will He leave us comfortless.

Thanks to Thy name, our dearest Lord,
For every promise in Thy word;
But, O! with this our hearts impress,
'I will not leave you comfortless.'

When we, at last, shall meet above,
In the blest world of joy and love,
Our raptured songs will then express,
He has not left us comfortless.

1348   Thomas à Kempis, tr. J Neale   LM
Because I live, ye shall live also.
John 14:19

Again the Lord's own day is here,
The day to Christian people dear,
As week by week it bids them tell
How Jesus rose from death and hell.

For by His flock their Lord declared
His resurrection should be shared;
And we who trust in Him to save
With Him are risen from the grave.

We, one and all, of Him possessed,
Are with exceeding treasures blest;
For all He did and all He bare
He gives us as our own to share.

Eternal glory, rest on high,
A blessèd immortality,
True peace and gladness, and a throne,
Are all His gifts and all our own.

And therefore unto Thee we sing,
O Lord of peace, eternal King;
Thy love we praise, Thy name adore,
Both on this day and evermore.

1349   Christian Gellert, tr. Frances Cox
                      78 78 4

Because I live, ye shall live also.
John 14:19

Jesus lives! thy terrors now
   Can, O death, no more appal us;
Jesus lives! by this we know
   Thou, O grave, canst not enthral us.

      Hallelujah!

Jesus lives! henceforth is death
   But the gate of life immortal;
This shall calm our trembling breath
   When we pass its gloomy portal.

Jesus lives! for us He died;
   Then, alone to Jesus living,
Pure in heart may we abide,
   Glory to our Saviour giving.

Jesus lives! our hearts know well
   Nought from us His love shall sever;
Life, nor death, nor powers of hell
   Tear us from His keeping ever.

Jesus lives! to Him the throne
   Over all the world is given;
May we go where He is gone,
   Rest and reign with Him in heaven.

1350   Samuel Medley   LM
Because I live, ye shall live also.
John 14:19

The Saviour lives no more to die!
He lives, the Lord enthroned on high!
He lives, triumphant o'er the grave!
He lives, eternally to save!

He lives, to still His people's fears!
He lives, to wipe away their tears!
He lives, to calm their troubled heart!
He lives, all blessings to impart!

He lives, all glory to His name!
He lives, unchangeably the same!
He lives, their mansions to prepare,
He lives, to bring them safely there!

1351   Anne Steele   LM
Because I live, ye shall live also.
John 14:19

When sins and fears prevailing rise,
   And fainting hope almost expires,
Jesus, to Thee I lift my eyes,
   To Thee I breathe my soul's desires.

Art Thou not mine, my living Lord?
   And can my hope, my comfort die,
Fixed on Thy everlasting word,
   That word which built the earth and sky?

If my immortal Saviour lives,
   Then my immortal life is sure;
His word a firm foundation gives;
   Here let me build and rest secure.

Here let my faith unshaken dwell;
   Immovable the promise stands;
Not all the powers of earth or hell
   Can e'er dissolve the sacred bands.

Here, O my soul, thy trust repose;
   If Jesus is for ever mine,
Not death itself, that last of foes,
   Shall break a union so divine.

1352 John Berridge   SM
He that hath My commandments, and keepeth them, he it is that loveth Me: and he that loveth Me shall be loved of my Father, and I will love him, and will manifest Myself to him.
John 14:21

The table now is spread;
   We meet around the board;
Dear Jesus, bless the wine and bread,
   And heavenly life afford.

O may the Lord appear,
   With looks divinely mild,
And whisper in each humble ear,
   'I love thee well, My child.'

1353 William Gadsby   88 88 D (anapaestic)
He that hath My commandments, and keepeth them, he it is that loveth Me.
John 14:21

I'll speak forth the love of my Lord,
   His praises my tongue shall employ;
He bought me with His precious blood,
   Nor Gabriel is loved more than I;
Though pure, He for me was made sin;
   Though rich, He for me became poor;
Though free, yet a debtor brought in;
   For me He has paid the long score.

These truths to my heart He proclaimed,
   When helpless I stood and distressed,
When I at the bar was arraigned,
   With law, sin, and terrors oppressed.
No hand to my help did appear;
   The witness against me was true;
Which filled me with horror and fear,
   Till Jesus, my Lord, came in view.

He saw me distressed, and He said,
   'Fear not, I procured thy discharge;
I'm Jesus, Who lives, and was dead,
   And now will I set thee at large.'
Not one in the court did object,
   But all gave a smile when He spoke;
He then took the yoke off my neck,
   And ravished my soul with His look.

What joy filled my soul, who can tell?
   But surely I ne'er shall forget;
My Jesus has all things done well,
   And therefore His love I'll repeat.
To Him all the glory belongs;
   My soul shall speak well of His name;
He now is the theme of my songs,
   And shall be for ever the same.

1354 Benjamin Francis   88 88 D (anapaestic)
He that hath my commandments, and keepeth them, he it is that loveth Me.
John 14:21

My gracious Redeemer I love;
   His praises aloud I'll proclaim,
And join with the armies above,
   To shout His adorable name.
To gaze on His glories divine
   Shall be my eternal employ;
And feel them incessantly shine,
   My boundless, ineffable joy.

He freely redeemed with His bood
   My soul from the confines of hell,
To live on the smiles of my God,
   And in His sweet presence to dwell;
To shine with the angels of light,
   With saints and with seraphs to sing;
To view with eternal delight
   My Jesus, my Saviour, my King.

In Meshech, as yet, I reside,
   A darksome and restless abode:
Molested with foes on each side,
   And longing to dwell with my God.
O when shall my spirit exchange
   This cell of corruptible clay
For mansions celestial, and range
   Through realms of ineffable day?

My glorious Redeemer! I long
   To see Thee descend on the cloud,
Amidst the bright numberless throng,
   And mix with the triumphing crowd.
O when wilt Thou bid me ascend,
   To join in Thy praises above,
To gaze on Thee, world without end,
   And feast on Thy ravishing love?

No sorrow, nor sickness, nor pain,
   Nor sin, nor temptation, nor fear,
Shall ever molest me again;
   Perfection of glory reigns there.
This soul and this body shall shine
   In robes of salvation and praise,
And banquet on pleasures divine,
   Where God His full beauty displays.

Ye palaces, sceptres, and crowns,
   Your pride with disdain I survey;
Your pomps are but shadows and sounds,
   And pass in a moment away.
The crown that my Saviour bestows,
   Yon permanent sun shall outshine;
My joy everlastingly flows;
   My God, my Redeemer, is mine!

1355   Frances Havergal   886
But the Comforter, which is the Holy Ghost, whom the Father will send in My name, He shall teach you all things.
John 14: 26

To Thee, O Comforter divine,
For all Thy grace and power benign,
    Sing we Hallelujah!

To Thee, whose faithful love had place
In God's great covenant of grace,
    Sing we Hallelujah!

To Thee, whose faithful voice doth win
The wandering from the ways of sin,
    Sing we Hallelujah!

To Thee, whose faithful power doth heal,
Enlighten, sanctify, and seal,
    Sing we Hallelujah!

To Thee, whose faithful truth is shown
By every promise made our own,
    Sing we Hallelujah!

To Thee, our Teacher and our Friend,
Our faithful Leader to the end,
    Sing we Hallelujah!

To Thee, by Jesus Christ sent down,
Of all His gifts the sum and crown,
    Sing we Hallelujah!

To Thee, who art with God the Son
And God the Father ever One,
    Sing we Hallelujah!

1356   Charles Wesley   87 87
But the Comforter, which is the Holy Ghost, whom the Father will send in My name, He shall teach you all things.
John 14: 26

Come, Thou everlasting Spirit,
    Bring to every thankful mind
All the Saviour's dying merit,
    All His sufferings for mankind.

True Recorder of His passion,
    Now the living faith impart,
Now reveal His great salvation,
    Preach His gospel to our heart.

Come, Thou Witness of His dying;
    Come, Remembrancer divine!
Let us feel Thy power, applying
    Christ to every soul, and mine!

1357   John Ellerton   10 10 10 10
Peace I leave with you, My peace I give unto you. *John 14:27*

Saviour, again to Thy dear name we raise
With one accord our parting hymn of praise;
We stand to bless Thee ere our worship cease,
Then, lowly kneeling, wait Thy word of peace.

Grant us Thy peace upon our homeward way;
With Thee began, with Thee shall end the day;
Guard Thou the lips from sin, the hearts from
        shame,
That in this house have called upon Thy name.

Grant us Thy peace, Lord, through the coming
        night,
Turn Thou for us its darkness into light;
From harm and danger keep Thy children free,
For dark and light are both alike to Thee.

Grant us Thy peace throughout our earthly life,
Our balm in sorrow, and our stay in strife;
Then, when Thy voice shall bid our conflict cease,
Call us, O Lord, to Thine eternal peace!

1358   Frances Havergal   65 65 D +refrain
Peace I leave with you, My peace I give unto you. *John 14:27*

Like a river glorious
    Is God's perfect peace,
Over all victorious
    In its bright increase;
Perfect, yet it floweth
    Fuller every day;
Perfect, yet it groweth
    Deeper all the way.

    Stayed upon Jehovah
        Hearts are fully blest;
    Finding, as He promised,
        Perfect peace and rest.

Hidden in the hollow
    Of His blessèd hand,
Never foe can follow,
    Never traitor stand;
We may trust Him fully
    All for us to do;
They who trust Him wholly
    Find Him wholly true.

1359 Augustus Toplady   CM
I am the true vine, and My Father is the husbandman. *John 15:1*

Jesus, immutably the same,
 Thou true and living Vine!
Around Thy all-supporting stem,
 My feeble arms I'd twine.

I can do nothing without Thee;
 My strength is wholly Thine;
Withered and barren should I be,
 If severed from the Vine.

Quickened by Thee, and kept alive,
 I'd flourish and bear fruit;
My life I'd from Thy sap derive,
 My vigour from Thy root.

Each moment watered by Thy care,
 And fenced with power divine;
Fruit to eternal life would bear,
 The feeblest branch of Thine.

1360 Joseph Lyne   96 96
Abide in Me, and I in you. *John 15:4*

Let me come closer to Thee, Lord Jesus,
 O closer day by day;
Let me lean harder on Thee, Lord Jesus,
 Yes, harder all the way.

Let me show forth Thy beauty, Lord Jesus,
 Like sunshine on the hills;
O let my lips pour forth Thy sweetness
 In joyous sparkling rills!

Yes, like a fountain, precious Lord Jesus,
 Make me and let me be;
Keep me and use me daily, Lord Jesus,
 For Thee, for only Thee.

In all my heart and will, O Lord Jesus,
 Be altogether King;
Make me a loyal subject, Lord Jesus,
 To Thee in everything.

Thirsting and hungering for Thee, Lord Jesus,
 With blessèd hunger here,
Looking for home on Zion's mountain:
 No thirst, no hunger there.

1361 William Longstaff   11 11 11 11
Abide in Me, and I in you. *John 15:4*

Take time to be holy, speak oft with thy Lord;
Abide in Him always, and feed on His word;
Make friends of God's children, help those who
 are weak;
Forgetting in nothing His blessing to seek.

Take time to be holy, the world rushes on;
Spend much time in secret with Jesus alone.
By looking to Jesus like Him thou shalt be;
Thy friends, in thy conduct, His likeness shall
 see.

Take time to be holy, let Him be thy Guide:
And run not before Him whatever betide:
In joy or in sorrow still follow thy Lord,
And, looking to Jesus, still trust in His word.

Take time to be holy, be calm in thy soul;
Each thought and each temper beneath His
 control.
Thus led by His Spirit and filled with His love,
Thou soon shalt be fitted for service above.

1362 John Ryland   77 77
Abide in Me, and I in you. *John 15:4*

Thou, who art the incarnate God,
In mine heart make Thine abode:
Come, dear Lord, and come to stay,
Not just smile and go away!

Let not clouds Thy face eclipse,
Let not anger seal Thy lips:
Thy fair countenance let me see;
With Thy sweet voice speak to me.

Rise then, Sun of Righteousness,
Me with Thy sweet beamings bless;
Winter then may stay or flee,
Lord, 'tis all alike to me.

If in life I have Thy grace,
And at death behold Thy face:
Life may stay, or life may flee,
Lord, 'tis all alike to me.

1363 Samuel Barnard CM
I am the vine, ye are the branches.
John 15:5

The Vine and branches are but one
  In God the Father's sight;
He views His people in His Son
  With infinite delight.

They all were chosen in Christ the Vine
  Before the world begun:
With Him they must in glory shine,
  For He and they are one.

This union is so firm and strong,
  That sin nor all their foes
Can never pluck them off, so long
  As Jesus doth oppose.

'Tis from this Vine they all receive
  Their sap while here below,
By which they to His glory live,
  Opposing every foe.

'Tis by this union, when they die,
  They will exalted be,
And praise their God above the sky,
  To all eternity.

1364 Frances Havergal 76 76 D
Without Me ye can do nothing. *John 15:5*

I could not do without Thee,
  O Saviour of the lost,
Whose precious blood redeemed me
  At such tremendous cost;
Thy righteousness, Thy pardon,
  Thy precious blood must be
My only hope and comfort,
  My glory and my plea.

I could not do without Thee,
  I cannot stand alone;
I have no strength nor goodness,
  No wisdom of my own:
But Thou, belovèd Saviour,
  Art all in all to me,
And perfect strength in weakness
  Is theirs who lean on Thee.

I could not do without Thee;
  No other friend can read
The spirit's strange deep longings,
  Interpreting its need;
No human heart could enter
  Each dim recess of mine
And soothe and hush and calm it,
  O blessèd Lord, but Thine.

I could not do without Thee,
  For years are fleeting fast,
And soon in solemn loneness
  The river must be passed.
But Thou wilt never leave me,
  And though the waves roll high,
I know Thou wilt be near me
  And whisper, 'It is I.'

1365 Joseph Hart 66 66 88
**As the Father hath loved Me, so have I loved
you: continue ye in My love.**
John 15:9

When Jesus undertook
  To rescue ruined man,
The realms of bliss forsook,
  And to relieve us ran;
He spared no pains, declined no load,
Resolved to buy us with His blood.

No harsh commands He gave,
  No hard conditions brought;
He came to seek and save,
  And pardon every fault.
Poor trembling sinners hear His call;
They come, and He forgives them all.

When thus we're reconciled,
  He sets no rigorous tasks;
His yoke is soft and mild,
  For love is all He asks.
E'en *that* from Him we first receive,
And well He knows we've none to give.

This pure and heavenly gift,
  Within our hearts to move,
The dying Saviour left
  These tokens of His love;
Which seem to say, ' While this you do,
Remember Him that died for you.'

1366 Joseph Hart 66 66 88
**Greater love hath no man than this, that a man
lay down his life for his friends**
John15:13

Join, every tongue, to sing
  The mercies of the Lord;
The love of Christ, our King,
  Let every heart record.
He saved us from the wrath of God,
And paid our ransom with His blood.

What wondrous grace was this!
  We sinned, and Jesus died;
He wrought the righteousness,
  And we were justified.
We ran the score to lengths extreme,
And all the debt was charged on Him.

Hell was our just desert,
　　And He *that* hell endured;
Guilt broke His guiltless heart
　　With wrath that we incurred;
We bruised His body, spilt His blood,
And both became our heavenly food.

1367　Ann Gilbert　　　　　　　LM
Greater love hath no man than this, that a man lay down his life for his friends.
John 15:13

Jesus, who lived above the sky,
Came down to be a man and die;
And in the Bible we may see,
How very good He used to be.

He went about, He was so kind,
To cure poor people who were blind;
And many who were sick and lame,
He pitied them, and did the same.

And more than that, He told them too,
The things that God would have them do;
And was so gentle and so mild,
He would have listened to a child.

But such a cruel death He died,
He was hung up and crucified;
And those kind hands that did such good,
They nailed them to a cross of wood.

And so He died, and this is why
He came to be a man and die:
The Bible says He came from heaven,
That men might have their sins forgiven.

He knew how wicked men had been,
And knew that God must punish sin,
So for His people Jesus said
He'd bear the punishment instead.

1368　William Gadsby　　　　77 77
Ye are My friends, if ye do whatsoever I command you. *John 15:14*

Jesus, we Thy name adore;
Thine the kingdom is and power;
Thou shalt reign on Zion's hill;
We would gladly do Thy will.

Thou hast bought our souls with blood,
And hast brought us home to God.
We would gladly Thee obey,
In Thy own appointed way.

We through grace are dead indeed,
And from our old husband freed,
But are married to the Lord,
And would gladly do His word.

Thou didst sink in floods of wrath,
Us to save from guilt and death;
And with such a scene in view,
We would Thy commandments do.

Thou hast claimed us as Thy bride;
Keep us near Thy wounded side;
Dead to every lord but Thee,
We would fain obedient be.

1369　Josiah Conder　　　　76 76 D
Ye have not chosen Me, but I have chosen you. *John 15:16*

'Tis not that I did choose Thee,
　　For, Lord, that could not be,
This heart would still refuse Thee,
　　But Thou hast chosen me:
Thou from the sin that stained me
　　Washed me and set me free,
And to this end ordained me,
　　That I should live to Thee.

'Twas sovereign mercy called me,
　　And taught my opening mind;
The world had else enthralled me,
　　To heavenly glories blind.
My heart owns none above Thee;
　　For Thy rich grace I thirst;
This knowing, if I love Thee,
　　Thou must have loved me first.

1370　Thomas Kelly　　　　　77 77
But when the Comforter is come.
John 15:26

Jesus is gone up on high;
　　But His promise still is here,
'I will all your wants supply;
　　I will send the Comforter.'

Let us now His promise plead,
　　Let us to His throne draw nigh;
Jesus knows His people's need,
　　Jesus hears His people's cry.

Send us, Lord, the Comforter,
　　Pledge and witness of Thy love;
Dwelling with Thy people here,
　　Leading them to joys above.

Till we reach the promised rest,
　　Till Thy face unveiled we see,
Of this blessèd hope possessed.
　　Teach us, Lord, to live to Thee!

1371 Charles Wesley 555 11
If I depart, I will send Him (the Comforter) unto you. *John 16:7*

Away with our fears,
Our troubles and tears,
The Spirit is come,
The witness of Jesus returned to His home.

The pledge of our Lord
To His heaven restored,
Is sent from the sky,
And tells us our Head is exalted on high.

Our Advocate there
By His blood and His prayer
The gift hath obtained,
For us He hath prayed, and the Comforter gained.

Our glorified Head
His Spirit hath shed,
With His people to stay,
And never again will He take Him away.

Our heavenly Guide
With us shall abide,
His comforts impart,
And set up His kingdom of love in the heart.

The heart that believes
His kingdom receives,
His power and His peace,
His life, and His joy's everlasting increase.

1372 John Berridge 88 88 88
And when He is come, He will reprove the world of sin, and of righteousness, and of judgment. *John 16:8*

No awful sense we find of sin,
The sinful life and sinful heart;
No loathing of the plague within,
Until the Lord that sense impart;
But when the Spirit of truth is come,
A sinner trembles at his doom.

Convinced and piercèd through and through,
He thinks himself the sinner chief;
And, conscious of his mighty woe,
Perceives at length his unbelief;
Good creeds may stock his head around,
But in his heart no faith is found.

No power his nature can afford
To change his heart, or purge his guilt;
No help is found but in the Lord,
No balm but in the blood He spilt;
A ruined soul, condemned he stands,
And unto Jesus lifts his hands.

So lift I up my hands and eyes,
And all my help in Jesus seek.
Lord, bring Thy purging sacrifice
To wash me white, and make me meek;
And give me more enlargèd faith,
To view the wonders of Thy death.

1373 Oswald Allen SM
Howbeit when He, the Spirit of truth, is come, He will guide you into all truth.
John 16:13

O Holy Spirit, come,
And Jesus' love declare:
O tell us of our heavenly home,
And guide us safely there.

Our unbelief remove
By Thine almighty breath:
O work the wondrous work of love,
The mighty work of faith.

Come with resistless power,
Come with almighty grace,
Come with the long-expected shower,
And fall upon this place.

1374 Charles Wesley DSM
Howbeit when He, the Spirit of truth, is come, He will guide you into all truth.
John 16:13

Spirit of faith, come down,
Reveal the things of God;
And make to us the Godhead known,
And witness with the blood.
'Tis Thine the blood to apply,
And give us eyes to see
Who did for guilty sinners die
Hath surely died for me.

No man can truly say
That Jesus is the Lord,
Unless Thou take the veil away,
And breathe the living word;
Then, only then, we feel
Our interest in His blood,
And cry, with joy unspeakable:
'Thou art my Lord, my God!'

O that the world might know
The all-atoning Lamb!
Spirit of faith, descend, and show
The virtue of His name;
The grace which all may find,
The saving power impart;
And testify to all mankind,
And speak in every heart.

Inspire the living faith,
Which whosoe'er receives,
The witness in himself he hath,
And consciously believes;
The faith that conquers all,
And doth the mountain move,
And saves whoe'er on Jesus call,
And perfects them in love.

1375   Joseph Hart   CM
He shall not speak of Himself. *John 16:13*

Whatever prompts the soul to pride,
  Or gives us room to boast,
Except in Jesus crucified,
  Is not the Holy Ghost.

That blessèd Spirit omits to speak
  Of what Himself has done,
And bids the enlightened sinner seek
  Salvation in the Son.

He never moves a man to say,
  'Thank God, I'm made so good,'
But turns His eye another way,
  To Jesus and His blood.

Great are the graces He confers,
  But all in Jesus' name;
He gladly dictates, gladly hears,
  'Salvation to the Lamb.'

1376   Samuel Medley   CM
These things I have spoken unto you, that in Me ye might have peace. *John 16:33*

Ye saints, attend the Saviour's voice,
  Spoke in His word of grace:
He says, and in it O rejoice!
  'In Me ye shall have peace.'

Though storms and tempests round you roar,
  And foes and fears increase,
He says, and what could He say more?
  'In Me ye shall have peace.'

What though afflictions still abound,
  Nor do temptations cease,
He says, and O how sweet the sound!
  'In Me ye shall have peace.'

What though your hearts with sorrow bleed,
  And sighs and tears increase,
He says, and O 'tis true indeed!
  'In Me ye shall have peace.'

Though you shall pass through death's cold flood,
  To gain your wished release,
He says, and sure He'll make it good,
  'In Me ye shall have peace.'

When you His face in glory view,
  Where joy can ne'er decrease,
Eternity shall prove it true:
  'In Him ye shall have peace.'

1377   William Cowper   LM
In the world ye shall have tribulation: but be of good cheer; I have overcome the world.
John 16:33

Dangers of every shape and name
Attend the followers of the Lamb,
Who leave the world's deceitful shore,
And leave it to return no more.

O Lord, the pilot's part perform,
And guide and guard me through the storm;
Defend me from, each threatening ill;
Control the waves; say, ' Peace! be still!'

Amidst the roaring of the sea,
My soul still hangs her hopes on Thee;
Thy constant love, Thy faithful care,
Is all that saves me from despair.

1378   Vernon Higham   CM
Father, the hour is come; glorify Thy Son, that Thy Son also may glorify Thee.
John 17:1

'The hour is come,' the Saviour cried,
  'To glorify Thy name:'
For us He lived, for us He died,
  To take away our shame.

The Father to the Son now gave
  His own to glorify;
His very own, that Christ might save
  This lovely legacy.

We hide within the Saviour's prayer,
  The shadow of His grace;
The sunshine of His costly care,
  For evermore embrace.

When all seemed lost and we alone
  At desolation stared;
This we believed, we were His own:
  He prayed because He cared.

Yes, we believe that we are Thine,
  The gifts of God to Thee,
And Thou art ours, our Friend divine
  To love eternally.

Eternal life Thou dost bestow
  To know Thee, and adore;
For heaven to us, is Thee to know,
  And dwell for evermore

© Author

1379   Vernon Higham   77 77 D
I pray for them: I pray not for the world, but for them which Thou hast given me; for they are Thine. And all Mine are Thine, and Thine are Mine; and I am glorified in them.
John 17:9,10

God eternal, can it be,
  From beyond the clouds of time,
Thou hast chosen even me,
  Named me in Thy courts sublime?
Timeless grace, immortal love
  Now in Christ has filled my soul,
With this knowledge from above,
  That He took sin's heavy toll.

Though I search, I cannot bring
  Any merit that will gain;
Tarnished, tainted, every thing
  Sin has touched, my spirit slain.
Was it, Lord, to such as I,
  Deep in sin's depravity,
That Thy mercy called to fly
  Out of darkness unto Thee?

Chosen by Thy grace alone,
  Hidden reasons to Thee known;
All I know, Thou didst atone,
  Claimed and took me as Thine own.
Chosen Saviour to redeem,
  Costly mission to perform,
Work peculiar, yet supreme,
  As He took our human form.

Thine I am, Thy prayer reveals,
  For the Father brought me nigh;
Such security appeals
  That Thy truth will sanctify.
Even me, how can it be
  That these lips should sing Thy praise?
Sweet Redeemer, now I see
  What it costs to grant this grace.
                              © *Author*

1380   Richard Burnham   CM
Those that Thou gavest Me I have kept, and none of them is lost. *John 17:12*

Though saints may fear each dread alarm,
  Tried and severely tossed,
Held by the Saviour's mighty arm,
  Not one can e'er be lost.

He'll lead them on in Zion's road,
  Though weary, weak, and faint;
And never shall they lose their God,
  Or God e'er lose a saint!

1381   Charles Coffin, tr. J Chandler   CM
That they all may be one. *John 17:21*

O Holy Spirit, Lord of grace,
  Eternal fount of love,
Inflame, we pray, our inmost hearts
  With fire from heaven above.

As Thou in bond of love dost join
  The Father and the Son,
So fill us all with mutual love,
  And knit our hearts in one.

All glory to the Father be,
  All glory to the Son,
All glory, Holy Ghost, to Thee,
  While endless ages run.

1382   John Kent   CM
I in them, and Thou in Me, that they may be made perfect in one. *John 17:23a*

Before the day-star knew its place,
  Or planets went their round,
The church, in bonds of sovereign grace,
  Were one with Jesus found.

In all that Jesus did on earth,
  His church an interest have:
Go, trace Him from His humble birth
  Down to the silent grave.

'Twas for His saints He tasted death;
  All glory to His name:
Yet, when He yields His dying breath,
  With Him His saints o'ercame.

With Him His members, on the tree,
  Fulfilled the law's demands:
'Tis 'I in them, and they in Me',
  For thus the union stands.

Since Jesus slept among the dead,
  His saints have nought to fear,
For with their glorious suffering Head,
  His members sojourned there.

When from the tomb we see Him rise
  Triumphant o'er His foes,
He bore His members to the skies,
  With Jesus they arose.

Ye saints, this union can't dissolve,
  By which all things are yours,
Long as eternal years revolve,
  Or Deity endures.

1383 William Tucker   LM
And that the world may know that Thou hast sent Me, and hast loved them, as Thou hast loved Me. *John 17:23b*

Deep in the everlasting mind
   The great mysterious purpose lay,
Of choosing some from lost mankind,
   Whose sins the Lamb should bear away.

Them, loved with an eternal love,
   To grace and glory He ordained;
Gave them a throne which cannot move,
   And chose them both to means and end.

In these He was resolved to make
   The riches of His goodness known;
These He accepts for Jesus' sake,
   And views them righteous in His Son.

No goodness God foresaw in His,
   But what His grace decreed to give;
No comeliness in them there is
   Which they did not from Him receive.

Faith and repentance He bestows
   On such as He designs to save;
From Him their soul's obedience flows,
   And He shall all the glory have.

1384 Augustus Toplady   CM
Father, I will that they also, whom Thou hast given Me, be with Me where I am; that they may behold My glory.
John 17:24a

Awake sweet gratitude, and sing
   The ascended Saviour's love;
Sing how He lives to carry on
   His people's cause above.

With cries and tears He offered up
   His humble plea below;
But with authority He asks,
   Enthroned in glory now.

For all that come to God by Him,
   Salvation He demands;
Points to their names upon His breast,
   And spreads His wounded hands.

His sweet atoning sacrifice
   Gives sanction to His claim:
'Father, I will that all My saints
   Be with Me where I am.'

Eternal life, at His request,
   To every saint is given;
Safety on earth, and, after death,
   The plenitude of heaven.

Founded on right, Thy prayer avails;
   The Father smiles on Thee;
And now Thou in Thy kingdom art,
   Dear Lord, remember me.

1385 C A Wellesley   87 87 D
For Thou lovedst Me before the foundation of the world. *John 17:24b*

Loved with love which knows no measure
   Save the Father's love to Thee,
Blessèd Lord, our hearts would treasure
   All the Father's thoughts of Thee.
All His joy, His rest, His pleasure,
   All His deepest heart's delight,
Lord, Thy heart alone can measure
   What Thou art in His pure sight.

How He set His love upon Thee,
   Called Thee His belovèd Son;
Yet for us He did not spare Thee,
   By Thy death our life was won.
Blood-bought people, saved and spotless,
   Here we come to show Thy grace;
Soon, presented by Thee faultless,
   We shall see Thee face to face.

O! the joy, the wondrous singing,
   When we see Thee as Thou art;
Thy blest name, Lord Jesus, bringing
   Sweetest music to God's heart.
Notes of gladness, songs unceasing,
   Hymns of everlasting praise;
Psalms of glory, joy increasing,
   Through God's endless day of days.

1386 Paulus Gerhardt, tr James Alexander
                     76 76 D
Then came Jesus forth, wearing the crown of thorns, and the purple robe.
John 19:5a

O sacred Head once wounded,
   With grief and pain weighed down,
How scornfully surrounded
   With thorns, Thine only crown!
How pale art Thou with anguish,
   With sore abuse and scorn!
How does that visage languish
   Which once was bright as morn!

O Lord of life and glory,
   What bliss till now was Thine!
I read the wondrous story,
   I joy to call Thee mine.
Thy grief and Thy compassion
   Were all for sinners' gain;
Mine, mine was the transgression,
   But Thine the deadly pain.

What language shall I borrow
  To praise Thee, heavenly Friend,
For this Thy dying sorrow,
  Thy pity without end?
Lord, make me Thine for ever,
  Nor let me faithless prove;
O let me never, never
  Abuse such dying love!

Be near me, Lord, when dying;
  O show Thyself to me;
And, for my succour flying,
  Come, Lord, to set me free:
These eyes, new faith receiving,
  From Jesus shall not move;
For he who dies believing
  Dies safely through Thy love.

PAULUS GERHARDT 1607-1676

1387   Thomas Ives   LM
And Pilate saith unto them, Behold the man!
John 19:5b

Behold the Man who lonely stands,
With body bared and fast-bound hands;
See on His head a crown of thorns;
Mark how His love the anguish scorns.

So kingly! yet so mocked and tried;
So gracious! yet by all denied!
O Man oppressed with human grief!
O Christ of all men Thou art chief!

Why stands He dumb before the crowd?
He hears their cry, relentless, loud:
'Away with Him: He shall not live;'
His silence doth the answer give.

'Behold your King!' His judges cry;
Time shows how true their mockery.
He was, and is, a King alway,
Unnumbered millions own His sway.

Jesus! Thou art the Prince of peace,
Thy reign of love shall never cease;
Though man's proud empires all decline,
An everlasting kingdom Thine.

1388   Charles Wesley   LM
And Pilate saith unto them, Behold the man!
John 19:5b

Ye that pass by, behold the Man!
  The Man of griefs condemned for you;
The Lamb of God for sinners slain,
  Weeping to Calvary pursue.

See there His temples crowned with thorns;
  His bleeding hands extended wide;
His streaming feet transfixed and torn;
  The fountain gushing from His side.

O Thou dear suffering Son of God,
  How does Thy heart to sinners move!
Sprinkle on me Thy precious blood;
  Help me to taste Thy dying love.

The rocks could feel Thy powerful death,
  And tremble, and asunder part;
O rend with Thy expiring breath,
  The harder marble of my heart.

1389   Vernon Higham   DCM
I thirst. *John 19:28*

I heard the cry of mercy mild
  Which broke my heart in two:
A voice so full for me His child —
  My soul towards Him flew.
'I thirst', He cried with parching heart,
  'Forgive them', was His song;
And heaven heard and hell did start,
  For He had done no wrong.

No sponge of wine with bitter stain
  His thirst could ever quench:
The ocean wide and clouds of rain
  This desert never drench.
For souls He called, for hearts He pined,
  This satisfaction strange:
He cried for me, and showed mankind
  The love that does not change.

His thirsty soul He satisfied,
  And called me by His name.
He drew me close to His dear side
  And told me why He came:
The eternal plan of God for man
  Fulfilled on painful tree;
His blood was shed, and showed the span
  Of love so wide and free.

Beyond the cross and bitter curse,
I see God's plan sublime:
He breaks the clouds of death for us —
Pours mercy into time.
Was ever agony like this,
That spread such life abroad?
For at the cross see mercy's kiss
Which drew us to the Lord.

© Author

1390   Jonathan Evans   87 87 47
It is finished. *John 19:30*

Hark! the voice of love and mercy
Sounds aloud from Calvary!
See, it rends the rocks asunder,
Shakes the earth and veils the sky:
'It is finished!'
Hear the dying Saviour cry!

'It is finished!' What assurance
Do the wondrous words afford!
Heavenly blessings, without measure,
Flow to us from Christ the Lord:
'It is finished!'
Saints, the dying words record.

Finished, all the types and shadows
Of the ceremonial law;
Finished all that God had promised;
Death and hell no more shall awe.
'It is finished!'
Saints, from hence your comfort draw.

Saints and angels shout His praises!
His great finished work proclaim;
All on earth, and all in heaven,
Join to bless Immanuel's name.
Hallelujah!
Endless glory to the Lamb!

1391   Charles Wesley   LM
It is finished. *John 19:30*

'Tis finished! the Messiah dies!
Cut off for sins, but not His own;
Accomplished is the sacrifice;
The great redeeming work is done.

Finished our vile transgression is,
And purged the guilt of all our sin;
And everlasting righteousness
Is brought, for all His people, in.

'Tis finished, all my guilt and pain.
I want no sacrifice beside.
For me, for me the Lamb was slain,
And I'm for ever justified.

Sin, death, and hell are now subdued;
All grace is now to sinners given;
And lo! I plead the atoning blood,
For pardon, holiness, and heaven.

1392   Henry Baker   SM
It is finished. *John 19:30*

O perfect life of love!
All, all is finished now,
All that He left His throne above
To do for us below.

No work is left undone
Of all the Father willed;
His toil, His sorrows, one by one,
The Scripture have fulfilled.

No pain that we can share
But He has felt its smart;
All forms of human grief and care
Have pierced that tender heart.

And on His thorn-crowned head,
And on His sinless soul,
Our sins in all their guilt were laid,
That He might make us whole.

In perfect love He dies;
For me He dies, for me!
O all-atoning Sacrifice,
I cling by faith to Thee.

In every time of need,
Before the judgment throne,
Thy work, O Lamb of God, I'll plead,
Thy merits, not my own.

Yet work, O Lord, in me,
As Thou for me hast wrought;
And let my love the answer be
To grace Thy love has brought.

1393   Charles Wesley   886 D
They shall look on Him whom they pierced.
John 19:37

O Thou who hast redeemed of old,
And bidst me of Thy strength take hold,
And be at peace with Thee;
Help me Thy benefits to own,
And hear me tell what Thou hast done,
O dying Lamb, for me.

Vouchsafe the eye of faith to see
The Man transfixed on Calvary,
To know Thee who Thou art,
The one eternal God and true!
And let the sight affect, subdue,
And break my stubborn heart.

Lover of souls, to rescue mine,
Reveal the charity divine
   That suffered in my stead;
That made Thy soul a sacrifice,
And quenched in death those gracious eyes,
   And bowed that sacred head.

The veil of unbelief remove;
And by Thy manifested love,
   And by Thy sprinkled blood,
Destroy the love of sin in me,
And get Thyself the victory,
   And bring me back to God.

1394   Venantius Fortunatus, tr. John Ellerton
                                 11 11 11 11 11
The first day of the week. *John 20:1*

'Welcome, happy morning!' age to age shall say;
Hell today is vanquished; Heaven is won today!
Lo! the Dead is living, God for evermore!
Him, their true Creator, all His works adore.
'Welcome, happy morning!' age to age shall say.

Maker and Redeemer, Life and Health of all,
Thou from heaven beholding human nature's fall,
Of the Father's Godhead true and only Son,
Manhood to deliver, manhood didst put on.
Hell today is vanquished; Heaven is won today!

Thou, of life the Author, death didst undergo,
Tread the path of darkness, saving strength to
   show:
Come, then, True and Faithful, now fulfil Thy
   word;
'Tis Thine own third morning! Rise, O buried Lord!
'Welcome, happy morning!' age to age shall say.

Loose the souls long prisoned, bound with Satan's
   chain;
All that now is fallen raise to life again,
Show Thy face in brightness, bid the nations see;
Bring again our daylight: day returns with Thee!
Hell today is vanquished; Heaven is won today!

1395   Vernon Higham   DCM
**Then went in also that other disciple, which
came first to the sepulchre, and he saw, and
believed.** *John 20:8*

Dawn of the resurrection day
   Has spread its glorious light,
And rolled the heavy stone away
   Of unbelief's sad night.
O joy of heaven, this sweet concord
   Of truth and mercy fair!
An empty grave, a living Lord
   Thy gospel will declare.

O stand amongst us, Son of God,
   And in our hearts grant grace
To be amidst the saints who trod
   The path of faith's swift race.
We have not seen Thy wounds and scar,
   We have not touched Thy side;
We have not followed Bethlehem's star;
   Yet in Thee we abide.

Light of our hearts, hope of our souls
   Is Jesus Christ today;
For in one mighty act, He rolls
   The weight of sin away.
We thank Thee here that Thou didst come
   To die for our disgrace,
To rise again and so confirm
   The surety of Thy grace.
                                   © *Author*

1396   James Allen, C. Batty and A.Toplady
                                           87 87
**But Mary stood without at the sepulchre
weeping: and as she wept, she stooped down,
and looked into the sepulchre.**
John 20:11

I no more at Mary wonder
   Dropping tears upon the grave,
Earnest asking all around her,
   'Where is He that died to save?'

Dying love her heart attracted.
   Soon she felt its rising power,
He who Mary thus affected,
   Bids His mourners weep no more.

1397   John Newton   77 77 D
**But Mary stood without at the sepulchre
weeping: and as she wept, she stooped down,
and looked into the sepulchre.**
John 20:11

Mary to her Saviour's tomb
   Hasted at the early dawn;
Spice she brought, and sweet perfume,
   But the Lord, she loved, was gone.
For awhile she weeping stood,
   Struck with sorrow and surprise;
Shedding tears, a plenteous flood,
   For her heart supplied her eyes.

Jesus, who is always near,
   Though too often unperceived;
Came, His drooping child to cheer,
   And enquired why she was grieved,
Though at first she knew Him not,
   When He called her by her name,
Then her griefs were all forgot,
   For she found He was the same.

Grief and sighing quickly fled
  When she heard His welcome voice;
Just before she thought Him dead,
  Now He bids her heart rejoice:
What a change His word can make,
  Turning darkness into day!
You who weep for Jesus' sake,
  He will wipe your tears away.

He who came to comfort her,
  When she thought her all was lost;
Will for your relief appear,
  Though you now are tempest-tossed;
On His word your burden cast,
  On His love your thoughts employ;
Weeping for awhile may last,
  But the morning brings the joy.

1398   Edwin Hatch   SM
Receive ye the Holy Ghost. *John 20:22*

Breathe on me, Breath of God,
  Fill me with life anew,
That I may love what Thou dost love,
  And do what Thou wouldst do.

Breathe on me, Breath of God,
  Until my heart is pure;
Until my will is one with Thine
  To do and to endure.

Breathe on me, Breath of God,
  Till I am wholly Thine;
Until this earthly part of me
  Glows with Thy fire divine.

Breathe on me, Breath of God,
  So shall I never die,
But live with Thee the perfect life
  Of Thine eternity.

1399   John Newton   LM
**Cast the net on the right side of the ship, and
ye shall find.** *John 21:6*

Now while the gospel net is cast.
  Do Thou, O Lord, the effort own;
From numerous disappointments past,
  Teach us to hope in Thee alone.

May this be a much favoured hour
  To souls in Satan's bondage led!
O clothe Thy word with sovereign power
  To break the rocks and raise the dead!

To mourners speak a cheerful word;
  On seeking souls vouchsafe to shine;
Let poor backsliders be restored,
  And all Thy saints in praises join.

1400   Philip Doddridge   CM
Lovest thou Me more than these?
John 21:15a

Do not I love Thee, dearest Lord?
  Behold my heart and see;
And cast each hated idol down,
  That dares to rival Thee.

Do not I love Thee from my soul?
  Then let me nothing love;
Dead be my heart to every joy,
  When Jesus cannot move.

Is not Thy name melodious still
  To my attentive ear?
Do I not in Thy word delight
  The Saviour's voice to hear?

Hast Thou a lamb in all Thy flock
  I would disdain to feed?
Hast Thou a foe before whose face
  I'd fear Thy cause to plead?

1401   William Featherstone   11 11 11 11
Thou knowest that I love Thee.
John 21:15b

Lord Jesus, I love Thee, I know Thou art mine!
For Thee all the pleasures of sin I resign;
My gracious Redeemer, my Saviour art Thou!
If ever I loved Thee, Lord Jesus, 'tis now!

I love Thee because Thou hast first lovèd me,
And purchased my pardon on Calvary's tree;
I love Thee for wearing the thorns on Thy brow;
If ever I loved Thee, Lord Jesus, 'tis now!

I will love Thee in life, I will love Thee in death,
And praise Thee as long as Thou lendest me
  breath;
And say when the death-dew lies cold on my
  brow;
If ever I loved Thee, Lord Jesus, 'tis now!

In mansions of glory and endless delight,
I'll ever adore Thee in heaven so bright;
I'll sing with the glittering crown on my brow;
If ever I loved Thee, Lord Jesus, 'tis now!

1402 William Cowper 77 77
Lovest thou Me? *John 21:17a*

Hark my soul! it is the Lord;
'Tis Thy Saviour, hear His word;
Jesus speaks, and speaks to thee:
'Say, poor sinner, lovest thou Me?'

'I delivered thee when bound,
And when wounded healed thy wound;
Sought thee wandering, set thee right,
Turned thy darkness into light.

'Can a woman's tender care
Cease towards the child she bare?
Yes, she may forgetful be,
Yet I will remember thee.

'Mine is an unchanging love,
Higher than the heights above;
Deeper than the depths beneath,
Free and faithful, strong as death.

'Thou shalt see My glory soon,
When the work of grace is done;
Partner of My throne shalt be;
Say, poor sinner, lovest thou Me?'

Lord, it is my chief complaint,
That my love is cold and faint;
Yet I love Thee and adore;
O for grace to love Thee more!

1403 Richard Burnham 87 87
Lord, Thou knowest all things. *John 21:17b*

Jesus, Thou omniscient Saviour,
    Known to Thee is all I do;
All my thoughts, and words, and actions,
    Lie before Thy piercing view.

All my various imperfections,
    Every sin and every fear,
Yea, my every secret evil
    Doth before Thy face appear.

Yet, O Lord, Thou know'st I love Thee;
    Love Thy name, and love Thy cause,
Love the sound of Thy rich gospel,
    Dearly love Thy glorious laws.

Love to fear Thee, love to serve Thee,
    Love to sing Thy matchless fame;
Love sincerely all Thy people,
    Love Thy saints of every name.

O Thou merciful Redeemer,
    Help me more Thy name to love;
Love Thee with intense affection.
    Love Thee as Thy saints above.

THOMAS HAWEIS 1734-1820

1404 Thomas Haweis CM
Wait for the promise of the Father.
Acts 1:4

Enthroned on high, almighty Lord,
    The Holy Ghost send down!
Fulfil in us Thy faithful word,
    And all Thy mercies crown.

Though on our heads no tongues of fire
    Their wondrous powers impart,
Grant, Saviour, what we most desire,
    Thy Spirit in our heart.

Spirit of life, and light, and love,
    Thy heavenly influence give!
Quicken our souls, born from above,
    In Christ, that we may live.

To our benighted minds reveal
    The glories of His grace,
And bring us where no clouds conceal
    The brightness of His face.

His love within us shed abroad,
    Life's ever-springing well!
Till God in us, and we in God,
    In love eternal dwell.

1405 Charles Wesley LM
Wait for the promise of the Father.
Acts 1:4

Our Jesus is gone up on high,
    For us the blessing to receive;
It now comes streaming from the sky,
    The Spirit comes, and sinners live.

Lord, we believe to us and ours
    The apostolic promise given;
We wait the Pentecostal powers,
    The Holy Ghost sent down from heaven.

Ah! leave us not to mourn below,
    Or long for Thy return to pine;
Now, Lord, the Comforter bestow,
    And fix in us the Guest divine.

Assembled here with one accord,
    Calmly we wait the promised grace,
The purchase of our dying Lord:
    Come, Holy Ghost, and fill the place.

If every one that asks may find,
    If still Thou dost on sinners fall,
Come as a mighty rushing wind;
    Great grace be now upon us all.

1406   Henry Fox   LM
Unto the uttermost part of the earth.
Acts 1:8

Send forth the gospel! let it run
    Southward and Northward, East and West;
Tell all the earth Christ died and lives
    Who giveth pardon, life, and rest.

Send forth Thy gospel, gracious Lord!
    Thine was the blood for sinners shed;
Thy voice still pleads in human hearts;
    To Thee Thine other sheep be led.

Send forth Thy gospel, holy Lord!
    Kindle in us love's sacred flame;
Love giving all and grudging nought
    For Jesus' sake, in Jesus' name.

Send forth the gospel! tell it out!
    Go, brothers, at the Master's call;
Prepare His way, who comes to reign
    The King of kings and Lord of all.

1407   Daniel Whittle   Irregular
**This same Jesus, which is taken up from you
into heaven, shall so come in like manner as
ye have seen Him go into heaven.** *Acts 1:11*

Jesus is coming! Sing the glad word!
Coming for those He redeemed by His blood,
Coming to reign as the glorified Lord!
    Jesus is coming again!

*Jesus is coming, is coming again!
    Jesus is coming again!
Shout the glad tidings o'er mountain and plain!
    Jesus is coming again!*

Jesus is coming! The dead shall arise,
Loved ones shall meet in a joyful surprise,
Caught up together to Him in the skies.
    Jesus is coming again!

Jesus is coming! His saints to release;
Coming to give to the warring earth peace:
Sinning, and sighing, and sorrow shall cease.
    Jesus is coming again!

Jesus is coming! The promise is true:
Who are the chosen, the faithful, the few,
Waiting and watching, prepared for review?
    Jesus is coming again!

1408   Jonathan Franklin   CM
**And when the day of Pentecost was fully
come, they were all with one accord in one
place.** *Acts 2:1*

Thy church, O Lord, that's planted here,
    O make it to increase
With numbers, blessed with filial fear,
    Enjoying heavenly peace.

O may we all, dear Lord, as one,
    United ever be,
Rejoicing in what Christ has done,
    Who groaned upon the tree.

May all each other's burdens bear;
    Be simple, meek, and kind;
And keep us safe from every snare,
    And all of humble mind.

1409   Andrew Reed   CM
**And suddenly there came a sound from
heaven as of a rushing mighty wind, and it
filled all the house where they were sitting.**
Acts 2:2

Spirit divine! attend our prayers,
    And make this house Thy home;
Descend with all Thy gracious powers,
    O come, great Spirit, come!

Come as the light, to us reveal
    Our emptiness and woe;
And lead us in those paths of life
    Where all the righteous go.

Come as the fire and purge our heart
    Like sacrificial flame;
Let our whole soul an offering be
    To our Redeemer's name.

Come as the dew and sweetly bless
    This consecrated hour;
May barrenness rejoice to own
    Thy fertilising power.

Come as the dove and spread Thy wings,
The wings of peaceful love;
And let the church on earth become
Blest as the church above.

Come as the wind, with rushing sound
And Pentecostal grace;
That all of women born may see
The glory of Thy face.

Spirit divine, attend our prayers;
Make a lost world Thy home;
Descend with all Thy gracious powers,
O come, great Spirit, come!

1410   Joseph Hart   CM
And there appeared unto them cloven tongues like as of fire, and it sat upon each of them.
Acts 2:3

The soul that with sincere desires
Seeks after Jesus' love,
That soul the Holy Ghost inspires
With breathings from above.

Not every one in like degree
The Spirit of God receives;
The Christian often cannot see
His faith, and yet believes.

So gentle sometimes is the flame,
That, if we take not heed,
We may unkindly quench the same,
We may, my friends, indeed.

Blest God! that once in fiery tongues
Cam'st down in open view,
Come, visit every heart that longs
To entertain Thee too.

And though not like a mighty wind,
Nor with a rushing noise,
May we Thy calmer comforts find,
And hear Thy still small voice.

Not for the gift of tongues we pray,
Nor power the sick to heal;
Give wisdom to direct our way,
And strength to do Thy will.

We pray to be renewed within,
And reconciled to God;
To have our conscience washed from sin
In the Redeemer's blood.

We pray to have our faith increased,
And O celestial Dove!
We pray to be completely blessed
With that rich blessing, love.

1411   James Montgomery   SM
And they were all filled with the Holy Ghost, and began to speak with other tongues, as the Spirit gave them utterance. *Acts 2:4*

Lord God the Holy Ghost,
In this accepted hour,
As on the day of Pentecost,
Descend in all Thy power.

We meet with one accord
In our appointed place,
And wait the promise of our Lord,
The Spirit of all grace.

Like mighty rushing wind
Upon the waves beneath,
Move with one impulse every mind,
One soul, one feeling, breathe.

The young, the old, inspire
With wisdom from above;
And give us hearts and tongues of fire,
To pray and praise and love.

Spirit of light, explore,
And chase our gloom away,
With lustre shining more and more,
Unto the perfect day.

Spirit of truth, be Thou
In life and death our Guide;
O Spirit of adoption, now
May we be sanctified.

1412   Alan Clifford   77 77 4
God hath made that same Jesus, whom ye have crucified, both Lord and Christ.
Acts 2:36

Blessèd Jesus! how Thy name
Fills my heart with holy flame;
Can there be such love as Thine,
Love so free and so divine?
   Hallelujah!

Blessèd Jesus, Son of God,
Who the lonely journey trod
From the court of heaven to earth,
That I might have heavenly birth.
   Hallelujah!

Blessèd Jesus, Son of Man,
Loyal to His Father's plan;
Dying sinners to release,
Living now to give them peace.
   Hallelujah!

Blessèd Jesus, glorious King,
All my praise to Thee I bring,
I am Thine, though once undone,
Thou hast conquered, mighty One!
    Hallelujah!

Blessèd Jesus, Saviour mine,
May I be for ever Thine,
Dwell with Thee, Thy glory see
Now and for eternity.
    Hallelujah!

© Author

1413   Richard Burnham   66 66 88
Repent, and be baptized every one of you in the name of Jesus Christ. *Acts 2:38*

'Repent and be baptized,'
   Saith your redeeming Lord:
Ye all are now apprised
   That 'tis your Saviour's word;
Arise, arise, without delay,
And His divine command obey.

Ye penitential race,
   Who fall at Jesus' feet,
Saved by His glorious grace,
   Come, to His will submit:
And be baptized without delay,
And His divine command obey.

Come, ye believing train,
   No more this truth withstand:
No longer think it vain
   To honour God's command:
But haste, arise without delay,
And be baptized in Jesus' way.

1414   Thomas Haweis   CM
For the promise is unto you, and to your children. *Acts 2:39*

Our children, Lord, in faith and prayer,
   We now present to Thee;
Let them Thy covenant mercies share
   And Thy salvation see.

Such helpless babes Thou didst embrace,
   While dwelling here below;
To us and ours, O God of grace,
   The same compassion show.

In early days their hearts secure
   From worldly snares, we pray;
O give them grace to persevere
   In every righteous way.

Before them let their parents live
   In godly faith and fear,
Then, Lord, to heaven their souls receive
   And bring their children there.

CHARLOTTE ELLIOTT 1789-1871

1415   Charlotte Elliott   888 4
Now Peter and John went up together into the temple at the hour of prayer.
Acts 3:1

My God, is any hour so sweet,
From blush of morn to evening star,
As that which calls me to Thy feet,
   The hour of prayer?

Then is my strength by Thee renewed;
Then are my sins by Thee forgiven;
Then dost Thou cheer my solitude
   With hope of heaven.

No words can tell what sweet relief
There for my every want I find,
What strength for warfare, balm for grief,
   What peace of mind!

Hushed is each doubt, gone every fear;
My spirit seems in heaven to stay;
And e'en the penitential tear
   Is wiped away.

Lord, till I reach yon blissful shore
No privilege so dear shall be
As thus my inmost soul to pour
   In prayer to Thee.

1416   George Briggs   87 87 D
God hath spoken by the mouth of all His holy prophets since the world began.
Acts 3:21

God hath spoken by His prophets,
  Spoken His unchanging word;
Each from age to age proclaiming
  God the One, the righteous Lord!
Mid the world's despair and turmoil
  One firm anchor holding fast,
God is on His throne eternal,
  He alone the first and last.

God hath spoken by Christ Jesus,
  Christ, the everlasting Son,
Brightness of the Father's glory,
  With the Father ever One;
Spoken by the Word Incarnate,
  God of God ere time began,
Light of Light, to earth descending,
  Man, revealing God to man.

God yet speaketh by His Spirit
  Speaking to the hearts of men,
In the age-long word declaring
  God's own message, now as then.
Through the rise and fall of nations
  One sure faith yet standeth fast:
God abides, His word unchanging,
  God alone the first and last.

God Hath Spoken by His Prophets
Words: George W. Briggs
Words © 1953, Ren. 1981 The Hymn Society
(Admin. Hope Publishing Company, Carol Stream, IL 60188).

1417   William Rees vs.1-3, W.Jones v.4,
         tr.W V. Higham   CM
Neither is there salvation in any other: for there is none other name under heaven given among men, whereby we must be saved.
Acts 4:12

There's none but Jesus, beauteous Lord,
  Can fill this heart of mine
With comforts sweet and kind accord,
  From depths of death divine.

No other one, with such delight,
  Can fill my troubled breast;
I often gaze upon that sight,
  And in His merits rest.

In His rich wounds I see a place
  My guilty head to hide,
For there I'll find sufficient grace,
  And in His arms abide.

The price He paid, my soul has found,
  And rests secure in love;
For there upon redemption ground,
  I'll claim my home above.

© Translator

1418   John Adams   87 87 47
Neither is there salvation in any other: for there is none other name under heaven given among men, whereby we must be saved.
Acts 4:12

Jesus Lover of Thy nation;
  Saviour of Thy people free!
Visit us with Thy salvation;
  Let us, Lord, Thy glory see;
    O revive us,
  That we may rejoice in Thee.

Let us find Thy love surrounding
  Us, Thy fickle children, here;
And Thy mighty grace abounding,
  Leading us in holy fear.
    Guide us, Jesus;
  To our souls be ever near.

May we never more forget Thee
  (Base ingratitude indeed!)
Keep us with Thy arm almighty,
  Us in verdant pastures lead.
    Be our Guardian,
  Till from this vain world we're freed.

Then, O sweetest, lovely Jesus!
  When in heaven we see Thy face,
Who from all our bondage freed us,
  We will give Thee all the praise.
    All the glory
  Shall redound to Thy free grace!

1419   William Gadsby   66 66 88
Neither is there salvation in any other: for there is none other name under heaven given among men, whereby we must be saved.
Acts 4:12

Where must a sinner fly,
  That feels himself undone?
On what kind hand rely,
  Eternal wrath to shun?
Can wit or reason help him out,
And bring a lasting peace about?

Reason no help can give,
  But leaves him in distress;
Nor can he be reprieved
  By works of righteousness;
The law as loud as thunder cries,
'The soul that sins against me, dies.'

Should creatures all agree,
 To give him settled rest,
They cannot set him free,
 Nor cheer his troubled breast;
No human arm his case can reach,
Nor men, nor angels heal the breach.

 Salvation is of God;
 Jehovah is His name;
 The Saviour shed His blood;
 The Lord of Life was slain;
And by His own atoning blood,
He made a precious way to God.

 Here sinners may draw near,
 With all their sin and guilt;
 Nor death nor danger fear,
 Since Jesus' blood was spilt;
A door of hope is opened wide,
In Jesus' bleeding hands and side.

1420   Christina Rossetti   8 10 10 4
**Neither is there salvation in any other: for
there is none other name under heaven given
among men, whereby we must be saved.**
Acts 4:12

None other Lamb, none other name,
 None other hope in heaven or earth or sea,
None other hiding-place from guilt and shame,
 None beside Thee!

My faith burns low, my hope burns low;
 Only my heart's desire cries out in me
By the deep thunder of its want and woe,
 Cries out to Thee.

Lord, Thou art life, though I be dead;
 Love's fire Thou art, however cold I be:
Nor heaven have I, nor place to lay my head,
 Nor home, but Thee.

1421   George Herbert   CM
**Neither is there salvation in any other: for
there is none other name under heaven given
among men, whereby we must be saved.**
Acts 4:12

There's not a man that's born of God,
 But readily will say,
'If ever my poor soul be saved,
 'Tis Christ must be the way.'

There's not a man that's born of God,
 But feels the plague of sin;
And though his outside be kept clean,
 He feels the fllth within.

The old man struggles hard to gain
 The conquest over grace;
And oft he seems to gain the field,
 When Jesus hides His face.

God knows we can do nothing well,
 He knows we are but dust;
He came to seek poor sinners out,
 And you and me the worst.

1422   Thomas Kelly   LM
**Neither is there salvation in any other: for
there is none other name under heaven given
among men, whereby we must be saved.**
Acts 4:12

There's not a name beneath the skies,
 Nor is there one in heaven above,
But that of Jesus, can suffice
 The sinner's burden to remove.

Sweet name, when once its virtue's known,
 How weak all other helps appear!
The sinner trusts to it alone,
 And finds the grand specific there.

'Twas long before I knew this truth,
 And learned to trust the Saviour's name;
In vanity I spent my youth;
 The thought now fills my heart with shame.

But since I've known the life and power
 With which His name is richly stored,
The world can keep my heart no more,
 Nor can its joys content afford.

The things I once esteemed the most
 I now account as worthless dross;
Thy name, dear Saviour, is my boast,
 For which the world appears but loss.

1423   Anne Steele   LM
**Neither is there salvation in any other: for
there is none other name under heaven given
among men, whereby we must be saved.**
Acts 4:12

Jesus, the spring of joys divine,
 Whence all our hopes and comforts flow,
Jesus, no other name but Thine
 Can save us from eternal woe.

In vain would boasting reason find
 The way to happiness and God;
Her weak directions leave the mind
 Bewildered in a dubious road.

No other name will heaven approve,
Thou art the true and living Way,
Ordained by everlasting love,
To the bright realms of endless day.

Here let our constant feet abide,
Nor from the heavenly path depart;
O let Thy Spirit, gracious Guide;
Direct our steps, and cheer our heart.

Safe lead us through this world of night,
And bring us to the blissful plains,
The regions of unclouded light,
Where perfect joy for ever reigns.

1424 Albert Midlane   77 77
And when they had prayed, the place was shaken where they were assembled together.
Acts 4:31

Lord, our waiting spirits bow,
In Thy blessèd presence now;
May the Holy Spirit be
Now our power to wait on Thee.

Power, O Lord, for power we cry!
Grant us each a rich supply,
That our longing souls may be
Fully satisfied by Thee.

Sweet the solemn hour of prayer,
Sweet to feed on heavenly fare,
Now let such our portion be,
Saviour, waiting upon Thee.

1425 Fanny Crosby   11 10 11 10
And when they had prayed, the place was shaken where they were assembled together.
Acts 4:31

Come, Holy Spirit, like a dove descending,
  Rest Thou upon us while we meet to pray;
Show us the Saviour, His great love revealing;
  Lead us to Him, the Life, the Truth, the Way.

Come, Holy Spirit, every cloud dispelling;
  Fill us with gladness, through the Master's
      name:
Bring to our memory words that He hath spoken;
  Then shall our tongues His wondrous grace
      proclaim.

Come, Holy Spirit, sent from God the Father,
  Thou Friend and Teacher, Comforter and Guide;
Our thoughts directing, keep us close to Jesus,
  And in our hearts for evermore abide.

1426 Samuel Medley   LM
Him hath God exalted with His right hand to be a Prince and a Saviour, for to give repentance to Israel, and forgiveness of sins. *Acts 5:31*

Join all who love the Saviour's name,
To sing His everlasting fame;
Great God! prepare each heart and voice
In Him for ever to rejoice.

Of Him what wondrous things are told!
In Him what glories I behold!
For Him I gladly all things leave;
To Him, my soul, for ever cleave.

In Him my treasure's all contained;
By Him my feeble soul's sustained;
From Him I all things now receive;
Through Him my soul shall ever live.

With Him I daily love to walk;
Of Him my soul delights to talk;
On Him I cast my every care;
Like Him one day I shall appear.

Bless Him, my soul, from day to day,
Trust Him to bring thee on thy way;
Give Him thy poor, weak, sinful heart;
With Him, O never, never part.

Take Him for strength and righteousness;
Make Him thy refuge in distress;
Love Him above all earthly joy,
And Him in everything employ.

Praise Him in cheerful, grateful songs;
To Him your highest praise belongs;
'Tis He who does your heaven prepare,
And Him you'll sing for ever there.

1427 Joseph Hart   87 87 D
Him hath God exalted with His right hand to be a Prince and a Saviour, for to give repentance to Israel, and forgiveness of sins. *Acts 5:31*

Lamb of God, we fall before Thee,
  Humbly trusting in Thy cross;
That alone be all our glory;
  All things else are dung and dross;
Thee we own a perfect Saviour,
  Only Source of all that's good:
Every grace and every favour
  Comes to us through Jesus' blood.

Jesus gives us true repentance,
  By His Spirit sent from heaven;
Jesus whispers this sweet sentence,
  'Son, thy sins are all forgiven.'

Faith He gives us to believe it;
  Grateful hearts His love to prize;
Want we wisdom? He must give it;
  Hearing ears, and seeing eyes.

Jesus gives us pure affections,
  Wills to do what He requires;
Makes us follow His directions,
  And what He commands inspires.
All our prayers and all our praises,
  Rightly offered in His name,
He that dictates them is Jesus;
  He that answers is the same.

When we live on Jesus' merit,
  Then we worship God aright,
Father, Son, and Holy Spirit,
  Then we savingly unite.
Hear the whole conclusion of it;
  Great or good, whate'er we call,
God, or King, or Priest, or Prophet,
  Jesus Christ is All in all.

1428 Frances Havergal 65 65 D + refrain
**Him hath God exalted with His right hand to be
a Prince and a Saviour, for to give repentance
to Israel, and forgiveness of sins.** *Acts 5:31*

Golden harps are sounding,
  Angel voices ring,
Pearly gates are opened,
  Opened for the King;
Christ, the King of glory,
  Jesus, King of love,
Is gone up in triumph
  To His throne above.

*All His work is ended,
  Joyfully we sing;
Jesus hath ascended;
  Glory to our King!*

He who came to save us,
  He who bled and died,
Now is crowned with glory
  At His Father's side;
Never more to suffer,
  Never more to die,
Jesus King of glory,
  Is gone up on high.

Praying for His children
  In that blessèd place,
Calling them to glory;
  Sending them His grace,
His bright home preparing,
  Faithful ones, for you,
Jesus ever liveth,
  Ever loveth too.

1429 Josiah Conder LM
**Wherefore, brethren, look ye out among you
seven men of honest report, full of the Holy
Ghost and wisdom, whom we may appoint
over this business.** *Acts 6:3*

Great King of saints! enthroned on high,
  Under Thy care Thy churches live:
Thou dost their various wants supply
  And well-appointed elders give.

For pastors may Thy name be blest,
  Who teach the doctrines of the Lord:
On deacons may Thy favour rest,
  Chosen according to Thy word.

While they their works assigned fulfil,
  O may their souls with grace be crowned!
And patience, sympathy and zeal,
  With meekness, in their lives abound.

Sound in the faith, in conscience clear,
  Ever may they in conduct prove,
Sober and just, devout, sincere,
  Guided by wisdom from above.

And when their service here is done,
  Their labours and their conflicts o'er,
Then may they wait before Thy throne
  In heaven to praise Thee evermore.

1430 John Rippon LM
**Wherefore, brethren, look ye out among you
seven men of honest report, full of the Holy
Ghost and wisdom, whom we may appoint
over this business.** *Acts 6:3*

Jesus our King, we suppliant bow,
  And hail the grace Thy church enjoys;
Her chosen deacons are Thine own,
  With all the gifts Thy love employs.

Up to Thy throne we lift our eyes,
  For blessings to attend our choice,
Of such whose generous, prudent zeal
  Shall make Thy favoured ways rejoice.

Happy in Jesus, their own Lord,
  May they His sacred table spread;
The table of their pastor fill,
  And fill the chosen poor with bread.

And when the work to them assigned,
  The work of love is fully done,
Call them from serving tables here,
  To sit around Thy glorious throne.

1431 Horatius Bonar DSM
The church in the wilderness. *Acts 7:38*

Far down the ages now,
Much of her journey done,
The pilgrim church pursues her way,
Until her crown be won;
The story of the past
Comes up before her view;
How well it seems to suit her still,
Old, and yet ever new!

'Tis the repeated tale
Of sin and weariness;
Of grace and love still flowing down
To pardon and to bless;
No wider is the gate,
No broader is the way,
No smoother is the ancient path,
That leads to light and day.

No sweeter is the cup,
Nor less our lot of ill;
'Twas tribulation ages since,
'Tis tribulation still;
No slacker grows the fight,
No feebler is the foe,
Nor less the need of armour tried,
Of shield and spear and bow.

Thus onward still we press,
Through evil and through good;
Through pain and poverty and want,
Through peril and through blood;
Still faithful to our God,
And to our Captain true,
We follow where He leads the way,
The Kingdom in our view.

1432 Richard Burnham CM
**They were baptized in the name of the Lord
Jesus.** *Acts 8:16*

Lord, may the messengers of peace
Thy every truth proclaim:
Swayed by the force of sovereign grace,
Baptize in Thy great name.

If twice ten thousand foes withstand,
Thy word is still the same:
Still we obey Thy great command,
Baptize in Thy great name.

Fearless of all that men can say,
We trace the heavenly Lamb:
Pursue Him in the watery way
Baptizing in His name.

Lord, while Thy saints thus follow Thee,
Thy glory is their aim;
Constrained by love, they long to be
Baptized in Thy great name.

Lord, bid our every fear be gone,
Support each weaker frame;
Blest with Thy presence we'll go on
Baptizing in Thy name.

1433 Adoniram Judson LM
**See, here is water; what doth hinder me to be
baptized?** *Acts 8:36*

Come, Holy Spirit, Dove divine,
On these baptismal waters shine,
And teach our hearts in highest strain
To praise the Lamb for sinners slain.

We love Thy name, we love Thy laws,
And joyfully embrace Thy cause,
We love Thy cross, the shame, the pain,
O Lamb of God, for sinners slain.

And as we rise with Thee to live,
O let the Holy Spirit give
The sealing unction from above,
The breath of life, the fire of love.

1434 John Cennick LM
Lord, what wilt Thou have me to do?
Acts 9:6

Be with me, Lord, where'er I go;
Teach me what Thou wouldst have me do;
Suggest whate'er I think or say;
Direct me in the narrow way.

Work in me, lest I harbour pride
Lest I in my own strength confide;
Show me my weakness, let me see
I have my power, my all, from Thee.

Assist and teach me how to pray;
Incline my nature to obey;
What Thou abhorrest let me flee,
And only love what pleases Thee.

1435 William Gadsby SM
Behold, he prayeth. *Acts 9:11*

The sinner born of God,
To God will pour his prayer,
In sighs, or groans, or words expressed,
Or in a falling tear.

The feelings of his heart
Ascend to the Most High;
And though the Lord awhile forbear,
His needs He will supply.

A form of words may please
A sinner dead in sin;
But quickened sinners want to pray
As prompted from within.

The Holy Ghost indites
All real vital prayer;
And prayer indited by the Lord,
The Lord will surely hear.

1436   Edward Perronet, J Rippon   CM
He is Lord of all. *Acts 10:36*

All hail the power of Jesus' name!
   Let angels prostrate fall;
Bring forth the royal diadem,
   To crown Him Lord of all.

Crown Him, ye martyrs of our God,
   Who from His altar call;
Extol Him in whose path ye trod,
   And crown Him Lord of all.

Ye seed of Israel's chosen race,
   Ye ransomed of the fall,
Hail Him who saves you by His grace,
   And crown Him Lord of all.

Sinners whose love can ne'er forget
   The wormwood and the gall,
Go, spread your trophies at His feet,
   And crown Him Lord of all.

Let every kindred, every tribe
   On this terrestrial ball,
To Him all majesty ascribe,
   And crown Him Lord of all.

O that, with yonder sacred throng,
   We at His feet may fall,
Join in the everlasting song,
   And crown Him Lord of all!

1437   Benjamin Beddome   CM
And he commanded them to be baptized in the name of the Lord. *Acts 10:48*

How great, how solemn is the work
   Which we attend today!
Now for a holy, solemn frame,
   O God, to Thee we pray.

O may we feel as once we felt,
   When pained and grieved at heart,
Thy kind, forgiving, melting look
   Relieved our every smart.

Let graces, then in exercise,
   Be exercised again;
And, nurtured by celestial power,
   In exercise remain.

Awake our love, our fear, our hope;
   Wake, fortitude and joy;
Vain world, begone; let things above
   Our happy thoughts employ.

Whilst Thee, our Saviour and our God,
   To all around we own,
Drive each rebellious, rival lust,
   Each traitor from Thy throne.

Instruct our minds; our wills subdue;
   To heaven our passions raise;
That hence our lives, our all may be
   Devoted to Thy praise.

1438   William Gadsby   LM
For he was a good man, and full of the Holy Ghost and of faith: and much people was added unto the Lord. *Acts 11:24*

By nature, none of Adam's race
   Can boast of goodness in God's sight;
Sin plunged them all in sad disgrace;
   Now nothing merely human's right.

Good men there are; but, be it known,
   Their goodness dwells in Christ their Head!
United to God's only Son,
   Their holiness can never fade.

In Him they stand complete and just;
   His righteousness He gives to them;
Of this they sing, of this they boast,
   Nor law nor Satan can condemn.

The One-in-Three, and Three-in-One,
   Sets up His kingdom in their breasts;
And there, to make His wonders known,
   He ever lives, and reigns, and rests.

Life, light, and holiness divine,
   From Jesus they by faith receive;
The Spirit makes His graces shine,
   And gives them power in Christ to live.

1439   Joseph Hart   87 87 D
So they, being sent forth by the Holy Ghost, departed unto Seleucia; and from thence they sailed to Cyprus. *Acts 13:4*

Holy Ghost, inspire our praises,
    Touch our hearts, and tune our tongues;
While we laud the name of Jesus,
    Heaven will gladly share our songs.
Hosts of angels, bright and glorious,
    While we hymn our common King,
Will be proud to join the chorus;
    And the Lord Himself shall sing.

Raise we, then, our cheerful voices
    To our God, who, full of grace,
In our happiness rejoices,
    And delights to hear His praise.
Whoso lives upon His promise,
    Eats His flesh and drinks His blood;
All that's past, and all to come, is
    For that soul's eternal good.

Happy soul, that hears and follows
    Jesus speaking in His word!
Paul, and Cephas, and Apollos,
    All are His in Christ the Lord.
Every state, howe'er distressing,
    Shall be profit in the end;
Every ordinance a blessing,
    Every providence a friend.

Christian, dost thou want a teacher,
    Helper, counsellor, or guide?
Wouldst thou find a proper preacher?
    Ask thy God, for He'll provide.
Build on no man's parts or merit,
    But behold the gospel plan;
Jesus sends His Holy Spirit,
    And the Spirit sends the man.

Bless, dear Lord, each labouring servant;
    Bless the work they undertake;
Make them able, faithful, fervent;
    Bless them, for Thy church's sake.
All things for our good are given:
    Comforts, crosses, staffs, or rods;
All is ours in earth and heaven;
    We are Christ's, and Christ is God's.

ROWLAND HILL 1744-1833

1440   Rowland Hill   LM
And when they had ordained them elders in every church, and had prayed with fasting, they commended them to the Lord, on whom they believed.
Acts 14:23

With heavenly power, O Lord, defend
Him whom we now to Thee commend;
His person bless, his soul secure;
And make him to the end endure.

Gird him with all-sufficient grace;
Direct his feet in paths of peace;
Thy truth and faithfulness fulfil,
And help him to obey Thy will.

Before him Thy protection send;
O love him, save him to the end!
Nor let him as Thy pilgrim rove
Without the convoy of Thy love.

Enlarge, inflame, and fill his heart;
In him Thy mighty power exert;
That thousands, yet unborn, may praise
The wonders of redeeming grace.

1441   Joseph Hart   SM
And put no difference between us and them, purifying their hearts by faith.
Acts 15:9

Faith's a convincing proof,
    A substance sound and sure,
That keeps the soul secured enough,
    But makes it not secure.

Notion's the harlot's test,
    By which the truth's reviled;
The child of fancy, finely dressed,
    But not the living child.

Faith is by knowledge fed,
And with obedience mixed,
Notion is empty, cold, and dead,
And fancy's never fixed.

True faith's the life of God;
Deep in the heart it lies;
It lives and labours under load;
Though damped, it never dies.

Opinions in the head,
True faith as far excels
As body differs from a shade,
Or kernels from the shells.

To see good bread and wine,
Is not to eat and drink;
So some who hear the word divine,
Do not believe, but think.

True faith refines the heart,
And purifies with blood;
Takes the whole gospel, not a part,
And holds the fear of God.

1442 Charles Wesley 10 10 11 11
**These men are the servants of the most high
God, which shew unto us the way of salvation.**
Acts 16:17

Ye servants of God, your Master proclaim,
And publish abroad His wonderful name;
The name all-victorious of Jesus extol,
His kingdom is glorious and rules over all.

God ruleth on high, almighty to save,
And still He is nigh, His presence we have;
The great congregation His triumph shall sing,
Ascribing salvation to Jesus our King.

'Salvation to God, who sits on the throne!'
Let all cry aloud and honour the Son;
The praises of Jesus let angels proclaim,
Fall down on their faces, and worship the Lamb.

Then let us adore, and give Him His right,
All glory and power, all wisdom and might,
All honour and blessing with angels above,
And thanks never ceasing and infinite love.

1443 John Fellows CM
**And he took them the same hour of the night,
and washed their stripes; and was baptized,
he and all his, straightway.**
Acts 16:33

What joy, dear Lord, our spirits feel,
From Thine increasing cause,
When households join to do Thy will,
And reverence Thy laws!

Thus, with believing love, of old
The happy jailor came,
And his instructed house enrolled
As followers of the Lamb.

Thus faithful Lydia's household too,
Believèd in the Lord,
And were baptized in open view,
According to His word.

We too, whom nature's ties combine,
In mutual love agree,
To own each ordinance divine,
And join ourselves to Thee.

1444 Anne Steele CM
**For in Him we live, and move, and have our
being; as certain also of your own poets have
said, For we are also His offspring.** Acts 17:28

Ye humble souls, approach your God
With songs of sacred praise,
For He is good, immensely good,
And kind are all His ways.

All nature owns His guardian care,
In Him we live and move;
But nobler benefits declare
The wonders of His love.

He gave His Son, His only Son,
To ransom rebel worms;
'Tis here He makes His goodness known
In its diviner forms.

To this dear refuge, Lord, we come;
'Tis here our hope relies:
A safe defence, a peaceful home,
When storms of trouble rise.

Thine eye beholds with kind regard
The soul that trusts in Thee;
Their humble hope Thou wilt reward
With bliss divinely free.

Great God, to Thy almighty love,
What honours shall we raise?
Not all the raptured songs above
Can render equal praise.

1445   Mary Peters   CM
When they heard this, they were baptized in the name of the Lord Jesus. *Acts 19:5*

A mighty mystery we set forth,
    A wondrous sign and seal;
Lord, give our hearts to know its worth,
    And all its truth to feel.

Death to the world we thus avow,
    Death to each sinful lust;
The risen life is our life now,
    The risen Christ our trust.

Baptized into the Father's name,
    We're children of our God;
Baptized into the Son we claim
    The ransom of His blood.

Baptized into the Holy Ghost
    In this accepted hour,
Give us to own the Pentecost,
    And the descending power.

1446   John Newton   LM
Then certain of the vagabond Jews, exorcists, took upon them to call over them which had evil spirits the name of the Lord Jesus, saying, We adjure you by Jesus whom Paul preacheth.
Acts 19:13

When the apostle wonders wrought,
    And healed the sick in Jesus' name;
The sons of Sceva vainly thought
    That they had power to do the same.

On one possessed they tried their art,
    And naming Jesus preached by Paul,
They charged the spirit to depart
    Expecting he'd obey their call.

The spirit answered, with a mock,
    'Jesus I know, and Paul I know;
I must have gone if Paul had spoke,
    But who are ye that bid me go?'

With fury then the man he filled,
    Who on the poor pretenders flew;
Naked and wounded, almost killed,
    They fled in all the people's view.

Jesus! that name, pronounced by faith,
    Is full of wonder-working power;
It conquers Satan, sin and death,
    And cheers in troubles darkest hour.

But they, who are not born again,
    Know nothing of it but the sound;
They do but take His name in vain
    When most their zeal and pains abound.

Satan their vain attempts derides,
    Whether they talk, or pray, or preach;
Long as the love of sin abides,
    His power is safe beyond their reach.

But you, believers, may rejoice,
    Satan well knows your mighty Friend;
He trembles at your Saviour's voice,
    And owns he cannot gain his end.

1447   Richard Burnham   CM
Serving the Lord with all humility of mind, and with many tears, and temptations. *Acts 20:19*

Humility the Lord beholds
    With an approving eye;
In humble souls He doth delight,
    For such on Him rely.

In their own views they nothing seem,
    For Christ is their great all;
And 'tis their highest happiness
    Before the cross to fall.

Thou humble Jesus, give us all
    Our nothingness to see;
Ne'er in ourselves we dare to boast,
    But humbly boast in Thee.

Lord, conquer pride, that swelling sin,
    Bid all its power depart;
May we all walk Thy sacred paths
    In lowliness of heart.

May we be more like saints above,
    Who all Thy glory see:
Who cast their crowns at Thy dear feet,
    And lose themselves in Thee.

1448   Benjamin Beddome, T Cotterill   LM
The gospel of the grace of God.
Acts 20:24

God, in the gospel of His Son,
Makes His eternal counsels known;
Where love in all its glory shines,
And truth is drawn in fairest lines.

Here sinners of a humble frame
May taste His grace, and learn His name;
May read, in characters of blood,
The wisdom, power, and grace of God.

The prisoner here may break his chains;
The weary rest from all his pains;
The captive feel his bondage cease;
The mourner find the way of peace.

Here faith reveals to mortal eyes
A brighter world beyond the skies;
Here shines the light which guides our way
From earth to realms of endless day.

O grant us grace, Almighty Lord,
To read and mark Thy holy word;
Its truths with meekness to receive,
And by its holy precepts live.

1449   Richard Burnham (alt)   87 87 D
The gospel of the grace of God.
Acts 20:24

O Thou great eternal Jesus,
    High and mighty Prince of Peace,
How Thy wonders shine resplendent
    In the gospel of Thy grace!
Sovereign good in vast abundance.
    Flows from this pure word of light;
Numerous blessings all immortal,
    Yielding infinite delight.

Thy rich gospel scorns conditions,
    Breathes salvation free as air;
Only breathes triumphant mercy,
    Baffling guilt, and all despair.
O the grandeur of the gospel,
    How it sounds the cleansing blood!
Shows the mercies of a Saviour,
    Shows the tender heart of God.

Only treats of love eternal,
    Swells the all-abounding grace,
Nothing knows but life and pardon,
    Full redemption, endless peace.
Thanks to God for such glad tidings,
    Thanks to great Immanuel's love;
Sing we now the free salvation.
    Soon shall sing in realms above.

1450   Jeremiah Rankin   98 89
**And now, brethren, I commend you to God,
and to the word of His grace.**
Acts 20:32

God be with you till we meet again!
    By His counsels guide, uphold you,
    With His sheep securely fold you;
God be with you till we meet again!

God be with you till we meet again!
    'Neath His wings securely hide you,
    Daily manna still provide you;
God be with you till we meet again!

God be with you till we meet again;
    When life's perils thick confound you,
    Put His loving arms around you;
God be with you till we meet again!

God be with you till we meet again!
    Keep love's banner floating o'er you,
    Smite death's threatening wave before you;
God be with you till we meet again!

1451   John Fawcett   87 87
**And now why tarriest thou? arise, and be
baptized, and wash away thy sins, calling on
the name of the Lord.** *Acts 22:16*

Humble souls, who seek salvation
    Through the Lamb's redeeming blood,
Hear the voice of revelation,
    Tread the path that Jesus trod.

Flee to Him, your only Saviour,
    In His mighty name confide;
In the whole of your behaviour
    Own Him as your sovereign Guide.

Hear the blest Redeemer call you,
    Listen to His heavenly voice:
Dread no ills that can befall you,
    While you make His ways your choice.

Jesus says, 'Let each believer
    Be baptizèd in My name';
Thus Himself in Jordan's river
    Was immersed beneath the stream.

Plainly here His footsteps tracing,
    Follow Him without delay,
Gladly His command embracing,
    Lo! your Captain leads the way.

View the rite with understanding,
    Jesus' grave before you lies;
Be interred at His commanding,
    After His example rise.

1452   Anon   SM
**They should repent and turn to God, and do
works meet for repentance.** *Acts 26:20*

'Tis not enough to say
    We're sorry and repent,
Yet still go on from day to day
    Just as we always went.

Repentance is to leave
    The sins we loved before,
And show that we in earnest grieve
    By doing so no more.

Lord, make us thus sincere,
    To watch as well as pray;
However sweet, however dear,
    Take all our sins away.

1453 Joseph Hoskins CM
And no small tempest lay on us.
Acts 27:20

None that embark at God's command,
  For heaven, can e'er be lost;
All safe escape to Canaan's land,
  However tempest-tossed.

Though winds may blow and storms may rise,
  And rocks and sands appear,
The Saviour to His people flies,
  And bids them not to fear.

Though seeming on destruction's brink,
  While the dread tempests roar.
However tossed, they shall not sink,
  But safely reach the shore.

Though neither sun nor stars appear
  For many days in sight,
Trust in the Lord, be of good cheer,
  And He shall guide you right.

Then let the saints in God confide,
  And on His promise rest;
They shall the storms of life outride,
  And be for ever blest.

1454 Alfred Smith, E Clark CM + refrain
**For there stood by me this night the angel of
God, whose I am, and whom I serve, saying,
Fear not, Paul.** *Acts 27:23,24*

I do not know what lies ahead,
  The way I cannot see;
Yet One stands near to be my Guide,
  He'll show the way to me:

  *I know who holds the future,
    And He'll guide me with His hand,
  With God things don't just happen,
    Everything by Him is planned;
  So as I face tomorrow
    With its problems large and small,
  I'll trust the God of miracles,
    Give to Him my all.*

I do not know how many days
  Of life are mine to spend;
But One who knows and cares for me
  Will keep me to the end:

I do not know the course ahead,
  What joys and griefs are there;
But One is near who fully knows,
  I'll trust His loving care:

1455 John Burton, Sr. 77 77
The holy scriptures. *Romans 1:2*

Holy Bible, book divine!
Precious treasure, thou art mine!
Mine, to tell me whence I came;
Mine, to teach me what I am.

Mine, to chide me when I rove;
Mine, to show a Saviour's love;
Mine art thou, to guide my feet;
Mine, to judge, condemn, acquit.

Mine, to comfort in distress,
Mine, with promise sweet to bless;
Mine, to show by living faith,
Man can triumph over death.

Mine, to tell of joys to come;
Mine, to show the sinner's doom;
Holy Bible, Book divine!
Precious treasure, thou art mine!

1456 Thomas Kelly LM
For I am not ashamed of the gospel of Christ.
Romans 1:16

I need not blush to own that He,
  On whom my hope of heaven is built,
Was crucified on yonder tree,
  Since 'tis His blood that cancels guilt.

Nor need I blush to call Him Lord,
  Whom heaven adores with all its hosts;
Yes, Jesus is by heaven adored,
  In Him the brightest seraph boasts.

What though the world no glory sees
  In Him my soul admires and loves,
I wonder not; how should He please
  The man who of himself approves?

I too could boast of merit once,
  And Jesus had no charms for me;
But all such claims I now renounce;
  No merit but in Him I see.

1457 Joseph Hart CM
Let God be true, but every man a liar.
Romans 3:4

The God I trust is true and just;
  His mercy has no end;
Himself has said my ransom's paid,
  And I on Him depend.

Then why so sad, my soul? though bad,
  Thou hast a Friend that's good;
He bought thee dear (abandon fear);
  He bought thee with His blood.

So rich a cost can ne'er be lost,
  Though faith be tried by fire;
Keep Christ in view; let God be true;
  And every man a liar.

1458 James Maxwell LM
All the world…guilty before God.
Romans 3:19

Here, Lord, my soul convicted stands
Of breaking all Thy ten commands;
And on me justly mightst Thou pour
Thy wrath in one eternal shower.

But, thanks to God, its loud alarms
Have warned me of approaching harms;
And now, O Lord, my wants I see;
Lost and undone, I come to Thee.

I see my fig-leaf righteousness
Can ne'er Thy broken law redress;
Yet in Thy gospel plan I see,
There's hope of pardon e'en for me.

Here I behold Thy wonders, Lord,
How Christ has to Thy law restored
Those honours, on the atoning day,
Which guilty sinners took away.

Amazing wisdom, power, and love,
Displayed to rebels from above!
Do Thou, O Lord, my faith increase,
To love and trust Thy plan of grace.

1459 Isaac Watts CM
All the world…guilty before God.
Romans 3:19

Vain are the hopes the sons of men
  On their own works have built;
Their hearts by nature all unclean,
  And all their actions guilt.

Let Jew and Gentile stop their mouths,
  Without a murmuring word;
And the whole race of Adam stand
  Guilty before the Lord.

In vain we ask God's righteous law
  To justify us now,
Since to convince and to condemn
  Is all the law can do.

Jesus, how glorious is Thy grace!
  When in Thy name we trust,
Our faith receives a righteousness
  That makes the sinner just.

1460 David Denham CM
But now the righteousness of God without the law is manifested.
Romans 3:21

The righteousness of God we prize,
  Which He in love reveals;
All that believe, He justifies,
  And by His Spirit seals.

The righteousness of God alone
  Can suit the sinner's case,
Which is unto all, and upon
  The heirs of sovereign grace.

The righteousness of God conveys
  Release from every charge;
Opens the heart in love and praise,
  And sets the soul at large.

The righteousness of God constrains
  To practise all that's good:
While Jesus in the conscience reigns,
  And sin's subdued in blood.

The righteousness of God insures
  Our triumph o'er the tomb:
From earth and hell it well secures,
  And leads to heaven—our home.

1461   Joseph Humphreys   77 77 77
Being justified freely by His grace through the redemption that is in Christ Jesus.
Romans 3:24

Blessèd are the sons of God,
They are bought with Christ's own blood;
They are ransomed from the grave
Life eternal they shall have:

With them numbered may we be,
Now, and through eternity.

They are justified by grace;
They enjoy the Saviour's peace;
All their sins are washed away;
They shall stand in God's great day:

They are lights upon the earth,
Children of the second birth;
One with God, with Jesus one,
Glory is in them begun:

They alone are truly blessed,
Heirs of God, joint heirs with Christ;
They with love and peace are filled,
They are by His Spirit sealed.

1462   Richard Burnham   LM
Being justified freely by His grace through the redemption that is in Christ Jesus.
Romans 3:24

Sinners are justified by grace,
Through the Redeemer's righteousness;
This is a glorious robe indeed,
And wrought for Abram's favoured seed.

Jehovah, in His wise decree,
Did all His chosen people see
As justified in His dear Son,
In Him from everlasting one.

When through the Spirit they believe,
The pleasing witness they receive;
And they are freely justified
Through the dear Man that groaned and died.

Yes, they rejoice in pardoning blood,
And triumph in the Son of God:
With joy and peace they all confess,
'Christ is the Lord our Righteousness.'

Now, Lord, our hearts in faith enlarge,
May we all see our great discharge,
Sing of Thy free forgiving love,
Till glorified with Thee above.

1463   Philip Doddridge, A Toplady   SM
Being justified freely by His grace through the redemption that is in Christ Jesus.
Romans 3:24

Grace! 'tis a charming sound,
Harmonious to the ear;
Heaven with the echo shall resound,
And all the earth shall hear.

Grace first contrived a way
To save rebellious man,
And all the steps that grace display
Which drew the wondrous plan.

Grace first inscribed my name
In God's eternal book;
'Twas grace that gave me to the Lamb,
Who all my sorrows took.

Grace taught my soul to pray,
And pardoning love to know;
'Twas grace that kept me to this day,
And will not let me go.

Grace all the work shall crown,
Through everlasting days;
It lays in heaven the topmost stone,
And well deserves the praise.

1464   William Gadsby   66 66 88
Being justified freely by His grace through the redemption that is in Christ Jesus.
Romans 3:24

The work of Christ I sing,
And glory in His name;
Immortal life to bring,
The Lord of Glory came;
He gave Himself for wretched me,
And sets my soul at liberty.

He magnified the law
And made an end of sin;
Without a single flaw,
A righteousness brought in.
Come, mourning souls, in Jesus trust;
His righteousness makes sinners just.

1465   William Tucker   LM
To declare, I say, at this time His righteousness. *Romans 3:26*

O Love beyond conception great,
That formed the vast stupendous plan,
Where all divine perfections meet,
To reconcile rebellious man.

There wisdom shines in fullest blaze
　And justice all her rights maintains;
Astonished angels stoop to gaze,
　While mercy o'er the guilty reigns.

Yes, mercy reigns, and justice too;
　In Christ they both harmonious meet;
He paid to justice all its due,
　And now He fills the mercy-seat.

Such are the wonders of our God,
　And the amazing depths of grace,
To save from wrath's vindictive rod,
　The chosen sons of Adam's race.

1466　Isaac Watts　LM
Blessed are they whose iniquities are forgiven, and whose sins are covered.
Romans 4:7

Blest is the man, for ever blest,
　Whose guilt is pardoned by his God;
Whose sins with sorrow are confessed,
　And covered with his Saviour's blood.

Blest is the man to whom the Lord
　Imputes not his iniquities;
He pleads no merit of reward,
　And not on works, but grace relies.

From guile his heart and lips are free:
　His humble joy, his holy fear,
With deep repentance well agree,
　And join to prove his faith sincere.

How glorious is that righteousness
　That hides and cancels all his sins!
While a bright evidence of grace
　Through his whole life appears and
　　shines.

1467　John Stevens　LM
Therefore it is of faith, that it might be by grace. *Romans 4:16*

Grace is Jehovah's sovereign will,
　In an eternal covenant sure;
Which for His seed He will fulfil,
　Longer than sun and moon endure.

Grace is a firm but friendly hand,
　Put forth by God to save His own;
And by that grace, through faith, we stand,
　Adoring at our Father's throne.

There grace its peaceful sceptre wields,
　Inviting souls to venture near;
There Christ His saving Spirit yields
　To those whose sins He deigned to bear.

Lord, help us on Thy grace to stand,
　And every trial firm endure;
Preservèd by Thy sovereign hand,
　And by Thy oath and covenant sure.

Thy willingness to save Thy seed,
　Is as they stand in Christ their Head;
No act Thy grace can supersede,
　For Thine must live, though they were
　　dead.

Thanks, everlasting thanks be given
　To God, to Christ, to matchless grace;
And to that Dove who seals for heaven
　All who shall sing Jehovah's praise!

1468　Samuel Tregelles　76 76 D
Therefore being justified by faith, we have peace with God through our Lord Jesus Christ. *Romans 5:1*

Lord Jesus, we believing,
　In Thee have peace with God;
Eternal life receiving,
　The purchase of Thy blood.
Our curse and condemnation
　Thou bearest in our stead;
Secure is our salvation
　In Thee, our risen Head.

The Holy Ghost, revealing
　Thy work, has made us blest;
Thy stripes have given us healing,
　Upon Thy love we rest.
In Thee the Father sees us
　Accepted and complete;
Thy blood from sin which frees us
　For glory makes us meet.

We know that nought can sever
　Our souls, O Lord, from Thee;
And thus united ever
　To all Thy saints are we.
We know Thy word declaring
　The Father's wondrous love,
In which we all are sharing
　With Thee, our Head above.

May we this love be showing
　To all Thy members here.
The channels for its flowing,
　Until Thou shalt appear;
Till all the church in union
　Around the Father's throne
Shall stand in blest communion,
　For ever joined in one.

1469   William Cowper (alt)   77 77
**We glory in tribulations also: knowing that
tribulation worketh patience.**
Romans 5:3

'Tis my happiness below,
  Not to live without the cross,
But the Saviour's power to know,
  Sanctifying every loss.

Trials must and will befall;
  But with humble faith to see
Love inscribed upon them all,
  This is happiness to me.

Trials make the promise sweet;
  Trials give new life to prayer;
Trials bring me to His feet,
  Lay me low and keep me there.

Did I meet no trials here,
  No chastisement by the way,
Might I not with reason fear
  I should be a castaway?

Worldlings may escape the rod,
  Sunk in earthly, vain delight;
But the true-born child of God
  Must not, would not if he might.

1470   John Berridge   CM
**We glory in tribulations also: knowing that
tribulation worketh patience.**
Romans 5:3

How simple are Thy children, Lord,
  Unskilled in what they pray;
Full oft they lift a hearty word,
  Yet know not what they say.

For patience when I raised a cry,
  Fresh burdens made me roar;
My foolish heart would then reply,
  For patience pray no more.

So much my Master seemed to blame,
  I thought to leave His school;
But now I learn to blush for shame,
  And see myself a fool.

I fancied patience would be brought
  Before my troubles rose;
And by such granted help I thought
  To triumph o'er my woes.

But Christ has cleared my misty sight,
  And, taught by Him, I find
That tribulations, working right,
  Produce a patient mind.

When our dear Master would bestow
  Much patience on His friends,
He loads their shoulders well with woe,
  And thus obtains His ends.

I must expect a daily cross;
  Lord, sanctify the pain;
Bid every furnace purge my dross
  And yield some patient gain.

1471   Richard Burnham   66 66 88
**We glory in tribulations also: knowing that
tribulation worketh patience.**
Romans 5:3

O Lord to us draw near,
  And Thy compassions show;
Make us with patience bear
  Affliction here below.
In patience may we all go on,
And say, 'O Lord, Thy will be done.'

Though pains we feel each day,
  Yet would we not rebel;
But cordially would say,
  'The Lord doth all things well:'
With patience bear our every loss,
And thus endure the sorest cross.

O God, may Thine elect
  E'er lean upon Thy breast,
And constantly reflect
  Upon a patient Christ:
Thus may we all more patient grow,
Under all trials here below.

1472   Adelaide Proctor   84 84 84
**We glory in tribulations also: knowing that
tribulation worketh patience.**
Romans 5:3

My God, I thank Thee, who hast made
  The earth so bright,
So full of splendour and of joy,
  Beauty and light;
So many glorious things are here,
  Noble and right.

I thank Thee, too, that Thou hast made
  Joy to abound,
So many gentle thoughts and deeds
  Circling us round,
That in the darkest spot of earth
  Some love is found.

I thank Thee more, that all our joy
　Is touched with pain,
That shadows fall on brightest hours,
　That thorns remain;
So that earth's bliss may be our guide
　And not our chain.

For Thou, who knowest, Lord, how soon
　Our weak heart clings,
Hast given us joys, tender and true,
　Yet all with wings,
So that we see, gleaming on high,
　Diviner things.

I thank Thee, Lord, that Thou hast kept
　The best in store:
We have enough, but not too much
　To long for more,
A yearning for a deeper peace
　Not known before.

I thank Thee, Lord, that here our souls,
　Though amply blest,
Can never find, although they seek,
　A perfect rest,
Nor ever shall, until they lean
　On Jesus' breast.

1473　Bianco D Siena, tr. Richard Littledale
66 11 D

The love of God is shed abroad in our hearts by the Holy Ghost which is given unto us.
Romans 5:5

　Come down O Love divine,
　Seek Thou this soul of mine,
And visit it with Thine own ardour glowing;
　O Comforter, draw near,
　Within my heart appear,
And kindle it, Thy holy flame bestowing.

　O let it freely burn,
　Till earthly passions turn
To dust and ashes, in its heat consuming;
　And let Thy glorious light
　Shine ever on my sight,
And clothe me round, the while my path illuming.

　Let holy charity
　Mine outward vesture be,
And lowliness become mine inner clothing;
　True lowliness of heart,
　Which takes the humbler part,
And o'er its own shortcomings weeps with
　　loathing.

And so the yearning strong,
　With which the soul will long,
Shall far outpass the power of human telling;
　For none can guess its grace,
　Till he become the place
Wherein the Holy Spirit makes His dwelling.

1474　William Gadsby　88 88 D
For when we were yet without strength, in due time Christ died for the ungodly.
Romans 5:6

Free grace is the theme of my song;
　A subject divinely sublime;
Though weak in myself, yet I'm strong,
　For Jehovah-Jesus is mine.
He's mine, and with pleasure I see,
　We both are united in one;
And such is my Jesus to me,
　I never can from Him be torn.

1475　Anne Steele　LM
For when we were yet without strength, in due time Christ died for the ungodly.
Romans 5:6

Stretched on the cross, the Saviour dies;
Hark! His expiring groans arise!
See, from His hands, His feet, His side,
Runs down the sacred crimson tide!

But life attends each deathful sound,
And flows from every bleeding wound;
The vital stream, how free it flows,
To save and cleanse His rebel foes!

To suffer in the traitor's place,
To die for man, surprising grace!
Yet pass rebellious angels by;
O why for man, dear Saviour, why?

Can I survey this scene of woe,
Where mingling grief and wonder flow?
And yet my heart unmoved remain,
Insensible to love or pain?

Come, dearest Lord, Thy power impart,
To warm this cold and stupid heart;
Till all its powers and feelings move
In melting grief and ardent love.

1476   John Newton   LM
For when we were yet without strength, in due time Christ died for the ungodly.
Romans 5:6

Jesus, who passed the angels by,
Assumed our flesh, to bleed and die;
And still He makes it His abode;
As man, He fills the throne of God.

Our next of kin, our Brother now,
Is He to whom the angels bow;
They join with us to praise His name,
But we the nearest interest claim.

But ah! how faint our praises rise!
Sure 'tis the wonder of the skies,
That we, who share His richest love,
So cold and unconcerned should prove.

O glorious hour! it comes with speed,
When we from sin and darkness freed,
Shall see the God who died for man,
And praise Him more than angels can.

1477   Vernon Higham   8 10 10 4
But God commendeth His love toward us, in that, while we were yet sinners, Christ died for us. *Romans 5:8*

O Son of Man, O Son of God,
Eternal grace Thy painful path had planned,
A heavy cross and agony of shame—
    The way ordained.

O death of Christ, O blood divine,
O perfect life He lived, all for our gain,
Fulfilling all the law's demands, and more,
    He did attain.

O bitter cup, O costly task,
To meet the wrath of God's own holiness!
The Saviour stood, and in my stead He died,
    My soul to bless.

O love of God, O wondrous grace,
That such an angry death of anguish sore
Should pay my penalty and make me whole—
    O boundless store!

O wondrous flood of grace and love,
Both mingled in the blood as He implored;
Can this be so, all this for me, my Lord?
    Thou art adored.

Peace through the blood of Christ alone,
Peace with my God and peace within my soul,
Peace in that day when He will come at last,
    My All in all.
                © Author

1478   Isaac Watts   SM
We also joy in God through our Lord Jesus Christ, by whom we have now received the atonement. *Romans 5:11*

Not all the blood of beasts
    On Jewish altars slain,
Could give the guilty conscience peace,
    Or wash away the stain.

But Christ, the heavenly Lamb,
    Takes all our sins away;
A sacrifice of nobler name
    And richer blood than they.

My faith would lay her hand
    On that dear head of Thine;
While like a penitent I stand,
    And there confess my sin.

My soul looks back to see
    The burdens Thou didst bear,
When hanging on the accursèd tree,
    And knows her guilt was there.

Believing, we rejoice
    To see the curse remove;
We bless the Lamb with cheerful voice,
    And sing His wondrous love.

1479   Isaac Watts   CM
Moreover the law entered, that the offence might abound. But where sin abounded, grace did much more abound.
Romans 5:20

Lord, how secure my conscience was,
    And felt no inward dread!
I was alive without Thy law,
    And thought my sins were dead.

My hopes of heaven were firm and bright,
    But since the precept came
With a convincing power and light,
    I find how vile I am.

My guilt appeared but small before,
    Till terribly I saw
How perfect, holy, just, and pure
    Was Thy eternal law!

Then felt my soul the heavy load;
    My sins revived again;
I had provoked a dreadful God,
    And all my hopes were slain.

Thy gracious throne I bow beneath;
    Lord, Thou alone canst save;
O break the yoke of sin and death,
    And thus redeem the slave.

JOHN KENT 1766-1843

1480 John Kent 886 D
Moreover the law entered, that the offence might abound. But where sin abounded, grace did much more abound.
Romans 5:20

Hark! how the blood-bought hosts above
Conspire to praise redeeming love,
  In sweet harmonious strains;
And while they strike the golden lyres,
This glorious theme each bosom fires,
  That grace triumphant reigns.

Join thou, my soul, for thou canst tell
How grace divine broke up thy cell,
  And loosed thy native chains;
And still, from that auspicious day,
How oft art thou constrained to say,
  That grace triumphant reigns.

Grace, till the tribes redeemed by blood,
Are brought to know themselves and God,
  Her empire shall maintain;
To call when He appoints the day,
And from the mighty take the prey,
  Shall grace triumphant reign.

When called to meet the king of dread,
Should love compose my dying bed,
  And grace my soul sustain,
Then, ere I quit this mortal clay,
I'll raise my fainting voice, and say,
  'Let grace triumphant reign.'

1481 Albert Midlane 87 87 47
Moreover the law entered, that the offence might abound. But where sin abounded, grace did much more abound.
Romans 5:20

Scripture says, 'Where sin abounded,
  There did grace much more abound.'
Thus has Satan been confounded,
  And his own discomfort found,
    Christ has triumphed!
  Spread the glorious news around.

Sin is strong, but grace is stronger;
  Christ than Satan more supreme;
Yield, oh, yield to sin no longer,
  Turn to Jesus, yield to Him;
    He has triumphed!
  Sinners, henceforth Him esteem.

1482 John Kent 87 87 47
Moreover the law entered, that the offence might abound. But where sin abounded, grace did much more abound.
Romans 5:20

Sovereign grace o'er sin abounding!
  Ransomed souls, the tidings swell;
'Tis a deep that knows no sounding;
  Who its breadth or length can tell?
    On its glories,
  Let my soul for ever dwell.

What from Christ that soul can sever,
  Bound by everlasting bands?
Once in Him, in Him for ever;
  Thus the eternal covenant stands.
    None shall pluck thee
  From the Strength of Israel's hands.

Heirs of God, joint-heirs with Jesus,
  Long ere time its race begun;
To His name eternal praises;
  O what wonders love has done!
    One with Jesus,
  By eternal union one.

On such love, my soul, still ponder,
  Love so great, so rich, so free;
Say, whilst lost in holy wonder,
  'Why, O Lord, such love to me?'
    Hallelujah!
  Grace shall reign eternally.

1483   John Newton (alt)   DCM
That as sin hath reigned unto death, even so might grace reign through righteousness unto eternal life by Jesus Christ our Lord.
Romans 5:21

Now may the Lord reveal His face,
   And teach our stammering tongues
To make His sovereign, reigning grace
   The subject of our songs.
No sweeter subject can invite
   A sinner's heart to sing,
Or more display the glorious right
   Of our exalted King.

Grace reigns to pardon crimson sins,
   To melt the hardest hearts;
And from the work it once begins
   It never once departs.
The world and Satan strive in vain
   Against the chosen few;
Secured by grace's conquering reign,
   They all shall conquer too.

Grace tills the soil, and sows the seeds,
   Provides the sun and rain;
Till from the tender blade proceeds
   The ripened harvest grain.
'Twas grace that called our souls at first;
   By grace thus far we're come;
And grace will help us through the worst,
   And lead us safely home.

Lord, when this charming life is past
   If we may see Thy face;
How we shall praise, and love, at last
   And sing the reign of grace!
Yet let us aim while here below
   Thy mercy to display;
And own at least the debt we owe,
   Although we cannot pay.

1484   Alan Clifford   77 77 D
That as sin hath reigned unto death, even so might grace reign through righteousness unto eternal life by Jesus Christ our Lord.
Romans 5:21

Gracious God, Thy praise we sing,
Praise to heaven's almighty King!
Once the sons of darkest night,
Now rejoicing in Thy light,
   Standing now before Thy throne,
   Saved by grace, we are Thine own!

   *Lord, like Thee, Thy grace shall be,
   Reigning to eternity!*

Gracious Father, we rejoice!
For in Christ, we are Thy choice;
Offspring of electing love,
We were formed to dwell above,
   There to worship and adore,
   Round Thy throne for evermore.

Gracious Saviour, humbled King,
At Thy cross we join to sing;
All Thy sacred tears and pain
Cannot, will not, be in vain!
   We were given, Lord, to Thee,
   Ransomed sons of God to be.

Gracious Spirit, light divine,
Life's renewing power is Thine;
All God's chosen lie in death,
Waiting for Thy quickening breath;
   Thine it is to purify!
   Thine it is to glorify!
                              © *Author*

1485   Isaac Watts   SM
What shall we say then? Shall we continue in sin, that grace may abound?
Romans 6:1

   Shall we go on to sin,
   Because Thy grace abounds?
Or crucify the Lord again,
   And open all His wounds?

   Forbid it, mighty God!
   Nor let it e'er be said
That we, whose sins are crucified,
   Should raise them from the dead.

   We will be slaves no more,
   Since Christ has made us free;
Has nailed our tyrants to His cross,
   And brought us liberty.

1486   Isaac Watts   LM
Know ye not, that so many of us as were baptized into Jesus Christ were baptized into His death? *Romans 6:3*

Do we not know that solemn word,
That we are buried with the Lord;
Baptized into His death, and then
Put off the body of our sin?

Our souls receive diviner breath,
Raised from corruption, guilt, and death;
So from the grave did Christ arise,
And lives to God above the skies.

No more let sin or Satan reign
Over our mortal flesh again;
The various lusts we served before,
Shall have dominion now no more.

1487   Mary Bowly   CM
**Know ye not, that so many of us as were
baptized into Jesus Christ were baptized into
His death?** *Romans 6:3*

O Lord, whilst we confess the worth
  Of this, the outward seal,
Teach us the truths herein set forth,
  Our very own to feel.

Death to the world we here avow,
  Death to each fleshly lust;
Newness of life our portion now,
  A risen Lord our trust.

And we, O Lord, who now partake
  Of Thine eternal life,
With every sin, for Thy dear sake,
  Would be at constant strife.

Baptized into the Father's name,
  We'd walk as sons of God;
Baptized in Thine, with joy we claim,
  The merits of Thy blood.

Baptized into the Holy Ghost,
  We'd prove His mighty power;
And making Thee our only boast,
  Obey Thee hour by hour.

1488   Joseph Hart   LM
**Know ye not, that so many of us as were
baptized into Jesus Christ were baptized into
His death?** *Romans 6:3*

Buried in baptism with our Lord,
We rise with Him, to life restored;
Not the bare life in Adam lost,
But richer far, for more it cost.

Water can cleanse the flesh, we own;
But Christ well knows, and Christ alone,
How dear to Him our cleansing stood,
Baptized with fire, and bathed in blood.

Not but we taste His bitter cup;
But only He could drink it up.
To burn for us was His desire;
And He baptizes us with fire.

This fire will not consume, but melt!
How soft, compared with that He felt!
Thus cleansed from filth, and purged from dross,
Baptizèd Christian, bear the cross.

1489   Philip Doddridge   CM
**Know ye not, that so many of us as were
baptized into Jesus Christ were baptized into
His death?** *Romans 6:3*

Hearken, ye children of your God,
  Ye heirs of glory, hear;
For accents so divine as these
  Might charm the dullest ear.

Baptized into your Saviour's death,
  Your souls to sin must die;
With Christ your Lord ye live anew,
  With Christ ascend on high.

There by His Father's hand He sits,
  Enthroned divinely fair;
Yet owns Himself your Brother still,
  And your Forerunner there.

Rise, from these earthly trifles, rise
  On wings of faith and love;
With Christ your choicest treasure lies,
  And be your hearts above.

But earth and sin will drag us down,
  When we attempt to fly;
Lord, send Thy strong attractive force
  To raise and fix us high.

1490   William Gadsby   SM
**Therefore we are buried with Him by baptism
into death: that like as Christ was raised up
from the dead by the glory of the Father, even
so we also should walk in newness of life.**
Romans 6:4

Jesus, our Lord and King,
  Thou art our hope and trust;
Thy boundless love and grace we sing,
  And of Thee we will boast.

As sinners saved by grace,
  And made alive to God,
Thy righteous laws we would embrace,
  And tread the heavenly road.

Thy wisdom did ordain
  This solemn rite, to show
How Thou wast plunged in wrath and pain,
  To save our souls from woe.

We come Thy name to own,
  And solemnly confess,
Thou art our Life, our Joy, our Crown,
  Our Strength, and Righteousness.

1491   Frederick Jackson   85 83
**Therefore we are buried with Him by baptism
into death.** *Romans 6:4*

Master, we Thy footsteps follow,
    We Thy word obey,
Hear us, Thy dear name confessing,
    While we pray.

Now into Thy death baptizèd,
    We ourselves would be
Dead to all the sin that made
    Thy Calvary.

Rising with Thee, make us like Thee,
    In Thy love and care,
In Thy zeal, and in Thy labour,
    And Thy prayer.

Let the love that knows no failing
    Cast out all our fears,
Let Thy pure and faithful Spirit
    Fill our years.

Till we hear the trumpets sounding
    On the other side,
And for ever, in Thy heaven
    We abide.

1492   John Fellows   87 87
**Therefore we are buried with Him by baptism
into death.** *Romans 6:4*

Jesus, mighty King in Zion!
    Thou alone our Guide shalt be,
Thy commission we rely on;
    We would follow none but Thee.

As an emblem of Thy passion,
    And Thy victory o'er the grave,
We, who know Thy great salvation,
    Are baptized beneath the wave.

Fearless of the world's despising,
    We the ancient path pursue;
Buried with our Lord, and rising
    To a life divinely new.

1493   Isaac Watts (alt)   SM
**Knowing that Christ being raised from the
dead dieth no more; death hath no more
dominion over Him.** *Romans 6:9*

Come all harmonious tongues,
    Your noblest music bring.
'Tis Christ the everlasting God,
    And Christ the Man, we sing.

Tell how He took our flesh,
    To take away our guilt;
Sing the dear drops of sacred blood,
    That hellish monsters spilt.

The waves of swelling grief
    Did o'er His bosom roll,
And mountains of almighty wrath,
    Lay heavy on His soul.

Down to the shades of death
    He bowed His awesome head;
Yet He arose to live and reign,
    When death itself is dead.

No more the bloody spear;
    The cross and nails no more;
For hell itself shakes at His name,
    And all the heavens adore.

There the Redeemer sits,
    High on His Father's throne;
The Father lays His vengeance by,
    And smiles upon His Son.

There His full glories shine,
    With uncreated rays;
And bless His saints' and angels' eyes,
    To everlasting days.

1494   William Gadsby   SM
**What then? shall we sin, because we are not
under the law, but under grace? God forbid.**
Romans 6:15

What, then! shall Christians sin,
    Because freed from the law?
Shall sinners, saved by grace divine,
    From holiness withdraw?

Shall grace seduce the mind,
    And lead the soul astray?
And souls who under grace are found,
    Delight to disobey?

Great God, forbid the thought!
    Preserve Thy saints in love,
While Pharisees set grace at nought,
    Saints shall Thy ways approve.

1495 John Newton LM
Being then made free from sin, ye became the servants of righteousness.
Romans 6:18

And dost Thou say, 'Ask what thou wilt?'
 Lord, I would seize the golden hour;
I pray to be released from guilt
 And freed from sin and Satan's power.

More of Thy presence, Lord, impart,
 More of Thine image let me bear;
Erect Thy throne within my heart,
 And reign without a rival there.

Give me to read my pardon sealed
 And from Thy joy to draw my strength,
To have Thy boundless love revealed,
 Its height and depth, its breadth and length.

Grant these requests, I ask no more,
 But to Thy care the rest resign;
Living or dying, rich or poor,
 All shall be well if Thou art mine.

1496 John Berridge 66 66 88
For the wages of sin is death; but the gift of God is eternal life through Jesus Christ our Lord. *Romans 6:23*

Where must a sinner fly,
 Who feels His guilty load,
And stands condemned to die,
 Out of the mouth of God?
Can any door of hope be found?
Not any sure, on nature's ground.

What if he mend his life,
 And pour out floods of tears,
And pray with fervent strife?
 These pay no past arrears.
The law, with unrelenting breath,
Declares the wage of sin is death.

Who then shall reconcile
 Such jarring things as these?
Say, how can Justice smile
 At Mercy on her knees?
Or how can Mercy lift her head,
If all the legal debt is paid?

Jesus, Thy helping hand
 Has made the contest cease,
Paid off each law demand,
 And bought the blest release;
Stern Justice, satisfied by Thee,
Bids Mercy bring the news to me.

O tidings sweet of grace,
 To sinners lost and poor,
Who humbly seek Thy face,
 And knock at Mercy's door;
Who taste the peace Thy blood imparts,
And feel the Saviour in their hearts.

All hail! we bless Thee now,
 Who bought us with Thy blood!
Our gracious Shepherd Thou,
 To bring us home to God.
On earth we sing Thy bleeding love,
And long to see Thy face above.

1497 John Berridge 77 77
For the wages of sin is death; but the gift of God is eternal life through Jesus Christ our Lord. *Romans 6:23*

Awful is Thy threatening, Lord;
Let me mark the solemn word;
What the righteous Ruler saith:
'Wages due to sin is death.'

Then I stand condemned to die
By the mouth of God most high.
Sins I have, a thousand too,
And a thousand deaths are due.

Should I spend my life in prayers,
Water all my couch with tears,
Turn from every evil past,
Still I am condemned and cast.

Lord, I own the sentence just,
Drop my head into the dust;
If my soul is cast to hell,
Thou, O Lord, art righteous still.

In myself I have no hope;
Justice every plea will stop;
Yet for mercy I may plead,
Springing from the church's Head.

Knock I may at Jesus' door,
Mercy for His sake implore,
Mercy, such as Thou wilt give;
Show it, Lord, and let me live.

1498   William Gadsby   886 D
**Wherefore, my brethren, ye also are become
dead to the law by the body of Christ; that ye
should be married to another.** *Romans 7:4*

My soul with holy wonder views
The love the Lord the Saviour shows,
   To wretched, dying man;
So strange, so boundless is His grace,
He takes the vilest of our race
   With Him to live and reign.

He'll charm them with a holy kiss,
And make them know what union is;
   He'll draw them to His breast;
A smiling eye upon them cast,
Which brings them to His feet in haste,
   Each singing, 'I am blest!

'I'm blest, I'm blest, for ever blest;
My rags are gone, and I am dressed
   In garments white as snow;
I'm married to the Lord the Lamb,
Whose beauties I can ne'er explain,
   Nor half His glory show.'

1499   William Cowper   CM
**For I was alive without the law once: but when
the commandment came, sin revived, and I
died.** *Romans 7:9*

No strength of nature can suffice
   To serve the Lord aright;
And what she has she misapplies,
   For want of clearer light.

How long beneath the law I lay,
   In bondage and distress!
I toiled the precept to obey,
   But toiled without success.

Then to abstain from outward sin
   Was more than I could do;
Now, if I feel its power within,
   I feel I hate it too.

Then, all my servile works were done
   A righteousness to raise;
Now, freely chosen in the Son,
   I freely choose His ways.

'What shall I do,' was then the word,
   'That I may worthier grow?
What shall I render to the Lord?'
   Is my inquiry now.

To see the law by Christ fulfilled,
   And hear His pardoning voice,
Changes a slave into a child,
   And duty into choice.

1500   Joseph Hart   SM
**For we know that the law is spiritual: but I am
carnal, sold under sin.** *Romans 7:14*

Though void of all that's good,
   And very, very poor,
Through Christ I hope to be renewed,
   And live for evermore.

I view my own bad heart,
   And see such evils there,
The sight with horror makes me start,
   And tempts me to despair.

Then with a single eye
   I look to Christ alone;
And on His righteousness rely,
   Though I myself have none.

By virtue of His blood,
   The Lord declares me clean.
Now serves my mind the law of God,
   My flesh the law of sin.

1501   John Newton   SM
**For that which I do I allow not: for what I
would, that do I not; but what I hate, that do I.**
Romans 7:15

I know the Lord is nigh,
   And would but cannot pray,
For Satan meets me when I try,
   And frights my soul away.

I would, but can't repent,
   Though I endeavour oft;
This stony heart can ne'er relent
   Till Jesus makes it soft.

I would, but cannot love,
   Though wooed by love divine;
No arguments have power to move
   A soul so base as mine.

I would, but cannot rest
   In God's most holy will;
I know what He appoints is best,
   Yet murmur at it still.

O could I but believe,
   Then all would easy be;
I *would*, but *cannot*; Lord, relieve!
   My help must come from Thee.

By nature prone to ill,
   Till Thy appointed hour,
I was as destitute of will
   As now I am of power.

Wilt Thou not crown at length
  The work Thou hast begun?
And with the will afford me strength
  In all Thy ways to run?

1502 Joseph Hart SM
O wretched man that I am! *Romans 7:24*

  How sore a plague is sin,
  To those by whom 'tis felt!
The Christian cries, '*Unclean, unclean!*'
  E'en though released from guilt.

  O wretched, wretched man!
  What horrid scenes I view!
I find, alas! do all I can,
  That I can nothing do.

  When good I would perform,
  Through fear or shame I stop.
Corruption rises like a storm,
  And blasts the promised crop.

  How long, dear Lord, how long
  Deliverance must I seek;
And fight with foes so very strong,
  Myself so very weak?

  I'll bear the unequal strife,
  And wage the war within;
Since death, that puts an end to life,
  Shall put an end to sin.

1503 Isaac Watts LM
**There is therefore now no condemnation to
them which are in Christ Jesus, who walk not
after the flesh, but after the Spirit.** *Romans 8:1*

Who shall the Lord's elect condemn?
  'Tis God that justifies their souls;
And mercy, like a mighty stream,
  O'er all their sins divinely rolls.

Who shall adjudge the saints to hell?
  'Tis Christ that suffered in their stead;
And the salvation to fulfil,
  Behold Him rising from the dead!

He lives! He lives! and sits above,
  For ever interceding there;
Who shall divide us from His love,
  Or what shall tempt us to despair?

Shall persecution, or distress,
  Famine, or sword, or nakedness?
He that has loved us bears us through,
  And makes us more than conquerors, too.

Faith has an overcoming power;
  It triumphs in the dying hour.
Christ is our life, our joy, our hope,
  Nor can we sink with such a prop.

Not all that men on earth can do,
  Nor powers on high, nor powers below,
Shall cause His mercy to remove,
  Or wean our hearts from Christ our love.

1504 John Wingrove 10 10 11 11
**There is therefore now no condemnation to
them which are in Christ Jesus, who walk not
after the flesh, but after the Spirit.** *Romans 8:1*

  Ye tempted and tried, to Jesus draw nigh,
  He suffered and died your wants to supply;
Trust Him for salvation; you need not to grieve;
'There's no condemnation to them that believe.'

  By day and by night His love is made known;
  It is His delight to succour His own;
He will have compassion; then why should you
    grieve?
'There's no condemnation to them that believe.'

  Though Satan will seek the sheep to annoy,
  The helpless and weak He ne'er shall destroy,
Christ is their salvation, and strength He will give;
'There's no condemnation to them that believe.'

1505 Samuel Barnard CM
**There is therefore now no condemnation to
them which are in Christ Jesus, who walk not
after the flesh, but after the Spirit.** *Romans 8:1*

No condemnation can be brought
  Against the sons of God;
Christ hath for them a clothing wrought,
  And washed them in His blood.

They righteous are in what He's done,
  And evermore will be;
They stand complete in Christ the Son,
  From condemnation free.

Justice demanded all the debt
  Of Christ, on whom it laid;
Just at the time the Saviour set,
  The debt He came and paid.

If Jesus had not paid the debt,
  Or suffered all the pain,
He ne'er had been at freedom set,
  He ne'er had rose again.

But when we see the Saviour rise,
  Triumphant from the dead,
Our hopes ascend above the skies,
  With our victorious Head.

1506   Robert Chapman   CM

There is therefore now no condemnation to them which are in Christ Jesus, who walk not after the flesh, but after the Spirit. *Romans 8:1*

No condemnation! O my soul!
  'Tis God that speaks the word;
Perfect in comeliness art thou
  In Christ, Thy glorious Lord.

In heaven His blood for ever speaks,
  In God the Father's ear;
His saints, the jewels on His heart,
  Jesus will ever bear.

No condemnation! precious words!
  Consider it, my soul:
Thy sins were all on Jesus laid:
  His stripes have made thee whole.

1507   John Kent   CM

For the law of the Spirit of life in Christ Jesus hath made me free from the law of sin and death. *Romans 8:2*

Jesus hath suffered once for sin,
  And now exalted reigns:
Ye sinners saved, His praise begin,
  In sweet harmonious strains.

No claims can law or justice crave
  From Jesus' mystic bride;
Full payment to the law He gave,
  When for her sins He died.

When Justice smote the Shepherd's head,
  The captive flock were free;
Beloved, when in transgression dead,
  Great God, and far from Thee.

Here, lost in thought, the seraphs gaze,
  The wondrous scene to scan;
What heights and depths of sovereign grace
  In wisdom's glorious plan!

Convinced of sin's demerit, we
  From self to Jesus fly;
Ourselves insolvent debtors see,
  And on His blood rely.

In vain we seek a fig-leaf dress,
  To hide our sin and shame;
But shelter in His righteousness,
  By whom salvation came.

This truth, by grace, we still maintain,
  And this conclusion draw,
That in the wounds of Jesus slain,
  'Tis sweet to read the law.

Made by an act of sovereign grace
  From legal bondage free,
As Thy own chosen, blood-bought race,
  Great God, we worship Thee.

1508   William Gadsby   LM

Because the carnal mind is enmity against God: for it is not subject to the law of God, neither indeed can be.
Romans 8:7

The carnal mind takes different ways,
And different objects she surveys;
She's pleased with things that suit her taste,
But hates the God of truth and grace.

No beauty in the Lord she views,
Nor is she charmed with gospel-news;
She sets at nought, with vain contempt,
The Man the Lord Jehovah sent.

She hates Him as the mighty God,
The church's Wisdom, Life, and Head;
His priestly office she disdains,
And wantons with His wounds and pains.

Whatever office Jesus bears,
Or in what glorious form appears,
She was, and is, and still will be
Against Him dreadful enmity.

Is this the case? Yes, Lord, 'tis true;
And I've a carnal nature too,
That fights, with all its hellish might,
Against the God of my delight.

Yet, bless the Lord, through grace I feel
I have a mind that loves Him well;
Nor shall the dreadful power of sin,
My better part from Jesus win.

May grace not only live and reign,
But may its powers be felt and seen;
Dear God, my every foe subdue,
And make me more than conqueror too.

1509   Isaac Watts   CM
**For as many as are led by the Spirit of God,
they are the sons of God.**
Romans 8:14

Why should the children of a King
   Go mourning all their days?
Great Comforter! descend and bring
   Some tokens of Thy grace.

Dost Thou not dwell in all the saints,
   And seal them heirs of heaven?
When wilt Thou banish my complaints,
   And show my sins forgiven?

Assure my conscience of her part
   In the Redeemer's blood;
And bear Thy witness with my heart,
   That I am born of God.

Thou art the earnest of His love,
   The pledge of joys to come;
And Thy soft wings, celestial Dove,
   Will safe convey me home.

1510   John Berridge   SM
**For ye have not received the spirit of bondage
again to fear; but ye have received the Spirit of
adoption, whereby we cry, Abba, Father.**
Romans 8:15

Well, canst thou read thy heart,
   And feel the plague of sin?
Does Sinai's thunder make thee start,
   And conscience roar within?

Expect to find no balm
   On nature's barren ground;
All human medicines will do harm;
   They only skin the wound.

To Jesus Christ repair,
   And knock at mercy's gate;
His blood alone can wash thee fair,
   And make thy conscience sweet.

In season due He seals
   A pardon on the breast;
The wounds of sin His Spirit heals,
   And brings the gospel-rest.

So comes the peace of God,
   Which cheers the conscience well
And love shed in the heart abroad,
   More sweet than we can tell.

Adopted sons perceive
   Their kindred to the sky;
The Father's pardoning love receive,
   And 'Abba, Father,' cry.

1511   Robert Hawker   87 87 D + refrain
**Ye have received the Spirit of adoption,
whereby we cry, Abba, Father.**
Romans 8:15

'Abba, Father,' Lord, we call Thee,
   Hallowed name! from day to day:
'Tis Thy children's right to know Thee,
   None but children 'Abba' say:
This high privilege we inherit,
   First by gift, then thro' Christ's blood,
God the Spirit, to our spirit,
   Witnesseth we're sons of God.

   *'Abba, Father,' still we call Thee,
     'Abba' sounds through all our hosts:
   All in heaven and earth adore Thee,
     Father, Son, and Holy Ghost.*

Abba's love first gave us being,
   When in Christ, in that vast plan;
Abba chose the church in Jesus
   Long before the world began.
O, what love the Father bore us!
   O how precious in His sight!
When He gave His church to Jesus,
   Jesus, His whole soul's delight.

All the choicest stores of pardon
   God sets forth in Christ His Son,
With the Spirit's grace to guide us,
   Safe to bring His children home:
'Abba, Father,' makes all certain,
   Both by word, by oath, and blood:
Abba saith, 'They are My people,'
   And they say, 'The Lord's my God,'

Hence, through all our changing seasons,
   Trouble, sorrow, sickness, woe,
Nothing changeth God's affections,
   Abba's love will bring us through.
Soon shall all Thy blood-bought children
   Round Thy throne their anthems raise,
And, in songs of rich salvation,
   Shout to Abba endless praise.

1512   Fanny Crosby   Irregular
And if children, then heirs; heirs of God, and joint-heirs with Christ; if so be that we suffer with Him, that we may be also glorified together. *Romans 8:17*

Blessèd assurance, Jesus is mine!
O what a foretaste of glory divine!
Heir of salvation, purchase of God;
Born of His Spirit, washed in His blood.

This is my story, this is my song,
Praising my Saviour all the day long.

Perfect submission, perfect delight,
Visions of rapture burst on my sight;
Angels descending, bring from above
Echoes of mercy, whispers of love.

Perfect submission, all is at rest,
I in my Saviour am happy and blest,
Watching and waiting, looking above,
Filled with His goodness, lost in His love.

1513   Richard Burnham   87 87
And if children, then heirs; heirs of God, and joint-heirs with Christ; if so be that we suffer with Him, that we may be also glorified together. *Romans 8:17*

Here the Christian meets with trials,
    Oft immersed in human woe;
Fierce temptations, various sorrows,
    Are his portion here below.

But the world to which he's travelling,
    Hath no evil to annoy;
There is nothing to molest him,
    Nothing to disturb his joy.

There he'll see the unfading beauties
    Of the dear Immanuel's face;
There behold the streaming glory,
    All the rising heights of grace.

Hark, my soul, they're sweetly singing!
    What a wondrous happy throng!
O what sounds of hallelujahs
    Echo in the noble song!

Come Lord Jesus, O come quickly,
    Let me to Thy throne arise,
Bear a part in that grand music,
    Join the chorus of the skies.

1514   John Stevens   87 87
For we are saved by hope: but hope that is seen is not hope: for what a man seeth, why doth he yet hope for? *Romans 8:24*

Every saint is saved by hoping
    In the great Redeemer's blood;
Round His footstool view them stooping,
    Humbly to adore their God.

Hope reviews the dying Saviour,
    Yields sweet succour to the saint;
E'er expects all promised favour,
    Never leaves the soul to faint.

Faith, and hope, and true affection,
    All are graces from the Lamb:
All designed to bring salvation;
    Hope expects it through His name.

While by faith the soul is reading,
    'Jesus died for sinful men,'
Hope desires, with fervent pleading,
    Feelingly to say 'Amen.'

These desires, all known in heaven,
    Shall not, cannot be denied:
Life eternal now is given;
    Hope shall say 'Amen,' when tried.

Thus by hope the saints are savèd,
    Living hope to Jesus goes;
Draws all life through Jesus' merit,
    And no other Saviour knows.

1515   *Gospel Magazine 1781*   77 77
Likewise the Spirit also helpeth our infirmities.
Romans 8:26

Blessèd Spirit from above,
    Teach, O teach me how to pray;
Fill my soul with heavenly love;
    Lead me the celestial way.

When temptations me surround,
    Help me, Lord, on Thee to call;
When iniquities abound,
    Save, O save me, or I fall.

When Thou hidest Thy lovely face,
    Till the cloud is passed away,
And I feel the sweets of peace,
    Never let me cease to pray.

When I feel my heart like stone,
    When I have no heart to pray,
At Thy feet, O God, I'd groan,
    'Take this stony heart away.'

Holy Spirit, on me shine;
  Make my evidences clear;
Then I'll say that God is mine!
  I shall with the Lord appear!

But O the blest day, and soon 'twill arise,
  When, freed from my clay, I mount to the skies;
Then gladly I'll enter my heavenly rest,
And there sing for ever, "Tis all for the best.'

1516 Joseph Swain   LM
The Spirit itself maketh intercession for us.
Romans 8:26

When some sweet promise warms our heart,
  And cheers us under every care,
It is the Spirit's gracious part
  To take that word and fix it there.

'Twas He that turned our hearts away
  From love of sin and hateful strife;
His all-creating beams display
  The dawn of everlasting life.

'Tis He that brings us comfort down,
  When we complain and mourn for sin;
And, while He shows our heavenly crown,
  Assures us sin no more shall reign.

Our great High Priest, before the throne,
  Presents the merits of His blood;
For our acceptance pleads His own,
  And proves our cause completely good.

When prayer or praise attempts to rise,
  And fain would reach Jehovah's ear,
His all-prevailing sacrifice
  Perfumes, and makes it welcome there.

1517 Samuel Medley   10 10 11 11
And we know that all things work together for good to them that love God.
Romans 8:28

My soul, now arise, my passions, take wing;
Look up to the skies, and cheerfully sing;
Let God be the Object in praises addressed,
And this be my subject, "Tis all for the best.'

Search all the world through, examine and see,
  And what canst thou view more suited to thee
Than this declaration, in Scripture expressed,
That God, thy Salvation, does all for the best?

Tho' here, day by day, His love shall see good
  Upon thee to lay His fatherly rod;
Yet be not dejected, however oppressed,
Though sorely afflicted, 'tis all for the best.

The beams of His grace are passing all worth,
  The smiles of His face are heaven on earth;
When to me He shows them, what joy fills my breast!
And when He withdraws them, 'tis all for the best.

1518 Mary Peters   84 84 888 4
And we know that all things work together for good to them that love God.
Romans 8:28

Through the love of God our Saviour
  All will be well;
Free and changeless is His favour,
  All, all is well:
Precious is the blood that healed us,
Perfect is the grace that sealed us,
Strong the hand stretched out to shield us,
  All must be well.

Though we pass through tribulation,
  All will be well;
Ours is such a full salvation,
  All, all is well:
Happy, still in God confiding,
Fruitful, if in Christ abiding,
Holy, through the Spirit's guiding,
  All must be well.

We expect a bright tomorrow,
  All will be well;
Faith can sing, through days of sorrow,
  All, all is well:
On our Father's love relying,
Jesus every need supplying,
Or in living or in dying,
  All must be well.

1519 Richard Burnham   LM
Moreover whom He did predestinate, them He also called. *Romans 8:30*

'Twas fixed in God's eternal mind
When His dear sons should mercy find;
From everlasting He decreed
When every good should be conveyed.

Determined was the manner how
Eternal favours He'd bestow;
Yea, He decreed the very place
Where He would show triumphant grace.

Also the means were fixed upon
Through which His sovereign love should run.
So time and place, yea, means and mode,
Were all determined by our God.

Vast were the settlements of grace
On millions of the human race;
And every favour, richly given,
Flows from the high decree of heaven.

In every mercy, full and free,
A sovereign God I wish to see;
To see how grace, free grace has reigned,
In every blessing He ordained.

Yes, dearest Lord, 'tis my desire
Thy wise appointments to admire;
And trace the footsteps of my God,
Through every path in Zion's road.

1520   Horatius Bonar   6 10 10 6
**What shall we then say to these things? If God
be for us, who can be against us?**
Romans 8:31

Blessèd be God, our God!
Who gave for us His well-beloved Son,
The gift of gifts, all other gifts in one;
Blessèd be God, our God!

What will He not bestow,
Who freely gave this mighty gift unbought,
Unmerited, unheeded, and unsought;
What will He not bestow?

He sparèd not His Son!
'Tis this that silences each rising fear;
'Tis this that bids the hard thought disappear;
He sparèd not His Son!

Who shall condemn us now?
Since Christ has died, and risen, and gone above,
For us to plead at the right hand of love,
Who shall condemn us now?

'Tis God that justifies!
Who shall recall the pardon or the grace,
Or who the broken chain of guilt replace?
'Tis God that justifies!

The victory is ours!
For us in might came forth the Mighty One;
For us He fought the fight, the triumph won;
The victory is ours!

1521   Benjamin Beddome   LM
**Who is He that condemneth? It is Christ that
died, yea rather, that is risen again.**
Romans 8:34

Who shall condemn to endless flames
   The chosen people of our God,
Since in the book of life their names
   Are fairly writ in Jesus' blood?

He, for the sins of all the elect,
   Hath a complete atonement made;
And Justice never can expect
   That the same debt should twice be paid.

Not tribulation, nakedness,
   The famine, peril, or the sword;
Not persecution, or distress,
   Can separate from Christ the Lord.

Nor life, nor death, nor depth, nor height,
   Nor powers below, nor powers above,
Nor present things, nor things to come,
   Can change His purposes of love.

His sovereign mercy knows no end,
   His faithfulness shall still endure;
And those who on His word depend
   Shall find His word for ever sure.

1522   Charles Wesley   LM
It is Christ that died. *Romans 8:34*

Jesus, the sinner's Friend, to Thee,
Lost and undone, for aid I flee;
Weary of earth, myself, and sin,
Open Thine arms and take me in.

Pity and heal my sin-sick soul;
'Tis Thou alone canst make me whole;
Fallen, till in me Thine image shine.
And lost I am, till Thou art mine.

At last I own it cannot be
That I should fit myself for Thee:
Here, then, to Thee I all resign;
Thine is the work, and only Thine.

What shall I say Thy grace to move?
Lord, I am sin, but Thou art love:
I give up every plea beside,
Lord, I am lost, but Thou hast died!

1523   James Montgomery   65 65 D
**It is Christ that died, yea rather, that is risen
again, who is even at the right hand of God,
who also maketh intercession for us.**
Romans 8:34

In the hour of trial,
   Jesus, pray for me,
Lest by base denial
   I depart from Thee;
When Thou seest me waver,
   With a look recall,
Nor, for fear or favour,
   Suffer me to fall.

With its 'witching pleasures
 Would this vain world charm,
Or its sordid treasures
 Spread to work me harm,
Bring to my remembrance
 Sad Gethsemane,
Or, in darker semblance,
 Cross-crowned Calvary.

If with sore affliction
 Thou in love chastise,
Pour Thy benediction
 On the sacrifice;
Then, upon Thine altar
 Freely offered up,
Though the flesh may falter,
 Faith shall drink the cup.

When in dust and ashes
 To the grave I sink,
While heaven's glory flashes
 O'er the shelving brink,
On Thy truth relying
 Through that mortal strife,
Lord, receive me, dying,
 To eternal life.

1524 Joseph Irons   CM
Who shall separate us from the love of Christ?
Romans 8:35

Blest truth! the church and Christ are one
 In bonds the most secure;
No separation can be known
 While endless years endure.

No separation! is proclaimed
 In God's unerring word;
Christ is not of His bride ashamed,
 Then let her own her Lord.

No separation! cheers my heart,
 And bids my fears subside;
My soul and Jesus cannot part,
 For me He lived and died.

No separation! precious thought!
 Then Christ is with me here;
And home to heaven I must be brought,
 For Jesus Christ is there.

No separation! this decree
 Of everlasting love
Is fixed by the eternal Three,
 And never can remove.

1525 Augustus Toplady   LM
Who shall separate us from the love of Christ?
Romans 8:35

Immovable our hope remains,
 Within the veil our anchor lies;
Jesus, who washed us from our stains,
 Shall bear us safely to the skies.

Strong in His strength, we boldly say,
 For us Immanuel shed His blood;
Who, then, shall tear our shield away,
 Or part us from the love of God?

Shall tribulation, or distress.
 Or pain, or persecution's sword?
Shall Satan rob us of our peace,
 Or prove too mighty for the Lord?

Founded in Christ, secure we stand,
 His love will order all things well;
We soon shall gain the promised land,
 Triumphant o'er the powers of hell.

The saints at all times are secure
 In Jesus' everlasting love;
Through Him they shall all storms endure,
 And with Him reign enthroned above.

1526 John Kent   SM
Nay, in all these things we are more than conquerors through Him that loved us.
Romans 8:37

 The conquest Jesus won
 O'er Satan, sin, and hell,
With all the wonders He has done,
 His saints shall sing and tell.

 On Him shall Zion place
 Her only hope for heaven,
And see, in His dear sacred face,
 Ten thousand sins forgiven.

 He passed within the veil,
 Did on His bosom bear
The worthless names that did prevail
 With Him to enter there.

 Worthy the slaughtered Lamb!
 Let ransomed mortals say;
For who shall sing His lovely name
 In higher notes than they?

1527 Vernon Higham DCM
**We are more than conquerors through Him
that loved us.** *Romans 8:37*

There is a fount of costly love
  Found in Thy heart sublime;
Redemption planned in heaven above,
  Fulfilled by Thee in time.
This painful sacrifice of grace,
  With message that He died,
Brings to my soul the smiling face
  Of justice satisfied.

There is a gentleness of peace
  Around Thy throne divine;
A place where grace will now release
  The flow of mercy's wine.
The peace of God is vast and pure,
  No words can ever tell;
It cannot fail, it will endure,
  Withstand the gates of hell.

There is a power of strength untold
  That comes from Thee alone,
Which gives me courage, makes me bold,
  Transforms my heart of stone.
I am persuaded now at last,
  When I behold Thy care,
That I am safe from Satan's blast:
  No more shall I despair.

In every thing and every place,
  In every changing wind,
I'll trust in Thee along life's race,
  And find Thee to be kind.
Thou liftest me by Thy great hand,
  By many foes oppressed;
As more than conqueror I stand:
  The victory of the blessed.

© Author

1528 William Dickinson 77 77 77
**Nor height, nor depth, nor any other creature,
shall be able to separate us from the love of
God, which is in Christ Jesus our Lord.**
Romans 8:39

Hallelujah! who shall part
Christ's own church from Christ's own heart?
  Sever from the Saviour's side
  Souls for whom the Saviour died?
Dash one precious jewel down
From Immanuel's blood-bought crown?

Hallelujah! shall the sword
Part us from our glorious Lord?
  Trouble dark or dire disgrace
  E'er the Spirit's seal efface?
Famine, nakedness or hate,
Bride and Bridegroom separate?

Hallelujah! life nor death,
Powers above nor powers beneath,
  Monarch's might nor tyrant's doom,
  Things that are nor things to come,
Men nor angels, e'er shall part
Christ's own church from Christ's own heart.

1529 Isaac Watts LM
**Hath not the potter power over the clay, of the
same lump to make one vessel unto honour,
and another unto dishonour?** *Romans 9:21*

Behold the potter and the clay;
  He forms His vessels as He please;
Such is our God, and such are we,
  The subjects of His high decrees.

Does not the workman's power extend
  O'er all the mass, which part to choose,
And mould it for a nobler end,
  And which to leave for viler use?

May not the sovereign Lord on high
  Dispense His favours as He will?
Choose some to life, while others die,
  And yet be just and gracious still?

What if, to make His terror known,
  He let His patience long endure,
Suffering vile rebels to go on,
  And seal their own destruction sure?

What if He mean to show His grace,
  And His electing love employs,
To mark out some of mortal race,
  And form them fit for heavenly joys?

Shall man reply against his Lord,
  And call his Maker's ways unjust,
The thunder of whose dreadful word
  Can crush a thousand worlds to dust?

But O my soul, if truths so bright
  Should dazzle and confound thy sight,
Yet still His written will obey,
  And wait the great decisive day.

Then shall He make His justice known,
  And the whole world before His throne,
With joy or terror shall confess
  The glory of His righteousness.

1530 John Berridge   886 D
Though the number of the children of Israel be
as the sand of the sea, a remnant shall be
saved. *Romans 9:27*

On wings of love the Saviour flies,
And freely left His native skies,
    To take a human birth;
The wise and righteous men go near,
His wonders see, His sermons hear,
    And think Him nothing worth,

A remnant small of humble souls
His grace mysteriously controls
    By sweet alluring call;
They hear it, and His person view,
They learn to love and follow too,
    And take Him for their all.

One of this remnant I would be,
A soul devoted unto Thee,
    Allurèd by Thy voice;
No more on gaudy idols gaze,
No longer tinsel grandeur praise,
    But fix on Thee my choice.

Thou knowest well my secret smart,
And readest all my aching heart,
    And hearest every sigh;
Can any creature give me rest,
Or any blessing make me blest,
    Unless my Lord is nigh?

While walking on the gospel-way,
I would see Jesus every day,
    And see in all His grace;
See Him my Prophet, Priest, and King;
See Him by faith, and praises sing;
    Then see Him face to face.

1531 William Gadsby   CM
How beautiful are the feet of them that preach
the gospel of peace.
Romans 10:15

What a divine harmonious sound
    The gospel-trumpet gives;
No music can with it compare;
    The soul that knows it lives.

Ten thousand blessings it contains,
    Divinely rich and free,
For helpless, wretched, ruined man,
    Though vile and base as we.

It speaks of pardon, full and free,
    Through Christ, the Lamb once slain;
Whose blood can cleanse the foulest soul,
    And take away all stain.

The vilest sinner out of hell,
    Who lives to feel his need,
Is welcome to a throne of grace,
    The Saviour's blood to plead.

The Lord delights to hear them cry,
    And knock at mercy's door;
'Tis grace that makes them feel their need,
    And pray to Him for more.

Nor will He send them empty back,
    Nor fright them from the door;
The Father has in Jesus stored
    All blessings for the poor.

1532 Isaac Watts   SM
How beautiful are the feet of them that preach
the gospel of peace, and bring glad tidings of
good things!
Romans 10:15

How beauteous are their feet
Who stand on Zion's hill!
Who bring salvation on their tongues
And words of peace reveal.

How charming is their voice!
How sweet the tidings are!
Zion, behold thy Saviour King,
He reigns and triumphs here!

How happy are our ears,
That hear this joyful sound,
Which kings and prophets waited for,
And sought but never found!

How blessèd are our eyes,
That see this heavenly light!
Prophets and kings desired it long
But died without the sight.

The watchmen join their voice,
And tuneful notes employ:
Jerusalem breaks forth in song
And deserts learn the joy.

The Lord makes bare His arm
Through all the earth abroad;
And every nation shall behold
Our Saviour and our God.

1533   James Allen   87 87 47
But they have not all obeyed the gospel. For Esaias saith, Lord, who hath believed our report? *Romans 10:16*

Sinners, will you scorn the message
  Sent in mercy from above?
Every sentence, oh, how tender!
  Every line is full of love:
    Listen to it:
  Every line is full of love.

Hear the heralds of the gospel
  News from Zion's King proclaim:
'Pardon to each rebel sinner;
  Free forgiveness in His name:'
    How important!
  'Free forgiveness in His name.'

Tempted souls, they bring you succour;
  Fearful hearts, they quell your fears;
And with news of consolation,
  Chase away the falling tears:
    Tender heralds!
  Chase away the falling tears.

Who hath our report believèd?
  Who received the joyful word?
Who embraced the news of pardon
  Spoken to you by the Lord?
    Can you slight it?
  Spoken to you by the Lord.

O ye angels, hovering round us,
  Waiting spirits, speed your way;
Haste ye to the court of heaven,
  Tidings bear without delay:
    Rebel sinners,
  Glad the message will obey.

1534   Joseph Hart   88 88 (anapaestic)
O the depth of the riches both of the wisdom and knowledge of God!
Romans 11:33

How good is the God we adore,
  Our faithful, unchangeable Friend!
His love is as great as His power
  And knows neither measure nor end!

'Tis Jesus the First and the Last,
  Whose Spirit shall guide us safe home;
We'll praise Him for all that is past;
  We'll trust Him for all that's to come.

1535   Vernon Higham   88 88 88
I beseech you therefore, brethren, by the mercies of God, that ye present your bodies a living sacrifice, holy, acceptable unto God, which is your reasonable service.
Romans 12:1

I saw an altar far away
With gentle Lamb that men did slay;
A costly place of bitter pain,
A cross the price that moved our stain.
  The wrath of God faced Christ alone,
  For sin of man He did atone.

O blessèd spot of joy and bliss,
A cleansing flow my heart did kiss;
A place where peace and mercy meet
In one embrace forever sweet.
  Almighty God, blest Trinity,
  For this my soul will worship Thee.

Then take my life for Thee alone,
And ever rule upon my throne,
As on the altar I recline,
A living sacrifice of Thine.
  Lord, keep me with Thy lovely grace,
  Transformed for all to see Thy face.

Fashions of earth now fade away,
Courses of evil must not stay:
Merciful Father, see Thy child,
Incline my heart with strength so mild.
  Always secure in Thee I find
  Sufficient grace and peace of mind.

Thy perfect will is my delight,
And in my heart renewing light:
Thus in my daily life I pray,
Delight in good, a holy way;
  Wonderful change, that all may see
  What God Almighty did for me.

                         © *Author*

1536   Frances Havergal   76 76
I beseech you therefore, brethren, by the mercies of God, that ye present your bodies a living sacrifice, holy, acceptable unto God, which is your reasonable service.
Romans 12:1

In full and glad surrender
  I give myself to Thee,
Thine utterly and only
  And evermore to be.

O Son of God, who lov'st me,
  I will be Thine alone;
And all I have and am, Lord,
  Shall henceforth be Thine own.

Reign over me, Lord Jesus;
O make my heart Thy throne!
It shall be Thine, dear Saviour,
It shall be Thine alone.

O come and reign, Lord Jesus;
Rule over everything!
And keep me always loyal
And true to Thee, my King.

1537 Handley Moule 77 77
**And be not conformed to this world: but be ye
transformed by the renewing of your mind,
that ye may prove what is that good, and
acceptable, and perfect, will of God.**
Romans 12:2

Lord and Saviour, true and kind,
Be the Master of my mind;
Bless and guide and strengthen still
All my powers of thought and will.

While I ply the scholar's task,
Jesus Christ, be near, I ask;
Help the memory, clear the brain,
Knowledge still to seek and gain.

Here I train for life's swift race;
Let me do it in Thy grace:
Here I arm me for life's fight;
Let me do it in Thy might.

Thou hast made me mind and soul;
I for Thee would use the whole;
Thou hast died that I might live;
All my powers to Thee I give.

Striving, thinking, learning still,
Let me follow thus Thy will,
Till my whole glad nature be
Trained for duty and for Thee.

1538 Elizabeth Charles SM
Rejoice with them that do rejoice.
Romans 12:15

Come and rejoice with me!
For once my heart was poor,
And I have found a treasury
Of love, a boundless store.

Come and rejoice with me!
I, once so sick at heart,
Have met with One who knows my case
And knows the healing art.

Come and rejoice with me!
For I was wearied sore,
And I have found a mighty arm
Which holds me evermore.

Come and rejoice with me!
My feet so wide did roam,
And One has sought me from afar
And beareth me safe home.

Come and rejoice with me!
For I have found a Friend
Who knows my heart's most secret depths
Yet loves me without end.

I knew not of His love;
And He had loved so long,
With love so faithful and so deep,
So tender and so strong.

1539 Joseph Hart LM
Be of the same mind one toward another.
Romans 12:16

To you who stand in Christ so fast,
Ye know your faith shall ever last;
The Lord, on whom that faith depends,
This kind, important message sends:

'If light, exulting thoughts arise,
Your weaker brethren to despise,
Remember all to Me are dear;
Who most is favoured most should bear.

'If strong thyself, support the weak;
If well, be tender to the sick;
To babes I oft reveal My mind,
And they who seek My face shall find.

'If faith be strong as well as true,
Then strive that love may be so too;
Boast not, but meek and lowly be;
The humblest soul is most like Me.

'Should I, displeased, My face but turn,
Ye sadly would your folly mourn;
Who now seemed best would soon be worst;
I often make the last the first.

'Encourage souls that on Me wait,
And stoop to those of low estate.
Contempt or slight I can't approve;
Be love your aim, for I am love.'

1540   James Montgomery   CM
Be of the same mind one toward another.
Romans 12:16

The glorious universe around,
    The heavens with all their train,
Sun, moon and stars are firmly bound
    In one mysterious chain.

God, in creation, thus displays
    His wisdom and His might;
While all His works with all His ways
    Harmoniously unite.

In one fraternal bond of love,
    One fellowship of mind,
The saints below and saints above
    Their bliss and glory find.

Here, in their house of pilgrimage,
    Thy statutes are their song:
There, through one bright, eternal age,
    Thy praises they prolong.

Lord, may our union form a part,
    Of that thrice happy whole:
Derive its pulse from Thee the heart,
    Its life from Thee the soul.

1541   Godfrey Thring   65 65 D
**Now is our salvation nearer than when we
believed.** *Romans 13:11*

Saviour, blessèd Saviour,
    Listen while we sing;
Hearts and voices raising
    Praises to our King:
All we have we offer,
    All we hope to be,
Body, soul, and spirit,
    All we yield to Thee.

Nearer, ever nearer,
    Christ, we draw to Thee,
Deep in adoration
    Bending low the knee:
Thou for our redemption
    Cam'st on earth to die;
Thou, that we might follow,
    Hast gone up on high.

Great, and ever greater,
    Are Thy mercies here;
True and everlasting
    Are the glories there,
Where no pain nor sorrow,
    Fear nor care, is known,
Where the angel legions
    Circle round Thy throne.

Higher then, and higher,
    Bear the ransomed soul,
Earthly toils forgotten,
    Saviour, to its goal;
Where, in joys unthought of,
    Saints with angels sing,
Never weary, raising
    Praises to their King.

1542   Thomas Kelly   11 11 11 11
The night is far spent, the day is at hand.
Romans 13:12

The night is far spent, the day is at hand;
    Already the dawn may be seen in the sky;
Rejoice, then, ye saints, it's your Lord's own
        command:
    Rejoice, for the coming of Jesus draws nigh.

How bright will it be when Jesus appears!
    How welcome to those who are saved by His
        cross!
A crown incorruptible then will be theirs,
    A rich compensation for suffering and loss.

Affliction is light when compared to that day,
    To the glory that then will from heaven be
        revealed!
'The Saviour is coming,' His people may say:
    'The Lord whom we look for, our Sun and our
        Shield!

'O kindle within us a holy desire,
    Like that which was found in Thy people of old,
Who felt all Thy love, and whose hearts were on
        fire,
    While they waited with longing Thy face to
        behold.'

1543   Richard Burnham   CM
**Wherefore receive ye one another, as Christ
also received us to the glory of God.**
Romans 15:7

O with what pleasure we behold
    Sinners to Canaan move,
Leaving the fleeting things of earth,
    For greater things above.

These saints have openly confessed
    The great Immanuel's name:
And with delight the church receives
    The lovers of the Lamb.

Lord, may they ever live to Thee,
    And grow in heavenly love;
Still may they fight the fight of faith,
    Till crowned with those above.

1544 Richard Burnham CM
Now the God of hope fill you with all joy and peace in believing, that ye may abound in hope, through the power of the Holy Ghost.
Romans 15:13

Our Jesus is the God of hope;
  He works it by His power;
It holds the weak believer up,
  In the distressing hour.

The darkest cloud hope pierces through,
  And waits upon the Lord,
Expects to prove that all is true
  Throughout the sacred word.

True hope looks out for blessings great;
  And, though they're long delayed,
Yet hope's determined still to wait,
  Until they are conveyed.

Hope long will wait, and wait again,
  And ne'er can give it up,
Till the blessed Lamb, who once was slain,
  Appears the God of hope.

1545 Horatius Bonar 10 10 10 10
God is faithful, by whom ye were called unto the fellowship of His Son Jesus Christ our Lord. *1 Corinthians 1:9*

Here O my Lord, I see Thee face to face;
  Here would I touch and handle things unseen,
Here grasp with firmer hand the eternal grace,
  And all my weariness upon Thee lean.

Here would I feed upon the bread of God,
  Here drink with Thee the royal wine of heaven;
Here would I lay aside each earthly load,
  Here taste afresh the calm of sin forgiven.

Mine is the sin, but Thine the righteousness;
  Mine is the guilt, but Thine the cleansing blood!
Here is my robe, my refuge and my peace—
  Thy blood, Thy righteousness, O Lord my God.

This is the hour of banquet and of song;
  This is the heavenly table spread for me;
Here let me feast, and, feasting, still prolong
  The brief, bright hour of fellowship with Thee.

Too soon we rise; the symbols disappear;
  The feast, though not the love, is past and gone;
The bread and wine remove, but Thou art here,
  Nearer than ever, still my Shield and Sun.

I have no help but Thine; nor do I need
  Another arm save Thine to lean upon;
It is enough, my Lord, enough indeed;
  My strength is in Thy might, Thy might alone.

Feast after feast thus comes and passes by,
Yet, passing, points to the glad feast above,
Giving sweet foretaste of the festal joy,
The Lamb's great bridal feast of bliss and love.

1546 Philip Doddridge SM
God is faithful, by whom ye were called unto the fellowship of His Son Jesus Christ our Lord. *1 Corinthians 1:9*

Our heavenly Father calls
  And Christ invites us near;
With both our friendship shall be sweet
  And our communion dear.

God pities all our griefs,
  He pardons every day,
Almightly to protect our souls
  And wise to guide our way.

How large His bounties are!
  What various stores of good,
Diffused from our Redeemer's hand
  And purchased with His blood!

Jesus our living Head,
  We bless Thy faithful care,
Our Advocate before the throne
  And our Forerunner there.

Here, fix, my roving heart,
  Here wait, my warmest love,
Till the communion be complete
  In nobler scenes above.

1547 Isaac Watts CM
For the preaching of the cross is to them that perish foolishness; but unto us which are saved it is the power of God.
1 Corinthians 1:18

Christ and His cross is all our theme;
  The mysteries that we speak
Are scandal in the Jew's esteem,
  And folly to the Greek.

But souls enlightened from above
  With joy receive the word;
They see what wisdom, power, and love
  Shine in their dying Lord.

The vital savour of His name
  Restores their fainting breath;
Believing, they rejoice in Him,
  The Antidote of death.

Till God diffuse His graces down,
  Like showers of heavenly rain,
In vain Apollos sows the ground,
  And Paul may plant in vain.

1548   Charles Wesley (alt)   88 88 88
**But we preach Christ crucified, unto the Jews
a stumblingblock, and unto the Greeks
foolishness.** *1 Corinthians 1:23*

O Love divine! what hast Thou done?
  The immortal God hath died for me!
The Father's co-eternal Son
  Bore all my sins upon the tree;
The immortal God for me hath died:
My Lord, my Love, is crucified!

Behold Him, ye that pass Him by,
  The bleeding Prince of life and peace!
Come, sinners, see your Maker die,
  And say, was ever grief like His?
Come, feel with me His blood applied:
My Lord, my Love is crucified.

Is crucified for me and you,
  To bring us rebels near to God:
Believe, believe the record true,
  The church is bought with Jesus' blood:
Pardon for sin flows from His side:
My Lord, my Love, is crucified.

Then let us sit beneath His cross.
  And gladly catch the healing stream,
All things for Him account but loss,
  And give up all our hearts to Him:
Of nothing think or speak beside:
My Lord, my Love, is crucified.

1549   Isaac Watts   CM
**But unto them which are called, both Jews and
Greeks, Christ the power of God, and the
wisdom of God.**
1 Corinthians 1:24

The Lord, descending from above,
  Invites His children near,
While power, and truth, and boundless love
  Display their glories here.

Here, in Thy gospel's wondrous frame,
  Fresh wisdom we pursue;
A thousand angels learn Thy name.
  Beyond whate'er they knew.

Thy name is writ in fairest lines;
  Thy wonders here we trace;
Wisdom through all the mystery shines,
  And shines in Jesus' face.

The law its best obedience owes
  To our incarnate God;
And Thy revenging justice shows
  Its honours in His blood.

But still the lustre of Thy grace
  Our warmer thoughts employs;
Gilds the whole scene with brighter rays,
  And more exalts our joys.

1550   Joseph Hart   CM
**But unto them which are called, both Jews and
Greeks, Christ the power of God, and the
wisdom of God.**
1 Corinthians 1:24

Believers own they are but blind;
  They know themselves unwise;
But wisdom in the Lord they find,
  Who opens all their eyes.

Unrighteous are they all, when tried:
  But God Himself declares
In Jesus they are justified;
  His righteousness is theirs.

That we're unholy needs no proof;
  We sorely feel the fall;
But Christ has holiness enough
  To sanctify us all.

Exposed by sin to God's just wrath,
  We look to Christ and view
Redemption in His blood by faith,
  And full redemption too.

Some this, some that, good virtue teach,
  To rectify the soul;
But we first after Jesus reach,
  And richly grasp the whole.

To Jesus joined, we all that's good
  From Him, our Head, derive.
We eat His flesh and drink His blood,
  And by and in Him live.

1551   Isaac Watts   CM
**For ye see your calling, brethren, how that not
many wise men after the flesh, not many
mighty, not many noble, are called.**
1 Corinthians 1:26

But few among the carnal wise,
  But few of noble race,
Obtain the favour of Thy eyes,
  Almighty King of grace!

He takes the men of meanest name
  For sons and heirs of God;
And thus He pours abundant shame
  On honourable blood.

He calls the fool and makes him know
  The mysteries of His grace,
To bring aspiring wisdom low,
  And all its pride abase,

Nature has all its glories lost,
  When brought before His throne;
No flesh shall in His presence boast,
  But in the Lord alone.

1552   William Styles   LM
**But of Him are ye in Christ Jesus, who of God
is made unto us wisdom, and righteousness,
and sanctification, and redemption.**
1 Corinthians 1:30

'Twas love divine that sanctified,
In Christ that church for which He died,
In Him her holiness was given,
Her meetness for the joys of heaven.

Jesus beheld her lost estate,
And for her bled without the gate,
There He her suffering Surety stood,
And sanctified her with His blood.

And Christ becomes our holiness,
Ruling our hearts by sovereign grace,
And we are sanctified by faith
In what our Lord and Saviour saith.

By unction from the Holy One,
We're sanctified to God alone,
The Holy Spirit dwells within,
And crucifies the love of sin.

Thrice-holy Lord, to Thee we raise
Our grateful songs of lofty praise,
Through cleansing blood and grace divine,
May we in Christ's own likeness shine.

1553   Irish c. 8th Cent, tr. M Byrne, edit. E Hull
         10 10 10 10 (dactylic) Irregular
**But of Him are ye in Christ Jesus, who of God
is made unto us wisdom, and righteousness,
and sanctification, and redemption.**
1 Corinthians 1:30

Be Thou my vision, O Lord of my heart;
Nought be all else to me, save that Thou art;
Thou my best thought, by day or by night,
Waking or sleeping, Thy presence my light.

Be Thou my wisdom, Thou my true word;
I ever with Thee, Thou with me, Lord;
Thou my great Father, I Thy true son;
Thou in me dwelling, and I with Thee one.

Be Thou my battle-shield, sword for the fight;
Be Thou my armour, be Thou my might;
Thou my soul's shelter, Thou my high tower;
Raise Thou me heavenward, O Power of my
  power.

Riches I heed not, nor man's empty praise;
Thou mine inheritance, now and always;
Thou and Thou only, first in my heart,
High King of heaven, my treasure Thou art.

High King of heaven, after victory won,
May I reach heaven's joy, O bright heaven's
  Sun!
Heart of my own heart, whatever befall,
Still be my vision, O Ruler of all.

1554   Charles Wesley   88 88 88
**And my speech and my preaching was not
with enticing words of man's wisdom, but in
demonstration of the Spirit and of power.**
1 Corinthians 2:4

I want the Spirit of power within,
  Of love, and of a healthful mind:
Of power, to conquer inbred sin;
  Of love, to Thee and all mankind;
Of health, that pain and death defies,
Most vigorous when the body dies.

When shall I hear the inward voice
  Which only faithful souls can hear?
Pardon, and peace, and heavenly joys
  Attend the promised Comforter:
O come! and righteousness divine,
And Christ, and all with Christ, are mine.

O that the Comforter would come!
  Nor visit as a transient Guest,
But fix in me His constant home,
  And take possession of my breast,
And fix in me His loved abode,
The temple of indwelling God.

Come, Holy Ghost, my heart inspire!
  Attest that I am born again;
Come, and baptize me now with fire,
  Nor let Thy former gifts be vain:
I cannot rest in sins forgiven;
Where is the earnest of my heaven?

Where the indubitable seal
  That ascertains the kingdom mine?
The powerful stamp I long to feel,
  The signature of love divine:
O shed it in my heart abroad,
Fulness of love, of heaven, of God!

1555   Thomas Kelly   LM
Which none of the princes of this world knew:
for had they known it, they would not have
crucified the Lord of glory.
1 Corinthians 2:8

The Lord of glory, moved by love,
Descends, in mercy, from above;
And He, before whom angels bow,
Is found a Man of grief below.

Such love is great, too great for thought,
Its length and breadth in vain are sought;
No tongue can tell its depth and height;
The love of Christ is infinite.

But though His love no measure knows,
The Saviour to His people shows
Enough to give them joy, when known,
Enough to make their hearts His own.

Constrained by this, they walk with Him,
His love their most delightful theme;
To glorify Him here, their aim,
Their hope, in heaven to praise His name.

1556   Isaac Watts   CM
Eye hath not seen, nor ear heard, neither have
entered into the heart of man, the things which
God hath prepared for them that love Him.
1 Corinthians 2:9

Nor eye hath seen, nor ear hath heard,
    Nor sense nor reason known,
What joys the Father has prepared
    For those who love His Son.

But the good Spirit of the Lord
    Reveals a heaven to come;
The beams of glory in His word,
    Allure and guide us home.

Pure are the joys above the sky,
    And all the region peace;
Nor wanton lips nor envious eye,
    Can see or taste the bliss.

Those holy gates for ever bar
    Pollution, sin, and shame:
None shall obtain admittance there
    But followers of the Lamb.

He keeps the Father's Book of Life;
    There all their names are found;
The hypocrite in vain shall strive
    To tread the heavenly ground.

1557   Anne Steele   CM
Eye hath not seen, nor ear heard, neither have
entered into the heart of man, the things which
God hath prepared for them that love Him.
1 Corinthians 2:9

Far from these narrow scenes of night
    Unbounded glories rise;
And realms of infinite delight,
    Unknown to mortal eyes.

Fair distant land! could mortal eyes
    But half its charms explore,
How would our spirits long to rise,
    And dwell on earth no more.

No cloud those blissful regions know,
    For ever bright and fair;
For sin, the source of mortal woe,
    Can never enter there.

Prepare us, Lord, by grace divine,
    For Thy bright courts on high:
Then bid our spirits rise, and join
    The chorus of the sky.

1558   John Kent   CM
But God hath revealed them unto us by His
Spirit: for the Spirit searcheth all things, yea,
the deep things of God.
1 Corinthians 2:10

Great God, how deep Thy counsels lie:
    Supreme in power art Thou;
All things to Thy omniscient eye,
    Are one eternal Now.

Thy thoughts of peace to Israel's race,
    From everlasting flowed;
And when Thou hid'st Thy lovely face
    Thou still art Israel's God.

In ties of blood, and nothing less,
    We view Thee as our own;
And God the eternal Spirit bless,
    Who makes the kindred known.

Long as the covenant shall endure,
    Made by the great Three-One,
Salvation is for ever sure,
    To every blood-bought son.

1559 John Newton 66 66 88
I have planted, Apollos watered; but God gave the increase. *1 Corinthians 3:6*

On what has now been sown,
    Thy blessing, Lord, bestow;
The power is Thine alone
    To make it spring and grow.
Do Thou the gracious harvest raise,
And Thou alone shalt have the praise.

1560 Richard Burnham CM
God gave the increase. *1 Corinthians 3:6*

Dear Saviour, may this church of Thine
    Flourish in all Thy ways,
Increase in love, abound in zeal,
    And grow in fervent praise.

May nothing break the bonds of love,
    Or hide Thy brighter face;
But all with growing warmth aspire,
    And pant for growth in grace.

May the dear pastor of the flock
    Be faithful and sincere;
Preach the whole counsel of the Lord,
    And firmly persevere.

O let him see the hand of love,
    Sealing the gospel word;
And feel an unction all divine
    Descending from the Lord.

May all the blessings of a God,
    In rich abundance fall;
Pastor and people all rejoice,
    And Christ be all in all.

1561 Joseph Hart 76 76 78 76
God gave the increase. *1 Corinthians 3:6*

Father, ere we hence depart,
    Send Thy good Spirit down,
To reside in every heart,
    And bless the seed that's sown;
Fountain of eternal love,
    Thou freely gavest Thy Son to die;
Send Thy Spirit from above,
    To quicken and apply.

1562 Samuel Stone 76 76 D
For other foundation can no man lay than that is laid, which is Jesus Christ.
1 Corinthians 3 :11

The church's one foundation
    Is Jesus Christ, her Lord;
She is His new creation
    By water and the word;
From heaven He came and sought her
    To be His holy bride,
With His own blood He bought her,
    And for her life He died.

Elect from every nation,
    Yet one o'er all the earth,
Her charter of salvation
    One Lord, one faith, one birth;
One holy name she blesses,
    Partakes one holy food,
And to one hope she presses
    With every grace endued.

Though with a scornful wonder
    Men see her sore oppressed,
By schisms rent asunder,
    By heresies distressed;
Yet saints their watch are keeping.
    Their cry goes up, 'How long?'
And soon the night of weeping
    Shall be the morn of song.

'Mid toil and tribulation
    And tumult of her war,
She waits the consummation
    Of peace for evermore;
Till with the vision glorious
    Her longing eyes are blest
And the great church victorious
    Shall be the church at rest.

Yet she on earth hath union
    With God the Three in One
And mystic sweet communion
    With those whose rest is won;
O happy ones and holy!
    Lord, give us grace that we,
Like them, the meek and lowly,
    On high may dwell with Thee.

1563 Charles Spurgeon SM
Know ye not that ye are the temple of God, and that the Spirit of God dwelleth in you?
1 Corinthians 3:16

The Holy Ghost is here,
    Where saints in prayer agree,
As Jesus' parting gift He's near
    Each pleading company.

Not far away is He,
To be by prayer brought nigh,
But here in present majesty,
As in His courts on high.

He dwells within our soul,
An ever welcome Guest;
He reigns with absolute control,
As Monarch in the breast.

Our bodies are His shrine,
And He the indwelling Lord;
All hail, Thou Comforter divine,
Be evermore adored.

Obedient to Thy will,
We wait to feel Thy power,
O Lord of life, our hope fulfil,
And bless this hallowed hour!

1564   Augustus Toplady   CM
**Know ye not that ye are the temple of God,
and that the Spirit of God dwelleth in you?**
1 Corinthians 3:16

O might this worthless heart of mine,
   The Saviour's temple be!
Emptied of every love but Thine,
   And shut to all but Thee!

I long to find Thy presence there,
   I long to see Thy face;
Almighty Lord, my heart prepare
   The Saviour to embrace.

1565   Isaac Watts   LM
**Therefore let no man glory in men. For all
things are yours.** *1 Corinthians 3:21*

How vast the treasure we possess!
How rich Thy bounty, King of grace!
This world is ours, and worlds to come;
Earth is our lodge, and heaven our home.

All things are ours: the gifts of God,
The purchase of a Saviour's blood;
While the good Spirit shows us how
To use and to improve them too.

If peace and plenty crown my days,
They help me, Lord, to speak Thy praise;
If bread of sorrows be my food,
Those sorrows work my lasting good.

I would not change my blest estate,
For all the world calls good or great;
And while my faith can keep her hold
I envy not the sinner's gold.

Father, I wait Thy daily will;
Thou shalt divide my portion still;
Grant me on earth what seems Thee best,
Till death and heaven reveal the rest.

1566   John Kent   77 77
**Therefore let no man glory in men. For all
things are yours.** *1 Corinthians 3:21*

Called by grace, the sinner see,
Rich, though sunk in poverty;
Rich in faith that God has given,
He's a legal heir of heaven.

All the searchless riches stored
In the person of our Lord:
Wisdom, truth, and glorious grace,
Everlasting love and peace.

All things that the cross procured
Stand eternally secured:
All are yours, ye heirs of bliss,
Cancelled sins, and righteousness.

All the promises we trace
In the records of His grace:
Richer far than mines of gold,
Half their wealth was never told.

Victory o'er the king of dread,
Strength the gloomy vale to tread;
Faith within the veil to see,
Jesus entered there for Thee.

All the bliss that seraphs know,
All the love that God can show,
All are yours, ye favoured few,
Mansions, thrones, and kingdoms too.

1567   William Gadsby   77 77
And ye are Christ's; and Christ *is* God's.
1 Corinthians 3:23

Sinners who on Jesus rest,
Must eternally be blest;
All Jehovah's love can give,
They from Jesus shall receive.

Loved of God, to Jesus given,
In the purposes of heaven;
They are bought with blood divine,
And they must in glory shine.

They are Jesus' flesh and bone,
Nor from Him shall e'er be torn;
Can a part be sent to hell,
And the whole in Zion dwell?

No! we bless the Lord on high,
Not a single joint can die;
Every member lives in Him;
He's the life of every limb.

They are Christ's by ties divine;
Here His brightest glories shine;
All creation must give place
To the subjects of His grace.

Matchless Jesus! may we be
Wholly taken up with Thee!
And, in every deep distress,
Lean upon Thy truth and grace.

1568   Joseph Hart   CM
For the kingdom of God is not in word, but in power. *1 Corinthians 4:20*

A form of words, though e'er so sound,
  Can never save a soul;
The Holy Ghost must give the wound,
  And make the wounded whole.

Though God's election is a truth,
  Small comfort there I see,
Till I am told by God's own mouth,
  That He has chosen me.

Sinners, I read, are justified,
  By faith in Jesus' blood;
But when to me that blood's applied,
  'Tis then it does me good.

To perseverance I agree;
  The thing to me is clear;
Because the Lord has promised me
  That I shall persevere.

Imputed righteousness I own
  A doctrine most divine;
For Jesus to my heart makes known
  That all His merit's mine.

That Christ is God I can avouch,
  And for His people cares,
Since I have prayed to Him as such,
  And He has heard my prayers.

That sinners black as hell, by Christ
  Are saved, I know full well;
For I His mercy have not missed,
  And I am black as hell.

Thus, Christians glorify the Lord,
  His Spirit joins with ours
In bearing witness to His word,
  With all its saving powers.

1569   John Bakewell, A Toplady   87 87 D
For even Christ our passover is sacrificed for us. *1 Corinthians 5:7*

Paschal Lamb, by God appointed,
  Loads of sin on Thee were laid;
By almighty love anointed,
  Thou hast full atonement made.
All Thy people are forgiven,
  Through the virtue of Thy blood;
Opened is the gate of heaven;
  Peace is made 'twixt man and God.

Jesus, hail! enthroned in glory,
  There for ever to abide!
All the heavenly hosts adore Thee,
  Seated at Thy Father's side.
For Thy people Thou art pleading;
  There Thou dost their place prepare;
Ever for them interceding,
  Till in glory they appear.

Riches, honour, strength, and blessing,
  Thou art worthy to receive;
Loudest praises, without ceasing,
  Meet it is for saints to give.
All the bright angelic spirits
  Bring their sweetest, noblest lays;
Help to sing the Saviour's merits;
  Help to chant the Saviour's praise.

1570   John Mason   CM
Therefore let us keep the feast.
1 Corinthians 5:8

My Lord, my love, was crucified,
  He all the pains did bear,
But in the sweetness of His rest
  He makes His servants share.

His blood was shed instead of ours,
  His soul our hell did bear;
He took our sin, gave us Himself;
  What an exchange is here!

His flesh is heavenly food indeed,
  His blood is drink divine,
His mouth most sweet my pardon seals,
  He tells me He is mine.

If now these feasts with Christ are sweet,
  And heaven on earth they prove,
O, what must full communion be
  With the whole church above!

1571   William Gadsby   CM
Therefore let us keep the feast.
1 Corinthians 5:8

Once more, like children, we are come,
    To banquet with our God;
May each one feel himself at home,
    And feast upon Thy love.

While we receive the bread and wine,
    As emblems of Thy death,
Lord, raise each soul above the sign,
    To feast on Christ by faith.

We would not come as strangers, Lord,
    Who only see the sign,
But, as the objects of Christ's love,
    Would feel we're one in Him.

Like free-born sons, we would be free
    From every legal chain;
Praise Him who brought our liberty,
    And ever with Him reign.

1572   John Kent   CM
And such were some of you: but ye are washed, but ye are sanctified, but ye are justified in the name of the Lord Jesus, and by the Spirit of our God.
1 Corinthians 6:11

Ye souls redeemed by Jesus' blood,
    Salvation's theme pursue;
Exalt the sovereign grace of God,
    For 'such were some of you!'

From head to foot defiled by sin,
    Deep in rebellion too;
This awful state mankind are in,
    'And such were some of you!'

Whilst they are sinners dead to God,
    Ye highly favoured few
Are washed from sin by Jesus' blood;
    For 'such were some of you!'

As ye are chosen from the rest,
    To grace the praise is due;
Be sovereign love for ever blest,
    For 'such were some of you!'

1573   John Burton, Jr.   87 87 (trochaic)
Ye are not your own. *1 Corinthians 6:19*

Saviour, while my heart is tender,
    I would yield that heart to Thee,
All my powers to Thee surrender,
    Thine and only Thine to be.

Take me now, Lord Jesus, take me;
    Let my contrite heart be Thine;
Thy devoted servant make me;
    Fill my soul with love divine.

Send me, Lord, where Thou wilt send me,
    Only do Thou guide my way;
May Thy grace through life attend me,
    Gladly then shall I obey.

Let me do Thy will or bear it;
    I would know no will but Thine;
Shouldst Thou take my life or spare it,
    I that life to Thee resign.

Thine I am, O Lord, for ever,
    To Thy service set apart;
Suffer me to leave Thee never;
    Seal Thine image on my heart.

1574   Joseph Swain   LM
For ye are bought with a price: therefore glorify God in your body, and in your spirit, which are God's. *1 Corinthians 6:20*

Great was the price to justice due
    When Jesus would redeem His bride;
Nothing but precious blood would do,
    And that must flow from His own side.

How glorious was the work He wrought
    While dwelling in this earthly globe,
When each good deed, and each pure thought,
    Conspired to weave our spotless robe!

Dressed in this robe, washed in this blood,
    And ransomed from the power of hell,
We now have free access to God,
    And justice likes the payment well.

Thus Jesus wrought our righteousness,
    Our guilt sustained, our sorrows bore;
Secured our everlasting peace,
    And triumphed o'er the serpent's power.

And now in heaven He lives to plead
    Before His holy Father's throne
What He has suffered in our stead,
    And sends us gifts and graces down.

And soon will this dear Saviour come,
    In majesty and glory dressed,
And take His ransomed children home
    To seats of everlasting rest.

1575   Frances Havergal   77 77
For ye are bought with a price: therefore glorify God in your body, and in your spirit, which are God's. *1 Corinthians 6:20*

Take my life and let it be
Consecrated, Lord, to Thee;
Take my moments and my days,
Let them flow in ceaseless praise.

Take my hands and let them move
At the impulse of Thy love;
Take my feet, and let them be
Swift and beautiful for Thee.

Take my voice and let me sing
Always, only, for my King;
Take my lips, and let them be
Filled with messages from Thee.

Take my silver and my gold,
Not a mite would I withhold;
Take my intellect, and use
Every power as Thou shalt choose.

Take my will and make it Thine;
It shall be no longer mine;
Take my heart, it is Thine own;
It shall be Thy royal throne.

Take my love, my Lord, I pour
At Thy feet its treasure store;
Take myself, and I will be
Ever, only, all, for Thee.

1576   Augustus Toplady   886 D
Ye are bought with a price; be not ye the servants of men. *1 Corinthians 7:23*

O Thou who didst Thy glory leave
Apostate sinners to retrieve
    From nature's deadly fall,
Me Thou hast purchased with a price.
Nor shall my crimes in judgment rise,
    For Thou hast borne them all.

Jesus was punished in my stead,
Without the gate my Surety bled
    To expiate my stain:
On earth the Godhead deigned to dwell,
And made of infinite avail
    The sufferings of the Man.

And was He for such rebels given?
He was; the Incarnate King of Heaven
    Did for His foes expire:
Amazed, O earth, the tidings hear;
He bore, that we might never bear
    His Father's righteous ire.

Ye saints, the Man of Sorrows bless,
The God for your unrighteousness
    Deputed to atone:
Praise Him, till with the heavenly throng,
Ye sing the never-ending song,
    And, see Him on His throne.

AUGUSTUS TOPLADY 1740-1778

1577   Augustus Toplady   77 77 77
That Rock was Christ. *1 Corinthians 10:4*

Rock of Ages, cleft for me;
Let me hide myself in Thee;
Let the water and the blood,
From Thy riven side which flowed,
    Be of sin the double cure,
    Cleanse me from its guilt and power.

Not the labour of my hands,
Can fulfil Thy law's demands;
Could my zeal no respite know,
Could my tears for ever flow,
    All for sin could not atone;
    Thou must save, and Thou alone.

Nothing in my hand I bring;
Simply to Thy cross I cling;
Naked, come to Thee for dress;
Helpless, look to Thee for grace;
    Foul, I to the fountain fly;
    Wash me, Saviour, or I die.

While I draw this fleeting breath,
When my eyelids close in death,
When I soar through tracts unknown,
See Thee on Thy judgment throne,
    Rock of Ages, cleft for me;
    Let me hide myself in Thee.

1578   Isaac Watts   SM
**The cup of blessing which we bless, is it not
the communion of the blood of Christ? The
bread which we break, is it not the communion
of the body of Christ?**
1 Corinthians 10:16

Jesus invites His saints
  To meet around His board;
Here pardoned rebels sit, and hold
  Communion with their Lord.

For food He gives His flesh;
  He bids us drink His blood;
Amazing favour, matchless grace
  Of our descending God!

By faith, the bread and wine
  Maintain our fainting breath,
By union with our living Lord,
  And interest in His death.

Our heavenly Father calls
  Christ and His members one;
We the young children of His love,
  And He the first-born Son.

We are but several parts
  Of the same broken bread;
One body has its several limbs,
  But Jesus is the Head.

Let all our powers be joined
  His gracious name to raise;
Pleasure and love fill every mind.
  And every voice be praise.

1579   William Gadsby   CM
**The cup of blessing which we bless, is it not
the communion of the blood of Christ? The
bread which we break, is it not the communion
of the body of Christ?**
1 Corinthians 10:16

With wondering eyes, Lord, we admire
  The feast prepared by grace;
Come, Lord, and set our souls on fire,
  And fill each heart with peace.

These emblems of Thy precious love,
  By faith may we receive!
And with a solemn pleasure prove,
  We in Thy name believe.

No goodness of our own we bring;
  We're sinners vile and base;
Christ is our all; of Christ we sing,
  And long to see His face.

O may we each, with heart and tongue
  Sing, 'Worthy is the Lamb';
To Him alone the praise belongs,
  And we'll adore His name.

1580   Charles Cole   SM
**For we being many are one bread, and one
body: for we are all partakers of that one
bread.** *1 Corinthians 10:17*

Of all the joys on earth
  Communion with the Lord
Is by the saints of heavenly birth,
  Preferred with one accord.

United as we are,
  One body and one bread,
We humbly claim an equal share
  In Christ, the living Head.

In Him we are complete,
  With Him we now commune:
His grace has made us truly great,
  And glory soon will come.

There we shall ever dwell
  In perfect love and peace,
And with transporting pleasure tell
  What full communion is.

1581   Charles Wesley   CM
**For we being many are one bread, and one
body: for we are all partakers of that one
bread.** *1 Corinthians 10:17*

How happy are Thy servants, Lord,
  Who thus remember Thee!
What tongue can tell our sweet accord,
  Our perfect harmony!

Who Thy mysterious supper share,
  Here at Thy table fed,
Many, and yet but one we are,
  One undivided bread.

One with the living bread divine,
  Which now by faith we eat;
Our hearts, and minds, and spirits join,
  And all in Jesus meet.

So dear the tie where souls agree
  In Jesus' dying love:
Then only can it closer be,
  When all are joined above.

1582 Isaac Watts CM

Whether therefore ye eat, or drink, or whatsoever ye do, do all to the glory of God.
1 Corinthians 10:31

Glory to God the Father's name,
Who, from our sinful race,
Chose out His favourites to proclaim
The honours of His grace.

Glory to God the Son be paid
Who dwelt in humble clay,
And, to redeem us from the dead,
Gave His own life away.

Glory to God the Spirit give,
From whose almighty power
Our souls their heavenly birth derive,
And bless the happy hour.

Glory to God that reigns above,
The eternal Three-in-One,
Who, by the wonders of His love,
Has made His nature known.

1583 George Herbert SM

Whether therefore ye eat, or drink, or whatsoever ye do, do all to the glory of God.
1 Corinthians 10:31

Teach me, my God and King,
In all things Thee to see;
And what I do in anything,
To do it as for Thee.

A man that looks on glass,
On it may stay his eye;
Or if he pleaseth, through it pass,
And then the heaven espy.

All may of Thee partake;
Nothing can be so mean,
Which with this tincture, 'For Thy sake,'
Will not grow bright and clean.

A servant with this clause
Makes drudgery divine;
Who sweeps a room, as for Thy laws,
Makes that and the action fine.

This is the famous stone
That turneth all to gold;
For that which God doth touch and own,
Cannot for less be told.

1584 John Cennick LM

Whether therefore ye eat, or drink, or whatsoever ye do, do all to the glory of God.
1 Corinthians 10:31

Be present at our table, Lord,
Be here and everywhere adored;
These mercies bless, and grant that we
May feast in paradise with Thee.

1585 Joseph Hart 76 76 78 76

Whether therefore ye eat, or drink, or whatsoever ye do, do all to the glory of God.
1 Corinthians 10:31

Hail, Thou Bridegroom, bruised to death,
Who hast the wine-press trod
Of the Almighty's burning wrath!
Hail, slaughtered Lamb of God;
Melt our hearts with love like Thine,
While we behold Thee on the tree,
Sweetly mourning o'er each sign,
In memory of Thee.

Hail, Thou mighty Saviour, blest
Before the world began
In the eternal Father's breast,
Hail, Son of God and man!
Thee we hymn in humble strains;
And to receive we now agree,
These blest symbols of Thy pains,
In memory of Thee.

Break, O break these hearts of stone,
By some endearing word.
Jesus, come! May every one
Behold his suffering Lord.
The Holy Ghost into us breathe;
Help us to take, from doubtings free,
These dear tokens of Thy death
In memory of Thee.

1586 James Montgomery CM

And when He had given thanks, He brake it, and said, Take, eat: this is My body, which is broken for you: this do in remembrance of Me.
1 Corinthians 11:24

According to Thy gracious word,
In meek humility,
This will I do, my dying Lord;
I will remember Thee.

Thy body, broken for my sake,
My bread from heaven shall be;
Thy cup of blessing I will take,
And thus remember Thee.

Can I Gethsemane forget?
    Or there Thy conflict see,
Thine agony and bloody sweat,
    And not remember Thee?

When to the cross I turn mine eyes
    And rest on Calvary,
O Lamb of God, my sacrifice,
    I must remember Thee.

Remember Thee, and all Thy pains,
    And all Thy love to me;
Yea, while a breath, a pulse, remains,
    Will I remember Thee.

And when these failing lips grow dumb,
    And mind and memory flee,
When Thou shalt in Thy kingdom come,
    Jesus, remember me.

1587   Horatius Bonar   777 6
And when He had given thanks.
1 Corinthians 11:24a

For the bread and for the wine,
For the pledge that seals Him mine,
For the words of love divine,
    We give our thanks, O Lord.

For the feast of love and peace,
Bidding all our sorrows cease,
Earnest of the kingdom's bliss,
    We give our thanks, O Lord.

Only bread and only wine,
Yet to faith the seal and sign
Of the heavenly and divine!
    We give our thanks, O Lord.

For the words that turn our eye
To the cross of Calvary,
Bidding us in faith draw nigh,
    We give our thanks, O Lord.

For the words that tell of home,
Pointing us beyond the tomb,
'Do ye this until I come,'
    We give our thanks, O Lord.

For that coming here foreshown,
For that day to man unknown,
For the glory and the throne,
    We give our thanks, O Lord.

1588   Samuel Stennett   CM
This do in remembrance of Me.
1 Corinthians 11:24b

Gracious Redeemer, how divine,
    How wondrous is Thy love,
The subject of th'eternal songs,
    Of blood-washed hosts above.

Join all your sacred harmony,
    Ye saints on earth below,
To praise Immanuel, from whose name
    All fragrant odours flow.

He left His crown, He left His throne,
    By His great Father's side,
He wore the thorn, He bore the cross,
    Was scourged and crucified.

Behold how every wound of His
    A precious balm distils,
Which heals the scars that sin had made,
    And cures all mortal ills.

Those wounds are mouths that preach His grace;
    The ensigns of His love;
The seals of our expected bliss
    In paradise above.

We see Thee at Thy table, Lord,
    By faith with great delight:
Oh how refined those joys will be
    When faith is turned to sight!

1589   Charles Wesley   SM
This do in remembrance of Me.
1 Corinthians 11:24b

Jesus, we thus obey
    Thy last and kindest word;
Here in Thine own appointed way
    We come to meet our Lord.

Our hearts we open wide,
    To make the Saviour room;
And lo! the Lamb, the Crucified,
    The sinner's Friend is come.

Thus we remember Thee,
    And take this bread and wine
As Thine own dying legacy,
    And our redemption's sign.

With high and heavenly bliss
    Thou dost our spirits cheer;
Thy house of banqueting is this,
    And Thou hast brought us here.

Thy presence makes the feast;
Now let our spirits feel
The glory not to be expressed,
The joy unspeakable.

Now let our souls be fed
With manna from above,
And over us Thy banner spread
Of everlasting love.

1590   Joseph Hart   77 77
**For as often as ye eat this bread, and drink
this cup, ye do shew the Lord's death till He
come.** *1 Corinthians 11:26*

Jesus once for sinners slain,
From the dead was raised again,
And in heaven is now set down
With His Father on His throne.

There He reigns a King supreme;
We shall also reign with Him;
Feeble souls, be not dismayed;
Trust in His almighty aid.

He has made an end of sin,
And His blood has washed us clean;
Fear not, He is ever near;
Now, e'en now, He's with us here.

Thus assembling, we, by faith,
Till He come, show forth His death:
Of His body bread's the sign,
And we drink His blood in wine.

Bread, thus broken, aptly shows
How His body God did bruise;
When the grape's rich blood we see,
Lord, we then remember Thee.

Saints on earth, with saints above,
Celebrate His dying love,
And let every ransomed soul
Sound His praise from pole to pole.

1591   Edward Bickersteth   77 77 77
**For as often as ye eat this bread, and drink
this cup, ye do shew the Lord's death till He
come.** *1 Corinthians 11:26*

'Till He come!' O let the words
Linger on the trembling chords!
Let the little while between
In their golden light be seen;
    Let us think how heaven and home
    Lie beyond that 'till He come!'

When the weary ones we love
Enter on their rest above,
Seems the earth so poor and vast,
All our life-joy overcast:
    Hush! be every murmur dumb,
    It is only till He come!

Clouds and conflicts round us press;
Would we have one sorrow less?
All the sharpness of the cross,
All that tells the world is loss,
    Death and darkness and the tomb,
    Only whisper, 'till He come!'

See, the feast of love is spread,
Drink the wine and break the bread;
Sweet memorials, till the Lord
Call us round His heavenly board;
    Some from earth, from glory some,
    Severed only till He come!

1592   George Rawson   888 4
**For as often as ye eat this bread, and drink
this cup, ye do shew the Lord's death till He
come.** *1 Corinthians 11:26*

By Christ redeemed, in Christ restored,
We keep the memory adored,
And show the death of our dear Lord,
    Until He come.

His body broken in our stead
Is seen in this memorial bread,
And so our feeble love is fed
    Until He come.

The drops of His dread agony,
His life-blood shed for us, we see,
The wine shall tell the mystery
    Until He come.

And thus that dark betrayal-night
With the last advent we unite,
By one blest chain of loving rite,
    Until He come.

Until the trump of God be heard,
Until the ancient graves be stirred,
And with the great commanding word
    The Lord shall come.

O blessèd hope! with this elate,
Let not our hearts be desolate,
But, strong in faith, in patience wait
    Until He come.

1593 Tobias Clausnitzer, tr. C Winkworth
78 78 88

No man can say that Jesus is the Lord, but by the Holy Ghost. *1 Corinthians 12:3*

Blessèd Jesus, at Thy word
  We are gathered all to hear Thee;
Let our minds and wills be stirred
  Now to seek and love and fear Thee;
By Thy teachings true and holy
Drawn from earth to love Thee solely.

All our knowledge, sense and sight,
  Lie in deepest darkness shrouded,
Till Thy Spirit breaks our night
  With the beams of truth unclouded;
Thou alone to God canst win us,
Thou must work all good within us.

Glorious Lord, Thyself impart,
  Light of Light, from God proceeding,
Open Thou each mind and heart,
  Help us by Thy Spirit's pleading.
Hear the cry Thy church now raises;
Lord, accept our prayers and praises.

1594 John Newton LM

And there are diversities of operations, but it is the same God which worketh all in all. *1 Corinthians 12:6*

O Thou, at whose almighty word
  The glorious light from darkness sprung,
Thy quickening influence afford,
  And clothe with power the preacher's tongue.

Though 'tis Thy truth he hopes to speak,
  He cannot give the hearing ear;
'Tis Thine the stubborn heart to break,
  And make the careless sinner fear.

As when of old, the water flowed
  Forth from the rock at Thy command;
Moses in vain had waved the rod,
  Without Thy wonder-working hand.

As when the walls of Jericho
  Down to the earth at once were cast;
It was Thy power that brought them low,
  And not the trumpets' feeble blast.

Thus, we would in the means be found,
  We thus, on Thee alone depend
To make the gospel's joyful sound
  Effectual to the promised end.

Now, while we hear Thy word of grace,
  Let self and pride before it fall;
And rocky hearts dissolve apace,
  In streams of sorrow at Thy call.

On all our youth assembled here
  The unction of Thy Spirit pour;
Nor let them lose another year,
  Lest Thou should strive and call no more.

1595 Christopher Wordsworth 777 5

Though I speak with the tongues of men and of angels, and have not charity, I am become as sounding brass, or a tinkling cymbal... *1 Corinthians 13:1*

Gracious Spirit, Holy Ghost,
Taught by Thee we covet most
Of Thy gifts at Pentecost,
  Holy, heavenly love.

Faith that mountains could remove,
Tongues of earth or heaven above,
Knowledge, all things, empty prove
  Without heavenly love.

Love is kind, and suffers long;
Love is meek, and thinks no wrong;
Love, than death itself more strong:
  Therefore give us love.

Prophecy will fade away,
Melting in the light of day;
Love will ever with us stay:
  Therefore give us love.

Faith and hope and love we see
Joining hand in hand agree;
But the greatest of the three,
  And the best, is love.

1596 Isaac Watts LM

And though I have all faith, so that I could remove mountains, and have not charity, I am nothing... *1 Corinthians 13:2*

Had I the tongues of Greeks and Jews,
And nobler speech than angels use,
If love be absent, I am found,
Like tinkling brass, an empty sound.

Were I inspired to preach and tell,
All that is done in heaven and hell;
Or could my faith the world remove,
Still I am nothing without love.

Should I distribute all my store
To feed the hungry and the poor;
Or give my body to the flame,
To win a martyr's glorious name;

If love to God, and love to men,
Be absent, all my hopes are vain;
Nor tongues, nor gifts, nor fiery zeal,
The work of love can e'er fulfil.

1597 Joseph Hart   SM
Charity never faileth. *1 Corinthians 13:8*

Of all that God bestows
  In earth or heaven above,
The best gift saint or angel knows,
  Or e'er will know, is love.

Love all defects supplies,
  Makes great obstructions small;
'Tis prayer, 'tis praise, 'tis sacrifice,
  'Tis holiness, 'tis all!

Descend celestial Dove,
  With Jesu's flock abide;
Give us that best of blessings:love,
  Whate'er we want beside.

1598 Isaac Watts   CM
**For now we see through a glass, darkly; but
then face to face: now I know in part; but then
shall I know even as also I am known.**
1 Corinthians 13:12

I love the windows of Thy grace,
  Through which my Lord is seen,
And long to meet my Saviour's face,
  Without a glass between.

O that the happy hour were come,
  To change my faith to sight!
I shall behold my Lord at home,
  In a diviner light.

Haste, my Belovèd, and remove
  These interposing days;
Then shall my passions all be love,
  And all my powers be praise.

1599 Isaac Watts   CM
**And now abideth faith, hope, charity, these
three; but the greatest of these is charity.**
1 Corinthians 13:13

Happy the heart where graces reign,
  Where love inspires the breast:
Love is the brightest of the train,
  And strengthens all the rest.

Knowledge, alas! 'tis all in vain,
  And all in vain our fear!
Our stubborn sins would fight and reign
  If love were absent there.

'Tis love that makes our cheerful feet
  In swift obedience move:
The devils know, and tremble too,
  But Satan cannot love.

This is the grace that lives and sings
  When faith and hope shall cease:
'Tis this shall strike our joyful strings
  In the bright realms of bliss.

Before we quite forsake our clay,
  Or leave this dark abode,
The wings of love bear us away
  To see our smiling God.

1600 Charles Wesley   76 76 77 76
**I will sing with the spirit, and I will sing with
the understanding also.**
1 Corinthians 14:15

Meet and right it is to sing!
  In every time and place,
Glory to our heavenly King,
  The God of truth and grace.
Join we then with sweet accord,
  All in one thanksgiving join
Holy, holy, holy Lord,
  Eternal praise be Thine.

Father, God, Thy love we praise,
  Which gave Thy Son to die;
Jesus, full of truth and grace,
  Alike we glorify:
Spirit, Comforter divine,
  Praise by all to Thee be given,
Till we in full chorus join,
  And earth is turned to heaven.

1601 Isaac Watts   CM
**For I delivered unto you first of all that which I
also received, how that Christ died for our sins
according to the scriptures.** *1 Corinthians 15:3*

Alas! and did my Saviour bleed?
  And did my Sovereign die?
Would He devote that sacred head
  For such a worm as I?

Was it for sins that I had done
  He groaned upon the tree?
Amazing pity! grace unknown!
  And love beyond degree!

Well might the sun in darkness hide,
  And shut His glories in,
When Christ, the mighty Maker, died
  For man the creature's sin.

Thus might I hide my blushing face,
  While His dear cross appears,
Dissolve my heart in thankfulness,
  And melt mine eyes to tears.

But drops of grief can ne'er repay
  The debt of love I owe:
Here, Lord, I give myself away:
  'Tis all that I can do.

1602 Wilbur Chapman

11 10 11 10 + refrain

Christ died for our sins according to the scriptures... *1 Corinthians 15:3,4*

One day when heaven was filled with His praises,
  One day when sin was as black as could be,
Jesus came forth to be born of a virgin—
  Dwelt amongst men, my example is He!

  Living, He loved me; dying, He saved me;
    Buried, He carried my sins far away!
  Rising, He justified freely for ever;
    One day He's coming — O glorious day!

One day they led Him up Calvary's mountain,
  One day they nailed Him to die on the tree;
Suffering anguish, despised and rejected;
  Bearing our sins, my Redeemer is He!

One day they left Him alone in the garden,
  One day He rested, from suffering free;
Angels came down o'er His tomb to keep vigil;
  Hope of the hopeless, my Saviour is He!

One day the grave could conceal Him no longer,
  One day the stone rolled away from the door;
He had arisen, o'er death He had conquered;
  Now is ascended, my Lord evermore!

One day the trumpet will sound for His coming,
  One day the skies with His glory will shine;
Wonderful day, His belovèd ones bringing;
  Glorious Saviour, this Jesus is mine!

1603 Joseph Radford LM

But by the grace of God I am what I am: and His grace which was bestowed upon me was not in vain. *1 Corinthians 15:10*

In vain, self-righteous sinners try
Themselves by works to justify;
But if I lisp a song of praise,
Each note shall echo, 'grace, free grace!'

'Twas grace that quickened me when dead,
'Twas grace my soul to Jesus led;
Grace brings a sense of pardoned sin,
And grace completes the work within.

Grace reconciles to every loss,
And sweetens every painful cross;
Defends my soul when danger's near;
By grace alone I persevere.

When from this world I soar above
To mansions of delight and love,
I'll cast my crown before His throne,
And shout, 'free grace, free grace alone!'

1604 William Bathurst CM

For He must reign, till He hath put all enemies under His feet.
1 Corinthians 15:25

'Tis past—that agonizing hour
  Of torture and of shame;
And Jesus is gone up with power,
  His promised throne to claim.

The Father heard Him when He cried
  From sorrow's deepest flood;
And gave Him those for whom He died,
  The purchase of His blood.

The first fruits have been gathered in,
  The work of love begun;
But brighter years shall soon begin
  Their glorious course to run.

The name of Jesus shall be known
  To earth's remotest bound;
Nations shall bow before His throne,
  And hail the joyful sound.

His summons shall awake the dead,
  And break the captive's chain,
Till o'er a ransomed world shall spread
  Christ's universal reign.

1605 Joseph Swain SM

So also is the resurrection of the dead. It is sown in corruption; it is raised in incorruption.
1 Corinthians 15:42

O what a wedding day
  Will that bright morning bring!
Our spirits married to this clay,
  And both to Zion's King!

  Praise for our bodies raised,
    And with our souls made one;
  Praise for our twofold nature, placed
    On Christ's immortal throne.

  Praise for the conquest won
    From sin, from death, and hell,
  By Him that sits upon the throne,
    Who has done all things well.

Praise for the conquest gained
By faith in Jesus' blood,
The grace which has our spirits trained
For fellowship with God.

Praise for the prospect sure
Of endless joy and peace,
And light, and life, and love as pure,
As God the Fountain is.

1606   Rowland Hill   88 88 88
**The trumpet shall sound, and the dead shall
be raised incorruptible, and we shall be
changed.** *1 Corinthians 15:52*

We sing His love who once was slain,
Who soon o'er death revived again,
That all His saints through Him might have
Eternal conquests o'er the grave.

*Soon shall the trumpet sound, and we
Shall rise to immortality.*

The saints who now in Jesus sleep,
His own almighty power shall keep,
Till dawns the bright illustrious day,
When death itself shall die away.

How loud shall our glad voices sing,
When Christ His risen saints shall bring
From beds of dust, and silent clay,
To realms of everlasting day!

When Jesus we in glory meet,
Our utmost joys shall be complete:
When landed on that heavenly shore.
Death and the curse will be no more!

Hasten, dear Lord, the glorious day,
And this delightful scene display:
When all Thy saints from death shall rise,
Raptured in bliss beyond the skies.

1607   From the Latin c. 12th cent., tr. F Pott
                                              888 4
Death is swallowed up in victory.
1 Corinthians 15:54

The strife is o'er, the battle done;
The victory of life is won;
The song of triumph has begun:
    Hallelujah!

The powers of death have done their worst,
But Christ their legions hath dispersed;
Let shouts of holy joy outburst:
    Hallelujah!

The three sad days have quickly sped:
He rises glorious from the dead;
All glory to our risen Head:
    Hallelujah!

He broke the bonds of death and hell;
The bars from heaven's high portals fell;
Let hymns of praise His triumph tell:
    Hallelujah!

Lord, by the stripes which wounded Thee,
From death's dread sting Thy servants free,
That we may live, and sing to Thee:
    Hallelujah!

1608   Christian Gellert, tr. J D Lang 78 78 77
**O death, where is thy sting? O grave, where is
thy victory?** *1 Corinthians 15:55*

Jesus lives and so shall I.
    Death! thy sting is gone for ever!
He who deigned for me to die,
    Lives, the bands of death to sever.
He shall raise me from the dust:
Jesus is my hope and trust.

Jesus lives and reigns supreme;
    And, His kingdom still remaining,
I shall also be with Him,
    Ever living, ever reigning.
God has promised: be it must:
Jesus is my hope and trust.

Jesus lives and by His grace,
    Victory o'er passions giving.
I will cleanse my heart and ways,
    Ever to His glory living.
Me He raises from the dust:
Jesus is my hope and trust.

Jesus lives! I know full well
    Nought from Him my heart can sever,
Life nor death nor powers of hell,
    Joy nor grief, henceforth for ever.
None of all His saints is lost:
Jesus is my hope and trust.

Jesus lives and death is now
    But my entrance into glory.
Courage, then, my soul, for thou
    Hast a crown of life before thee;
Thou shalt find thy hopes were just:
Jesus is the Christian's trust.

1609   Vernon Higham   66 84 D
O death, where is thy sting? O grave, where is thy victory?
1 Corinthians 15:55

See Christ the Victor raised
In resurrection life,
The mighty arm of God displayed,
    Who ends the strife.
He is the Lord of all,
Whose arm is shortened not;
See devils' flight, and Satan's fall,
    And hell their lot.

What miracle of grace
To mortal life's brief span,
So marred by sin and hell's disgrace,
    A glorious plan!
The Father on me looked,
And saw my great distress;
He wove a gown, He only could,
    Immortal dress

The sting of death is sin,
The power of law declares;
But Jesus Christ the Son doth win —
    Our guilt He bears.
Behold, ye sinners, now,
And look to Christ alone;
Behold the blood upon His brow —
    He did atone.

Be steadfast in life's race,
Abounding in His way,
For all we do is by His grace,
    For we would stray.
He took mortality
With sin's corrupting blight,
And nailed it all to Calvary's tree,
    To give us light.

Immortal is my dress,
Corruption fled away;
Now robed in Him, yes, nothing less,
    In bright array.
O death, where is thy sting?
O grave, thy victory?
The living Christ on mercy's wing
    Grants peace to me.

© Author

1610   Venantius Fortunatus, tr. A Nelson
    87 87 87
O death, where is thy sting? O grave, where is thy victory? *1 Corinthians 15:55*

Praise the Saviour, now and ever,
    Praise Him, all beneath the skies;
Prostrate lying, suffering, dying,
    On the cross a sacrifice;
Victory gaining, life obtaining,
    Now in glory He doth rise.

Man's work faileth, Christ availeth,
    He is all our righteousness;
He, our Saviour, has for ever
    Set us free from dire distress.
Through His merit we inherit
    Life and peace and happiness.

Sin's bonds severed, we're delivered;
    Christ has bruised the serpent's head.
Death no longer is the stronger;
    Hell itself is captive led.
Christ has risen from death's prison;
    O'er the tomb He light has shed.

For His favour, praise for ever
    Unto God the Father sing.
Praise the Saviour, praise Him ever,
    Son of God, our Lord and King.
Praise the Spirit; through Christ's merit
    He doth our salvation bring.

1611   Edmond Budry, tr. Richard Hoyle
    10 11 11 11 + refrain
But thanks be to God, which giveth us the victory through our Lord Jesus Christ.
1 Corinthians 15:57

Thine be the glory, risen, conquering Son,
Endless is the victory Thou o'er death hast won;
Angels in bright raiment rolled the stone away,
Kept the folded grave-clothes where Thy body lay.

Thine be the glory, risen, conquering Son,
Endless is the victory Thou o'er death hast won!

Lo, Jesus meets us, risen from the tomb!
Lovingly He greets us, scatters fear and gloom;
Let the church with gladness hymns of triumph
    sing,
For her Lord now liveth, death hath lost its sting.

No more we doubt Thee, glorious Prince of life;
Life is nought without Thee: aid us in our strife;
Make us more than conquerors, through Thy
    deathless love:
Bring us safe through Jordan to Thy home above.

1612   Samuel Stennett   LM
Upon the first day of the week let every one of you lay by him in store, as God hath prospered him, that there be no gatherings when I come.
1 Corinthians 16:2

Another six days' work is done,
Another Sabbath is begun;
Return, my soul, enjoy thy rest,
Improve the day thy God hath blest.

Come, bless the Lord, whose love assigns
So sweet a rest to wearied minds;
Provides an antepast of heaven,
And gives this day the food of seven.

O that our thoughts and thanks may rise
As grateful incense to the skies;
And draw from heaven that sweet repose
Which none but he that feels it knows.

This heavenly calm within the breast,
Is the dear pledge of glorious rest,
Which for the church of God remains,
The end of cares, the end of pains.

In holy duties let the day
In holy pleasures pass away;
How sweet a Sabbath thus to spend
In hope of one that ne'er shall end!

1613   Frank Houghton   LM
**For a great door and effectual is opened unto
me, and there are many adversaries.**
1 Corinthians 16:9

Father, we come before Thy throne,
    Ready to hearken and obey
The clear commands of Christ alone,
    Thy Son, the Life, the Truth, the Way.

Where doors are open, give us grace
    To enter with the Spirit's sword,
There to proclaim in every place
    The saving name of Christ the Lord.

Should doors be barred, in simple trust,
    Alert we wait the trumpet call,
And follow Christ because we must:
    His mighty love constrains us all.

So in the challenge of this hour
    Thy servants worship and adore!
Thine is the kingdom, Thine the power
    And Thine the glory evermore!

© *Overseas Missionary Fellowship*

1614   George Duffield   76 76 D
**Watch ye, stand fast in the faith, quit you like
men, be strong.**
1 Corinthians 16:13

Stand up, stand up for Jesus,
    Ye soldiers of the cross!
Lift high His royal banner,
    It must not suffer loss.
From victory unto victory
    His army shall He lead,
Till every foe is vanquished
    And Christ is Lord indeed

.

Stand up, stand up for Jesus!
    The trumpet call obey;
Forth to the mighty conflict
    In this His glorious day.
Ye that are men, now serve Him
    Against unnumbered foes;
Let courage rise with danger
    And strength to strength oppose.

Stand up, stand up for Jesus!
    Stand in His strength alone;
The arm of flesh will fail you
    Ye dare not trust your own.
Put on the gospel armour,
    Each piece put on with prayer;
Where duty calls, or danger,
    Be never wanting there!

Stand up, stand up for Jesus!
    The strife will not be long;
This day the noise of battle,
    The next the victor's song.
To him that overcometh
    A crown of life shall be;
He with the King of glory
    Shall reign eternally.

1615   Isaac Watts   LM
**Blessed be God, even the Father of our Lord
Jesus Christ, the Father of mercies, and the
God of all comfort.**
2 Corinthians 1:3

To God the Father, God the Son,
And God the Spirit, Three in One,
Be honour, praise and glory given,
By all on earth, and all in heaven.

1616   Daniel Herbert   CM
Ye also helping together by prayer for us.
2 Corinthians 1:11

Lord, fill Thy servant's soul today
    With pure seraphic fire,
And set his tongue at liberty,
    And grant his soul's desire.

O may he preach the word of God
    With energy and power;
May gospel-blessings spread around,
    Like a refreshing shower.

May God's eternal love and grace
    Be sweetly felt within;
While he is preaching Christ the Lord,
    Who bore our curse and sin.

May burdened sinners lose their load,
  And downcast souls rejoice;
May doubting souls believe today
  They are Jehovah's choice.

May Christ be first, and Christ be last,
  And Christ be all in all,
Who died to make salvation sure,
  And raise us from the fall.

O may Thy servant now today
  Proclaim salvation free,
As finished by the Son of God,
  For such poor souls as we.

1617   Robert Hawker   886 D + refrain
**For all the promises of God in Him are yea,
and in Him Amen, unto the glory of God by us.**
2 Corinthians 1:20

We bless Thee, O! Thou great Amen,
Jehovah's pledge to sinful men,
  Confirming all His word;
No promises are doubtful then,
For all are Yea and all Amen,
  In Jesus Christ our Lord.

  *Secured in this, the church on high,
  And all below, unceasing cry
    'Amen! Amen! Amen!'
  To Thee, O Lord! all praise is given,
  The loud response of earth and heaven,
    'All hail, Thou great Amen!'*

Sweet ordinance of God to bless,
By Him, the Lord our Righteousness,
  By Him, I say again:
This mighty Him makes all things sure,
Through life, in death, and evermore,
  In Him, the great Amen.

O faithful witness of our God,
Who came by water and by blood,
  Proving the Holy One!
Thy record must for ever stand,
Of life eternal from God's hand,
  And all in Thee, His Son.

Sweetly Thy verilys we hear,
For God's Amen dispels all fear,
  Thy faithfulness it proves:
And while such grace from God is shown,
To God's Amen we add our own,
  Our 'so be it' God loves.

Ye saints of God, in age or youth,
Who swear by Him, the God of truth,
  By Him, I say again:
Make Him whom God hath made to you,
Your Alpha and Omega too—
  God's Christ is your Amen.

Nor less above, ye heavenly host,
To Father, Son, and Holy Ghost
  Give praise, through Him, with men:
For of Him, through Him, by Him, sure,
The church shall glory evermore,
  In Him, the great Amen.

1618   Joseph Hoskins   77 77
**Not for that we have dominion over your faith,
but are helpers of your joy: for by faith ye
stand.** *2 Corinthians 1:24*

Strangers, pilgrims, here below,
  Travelling to fair Canaan's land,
Lean on Jesus as you go,
  For by faith alone ye stand.

Keep the cross of Christ in view;
  'Tis an object truly grand;
This will bear you safely through,
  For by faith alone ye stand.

Glory in the Saviour's name,
  Join with all the ransomed band,
Trust the Lord, He's still the same,
  For by faith alone ye stand.

Trust the Lord in life and death,
  Trust your all in Jesus' hand;
Trust Him with your latest breath,
  For by faith alone ye stand.

Then will faith be turned to sight;
  With the Lord you'll ever be,
And in infinite delight,
  Spend a vast eternity.

1619   John Newton   888
**Now thanks be unto God, which always
causeth us to triumph in Christ, and maketh
manifest the savour of His knowledge by us in
every place.**
2 Corinthians 2:14

Why should I fear the darkest hour,
Or tremble at the tempter's power?
Jesus vouchsafes to be my Tower.

Though hot the fight, why quit the field?
Why must I either flee or yield
Since Jesus is my mighty Shield?

When creature comforts fade and die,
Worldlings may weep, but why should I?
Jesus still lives and still is nigh.

Though all the flocks and herds were dead,
My soul a famine need not dread,
For Jesus is my living Bread.

I know not what may soon betide,
Or how my wants shall be supplied;
But Jesus knows and will provide.

Though sin would fill me with distress,
The throne of grace I dare address,
For Jesus is my Righteousness.

Though faint my prayers and cold my love,
My steadfast hope shall not remove
While Jesus intercedes above.

Against me earth and hell combine;
But on my side is power divine;
Jesus is all and He is mine.

1620 John Berridge 886 886
**Not that we are sufficient of ourselves to think
any thing as of ourselves; but our sufficiency
is of God.** *2 Corinthians 3:5*

O Lord, with shame I do confess
My universal emptiness,
    My poverty and pride;
I cannot keep Thee in my sight,
Nor can I think one thought aright,
    Unless Thy Spirit guide.

I cannot from my idols part,
Nor love the Lord with all my heart,
    Nor can myself deny;
I cannot pray, and feel Thee near,
Nor can I sing with heavenly cheer,
    Unless the Lord be nigh.

Since Adam from God's image fell,
On spiritual things we cannot dwell;
    The heart is turned aside;
And none can raise to life the dead
But He who raised Himself indeed,
    And for dead sinners died.

Then let this mighty Jesus be
An all-sufficient help for me,
    Creating power and will;
Thy grace sufficèd saints of old;
It made them strong and made them bold,
    And it suffices still.

1621 John Kent CM
The letter killeth, but the spirit giveth life.
2 Corinthians 3:6

Behold how Adam's helpless race
    Are striving, though in vain;
Who think by works, and not by grace,
    Salvation to obtain!

Though dead in sin, they struggle hard,
    And seek to enter in
The gate, that flaming cherubs guard,
    For ever shut by sin.

But when the killing law takes place,
    It makes their efforts null;
Salvation then appears of grace,
    Abundant, free, and full.

Now from the precept to the cross,
    His eyes the sinner turns;
His brightest deeds he counts as dross,
    And o'er his vileness mourns.

God, on the table of his heart,
    Inscribes His love and fear;
He loves the law in every part,
    But takes no refuge there.

Give us, O God, Thy grace to see
    The only Fountain Thou;
Then shall we own salvation free,
    And at Thy footstool bow.

1622 Isaac Watts LM
**For God, who commanded the light to shine
out of darkness, hath shined in our hearts, to
give the light of the knowledge of the glory of
God in the face of Jesus Christ.**
2 Corinthians 4:6

Now to the Lord a noble song!
Awake, my soul; awake, my tongue!
Hosanna to the eternal name,
And all His boundless love proclaim!

See where it shines in Jesus' face,
The brightest image of His grace!
God, in the person of His Son,
Has all His mightiest works outdone.

The spacious earth and spreading flood
Proclaim the wise, the powerful God;
And Thy rich glories from afar
Sparkle in every rolling star.

But in His looks a glory stands,
The noblest labour of Thy hands;
The pleasing lustre of His eyes
Outshines the wonders of the skies.

Grace! 'tis a sweet, a charming theme!
My thoughts rejoice at Jesus' name!
Ye angels, dwell upon the sound!
Ye heavens, reflect it to the ground!

O may I live to reach the place
Where He unveils His lovely face,
There all His beauties to behold,
And sing His name to harps of gold!

1623   William Tucker   LM
**For God, who commanded the light to shine
out of darkness, hath shined in our hearts, to
give the light of the knowledge of the glory of
God in the face of Jesus Christ.**
2 Corinthians 4:6

Amidst ten thousand anxious cares,
The world and Satan's deep-laid snares,
This my incessant cry shall be,
'Jesus, reveal Thyself to me.'

When Sinai's awful thunder rolled,
And struck with terror all my soul,
No gleam of comfort could I see,
Till Jesus was revealed to me.

When by temptations sore oppressed,
Distressful anguish fills my breast!
All, all is grief and misery,
Till Jesus is revealed to me.

When various lusts imperious rise,
And my unguarded soul surprise;
I'm captive led, nor can get free,
Till Christ reveals Himself to me.

When darkness, thick as beamless night,
Hides the loved Saviour from my sight,
Nothing but this my ardent plea,
'Jesus, reveal Thyself to me.'

'Tis He dispels the dismal gloom;
Gives light and gladness in its room;
Then have I joy and liberty
As Christ reveals Himself to me.

1624   Samuel Medley   CM
**Persecuted, but not forsaken; cast down, but
not destroyed.** *2 Corinthians 4:9*

Now, in Thy praise, eternal King,
   Be all Thy saints employed;
Whilst of this precious truth they sing
   'Cast down, but not destroyed.'

Oft the united powers of hell
   Our souls have sore annoyed;
And yet we live this truth to tell,
   'Cast down, but not destroyed.'

In all the paths and trials past
   Much mercy we've enjoyed;
And this shall be our song at last
   'Cast down, but not destroyed.'

1625   Joseph Hart   LM
**For which cause we faint not; but though our
outward man perish, yet the inward man is
renewed day by day.**
2 Corinthians 4:16

When pining sickness wastes the frame,
   Acute disease, or tiring pain;
When life fast spends her feeble flame,
   And all the help of man proves vain;

Then, then to have recourse to God,
   To pour a prayer in time of need,
And feel the balm of Jesus' blood,
   This is to find a Friend indeed.

And this, O Christian, is thy lot,
   Who cleavest to the Lord by faith;
He'll never leave thee (doubt it not)
   In pain, in sickness, or in death.

Himself shall be thy helping Friend,
   Thy good Physician and thy nurse;
To make thy bed shall condescend,
   And from the affliction take the curse.

Shouldst thou a moment's absence mourn;
   Should some short darkness intervene;
He'll give thee power, till light return,
   To trust Him, with the cloud between.

1626   William Hurn   CM
**For our light affliction, which is but for a
moment, worketh for us a far more exceeding
and eternal weight of glory.**
2 Corinthians 4:17

There's an exceeding weight of bliss,
   Eternal, unexplored;
'Tis glory—O my soul, rejoice
   At that transporting word.

Glory! What thought can rise so high?
   What tongue can that explain?
A kingdom 'tis for us prepared,
   Where all the saints shall reign.

There they enjoy eternal rest,
  Secure from grief and fear;
And glory's bright unfading crown
  They shall for ever wear.

Though cruel foes shall vex us now,
  And persecutions flame,
O! these are nothing, when compared
  To glory near the Lamb.

No foes can separate our souls
  From Christ our living Head;
Our sufferings here are light and short,
  And they to glory lead.

When He, the righteous Judge, shall come,
  Triumphant in the skies,
Our bodies, now in vileness sown,
  Shall in His glory rise.

1627   Isaac Watts   CM
We have a building of God, an house not made with hands, eternal in the heavens.
2 Corinthians 5:1

There is a house not made with hands,
  Eternal and on high,
And here my spirit waiting stands
  Till God shall bid it fly.

Shortly this prison of my clay
  Must be dissolved and fall:
Then, O my soul! with joy obey
  Thy heavenly Father's call.

'Tis He, by His almighty grace,
  That forms Thee fit for heaven,
And, as an earnest of the place,
  Has His own Spirit given.

We walk by faith of joys to come,
  Faith lives upon His word:
But while the body is our home,
  We're absent from the Lord.

'Tis pleasant to believe Thy grace,
  But we had rather see;
We would be absent from the flesh,
  And present, Lord with Thee.

1628   Vernon Higham   SM
We have a building of God, an house not made with hands, eternal in the heavens.
2 Corinthians 5:1

  The God of grace and love,
    Who holds me to His breast:
My present peace, my home above
    In His protection rest.

But for a moment brief
  Sorrows surround my days;
Yet with a glorious glad belief
  I see my hope and stay.

Exceeding is the weight
  Of glory for the saint;
Surpassing thought, celestial sight
  For those who will not faint.

I have a mansion fair,
  A home not made by hand,
A place prepared with holy care,
  Designed by His command.

Whilst in this body worn,
  My spirit groans for Thee;
Yet in my heart a hope is born —
  Immortal I shall be.

Then shall I praise His name,
  Sweet melody of grace;
Fashioned anew, in glorious frame,
  I shall behold His face.

© Author

1629   Anne Steele   LM
For we that are in this tabernacle do groan, being burdened: not for that we would be unclothed, but clothed upon, that mortality might be swallowed up of life. *2 Corinthians 5:4*

Sad prisoners in a house of clay,
  With sins, and griefs, and pains oppressed,
We groan the lingering hours away,
  And wish and long to be released.

Nor is it liberty alone,
  Which prompts our restless, ardent sighs;
For immortality we groan,
  For robes and mansions in the skies.

Eternal mansions! bright array!
  O blest exchange! transporting thought!
Free from the approaches of decay,
  Or the least shadow of a spot.

Bright world of bliss, O could I see
  One shining glimpse, one cheerful ray,
(Fair dawn of immortality)
  Break through these tottering walls of clay.

Jesus, in Thy dear name I trust,
  My life, my light, my Saviour, God;
When this frail house dissolves in dust,
  O raise me to Thy bright abode.

1630 John Newton CM
That mortality might be swallowed up of life.
2 Corinthians 5:4

In vain my fancy tries to paint
   The moment after death,
The glories that surround the saints
   When yielding up their breath.

One gentle sigh each fetter breaks,
   We scarce can say, 'They're gone,'
Before the willing spirit takes
   Her mansion near the throne.

Faith strives, but all its efforts fail,
   To trace her in her flight:
No eye can pierce within the veil
   Which hides that world of light.

Thus much (and this is all) we know:
   They are completely blest,
Have done with sin, and care, and woe,
   And with their Saviour rest.

1631 John Gurney 88 88 88
For we walk by faith, not by sight.
2 Corinthians 5:7

We saw Thee not when Thou didst come
   To this poor world of sin and death;
Nor e'er beheld Thy cottage home,
   In that despisèd Nazareth;
But we believe Thy footsteps trod
Its streets and plains, Thou Son of God.

We saw Thee not upon the wave,
   When Thou the stormy sea didst bind,
Nor marked the health Thy blessing gave
   To lame and sick, to deaf and blind;
But we believe the fount of light
Could give the darkened eyeball sight.

We were not with the faithful few
   Who stood Thy bitter cross around,
Nor heard Thy prayer for them that slew,
   Nor felt the earthquake rock the ground;
We saw no spear-wound pierce Thy side;
But we believe that Thou hast died.

We stood not by the empty tomb,
   Where late Thy sacred body lay;
Nor sat within that upper room,
   Nor met Thee in the open way;
But we believe that angels said,
'Why seek the living with the dead?'

We did not mark the chosen few,
   When Thou didst through the clouds ascend,
First lift to heaven their wondering view,
   Then to the earth all prostrate bend;
Yet we believe that mortal eyes
Beheld Thee rising to the skies.

And now that Thou dost reign on high,
   And thence Thy waiting people bless,
No ray of glory from the sky
   Doth shine upon our wilderness;
But we believe that Thou art there,
And seek Thee, Lord, in praise and prayer.

1632 Isaac Watts LM
**We are confident, I say, and willing rather to
be absent from the body, and to be present
with the Lord.** *2 Corinthians 5:8*

Absent from flesh! O blissful thought!
   What unknown joys that moment brings!
Freed from the mischiefs sin has wrought,
   From pains, and fears, and all their springs.

Absent from flesh! illustrious day!
   Surprising scene! triumphant stroke,
That rends the prison of my clay,
   And I can feel my fetters broke.

Absent from flesh! then rise, my soul,
   Where feet, nor wings, could ever climb,
Beyond the heavens, where planets roll,
   Measuring the cares and joys of time.

I go where God and glory shine,
   His presence makes eternal day:
All that is mortal I resign,
   For angels wait and point my way.

1633 William Gadsby 87 87 47
For the love of Christ constraineth us.
2 Corinthians 5:14

High beyond imagination
   Is the love of God to man;
Far too deep for human reason;
   Fathom that it never can;
     Love eternal
   Richly dwells in Christ the Lamb.

Love like Jesus' none can measure,
   Nor can its dimensions know;
'Tis a boundless, endless river,
   And its waters freely flow.
     O ye thirsty,
   Come and taste its streams below.

Jesus loved, and loves for ever;
  Zion on His heart does dwell;
He will never, never, never
    Leave His church a prey to hell.
      All is settled,
  And my soul approves it well.

1634   Charles Wesley (altered)   SM
For the love of Christ constraineth us.
2 Corinthians 5:14

When shall Thy love constrain
  This heart Thy own to be?
When shall the wounded spirit gain
  A healing rest in Thee?

Ah! what avails my strife,
  My wandering to and fro?
Thou hast the words of endless life;
  Lord, whither shall I go?

My worthless heart to gain,
  The God who gave me breath
Was found in fashion as a man,
  And died a cursèd death!

Then may I sin forsake,
  The world for Thee resign;
Gracious Redeemer, take, O take,
  And seal me ever Thine!

JOHN WESLEY 1703-1791

1635   Paulus Gerhardt, tr. John Wesley
                         88 88 88
For the love of Christ constraineth us.
2 Corinthians 5:14

Jesus, Thy boundless love to me
  No thought can reach, no tongue declare;
O knit my thankful heart to Thee
  And reign without a rival there;
Thine, wholly Thine, alone I'd live;
Myself to Thee entirely give.

O grant that nothing in my soul
  May dwell, but Thy pure love alone;
O may Thy love possess me whole,
  My joy, my treasure and my crown;
All coldness from my heart remove;
My every act, word, thought, be love.

O Love, how cheering is Thy ray!
  All pain before Thy presence flies;
Care, anguish, sorrow, melt away,
  Where'er Thy healing beams arise;
O Jesus, nothing may I see,
Nothing desire or seek but Thee.

Unwearied may I this pursue,
  Dauntless to the prize aspire;
Hourly within my soul renew
  This holy flame, this heavenly fire;
And day and night be all my care
To guard the sacred treasure there.

In suffering be Thy love my peace,
  In weakness be Thine arm my strength;
And when the storms of life shall cease
  And Thou from heaven shalt come at length,
Lord Jesus, then this heart shall be
For ever satisfied with Thee.

1636   Charles Wesley   88 88 88
For the love of Christ constraineth us.
2 Corinthians 5:14

Give me the faith which can remove
  And sink the mountain to a plain;
Give me the childlike praying love
  Which longs to build Thy house again;
Thy love, let it my heart o'erpower
And fill me from this very hour.

I would the precious time redeem
  And longer live for this alone,
To spend and to be spent for them
  Who have not yet my Saviour known;
Fully on these my mission prove
And only breathe to breathe Thy love.

My talents, gifts and graces, Lord,
  Into Thy blessèd hands receive,
And let me live to preach Thy word,
  And let me to Thy glory live;
My every sacred moment spend
In publishing the sinners' Friend.

Enlarge, inflame and fill my heart
  With boundless charity divine;
So shall I all my strength exert
  And love them with a zeal like Thine;
And lead them to Thy open side,
The sheep for whom their Shepherd died.

1637   Vernon Higham   **CM**
Therefore if any man be in Christ, he is a new creature: old things are passed away; behold, all things are become new.
2 Corinthians 5:17

What is this stirring in my breast
   That draws me, Lord, to Thee,
To seek the things I did detest,
   And long Thy face to see?

It must have been Thy hand alone
   That caused my heart to mourn,
And showed me One who did atone
   And all my sins has borne.

Amazing is Thy gentle way:
   Although inflicting pain,
It is Thy hand that does allay,
   To take away my stain.

O Holy Ghost, this is Thy sphere,
   To help my soul abide,
Rich wounds to show and thrust of spear
   In His dear, blessèd side.

My heart is full: I thank Thee now
   For all that Thou hast done;
With mercy rich, Thou didst endow;
   My soul with grace has won.

O satisfy, my soul delight,
   In holy pastures pure,
To learn of Thee, to walk aright,
   And to the end endure.

Thy holy unction to the meek,
   Bestowed at Pentecost,
I long to know, that I may speak
   To win for Thee the lost.

© Author

1638   Samuel Stennett   **DSM**
Therefore if any man be in Christ, he is a new creature: old things are passed away; behold, all things are become new.
2 Corinthians 5:17

How various and how new
   Are Thy compassions, Lord!
Each morning shall Thy mercies show,
   Each night Thy truth record.
   Thy goodness, like the sun,
   Dawned on our early days,
Ere infant reason had begun
   To form our lips to praise.

Each object we beheld
   Gave pleasure to our eyes;
And nature all our senses held
   In bands of sweet surprise;
   But pleasures more refined
   Awaited that blest day,
When light arose upon our mind,
   And chased our sins away.

How new Thy mercies, then!
   How sovereign, and how free!
Our souls that had been dead in sin,
   Were made alive to Thee.
   Now we expect a day
   Still brighter far than this,
When death shall bear our souls away
   To realms of light and bliss.

There rapturous scenes of joy
   Shall burst upon our sight;
And every pain, and tear, and sigh,
   Be drowned in endless light.
   Beneath Thy balmy wing,
   O Sun of Righteousness,
Our happy souls shall sit and sing
   The wonders of Thy grace.

Nor shall that radiant day,
   So joyfully begun,
In evening shadows die away,
   Beneath the setting sun.
   How various and how new
   Are Thy compassions, Lord!
Eternity Thy love shall show,
   And all Thy truth record

1639   Charles Wesley   **76 76 77 76**
God was in Christ, reconciling the world unto Himself. *2 Corinthians 5:19*

God of unexampled grace,
   O Saviour of mankind,
Matter of eternal praise
   We in Thy passion find:
Still our choicest strains we bring,
   Still the joyful theme pursue,
Thee the Friend of sinners sing,
   Whose love is ever new.

Endless scenes of wonder rise
   From that mysterious tree,
Crucified before our eyes,
   Where we our Maker see:
Jesus, Lord, what hast Thou done?
   Publish we the death divine,
Stop, and gaze, and fall, and own
   Was never love like Thine!

Never love nor sorrow was
　Like that my Saviour showed:
See Him stretched on yonder cross,
　And crushed beneath our load!
Now discern the Deity,
　Now His heavenly birth declare!
Faith cries out: "Tis He, 'tis He,
　My God, that suffers there!"

1640　William Gadsby　SM
For He hath made Him to be sin for us, who knew no sin; that we might be made the righteousness of God in Him.
2 Corinthians 5:21

The Lord my Saviour is;
　For me He shed His blood;
And shall I scorn His name to own?
　Forbid it, mighty God.

With me upon His heart,
　He stooped to bleed and die;
And when my guilt was to Him charged,
　The charge did not deny.

The debt, though great, He paid,
　That I might be set free;
No charge against me can be brought,
　For Jesus died for me.

'Midst all His vast concerns,
　He could not me forget;
Then let my heart, my soul, my tongue,
　His dying love repeat.

1641　William Gadsby　LM
He hath made Him to be sin for us.
2 Corinthians 5:21

Behold a scene of matchless grace,
'Tis Jesus in the sinner's place;
Heaven's brightest Glory sunk in shame,
That rebels might adore His name.

Tremendous clouds of wrath and dread,
In vengeance burst upon His head;
Ten thousand horrors seize His soul,
And vengeful mountains on Him roll.

He sighed; He groaned; He sweat; He cried;
Through awful floods He passed and died;
All penal wrath to Zion due,
Infinite justice on Him threw.

He rose in triumph from the dead;
Justice declared the debt was paid;
Then Christ with kingly grandeur flew,
And took His throne in glory too.

Come, saints, with solemn pleasure trace
The boundless treasures of His grace;
He bore almighty wrath for you,
That you might all His glory view.

1642　Joseph Humphreys　CM
Now is the day of salvation.
2 Corinthians 6:2

Come guilty souls, and flee away
　To Christ, and heal your wounds;
This is the welcome gospel-day
　Wherein free grace abounds.

God loved the church, and gave His Son
　To drink the cup of wrath;
And Jesus says He'll cast out none
　That come to Him by faith.

1643　Thomas Kelly　77 77
Be ye separate, saith the Lord.
2 Corinthians 6:17

Lord, behold us in Thy grace,
　Humbly at Thy feet we fall,
See, we come to seek Thy face:
　Deign, O deign to hear our call!

When we lay in sin and death,
　Thou didst pass and bid us live,
Thou didst give Thy people faith,
　Thou didst all our sins forgive.

Jesus, Thou didst shed Thy blood:
　On this rock our hope we raise;
Thou hast brought us near to God:
　Thine the work, and Thine the praise.

'Tis Thy will that we should be
　Separate from all around,
Let our will with Thine agree,
　Let Thy people thus be found.

Let us bear each other's load,
　Faithful to each other prove;
Till we gain the saints' abode,
　Till we take our place above—

There to see without a cloud—
　There with zeal untired to sing;
Mix with heaven's triumphant crowd,
　And for ever praise our King.

1644   Ann Gilbert   LM
A Father unto you. *2 Corinthians 6:18*

Great God! and wilt Thou condescend
To be my Father and my Friend?
I, a poor child, and Thou so high,
The Lord of earth and air and sky.

Art Thou my Father? Canst Thou bear
To hear my poor imperfect prayer?
Or wilt Thou listen to the praise
That such a little one can raise?

Art Thou my Father? Let me be
A meek obedient child to Thee,
And try, in word and deed and thought,
To serve and please Thee as I ought.

Art Thou my Father? I'll depend
Upon the care of such a Friend,
And only wish to do and be
Whatever seemeth good to Thee.

Art Thou my Father? Then at last,
When all my days on earth are past,
Send down and take me in Thy love
To be Thy better child above.

1645   Joseph Hart   CM
For godly sorrow worketh repentance.
2 Corinthians 7:10

Repentance is a gift bestowed
   To save a soul from death;
Gospel repentance towards God
   Is always joined to faith.

Not for an hour, or day, or week,
   Do saints repentance own;
But all the time the Lord they seek,
   At sin they grieve and groan.

Nor is it such a dismal thing
   As 'tis by some men named;
A sinner may repent and sing,
   Rejoice and be ashamed.

'Tis not the fear of hell alone,
   For that may prove extreme;
Repenting saints the Saviour own,
   And grieve for grieving Him.

If penitence be quite left out,
   Religion is but halt;
And hope, though e'er so clear of doubt,
   Like offerings without salt.

1646   John Fawcett   CM
**For behold this selfsame thing, that ye
sorrowed after a godly sort, what carefulness
it wrought in you.**
2 Corinthians 7:11a

O may my heart by grace renewed,
   Be my Redeemer's throne:
And be my stubborn will subdued,
   His government to own!

Let deep repentance, faith, and love,
   Be joined with godly fear;
And all my conversation prove
   My heart to be sincere.

Preserve me from the snares of sin
   Through my remaining days;
And in me let each virtue shine
   To my Redeemer's praise.

Let lively hope my soul inspire;
   Let warm affections rise;
And may I wait with strong desire,
   To mount above the skies.

1647   John Newton   CM
Yea, what zeal. *2 Corinthians 7:11b*

Zeal is that pure and heavenly flame,
   The fire of love supplies;
While that which often bears the name,
   Is self in a disguise.

True zeal is merciful and mild,
   Can pity and forbear;
The false is headstrong, fierce and wild,
   And breathes revenge and war.

While zeal for truth the Christian warms,
   He knows the worth of peace;
But self contends for names and forms,
   Its party to increase.

Zeal has attained its highest aim,
   Its end is satisfied;
If sinners love the Saviour's name,
   Nor seeks it ought beside.

But self, however well employed,
   Has its own ends in view;
And says, as boasting Jehu cried,
   'Come, see what I can do.'

Self may its poor reward obtain,
   And be applauded here;
But zeal the best applause will gain,
   When Jesus shall appear.

Dear Lord, the idol self dethrone,
    And from our hearts remove;
And let no zeal by us be shown,
    But that which springs from love.

1648   Baptist Noel   LM
And this they did, not as we hoped, but first
gave their own selves to the Lord, and unto us
by the will of God.
2 Corinthians 8:5

Glory to God, whose Spirit draws
Fresh soldiers to the Saviour's cause,
Who thus, baptized into His name,
His goodness and their faith proclaim.

For these now added to the host,
Who in their Lord and Saviour boast,
And consecrate to Him their days,
Accept, O God, our grateful praise.

Thus may Thy mighty Spirit draw
All here to love and keep His law;
Themselves His subjects to declare
And place themselves beneath His care.

Lead them at once their Lord to own,
To glory in His cross alone;
And then, baptized, His truth to teach,
His love to share, His heaven to reach.

1649   Fanny Crosby   87 87 D
For ye know the grace of our Lord Jesus
Christ., that, though He was rich, yet for your
sakes he became poor, that ye through his
poverty might be rich. *2 Corinthians 8:9*

Tell me the story of Jesus,
    Write on my heart every word;
Tell me the story most precious,
    Sweetest that ever was heard;
Tell how the angels in chorus
    Sang, as they welcomed His birth,
'Glory to God in the highest,
    Peace and good tidings to earth!'

Tell me the story of Jesus,
    Write on my heart every word;
Tell me the story most precious,
    Sweetest that ever was heard;

Fasting alone in the desert,
    Tell of the days that He passed;
How He was tried and was tempted,
    Yet was triumphant at last:
Tell of the years of His labour,
    Tell of the sorrows He bore;
He was despised and rejected,
    Homeless, afflicted and poor.

Tell of the cross where they nailed Him;
    Tell of His anguish and pain;
Tell of the grave where they laid Him,
    Tell how He liveth again:
Love, in that story so tender,
    Clearer than ever I see:
Glory for ever to Jesus!
    He paid the ransom for me.

1650   Norman Perry   76 76 D
For ye know the grace of our Lord Jesus
Christ., that, though He was rich, yet for your
sakes he became poor, that ye through his
poverty might be rich. *2 Corinthians 8:9*

O tender heart of Jesus,
    So warm, so true and pure;
Only Thy sweet compassion
    Can wandering hearts allure;
As o'er the ancient city,
    As by the solemn tomb;
Thy tears revealed Thy pity,
    God's heartbeats in the gloom.

O lovely hands of Jesus,
    Unsoiled by evil deed,
Dispensing nought but blessings
    To satisfy all need.
The darkened eyes were opened,
    The sick ones felt Thy touch;
Thou art the good Physician
    Because Thou lovest much.

O blessèd feet of Jesus,
    That trod no sinful way;
Come near as in past ages,
    We need Thee day by day;
As walking on the waters,
    Lord of the raging wave;
Or journeying out to Sychar,
    Poor wearied ones to save.

O wondrous love of Jesus,
    How precious is the thought
That on the cross so bitter,
    Thy blood our pardon bought;
O lead us to the fountain
    And cleanse us in the blood
That from Thy heart, Lord Jesus,
    Streamed forth a healing flood.

© Mrs R Westmacott

1651   Frank Houghton   98 98 98

He was rich, yet for your sakes He became poor. *2 Corinthians 8:9*

Thou who wast rich beyond all splendour,
   All for love's sake becamest poor;
Thrones for a manger didst surrender,
   Sapphire-paved courts for stable floor.
Thou who wast rich beyond all splendour,
   All for love's sake becamest poor.

Thou who art God beyond all praising,
   All for love's sake becamest Man;
Stooping so low, but sinners raising
   Heavenwards by Thine eternal plan.
Thou who art God beyond all praising,
   All for love's sake becamest Man.

Thou who art love beyond all telling,
   Saviour and King, we worship Thee.
Immanuel, within us dwelling,
   Make us what Thou wouldst have us be.
Thou who art love, beyond all telling,
   Saviour and King, we worship Thee.

© Overseas Missionary Fellowship

1652   Tr.from Martin Luther   LM

He became poor. *2 Corinthians 8:9*

All praise to Thee, eternal Lord,
Clothed in a garb of flesh and blood;
Choosing a manger for Thy throne,
While worlds on worlds are Thine alone.

Once did the skies before Thee bow;
A virgin's arms contain Thee now;
Angels who did in Thee rejoice
Now listen for Thine infant voice.

A little Child, Thou art our Guest,
That weary ones in Thee may rest;
Forlorn and lowly is Thy birth,
That we may rise to heaven from earth.

Thou comest in the darksome night
To make us children of the light,
To make us, in the realms divine,
Like Thine own angels round Thee shine.

All this for us Thy love hath done;
By this to Thee our love is won:
For this we tune our cheerful lays,
And shout our thanks in ceaseless praise.

1653   John Kent   LM

The exceeding grace of God in you. *2 Corinthians 9:14*

Great source of all the eternal grace,
That saints shall know or angels trace
Thee we'll attempt in songs to praise
For acts of grace in ancient days.

Long ere the day that Adam fell,
The covenant stood in all things well;
Grace had secured in Jesus then
Millions untold of chosen men.

By grace their crimes were all removed,
When Jesus bled for those He loved:
That awful, black, tremendous score
Sunk in the deep to rise no more.

'Twas all of grace, from first to last,
The deed was done, the pardon passed.
Secure in Christ were all its heirs,
The curse was His, and pardon theirs.

Great God of grace, forgive the lays
That fall so far beneath Thy praise:
By grace we hope to sing ere long
Eternal love in sweeter song.

1654   Benjamin Beddome   LM

Thanks be unto God for His unspeakable gift. *2 Corinthians 9:15*

Jesus, my Lord, my chief delight,
   For Thee I long, for Thee I pray,
Amid the shadows of the night,
   Amid the business of the day.

When shall I see Thy smiling face,
   That face which often I have seen?
Arise, Thou Sun of Righteousness,
   Scatter the clouds that intervene.

Thou art the glorious gift of God
   To sinners weary and distressed;
The first of all His gifts bestowed,
   And certain pledge of all the rest.

Could I but say this gift is mine,
   The world should lie beneath my feet;
Though poor, no more would I repine,
   Or look with envy on the great.

The precious jewel I would keep,
   And lodge it deep within my heart;
At home, abroad, awake, asleep,
   It never should from thence depart!

1655   Isaac Watts   LM
**My grace is sufficient for thee: for My strength
is made perfect in weakness.**
2 Corinthians 12:9

Let me but hear my Saviour say,
'Strength shall be equal to thy day';
Then I rejoice in deep distress,
Leaning on all-sufficient grace.

I glory in infirmity,
That Christ's own power may rest on me;
When I am weak, then am I strong;
Grace is my shield, and Christ my song.

I can do all things, or can bear
All sufferings, if my Lord be there;
Sweet pleasures mingle with the pains
While His left hand my head sustains.

But if the Lord be once withdrawn,
And we attempt the work alone,
When new temptations spring and rise,
We find how great our weakness is.

1656   Vernon Higham   DCM
**My grace is sufficient for thee: for My strength
is made perfect in weakness.**
2 Corinthians 12:9

Thy tender grace I've sought so long,
   Thy gentle touch to feel;
To know within my heart a song
   Thy mercy will reveal.
O gaze upon my aching soul,
   And hasten to restore;
O tell me Thou canst make me whole,
   Cause me to love Thee more.

What are the hindrances in me
   That turn my gaze away,
And make my soul to flee from Thee
   Who art my hope and stay?
Thy Spirit showed me depths within
   Of deep rebellious ways,
And taught me more about my sin
   By His exposing rays.

O rouse my soul to call on Thee
   On whom my sin was laid;
Remind my heart of Calvary
   Where my great debt was paid.
How could I ever Thee forget,
   Or roam from Thy dear side?
Forgive me, Lord, for my neglect;
   In Thee let me abide.

At last my soul in Thee hath found
   All, all sufficient grace,
And I shall be in mercy bound,
   And dwell in Thine embrace.
I'll seek Thee more, and find Thee still
   All Thou hast claimed to be;
O grant that now, unhindered, will
   Thy grace fill even me.

© Author

1657   John Needham   CM
**My grace is sufficient for thee: for My strength
is made perfect in weakness.**
2 Corinthians 12:9

Kind are the words that Jesus speaks
   To cheer the struggling saint;
'My grace sufficient is for you,
   Though nature's powers may faint.

'My grace its glories shall display,
   And make your griefs remove;
Your weakness shall the triumphs tell
   Of boundless power and love.'

What though my griefs are not removed,
   Yet why should I despair?
While Jesus' gracious arms support,
   I can the burden bear.

Jesus, my Saviour and my Lord,
   'Tis good to trust Thy name;
Thy power, Thy faithfulness and love
   Will ever be the same.

Weak as I am, yet through Thy grace
   I all things can perform;
And, smiling, triumph in Thy name
   Amid the raging storm.

1658   Samuel Medley (alt)   LM
Though I be nothing. *2 Corinthians 12:11*

Jehovah's awesome name revere,
In humble praise, with holy fear;
In glory throned, divinely bright,
All worlds are nothing in His sight.

The numerous proud, self-righteous host,
Who fondly of their something boast,
Will find their something nothing more
Than what will prove them blind and poor.

O may my soul such folly shun,
Nor ever boast what I have done;
But at God's footstool humbly fall,
And Jesus be my All in all.

Though of myself I nothing am,
I'm dear to God and to the Lamb;
Though I have nothing, I confess,
All things in Jesus I possess.

I can do nothing, Lord, 'tis true,
Yet in Thy strength can all things do;
Nothing I merit, Lord, I own,
Yet shall possess a heavenly throne.

Thus something, Saviour, may I be,
Nothing in self, but all in Thee;
And when in glory I appear,
Be something, and yet nothing, there.

1659 Horatius Bonar LM
And I will very gladly spend and be spent for you; though the more abundantly I love you, the less I be loved.
2 Corinthians 12:15

Go, labour on; spend and be spent,
  Thy joy to do the Father's will;
It is the way the Master went;
  Should not the servant tread it still?

Go, labour on; 'tis not for nought;
  Thy earthly loss is heavenly gain;
Men heed thee, love thee, praise thee not;
  The Master praises—what are men?

Go, labour on; your hands are weak,
  Your knees are faint, your soul cast down;
Yet falter not; the prize you seek
  Is near—a kingdom and a crown.

Go, labour on while it is day:
  The world's dark night is hastening on:
Speed, speed Thy work, cast sloth away;
  It is not thus that souls are won.

Toil on, faint not, keep watch and pray;
  Be wise the erring soul to win;
Go forth into the world's highway,
  Compel the wanderer to come in.

Toil on and in thy toil rejoice;
  For toil comes rest, for exile home;
Soon shalt thou hear the Bridegroom's voice,
  The midnight cry, 'Behold, I come!'

1660 John Newton 87 87
The grace of the Lord Jesus Christ, and the love of God, and the communion of the Holy Ghost, be with you all.
2 Corinthians 13:14

May the grace of Christ, our Saviour,
  And the Father's boundless love,
With the Holy Spirit's favour,
  Rest upon us from above.

Thus may we abide in union
  With each other and the Lord;
And possess, in sweet communion,
  Joys which earth cannot afford.

1661 John Monsell 87 87
Who gave Himself for our sins, that He might deliver us from this present evil world, according to the will of God and our Father.
Galatians 1:4

Mercy, mercy, God the Father!
  God the Son, be Thou my plea!
God the Holy Spirit, comfort!
  Triune God, deliver me!

Not my sins, O Lord, remember,
  Not Thine own avenger be;
But, for Thy great tender mercies,
  Saviour God, deliver me!

By Thy cross, and by Thy passion,
  Bloody sweat and agony,
By Thy precious death and burial,
Saviour God, deliver me!

By Thy glorious resurrection,
  Thine ascent in heaven to be,
By Thy Holy Spirit's coming,
  Saviour God, deliver me!

In all time of tribulation,
  In all time of wealth, in the
Hour of death, and day of judgement,
  Saviour God, deliver me!

1662 William Gadsby 10 10 11 11
For I through the law am dead to the law, that I might live unto God. *Galatians 2:19*

Thanks be to my Head, the great King of kings,
My life from the dead, the death of my sins;
Who took all my woes, and was made sin for me;
Who died, and who rose, and from sin set me
    free.

His Spirit He sent, to soften my heart;
The old veil to rend, and life to impart;
To bring me from darkness to light in the Lord,
And kill me to Moses, to sin, and the world.

Thus I, through the law, dead to the law am,
Yet married am I to Jesus the Lamb!
This union is sealèd, all heaven's agreed;
From sin and from Moses I henceforth am freed.

My soul, then, rejoice; let Christ be thy song;
With heart and with voice, with lip and with
    tongue,
Before men or angels, sing, 'Worthy's the Lamb
Of unceasing praises, for ever. Amen.'

1663   John Newton   LM
I am crucified with Christ. *Galatians 2:20*

When on the cross my Lord I see
Bleeding to death, for wretched me;
Satan and sin no more can move,
For I am all transformed to love.

His thorns, and nails, pierce through my heart,
In every groan I bear a part;
I view His wounds with streaming eyes,
But see! He bows His head and dies!

Come, sinners, view the Lamb of God,
Wounded and dead, and bathed in blood;
Behold His side, and venture near,
The well of endless life is here.

Here I forget my cares and pains;
I drink, yet still my thirst remains;
Only the Fountain-head above,
Can satisfy the thirst of love.

O, that I thus could always feel!
Lord, more and more Thy love reveal!
Then my glad tongue shall loud proclaim
The grace and glory of Thy name.

His name dispels my guilt and fear,
Revives my heart, and charms my ear,
Affords a balm for every wound,
And Satan trembles at the sound.

1664   Augustus Toplady   CM
I live; yet not I, but Christ liveth in me.
Galatians 2:20

Supreme High Priest, the pilgrim's light,
  My heart for Thee prepare,
Thine image stamp, and deeply write
  Thy superscription there.

Ah! let my forehead bear Thy seal,
  My arm Thy badge retain,
My heart the inward witness feel
  That I am born again.

Ah! give me, Lord, the single eye
  Which aims at nought but Thee;
I fain would live, and yet not I:
  Let Jesus live in me.

1665   Michael Saward   66 11 D
**I am crucified with Christ: nevertheless I live;
yet not I, but Christ liveth in me: and the life
which I now live in the flesh I live by the faith
of the Son of God, who loved me, and gave
Himself for me.** *Galatians 2:20*

    Lord of the cross of shame,
    Set my cold heart aflame
With love for You, my Saviour and my Master;
    Who on that lonely day
    Bore all my sins away,
And saved me from the judgment and disaster.

    Lord of the empty tomb,
    Born of a virgin's womb,
Triumphant over death, its power defeated;
    How gladly now I sing
    Your praise, my risen King,
And worship You, in heaven's splendour seated.

    Lord of my life today,
    Teach me to live and pray
As one who knows the joy of sins forgiven;
    So may I ever be,
    Now and eternally,
United with the citizens of heaven.

*Words: M. Saward © Mrs E. R. Hudson /
The Jubilate Group. www.jubilate.co.uk
USED BY PERMISSION*

1666   John Newton   CM
**The life which I now live in the flesh I live by
the faith of the Son of God, who loved me, and
gave Himself for me.**
Galatians 2:20

Sight, hearing, feeling, taste, and smell,
  Are gifts we highly prize;
But faith doth singly each excel,
  And all the five comprise.

More piercing than the eagle's sight,
  Faith views the worlds unknown,
Surveys the glorious realms of light,
  And Jesus on the throne.

It hears the mighty voice of God,
   And ponders what He saith;
His word and works, His gifts and rod,
   Have each a voice to faith.

It feels the touch of heavenly power,
   And from that boundless source,
Derives fresh vigour every hour,
   To run its daily course.

The truth and goodness of the Lord
   Are suited to its taste;
Mean is the worldling's festive hoard
   To faith's perpetual feast.

It smells the dear Redeemer's name
   Like ointment pourèd forth,
Faith only knows, or can proclaim,
   Its savour or its worth.

Till saving faith possess the mind,
   In vain of sense we boast;
We are but senseless, tasteless, blind
   And deaf, and dead, and lost.

1667   Horatius Bonar   LM
The Son of God, who loved me.
Galatians 2:20

The Son of God, in mighty love,
   Came down to Bethlehem for me,
Forsook His throne of light above,
   An infant upon earth to be.

In love, the Father's sinless Child
   Sojourned at Nazareth for me;
With sinners dwelt the Undefiled,
   The Holy One in Galilee.

Jesus, whom angel-hosts adore,
   Became a Man of griefs for me:
In love, though rich, becoming poor,
   That I, through Him, enriched might be.

Though Lord of all, above, below,
   He went to Olivet for me;
He drank my cup of wrath and woe,
   And bled in dark Gethsemane.

The ever-blessèd Son of God
   Went up to Calvary for me;
There paid my debt, there bore my load
   In His own body on the tree.

Jesus, whose dwelling is the skies,
   Went down into the grave for me;
There overcame my enemies,
   There won the glorious victory.

'Tis finished all: the veil is rent,
   The welcome sure, the access free;
Now then, we leave our banishment,
   O Father, to return to Thee!

1668   Fergus Ferguson   10 10 10 10
**The Son of God, who loved me, and gave
himself for me.** *Galatians 2:20*

He lovèd me, and gave Himself for me;
   Amazing love, amazing sacrifice!
I'll take my harp down from the willow tree,
   And bid its note in praise of Jesus rise.

He lovèd me, and gave Himself for me;
   And surely I myself to Him will give;
None, Jesus, will I ever love like Thee,
   And to Thy glory only will I live.

O when I stand 'mid yonder shining throng,
   And on fair Canaan's coast my Saviour see,
I'll add this chorus to the swelling song,
   'He lovèd me, and gave Himself for me.'

1669   Francis Rawley   87 87 D
**The Son of God, who loved me, and gave
himself for me.** *Galatians 2:20*

I will sing the wondrous story
   Of the Christ who died for me;
How He left the realms of glory
   For the cross on Calvary.
Yes, I'll sing the wondrous story
   Of the Christ who died for me;
Sing it with His saints in glory,
   Gathered by the crystal sea.

I was lost, but Jesus found me,
   Found the sheep that went astray,
Raised me up and gently led me
   Back into the narrow way.
Days of darkness still may meet me,
   Sorrow's paths I oft may tread;
But His presence still is with me,
   By His guiding hand I'm led.

He will keep me till the river
   Rolls its waters at my feet;
Then He'll bear me safely over,
   Made by grace for glory meet.
Yes, I'll sing the wondrous story
   Of the Christ who died for me;
Sing it with His saints in glory,
   Gathered by the crystal sea.

1670   Cecil Alexander   CM
The Son of God, who loved me, and gave himself for me. *Galatians 2:20*

There is a green hill far away,
  Outside a city wall,
Where the dear Lord was crucified,
  Who died to save us all.

We may not know, we cannot tell,
  What pains He had to bear;
But we believe it was for us
  He hung and suffered there.

He died that we might be forgiven,
  He died to make us good,
That we might go at last to heaven,
  Saved by His precious blood.

There was no other good enough
  To pay the price of sin;
He only could unlock the gate
  Of heaven, and let us in.

O dearly, dearly has He loved!
  And we must love Him too,
And trust in His redeeming blood
  And try His works to do.

1671   Charles Wesley   CM
The Son of God, who loved me, and gave himself for me. *Galatians 2:20*

For ever here my rest shall be,
  Close to Thy bleeding side;
This all my hope and all my plea,
  For me the Saviour died.

My dying Saviour and my God,
  Fountain for guilt and sin,
Sprinkle me ever with Thy blood,
  And cleanse and keep me clean.

Wash me and make me thus Thine own,
  Wash me and mine Thou art,
Wash me but not my feet alone,
  My hands, my head, my heart.

The atonement of Thy blood apply,
  Till faith to sight improve,
Till hope in full fruition die
  And all my soul be love.

1672   Anne Cousin   86 86 86
Christ hath redeemed us from the curse of the law, being made a curse for us.
Galatians 3:13

O Christ, what burdens bowed Thy head!
  Our load was laid on Thee;
Thou stoodest in the sinner's stead,
  Didst bear all ill for me.
A victim led, Thy blood was shed!
  Now there's no load for me.

Death and the curse were in our cup:
  O Christ, 'twas full for Thee!
But Thou hast drained the last dark drop,
  'Tis empty now for me:
That bitter cup, love drank it up,
  Now blessing's draught for me.

Jehovah lifted up His rod:
  O Christ, it fell on Thee!
Thou wast sore stricken of Thy God;
  There's not one stroke for me.
Thy tears, Thy blood, beneath it flowed;
  Thy bruising healeth me.

Jehovah bade His sword awake:
  O Christ, it woke 'gainst Thee;
Thy blood the flaming blade must slake,
  Thy heart its sheath must be.
All for my sake, my peace to make:
  Now sleeps that sword for me.

For me, Lord Jesus, Thou hast died,
  And I have died in Thee:
Thou'rt risen, my bands are all untied,
  And now Thou livest in me;
When purified, made white, and tried,
  Thy glory then for me.

1673   William Williams   SM
Christ hath redeemed us from the curse of the law, being made a curse for us.
Galatians 3:13

  Awake, my soul, and rise
  Amazed, and yonder see
How hangs the mighty Saviour God
  Upon a cursèd tree!

  How gloriously fulfilled
  Is that most ancient plan,
Contrived in the eternal mind
  Before the world began.

  Here depths of wisdom shine,
  Which angels cannot trace;
The highest rank of cherubim
  Still lost in wonder gaze.

Here free salvation reigns,
And carries all before;
And this shall for the guilty race
Be refuge evermore.

Now hell in all her strength,
Her rage, and boasted sway,
Can never snatch a wandering sheep
From Jesus' arms away.

1674   Paulus Gerhardt, tr. J Wesley   LM
Christ hath redeemed us from the curse of the law, being made a curse for us.
Galatians 3:13

Extended on a cursèd tree,
Besmeared with dust, and sweat, and blood,
See there, the King of glory see!
Sinks and expires the Son of God.

Who, who, my Saviour, this hath done?
Who could Thy sacred body wound?
No guilt Thy spotless heart hath known,
No guile hath in Thy lips been found.

I, I alone, have done the deed!
'Tis I Thy sacred flesh have torn;
My sins have caused Thee, Lord, to bleed,
Pointed the nail, and fixed the thorn.

The burden, for me to sustain
Too great, on Thee, my Lord, was laid;
To heal me, Thou hast borne my pain;
To bless me, Thou a curse wast made.

My Saviour, how shall I proclaim?
How pay the mighty debt I owe?
Let all I have and all I am,
Ceaseless to all Thy glory show.

Too much to Thee I cannot give;
Too much I cannot do for Thee;
Let all Thy love, and all Thy grief,
Graven on my heart for ever be!

The meek, the still, the lowly mind,
O may I learn from Thee, my God,
And love, with softest pity joined,
For those that trample on Thy blood!

Still let Thy tears, Thy groans, Thy sighs,
O'erflow my eyes, and heave my breast,
Till loose from flesh and earth I rise,
And ever in Thy bosom rest.

1675   Charles Wesley, T Davis   77 77
Ye are all one in Christ Jesus.
Galatians 3:28

Lord, we all look up to Thee,
As one flock, one family:
May all strife between us cease,
As we love Thee, Prince of Peace.

Make us of one heart and mind,
Gentle, meek, forgiving, kind,
Lowly both in thought and word,
Like Thyself, belovèd Lord.

Let us for each other care;
Each the other's burden bear:
Each to each by love endear;
One in faith, and hope, and fear.

Free from all that hearts divide,
Let us thus in Thee abide;
All the depths of love express,
All the heights of holiness.

1676   John Kent   SM
Ye are all one in Christ Jesus.
Galatians 3:28

In union with the Lamb,
From condemnation free,
The saints from everlasting were;
And shall for ever be.

In covenant from of old,
The sons of God they were;
The feeblest lamb in Jesus' fold
Was blessed in Jesus there.

Its bonds shall never break,
Though earth's old columns bow;
The strong, the tempted, and the weak.
Are one in Jesus now.

When storms or tempests rise,
Or sins your peace assail,
Your hope in Jesus never dies;
'Tis cast within the veil.

Here let the weary rest,
Who love the Saviour's name;
Though with no sweet enjoyments blessed,
This covenant stands the same.

1677 John Stevens   11 11 11 11
To redeem them that were under the law, that we might receive the adoption of sons.
Galatians 4:5

Great Father of glory, how rich is Thy grace!
What wonderful love is displayed in Thy face!
In Jesus Thy image with brightness we view,
And hope to be formed to that likeness anew.

By favour adopted, Thy sons we appear,
And led by Thy Spirit, we boldly draw near;
In Jesus belovèd, and washed in His blood,
With hope we adore at the footstool of God.

The man who is blessed with hope in the cross,
Is freed from the bondage of guilt and the curse;
The blood of his Surety by faith he reviews,
While hope in that fountain his spirit renews.

The world knows us not; but in this we rejoice,
To God we're no strangers, but objects of choice.
His love from eternity gave us a home,
Where now we are hoping in safety to come.

Arrayed in obedience, all wrought by the Lamb,
By Christ our Jehovah, the ancient I AM;
With boldness we journey, while Christ leads us on,
And hope soon in glory to praise the Three-One.

1678 From the Latin, tr. J Neale   88 88 88
To redeem them that were under the law, that we might receive the adoption of sons.
Galatians 4:5

O come, O come, Immanuel,
And ransom captive Israel,
That mourns in lonely exile here
Until the Son of God appear.

Rejoice! rejoice! Immanuel
Shall come to thee, O Israel.

O come, O come, Thou Lord of might,
Who to Thy tribes on Sinai's height
In ancient times didst give the law
In cloud and majesty and awe.

O come, Thou Rod of Jesse, free
Thine own from Satan's tyranny;
From depths of hell Thy people save,
And give them victory o'er the grave.

O come, Thou Dayspring, come and cheer
Our spirits by Thine advent here;
Disperse the gloomy clouds of night,
And death's dark shadows put to flight.

O come, Thou Key of David, come
And open wide our heavenly home;
Make safe the way that leads on high,
And close the path to misery.

1679 Samuel Stennett   LM
To redeem them that were under the law, that we might receive the adoption of sons.
Galatians 4:5

Not all the nobles of the earth,
Who boast the honours of their birth,
Such real dignity can claim
As those who bear the Christian name.

To them the privilege is given
To be the sons and heirs of heaven,
The sons of God who reigns on high,
And heirs of joy beyond the sky.

On them, a happy chosen race,
Their Father pours His richest grace,
To them His counsels He imparts,
And stamps His image on their hearts.

When, through temptation, they rebel,
His chastening rod He makes them feel;
Then, with a Father's tender heart,
He soothes the pain and heals the smart.

Their daily wants His hands supply,
Their steps He guards with watchful eye,
Leads them from earth to heaven above,
And crowns them with eternal love.

1680 Johann Lavater, tr. E Smith   CM
My little children, of whom I travail in birth again until Christ be formed in you.
Galatians 4:19

O Jesus Christ, grow Thou in me
    And all things else recede:
My heart be daily nearer Thee,
    From sin be daily freed.

Each day let Thy supporting might
    My weakness still embrace;
My darkness vanish in Thy light,
    Thy life my death efface.

In Thy bright beams which on me fall
    Fade every evil thought;
That I am nothing, Thou art all,
    I would be daily taught.

More of Thy glory let me see,
    Thou Holy, Wise and True!
I would Thy living image be
    In joy and sorrow too.

Fill me with gladness from above,
    Hold me by strength divine!
Lord, let the glow of Thy great love
    Through my whole being shine.

Make this poor self grow less and less,
    Be Thou my life and aim:
O make me daily, through Thy grace,
    More meet to bear Thy name!

1681   Charles Wesley   88 88 88
Christ hath made us free. *Galatians 5:1*

And can it be that I should gain
    An interest in the Saviour's blood?
Died He for me, who caused His pain?
    For me, who Him to death pursued?
Amazing love! how can it be
That Thou, my God, shouldst die for me?

'Tis mystery all! The Immortal dies!
    Who can explore His strange design?
In vain the first-born seraph tries
    To sound the depths of love divine!
'Tis mercy all! let earth adore,
Let angel minds inquire no more.

He left His Father's throne above,
    So free, so infinite His grace;
Emptied Himself of all but love,
    And bled for Adam's helpless race;
'Tis mercy all, immense and free;
For, O my God, it found out me.

Long my imprisoned spirit lay
    Fast bound in sin and nature's night;
Thine eyes diffused a quickening ray,
    I woke, the dungeon flamed with light;
My chains fell off, my heart was free;
I rose, went forth, and followed Thee.

No condemnation now I dread;
    Jesus, and all in Him, is mine!
Alive in Him, my living Head,
    And clothed in righteousness divine,
Bold I approach the eternal throne,
And claim the crown, through Christ my own.

1682   John Newton   88 88 88
For the flesh lusteth against the Spirit, and the Spirit against the flesh.
Galatians 5:17

Strange and mysterious is my life;
    What opposites I feel within!
A stable peace, a constant strife;
    The rule of grace, the power of sin;
Too often I am captive led,
Yet often triumph in my Head.

I prize the privilege of prayer,
    But O what backwardness to pray!
Though on the Lord I cast my care,
    I feel its burden every day;
I'd seek His will in all I do,
Yet find my own is working too.

I call the promises my own,
    And prize them more than mines of gold;
Yet though their sweetness I have known,
    They leave me unimpressed and cold;
One hour upon the truth I feed,
The next I know not what I read.

Thus different powers within me strive,
    And grace and sin by turns prevail;
I grieve, rejoice, decline, revive,
    And victory hangs in doubtful scale;
But Jesus has His promise passed
That grace shall overcome at last.

1683   William Parker   65 65
For the flesh lusteth against the Spirit, and the Spirit against the flesh.
Galatians 5:17

Holy Spirit, hear us;
    Help us while we sing;
Breathe into the music
    Of the praise we bring.

Holy Spirit, prompt us
    When we kneel to pray;
Nearer come, and teach us
    What we ought to say.

Holy Spirit, shine Thou
    On the book we read;
Gild its holy pages
    With the light we need.

Holy Spirit, give us
    Each a lowly mind;
Make us more like Jesus,
    Gentle, pure and kind.

Holy Spirit, keep us
    Safe from sins which lie
Hidden by some pleasure
    From our youthful eye.

Holy Spirit, help us
  Daily, by Thy might,
What is wrong to conquer,
  And to choose the right.

1684   William Gadsby   CM
**But God forbid that I should glory, save in the
cross of our Lord Jesus Christ.** *Galatians 6:14*

Dear Lord, forbid that we should boast,
  Save in the cross of Christ,
Here may we confidently trust,
  And solemnly rejoice.

A triune God is here displayed
  In all His glorious hue;
Here sinners may approach and live,
  Behold and love Him too.

Here we have power to plead with God,
  And call the Lord our own;
With pleasure view our Father sit
  Upon a smiling throne.

Lose sight of Jesus and His cross,
  And soon we fall a prey;
Our lust and pride, by power or craft,
  Will carry us away.

But when, by faith, the cross we view,
  Such is its mighty power,
Though earth and hell unite with sin,
  We conquer and adore.

1685   Samuel Barnard   LM
**But God forbid that I should glory, save in the
cross of our Lord Jesus Christ.**
Galatians 6:14

Ye ransomed souls, arise and sing
The love of Christ, your heavenly King,
Who bore your sin, your shame, your loss,
And glory only in His cross.

O! let His love your songs employ,
And His salvation be your joy;
Yea, count all other things but dross,
And glory only in His cross.

'Tis through the cross on which He died,
The world to you is crucified;
And you to it— O happy loss!
Then glory only in His cross.

At last with Him you shall appear,
And join the joy and triumph there;
In endless songs His love applause,
And ever glory in His cross.

1686   Thomas Kelly   LM
**But God forbid that I should glory, save in the
cross of our Lord Jesus Christ.**
Galatians 6:14

We sing the praise of Him who died,
  Of Him who died upon the cross;
The sinner's hope let men deride,
  For this we count the world but loss.

Inscribed upon the cross we see,
  In shining letters 'God is love;'
He bears our sins upon the tree;
  He brings us mercy from above.

The cross! it takes our guilt away;
  It holds the fainting spirit up;
It cheers with hope the gloomy day,
  And sweetens every bitter cup.

It makes the coward spirit brave,
  And nerves the feeble arm for fight;
It takes the terror from the grave,
  And gilds the bed of death with light;

The balm of life, the cure of woe,
  The measure and the pledge of love,
The sinner's refuge here below,
  The angels' theme in heaven above.

1687   John Bowring   87 87 (trochaic)
**But God forbid that I should glory, save in the
cross of our Lord Jesus Christ.**
Galatians 6:14

In the cross of Christ I glory,
  Towering o'er the wrecks of time;
All the light of sacred story
  Gathers round its head sublime.

When the woes of life o'ertake me,
  Hopes deceive and fears annoy,
Never shall the cross forsake me;
  Lo! it glows with peace and joy.

When the sun of bliss is beaming
  Light and love upon my way,
From the cross the radiance streaming
  Adds more lustre to the day.

Bane and blessing, pain and pleasure,
  By the cross are sanctified;
Peace is there that knows no measure,
  Joys that through all time abide.

In the cross of Christ I glory,
  Towering o'er the wrecks of time;
All the light of sacred story
  Gathers round its head sublime.

1688 Augustus Toplady 88 88 88
But God forbid that I should glory, save in the cross of our Lord Jesus Christ.
Galatians 6:14

Redeemer! whither should I flee,
    Or how escape the wrath to come?
The weary sinner flies to Thee
    For shelter from impending doom;
Smile on me, gracious Lord, and show
Thyself the Friend of sinners now.

Beneath the shadow of Thy cross
    The heavy-laden soul finds rest;
I would esteem the world but dross
    So I might be of Christ possessed.
I'd seek my every joy in Thee,
Be Thou both life and light to me.

Close to the ignominious tree,
    Jesus, my humbled soul would cleave;
Despised and crucified with Thee,
    With Thee resolved to die and live;
This prayer and this ambition mine,
Living and dying to be Thine.

There, fastened to the rugged wood
    By holy love's resistless chain,
And life deriving from Thy blood,
    Never to wander wide again,
There may I bow my suppliant knee,
And own no other Lord but Thee.

1689 Horatius Bonar Irregular
But God forbid that I should glory, save in the cross of our Lord Jesus Christ.
Galatians 6:14

The cross it standeth fast:
    Hallelujah! Hallelujah!
Defying every blast:
    Hallelujah! Hallelujah!
The winds of hell have blown,
    The world its hate hath shown,
Yet it is not overthrown,
    Hallelujah for the cross!

    Hallelujah, hallelujah,
      Hallelujah for the cross!
    Hallelujah, hallelujah,
      It shall never suffer loss!

It is the old cross still:
    Hallelujah! Hallelujah!
Its triumph let us tell:
    Hallelujah! Hallelujah!
The grace of God here shone,
    Through Christ the blessed Son,
Who did for sin atone:
    Hallelujah for the cross!

'Twas here the debt was paid:
    Hallelujah! Hallelujah!
Our sins on Jesus laid:
    Hallelujah! Hallelujah!
So round the cross we sing
    Of Christ our offering,
Of Christ our living King:
    Hallelujah for the cross!

1690 Fanny Crosby 76 76 + refrain
But God forbid that I should glory, save in the cross of our Lord Jesus Christ.
Galatians 6:14

Jesus, keep me near the cross;
    There a precious fountain,
Free to all, a healing stream,
    Flows from Calvary's mountain.

    In the cross, in the cross,
    Be my glory ever;
    Till my raptured soul shall find
      Rest beyond the river.

Near the cross, a trembling soul,
    Love and mercy found me;
There the Bright and Morning Star
    Shed its beams around me.

Near the cross! O Lamb of God
    Bring its scenes before me;
Help me walk from day to day
    With its shadow o'er me.

Near the cross I'll watch and wait,
    Hoping, trusting ever,
Till I reach the golden strand
    Just beyond the river.

1691 William Gadsby (alt) LM
Blessed be the God and Father of our Lord Jesus Christ, who hath blessed us with all spiritual blessings in heavenly places in Christ. *Ephesians 1:3*

What joyful news the gospel is,
To guilty sinners in distress!
It speaks of mercy, rich and free,
For such sinful souls as we.

Jesus, my Shepherd, lived and died,
Rose, and now lives to intercede;
He bears my name upon His heart,
Nor will He ever with me part.

For me He bore the wrath of God;
For me He in the wine-press trod;
He magnified the law for me,
And I for ever am set free.

He loved me ere the world began;
Nor did my Saviour love alone;
The Spirit and the Father joined,
As one Jehovah, in one mind.

In endless love, the Holy Three
All blessings have secured for me;
All good that's worthy of a God,
For me in Jesus Christ is stored.

What glory, yea, what matchless grace,
Appears in my Redeemer's face!
All Deity can there agree
To smile upon a soul like me.

1692 *Gospel Magazine* 1777   87 87 47
**Blessed be the God and Father of our Lord
Jesus Christ, who hath blessed us with all
spiritual blessings in heavenly places in
Christ...** *Ephesians 1:3-7*

Sons we are, through God's election,
    Who in Jesus Christ believe;
By eternal destination,
    Saving grace we here receive;
        Our Redeemer
    Does both grace and glory give.

Every soul of man, by sinning,
    Merits everlasting pain;
But Thy love, without beginning,
    Formed and fixed salvation's plan.
        Countless millions
    Shall in life through Jesus reign.

Pause, my soul! adore and wonder!
    Ask, 'O why such love to me?'
Grace has put me in the number
    Of the Saviour's family;
        Hallelujah!
    Thanks, Eternal Love, to Thee!

These are springs of consolation,
    To converted sons of grace;
Finished, free, and full salvation
    Shining in the Saviour's face!
        Free grace only
    Suits the wretched sinner's case.

When in that blest habitation,
    Which my God for me ordained;
When in glory's full possession,
    I with saints and angels stand;
        Free grace only
    Shall resound through Canaan's land!

1693 Isaac Watts   66 66 88
**Blessed be the God and Father of our Lord
Jesus Christ, who hath blessed us with all
spiritual blessings in heavenly places in
Christ...** *Ephesians 1:3,4*

To Him that chose us first,
    Before the world began;
To Him that bore the curse,
    To save rebellious man;
To Him that formed our hearts anew,
Is endless praise and glory due.

The Father's love shall run
    Through our immortal songs;
We bring to God the Son,
    Hosannas on our tongues;
Our lips address the Spirit's name,
With equal praise and zeal the same.

Let every saint above,
    And angel round the throne,
For ever bless and love
    The sacred Three-in-One;
Thus heaven shall raise His honours high,
When earth and time grow old and die.

1694 David Denham   CM
**According as He hath chosen us in Him before
the foundation of the world, that we should be
holy and without blame before Him in love.**
Ephesians 1:4

Chosen of God ere time begun,
    His sovereignty we prove;
With Christ our Head accounted one
    In bonds of covenant love!

Chosen as sons and heirs of God,
    Our names are writ in heaven;
Chosen to life through Jesus' blood,
    Our sins are all forgiven.

Chosen as witnesses, we speak
    Of all our God hath done;
Chosen to holiness, we seek
    Our all in Christ alone.

Chosen to run the heavenly race,
    The glorious prize to gain;
Chosen to persevere through grace,
    We shall the crown obtain.

Thus chosen, we shall surely meet
    On Zion's heights above;
And stand before the Lord complete,
    Unblameable in love.

1695   William Gadsby   CM
**According as He hath chosen us in Him before
the foundation of the world, that we should be
holy and without blame before Him in love...**
Ephesians 1:4-9

Election is a truth divine,
   As absolute as free;
Works ne'er can make the blessing mine;
   'Tis God's own wise decree.

Before Jehovah built the skies,
   Or earth, or seas, or sun,
He chose a people for His praise,
   And gave them to His Son.

Eternal was the choice of God,
   A sovereign act indeed;
And Jesus, the incarnate Word,
   Secures the chosen seed.

He loved and chose because He would;
   Nor did His choice depend
On sinners' work, or bad or good,
   But on His sovereign mind.

Nor law, nor death, nor hell, nor sin,
   Can alter His decree;
The elect eternal life shall win,
   And all God's glory see.

His counsel stands for ever sure,
   Immortal and divine;
And justice, mercy, truth, and power,
   Unite to make it mine.

1696   William Tucker   LM
**Having predestinated us unto the adoption of
children by Jesus Christ to Himself, according
to the good pleasure of His will.** *Ephesians 1:5*

Expand my soul, arise and sing
The matchless grace of Zion's King;
Whose love, as ancient as His name,
Let all thy powers aloud proclaim.

Chosen of old, of old approved:
In Christ th' eternal Son beloved:
Adopted too, and children made,
Ere sin its harmful poison spread.

Though sin and guilt infest them here,
In Christ they all complete appear;
For all that justice e'er demands,
Received full payment from His hands.

In Him the Father never saw
The least transgression of His law;
Perfection then in Him we view,
And saints in Him are perfect too.

Then let our souls in Him rejoice,
As favoured objects of His choice;
Redeemed, and saved by grace, we sing
Eternal praise to Christ our King.

1697   Catherine Pennefather   SM
To the praise of the glory of His grace.
Ephesians 1:6

Jesus, the sinner's Friend!
   We hide ourselves in Thee;
God looks upon Thy sprinkled blood;
   It is our only plea.

He hears Thy precious name,
   We claim it as our own;
The Father must accept and bless
   His well-belovèd Son.

He sees Thy spotless robe:
   It covers all our sin;
The golden gates have welcomed Thee,
   And we may enter in.

Thou hast fulfilled the law,
   And we are justified;
Ours is the blessing, Thine the curse:
   We live, for Thou hast died.

Jesus, the sinner's Friend!
   We cannot speak Thy praise,
No mortal voice can sing the song
   That ransomed hearts would raise.

But when before the throne,
   Upon the glassy sea,
Clothed in our blood-bought robes of white
   We stand complete in Thee,

Jesus, we'll give Thee then
   Such praises as are meet,
And cast ten thousand golden crowns,
   Adoring at Thy feet.

1698   Emmanuel Sibomana, tr. R Guillebaud
64 64 67 64
To the praise of the glory of His grace.
Ephesians 1:6

O how the grace of God
   Amazes me!
It loosed me from my bonds
   And set me free!
What made it happen so?
   'Twas His will, this much I know
Set me, as now I show,
   At liberty.

My God has chosen me,
   Though one of nought,
To sit beside my King
   In heaven's court.
Hear what my Lord has done;
   O the love that made Him run
To meet His erring son!
   This has God wrought.

Not for my righteousness,
   For I have none,
But for His mercy's sake,
   Jesus, God's Son,
Suffered on Calvary's tree,
   Crucified with thieves was He,
Great was His grace to me,
   His wayward one!

And when I think of how,
   At Calvary,
He bore sin's penalty
   Instead of me,
Amazed, I wonder why
   He, the sinless One, should die
For one so vile as I:
   My Saviour He!

Now all my heart's desire
   Is to abide
In Him, my Saviour dear,
   In Him to hide.
My shield and buckler He,
   Covering and protecting me:
From Satan's darts I'll be
   Safe at His side.

Lord Jesus, hear my prayer,
   Thy grace impart;
When evil thoughts arise
   Through Satan's art,
O, drive them all away
   And do Thou, from day to day,
Keep me beneath Thy sway,
   King of my heart.

Come now the whole of me,
   Eyes, ears and voice,
Join me, creation all,
   With joyful noise:
Praise Him who broke the chain
   Holding me in sin's domain,
And set me free again!
   Sing and rejoice!

1699   William Gadsby   88 88 D
**In whom we have redemption through His
blood, the forgiveness of sins, according to
the riches of His grace.** *Ephesians 1:7*

Free grace is the joy of my heart;
   Its glories, with wonder, I trace;
To me it does freely impart
   Rich blessings, just suiting my case;
No monster more wretched could be,
   Nor less of God's favour deserve;
Yet such is free grace unto me,
   I never, no never can starve.

Grace takes all my ruin and woe,
   Nor murmurs my burdens to bear;
And grace in return makes me know
   In Jesus I'm comely and fair.
In self I'm polluted and vile;
   But grace sweetly speaks unto me,
It tells me, and that with a smile,
   In Jesus I'm perfect and free.

Its blessings, though rich and divine,
   Are all without money and price;
A soul, though as wretched as mine,
   May venture to hope and rejoice;
Its highest delight is to give
   True riches to sinners undone;
Nor can it, nor will it deceive,
   The soul that with Jesus is one.

1700   William Williams, tr. Vernon Higham
                     73 73 77 73 73
**In whom we have redemption through His
blood, the forgiveness of sins, according to
the riches of His grace.** *Ephesians 1:7*

There is a path of pardon
   In His blood;
There is a sure salvation
   In His blood.
The law's full consummation,
A Father's approbation—
Hear Zion's acclamation!
   In His blood—
Atonement and redemption
   In His blood!

O come, ye sons of Adam,
   And rejoice!
Now trust the God of Abraham
   And rejoice!
O hasten, happy sinner,
To life in Christ for ever,
To bonds that nought can sever:
   O rejoice!
In full and glad surrender
   Come, rejoice!

1701 John Kent   LM
In whom we have redemption through His
blood, the forgiveness of sins, according to
the riches of His grace. *Ephesians 1:7*

God, in the riches of His grace,
   Did from eternity ordain
A seed elect of Adam's race,
   Eternal glory should obtain.

God, in the riches of His grace,
   Hath Christ exalted over all;
His goings forth of old we trace,
   The sinner's Surety in the fall.

God, in the riches of His grace,
   Hath to the charge of Jesus laid
The sin of all that chosen race,
   Whose debt of suffering Jesus paid.

God, in the riches of His grace,
   Hath in the gospel Christ displayed,
Whose blood hath sealed the sinner's peace,
   And bruised th'envenomed serpent's head.

God, in the riches of His grace,
   We'll to eternity adore,
And wonders still on wonders trace,
But ne'er His depth of love explore.

1702 John Kent   CM
In whom also we have obtained an inheritance.
Ephesians 1:11

Arise, my thoughts, and trace the spring
   From whence salvation came;
Do Thou, celestial Spirit, bring
   Thy soul-expanding flame.

'Twas settled in Jehovah's grace,
   That deep the most profound,
Before He gave the hills their place,
   Or fixed creation's bound.

Great God! How deep Thy counsels lie,
   Supreme in power art Thou;
All things, to Thine omniscient eye,
   Are one eternal now.

Thy thoughts of peace to Israel's race
   From everlasting flowed;
And when Thou hid'st Thy lovely face,
   Thou still art Israel's God.

In ties of blood, and nothing less,
   We claim Thee as our own;
And God th' eternal Spirit bless
   Who makes the kinship known.

Long as the covenant shall endure,
   Made by the Great Three-One,
Salvation is for ever sure
   To every blood-bought son.

1703 Ellen Burman   10 10 10 10
That we should be to the praise of His glory,
who first trusted in Christ.
Ephesians 1:12

Teach me to live, 'tis easier far to die,
   Gently and silently to pass away,
On earth's long night to close the heavy eye
   And waken in the realms of glorious day.

Teach me that harder lesson, how to live,
   To serve Thee in the darkest paths of life;
Arm me for conflict now, fresh vigour give
   And make me more than conqueror in the strife.

Teach me to live, Thy purpose to fulfil;
   Bright for Thy glory let my taper shine!
Each day renew, remould the stubborn will;
   Closer round Thee my heart's affections twine.

Teach me to live! no idler let me be,
   But in Thy service hand and heart employ,
Prepared to do Thy bidding cheerfully,
   Be this my highest, this my holiest joy.

Teach me to live! with kindly words for all,
   Wearing no cold, repulsive brow of gloom;
Waiting, with cheerful patience, till Thy call
   Summons my spirit to her heavenly home.

1704 Martin Luther, tr. C Winkworth   LM
In whom also after that ye believed, ye were
sealed with that holy Spirit of promise.
Ephesians 1:13

Come, Holy Spirit, God and Lord!
Be all Thy graces now outpoured
On the believer's mind and soul,
To strengthen, save, and make us whole.

Thou strong Defence, Thou holy Light,
Teach us to know our God aright,
And call Him Father from the heart;
The word of life and truth impart;

That we may love no stranger's creed,
Nor follow other teacher's lead,
But Jesus for our Master own,
And put our trust in Him alone.

From every error keep us free;
Let none but Christ our Master be,
That we in living faith abide,
In Him with all our might confide.

1705 Vernon Higham SM
**The eyes of your understanding being
enlightened.** *Ephesians 1:18*

Lord, open Thou my eyes,
Wonderful grace to see,
Where Jesus Christ is nailed and dies
There on a hill for me.

Lord, open Thou my mind,
More of Thy wealth to know;
Furnish my life with grace so kind
From Thine abundant flow.

Lord, open Thou my heart;
Graciously now enfold;
Stir up my love and never part
From this eternal hold.

Lord, open Thou my hand
To take Thy grace as mine,
That in that day in Christ I'll stand
In righteousness divine.

Lord, Thou hast touched my soul,
Thy gentle hand I feel;
With healing that has made me whole,
Thy grace did o'er me steal.

Praise to Thy name, O Lord,
Wondrous, immortal Three!
Now I shall sing in sweet accord
Wonderful grace in me.

© Author

1706 William Gadsby CM
**And hath put all things under His feet, and
gave Him to be the head over all things to the
church.** *Ephesians 1:22*

The Lord on high His love proclaims,
And makes His goodness known;
To men deserving endless pains
He gave His only Son.

He gave His Son their life to be,
To save them from despair;
From death and hell to set them free,
In glory to appear.

All real good in Jesus dwells,
And freely is bestowed
On such as cannot help themselves,
And cry for help to God.

Then, mourning souls, dry up your tears;
Though wretched be your case,
His love shall banish all your fears;
He'll save you by His grace.

1707 Samuel Medley LM
**Which is His body, the fulness of Him that
filleth all in all.** *Ephesians 1:23*

Sinners who have believed through grace,
Although the vilest of our race,
In this agree, both great and small,
That Jesus Christ is All in all.

The Greek, the Jew, and such as we,
Barbarian, Scythian, bond, or free,
Here find no separating wall;
For Jesus is our All in all.

He is our life from day to day,
He is our strength through all the way,
He saves from bondage, sin, and thrall,
And is to us our All in all.

He is the Lord our Righteousness,
He is our refuge in distress,
He hears when we upon Him call,
And thus appears our All in all.

In heaven this truth will best be known,
When we surround His glorious throne,
And with th' adoring armies fall,
And Jesus sing, our All in all.

1708 Vernon Higham LM
**And you hath He quickened, who were dead in
trespasses and sins.**
Ephesians 2:1

O blessèd day, O wondrous dawn,
When Thou O Holy Spirit came
And touched my heart, and I was born
To life with God, to end my shame.

No more to roam the realms of sin,
Blind to my state and Satan's hold;
Called by my God to live with Him,
And leave the depths of death untold.

By grace I rise and turn to Thee,
And leave the idols of desire;
Through faith I come to Calvary
And see my Saviour there expire.

O tender love, extended there
  Upon a cross, for sin He paid.
O wondrous wounds to One so fair:
  For all my sin on Him was laid.

I lift my gaze to His dear face,
  And stand forgiven in His sight;
He took away my sad disgrace
  And looked upon me with delight.

O blessèd Jesus, grace does share;
  As God, as man, His love He shows;
Robed in His beauty, now I wear
  The righteousness He thus bestows.

Safe, safe am I in arms of grace,
  A place prepared by love divine;
One day to see His lovely face
  And hear Him tell me 'thou art Mine'.
                                    © Author

1709   William Gadsby   77 77
By grace ye are saved. *Ephesians 2:5*

Saved and saved alone by grace;
Saved to see my Saviour's face;
Saved from Satan's iron yoke,
And the law that I had broke.

Saved from sin, that hateful foe
That has millions plunged in woe,
Saved from all its reigning power;
Saved to serve my lusts no more.

Saved, nor can I be condemned;
Jesus Christ, the sinner's Friend,
Took my place and vengeance bore,
Me to save for evermore.

Death, nor hell, nor world, nor sin,
Foes without, nor foes within,
Ever can my soul destroy;
I am saved eternally.

1710   Christian Scheidt   98 98 88
By grace ye are saved. *Ephesians 2:5*

By grace I'm saved, grace free and boundless;
  My soul, believe and doubt it not.
Why stagger at this word of promise?
  Hath Scripture ever falsehood taught?
No! then this word must true remain:
By grace thou, too, shalt heaven obtain.

By grace! None dare lay claim to merit;
  Our works and conduct have no worth.
God in His love sent our Redeemer,
  Christ Jesus, to this sinful earth;
His death did for our sins atone
And we are saved by grace alone.

By grace! O mark this word of promise
  When thou art by thy sins oppressed,
When Satan plagues thy troubled conscience
  And when thy heart is seeking rest.
What reason cannot comprehend
God by His grace to thee doth send.

By grace! This ground of faith is certain;
  So long as God is true, it stands.
What saints have penned by inspiration,
  What in His word our God commands,
What our whole faith must rest upon,
Is grace alone, grace in His Son.

1711   William Matson   LM
By grace ye are saved. *Ephesians 2:5*

Lord! I was blind, I could not see
  In Thy marred visage any grace;
  But now the beauty of Thy face
In radiant vision dawns on me.

Lord! I was deaf, I could not hear
  The thrilling music of Thy voice;
  But now I hear Thee and rejoice
And sweet are all Thy words, and dear!

Lord! I was dumb, I could not speak
  The grace and glory of Thy name;
  But now, as touched with living flame,
My lips Thine eager praises wake!

Lord! I was dead, I could not stir
  My lifeless soul to come to Thee;
  But now since Thou hast quickened me
I rise from sin's dark sepulchre!

For Thou hast made the blind to see,
  The deaf to hear, the dumb to speak,
  The dead to live; and Thou didst break
The chains of my captivity!

1712 *Gospel Magazine* 1777 CM
For by grace are ye saved through faith; and
that not of yourselves: it is the gift of God.
Ephesians 2:8

How sovereign is the love of God
   To Israel's favoured race!
Paid is the mighty debt they owed;
   Salvation is of grace.

His love, without beginning, knew
   Each chosen sinner's case;
And sent His equal Son to show
   Salvation is of grace.

Immanuel had not bled and died,
   Nor suffered in our place,
But for this truth (O sound it wide!),
   Salvation is of grace.

We had not known and loved the Son,
   Nor sung His worthy praise,
But that Himself the work begun;
   Salvation is of grace.

1713 Benjamin Beddome SM
For by grace are ye saved through faith; and
that not of yourselves: it is the gift of God.
Ephesians 2:8

Faith! 'tis a precious grace,
   Where'er it is bestowed;
It boasts of a celestial birth,
   And is the gift of God.

Jesus it owns as King,
   An all-atoning Priest;
It claims no merits of its own,
   But looks for all in Christ.

To Him it leads the soul,
   When filled with deep distress;
Flies to the fountain of His blood,
   And trusts His righteousness.

Since 'tis Thy work alone,
   And that divinely free,
Come, Holy Spirit, and make known
   The power of faith in me.

JOHN NEWTON 1725-1807

1714 John Newton CM
For by grace are ye saved through faith; and
that not of yourselves: it is the gift of God.
Ephesians 2:8

Amazing grace! how sweet the sound
   That saved a wretch like me;
I once was lost, but now am found;
   Was blind, but now I see.

'Twas grace that taught my heart to fear,
   And grace my fears relieved;
How precious did that grace appear
   The hour I first believed!

Through many dangers, toils, and snares,
   I have already come;
'Tis grace has brought me safe thus far,
   And grace will lead me home.

The Lord has promised good to me,
   His word my hope secures;
He will my Shield and Portion be,
   As long as life endures.

Yes, when this flesh and heart shall fail,
   And mortal life shall cease,
I shall possess, within the veil,
   A life of joy and peace.

The earth shall soon dissolve like snow,
   The sun forbear to shine;
But God, who called me here below,
   Will be for ever mine.

Alternative 6th verse:
   Anon 1910

When we've been there ten thousand years,
   Bright shining as the sun,
We've no less days to sing God's praise
   Than when we first begun.

1715   Horatius Bonar   CM
**For by grace are ye saved through faith; and
that not of yourselves: it is the gift of God.**
Ephesians 2:8

All that I was: my sin, my guilt,
   My death was all my own;
All that I am I owe to Thee,
   My gracious God, alone.

The evil of my former state
   Was mine, and only mine;
The good in which I now rejoice
   Is Thine, and only Thine.

The darkness of my former state,
   The bondage, all was mine;
The light of life in which I walk,
   The liberty is Thine.

The grace that made me feel my sin,
   Bade me in Christ believe;
Then, in believing, peace I found,
   And now in Christ I live.

All that I am even here on earth,
   All that I hope to be,
When Jesus comes and glory dawns,
   I owe it, Lord, to Thee.

1716   Augustus Toplady (alt)   CM
Not of works, lest any man should boast.
Ephesians 2:9

Not for the works which we have done,
   Or shall hereafter do,
Hath God decreed on sinful souls
   Salvation to bestow.

The glory, Lord, from first to last,
   Is due to Thee alone:
Aught to ourselves we dare not take,
   Or rob Thee of Thy crown.

Our glorious Surety undertook
   To satisfy for man,
And grace was given us in Him
   Before the world began.

This is Thy will, that in Thy love
   We ever should abide;
And lo, we earth and hell defy
   To make Thy counsel void.

Not one of all the chosen race
   But shall to heaven attain;
Partake on earth the purposed grace,
   And then with Jesus reign.

Of Father, Son, and Spirit, we
   Extol the threefold care;
Whose love, whose merit, and whose power
   Unite to lift us there.

1717   John Kent   77 77
For He is our peace. *Ephesians 2:14*

Sons of peace redeemed by blood,
Raise your songs to Zion's God;
Made from condemnation free,
Grace triumphant sing with me.

Calvary's summit let us trace.
View the heights and depths of grace;
Count the purple drops, and say,
'Thus my sins were borne away.'

Now no more His wrath we dread,
He hath thus to Zion said,
'Since thy Surety paid thy score
I behold thy sins no more.'

Sunk, as in a shoreless flood,
Lost, as in a Saviour's blood,
Zion, O! how blest art thou,
Justified from all things now!

Once, in vain, this peace we sought
From the law, but found it not;
Filled with sorrow, guilt, and shame,
We at length to Calvary came.

Here we stood at peace with heaven,
Found the sweets of sins forgiven,
Wept as pardoned sinners do,
Felt the blood of sprinkling too.

Here we saw the curse removed,
Sin condemned, and sinners loved!
O! how sweet to feel the same,
Passing tribulation's flame!

Will our God this peace reveal,
When our heart and flesh shall fail?
Then we'll sing in Jordan's flood,
Sweet's the peace that's sealed by blood.

1718 Horatius Bonar   66 86 10 12
For He is our peace. *Ephesians 2:14*

No blood, no altar now:
The sacrifice is o'er;
No flame, no smoke ascends on high,
The lamb is slain no more.
But richer blood has flowed from nobler veins,
To purge the soul from guilt and cleanse the
reddest stains.

We thank Thee for the blood,
The blood of Christ, Thy Son;
The blood by which our peace is made,
The victory is won;
Great victory o'er hell and sin and woe,
That needs no second fight and leaves no second
foe.

We thank Thee for the grace,
Descending from above,
That overflows our widest guilt—
The eternal Father's love,
Love of the Father's everlasting Son,
Love of the Holy Ghost—Jehovah, Three in One.

1719

John Newton   CM
**For through Him we both have access by one
Spirit unto the Father.**
Ephesians 2:18

Great God! from Thee there's nought concealed,
Thou seest my inward frame;
To Thee I always stand revealed
Exactly as I am!

Since I can hardly, therefore, bear
What in myself I see;
How vile and black must I appear,
Most holy God, to Thee!

But since my Saviour stands between,
In garments dyed in blood,
'Tis He, instead of me is seen,
When I approach to God.

Thus, though a sinner, I am safe;
He pleads, before the throne,
His life and death in my behalf,
And calls my sins His own.

What wondrous love, what mysteries,
In this appointment shine!
My breaches of the law are His,
And His obedience mine.

1720 Charles Wesley   CM
**Now therefore ye are no more strangers and
foreigners, but fellowcitizens with the saints,
and of the household of God.**
Ephesians 2:19

Happy the souls to Jesus joined
And saved by grace alone;
Walking in all His ways, they find
Their heaven on earth begun.

The church triumphant in Thy love,
Their mighty joys we know;
They sing the Lamb in hymns above,
And we in hymns below.

Thee in Thy glorious realm they praise
And bow before Thy throne;
We in the kingdom of Thy grace;
The kingdoms are but one.

The holy to the holiest leads;
From thence our spirits rise
And he that in Thy statutes treads
Shall meet Thee in the skies.

1721 David Denham   CM
**Now therefore ye are no more strangers and
foreigners, but fellowcitizens with the saints,
and of the household of God.**
Ephesians 2:19

No more a stranger to the Lord,
In Satan's power enslaved;
But quickened by Jehovah's word,
I sing a sinner saved.

No more a stranger to His grace,
I feel its power within;
Walk in the light of Jesus' face,
Freed from the reign of sin.

No more a stranger to His blood,
Its cleansing power I prove;
Pardoned and justified by God,
I'm happy in His love.

No more a stranger to His rest,
He bids my sorrows cease;
With life and righteousness possessed,
In Christ I've perfect peace.

No more a stranger to His throne,
I give myself to prayer;
I trust His faithfulness alone,
And seek all succour there.

No more a stranger, but a son,
An heir of joys to come;
With Father, Son, and Spirit one,
And heaven my glorious home.

1722   From the Latin, tr. John Chandler

66 66 44 44

And are built upon the foundation of the apostles and prophets, Jesus Christ Himself being the chief corner stone.
Ephesians 2:20

Christ is our Corner-stone,
  On Him alone we build;
With His true saints alone
  The courts of heaven are filled;
    On His great love
      Our hopes we place
      Of present grace
    And joys above.

O, then with hymns of praise
  These hallowed courts shall ring;
Our voices we will raise
  The Three in One to sing;
    And thus proclaim
      In joyful song,
      Both loud and long,
    That glorious name.

Here, gracious God, do Thou
  For evermore draw nigh;
Accept each faithful vow,
  And mark each suppliant sigh;
    In copious shower
      On all who pray
      Each holy day
    Thy blessings pour.

Here may we gain from heaven
  The grace which we implore;
And may that grace, once given,
  Be with us evermore,
    Until that day
      When all the blest
      To endless rest
    Are called away.

1723   Charles Wesley   CM
Of whom the whole family in heaven and earth is named. *Ephesians 3:15*

Come, let us join our friends above,
  That have obtained the prize,
And on the eagle wings of love
  To joys celestial rise.

Let saints below in concert sing
  With those to glory gone;
For all the servants of our King
  In earth and heaven are one.

One family we dwell in Him,
  One church, above, beneath,
Though now divided by the stream,
  The narrow stream, of death.

One army of the living God
  To His command we bow,
Part of His host hath crossed the flood
  And part is crossing now.

E'en now by faith we join our hands
  With those that went before;
And greet the blood-besprinkled bands
  On the eternal shore.

O that we now might grasp our Guide!
  O that the word were given!
Come, Lord of Hosts, the waves divide
  And land us all in heaven.

1724   Samuel Longfellow   77 77
That He would grant you, according to the riches of His glory, to be strengthened with might by His Spirit in the inner man.
Ephesians 3:16

Holy Spirit, Truth divine!
Dawn upon this soul of mine;
Word of God and inward Light,
Wake my spirit, clear my sight.

Holy Spirit, Love divine!
Glow within this heart of mine;
Kindle every high desire;
Perish self in Thy pure fire!

Holy Spirit, Power divine!
Fill and nerve this will of mine;
By Thee may I strongly live,
Bravely bear and nobly strive!

Holy Spirit, Right divine!
King within my conscience reign;
Be my Lord, and I shall be
Firmly bound, for ever free.

Holy Spirit, Peace divine!
Still this restless heart of mine;
Speak to calm this tossing sea,
Stayed in Thy tranquillity.

Holy Spirit, Joy divine!
Gladden Thou this heart of mine;
In the desert ways I sing:
Spring, O Well, for ever spring!

1725 William Rozzel   LM
Strengthened with might by His Spirit in the inner man. *Ephesians 3:16*

As through this vale of tears I go,
And walk through various scenes of woe,
The Lord in mercy scatters round
His manna on the barren ground.

Bids me the gracious blessings taste,
That lie upon the dreary waste:
His invitations I obey,
Eat the sweet food, and urge my way.

Strengthened by bread of heavenly make,
I rise refreshed, and courage take,
Pursue my course, though rough the way,
And press towards the realms of day.

The Spirit's word I grasp and hold,
The Spirit's influence makes me bold;
The foe's great Conqueror by me stands,
And bids me fight and nerves my hands.

Thus, heaven-supported, every foe
In vain assaults me as I go;
Since He who bids my feet to move,
Loves with an everlasting love.

1726 Samuel Trevor Francis   87 87 D
And to know the love of Christ, which passeth knowledge, that ye might be filled with all the fulness of God.
Ephesians 3:19

O, the deep, deep love of Jesus!
    Vast, unmeasured, boundless, free;
Rolling as a mighty ocean
    In its fulness over me.
Underneath me, all around me,
    Is the current of Thy love;
Leading onward, leading homeward,
    To my glorious rest above.

O, the deep, deep love of Jesus!
    Spread His praise from shore to shore;
How He loveth, ever loveth,
    Changeth never, nevermore;
How He watches o'er His loved ones,
    Died to call them all His own;
How for them He intercedeth,
    Watcheth o'er them from the throne.

O, the deep, deep love of Jesus!
    Love of every love the best:
'Tis an ocean vast of blessing,
    'Tis a haven sweet of rest.
O, the deep, deep love of Jesus!
    'Tis a heaven of heavens to me;
And it lifts me up to glory,
    For it lifts me up to Thee.

1727 Charles Wesley   66 66 88
And to know the love of Christ, which passeth knowledge, that ye might be filled with all the fulness of God.
Ephesians 3:19

Author of life divine,
    Who hast a table spread,
Furnished with mystic wine
    And everlasting bread,
Preserve the life Thyself hast given,
And feed and train us up for heaven.

Our needy souls sustain
    With fresh supplies of love,
Till all Thy life we gain
    And all Thy fulness prove,
And, strengthened by Thy perfect grace,
Behold without a veil Thy face.

1728 Vernon Higham   CM
And to know the love of Christ, which passeth knowledge, that ye might be filled with all the fulness of God.
Ephesians 3:19

There is a love that Christ alone
    Can give to hearts that seek:
A love that fills and keeps His own,
    And makes the mighty meek.

Such meekness, Lord, is strength divine,
    That leads to paths of grace:
That tells my heart that I am Thine,
    And shall behold Thy face.

The length and breadth no more can tell
    The depth and height of love:
It passes knowledge, like the swell
    Of gracious waves above.

There is a place where I may find
    The fulness of God's grace:
A path of faith and love, to bind
    God's promise and embrace.

O let me, Lord, pursue Thee now,
    The Christ of Calvary:
O stir my soul that I may bow,
    And plead my cause to Thee.

This promise, Thou wilt honour, Lord,
    To hearts that Thou hast moved:
O leave me not, but grace afford,
    And let Thy name be proved.

Exalt Thy name in hearts of stone,
Now stirred to love Thy name:
For Thou art God, and Thou alone
Canst spread Thy royal fame.

© Author

1729   Lucy Bennett   76 76 D
And to know the love of Christ, which passeth knowledge, that ye might be filled with all the fulness of God.
Ephesians 3:19

O teach me what it meaneth,
That cross uplifted high,
With One, the Man of Sorrows,
Condemned to bleed and die,
O teach me what it cost Thee
To make a sinner whole;
And teach me, Saviour, teach me
The value of a soul!

O teach me what it meaneth,
That sacred crimson tide,
The blood and water flowing
From Thine own wounded side.
Teach me that if none other
Had sinned, but I alone,
Yet still Thy blood, Lord Jesus,
Thine only, must atone.

O teach me what it meaneth,
Thy love beyond compare,
The love that reacheth deeper
Than depths of self-despair!
Yes teach me, till there gloweth
In this cold heart of mine
Some feeble, pale reflection
Of that pure love of Thine.

O teach me what it meaneth,
For I am full of sin;
And grace alone can reach me
And love alone can win.
O teach me, for I need Thee,
I have no hope beside—
The chief of all the sinners
For whom the Saviour died!

O infinite Redeemer!
I bring no other plea
Because Thou dost invite me
I cast myself on Thee;
Because Thou dost accept me
I love and I adore;
Because Thy love constraineth
I'll praise Thee evermore!

1730   Mary Shekleton   10 10 10 10 4
And to know the love of Christ, which passeth knowledge, that ye might be filled with all the fulness of God.
Ephesians 3:19

It passes knowledge that dear love of Thine,
My Jesus, Saviour; yet this soul of mine
Would of Thy love, in all its breadth and length,
Its height and depth, its everlasting strength,
Know more and more.

It passes telling, that dear love of Thine,
My Jesus, Saviour; yet these lips of mine
Would fain proclaim to sinners, far and near,
A love which can remove all guilty fear
And love beget.

It passes praises, that dear love of Thine,
My Jesus, Saviour; yet this heart of mine
Would sing that love, so full, so rich, so free,
Which brings a rebel sinner, such as me,
Nigh unto God.

But though I cannot sing, or tell, or know
The fulness of Thy love, while here below,
My empty vessel I may freely bring;
O Thou, who art of love the living spring,
My vessel fill.

O fill me, Jesus, Saviour, with Thy love!
Lead, lead me to the living fount above;
Thither may I, in simple faith, draw nigh,
And never to another fountain fly,
But unto Thee.

And when my Jesus face to face I see,
When at His lofty throne I bow the knee;
Then of His love, in all its breadth and length,
Its height and depth, its everlasting strength,
My soul shall sing.

1731   Anne Steele (alt)   CM
And to know the love of Christ, which passeth knowledge, that ye might be filled with all the fulness of God.
Ephesians 3:19

Triumphant, Christ ascends on high,
The glorious work complete;
Sin, death and hell low vanquished lie
Beneath His awesome feet.

There, with eternal glory crowned,
The Lord, The Conqueror, reigns,
His praise the heavenly choirs resound,
In their immortal strains.

Amid the splendours of His throne
  Unchanging love appears;
The names He purchased for His own
  Still on His heart He bears.

O the rich depths of love divine!
  Of bliss, a boundless store:
Dear Saviour, let me call Thee mine,
  I cannot wish for more.

On Thee alone my hope relies,
  Beneath Thy cross I fall,
My Lord, my life, my sacrifice,
  My Saviour and my All.

1732   David Denham   CM
**Now unto Him that is able to do exceeding
abundantly above all that we ask or think,
according to the power that worketh in us.**
Ephesians 3:20

The Lord is able to exceed,
  And answer every cry,
He is our help in every need,
  Our Refuge ever nigh.

He's able to maintain His right,
  His sovereignty make known,
To turn from darkness into light,
  And seek and save His own.

He's able to remove our fears,
  To show our sins forgiven,
To strengthen faith, to dry our tears,
  And make us meet for heaven.

He's able to preserve in peace,
  And make us always blest:
From sin and sorrows to release,
  And take us to His rest.

1733   *Silver St Collection* 1821   CM
**Unto Him be glory in the church by Christ
Jesus throughout all ages, world without end.
Amen.** *Ephesians 3:21*

'Glory to God!' the angel said,
  'Good tidings, lo! I bring;
In David's city is a babe—
  Your Lord and Saviour-King.'

Glory to God, and peace on earth,
  Goodwill to man is shown;
Let heavenly joy at Jesus' birth
  Be through the nations known.

'Glory to God!' let man reply,
  For Christ the Lord is come;
Behold Him in a manger lie—
  A stable is His home.

Glory to God! for love so mild;
  How wonderful the plan,
That Jesus once became a child,
  To save rebellious man!

'Glory to God!' let all the earth
  Join in the heavenly song,
And praise Him for the Saviour's birth,
  In every land and tongue.

JOHN FAWCETT 1740-1817

1734   John Fawcett   SM
**Endeavouring to keep the unity of the Spirit in
the bond of peace.**
Ephesians 4:3

  Blest be the tie that binds
    Our hearts in Christian love;
The fellowship of kindred minds
    Is like to that above.

  Before our Father's throne
    We pour our ardent prayers;
Our fears, our hopes, our aims are one,
    Our comforts and our cares.

  We share our mutual woes,
    Our mutual burdens bear
And often for each other flows
    The sympathising tear.

  When for awhile we part,
    This thought will soothe our pain,
That we shall still be joined in heart
    And hope to meet again.

  This glorious hope revives
    Our courage by the way,
While each in expectation lives
    And longs to see the day.

  From sorrow, toil and pain
    And sin we shall be free;
And perfect love and friendship reign
    Through all eternity.

1735   William Gadsby   SM
One Lord, one faith, one baptism.
Ephesians 4:5

Of one Lord will we sing,
   And spread His fame abroad,
Jehovah Jesus is our King,
   And be His name adored.

One living, vital faith,
   Each Christian will approve;
A faith that triumphs over death,
   And sweetly works by love.

One baptism we own;
   A sacred, solemn sign
Of what the Saviour's undergone,
   To wash away our sin.

His overwhelming pain,
   And burial we see;
His rising from the grave again,
   To set His children free.

Here we by faith may view,
   That every Christian's dead
To Satan, sin, and Moses too,
   Through Christ, our living Head.

In rising from the flood,
   Saints solemnly proclaim
Their life is hid with Christ in God,
   And they shall with Him reign.

1736   Charles Wesley   66 66 88
**Wherefore He saith, When He ascended up on
high, He led captivity captive, and gave gifts
unto men.** *Ephesians 4:8*

God is gone up on high
   With a triumphant noise;
The clarions of the sky
   Proclaim the angelic joys!

   Join all on earth, rejoice and sing;
   Glory ascribe to glory's King.

God in the flesh below,
   For us He reigns above:
Let all the nations know
   Our Jesus' conquering love!

All power to our great Lord
   Is by the Father given;
By angel hosts adored,
   He reigns supreme in heaven:

High on His holy seat
   He bears the righteous sway;
His foes beneath His feet
   Shall sink and die away:

His foes and ours are one,
   Satan, the world, and sin:
But He shall tread them down,
   And bring His kingdom in:

Till all the earth, renewed
   In righteousness divine,
With all the hosts of God
   In one great chorus join:

1737   Arthur Russell   887 D (iambic)
**He that descended is the same also that
ascended up far above all heavens, that He
might fill all things.** *Ephesians 4:10*

The Lord ascendeth up on high,
The Lord hath triumphed gloriously,
   In power and might excelling;
The grave and hell are captive led,
Lo! He returns, our glorious Head,
   To His eternal dwelling.

The heavens with joy receive their Lord,
By saints, by angel hosts adored;
   O day of exultation!
O earth, adore thy glorious King!
His rising, His ascension sing
   With grateful adoration!

Our great High Priest hath gone before,
Now on His church His grace to pour,
   And still His love He giveth:
O may our hearts to Him ascend;
May all within us upward tend
   To Him who ever liveth!

1738   Charles Wesley   77 44 7
**But speaking the truth in love, may grow up
into Him in all things, which is the head, even
Christ.** *Ephesians 4:15*

Head of the church triumphant,
   We joyfully adore Thee;
Till Thou appear, Thy members here
   Shall thirst for greater glory.

We lift our hearts and voices,
   With blest anticipation;
And cry aloud, and give to God
   The praise of our salvation.

While in affliction's furnace,
And passing through the fire,
Thy love we praise, which tries our ways,
And ever brings us higher.

We lift our hands, exulting
In Thy almighty favour;
The love divine which made us Thine
Shall keep us Thine for ever.

By faith we see the glory
To which Thou shalt restore us,
The world despise for that high prize
Which Thou hast set before us.

And if Thou count us worthy,
We each, as dying Stephen,
Shall see Thee stand at God's right hand,
To take us up to heaven.

1739   Margaret Clarkson   65 65 D

And grieve not the holy Spirit of God, whereby ye are sealed unto the day of redemption.
Ephesians 4:30

God the Holy Spirit,
   Reign within my heart;
Banish sin and sorrow;
   Bid all fear depart.
Rule o'er all my being,
   All that's wrong subdue;
Make me like my Saviour,
   Holy, strong and true.

God, the Holy Spirit,
   Help me as I pray;
Make me mean most truly
   All the words I say.
Help me trust Thy promise
   Thou wilt hear my prayer;
Help me leave the answers
   In Thy holy care.

God, the Holy Spirit,
   Teach Thy word to me;
All its heavenly beauty
   Give me eyes to see.
Help me feed my spirit
   On Thy truth each day;
And what Thou dost teach me
   Help me to obey.

God, the Holy Spirit,
   Mould me to Thy will;
All my Saviour's pleasure
   In my life fulfil.
Heart and soul and body,
   All to Thee I bring:
Use me in the service
   Of my glorious King!

1740   William Gadsby   77 77

And walk in love, as Christ also hath loved us, and hath given Himself for us an offering and a sacrifice to God for a sweet smelling savour.
Ephesians 5:2

Lord, we fain would walk in love,
But, alas! how slow we move;
Pride, that haughty monster, pride,
Often makes us start aside.

Lamb of God, Thy power make known;
Sweetly draw, and we will run;
Make our love to Thee and Thine
Like the sun at noon-day shine.

As the purchase of Thy blood,
May we seek each other's good;
And be it our great concern,
Thee to view, of Thee to learn.

May we mourn with those that mourn;
Make each other's cause our own;
Ever keeping this in mind,
We are to each other joined.

Flesh of flesh, and bone of bone,
With the King of glory one;
Of one body each a part,
Jesus, make us one in heart.

King of kings, enthroned above,
Come and shed abroad Thy love;
Fill us with that source of joy,
Which can never, never cloy.

1741   Jane Crewdson   888 6

And walk in love, as Christ also hath loved us, and hath given Himself for us an offering and a sacrifice to God for a sweet smelling savour.
Ephesians 5:2

O Saviour, I have nought to plead,
   In earth beneath or heaven above,
But just my own exceeding need
   And Thy exceeding love.

The need will soon be past and gone,
   Exceeding great, but quickly o'er;
The love unbought is all Thine own,
   And lasts for evermore.

1742   John Kent   CM
**For ye were sometimes darkness, but now are
ye light in the Lord: walk as children of light.**
Ephesians 5:8

'Till God the Spirit's rising beam
   Breaks on the sinner's eyes,
He hates the glorious gospel scheme,
   And Jesus will despise.

Self is the god that he adores,
   And sin his only food;
He seeks no healing for his sores,
   In Jesus' precious blood.

While such at sovereign mercy spurn,
   And boast how good they are,
We'll to the cross of Jesus turn,
   And seek salvation there.

Jesus, as Thou hast made us free,
   We boast not in our shame;
Yet every song shall tell of Thee,
   And speak Thy lovely name.

Nothing we plead before our God,
   By nature all depraved;
Yet in the Lamb's redeeming blood,
   We boast a sinner saved.

Sinner, 'tis only in the Lamb,
   Jehovah smiles on Thee;
Beneath the skies, no other name
   Can set the guilty free.

1743   James Seddon   76 76 D
**And be not drunk with wine, wherein is
excess; but be filled with the Spirit.**
Ephesians 5:18

The Spirit came, as promised,
   In God's appointed hour;
And now to each believer
   He comes in love and power.
And by His Holy Spirit,
   God seals us as His own;
And, through the Son and Spirit
   Makes access to His throne.

The Spirit makes our bodies
   The temple of the Lord.
He binds us all together
   In faith and true accord.
The Spirit in His greatness,
   Brings power from God above,
And with the Son and Father
   Dwells in our hearts in love.

He bids us live together
   In unity and peace;
Employ His gifts in blessing,
   And let base passions cease.
We should not grieve the Spirit
   By open sin or shame;
Nor let our words and actions
   Deny His holy name.

The word, the Spirit's weapon,
   Will bring all sin to light;
And prayer, by His directing,
   Will add new joy and might.
Be filled then with His Spirit,
   Live out God's will and word;
Rejoice with hymns and singing,
   Make music to the Lord.

*Words: J. E. Seddon © Mrs M. Seddon /
The Jubilate Group. www.jubilate.co.uk
USED BY PERMISSION*

1744   Vernon Higham   66 84 D
**Speaking to yourselves in psalms and hymns
and spiritual songs, singing and making
melody in your heart to the Lord.**
Ephesians 5:19

With thankful heart I praise
   The God who reigns supreme:
His providence and sweetest grace
   My constant theme.
The storm and wind may blow,
   My life in turmoil be,
But I believe, and this I know—
   He pilots me.

Submissive to His will
   Are land and sea and sky,
When He commands the waves are still,
   They hear His cry.
The Lord who shaped the earth,
   And called a world to sight,
Who brought about a mighty birth,
   Is Lord of light.

I trust this Mighty One
   Who took my guilt away;
He saw the suffering of His Son,
   My sin did slay.
What wondrous love I see
   That took my shame and loss;
For Jesus Christ the penalty
   Paid on the cross.

Whatever life may hold
In joy or burden sad,
My God will all my time unfold,
 And make me glad.
He is the God of grace,
Who rules my span of life;
His sovereign power and sweet embrace
 Remove the strife.

All things are in His hand,
I thankfully rejoice;
His mercy grants me strength to stand,
 And heed His voice.
A song of joy within,
Inspired by Calvary—
This act divine my heart did win—
 Sweet melody.

© Author

1745 Dorothy Gurney   11 10 11 10
**Husbands, love your wives, even as Christ
also loved the church, and gave Himself for it.**
Ephesians 5:25

O perfect Love, all human thought transcending,
 Lowly we kneel in prayer before Thy throne,
That theirs may be the love which knows no
  ending
 Whom Thou for evermore dost join in one.

O perfect Life, be Thou their full assurance
 Of tender charity and steadfast faith,
Of patient hope and quiet, brave endurance,
 With childlike trust that fears nor pain nor death.

Grant them the joy which brightens earthly sorrow,
 Grant them the peace which calms all earthly
  strife;
And to life's day the glorious unknown morrow
 That dawns upon eternal love and life.

Hear us, O Father, gracious and forgiving,
 Through Jesus Christ Thy co-eternal Word,
Who, with the Holy Ghost, by all things living
 Now and to endless ages art adored.

1746 Vernon Higham   CM
**That He might present it to Himself a glorious
church, not having spot, or wrinkle, or any
such thing; but that it should be holy and
without blemish.**
Ephesians 5:27

Glory to Thee, O God above,
 For Thou hast loved Thine own.
Thy blessèd Son with costly love,
 Has made us Thine alone.

Thy glorious church while here on earth,
 Is purchased as His bride,
Robed in a righteousness of worth
 Is heaven's delight and pride.

Sweet is the covenant of grace
 Uniting two in Thee;
Love and obedience now embrace
 In happy harmony.

What God has joined for His name's sake
 No man shall separate;
Sacred the promises we make
 Ourselves to consecrate.

One with each other and with Thee
 In holy unity,
Our lives upon Thine altar be
 In love's captivity.

O grant the presence of the Lord
 To seal the promise rare,
And give the blessing of Thy word
 With everlasting care.

© Author

1747 Henry White   77 77
**Finally, my brethren, be strong in the Lord,
and in the power of His might.**
Ephesians 6:10

Oft in danger, oft in woe,
Onward, Christians, onward go;
Bear the toil, maintain the strife,
Strengthened with the Bread of life.

Onward, Christians, onward go!
Join the war and face the foe;
Will ye flee in danger's hour?
Know ye not your Captain's power?

Let your drooping hearts be glad;
March in heavenly armour clad;
Fight, nor think the battle long;
Victory soon shall tune your song.

Let not sorrow dim your eye,
Soon shall every tear be dry;
Let not fears your course impede,
Great your strength, if great your need.

Onward then in battle move;
More than conquerors ye shall prove;
Though opposed by many a foe,
Christian soldiers, onward go.

1748   Charles Wesley   SM
**Put on the whole armour of God, that ye may
be able to stand against the wiles of the devil.**
Ephesians 6:11

Soldiers of Christ, arise
And put your armour on;
Strong in the strength which God supplies
   Through His eternal Son;

Strong in the Lord of hosts
And in His mighty power;
Who in the strength of Jesus trusts
   Is more than conqueror.

Stand, then, in His great might
With all His strength endued;
And take, to arm you for the fight,
   The panoply of God.

Leave no unguarded place,
No weakness of the soul;
Take every virtue, every grace
   And fortify the whole.

From strength to strength go on;
Wrestle and fight and pray;
Tread all the powers of darkness down
   And win the well-fought day.

That, having all things done
And all your conflicts past,
Ye may o'ercome, through Christ alone
   And stand complete at last.

1749   Joseph Hart   LM
**Praying always with all prayer and
supplication in the Spirit, and watching
thereunto with all perseverance and
supplication for all saints.**
Ephesians 6:18

Prayer was appointed to convey
   The blessings God designs to give.
Long as they live should Christians pray;
   For only while they pray they live.

The Christian's heart his prayer indites;
   He speaks as prompted from within;
The Spirit his petition writes,
   And Christ receives and gives it in.

'Tis prayer supports the soul that's weak,
   Though thought be broken, language
      lame,
Pray, if thou canst or canst not speak;
   But pray with faith in Jesus' name.

Depend on Him, thou canst not fail;
   Make all thy wants and wishes known;
Fear not, His merits must prevail;
   Ask what thou wilt, it shall be done.

1750   Augustus Toplady
                           88 88 D (anapaestic)
**Being confident of this very thing, that He
which hath begun a good work in you will
perform it until the day of Jesus Christ.**
Philippians 1:6

A debtor to mercy alone,
   Of covenant mercy I sing;
Nor fear, with Thy righteousness on,
   My person and offerings to bring.
The terrors of law and of God
   With me can have nothing to do;
My Saviour's obedience and blood
   Hide all my transgressions from view.

The work which His goodness began,
   The arm of His strength will complete;
His promise is 'Yea and Amen,'
   And never was forfeited yet.
Things future, nor things that are now,
   Not all things below nor above,
Can make Him His purpose forego,
   Or sever my soul from His love.

My name from the palms of His hands
   Eternity will not erase,
Impressed on His heart it remains,
   In marks of indelible grace;
Yes, I to the end shall endure,
   As sure as the earnest is given;
More happy, but not more secure,
   The glorified spirits in heaven.

1751   Joseph Swain   CM
**And this I pray, that your love may abound yet
more and more in knowledge and in all
judgment.** *Philippians 1:9*

How sweet, how heavenly is the sight,
   When those that love the Lord,
In one another's peace delight,
   And so fulfil His word!

When each can feel his brother's sigh,
   And with him bear a part;
When sorrow flows from eye to eye,
   And joy from heart to heart.

When free from envy, scorn, and pride,
   Our wishes all above,
Each can his brother's failings hide,
   And show a brother's love.

When love in one delightful stream
  Through every bosom flows;
When union sweet and dear esteem
  In every action glows!

Love is the golden chain that binds
  The happy souls above;
And he's an heir of heaven that finds
  His bosom glow with love.

1752   Richard Burnham   66 66 88
**That ye may approve things that are excellent;
that ye may be sincere and without offence till
the day of Christ.**
Philippians 1:10

O God, Thou glorious King,
  Thine eyes pierce through the world,
And every secret thing
  Thou clearly dost behold:
Our hearts are open to Thy view,
Make us sincere in all we do.

Then may we ever dread
  To trifle with Thy word,
And ever be afraid
  To sin against the Lord;
O may our hearts be right with Thee,
Sincere, and from deception free.

May we be kept sincere,
  And after Jesus breathe,
Still walk in godly fear,
  And close to Jesus cleave;
In all sincerity rejoice,
And hear Thy kind approving voice.

1753   Carl Spitta, tr. J Borthwick   DCM
**But I would ye should understand, brethren,
that the things which happened unto me have
fallen out rather unto the furtherance of the
gospel.** *Philippians 1:12*

How blessèd, from the bonds of sin
  And earthly fetters free,
In singleness of heart and aim,
  Thy servant, Lord, to be;
The hardest toil to undertake
  With joy at Thy command,
The meanest office to receive
  With meekness at Thy hand.

With willing heart and longing eyes
  To watch before Thy gate,
Ready to run the weary race,
  To bear the heavy weight;
No voice of thunder to expect,
  But follow, calm and still;
For love can easily divine
  The One Beloved's will.

Thus may I serve Thee, gracious Lord,
  Thus ever Thine alone,
My soul and body given to Thee,
  The purchase Thou hast won;
Through evil or through good report
  Still keeping by Thy side,
By life or death, in this poor flesh
  Let Christ be magnified.

How happily the working days
  In this dear service fly;
How rapidly the closing hour,
  The time of rest draws nigh,
When all the faithful gather home,
  A joyful company,
And ever where the Master is
  Shall His blest servants be.

1754   William Horne   CM
For to me to live is Christ, and to die is gain.
Philippians 1:21

Death is no more a frightful foe;
  Since I with Christ shall reign,
With joy I leave this world of woe;
  For me to die is gain.

To darkness, doubts, and fears, adieu;
  Adieu, thou world so vain;
Then shall I know no more of you;
  For me to die is gain.

No more shall Satan tempt my soul,
  Corruption shall be slain;
And tides of pleasure o'er me roll;
  For me to die is gain.

Nor shall I know a Father's frown,
  But ever with Him reign,
And wear an everlasting crown,
  For me to die is gain.

Sorrow for joy I shall exchange,
  For ever freed from pain;
And o'er the plains of Canaan range;
  For me to die is gain.

Fain would my raptured soul depart,
  Nor longer here remain,
But dwell, dear Jesus, where Thou art;
  For me to die is gain.

1755 Theodore Monod   87 887
For to me to live is Christ, and to die is gain.
Philippians 1:21

O the bitter shame and sorrow,
   That a time could ever be,
When I let the Saviour's pity
Plead in vain and proudly answered,
   'All of self and none of Thee!'

Yet He found me; I beheld Him
   Bleeding on the accursèd tree,
Heard Him pray, 'Forgive them, Father!'
And my wistful heart said faintly
   'Some of self and some of Thee.'

Day by day His tender mercy,
   Healing, helping, full and free,
Sweet and strong and, O so patient,
Brought me lower, while I whispered,
   'Less of self and more of Thee.'

Higher than the highest heavens,
   Deeper than the deepest sea,
Lord, Thy love at last hath conquered;
Grant me now my supplication
   'None of self and all of Thee.'

1756 *Prust's H/B* 1869   LM
For to me to live is Christ, and to die is gain.
Philippians 1:21

How blest is life if lived for Thee,
   My loving Saviour and my Lord;
No pleasures that the world can give
   Such perfect gladness can afford.

To know I am Thy ransomed child,
   Bought by Thine own most precious blood
And from Thy loving hand to take
   With grateful heart each gift of good;

All day to walk beneath Thy smile,
   Watching Thine eye to guide me still,
To rest at night beneath Thy care,
   Guarded by Thee from every ill;

To feel that though I journey on
   By stony paths and rugged ways,
Thy blessèd feet have gone before
   And strength is given for weary days.

Such love shall ever make me glad,
   Strong in Thy strength to work or rest,
Until I see Thee face to face
   And in Thy light am fully blest.

1757 Henri Malan, tr.G Bethune   SM
For to me to live is Christ, and to die is gain.
Philippians 1:21

It is not death to die,
   To leave this weary road,
And midst the family on high,
   To be at home with God.

It is not death to close
   The eye long dimmed by tears,
And wake in glorious repose
   To spend eternal years.

It is not death to bear
   The wrench that sets us free
From dungeon-chains to breathe the air
   Of boundless liberty.

It is not death to fling
   Aside this sinful dust,
And rise on strong, exulting wing,
   To live among the just.

Jesus, Thou Prince of life,
   Thy chosen cannot die;
Like Thee, they conquer in the strife
   To reign with Thee on high.

1758 Richard Baxter   CM
Yet what I shall choose I wot not.
Philippians 1:22

Lord, it belongs not to my care
   Whether I die or live;
To love and serve Thee is my share
   And this Thy grace must give.

If life be long, I will be glad
   That I may long obey;
If short, yet why should I be sad
   To soar to endless day?

Christ leads me through no darker rooms
   Than He went through before;
And He that to God's kingdom comes
   Must enter by this door.

Come, Lord, when grace has made me meet
   Thy blessèd face to see,
For if Thy work on earth be sweet,
   What will Thy glory be?

My knowledge of that life is small,
   The eye of faith is dim;
But 'tis enough that Christ knows all
   And I shall be with Him.

1759   Isaac Watts   CM

For I am in a strait betwixt two, having a desire to depart, and to be with Christ; which is far better. *Philippians 1:23*

Father, I long, I faint to see
  The place of Thy abode;
I'd leave Thy earthly courts and flee
  Up to Thy seat, my God!

Here I behold Thy distant face,
  And 'tis a pleasing sight;
But to abide in Thy embrace
  Is infinite delight.

I'd part with all the joys of sense
  To gaze upon Thy throne;
Pleasure springs fresh for ever thence,
  Unspeakable, unknown.

The more Thy glories strike my eyes;
  The humbler I shall lie;
Thus, while I sink, my joys shall rise
  Unmeasurably high.

1760   Alan Clifford   66 66 44 44

If there be therefore any consolation in Christ, if any comfort of love, if any fellowship of the Spirit, if any bowels and mercies.
Philippians 2:1

Let joyful tongues unite
  And sing with fervent voice,
To praise our Saviour's might
  And His triumphant grace!
    Rejoice with awe,
      For through His love
      We'll dwell above,
    For evermore!

He left His courts on high,
  His Father's peace to bring,
That through His blood brought nigh,
  We'd to His mercy sing;
    Our guilty souls,
      Though bound for hell,
      To Zion's hill
    Are brought, with praise!

Behold the cruel cross
  On which the Saviour died;
His suffering ends our loss,
  God's law is satisfied;
    His mercy's just,
      So at His throne
      His love we own,
    We can Him trust.

We'll sing eternally
  And bless that sacred name;
With joy we bend the knee
  To Him who took our shame;
    We worship bring!
      O may our days
      Be full of praise,
    Immortal King!

                   © *Author*

1761   Caroline Noel   65 65 D

Let this mind be in you, which was also in Christ Jesus... *Philippians 2:5-11*

At the name of Jesus
  Every knee shall bow,
Every tongue confess Him
  King of glory now;
'Tis the Father's pleasure
  We should call Him Lord,
Who from the beginning
  Was the mighty Word.

At His voice creation
  Sprang at once to sight,
All the angel faces,
  All the hosts of light;
Thrones and dominations,
  Stars upon their way,
All the heavenly orders
  In their great array.

Humbled for a season
  To receive a name
From the lips of sinners,
  Unto whom He came;
Faithfully He bore it
  Spotless to the last;
Brought it back victorious
  When from death He passed.

In your hearts enthrone Him;
  There let Him subdue
All that is not holy,
  All that is not true;
Crown Him as your Captain
  In temptation's hour,
Let His will enfold you
  In its light and power.

Brothers, this Lord Jesus
  Shall return again,
With His Father's glory,
  With His angel train;
For all wreaths of empire
  Meet upon His brow,
And our hearts confess Him
  King of glory now.

1762 Katie Wilkinson 87 85
Let this mind be in you, which was also in Christ Jesus. *Philippians 2:5*

May the mind of Christ my Saviour
　Live in me from day to day,
By His love and power controlling
　All I do and say.

May the word of God dwell richly
　In my heart from hour to hour,
So that all may see I triumph
　Only through His power.

May the peace of God my Father
　Rule my life in everything,
That I may be calm to comfort
　Sick and sorrowing.

May the love of Jesus fill me
　As the waters fill the sea;
Him exalting, self abasing,
　This is victory.

May I run the race before me,
　Strong and brave to face the foe,
Looking only unto Jesus
　As I onward go.

May His beauty rest upon me
　As I seek the lost to win,
And may they forget the channel,
　Seeing only Him.

1763 James Montgomery 77 77
Let this mind be in you, which was also in Christ Jesus. *Philippians 2:5*

Father of eternal grace,
　May we all resemble Thee;
Meekly beaming in our face,
　May the world Thine image see.

Happy only in Thy love,
　Poor, unfriended, or unknown;
Fix our thoughts on things above,
　Stay our hearts on Thee alone.

Humble, holy, all resigned
　To Thy will; Thy will be done!
Give us, Lord, the perfect mind
　Of Thy well-belovèd Son.

Counting gain and glory loss,
　May we tread the path He trod:
Bear with Him on earth our cross,
　Rise with Him to Thee, our God.

SAMUEL STENNETT 1727-1795

1764 Samuel Stennett 66 66 88
Who, being in the form of God, thought it not robbery to be equal with God.
Philippians 2:6

Come, every gracious heart,
　That loves the Saviour's name,
Your noblest powers exert,
　To celebrate His fame;
Tell all who fear the Lord below,
The debt of love to Him you owe.

He left His starry crown,
　And laid His robes aside,
On wings of love came down,
　And wept, and bled, and died;
What He endured no tongue can tell,
To save our souls from death and hell.

From the dark grave He rose,
　The mansion of the dead;
And thence His mighty foes
　In glorious triumph led;
Up through the sky the Conqueror rode,
And reigns on high, the Saviour, God.

From thence He'll quickly come;
　His chariots will not stay;
And bear our spirits home,
　To realms of endless day.
There shall we see His lovely face,
And ever dwell in His embrace.

1765   Vernon Higham   CM

Who, being in the form of God, thought it not robbery to be equal with God.
Philippians 2:6

Lord Jesus Christ, I worship Thee,
 Thou King of love and grace;
For Thou hast whispered I may see
 The glory of Thy face.

My Saviour gave Himself for me,
 With reputation, none!
O, such a death and agony
 Has my pure pardon won!

Nothing I give can Him repay,
 My Saviour and my joy;
Nothing I have can I display,
 Will ever grace employ.

Yet freely of Thy grace alone,
 I stand on ground secure;
Thou hast atoned and moved the stone
 To gates of life so sure.

O let me bring to Thee my love,
 The tithes of my own heart;
To give, and give, to Thee above,
 This holy, blessèd part.

How can these hands forget so soon
 Those piercèd on a cross?
How can this heart refuse a room
 And suffer such a loss?

O teach me Lord to understand
 How Thou dost blessing give;
Fill Thou Thy storehouse by Thy hand,
 And show me how to live!

© Author

1766   Anne Steele   CM

But made Himself of no reputation, and took upon Him the form of a servant, and was made in the likeness of men.
Philippians 2:7

To our Redeemer's glorious name,
 Awake the sacred song;
O may His love (immortal flame!)
 Tune every heart and tongue.

His love, what mortal thought can reach,
 What mortal tongue display?
Imagination's utmost stretch
 In wonder dies away!

He left His radiant throne on high!
 Left the bright realms of bliss!
And came to earth to bleed and die!
 Was ever love like this?

Dear Lord, while we adoring pay
 Our humble thanks to Thee,
May every heart with rapture say,
 'The Saviour died for me.'

1767   Cecil Alexander   87 87 77

But made Himself of no reputation, and took upon Him the form of a servant, and was made in the likeness of men.
Philippians 2:7

Once in royal David's city
 Stood a lowly cattle-shed,
Where a mother laid her baby
 In a manger for His bed.
Mary was that mother mild,
Jesus Christ her little Child.

He came down to earth from heaven,
 Who is God and Lord of all;
And His shelter was a stable,
 And His cradle was a stall:
With the poor and mean and lowly
Lived on earth our Saviour holy.

And through all His wondrous childhood
 He would honour and obey,
Love, and watch the lowly mother
 In whose gentle arms He lay:
Christian children all must be
Mild, obedient, good as he.

For He is our childhood's pattern:
 Day by day like us He grew;
He was little, weak, and helpless,
 Tears and smiles like us He knew;
And He feeleth for our sadness,
And He shareth in our gladness.

And our eyes at last shall see Him,
 Through His own redeeming love;
For that Child so dear and gentle
 Is our Lord in heaven above;
And He leads His children on
To the place where He is gone.

Not in that poor lowly stable,
 With the oxen standing by,
We shall see Him, but in heaven,
 Set at God's right hand on high,
When, like stars, His children crowned,
All in white shall wait around.

1768   Anne Steele (alt)   CM
**And being found in fashion as a man, He
humbled Himself, and became obedient unto
death, even the death of the cross.**
Philippians 2:8

And did the Holy and the Just,
  The Sovereign of the skies,
Stoop down to wretchedness and dust,
  That guilty ones might rise?

Yes, the Redeemer left His throne,
  His radiant throne on high,
Surprising mercy! Love unknown!
  To suffer, bleed, and die!

He took the dying traitor's place,
  And suffered in his stead;
For man O miracle of grace!
  For man the Saviour bled.

Dear Lord, what heavenly wonders dwell
  In Thy atoning blood!
By this are sinners snatched from hell,
  And rebels brought to God.

What glad return can I impart
  For favours so divine?
O take my all, this worthless heart,
  And make it wholly Thine.

1769   Benjamin Hanby   77 + refrain
**And being found in fashion as a man, He
humbled Himself, and became obedient unto
death, even the death of the cross.**
Philippians 2:8

Who is He in yonder stall,
At whose feet the shepherds fall?

  *'Tis the Lord! O wondrous story!
  'Tis the Lord, the King of glory!
    At His feet we humbly fall—
    Crown Him! crown Him, Lord of all!*

Who is He in deep distress
Fasting in the wilderness?

Who is He to whom they bring
All the sick and sorrowing?

Who is He the gathering throng
Greet with loud triumphant song?

Who is He on yonder tree
Dies in shame and agony?

Who is He who from the grave
Comes to heal and help and save?

Who is He that from His throne
Rules through all the worlds alone?

1770   Charles Wesley   66 66 88
**And being found in fashion as a man, He
humbled Himself, and became obedient unto
death, even the death of the cross.**
Philippians 2:8

  Let earth and heaven combine,
    Angels and men agree,
  To praise in songs divine
    The incarnate Deity;
Our God contracted to a span,
Incomprehensibly made man.

  He laid His glory by,
    He wrapped Him in our clay;
  Unmarked by human eye,
    The latent Godhead lay;
Infant of days He here became,
And bore the mild Immanuel's name.

  Unsearchable the love
    That hath the Saviour brought;
  The grace is far above
    Mankind's or angel's thought:
Suffice for us that God, we know,
Our God, is manifest below.

  He deigns in flesh to appear,
    Widest extremes to join;
  To bring our vileness near,
    And make us all divine:
And we the life of God shall know,
For God is manifest below.

  Made perfect first in love,
    And sanctified by grace,
  We shall from earth remove,
    And see His glorious face:
Then shall His love be fully showed,
And man shall then be lost in God.

1771   Isaac Watts   66 66 88
**Wherefore God also hath highly exalted Him,
and given Him a name which is above every
name.** *Philippians 2:9*

  Join all the glorious names
    Of wisdom, love, and power,
  That ever mortals knew,
    That angels ever bore;
All are too mean to speak His worth,
Too mean to set my Saviour forth.

Great Prophet of my God,
My tongue would bless Thy name;
By Thee the joyful news
Of our salvation came;
The joyful news of sins forgiven,
Of hell subdued, and peace with heaven.

Jesus, my great High Priest,
Offered His blood and died;
My guilty conscience seeks
No sacrifice beside.
His powerful blood did once atone,
And now it pleads before the throne.

My Saviour and my Lord,
My Conqueror and my King,
Thy sceptre and Thy sword,
Thy reigning grace I sing;
Thine is the power; behold, I sit,
In willing bonds, beneath Thy feet.

Should all the hosts of death,
And powers of hell unknown,
Put their most dreadful forms
Of rage and mischief on,
I shall be safe, for Christ displays
Superior power and guardian grace.

THOMAS KELLY 1769-1855

1772 Thomas Kelly   CM
**Wherefore God also hath highly exalted Him,
and given Him a name which is above every
name.** *Philippians 2:9*

The head that once was crowned with thorns
Is crowned with glory now;
A royal diadem adorns
The mighty Victor's brow.

The highest place that heaven affords
Is His by sovereign right,
The King of kings, the Lord of lords,
And heaven's eternal Light.

The joy of all who dwell above,
The joy of all below,
To whom He manifests His love,
And grants His name to know.

To them the cross, with all its shame,
With all its grace, is given;
Their name an everlasting name,
Their joy the joy of heaven.

They suffer with their Lord below,
They reign with Him above;
Their profit and their joy to know
The mystery of His love.

The cross He bore is life and health,
Though shame and death to Him:
His people's hope, His people's wealth,
Their everlasting theme.

1773 Anon 15th Cent, tr. J Neale   87 87 87
**Wherefore God also hath highly exalted Him,
and given Him a name which is above every
name.** *Philippians 2:9*

To the name of our salvation,
Praise and honour let us pay,
Which for many a generation
Hid in God's foreknowledge lay,
But with holy exultation
We may sing aloud today.

Jesus is the name we treasure,
Name beyond what words can tell;
Name of gladness, name of pleasure,
Ear and heart delighting well;
Name of sweetness, passing measure,
Saving us from sin and hell.

Jesus is the name exalted
Over every other name;
In this name, whene'er assaulted,
We can put our foes to shame;
Strength to them who else had halted,
Eyes to blind, and feet to lame.

Therefore we, in love adoring,
This most blessèd name revere:
Holy Jesus, Thee imploring
So to write it in us here,
That, hereafter heavenward soaring,
We may sing with angels there.

JOSIAH CONDER 1789-1855

1774   Josiah Conder   86 86 88
That at the name of Jesus every knee should bow, of things in heaven, and things in earth, and things under the earth. *Philippians 2:10*

Thou art the everlasting Word,
  The Father's only Son;
God manifestly seen and heard,
  And Heaven's belovèd One:

    Worthy, O Lamb of God, art Thou
    That every knee to Thee should bow.

In Thee most perfectly expressed
  The Father's glories shine;
Of the full Deity possessed,
  Eternally divine:

True image of the Infinite,
  Whose essence is concealed;
Brightness of uncreated light;
  The heart of God revealed:

But the high mysteries of Thy Name
  An angel's grasp transcend;
The Father only—glorious claim!—
  The Son can comprehend:

Throughout the universe of bliss,
  The centre Thou, and sun;
The eternal theme of praise is this,
  To Heaven's belovèd One:

1775   Frederick Whitfield   CM
That at the name of Jesus every knee should bow, of things in heaven, and things in earth, and things under the earth. *Philippians 2:10*

There is a Name I love to hear,
  I love to sing its worth,
It sounds like music in mine ear,
  The sweetest Name on earth.

It tells me of a Saviour's love,
  Who died to set me free,
It tells me of His precious blood,
  The sinner's perfect plea.

It bids my trembling sou! rejoice,
  And dries each rising tear;
It tells me in a still small voice,
  To trust and never fear.

Jesus, the name I love so well,
  The name I love to hear,
No saint on earth its worth can tell,
  No heart conceive how dear.

This name shall shed its fragrance still
  Along this thorny road,
Shall sweetly smooth the rugged hill
  That leads me up to God.

And there, with all the blood-bought throng,
  From sin and sorrow free,
I'll sing the new eternal song
  Of Jesus' love to me.

1776   Edward Osler   886 D
But I trust in the Lord Jesus to send Timotheus shortly unto you, that I also may be of good comfort, when I know your state.
Philippians 2:19

Lord of the church, we humbly pray
For those who guide us in Thy way,
  And speak Thy holy word;
With love divine their hearts inspire,
And touch their lips with hallowed fire,
  And needful grace afford.

Help them to preach the truth of God,
Redemption through the Saviour's blood;
  Nor let Thy Spirit cease
On all the church His gifts to shower—
To them, a messenger of power,
  To us, of life and peace.

So may they live to Thee alone;
Then hear the welcome word 'Well done!'
  And take their crown above;
Enter into their Master's joy,
And all eternity employ
  In praise and bliss and love!

1777   James Montgomery   LM
Receive him therefore in the Lord with all gladness; and hold such in reputation.
Philippians 2:29

We bid thee welcome in the name
  Of Jesus our exalted Head;
Come as a servant, so He came,
  And we receive Him in our stead.

Come as a shepherd; guard and keep
  This fold from hell, and earth, and sin;
Nourish the lambs, and feed the sheep,
  The wounded heal, the lost bring in.

Come as an angel; hence to guide
  A band of pilgrims on their way;
That safely walking at thy side,
  We faint not, fail not, turn, nor stray.

Come as a teacher sent from God,
  Charged His whole counsel to declare;
Lift o'er our ranks the prophet's rod,
  While we uphold thy hands with prayer.

Come as a messenger of peace,
  Filled with the Spirit, fired with love;
Live to behold our large increase,
  And die to meet us all above.

1778   Isaac Watts   CM
For we are the circumcision, which worship God in the spirit, and rejoice in Christ Jesus, and have no confidence in the flesh.
Philippians 3:3

Come Holy Spirit, heavenly Dove,
  With Thy all-quickening powers;
Kindle a flame of sacred love
  In these cold hearts of ours.

In vain we tune our formal songs,
  In vain we strive to rise;
Hosannas languish on our tongues,
  And our devotion dies.

Dear Lord, and shall we ever live
  At this poor dying rate?
Our love so faint, so cold to Thee,
  And Thine to us so great?

Come, Holy Spirit, heavenly Dove,
  With Thy all-quickening powers;
Come shed abroad a Saviour's love,
  And that shall kindle ours.

1779   Richard Burnham   LM
But what things were gain to me, those I counted loss for Christ. *Philippians 3:7*

To know my Jesus crucified,
By far excels all things beside;
All earthly good I count but loss,
And triumph in my Saviour's cross.

Knowledge of all terrestrial things
Ne'er to my soul true pleasure brings;
No peace, but in the Son of God;
No joy, but through His pardoning blood.

O could I know and love Him more,
And all His wondrous grace explore,
Ne'er would I covet man's esteem,
But part with all, and follow Him.

Lord, may I bear my every loss;
Be patient under every cross;
Never may I my Saviour blame,
Though I'm despised for His dear name.

Thus make me willing, glorious Lamb,
To suffer all things for Thy name;
At last be where my Jesus is,
And rise to everlasting bliss.

1780   Isaac Watts   LM
I count all things but loss for the excellency of the knowledge of Christ Jesus my Lord.
Philippians 3:8

When I survey the wondrous cross
  On which the Prince of glory died,
My richest gain I count but loss,
  And pour contempt on all my pride.

Forbid it, Lord, that I should boast,
  Save in the cross of Christ my God:
All the vain things that charm me most,
  I sacrifice them to His blood.

See from His head, His hands, His feet,
  Sorrow and love flow mingled down:
Did e'er such love and sorrow meet,
  Or thorns compose so rich a crown?

Were the whole realm of nature mine,
  That were an offering far too small;
Love so amazing, so divine,
  Demands my soul, my life, my all!

1781 Isaac Watts LM
**I count all things but loss for the excellency of
the knowledge of Christ Jesus my Lord.**
Philippians 3:8

No more, my God, I boast no more
  Of all the duties I have done;
I quit the hopes I held before,
  To trust the merits of Thy Son.

Now, for the love I bear His name,
  What was my gain I count my loss;
My former pride I call my shame,
  And nail my glory to His cross.

Yes, and I must and will esteem
  All things but loss for Jesus' sake;
O may my soul be found in Him,
  And of His righteousness partake!

The best obedience of my hands
  Dares not appear before Thy throne;
But faith can answer Thy demands,
  By pleading what my Lord has done.

1782 Richard Burnham 66 66 88
**I count all things but loss for the excellency of
the knowledge of Christ Jesus my Lord.**
Philippians 3:8

To know that Christ is mine;
  To view His smiling face;
To see His glory shine,
  Gives pure and perfect peace;
O may I ever sing and say,
'Jesus the Saviour died for me.'

To me, how wondrous kind!
  On me what blessings fall!
His cross delights my mind,
  His love transports my soul;
While on His bosom I recline,
He tells me all He has is mine.

Mine His atoning blood,
  And mine His righteousness!
Mine all the grace of God,
  And mine the gospel peace!
Mine, every promise in the word,
And mine the fulness of the Lord!

Jesus I now adore,
  Salvation now I prove;
Lord, may I never more
  Suspect Thy dying love:
Let none deprive me of this plea,
'The great Redeemer died for me.'

1783 Vernon Higham LM
**I count all things but loss for the excellency of
the knowledge of Christ Jesus my Lord.**
Philippians 3:8

I once believed my life a gain,
And thought that I would grace attain:
The Spirit showed me all the dross,
And now I see it all but loss.

Then I beheld the Saviour's face,
And looked upon a life of grace:
When I compared my feeble chart,
Shame and remorse then filled my heart.

O to be found in Christ alone,
For on the cross He did atone:
He took my sin and nailed it there,
And gave a gown of grace to wear.

Now I dismiss my foolish pride,
Covered in Christ, in whom I hide:
All this by faith that will not fail,
Granted by God, I will prevail.

O wondrous joy the Lord to know,
I will delight Thy name to show:
Yet, I desire to know Thee more,
I hunger for Thy boundless store.

Thy risen power I long to prove,
Fully enabled in each move:
Through fellowship of suffering sweet,
I worship Thee and ever greet.

Confirm me now in image strange;
Death worketh life, what great exchange!
Yet I believe in Thine increase;
Lord, evermore may I decrease.

Lord, all my life to do Thy will,
This by Thy grace I will fulfill:
Then Thou wilt change my body vile,
Fashioned in Christ— I wait awhile.
© Author

W. VERNON HIGHAM. 1926-

1784   Vernon Higham   DCM

That I may know Him, and the power of His resurrection, and the fellowship of His sufferings, being made conformable unto His death. *Philippians 3:10*

Deep in my heart there is a sigh,
   A longing, Lord, for Thee;
To know the depths that in Thee lie,
   The grace of Calvary.
O grant that I might understand
   Thy glorious mystery,
More of Thyself, and by Thy hand
   Obedience stir in me.

Thy living power I long to prove
   In resurrection might,
With overcoming grace to move
   Each sin that dims this light.
O grant that I may find the source
   Of hidden strength and stay,
Which flows from Thee, and on its course
   O draw my soul each day.

There is a fellowship of pain
   Deep in Thy heart of love,
Of suffering sweet, eternal gain,
   The tears of heaven above.
O grant me, Lord, to feel this joy,
   These tremors of Thy grace;
Engraved by Thee, none can destroy
   The riches I embrace.

Then lead me in this wondrous way
   To die to self and sin;
And take me, Lord, when Thou dost slay,
   And drive Thy grace within.
O grant me now an image sweet
   Impressed upon my heart;
With joy I lie beneath Thy feet,
   To weep and not depart.

© Author

1785   Richard Lee   LM

That I may know Him, and the power of His resurrection, and the fellowship of His sufferings, being made conformable unto His death. *Philippians 3:10*

'Tis life to know the dying Lamb,
Eternal life is in His name;
O may I in this knowledge grow,
And daily more of Jesus know!

Know Him to wash me in His blood;
Know Him to make my peace with God;
Know Him for strength and righteousness;
And know Him for renewing grace.

Know Him as my exceeding joy;
Know Him, my praises to employ;
Know Him in all the heights of bliss;
And know and see Him as He is.

1786   John Berridge   886 D

I follow after. *Philippians 3:12*

If unto Jesus thou art bound,
A crowd about Him will be found;
   Attending day and night;
A worldly crowd to din thy ears,
And crowds of unbelieving fears,
   To hide Him from thy sight.

Yet all the vain and noisy crowd
Is but a thin and lowering cloud,
   A mist before thy eyes;
If thou press on, the crowds will fly,
Or if thou faint, to Jesus cry,
   And He will send supplies.

This only way can pilgrims go,
And all complain, as thou wilt do,
   Of crowds that daily come;
Yet though beset by crafty foes,
And passing through a thousand woes,
   They get securely home.

O Lord, a cheering look bestow,
Or lend a hand to help me through,
   And draw me up to Thee;
And when, through fear, I only creep,
Or dare not move a single step,
   Yet Thou canst come to me.

1787   Charles Wesley   77 77 D
**I beseech Euodias, and beseech Syntyche,
that they be of the same mind in the Lord.**
Philippians 4:2

Lord from whom all blessings flow,
Perfecting the church below,
  Steadfast may we cleave to Thee,
  Love, the mystic union be:
Join our faithful spirits, join
Each to each, and all to Thine;
  Lead us through the paths of peace
  On to perfect holiness.

Move and actuate and guide;
Various gifts to each divide:
  Placed according to Thy will
  Let us all our work fulfil;
Never from our office move;
Needful to each other prove;
  Use the grace on each bestowed
  Tempered by the art of God.

Sweetly may we all agree
Touched with softest sympathy:
  There is neither bond nor free,
  Great nor servile, Lord, in Thee:
Love like death hath all destroyed,
Rendered all distinctions void:
  Names and sects and parties fall,
  Thou, O Christ, art All in all.

1788   William Gadsby   SM
**Rejoice in the Lord alway: and again I say,
Rejoice.** *Philippians 4:4*

  Let saints lift up their hearts,
  And, with a cheerful voice,
The wonders of their King proclaim,
  And in the Lord rejoice.

  Whatever be thy frame,
  Though dark and cold as ice,
No change has taken place in Him;
  Then in the Lord rejoice.

  Till God can change His mind,
  And swear He has no choice,
The soul that in the Lord believes,
  Shall in the Lord rejoice.

  As sure as God is God,
  And Abra'm heard His voice,
He'll love His saints unto the end,
  Then let them all rejoice.

  Nor sin, nor death, nor hell,
  Can make Him hate His choice;
The cause of love is in Himself;
  And in Him we'll rejoice.

He made an end of sin,
  And bought us with a price;
Our life, our hope, our all's in Him,
  And we'll in Him rejoice.

CHARLES WESLEY 1707-88

1789   Charles Wesley   CM
**Rejoice in the Lord alway: and again I say,
Rejoice.** *Philippians 4:4*

O for a thousand tongues to sing
  My dear Redeemer's praise,
The glories of my God and King,
  The triumphs of His grace!

Jesus! the name that charms our fears,
  That bids our sorrows cease;
'Tis music in the sinner's ears,
  'Tis life, and health, and peace.

He breaks the power of cancelled sin,
  He sets the prisoner free;
His blood can make the foulest clean,
  His blood availed for me.

He speaks, and, listening to His voice,
  New life the dead receive,
The mournful, broken hearts rejoice,
  The humble poor believe.

Hear Him, ye deaf; His praise, ye dumb,
  Your loosened tongues employ;
Ye blind, behold your Saviour come;
  And leap, ye lame, for joy!

My gracious Master and my God,
  Assist me to proclaim,
To spread through all the earth abroad
  The honours of Thy name.

1790   William Gadsby   87 87 47
The Lord is at hand. *Philippians 4:5*

Pause my soul! and ask the question,
   'Art thou ready to meet God?'
Am I made a real Christian,
   Washed in the Redeemer's blood?
     Have I union
To the church's living Head?

Am I quickened by His Spirit;
   Live a life of faith and prayer?
Trusting wholly to His merit;
   Casting on Him all my care?
     Daily panting,
In His likeness to appear?

If my hope on Christ is stayèd,
   Let Him come when He thinks best;
O my soul! be not dismayèd,
   Lean upon His loving breast;
     He will cheer Thee
With the smilings of His face.

But, if still a total stranger
   To His precious name and blood,
Thou art on the brink of danger;
   Canst thou face a holy God?
     Think and tremble,
Death is now upon the road.

1791   James Montgomery   CM
**Be careful for nothing; but in every thing by
prayer and supplication with thanksgiving let
your requests be made known unto God.**
Philippians 4:6

Prayer is the soul's sincere desire,
   Uttered or unexpressed;
The motion of a hidden fire
   That trembles in the breast.

Prayer is the burden of a sigh,
   The falling of a tear;
The upward glancing of an eye,
   When none but God is near.

Prayer is the simplest form of speech
   That infant lips can try;
Prayer the sublimest strains that reach
   The Majesty on high.

Prayer is the contrite sinner's voice,
   Returning from his ways;
While angels in their songs rejoice,
   And cry, 'Behold, he prays!'

Prayer is the Christian's vital breath,
   The Christian's native air;
His watchword at the gates of death;
   He enters heaven with prayer.

Nor prayer is made on earth alone,
   The Holy Spirit pleads,
And Jesus, on the eternal throne,
   For sinners intercedes.

O Thou by whom we come to God,
   The Life, the Truth, the Way,
The path of prayer Thyself hast trod;
   Lord, teach us how to pray.

1792   Thomas Kelly   LM
**Be careful for nothing; but in every thing by
prayer and supplication with thanksgiving let
your requests be made known unto God.**
Philippians 4:6

The privilege I greatly prize
   Of casting all my care on Him,
The mighty God, the only wise,
   Who reigns in heaven and earth supreme.

How sweet to be allowed to call
   The God whom heaven adores, my Friend!
To tell my thoughts, to tell Him all,
   And then to know my prayers ascend!

Yes, they ascend: the feeblest cry
   Has wings that bear it to His throne;
The prayer of faith ascends the sky,
   And brings a gracious answer down.

Then let me banish anxious care,
   Confiding in my Father's love:
To Him make known my wants in prayer,
   Prepared His answer to approve.

My Father's wisdom cannot err,
   His love no change nor failure knows;
Be mine His counsel to prefer,
   And acquiesce in all He does.

1793   Horatius Bonar   CM
And the peace of God, which passeth all understanding, shall keep your hearts and minds through Christ Jesus.
Philippians 4:7

Calm me, my God, and keep me calm
  While these hot breezes blow;
Be like the night dew's cooling balm
  Upon earth's fevered brow.

Yes, keep me calm, though loud and rude
  The sounds my ear that greet,
Calm in the closet's solitude,
  Calm in the bustling street;

Calm in the hour of buoyant health,
  Calm in my hour of pain;
Calm in my poverty or wealth,
  Calm in my loss or gain;

Calm in the suffering of wrong
  Like Him who bore my shame;
Calm 'mid the threatening, taunting throng
  Who hate Thy holy name;

Calm as the ray of sun or star
  Which storms assail in vain,
Moving unruffled through earth's war
  The eternal calm to gain.

1794   John Newton   LM
And the peace of God, which passeth all understanding, shall keep your hearts and minds through Christ Jesus. *Philippians 4:7*

The peace which God alone reveals,
  And by His word of grace imparts,
Which only the believer feels,
  Direct, and keep, and cheer our hearts.

And may the holy Three-in-One,
  The Father, Word, and Comforter,
Pour an abundant blessing down
  On every soul assembled here.

1795   Charles Wesley   DSM
I can do all things through Christ which strengtheneth me. *Philippians 4:13*

  Jesus, my strength, my hope,
    On Thee I cast my care,
With humble confidence look up
    And know Thou hearest my prayer.
    Give me on Thee to wait
    Till I can all things do,
  On Thee, almighty to create,
    Almighty to renew.

  I want a godly fear,
    A quick-discerning eye
That looks to Thee when sin is near
    And sees the tempter fly:
    A spirit still prepared
    And armed with jealous care,
For ever standing on its guard
    And watching unto prayer.

  I want a true regard,
    A single, steady aim,
Unmoved by threatening or reward
    To Thee and Thy great name;
    A jealous, just concern
    For Thine immortal praise;
A pure desire that all may learn
    And glorify Thy grace.

  I rest upon Thy word;
    The promise is for me;
My succour and salvation, Lord,
    Shall surely come from Thee;
    But let me still abide,
    Nor from my hope remove,
Till Thou my patient spirit guide
    Into Thy perfect love.

1796   John Newton   77 77
But my God shall supply all your need according to His riches in glory by Christ Jesus. *Philippians 4:19*

Now I see, whate'er betide,
  All is well if Christ be mine;
He has promised to provide;
  May He teach me to resign.

When a sense of sin and thrall
  Forced me to the sinner's Friend,
He engaged to manage all,
  By the way and to the end.

'Cast,' He said, 'on Me thy care;
  ''Tis enough that I am nigh;
I will all thy burdens bear;
  I will all thy needs supply.'

Lord, I would indeed submit;
  Gladly yield my all to Thee;
What Thy wisdom sees most fit,
  Must be surely best for me.

Only when the way is rough,
  And the coward flesh would start,
Let Thy promise and Thy love
  Cheer and animate my heart.

1797   Isaac Watts   CM
**But my God shall supply all your need
according to His riches in glory by Christ
Jesus.** *Philippians 4:19*

My Shepherd will supply my need;
   Jehovah is His name.
In pastures fresh He makes me feed,
   Beside the living stream.

He brings my wandering spirit back,
   When I forsake His ways;
And leads me, for His mercy's sake,
   In paths of truth and grace.

When I walk through the shades of death,
   Thy presence is my stay;
A word of Thy supporting breath
   Drives all my fears away.

Thy hand, in sight of all my foes,
   Does still my table spread;
My cup with blessings overflows;
   Thy oil anoints my head.

The sure provisions of my God
   Attend me all my days.
O may Thy house be my abode,
   And all my work be praise!

There would I find a settled rest,
   While others go and come.
No more a stranger or a guest,
   But like a child at home.

1798   Anne Steele   CM
**But my God shall supply all your need
according to His riches in glory by Christ
Jesus.** *Philippians 4:19*

When I survey life's varied scene
   Amid the darkest hours,
Sweet rays of comfort shine between,
   And thorns are mixed with flowers.

Lord, teach me to adore the hand
   Whence all my comforts flow,
And let me in this desert land
   A glimpse of Canaan know.

And O whate'er of earthly bliss
   Thy sovereign will denies,
Accepted at Thy throne of grace
   Let this petition rise:

'Give me a calm, a thankful heart,
   From every murmur free;
The blessings of Thy grace impart,
   And let me live to Thee.

'Let the sweet hope that Thou art mine
   My path of life attend,
Thy presence through my journey shine,
   And crown my journey's end.'

1799   Philip Doddridge   CM
**But my God shall supply all your need
according to His riches in glory by Christ
Jesus.** *Philippians 4:19*

My God! how cheerful is the sound!
   How pleasant to repeat!
Well may that heart with pleasure bound,
   Where God hath fixed his seat.

What want shall not our God supply
   From His abundant stores?
What streams of mercy from on high
   An arm almighty pours!

From Christ the ever-living spring,
   These ample blessings flow:
Prepare, my lips, His name to sing,
   Whose heart has loved us so.

Now to our Father and our God
   Be endless glory given,
Through all the realms of man's abode,
   And through the highest heaven.

1800   *Gospel Magazine 1796*   LM
**For the hope which is laid up for you in
heaven, whereof ye heard before in the word
of the truth of the gospel.**
Colossians 1:5

In heaven my choicest treasure lies,
My hopes are placed above the skies;
'Tis Christ, the bright and Morning Star,
Draws my affections from afar.

O that my anxious mind were free
From this vile tenement of clay,
That I might view the immortal Word,
And live and reign with Christ my Lord.

Then should I see, and feel, and know,
What 'tis to rest from sin and woe;
And all my soul be tuned to sing
The praises due to Christ my King.

Hail, blessèd time! Lord, bid me come,
And enter my celestial home,
And drown the sorrows of my breast,
In seas of unmolested rest.

1801 Isabel Stevenson   85 83

We...desire that ye might be filled with the knowledge of His will in all wisdom and spiritual understanding.
Colossians 1:9

Holy Father, in Thy mercy,
  Hear Thy children's prayer;
Keep our loved ones, in their absence,
    'Neath Thy care.

Jesus, Saviour, let Thy presence
  Be their light and guide;
Keep, O keep them, in their weakness,
    At Thy side.

When in sorrow, when in danger,
  When in loneliness,
In Thy love look down and comfort
    Their distress.

May the joy of Thy salvation
  Be their strength and stay;
May they love and may they praise Thee
    Day by day.

Holy Spirit, let Thy teaching
  Sanctify their life;
Send Thy grace that they may conquer
    In the strife.

Father, Son and Holy Spirit,
  God the One in Three,
Bless them, guide them, save them, keep them
    Near to Thee.

1802 *Book of Hours* 1514   Irregular

We...desire that ye might be filled with the knowledge of His will in all wisdom and spiritual understanding.
Colossians 1:9

God be in my head,
  And in my understanding;
God be in mine eyes,
  And in my looking;
God be in my mouth,
  And in my speaking;
God be in my heart,
  And in my thinking;
God be at mine end,
  And at my departing.

1803 William Gadsby   66 66 88

That ye might walk worthy of the Lord unto all pleasing, being fruitful in every good work, and increasing in the knowledge of God.
Colossians 1:10

Ye souls, redeemed with blood,
  And called by grace divine,
Walk worthy of your God,
  And let your conduct shine;
Keep Christ, your living Head, in view,
In all you say, in all you do.

Has Jesus made you free?
  Then you are free indeed;
Ye sons of liberty,
  Ye chosen royal seed,
Walk worthy of your Lord, and view
Your glorious Head, in all you do.

Shall sons of heavenly birth
  Their dignity debase?
Unite with sons of earth,
  And take a servant's place?
The slaves to sin and Satan too
Forget to keep their Lord in view?

Forbid it, mighty God!
  Preserve us in Thy fear;
Uphold with staff and rod,
  And guard from every snare;
Teach us to walk with Christ in view,
And honour Him in all we do.

Increase our faith and love,
  And make us watch and pray;
O fix our souls above,
  Nor let us ever stray;
Dear Lord, do Thou our strength renew,
And lead us on with Christ in view.

WILLIAM SLEEPER 1819-1904

1804 William Sleeper Irregular
Who hath delivered us from the power of darkness, and hath translated us into the kingdom of His dear Son. *Colossians 1:13*

Out of my bondage, sorrow and night,
  Jesus, I come! Jesus, I come!
Into Thy freedom, gladness and light,
  Jesus, I come to Thee!
Out of my sickness into Thy health,
Out of my want and into Thy wealth,
Out of my sin and into Thyself,
  Jesus, I come to Thee!

Out of my shameful failure and loss,
  Jesus, I come! Jesus, I come!
Into the glorious gain of Thy cross,
  Jesus, I come to Thee!
Out of earth's sorrows into Thy balm,
Out of life's storm and into Thy calm,
Out of distress to jubilant psalm,
  Jesus, I come to Thee!

Out of unrest and arrogant pride,
  Jesus, I come! Jesus, I come!
Into Thy blessèd will to abide,
  Jesus, I come to Thee!
Out of myself to dwell in Thy love,
Out of despair into raptures above,
Upward for aye on wings like a dove,
  Jesus, I come to Thee!

Out of the fear and dread of the tomb,
  Jesus, I come! Jesus, I come!
Into the joy and light of Thy home,
  Jesus, I come to Thee!
Out of the depths of ruin untold,
Into the peace of Thy sheltering fold,
Ever Thy glorious face to behold,
  Jesus, I come to Thee!

1805 Johann Rothe, tr. J Wesley 88 88 88
In whom we have redemption through His blood, even the forgiveness of sins.
Colossians 1:14

Now I have found the ground wherein
  Sure my soul's anchor may remain—
The wounds of Jesus, for my sin
  Before the world's foundation slain;
Whose mercy shall unshaken stay,
When heaven and earth are fled away.

Father, Thine everlasting grace
  Our scanty thought surpasses far,
Thy heart still melts with tenderness,
  Thine arms of love still open are
Returning sinners to receive,
That mercy they may taste and live.

O Love, Thou bottomless abyss,
  My sins are swallowed up in Thee!
Covered is my unrighteousness,
  Nor spot of guilt remains on me,
While Jesus' blood, through earth and skies,
Mercy, free, boundless mercy cries.

With faith I plunge me in this sea,
  Here is my hope, my joy, my rest;
Hither, when hell assails, I flee,
  I look into my Saviour's breast:
Away, sad doubt and anxious fear!
Mercy is all that's written there.

Though waves and storms go o'er my head,
  Though strength, and health, and friends
    be gone,
Though joys be withered all and dead,
  Though every comfort be withdrawn,
On this my steadfast soul relies—
Father, Thy mercy never dies!

Fixed on this ground will I remain,
  Though my heart fail and flesh decay;
This anchor shall my soul sustain,
  When earth's foundations melt away:
Mercy's full power I then shall prove,
Loved with an everlasting love.

1806 Margaret Clarkson 66 66 88
And He is before all things, and by Him all things consist. *Colossians 1:17*

We come, O Christ, to Thee,
  True Son of God and man,
By whom all things consist,
  In whom all life began:
In Thee alone we live and move,
And have our being in Thy love.

Thou art the Way to God,
  Thy blood our ransom paid;
In Thee we face our Judge
  And Maker unafraid.
Before the throne absolved we stand:
Thy love has met Thy law's demand.

Thou art the living Truth,
  All wisdom dwells in Thee;
Thou source of every skill,
  Eternal verity!
Thou great I AM! In Thee we rest,
True answer to our every quest.

Thou only art true Life,
  To know Thee is to live
The more abundant life
  That earth can never give:
O risen Lord! We live in Thee
And Thou in us eternally!

We worship Thee, Lord Christ,
  Our Saviour and our King;
To Thee our youth and strength
  Adoringly we bring:
So fill our hearts that men may see
Thy life in us, and turn to Thee!

1807 William Cowper LM
**And He is before all things, and by Him all
things consist.** *Colossians 1:17*

MY song shall bless the Lord of all;
  My praise shall climb to His abode;
Thee, Saviour, by that name I call,
  The great Supreme, the mighty God.

Without beginning or decline,
  Object of faith, and not of sense;
Eternal ages saw Him shine;
  He shines eternal ages hence.

As much when in the manger laid
  Almighty Ruler of the sky,
As when the six days' work He made
  Filled all the morning stars with joy.

Of all the crowns Jehovah wears,
  Salvation is His dearest claim;
That gracious sound well-pleased He hears,
  And owns Immanuel for His name.

A cheerful confidence I feel,
  My well-placed hopes with joy I see;
My bosom glows with heavenly zeal
  To worship Him who died for me.

As man, He pities my complaint,
  His power and truth are all divine;
He will not fail, He cannot faint,
  Salvation's sure, and must be mine.

1808 Philip Doddridge LM
**And He is before all things, and by Him all
things consist.** *Colossians 1:17*

High on His Father's royal throne,
Jesus in highest glory shone.
Ere Adam's clay with life was warmed,
Or the angelic hosts were formed.

Ages shall pass away, but He
The same has been; the same shall be:
Eternal radiance gilds His head,
While stars and suns wax old and fade.

Nature shall change, and fade, and die;
Jesus shall raise His chosen high,
And seat them with Him on His throne.
In glory changeless as His own.

1809 James Deck 886 D
And He is the head of the body, the church.
Colossians 1:18

O blessèd Jesus, Lamb of God,
Who hast redeemed us by Thy blood,
  From sin, and death, and shame—
With joy and praise Thy people see
The crown of glory won by Thee,
  And worthy Thee proclaim.

Exalted by the Father's love,
All thrones, and powers, and names above,
  In earth below or heaven;
Wisdom and riches, power divine,
Blessing and honour, Lord, are Thine,
  All things to Thee are given.

Head of Thy church, Thou sittest there,
Thy bride shall all Thy glory share,
  Thy fulness, Lord, is ours;
Our life thou art, Thy grace sustains,
Thy strength in us the victory gains
  O'er sin and Satan's powers.

Soon shall the day of glory come,
Thy bride shall reach the Father's home,
  And all Thy glory see;
And, O! what joy to see Thee shine,
To hear Thee own us, Lord, as Thine,
  And ever dwell with Thee.

1810 William Williams LM
Peace through the blood of his cross.
Colossians 1:20

Beneath Thy cross I lay me down,
And mourn to see Thy thorny crown;
Love drops in blood from every vein,
Love is the spring of all Thy pain.

Here, Jesus, I shall ever stay,
And spend my longing hours away,
Think on Thy bleeding wounds and pain,
And contemplate Thy woes again.

The rage of Satan and of sin,
Of foes without and fears within,
Shall ne'er my conquering soul remove,
Or from thy cross, or from Thy love.

Secured from harms beneath Thy shade,
Here death and hell shall ne'er invade,
Nor Sinai, with its thundering noise,
Shall e'er disturb my happier joys.

O, unmolested happy rest
Where inward fears are all suppressed!
Here I shall love and live secure,
And patiently my cross endure.

1811   William Gadsby   CM
Christ in you, the hope of glory.
Colossians 1:27

Jesus the Lord, my Saviour is,
   My Shepherd, and my God;
My light, my strength, my joy, my bliss;
   And I His grace record.

Whate'er I need in Jesus dwells,
   And there it dwells for me;
'Tis Christ my earthen vessel fills
   With treasures rich and free.

Mercy and truth and righteousness,
   And peace, most richly meet
In Jesus Christ, the King of grace,
   In whom I stand complete.

As through the wilderness I roam,
   His mercies I'll proclaim;
And when I safely reach my home,
   I'll still adore His name.

'Worthy the Lamb,' shall be my song,
   'For He for me was slain;'
And with me all the heavenly throng
   Shall join, and say, 'Amen.'

1812   8th Cent, tr. J Chandler   CM
Christ in you, the hope of glory.
Colossians 1:27

O Christ, our hope, our hearts' desire,
   Redemption's only spring;
Creator of the world art Thou,
   Its Saviour and its King.

How vast the mercy and the love
   Which laid our sins on Thee,
And led Thee to a cruel death
   To set Thy people free.

But now the bonds of death are burst,
   The ransom has been paid;
And Thou art on Thy Father's throne
   In glorious robes arrayed.

O may Thy mighty love prevail
   Our sinful souls to spare;
O may we come before Thy throne
   And find acceptance there!

O Christ, be Thou our present joy,
   Our future great reward;
Our only glory may it be
   To glory in the Lord.

All praise to Thee, ascended Lord;
   All glory ever be
To Father, Son, and Holy Ghost,
   Through all eternity.

1813   Benjamin Beddome   CM
Christ in you, the hope of glory.
Colossians 1:27

If Christ is mine, then all is mine,
   And more than angels know;
Both present things, and things to come
   And grace and glory too.

If He is mine, then though He frown
   He never will forsake;
His chastisements all work for good,
   And but His love bespeak.

If He is mine, I need not fear
   The rage of earth and hell;
He will support my feeble frame,
   And all their power repel.

If He is mine, let friends forsake
   And earthly comforts flee,
He, the Dispenser of all good,
   Is more than all to me.

If He is mine, unharmed I pass
   Through death's most gloomy vale,
He'll be my comfort and my stay,
   When heart and flesh shall fail.

Let Christ assure me He is mine,
   I nothing want beside;
My soul shall at the fountain live,
   When all the streams are dried.

1814   Isaac Watts   LM
Knit together in love. *Colossians 2:2*

Blest be the Father and His love,
   To whose celestial source we owe
Rivers of endless joy above,
   And rills of comfort here below.

Glory to Thee, great Son of God,
  From whose dear wounded body rolls
A precious stream of vital blood,
  Pardon and life for dying souls.

We give Thee, sacred Spirit, praise,
  Who in our hearts of sin and woe
Makes living springs of grace arise,
  And into boundless glory flow.

Thus God the Father, God the Son,
  And God the Spirit we adore;
That sea of life and love unknown,
  Without a bottom or a shore.

1815 William Hurn CM
**In whom are hid all the treasures of wisdom
and knowledge.** *Colossians 2:3*

Christ is the uncreated light,
  The everlasting Word;
And wisdom's precious mines in Him
  Are all divinely stored.

In ancient days the holy seers
  Were by His Spirit filled,
And wondering, sought to understand
  The glory they beheld.

To sinners He reveals His love,
  And makes His gospel known;
And saints are taught and kept by Him
  Till they obtain the crown.

He shows us, in His providence,
  Where all our safety lies.
And in affliction's gracious school,
  He makes His people wise.

He teaches youth and childhood too,
  That they may know His ways;
To babes His glory He unfolds,
  And perfects there His praise.

Great Prophet, we would praise Thy name,
  And in Thy grace confide:
O condescend to teach us here!
  And be our constant Guide.

1816 Emily Symons SM
**As ye have therefore received Christ Jesus the
Lord, so walk ye in Him.**
Colossians 2:6

  I give myself to Thee,
    My Saviour and my God,
To be Thine own for evermore,
    The purchase of Thy blood.

  I give myself to Thee,
    My Father and my Friend,
To walk in all Thy perfect way,
    Until my life shall end.

  O help me to renounce
    The hateful works of sin,
The empty vanities of life,
    The flesh that strives within.

  O help me to obey
    The law which Thou hast given,
And daily by Thy grace to tread
    The path that leads to heaven.

  And ever more and more,
    Lord, let Thy servant prove
The riches of redeeming grace,
    The wonders of Thy love.

  Thus rooted in Thy love
    And steadfast in Thy faith,
Joyful through hope may I remain
    Still faithful unto death.

1817 Charles Wesley 88 88 88
**For in Him dwelleth all the fulness of the
Godhead bodily.** *Colossians 2:9*

My heart is full of Christ, and longs
  Its glorious matter to declare!
Of Him I make my loftier songs,
  I cannot from His praise forbear;
My ready tongue makes haste to sing
The glories of my heavenly King.

Fairer than all the earth-born race,
  Perfect in comeliness Thou art;
Replenished are Thy lips with grace,
  And full of love Thy tender heart:
God ever blest! we bow the knee,
And own all fulness dwells in Thee.

Gird on Thy thigh the Spirit's sword,
  And take to Thee Thy power divine;
Stir up Thy strength, Almighty Lord,
  All power and majesty are Thine:
Assert Thy worship and renown;
O all-redeeming God, come down!

Come, and maintain Thy righteous cause,
  And let Thy glorious toil succeed;
O spread the victory of Thy cross,
  Ride on, and prosper in Thy deed!
Through earth triumphantly ride on,
And reign in every heart alone.

1818 Joseph Hart   CM
And ye are complete in Him.
Colossians 2:10

When is it Christians all agree,
    And let distinctions fall?
When, nothing in themselves, they see
    That Christ is All in all.

But strife and difference will subsist
    While men will something seem;
Let them but singly look to Christ
    And all are one in Him.

The infant and the agèd saint,
    The worker and the weak,
They who are strong and seldom faint,
    And they who scarce can speak.

Eternal life's the gift of God;
    It comes through Christ alone;
'Tis His, He bought it with His blood;
    And therefore gives His own.

We have no life, no power, no faith,
    But what by Christ is given;
We all deserve eternal death,
    And thus we are all even.

1819 William Horne   SM
And ye are complete in Him.
Colossians 2:10

Union with Christ the Lord,
    O! how divinely sweet!
All consolation's here enjoyed,
    And here all blessings meet.

The church in Him complete,
    With Him for ever one.
Shall all its mighty foes defeat,
    And in His strength go on.

His bride He'll ne'er disown,
    Nor from His heart remove;
The bond that makes and keeps them one
    Is everlasting love.

Christ is the glorious Head,
    The blessèd members we;
And children by adoption made
    Of His own family.

Who can asunder part.
    Or who shall e'er destroy
This darling of His loving heart,
    This apple of His eye?

The church in Him complete,
    With Him for ever one,
Shall all its mighty foes defeat.
    And in His strength go on.

1820 Maria De Fleury, C H Spurgeon v3   CM
**Buried with Him in baptism, wherein also ye
are risen with Him.** *Colossians 2:12*

Come, ye who bow to sovereign grace,
    Record Imannuel's love;
Join in a song of noble praise
    To Him who reigns above.

Once in the gloomy grave He lay,
    But, by His rising power,
He bore the gates of death away,
    Hail! mighty Conqueror!

Buried with Him beneath this flood,
    We glory in His death:
We own our great incarnate God,
    And rise with Him by faith.

As saints of old confessed His name
    In Jordan's flowing tide,
So we adore the bleeding Lamb,
    Renouncing all beside.

No trust in water do we place,
    'Tis but an outward sign;
The great reality is grace,
    The fountain, blood divine.

1821 James Deck   76 76 D
**Buried with Him in baptism, wherein also ye
are risen with Him.** *Colossians 2:12*

Around Thy grave, Lord Jesus,
    Thine empty grave, we stand,
With hearts all full of praises,
    To keep Thy blessed command:
By faith our souls rejoicing,
    To trace Thy path of love
Through death's dark angry billows,
    Up to the throne above.

Lord Jesus, we remember
    The travail of Thy soul,
When in Thy love's deep pity
    The waves did o'er Thee roll:
Baptized in death's cold waters,
    For us Thy blood was shed;
For us the Lord of Glory
    Was numbered with the dead.

O Lord, Thou now art risen,
  Thy travail all is o'er,
For sin Thou once hast suffered,
  Thou livest to die no more;
Sin, death, and hell are vanquished
  By Thee, Thy church's Head:
And lo! we share Thy triumphs.
  Thou First-born from the dead.

Into Thy death baptizèd,
  We own with Thee we died;
With Thee, our life, are risen,
  And in Thee glorified;
From sin, the world, and Satan,
  We're ransomed by Thy blood,
And now would walk as strangers
  Alive with Thee to God.

1822   Isaac Watts   CM
**And having spoiled principalities and powers,
He made a shew of them openly, triumphing
over them in it.**
Colossians 2:15

Hosanna! to the Prince of light,
  Who clothed Himself in clay,
Entered the iron gates of death,
  And tore the bars away!

Death is no more the king of dread,
  Since our Immanuel rose;
He took the tyrant's sting away.
  And spoiled our hellish foes.

See how the Conqueror mounts aloft,
  And to His Father flies,
With scars of honour in His flesh,
  And triumph in His eyes.

There our exalted Saviour reigns,
  And scatters blessings down;
His Father well rewards His pains,
  And bids Him wear the crown.

Bright angels, strike your loudest strings,
  Your sweetest voices raise:
Let heaven and all created things
  Sound our Immanuel's praise.

1823   William Cowper   66 66 88
**Which are a shadow of things to come; but the
body is of Christ.** *Colossians 2:17*

Israel, in ancient days,
  Not only had a view
Of Sinai in a blaze,
  But learned the gospel too;
The types and figures were a glass,
In which they saw the Saviour's face.

The paschal sacrifice
  And blood-besprinkled door,
Seen with enlightened eyes,
  And once applied with power,
Would teach the need of other blood
To reconcile an angry God.

The lamb, the dove, set forth
  His perfect innocence,
Whose blood of matchless worth
  Should be the soul's defence;
For He who can for sin atone,
Must have no failings of His own.

The scape-goat on his head
  The people's trespass bore,
And to the desert led,
  Was to be seen no more;
In him our Surety seemed to say
'Behold, I bear your sins away.'

Dipped in his fellow's blood,
  The living bird went free;
The type, well understood,
  Expressed the sinner's plea,
Described a guilty soul enlarged,
And by a Saviour's death discharged.

Jesus, I love to trace
  Throughout the sacred page,
The footsteps of Thy grace,
  The same in every age;
O grant that I may faithful be,
To clearer light vouchsafed to me.

1824   Paul Cook   87 87 D
**If ye then be risen with Christ, seek those
things which are above.** *Colossians 3:1*

Rise with me— my soul in triumph
  Mounts to see the Prince of kings;
Draw with me the flood which issues
  From the boundless heavenly springs.
There together let us wonder,
  Gaze upon the Lamb that died;
Bow before the Victor reigning,
  Glory in the flowing tide.

O how mighty are the riches
  Of a grace so large and free,
Full of virtue and redemption,
  Bought by grief and agony!
There for sinners interceding
  Sits the Man of Sorrows now,
Glory, honour, praise eternal
  Circle round His noble brow.

Stay with me, while here I glory,
  Raptured by His lovely face;
Praise with me the King of beauty,
  All the lines of favour trace.
King eternal, may Thy mercy
  Move our souls Thy grace to adore;
Streams all-flowing, love abounding
  Satisfy for evermore.

© Author

1825 Joseph Hart 66 66 88
**Set your affection on things above, not on
things on the earth.** *Colossians 3:2*

  Come, raise your thankful voice,
    Ye souls redeemed with blood;
  Leave earth and all its toys,
    And mix no more with mud.

  *Dearly we're bought, highly esteemed;
  Redeemed, with Jesus' blood redeemed.*

  Christians are priests and kings,
    All born of heavenly birth;
  Then think on nobler things,
    And grovel not on earth.

  With heart, and soul, and mind,
    Exalt redeeming love;
  Leave worldly cares behind,
    And set your minds above.

  Lift up your ravished eyes,
    And view the glory given;
  All lower things despise,
    Ye citizens of heaven.

  Be to this world as dead,
    Alive to that to come;
  Our life in Christ is hid,
    Who soon shall call us home.

1826 John Newton (alt) CM
**Set your affection on things above, not on
things on the earth.** *Colossians 3:2*

Let worldly minds the world pursue,
  It has no charms for me;
Once I admired its trifles too,
  But grace has set me free.

Its pleasures now no longer please,
  No more content afford;
Far from my heart be joys like these,
  Now I have seen the Lord.

As by the light of opening day
  The stars are all concealed;
So earthly pleasures fade away,
  When Jesus is revealed.

Creatures no more divide my choice;
  I bid them all depart;
His name, and love, and gracious voice,
  Have fixed my roving heart.

Now, Lord, I would be Thine alone,
  And wholly live to Thee;
But may I hope that Thou wilt own
  A sinful soul like me?

Yes; though of sinners I'm the worst,
  I cannot doubt Thy will;
For if Thou hadst not loved me first,
  I Thee had hated still.

1827 Vernon Higham DCM
**Set your affection on things above, not on
things on the earth.** *Colossians 3:2*

Wean my sad heart from things on earth;
  From deep rebellion draw
My disobedience and the dearth
  In me of all Thy law.
Show me the beauty of Thy Son—
  Immortal, born in time;
Salvation to my soul who won,
  And brought me peace sublime.

O guide me into depths of light
  To know and feel Thy gaze,
When pardon flows and moves the night,
  And sets my soul ablaze.
A saving hope within me now,
  A beacon on a hill,
The rays of Calvary endow
  The joy of heaven still.

Set my affections now on high
  To seek things that are Thine,
A holy hunger and a cry
  To call on the Divine.
O teach me how to feed on Thee,
  To live upon Thy word,
And prove the vast resourceful sea
  Thou hast for me reserved.

Cause the desires of my heart
  To long for Thee alone,
And in my mind a seeking start
  With Thee upon the throne.
Control and guide with tender touch
  My frailty, with Thy care;
In realms of grace I long so much
  To dwell, and glory share.

© Author

JAMES DECK 1807-1884

1828 James Deck   CM
For ye are dead, and your life is hid with Christ in God. *Colossians 3:3*

Lord Jesus, are we one with Thee?
  O height, O depth of love!
Thou one with us on Calvary,
  We one with Thee above?

Such was Thy grace, that for our sake
  Thou didst from heaven come down;
Our mortal flesh and blood partake,
  In all our misery one.

Our sins, our guilt, in love divine,
  Confessed and borne by Thee:
The sting, the curse, the wrath were Thine
  To set Thy members free.

Ascended now, in glory bright,
  Still one with us Thou art;
Nor life nor death, nor depth nor height
  Thy saints and Thee can part.

O teach us, Lord, to know and own
  This wondrous mystery,
That Thou with us art truly one,
  And we are one with Thee!

Soon, soon shall come that glorious day,
  When, seated on Thy throne,
Thou shalt to wondering worlds display,
  That Thou with us art one.

1829 Horatius Bonar   SM
For ye are dead, and your life is hid with Christ in God. *Colossians 3:3*

Our life is hid with Christ,
  With Christ in God above;
Upward our hearts would go to Him,
  Whom, seeing not, we love.

He liveth and we live;
  His life for us prevails;
His fulness fills our emptiness,
  His strength for us avails.

Life worketh in us now,
  And shall for evermore;
Death shall be swallowed up of life,
  The grave its trust restore.

When He who is our life
  In glory shall appear,
We too shall be revealed with Him,
  And His bright raiment wear.

In Him we then shall be
  Transformed and glorified,
For we shall see Him as He is,
  And in His light abide.

1830 Horatius Bonar   SM
For ye are dead, and your life is hid with Christ in God. *Colossians 3:3*

I bless the Christ of God;
  I rest on love divine;
And with unfaltering lip and heart,
  I call this Saviour mine.

His cross dispels each doubt;
  I bury in His tomb
Each thought of unbelief and fear,
  Each lingering shade of gloom.

I praise the God of grace;
  I trust His truth and might;
He calls me His, I call Him mine,
  My God, my joy, my light.

In Him is only good,
  In me is only ill;
My ill but draws His goodness forth,
  And me He loveth still.

'Tis He who saveth me,
  And freely pardon gives;
I love because He loveth me,
  I live because He lives.

My life with Him is hid,
  My death has passed away,
My clouds have melted into light,
  My midnight into day.

1831 Isaac Watts   LM
When Christ, who is our life, shall appear, then shall ye also appear with Him in glory.
Colossians 3:4

Descend from heaven, immortal Dove,
    Stoop down and take us on Thy wings,
And mount and bear us far above
    The reach of these inferior things;

Beyond, beyond this lower sky,
    Up where eternal ages roll,
Where solid pleasures never die,
    And fruits immortal feast the soul.

O for a sight, a pleasing sight,
    Of our almighty Father's throne;
There sits our Saviour crowned with light,
    Clothed in a body like our own.

Adoring saints around Him stand,
    And thrones and powers before Him fall:
The God shines gracious through the Man,
    And sheds sweet glories on them all.

O what amazing joys they feel,
    While to their golden harps they sing
And sit on every heavenly hill,
    And spread the triumphs of their King!

When shall the day, dear Lord, appear,
    That I shall mount to dwell above,
And stand and bow amongst them there
    And view Thy face, and sing Thy love?

1832 John Adams   LM
Christ is all, and in all. *Colossians 3:11*

Christ is my All, my sure Defence,
Nor shall my soul depart from thence;
He is my Rock, my Refuge too,
In spite of all my foes can do.

Christ is my All, and He will lead
My soul in pastures green to feed;
'Tis He supplies my every want,
And will all needful blessings grant.

Christ is my All! where should I go?
Without Him I can nothing do.
Helpless and weak, a sinner great,
Yet in His righteousness complete.

1833 William Gadsby   88 88 D
Christ is all, and in all. *Colossians 3:11*

Ye famishing, naked, and poor,
    Distressèd, tormented, forlorn,
In Christ is a suitable store,
    For all that unto Him will come;
He's Bread, and the Bread of Life too;
    Well suited the hungry to fill;
Nor one that unto Him shall go,
    But what will approve the Bread well.

Yes, He is the true paschal Lamb,
    Of which all His Israel must eat;
Not sodden, but roast in the flame
    Of Sinai's most horrible heat.
This, this is the true fatted calf
    The Father gave orders to kill,
That prodigals might have enough
    When feasting on fair Zion's hill.

The Wine of the Kingdom is Christ,
    Provided for beggars distressed!
Which makes broken hearts to rejoice,
    When with it the soul is refreshed.
He's Water to cleanse and to heal;
    The thirsty are welcome to drink;
A River that never can fail;
    A Fountain that never can sink.

It always is full to the brim,
    Of water of life and of peace;
From which blessings flow like a stream,
    As free as the sun runs its race.
He's marrow and fatness as well,
    A fulness of every good;
Nor Gabriel is able to tell,
    The blessings that in Him are stored.

1834 Charles Wesley   LM
Christ is all, and in all. *Colossians 3:11*

When gracious Lord, when shall it be
That I shall find my all in Thee?
The fulness of Thy promise prove,
The seal of Thy eternal love?

Thee, only Thee, I fain would find,
And cast the world and sin behind;
A helpless soul, I come to Thee,
With only sin and misery.

Lord, I am sick— my sickness cure;
I want— do Thou enrich the poor;
Under Thy mighty hand I stoop—
O lift the abject sinner up!

Lord, I am blind— be Thou my sight;
Lord, I am weak— be Thou my might;
A helper of the helpless be,
And let me find my all in Thee.

1835   Charles Wesley   77 77 77
Christ is all, and in all. *Colossians 3:11*

Weary souls, that wander wide
    From the central point of bliss,
Turn to Jesus crucified,
    Fly to those dear wounds of His:
Sink into the cleansing flood;
Rise into the life of God!

Find in Christ the way of peace,
    Peace unspeakable, unknown;
By His pain He gives you ease,
    Life by His expiring groan;
Rise, exalted by His fall,
Find in Christ your All in all.

O believe the record true:
    God to you His Son hath given!
Ye may now be happy too,
    Find on earth the life of heaven,
Live the life of heaven above,
All the life of glorious love.

1836   Richard Burnham   88 88 D
**For our gospel came not unto you in word
only, but also in power, and in the Holy Ghost,
and in much assurance.**
1 Thessalonians 1:5

The gospel's a message of peace,
    We oft by experience have felt;
'Tis filled with Immanuel's grace,
    And sweeps away mountains of guilt.
O sweet revelation divine!
    Delighted, we've heard its contents;
All through it our Jesus does shine,
    A lover of all His dear saints.

Through various scenes of distress,
    Perplexèd with sin, guilt, and fear;
This glorious message of grace
    Has frequently yielded good cheer.
Dear Lord, may we prize the rich peace,
    The peace so abundantly given:
It flows through the word of Thy grace,
    And makes us anticipate heaven.

1837   Augustus Toplady   CM
**For God hath not called us unto uncleanness,
but unto holiness.**
1 Thessalonians 4:7

How vast the benefits divine,
    Which we in Christ possess!
We're saved from guilt and every sin
    And called to holiness.

It's not for works which we have done,
    Or shall hereafter do,
But He of His abounding love
    Salvation does bestow.

The glory, Lord, from first to last,
    Is due to Thee alone;
Aught to ourselves we dare not take
    Or rob Thee of Thy crown.

Our glorious Surety undertook
    Redemption's wondrous plan;
And grace was given us in Him
    Before the world began.

Not one of all the chosen race,
    But shall to heaven attain:
Partake on earth the purposed grace
    And then with Jesus reign.

1838   Isaac Watts   CM
**Sorrow not, even as others which have no
hope.** *1 Thessalonians 4:13*

Why do we mourn departed friends,
    Or shake at death's alarms?
'Tis but the voice that Jesus sends,
    To call them to His arms.

Are we not tending upward too,
    As fast as time can move?
Nor should we wish the hours more slow,
    To keep us from our love.

Why should we tremble to convey
    Their bodies to the tomb?
There the dear flesh of Jesus lay,
    And left a long perfume.

The graves of all His saints He blessed,
    And softened every bed;
Where should the dying members rest,
    But with their dying Head?

Thence He arose, ascending high,
    And showed our feet the way;
Up to the Lord our flesh shall fly,
    At the great rising day.

Then let the last loud trumpet sound,
And bid our kindred rise;
Awake, ye nations under ground;
Ye saints, ascend the skies.

1839   James Montgomery   DSM
So shall we ever be with the Lord.
1 Thessalonians 4:17

'For ever with the Lord!'
Amen, so let it be!
Life from the dead is in that word,
'Tis immortality.
Here in the body pent,
Absent from Him I roam,
Yet nightly pitch my moving tent
A day's march nearer home.

My Father's house on high,
Home of my soul, how near
At times to faith's foreseeing eye
Thy golden gates appear!
Ah! then my spirit faints
To reach the land I love,
The bright inheritance of saints,
Jerusalem above.

'For ever with the Lord!'
Father, if 'tis Thy will,
The promise of that faithful word
E'en here to me fulfil.
Be Thou at my right hand,
Then I can never fail;
Uphold Thou me and I shall stand;
Fight and I must prevail.

So when my latest breath
Shall rend the veil in twain,
By death I shall escape from death
And life eternal gain.
That resurrection-word,
That shout of victory;
Once more, 'For ever with the Lord!'
Amen, so let it be!

1840   Thomas Kelly   87 87 77
But ye, brethren, are not in darkness, that that day should overtake you as a thief.
1 Thessalonians 5 v4

Nothing know we of the season
When the world shall pass away;
But we know, the saints have reason
To expect a glorious day;
When the Saviour will return,
And His people cease to mourn.

O what sacred joys await them!
They shall see the Saviour then;
Those who now oppose and hate them,
Never can oppose again.
Brethren, let us think of this:
All is ours if we are His.

Waiting for our Lord's returning,
Be it ours His word to keep;
May our lamps be always burning,
May we watch while others sleep.
We're no longer of the night;
We are children of the light.

Being of the favoured number,
Whom the Saviour calls His own,
'Tis not meet that we should slumber;
Nothing should be left undone.
This should be His people's aim,
Still to glorify His name.

1841   William Gadsby   11 11 11 11
Let us watch and be sober.
1 Thessalonians 5:6

Watch, watch, and be sober, ye children of God;
Your wonderful Lover has bought you with blood,
Your Husband and Saviour for you gave His life;
Then be your behaviour becoming His wife.

O watch against trusting to your native strength;
Behold Peter boasting, but o'ercome at length;
Your strength will forsake you, and leave you to fall,
Unless the Lord make you to trust Him for all.

Treat all as deceivers that lead not to Christ;
As holy believers, rely on your Priest;
Watch ye against sleeping, and stand to your post,
Lest you should go weeping, while Canaanites boast.

By awful temptations attacked and distressed,
Though thousand vexations each moment molest,
Yet watch against falling, and yield not to doubt,
On Christ your Lord calling, your foes you shall rout.

1842 Isaac Watts CM
For God hath not appointed us to wrath, but to obtain salvation by our Lord Jesus Christ.
1 Thessalonians 5:9

Father, I sing Thy wondrous grace
   I bless my Saviour's name,
He wrought salvation for the poor,
   And bore the sinner's shame.

His deep distress has raised us high,
   His duty and His zeal
Fulfilled the law which mortals broke,
   And finished all Thy will.

His dying groans, His living songs,
   Shall better please my God,
Than harp or trumpet's solemn sound,
   Than goats' or bullocks' blood.

This shall His humble followers see,
   And set their hearts at rest:
They by His death draw near to Thee,
   And live for ever blest.

Zion is Thine, most Holy God;
   Thy Son shall bless her gates,
And glory purchased by His blood
   For Thine own Israel waits.

1843 William Gadsby 66 66 88
Rejoice evermore. *1 Thessalonians 5:16*

   Rejoice ye saints, rejoice,
      In Christ, your glorious Head;
   With heart, and soul, and voice,
      His matchless honours spread;
Exalt His love, proclaim His name,
And sweetly sing the Lamb once slain.

   The blood and righteousness
      Of the incarnate Word;
   The wisdom, truth, and grace,
      Of your exalted Lord,
Unite, with one immortal voice,
To bid the saints of God rejoice.

   God's promise and His oath,
      And covenant of grace,
   Abide secure enough,
      To all the chosen race;
And with a solemn, heavenly voice
Invite believers to rejoice.

The whole of Deity,
   With all His grace contains,
In sweetest harmony
   A solemn joy proclaims;
The Father, Word, and Spirit's voice
Unite to bid the saints rejoice.

1844 Thomas Powell LM
Brethren, pray for us.
1 Thessalonians 5:25

Bow down Thine ear, Almighty Lord,
   And hear Thy church's suppliant cry
For all who preach Thy saving word,
   And wait upon Thy ministry.

In mercy, Father, now give heed
   And pour Thy quickening Spirit's breath
On those whom Thou hast called to feed
   Thy flock redeemed by Jesus' death.

O Saviour, from Thy piercèd hand
   Shed o'er them all Thy gifts divine;
That those who in Thy presence stand
   May do Thy will with love like Thine.

Blest Spirit, in their hearts abide
   And give them grace to watch and pray;
That as they seek Thy flock to guide,
   Themselves may keep the narrow way.

O God, Thy strength and mercy send
   To shield them in their strife with sin;
Grant them, enduring to the end,
   The crown of life at last to win.

1845 Anon (alt), *Lady Huntingdon's Hymn Book*
886 D
He shall come to be glorified in His saints.
2 Thessalonians 1:10

When Thou, my righteous Judge, shalt come
To take Thy ransomed people home,
   Shall I among them stand?
Shall such a sinful soul as I,
Who sometimes am afraid to die,
   Be found at Thy right hand?

I love to meet among them now,
Before Thy gracious feet to bow,
   Though vilest of them all;
But can I bear the piercing thought:
What if my name should be left out,
   When Thou for them shalt call?

Prevent, prevent it by Thy grace;
Be Thou, dear Lord, my hiding-place,
    In this the accepted day;
Thy pardoning voice, O let me hear,
To still my unbelieving fear;
    Nor let me fall, I pray.

Let me among Thy saints be found
Whene'er the archangel's trump shall sound,
    To see Thy smiling face;
Then loudest of the crowd I'll sing,
While heaven's resounding mansions ring
    With shouts of sovereign grace.

1846   Richard Burnham   LM
**God hath from the beginning chosen you to
salvation.** *2 Thessalonians 2:13*

I hear the great Jehovah's voice;
He speaks His everlasting choice,
Tells me its spring is sovereign grace,
Its end a world of perfect bliss.

When the Lord chose the numerous seed,
He viewed them in their glorious Head;
He clearly saw their awful fall,
But made provision for them all.

For He determined ne'er to lose
The objects He had loved and chose;
From His dear sons He ne'er could part,
They lay so near His gracious heart.

Therefore in wisdom He decreed,
A way to save the chosen seed;
Jesus their loving Surety stands,
And answers all the law's demands.

Jesus, to Thee we now would fly,
And on Thy precious blood rely;
Find through the conduct of Thy grace,
That we're among the chosen race.

1847   John Kent   CM
**God hath from the beginning chosen you to
salvation.** *2 Thessalonians 2:13*

Saved from the power and guilt of sin,
    The law's tremendous curse,
We'll now the sacred song begin,
    Where God began with us.

We'll sing the vast unmeasured grace,
    Which, from the days of old,
Did all His Son's elect embrace,
    As sheep within His fold.

The basis of eternal love
    Shall mercy's frame sustain;
Earth, hell, or sin, the same to move,
    Shall all conspire in vain.

Sing, O ye sinners bought with blood:
    Hail the great Three-in-One;
Tell how secure the covenant stood
    Ere time its race begun.

Ne'er had ye felt the guilt of sin,
    Nor sweets of pardoning love,
Unless your worthless names had been
    Enrolled to life above.

O what a sweet exalted song
    Shall rend the vaulted skies,
When, shouting 'Grace', the blood-washed
    throng
    Shall see the top-stone rise.

1848   Richard Burnham   CM
Through sanctification of the Spirit.
2 Thessalonians 2:13

Sin is the source of every ill,
    It draws the heart from God;
Darkens the mind, perverts the will,
    And leads the downward road.

'Tis the sure harbinger of pain,
    Peace it can ne'er afford;
And while the sinner lives in sin,
    He ne'er can see the Lord.

No, not a soul can see His face,
    Or after Him pursue,
Till sanctified by sovereign grace,
    And formed divinely new.

But every heaven-born son of God
    His every sin bewails;
Looks at the Saviour's flowing blood,
    And holiness prevails.

Lord, while we look may we enjoy
    More sanctifying grace;
Then shall our spirits soar on high,
    And feel more solid peace.

HORATIUS BONAR 1808-89

1849   Horatius Bonar   LM
**Now our Lord Jesus Christ Himself, and God,
even our Father, which hath loved us, and
hath given us everlasting consolation and
good hope through grace.**
2 Thessalonians 2:16

O love of God, how strong and true;
Eternal, and yet ever new;
Uncomprehended and unbought,
Beyond all knowledge and all thought!

O love of God, how deep and great,
Far deeper than man's deepest hate;
Self-fed, self-kindled like the light,
Changeless, eternal, infinite!

O heavenly love, how precious still,
In days of weariness and ill,
In nights of pain and helplessness,
To heal, to comfort, and to bless!

O wide-embracing, wondrous love,
We read thee in the sky above;
We read thee in the earth below,
In seas that swell and streams that flow.

We read thee best in Him who came
To bear for us the cross of shame,
Sent by the Father from on high,
Our life to live, our death to die.

We read thy power to bless and save,
E'en in the darkness of the grave;
Still more in resurrection light
We read the fulness of thy might.

O love of God, our shield and stay
Through all the perils of our way;
Eternal love, in thee we rest,
For ever safe, for ever blest.

1850   John Stevens   886 D
Good hope through grace.
2 Thessalonians 2:16

Good hope, through grace, the saints possess,
The fruit of Jesus' righteousness,
   And by His Spirit given;
Faith eyes the promise firm and sure,
And hope expects for evermore
   To dwell with Christ in heaven.

Good hope is born of sovereign grace,
And lives in Jesus' righteousness,
   With faith, and peace, and love;
What faith believes good hope desires,
And after perfect bliss aspires,
   In the bright world above.

All through the wilderness below,
Good hope expects more good to know;
   And thus is kept alive.
The soul, that many a trial bears,
And conflicts hard with doubts and fears,
   Till joy and peace arrive.

When sore temptations haunt the soul,
Good hope shall all their power control,
   And save from sad despair;
While faith looks up to Jesus' blood,
Good hope rides safely o'er the flood;
   Nor dreads destruction there.

When gloomy death, in dread array,
Appears to call the saint away,
   Faith looks beyond the flood,
And when the soul to march prepares,
Good hope sends out her fervent prayers,
   And dies in peace with God.

1851   Samuel Parrott   SM
Good hope through grace.
2 Thessalonians 2:16

   Hope is a taste begun,
   Of great Jehovah's grace;
Revealed in Jesus Christ the Son,
   To all the chosen race.

   Hope is a lively act
   Of Jesus' life within.
And grounded in the gospel fact,
   That Jesus died for sin.

   Hope purifies the heart,
   Through Jesus' cleansing blood,
Performs, like faith, a saving part,
   Beneath the throne of God.

Good hope expects to meet
  In Christ a rich supply,
And humbly waits around His seat
  With holy peace and joy.

Through grace good hope abides,
  And shields us from despair;
Yields cordials to the heart besides,
  And helps the saints in prayer.

Hope comforts through the cross,
  Speaks sweetly of the Lamb;
And gospel hope will suffer loss,
  To serve the great I AM.

1852   David Denham   CM
But the Lord is faithful.
2 Thessalonians 3:3

The Lord is faithful to secure
  His saints where'er they go;
The Lord is faithful to ensure
  Both grace and glory too.

The Lord is faithful to maintain
  His work of grace within;
The Lord is faithful to restrain
  The love and power of sin.

The Lord is faithful still to guide,
  And guard us night and day;
The Lord is faithful to provide,
  And keep us lest we stray.

The Lord is faithful to perform
  All His designs of love;
Faithful to shield in every storm,
  And make us conquerors prove.

1853   Frank Houghton   LM
And the Lord direct your hearts into the love of God, and into the patient waiting for Christ.
2 Thessalonians 3:5

O Thou who dost direct my feet
  To right or left where pathways part,
Wilt Thou not, faithful Paraclete,
  Direct the journeying of my heart?

Into the love of God, I pray,
  Deeper and deeper let me press,
Exploring all along the way
  Its secret strength and tenderness.

Into the steadfastness of One
  Who patiently endured the cross,
Of Him who, though He were a Son,
  Came to His crown through bitter loss.

This is the road of my desire:
  Learning to love as God loves me,
Ready to pass through flood or fire
  With Christ's unwearying constancy.

© *Overseas Missionary Fellowship*

1854   Gerhard Tersteegen, tr. John Wesley
      88 88 88
And the Lord direct your hearts into the love of God, and into the patient waiting for Christ.
2 Thessalonians 3:5

Thou hidden love of God, whose height,
  Whose depth unfathomed, no man knows,
I see from far Thy beauteous light,
  And inly sigh for Thy repose;
My heart is pained, nor can it be
At rest, till I find rest in Thee.

Is there a thing beneath the sun,
  That strives with Thee my heart to share?
Ah! tear it thence, and reign alone,
  And govern every motion there.
Then shall my heart from earth be free.
When it has found its all in Thee.

O crucify this self, that I
  No more, but Christ in me, may live;
Bid all my vile affections die,
  Nor let one hateful lust survive.
In all things nothing may I see,
Nothing desire, or seek, but Thee.

Lord, draw my heart from earth away,
  And make it only know Thy call;
Speak to my inmost soul, and say,
  'I am thy Saviour God, thy All!'
O dwell in me, fill all my soul,
And all my powers by Thine control.

1855   William Gadsby   CM
The Lord be with you all.
2 Thessalonians 3:16

The Lord Himself be with you all,
  To teach you His own will;
And guide you safe from every thrall,
  To Zion's heavenly hill.

Be with you to unfold His grace,
  And prove His truth divine;
Unveil the glories of His face,
  And make His counsels shine.

Whatever be your state or case,
  The Lord Himself be near;
Support, protect, defend, embrace,
  And make your passage clear.

Thus may you prove His promise true,
   And glorify His name;
And every day your songs renew,
   While life and breath remain.

The Lord be with you to the end,
   And land you safe above;
A long eternity to spend
   In singing, 'God is love.'

Come, all ye pining, hungry poor,
   The Saviour's bounty taste;
Behold a never-failing store
   For every willing guest.

Here shall your numerous wants receive
   A free, a full supply;
He has unmeasured bliss to give,
   And joys that never die.

1856   William Gadsby   10 10 11 11

But we know that the law is good, if a man use it lawfully. *1 Timothy 1:8*

The law of the Lord is perfect and good,
   But cannot afford nor comfort nor food,
To sinners distressèd, o'erwhelmèd with fear,
But Jesus the blessèd can yield them good cheer.

The sinner may toil with care and with pain,
   Some comfort to bring from Sinai's flame,
Spend long nights in sorrow, and days in distress,
Yet find on the morrow the law does him curse.

Where then can he flee for help or relief?
   A sinner is he, a rebel in chief.
He feels himself guilty, and what can he do?
He's unsound and filthy, and no good can show.

Thanks be to the Lamb, the great King of kings,
   Who comes just in time, and glad tidings brings,
Applies peace and pardon, with power from
     above,
The poor soul to gladden, and calls him His love.

These tidings Christ brings, and they reach the
   heart;
   The Spirit He sends His truth to impart;
The sweet Spirit seals him a son and an heir,
And comforts and cheers him, and banishes fear.

Then ravished with joy, and o'ercome with love
   'Abba, Father,' he'll cry, 'my Lord and my God,
My Friend and my Portion, my Head and my All;
Thou art my Salvation from guilt, sin, and thrall.'

1857   Anne Steele   CM

The grace of our Lord was exceeding abundant... 1 Timothy 1:14

Lord, we adore Thy boundless grace,
   The heights and depths unknown,
Of pardon, life, and joy, and peace,
   In Thy belovèd Son.

O wondrous gifts of love divine,
   Dear Source of every good;
Jesus, in Thee what glories shine!
   How rich Thy flowing blood!

1858   Henry Paice   LM

And the grace of our Lord was exceeding abundant... *1 Timothy 1:14*

Ah! but for free and sovereign grace,
   I still had lived estranged from God,
Till hell had proved the destined place
   Of my deserved, but dread abode!

But O! amazed, I see the hand
   That stopped me in my wild career;
A miracle of grace I stand:
   The Lord hath taught my heart to fear.

To fear His name, to trust His grace,
   To learn His will be my employ,
Till I shall see Him face to face,
   Himself my heaven, Himself my joy.

1859   Thomas Kelly   CM

This is a faithful saying, and worthy of all acceptation, that Christ Jesus came into the world to save sinners; of whom I am chief. *1 Timothy 1:15*

The gospel comes with welcome news
   To sinners lost like me;
Their various schemes let others choose,
   Saviour, I come to Thee.

Of sinners sure I am the chief,
   But grace is rich and free;
This welcome truth affords relief
   To sinners, e'en to me.

Of merit now let others speak,
   But merit I have none;
For merit 'tis in vain to seek,
   I'm saved by grace alone.

'Twas grace my wayward heart first won,
   'Tis grace that holds me fast,
Grace will complete the work begun,
   And save me to the last.

Then shall my soul with rapture trace
   What God has done for me:
And celebrate redeeming grace
   Throughout eternity.

1860 Dora Greenwell   888 7

This is a faithful saying, and worthy of all acceptation, that Christ Jesus came into the world to save sinners; of whom I am chief.
1 Timothy 1:15

I am not skilled to understand
What God hath willed, what God hath planned;
I only know at His right hand
    Stands One who is my Saviour!

I take Him at His word indeed;
Christ died for sinners, this I read;
And in my heart I find a need
    Of Him to be my Saviour!

That He should leave His place on high,
And come for sinful man to die,
You count it strange? So once did I
    Before I knew my Saviour!

And O that He fulfilled may see
The travail of His soul in me,
And with His work contented be
    As I with my dear Saviour.

Yes, living, dying, let me bring
My strength, my solace from this spring,
That He who lives to be my King
    Once died to be my Saviour.

1861 Walter Smith   11 11 11 11

Now unto the King eternal, immortal, invisible, the only wise God, be honour and glory for ever and ever. Amen.
1 Timothy 1:17

Immortal, invisible, God only wise,
In light inaccessible hid from our eyes,
Most blessèd, most glorious, the Ancient of Days,
Almighty, victorious, Thy great name we praise.

Unresting, unhasting, and silent as light,
Nor wanting, nor wasting, Thou rulest in might;
Thy justice like mountains high soaring above,
Thy clouds which are fountains of goodness and
    love.

Great Father of glory, pure Father of light,
Thine angels adore Thee, all veiling their sight;
All praise we would render, O help us to see
'Tis only the splendour of light hideth Thee.

Immortal, invisible, God only wise,
In light inaccessible hid from our eyes,
Most blessèd, most glorious, the Ancient of Days,
Almighty, victorious, Thy great Name we praise.

1862 Henry Baker   LM

For kings, and for all that are in authority; that we may lead a quiet and peaceable life in all godliness and honesty.
1 Timothy 2:2

O God of love, O King of peace,
Make wars throughout the world to cease;
The wrath of sinful man restrain;
Give peace, O God, give peace again.

Remember, Lord, Thy works of old,
The wonders that our fathers told;
Remember not our sin's dark stain;
Give peace, O God, give peace again.

Whom shall we trust but Thee, O Lord?
Where rest but on Thy faithful word?
None ever called on Thee in vain;
Give peace, O God, give peace again.

Where saints and angels dwell above,
All hearts are knit in holy love;
O bind us in that heavenly chain;
Give peace, O God, give peace again.

1863 David Denham   LM

For there is one God, and one Mediator between God and men, the Man Christ Jesus.
1 Timothy 2:5

The Mediator's glorious name,
My soul with all the saints proclaim;
Sing of His goings forth of old,
Whose thoughts of peace can ne'er be told.

O sing the Mediator's love,
Which brought Him from His throne above;
Moved Him in covenant to agree
To suffer, bleed, and die for me.

Here wisdom, justice, power, and grace
Shine in the Mediator's face;
Jehovah's just, yet justifies
All that to Christ for refuge flies.

In Christ, our medium of access,
We've pardon, rest, and righteousness:
The Father draws, the Spirit seals
And everlasting life reveals.

Thus all who in the Lord believe,
The witness in their souls receive;
Through grace are made for glory meet,
And stand in Christ their Head complete.

1864　Vernon Higham

10 10 10 10 + refrain
Great is the mystery of godliness.
1 Timothy 3:16

Great is the gospel of our glorious God,
Where mercy met the anger of God's rod;
A penalty was paid and pardon bought,
And sinners lost at last to Him were brought:

O let the praises of my heart be Thine,
For Christ has died that I may call Him mine,
That I may sing with those who dwell above,
Adoring, praising Jesus, King of love.

Great is the mystery of godliness,
Great is the work of God's own holiness;
It moves my soul, and causes me to long
For greater joys than to the earth belong:

The Spirit vindicated Christ our Lord,
And angels sang with joy and sweet accord;
The nations heard, a dark world flamed with
　light—
When Jesus rose in glory and in might:
© Author

1865　Gill Timms　　　CM

But godliness with contentment is great gain.
1 Timothy 6:6

Happy the men whose bliss supreme
　Flows from a source on high,
And flows in one continual stream,
　When earthly springs are dry.

Contentment makes their little more,
　And sweetens good possessed;
While faith foretastes the joys in store,
　And makes them doubly blessed.

If providence their comforts shroud,
　And dark distresses lower,
Hope paints its rainbow on the cloud,
　And grace shines through the shower.

What troubles can their hearts o'erwhelm,
　Who view a Saviour near,
Who ever sits and guides the helm,
　Whose voice forbids their fear?

God is their joy and portion still,
　When earthly good retires,
And shall their hearts sustain and fill,
　When time itself expires.

JOHN MONSELL 1811-75

1866　John Monsell　　　LM

Fight the good fight of faith.
1 Timothy 6:12

Fight the good fight with all thy might,
Christ is thy strength, and Christ thy right;
Lay hold on life, and it shall be
Thy joy and crown eternally.

Run the straight race, through God's good grace,
Lift up thine eyes, and seek His face;
Life with its path before thee lies,
Christ is the way and Christ the prize.

Cast care aside; upon thy Guide
Lean, and His mercy will provide:
Lean, and the trusting soul shall prove,
Christ is its life and Christ its love.

Faint not, nor fear, His arm is near;
He changeth not, and thou art dear;
Only believe, and thou shalt see
That Christ is All in all to thee.

1867　Thomas Kelly　　　87 87 47

The King of kings, and Lord of lords.
1 Timothy 6:15

Look ye saints! the sight is glorious!
　See the exalted Saviour now,
From the fight returned victorious;
　Every knee to Him shall bow.
　　Crown Him, crown Him!
　Crowns become the Victor's brow!

Crown the Saviour; saints, adore Him;
　Rich the trophies Jesus brings!
Saints and angels bow before Him,
　While the vault of heaven rings;
　　Crown Him, crown Him!
　Crown the Saviour King of kings!

Sinners in derision crowned Him,
　Mocking thus the Saviour's claim;
Saints and angels throng around Him,
　Own His title, praise His name:
　　Crown Him! Crown Him!
　Spread abroad the Victor's fame!

Hark! those bursts of acclamation,
　Hark! those loud triumphant chords!
Jesus takes the highest station;
　O what joy the sight affords!
　　Crown Him, crown Him!
　King of kings, and Lord of lords!

CHRISTOPHER WORDSWORTH 1807-1885

1868　Joseph Hart　　　　　　　SM
**Trust... in the living God, who giveth us richly
all things to enjoy.** *1 Timothy 6:17*

　Remember, man, thy birth;
　　Set not on gold thy heart;
　Naked thou cam'st upon the earth,
　　And naked must depart.

　This world's vain wealth despise;
　　Happiness is not here;
　To Jesus lift thy longing eyes,
　　And seek thy treasure there.

　If profit be thy scope,
　　Diffuse thy alms about;
　The worldling prospers laying up,
　　The Christian laying out.

　Returns will not be scant
　　With honour in the highest;
　For who relieves his brethren's want,
　　Bestows his alms on Christ.

　Give gladly to the poor,
　　'Tis lending to the Lord;
　In secret so increase thy store,
　　And hide in heaven the hoard.

　There thou mayest fear no thief,
　　No rankling rust or moth;
　Thy treasure and thy heart are safe;
　　Where one is, will be both.

1869　Christopher Wordsworth　　888 4
God, who giveth us richly all things to enjoy.
1 Timothy 6 v17

　O Lord of heaven and earth and sea,
　To Thee all praise and glory be;
　How shall we show our love to Thee,
　　Giver of all?

　The golden sunshine, vernal air,
　Sweet flowers and fruits, Thy love declare;
　Where harvests ripen, Thou are there,
　　Giver of all.

　For peaceful homes and healthful days,
　For all the blessings earth displays,
　We owe Thee thankfulness and praise,
　　Giver of all.

　Thou didst not spare Thine only Son,
　But gav'st Him for a world undone,
　And freely with that blessèd One
　　Thou givest all.

　For souls redeemed, for sins forgiven,
　For means of grace and hopes of heaven,
　Father, what can to Thee be given,
　　Who givest all?

　We lose what on ourselves we spend,
　We have as treasure without end
　Whatever, Lord, to Thee we lend,
　　Who givest all.

　To Thee, from whom we all derive
　Our life, our gifts, our power to give:
　O may we ever with Thee live,
　　Giver of all!

1870   Vernon Higham   64 64 66 64

Wherefore I put thee in remembrance that thou stir up the gift of God, which is in thee by the putting on of my hands.
2 Timothy 1:6

Persuaded by Thy word,
  I worship Thee,
Constrained to seek my Lord
  At Calvary.
A burden gone away,
And blessedness to stay,
Removing all dismay:
  I will not flee.

No shame shall wound my heart,
  For Thine embrace
Of peace and power impart
  Sufficient grace.
My life I now commit,
My will to Thee submit,
And at Thy feet I'll sit,
  To seek Thy face.

O grant me strength to hold
  The gospel sweet;
A spirit true and bold
  I gladly greet.
Committed to my care,
A truth beyond compare,
O give me grace to bear,
  Thy foes defeat.

When error comes to lie,
  O keep me, Lord;
Then stir Thy gift in me,
  And power afford.
Declare Thy gospel sound,
Destroy when lies abound;
O Jesus, I have found
  Thy word a sword.

© Author

1871   John Ellerton   66 66 D

For God hath not given us the spirit of fear; but of power, and of love, and of a sound mind. *2 Timothy 1:7*

Shine Thou upon us, Lord,
  True Light of men, today;
And through the written word
  Thy very self display;
That so, from hearts which burn
  With gazing on Thy face,
The little ones may learn
  The wonders of Thy grace.

Breathe Thou upon us, Lord,
  Thy Spirit's living flame,
That so with one accord
  Our lips may tell Thy name;
Give Thou the hearing ear,
  Fix Thou the wandering thought,
That those we teach may hear
  The great things Thou hast wrought.

Speak Thou for us, O Lord,
  In all we say of Thee;
According to Thy word
  Let all our teaching be;
That children come to know
  The one true Shepherd's voice,
Where'er He leads them go,
  And in His love rejoice.

Live Thou within us, Lord;
  Thy mind and will be ours;
Be Thou beloved, adored,
  And served with all our powers;
That so our lives may teach
  The children what Thou art,
And plead, by more than speech,
  For Thee with every heart.

1872   Isaac Watts   LM

Who hath saved us, and called us with an holy calling, not according to our works, but according to His own purpose and grace, which was given us in Christ Jesus before the world began.
2 Timothy 1:9

Now to the power of God supreme
  Be everlasting honour given;
He saves from hell (we bless His name),
  He calls our wandering feet to heaven.

Not for our duties or deserts,
  But of His own abounding grace,
He works salvation in our hearts,
  And forms a people for His praise.

'Twas His own purpose that began
  To rescue rebels doomed to die;
He gave us grace in Christ His Son,
  Before He spread the starry sky.

Jesus the Lord appears at last,
  And makes His Father's counsels known;
Declares the great transactions past,
  And brings immortal blessings down.

He dies! and in that dreadful night
  Did all the powers of hell destroy.
Rising, He brought our heaven to light,
  And took possession of the joy.

1873 John Adams   87 87 47
Who hath saved us. *2 Timothy 1:9*

Jesus is our great salvation,
 Worthy of our best esteem;
He has saved His favourite nation;
 Join to sing aloud of Him.
  He has saved us!
 Christ alone could us redeem.

When involved in sin and ruin,
 And no helper there was found,
Jesus our distress was viewing;
 Grace did more than sin abound
  He has called us,
 With salvation in the sound.

Let us never, Lord, forget Thee;
 Make us walk as children here.
We will give Thee all the glory
 Of that love that brought us near.
  Bid us praise Thee,
 And rejoice with holy fear.

Free election, known by calling,
 Is a privilege divine;
Saints are kept from final falling;
 All the glory, Lord, be Thine!
  All the glory,
 All the glory, Lord, is Thine!

O blessèd soul that lies
 Within redemption;
Reposes and relies
 In safe salvation.
O happy my estate,
Where grace does not abate;
Then enter through that gate
 Of full salvation.

Then to behold Thy face
 Of peace and beauty,
Forever Thee embrace,
 O Lord of mercy.
Then shall I know as known
And love my Lord's renown,
Thy majesty to crown,
 O King of glory.

© Author

1874 Vernon Higham   65 65 66 65
**The appearing of our Saviour Jesus Christ,
who hath abolished death.**
2 Timothy 1:10

O Saviour of my soul
 Let me adore Thee,
When life has left its toll,
 And I am empty.
It is Thy hand of love
That lifts me far above:
O blessèd Holy Dove,
 Who shows me glory!

Christ hath abolished death,
 O conquest glorious,
Through life of living breath,
 My King victorious.
For Thou hast brought to light
Immortal life so bright,
That I may claim the sight
 Of heights so wondrous!

DANIEL WHITTLE 1840-1901

1875 Daniel Whittle   CM + refrain
**I know whom I have believed, and am
persuaded that He is able to keep that which I
have committed unto Him against that day.**
2 Timothy 1:12

I know not why God's wondrous grace
 To me hath been made known;
Nor why, unworthy as I am,
 He claimed me for His own.

 *But 'I know whom I have believèd; And am
 persuaded that He is able to keep that which
 I've committed unto Him against that day.'*

I know not how this saving faith
 To me He did impart;
Or how believing in His word
 Wrought peace within my heart.

I know not how the Spirit moves,
 Convincing men of sin;
Revealing Jesus through the word,
 Creating faith in Him.

I know not what of good or ill
  May be reserved for me,
Of weary ways or golden days,
  Before His face I see.

I know not when my Lord may come;
  I know not how, nor where;
If I shall pass the vale of death,
  Or meet Him in the air.

Dost thou, by faith, to Jesus flee?
Is his dear image stamped on thee?
If so, let nothing thee dismay,
Thou shalt find mercy in that day.

Eternal Judge! Almighty Lord!
Seal home and bless Thy solemn word;
And O that we poor sinners may
Of Thee find mercy in that day!

1876   Isaac Watts   CM
I know whom I have believed, and am
persuaded that He is able to keep that which I
have committed unto Him against that day.
2 Timothy 1:12

I'm not ashamed to own my Lord,
  Or to defend His cause,
Maintain the honour of His word,
  The glory of His cross.

Jesus, my God, I know His name,
  His name is all my trust;
Nor will He put my soul to shame,
  Nor let my hope be lost.

Firm as His throne His promise stands,
  And He can well secure
What I've committed to His hands,
  Till the decisive hour.

Then will He own my worthless name
  Before His Father's face,
And in the new Jerusalem
  Appoint my soul a place.

1877   Samuel Medley   LM
The Lord grant unto him that he may find
mercy of the Lord in that day.
2 Timothy 1:18

Great Judge of all! that day will come
When mortals must receive their doom;
O, hear our cry, and grant we may
Of Thee find mercy in that day!

The wicked tremble, saints rejoice,
One dreads, the other loves the voice;
The wicked fear, believers sing,
The coming of their God and King.

Think, O my soul, thou must appear,
And pass the judgment at this bar!
What now does God and conscience say?
Wilt thou find mercy in that day?

1878   John Bunyan   65 65 66 65
Thou therefore, my son, be strong in the grace
that is in Christ Jesus.
2 Timothy 2:1

He who would valiant be
  'Gainst all disaster,
Let him in constancy,
  Follow the Master.
There's no discouragement
Shall make him once relent
His first avowed intent
  To be a pilgrim.

Who so beset him round
  With dismal stories,
Do but themselves confound;
  His strength the more is.
No foes shall stay his might,
Though he with giants fight:
He will make good his right
  To be a pilgrim.

Since, Lord, Thou dost defend
  Us with Thy Spirit.
We know we at the end
  Shall life inherit.
Then fancies flee away!
I'll fear not what men say,
I'll labour night and day
  To be a pilgrim.

1879   Richard Burnham   CM
Therefore I endure all things for the elect's
sakes, that they may also obtain the salvation
which is in Christ Jesus with eternal glory.
2 Timothy 2:10

The name of Jesus, O how sweet!
  How it removes my pain,
Calms the great tumults of my soul,
  And makes it all serene!

When His all-glorious name I hear,
My rising joys abound;
Salvation from my every sin,
Flows from the blissful sound.

Saved from the love and power of sin,
Saved from the wrath of God:
Saved to the glory of His grace,
Through the Redeemer's blood.

Now, O ye saints, arise and sing,
Sing the dear Saviour's worth;
Let His salvation be your theme,
And sound it through the earth.

1880   Thomas Greene   CM
If we believe not, yet He abideth faithful: He cannot deny Himself. *2 Timothy 2:13*

Why should my fears so far prevail,
When they my hopes accost?
My faith, though weak, can never fail,
Nor shall my hopes be lost.

A thousand promises are wrote
In characters of blood;
And those emphatic lines denote
The ever-faithful God.

Through those dear promises I range;
And, blessèd be His name,
Though I, a feeble mortal, change,
His love is still the same.

1881   Thomas Haweis   77 77 77
The foundation of God standeth sure, having this seal, The Lord knoweth them that are His.
2 Timothy 2:19

God's foundation standeth sure,
We shall to the end endure;
Safely will the Shepherd keep
Those He purchased for His sheep.

God's foundation standeth sure,
We shall to the end endure.

Known to Him before the sun
First began his course to run;
Chosen, callèd from above,
Objects of eternal love.

Every evil, Lord, subdue,
By Thy grace our souls renew;
Then, from base affections free,
Dead to sin, we'll live to Thee.

1882   Elsie Yale   65 65 D + refrain
Meet for the master's use, and prepared unto every good work. *2 Timothy 2:21*

There's a work for Jesus
Ready at your hand,
'Tis a task the Master
Just for you has planned.
Haste to do His bidding,
Yield Him service true;
There's a work for Jesus
None but you can do.

Work for Jesus, day by day,
Serve Him ever, falter never, Christ obey.
Yield Him service, loyal, true;
There's a work for Jesus none but you can do.

There's a work for Jesus,
Humble though it be,
'Tis the very service
He would ask of thee.
Go where fields are whitened
And the labourers few;
There's a work for Jesus
None but you can do.

There's a work for Jesus
Precious souls to bring,
Tell them of His mercies,
Tell them of your King.
Faint not, grow not weary,
He will strength renew;
There's a work for Jesus
None but you can do.

1883   Maria Penstone   Irregular
All Scripture is given by inspiration of God, and is profitable for doctrine, for reproof, for correction, for instruction in righteousness.
2 Timothy 3:16

God has given us a book full of stories,
Which was made for His people of old,
It begins with the tale of a garden,
And ends with the city of gold.

But the best is the story of Jesus,
Of the Babe with the ox in the stall,
Of the song that was sung by the angels,
The most beautiful story of all.

There are stories for parents and children,
For the old who are ready to rest,
But for all who can read them or listen,
The story of Jesus is best.

For it tells how He came from the Father,
His far-away children to call,
To bring the lost sheep to their Shepherd—
The most beautiful story of all.

1884 Joseph Hart SM
All Scripture is given by inspiration of God, and is profitable for doctrine, for reproof, for correction, for instruction in righteousness.
2 Timothy 3:16

Say Christian, wouldst thou thrive
In knowledge of thy Lord?
Against no Scripture ever strive,
But tremble at His word.

Revere the sacred page;
To injure any part
Betrays, with blind and feeble rage,
A hard and haughty heart.

If aught there dark appear,
Bewail thy want of sight;
No imperfection can be there,
For all God's words are right.

The Scriptures and the Lord
Bear one tremendous name;
The written and the incarnate Word
In all things are the same.

1885 Isaac Watts CM
I have fought a good fight, I have finished my course, I have kept the faith.
2 Timothy 4:7

Are we the soldiers of the cross,
The followers of the Lamb?
And shall we fear to own His cause,
Or blush to speak His name?

No! we must fight if we would reign:
Increase our courage, Lord;
We'll bear the toil, endure the pain,
Supported by Thy Word.

Thy saints in all this glorious war
Shall conquer, though they're slain;
They see the triumph from afar,
And shall with Jesus reign.

When that illustrious day shall rise,
And all Thine armies shine
In robes of victory through the skies,
The glory shall be Thine.

1886 Isaac Watts CM
I have fought a good fight, I have finished my course, I have kept the faith.
2 Timothy 4:7

With heavenly weapons I have fought
The battles of the Lord:
Finished my course, and kept the faith,
And wait the sure reward.

God hath laid up in heaven for me
A crown which cannot fade;
The righteous Judge at that great day
Shall place it on my head.

Nor hath the King of grace decreed
This prize for me alone:
But all that love, and long to see
The appearance of His Son.

Jesus, the Lord, shall guard me safe
From every ill design;
And to His heavenly kingdom keep
This feeble soul of mine.

God is my everlasting aid,
And hell shall rage in vain;
To Him be highest glory paid,
And endless praise—Amen.

1887 John Kent LM
In hope of eternal life, which God, that cannot lie, promised before the world began. *Titus 1:2*

In hope of life eternal given,
Behold a pardoned sinner dies;
A legal blood-bought heir of heaven
Called to his mansion in the skies.

He left the world with all its toys,
For better, brighter worlds on high;
His faith embraced substantial joys,
Soaring beyond the starry sky.

Methinks I see him now at rest
In the bright mansion love ordained;
His head reclines on Jesus' breast,
No more by sin or sorrow pained.

Why should our eyes with sorrow flow?
Or bosoms heave the painful sigh?
When Jesus calls, the saint must go;
'Twas his eternal gain to die.

Fearless he entered Jordan's flood,
At peace with heaven he closed his eyes,
His only trust was Jesus' blood,
In sure and certain hope to rise.

1888 Isaac Watts LM

That they may adorn the doctrine of God our Saviour in all things. *Titus 2:10*

So let our lips and lives express
The holy gospel we profess;
So let our works and virtues shine,
To prove the doctrine all divine.

Thus shall we best proclaim abroad
The honours of our Saviour God,
When His salvation reigns within,
And grace subdues the power of sin.

Our flesh and sense must be denied,
Passion and envy, lust and pride,
While justice, temperance, truth and love,
Our inward godliness approve.

Religion bears our spirits up,
While we expect that blessèd hope,
The bright appearance of the Lord:
And faith stands leaning on His word.

1889 William Gadsby CM

For the grace of God that bringeth salvation hath appeared to all men.
Titus 2:11

God is a Spirit, just and wise;
    His footsteps who can trace?
His love, more ancient than the skies,
    Breaks forth in boundless grace.

In vast eternity He chose
    A people for His praise;
And saves them from their guilt and woes,
    By His almighty grace.

Redeemed, with Jesus' blood redeemed,
    His beauties called to trace,
No angel can be more esteemed
    Than sinners saved by grace.

The work begun is carried on,
    Nor hell can it deface;
The whole elect with Christ are one
    And must be saved by grace.

Where Jesus is, there they must be,
    And view His lovely face;
And sit to all eternity,
    In chanting forth His grace.

1890 Joseph Hart LM

But after that the kindness and love of God our Saviour toward man appeared.
Titus 3:4

To comprehend the great Three-One,
    Is more than highest angels can;
Or what the Trinity has done
    From death and hell to ransom man.

But all true Christians this may boast,
    A truth from nature never learned,
That Father, Son, and Holy Ghost,
    To save our souls are all concerned.

The Father's love in this we find,
    He made His Son our sacrifice;
The Son in love His life resigned;
    The Spirit of love His blood applies.

Thus we the Trinity can praise
    In unity through Christ our King;
Our grateful hearts and voices raise
    In faith and love, while thus we sing:

'Glory to God the Father be,
    Because He sent His Son to die;
Glory to God the Son, that He
    Did with such willingness comply.'

1891 Isaac Watts CM

Not by works of righteousness which we have done, but according to His mercy He saved us.
Titus 3:5

'Tis not by works of righteousness
    Which our own hands have done,
But we are saved by sovereign grace,
    Abounding through the Son.

'Tis from the mercy of our God
    That all our hopes begin;
'Tis by the water and the blood
    Our souls are washed from sin.

'Tis through the purchase of His death
    Who hung upon the tree,
The Spirit is sent down to breathe
    On such dry bones as we.

Raised from the dead, we live anew;
    And, justified by grace,
We shall appear in glory too,
    And see our Father's face.

'Glory to God the Holy Ghost,
    Who to our hearts this love reveals;'
Thus God Three-One, to sinners lost
    Salvation sends, procures, and seals.

1892   Horatius Bonar   66 66 88
Not by works of righteousness which we have done, but according to His mercy He saved us.
Titus 3:5

Thy works, not mine, O Christ,
  Speak gladness to this heart;
They tell me all is done,
  They bid my fear depart.

To whom save Thee, who canst alone
For sin atone, Lord, shall I flee?

Thy wounds, not mine, O Christ,
  Can heal my bruisèd soul;
Thy stripes, not mine, contain
  The balm that makes me whole.

Thy cross, not mine, O Christ,
  Has borne the awful load
Of sins that none could bear
  But the incarnate God.

Thy death, not mine, O Christ,
  Has paid the ransom due;
Ten thousand deaths like mine
  Would have been all too few.

Thy righteousness, O Christ,
  Alone can cover me;
No righteousness avails
  Save that which is of Thee:

1893   John Newton   77 77
The grace of our Lord Jesus Christ be with you. *Philemon 1:25*

For a season called to part,
  Let us now ourselves commend
To the gracious eye and heart
  Of our ever-present Friend.

Jesus, hear our humble prayer,
  Tender Shepherd of Thy sheep;
Let Thy mercy and Thy care
  All our souls in safety keep.

In Thy strength may we be strong;
  Sweeten every cross and pain;
Give us, if we live, ere long,
  Here to meet in peace again.

1894   Gerhard Tersteegen, tr. E Bevan 77 77
Being made so much better than the angels, as He hath by inheritance obtained a more excellent name than they. *Hebrews 1:4*

Name of Jesus! highest name!
  Name that earth and heaven adore!
From the heart of God it came,
  Leads me to God's heart once more.

Name of Jesus! living tide!
  Days of drought for me are past;
How much more than satisfied
  Are the thirsty lips at last!

Name of Jesus! dearest name!
  Bread of heaven and balm of love:
Oil of gladness, surest claim
  To the treasures stored above.

Jesus gives forgiveness free,
  Jesus cleanses all my stains;
Jesus gives His life to me,
  Jesus always He remains.

Only Jesus! fairest name!
  Life and rest and peace and bliss,
Jesus, evermore the same,
  He is mine and I am His.

1895   Samuel Wesley   CM
But unto the Son He saith, Thy throne, O God, is for ever and ever: a sceptre of righteousness is the sceptre of Thy kingdom.
Hebrews 1 :8

Hail! God the Son, with glory crowned
  Ere time began to be!
Throned with the Father, through the round
  Of vast eternity.

Whose wondrous love, in mystery showed
  That mystery who can scan?
The co-eternal Son of God,
  The mortal Son of man.

Our feeble nature He assumes.
  And, full of truth and grace.
By His imputed work becomes
  The Lord our Righteousness.

To lift us from our lost estate,
  Behold His life-blood stream!
Hail, Lord, almighty to create!
  Almighty to redeem!

The Mediator's God-like sway
  His church below sustains,
Till nature shall her Judge survey,
  The King Messiah reigns.

1896   Richard Burnham   CM
**And as a vesture shalt Thou fold them up, and
they shall be changed: but Thou art the same,
and Thy years shall not fail.**
Hebrews 1:12

Through all the changes here below,
  I'd prize the Saviour's name;
His heart no change can ever know,
  For He is e'er the same.

Though foes, and friends, and saints unite
  To clothe my soul with shame,
I turn to Christ, the Prince of light,
  Whose love is e'er the same.

And if my Lord should seem to frown,
  And disregard my name,
In purest love He soon comes down,
  And says He's still the same.

And though my firmest faith should fail,
  And low is all my frame,
His tender mercies still prevail,
  For Jesus is the same.

And when I'm closed in death's embrace,
  With joy I'd then proclaim
The wonders of abounding grace,
  And Jesus still the same.

1897   Matthew Wilks   77 77 77
**And as a vesture shalt Thou fold them up, and
they shall be changed: but Thou art the same,
and Thy years shall not fail.**
Hebrews 1:12

Brethren let us look around
To creation's utmost bound;
  Lo, this beauteous fabric shall
  Into dire confusion fall:
But our Christ is still the same,
Endless blessings on His name!

Each dear object of our love,
Rending thought, must soon remove!
  Wealth, with all its glittering show,
  Shortly will forsake us too:
But our Christ is still the same,
Endless blessings on His name!

Abraham's bold rebellious race
Found Him full of truth and grace
  Priests and prophets all have told
  What He did for saints of old:
Jesus Christ is still the same,
Endless blessings on His name!

Will He now His grace deny?
Lay His wonted kindness by?
  Will He, can He, say, 'Depart,'
  To the humble, contrite heart?
No, our Christ is still the same,
Endless blessings on His name!

What can creatures further say?
Is He not the same today?
  Shall He not for ever prove
  Jesus Christ the same above?
Yes, in heaven He'll prove the same,
Endless blessings on His name!

1898   John Stevens   CM
But we see Jesus. *Hebrews 2:9*

How great and solemn is the thing,
  For which we here are come;
To view the death of Zion's King,
  And gaze upon His tomb.

To see Him, under death's arrest,
  Enter the dismal grave;
Awhile in that dark cell to rest,
  Our mortal flesh to save;

To see Him in His grave-clothes lie,
  His life and glory gone;
To ask ourselves the reason why
  This wondrous deed was done.

To view the wounds of which He died
  And own our sins the cause;
To honour Christ the crucified,
  Adhering to His laws.

To trace Him rising from the tomb
  In victory over all;
The first-born Son of nature's womb,
  That rose no more to fall.

Here, humble saints, your tribute pay;
  A risen Saviour sing;
Come, be baptized without delay,
  In honour of your King.

1899   Charles Wesley   CM
**For both He that sanctifieth and they who are
sanctified are all of one: for which cause He is
not ashamed to call them brethren.**
Hebrews 2:11

Jesus, my life, Thyself apply,
   Thine hallowing Spirit breathe;
My vile affections crucify,
   Conform me to Thy death.

Conqueror of hell, and earth, and sin,
   Thy work in me revive;
Enter my soul and reign within,
   And kill and make alive.

Rule in me, Lord; Thy foes control
   Which would not own Thy sway;
Diffuse Thy likeness through my soul,
   Shine to the perfect day.

O save me from the power of sin,
   And seal me Thine abode;
Thine image stamp, and make me shine,
   A temple meet for God.

My inward holiness Thou art,
   Almighty to refine;
With all Thy fulness fill my heart,
   Till all my heart is Thine.

1900   Joseph Hart   LM
**That through death He might destroy him that
had the power of death, that is, the devil.**
Hebrews 2:14

Ye Christians, hear the joyful news,
Death has received a deadly bruise;
Our Lord has made his empire fall,
And conquered him that conquered all.

Though doomed are all men once to die,
Yet we by faith death's power defy;
We soon shall feel his bands unbound,
Awakened by the Archangel's sound.

The trump of God shall rend the rocks,
And open adamantine locks;
Come forth the dead from death's dark dome,
And Jesus call His ransomed home.

1901   William Gadsby   77 77
**Consider the Apostle and High Priest of our
profession, Christ Jesus.**
Hebrews 3:1

Jesus is my great High Priest;
Bears my name upon His breast;
And that we may never part,
I am sealed upon His heart.

All my sins were on Him thrown:
He for them did once atone;
He did all my debts discharge,
And has set my soul at large.

By His own atoning blood,
He my wounded spirit cured;
Washed and made me white as snow;
Cleansed me well from top to toe.

He the veil has rent in twain;
Through His flesh I enter in;
And with Him for ever rest,
In the Lord's most holy place.

He has bought me with His blood;
Reconciled my soul to God;
Made me meet for glory too,
And will bring me safely through.

1902   David Denham   CM
For we which have believed do enter into rest.
Hebrews 4:3

How may the chosen of our God
   With faith in Christ be blest;
Wash in the fountain of His blood,
   And enter into rest?

Though oft through unbelief we pine,
   With anxious cares oppressed;
Yet when the Lord is pleased to shine,
   We enter into rest.

The gospel trumpet shall be blown,
   That souls by sin distressed
May see they are with Jesus one,
   And enter into rest.

Soon all the friends of Christ shall meet
   Where foes shall ne'er molest;
Stand in the last great day complete,
   And enter into rest.

1903   William Gadsby   886 D
For if Jesus had given them rest, then would
He not afterward have spoken of another day.
Hebrews 4:8

The Sabbath was a day of rest;
The day the Lord Jehovah blest;
   A lively type of Christ;
The labouring poor may venture here;
The guilty banish all their fear,
   And lean on Jesus' breast.

When foes without, and foes within,
Wrath, law, and Satan, guilt and sin,
   The child of God molest;
Fatigued with sin, distressed with fear,
He enters into Christ, and there
   He finds a settled rest.

Jesus is Zion's only rest;
Thrice happy is the man, and blest,
   That into Him believes;
His six days' toil is finished then;
His slavish fear for ever gone;
   By faith in Christ He lives.

A precious resting-place indeed;
Whatever weary pilgrims need
   Is richly treasured here.
Here sinners may commune with God,
And drink full draughts of heavenly love,
   Nor death nor danger fear.

O may I ever rest in Him,
And never, never stray again,
   Nor after strangers roam;
Dear Jesus, fix my roving heart,
Nor ever let me from Thee start,
   Till Thou shalt take me home.

1904   Charles Wesley   CM
There remaineth therefore a rest to the people
of God. *Hebrews 4:9*

Lord, I believe a rest remains
   To all Thy people known;
A rest where pure enjoyment reigns,
   And Thou art loved alone.

O that I now the rest might know,
   Believe and enter in!
Dear Saviour, now the power bestow,
   And let me cease from sin.

Remove this hardness from my heart,
   This unbelief remove;
To me the rest of faith impart,
   The Sabbath of Thy love.

Come, Thou dear Saviour, come away!
   Into my soul descend;
No longer from Thy creature stay,
   My Author and my End.

1905   William Williams   87 87
There remaineth therefore a rest to the people
of God. *Hebrews 4:9*

Jesus lead me by Thy power
   Safe into the promised rest;
Hide my soul within Thy arms;
   Make me lean upon Thy breast.

Be my Guide in every peril,
   Watch me hourly, night and day;
Else my foolish heart will wander
   From Thy Spirit far away.

In Thy presence I am happy;
   In Thy presence I'm secure;
In Thy presence all afflictions
   I can easily endure.

In Thy presence I can conquer,
   I can suffer, I can die;
Far from Thee, I faint and languish
   O Thou Saviour, keep me nigh.

1906   Thomas Kelly   LM
There remaineth therefore a rest to the people
of God. *Hebrews 4:9*

For weary saints a rest remains
In heaven from all their toil and pains,
Where seas of joy eternal flow
Without a taint of mortal woe.

There, from all sin and sorrow free,
They spend a long eternity;
No more to strive with flesh and blood,
But cease from sin and rest in God.

Eternal love this rest ordained,
To soothe the breast with sorrows pained,
And fold His lambs from harm secure,
Long as eternal years endure.

O sacred rest, for thee we groan;
And bid the wheels of time roll on,
To bring that hour when we shall rise
To join the chorus of the skies.

Immortal love shall then repay
The transient sorrow of the way,
And Jesus' name swell every song,
A whole eternity along.

1907   Vernon Higham   DSM
**There remaineth therefore a rest to the people
of God.** *Hebrews 4:9*

There is a rest prepared
That we may enter in,
A place of peace where love has cared
And dealt with all our sin.
The power of hell is stayed;
The path of life is shown;
The dreadful penalty is paid:
For sin did Christ atone.

There is a path prepared,
Paved by the grace of heaven,
A place of joy and mercy shared,
And sheltered from all harm.
We rest our weary souls,
We cast our burdens here;
And find that Jesus Christ controls,
Is King in every sphere.

There is a peace prepared,
That silences the storm,
When all the elements have raged
And left our souls forlorn.
This peace will now abide
And drive away our fears;
Then draw us to Thy blessèd side,
And wipe away our tears.

There is a place prepared,
And Thou wilt bring us in;
Crush unbelief where sin has dared
To enter such a scene.
O place our faith secure,
And tell us we are blessed;
O grant a vision to endure,
Our final Sabbath rest.

© *Author*

1908   Joseph Hart (alt)   77 77 77
**Let us labour therefore to enter into that rest,
lest any man fall after the same example of
unbelief.** *Hebrews 4:11*

Lord, we lie before Thy feet;
Look on all our deep distress;
Thy rich mercy may we meet;
Clothe us with Thy righteousness;
Stretch forth Thy almighty hand;
Hold us up, and we shall stand.

O that closer we could cleave
To Thy bleeding, dying breast!
Give us firmly to believe,
And to enter into rest;
Lord increase, increase our faith;
Make us faithful unto death.

Make Thy mighty wonders known;
Let us see Thy sufferings plain;
Let us hear Thee sigh and groan,
Till we sigh and groan again;
Rend, O rend the veil between;
Open wide the sacred scene.

Let us trust Thee evermore;
Every moment on Thee call,
For new life, new will, new power;
Let us trust Thee, Lord, for all;
May we nothing know beside
Jesus, and Him crucified.

1909   Frank Houghton   LM
**For the word of God is quick, and powerful,
and sharper than any
two-edged sword.** *Hebrews 4:12*

My Lord, who in the desert fed
On soul-sustaining heavenly bread,
Words that were meat and drink to Thee;
O let them daily nourish me!

And since the sword that served Thee well
In battling with the powers of hell
Is even now at hand for me,
Help me to wield it manfully.

But first, O holy, gracious Lord,
I pray Thee, let Thy Spirit's sword
Pierce heart and conscience, till I see
Both what I am and ought to be.

Thy word my rule and my delight,
My strength for service and for fight!
For this exhaustless treasure-store,
My Lord, I praise Thee and adore!

© *Overseas Missionary Fellowship*

1910   Thomas Mackellar   87 84
**For the word of God is quick, and powerful,
and sharper than any
two-edged sword.** *Hebrews 4:12*

Book of grace and book of glory!
  Gift of God to age and youth,
Wondrous is thy sacred story,
  Bright, bright with truth!

Book of love! in accents tender
  Speaking unto such as we;
May it lead us, Lord, to render
  All, all to Thee.

Book of hope! the spirit sighing,
  Sweetest comfort finds in thee,
As it hears the Saviour crying
  'Come, come to Me!'

Book of peace! when nights of sorrow
  Fall upon us drearily,
Thou wilt bring a shining morrow,
  Full, full of Thee.

Book of life! when we, reposing,
  Bid farewell to friends we love,
Give us, for the life then closing,
  Life, life above.

1911   John Newton   SM
**For the word of God is quick, and powerful,
and sharper than any
two-edged sword.** *Hebrews 4:12*

  The word of Christ, our Lord,
  With whom we have to do;
Is sharper than a two-edged sword,
  To pierce the sinner through!

  Swift as the lightnings blaze
  When awful thunders roll,
It fills the conscience with amaze,
  And penetrates the soul.

  No heart can be concealed
  From His all-piercing eyes;
Each thought and purpose stands revealed,
  Naked, without disguise.

  He sees His people's fears,
  He notes their mournful cry;
He counts their sighs and falling tears,
  And helps them from on high.

Though feeble is their good,
  It has His kind regard;
Yea, all they would do, if they could,
  Shall find a sure reward.

He sees the wicked too,
  And will repay them soon,
For all the evil deeds they do,
  And all they would have done.

Since all our secret ways
  Are marked and known by Thee;
Afford us, Lord, Thy light of grace
  That we ourselves may see.

1912   Michael Bruce   LM
**Seeing then that we have a great High Priest,
that is passed into the heavens, Jesus the Son
of God, let us hold fast our profession.**
Hebrews 4:14

Where high the heavenly temple stands,
The house of God, not made with hands,
A great High Priest our nature wears,
The Guardian of mankind appears.

He who for men their Surety stood,
And poured on earth His precious blood,
Pursues in heaven His mighty plan,
The Saviour and the Friend of man.

Though now ascended up on high,
He bends on earth a Brother's eye;
Partaker of the human name,
He knows the frailty of our frame.

Our fellow-sufferer yet retains
A fellow-feeling of our pains;
And still remembers, in the skies,
His tears, and agonies, and cries.

In every pang that rends the heart,
The Man of Sorrows had a part;
He sympathises with our grief,
And to the sufferer sends relief.

With boldness, therefore, at the throne,
Let us make all our sorrows known;
And ask the aid of heavenly power,
To help us in the evil hour.

1913   Christopher Idle   87 87 77
**Seeing then that we have a great High Priest,
that is passed into the heavens, Jesus the Son
of God, let us hold fast our profession.**
Hebrews 4:14

Since our great High Priest, Christ Jesus,
  Bears the name above all names,
Reigning Son of God, surpassing
  Other titles, powers, and claims—
Since to heaven our Lord has passed;
Let us hold our witness fast!

Since we have a Priest who suffered,
  Knowing weakness, tears, and pain;
Who, like us, was tried and tempted;
  Unlike us, without a stain—
Since He shared our lowly place;
Let us boldly seek His grace!

Sacrifice and suffering over,
  Now He sits at God's right hand
Crowned with praise, no more an outcast,
  His pre-eminence long-planned;
Such a great High Priest we have,
Strong to help, supreme to save!

Love's example, hope's attraction,
  Faith's beginning and its end,
Pioneer of our salvation,
  Mighty Advocate and Friend,
Jesus, now in glory raised,
Our ascended Lord be praised!

*Words: © C. Idle / The Jubilate Group.
www.jubilate.co.uk USED BY PERMISSION*

1914   Joseph Hart   87 87 D
**Seeing then that we have a great High Priest,
that is passed into the heavens, Jesus the Son
of God, let us hold fast our profession.**
Hebrews 4:14

Great High Priest, we view Thee stooping
  With our names upon Thy breast,
In the garden groaning, drooping,
  To the ground with horrors pressed;
Weeping angels stood confounded,
  To behold their Maker thus;
And can we remain unmovèd,
  When we know 'twas all for us?

On the cross Thy body broken,
  Cancels every penal tie;
Tempted souls, produce this token,
  All demands to satisfy.
All is finished; do not doubt it,
  But believe your dying Lord;
Never reason more about it,
  Only take Him at His word.

Lord, we fain would trust Thee solely;
  'Twas for us Thy blood was spilt;
Bruisèd Bridegroom, take us wholly,
  Take, and make us what Thou wilt.
Thou hast borne the bitter sentence
  Passed on man's devoted race;
True belief and true repentance,
  Are Thy gifts, Thou God of grace.

1915   Horatius Bonar   66 66 88
**Seeing then that we have a great High Priest,
that is passed into the heavens, Jesus the Son
of God, let us hold fast our profession.**
Hebrews 4:14

Done is the work that saves,
  Once and for ever done;
Finished the righteousness
  That clothes the unrighteous one.
The love that blesses us below
Is flowing freely to us now.

The sacrifice is o'er,
  The veil is rent in twain,
The mercy-seat is red
  With blood of Victim slain;
Why stand ye then without, in fear?
The blood divine invites us near.

The gate is open wide;
  The new and living way
Is clear and free and bright
  With love and peace and day.
Into the holiest now we come,
Our present and our endless home.

Upon the mercy-seat
  The High Priest sits within;
The blood is in His hand
  Which makes and keeps us clean.
With boldness let us now draw near;
That blood has banished every fear.

Then to the Lamb once slain
  Be glory, praise and power,
Who died and lives again,
  Who liveth evermore,
Who loved and washed us in His blood,
Who makes us kings and priests to God.

1916 Gerhard Tersteegen   SM
tr. in Leifchild's Original Hymns 1842
Seeing then that we have a great High Priest, that is passed into the heavens, Jesus the Son of God, let us hold fast our profession.
Hebrews 4:14

How gracious, kind and good,
  My great High Priest, art Thou!
As Aaron in the holiest stood,
  So Christ in heaven now.

When conscience would despair,
  By reason of my sin,
Thy blood can banish all its care,
  And peace restore within.

It gives the anxious mind
  A confidence in Thee;
Though nothing in ourselves we find,
  But insufficiency.

Whene'er my footsteps slide,
  And when my spirit fails,
I flee to Thy dear bleeding side,
  And humble faith prevails.

Then feels my deepest smart
  The soul-reviving power,
And gently rests my troubled heart
  Beneath the crimson shower.

1917 Isaac Watts   CM
For we have not an High Priest which cannot be touched with the feeling of our infirmities; but was in all points tempted like as we are, yet without sin.
Hebrews 4:15

With joy we meditate the grace
  Of our High Priest above;
His heart is made of tenderness;
  His mercies melt with love.

Touched with a sympathy within,
  He knows our feeble frame;
He knows what sore temptations mean,
  For He has felt the same.

But spotless, innocent, and pure,
  The great Redeemer stood,
While Satan's fiery darts He bore,
  And did resist to blood.

He, in the days of feeble flesh,
  Poured out His cries and tears;
And, in His measure, feels afresh
  What every member bears.

He'll never quench the smoking flax,
  But raise it to a flame;
The bruisèd reed He never breaks,
  Nor scorns the meanest name.

Then let our humble faith address
  His mercy and His power;
We shall obtain delivering grace,
  In the distressing hour.

1918 Jane Crewdson   CM
For we have not an High Priest which cannot be touched with the feeling of our infirmities; but was in all points tempted like as we are, yet without sin.
Hebrews 4:15

There is no sorrow, Lord, too light
  To bring in prayer to Thee;
There is no anxious care too slight
  To wake Thy sympathy.

Thou who hast trod the thorny road
  Wilt share each small distress;
The love which bore the greater load
  Will not refuse the less.

There is no secret sigh we breathe
  But meets Thine ear divine,
And every cross grows light beneath
  The shadow, Lord, of Thine.

Life's ills without, sin's strife within,
  The heart would overflow,
But for that Love which died for sin,
  That Love which wept for woe.

1919 Samuel Medley   CM
Let us therefore come boldly unto the throne of grace, that we may obtain mercy, and find grace to help in time of need. *Hebrews 4:16*

Dear Lord! to us assembled here
  Reveal Thy smiling face,
While we, by faith, with love and fear,
  Approach the throne of grace.

Thy house is called the house of prayer,
  A solemn sacred place;
O let us now Thy presence share,
  While at the throne of grace.

With holy boldness may we come,
  Though of a sinful race,
Thankful to find there yet is room
  Before the throne of grace.

Our earnest, fervent cry attend,
    And all our faith increase,
While we address our heavenly Friend
    Upon the throne of grace.

His tender pity and His love
    Our every fear will chase;
And all our help, we then shall prove,
    Comes from the throne of grace.

Dear Lord, our many wants supply;
    Attend to every case;
While humbled in the dust we lie,
    Low at the throne of grace.

We bless Thee for Thy word and laws;
    We bless Thee for Thy peace;
And we do bless Thee, Lord, because
    There is a throne of grace.

1920   George Herbert   CM
Let us therefore come boldly unto the throne of grace, that we may obtain mercy, and find grace to help in time of need. *Hebrews 4:16*

Come boldly to a throne of grace,
    Ye wretched sinners, come;
And lay your load at Jesus' feet,
    And plead what He has done.

'How can I come?' some soul may say,
    'I'm lame, and cannot walk;
My guilt and sin have stopped my mouth;
    I sigh, but dare not talk.'

Come boldly to the throne of grace,
    Though lost, and blind, and lame;
Jehovah is the sinner's Friend,
    And ever was the same.

He makes the dead to hear His voice;
    He makes the blind to see;
The sinner lost He came to save,
    And set the prisoner free.

Come boldly to the throne of grace,
    For Jesus fills the throne;
And those He kills He makes alive;
    He hears the sigh or groan.

Poor bankrupt souls, who feel and know
    The hell of sin within,
Come boldly to the throne of grace;
    The Lord will take you in.

1921   Frederick Whitfield   76 76 D
Let us therefore come boldly unto the throne of grace, that we may obtain mercy, and find grace to help in time of need. *Hebrews 4:16*

I need Thee, precious Jesus!
    For I am full of sin:
My soul is dark and guilty,
    My heart is dead within:
I need the cleansing fountain,
    Where I can always flee,
The blood of Christ most precious,
    The sinner's perfect plea.

I need Thee, precious Jesus!
    For I am very poor;
A stranger and a pilgrim,
    I have no earthly store:
I need the love of Jesus
    To cheer me on my way,
To guide my doubting footsteps,
    To be my strength and stay.

I need Thee, precious Jesus!
    I need a Friend like Thee;
A Friend to soothe and comfort,
    A Friend to care for me:
I need the heart of Jesus
    To feel each anxious care,
To tell my every trouble
    And all my sorrows share.

I need Thee, precious Jesus!
    And hope to see Thee soon,
Encircled with the rainbow,
    And seated on Thy throne;
There with Thy blood-bought children
    My joy shall ever be,
To sing Thy praise, Lord Jesus,
    To gaze, my Lord, on Thee.

1922   Isaac Watts   LM
Wherein God, willing more abundantly to shew unto the heirs of promise the immutability of His counsel, confirmed it by an oath.
Hebrews 6:17

How oft have sin and Satan strove
    To rend my soul from Thee, my God!
But everlasting is Thy love,
    And Jesus seals it with His blood.

The oath and promise of the Lord
    Join to confirm the wondrous grace,
Eternal power performs the word,
    And fills all heaven with endless praise.

Amidst temptations sharp and long,
  My soul to this dear refuge flies;
Hope is my anchor, firm and strong,
  While tempests blow and billows rise.

The gospel bears my spirit up;
  A faithful and unchanging God
Lays the foundation of my hope
  In oaths, and promises, and blood.

1923 John Berridge   SM

**That by two immutable things, in which it was
impossible for God to lie, we might have a
strong consolation, who have fled for refuge
to lay hold upon the hope set before us.**
Hebrews 6:18

No help in self I find,
  And yet have sought it well;
The native treasure of my mind
  Is sin, and death, and hell.

To Christ for help I fly,
  The Friend of sinners lost,
A refuge sweet, and sure, and nigh,
  And there is all my trust.

Lord, grant me free access
  Unto Thy piercèd side,
For there I seek my dwelling-place,
  And there my guilt would hide.

In every time of need,
  My helpless soul defend,
And save me from all evil deed,
  And save me to the end.

And when the hour is near
  That flesh and heart will fail,
Do Thou in all Thy grace appear,
  And bid my faith prevail.

1924 Priscilla Owens   Irregular

**Which hope we have as an anchor of the soul,
both sure and stedfast, and which entereth
into that within the veil.**
Hebrews 6:19

Will your anchor hold in the storms of life?
When the clouds unfold their wings of strife,
When the strong tides lift and the cables strain,
Will your anchor drift or firm remain?

*We have an anchor that keeps the soul
Steadfast and sure while the billows roll,
Fastened to the Rock which cannot move,
Grounded firm and deep in the Saviour's love!*

Will your anchor hold in the straits of fear?
When the breakers roar and the reef is near;
While the surges rave and the wild winds blow,
Shall the angry waves then your barque o'erflow?

Will your anchor hold in the floods of death,
When the waters cold chill your latest breath?
On the rising tide you can never fail
While your anchor holds within the veil!

Will your eyes behold through the morning light
The city of gold, and the harbour bright?
Will you anchor safe by the heavenly shore,
When life's storms are past for evermore?

1925 Vernon Higham   64 64 66 64

**Which hope we have as an anchor of the soul,
both sure and stedfast, and which entereth
into that within the veil.**
Hebrews 6:19

Wonderful truth unfold
  Grace to declare;
Beautiful words now told
  Mercy doth bear.
Thou art adorable,
Thy grace unchangeable,
Thy word immutable,
  Beyond compare.

Where shall my soul recline,
  Except in Thee?
How shall this heart of mine
  Find Calvary?
Take my unrighteousness
In Thy great tenderness;
Remove my foolishness;
  This is my plea.

Then in tempestuous sea,
  In storm or gale,
If I forgotten be,
  Thou wilt prevail.
Anchor my soul to Thee,
Fastened to Calvary,
Holding eternally,
  Never to fail.

Then I shall enter in
  Drawn by Thy grace,
When all are gathered in
  To see Thy face.
Now to adore Thy name,
Discarding all my shame,
Grant me a living frame,
  Thee to embrace.

© Author

1926   Samuel Medley   LM
Whither the forerunner is for us entered, even Jesus, made an High Priest for ever after the order of Melchisedec.
Hebrews 6:20

Far, far beyond these lower skies,
  Up to the glories all His own.
Where we by faith lift up our eyes.
  There Jesus, our Forerunner's gone.

Amidst the shining hosts above,
  Where His blessed smile new pleasure gives;
Where all is wonder, joy, and love,
  There Jesus, our Forerunner, lives.

He lives, salvation to impart,
  From sin, and Satan's cursèd wiles,
With love eternal in His heart,
  There Jesus, our Forerunner, smiles.

Before His heavenly Father's face
  For every saint He intercedes,
And, with infallible success,
  There Jesus, our Forerunner, pleads.

But, O 'tis this completes the whole,
  And all its bliss and glory proves;
That, while eternal ages roll,
  There Jesus, our Forerunner, loves.

We shall, when we in heaven appear,
  His praises sing, His wonders tell;
And, with our great Forerunner, there
  For ever, yes, for ever dwell.

1927   Philip Doddridge   LM
Whither the forerunner is for us entered, even Jesus, made an High Priest for ever after the order of Melchisedec.
Hebrews 6:20

Jesus, the Lord, our souls adore,
A painful sufferer now no more;
High on His Father's throne He reigns,
O'er earth and heaven's extensive plains.

His race for ever is complete;
For ever undisturbed His seat;
Myriads of angels round Him fly,
And sing His well-gained victory.

Yet, midst the honours of His throne,
He joys not for Himself alone:
His meanest servants share their part,
Share in that royal tender heart.

Raise, raise, my soul, Thy raptured sight
With sacred wonder and delight;
Jesus, thine own Forerunner see
Entered beyond the veil for thee.

Loud let the howling tempest yell,
And foaming waves to mountains swell,
No shipwreck can my vessel fear,
Since hope hath fixed her anchor here.

1928   David Denham   77 77
By so much was Jesus made a surety of a better testament. *Hebrews 7:22*

Now, ye ransomed of the Lord,
Praise the great incarnate Word:
View Him in our place and stead,
As a Lamb to slaughter led.

He the righteous law obeyed,
And for us a curse was made;
Justice had its full demands
At our Surety's holy hands.

He for us the wine-press trod,
He endured the Father's rod;
Blotting out His people's sin,
Righteousness and peace brought in.

He alone the breach could heal,
And in all points for us feel,
He was tempted and oppressed,
That He might become our rest.

He for us abolished death,
Conquering with His dying breath;
We shall soon His triumphs swell,
Rescued from the jaws of hell.

1929   Samuel Medley   CM
Wherefore He is able also to save them to the uttermost that come unto God by Him, seeing He ever liveth to make intercession for them.
Hebrews 7:25

Wherewith shall we approach the Lord,
  And bow before His throne?
By trusting in His faithful word,
  And pleading Christ alone.

The blood, the righteousness, and love
  Of Jesus, will we plead;
He lives within the veil above,
  For us to intercede.

Sure ground, and sure foundation too,
  We find in Jesus' name;
Herein we every blessing view,
  And every favour claim.

Then let His name for ever be
  To us supremely dear;
Our only, all-prevailing plea,
  For all our hope is there.

This is the name the Father loves
  To hear His children plead;
And all such pleading He approves,
  And blesses them indeed.

1930 Charitie Bancroft   LM
Wherefore He is able also to save them to the
uttermost that come unto God by Him, seeing
He ever liveth to make intercession for them.
Hebrews 7:25

Before the throne of God above
  I have a strong, a perfect plea;
A great High Priest, whose name is Love,
  Who ever lives and pleads for me.

My name is graven on His hands,
  My name is written on His heart;
I know that, while in heaven He stands,
  No tongue can bid me thence depart.

When Satan tempts me to despair,
  And tells me of the guilt within,
Upward I look, and see Him there
  Who made an end of all my sin.

Because the sinless Saviour died,
  My sinful soul is counted free;
For God, the Just, is satisfied
  To look on Him, and pardon me.

Behold Him there! the bleeding Lamb!
  My perfect, spotless Righteousness,
The great unchangeable, I AM,
  The King of glory and of grace.

One with Himself, I cannot die,
  My soul is purchased by His blood;
My life is hid with Christ on high,
  With Christ, my Saviour and my God.

1931 John Kent   87 87
Wherefore He is able also to save them to the
uttermost that come unto God by Him, seeing
He ever liveth to make intercession for them.
Hebrews 7:25

'Tis the gospel's joyful tidings,
  Full salvation sweetly sounds;
Grace to heal thy foul backslidings,
  Sinner, flows from Jesus' wounds.

Are thy sins beyond recounting,
  Like the sand the ocean laves?
Jesus is of life the fountain;
  He unto the utmost saves.

Hail the Lamb who came to save us;
  Hail the love that made Him die!
'Tis the gift that God has given us;
  We'll proclaim His honours high.

When we join the general chorus
  Of the royal blood-bought throng,
Who to glory went before us,
  Saved from every tribe and tongue,

Then we'll make the blissful regions
  Echo to our Saviour's praise;
While the bright angelic legions
  Listen to the charming lays.

1932 Anne Steele   LM
Wherefore He is able also to save them to the
uttermost that come unto God by Him, seeing
He ever liveth to make intercession for them.
Hebrews 7:25

He lives, the great Redeemer lives,
(What joy the blest assurance gives!)
And now, before His Father God,
Pleads the full merit of His blood.

Repeated crimes awake our fears,
And justice armed with frowns appears;
But in the Saviour's lovely face.
Sweet mercy smiles, and all is peace.

Hence, then, ye black despairing thoughts;
Above our fears, above our faults,
His powerful intercessions rise,
And guilt recedes, and terror dies.

In every dark distressful hour,
When sin and Satan join their power,
Let this dear hope repel the dart,
That Jesus bears us on His heart.

Great Advocate, almighty Friend;
On Him our humble hopes depend:
Our cause can never, never fail,
For Jesus pleads, and must prevail.

1933 Charles Wesley   LM
Wherefore He is able also to save them to the uttermost that come unto God by Him, seeing He ever liveth to make intercession for them.
Hebrews 7:25

Wherewith, O God, shall I draw near,
 And bow myself before Thy face?
How in Thy purer eyes appear?
 What shall I bring to gain Thy grace?

Whoe'er to Thee themselves approve
 Must take the path Thy word hath showed,
Justice pursue, and mercy, love,
 And humbly walk by faith with God.

But though my life henceforth be Thine,
 Present for past can ne'er atone;
Though I to Thee the whole resign,
 I only give back Thine own.

What have I then wherein to trust?
 I nothing have, I nothing am;
Excluded is my every boast,
 My glory swallowed up in shame.

Guilty I stand before Thy face,
 On me I feel Thy wrath abide;
'Tis just the sentence should take place;
 'Tis just— but O Thy Son hath died!

Jesus, the Lamb of God, hath bled;
 He bore our sins upon the tree;
Beneath our curse He bowed His head;
 'Tis finished! He hath died for me!

See where before the throne He stands,
 And pours the all-prevailing prayer,
Points to His side, and lifts His hands,
 And shows that I am graven there.

He ever lives for me to pray;
 He prays that I with Him may reign:
Amen to what my Lord doth say!
 Jesus, Thou canst not pray in vain.

1934 Charlotte Elliott   888 6
Wherefore He is able also to save them to the uttermost that come unto God by Him, seeing He ever liveth to make intercession for them.
Hebrews 7:25

O Thou, the contrite sinner's Friend,
Who, loving, lovest him to the end,
On this alone my hopes depend.
 That Thou wilt plead for me.

When weary in the Christian race,
Far off appears my resting-place,
And fainting I mistrust Thy grace,
 Then, Saviour, plead for me.

When I have erred and gone astray
Afar from Thine and wisdom's way,
And see no glimmering guiding ray,
 Still, Saviour, plead for me.

And when my dying hour draws near,
Then, to preserve my soul from fear,
Lord, to my fading sight appear,
 Pleading in heaven for me.

When the full light of heavenly day
Reveals my sins in dread array,
Say, 'I have washed them all away,
 I plead, yea, plead for thee.'

1935 William Gadsby   77 77
For such an High Priest became us, who is holy, harmless, undefiled, separate from sinners, and made higher than the heavens.
Hebrews 7:26

Jesus, as my great High Priest,
Bears my name upon His breast;
And that we may never part,
I am sealed upon His heart.

Light and love from Jesus flow,
He is my perfection too;
I upon His shoulders rest;
With His counsel I am blest.

I to Him my sins confess;
Carry to Him my distress;
And though great my evils are,
He preserves me from despair.

He the veil has rent in twain,
Through His flesh I enter in;
And with Him for ever rest,
In His full atonement blessed.

Jesus ever, ever lives,
As my Advocate He pleads;
I can never, never die,
While He lives enthroned on high.

1936 Philip Doddridge   CM
For such an High Priest became us, who is holy, harmless, undefiled, separate from sinners, and made higher than the heavens.
Hebrews 7:26

Now let our cheerful eyes survey
 Our great High Priest above,
And celebrate His constant care,
 And sympathetic love.

Though raised to a superior throne,
  Where angels bow around,
And high o'er all the shining train,
  With matchless honours crowned;

The names of all His saints He bears
  Deep graven on His heart;
Nor shall the meanest Christian say,
  That he hath lost his part.

Those characters shall fair abide,
  Our everlasting trust,
When gems, and monuments, and crowns,
  Are mouldered down to dust.

So, gracious Saviour, on my breast
  May Thy dear name be worn,
A sacred ornament and guard,
  To endless ages borne.

1937 John Cennick   66 66 88
But Christ being come an High Priest of good things to come. *Hebrews 9:11*

A good High Priest is come,
  Supplying Aaron's place,
And taking up his room,
  Dispensing life and grace.
The law by Aaron's priesthood came;
But grace and truth by Jesus' name.

My Lord a Priest is made
  (As sware the mighty God)
To Israel and His seed:
  Ordained to offer blood
For sinners, who His mercy seek
A Priest, as was Melchizedek.

He once temptation knew
  Of every sort and kind,
That He might succour show
  To every tempted mind;
In every point the Lamb was tried
Like us, and then for us He died.

He died, but lives again,
  And by the altar stands;
There shows how He was slain,
  Opening His piercèd hands:
Our Priest abides, and pleads the cause
Of us, who have transgressed His laws.

I other priests disclaim,
  And laws and offerings too:
None but the bleeding Lamb
  The mighty work can do.
He shall have all the praise; for He
Hath loved, and lived, and died for me.

1938 Augustus Toplady   CM
Neither by the blood of goats and calves, but by His own blood He entered in once into the holy place, having obtained eternal redemption for us. *Hebrews 9:12*

O precious blood, O glorious death,
  By which the sinner lives!
When stung with sin this blood we view,
  And all our joy revives.

Our scarlet crimes are made as wool,
  And we brought nigh to God,
Thanks to that wrath-appeasing death—
  That heaven-procuring blood.

The blood that makes His glorious church
  From every blemish free;
And O the riches of His love!
  He poured it out for me.

Guilty and worthless as I am,
  It all for me was given;
And boldness, through His blood, I have
  To enter into heaven.

1939 William Styles   886 D
And almost all things are by the law purged with blood; and without shedding of blood is no remission. *Hebrews 9:22*

When Cain of old acceptance sought,
An offering of fruit he brought,
  To make his peace with heaven;
In vain: no sacred fire came down;
He stood before Jehovah's frown,
  A sinner unforgiven.

But Abel, pardon to obtain,
Came with a lamb that he had slain,
  To offer to his God.
And all was well; for then, as now,
No access could the Lord allow,
  But by atoning blood.

Nought that to man as man belongs—
Love, kindness, patience under wrongs,
  Virtue however bright,
Avails to cancel human sin;
Or ever can acceptance win,
  In God's most holy sight.

1940   Charles Wesley   66 66 88
**For Christ is not entered into the holy places
made with hands, which are the figures of the
true; but into heaven itself, now to appear in
the presence of God for us.** *Hebrews 9:24*

Arise, my soul, arise,
    Shake off thy guilty fears:
The perfect Sacrifice
    In my behalf appears:
Before the throne my Surety stands,
My name is written on His hands.

He ever lives above,
    For me to intercede,
His all-redeeming love,
    His precious blood, to plead;
His blood atoned for every race,
And sprinkles now the throne of grace.

The Father hears Him pray,
    His dear anointed One;
He cannot turn away
    The presence of His Son:
His Spirit answers to the blood,
And tells me I am born of God.

My God is reconciled,
    His pardoning voice I hear;
He owns me for His child,
    I can no longer fear;
With confidence I now draw nigh,
And 'Father, Abba, Father!' cry.

1941   Thomas Kelly   66 66 88
**For Christ is not entered into the holy places
made with hands, which are the figures of the
true; but into heaven itself, now to appear in
the presence of God for us.** *Hebrews 9:24*

The atoning work is done;
    The Victim's blood is shed;
And Jesus now is gone,
    His people's cause to plead.
He stands in heaven, their great High Priest,
And bears their names upon His breast.

He sprinkles with His blood
    The mercy-seat above;
Else justice had withstood
    The purposes of love;
But justice now objects no more,
And mercy yields her boundless store.

No temple made with hands
    His place of service is;
In heaven itself He stands—
    A heavenly Priesthood His!
In Him the shadows of the law
Are all fulfilled, and now withdraw.

And, though awhile He be
    Hid from the eyes of men,
His people look to see
    Their great High Priest again;
In brightest glory He will come,
And take His waiting people home.

1942   Isaac Watts   CM
**But now once in the end of the world hath He
appeared to put away sin by the sacrifice of
Himself.** *Hebrews 9:26*

How is our nature marred by sin!
    Nor can it ever find
A way to make the conscience clean,
    Or heal the wounded mind.

In vain we seek for peace with God,
    By methods of our own;
Jesus, there's nothing but Thy blood
    Can bring us near the throne.

The threatenings of the broken law
    Impress our souls with dread;
If God His sword of vengeance draw,
    It strikes our spirits dead.

But Thy illustrious sacrifice
    Has answered these demands;
And peace and pardon from the skies
    Come down by Jesus' hands.

'Tis by Thy death we live, O Lord!
    'Tis on Thy cross we rest;
For ever be Thy love adored,
    Thy name for ever blest.

1943   Philip Doddridge   CM
**And as it is appointed unto men once to die,
but after this the judgment.**
Hebrews 9:27

Heaven has confirmed the great decree
    That Adam's race must die;
One general ruin sweeps them down,
    And low in dust they lie.

Ye living men, the tomb survey
    Where you must quickly dwell;
Hark! how the awful summons sounds
    In every funeral knell.

Once you must die, and once for all
    The solemn purport weigh,
For know that heaven or hell are hung
    On that important day.

Those eyes, so long in darkness veiled,
   Must wake, the Judge to see,
And every word and every thought
   Must pass His scrutiny.

O, may I in the Judge behold
   My Saviour and my Friend,
And, far beyond the reach of death,
   With all His saints ascend.

1944   The Clifton Hymnal   LM
For the law having a shadow of good things to come.
Hebrews 10:1

By types and figures through the year
God taught His church that Christ drew near
And in them darkly may they see
A shadow of good things to be.

The Paschal Lamb at evening slain,
With bone unbroken, without stain,
The blood on door and lintel shed,
The hyssop and the unleavened bread.

The scape-goat bearing far away
The sins that on his head they lay,
The daily sacrifice that bled,
Morning and evening in man's stead;

The brazen serpent, set on high,
That Israel looking might not die
Pointed to Him that should arise,
To be the sinner's Sacrifice.

The manna that at break of day
About the tents of Israel lay,
Told of that true and living Bread
Wherewith God's holy church is fed.

The cloven rock whence streams were sent
Following the people as they went,
Day after day their thirst sufficed
Unfailing, and that Rock was Christ.

1945   Alice Janvrin   85 83
From henceforth expecting till His enemies be made His footstool.
Hebrews 10:13

He expecteth, He expecteth!
   As the hour draws near,
When the King, in all His glory,
    Shall appear.

He is waiting with long patience
   For His crowning day,
For that kingdom which shall never
    Pass away.

And till every tribe and nation
   Bow before His throne,
He expecteth loyal service
    From His own.

Shall we, dare we, disappoint Him?
   Brethren, let us rise!
He who died for us is watching
    From the skies—

Watching till His royal banner
   Floateth far and wide,
Till He seeth of His travail:
    Satisfied!

1946   John Burton, Jr.   SM
Let us draw near with a true heart in full assurance of faith, having our hearts sprinkled from an evil conscience, and our bodies washed with pure water.
Hebrews 10:22

I often say my prayers,
   But do I ever pray?
And do the wishes of my heart
   Go with the words I say?

I may as well kneel down
   And worship gods of stone,
As offer to the living God
   A prayer of words alone.

For words without the heart
   The Lord will never hear;
Nor will He to those lips attend
   Whose prayers are not sincere.

Lord, teach me what I need
   And teach me how to pray;
And do not let me seek Thy grace
   Not meaning what I say.

1947   Bryn Rees   SM
Let us hold fast the profession of our faith without wavering; (for He is faithful that promised.) *Hebrews 10:23*

Have faith in God, my heart,
   Trust and be unafraid;
God will fulfil in every part
   Each promise He has made.

Have faith in God, my mind,
   Though oft thy light burns low;
God's mercy holds a wiser plan
   Than thou canst fully know.

Have faith in God, my soul,
His cross for ever stands;
And neither life nor death can pluck
His children from His hands.

Lord Jesus, make me whole;
Grant me no resting place,
Until I rest, heart, mind and soul,
The captive of Thy grace.

© Alexander Scott

1948   William Gadsby   SM
Now the just shall live by faith.
Hebrews 10:38

The just by faith shall live,
Nor fear the powers of hell;
All blessings that a God can give,
In Christ most richly dwell.

By faith in Jesus' blood,
The just shall live indeed;
Shall have a settled peace with God,
And from their sins be freed.

When sense and reason fail,
And all things dark appear,
By faith, the just shall say, ''Tis well,
Jehovah will appear.'

If providence should frown,
And crosses still increase;
By faith, the just shall live and own
God their salvation is.

By faith in Christ, as God,
As Prophet, Priest, and King,
The just shall live, and live to prove,
That death has lost its sting.

1949   Isaac Watts   CM
Now faith is the substance of things hoped for, the evidence of things not seen. *Hebrews 11:1*

Faith is the brightest evidence
Of things beyond our sight;
Breaks through the clouds of flesh and sense,
And dwells in heavenly light.

It sets time past in present view,
Brings distant prospects home,
Of things a thousand years ago,
Or thousand years to come.

By faith we know the worlds were made
By God's almighty word;
Abram, to unknown countries led,
By faith obeyed the Lord.

He sought a city fair and high,
Built by the eternal hands;
And faith assures us, though we die,
That heavenly building stands.

1950   John Matlock   SM
For he looked for a city which hath foundations, whose builder and maker is God.
Hebrews 11:10

What is this world to me?
This world is not my home;
A scene of pain, of grief, and woe;
When will my Saviour come?

Come, O Thou Saviour dear,
And cheer my fainting soul!
Appear, O gracious Lord, appear,
And make the sinner whole.

Give me, O Lord, to prove
Thy pardoning love so sweet,
That I may ever lay my soul
At the dear Saviour's feet.

Give me Thy lowly mind,
Thy love to me impart,
And grant that I may ever find
The Saviour in my heart.

1951   William Gadsby   77 77
Esteeming the reproach of Christ greater riches than the treasures in Egypt.
Hebrews 11:26

Precious Jesus! must it be,
Is it Thy all-wise decree,
That afflictions must attend
Zion to her journey's end?

Yes, affliction is their lot;
Earth is a polluted spot,
Where a million evils dwell,
All in league with death and hell.

Pains and sorrows, sins and woes,
Will the Christian's way oppose;
Every day brings something new,
Zion's troubles to renew.

Yet, when faith is strong and true,
They with cheerfulness go through,
Scorning all created good,
When opposed to Christ, their God.

Living faith will still esteem
The reproaches of the Lamb,
Greater riches than this earth
Can afford the sons of mirth.

O for faith this choice to make,
And endure, for Jesus' sake,
The reproaches of His cross,
Counting all things else but dross!

1952   Isaac Watts   CM
**Let us run with patience the race that is set
before us.** *Hebrews 12:1*

Give me the wings of faith to rise
    Within the veil, and see
The saints above, how great their joys,
    How bright their glories be.

Once they were mourning, here below,
    And wet their couch with tears;
They wrestled hard, as we do now,
    With sins, and doubts, and fears.

I ask them whence their victory came,
    They with united breath,
Ascribe their conquest to the Lamb,
    Their triumph to His death.

They marked the footsteps that He trod,
    His zeal inspired their breast;
And following their incarnate God,
    Possess the promised rest.

Our glorious Leader claims our praise
    For His own pattern given;
While the long cloud of witnesses
    Shows the same path to heaven.

1953   John Stevens   CM
**Looking unto Jesus the author and finisher of
our faith.** *Hebrews 12:2*

Faith owes its birth to sovereign grace,
    And lives beneath the throne,
Where grace maintains her dwelling-place,
    And reigns supreme alone.

The precious cleansing blood of Christ
    Is a delightful theme;
When faith is lifted up the highest,
    She sings of none but Him.

Faith owns the sceptre through the cross,
    And yields obedience true;
Counts all things else but earth and dross,
    To keep the Lamb in view.

To live upon His precious death
    Is faith's divine repast;
The language of His dying breath,
    See how she holds it fast!

Faith views Him dead upon the tree;
    Then buried in the grave;
And waits around the tomb to see
    Him rise with power to save.

Then to the Mount of Olives go;
    There faith, with eager eye,
Beholds her Lord leave all below,
    To dwell and reign on high.

With tears of joy, faith now believes
    The day will surely come,
When He who Jesus' cross receives
    Shall see Him crowned at home.

1954   Ray Palmer   664 6664
**Looking unto Jesus the author and finisher of
our faith.** *Hebrews 12:2*

My faith looks up to Thee,
Thou Lamb of Calvary,
    Saviour divine:
Now hear me while I pray;
Take all my guilt away;
O let me from this day
    Be wholly Thine.

May Thy rich grace impart
Strength to my fainting heart,
    My zeal inspire;
As Thou hast died for me,
O may my love to Thee
Pure, warm, and changeless be,
    A living fire.

While life's dark maze I tread
And griefs around me spread,
    Be Thou my Guide;
Bid darkness turn to day,
Wipe sorrow's tears away,
Nor let me ever stray
    From Thee aside.

When ends life's transient dream,
When death's cold, sullen stream
    Shall o'er me roll,
Blest Saviour, then, in love,
Fear and distrust remove;
O bear me safe above,
    A ransomed soul.

1955   Samuel Medley   LM
Looking unto Jesus the author and finisher of our faith. *Hebrews 12:2*

For us, our gracious God, appear,
     And all our souls with comfort fill,
That we in grace may persevere,
     Looking by faith to Jesus still.

With patience, zeal, and holy love,
     May we the appointed race fulfil,
And all our hearts be fixed above,
     Looking by faith to Jesus still.

We'll welcome life, or welcome death,
     Just as it please Thy sovereign will;
With joy we'll live, or yield our breath,
     Looking by faith to Jesus still.

Ere long we hope His face to see,
     And sing on Zion's heavenly hill;
Where this our happiness will be,
     Looking with joy to Jesus still.

1956   James Montgomery   77 77 77
For consider Him that endured such contradiction of sinners against Himself, lest ye be wearied and faint in your minds.
Hebrews 12:3

Go to dark Gethsemane,
     Ye that feel the tempter's power;
Your Redeemer's conflict see,
     Watch with Him one bitter hour!
Turn not from His griefs away;
Learn of Jesus Christ to pray.

Follow to the judgment-hall:
     View the Lord of Life arraigned.
O the wormwood and the gall!
     O the pangs His soul sustained!
Shun not suffering, shame, or loss,
Learn of Him to bear the cross.

Calvary's mournful mountain climb;
     There, adoring at His feet,
Mark that miracle of time:
     God's own sacrifice complete.
'It is finished!' hear Him cry:
Learn of Jesus Christ to die.

Early hasten to the tomb,
     Where they laid His breathless clay;
All is solitude and gloom:
     Who hath taken Him away?
Christ is risen: He seeks the skies,
Saviour, teach us so to rise!

1957   Timothy Dudley-Smith   LM
For consider Him that endured such contradiction of sinners against Himself, lest ye be wearied and faint in your minds.
Hebrews 12:3

Consider Him, our Saviour Christ,
The Father's gift of love unpriced,
By whom the world is reconciled;
Consider Him, the holy Child.

Consider Him, to whom there came
The sick, the helpless and the lame,
The poor, the blind, the deaf and dumb:
Consider Him, who bids us come.

Consider Him when put to scorn
With purple robe and crown of thorn,
Who paths of pain and sorrow trod:
Consider Him, the Lamb of God.

Consider Him as, lifted high,
He hung upon that cross to die;
The sinners' Friend, for us He died:
Consider Him, the Crucified.

Consider Him who, strong to save,
Has vanquished sin and death and grave;
Who freed our fetters, burst our chains,
And in His glory lives and reigns!

Consider Him, as day by day
We strive to walk the narrow way;
And, lest our love of Christ grow dim,
Consider Him, consider Him.

'Consider him, our Saviour Christ' by Timothy Dudley-Smith (b.1926). © Timothy Dudley-Smith in Europe and Africa. © Hope Publishing Company in the United States of America and the rest of the world. Reproduced by permission of Oxford University Press . All rights reserved.

1958   Joseph Hart   CM
My son, despise not thou the chastening of the Lord. *Hebrews 12:5*

Happy the man that bears the stroke
     Of His chastising God;
Nor stubbornly rejects His yoke,
     Nor faints beneath His rod.

They who the Lord's correction share
     Have favour in His eyes;
As kindest fathers will not spare
     Their children to chastise.

Thy Lord for nothing would not chide;
　Thou highly shouldst esteem
The cross that's sent to purge thy pride,
　And make thee more like Him.

For this correction render praise;
　'Tis given thee for thy good.
The lash is steeped He on thee lays,
　And softened in His blood.

Then kiss the rod; thy sins confess;
　It shall a blessing prove;
And yield the fruits of righteousness:
　Humility and love.

1959　William Gadsby　77 77
For whom the Lord loveth He chasteneth.
Hebrews 12:6

Whom the Lord Jehovah loves,
He in various ways reproves;
'Tis His settled, wise decree,
That His sons chastised shall be.

Them to wean from self and sin,
Try the grace He works within;
Strip them of each idol god;
Make them prize the Saviour's blood;

Teach them what and where they are;
Draw forth patience, faith, and prayer;
Make them closer cling to Christ,
And in Him alone rejoice;

These are ends He has in view,
And He'll them accomplish too;
Nor shall our poor peevish heart
Make Him from His purpose start.

Father, make us clearly view
What Thy love designs to do;
And in every trying case,
Trust Thy faithfulness and grace.

1960　Philip Bliss　11 11 11 11
**Follow peace with all men, and holiness,
without which no man shall see the Lord.**
Hebrews 12:14

More holiness give me, more strivings within;
More patience in suffering, more sorrow for sin;
More faith in my Saviour, more sense of His care;
More joy in His service, more purpose in prayer.

More gratitude give me, more trust in the Lord;
More zeal for His glory, more hope in His word;
More tears for His sorrows, more pain at His grief;
More meekness in trial, more praise for relief.

More purity give me, more strength to o'ercome;
More freedom from earth-stains, more longings for
　home;
More fit for the kingdom, more used would I be;
More blessèd and holy, more, Saviour, like Thee.

1961　John Newton　77 77
**For ye are not come unto the mount that might
be touched, and that burned with fire, nor unto
blackness, and darkness, and tempest.**
Hebrews 12:18

Not to Sinai's dreadful blaze,
But to Zion's throne of grace,
By a way marked out with blood,
Sinners now approach to God.

Not to hear the fiery law,
But with humble joy to draw
Water, by that well supplied
Jesus opened when He died.

Lord, there are no streams but Thine
Can assuage a thirst like mine!
'Tis a thirst Thyself didst give;
Let me, therefore, drink and live!

1962　Isaac Watts　CM
But ye are come unto mount Zion.
Hebrews 12:22

Not to the terrors of the Lord,
　The tempest, fire, and smoke;
Not to the thunder of that word
　Which God on Sinai spoke:

But we are come to Zion's hill,
　The city of our God,
Where milder words declare His will,
　And spread His love abroad.

Behold th' innumerable host
　Of angels clothed in light!
Behold the spirits of the just
　Whose faith is turned to sight!

Behold the blessed assembly there,
　Whose names are writ in heaven;
And God, the Judge of all, declares
　Their vilest sins forgiven.

The saints on earth, and all the dead,
　But one communion make;
All join in Christ, their living Head,
　And of His grace partake.

In such society as this
My weary soul would rest:
The man that dwells where Jesus is,
Must be for ever blessed.

1963   William Gadsby   77 77
**And to Jesus the Mediator of the new
covenant, and to the blood of sprinkling, that
speaketh better things than that of Abel.**
Hebrews 12:24

Mercy speaks by Jesus' blood;
Hear and sing, ye sons of God;
Justice satisfied indeed;
Christ has full atonement made.

Jesus' blood speaks loud and sweet;
Here all Deity can meet,
And, without a jarring voice,
Welcome Zion to rejoice.

Should the law against her roar,
Jesus' blood still speaks with power,
'All her debts were cast on Me,
And she must and shall go free.'

Peace of conscience, peace with God,
We obtain through Jesus' blood;
Jesus' blood speaks solid rest;
We believe, and we are blest.

1964   John Berridge   LM
**And to Jesus the Mediator of the new
covenant, and to the blood of sprinkling, that
speaketh better things than that of Abel.**
Hebrews 12:24

Dear dying Friend, we look on Thee,
And own our foul offences here;
We built Thy cross on Calvary,
And nailed and pierced Thy body there.

Yet, let the blood our hands have spilt
Be sprinkled on each guilty heart,
To purge the conscience well from guilt,
And everlasting life impart.

So will we sing Thy lovely name,
For grace so rich and freely given;
And tell Thy love, and tell our shame,
That One we murdered gives us heaven.

1965   John Needham   CM
**Let us have grace, whereby we may serve God
acceptably with reverence and godly fear.**
Hebrews 12:28

Happy beyond description he
Who fears the Lord his God,
Who hears His threats with holy awe,
And trembles at His rod.

Fear is a grace which ever dwells
With its fair partner, love;
Blending their beauties, both proclaim
Their source is from above.

Let terrors fright th' unwilling slave
The child with joy appears;
Cheerful he does his Father's will,
And loves as much as fears.

Let fear and love, most holy God!
Possess this soul of mine;
Then shall I worship Thee aright,
And taste Thy joys divine.

1966   Charles Wesley   CM
**Let us have grace, whereby we may serve God
acceptably with reverence and godly fear.**
Hebrews 12:28

I want a principle within
Of jealous, godly fear;
A sensibility of sin,
A pain to feel it near.

I want the first approach to feel
Of pride, or fond desire;
To catch the wandering of my will,
And quench the kindling fire.

That I from Thee no more may part,
No more Thy goodness grieve,
The filial awe, the fleshy heart,
The tender conscience, give.

Quick as the apple of an eye,
O God, my conscience make!
Awake my soul, when sin is nigh,
And keep it still awake.

If to the right or left I stray,
That moment, Lord, reprove;
And let me weep my life away,
For having grieved Thy love.

O may the least omission pain
My well-instructed soul;
And drive me to the blood again,
Which makes the wounded whole!

JOHN BERRIDGE 1716-93

1967   John Berridge   CM
Marriage is honourable in all.
Hebrews 13:4

Our Jesus freely did appear
   To grace a marriage feast;
And, Lord, we ask Thy presence here
   To make a wedding-guest.

Upon the bridal pair look down;
   Who now have plighted hands;
Their union with Thy favour crown,
   And bless the nuptial bands.

In purest love their souls unite,
   And linked in kindly care,
To render family burdens light,
   By taking mutual share.

With gifts of grace their hearts endow;
   Of all rich dowries best!
Their substance bless, and peace bestow,
   To sweeten all the rest.

1968   John Moore   Irregular
**He hath said, I will never leave thee, nor
forsake thee.** *Hebrews 13:5*

Days are filled with sorrow and care,
   Hearts are lonely and drear;
Burdens are lifted at Calvary,
   Jesus is very near.

   *Burdens are lifted at Calvary,
   Calvary, Calvary;
   Burdens are lifted at Calvary,
   Jesus is very near.*

Cast your care on Jesus today,
   Leave your worry and care;
Burdens are lifted at Calvary
   Jesus is very near.

Troubled soul, the Saviour can see,
   Every heartache and tear;
Burdens are lifted at Calvary,
   Jesus is very near.

1969   John Newton   77 77
**He hath said, I will never leave thee, nor
forsake thee.** *Hebrews 13:5*

As the sun's enlivening eye
   Shines on every place the same;
So the Lord is always nigh
   To the souls that love His name.

When they move at duty's call,
   He is with them by the way:
He is ever with them all,
   Those who go, and those who stay.

From His holy mercy-seat
   Nothing can their souls confine,
Still in spirit they may meet,
   Still in sweet communion join.

For a season called to part,
   Let us then ourselves commend
To the gracious eye and heart
   Of our ever-present Friend.

Jesus, hear our humble prayer!
   Tender Shepherd of Thy sheep!
Let Thy mercy and Thy care
   All our souls in safety keep.

In Thy strength may we be strong!
   Sweeten every cross and pain:
Give us, if we live, ere long
   Here to meet in peace again.

1970   Vernon Higham   98 98 (anapaestic)
He hath said, I will never leave thee, nor forsake thee. *Hebrews 13:5*

I saw a new vision of Jesus,
   A view I'd not seen here before,
Beholding in glory so wondrous
   With beauty I had to adore.
I stood on the shores of my weakness,
   And gazed at the brink of such fear;
'Twas then that I saw Him in newness,
   Regarding Him fair and so dear.

My Saviour will never forsake me,
   Unveiling His merciful face,
His presence and promise almighty,
   Redeeming His loved ones by grace.
In shades of the valley's dark terror,
   Where hell and its horror hold sway,
My Jesus will reach out in power,
   And save me by His only way.

For yonder a light shines eternal,
   Which spreads through the valley of gloom;
Lord Jesus, resplendent and regal,
   Drives fear far away from the tomb.
Our God is the end of the journey,
   His pleasant and glorious domain;
For there are the children of mercy,
   Who praise Him for Calvary's pain.

© Author

1971   William Gadsby   CM
The Lord is my helper. *Hebrews 13:6*

The Lord's my Helper and Support,
   My Saviour and my Friend;
He bears my sinking spirits up,
   And will my soul defend.

Though earth, and hell, and sin agree,
   My comfort to destroy,
The Lord of glory fights for me,
   Nor will He let me die.

1972   Thomas Kelly   66 86 47
For here have we no continuing city, but we seek one to come. *Hebrews 13:14*

   From Egypt lately come,
     Where death and darkness reign,
We seek our new, our better home,
     Where we our rest shall gain.

     Hallelujah!
     We are on our way to God.

To Canaan's sacred bound,
   We haste with songs of joy;
Where peace and liberty are found,
   And sweets that never cloy.

Our toils and conflicts cease
   On Canaan's happy shore:
We there shall dwell in endless peace,
   And never hunger more.

But hark! those distant sounds
   That strike our listening ears;
They come from Canaan's happy bounds
   Where God our King appears.

There, in celestial strains,
   Enraptured myriads sing:
There love in every bosom reigns,
   For God Himself is King.

We soon shall join the throng,
   Their pleasures we shall share;
And sing the everlasting song,
   With all the ransomed there.

How sweet the prospect is!
   It cheers the pilgrim's breast;
We're journeying through the wilderness,
   But soon shall gain our rest.

1973   Thomas Kelly   LM
For here have we no continuing city, but we seek one to come. *Hebrews 13:14*

'We've no abiding city here;'
   This may distress the worldling's mind;
But should not cost the saint a tear,
   Who hopes a better rest to find.

2 'We've no abiding city here;'
   Sad truth, were this to be our home;
But let the thought our spirits cheer,
   'We seek a city yet to come.'

'We've no abiding city here;'
   Then let us live as pilgrims do;
Let not the world our rest appear,
   But let us haste from all below.

'We've no abiding city here,'
   We seek a city out of sight,
Zion its name—the Lord is there;
   It shines with everlasting light.

O sweet abode of peace and love,
   Where pilgrims freed from toil are blest;
Had I the pinions of the dove,
   I'd fly to Thee, and be at rest.

1974 Philip Doddridge CM
Obey them that have the rule over you, and submit yourselves: for they watch for your souls. *Hebrews 13:17*

Let Zion's watchmen all awake,
    And take th' alarm they give;
Now let them from the mouth of God
    Their solemn charge receive.

'Tis not a cause of small import
    The pastor's care demands;
But what might fill an angel's heart,
    And filled a Saviour's hands.

They watch for souls, for which the Lord
    Did heavenly bliss forego;
For souls which must for ever live
    In raptures or in woe.

May they that Jesus whom they preach,
    Their own Redeemer see;
And watch Thou daily o'er their souls,
    That they may watch for Thee.

1975 John Newton 77 77
Now the God of peace, that brought again from the dead our Lord Jesus, that great Shepherd of the sheep, through the blood of the everlasting covenant.
Hebrews 13:20

Now may He who from the dead
    Brought the Shepherd of the sheep,
Jesus Christ, our King and Head,
    All our souls in safety keep.

May He teach us to fulfil
    What is pleasing in His sight;
Perfect us in all His will,
    And preserve us day and night.

To that dear Redeemer's praise,
    Who the covenant sealed with blood,
Let our hearts and voices raise
    Loud thanksgivings to our God.

1976 Horatio Palmer
11 11 11 12 + refrain
Blessed is the man that endureth temptation.
James 1:12

Yield not to temptation, for yielding is sin;
Each victory will help you some other to win;
Fight manfully onward; dark passions subdue;
Look ever to Jesus, He will carry you through.

Ask the Saviour to help you,
Comfort, strengthen, and keep you;
He is willing to aid you,
He will carry you through.

Shun evil companions; bad language disdain;
God's name hold in reverence, nor take it in vain;
Be thoughtful and earnest, kind-hearted and true;
Look ever to Jesus, He will carry you through.

To him that o'ercometh God giveth a crown;
Through faith we shall conquer, though often cast
    down;
He who is our Saviour our strength will renew;
Look ever to Jesus, He will carry you through.

1977 Folliott Pierpoint 77 77 77
Every good gift and every perfect gift is from above. *James 1:17*

For the beauty of the earth,
    For the beauty of the skies,
For the love which from our birth
    Over and around us lies;
Father, unto Thee we raise
This, our sacrifice of praise.

For the beauty of each hour
    Of the day and of the night,
Hill and vale, and tree and flower,
    Sun and moon, and stars of light;
Father, unto Thee we raise
This, our sacrifice of praise.

For the joy of human love,
    Brother, sister, parent, child,
Friends on earth, and friends above,
    For all gentle thoughts and mild;
Father, unto Thee we raise
This, our sacrifice of praise.

For Thy church that evermore
    Lifteth holy hands above,
Offering up on every shore
    Its pure sacrifice of love;
Father, unto Thee we raise
This, our sacrifice of praise.

1978 Jane Taylor CM
Every good gift and every perfect gift is from above. *James 1:17*

Lord, I would own Thy tender care,
    And all Thy love to me;
The food I eat, the clothes I wear,
    Are all bestowed by Thee.

'Tis Thou preservest me from death
    And dangers every hour;
I cannot draw another breath
    Unless Thou give me power.

My health and friends and parents dear
    To me by God are given;
I have not any blessing here
    But what is sent from heaven.

Kind angels guard me every night,
    As round my bed they stay;
Nor am I absent from Thy sight
    In darkness or by day.

Such goodness, Lord, and constant care,
    I never can repay;
But may it be my daily prayer,
    To love Thee and obey.

1979 William Gadsby 88 88 D
The perfect law of liberty. *James 1:25*

The gospel's the law of the Lamb;
    My soul of its glories shall sing;
With pleasure my tongue shall proclaim
    The law of my Saviour and King;
A sweet law of liberty this;
    A yoke that is easy and mild;
Of love it the precious law is,
    Unknown unto all but a child.

The law of the Spirit of life,
    That takes the old yoke from our neck,
Proves Zion to be the Lamb's wife,
    And Zion with beauty does deck;
Provides her a clothing divine,
    And makes her all-glorious within;
Nor angels are clothèd more fine,
    Nor can it be sullied with sin.

Its beauties all centre in Christ,
    For Christ is the substance of it;
It makes broken hearts to rejoice,
    And insolvent debtors will fit.
'Tis wisdom, 'tis strength, and 'tis love,
    'Tis all that a sinner can need;
And all that are born from above,
    By Jesus from Moses are freed.

This law is the poor pilgrim's rule;
    With boldness this truth I'll maintain;
Thrice happy's the man, though a fool,
    That in it can look and remain;
This man shall be blest in his deed,
    For Jesus and he are but one;
He'll therefore supply all his need,
    For ever and ever. Amen.

1980 Katherine Hankey 76 76 D + refrain
He being not a forgetful hearer.
James 1:25

Tell me the old, old story
    Of unseen things above,
Of Jesus and His glory,
    Of Jesus and His love:
Tell me the story simply,
    As to a little child,
For I am weak and weary,
    And helpless and defiled.

Tell me the old, old story,
Tell me the old, old story,
Tell me the old, old story
Of Jesus and His love.

Tell me the story slowly,
    That I may take it in,
That wonderful redemption,
    God's remedy for sin.
Tell me the story often,
    For I forget so soon;
The early dew of morning
    Has passed away at noon.

Tell me the story softly,
    With earnest tones and grave:
Remember, I'm the sinner
    Whom Jesus came to save.
Tell me that story always,
    If you would really be
In any time of trouble
    A comforter to me.

Tell me the same old story
    When you have cause to fear
That this world's empty glory
    Is costing me too dear.
Yes, and when that world's glory
    Is dawning on my soul,
Tell me the old, old story:
    'Christ Jesus makes thee whole.'

1981   Annie J Flint   12 11 12 11 + refrain
He giveth more grace. *James 4:6*

He giveth more grace when the burdens grow
   greater,
  He sendeth more strength when the labours
   increase;
To added affliction He addeth His mercy,
  To multiplied trials, His multiplied peace.

His love has no limit, His grace has no measure,
  His power has no boundary known unto men;
For out of His infinite riches in Jesus
  He giveth, and giveth, and giveth again!

When we have exhausted our store of endurance,
  When our strength has failed ere the day is half
   done,
When we reach the end of our hoarded resources,
  Our Father's full giving is only begun.

1982   Fanny Crosby   64 64 66 64
**Draw nigh to God, and He will draw nigh to
you.** *James 4:8*

Here from the world we turn,
  Jesus to seek;
Here may His loving voice
  Tenderly speak.
Jesus, our dearest Friend,
While at Thy feet we bend,
O, let Thy smile descend!
  'Tis Thee we seek.

Come, Holy Comforter,
  Presence Divine,
Now in our longing hearts
  Graciously shine;
O, for Thy mighty power!
O, for a blessèd shower,
Filling this hallowed hour
  With joy divine!

Saviour, Thy work revive,
  Here may we see
Those who are dead in sin
  Quickened by Thee;
Come to our hearts' delight,
Make every burden light,
Cheer Thou our waiting sight;
  We long for Thee.

1983   Benjamin Beddome   CM
**Draw nigh to God, and He will draw nigh to
you.** *James 4:8*

When God inclines the heart to pray,
  He hath an ear to hear;
To Him there's music in a groan,
  And beauty in a tear.

The humble suppliant cannot fail
  To have his wants supplied.
Since He for sinners intercedes,
  Who once for sinners died.

1984   Thomas Kelly   87 87 D
**For what is your life? It is even a vapour, that
appeareth for a little time, and then vanisheth
away.** *James 4:14*

What is life? 'Tis but a vapour,
  Soon it vanishes away;
Life is like a dying taper;
  O my soul, why wish to stay?
Why not spread thy wings and fly
Straight to yonder world of joy?

See that glory, how resplendent,
  Brighter far than fancy paints!
There in majesty transcendent,
  Jesus reigns, the King of saints:
Spread thy wings, my soul, and fly
Straight to yonder world of joy.

Joyful crowds His throne surrounding,
  Sing with rapture of His love;
Through the heavens His praise resounding,
  Fills the blissful courts above;
Spread thy wings, my soul, and fly
Straight to yonder world of joy.

Go and share His people's glory,
  Midst the ransomed crowd appear;
Thine a joyful, wondrous story,
  One that angels love to hear;
Spread thy wings, my soul, and fly
Straight to yonder world of joy.

1985   Andrew Reed   CM
**For what is your life? It is even a vapour, that
appeareth for a little time, and then vanisheth
away.** *James 4:14*

There is an hour when I must part
    With all I hold most dear;
And life with its best hopes will then
    As nothingness appear.

There is an hour when I must sink
    Beneath the stroke of death,
And yield to Him, who gave it first,
    My struggling vital breath.

There is an hour when I must stand
    Before the judgement-seat,
And all my sins, and all my foes,
    In awful vision meet.

There is an hour when I must look
    On one eternity;
And nameless woe, or blissful life,
    My endless portion be.

O Saviour, then, in all my need,
    Be near, be near to me;
And let my soul by stedfast faith
    Find life and heaven in Thee.

1986   William Cowper   LM
**Is any among you afflicted? let him pray. Is
any merry? let him sing psalms.**
James 5:13

God of my life, to Thee I call;
Afflicted at Thy feet I fall;
When the great water-floods prevail,
Leave not my trembling heart to fail.

Friend of the friendless and the faint,
Where should I lodge my deep complaint?
Where but with Thee, whose open door
Invites the helpless and the poor?

Did ever mourner plead with Thee,
And Thou refuse that mourner's plea?
Does not the word still fixed remain,
That none shall seek Thy face in vain?

That were a grief I could not bear,
Didst Thou not hear and answer prayer;
But a prayer-hearing, answering God
Supports me under every load.

Poor though I am, despised, forgot,
Yet God, my God, forgets me not;
And He is safe, and must succeed,
For whom the Lord vouchsafes to plead.

AMY CARMICHAEL 1867-1951

1987   Amy Carmichael   64 64
Let them pray over him. *James 5:14*

Dear Lord, for all in pain
    We pray to Thee;
O come and smite again
    Thine enemy.

Give to Thy servants skill
    To soothe and bless,
And to the tired and ill
    Give quietness.

And, Lord, to those who know
    Pain may not cease,
Come near, that even so
    They may have peace.

1988   Augustus Toplady   87 87 87 87
**Elect according to the foreknowledge of God
the Father.** *1 Peter 1:2*

For Thy free electing favour,
    Thee, O Father, we adore!
Jesus, our atoning Saviour,
    Thee we worship evermore!
Holy Ghost from both proceeding,
    Let Thy praise our breath employ;
Earnest of our future heaven,
    Source of holiness and joy!

1989 Isaac Watts CM
Blessed be the God and Father of our Lord Jesus Christ, which according to His abundant mercy hath begotten us again unto a lively hope by the resurrection of Jesus Christ from the dead. *1 Peter 1:3*

Bless'd be the everlasting God,
  The Father of our Lord;
Be His abounding mercy praised,
  His majesty adored.

When from the dead He raised His Son,
  And called Him to the sky,
He gave our souls a lively hope
  That they should never die.

What though our inbred sins require
  Our flesh to see the dust;
Yet as the Lord our Saviour rose,
  So all His followers must.

There's an inheritance divine
  Reserved against that day;
'Tis uncorrupted, undefiled,
  And cannot fade away.

Saints by the power of God are kept
  Till the salvation come;
We walk by faith, as strangers here,
  Till Christ shall call us home.

1990 John Newton CM
A lively hope by the resurrection of Jesus Christ from the dead. *1 Peter 1:3*

My soul, this curious house of clay,
  Thy present frail abode,
Must quickly fall to worms a prey,
  And Thou return to God.

Canst thou, by faith, survey with joy,
  The change before it come,
And say, 'Let death this house destroy,
  I have a heavenly home?'

The Saviour, whom I then shall see,
  With new admiring eyes,
Already has prepared for me
  A mansion in the skies.

I feel this mud-walled cottage shake,
  And long to see it fall;
That I my willing flight may take
  To Him who is my All.

Burdened and groaning then no more,
  My rescued soul shall sing,
As up the shining path I soar,
  'Death, thou hast lost thy sting.'

Dear Saviour, help us now to seek,
  And grant Thy Spirit's power;
That we may all this language speak,
  Before the dying hour.

1991 Isaac Watts SM
Whom having not seen, ye love; in whom, though now ye see Him not, yet believing, ye rejoice with joy unspeakable and full of glory. *1 Peter 1:8*

Not with our mortal eyes
  Have we beheld the Lord;
Yet we rejoice to hear His name,
  And love Him in His word.

On earth we want the sight
  Of our Redeemer's face;
Yet, Lord, our inmost thoughts delight
  To dwell upon Thy grace.

And when we taste Thy love,
  Our joys divinely grow
Unspeakable, like those above
  And heaven begins below.

1992 Ray Palmer CM
Whom having not seen, ye love; in whom, though now ye see Him not, yet believing, ye rejoice with joy unspeakable and full of glory. *1 Peter 1:8*

Jesus, these eyes have never seen
  That radiant form of Thine;
The veil of sense hangs dark between
  Thy blessèd face and mine.

I see Thee not, I hear Thee not,
  Yet art Thou oft with me;
And earth hath ne'er so dear a spot
  As where I meet with Thee.

Yet, though I have not seen and still
  Must rest in faith alone,
I love Thee, dearest Lord, and will,
  Unseen, but not unknown.

When death these mortal eyes shall seal
  And still this throbbing heart,
The rending veil shall Thee reveal,
  All glorious as Thou art.

1993 Vernon Higham 77 77 D

Whom having not seen, ye love; in whom, though now ye see Him not, yet believing, ye rejoice with joy unspeakable and full of glory.
1 Peter 1:8

Let my soul for ever praise
  What Thou art, O God above,
Worship Thee with joy and raise
  Glorious anthems of Thy love.
Listen to my soul acclaim
  Wondrous stories of Thy care,
Thanking Thee for Him who came
  Ever more this joy to share.

Joy unspeakable is mine,
  Full of glory, full of grace,
Gift of mercy, love divine,
  Radiance of my Saviour's face!
Let this joy for ever flow,
  Till my being glows with Thee;
Let this radiance in me show
  Glimpses of eternity.

Who are these arrayed around,
  Breathing vengeance on my soul—
Fiery trials that surround,
  Testing hard if I am whole?
Yet my joy in Thee will stay;
  Knowing of Thy tenderness,
Nothing shall my heart dismay,
  Or remove Thy faithfulness.

Glorious joy, a gift from Thee
  Born in heaven, a child of grace,
Shows a gentleness to me
  With a smile from Thy dear face.
When I tremble in distress,
  And my heart cries out in pain,
Thou, my God, wilt ever bless,
  And this joy shall firm remain.

Then Thy ransomed shall be brought
  Unto Thine eternal fold,
Every soul that Thou hast bought,
  Fashioned, burnished in Thy mold.
Hear my heart rejoice in Thee;
  Overflowing grace abound;
Now and then my glory be,
  For in Christ my soul is found.

© Author

1994 William Williams, tr. Vernon Higham
  87 87 D

Whom having not seen, ye love; in whom, though now ye see Him not, yet believing, ye rejoice with joy unspeakable and full of glory.
1 Peter 1:8

Lord of grace and power, I love Thee,
  Yet unseen to human sight:
Thou didst draw my soul with mercy
  From its dearest false delight.
In a moment Thou didst conquer
  What the world could not achieve;
Now enthroned in silent splendour
  In my heart as I believe.

Heart and mind and sight and hearing,
  Never thought or ever knew
Of the wonder of Thy Being,
  Absolute, profound and true.
Yet I find my heart doth love Thee,
  More than all in nature's world;
Greater news and sweeter mercy,
  Is Thy Person to behold.

Highest heaven is Thy abiding,
  Far above the span of mind.
Sinful depths of sorrow hiding
  In the home of man I find.
Yet I know my soul is nearer
  To my Lord, and stranger still
Is Thy promise, and far dearer
  Than the world with all its skill.

© Translator

1995 Vernon Higham 66 66 88

Receiving the end of your faith, even the salvation of your souls. *1 Peter 1:9*

Enable me to see
  By faith my heavenly home,
A land of love to me,
  Secured by grace alone:
For God Himself will wipe away
All tears of pain and death's decay.

Enable me to know
  The depths of Thine embrace;
The hope of heaven below,
  Inheritance of grace:
For God is good in all His ways
And every promise love displays.

Enable me to live
  Believing in Thy word,
Whate'er my lot will give
  My heart Thy truth has heard.
Forever has Thy truth maintained
A myriad souls in His domain.

Enable me to feel
That Thou art ever near.
I at Thy throne appeal
And ever will appear;
For there Thy mercy I obtain,
Until my soul shall heaven attain.

Enable me to love,
O God of love, Thy Son;
Graced by Thy holy Dove,
The love that makes us one:
That I may know and love for Thee,
Beneath the cross of Calvary.

© Author

1996   Isaac Watts   LM
**The sufferings of Christ, and the glory that
should follow.** *1 Peter 1:11*

Deep in our hearts let us record
The deeper sorrows of our Lord,
Behold the rising billows roll,
To overwhelm His holy soul.

In loud complaints He spends His breath,
While hosts of hell and powers of death,
And all the sons of malice join
To execute their cursed design.

Yet, gracious God! Thy power and love
Have made the curse a blessing prove;
Those dreadful sufferings of Thy Son
Atoned for sins which we had done.

The pangs of our expiring Lord,
The honours of Thy law restored;
His sorrows made Thy justice known,
And paid for follies not His own.

O for His sake our guilt forgive,
And let the mourning sinner live.
The Lord will hear us in His name,
Nor shall our hope be turned to shame.

1997   Philip Doddridge   CM
**The sufferings of Christ, and the glory that
should follow.** *1 Peter 1:11*

Awake my soul, stretch every nerve,
And press with vigour on;
A heavenly race demands Thy zeal,
And an immortal crown.

A cloud of witnesses around
Hold Thee in full survey:
Forget the steps already trod,
And onward urge Thy way.

'Tis God's all-animating voice
That calls Thee from on high;
'Tis His own hand presents the prize
To Thine aspiring eye.

Blest Saviour, introduced by Thee,
Have I my race begun;
And, crowned with victory, at Thy feet
I'll lay my honours down.

JOSEPH IRONS 1785-1852

1998   Joseph Irons   CM
**Ye were not redeemed with corruptible things,
as silver and gold, from your vain
conversation received by tradition from your
fathers, but with the precious blood of Christ.**
1 Peter 1:18,19

What sacred fountain yonder springs
Up from the throne of God,
And all new covenant blessing brings?
'Tis Jesus' precious blood.

What mighty sum paid all my debt
When I a bondman stood,
And has my soul at freedom set?
'Tis Jesus' precious blood.

What stream is that which sweeps away
My sins just like a flood,
Nor lets one guilty blemish stay?
'Tis Jesus' precious blood.

What voice is that which speaks for me
In heaven's high court for good,
And from the curse has made me free?
'Tis Jesus' precious blood.

What theme, my soul, shall best employ
Thy song before thy God,
And make all heaven to ring with joy?
'Tis Jesus' precious blood.

1999   Spencer Walton   Irregular
But with the precious blood of Christ.
1 Peter 1:19

In tenderness He sought me,
   Weary and sick with sin
And on His shoulders brought me
   Back to His fold again;
While angels in His presence sang
Until the courts of heaven rang.

   O the love that sought me!
   O the blood that bought me!
O the grace that brought me to the fold!
Wondrous grace that brought me to the fold!

He found me bruised and dying
   And poured in oil and wine;
He whispered to assure me,
   'I've found thee; thou art Mine!'
I never heard a sweeter voice,
It made my aching heart rejoice.

He pointed to the nail-prints;
   For me His blood was shed;
A mocking crown so thorny
   Was placed upon His head:
I wondered what He saw in me
To suffer such deep agony.

I'm sitting in His presence,
   The sunshine of His face;
While with adoring wonder
   His blessings I retrace.
It seems as if eternal days
Are far too short to sound His praise.

So while the hours are passing,
   He gives me perfect rest;
I'm waiting for the morning,
   The brightest and the best,
When He will call us to His side,
To be with Him, His spotless bride.

2000   Henry Baker   66 66 *trochaic*
The word of God, which liveth and abideth for ever. *1 Peter 1:23*

Lord, Thy word abideth,
And our footsteps guideth;
Who its truth believeth
Light and joy receiveth

When our foes are near us,
Then Thy word doth cheer us,
Word of consolation,
Message of salvation.

When the storms are o'er us,
And dark clouds before us,
Then its light directeth,
And our way protecteth.

Who can tell the pleasure,
Who recount the treasure,
By Thy word imparted
To the simple-hearted?

Word of mercy, giving
Succour to the living;
Word of life, supplying
Comfort to the dying.

O, that we discerning
Its most holy learning,
Lord, may love and fear Thee,
Evermore be near Thee!

2001   Frederick Jackson   86 86 88 86
**But the word of the Lord endureth for ever.
And this is the word which by the gospel is
preached unto you.** *1 Peter 1:25*

There is a book that comes to me,
   From One who spake of old,
Who calls with shepherd-voice the flock
   That wanders from the fold.

   'Tis old, 'tis old, yet ever new,
   'Tis old, 'tis old, yet ever true,
   'Tis fresh, 'tis fresh as morning dew,
     The story old but new.

There is a book whose pages white
   A wondrous love reveal:
A love once wounded unto death,
   The wounds of sin to heal.

There is a book whose promises
   I all my life may plead;
They shine like stars above the night
   Of my exceeding need.

There is a book whose pilgrim songs
   Are sweet as songs of spring:
I hope to sing them till the day
   When I shall see the King.

2002   Esther Grünbeck, tr. C Kinchin   CM
**If so be ye have tasted that the Lord is
gracious.** *1 Peter 2:3*

Grace, how exceeding sweet to those
   Who feel they sinners are!
Sunk and distressed, they taste and know
   Their heaven is only there.

Thus grace, free grace most sweetly calls
   Directly come who will;
Just as you are, for Christ receives
   Poor helpless sinners still.

We thirst, O Lord, give us each day
  To taste more of this grace!
More of that stream which from the rock
  Flowed through the wilderness.

Where'er eternal life is given,
  This thirst the same will be;
The heart will after Jesus pant,
  To all eternity.

'Tis grace alone that feeds our souls,
  Grace keeps us inly poor;
And oh, that nothing else but grace
  May rule for evermore!

2003   Samuel Medley   LM
**To whom coming, as unto a living stone,
disallowed indeed of men, but chosen of God,
and precious.** *1 Peter 2:4*

Come, happy souls, who know the Lord,
Who love and trust His sacred word;
With songs of praise address His throne,
And Jesus sing, the living Stone.

Chosen of God, and precious too
He is, in each believer's view:
Built upon Him, and 'stablished here,
They all as living stones appear.

No other trust shall intervene,
To Him I'll look, on Him I'll lean;
And all foundations I'll disown,
But Him who is the living Stone.

Though sins and sorrows o'er me roll,
He quickens and restores my soul:
My life and comforts, all I own,
Flow only from this living Stone.

Here my salvation stands secure,
This Rock of Ages must endure;
Nor shall my hope be overthrown,
Built upon Christ, the living Stone.

2004   7th Cent., tr. J Neale (alt)   87 87 87
**Behold, I lay in Zion a chief corner stone,
elect, precious.** *1 Peter 2:6*

Christ is made the sure Foundation,
  Christ the Head and Corner-stone,
Chosen of the Lord, and precious,
  Binding all the church in one,
Holy Zion's help for ever
  And her confidence alone

All that dedicated city
  Dearly loved of God on high,
In exultant jubilation
  Pours perpetual melody,
God the One in Three adoring
  In glad hymns eternally.

To this temple, where we call Thee,
  Come, O Lord of hosts, today;
With Thy wonted loving-kindness
  Hear Thy servants as they pray;
And Thy fullest benediction
  Shed within its walls alway.

Here vouchsafe to all Thy servants
  What they ask of Thee to gain,
What they gain from Thee for ever
  With the blessèd to retain,
And hereafter in Thy glory
  Evermore with Thee to reign.

Praise and honour to the Father,
  Praise and honour to the Son,
Praise and honour to the Spirit,
  Ever Three and ever One;
One in might, and One in glory,
  While unending ages run.

2005   Philip Doddridge   CM
**Unto you therefore which believe He is
precious.** *1 Peter 2:7*

Jesus I love Thy charming name;
  'Tis music in my ear;
Fain would I sound it out so loud,
  That earth and heaven might hear.

Yes, Thou art precious to my soul,
  My transport and my trust;
Jewels to Thee are gaudy toys,
  And gold is sordid dust.

O may Thy name upon my heart
  Shed a rich fragrance there;
The noblest balm of all my wounds,
  The cordial of my care.

I'll speak the honours of Thy name
  With my last labouring breath;
And, dying, clasp Thee in my arms,
  The Antidote of death!

2006   Bernard of Clairvaux, tr. E Caswall CM
**Unto you therefore which believe He is
precious.** *1 Peter 2:7*

Jesus, the very thought of Thee
  With sweetness fills my breast;
But sweeter far Thy face to see,
  And in Thy presence rest.

Nor voice can sing, nor heart can frame,
  Nor can the memory find
A sweeter sound than Thy blest name,
  O Saviour of mankind!

O hope of every contrite heart,
  O joy of all the meek;
To those who fall, how kind Thou art!
  How good to those who seek!

But what to those who find? Ah! this
  Nor tongue nor pen can show;
The love of Jesus, what it is
  None but His loved ones know.

Jesus, our only joy be Thou,
  As Thou our prize wilt be;
Jesus, be Thou our glory now,
  And through eternity.

2007   Vernon Higham   87 87 D (iambic)
**Unto you therefore which believe He is
precious.** *1 Peter 2:7*

I have not seen Thy face, O Lord,
  Yet with my heart I love Thee;
For Thou hast plucked each tender cord
  With pleasing touch of mercy.
O Saviour, Lord, my King and Friend,
  I worship Thee with gladness;
And by Thy grace I will defend
  Thy name that brought me kindness.

I have not known Thee here on earth,
  Yet with my soul I trust Thee;
For Thou hast stirred my thought to birth
  Of God and heaven and glory.
O precious Saviour, hear my praise
  With songs of joy and wonder;
For Thou hast taught my lips to raise
  A theme of words so tender.

Now I have seen Thy glorious face,
  With eyes of faith unveiling
The splendour of the theme of grace,
  All to my mind revealing.
Such bliss and happiness is mine
  To know the God of glory;
For who could call the Lord divine
  But for Thy grace and mercy?

© *Author*

2008   Charles Wesley   88 88 88
**For so is the will of God, that with well doing
ye may put to silence the ignorance of foolish
men.** *1 Peter 2:15*

Watched by the world with jealous eye,
  That fain would see our sin and shame,
As servants of the Lord most high,
  As zealous for His glorious name,
May we in all His footsteps move
With holy fear and humble love.

That wisdom, Lord, on us bestow,
  From every evil to depart;
To stop the mouth of every foe
  By upright walk, and lowly heart;
The proofs of godly fear to give;
And show the world how Christians live.

2009   William Enfield   CM
**Christ also suffered for us, leaving us an
example, that ye should follow His steps.**
1 Peter 2:21

Behold, where, in the Friend of man
  Appears each grace divine;
The virtues all in Jesus meet,
  With mildest radiance shine.

To spread the rays of heavenly light,
  To give the mourner joy,
To preach glad tidings to the poor,
  Was His divine employ.

Lowly in heart to all His friends,
  A Friend and Servant found;
He washed their feet, He wiped their tears,
  And healed each bleeding wound.

Midst keen reproach and cruel scorn,
  Patient and meek He stood;
His foes, ungrateful, sought His life—
  He laboured for their good.

In the last hour of deep distress,
  Before His Father's throne,
With soul resigned, He bowed, and said,
  'Thy will, not Mine, be done.'

Be Christ our pattern and our guide;
  His image may we bear!
O may we tread His sacred steps,
  And His bright glories share.

2010   Samuel Preiswerk, tr. F Houghton
86 86 88 886
Christ also suffered for us, leaving us an example, that ye should follow His steps.
1 Peter 2:21

Lord Jesus Christ, the work is Thine;
  Not ours, but Thine alone;
And prospered by Thy power divine
  Can ne'er be overthrown.
Before it pushes to the light
The corn of wheat is hid from sight.
    Deep in the silent earth it lies,
    Its very self decays and dies,
    Losing itself it dies.

To glory Thou didst rise through pain,
  Jesus, our risen Head,
And all who follow in Thy train
  The selfsame path must tread.
So in Thy fellowship we go,
Refusing not to share Thy woe,
    If only Thou dost lead us through
    The gates of death to life anew,
    Through death to life anew.

Thou as a corn of wheat didst die
  And sink into the grave.
'Now quicken, Fount of life', we cry,
  'The dead Thou cam'st to save!
O send Thy heralds everywhere
The tidings of Thy name to bear:
    And till its fame is fully shown,
    We pledge ourselves to make it known,
    We live to make it known!'

© Overseas Missionary Fellowship

2011   Augustus Toplady   77 77 77
Who His own self bare our sins in His own body on the tree. *1 Peter 2:24*

Surely Christ thy griefs hath borne,
Weeping soul, no longer mourn;
  View Him bleeding on the tree,
  Pouring out His life for thee:
There thy every sin He bore;
Weeping soul, lament no more.

Cast thy guilty soul on Him,
Find Him mighty to redeem;
  At His feet thy burden lay;
  Look thy doubts and cares away;
Now by faith the Son embrace;
Plead His promise, trust His grace.

Lord, Thy arm must be revealed,
Ere I can by faith be healed;
  Since I scarce can look to Thee,
  Cast a gracious eye on me!
At Thy feet myself I lay;
Shine, O shine my fears away!

RICHARD BURNHAM 1749-1810

2012   Richard Burnham   CM
Heirs together of the grace of life.
1 Peter 3:7

Great God of order, truth, and grace,
  Fountain of social joys,
Shine with Thy sweet approving smile,
  And crown the nuptial ties.

Look on the now united pair,
  And O the union bless;
Here may true friendship ever reign
  In firmest bonds of peace.

May each the other kindly help
  To run the shining road;
Join with delight in prayer and praise,
  And ever cleave to God.

May both be fired with one concern
  For one eternal prize;
And warmest zeal their souls inflame
  For joys beyond the skies.

One be their views, their aim, their end,
  Pure heavenly bliss to prove,
Meeting at last around the throne,
  To reign in realms of love.

There may we all with them unite
  In one harmonious song;
And one pure anthem swell the joys
  Of one celestial throng.

2013   Anon   87 87 (trochaic)
Heirs together of the grace of life.
1 Peter 3:7

Gracious Father, we entreat Thee
  For a blessing rich and free;
On Thy children now united;
  May they serve and follow Thee.

Grant them, Lord, Thy richest blessings;
  May they each Thy presence know,
Shedding life and light and sunshine
  On their pathway here below.

Grant them joy and peace and gladness;
  Give them grace and power divine;
Guard their hearts from care and sadness;
  Make them truly, wholly Thine.

Heirs through grace of life eternal,
  While as strangers wandering here,
May their prayers ascend unhindered
  To a gracious Father's ear.

May they, hand in hand together,
  Tread in faith life's brief career;
Looking, longing, watching, waiting,
  Till their Saviour doth appear.

2014   Henry Ware   CM
Heirs together of the grace of life.
1 Peter 3:7

Happy the home when God is there,
  And love fills every breast;
When one their wish, and one their prayer,
  And one their heavenly rest.

Happy the home where Jesus' name
  Is sweet to every ear;
Where children early lisp His fame,
  And parents hold Him dear.

Happy the home where prayer is heard,
  And praise is wont to rise;
Where parents love the sacred word
  That makes us truly wise.

Lord, let us in our homes agree,
  This blessèd peace to gain;
Unite our hearts in love to Thee,
  And love to all will reign.

2015   Thomas Kelly   87 87 47
**Finally, be ye all of one mind, having
compassion one of another, love as brethren,
be pitiful, be courteous.**
1 Peter 3:8

Brethren let us walk together
  In the bonds of love and peace;
Can it be a question whether
  Brethren should from conflict cease?
    'Tis in union
  Hope, and joy, and love increase.

While we journey homeward, let us
  Help each other in the road;
Foes on every side beset us;
  Snares through all the way are strewed;
    It behoves us
  Each to bear a brother's load.

When we think how much our Father
  Has forgiven, and does forgive,
Brethren, we should learn the rather
  Free from wrath and strife to live,
    Far removing
  All that might offend or grieve.

Then, let each esteem his brother
  Better than himself to be;
And let each prefer another,
  Full of love, from envy free;
    Happy are we,
  When in this we all agree.

2016   Joseph Scriven   87 87 D
His ears are open unto their prayers.
1 Peter 3:12

What a Friend we have in Jesus,
  All our sins and griefs to bear!
What a privilege to carry
  Everything to God in prayer!
O what peace we often forfeit!
  O what needless pain we bear!
All because we do not carry
  Everything to God in prayer.

Have we trials and temptations?
  Is there trouble anywhere?
We should never be discouraged;
  Take it to the Lord in prayer.
Can we find a friend so faithful
  Who will all our sorrows share?
Jesus knows our every weakness;
  Take it to the Lord in prayer.

Are we weak and heavy-laden,
Cumbered with a load of care?
Precious Saviour, still our refuge
Take it to the Lord in prayer.
Do thy friends despise, forsake thee?
Take it to the Lord in prayer;
In His arms He'll take and shield thee
Thou wilt find a solace there.

2017 John Newton LM
And who is he that will harm you, if ye be followers of that which is good?
1 Peter 3:13

That man no guard or weapon needs,
Whose heart the blood of Jesus knows;
But safe may pass, if duty leads,
Through burning sands or mountain snows.

Released from guilt, he feels no fear,
Redemption is his shield and tower;
He sees his Saviour always near
To help in every trying hour.

Though I am weak and Satan strong,
And often to assault me tries,
When Jesus is my Shield and Song,
Abashed the wolf before me flies.

His love possessing, I am blest,
Secure, whatever change may come;
Whether I go to East or West,
With Him I still shall be at home.

If placed beneath the northern pole,
Though winter reigns with rigour there;
His gracious beams would cheer my soul,
And make a spring throughout the year.

Or if the desert's sun-burnt soil,
My lonely dwelling e'er should prove;
His presence would support my soul,
Whose smile is life, whose voice is love.

2018 Richard Burnham LM
Be ready always to give an answer to every man that asketh you a reason of the hope that is in you with meekness and fear. *1 Peter 3:15*

Now we are met in holy fear,
To hear the happy saints declare
The free compassions of a God,
The virtues of a Saviour's blood.

Jesus, assist them now to tell
What they have felt, and how they feel;
O Saviour, help them to express
The wonders of triumphant grace.

While to the church they freely own
What for their souls the Lord hath done,
We'd join to praise eternal love,
And heighten all the joys above.

2019 Richard Burnham 77 77
But the end of all things is at hand: be ye therefore sober, and watch unto prayer.
1 Peter 4:7

Jesus, Sovereign of the skies,
'Tis to Thee we lift our eyes;
All our supplications hear,
Answer every fervent prayer.

Jesus, come, do not delay,
Show us mercy while we pray;
Show us now Thy tender heart,
All Thy kindness now impart.

Rain down blessings from above,
Let it be a time of love;
Then we'll all rejoice, and say,
'O! 'tis good, 'tis good to pray.'

2020 *Carne's Collection* 77 77
If ye be reproached for the name of Christ, happy are ye. *1 Peter 4:14*

Happy Christian! God's own child,
Chosen, callèd, reconciled;
Once a rebel, full of taint,
Now a duteous humble saint.

Happy Christian! look on high,
See thy portion in the sky!
Fixed by everlasting love,
Who that portion can remove?

Happy Christian! though the earth
Cannot know thy gracious worth,
Yet thy God shall soon proclaim
Through all heaven thy blessèd name.

Happy Christian! angels say,
'Hither, brother, come away:
Leave the world, and all its woes;
Take with us thy sweet repose.'

Happy Christian! upwards fly;
Rise, the kingdom now is nigh:
Fill thy place before the throne;
On thy Saviour put the crown.

2021   Richard Burnham   CM
Humble yourselves therefore under the mighty hand of God, that He may exalt you in due time. *1 Peter 5:6*

Lord, may we feel Thy humbling hand
   On all our powers within:
And while Thy judgments are abroad,
   Forgive our nation's sin.

Counsel the rulers of the land,
   Yea, Lord, instruct us all;
O may we now in heart unite
   On Thy dear name to call.

Now may we each with tears confess
   The judgment long deserved:
But still admire, rejoice, and sing
   That still we are preserved.

May all around awake and hear
   The sovereign voice of God,
And fly from each delusive dream,
   And wash in Calvary's blood.

May Britain's truly favoured isle
   Be crowned with lasting peace,
Own the eternal Saviour's arm,
   And sing of saving grace.

2022   Joseph Anstice   886 D
Casting all your care upon Him; for He careth for you. *1 Peter 5:7*

O Lord, how happy should we be
If we could cast our care on Thee,
   If we from self could rest,
And feel at heart that One above,
In perfect wisdom, perfect love,
   Is working for the best.

Could we but kneel and cast our load
Even while we pray, upon our God;
   Then rise with lightened cheer,
Sure that the Father, who is nigh
To still the famished raven's cry,
   Will hear in that we fear.

We do not trust Him as we should;
So chafes weak nature's restless mood
   To cast its peace away;
But birds and flowers around us preach
And all the present evil teach
   Sufficient for the day.

Lord, make these faithless hearts of ours
Such lessons learn from birds and flowers;
   Make them from self to cease,
Leave all things to a Father's will
And taste, before Him lying still,
   Even in affliction, peace.

2023   Sarah Rhodes   56 64
Casting all your care upon Him; for He careth for you. *1 Peter 5:7*

God, who made the earth,
   The air, the sky, the sea,
Who gave the light its birth,
   Careth for me.

God, who made the grass,
   The flower, the fruit, the tree,
The day and night to pass,
   Careth for me.

God, who made the sun,
   The moon, the stars, is He
Who, when life's clouds come on,
   Careth for me.

God, who sent His Son
   To die on Calvary,
He, if I lean on Him,
   Will care for me.

When in heaven's bright land
   I all His loved ones see,
I'll sing with that blest band,
   'God cared for me.'

2024   Philip Doddridge   SM
Casting all your care upon Him; for He careth for you. *1 Peter 5:7*

How gentle God's commands,
   How kind His precepts are!
Come, cast your burdens on the Lord,
   And trust His constant care.

While providence supports,
   Let saints securely dwell;
That hand which bears all Nature up
   Shall guide His children well.

Why should this anxious load
   Press down your weary mind?
Haste to your heavenly Father's throne,
   And sweet refreshment find.

His goodness stands approved,
Down to the present day;
I'll drop my burden at His feet,
And bear a song away.

2025   William Gadsby   SM
Precious faith. *2 Peter 1:1*

Faith 'tis a grace divine,
A gift both rich and free;
'Twas grace that made this blessing mine,
From guilt to set me free.

The faith of God's elect
Is precious, pure, and good;
Such is its power, and its effect,
True faith prevails with God.

To Jesus and His blood,
It looks for life and peace;
The oaths and promises of God,
Its power and zeal increase.

When saints in darkness roam
With sin and guilt distressed,
Faith in Christ's righteousness alone
Can set the soul at rest.

Faith lives in spite of hell;
And, when the soul's oppressed
With miseries more than tongue can tell,
It leans on Jesus' breast.

Though death and dangers fly
Like lightning from the skies;
He that believes shall never die;
Faith must obtain the prize.

2026   'K' in *Rippon's Collection* 1787
11 11 11 11
Exceeding great and precious promises.
2 Peter 1:4

How firm a foundation, ye saints of the Lord,
Is laid for your faith in His excellent word!
What more can He say than to you He has said,
You who unto Jesus for refuge have fled?

In every condition—in sickness, in health,
In poverty's vale, or abounding in wealth;
At home, or abroad, on the land, on the sea,
'As thy days may demand, shall thy strength ever
be.

'Fear not, I am with thee; O be not dismayed;
I, I am thy God, and will still give thee aid;
I'll strengthen thee, help thee, and cause
thee to stand,
Upheld by My righteous, omnipotent hand.

'When through the deep waters I cause thee to
go,
The rivers of woe shall not thee overflow;
For I will be with thee, thy troubles to bless,
And sanctify to thee thy deepest distress.

'When thro' fiery trials thy pathway shall lie,
My grace all-sufficient shall be thy supply;
The flame shall not hurt thee: I only design
Thy dross to consume, and thy gold to refine.

'E'en down to old age, all My people shall prove
My sovereign, eternal, unchangeable love;
And when hoary hairs shall their temples adorn,
Like lambs they shall still in My bosom be borne.

'The soul that on Jesus has leaned for repose,
I will not, I will not desert to his foes;
That soul, though all hell should endeavour to
shake,
I'll never, no never, no never forsake.'

2027   Charles Wesley   CM
**And this voice which came from heaven we
heard, when we were with Him in the holy
mount.** *2 Peter 1:18*

Speak to us, Lord, Thyself reveal,
While here on earth we rove;
Speak to our hearts and let us feel
The kindling of Thy love.

With Thee conversing, we forget
All time and toil and care;
Labour is rest and pain is sweet,
If Thou, my God, art here.

Here then, my God, vouchsafe to stay
And bid my heart rejoice;
My bounding heart shall own Thy sway
And echo to Thy voice.

Thou callest me to seek Thy face;
'Tis all I wish to seek;
To attend the whispers of Thy grace
And hear Thee inly speak.

Let this my every hour employ,
Till I Thy glory see;
Enter into my Master's joy
And find my heaven in Thee.

2028 Charles Wesley CM
Holy men of God spake as they were moved by the Holy Ghost. *2 Peter 1:21*

Come Holy Ghost, our hearts inspire
　Let us Thine influence prove,
Source of the old prophetic fire,
　Fountain of light and love.

Come, Holy Ghost, for moved by Thee
　The prophets wrote and spoke;
Unlock the truth, Thyself the key,
　Unseal the sacred book.

Expand Thy wings, celestial Dove,
　Brood o'er our nature's night;
On our disordered spirits move,
　And let there now be light.

God, through Himself, we then shall know
　If Thou within us shine,
And sound, with all Thy saints below,
　The depths of love divine.

2029 Percy Dearmer 888 7 (trochaic)
But grow in grace, and in the knowledge of our Lord and Saviour Jesus Christ.
2 Peter 3:18

Jesus, good above all other,
Gentle Child of gentle mother,
In a stable born our Brother,
　Give us grace to persevere.

Jesus, cradled in a manger,
For us facing every danger,
Living as a homeless stranger,
　Make we Thee our King most dear.

Jesus, for Thy people dying,
Risen Master, death defying,
Lord in heaven, Thy grace supplying,
　Keep us to Thy presence near.

Jesus, who our sorrows bearest,
All our thoughts and hopes Thou sharest;
Thou to man the truth declarest;
　Help us all Thy truth to hear.

Lord, in all our doings, guide us;
Pride and hate shall ne'er divide us;
We'll go on with Thee beside us
　And with joy we'll persevere!

2030 Thomas Kelly 87 87 47
To Him be glory both now and for ever. Amen.
2 Peter 3:18

Glory, glory everlasting
　Be to Him who bore the cross!
Who redeemed our souls by tasting
　Death, the death deserved by us;
　　Spread His glory,
　Who redeemed His people thus.

His is love, 'tis love unbounded,
　Without measure, without end:
Human thought is here confounded,
　'Tis too vast to comprehend,
　　Praise the Saviour!
　Magnify the sinner's Friend.

While we hear the wondrous story
　Of the Saviour's cross and shame,
Sing we, 'everlasting glory
　Be to God and to the Lamb!
　　Saints and angels,
　Give ye glory to His name!'

2031 David Denham CM
Truly our fellowship is with the Father, and with His Son Jesus Christ. *1 John 1:3*

Enriched by everlasting love
　And washed in Jesus' blood,
Through justifying grace we prove
　Our fellowship with God.

Complete in Christ, our glorious Head,
　Who hath the winepress trod:
Sealed by the Spirit, we are led
　To fellowship with God.

When pressed with sorrow, sin, and fear,
　Beneath affliction's rod,
The darkest paths are all made clear
　By fellowship with God.

O for more faith, more love to soar
　Above this earthly clod,
And there enjoy, for evermore,
　True fellowship with God.

2032 Thomas Binney 86 886
God is light, and in Him is no darkness at all.
1 John 1:5

Eternal Light! Eternal Light!
　How pure the soul must be,
When, placed within Thy searching sight,
It shrinks not, but with calm delight,
　Can live and look on Thee.

The spirits that surround Thy throne
May bear the burning bliss;
But that is surely theirs alone,
Since they have never, never known
A fallen world like this.

O how shall I, whose native sphere
Is dark, whose mind is dim,
Before the ineffable appear,
And on my naked spirit bear
The uncreated beam?

There is a way for man to rise
To that sublime abode;
An offering and a sacrifice,
A Holy Spirit's energies,
An Advocate with God.

These, these prepare us for the sight
Of holiness above;
The sons of ignorance and night
Can dwell in the eternal light,
Through the eternal love.

2033 Charles Wesley 76 76 78 76
But if we walk in the light, as He is in the light, we have fellowship one with another, and the blood of Jesus Christ His Son cleanseth us from all sin.
1 John 1:7

Let the world their virtue boast,
And works of righteousness,
I, a wretch undone and lost,
Am freely saved by grace.
Take me, Saviour, as I am,
And let me lose my sins in Thee.
Friend of sinners, spotless Lamb,
Thy blood was shed for me.

Full of truth and grace Thou art,
And here is all my hope;
False and foul as hell, my heart
To Thee I offer up.
Thou wast given to redeem
My soul from all iniquity.
Friend of sinners, spotless Lamb,
Thy blood was shed for me.

Nothing have I, Lord, to pay,
Nor can Thy grace procure,
Empty send me not away,
For I, Thou know'st, am poor.
Dust and ashes is my name,
My all is sin and misery.
Friend of sinners, spotless Lamb,
Thy blood was shed for me.

2034 Horatius Bonar 64 64 664
But if we walk in the light, as He is in the light, we have fellowship one with another, and the blood of Jesus Christ His Son cleanseth us from all sin.
1 John 1:7

No, not despairingly
Come I to Thee;
No, not distrustingly
Bend I the knee:
Sin hath gone over me,
Yet is this still my plea,
Jesus hath died.

Lord, I confess to Thee
Sadly my sin;
All I am tell I Thee,
All I have been:
Purge Thou my sin away,
Wash Thou my soul this day;
Lord, make me clean.

Faithful and just art Thou,
Forgiving all;
Loving and kind art Thou
When poor ones call:
Lord, let the cleansing blood,
Blood of the Lamb of God,
Pass o'er my soul.

Then all is peace and light
This soul within;
Thus shall I walk with Thee,
The loved Unseen;
Leaning on Thee, my God,
Guided along the road,
Nothing between.

2035 Bernard Barton CM
But if we walk in the light, as He is in the light, we have fellowship one with another, and the blood of Jesus Christ His Son cleanseth us from all sin.
1 John 1:7

Walk in the light, so shalt thou know
That fellowship of love
His Spirit only can bestow
Who reigns in light above.

Walk in the light and sin abhorred
Shall not defile again;
The blood of Jesus Christ thy Lord
Shall cleanse from every stain.

Walk in the light and thou shalt find
Thy heart made truly His
Who dwells in cloudless light enshrined,
In whom no darkness is.

Walk in the light and thou shalt own
  Thy darkness passed away,
Because that light hath on thee shone
  In which is perfect day.

Walk in the light and then the tomb
  No fearful shade shall wear;
Glory shall chase away its gloom,
  For Christ hath conquered there.

Walk in the light and thine shall be
  A path, though thorny, bright;
For God, by grace, shall dwell in thee
  And God Himself is Light.

2036   Charles Wesley   886 D
My little children, these things write I unto you, that ye sin not. And if any man sin, we have an advocate with the Father, Jesus Christ the righteous. *1 John 2:1*

Thou sinner's Advocate with God,
My only trust is in Thy blood,
  Thou all-atoning Lamb;
The virtue of Thy death impart,
Speak comfort to my drooping heart,
  And tell me all Thy name.

Speak, Lord, and let me find Thee near;
O come and dissipate my fear;
  Declare my sins forgiven;
Return, Thou Prince of Peace; return,
Thou Comforter of all that mourn,
  And guide me safe to heaven.

2037   Isaac Watts   SM
Behold, what manner of love the Father hath bestowed upon us, that we should be called the sons of God. *1 John 3:1*

  Behold what wondrous grace
    The Father has bestowed
On sinners of a mortal race,
    To call them sons of God.

  'Tis no surprising thing
    That we should be unknown;
The Jewish world knew not their King,
    God's everlasting Son.

  Nor does it yet appear
    How great we must be made;
But when we see our Saviour there,
    We shall be like our Head.

  A hope so much divine
    May trials well endure,
For we, as sons in Christ, are made
    As pure as He is pure.

If in my Father's love
  I share a filial part,
Send down Thy Spirit, like a dove,
  To rest upon my heart.

We would no longer lie
  Like slaves before Thy throne;
Our faith shall 'Abba, Father', cry,
  And Thou the kindred own.

2038   *Psalter* 1781   CM
Behold, what manner of love the Father hath bestowed upon us, that we should be called the sons of God. *1 John 3:1*

Behold the amazing gift of love
  The Father has bestowed
On us, the sinful sons of men,
  To call us sons of God.

Concealed as yet this honour lies,
  By this dark world unknown,
A world that knew not, when He came,
  Even God's eternal Son.

High is the rank we now possess,
  But higher we shall rise;
Though what we shall hereafter be
  Is hid from mortal eyes.

Our souls, we know, when He appears,
  Shall bear His image bright;
For all His glory, full disclosed,
  Shall open to our sight.

A hope so great and so divine
  May trials well endure,
And purge the soul from sense and sin
  As Christ Himself is pure.

2039   Elizabeth Mills   88 88 (anapaestic)
We know that, when He shall appear, we shall be like Him; for we shall see Him as He is.
1 John 3:2

We speak of the realms of the blest,
  That country so bright and so fair;
And oft are its glories confessed;
  But what must it be to be there?

We speak of its pavements of gold,
  Its walls decked with jewels so rare;
Its wonders and beauties untold;
  But what must it be to be there?

We speak of its freedom from sin,
  From sorrow, temptation and care;
From trials without and within;
  But what must it be to be there?

We speak of its service of love,
The robes which the glorified wear;
The church of the first-born above;
But what must it be to be there?

Do Thou, Lord, midst pleasure and woe,
For heaven our spirits prepare;
And shortly we also shall know
And feel what it is to be there.

2040   Charles Gabriel   10 10 10 10 + refrain
**We know that, when He shall appear, we shall
be like Him; for we shall see Him as He is.**
1 John 3:2

When all my labours and trials are o'er
And I am safe on that beautiful shore,
Just to be near the dear Lord I adore,
Will through the ages be glory for me.

*O that will be glory for me,
Glory for me, glory for me,
When by His grace I shall look on His face,
That will be glory, be glory for me!*

When by the gift of His infinite grace
I am accorded in heaven a place,
Just to be there and to look on His face,
Will through the ages be glory for me.

Friends will be there I have loved long ago;
Joy like a river around me will flow;
Yet just a smile from my Saviour, I know,
Will through the ages be glory for me.

2041   Joseph Swaine   LM
We shall be like Him. *1 John 3:2*

And am I blest with Jesus' love?
And shall I dwell with Him above?
And will the joyful period come
When I shall call the heavens my home?

Think, O my soul, what must it be,
A world of glorious minds to see:
Drink at the fountain-head of peace,
And bathe in everlasting bliss!

To hear them all at once proclaim
Eternal glories to the Lamb,
And join, with joyful heart and tongue,
That new and never-ending song!

And does the happy hour draw near
When Christ will in the clouds appear,
And I without a veil shall see
The God, the Man that bled for me?

If in my soul such joy abounds,
While weeping faith explores His wounds,
How glorious will those scars appear,
When perfect bliss forbids a tear!

Think, O my soul, if 'tis so sweet
On earth to sit at Jesus' feet,
What must it be to wear a crown,
And sit with Jesus on His throne!

2042   Thomas Lynch   77 77 77
**And hereby we know that He abideth in us, by
the Spirit which He hath given us.** *1 John 3:24*

Gracious Spirit, dwell with me!
I myself would gracious be,
And with words that help and heal
Would Thy life in mine reveal;
And with actions bold and meek
Would for Christ, my Saviour, speak.

Truthful Spirit, dwell with me!
I myself would truthful be,
And with wisdom kind and clear
Let Thy life in mine appear;
And with actions brotherly
Speak my Lord's sincerity.

Tender Spirit, dwell with me!
I myself would tender be;
Shut my heart up like a flower
In temptation's darksome hour;
Open it when shines the sun,
And His love by fragrance own.

Mighty Spirit, dwell with me!
I myself would mighty be,
Mighty so as to prevail
Where unaided man must fail,
Ever by a mighty hope
Pressing on and bearing up.

Holy Spirit, dwell with me!
I myself would holy be,
Separate from sin, I would
Choose and cherish all things good;
And whatever I can be
Give to Him who gave me Thee.

2043   Horatius Bonar   10 10 10 10
**And hereby we know that He abideth in us, by
the Spirit which He hath given us.**
1 John 3:24

Not what I am, O Lord, but what Thou art!
    That, that alone can be my soul's true rest,
Thy love, not mine, bids fear and doubt depart
    And stills the tempest of my throbbing breast.

Thy name is Love! I hear it from the cross;
    Thy name is Love! I hear it in the tomb;
All meaner love is perishable dross,
    But this shall light me through time's thickest
        gloom.

'Tis what I know of Thee, my Lord and God,
    That fills my soul with peace, my lips with song;
Thou art my health, my joy, my staff, my rod,
    Leaning on Thee, in weakness I am strong.

More of Thyself, O show me hour by hour,
    More of Thy glory, O my God and Lord;
More of Thyself, in all Thy grace and power;
    More of Thy love and truth, Incarnate Word!

2044   Richard Burnham   CM
**Beloved, let us love one another: for love is of
God.** *1 John 4:7*

When truth displays eternal love,
    Through Calvary's healing blood,
The sinner's heart ascends above,
    Transported with his God.

O how he loves his loving Lord,
    What ardent love he feels!
O how he loves the sacred word,
    That such great love reveals!

This love makes every callèd sheep
    Look lovely in his sight;
With Jesus' flock he loves to keep,
    And 'tis his great delight.

Lord, may the shining beams of love
    Afford us constant peace,
And may we all go on to prove
    The riches of Thy grace.

Now, dearest Lord, we Thee implore
    To send Thy heavenly Dove,
And bless our souls for evermore
    With pure increasing love.

2045   Horatius Bonar   64 64
**Beloved, let us love one another: for love is of
God.** *1 John 4:7*

Belovèd, let us love:
    Love is of God;
In God alone hath love
    Its true abode.

Belovèd, let us love:
    For they who love,
They only, are His sons,
    Born from above.

Belovèd, let us love:
    For love is rest,
And he who loveth not
    Abides unblest.

Belovèd, let us love:
    In love is light,
And he who loveth not,
    Dwelleth in night.

Belovèd, let us love:
    For only thus
Shall we behold that God
    Who loveth us.

2046   George Burder   CM
**He that loveth not knoweth not God; for God is
love.** *1 John 4:8*

Come, ye that know and fear the Lord,
    And lift your souls above;
Let every heart and voice accord,
    To sing that God is love!

This precious truth His word declares,
    And all His mercies prove;
Jesus, the Gift of gifts appears,
    To show that God is love!

Behold His patience lengthened out,
    To those who from Him rove;
And calls effectual reach their hearts,
    To teach them God is love!

The work begun is carried on
    By power from heaven above;
And every step, from first to last,
    Proclaims that God is love!

O may we all, while here below,
    This best of blessings prove;
Till warmer hearts in brighter worlds,
    Shall shout that God is love!

2047   Zion's Trumpet 1838   87 87
He that loveth not knoweth not God; for God is love. *1 John 4:8*

What is love? My soul would answer,
  Nought deserves the endearing name
But the God of love, the Saviour,
  Whose dear heart's a constant flame.

View Him prostrate in the garden,
  Wet His locks with dews of night,
Grappling with the powers of darkness,
  Sweating blood, amazing sight!

Hear His groans, till He, expiring,
  Cries triumphant, 'It is done;'
Bearing all the wrathful anger
  Which to us was due alone.

What is love? My soul would echo
  With the saints in heaven above.
Who, through Jesus, gone to glory,
  Sing in concert, 'This is love!'

2048   from the Polish, tr. E Reed   Irregular
In this was manifested the love of God toward us, because that God sent His only begotten Son into the world, that we might live through Him. *1 John 4:9*

    Infant holy,
    Infant lowly,
For His bed a cattle stall;
    Oxen lowing,
    Little knowing
Christ the babe is Lord of all.
    Swift are winging
    Angels singing,
    Nowells ringing,
    Tidings bringing,
Christ the babe is Lord of all.

    Flocks were sleeping,
    Shepherds keeping
Vigil till the morning new
    Saw the glory,
    Heard the story,
Tidings of a gospel true.
    Thus rejoicing,
    Free from sorrow,
    Praises voicing
    Greet the morrow,
Christ the babe was born for you!

2049   Anon and J Deck vs 3,4   87 87 47
Herein is love, not that we loved God, but that He loved us, and sent His Son to be the propitiation for our sins. *1 John 4:10*

Father, 'twas Thy love that knew us
  Earth's foundations long before;
That same love to Jesus drew us
  By its sweet constraining power,
    And will keep us
Safely now, and evermore.

Pause, my soul, adore and wonder!
  Ask, 'O why such love to me?'
Grace hath put me in the number
  Of the Saviour's family;
    Hallelujah!
Thanks, eternal thanks, to Thee!

Since that love had no beginning,
  And shall never, never cease;
Keep, O keep me, Lord, from sinning,
  Guide me in the way of peace!
    Make me walk in
All the paths of holiness.

God of love, our souls adore Thee!
  We would still Thy grace proclaim,
Till we cast our crowns before Thee,
  And in glory praise Thy name:
    Hallelujah!
Be to God and to the Lamb!

2050   William Penn   CM
Herein is love, not that we loved God, but that He loved us, and sent His Son to be the propitiation for our sins. *1 John 4:10*

Enthrone thy God within thy heart,
  Thy being's inmost shrine;
He doth to thee the power impart
  To live the life divine.

Seek truth in Him with Christ-like mind;
  With faith His will discern;
Walk on life's way with Him, and find
  Thy heart within thee burn.

With love that overflows thy soul
  Love Him who first loved thee;
Is not His love thy life, thy goal,
  Thy soul's eternity?

Serve Him in His sufficing strength:
  Heart, mind and soul employ;
And He shall crown thy days at length
  With everlasting joy.

2051 William How   LM
We love him, because he first loved us.
1 John 4:19

It is a thing most wonderful,
   Almost too wonderful to be,
That God's own Son should come from heaven,
   And die to save a child like me.

And yet I know that it is true:
   He chose a poor and humble lot,
And wept, and toiled, and mourned, and died,
   For love of those who loved Him not.

I cannot tell how He could love
   A child so weak and full of sin;
His love must be most wonderful,
   If He could die my love to win.

I sometimes think about the cross,
   And shut my eyes, and try to see
The cruel nails and crown of thorns,
   And Jesus crucified for me.

But even could I see Him die,
   I could but see a little part
Of that great love, which, like a fire,
   Is always burning in His heart.

It is most wonderful to know
   His love to me so free and sure;
But 'tis more wonderful to see
   My love for Him so faint and poor.

And yet I want to love Thee, Lord;
   O light the flame within my heart,
And I will love Thee more and more,
   Until I see Thee as Thou art.

2052 *Pilgrim Hymnal* 1904   10 10 10 6
We love Him, because He first loved us.
1 John 4:19

I sought the Lord and afterward I knew
He moved my soul to seek Him, seeking me;
It was not I that found, O Saviour true;
   No, I was found by Thee.

Thou didst reach forth Thy hand and mine enfold;
I walked and sank not on the storm-vexed sea;
'Twas not so much that I on Thee took hold
   As Thou, dear Lord, on me.

I find, I walk, I love, but O the whole
Of love is but my answer, Lord, to Thee!
For Thou wert long beforehand with my soul;
   Always Thou lovèdst me.

2053 Jane Leeson   77 77
We love Him, because He first loved us.
1 John 4:19

Saviour, teach me day by day,
Love's sweet lesson to obey;
Sweeter lesson cannot be,
Loving Him who first loved me.

With a young, glad heart of love,
At Thy bidding may I move,
Prompt to serve and follow Thee,
Loving Him who first loved me.

Teach me all Thy steps to trace,
Strong to follow in Thy grace;
Learning how to love from Thee,
Loving Him who first loved me.

Love, in loving, finds employ,
In obedience all her joy,
Ever new that joy will be,
Loving Him who first loved me.

Thus may I rejoice to show
That I feel the love I owe;
Singing, till Thy face I see,
Of His love who first loved me.

2054 William Gadsby   SM
**For whatsoever is born of God overcometh the
world: and this is the victory that overcometh
the world, even our faith.** *1 John 5:4*

When faith to Sinai looks,
   It fills the heart with dread;
And justifies the dreadful stroke
   That strikes the sinner dead.

And when by faith we trace
   Christ is the only way
From endless wrath to endless bliss,
   We for the blessing pray.

But when faith views the Lamb,
   As my atoning Priest,
It magnifies His precious name,
   And sets the heart at rest.

How precious is the faith
   That God to Zion gives!
It triumphs over sin and death.
   And in Jehovah lives.

2055   Edward Cooper   LM
**For there are three that bear record in heaven,
the Father, the Word, and the Holy Ghost: and
these three are one.**
1 John 5:7

Father of heaven! whose love profound
A ransom for our souls hath found:
Before Thy throne we sinners bend:
To us Thy pardoning love extend.

Almighty Son! Incarnate Word!
Our Prophet, Priest, Redeemer, Lord!
Before Thy throne we sinners bend:
To us Thy saving grace extend.

Eternal Spirit! by whose breath
The soul is raised from sin and death;
Before Thy throne we sinners bend:
To us Thy quickening power extend.

Jehovah! Father, Spirit, Son!
Mysterious Godhead! Three in One!
Before Thy throne we sinners bend:
Grace, pardon, life to us extend.

2056   Anon   77 77
**For there are three that bear record in heaven,
the Father, the Word, and the Holy Ghost: and
these three are one.**
1 John 5:7

Holy Father, God of love!
Throned in majesty above,
Just and true are all Thy ways,
Worthy of eternal praise.

Fill my heart with Thy rich grace;
Then with joy I'll run my race;
Christ's fair image on me seal,
And Thy love in Him reveal.

Holy Jesus, Lamb of God,
Send Thy healing word abroad;
Show how strong and kind Thou art,
Let me see Thy loving heart.

Holy Spirit, quickening breath!
Work in us Thy precious faith;
Bless our hearts with gospel peace,
Furnish us with every grace.

Breathe upon us from above,
Teach us truth, and give us love;
All that feel Thy quickening flame,
Will adore and bless Thy name.

2057   Nahum Tate, Nicholas Brady   CM
**For there are three that bear record in heaven,
the Father, the Word, and the Holy Ghost: and
these three are one.**
1 John 5:7

To Father, Son, and Holy Ghost,
    One God, whom we adore,
Be glory as it was, is now,
    And shall be evermore.

2058   Augustus Toplady   LM
**He that believeth on the Son of God hath the
witness in himself.** *1 John 5:10*

Witness of Christ within my heart,
    My interest in His love display;
My interest in that better part,
    Which none can ever take away.

Thy Word and Spirit both conspire
    To tell Thy church she is forgiven;
O lift me daily higher and higher,
    Till all my joys are crowned with heaven.

2059   David Denham   CM
**He that hath the Son hath life; and He that hath
not the Son of God hath not life.**
1 John 5:12

He that hath Christ by precious faith
    Hath life for evermore;
Shall triumph over sin and death,
    And then to glory soar.

He that hath Christ for righteousness,
    Renounceth all His own;
Flees to His refuge in distress,
    And trusts His grace alone.

He that hath Christ in Jordan's flood,
    Shall more than conqueror prove;
Supported by the arm of God,
    And filled with peace and love.

He that hath Christ is always blest,
    From Him we cannot fall;
Christ is our Life, our Joy, our Rest,
    Our God, our Strength, our All.

2060 David Denham CM
And we know that the Son of God is come.
1 John 5:20

By faith we know the Son of God,
In human form revealed;
We know He shed for us His blood,
By peace and pardon sealed.

We know He wrought our righteousness,
And magnified the law;
We know He comforts in distress,
From whom all help we draw.

We know His all-sufficient grace
Can heal our broken hearts;
We know His fulness suits our case,
And heavenly joy imparts.

We know and love His gracious voice
Which draws the soul to rest;
We know, and in His name rejoice,
And are completely blest.

We know He resteth in His love,
Omnipotent to save;
And with Him we shall reign above,
Triumphant o'er the grave.

2061 James Montgomery 66 66 88
Now I beseech thee...that we love one another.
2 John 1:5

How beautiful the sight
Of brethren who agree
In friendship to unite,
And bonds of charity!
'Tis like the precious ointment shed
O'er all his robes from Aaron's head.

'Tis like the dews that fill
The cups of Hermon's flowers;
Or Zion's fruitful hill,
Bright with the drops of showers,
When mingling odours breathe around,
And glory rests on all the ground.

For there the Lord commands
Blessings, a boundless store,
From His unsparing hands,
Yea, life for evermore:
Thrice happy they who meet above
To spend eternity in love!

2062 John Newton 87 87 47
The judgment of the great day. *Jude 1:6*

Day of judgment, day of wonders!
Hark! the trumpet's awful sound,
Louder than a thousand thunders,
Shakes the vast creation round!
How the summons
Will the sinner's heart confound!

See the Judge our nature wearing,
Clothed in Majesty divine
You who long for His appearing,
Then shall say, 'This God is mine!'
Gracious Saviour,
Own me in that day for Thine.

At His call the dead awaken,
Rise to life from earth and sea!
All the powers of nature, shaken
By His looks, prepare to flee!
Careless sinner,
What will then become of thee?

But to those who have confessèd,
Loved, and served the Lord below,
He will say, 'Come near, ye blessèd,
See the kingdom I bestow;
You for ever
Shall My love and glory know.'

2063 Samuel Medley CM
Praying in the Holy Ghost. *Jude 1:20*

Eternal Spirit! mighty Lord!
Jehovah is Thy name;
Thy glories here will we record,
And sing Thy wondrous fame.

'Twas Thy almighty power and love
Which called our souls from death;
O! raise our hearts to Thee above
In praise, while we have breath.

Of heavenly love Thou art the pledge,
The witness, and the seal;
O that in prayer, when we engage,
We may Thine influence feel.

Help our infirmities, we pray,
Our ignorance remove;
O smile our darkness into day,
And fill us with Thy love.

Our faint attempts, Lord, kindly own,
   And for us intercede;
Hear every sigh, and every groan
   Which from our hearts proceed.

2064   Isaac Watts   SM

**Now unto Him that is able to keep you from
falling, and to present you faultless before the
presence of His glory with exceeding joy.**
Jude 1:24

To God the only wise,
   Our Saviour and our King,
Let all the saints below the skies
   Their humble praises bring.

'Tis His almighty love,
   His counsel and His care,
Preserves us safe from sin and death,
   And every hurtful snare.

He will present our souls
   Unblemished and complete
Before the glory of His face,
   With joys divinely great.

Then all the chosen seed
   Shall meet around the throne;
Shall bless the conduct of His grace,
   And make His wonders known.

To our Redeemer, God,
   Wisdom and power belongs;
Immortal crowns of majesty,
   And everlasting songs.

2065   Leonard Hills   76 86 D

**Now unto Him that is able to keep you from
falling, and to present you faultless before the
presence of His glory with exceeding joy.**
Jude 1:24

O keep my feet, Lord Jesus,
   That I may follow Thee
And never stumble in the way
   However rough it be.
O keep my hands, Lord Jesus,
   That I may ready be
To help the weak and helpless,
   And joyously for Thee.

O keep my ears, Lord Jesus,
   Alert for Thine own word
'Mid all the noise of daily strife
   May Thy voice first be heard.
O keep my eyes, Lord Jesus,
   That I may ever see
The marks of Thine own leading,
   Wherever I may be.

O keep my tongue, Lord Jesus,
   And use it just for Thee;
When tempted to say unkind things,
   Then let me silent be.
O keep my heart, Lord Jesus,
   And fill it with Thy love,
And use me every day until
   I rest with Thee above.

2066   Thomas Kelly   87 87 47

**Now unto Him that is able to keep you from
falling, and to present you faultless before the
presence of His glory with exceeding joy.**
Jude 1:24

Keep us, Lord, O keep us ever!
   Vain our hope if left by Thee:
We are Thine, O leave us never,
   Till Thy face in heaven we see!
      There to praise Thee
   Through a bright eternity.

All our strength at once would fail us,
   If deserted, Lord, by Thee;
Nothing then could aught avail us,
   Certain our defeat would be:
      Those who hate us
   Thenceforth their desire would see.

But we look to Thee as able,
   Grace to give in time of need;
Heaven we know is not more stable
   Than the promise which we plead:
      'Tis Thy promise
   Gives Thy people hope indeed.

2067   Edmund Sears   11 11 11 11

**Grace be unto you, and peace, from Him which
is, and which was, and which is to come.**
Revelation 1:4

Unchangeable Jesus, Thy praises we sing,
And own Thee our Prophet, our Priest, and our
   King,
O, give us while singing sweet tastes of Thy
   love,
To raise our affections to treasures above!

Unchangeable Jesus, our waverings we own,
Acknowledge with sorrow our sins at Thy throne,
We surely should perish, so changing are we
But that Thy free favour is firm as 'tis free.

Unchangeable Jesus, O teach us at length,
In no way to lean on our wisdom and strength!
Since, moon-like, our graces now wax and now
   wane,
But, sun-like, Thy favour is ever the same.

Unchangeable Jesus, in whom we'd confide,
Thy sunshine of goodness does ever abide;
O, give us on Thee and Thy promise to lean,
And trust Thou art shining when clouds intervene!

Unchangeable Jesus, the day will soon come,
When all Thy dear loved ones shall see Thee at
   home;
O, then may our voices add strength to the song,
That rolls through long ages Thy praises along!

2068   John Newton   87 87 77
**Unto Him that loved us, and washed us from
our sins in His own blood.**
Revelation 1:5

Let us *love* and *sing*, and *wonder*;
   Let us *praise* the Saviour's name!
He has hushed the Law's loud thunder;
   He has quenched Mount Sinai's flame;
He has washed us with His blood;
He has brought us nigh to God.

Let us *love* the Lord who bought us;
   Pitied us when enemies;
Called us by His grace, and taught us;
   Gave us ears, and gave us eyes;
He has washed us with His blood;
He presents our souls to God!

Let us *sing* though fierce temptations
   Threaten hard to bear us down!
For the Lord, our strong salvation;
   Holds in view the conqueror's crown;
He who washed us with His blood;
Soon will bring us home to God!

Let us *wonder*; grace and justice
   Join and point to mercy's store;
When, through grace, in Christ our trust is,
   Justice smiles, and asks no more;
He has washed us with His blood;
Has secured our way to God!

Let us *praise*, and join the chorus
   Of the saints enthroned on high;
Here they trusted Him before us,
   Now their praises fill the sky:
'Thou hast washed us with Thy blood;
Thou art worthy, Lamb of God!'

2069   Joseph Hart (alt)   77 77
**Unto Him that loved us, and washed us from
our sins in His own blood.**
Revelation 1:5

Jesus Christ, God's holy Lamb,
We will praise Thy lovely name;
We were saved by God's decree,
And our debt was paid by Thee.

Thou hast washed us in Thy blood,
Made us kings and priests to God;
Take this tribute of the poor;
Less we can't, we can't give more.

Souls redeemed, your voices raise,
Sing your dear Redeemer's praise;
Worthy Thou of love and laud,
King of saints, incarnate God.

Righteous are Thy ways, and true;
Endless honours are Thy due;
Grace and glory in Thee shine;
Matchless mercy, love divine.

We for whom Thou once wast slain,
We Thy ransomed sinner-train,
In this one request agree,
'Make us more resemble Thee.'

2070   Arthur Pierson   11 12 + refrain
**Unto Him that loved us, and washed us from
our sins in His own blood.**
Revelation 1:5

With harps and with viols there stand a great
   throng
In the presence of Jesus and sing this new song:

   *'Unto Him who hath loved us and washed us
     from sin,
   Unto Him be the glory for ever! Amen.'*

All these once were sinners, defiled in His sight,
Now arrayed in pure garments in praise they
    unite:

He maketh the rebel a priest and a king,
He hath bought us and taught us this new song to
    sing:

How helpless and hopeless we sinners had been
If He never had loved us till cleansed from our sin!

Aloud in His praises our voices shall ring,
So that others believing, this new song shall sing:

2071   Albert Midlane   87 87
**Behold, He cometh with clouds; and every eye
shall see Him, and they also which pierced
Him.** *Revelation 1:7*

Hark! the cry, 'Behold, He cometh,'
   Hark! the cry, 'The Bridegroom's near,'
These are accents falling sweetly
   On the ransomed sinner's ear.

Man may disbelieve the tidings,
   Or in anger turn away;
'Tis foretold there shall be scoffers
   Rising in the latter day.

But He'll come, the Lord from heaven,
   Not to suffer or to die;
But to take His waiting people
   To their glorious rest on high.

Happy they who stand expecting
   Christ, the Saviour, to appear:
Sad for those who do not love Him,
   Those who do not wish Him here.

But in mercy still He lingers.
   Lengthening out the day of grace;
Till He comes, inviting sinners
   To His welcome, fond embrace.

2072   Benjamin Francis   87 87 D
**Behold, He cometh with clouds; and every eye
shall see Him, and they also which pierced
Him.** *Revelation 1:7*

I am waiting for the dawning
   Of the bright and blessèd day
When the darksome night of sorrow
   Shall have vanished far away.
When for ever with the Saviour,
   Far beyond this vale of tears,
I shall swell the song of worship,
   Through the everlasting years.

I am looking at the brightness
   See, it shineth from afar
Of the clear and joyous beaming
   Of the Bright and Morning Star.
Through the dark grey mist of morning
   Do I see its glorious light;
Then away with every shadow
   Of this sad and weary night.

I am waiting for the coming
   Of the Lord who died for me;
O! His words have thrilled my spirit:
   'I will come again for Thee.'
I can almost hear His footfall
   On the threshold of the door;
And my heart, my heart is longing
   To be His for evermore.

2073   John Cennick, C Wesley   87 87 47
**Behold, He cometh with clouds; and every eye
shall see Him, and they also which pierced
Him.** *Revelation 1:7*

Lo! He comes with clouds descending,
   Once for favoured sinners slain;
Thousand thousand saints attending,
   Swell the triumph of His train:
     Hallelujah!
   God appears; on earth to reign.

Every eye shall now behold Him
   Robed in dreadful majesty;
Those who set at nought and sold Him,
   Pierced and nailed Him to the tree,
     Deeply wailing,
   Shall the true Messiah see.

Every island, sea, and mountain,
   Heaven and earth, shall flee away;
All who hate Him must, confounded,
   Hear the trump proclaim the day:
     Come to judgment!
   Come to judgment! Come away!

Now redemption, long expected,
   See in solemn pomp appear;
All His saints, by man rejected,
   Now shall meet Him in the air:
     Hallelujah!
     See the day of God appear!

2074   Christopher Wordsworth   76 76 D
I was in the Spirit on the Lord's day, and heard behind me a great voice, as of a trumpet.
Revelation 1:10

O day of rest and gladness!
  O day of joy and light!
O balm of care and sadness!
  Most beautiful, most bright;
On thee, the high and lowly,
  Through ages joined in tune,
Sing, 'Holy, Holy, Holy,'
  To the great God Triune!

On thee, at the creation,
  The light first had its birth;
On thee, for our salvation,
  Christ rose from depths of earth;
On thee our Lord victorious,
  The Spirit sent from heaven;
And thus on thee, most glorious,
  A triple light was given.

Today on weary nations
  The heavenly manna falls;
To holy convocations
  The silver trumpet calls,
Where gospel-light is glowing
  With pure and radiant beams,
And living water flowing
  With soul-refreshing streams.

New graces ever gaining
  From this our day of rest,
We reach the rest remaining
  To spirits of the blest:
To Holy Ghost be praises,
  To Father, and to Son;
The church her voice upraises
  To Thee, blest Three in One!

2075   Timothy Dudley-Smith   86 8886
And I turned to see the voice that spake with me. And being turned, I saw seven golden candlesticks. *Revelation 1:12*

He walks among the golden lamps
  On feet like burnished bronze:
His hair as snows of winter white,
His eyes with fire aflame, and bright
His glorious robe of seamless light
  Surpassing Solomon's.

And in His hand the seven stars
  And from His mouth a sword:
His voice the thunder of the seas;
All creatures bow to His decrees
Who holds the everlasting keys
  And reigns as Sovereign Lord.

More radiant than the sun at noon,
  Who was, and is to be:
Who was, from everlasting days;
Who lives, the Lord of all our ways;
To Him be majesty and praise
  For all eternity.

'He walks among the golden lamps' by Timothy Dudley-Smith (b.1926). © Timothy Dudley-Smith in Europe and Africa. © Hope Publishing Company in the United States of America and the rest of the world. Reproduced by permission of Oxford University Press . All rights reserved.

2076   Anne Steele   CM
And when I saw Him, I fell at His feet as dead.
Revelation 1:17

Dear Saviour, when my thoughts recall
  The wonders of Thy grace,
Low at Thy feet ashamed I fall,
  And hide this wretched face.

Should love like Thine be thus repaid?
  Ah, vile, ungrateful heart!
By earth's low cares detained, betrayed,
  From Jesus to depart.

From Jesus, who alone can give
  True pleasure, peace, and rest:
When absent from my Lord I live
  Unsatisfied, unblest.

But He, for His own mercy's sake,
  My wandering soul restores:
He bids the mourning heart partake
  The pardon it implores.

O while I breathe to Thee, my Lord,
  The penitential sigh,
Confirm the kind forgoing word
  With pity in Thine eye.

Then shall the mourner at Thy feet
  Rejoice to seek Thy face:
And grateful own how kind, how sweet,
  Thy condescending grace.

2077 Arthur Russell 76 76 D

I am He that liveth, and was dead; and, behold, I am alive for evermore, Amen; and have the keys of hell and of death. *Revelation 1:18*

O Jesus, we adore Thee,
   Upon the cross, our King!
We bow our hearts before Thee,
   Thy gracious name we sing.
That name hath brought salvation,
   That name in life our stay,
Our peace, our consolation,
   When life shall fade away.

Yet doth the world disdain Thee,
Still passing by the cross;
Lord, may our hearts retain Thee;
   All else we count but loss.
Ah, Lord, our sins arraigned Thee,
   And nailed Thee to the tree:
Our pride, our Lord, disdained Thee
   Yet deign our hope to be.

O glorious King, we bless Thee,
   No longer pass Thee by;
O Jesus, we confess Thee
   The Son enthroned on high.
Lord, grant to us remission;
   Life through Thy death restore;
Yea, grant us the fruition
   Of life for evermore.

2078 Russell Hurditch
11 10 11 10 + refrain

I am He that liveth, and was dead; and, behold, I am alive for evermore, Amen; and have the keys of hell and of death. *Revelation 1:18*

He dies! He dies! the lowly Man of sorrows,
   On whom were laid our many griefs and woes;
Our sins He bore, beneath God's awful billows,
   And He hath triumphed over all our foes.

*   I am He that liveth, that liveth, and was dead;*
*   I am He that liveth, that liveth, and was dead;*
*   And behold, I am alive for evermore,*
*   Behold, I am alive for evermore,*
*   I am He that liveth, that liveth, and was dead;*
*   And behold, I am alive for evermore.*

He lives! He lives! what glorious consolation!
   Exalted at His Father's own right hand;
He pleads for us, and by His intercession,
   Enables all His saints by grace to stand.

He comes! He comes! O blest anticipation!
   In keeping with His true and faithful word;
To call us to our heavenly consummation;
   Caught up, to be for ever with the Lord.

2079 Thomas Kelly 77 77

I am He that liveth, and was dead; and, behold, I am alive for evermore, Amen; and have the keys of hell and of death.
Revelation 1:18

Crowns of glory, ever bright,
   Rest upon the Victor's head;
Crowns of glory are His right,
   Him who liveth and was dead.

Jesus fought and won the day;
   Such a fight was never fought;
Well His people now may say,
   'See what God, our God, has wrought.'

He subdued the powers of hell;
   In the fight He stood alone;
All His foes before Him fell,
   By His single arm o'erthrown.

They have fallen to rise no more;
   Final is the foe's defeat:
Jesus triumphed by His power,
   And His triumph is complete.

2080 Richard Burnham 87 87

I am He that liveth, and was dead; and, behold, I am alive for evermore, Amen; and have the keys of hell and of death. *Revelation 1:18*

Now I know the great Redeemer,
   Know He lives, and spreads His fame;
Lives, and all the heavens adore Him;
   Lives, and earth resounds His name.

Yes, I know Messiah liveth,
   Lives, and prays, and pleads for me;
Lives, and loves, and smiles, and blesses;
   Lives, and sets my spirit free.

My Redeemer lives within me,
   Lives, and heavenly love conveys;
Lives, and glory now surrounds me;
   Lives, and I His name shall praise.

Pardon, peace, and full salvation,
   From my living Saviour flow;
Light, and life, and consolation,
   All the good I e'er can know.

Ah, how kind is my Redeemer,
   He's my ever-living Friend;
He will never, never leave me,
   But will love me to the end.

Soon shall I behold my Saviour,
   He who lives and reigns above;
Lives, and I shall live for ever;
   Live and sing redeeming love.

2081   Joseph Swain   CM
To Him that overcometh will I give to eat of the tree of life, which is in the midst of the paradise of God. *Revelation 2:7*

O what a garden will be seen,
   When all the flowers of grace
Appear in everlasting green,
   Before the Planter's face!

No more exposed to burning skies,
   Or winter's piercing cold;
What never-dying sweets will rise
   From every opening fold!

No want of sun or showers above,
   To make the flowers decline!
Fountains of life and beams of love
   For ever spring and shine.

No more they need the quickening air,
   Or gently rising dew;
Unspeakable their beauties are,
   And yet for ever new.

Christ is their shade, and Christ their sun;
   Among them walks the King,
Whose presence is eternal noon,
   His smiles, eternal spring.

2082   Vernon Higham   DSM
Be Thou faithful unto death, and I will give Thee a crown of life. *Revelation 2:10*

Thanks be to Thee, my God,
   My heart and soul rejoice,
And praises blend in sweet accord
   In anthems of Thy choice.
   O hear the gospel song,
   Our Saviour did atone,
With full forgiveness for my wrong,
   Saved by His grace alone.

Was ever grace like Thine
   Which always finds its own,
Is satisfied when Thou art mine,
   And turns me to Thy throne?
   I'm saved by grace, I know,
   Embraced eternally
By arms of mercy here below,
   The folds of Calvary.

This confidence I bring
   That fears will all allay,
As tears of sorrow by this King
   Are gently wiped away.
   I'll turn my gaze to see
   My risen glorious Lord,
And thank Him for the victory,
   The promise of His word.

The end of faith He shows,
   The fulness of His love,
And how He spares me from my foes
   In bringing me above.
   This is my home at last,
   Where Jesus will me greet;
The crown He gives, I gladly cast
   Beneath His feet.

           © *Author*

2083   John Newton   CM
He that hath an ear, let him hear what the Spirit saith unto the churches; He that overcometh shall not be hurt of the second death. *Revelation 2:11*

The message first to Smyrna sent,
   A message full of grace;
To all the Saviour's flock is meant,
   In every age and place.

Thus to His church, His chosen bride,
   Saith the great First and Last;
Who ever lives, though once He died,
   'Hold Thy profession fast.

'Thy works and sorrows well I know,
   Performed and borne for Me;
Poor though thou art, despised and low,
   Yet who is rich like thee?

'I know thy foes, and what they say,
   How long they have blasphemed;
The synagogue of Satan, they,
   Though they would Jews be deemed.

'Though Satan for a season rage,
   And prisons be your lot;
I am your Friend, and I engage
   You shall not be forgot.

'Be faithful unto death, nor fear
   A few short days of strife;
Behold! the prize you soon shall wear,
   A crown of endless life!'

Hear what the holy Spirit saith
   Of all who overcome;
'They shall escape the second death,
   The sinner's awful doom!'

2084   William Cowper   76 76 77 76
I know Thy works, that Thou hast a name that
Thou livest, and art dead…
Revelation 3:1-6

'Write to Sardis,' saith the Lord,
    And write what He declares;
He whose Spirit, and whose word,
    Upholds the seven stars:
'All thy works and ways I search,
    Find thy zeal and love decayed;
Thou art called a living church,
    But thou art cold and dead.

'Watch, remember, seek and strive,
    Exert thy former pains;
Let thy timely care revive,
    And strengthen what remains:
Cleanse thine heart, thy works amend,
    Former times to mind recall;
Lest My sudden stroke descend,
    And finish thee once for all.

'Yet I number now, in thee,
    A few that are upright;
These My Father's face shall see,
    And walk with Me in white:
When in judgment I appear,
    They for Mine shall be confessed;
Let My faithful servants hear,
    And woe be to the rest.'

2085   Anne Steele   LM
He that overcometh, the same shall be clothed
in white raiment; and I will not blot out his
name out of the book of life, but I will confess
his name before My Father, and before His
angels.
Revelation 3:5

To Jesus, our victorious Lord,
    The praises of our lives belong;
For ever be His name adored;
    Sweet theme of every thankful song.

Lost in despair, beset with foes,
    Undone, and perishing we lay;
His pity melted o'er our woes,
    And saved the trembling, dying prey.

He fought, He conquered though He fell,
    While with His last expiring breath,
He triumphed o'er the powers of hell,
    And by His dying vanquished death.

Though still reviving foes arise,
    Temptations, sins, and doubts appear,
And pain our hearts, and fill our eyes
    With many a groan, and many a tear;

Still may we fight, and still prevail,
    In our Almighty Leader's name;
His strength, whene'er our spirits fail,
    Can all our active powers inflame.

2086   John Newton   LM
These things saith He that is holy, He that is
true, He that hath the key of David…
Revelation 3:7-13

Thus saith the holy One and true,
To His belovèd faithful few;
'Of heaven and hell I hold the keys,
To shut, or open, as I please.

'I know thy works, and I approve,
Though small thy strength, sincere thy love;
Go on, My word and name to own,
For none shall rob thee of thy crown.

'Before thee see My mercy's door
Stands open wide to shut no more;
Fear not temptation's fiery day,
For I will be thy strength and stay.

'Thou hast My promise, hold it fast,
The trying hour will soon be past;
Rejoice, for lo! I quickly come,
To take thee to My heavenly home.

'A pillar there, no more to move,
Inscribed with all My names of love;
A monument of mighty grace,
Thou shalt for ever have a place.'

Such is the conqueror's reward,
Prepared and promised by the Lord!
Let him that has the ear of faith,
Attend to what the Spirit saith.

2087　John Newton　LM
These things saith the Amen, the faithful and true witness, the beginning of the creation of God... *Revelation 3:14-20*

Hear what the Lord, the great Amen,
　The true and faithful Witness says!
He formed the vast creation's plan,
　And searches all our hearts and ways.

To some He speaks as once of old,
　'I know thee, thy profession's vain;
Since thou art neither hot nor cold,
　I'll spit thee from Me with disdain.

'Thou boastest, 'I am wise and rich,
　Increased in goods and nothing need;'
And dost not know thou art a wretch,
　Naked and poor, and blind and dead.

'Yet while I thus rebuke, I love,
　My message is in mercy sent;
That thou mayest My compassion prove,
　I can forgive, if thou repent.

'Wouldst thou be truly rich and wise?
　Come, buy My gold in fire well tried,
My ointment to anoint thine eyes,
　My robe, thy nakedness to hide.

'See at thy door I stand and knock!
　Poor sinner, shall I wait in vain?
Quickly thy stubborn heart unlock,
　That I may enter with My train.

'Thou canst not entertain a king,
　Unworthy thou of such a Guest!
But I My own provisions bring,
　To make thy soul a heavenly feast.'

2088　Isaac Watts　LM
As many as I love, I rebuke and chasten: be zealous therefore, and repent. *Revelation 3:19*

Awake my zeal, awake my love,
　To serve my Saviour here below,
In works which perfect saints above,
　And holy angels cannot do.

Awake my charity, to feed
　The hungry soul, and clothe the poor:
In heaven are found no sons of need,
　There all these duties are no more.

Subdue thy passions, O my soul!
　Maintain the fight, thy work pursue;
Daily thy rising sins control,
　And be thy victories ever new.

The land of triumph lies on high,
　There are no fields of battle there;
Lord, I would conquer till I die,
　And finish all the glorious war.

Let every flying hour confess
　I gain Thy gospel fresh renown;
And when my life and labours cease,
　May I possess the promised crown!

2089　John Newton　CM
To him that overcometh will I grant to sit with Me in My throne, even as I also overcame, and am set down with My Father in His throne. *Revelation 3:21*

Rejoice, believer, in the Lord,
　Who makes your cause His own;
The hope that's built upon His word
　Can ne'er be overthrown.

Though many foes beset your road
　And feeble is your arm,
Your life is hid with Christ in God
　Beyond the reach of harm.

Weak as you are, you shall not faint;
　Or fainting, shall not die;
Jesus, the strength of every saint,
　Will aid you from on high.

Though unperceived by mortal sense,
　Faith sees Him always near,
A guide, a glory, a defence;
　Then what have you to fear?

As surely as He overcame
　And triumphed once for you;
So surely you that love His name
　Shall triumph in Him too.

2090　Reginald Heber　11 12 12 10
Holy, holy, holy, Lord God Almighty, which was, and is, and is to come. *Revelation 4:8*

Holy, holy, holy! Lord God Almighty;
Gratefully adoring, our songs shall rise to Thee:
Holy, holy, holy! merciful and mighty,
God in three Persons, blessèd Trinity!

Holy, holy, holy! all the saints adore Thee,
Casting down their golden crowns around the
　glassy sea;
Cherubim and seraphim falling down before Thee,
Who wast, and art, and evermore shalt be.

Holy, holy, holy! though the darkness hide Thee,
Though the eye of sinful man Thy glory may not
  see;
Only Thou art holy: there is none beside Thee,
Perfect in power, in love, and purity.

Holy, holy, holy! Lord God Almighty,
All Thy works shall praise Thy name, in earth, and
  sky, and sea;
Holy, holy, holy! merciful and mighty,
God in three Persons, blessèd Trinity!

2091   Joseph Hoskins   LM
Who liveth for ever and ever.
Revelation 4:9

Ye mourning souls, dry up your tears
Dismiss your gloomy, groundless fears,
And let your hearts with this revive,
That Jesus Christ is yet alive.

His saints He loves, and never leaves;
The chief of sinners He receives;
Let then your hearts with this revive,
The sinner's Friend is yet alive.

He'll guard your souls from every ill,
His largest promises fulfil;
Then let your hearts with this revive,
That Jesus Christ is yet alive.

What though you fear to launch away,
And quit this tenement of clay:
O, let your hearts with this revive,
That Jesus Christ is yet alive!

Abundant grace He will afford,
Till you are present with the Lord;
And prove what you have heard before
That Jesus lives for evermore.

2092   Anne Steele   LM
**The four and twenty elders fall down before
Him.** *Revelation 4:10*

O for a sweet inspiring ray,
  To animate our feeble strains,
From the bright realms of endless day,
  The blissful realms where Jesus reigns.

There, low before His glorious throne,
  Adoring saints and angels fall;
And with delightful worship, own
  His smile their bliss, their heaven, their all.

Immortal glories crown His head;
  While tuneful hallelujahs rise,
And love, and joy, and triumph spread
  Through all th' assemblies of the skies.

He smiles, and seraphs tune their songs
  To boundless rapture while they gaze:
Ten thousand thousand joyful tongues
  Resound His everlasting praise.

Dear Saviour! let Thy Spirit seal
  Our interest in that blissful place;
Till death remove the mortal veil,
  And we behold Thy lovely face.

2093   Isaac Watts   CM
**And I beheld, and, lo, in the midst of the
throne and of the four beasts, and in the midst
of the elders, stood a Lamb as it had been
slain.** *Revelation 5:6*

Behold the glories of the Lamb,
  Amidst His Father's throne;
Prepare new honours for His name,
  And songs before unknown.

Let elders worship at His feet;
  The church adore around;
With vials full of odours sweet,
  And harps of sweeter sound.

Those are the prayers of the saints,
  And these the hymns they raise
Jesus is kind to our complaints,
  He loves to hear our praise.

Eternal Father, who shall look
  Into Thy secret will?
Who but the Son shall take that book,
  And open every seal?

He shall fulfil Thy great decrees;
  The Son deserves it well;
Lo! in His hands the sovereign keys
  Of heaven, and death, and hell.

Now to the Lamb that once was slain,
  Be endless blessings paid;
Salvation, glory, joy remain
  For ever on Thy head.

Thou hast redeemed our souls with blood,
  Hast set the prisoners free,
Hast made us kings and priests to God,
  And we shall reign with Thee.

The worlds of nature and of grace
  Are put beneath Thy power;
Then shorten these delaying days,
  And bring the promised hour.

2094   Joseph Hart   CM
**And I beheld, and, lo, in the midst of the
throne and of the four beasts, and in the midst
of the elders, stood a Lamb as it had been
slain.** *Revelation 5:6*

We sing Thy praise, exalted Lamb,
  Who sitt'st upon Thy throne;
Ten thousand blessings on Thy name,
  Who worthy art alone.

Thy bruisèd, broken body bore
  Our sins upon the tree;
And now Thou liv'st for evermore,
  And now we live through Thee.

Poor sinners, sing the Lamb that died;
  What theme can sound so sweet?
His drooping head, His streaming side,
  His piercèd hands and feet.

With all that scene of suffering love
  Which faith presents to view:
For now He lives and reigns above,
  And lives and reigns for you.

Was ever grace, Lord, rich as Thine?
  Can aught be with it named?
What powerful beams of love divine
  Thy tender heart inflamed!

Ye angels, hymn His glorious name,
  Who loved and conquered thus;
And we will likewise praise the Lamb,
  For He was slain for us.

2095   Richard Burnham   88 88 D
**And I beheld, and, lo, in the midst of the
throne and of the four beasts, and in the midst
of the elders, stood a Lamb as it had been
slain.** *Revelation 5:6*

Come, all ye redeemed and unite
  In high hallelujahs to God;
And sing with increasing delight,
  O sing of the Lamb and His blood!
Sing, sing His superlative worth,
  Till we His full glory obtain;
The chorus resound through the earth,
  Of 'Worthy the Lamb that was slain!'

We'll sing of the conquest complete.
  Obtained by His wonderful hand;
A conquest eternally great,
  And shall to eternity stand.
We'll sing the grand Conqueror's praise,
  And never, O never refrain;
The chorus to heaven we'll raise,
  Of 'Worthy the Lamb that was slain!'

We'd sing, and exult, and go on,
  And wonder, and love, and admire;
Still sing the atonement alone,
  And sing till our souls are on fire:
And when the high throne we surround,
  Releasèd from darkness and pain,
All heaven shall swell with the sound.
  Of 'Worthy the Lamb that was slain!'

2096   William Dix   87 87 D
**And they sung a new song, saying, Thou art
worthy to take the book, and to open the seals
thereof.** *Revelation 5:9*

Hallelujah! sing to Jesus,
  His the sceptre, His the throne;
Hallelujah! His the triumph,
  His the victory alone;
Hark the songs of peaceful Zion
  Thunder like a mighty flood;
Jesus out of every nation
  Hath redeemed us by His blood.

Hallelujah! not as orphans
  Are we left in sorrow now;
Hallelujah! He is near us,
  Faith believes, nor questions how:
Though the cloud from sight received Him
  When the forty days were o'er.
Shall our hearts forget His promise,
  'I am with you evermore'?

Hallelujah! bread of heaven!
  Thou on earth our food, our stay;
Hallelujah! here the sinful
  Flee to Thee from day to day;
Intercessor, Friend of sinners,
  Earth's Redeemer, plead for me,
Where the songs of all the sinless
  Sweep across the crystal sea.

Hallelujah! Hallelujah!
  Glory be to God on high;
To the Father, and the Saviour,
  Who has gained the victory;
Glory to the Holy Spirit,
  Fount of love and sanctity;
Hallelujah! Hallelujah!
  To the triune Majesty.

2097   Joseph Swain   LM
**And they sung a new song, saying, Thou art
worthy to take the book, and to open the seals
thereof.** *Revelation 5:9*

To Him that loved us, ere we lay
Concealed within the passive clay;
To Him that loved us though we fell,
And saved us from the pains of hell!

To Him that found us dead in sin,
And planted holy life within;
To Him that taught our feet the way
From endless night to endless day;

To Him that wrought our righteousness,
And sanctified us by His grace;
To Him that brought us back to God,
Through the red sea of His own blood:

To Him that sits upon the throne,
The great eternal Three in One;
To Him let saints and angels raise
An everlasting song of praise.

2098   Katherine Hankey   76 76 D + refrain
And they sung a new song, saying, Thou art worthy to take the book, and to open the seals thereof. *Revelation 5:9*

I love to tell the story
Of unseen things above,
Of Jesus and His glory,
Of Jesus and His love;
I love to tell the story,
Because I know it's true;
It satisfies my longings,
As nothing else would do.

I love to tell the story,
'Twill be my theme in glory,
To tell the old, old story
Of Jesus and His love.

I love to tell the story:
'Tis pleasant to repeat
What seems, each time I tell it,
More wonderfully sweet;
I love to tell the story:
For some have never heard
The message of salvation
From God's own holy word.

I love to tell the story:
For those who know it best
Seem hungering and thirsting
To hear it like the rest;
And when in scenes of glory
I sing the new, new song,
'Twill be the old, old story
That I have loved so long.

2099   Henry Alford   76 86 D
And I beheld, and I heard the voice of many angels round about the throne and the beasts and the elders: and the number of them was ten thousand times ten thousand, and thousands of thousands. *Revelation 5:11*

Ten thousand times ten thousand
In sparkling raiment bright;
The armies of the ransomed saints
Throng up the steeps of light:
'Tis finished, all is finished,
Their fight with death and sin;
Fling open wide the golden gates
And let the victors in.

What rush of hallelujahs
Fills all the earth and sky!
What ringing of a thousand harps
Bespeaks the triumph nigh!
O day, for which creation
And all its tribes were made!
O joy, for all its former woes
A thousandfold repaid!

O then what raptured greetings
On Canaan's happy shore,
What knitting severed friendships up
Where partings are no more!
Then eyes with joy shall sparkle
That brimmed with tears of late;
Orphans no longer fatherless,
Nor widows desolate.

Bring near Thy great salvation,
Thou Lamb for sinners slain;
Fill up the roll of Thine elect,
Then take Thy power and reign!
Appear, Desire of nations,
Thine exiles long for home;
Show in the heavens Thy promised sign;
Thou Prince and Saviour, come!

2100   James Allen, C Batty   664 6664
Worthy is the Lamb that was slain to receive power, and riches, and wisdom, and strength, and honour, and glory, and blessing.
Revelation 5:12

Glory to God on high!
Let earth and skies reply,
Praise ye His name!
His love and grace adore,
Who all our sorrow bore;
Sing aloud evermore,
'Worthy the Lamb!'

Jesus, our Lord and God,
Bore sin's tremendous load!
　Praise ye His name!
Tell what His arm has done,
What spoils from death He won;
Sing His great name alone;
　'Worthy the Lamb!'

While they around the throne
Cheerfully join in one,
　Praising His name,
Ye who have felt His blood
Sealing your peace with God,
Sound His dear fame abroad;
　'Worthy the Lamb!'

ISAAC WATTS 1674-1748

2101　John Bakewell　　　87 87 D
Worthy is the Lamb that was slain to receive power, and riches, and wisdom, and strength, and honour, and glory, and blessing.
Revelation 5:12

Hail, Thou once despisèd Jesus!
　Hail, Thou Galilean King!
Thou didst suffer to release us;
　Thou didst free salvation bring.
Hail, Thou agonizing Saviour,
　Bearer of our sin and shame!
By Thy merits we find favour;
　Life is given through Thy name.

Paschal Lamb, by God appointed,
　All our sins on Thee were laid;
By almighty love anointed,
　Thou hast full atonement made:
All Thy people are forgiven
　Through the virtue of Thy blood;
Opened is the gate of heaven;
　Peace is made 'twixt man and God.

Jesus, hail! enthroned in glory,
　There for ever to abide;
All the heavenly host adore Thee,
　Seated at Thy Father's side;
There for sinners Thou art pleading,
　There Thou dost our place prepare,
Ever for us interceding,
　Till in glory we appear.

Worship, honour, power and blessing,
　Thou art worthy to receive;
Loudest praises without ceasing,
　Meet it is for us to give.
Help, ye bright, angelic spirits!
　Bring your sweetest, noblest lays;
Help to sing our Saviour's merits,
　Help to chant Immanuel's praise!

2102　Isaac Watts　　　　　CM
Worthy is the Lamb that was slain to receive power, and riches, and wisdom, and strength, and honour, and glory, and blessing.
Revelation 5:12

Come let us join our cheerful songs
　With angels round the throne;
Ten thousand thousand are their tongues,
　But all their joys are one.

'Worthy the Lamb that died,' they cry,
　'To be exalted thus.'
'Worthy the Lamb,' our lips reply,
　'For He was slain for us.'

Jesus is worthy to receive
　Honour and power divine;
And blessings more than we can give,
　Be, Lord, for ever Thine.

Let all that dwell above the sky,
　And air, and earth, and seas,
Conspire to lift Thy glories high,
　And speak Thy endless praise.

The whole creation join in one,
　To bless the sacred name
Of Him that sits upon the throne,
　And to adore the Lamb.

2103　John Kent　　　84 84 888 4
Worthy is the Lamb. *Revelation 5:12*

'Tis the church triumphant singing,
　　'Worthy the Lamb!'
Heaven throughout with praises ringing,
　　'Worthy the Lamb!'
Thrones and powers before Him bending,
Odours sweet with voice ascending
Swell the chorus never ending,
　　'Worthy the Lamb!'

Every kindred, tongue and nation—
  'Worthy the Lamb!'
Join to sing the great salvation;
  'Worthy the Lamb!'
Loud as mighty thunders roaring,
Floods of mighty waters pouring,
Prostrate at His feet adoring,
  'Worthy the Lamb!'

Harps and songs for ever sounding
  'Worthy the Lamb!'
Mighty grace o'er sin abounding;
  'Worthy the Lamb!'
By His blood He dearly bought us;
Wandering from the fold He sought us
And to glory safely brought us:
  'Worthy the Lamb!'

Sing with blest anticipation,
  'Worthy the Lamb!'
Through the vale of tribulation,
  'Worthy the Lamb!'
Sweetest notes, all notes excelling,
On the theme for ever dwelling,
Still untold, though ever telling,
  'Worthy the Lamb!'

2104   Timothy Dudley-Smith   87 87 D
Blessing, and honour, and glory, and power, be unto Him that sitteth upon the throne, and unto the Lamb for ever and ever.
Revelation 5:13

Heavenly hosts in ceaseless worship
  'Holy, holy, holy' cry;
'He who is, who was and will be,
  God Almighty, Lord most high.'
Praise and honour, power and glory,
  Be to Him who reigns alone!
We, with all His hands have fashioned,
  Fall before the Father's throne.

All creation, all redemption,
  Join to sing the Saviour's worth;
Lamb of God, whose blood has bought us,
  Kings and priests, to reign on earth.
Wealth and wisdom, power and glory,
  Honour, might, dominion, praise,
Now be His from all His creatures
  And to everlasting days!

'Heavenly hosts in ceaseless worship' by Timothy Dudley-Smith (b.1926). © Timothy Dudley-Smith in Europe and Africa. © Hope Publishing Company in the United States of America and the rest of the world. Reproduced by permission of Oxford University Press . All rights reserved.

2105   William Williams, tr W Howells   87 87 D
He went forth conquering, and to conquer.
Revelation 6:2

Onward march, all-conquering Jesus,
  Gird Thee on Thy mighty sword;
Sinful earth can ne'er oppose Thee;
  Hell itself quails at Thy word.
Thy great name is so exalted,
  Every foe shrinks back in fear;
Terror creeps through all creation,
  When it knows that Thou art near.

Free my soul from sin's foul bondage;
  Hasten now the glorious dawn;
Break proud Babel's gates in sunder;
  Let the massive bolts be drawn.
Forth, like ocean's heaving surges,
  Bring in myriads ransomed slaves,
Host on host, with shouts of triumph,
  Endless, countless as the waves.

Even today I hear sweet music,
  Praises of a blood-freed throng;
Full deliverance, glorious freedom,
  Are their themes for endless song;
Whiter than the snow their raiment,
  Victor palms they wave on high,
As they pass, with fullest glory,
  Into life's felicity.

How my raptured soul rejoices
  That the jubilee is near;
Every word will be accomplished
  Spoken by our Saviour here.
North and South, in countless myriads,
  From earth's darkest ends they come,
With the dance and gladsome music,
  Into heaven's eternal home.

2106   Isaac Watts   66 66 88
He went forth conquering, and to conquer.
Revelation 6:2

My dear Almighty Lord,
  My Conqueror and my King!
Thy sceptre and Thy sword,
  Thy reigning grace I sing:
Thine is the power; behold I sit,
In willing bonds beneath Thy feet.

Now let my soul arise,
  And tread the tempter down;
My Captain leads me forth
  To conquest and a crown:
A feeble saint shall win the day,
Though death and hell obstruct the way.

Should all the hosts of death,
  And powers of hell unknown,
Put their most dreadful forms
  Of rage and mischief on,
I shall be safe; for Christ displays
Superior power, and guardian grace.

2107   Charitie Bancroft   76 76
Clothed with white robes.
Revelation 7:9

O for the robe of whiteness,
  O for the tearless eyes;
O for the glorious brightness
  Of the unclouded skies!

O for the 'no more weeping'
  Within the land of love:
The endless joy of keeping
  The bridal feast above.

O for the hour of seeing
  My Saviour face to face:
The joy of ever being
  In that sweet meeting-place.

Jesus, Thou King of glory,
  I soon shall dwell with Thee;
And sing the wondrous story
  Of all Thy love to me.

2108   Josiah Conder   77 77 77
**And all the angels stood round about the
throne, and about the elders and the four
beasts, and fell before the throne on their
faces, and worshipped God.**
Revelation 7:11

Now with angels round the throne,
  Cherubim and seraphim,
And the church, which still is one,
  Let us swell the solemn hymn;
Glory to the great I AM!
Glory to the Victim-Lamb.

Blessing, honour, glory, might,
  And dominion infinite.
To the Father of our Lord,
  To the Spirit and the Word:
As it was all worlds before,
Is, and shall be evermore.

2109   Isaac Watts, William Cameron   CM
**And one of the elders answered, saying unto
me, What are these which are arrayed in white
robes? and whence came they?...**
Revelation 7:13-17

How bright these glorious spirits shine!
  Whence all their white array?
How came they to the blissful seats
  Of everlasting day?

Lo! these are they from sufferings great,
  Who came to realms of light;
And in the blood of Christ have washed
  Those robes that shine so bright.

Now with triumphal palms they stand
  Before the throne on high
And serve the God they love, amidst
  The glories of the sky.

Hunger and thirst are felt no more,
  Nor such with scorching ray;
God is their Sun, whose cheering beams
  Diffuse eternal day.

The Lamb, who dwells amidst the throne,
  Shall o'er them still preside,
Feed them with nourishment divine
  And all their footsteps guide.

'Midst pastures green He'll lead His flock,
  Where living streams appear;
And God the Lord from every eye
  Shall wipe away each tear.

To Father, Son and Holy Ghost,
  The God whom we adore,
Be glory, as it was, is now
  And shall be evermore.

2110   Charles Wesley   77 77
**And one of the elders answered, saying unto
me, What are these which are arrayed in white
robes? and whence came they?**
Revelation 7:13

Who are these arrayed in white,
  Brighter than the noonday sun,
Foremost of the sons of light,
  Nearest the eternal throne?

These are they who bore the cross,
  Faithful to their Master died,
Suffered in His righteous cause,
  Followers of the Crucified.

Out of great distress they came,
    And their robes by faith below,
In the blood of Christ the Lamb,
    They have washed as white as snow.

More than conquerors at last,
    Here they find their trials o'er:
They have all their sufferings passed,
    Hunger now and thirst no more.

He that on the throne doth reign
    Them for evermore shall feed,
With the tree of life sustain,
    To the living fountain lead.

He shall all their griefs remove,
    He shall all their wants supply;
God Himself, the God of love,
    Tears shall wipe from every eye.

2111   Anne Shepherd   CM + refrain

Therefore are they before the throne of God, and serve Him day and night in His temple: and He that sitteth on the throne shall dwell among them. *Revelation 7:15*

Around the throne of God in heaven
    Thousands of children stand,
Children whose sins are all forgiven,
    A holy, happy band:

    Singing 'glory, glory, glory!'
    Singing 'glory, glory, glory!'

In flowing robes of spotless white
    See everyone arrayed:
Dwelling in everlasting light,
    And joys that never fade.

Once they were little ones like you
    And lived on earth below,
They could not praise as they do now
    The Lord who loved them so.

What brought them to that world above,
    That heaven so bright and fair,
Where all is peace and joy and love?
    How came those children there?

Because the Saviour shed His blood
    To wash away their sin;
Bathed in that pure and precious flood,
    Behold them white and clean!

On earth they sought the Saviour's grace,
    On earth they loved His name;
So now they see His blessèd face
    And stand before the Lamb.

2112   Joseph Hart   CM

Therefore are they before the throne of God, and serve Him day and night in His temple: and He that sitteth on the throne shall dwell among them. *Revelation 7:15*

Ye souls that trust in Christ, rejoice;
    Your sins are all forgiven;
Let every Christian lift His voice,
    And sing the joys of heaven.

Heaven is that holy, happy place,
    Where sin no more defiles;
Where God unveils His blissful face,
    And looks, and loves, and smiles;

Lord, as Thou show'st Thy glory there,
    Make known Thy grace to us;
And heaven will not be wanting here
    While we can hymn Thee thus:

'Jesus, our dear Redeemer, died
    That we might be forgiven;
Rose that we might be justified,
    And sends the Spirit from heaven.'

2113   Robert Elliott, A Toplady   CM

Therefore are they before the throne of God, and serve Him day and night in His temple: and He that sitteth on the throne shall dwell among them. *Revelation 7:15*

How happy are the souls above,
    From sin and sorrow free!
With Jesus they are now at rest,
    And all His glory see.

'Worthy the Lamb!' aloud they cry,
    'That brought us here to God!'
In ceaseless hymns of praise they shout
    The merits of His blood.

With wondering joy they recollect
    Their fears and dangers past;
And bless the wisdom, power, and love
    Which brought them safe at last.

They follow the exalted Lamb
    Where'er they see Him go;
And at the footstool of His grace
    Their blood-bought crowns they throw.

Lord, let the merit of Thy death
    To me be likewise given;
And I with them will shout Thy praise
    Through all the courts of heaven.

2114   Charles Wesley   87 87
For the Lamb which is in the midst of the throne shall feed them, and shall lead them unto living fountains of waters: and God shall wipe away all tears from their eyes.
Revelation 7:17

Happy soul! thy days are ended,
   All thy mourning hours below;
Go, by angel guards attended,
   To thy waiting Saviour, go!

Anxious to receive thy spirit,
   Lo! Immanuel dwells above;
Pleads the value of His merit,
   Reaches out the crown of love.

Struggle through thy latest passion;
   Let no fear alarm thy breast:
God shall bring thee full salvation,
   God shall give thee endless rest.

For the joy He sets before thee,
   Bear a momentary pain;
Die to lead a life of glory!
   Suffer, with thy Lord to reign.

2115   James Montgomery   77 77 D
The kingdoms of this world are become the kingdoms of our Lord, and of His Christ; and He shall reign for ever and ever.
Revelation 11:15

Hark! the song of jubilee,
   Loud as mighty thunders' roar,
Or the fulness of the sea
   When it breaks upon the shore:
Hallelujah! for the Lord
   God Omnipotent shall reign;
Hallelujah! let the word
   Echo round the earth and main.

Hallelujah! hark! the sound,
   From the centre to the skies,
Wakes above, beneath, around,
   All creation's harmonies:
See Jehovah's banner furled,
   Sheathed His sword: He speaks, it's done;
And the kingdoms of this world
   Are the kingdom of His Son.

He shall reign from pole to pole
   With illimitable sway;
He shall reign when, like a scroll,
   Yonder heavens have passed away:
Then the end: beneath His rod
   Man's last enemy shall fall;
Hallelujah! Christ in God,
   God in Christ, is All in all.

2116   John Kent   LM
And I looked, and, lo, a Lamb stood on the mount Zion, and with Him an hundred forty and four thousand, having His Father's name written in their foreheads.
Revelation 14:1

On Zion's glorious summit stood
A numerous host redeemed by blood;
They hymned their King in strains divine,
I heard the song and strove to join.

Here all who suffered sword and flame,
For truth, and Jesus' lovely name,
Shout victory now, and hail the Lamb,
And bow before the great I AM.

While everlasting ages roll,
Eternal love shall feast their soul;
And scenes of bliss, for ever new,
Rise in succession to their view.

Here Mary and Manasseh view,
The dying thief, and Abraham too;
With equal love their spirits flame,
The same their joy, their song the same.

O sweet employ, to sing and trace
The amazing heights and depths of grace;
And spend, from sin and sorrow free,
A blissful vast eternity!

O what a sweet exalted song,
When every tribe and every tongue,
Redeemed by blood, with Christ appear,
And join in one full chorus there!

My soul anticipates the day,
Would stretch her wings and soar away,
To aid the song, a palm to bear,
And bow, the chief of sinners, there.

2117   Thomas Kelly   87 87 77
I heard the voice of harpers harping with their harps. *Revelation 14:2*

Hark, ten thousand harps and voices
   Sound the note of praise above!
Jesus reigns, and heaven rejoices;
   Jesus reigns, the God of love;
See, He fills yon azure throne!
Jesus rules the world alone.

Come, ye saints, unite your praises
   With the angels round His throne;
Soon we hope the Lord will raise us
   To the place where He is gone.
Meet it is that we should sing,
Glory, glory to our King!

Sing how Jesus came from heaven,
 How He bore the cross below;
How all power to Him is given;
 How He reigns in glory now:
It's a great and endless theme!
O, it's sweet to sing of Him!

King of Glory, reign for ever!
 Thine an everlasting crown!
Nothing from Thy love shall sever
 Those whom Thou hast made Thine own
Happy objects of Thy grace,
Destined to behold Thy face,

Saviour, hasten Thine appearing;
 Bring, O bring the glorious day;
When, the awful summons hearing,
 Heaven and earth shall pass away;
Then, with golden harps we'll sing,
'Glory, glory to our King!'

2118 John Kent   886 D
**And they sung as it were a new song before
the throne.** *Revelation 14:3*

Come Christians, in our songs record,
The honours of our dying Lord,
 Triumphant over sin;
How sweet the song there's none can say,
But those whose sins are washed away,
 Who feel the same within.

We claim no merit of our own,
But, self-condemned before Thy throne,
 Our hopes on Jesus place;
Though once in heart and life depraved,
We now can sing as sinners saved,
 And praise redeeming grace.

We'll sing the same while life shall last,
And when, at the archangel's blast,
 Our sleeping dust shall rise,
Then in a song for ever new,
The glorious theme we'll still pursue
 Throughout the azure skies.

Prepared of old, at God's right hand
Bright everlasting mansions stand
 For all the blood-bought race;
And till we reach those seats of bliss,
We'll sing no other song but this,
 'Salvation all of grace.'

2119 John Bode   76 76 D
**These are they which follow the Lamb
whithersoever He goeth.** *Revelation 14:4*

O Jesus, I have promised
 To serve Thee to the end;
Be Thou for ever near me,
 My Master and my Friend;
I shall not fear the battle
 If Thou art by my side,
Nor wander from the pathway
 If Thou wilt be my Guide.

O let me feel Thee near me;
 The world is ever near;
I see the sights that dazzle,
 The tempting sounds I hear;
My foes are ever near me,
 Around me and within;
But, Jesus, draw Thou nearer,
 And shield my soul from sin.

O let me hear Thee speaking
 In accents clear and still,
Above the storms of passion,
 The murmurs of self-will;
O speak to reassure me,
 To hasten, or control;
O speak, and make me listen,
 Thou Guardian of my soul.

O Jesus, Thou hast promised
 To all who follow Thee
That where Thou art in glory
 There shall Thy servant be;
And, Jesus, I have promised
 To serve Thee to the end;
O give me grace to follow
 My Master and my Friend.

O let me see Thy footmarks,
 And in them plant mine own;
My hope to follow duly
 Is in Thy strength alone.
O guide me, call me, draw me,
 Uphold me to the end;
And then in heaven receive me,
 My Saviour and my Friend.

2120 Joseph Hart 77 77 D
**These are they which follow the Lamb
whithersoever He goeth.** *Revelation 14:4*

Come ye humble sinner-train,
Souls for whom the Lamb was slain,
  Cheerful let us raise our voice;
  We have reason to rejoice.
Let us sing, with saints in heaven,
Life restored, and sin forgiven;
  Glory and eternal laud
  Be to our incarnate God.

Now look up with faith and see
Him that bled for you and me,
  Seated on His glorious throne,
  Interceding for His own.
What can Christians have to fear,
When they view the Saviour there?
  Hell is vanquished, heaven appeased,
  God is satisfied and pleased.

Snares and dangers may beset,
For we are but travellers yet.
  As the way, indeed, is hard,
  May we keep a constant guard.
Neither lifted up with air,
Nor dejected to despair;
  Always keeping Christ in view;
  He will bring us safely through.

2121 Isaac Watts CM
Blessed are the dead which die in the Lord.
Revelation 14:13

Hear what the voice from heaven proclaims
  For all the pious dead,
Sweet is the savour of their names,
  And soft their sleeping bed.

They die in Jesus, and are blessed;
  How kind their slumbers are!
From sufferings and from sins released,
  And freed from every snare.

Far from this world of toil and strife,
  They're present with the Lord:
The labours of their mortal life
  End in a large reward.

2122 William Hammond SM
**And they sing the song of Moses the servant
of God, and the song of the Lamb.**
Revelation 15:3

  Awake, and sing the song
  Of Moses and the Lamb;
Wake every heart and every tongue
  To praise the Saviour's name.

  Sing of His dying love;
  Sing of His rising power;
Sing how He intercedes above
  For those whose sins He bore.

  Ye pilgrims, on the road
  To Zion's city, sing;
Rejoice ye in the Lamb of God,
  In Christ, the eternal King.

  Soon shall we hear Him say,
  'Ye blessèd children, come!'
Soon will He call us hence away,
  And take His wanderers home.

  There shall each raptured tongue
  His endless praise proclaim,
And sing in sweeter notes the song
  Of Moses and the Lamb.

2123 Isaac Watts LM
For He is Lord of lords, and King of kings.
Revelation 17:14

Jesus, Thou everlasting King,
Accept the tribute which we bring;
Accept the well-deserved renown,
And wear our praises as Thy crown.

Let every act of worship be
Like our espousals, Lord, to Thee;
Like the dear hour when from above
We first received Thy pledge of love.

The gladness of that happy day—
Our hearts would wish it long to stay;
Nor let our faith forsake its hold,
Nor comfort sink, nor love grow cold.

Each following minute as it flies,
Increase Thy praise, improve our joys,
Till we are raised to sing Thy name
At the great Supper of the Lamb.

O that the months would roll away
And bring that coronation day!
The King of grace shall fill the throne,
His Father's glory all His own.

2124   Thomas Kelly   87 87 47
Alleluia; Salvation, and glory, and honour, and power, unto the Lord our God. *Revelation 19:1*

Praise the Lord who died to save us,
    Praise His name for ever dear!
Praise His blessèd name who gave us
    Eyes to see and ears to hear!
        Praise the Saviour,
    Object of our love and fear!

Grace it was, and grace abounding,
    Brought Him down to save the lost;
You above, His throne surrounding,
    Praise Him, praise Him, all His host!
        Saints adore Him!
    You are they who owe Him most.

You, of all His hand created,
    Objects are of grace alone;
Aliens once but reinstated,
    Destined now to fill a throne:
        Sing with wonder!
    Sing of what our Lord has done.

Praise His name who died to save us,
    'Tis by Him His people live!
And in Him the Father gave us
    All that boundless love could give;
        Life eternal
    In our Saviour we receive.

2125   Joseph Irons   CM
And again they said, Alleluia. *Revelation 19:3*

Hark! how the choir around the throne
    Adore their glorious King!
They drink full draughts of bliss unknown
    And hallelujah sing!

They range through heaven's unmeasured
        plain
    And find new cause for praise:
See more of Jesus, and again
    Loud hallelujahs raise!

Anon the pearly gates unfold,
    An heir of bliss draws nigh;
Again they strike their harps of gold
    And hallelujah cry!

Another sinner, born of God,
    Makes heaven's vast concave ring;
Again they Jesus' love record
    And hallelujah sing!

At last the ransomed throng, complete,
    Is glorified throughout;
Again they bow at Jesus' feet
    And hallelujah shout!

Ere long I hope to join the throng
    Who bow before the King:
And, in one everlasting song,
    My hallelujah bring!

2126   Isaac Watts (alt)   LM
And a voice came out of the throne, saying, Praise our God, all ye His servants, and ye that fear Him, both small and great. *Revelation 19:5*

Praise, everlasting praise, be paid
To Him that earth's foundation laid;
Praise to the God, whose strong decrees,
Sway the creation as He please.

Praise to the goodness of the Lord,
Who rules His people by His word;
And there, as strong as His decrees,
He sets His kindest promises.

Firm are the words His prophets give,
Sweet words, on which His children live:
Each of them is the voice of God,
Who spoke, and spread the skies abroad.

Each of them powerful as that sound
That bid the new-made world go round;
And stronger than the solid poles
On which the wheel of nature rolls.

O, for a strong, a lasting faith,
To credit what th' Almighty saith!
Embrace the message of His Son,
And call the joys of heaven our own.

Then should the earth's old pillars shake,
And all the wheels of nature break.
Our steady souls should fear no more
Than solid rocks when billows roar.

Our everlasting hopes arise
Above the ruinable skies,
Where th' eternal Builder reigns,
And His own courts His power sustains.

2127   Josiah Conder   LM
Alleluia: for the Lord God omnipotent reigneth.
Revelation 19:6

The Lord is King! lift up your voice,
O earth, and all ye heavens, rejoice!
From world to world the joy shall ring,
'The Lord omnipotent is King!'

The Lord is King! who then shall dare
Resist His will, distrust His care,
Or murmur at His wise decrees,
Or doubt His royal promises?

The Lord is King! child of the dust,
The Judge of all the earth is just;
Holy and true are all His ways;
Let every creature speak His praise.

He reigns! ye saints, exalt your strains;
Your God is King, your Father reigns;
And He is at the Father's side,
The Man of love, the Crucified.

Come, make your wants, your burdens known:
He will present them at the throne;
And angel bands are waiting there,
His messages of love to bear.

One Lord, one empire, all secures;
He reigns, and life and death are yours;
Through earth and heaven one song shall ring,
'The Lord omnipotent is King!'

2128   Charles Wesley   10 10 11 11
Alleluia: for the Lord God omnipotent reigneth.
Revelation 19:6

Omnipotent Lord, my Saviour and King,
  Thy succour afford, Thy righteousness bring.
Thy promises bind Thee compassion to have;
Now, now let me find Thee almighty to save.

Lord, Thou art my hope; o'erwhelmèd with grief,
  To Thee I look up for certain relief;
I dread no denial, no danger I fear,
Nor start from the trial if Jesus be here.

Yes! God is above men, devils, and sin;
  My Jesus's love the battle shall win;
So wonderfully glorious His coming shall be,
His love all victorious shall conquer for me.

2129   Matthew Bridges, Godfrey Thring DSM
**His eyes were as a flame of fire, and on His
head were many crowns; and He had a name
written, that no man knew, but He Himself.**
Revelation 19:12

Crown Him with many crowns,
  The Lamb upon His throne;
Hark, how the heavenly anthem drowns
  All music but its own!
  Awake, my soul, and sing
  Of Him who died for Thee,
And hail Him as Thy matchless King,
  Through all eternity.

Crown Him the Son of God,
  Before the worlds began,
And ye who tread where He hath trod,
  Crown Him the Son of Man;
  Who every grief hath known
  That wrings the human breast
And takes and bears them for His own,
  That all in Him may rest.

Crown Him the Lord of life,
  Who triumphed o'er the grave,
And rose victorious in the strife
  For those He came to save:
  His glories now we sing
  Who died, and rose on high;
Who died eternal life to bring,
  And lives that death may die.

Crown Him the Lord of love;
  Behold His hands and side,
Those wounds yet visible above
  In beauty glorified:
  No angel in the sky
  Can fully bear that sight,
But downward bends His burning eye
  At mysteries so bright.

Crown Him the Lord of peace,
  Whose power a sceptre sways
From pole to pole, that wars may cease,
  And all be prayer and praise:
  His reign shall know no end,
  And round His piercèd feet
Fair flowers of Paradise extend
  Their fragrance ever sweet.

Crown Him the Lord of years,
  The Potentate of time,
Creator of the rolling spheres,
  Ineffably sublime!
  All hail, Redeemer, hail!
  For Thou hast died for me;
Thy praise shall never, never fail
  Throughout eternity.

2130 Thomas Kelly (alt) 77 77
And He hath on His vesture and on His thigh a name written, KING OF KINGS, AND LORD OF LORDS. *Revelation 19:16*

'King of kings, and Lord of lords!'
These are great and awesome words;
'Tis to Jesus they belong;
Let His people raise their song.

Rich in glory, Thou didst stoop;
Thou that art Thy people's hope;
Thou wast poor, that they might be
Rich in glory, Lord, with Thee.

When we think of love like this,
Joy and shame our hearts possess;
Joy, that Thou couldst pity thus;
Shame, for such returns from us.

Yet we hope the day to see,
When we shall from earth be free;
Borne aloft, to heaven be brought,
There to praise Thee as we ought.

While we still continue here,
Let this hope our spirits cheer.
Till in heaven Thy face we see,
Teach us, Lord, to live to Thee.

2131 Vernon Higham 88 88 88
And I saw a great white throne, and Him that sat on it, from whose face the earth and the heaven fled away; and there was found no place for them. *Revelation 20:11*

What wondrous sight now fills the skies,
    The terror of the Lord displayed?
The final breath of time now dies,
    And all the scenes of life are played;
The sea gives up its ancient dead,
And shrill the call of trumpet dread.

Sad lake, its waters full of gall,
    Within its depths the second death;
I saw the dead both great and small,
    Before the God of life and breath,
With book of doom condemning men,
And book of life, the grace of heaven.

O God of love and justice pure,
    Cover my soul with righteousness;
Send to my heart the wondrous cure,
    Thy precious blood and cleansing dress,
That I may stand in bold array,
And sing with joy on Judgement Day.
© *Author*

2132 Bernard of Cluny 12th Cent., tr. J Neale
76 76 D
And I John saw the holy city, new Jerusalem. *Revelation 21:2*

Jerusalem, the golden,
    With milk and honey blest,
Beneath thy contemplation
    Sink heart and voice oppressed;
I know not, O I know not,
    What joys are waiting there,
What radiancy of glory,
    What bliss beyond compare!

They stand, those halls of Zion,
    All jubilant with song
And bright with many an angel
    And all the martyr throng.
The Prince is ever with them,
    The daylight is serene,
The pastures of the blessèd
    Are decked with living green.

There is the throne of David
    And there, from care released,
The song of them that triumph,
    The shout of them that feast,
And they who, with their leader,
    Have conquered in the fight,
For ever and for ever
    Are clad in robes of white.

O sweet and blessèd country,
    The home of God's elect!
O sweet and blessèd country,
    That eager hearts expect!
Jesus, in mercy bring us
    To that dear land of rest,
Who art, with God the Father
    And Spirit, ever blest!

2133   Vernon Higham   CM
And I John saw the holy city, new Jerusalem,
coming down from God out of heaven,
prepared as a bride adorned for her husband.
Revelation 21:2

There is a home with God above,
　A place of peace and joy;
A sweet inheritance of love
　Which nothing can destroy.

At last my soul shall enter in
　And join the happy throng;
A ransom paid for all my sin
　Shall be my joy and song.

Such sacrifice of costly grace;
　The Saviour died for me:
Enabled me to see His face,
　To live eternally.

Surrounded by such loveliness,
　My heart has lost all fear;
I see the Father's tenderness
　Who wipes away each tear.

Time and decay shall reign no more,
　For death has lost its sting.
The Victor rules forevermore,
　My Lord and glorious King.

The wonder of God's grace untold,
　The mysteries of His will,
He tenderly will now unfold,
　And show His sovereign skill.

The freedom of His presence gives
　Each precious soul delight,
And happy is the soul that lives
　To see this vision bright.
                              © *Author*

2134   Samuel Medley   CM
I will give unto him that is athirst of the
fountain of the water of life freely.
Revelation 21:6

O what amazing words of grace
　Are in the gospel found!
Suited to every sinner's case
　Who knows the joyful sound.

Come, then, with all your wants and wounds,
　Your every burden bring;
Here love, eternal love, abounds,
　A deep celestial spring.

'Whoever wills', O gracious word!
　'Shall of this stream partake;'
Come thirsty souls, and bless the Lord,
　And drink for Jesu's sake.

This spring with living water flows,
　And living joy imparts;
Come, thirsty souls, your wants disclose,
　And drink with thankful hearts.

To sinners poor, like me and you,
　He says He'll 'freely give',
Come, thirsty souls, and prove it true,
　Drink, and for ever live.

2135   Joseph Bromehead   CM
That great city, the holy Jerusalem,
descending out of heaven from God.
Revelation 21:10

Jerusalem my happy home!
　Name ever dear to me;
When shall my labours have an end
　In joy, and peace, and thee?

When shall these eyes thy heaven-built walls
　And pearly gates behold;
Thy bulwarks and salvation strong,
　And streets of shining gold?

Why should I shrink at pain or woe,
　Or feel at death dismay?
I've Canaan's goodly land in view,
　And realms of endless day.

Apostles, prophets, martyrs there
　Around my Saviour stand;
And soon my friends in Christ below
　Will join the glorious band.

Jerusalem, my happy home!
　My soul still pants for thee;
Then shall my labours have an end,
　When I thy joys shall see.

2136   Mary Deck   66 55 6
They which are written in the Lamb's book of
life. *Revelation 21:27*

There is a city bright,
Closed are its gates to sin;
　Nought that defileth,
　Nought that defileth,
Can ever enter in.

Saviour, I come to Thee!
O Lamb of God, I pray,
  Cleanse me and save me,
  Cleanse me and save me,
Wash all my sins away.

Lord, make me from this hour
Thy loving child to be,
  Kept by Thy power,
  Kept by Thy power,
From all that grieveth Thee.

Till in the snowy dress
Of Thy redeemed I stand;
  Faultless and stainless,
  Faultless and stainless,
Safe in that happy land!

What does He show to God
  That satisfies His heart,
That stems His wrath, and stays His rod,
  And bids me not depart?
It is His righteousness,
  Displayed in Christ His Son,
Has granted me this blessedness,
  That Christ alone has won.

Then I shall praise His name
  With songs that come from Him;
He granted me a heart aflame
  That sin can never dim.
  Rejoice, my soul, rejoice!
  O glorious Trinity,
My cup is full, and fills my voice
  With gratitude to Thee.

© Author

2137   Vernon Higham   DSM
They which are written in the Lamb's book of life. *Revelation 21:27*

I heard the Father's cry,
  Who turns away from sin:
He shuts the gates, and those who try
  Can never enter in.
  Then heaven is barred to me,
  My fancied merit, loss:
My woeful lot— where can I flee
  And rid my soul of dross?

How shall I find a way
  To come to God above;
When all my efforts lead astray,
  My poor soul pants for love?
  'Tis then I see His grace,
  Revealing mercy's part;
Then all my sin and life's disgrace
  I lay on Jesus' heart.

O Saviour now so kind,
  What heart of love is Thine!
For all my sin and stain I find
  On Christ the King divine.
  What can I say, my Lord?
  What tongue can ever tell?
The gift of grace does now afford
  A path that passes hell.

My Saviour's merit pleads
  A place for me to stand;
An Advocate who intercedes
  My Hope, at God's right hand.
  Who is this Friend I need,
  Who shed His blood for me?
Behold the Christ, whose death and deed
  Forgive eternally!

2138   Francis Knollis   SM
And there shall be no night there.
Revelation 22:5

There is no night in heaven;
  In that blest world above
Work never can bring weariness,
  For work itself is love.

There is no grief in heaven;
  For life is one glad day;
And tears are of those former things
  Which all have passed away.

There is no sin in heaven;
  Behold that blessèd throng,
All holy is their spotless robe,
  All holy is their song!

There is no death in heaven;
  For they who gain that shore
Have won their immortality
  And they can die no more.

Lord Jesus, be our Guide;
  O lead us safely on,
Till night and grief and sin and death
  Are past and heaven is won!

2139 Albert Midlane   CM
And they shall reign for ever and ever.
Revelation 22:5

Where God begins His gracious work,
   That work He will complete,
For round the objects of His love,
   All power and mercy meet.

Man may repent him of his work,
   And fail in his intent;
God is above the power of change,
   He never can repent.

Each object of His love is sure
   To reach the heavenly goal;
For neither sin nor Satan can
   Destroy the blood-washed soul.

Satan may vex, and unbelief
   The saved one may annoy,
But He *must* conquer; yes, as sure
   As Jesus reigns in joy.

The precious blood of God's dear Son
   Shall ne'er be spilt in vain;
The soul on Christ believing, must
   With Christ for ever reign.

2140 Samuel Medley   LM
The bright and morning star.
Revelation 22:16

With joy, ye saints, attend and raise
Your voices in harmonious praise!
Blessed Spirit! every heart prepare
To sing the bright, the Morning Star!

In glory bright the Saviour reigns,
And endless grandeur there sustains;
We view His beams, and from afar
Hail Him the bright, the Morning Star!

Blessed Star! where'er His lustre shines,
He all the soul with grace refines;
And makes each happy saint declare
He is the bright, the Morning Star!

Sweet Star! His influence is divine;
Life, peace, and joy, attending shine:
Death, hell, and sin, before Him flee;
The bright, the Morning Star is He.

Eternal Star! our songs shall rise,
When we shall meet Thee in the skies;
And in eternal anthems, there
Praise Thee, the bright, the Morning Star.

2141 William Gadsby   SM
And whosoever will, let him take the water of life freely. *Revelation 22:17*

   Come, whosoever will,
   Nor vainly strive to mend;
Sinners are freely welcome still
   To Christ, the sinner's Friend.

   The gospel-table's spread
   And richly furnished too,
With wine and milk, and living bread,
   And dainties not a few.

   The guilty, vile, and base,
   The wretched and forlorn,
Are welcome to the feast of grace,
   Though goodness they have none.

   No goodness He expects;
   He came to save the poor;
Poor helpless souls He ne'er neglects,
   Nor sends them from His door.

   His tender, loving heart
   The vilest will embrace;
And freely to them will impart
   The riches of His grace.

2142 Anne Steele   CM
And whosoever will, let him take the water of life freely. *Revelation 22:17*

The Saviour calls! let every ear
   Attend the heavenly sound;
Ye doubting souls, dismiss your fear,
   Hope smiles reviving round.

For every thirsty, longing heart,
   Here streams of bounty flow;
And life and health and bliss impart
   To banish mortal woe.

Ye sinners, come, 'tis mercy's voice,
   The gracious call obey;
Mercy invites to heavenly joys
   And can you yet delay?

Dear Saviour, draw reluctant hearts;
   To Thee let sinners fly
And take the bliss Thy love imparts
   And drink and never die.

2143 George Herbert CM
**And whosoever will, let him take the water of
life freely.** *Revelation 22:17*

Ho, poor distressèd, thirsty soul,
  The fountain is just by,
Whose waters run both full and free;
  Come, drink, and never die.

O come, poor helpless thirsty soul,
  The call is made to you;
That God who made you feel your thirst
  Will prove His promise true.

O ye who long to feel and see
  Your interest in His blood,
This thing is proved beyond a doubt,
  Because you thirst for God.

There's not a sinner out of hell,
  The vilest of the base,
If he is made to trust in Christ,
  Who shall not see His face.

2144 Frances Havergal 87 887 77 77
**He which testifieth these things saith, Surely I
come quickly. Amen. Even so, come, Lord
Jesus.** *Revelation 22:20*

Thou art coming, O my Saviour,
  Thou art coming, O my King;
In Thy beauty all-resplendent,
In Thy glory all-transcendent;
  Well may we rejoice and sing.
Coming! in the opening East
  Herald brightness slowly swells;
Coming! O my glorious Priest,
  Hear we not Thy golden bells?

Thou art coming, Thou art coming;
  We shall meet Thee on Thy way,
We shall see Thee, we shall know Thee,
We shall bless Thee, we shall show Thee
  All our hearts could never say.
What an anthem that will be,
  Ringing out our love to Thee,
Pouring out our rapture sweet
  At Thine own all-glorious feet!

O the joy to see Thee reigning,
  Thee, my own belovèd Lord!
Every tongue Thy name confessing,
Worship, honour, glory, blessing
  Brought to Thee with glad accord—
Thee, my Master and my Friend,
  Vindicated and enthroned,
Unto earth's remotest end
  Glorified, adored, and owned!

2145 John Newton 66 66 88
**He which testifieth these things saith, Surely I
come quickly. Amen. Even so, come, Lord
Jesus.** *Revelation 22:20*

To Thee our wants are known,
  From Thee are all our powers;
Accept what is Thine own,
  And pardon what is ours:
Our praises, Lord, and prayers receive,
And to Thy word a blessing give.

O grant that each of us,
  Now met before Thee here,
May meet together thus
  When Thou and Thine appear!
And follow Thee to heaven our home,
E'en so, Amen, Lord Jesus, come.

2146 Horatius Bonar SM
**He which testifieth these things saith, Surely I
come quickly. Amen. Even so, come, Lord
Jesus.** *Revelation 22:20*

Come, Lord, and tarry not;
  Bring the long-looked-for day;
O, why these years of waiting here,
  These ages of delay?

Come, for Thy saints still wait;
  Daily ascends their sigh;
The Spirit and the bride say, 'Come;'
  Dost Thou not hear the cry?

Come, for creation groans,
  Impatient of Thy stay,
Worn out with these long years of ill,
  These ages of delay.

Come, for the corn is ripe,
  Put in Thy sickle now,
Reap the great harvest of the earth;
  Sower and Reaper Thou!

Come, in Thy glorious might,
  Come with the iron rod,
Scattering Thy foes before Thy face,
  Most mighty Son of God.

Come and make all things new,
  Build up this ruined earth,
Restore our faded Paradise,
  Creation's second birth.

Come, and begin Thy reign
  Of everlasting peace;
Come, take the kingdom to Thyself,
  Great King of Righteousness.

AUTHORS

Adams, John (1751-1835)	90	687	1315	1418	1832	1873	
Addison, Joseph (1672-1719)	477	794					
Alexander, Cecil (1818-1895)	679	912	1019	1337	1670	1767	
Alford, Henry (1810-1871)	1046	1065	2099				
Allen, James (1734-1804)	990	1396	1533	2100			
Allen, William (1784-1868)	387						
Allen, Oswald (1816-1878)	1373						
Alstyne, Frances Jane Van (1820-1915)	48	82	184	333	529	592	684	791
(Crosby Fanny J. was her pen-name)	1073	1297	1425	1512	1649	1690	1982	
Ambrose (c 339-397)	641						
Anonymous	121	156	828	1166	1233	1452	1714	1773
	1845	2013	2049	2056			
Anstice, Joseph (1808-1836)	2022						
Auber, Harriet (1773-1862)	225	287	415	437	443	451	497	504
	537	1342					
B—R, James, 1780	1187						
Bailey, John, 1811	426						
Baker, Henry W. (1821-1877)	254	600	1044	1392	1862	2000	
Bakewell, John (1721-1819)	1569	2101					
Baldwin, Thomas (1753-1825)	1117						
Bancroft, Charitie L. (1841-1923)	1930	2107					
Baring-Gould, Sabine (1834-1924)	654	1077					
Barnard, Samuel,.1799	766	1051	1363	1505	1685		
Barton, Bernard (1784-1849)	571	2035					
Barton, William (1597-1678)	260						
Bathurst, William H. (1796-1877)	155	1226	1604				
Batty, Christopher (1715-1797)	1396	2100					
Baughen, Michael (1930-)	199						
Baxter, Richard (1615-1691)	502	1758					
Beaumont, John (1762-1822)	596	622	626				
Beddome, Benjamin (1717-95)	87	128	273	290	392	688	785	902
	970	1071	1158	1234	1321	1326	1437	1448
	1521	1654	1713	1813	1983		
Bell, James (1851-1916)	120						
Bennett, William, 1790	393						
Bennett, Lucy A. (1850-1927)	1729						
Bernard of Clairvaux (1091-1153)	2006						
Bernard of Cluny (1100-1199,e.)	2132						
Berridge, John (1716-1793)	70	103	110	124	228	248	285	301
	315	342	397	567	580	655	662	670
	675	701	710	748	802	829	858	894
	905	1043	1054	1214	1225	1230	1242	1269
	1352	1372	1470	1496	1497	1510	1530	1620
	1786	1923	1964	1967			
Bevan, Emma (1827-1909)	887						
Bickersteth, Edward H. (1825-1906)	760	1131	1156	1591			
Binney, Thomas (1798-1874)	2032						
Bliss, Philipp P. (1838-1876)	247	817	1960				
Bode, John E. (1816-1874)	2119						
Boden, James (1757-1841)	652						
Bonar, Horatius (1808-1889)	13	65	153	321	360	799	822	950
	951	1212	1431	1520	1545	1587	1659	1667
	1689	1715	1718	1793	1829	1830	1849	1892
	1915	2034	2043	2045	2146		

Duffield, George (1818-1888)	1614						
Duncan, Mary (1814-1840)	256						
Dwight, Timothy (1752-1817)	88						
Edmeston, James (1791-1867)	57						
Ellerton, John (1826-1893)	546	593	1152	1357	1871		
Elliott, Charlotte (1789-1871)	412	1107	1108	1147	1167	1292	1415	1934
	1159						
Elliott, Robert, 1761	2113						
Enfield, William (1741-1797)	2009						
Erskine, Ralph (1685-1752)	826	1183	1265	1225			
Evans, Jonathan (1748-1809)	668	672	1064	1310	1390		
Everest, Charles W. (1814-1877)	1078						
Faber, Frederick W. (1814-1863)	97	835	1150				
Fawcett, John (1740-1817)	58	72	83	92	268	302	573	833
	1075	1263	1295	1334	1451	1646	1734	
Featherstone, William R. (1842-1870)	1401						
Felkin, Ellen T. (1860-1929)	406						
Fellows, John (d. 1785)	1015	1099	1182	1267	1443	1492	
Ferguson, Fergus (1824-1897)	1668						
Flint, Annie Johnson (1866-1932)	1981						
Flowerdew, Alice (1759-1830)	7						
Fortunatus, Venantius (530-609)	1394	1610					
Fowler, Henry (1779-1838)	99	182	421				
Fox, Henry E. (1841-1926)	1406						
Francis, Benjamin (1734-1799)	157	1354	2072				
Francis, Samuel Trevor (1834-1925)	1726						
Franklin, Jonathan (1760-1833)	288	1408					
Gabb, James (1830-1900)	1137						
Gabriel, Charles H. (1856-1932)	1240	2040					
Gadsby, William (1773-1844)	59	61	62	106	114	123	135	227
	265	279	286	339	396	465	479	507
	521	646	660	661	719	745	772	777
	779	789	798	843	848	851	867	875
	881	884	898	921	936	952	965	995
	1000	1016	1034	1062	1097	1105	1206	1213
	1305	1316	1330	1339	1353	1368	1419	1435
	1438	1464	1474	1490	1494	1498	1508	1531
	1567	1571	1579	1633	1640	1641	1662	1684
	1691	1695	1699	1706	1709	1735	1740	1788
	1790	1803	1811	1833	1841	1843	1855	1856
	1889	1901	1903	1935	1948	1951	1959	1963
	1971	1979	2025	2054	2141			
Gates, Mary C., 1886	1200						
Gellert, Christian F. (1715-1769)	1349	1608					
Gerhardt, Paulus (1607-1676)	320	505	1174	1319	1386	1635	1674	
Gibbons, Thomas (1720-1785)	77	885					
Gilbert, Ann (1782-1866)	1644	1367					
Giles, John E. (1805-1875)	1079						
Gill, Thomas H. (1819-1906)	38	487	1208				
Gilmore, Joseph H. (1834-1918)	532						
Gladden, Washington (1836-1918)	1126						
Goode, William (1762-1816)	200	448					
Grant, Robert (1779-1838)	523	830					
Greene, Thomas, 1780	118	1880					
Greenwell, Dora (1821-1882)	1860						

INDEX OF OTHER SOURCES OF WORDS

Anabaptist Ausbund	1036	Psalter 1912	258
Anon, Sankey's Songs and Solos	1233	312 562 569	
Carne's Collection	2020	Psalter Hymnal 1927	617
Dobell's Selection	104	Scottish Psalter 1615	565
Gospel Magazine 1777	1692	579	
1712		Scottish Psalter 1650	255
Gospel Magazine 1778	81	329 344 414 528	
Gospel Magazine 1781	306	Scottish Version 1641	317
1515		514 581	
Gospel Magazine 1796	1800	Silver St Collection 1821	1733
Lady Huntingdon's Hymn Book 1774	1845	The Clifton Hymnal	1944
Lady Huntingdon's Selection 1764	560	The Sower 1878	501
Old and New Versions	251	Leifchild's Original Hymns 1842	
Oligos, Christian Magazine 1790	30	(translation)	1916
Original 1790	568	Traditional 17th Cent.	1010
Pilgrim Hymnal 1904	2052	Young People's Hymnal	31
Prust's Supplementary H/book 1869	1756	32	
Psalter 1781	2038	Zion's Trumpet 1838	2047

TRANSLATOR INDEX

Alexander, James W. (1804-59)	1386	Hine, Stuart K. (1899-1989)	524
Bethune, George W. (1805-1862)	1757	Houghton, Frank (1894-1972)	2010
Bevan, Emma F. (1827-1909)	1220	Howells, William (1855-1932)	2105
1894		Hoyle, Richard B. (1875-1939)	1611
Borthwick, Jane L. (1813-97)	244	Hull. Eleanor H. (1860-1935) editor	1553
357 1753		Jackson, Samuel (1786-1861)	623
Bridges, Robert. (1844-1930)	820	Jones, Robert Maynard (1929-)	717
Byrne, Mary E. (1880-1931)	1553	Kinchin, C. (1711-1742)	2002
Campbell, Jane M. (1817-1878)	636	Lang, J. D. (1799-1878)	1608
Carlyle, Thomas (1795-1881)	353	Littledale, Richard F. (1833-1890)	1473
Caswall, Edward (1814-1878)	432	MacBean, Lachlan (1853-1931)	737
2006		Neale, John M. (1818-1866)	983
Chandler, John (1806-1876)	1381	1348 1678 1773 2004 2132	
1722 1812		Nelson Augustus (1863-1949)	1610
Chatfield, Allen W. (1808-1896)	578	Oakley, Frederick (1802-1880)	1170
Clemens, Christian G. (1743- 1815)	126	Palmer, Ray (1808-1887)	533
Collyer, William B. (1782-1854)	940	Payne, Ernest (1902-1980)	1036
Cotterill, Thomas. (1779-1823)	940	Pott, Francis (1832-1909)	1607
Cox, Frances E. (1812-1897)	1349	Reed, Edith M. G. (1885-1933)	2048
Dearmer, Percy (1867-1936)	1012	Smith, Elizabeth L. (1817-1898)	1680
Döving, Carl (1867-1937)	335	Wesley, Charles (1707-1788)	641
Edwards, William (1848-1929)	1273	Wesley, John (1703-1791)	23
Ellerton, John (1826-1893)	1394	241 320 505 632 846 882	
Findlater, Sarah L. (1823-1907)	556	1335 1635 1674 1805 1854	
Guillebaud, Rosemary (1915-2002)	1698	Williams, Peter (1721-1796)	447
Harrison, Graham S. (1935-2013)	391	Winkworth, Catherine (1827-1878)	262
Higham, William Vernon (1926-)	1700	318 590 599 650 1164 1174	
1994		1175 1593	

Acknowledgment:
Some of the details and dates in the indexes were obtained from www.hymnary.org.